Putnam's Contemporary Dictionaries

Spanish-English
Inglés-Español

Putnam's

Contemporary Dictionaries

Spanish-English

Inglés-Español

R. F. BROWN, M.A., Ph.D.
Professor of Spanish Language
and Literature, the University of Leeds

Revised by:
J. M. CASSERLY, M.A.
Lecturer in Spanish,
University of Strathclyde

CARLOS REYES OROZCO
Universidad Autónoma de México

CHARLES BERLITZ
CATHERINE WILSON
Special Editors to the American Edition

G. P. PUTNAM'S SONS New York

First American edition, 1972

Library of Congress Catalog Card Number: 72–88104
SBN: 399–11041–0

Published by arrangement
with William Collins Sons & Co., Ltd., London and Glasgow

Printed in the United States of America

General Editor: J. B. Foreman, M.A.
Executive Editor: Iseabail C. Macleod, M.A.

Contents

Indice de Materias

Introduction

In this edition a number of words in current use in Latin America have been included. The assistance of our Spanish, Latin American, American and British collaborators in this matter has been invaluable. We have also included the grammatical forms of the articles, pronouns, possessives, demonstratives etc. for the benefit of the complete beginner.

Abbreviations Used in the Dictionary—Abreviaturas Usadas en el Diccionario

Español	Abreviatura	English
adjetivo	**a**	adjective
académico	**acad**	academic
adverbio	**ad**	adverb
adjetivo y nombre femenino	**a f**	adjective and noun feminine
adjetivo y nombre masculino	**a m**	adjective and noun masculine
adjetivo y nombre	**an**	adjective and noun
anatomía	**anat**	anatomy
andaluz	**Andal**	Andalusian
adjetivo plural	**a pl**	adjective plural
adjetivo y pronombre	**a pn**	adjective and pronoun
aproximadamente	**approx**	approximately
arcaico	**arch**	archaic
arquitectura	**archit**	architecture
Argentina	**Arg**	Argentina
astronomía	**astr**	astronomy
automóviles	**aut**	automobile
aviación	**av**	aviation
Bolivia	**Bol**	Bolivia
Centro América	**CA**	Central America
carpintería	**carp**	carpentry
compárese	**cf**	compare
Chile	**Chi**	Chile
conjunción	**cj**	conjunction
Colombia	**Col**	Colombia
comercio	**com**	commerce
comparativo	**comp**	comparative
Costa Rica	**CR**	Costa Rica
Cuba	**Cub**	Cuba
artículo definido	**def art**	definite article
demostrativo	**dem**	demonstrative
Ecuador	**Ec**	Ecuador
eclesiástico	**eccles**	ecclesiastical
electricidad	**el**	electricity
equivalente	**equiv**	equivalent
especialmente	**esp**	especially
exclamación	**excl**	exclamation
(nombre) femenino	**f**	feminine (noun)
familiar	**fam**	familiar
figurativamente	**fig**	figuratively
femenino plural	**f pl**	feminine plural
genitivo	**gen**	genitive
geología	**geol**	geology
Guatemala	**Guat**	Guatemala
heráldica	**her**	heraldry
Honduras	**Hond**	Honduras
impersonal	**impers**	impersonal
artículo indefinido	**indef art**	indefinite article
interrogativo	**inter**	interrogative
invariable	**inv**	invariable
irregular	**ir**	irregular
(nombre) masculino	**m**	masculine (noun)
matemática	**math**	mathematics

mecánica	**mec**	mechanics
medicina	**med**	medicine
México	**Mex**	Mexico
nombre masculino y femenino	**mf**	noun masculine and feminine
militar	**mil**	military
minería	**min**	mining
masculino plural	**m pl**	masculine plural
música	**mus**	music
nombre	**n**	noun
náutico	**naut**	nautical
negativo	**neg**	negative
Nicaragua	**Nic**	Nicaragua
número	**num**	numeral
ornitología	**orni**	ornithology
sí mismo	**o.s.**	oneself
Panamá	**Pan**	Panama
fotografía	**phot**	photography
plural	**pl**	plural
pronombre	**pn**	pronoun
pronombre y adjetivo	**pn a**	pronoun and adjective
poético	**poet**	poetry
político	**pol**	political
posesivo	**pos**	possessive
participio pasado	**pp**	past participle
Peru	**Per**	Peru
Puerto Rico	**PR**	Puerto Rico
pronombre y nombre	**pr n**	pronoun and noun
preposición	**prep**	preposition
reflexivo	**refl**	reflexive
relativo	**rel**	relative
religión	**relig**	religion
ferrocarril	**rl**	railway
región de la Plata	**RP**	Río de la Plata Region
singular	**s**	singular
Sudamérica	**SA**	Spanish America
Santo Domingo	**SD**	Santo Domingo
costura	**sew**	sewing
vulgarismo	**sl**	slang
alguien	**s.o.**	someone
algo	**sth**	something
superlativo	**sup**	superlative
técnico	**tec**	technical
teatro	**theat**	theater
Uruguay	**Urug**	Uruguay
Estados Unidos	**US**	United States
generalmente	**usu**	usually
verbo	**v**	verb
verbo auxiliar	**v aux**	auxiliary verb
verbo intransitivo	**vi**	verb intransitive
verbo impersonal	**v imp**	verb impersonal
verbo intransitivo y reflexivo	**vir**	verb intransitive and reflexive
verbo reflexivo	**vr**	verb reflexive
verbo transitivo	**vt**	verb transitive
verbo transitivo e intransitivo	**vti**	verb transitive and intransitive
verbo transitivo, intransitivo y reflexivo	**vtir**	verb transitive, intransitive and reflexive
verbo transitivo y reflexivo	**vtr**	verb transitive and reflexive
Venezuela	**Ven**	Venezuela
grosero	**vulg**	vulgar
zoología	**zool**	zoology

Spanish Pronunciation—Pronunciación Española

Letter	*As in*	*Nearest english equivalent*	*Remarks*
a	**ala**	father	
b	**bobo**	soft **b**	
c	capa	cat	
	codo	cot	**k** sound before a, o, u
	cuna	cut	
	cero	think	**th** sound before e, i
	cinco	think	
ch	**ch**ulo	**ch**ur**ch**	
d	dama	soft **d**	
	codo	though	**th** sound between vowels
e	mesa	fate	when final letter in syllable—me-sa
	hotel	set	when followed by consonant in same syllable—ho-tel
f	faro	father	
g	gafas	garden	rule same as for **c**:
	golfo	gone	hard sound before a, o, u
	gusano	good	soft sound before e, i
	gemelo	**ch** as in lo**ch**	-**ch** as in Scottish loch
	girasol	**ch** as in lo**ch**	
h	haba	never pronounced	ato and hato are pronounced exactly the same
i	isla	feet	always
j	jabón	**ch** as in lo**ch**	
k	kilómetro	kick	rare
l	luna	look	
ll	pollo	**lli** as in mi**lli**on	
m	mapa	man	
n	nota	note	
ñ	señor	**ny** as in ca**ny**on	
o	libro	so	when final letter in syllable—li-bro
	cortina	cot	when followed by consonant in same syllable—cor-ti-na
p	pino	pin	
q(u)	queso	cake	always followed by u = k
r	reloj	trilled **r**	
rr	perro	strongly trilled **r**	
s	dos	so	always soft, not z
t	tres	tree	
u	uno	boot	never English u as in cube; always oo
v	vaca	**b**asket	like b—a sound somewhere between the b and v
w	wagón	van	very rare
x	xilófono	soft	rare
y	ya	yes	
z	zorro	think	

Stress

1. Words ending in a vowel and N or S take the stress on the vowel before the last, e.g. chico, hablan, antes.
2. Words ending in a consonant (except N or S) take the stress on the last vowel, e.g. hotel, cantar, precoz.
3. In all exceptions to the above two rules the stressed vowel is marked with an accent.

Spanish-American Pronunciation

In the Spanish-speaking countries of Central and South America:

z	**z**orro	s as in sink
c	**c**inco	s as in sink (before e or i)
ll	**ll**ama	yawn or like the s in treasure

Pronunciación Inglesa—English Pronunciation

Se debe notar la casi imposibilidad de explicar de modo satisfactorio los sonidos de una lengua en términos de otra. Lo que sigue no pretende ser más que una aproximación a los sonidos ingleses, y una ayuda general.

Vocales y Diptongos—Vowels and Diphthongs

	inglés	*sonido parecido en el español*
[ɑː]	f**a**ther ['fɑːðə]	p**a**dre (prolongado)
[ʌ]	b**u**tter ['bʌtə]	p**ú**a
[æ]	m**a**n [mæn]	c**a**sa (más cerrado)
[ɛə]	th**ere** [ðɛə]	p**e**rro (más abierto)
[ai]	fl**y** [flai]	b**ai**le
[au]	h**ou**se [haus]	c**au**sa
[ei]	n**a**m**e** [neim]	r**ey**
[e]	g**e**t [get]	hot**e**l
[ə]	**a**go [ə'gou]	(parecido al sonido francés j**e**, l**e**)
[əː]	b**ir**d [bəːd]	(parecido al sonido francés b**eu**rre)
[i]	b**i**g [big]	(sonido entre **e** en mesa e **i** en cinco)
[iː]	t**ea** [tiː]	m**i**sa
[iə]	h**ere** [hiə]	simpat**ía**
[ou]	n**o**t**e** [nout]	c**o**sa (suena como si la siguiese una [u] débil)
[ɔ]	h**o**t [hɔt]	p**o**rra
[ɔː]	t**a**ll [tɔːl]	p**o**r
[ɔi]	b**oi**l [bɔil]	h**oy**
[u]	l**oo**k [luk]	b**u**rro (muy rápido, y más cerrado)
[uː]	f**oo**l [fuːl]	d**u**da
[uə]	p**ure** [pjuə]	p**úa** (suena como [u], seguido por [ə])

Consonantes—Consonants

	inglés	*sonido parecido en el español*
[b]	**b**ook [bʌk]	cam**b**iar
[d]	**d**ate [deit]	an**d**ar
[f]	**f**ool [fuːl]	**f**az
[g]	**g**ape [geip]	**g**orra
[h]	**h**ot [hɔt]	**j**ota (sin la aspereza gutural de la jota)
[j]	**y**ou [juː]	su**y**o
[k]	**c**at [kæt]	**c**asa

[l]	**all** [ɔːl]	**l**una
[m]	**m**uch [mʌtʃ]	**m**adre
[n]	**n**oo**n** [nuːn]	**n**ada
[p]	**p**ush [puʃ]	**p**adre
[r]	**r**ed [red]	pe**r**o (menos fuerte)
[s]	**s**tand [stænd]	ca**s**a
[t]	**t**ennis [tenis]	**t**al
[v]	**v**ery [veri]	(no existe en español; más parecido a la 'f' en **f**ácil que a **b** o **v** en español)
[w]	**w**ater [wɔːtə]	**hu**eso
[z]	hi**s** [hiz]	de**s**de
[ʒ]	vi**s**ion [viʒən]	(parecido al sonido francés **je**, **g**énéral)
[ʃ]	**sh**all [ʃæl]	(como **ch** en la palabra francesca *chose*)
[θ]	**th**ing [θiŋ]	**z**orro
[ð]	**th**ere	to**d**o
[ŋ]	si**ng** [siŋ]	ci**n**co
[x]	lo**ch** (*Scot*) [lox]	**j**amás

Spanish - English

A

a *prep* to, in, at, by.
abacero *m* grocer.
abacorar *vt Ven* to pursue, attack; *Ec* to hatch, brood.
abad *m* abbot.
abadejo *m* codfish.
abadía *f* abbey.
abajeño *m Mex, PR* person from lowlands.
abajera *f Arg* horse blanket.
abajino *m Chi* inhabitant of northern territories.
abajo *ad* under, below; downstairs.
abalanzar *vt* to balance, weigh; *vr* to rush on; — **sobre** to hurl oneself on.
abanderado *m* ensign.
abandonado *a* forlorn; slovenly, careless, left behind; desolate.
abandonar *vt* to abandon, give up, leave, desert.
abandono *m* abandonment; ease, indolence; abandon.
abanicar *vt* to fan; *vr* to fan oneself.
abanico *m* fan; derrick.
abaratar *vt* to cheapen.
abarca *f* (peasant) sandal.
abarcar *vt* to embrace (*with vision, ambition etc*); to include, contain.
abarrotar *vt* to stow a cargo; to overstock.
abarrotero *m SA* grocer.
abarrotes *m pl SA* groceries.
abastecer *vt* to supply (*town with water etc*), purvey.
abastecimiento *m* supply, provisions.
abastero *m Cub, Chi* purveyor of livestock, vegetables.
abasto *m* supply, provision; *pl* **—s** rations.
abatatar(se) *vr SA* to frighten, depress, intimidate.
abate *m* abbé, minor cleric.
abatí *m Arg, Par* maize, corn; liqueur of maize.
abatido *a* depressed, dejected; spiritless; dull; crestfallen.
abatimiento *m* depression; low spirits.
abatir *vt* to knock down; to discourage, depress; to humble.
abdicación *f* abdication.
abdicar *vt* to abdicate; to abandon (*rights etc*).
abdomen *m* abdomen, belly.
abecedario *m* alphabet card; primer.
abedul *m* birch tree.
abeja *f* bee; — **reina** queen.
abejón *m* bumblebee, drone.
aberración *f* aberration; error.
abertura *f* opening, crevice; aperture, fissure
abeto *m* silver fir, spruce.
abierto *a* open, frank; candid.
abigarrado *a* motley, variegated.
abintestato *a* intestate; *m* intestacy.
abiselar *vt* to bevel.
abisinio *an* Abyssinian.
abismado *a* dejected, lost (*in thoughts etc*).
abismar *vt* to depress; *vr* — **en** to lose o.s. in (*thought etc*).
abismo *m* abyss, gulf; hell; depths.
abjuración *f* abjuration, recantation.
abjurar *vt* to abjure, forswear.
ablandar *vt* to soften; to mollify; to mitigate.
ablución *f* ablutions (*usually religious*).
abnegación *f* abnegation, self-sacrifice.
abnegar(se) *vr* to renounce, sacrifice o.s.
abobado *a* silly, stupid, stupefied.
abocar *vt* to catch with the mouth; *vr* — **con** to meet, to discuss a problem.
abochornar *vt* to shame; *vr* to be covered with shame.
abochornado *a* mortified, shamed.
abofetear *vt* to box; to cuff, slap.
abogacía *f* profession of a lawyer.
abogaderas *f pl SA* cunning reasoning or arguments.
abogado *m* lawyer, advocate, barrister.
abogar *vi* — **por** to advocate, plead support.
abolengo *m* ancestry, lineage; inheritance.
abolición *f* abolition, extinction.
abolir *vt* to abolish, annul.
abolladura *f* unevenness; dent, bruise.
abollar *vt* to emboss, dent.
abombarse *vr SA* to rot, putrify.
abominación *f* abhorrence, hateful thing, abomination.
abonado *m* subscriber, season-ticket holder; *a* well-accredited; fertilized (with manure).
abonanzar *vi* to clear up, to calm (*of weather*).
abonar *vt* to credit; to subscribe; to stand surety for; to manure.
abono *m* guarantee; manure; season ticket.
abordar *vt* to board, to tie up (*of ship*); to accost.
abordo *m* boarding (*a ship*), attack.

aborígenes *m or f pl* aborigines.
aborlonado *a Chi, Col* ribbed, striped.
aborrecer *vt* to hate, abhor.
aborrecible *a* hateful.
abortar *vi* to miscarry; to fail, to come to nothing.
aborto *m* miscarriage, abortion; monster.
abotonar *vt* to button; *vi* to bud.
abovedado *a* arched, vaulted.
abra *f* bay, cove, gorge.
abracar *vt SA* to seize, embrace.
abrasar *vt* to burn; *vr* to be consumed (*passion*).
abrazar *vt* to embrace, clasp; to comprise, include.
abrazo *m* embrace, warm greetings (*in letters*).
abrevadero *m* watering place.
abrevar *vt* to water (*cattle*).
abreviar *vt* to abbreviate, cut short, abridge; to hasten.
abreviatura *f* abbreviation.
abrigar *vt* to shelter, cover, shield; to cherish (*hopes etc*).
abrigo *m* shelter, protection, cover; overcoat; **al — de** protected by, under (the) shelter of.
abril *m* April.
abrir *vt* to open; to unfold; to begin; to cleave, split.
abrochador *m* buttonhook.
abrochar *vt* to button, fasten; *Chi, Ec* to punish, chastise.
abrogación *f* abrogation, repeal.
abrogar *vt* to repeal, annul.
abrojo *m* thistle; thorn.
abrumado *a* weary, oppressed, overwhelmed.
abrumar *vt* to overwhelm, crush, weigh down.
abrupto *a* rugged, steep.
absceso *m* abscess.
ábside *f* apse.
absolución *f* absolution, acquittal.
absolutismo *m* absolutism, despotism.
absoluto *a* absolute; **en—** not at all, certainly not.
absolver (ue) *vt* to absolve, acquit.
absorber *vt* to absorb, imbibe, take in.
absorción *f* absorption.
absorto *a* amazed, absorbed.
abstemio *a* abstemious.
abstención *f* abstention.
abstenerse *vr* to abstain, refrain.
abstinencia *f* abstinence, forbearance; **día de—** fast day.
abstracción *f* omission; absence of mind.
abstraer *vt* to abstract; *vr* to become thoughtful.
abstraído *a* withdrawn.
abstruso *a* abstruse.
absuelto *a* acquitted, absolved.
absurdo *a* absurd, stupid, pointless; *m* absurdity.
abuchear *vt* to boo, hoot.
buela *f* grandmother.
abulense *m* (*native*) of Avila.
abuelita *f Col* cradle; *Chi* baby's bonnet.
abuelo *m* grandfather; *pl* **—s** grandparents.
abuinche *m Col* machete.
abultado *a* bulky, swollen.
abultar *vt* to increase in size, in appearance; to enlarge, fill out.
abundancia *f* plenty, abundance.
abundante *a* abundant, plentiful, copious.
abundar *vi* to abound, be full, plenty of.
aburrición *f SA* boredom.
aburrido *a* weary, bored; tedious, boring.
aburrimiento *m* weariness, tediousness, boredom.
aburrir *vt* to bore, annoy, weary; *vr* to become weary.
abusar *vi* to take undue advantage of, trespass, misuse; to abuse.
abuso *m* misusage, misuse; abuse.
abyecto *a* abject.
acá *ad* here, hither;**— y allá** here and there.
acabado *a* perfect, faultless.
acabar *vt* to finish, conclude, end; **— con** to finish off; **— de** to have just; **— en** to end (in, by).
academia *f* academy.
académico *m* scholar, academician; *a* academic.
acaecer *vi* to happen.
acalaca *f SA* ant.
acalenturado *a Mex* feverish.
acallar *vt* to silence; to assuage (*pain*).
acaloramiento *m* heat (*of argument*).
acalorar *vt* to warm, heat; to inflame, promote; *vr* to grow excited.
acamastronarse *vr Per* to become sly, crafty.
acampanado *a* bell-shaped.
acampar *vt* to encamp.
acanalado *a* grooved, fluted; corrugated.
acanalar *vt* to groove.
acantilado *m* (*sea*) cliff; *a* steep.
acantonar *vt* to quarter troops.
acaparamiento *m* cornering, monopoly, monopolizing.
acaparar *vt* to monopolize, corner, buy up.
acariciar *vt* to caress, fondle; to cherish (*ideas etc*).
acarrear *vt* to carry, transport; to occasion; to cause.
acarreo *m* transport; conveyance.
acaserarse *vr Chi, Per* to become a regular customer.
acaso *ad* perhaps, by chance; *m* chance, destiny.
acatamiento *m* reverence, respect, esteem; obedience to.
acatar *vt* to respect, revere; to acknowledge, accept (*ruling etc*).
acatarrarse *vr* to catch a cold.
acaudalado *a* wealthy.

acaudalar *vt* to hoard up (*riches*).
acaudillar *vt* to head, command (*troops*).
acceder *vi* to agree, accede; to comply, give way to (*pleas etc*).
accesible *a* accessible.
acceso *m* access, admittance.
accesorio *a* accessory, incidental.
accidentado *a* rough, uneven.
accidental *a* accidental, casual.
accidente *m* accident.
acción *f* action; feat; battle; plot (*of play*); stock; lawsuit; **— de gracias** thanksgiving.
accionar *vt* to gesticulate; to operate (*a machine*).
accionista *m* shareholder.
acebo *m* holly tree.
acebuche *m* wild olive tree.
acecinar *vt* to salt and dry meat.
acechar *vt* to waylay; *vi* to lie in ambush, wait (*for an opportunity*).
acecho *m* waylaying, lurking; **en —** in ambush.
acedía *f* sourness, acidity.
acedo *a* sour, acid.
aceitar *vt* to oil, lubricate.
aceite *m* (olive) oil; **— mineral** petroleum.
aceitera *f* oil jar, oil cruet; oil can.
aceitoso *a* oily, greasy.
aceituna *f* olive.
aceitunado *a* olive-colored.
acelerar *vt* to accelerate, hurry, expedite.
acémila *f* mule, beast of burden.
acendrado *a* purified, noble, exalted, finely-wrought, devoted, selfless.
acendrar *vt* to refine (*metals*); to purify.
acento *m* accent, stress.
acentuar *vt* to accentuate, lay stress on.
acepción *f* meaning, acceptation.
aceptación *f* acceptation; acceptance; approbation.
aceptar *vt* to accept, agree.
acequia *f* irrigation ditch, drain, canal.
acera *f* pavement, sidewalk.
acerado *a* steel; caustic (*comment*).
acerbo *a* bitter; sharp, cruel, harsh.
acerca de *prep* about, relating to, concerning.
acercar *vt* to approach; put, place near, bring near; *vr* **— a** to come near.
acero *m* steel, sword; **— fundido** cast steel.
acérrimo *a* bitter, fierce, out-and-out, staunch (*partisan etc*).
acertado *a* just right, to the point, correct.
acertar (ie) *vt* to hit the mark; to succeed; to be right, successful.
acervo *m* heap, store.
acético *a* acetic.
aciago *a* unfortunate, of ill omen, lowering.
acíbar *m* aloes; bitterness.
acibarar *vt* to make bitter.
acicalar *vt* to polish; *vr* to spruce up.
acicate *m* spur; stimulant.
acicatear *vt Ven* to spur.
acidez *f* acidity; sourness.
ácido *m* acid; *a* sour, tart.
acierto *m* success, knack; good (*hit, thing, point*).
acigarrado *a Chi* rough, (*voice*) hoarse.
acivilarse *vr Chi* to marry before a registrar.
aclamación *f* acclamation, applause; **por —** unanimously.
aclamar *vt* to applaud, acclaim.
aclaración *f* explanation.
aclarar *vt* to make clear, explain; to clarify.
aclimatación *f* acclimatization.
aclimatar *vt* to acclimatize.
acobardar *vt* to intimidate, daunt.
acocil *m Mex* shrimp.
acocote *m SA* foolishness, stupidity.
acogedor *a* welcoming, hospitable.
acoger *vt* to receive; to admit; *vr* to take refuge, shelter; to shelter.
acogida *f* reception, welcome.
acolchar *vt* to quilt.
acolchonar *vt SA* to quilt, cushion.
acólito *m* acolyte.
acomedido *a SA* obsequious, compliant.
acomedirse *vr SA* to offer oneself, volunteer.
acometer *vt* to assault, attack; to undertake.
acometida *f* attack, assault.
acomodado *a* well-to-do.
acomodador *m* usher; (*lit*) adaptor.
acomodar *vt* to accommodate; to make comfortable, to reconcile.
acomodarse *vr SA* to sit down; *Arg* to obtain a job through friends, marry a wealthy woman.
acomodo *m* employment; compromise, arrangement, bribe.
acompañamiento *m* attendance, retinue; accompaniment.
acompañar *vt* to accompany, go with; to keep company.
acondicionar *vt* to arrange, prepare.
acongojar *vt* to afflict, oppress, grieve.
aconsejar *vt* to advise, counsel.
acontecer *vi* to happen, occur.
acontecimiento *m* event.
acopio *m* gathering, collecting.
acoplamiento *m* coupling.
acoplar *vt* to join, couple.
acorazado *m* ironclad (*battleship*).
acordar (ue) *vt* to agree to; to concert; to tune; *vr* **— de** to remember, recollect.
acorde *a* in conformity with; *m* chord.
acordeón *m* accordion.
acordonado *a Mex* lean, (*animals*) thin.
acorralar *vt* to shut up cattle, corral; to corner.

acortar *vt* to shorten, cut short.
acosar *vt* to pursue closely; to importune, harass.
acostar (ue) *vt* to lay down; put to bed ; *vr* to go to bed, to lie down.
acostumbrar *vt* to use, to accustom; *vi* to be in the habit; *vr* **— a** to get used to.
acotación *f* marginal note; annotation.
acotar *vt* to set the bounds (*of land*).
acre *a* bitter, sour; acrid (*smoke*); mordant; *m* acre.
acrecentar *vt* to increase.
acreditar *vt* to credit; to give assurance; to establish, answer for; to prove.
acreedor *m* creditor;**— de** worthy of, deserving.
acribar *vt* to sieve.
acribillar *vt* to riddle (with bullets); to pierce.
acriollarse *vr SA* to become like a native.
acrisolar *vt* to assay (*metals*); to purify, put to the test.
acritud *f* sourness; mordancy, bitterness.
acta *f* record, minute; election return; *pl* **libro de —s** minute book; **levantar acta** draw up affidavit etc.
actitud *f* attitude.
activar *vt* to speed up, set in motion.
actividad *f* activity; quickness.
activo *a* active; diligent, nimble; *m* assets, credit balance.
acto *m* act, action: **— continuo** immediately afterwards; **en el —** at once.
actor *m* actor; plaintiff, claimant.
actriz *f* actress.
actuación *f* acting, performance of judicial or legal acts, rôle.
actual *a* present day, topical.
actualidades *f pl* news; **en la actualidad** nowadays.
actualizar *vt* to bring up to date.
actuar *vt* to act; to discharge (*duty*); to put in action.
actuario *m* actuary, clerk (*in court*).
acuarela *f* watercolor.
acuático *a* aquatic, water-.
acuciar *vt* to drive on; to long for; to be persecuted by (*remorse etc*).
acucioso *a* diligent, zealous, eager.
acuclillarse *vr* to squat, crouch.
acudir *vi* to have recourse to; to gather around; *vt* to assist, succor; to come.
acueducto *m* aqueduct.
acuerdo *m* agreement; decree; resolution; **¡de —!** right!
acullá *ad* yonder.
acumulación *f* accumulation.
acumulador *m* accumulator, car battery.
acumular *vt* to accumulate; to heap up.
acuñar *vt* to coin, mint; to wedge.
acuoso *a* watery, aqueous.
acure *m Col, Ven* guinea pig.
acurrucarse *vr* to curl up.
acusación *f* accusation, charge.
acusar *vt* to accuse, blame;**— recibo** to acknowledge receipt.
acusete *m SA* informer, talebearer.
acústica *f* acoustics.
achacar *vt* to impute, blame, lay blame on.
achacoso *a* sickly, full of ailments, ailing.
achancharse *vr Per* to become lazy
achaque *m* ailment; habitual in disposition; weakness.
achicar *vt* to diminish; *vr* to eat humble pie.
achicharrar *vt* to cook crisp.
achiguarse *vr Arg, Chi* to warp bulge, sag.
achichinque *m Mex* servile supporter.
achicopalarse *vr Mex* to dishearten, discourage.
achicoria *f* chicory.
acholado *an SA* half Indian; half-breed.
acholar *vt Chi, Per* to disconcert; shame.
acholo *m Chi* embarrassment.
achucutarse *vr CA* to become disheartened.
achunchar *vt Chi* to foil, frustrate.
achurador *m RP* slaughterer, murderer; opportunist.
achuras *f pl* giblets.
achurero *m RP* tripe and giblet vendor.
adagio *m* proverb, saying, adage.
adalid *m* leader, champion.
Adán *m* Adam.
adaptación *f* adaptation.
adaptar *vt* to adapt, fit.
adarga *f* shield.
adecuado *a* adequate, fit, appropriate, seemly.
adefesio *m* nonsense; ridiculous person.
adefesioso *a SA* nonsensical, extravagant.
adelantado *a* advanced; *m* governor (*of province*).
adelantamiento *m* progress, advance.
adelantar *vt* to advance, go ahead; *vr* to go forward, take the lead.
adelante *ad* forward, onward; **¡—!** come in!; **en —** henceforth, from now on.
adelanto *m* progress; advance (*payment*).
adelfa *f* rose-bay.
adelgazar *vt* to attenuate, make thin, slim.
ademán *m* gesture, look; *pl* manners.
además *ad* besides, moreover, further.
adentro *ad* inside, within.
adepto *m* adept.
aderezar *vt* to prepare, adorn, make ready, dress (*salad*).

aderezo *m* dressing; set of jewels.
adeudar *vt* to debit, charge; to be in debt.
adherir *vi* to adhere, stick.
adhesión *f* adhesion; support.
adición *f* addition, sum; *f SA* check, bill.
adicionar *vt* to add; to make additions.
adicto *a* addicted, attached; *n* supporter.
adiestrar *vt* to train; to teach; to make skillful.
adinerado *a* wealthy, moneyed.
adiós *excl* good-bye, adieu.
aditamento *m* increase, addition.
aditivo *m* additive.
adivinanza *f* guess; riddle.
adivinar *vt* to foretell the future, guess; to solve (riddle).
adivino *m* soothsayer.
adjudicación *f* adjudication, allotment.
adjudicar *vt* to allot, to adjudge, award.
adjuntar *vt* to enclose, attach (*in letter*).
adjunto *a* joined, attached, enclosed (*in letter*); *m* assistant.
administración *f* management, administration; **en—** in trust.
administrador *m* manager, administrator, trustee.
administrar *vt* to manage, govern, administer.
administrativo *a* administrative.
admirable *a* admirable.
admiración *f* wonder, admiration.
admirar *vt* to admire; to astonish; *vr* to be surprised.
admisible *a* admissible.
admitir *vt* to admit, concede; to receive.
admonición *f* warning.
adobar *vt* to dress (*food*); to pickle.
adobe *m Mex* sun-dried brick, adobe.
adobo *m* (*seasoning, dressing*) ingredients.
adolecer *vi* to ail, be ill; to be subject to; to suffer from.
adolescente *an* adolescent.
adonde *ad* whither, where.
adopción *f* adoption.
adoptar *vt* to adopt.
adoquín *m* paving stone; *Arg* cobblestone.
adoración *f* adoration; worship.
adorar *vt* to adore, worship.
adormecer *vt* to lull one asleep; *vi* to fall asleep.
adormidera *f* poppy.
adornar *vt* to adorn, ornament; to garnish.
adorno *m* ornament, finery.
adquirir *vt* to acquire, get.
adquisición *f* acquisition, attainment, acquiring, getting.
adrede *ad* on purpose, purposely.
adscribir *vt* to ascribe; to appoint (*to a post*).
aduana *f* customhouse; *pl* customs.
aduanero *a* customs; *m* customs officer.
aduar *m* horde (*gypsies etc*); *SA* Indian settlement.
aducir *vt* to bring forward, adduce, cite.
adueñarse *vr* to take possession of, lay hold of; to seize.
adulación *f* flattery.
adular *vt* to flatter, compliment; fawn on.
adulete *m SA* flatterer.
adulteración *f* adulteration.
adulterar *vr* to adulterate, falsify, corrupt.
adulterio *m* adultery.
adulto *m* adult, grown up.
adusto *a* gloomy, doleful; austere, severe.
advenedizo *m* upstart, newcomer; *a* parvenu, foreign, upstart.
advenimiento *m* advent, arrival, coming.
adventicio *a* adventitious.
adverbio *m* adverb.
adversario *m* opponent, adversary.
adversidad *f* misfortune, calamity.
adverso *a* adverse, contrary.
advertencia *f* advice, warning; (*in book*) foreword.
advertir (**ie**) *vt* to advise, warn; to notice, note; to instruct, give warning.
adviento *m* advent.
adyacente *a* adjacent.
aéreo *a* aerial, fantastic; **correo —** airmail.
aeronáutica *f* aeronautics.
aeroplano *m* airplane.
aeropuerto *m* airport.
afabilidad *f* affability, courtesy, courteousness, kindliness.
afable *a* courteous, affable, condescending.
afamado *a* renowned, celebrated, famous.
afán *m* anxiety, solicitude; eagerness, desire.
afanaduría *f Mex* casualty ward.
afanar *vi* to try hard, strive; to toil, labor; *Arg* to steal.
afanoso *a* anxious, solicitous, restive, painstaking.
afear *vt* to deform, make ugly; to condemn, decry.
afección *f* fondness; disease, infection.
afectación *f* affectation, daintiness.
afectado *a* conceited; *Arg* hurt, ill.
afectar *vt* to affect; to produce effect; to feign.
afecto *m* affection, fondness; *a* affectionate, inclined.
afectuoso *m* loving, affectionate.
afeitar *vt* to shave; to make up; to embellish.
afeite *m* paint, rouge; *pl* personal adornments.
afeminado *a* effeminate.

afeminar *vt* to make effeminate, lose virility; *vr* to become effeminate.
aferrado *a* headstrong, obstinate; deeply attached to.
aferrar *vt* to grapple, grasp.
afianzamiento *m* security, bail.
afianzar *vt* to fasten, fix; to secure (*by bond*), go bail; to guarantee.
afición *f* interest; liking, affection.
aficionado *m* amateur, fan; *a* fond of, interested in.
aficionarse *vr* to take a liking, a fancy to.
afilado *a* keen, sharp; tapering.
afilar *vt* to sharpen; to whet; to taper; *Arg* (*sl*) to court.
afiliación *f* affiliation.
afiliar *vt* to affiliate; join (*society*).
afiligranado *a* filigree; delicate.
afín *a* related, akin; *m* relation by affinity.
afinación *f* tuning (*of instruments*).
afinar *vt* to make fine, purify; (*mus*) to tune.
afinidad *f* affinity; resemblance.
afirmación *f* assertion, positive statement; declaration.
afirmar *vt* to affirm, state positively, insist; to make fast.
afirmativo *a* positive, affirmative.
aflicción *f* grief, sorrow, anguish.
afligir *vt* to grieve, afflict, pain.
aflojar *vt* to loosen, relax, slacken.
afloramiento *m* outcrop (*coal etc*).
afluencia *f* gathering together (*of people*), crowd.
afluente *a* copious; *m* tributary, stream.
afluir *vi* to flow in, run into; to stream; to congregate.
afonía *f* loss of voice.
aforismo *m* aphorism.
afortunado *a* lucky, fortunate, happy.
afrancesado *m* Frenchified Spaniard.
afrecho *m SA* sawdust; *Arg* brain.
afrenta *f* affront, insult, disgrace.
afrentar *vt* to affront, abuse.
afrentoso *a* ignominious.
África *f* Africa.
africano *an* African.
afrontar *vt* to confront, put face to face.
afuera *ad* outside, abroad; *f pl* outskirts, environs, suburbs.
afutrarse *vr SA* to dress in style.
agacharse *vr* to stoop, squat, crouch.
agalla *f* gill (*of fish*); *pl* **—s** (*fam*) guts.
agalludo *a SA* cunning, astute.
agape *m* banquet.
agarradera *f* handle; **tener buenas —s** to have influence, pull.
agarradero *m* anchorage; handle, haft.
agarrado *a* closefisted, mean.
agarrar *vt* to grasp, seize, lay hold of, grip.
agarrotar *vt* to pinion, bind tightly.
agasajar *vt* to entertain, regale, fête.
agasajo *m* kind reception, present, hospitality, party.
agazapar *vt* to grasp, seize; *vr* to vouch.
agencia *f* agency.
agenciar *vt* to manage; to get; to negotiate.
agenda *f* memorandum.
agente *m* agent; traffic policeman; **— de cambios** stockbroker; **— de policía** policeman.
agigantado *a* gigantic.
ágil *a* nimble, agile, brisk, alert.
agio *m* usury.
agiotista *m* usurer.
agitación *f* agitation, disturbance, uneasiness.
agitar *vt* to agitate, ruffle; to wave (*hands etc*); *vr* to be upset; to flutter.
aglomerar *vt* to agglomerate, heap up.
agnóstico *an* agnostic.
agobiar *vt* to oppress, weigh down.
agolparse *vr* to crowd together.
agonía *f* agony, violent pain; death pangs.
agonizante *mf* dying person.
agonizar *vi* to be dying.
agorero *m* soothsayer, diviner.
agostar *vt* to parch, wither.
agosto *m* August; harvest; **hacer su —** to feather one's nest.
agotado *a* tired out, worn out.
agotar *vt* to exhaust; to drain off (*liquid*); *vr* to be sold out (*of edition etc*).
agraciar *vt* to adorn, make graceful; to grant a favor; to grace.
agradable *a* agreeable, enjoyable, pleasant.
agradar *vt* to please; to like; to gratify.
agradecer *vt* to thank, be grateful, thankful for.
agradecimiento *m* gratitude, thanks.
agrado *m* pleasure; agreeableness; **de mi —** what I like.
agrandar *vt* to enlarge, increase.
agrario *a* of the land, agrarian.
agravar *vt* to make heavier; to aggravate.
agraviar *vt* to wrong, offend.
agravio *m* offense, insult.
agravión *a Chi* sensitive, touchy.
agraz *m* unripe grape; juice of this grape; **en —** unseasonably.
agredir *vt* to attack, assault.
agregado *m* attaché; aggregate; *Arg, Col, Ven* tenant farmer.
agregar *vt* to add, aggregate.
agresión *f* aggression, assault, attack (*personal*).
agresivo *a* aggressive.
agreste *a* rustic, wild.
agriar *vt* to make sour; *vr* to become sour.
agrícola *a* agricultural.
agricultor *m* farmer.
agridulce *a* bittersweet.

agrietarse *vr* to crack, split.
agringarse *vr SA* to become like North American, foreigner.
agrio *a* sour; rough; bitter, tart.
agronomía *f* rural economy, husbandry.
agrónomo *m* agricultural expert.
agrupación *f* cluster, group, association.
agrupar *vt* to group, cluster.
agua *f* water; **— dulce** fresh water; **— potable** drinking water; **— salada** salt water; **— de manantial** spring water.
aguacate *m* avocado pear; *SA* foolishness, stupidity.
aguacero *m* heavy shower, squall.
aguachar *vt Chi* to tame horses.
aguada *f* watercolor.
aguado *a* watered (*of wine etc*).
aguador *m* water carrier.
aguaitar *vt SA* to lie in ambush, spy, watch.
aguafiestas *mf* wet blanket, killjoy.
aguamala *f Mex* jellyfish.
aguamanil *m* ewer, water jug; washstand.
aguamarina *f* aquamarine.
aguantada *f SA* suffering, enduring.
aguantar *vt* to endure, bear, (with-) stand; *vr* to contain o.s.
aguar *vt* to dilute, water.
aguardar *vt* to wait, expect, await.
aguardiente *m* spirit similar to brandy, whisky.
aguarrás *m* turpentine.
agudeza *f* sharpness, keenness; subtlety; witticism, repartee.
agudo *a* sharp, keen; witty; penetrating.
agüero *m* omen, prognostication.
aguijar *vt* to spur, incite.
aguijón *m* sting (*of wasp etc*); **dar coces contra el—** to kick against the pricks.
aguijonear *vt* to spur on.
águila *f* eagle.
aguileño *a* aquiline, hawk-nosed.
aguilucho *m* eaglet.
aguinaldo *m* Christmas (*or* Epiphany) present.
aguja *f* needle; hand (*of watch*); (*rl*) point, switch; steeple.
agujerear *vt* to make holes; to bore, pierce.
agujero *m* hole.
agujetas *f* shoelaces; pins and needles, cramp.
agustino *m* Augustinian.
aguzar *vt* to sharpen; **— las orejas** to prick up the ears.
aherrojar *vt* to chain, put in irons.
ahí *ad* there, in that place.
ahijado *m* godson.
¡ahijuna! *excl Arg, Chi* interjection expressing surprise, admiration.
ahinco *m* earnestness, eagerness, ardor.
ahijar *vt* to adopt.
ahito *m* indigestion, surfeit; *a* satiated.
ahogar *vt* to suffocate, smother, drown; to quench; *vr* to be drowned.
ahogo *m* anguish, affliction.
ahondar *vi* to go deep, investigate.
ahora *ad* now, at present; **por —** for the moment; **— mismo** right now.
ahorcajadas *ad* **a —** astride (*horse*).
ahorcar *vt* to hang (*a man*).
ahorita *ad* just now, soon.
ahorrar *vt* to save (*money, trouble*).
ahorro *m* saving, thrift; **caja de —s** savings bank.
ahuecar *vt* to hollow, to make hollow; to deepen (*voice*).
ahuizote *m Mex* nuisance, troublesome person.
ahumar *vt* to smoke (*fish etc*).
ahuyentar *vt* to drive away, banish (*care etc*).
aindiado *a SA* person who resembles an Indian.
airado *a* furious, wrathful.
airarse *vr* to grow angry.
aire *m* air, aspect, look; **al — libre** in the open air.
airoso *a* graceful; airy; successful; **salir — de** to emerge with credit from.
aislador *m* insulator.
aislar *vt* to isolate, cut off; to insulate.
ajar *vt* to fade, tarnish; to spoil.
ajedrez *m* chess.
ajenjo *m* wormwood; absinth.
ajeno *a* another's; foreign, strange, remote.
ajetreo *m* much coming and going.
ají *m* red pepper.
ajicero *m Chi* seller of chili; jar for chili.
ajo *m* garlic.
ajolote *m Mex* mud puppy.
ajonjolí *m* sesame.
ajorca *f* bracelet.
ajuar *m* apparel; household furniture; trousseau.
ajustado *a* exact, right; (*clothes*) close-fitting, tight.
ajustar *vt* to adjust, agree, concert, settle; to hire (*servant etc*); to fit (*clothes*).
ajuste *m* agreement, settlement; fit; engagement (*of maid etc*).
ajusticiar *vt* to put to death, execute.
ala *f* wing; brim (*of hat*).
alabanza *f* praise.
alabar *vt* to praise, extol.
alabarda *f* halberd.
alabastro *m* alabaster.
alabearse *vr* to warp.
alacena *f* cupboard, closet, locker.
alacrán *m* scorpion.
alado *a* winged; feathered; light.
alambicado *a* distilled; euphuistic.
alambicar *vt* to distill.
alambique *m* still.
alambre *m* wire; **— para cercas** fencing wire; **— erizado** barbed wire.

alameda *f* poplar grove, promenade, avenue.
álamo *m* poplar; **— temblón** aspen.
alano *m* mastiff.
alar *m* overhanging roof; *m Col* sidewalk.
alarde *m* ostentation, boasting; **hacer — de** to boast of, show off, display.
alargar *vt* to lengthen; to prolong; to put out (*hand*).
alarido, a *m* shout, outcry; *f* hue and cry.
alarma *m* alarm.
alba *f* dawn.
albacea *m* testamentary executor.
albañal *m* sewer.
albañil *m* mason, bricklayer.
albarca *f* (*peasant*) sandal. *see* **abarca.**
albarda *f* packsaddle.
albaricoque *m* apricot.
albazo *m Ec, Mex* reveille.
albedrío *m* free will.
albéitar *m* farrier, veterinary surgeon.
alberca *f* pond, pool, tank, vat.
albérchigo *m* peach.
albergar *vt* to lodge, shelter, harbor (*hopes etc*).
albergue *m* shelter, (mountain) hut, refuge.
Alberto *m* Albert.
albis: quedarse en — to draw a blank, to remain as ignorant (*after explanation etc*).
albo *a* white.
albóndiga *f* spiced meatball.
albor *m* whiteness; dawn.
alborada *f* dawn of day; reveille.
alborear *vi* to dawn.
albornoz *m* burnoose.
alborotar *vt* to disturb, make noise; *vr* to get excited, riot.
alboroto *m* hubbub, row, riot.
alborozar *vt* to exhilarate; *vr* t[illegible] merry.
alborozo *m* merriment; noisy joy, merrymaking.
albricias *f pl* reward for good news; *excl* what joy!
álbum *m* album.
albur *m* dace; *SA* risk, chance.
alcachofa *f* artichoke.
alcahuete, a *m* pimp, procurer; *f* bawd.
alcaide *m* jailer; governor of a castle.
alcalde *m* mayor.
alcaldía *f* office, jurisdiction and house of mayor.
alcance *m* overtaking; deficit; reach; range; supplement; **al — de** within reach of; *pl* capacity.
alcanforarse *m SA, Hond, Ven* to disappear, evaporate.
alcantarilla *f* drain; sewer.
alcanzar *vt* to reach; to attain, obtain; to overtake; to be sufficient.
alcatraz *m* gannet, solan goose.
alcázar *m* castle; fortress; quarterdeck.
alcoba *f* bedroom; alcove.
alcohol *m* alcohol.
alcornoque *m* cork tree; blockhead.
alcubilla *f* reservoir, water tank.
alcurnia *f* lineage, race.
alcuza *f* olive-oil container.
aldaba *f* knocker, door handle, latch.
aldabazo *f* knock (*on the door*).
aldea *f* village, hamlet.
aldeano *m* villager, countryman.
aleación *f* alloy.
aleccionar *vt* to teach, teach a lesson to.
aledaño *m* boundary (*of estate*).
alegación *f* argument; allegation.
alegar *vt* to allege, maintain, adduce.
alegato *m* allegation.
alegoría *f* allegory.
alegrar *vt* to make merry, enliven; *vr* to rejoice, be happy, be glad.
alegre *a* merry, gay, in high spirits.
alegría *f* merriment, mirth, joy.
alejamiento *m* removal, withdrawal.
alejar *vt* to remove (to a distance), take away, separate; *vr* to go away.
aleluya *m* alleluia; cheap verse.
alemán *an* German.
Alemania *f* Germany.
alentado *a* brave, spirited; encouraged.
alentar (ie) *vt* to breathe; to encourage, cheer.
alerce *m* larch tree.
alergia *f* allergy.
alero *m* eaves, gable end; (*aut*) mudguard, fender; overhanging roof.
alerta *ad* vigilantly; **estar —** to be on the watch.
aleta *f* small wing; fin (*of fish*).
aletargar *vt* to benumb; *vr* to fall into a lethargy.
aletear *vi* to flutter.
aleve *a* treacherous, perfidious.
alevosía *f* perfidy, treachery, breach of faith.
alfabeto *m* alphabet.
alfandoque *m SA* paste made with molasses, cheese and ginger.
alfanje *m* cutlass, scimitar.
alfarero *m* potter.
alfeñique *m* sugar paste; delicate person.
alférez *m* ensign, 2nd Lieutenant; standard bearer.
alfil *m* bishop (*in chess*).
alfiler *m* pin; **— de gancho** safety pin.
alfombra *f* carpet; floor carpet.
alfombrar *vt* to carpet; to spread carpet.
alfombrilla *f* rug.
alforja *f* saddlebag.
alforza *f* plait, tuck; scar.
alga *f* seaweed.
algarabía *f* gabble, clamor.
algarroba *f* carob.
algazara *f* noise of a crowd, hubbub.
álgido *a* cold, chilly.
algo *pn* something; *ad* somewhat.
algodón *m* cotton, cotton wool,

absorbent cotton; **géneros de —** cotton goods.
algodonero *m* cotton plant.
alguacil *m* constable, bailiff.
alguien *pn* somebody, someone.
alguno *pn a* some person, something; some; **alguna vez** sometimes; **— que otro** a few, quite a few.
alhaja *f* jewel.
alhajero *m* jewel case.
alharaquiento *a Mex* fussy; strident, clamorous.
alhóndiga *f* public granary.
aliado *m* ally.
aliaga *f* furze.
alianza *f* alliance, league.
aliarse *vr* to be allied, to enter a league.
alias *ad* otherwise, alias.
alicaído *a* weak, crestfallen, downcast.
alicantino *an* of Alicante.
alicates *m pl* pincers; nail trimmers, clippers.
aliciente *m* incitement, inducement.
alienación *f* alienation (*of mind*).
aliento *m* breath; courage.
aligerar *vt* to alleviate, lighten.
alijador *m* docker.
alimaña *f* vermin (*foxes etc*).
alimentación *f* nourishment; nutrition; feeding; **de mucha —** very nourishing.
alimentar *vt* to feed, nourish; to nurture.
alimenticio *a* nourishing.
alimento *m* food, nourishment, nutriment; *pl* alimony, pension.
alinear *vt* to line up; (*mil*) to dress (*ranks*); to straighten (*a line*).
aliñar *vt* to dress, season (*food*); to arrange.
aliño *m* dress, preparation, condiment; cleanliness.
alisar *vt* to plane; to polish, smooth; to slick (hair).
aliso *m* alder.
alistamiento *m* enrollment; conscription.
alistar *vtr* to prepare, make ready; to enlist.
aliviar *vt* to lighten, alleviate, soothe.
alivio *m* alleviation, ease; recovery, relief.
aljibe *m* raintank, rainwater cistern, well.
aljofaina *f* washbasin.
alma *f* soul, strength; inhabitant; **llegar al —** to strike home.
almacén *m* store, shop; warehouse, depository; *RP* grocer's (shop).
almacenar *vt* to store, hoard.
almacenero *m RP* grocer.
almáciga *f* seedbed.
almadraba *f* tunny-fishing net.
almanaque *m* almanac; *Arg* calendar.
almeja *f* mussel.
almena *f* battlement.
almendra *f* almond, kernel; *pl* **—s garapiñadas** sugared almonds; **—s de cacao** cocoa beans.
almendro *m* almond tree.
almiar *m* haystack.
almíbar *m* sugar syrup.
almibarado *a* endearing, coaxing; **lenguaje —** honeyed words.
almidón *m* starch.
almidonar *vt* to starch.
almirantazgo *m* admiralty.
almirante *m* admiral.
almohada *f* pillow, cushion.
almohadilla *f* cushion; pad; hassock.
almoneda *f* auction.
almorzar (ue) *vi* to lunch.
almuerzo *m* luncheon.
alnado, a *mf* stepchild.
alocado *a* crazed, wild.
alocución *f* allocution.
alojamiento *m* lodging; billet.
alojar *vt* to lodge; to quarter troops.
alondra *f* lark.
alpargata *f* hemp-soled sandal.
alpargatería *f* sandal factory.
Alpes, los *m pl* the Alps.
alpiste *m* canary seed.
alquería *f* grange, country house.
alquilar *vt* to let, hire, rent.
alquiler *m* letting, hiring; hire, rent.
alquimia *f* alchemy.
alquimista *m* alchemist.
alquitrán *m* tar; liquid pitch.
alrededor *ad* around, about; **— de** about.
alrededores *m pl* environs, outskirts; surroundings.
alta *f* discharge certificate (*hospital*); **dar de —** to discharge.
altavoz *m* loudspeaker.
altanería *f* hawking; haughtiness, pride, arrogance.
altanero *a* haughty, arrogant, high-handed.
altar *m* altar.
alterable *a* alterable.
alteración *f* alteration, change; strong emotion, perturbation; debasing (*coinage*).
alterar *vt* to alter; to upset, disturb; *vr* to be disconcerted.
altercado *m* controversy, wrangle, quarrel; strife.
alternar *vti* to alternate, take turns.
alternativa *f* alternative; **tomar la —** to become a fully-qualified matador.
alternativo *a* alternate.
alteza *f* highness; sublimity, excellence.
altibajo *m* unevenness (*of ground*); *pl* ups and downs.
altillo *m* attic.
altisonante *a* high-sounding.
altivez *f* haughtiness, pride.
altivo *a* haughty, proud, arrogant.
alto *a* high, tall, elevated; loud; *m* height; halt; **pasar por —** to omit, overlook.
altiplanicie *f* plateau.
altoparlante *m* loudspeaker.

altura *f* height; *pl* **en las —s de** in the latitude of.
alubia *f* kidney bean, French bean.
alucinación *f* hallucination.
alud *m* avalanche.
aludir *vi* to allude, refer to.
alumbrado *m* lighting, illumination; **— público** public lighting.
alumbramiento *m* (child)birth.
alumbrar *vt* to light, enlighten.
aluminio *m* aluminium.
alumno *m* pupil, student.
alusión *f* allusion, reference.
alusivo *a* allusive, referring to.
aluvión *m* alluvion.
alverja *f SA* pea.
alza *f* rise, advance in price; sights (*on rifle*).
alzada *f* height (*of horses*); **juez de —s** judge of appeal.
alzamiento *m* (the act of) lifting; uprising, revolt.
alzar *vt* to raise, lift up; to repeal; to cut (*cards*); *vr* to rise in rebellion; to get up.
allá *ad* there, yonder.
allanar *vt* to make even, level; to remove difficulties; *vr* to acquiesce.
allegado *m* relative; supporter.
allegar *vt* to gather, collect.
allende *ad* on the other side, beyond.
allí *ad* there; in that place.
ama *f* mistress (of a house), landlady; **— de llaves** housekeeper.
amabilidad *f* amiability, kindness, friendliness.
amable *a* kind.
amachinarse *vr CA, Col, Ven* to live in concubinage.
amaestrar *vt* to train, teach; to break in (*animals*).
amagar *vt* to presage, threaten, portend.
amago *m* foreboding, threat.
amainar *vt* to relax; to lower the sails; *vi* to lessen (*of wind*).
amalgama *f* amalgam.
amalgamar *vt* to amalgamate.
amamantar *vt* to give suck, nurse.
amanecer *vi* to dawn; **al —** at daybreak.
amansador *m SA* horse-breaker.
amansar *vt* to tame; to pacify.
amante *m f* lover.
amanzanar *vt Arg* to divide a plot of land into squares.
amapola *f* poppy.
amar *vt* to love, be fond of, cherish.
amargado *a* embittered, soured.
amargar *vt* to make bitter; to embitter.
amargo *a* bitter; acrid; embittered.
amargura *f* bitterness; affliction.
amarillento *a* yellowish, golden.
amarillo *a* yellow.
amarrar *vt* to lash, fasten; to bind; to tie up (*of ship*).
amartelar *vt* to enamor, court.
amartillar *vt* to hammer; to cock (*pistol*).
amasar *vt* to knead.
amasijo *m* dough; mash.
amatista *f* amethyst.
amazona *f* amazon; riding skirt.
Amazonas, el Río *m* the River Amazon.
ambajes *m pl* circumlocution, roundabout phrases; **sin —** openly, to the point; **habla sin —** don't beat about the bush.
ámbar *m* amber.
ambición *f* ambition; aspiration.
ambicionar *vt* to covet, desire strongly.
ambicioso *a* ambitious, aspiring.
ambidextro *a* ambidextrous.
ambiente *m* atmosphere, air, surroundings, aura; *Arg, Urug* room.
ambigüedad *f* ambiguity, double meaning.
ambiguo *a* ambiguous, doubtful, undefined.
ámbito *m* compass, area.
ambos, ambas *a pl* both; the one and the other.
ambulancia *f* field hospital; ambulance.
ambulante *a* roving, itinerant.
amedrentar *vt* to frighten, intimidate.
amenaza *f* threat, menace.
amenazar *vt* to threaten; to be impending.
amenidad *f* amenity, agreeableness.
amenizar *vt* to render pleasant or agreeable, to add a pleasant variety to.
amenguar *vt* to diminish.
ameno *a* pleasant, delightful; varied.
América del Norte *f* North America.
América del Sur *f* South America.
América latina *f* Latin America.
americana *f* jacket, lounge coat.
americano *an* American, South-American.
ametralladora *f* machine-gun.
amigable *a* friendly; amicable.
amigo *m* friend.
amilanar *vt* to terrify, cow.
aminorar *vt* to lessen.
amistad *f* friendship, amity.
amistoso *a* friendly, cordial.
amnistía *f* amnesty.
amo *m* master, proprietor; overseer, boss.
amodorrarse *vr* to grow drowsy.
amolar *vt* to whet, grind, sharpen.
amoldar *vt* to mold, fashion; *vr* to adapt o.s., fit into.
amonestación *f* admonition, warning; banns.
amonestar *vt* to warn, admonish.
amontonar *vt* to heap up, hoard.
amor *m* love, affection; fondness; **— propio** conceit.
amoratado *a* livid, bruised.
amordazar *vt* to gag, muzzle.

amorío *m* love-making; flirtation; love affair.
amoroso *a* loving, affectionate.
amortajar *vt* to shroud (*corpse*).
amortiguar *vt* to temper, weaken; *vi* to deaden.
amortización *f* amortization; redemption; **fondo de —** sinking fund.
amotinar *vt* to excite rebellion; *vr* to mutiny.
amparar *vt* to shelter, protect.
amparo *m* shelter, protection, asylum.
ampliación *f* enlargement, broadening.
ampliar *vt* to amplify, enlarge, extend.
amplificación *f* amplification, enlargement.
amplificar *vt* to amplify, enlarge.
amplio *a* ample, wide, large, broad, full.
amplitud *f* largeness, width, fullness.
ampolla *f* blister; cruet.
ampulosidad *f* verbosity, pompousness.
amueblar *vt* to furnish.
amurallar *vt* to wall, surround with ramparts.
Ana *f* Anne, Hannah.
anacoreta *m* anchorite.
anacronismo *m* anachronism.
ánade *mf* duck.
anales *m pl* annals.
analfabeto *m* illiterate person.
análisis *f* analysis.
analítico *a* analytic.
analizar *vt* to analyze; to parse.
analogía *f* analogy.
análogo *a* analogous; similar.
ananá *f* (*or* **ananás** *m*) pineapple; *see* **piña.**
anaquel *m* shelf.
anaranjado *a* orange-colored.
anarquía *f* anarchy.
anárquico *a* anarchic, anarchical.
anatema *m* anathema, excommunication.
anatomía *f* anatomy.
anca *f* croup; rump, haunch.
anciano *a* old, ancient; *m* old man.
ancla *f* anchor; *pl* **levar —s** to weigh anchor.
ancladero *m* anchorage, anchoring place.
anclar *vt* to anchor.
ancuviña *f SA* grave of the Chilean Indians.
ancho *a* wide, broad; loose-fitting, slack.
anchoa *f* anchovy.
anchura *f* width, breadth, latitude.
anchuroso *a* spacious, broad.
anda *f Chi, Guat, Per* stretcher, litter, bier.
andada *f* track, haunt; *pl* **volver a las —s** to return to the old game (*vice etc*).
andadura *f* gait, pacing; amble.
Andalucía *f* Andalusia.
andaluz *an* Andalusian.
andamio *m* scaffolding.
andanada *f* broadside; reprimand.
andar *vi* to go, walk, move along; to elapse; **a poco —** within a short time; **— de cabeza** to be topsy-turvy.
andariego *a* roving, restless.
andarín *a* very fond of walking.
andas *f pl* litter, bier.
andén *m* (*rl*) platform; horse path.
andrajo *m* rag.
andrajoso *a* ragged, in tatters.
Andrés *m* Andrew.
anécdota *f* anecdote, tale.
andurriales *m pl* by-roads, out-of-the-way place; muddy patch.
anegar *vt* to inundate, flood, drown (*sorrow etc*).
anejo *a* dependent, subsidiary.
anexar *vt* to annex; to join.
anexión *f* annexation, union.
anexo *a* annexed; *m* schedule.
anfibio *a* amphibious.
anfiteatro *m* amphitheater; (*theat fam*) top balcony.
anfitrión *m* host.
ángel *m* angel; **tener —** to be very charming.
angélico *a* angelic; benevolent, very kind.
angina *f* quinsy; pharyngitis; **— de pecho** angina pectoris.
anglicano *an* Anglican.
angosto *a* narrow, limited.
angostura *f* narrowness; distress.
anguila *f* eel.
angular *a* angular; **piedra —** corner stone.
ángulo *m* angle.
angustia *f* anguish, anxiety, affliction.
angustiar *vt* to cause anguish, afflict, distress.
anhelante *a* eager, yearning.
anhelar *vt* to long; to covet, desire.
anhelo *m* longing, eagerness, desire.
anidar *vi* to nestle; to dwell.
anilina *f* aniline.
anillo *m* (*plain*) ring; small hoop; **— de boda** wedding ring; **— de compromiso** engagement ring.
ánima *f* soul, ghost; spirit; *pl* **día de las —s** All Souls' Day.
animación *f* animation, liveliness, bustle.
animado *a* lively; enthusiastic, keen.
animadversión *f* animadversion, critical comment, pointed remark.
animal *m* animal; brute; blockhead.
animar *vt* to encourage, incite, animate, enliven; *vr* to gain confidence, be reassured, take courage.
ánimo *m* courage; mind, intention; enthusiasm.
animosidad *f* animosity, courage, valor, boldness.

animoso *a* brave, enthusiastic, spirited.
aniquilación *f* annihilation, extinction.
aniquilar *vt* to annihilate, destroy, crush.
anís *m* aniseed; anise; anise liqueur.
anisado *m* aniseed brandy; aniseed spirit.
aniversario *m* anniversary.
ano *m* anus.
anoche *ad* last night.
anochecer *vi* to grow dark; **al —** at nightfall; **anochece** night is falling, it is growing dark.
anodino *a* anodyne; pale, colorless.
anomalía *f* anomaly; irregularity.
anómalo *a* anomalous, irregular.
anonadamiento *m* bewilderment, stupefaction.
anonadar *vt* to annihilate, stun, overwhelm.
anónimo *a* anonymous.
anormal *a* abnormal.
anotación *f* note; annotation.
anotar *vt* to note down; to comment.
ansia *f* anxiety; longing, ardent desire; greediness.
ansiar *vt* to desire anxiously, long for, hanker after.
ansiedad *f* anxiety; longing.
ansioso *a* anxious; desirous.
antagónico *a* antagonistic.
antagonista *m* antagonist; competitor.
antaño *ad* last year; in olden times, of old.
ante *prep* before; **— todo to begin** with, above all; *m* dressed buckskin; *Per* kind of beverage; *Mex* kind of dessert.
anteanoche *ad* night before last.
anteayer *ad* day before yesterday.
antebrazo *m* forearm.
antecámara *f* antechamber; lobby.
antecedente *a m* antecedent; *a* previous, earlier.
anteceder *vt* to precede, go before.
antecesor *m* predecessor, forefather.
antedicho *a* aforesaid; above-mentioned.
antelación *f* precedence (in order of time).
antemano *ad* beforehand; **de —** beforehand, previously.
antena *f* lateen yard; (*television*) aerial; feeler (*of insect*).
antenoche *ad* night before last.
anteojo *m* spyglass; *m pl* eyeglasses, spectacles.
antepasados *m pl* forefathers, ancestors.
antepecho *m* breastwork, parapet, sill, balcony.
anteponer *vt* to put before; to prefer.
anteportada *f* flyleaf.
anterior *a* former, earlier, previous.
anterioridad *f* priority; **con —** previously.
antes *ad* before; rather.
antesala *f* antechamber.
anticipación *f* anticipation, foretaste.
anticipado *a* premature, in advance.
anticipar *vt* to anticipate; to advance (*money*); to forestall.
anticuado *a* antiquated, obsolete.
anticuario *m* antiquarian, antique dealer.
antídoto *m* antidote; counterpoison.
antifaz *m* veil, mask.
antífona *f* antiphony, anthem.
antigualla *f* antique; a fright, outmoded clothes *etc*.
antiguamente *ad* in olden times, formerly.
antigüedad *f* antiquity, oldness; seniority; *pl* antiques.
antiguo *a* ancient, old, antique; former.
antílope *m* antelope.
antillano *an* Antillian, West Indian.
Antillas *f pl* West Indies, Antilles.
antipara *f* screen.
antipatía *f* antipathy, aversion, lack of appeal, dislike.
antipático *a* displeasing; repugnant, disagreeable, unpleasant, not congenial.
antípodas *m pl* antipodes.
antiquísimo *a* very ancient.
antítesis *f* antithesis; opposition; opposite, contrary.
antojadizo *a* whimsical, capricious, faddy, difficult to please.
antojarse *vr* to desire, long, have a fancy for; to assume, to think.
antojo *m* whim, vehement desire, caprice, fancy.
antología *f* anthology.
Antonio *m* Anthony.
antorcha *f* torch, taper.
antro *m* cavern, cave, den.
antropófago *m* cannibal.
antropología *f* anthropology.
anual *a* annual; yearly.
anualidad *f* annuity; annual recurrence.
anuario *m* annual; year book.
anublar *vt* to cloud; to darken, obscure.
anudar *vt* to knot; to unite.
anulación *f* annulment, cancellation, abrogation.
anular *vt* to annul, rescind; *a* annular.
anunciación *f* annunciation.
anunciar *vt* to announce, state; to advertise.
anuncio *m* announcement, omen, forerunner; advertisement, notice.
anverso *m* obverse.
anzuelo *m* fish hook; bait; **tragar el —** to be duped, swallow the bait.
añadido *m* hair switch.
añadidura *f* addition.
añadir *vt* to add, join.
añejo *a* old, musty, rich old (*wine*).
añicos *m pl* small pieces: bits;

hacerse — to wear oneself to a shred.
año *m* year; **— bisiesto** leap year.
añoranza *f* homesickness, nostalgia, longing.
añoso *a* aged, stricken in years.
aojar *vt* to bewitch.
apacentamiento *m* grazing (*of cattle*).
apacentar (ie) *vt* to graze, feed.
apacible *a* peaceable, meek, serene, calm.
apaciguamiento *m* pacification, calming.
apaciguar *vt* to appease, pacify; *vi* to abate, grow calm.
apachurrar *vt SA* to crush, flatten.
apadrinar *vt* to act as godfather, as second (*in duel*); to support.
apagado *a* (*colors*) sober, lusterless, dull, (*sound*) dull, muted; (*fire*) out.
apagar *vt* to put out, quench; to soften (*colors*).
apalabrar *vt* to agree verbally, to engage beforehand.
apalear *vt* to beat, cudgel; to winnow.
apaleo *m* beating.
apandillarse *vr* to band together (*in league or faction*).
apañado *a* skillful.
apañar *vt* to seize, grasp.
aparador *m* sideboard, buffet.
aparato *m* apparatus, instrument; ostentation, show.
aparatoso *a* showy, pompous.
aparecer *vi* to appear; to come up, turn up.
aparecido *m* ghost.
aparejado *a* ready, fit, equipped.
aparejar *vt* to get ready; to saddle or harness (*horses*), to rig (*ship*).
aparejo *m* apparel, harness, gear; *pl* tools.
aparentar *vt* to affect, feign, to seem (*to have etc*).
aparente *a* apparent; evident.
aparición *f* apparition, appearance.
apariencia *f* appearance, aspect; **salvar las —s** to keep up appearances.
apartado — postal *m* P.O. box number; *a* retired, secluded, out of touch.
apartamento *m SA* flat, apartment.
apartamiento *m* isolation, separation.
apartar *vt* to separate, put (aside, on one side); to divide.
aparte *m* break (*in line, paragraph*); an aside (*theat*); *ad* separately, outside of, distant.
apasionado *a* passionate.
apasionar *vt* to inspire passion; *vr* to become impassioned; to become passionately fond of.
apaste *m Guat, Hond, Mex* earthenware tub with handles.
apatía *f* apathy.
apático *a* apathetic.
apeadero *m* halt, stop (*on railway*).
apearse *vr* to alight, dismount.
apechugar *vt* to undertake with spirit, to tackle.
apedrear *vt* to stone.
apegarse *vr* to adhere to; to be much taken by a thing.
apego *m* attachment, fondness.
apelación *f* appeal.
apelante *m* apellant.
apelar *vt* to appeal, have recourse to.
apellidar *vt* to call by name.
apellido *m* surname; family name.
apenado *a* sorry; troubled.
apenar *vt* to cause pain; *vr* to grieve.
apenas *a* scarcely, hardly; no sooner than.
apéndice *m* appendix, supplement.
apercibimiento *m* preparation; providing; summons (*law*).
apercibir *vt* to make ready; to provide.
aperitivo *a m* appetizer, aperitif.
apero *m* equipment; implements, tools.
aperos *m pl SA* riding accouterments.
apertura *f* opening.
apesadumbrar *vt* to afflict; grieve, vex.
apestar *vt* to infect (*with disease*); to emit offensive smell; to nauseate.
apetecer *vt* to wish, long for, have a taste, urge (for, to).
apetecible *a* desirable, tasty, appetizing.
apetencia *f* appetite; desire.
apetito *m* appetite, hunger.
apetitoso *a* appetizing, savory, desirable.
apiadarse *vr* to pity, have mercy on.
ápice *m* apex, summit; smallest detail, shred.
apiñar *vt* to press together; *vr* to crowd.
apio *m* celery.
apisonar *vt* to ram down, flatten.
aplacar *vt* to placate, appease.
aplanamiento *m* levelling.
aplanar *vt* to make even, level, roll; to dismay.
aplastar *vt* to crush, flatten; to floor (*opponent*).
aplaudir *vt* to applaud.
aplauso *m* applause, praise.
aplazamiento *m* postponement, adjournment; convocation, citation.
aplazar *vt* to adjourn, put off, postpone.
aplicación *f* assiduity, industry, diligence; employment, use, application.
aplicado *a* studious, hard-working.
aplicar *vt* to apply; *vr* to devote oneself to; to put to use.
aplomo *m* self-possession, coolness.
apocado *a* pusillanimous, cowardly, spiritless, spineless.
apocalipsis *m* Apocalypse.

apocamiento *m* bashfulness, meanness of spirit.
apocar *vt* to lessen, cramp; *vr* to humble oneself.
apócrifo *a* apocryphal.
apodar *vt* to give nickname.
apoderado *m* attorney, proxy; with authority to sign; *a* empowered, authorized.
apoderar *vt* to empower, grant a power of attorney; *vr* to take possession of, seize.
apodo *m* nickname.
apogeo *m* summit, height (*of success etc*).
apolítico *a* apolitical, non-political.
apolillarse *vr* to become moth eaten.
apología *f* defense (*in speech, writing*) of (*person, idea etc*); eulogy.
apoplejía *f* apoplexy.
apoplético *a* apoplectic.
apoquinar *vt Mex* to come across, (*fam*) cough up.
aporrear *vt* to beat, cudgel.
aporreo *m* beating, pommelling.
aportar *vt* to bring.
aposentar (ie) *vt* to lodge; *vr* to take a lodging.
aposento *m* chamber, room, apartment.
aposta *ad* intentionally.
apostar *vt* to bet; *Arg* to contribute (*money*); to post soldiers; *vr* to emulate.
apostasía *f* apostasy.
apostilla *f* marginal note.
apóstol *m* apostle.
apóstrofe *m* apostrophe.
apostura *f* gentleness, neatness (*in appearance*).
apotegma *m* apothegm, maxim.
apoteosis *f* apotheosis.
apoyar *vt* to support, corroborate, back up; *vr* to rest on, lean; to base.
apoyo *m* support, protection, help, backing.
apozarse *vr Col, Chi* to form a pool, accumulate.
apreciable *a* appreciable, respectable, valued.
apreciación *f* estimation.
apreciar *vt* to appreciate, value, appraise, assess.
aprecio *m* esteem; appreciation.
aprehender *vt* to apprehend, seize.
aprehensión *f* apprehension, misgiving; seizure; acuteness.
apremiante *a* urgent, pressing.
apremiar *vt* to press, compel, urge.
apremio *m* pressure, constriction; judicial compulsion.
aprender *vt* to learn.
aprendiz *m* apprentice; beginner, novice.
aprendizaje *m* apprenticeship.
aprensión *f* apprehension, scruple, unfounded fear, misapprehension.
aprensivo *a* apprehensive, fearful.
apresamiento *m* capture.
apresar *vt* to seize, to grasp, capture; to take (*ship*) as prize.
aprestar *vt* to prepare; *vr* to get ready.
apresto *m* preparation, starch.
apresurado *a* brief, hasty, hurried.
apresuramiento *m* hurry.
apresurar *vt* to accelerate, hurry on; *vr* to make haste.
apretado *a* tight, fast; close, mean; dangerous; thick (*growth etc*).
apretar (ie) *vt* to compress, tighten, press down; (*hands*) to squeeze, shake; to harass, to constrain; **— el paso** to hurry on.
apretón *m* pressure; **— de manos** handshake.
apretura *f* crowd; narrowness, tightness.
aprieto *m* stringency, (*fam*) jam, difficulty; **hallarse en un —** to be in a fix.
aprisa *ad* hurriedly, fast, promptly.
aprisionar *vt* to imprison; to bind, confine.
aprobación *f* approval, consent.
aprobar (ue) *vt* to approve; to pass (*examination*).
aprontar *vt* to prepare quickly, get ready.
apropiación *f* appropriation.
apropiado *a* proper, convenient, fit, suitable.
apropiar *vt* to appropriate; *vr* to appropriate.
aprovechado *a* thrifty; industrious, clever; enterprising.
aprovechamiento *m* advantage, profit, progress.
aprovechar *vt* to profit by, to take advantage of; *vr* to avail oneself, make good use of.
aprovisionar *vt* to supply.
aproximación *f* approximation.
aproximado *a* close.
aproximar *vtr* to approach, draw on, draw nearer; to be close to.
aptitud *f* aptitude, fitness, ability, gift (for).
apto *a* apt, competent, able, likely, suitable.
apuesta *f* bet, wager.
apuesto *a* spruce, genteel.
apuntación *f* annotation, note, memorandum, remark.
apuntador *m* prompter; marker.
apuntalar *vt* to prop, reinforce, underpin.
apuntar *vt* to aim; to point out; to note, write down; to prompt (*theat*).
apunte *m* note; *pl* **sacar —s** to take notes.
apuñalar *vt* to stab.
apupar *vt Ec* to carry on one's back.
apurado *a* hard up; in trouble; exhausted; distracted.
apurar *vt* to exhaust, consume, drain; to urge, press; to hurry, rush; *vr* to worry; to strive, be at great pains to.

apuro *m* want; trouble; quandary, dilemma, straits.
aquejar *vt* to afflict, ail; to suffer from.
aquél *pn* that, that one, the former.
aquí *ad* here, in this place; **de — en adelante** henceforth, hereafter; **he —** behold.
aquiescencia *f* consent, acquiescence.
aquietar *vt* to quiet down, allay; *vr* to be quiet.
aquilatar *vt* to examine closely; to assay; to appraise.
ara *f* altar.
árabe *an* Arabian, Arabic.
arado *m* plow.
aragonés *an* Aragonese.
arana *f SA* trick, cheat.
arancel *m* tariff (*of duties, fees etc*).
araña *f* spider; chandelier, luster.
arañar *vt* to scratch, scrabble.
arañazo *m* deep scratch.
araño *m* scratch.
arar *vt* to plow.
arbitraje *m* arbitration.
arbitrar *vt* to arbitrate; to award.
arbitrariedad *f* arbitrariness.
arbitrario *a* arbitrary.
arbitrio *m* free will; expedient; resource.
árbitro *m* arbitrator; arbiter; (*sport*) referee.
árbol *m* tree; mast; shaft.
arbolado *m* woodland; *a* wooded.
arboladura *f* mast and yards (*ship*).
arbolar *vt* to hoist.
arboleda *f* grove, plantation, avenue.
arbotante *m* flying buttress.
arbusto *m* shrub.
arca *f* chest, coffer, safe; ark.
arcada *f* arcade; nausea.
árcade *a* Arcadian.
arcaduz *m* conduit pipe.
arcaico *a* archaic, antiquated.
arcángel *m* archangel.
arcano *m* arcanum, mystery.
arce *m* maple tree.
arcediano *m* archdeacon.
arcilla *f* clay.
arco *m* arch; bow; hoop; **— iris** rainbow.
arcón *m* large chest, bunker.
archipiélago *m* archipelago.
archivar *vt* to file, deposit in an archive; to store away.
archivo *m* archives.
arder *vi* to burn, glow with fire.
ardid *m* trick, stratagem.
ardido *a* brave, courageous; *Arg* fermented.
ardiente *a* burning; fervid.
ardilla *f* squirrel.
ardor *m* ardor, enthusiasm, valor.
ardoroso *a* fiery, fervid, ardent.
arduo *a* arduous, difficult.
área *f* area; 100 square meters.
arena *f* sand; arena.
arenal *m* sandy ground, sandy beach; sand bank.
arenga *f* harangue.
arengar *vti* to harangue; to hold forth.
arenisca *f* sandstone.
arenisco *a* gritty.
arenoso *a* sandy, gravelly.
arenque *m* herring.
argamasa *f* cement, mortar.
argamasar *vt* to mix cement.
argelino *an* Algerian.
argentino *a* Argentine; silver; *m* Argentinian.
argolla *f* iron ring.
argucia *f* subtlety, sophistry.
argüir *vi* to argue; infer.
argumentación *f* argument.
argumentar *vi* to argue, dispute.
argumento *m* argument; plot (*of book*).
aridez *f* aridity; dryness.
árido *a* arid, dry.
ariete *m* battering ram.
ario *an* Aryan.
arisco *a* shy, wild, surly, coltish.
arista *f* edge.
aristócrata *m* aristocrat.
aritmética *f* arithmetic.
arlequín *m* harlequin, buffoon; ice cream.
arma *f* arm, weapon; *pl* armorial ensigns; **— blanca** steel arms, cold steel.
armada *f* navy, fleet.
armado *a* armed; set.
armadura *f* framework, structure; armor.
armamento *f* armament.
armar *vt* to arm; to put together, mount; to fit out (*ship*); **— caballero** to knight; *vr* to arm oneself.
armario *m* cupboard; commode, cabinet.
armatoste *m* unwieldy furniture, unwieldy object.
armazón *f* frame, skeleton.
armella *f* eyebolt, screweye.
armería *f* armory, arsenal.
armiño *m* ermine, stoat.
armisticio *m* armistice.
armonía *f* harmony; peace; chord.
armonioso *a* harmonious, pleasing.
armonizar *vt* to harmonize, match, bring into agreement.
arnés *m* harness, gear; defensive armor.
aro *m* hoop; staple; *RP* earring.
aroma *m* aroma, scent, fragrance.
aromático *a* aromatic, fragrant.
arpa *f* harp.
arpía *f* harpy; shrew.
arpista *m Chi* thief.
arpón *m* harpoon, harping iron.
arquear *vt* to arch; to gauge (*ships*).
arqueo *m* arching; tonnage (*of ship*).
arqueología *f* archæology.
arquero *m* archer.
arquitecto *m* architect.
arquitectónico *a* architectural.
arrabal *m* suburb; *pl* outskirts.
arracada *f* earring with pendant.
arracimarse *vr* to cluster.

arraigado *a* rooted, inveterate.
arraigar *vi* to root, take root; *vr* to establish; to settle down.
arrancar *vt* to uproot; to pull out; *vi* to originate; to proceed; to set off (*of train*).
arranque *m* extirpation; (*of feeling*) burst; start; (*aut*) starter.
arranquera *f Cub, Mex* financial difficulty.
arras *f pl* earnest money, pledge; dowry.
arrasar *vt* to demolish, to level, to raze; *vr* — **en lágrimas** to weep copiously, be blinded with tears.
arrastrado *a* rascally; **vida —a** hand-to-mouth existence.
arrastrar *vt* to drag; to carry away; to lead a trump (*card*); *vr* to crawl.
arrayán *m* myrtle.
arrear *vt* to drive, round up (*mules, horses or cattle*); *Arg, Mex* to steal cattle; to put on trappings.
arrebatado *a* rapid; rash, violent, impetuous.
arrebatar *vt* to carry off, snatch; *vr* to be carried away by passion.
arrebato *m* sudden attack; surprise, start; paroxysm; sudden fit of passion, rapture.
arrebol *m* glow of the sky; red (pink) glow; rouge, cosmetic.
arrebujarse *vr* to wrap o.s. up in the bedclothes.
arreciar *vi* to grow stronger, increase in strength (*of fever, wind*).
arrecife *m* causeway; reef.
arreglado *a* in order, ordered, moderate; arranged, settled.
arreglar *vt* to arrange, settle, regulate; to mend, put right; to make tidy, to tidy; to settle, pay (*debt*).
arreglo *m* arrangement, settlement; order; **con — a** according to.
arremangar *vt* to roll up, turn up (*sleeves*).
arremedar *vt Cub, Mex* to imitate, ape.
arremeter *vt* attack, assail, rush at.
arremetida *f* attack, assault.
arrendador *m* landlord; lessor.
arremolinar *vti* to eddy, whirl around.
arremueco *m Col* caress, fondling.
arrendamiento *m* lease, renting, letting.
arrendar (ie) *vt* to rent, lease.
arrendatario *m* tenant, lessee.
arreo *m* ornament; *pl* trappings, harness, equipment.
arrepentimiento *m* repentance.
arrepentirse *vr* to repent, regret, rue.
arrestado *a* intrepid, daring.
arrestar *vt* to arrest, detain, imprison.
arresto *m* detention.
arriar *vt* to lower, to strike (*sails, colors*).
arriate *m* flowerbed.
arriba *ad* above, over, on top; **de — abajo** from top to bottom.
arribar *vi* to arrive; to put into a harbor.
arribeño *m Mex, Arg, Per* person from highlands.
arribo *m* arrival.
arriendo *m* lease, rental.
arriero *m* muleteer.
arriesgado *a* perilous, dangerous, daring.
arriesgar *vt* to hazard, risk, venture; *vr* to expose oneself to danger; to dare.
arrimar *vt* to put close(r); to lay aside; — **el hombro** to put one's shoulder to the wheel; *vr* to lean upon; to draw up to (*fire etc*).
arrimo *m* shelter, protection.
arrinconado *a* put away, neglected, discarded, cornered.
arrinconar *vt* to put in a corner; to corner.
arrizar *vt* to stow.
arroba *f* quarter (*of wheat etc*).
arrobamiento *m* rapture, bliss, ecstasy.
arrodillarse *vr* to kneel down.
arrogancia *f* arrogance.
arrogante *a* arrogant, spirited, haughty.
arrogarse *vr* to arrogate, claim, usurp, assume.
arrojado *a* daring, rash, intrepid.
arrojar *vt* to throw, throw away, fling; to emit, shoot out; *SA* to vomit; *vr* to venture on, hurl o.s. into.
arrojo *m* boldness, audacity.
arrollar *vt* to roll up, roll (around, along, back); to rout.
arropar *vt* to wrap up well, swathe, dress.
arrope *m* (*fruit*) syrup.
arroró *m Arg* lullaby.
arrostrar *vt* to face, face up to, confront; *vr* — **con** to fight face to face.
arroyo *m* rivulet, stream; gutter.
arroz *m* rice.
arrozal *m* rice field.
arruga *f* wrinkle, crease, line (on face); corrugation.
arrugar *vt* to crease, fold, wrinkle; — **la frente** to frown.
arruinar *vt* to ruin, demolish.
arrullar *vt* to lull; to bill and coo (*doves*); to woo.
arrullo *m* lullaby; cooing.
arrumaco *m* flattery; show of affection.
arrurruz *m* arrowroot.
arsenal *m* arsenal, dockyard.
arsénico *m* arsenic.
arte *m* art, skill, ability; *f pl* arts, means; **malas —** trickery, cunning, skill; **bellas —** fine arts.
artefacto *m* manufacture; handiwork; machine; contraption.

artejo *m* joint, knuckle.
arteria *f* artery.
artería *f* cunning; artifice, stratagem.
artesa *f* kneading trough; canoe.
artesano *m* artisan; mechanic.
artesonado *m* paneled (*ceiling*).
ártico *a* Arctic.
articulación *f* joint; pronunciation.
articulado *a* articulate; jointed.
articular *vt* to articulate; to pronounce distinctly; to put together.
artículo *m* article, condition; joint.
artífice *m* artificer, maker, artist.
artificio *m* artifice, trick; workmanship, craft, skill.
artificioso *a* artful, crafty, ingenious, deceitful, specious.
artillería *f* artillery.
artillero *m* gunner, artilleryman.
artimaña *f* trap, snare.
artista *mf* artist; artiste.
artístico *a* artistic.
artritis *f* arthritis, gout.
Arturo *m* Arthur.
arveja *f* pea.
arzobispado *m* archbishopric.
arzobispo *m* archbishop.
arzón *m* bow of a saddle; saddle tree.
as *m* ace.
asa *f* handle.
asado *m* roast; *Arg* barbecue.
asador *m* spit, roasting jack.
asalariar *vt* to put on a salary; to pay a fixed salary, hire.
asaltador *m* assailant, highwayman.
asaltar *vt* to assail, fall upon, assault.
asalto *m* surprise attack; bout (*fencing*); **guardias de —** riot police.
asamblea *f* assembly, meeting.
asar *vt* to roast; *vr* to be roasting.
asaz *ad* enough; quite.
asbesto *m* asbestos.
ascendencia *f* ancestry, origins.
ascender *vi* to be promoted, rise (*in rank*), to climb; **— a** to amount to.
ascendiente *m* ancestor; ascendency, influence.
ascensión *f* ascension.
ascenso *m* promotion.
ascensor *m* lift; elevator.
asceta *m* ascetic.
ascético *a* ascetic.
asco *m* disgust; nausea; **dar —** to be revolting.
ascua *f* red-hot coal; **estar en —s** to be jumpy.
aseado *a* neat, tidy, clean.
asear *vt* to clean; to polish.
asechanza *f* waylaying, trap.
asechar *vt* to lie in ambush; to watch.
asediar *vt* to besiege, to importune.
asedio *m* blockade, siege.
asegurado *m* insured party; *a* assured, decided.
asegurador *m* insurer, underwriter.
asegurar *vt* to insure, assure; to ensure; to secure, fasten; *vr* to make sure, be certain.
asemejarse *vr* to resemble.
asendereado *a* frequented, beaten (*track*).
asentado *a* settled, fixed, agreed.
asentar *vt* to place, affirm, establish; to book, to enter; to seat; to settle; to set down; **— los cimientos** to lay the foundations.
asentimiento *m* assent, consent.
asentir *vi* to assent, acquiesce; to be of the same opinion.
aseo *m* cleanliness, neatness.
asequible *a* attainable, obtainable, available.
aserción *f* assertion.
aserrado *a* serrated, toothed, jagged.
aserrar (ie) *vt* to saw.
aserrín *m* sawdust.
aserto *m* assertion, the act of asserting.
asesinar *vt* to assassinate, murder.
asesinato *m* murder.
asesino *m* assassin, murderer, cutthroat.
asesor *m* counselor, adviser, assessor.
asesorarse *vr* to take the advice or assistance of counsel; to be advised; to take stock of.
asestar *vt* to aim, point; to strike (*with a weapon*).
aseveración *f* asseveration.
aseverar *vt* to affirm, to declare solemnly.
asfalto *m* asphalt.
asfixiar *vt* to suffocate.
así *ad* so, thus; therefore; **— que** as soon as.
asiático *an* Asiatic.
asidero *m* handle; occasion, pretext.
asiduidad *f* assiduousness.
asiduo *a* assiduous, steady, regular.
asiento *m* seat, chair; situation; treaty; sediment; prudence.
asignación *f* assignment, distribution.
asignar *vt* to assign, ascribe.
asignatura *f* subject (*of study*), curriculum.
asilo *m* asylum, shelter, home (*for aged, helpless etc*).
asimilación *f* assimilation.
asimilar *vt* to assimilate; to make one thing like another; *Arg* to digest.
asimismo *ad* equally, likewise.
asir *vt* to grasp, seize.
asistencia *f* those present, audience; help, assistance; **— pública** *Arg, Urug, Par* state hospital.
asistir *vi* to be present, to follow suit (*cards*); *vt* to help, assist; to attend (*the sick*).
asno *m* ass, donkey.
asociación *f* association; society; fellowship.
asociado *m* associate, comrade.
asociar *vt* to associate, put together; *vr* to associate with.

asolación *f* desolation, devastation.
asolar *vt* to level with the ground, raze; to make desolate, devastate.
asolear *vt* to sun; *vr* to expose o.s. to the sun, get sunburnt.
asomar *vi* to appear; *vr* to put (stick, look) out.
asombrar *vt* to frighten; to astonish, amaze.
asombro *m* amazement; dread.
asombroso *a* wonderful, amazing, astonishing.
asomo *m* sign, token, hint, inkling, suspicion.
asonada *f* riot, commotion.
asonancia *f* assonance.
asorcharse *vr SA* to blush.
aspa *f* sail (*of windmill*); (propeller) blade; reel (*for winding yarn*).
aspar *vt* to wind (*wool*).
aspaviento *m* forced or exaggerated display (*of wonder etc*).
aspecto *m* aspect; appearance, looks; outlook.
aspereza *f* asperity; gruffness, harshness.
áspero *a* rough, harsh, raw, severe.
aspersión *f* aspersion, sprinkling.
áspid *m* aspic, asp.
aspillera *f* battlement, embrasure.
aspiración *f* aspiration; desire.
aspirar *vt* to draw in breath; to aspire; to aim at, covet.
asquerosidad *f* foulness, filthiness.
asqueroso *a* nasty, disgusting, loathsome.
asta *f* horn, antler; staff, pole, flagstaff; shaft (*of lance etc*).
astilla *f* splinter; splint; **de tal palo, tal —** a chip off the old block.
astillero *m* shipwright's yard, dockyard; rack (*for lances, pikes etc*); *Mex* clearing, open space.
astringente *a* astringent.
astringir *vt* to contract; to compress.
astro *m* star, planet; *SA* actor.
astrólogo *m* astrologer.
astronomía *f* astronomy.
astrónomo *m* astronomer.
astucia *f* cunning; slyness.
asturiano *a m* Asturian.
astuto *a* astute, cunning, sly, crafty.
asueto *m* short holiday, break; **día de —** day off.
asumir *vt* to assume, take up, adopt.
asunción *f* assumption, elevation.
asunto *m* subject; subject matter; affair, business; **—s exteriores** foreign affairs.
asustadizo *a* shy; timid; easily frightened.
asustar *vt* to frighten, startle, scare; *vr* to be frightened.
atabal *m* tympanum, drum.
atacar *vt* to attack, storm.
atado *m* bundle, parcel.
atadura *f* tying; ligature; knot.
atajar *vi* to take a short cut; *vt* to intercept; to obstruct; to cut short (*speech etc*).
atajo *m* short cut.
atalaya *f* watch tower; *m* watchman.
atañer *vi* to appertain.
ataque *m* attack, assault; fit (*of illness*).
atar *vt* to tie; to bind; **loco de —** raving lunatic.
atarantar *vt SA* to stun, daze.
atareado *a* exceedingly busy.
atarear *vt* to task; to exercise; *vr* to be very busy, work hard.
atarjea *f* drainpipe, sewer.
atarugar *vt* to fasten, wedge, plug; *Mex* to get confused.
atasajar *vt* to cut meat into pieces; to jerk (*beef*).
atascamiento *m* impediment, obstruction.
atascar *vt* to stop a leak; to stop up (*pipes*); *vr* to get bogged down; to get stopped up.
ataúd *m* coffin.
ataviado *a* embellished; ornamented, adorned.
ataviar *vt* to embellish, ornament, trim, dress up.
atavío *m* embellishment; dress, ornament.
atavismo *m* atavism.
atejo *m Col* parcel, bundle.
atemorizar *vt* to frighten, daunt.
atemperar *vt* to temper, allay, assuage.
atención *f* attention; civility; care; *excl* look out!, beware!
atender *vti* to attend; to look after; to take care, mind, heed.
ateneo *m* Athenæum; *a* Athenian.
atenerse *vr* to adhere; to depend upon; to abide by.
atentado *m* transgression; attempt, offense, crime, attack.
atentar *vt* to attempt or to make an attempt on (*as a crime*); to attack.
atento *a* attentive, polite.
atenuación *f* attenuation; extenuation.
atenuante *a* extenuating.
atenuar *vt* to attenuate, extenuate, to diminish.
ateo *m* atheist.
aterido *a* stiff with cold.
aterrador *a* frightful, terrible.
aterrar *vt* to frighten, scare.
aterrizar *vti* to land (*airplane*).
aterrorizar *vt* to terrify, terrorize.
atesorar *vt* to treasure, hoard up.
atestación *f* testimony, affidavit.
atestar *vt* to fill up; to cram, stuff; to testify, substantiate.
atestiguar *vt* to depose, give evidence.
atezar (ie) *vt* to blacken.
atiborrar *vt* to stuff, cram, gorge.
ático *m* attic; *a* of Athens, Athenian.
atildamiento *m* tidiness, nicety.
atildar *vt* to censure; to place a 'tilde' on a letter; to adorn.
atinado *a* pertinent, apposite, shrewd.

atinar *vt* to hit the mark; to guess accurately.
atisbar *vt* to pry; to scrutinize; to waylay.
atizar *vt* to stir the fire; to stir up, arouse.
atlántico *a m* Atlantic.
atlas *m* atlas.
atleta *m* athlete, wrestler.
atlético *a* athletic, robust.
atmósfera *f* atmosphere, air.
atole *m Mex* hot drink made of corn meal.
atolladero *m* quagmire; blind alley, deadlock.
atollarse *vr* to fall into the mire, get into difficulties.
atolón *m* atoll.
atolondrado *a* harebrained, thoughtless, giddy.
atolondramiento *m* confusion, amazement; witlessness.
átomo *m* atom.
atónito *a* amazed, astonished, stunned.
atontado *a* stunned, stupefied, knocked silly.
atontar *vt* to stun; to confound, confuse.
atorarse *vr Arg* to choke; to get confused.
atormentador *m* tormentor.
atormentar *vt* to torment; torture, cause affliction.
atornillar *vt* to screw.
atorrante *m Arg* vagabond, loafer.
atosigar *vt* to harass, bother; to poison.
atrabiliario *a* bad-tempered.
atrabilis *f* black bile; bad temper.
atracar *vr* to glut; to stuff oneself with food; *vt* to come alongside (*of ship*); to moor; to assault (a person).
atracción *f* attraction, appeal.
atraco *m* holdup.
atractivo *a* attractive; *m* charm, delight.
atraer *vt* to attract, allure; to draw in, bring in.
atrancar *vt* to bar a door; to obstruct.
atrapar *vt* to trap.
atrás *a* backwards; behind; *excl* stand back!
atrasado *a* late; backward, behindhand.
atrasar *vt* to retard; *vr* to be late; to go slow (*clock*).
atraso *m* backwardness; arrears; delay.
atravesar (ie) *vt* to cross; to pass over; to run through; to go over, through.
atrayente *a* attractive.
atrenzo *m SA* conflict, difficulty.
atreverse *vr* to dare, venture.
atrevido *a* daring, bold; insolent.
atrevimiento *m* boldness, audacity, effrontery.
atribución *f* attribution; competence.
atribuir *vt* to attribute, ascribe; *vr* to assume.
atribular *vt* to vex.
atributo *m* attribute; inherent quality.
atril *m* lectern.
atrincherar *vt* to entrench; *vr* to dig oneself in.
atrio *m* porch (*of church*), portico, courtyard.
atrocidad *f* atrocity, horror.
atrofiarse *vr* to waste away; to be atrophied.
atronar (ue) *vt* to stun, stupefy.
atropellado *a* hasty, hurried, jumbled.
atropellar *vt* to run over; knock down; to beat down, insult; *vr* to be in haste.
atropello *m* outrage, insult; accident (*s.o. run over*).
atroz *a* atrocious, inhuman, heinous.
atún *m* tuna fish.
aturdido *a* thoughtless; unnerved, dumbfounded, bewildered.
aturdir *vt* to stupefy, bewilder, render speechless.
aturrullar *vt* to confuse, set at sixes and sevens.
atusar *vt* to trim (*hair, plants*).
audacia *f* boldness, effrontery.
audaz *a* bold, audacious, fearless.
audiencia *f* audience, reception, hearing.
auditor *m* auditor; judge.
auditorio *m* audience, auditory.
auge *m* great prosperity, boom; acme, highest point; **estar en —** to be flourishing.
augurar *vt* to prognosticate; to augur.
aula *f* classroom, lecture hall.
aulaga *f* furze, gorse.
aullar *vi* to howl (*of dogs etc*).
aullido *m* howl, cry (*of horror, pain*).
aumentar *m* to increase, enlarge.
aumento *m* increase, augmentation; **ir en —** to go on increasing.
aun (aún) *a* yet, still, even, further.
aunar *vt* to join together, unite, confederate.
aunque *cj* nevertheless, yet, although.
aura *f* gentle breeze, aura; **— popular** popular favor.
áureo *a* golden.
aureola *f* halo.
auricular *a* ear; *m* (telephone) receiver.
aurífero *a* auriferous, gold-bearing.
aurora *f* dawn.
ausencia *f* absence.
ausentarse *vt* to absent oneself, stay away.
ausente *a* absent.
auspicio *m* auspice, patronage; presage.
austeridad *f* austerity.
austero *a* austere; stern, rigid, severe.
austral *a* austral, southern.
australiano *an* Australian.

austríaco *an* Austrian.
autenticar *vt* to authenticate, attest.
auténtico *a* authentic, real, genuine.
auto *m* judicial decree; edict; — **de prisión** warrant, writ; — **sacramental** allegorical play on the Eucharist; (motor) car; *pl* (*legal*) proceedings.
autócrata *m* autocrat.
autógrafo *m* autograph.
autómata *m* automaton; robot.
automático *m* automatic.
automotor *a SA* of cars, automobile; *m* car, automobile.
automóvil *m* motorcar, automobile.
autonomía *f* autonomy; home rule.
autónomo *m* autonomous; free.
autopsia *f* autopsy, post-mortem.
autor *m* author; writer; composer.
autoridad *f* authority, power, capacity.
autorización *f* authority, authorization, power.
autorizado *a* commendable, expert; empowered.
autorizar *vt* to authorize; to legalize; to approve.
autoservicio *m SA* self-service.
auxiliar *vt* to help, aid, assist; *a* auxiliary; *m* assistant.
auxilio *m* aid, help; assistance; — **social** public assistance.
avalancha *f* avalanche.
avalentonado *m* braggart; *a* boastful, overweening.
avalorar *vt* to appraise, value.
avaluar *vt* to evaluate.
avance *m* advance; payment in advance.
avanzada *f* van; outpost.
avanzar *vi* to advance, go forward.
avaricia *f* cupidity, avarice, greed.
avariento *a* avaricious, niggard, miserly.
avaro *m* miser.
avasallar *vt* to subdue, enslave.
ave *f* (*large*) bird; fowl; — **de rapiña** bird of prey; — **negra** *Arg* dishonest lawer.
avecinarse *vr* to come nearer.
avecindar *vt* to make a citizen; to settle; to become a resident, a citizen.
avellana *f* hazelnut, filbert.
avellanar *vr* to countersink.
avellaneda *f* hazel plantation.
avellano *m* hazelnut tree.
ave maría *excl* Goodness gracious!; Peace on this house!
avena *f* oats.
avenencia *f* agreement, accord.
avenida *f* flood, inundation; avenue.
avenimiento *m* agreement, understanding.
avenir *vt* to bring together, reconcile; *vr* — **con** to get along well with.
aventajado *a* outstanding, notable; profitable.
aventajar *vt* to surpass, excel; to improve.
aventamiento *m* winnowing.
aventar (ie) *vt* to winnow; to fan, pass air over.
aventón *m Mex* push, shove; (*fam*) **dar un** — to give someone a lift.
aventura *f* adventure; event; venture.
aventurado *a* risky, hazardous.
aventurero *m* adventurer.
avergonzar *vt* to shame; *vr* to feel ashamed, be ashamed.
avería *f* damage; (*mech*) breakdown, failure; (*naut*) average; **hombre de** — *Arg* delinquent.
averiado *a* damaged, spoiled, broken down.
averiarse *vr* to become damaged.
averiguación *f* inquiry, inquest.
averiguar *vt* to ascertain, find out, investigate.
averno *m* (*poet*) hell.
aversión *f* aversion; reluctance; **cobrar** — **a** to loathe.
avestruz *m* ostrich.
aviación *f* aviation.
aviador *m* aviator, airman, pilot.
avidez *f* covetousness, avidity.
ávido *a* greedy, covetous; eager.
avieso *a* crooked; perverse.
avigorar *vt* to invigorate.
avinagrado *a* stale, sour; harsh, embittered, crabbed.
avinagrar *vt* to make sour; *vr* to become sour.
avío *m* preparation, provision; *SA* money lent; *pl* utensils; — **de coser** sewing materials.
avión *m* airplane; — **a chorro** *Arg, Urug, Par* jet.
avisado *a* cautious, prudent, wise, sharp, clear-sighted.
avisar *vt* to inform, advise; to notify.
aviso *m* notice, information, announcement.
avispa *f* wasp.
avispado *a* lively, brisk, clever.
avispar *vt* to rouse, enliven.
avispero *m* wasp's nest; swarm of bees, wasps.
avistar *vt* to descry, catch sight of *vr* — **con** to interview.
avituallar *vt* to victual.
avivar *vt* to enliven, encourage, hasten; to heighten (*colors*); *vi* to revive.
avizorar *vt* to keep sharp lookout on.
axioma *m* axiom.
¡ay! *excl* alas!
aya *f* governess, instructress.
ayecahue *m Chi* nonsense, absurdity.
ayer *ad* yesterday.
ayo *m* tutor, governor.
ayocote *m Mex* kidney bean.
ayuda *f* aid, help, assistance; — **de cámara** valet.
ayudante *m* aide-de-camp; assistant.
ayudar *vt* to help, assist, aid.
ayunar *vi* to fast.
ayuno *m* fast, abstinence; *ad* **en**

ayunas fasting; **quedarse en —** to be not a wit wiser.
ayuntamiento *m* municipal council or government; town hall.
azabache *m* jet.
azada *f* hoe.
azadazo *m* blow with a spade or hoe.
azadón *m* large hoe; **— de pico** pickax.
azafata *f* air hostess, lady-in-waiting.
azafate *m* flat basket; tray.
azafrán *m* saffron.
azahar *m* orange or lemon blossom.
azar *m* hazard, chance; unforeseen disaster; unlucky throw (*at cards etc*); disappointment.
azarearse *vr* to become embarrassed, get muddled; *Guat, Hond* to get angry.
azaroso *a* unlucky, hazardous.
ázimo *a* unleavened.
azogue *m* quicksilver; **es un —** he's a restless creature.
azor *m* goshawk.
azoramiento *m* confusion, perturbation, bewilderment.
azorar *vt* to confound, terrify.
azotar *vt* to flog, whip, flagellate.
azote *m* whip; lash; scourge.
azotea *f* flat roof.
azteca *an* Aztec.
azúcar *m* sugar; **— de pilón** lump sugar; **— rosado** caramel sugar.
azucarado *a* sweetened, candied; (*of words*) honeyed.
azucarero *m* sugar bowl; *a* sugar, of sugar.
azucarillo *m* (kind of) meringue.
azucena *f* white lily.
azúd *f* sluice, waterwheel.
azufre *m* sulphur, brimstone.
azul *a* blue; **— turquí** indigo.
azulejo *m* glazed tile.
azumbre *m* (*equivalent*) half a gallon.
azuzar *vt* to set (*dogs*) on; to irritate.

B

baba *f* slaver, spittle, drivel.
bable *m* Asturian dialect.
babor *m* port, larboard.
baboso *a* slobbery; immature.
babucha *f* (soft, ornamented) slipper.
bacalao *m* codfish.
bacilo *m* bacillus.
bacín *m* chamberpot.
Baco *m* Bacchus.
baculacada *f Chi, Per* unfair action.
báculo *m* staff; support; walking stick; **— pastoral** bishop's crozier.
bache *m* pothole (*in road*).
bachiller *m* B.A., bachelor (*degree*); babbler.
badajo *m* (bell) clapper; tonguewagger.
badajocense *an* (*native*) of Badajoz.
badulaque *m* (*fam*) nitwit, featherbrain, unreliable person.
bagaje *m* baggage.
bagatela *f* trifle, bagatelle.
bagazo *m* bagasse; pressed pulp.
bagual *a Arg* wild, unbroken (*of horse*).
bahía *f* bay.
bailar *vi* to dance.
baile *m* dance, ball; **— de San Vito** St. Vitus's dance, chorea.
baja *f* fall, diminution in price; casualty (*in battle, accident*); **darse de —** to resign.
bajá *m* pasha.
bajada *f* descent, slope.
bajamar *m* low tide.
bajar *vi* to decline, fall, come down, go down; *vt* to lower.
bajel *m* vessel, craft.
bajeza *f* meanness; abjectness.
bajial *m Per* marsh.
bajío *m* shoal; submerged sandbank.
bajo *a* low, abject, mean, lowered; *ad* below; **hablar —** to speak softly; *prep* under; *m* bass; *pl* petticoats.
bajorrelieve *m* bas-relief.
bajón *m* bassoon, bassoon player.
bala *f* bullet; bale.
baladí *a* trifling, unimportant, worthless.
baladrón *m* boaster.
baladronada *f* boast, brag.
balance *m* equilibrium; balance; balance sheet; *Col* affair, business; **echar un —** to draw up a balance.
balancear *vt* to balance, to settle accounts; to rock, balance, dandle (*baby*).
balanceo *m* oscillation, rocking, swaying.
balandra *f* sloop.
balandro *m* schooner.
balanza *f* scale; pair of scales.
balar *vi* to bleat.
balaustrada *f* balustrade.
balay *m SA* wicker basket.
balazo *m* shot; bullet wound.
balbucear, balbucir *vi* to babble, mumble, stutter, make (first) sounds.
balcarrotas *f pl SA* plaited hair.
balcón *m* balcony, veranda.
baldar *vt* to cripple, obstruct; to trump (*cards*).
balde *m* wide-bottomed bucket; **de —** free, without paying; **en —** in vain.
baldear *vi* (*naut*) to swill decks.
baldío *a* uncultivated; idle; *m* waste land.
baldón *m* opprobrium, affront, blot (on escutcheon).
baldosa *f* square paving tile; flagstone.
balduque *m* red tape.
balear *a* Balearic.
balido *m* bleating.
balneario *a* of baths; *m* spa, health resort.
balón *m* large bundle; bale; (*inflated*) (foot)ball.
balsa *f* pool, raft.

balsámico *a* balsamic.
bálsamo *m* balsam, balm.
baluarte *m* bastion; bulwark.
ballena *f* whale; whalebone.
ballenero *m* whaler, whaling ship.
ballesta *f* crossbow.
ballestero *m* archer; crossbowman.
bambolear *vi* to stagger, reel; to oscillate; to totter.
bambolla *f* (*fam*) showiness, ostentation, swank.
bambú *m* bamboo; bamboo cane.
banca *f* bench, long wooden seat; Philippine canoe; banking; **— de hielo** ice field; *Arg, Urug* influence, power, ascendancy.
bancario *a* banking.
bancarrota *f* bankruptcy, failure.
banco *m* bench, form; bank; shoal (*of fish*).
banda *f* band; (brass, military) band; sash; gang, party; side (*of ship*); cushion (*billiards*).
bandada *f* flock; covey, flight.
bandear *vt Arg, Par, Urug* to cross (*river etc*); *Arg* (*pol*) to join most successful party.
bandeja *f* tray, platter.
bandera *f* (*national*) flag, ensign, banner, standard; **arriar la —** to strike the colors, to surrender; *pl* **con —s desplegadas** with flying colors.
banderilla *f* barbed stick used in bullfighting.
banderillero *m* man who jabs banderillas into bull's neck.
banderín *m* flag; signal (*rl*); recruiting post.
banderizo *a* partisan.
bandido *m* bandit, outlaw, highwayman.
bando *m* proclamation, edict; faction, side, persuasion.
bandolera *f* bandoleer, shoulder belt (*for gun*).
bandolero *m* highwayman, robber.
bandurria *f* musical instrument (*like small guitar, with six double strings*).
banquero *m* banker, manager.
banqueta *f* stool; *SA* pavement, sidewalk.
banquete *m* dock (*in court*); banquet.
bañadera *f SA* bathtub.
bañado *m SA* marsh land.
bañar *vt* to bathe, dip, wash; irrigate.
bañera *f* bathtub.
baño *m* bath, bathing; bathtub; coat (*of paint etc*).
baqueta *f* ramrod; switch; *pl* drumsticks.
baquetear *vt* to vex, annoy.
baquetudo *a Cub* slow, sluggish.
barata *f Mex* sale bargain.
baraja *f* pack of cards.
barajar *vt* to shuffle (*cards*); *Arg, Par, Urug* to catch (*ball etc*) in the air; **paciencia y —** let's wait and see.
baranda *f* railing.
barandilla *f* rail, railing.
baratija *f* trifle, bauble; toy, trinket.
baratillo *m* secondhand shop; remnant sale.
barato *a* cheap, inexpensive; *ad* cheaply.
baratura *f* cheapness.
baraúnda *f* hubbub; confusion, scrum.
barba *f* chin, beard; actor who plays old men's parts; **por —** ahead, apiece; **hacer la —** to shave.
barbacoa *f* barbecue.
barbaján *m Cub, Mex* coarse, clumsy.
bárbara *f* (*naut*) **santa —** powder magazine.
barbaridad *f* barbarity, cruelty; **¡qué —!** how frightful!; **una —** excessive quantity.
barbarie *f* barbarism; incivility (of manners).
bárbaro *m* barbarian; *a* barbarous, rough, rude, clumsy, crude; (*fam*) great, stunning; *Arg* excessive.
barbear *vt* to shave; to flatter.
barbecho *m* fallow.
barbero *m* barber.
barbijo *m Arg* chinstrap; scar on face.
barbilampiño *a* callow, baby-faced (*youth*); *m* youngling, stripling, beginner.
barbilla *f* chin.
barbiquejo *m Mex* chinstrap.
barbotar *vt* to mutter, mumble.
barca *f* (*small*) boat, barge, ferryboat.
barcaza *f* lighter, barge.
barcelonés *an* (*inhabitant*) of Barcelona.
barco *m* boat, ship; barge; vessel.
barda *f* fence.
bardar *vt* to thatch.
bardo *m* (*also* **barda** *f*) bard, poet.
barítono *m* baritone.
barlovento *m* windward; weather side.
barniz *m* varnish; superficial coat, veneer.
barnizar *vt* to varnish, glaze, lacquer.
barómetro *m* barometer.
barón *m* baron.
baronesa *f* baroness.
barquero *m* boatman; ferryman.
barquillo *m* small boat; sweet wafer.
barra *f* bar, stick, length (*of wood etc*); iron lever; metal ingot; sandbank.
barrabasada *f* devilishness; fiendish act.
barraca *f* hut, cabin; (*market*) stall; (*Valencian*) cottage; barrack; *SA* storage, warehouse.
barranca *f see* **barranco.**
barranco *m* ravine, gorge.
barredura *f* sweepings.
barreminas *m SA* minesweeper.
barrenar *vt* to bore, drill; to scuttle (*a ship*).

barrer *vt* to sweep, sweep away, carry off the whole; to rake (*with a volley etc*).
barrera *f* barrier, fence; clay pit.
barricada *f* barricade.
barriga *f* belly, abdomen.
barrigudo *a* fat-bellied.
barril *m* barrel, water cask.
barrilero *m* cooper.
barrio *m* ward, district, quarter, suburb.
barro *m* clay, mud; **— cocido** terra-cotta; *pl* pimples.
barroco *a* baroque.
barroso *a* muddy, clay-colored; pimply.
barruntar *vt* to guess, anticipate, conjecture, suspect.
barrunto *m* conjecture, foresight.
bártulos *m pl* tools, household goods, chattels.
barullo *m* confusion, disorder, row; *Arg* noise, din.
basa *f* pedestal, basis, foundation.
basalto *m* basalt.
basar *vi* to base, set up, found.
basca *f* nausea.
báscula *f* lever scale, weighing scales.
base *f* basis, foundation, ground; **— aérea** air base.
básico *a* basic.
basilisco *m* basilisk.
basta *excl* enough; halt, stop; *f* (*sew*) basting.
bastante *ad* enough, sufficiently, quite, rather; *a* sufficient.
bastar *vi* to suffice, be enough.
bastardilla *f* italics (*print*).
bastardo *a* bastard, spurious; *m* bastard.
bastidor *m* embroidery frame; **entre bastidores** (*theat*) in the wings.
bastimento *m* provisions, food.
bastión *m* bastion; bulwark.
basto *a* rough, crude, coarse; *m* packsaddle; *pl* clubs (*cards*).
bastón *m* cane, stick.
bastonero *m* cane maker *or* seller; cotillion leader (*at dance*).
basura *f* sweepings, dung, refuse, garbage.
basurero *m* garbage man, garbage or rubbish dump.
bata *m* dressing gown, housecoat, wrap.
bataclán *m SA* striptease, burlesque show.
batahola *f* bustle, clamor, hurly-burly.
batalla *f* battle, fight.
batallar *vi* to battle, fight.
batallón *m* battalion.
batata *f* sweet potato; *Arg, Par, Urug* fright, shyness.
batea *f* wooden, painted tray; punt.
batel *m* small vessel.
batelero *m* boatman.
batería *f* battery, set of drums; **— de cocina** kitchen utensils.
batey *m Cub* sugar plant.
batiboleo *m Mex* bustle, stir.
batida *f* hunting party; battue; *Arg* police raid.
batido *a* (*of silk*) shot; *m* batter (*of flour etc*); (*of hair*) back-combed.
batidor *m* scout; beater; outrider; hempdresser.
batiente *m* jamb, leaf *or* post (*of door*).
batifondo *m Arg, Par, Urug* uproar, noise, din.
batir *vt* to beat (*eggs etc*); clap; demolish; coin (*money*); (*mil*) reconnoitre; *vr* to fight, engage in a duel.
batista *f* lawn, cambric.
batuquear *vi Col, Ven* to flap.
batuta *f* baton; **llevar la —** to lead, preside, be in charge.
baúl *m* trunk, chest, box.
bautismo *m* baptism.
bautizar *vt* to christen, baptize; to water wine.
bautizo *m* christening.
baya *f* berry.
bayeta *f* baize; thick, rough woolen cloth.
bayetón *m SA* long poncho.
bayo *a* bay; yellowish color.
bayoneta *f* bayonet; **— calada** fixed bayonet.
bayonetazo *m* bayonet thrust.
bayote *m SA* ring worn by Indians on lower lip.
bayú *m Cub* brothel.
baza *f* trick (*at cards*); **meter —** to get a word in; to intervene.
bazar *m* bazaar.
bazo *m* spleen.
bazofia *f* hogwash; remnants.
beata *f* (often) pious old maid; woman engaged in works of piety; hypocrite; churchgoer; devout lady.
beatificar *vt* to beatify.
beatitud *f* blessedness, holiness.
beato *a* blessed, happy.
Beatriz *f* Beatrice.
bebé *m* baby.
bebedero *m* drinking vessel, trough, bird bath; *a* potable.
bebedizo *m* potion, philter, poisoned drink.
bebedor *m* toper, drinker.
beber *vt* & *vi* to drink, swallow, imbibe; **— los vientos por** to be mad for love of.
bebida *f* drink, beverage, potion.
beca *f* scholarship, grant, fellowship.
becada *f* woodcock.
becerro *m* yearling calf; tanned calfskin; church register; book bound in calfskin; **— marino** seal.
bedel *m* beadle, (*university*) porter.
beduino *an* Bedouin.
befa *f* taunt, jeer, mockery, scorn.
befar *vt* to scoff, laugh at.
befo *a* knock-kneed; thick-lipped.
beldad *f* beauty; loveliness.
belén *m* Bethlehem; nativity scene, crèche; confusion, bedlam.

beleño *m* henbane.
belga *an* Belgian.
Bélgica *f* Belgium.
bélico *m* warlike, martial.
belicoso *a* warlike, pugnacious.
beligerante *a m* belligerent.
bellaco *m* rogue, knave, sly one.
bellaquería *f* knavery, act of cunning.
belleza *f* beauty, loveliness; flourish, ornament.
bello *a* beautiful, handsome, fair, lovely.
bellota *f* acorn.
bembo *a SA* thick-lipped.
bemol *m* (*mus*) flat.
bendecir *vt* to bless, consecrate.
bendición *f* benediction; *pl* marriage ceremony.
bendito *a* blessed; *m* simpleton; saint.
benedictino *an* Benedictine.
beneficencia *f* beneficence, kindness, charity.
beneficiar *vt* to benefit, cultivate, improve; to reward; to confer a sinecure; *vr* to make profit, to improve oneself.
beneficio *m* benefit, profit; favor, kindness; (*eccles*) living.
beneficioso *a* beneficial, advantageous.
benéfico *a* kind, charitable.
benemérito *a* worthy, meritorious; *f fam* = Guardia Civil.
beneplácito *m* approbation, consent, good will.
benevolencia *f* benevolence, good will.
benévolo *a* kind-hearted, amiable, benevolent.
benignidad *f* kindness, benignity.
benigno *a* benign, clement, kind; mild (*weather*); (*influence*) softening, gentle.
benito *an* Benedictine.
beodo *m* drunken, soused (*in drink*).
berenjena *f* eggplant, aubergine.
bergantín *m* brig, brigantine.
berlina *f* landau; front compartment of stagecoach.
bermejo *a* bright red, vermilion.
bermellón *m* vermilion.
berrear *vi* to low (*like a calf*); *SA* to cry loudly, howl.
berrido *m* lowing (*of a calf*); (*fig*) howl, screaming (*of child*).
berrinche *m* fury, temper (*of small boys*).
berrinchudo *a Guat, Mex* cross, irascible.
berro *m* watercress.
berza *f* cabbage; — **lombarda** red cabbage.
besamanos *m* levée, court day; compliment.
besar *vt* to kiss.
beso *m* kiss.
bestia *f* beast; stupid person, clod, idiot.
bestialidad *f* bestiality, brutality.
besugo *m* seabream.
besuquear *vt* to slobber over (with kisses), cover with kisses.
betún *m* bitumen; shoe blacking.
biberón *m* (*infant's*) feeding bottle.
biblia *f* Bible.
bíblico *a* biblical.
bibliófilo *m* booklover, bibliophile.
bibliógrafo *m* bibliographer.
biblioteca *f* library; public library; *RP* bookcase.
bibliotecario *m* librarian.
bicicleta *f* bicycle.
bicho *m* insect, grub, 'thing' (*i.e. small animal*); *pl* vermin.
bielda *f* pitchfork.
bieldo *m* winnowing fork.
bien *m* good, utility; darling, loved one; **no** — as soon as; *pl* **—es muebles** goods and chattels; **—es de consumo** consumer goods; **—es raíces** real estate; *ad* well, right, indeed, easily, although.
bienal *a* biennial.
bienandanza *f* prosperity, fortune, success, good luck.
bienaventurado *a* happy, fortunate, blessed.
bienestar *m* comfort, well-being; welfare.
bienhadado *a* happy, lucky.
bienhallado *a* well met, glad to be here.
bienhecho *a* well-built, well done.
bienhechor *m* benefactor.
bienio *m* two-year space *or* period, the two years.
bienquisto *a* well-beloved, well-liked.
bienvenida *f* welcome; **dar la** — to welcome.
bife *m SA* steak; *Arg, Urug* slap.
biftec *m* steak.
bifurcación *f* forking, fork, branching (*of roads etc*).
bígamo *m* bigamist.
bigote *m* moustache, whisker.
bilbaíno *an* of Bilbao.
bilingüe *a* bilingual.
bilioso *a* bilious, liverish.
bilis *f* bile.
billar *m* billiards; billiard table; **sala de** — billiard hall.
billete *m* ticket; note, brief letter, love letter; — **de banco** bank note; — **sencillo** single ticket; — **de ida y vuelta** return ticket.
billetera *f Arg, Chi* wallet, billfold.
billón *m* billion.
bimbalete *m Mex* prop; buttress, pillar.
bimensual *a* twice monthly, fortnightly.
bimestral *a* every two months, two monthly.
bimotor *a* twin-engined (*plane*).
binóculo *m* binocular(s).
biografía *f* biography.

biógrafo *m* biographer.
biombo *m* (fire) screen.
biplano *m* biplane.
birlar *vt* to bowl (*a ball*) a second time; to knock down; to kill at one blow; snatch away.
birlibirloque *m* **por arte de —** by signs and spells.
birlocha *f* paper kite.
Birmania *f* Burma.
birreta *f* cardinal's red cap.
birrete *m* cap, bonnet.
birria *f* **¡que —!** what a sight! what a mess!
bisabuelo, a *mf* great-grandfather, great-grandmother.
bisagra *f* hinge.
bisel *m* bevel, bevelled edge.
bisiesto *a* **año —** leap year.
bisnieto, a *mf* great-grandson, great-granddaughter.
bisoño *a* novice, inexperienced; *m* raw recruit.
bisturí *m* bistoury, scalpel.
bizarría *f* gallantry, dash, swagger; liberality, splendidness.
bizarro *a* gallant, dashing, brave; generous; rare.
bizcacha *f SA* rodent.
bizco *a* squint-eyed, cross-eyed.
bizcocho *m* sponge cake, sponge biscuit; biscuit.
bizcorneto *a Col* cross-eyed, squinting.
bizma *f* poultice.
blanca *f* (*equiv*) brass farthing; (*mus*) minim; **sin—** broke, without a cent.
blanco *a* white; *m* lacuna, blank; goal, target, aim; white star spot (*on horses*); **arma —a** (*cold*) steel (weapons); **dar en el —** to hit the mark; **dejar en—** to leave blank.
blancura *f* whiteness.
blandir *vt* to brandish.
blando *a* soft, pliant, mild, tractable, gentle.
blandón *m* wax taper.
blandura *f* softness, mildness, gentleness.
blanquear *vt* to whiten; to bleach; to whitewash; *vi* to be bleached, go white.
blanquecino *a* whitish.
blanquete *m* whitewash; white cosmetic.
blanquillo *m SA* small fish; *Mex* egg.
blasfemar *vi* to blaspheme; to curse.
blasfemia *f* blasphemy, curse.
blasón *m* heraldry, escutcheon, shield, armorial bearings; pride, proud boast.
blasonar *vt* to blazon; *vi* to be ostentatious; **— de** to boast of.
bledo *m* wild amaranth; **no me importa un—**I don't care one bit.
blindado *a* armored (*tanks, cars etc*).
blindaje *m* blindage; armor plate.
blindar *vt* to protect with armor plating.
bloque *m* block.
bloquear *vt* to blockade, besiege, invest.
bloqueo *m* blockade.
blusa *f* blouse, smock.
boa *f* boa.
boato *m* show, flourish, pomp, panache, ostentation.
bobada *f* foolishness.
bobalicón *m* blockhead.
bobería *f* stupidity; foolishness, doltishness.
bobina *f* bobbin.
bobo *m* dunce, dolt, clown, fool; *a* silly, simple, innocent.
boca *f* mouth; entrance, bung, hole; nozzle: **a — de jarro** point-blank, very close; **— arriba** face upward; **— abajo** on one's face, face downward; **hacer —** to take an appetizer; **no decir esta — es mía** to keep mum; **de manos a —** unexpectedly, out of the blue.
bocacalle *f* crossing, junction, opening, end (of street).
bocadillo *m* sandwich; snack; narrow ribbon.
bocado *m* morsel, bite; **— de rey** titbit, delicacy.
bocanada *f* puff (*of smoke*), mouthful (*of liquid*); **— de viento** gust, blast; **— de gente** crush, crowd.
boceto *m* sketch, unfinished drawing.
bocina *f* horn (*of car*), trumpet, megaphone, foghorn.
bocoy *m* hogshead.
bochinche *m* row, tumult, uproar.
bochorno *m* sultry weather; disgrace, stigma, obloquy, dishonor; blush; shame, blot (*on reputation*).
bochornoso *a* stifling, sultry, thundery; shameful; vile, infamous, scandalous, degrading.
boda *f* wedding, marriage ceremony.
bodega *f* cellar, wine vault; storeroom: hold (*of ship*); bar, pub.
bodegaje *m SA* warehousing.
bodegón *m* tavern; eating house; still-life painting.
bodegonero *m* tavern keeper.
bodeguero *m* storekeeper.
bofe *m* lung, lights; **echar el — to** pant heavily.
bofetada *f* slap; *pl* **a —s** with (*his*) fists.
bofetón *m* cuff, heavy blow on face.
boga *f* rowing; **estar en —** to be fashionable; *m* rower in a canoe.
bogar *vi* to row.
bogotano *an* (*inhabitant*) of Bogota.
bohardilla *f* attic.
bohemio *an* Bohemian, bohemian, gypsy.
bohío *m SA* Indian hut.
boina *f* beret.
boj *m* box tree, boxwood.
bojote *m Col, Hond, Ven* bundle, parcel.
bojotero *m Col* worker in sugar mill.
bola *f* (*solid*) ball; bowl, bowling; (*fam*) he; *Arg* weighted lariat.

bolero *m* Spanish dance; woman's short jacket.
boleta *f* ticket; soldiers' billet.
boletería *m SA* box office, booking office.
boletín *m* official gazette, bulletin.
boleto *m SA* ticket.
boliche *m* jack (*in bowls*); cup-and-ball (*game*); dragnet; *Arg* small café.
bolígrafo *m* ballpoint pen.
bolívar *m Ven* silver coin.
boliviano *an* Bolivian.
bolo *m* a nine-pin, skittle, cushion (*for lacemaking*); bolus, large pill.
bolsa *f* purse; money; Exchange.
bolsillo *m* pocket; purse.
bolsista *m* speculator, stockbroker.
bolla *f SA* great wealth.
bollo *m* small loaf, small (*sponge*) cake; dent, lump.
bomba *f* pump; bomb; lamp chimney; **— atómica** atom bomb; **— de hidrógeno** hydrogen bomb; **— nuclear** nuclear bomb.
bombacha *f Arg, Par, Urug* wide trousers worn by peasants; panties.
bombardear *vt* to bomb.
bombardeo *m* bombardment, bombing.
bombear *vt* to pump.
bombero *m* fireman.
bombilla *f* bulb (*electric light*); *SA* tube for drinking maté.
bonachón *a* good-natured, easy-going.
bonaerense *an* from Buenos Aires.
bonancible *a* calm, fair, quiet.
bonanza *f* calm, fair weather at sea; prosperity.
bondad *f* goodness; kindness.
bondadoso *a* kind-hearted, helpful.
bonete *m* cap, bonnet (*eccles* & *acad*).
bonetería *f* haberdashery, notions.
bongo *m* CA Indian canoe.
bonito *a* pretty, nice, graceful; *m* striped tuna.
bono *m* bond, certificate, security; **— del tesoro** exchequer bill, Treasury bill.
boquear *vt* to gasp; to breathe one's last.
boquerón *m* wide opening, hole; anchovy.
boquete *m* gap, narrow entrance.
boquiabierto *a* gaping, open-mouthed; *m* gaper.
boquilla *f* (*mus*) mouthpiece; cigarette holder; gas jet.
boquirroto *a* loquacious, garrulous.
borbollar *vi* to gush out, to bubble (*when boiling*).
borbotar *vi* to bubble, flow in spurts (*blood from wound etc*).
borbotón *m* **hablar a —es** to talk impetuously.
borceguí *m* buskin; laced boot.
borda *f* hut, cottage; gunwale (*of ship*).
bordado *m* embroidery.
bordar *vt* to embroider.
borde *m* border, edge, fringe; hem; brim.
bordelés *an* of Bordeaux.
bordo *m* side of a ship; **a —** on board.
bordón *m* staff; walking stick; bass string; refrain (*of song*); *pl* outriggers.
boreal *a* boreal, northern.
borinqueño *an* Puerto Rican.
borla *f* tassel, tuft; (*acad*) doctor's bonnet; **tomar la —** to take a doctorate.
borona *f SA* crumb.
borra *f* yearling ewe; floss silk; nap (*on cloth*); flock wool; lees, waste; idle chatter.
borrachera *f* drunkenness; carousal, spree.
borracho *a m* drunk, intoxicated.
borrado *a Per* pock-marked.
borrador *m* rough draft; rough notebook, scribbling pad, scratch pad; eraser, duster.
borrajear *vi* to scribble, scrawl.
borrar *vt* to cross out, rub out scratch out; to obscure, obliterate, smudge.
borrasca *f* squall, tempest.
borrascoso *a* squally.
borrego *m* yearling lamb; simpleton.
borrica *f* she ass.
borricada *f* a drove of asses; donkey-ride.
borrico *m* ass; fool.
borrón *m* blot (*of ink*); blur; blemish, blot (*on reputation etc*).
borroso *a* (*weather*) thick, turbid; illegible; obscure (*of writing*).
boruquiento *a Mex* noisy, boisterous.
bosque *m* wood, forest, grove.
bosquejar *vt* to sketch, model.
bosquejo *m* sketch; rough plan.
bosta *f RP* dung.
bostezar *vi* to yawn, gape.
bostezo *m* yawn.
bota *f* topboot; leather wine bag.
botador *m* pitcher (*in games*); boat-hook.
botadura *f* launching (*of ship*).
botánica *f* botany.
botánico *a* botanical; *m* botanist.
botar *vt* to fling; squander; to launch (*ship*); to bounce.
botarate *m* scatterbrain.
bote *m* boat; (*lance*) thrust; jump; rebound; bounce (*of ball*); **de — en —** full up (*with people*), chock-full.
botella *f* bottle, flask.
botica *f* chemist's (shop), apothecary's (shop).
boticario *m* chemist, pharmacist.
botija *f* (round earthenware) jug; *Urug* small child.
botijo *m* earthen jar (with spout and handle).
botillo *vi* small wineskin.
botín *m* buskin; gaiter; booty, spoils.
botón *m* button; tip; knob; (*el*)

switch; bud; sprout; *Arg, Chi, Urug* policeman; **botones** pageboy, bellhop.
bototo *m SA* gourd for water.
bóveda *f* arched roof, vault; cave.
bovino *a* bovine; of cattle.
boxeo *m* boxing.
boya *f* buoy.
boyante *a* buoyant; afloat, prosperous.
boyero *m* oxdriver, cowherd.
bozal *m* muzzle.
bozo *m* down (*on upper lip*).
braceaje *m* depth of water (*in fathoms*).
bracear *vi* to move one's arms; to swim hand over hand; (*naut*) to brace.
bracero *m* day laborer; **de —** arm in arm.
bracete *m* **de —** arm in arm.
braga *f* breeches, knickerbockers.
bragazas *f pl* wide breeches; *m* henpecked man.
bragueta *f* (*trouser*) fly.
bramar *vi* to roar, bellow, groan.
bramido *m* howl(ing), roar(ing).
brasa *f* live coal; *pl* **estar en —s** to be like a cat on hot bricks.
brasero *m* brazier; *Mex* hearth, fireplace.
brasileño *an* Brazilian.
bravata *f* boast, an act, showing off; threat.
braveza *f* courage; vigor; ferocity; fury (*of elements*).
bravío *a* savage, untamed.
bravo *a* hardy, courageous, valiant; wild; **toro —** bull for bullfights; *excl* hurrah!
bravura *f* courage; manliness; boastfulness.
braza *f* fathom.
brazada *f* armful.
brazado *m see* **brazada.**
brazalete *m* armlet, bracelet.
brazo *m* arm; branch; **— secular** temporal authority; *pl* **los —s cruzados** with folded arms (*idle*); **luchar a — partido** to fight with bare fists; **ser el — derecho de** to be the right hand man of.
brea *f* pitch, tar; coarse canvas
brebaje *f* medicine, draft, beverage; (*naut*) grog.
brecha *f* breach, opening; **batir en—** to make a breach in.
brega *f* struggle, strife; contest; pun.
bregar *vi* to struggle, wrestle (*with*), contend; to work dough with rolling pin.
breña *f* rough scrub, waste moorland.
breñal *m see* **breña.**
breva *f* early fig; large early acorn; choice cigar; *Arg, Urug* **pecar la —** to rob, steal.
breve *a* brief, short, concise; *m* apostolic brief; *f* (*mus*) breve; **en —** soon.
brevedad *f* brevity, conciseness.
breviario *m* breviary; epitome.
brezal *m* heath, field of heather.
brezo *m* heath; heather.
bribón *m* scoundrel, vagrant.
bribonear *vi* to loaf, lead a vagabond life.
brida *f* bridle; curb; flange.
brigada *f* brigade.
brillante *a* brilliant, bright; *m* brilliant, diamond.
brillar *vi* to shine, glitter; be outstanding (*in talents etc*).
brillo *m* shine; resplendence, splendor; distinction; polish.
brincar *vi* to frisk, hop, leap.
brinco *m* jump, hop, bound.
brindar *vi* to drink *or* toast health; to promise, offer a prospect of; *vt* to offer willingly, proffer.
brindis *m* toast; health; dedication.
brío *m* strength, fire; nerve, spirit, liveliness.
brioso *a* fiery, vigorous, lively.
brisa *f* breeze, soft wind.
brisca *f* bezique.
británico *a* British.
brizna *f* particle, fragment, chip; blade, sprig (*grass etc*).
brocado *m* brocade.
brocal *m* curbstone (of a well).
brocha *f* painter's brush; **de— gorda** roughhewn, slapdash, rough and ready fashion.
broche *m* clasp; brooch; hook and eye.
broma *f* practical joke, jest; **— pesada** joke taken too far; **de —** in fun, not in earnest.
bromear *vi* to jest.
bromista *m* merry jester; practical joker.
bronca *f* row; **se armó una —** there was no end of a row.
bronce *m* bronze; (*mus*) trumpet.
bronceado *a* brazen, of brass; *m* bronzing.
bronco *a* rough, coarse; peevish; hoarse.
bronquial *a* bronchial.
bronquitis *f* bronchitis.
broquel *m* buckler, shield.
brotar *vi* to shoot, sprout, bud; to spring (*from*).
brote *m* bud, shoot.
broza *f* thicket; dead wood, rubbish; idle talk painter's brush.
bruces *ad* **de —** face downward, headlong.
bruja *f* witch, hag, sorceress.
brujería *f* witchcraft.
brujo *m* magician, sorcerer; *a Cub, Mex, PR* poor.
brújula *f* compass; sea compass.
brujulear *vt* to find out by guesswork; to conjecture.
bruma *f* mist, haze.
brumoso *a* hazy, foggy, misty; vague.
bruñido *m* polish: *a* burnished.

bruñir *vt* to polish, burnish.
brusco *a* rude, forward, rough, sharp, brusque.
brutal *a* brutal, vicious, savage.
brutalidad *f* brutality, savageness.
bruto *m* brute; ignorant person; *a* unpolished, crude; **peso —** gross weight; **en —** as grown, mined *etc*, unrefined, (*stone*) undressed.
buba *f* pustule, small tumor.
bucanero *m* buccaneer.
bucear *vi* to dive; to search below the surface.
buceo *m* diving.
bucle *m* curl, ringlet.
bucólico *a* bucolic.
buche *m* maw, crop; foal; pucker (*in clothes*); **sacar a uno el —** to worm secrets out of one.
Buda *m* Buddha.
budare *m Ven* baking pan.
budín *m* pudding; sultana cake; *Arg* (*sl*) pretty woman.
buenamente *ad* spontaneously, easily.
buenaventura *f* good luck, fortune.
bueno *a* good; plain, honest; sound, healthy; appropriate; *ad* well; **de buenas a primeras** straight away; **a buenas** with good will, right.
buey *m* ox; **— marino** sea cow; **— de agua** gush of water from spring *etc.*
búfalo *m* buffalo.
bufanda *f* muffler, scarf.
bufar *vi* to snort.
bufete *m* desk; sideboard; writing table; lawyer's office; **abrir —** to set up as a lawyer.
bufido *m* snorting; huff, h'mph!
bufo *m* buffoon; *a* grotesque, comic (*opera*).
bufón *m* buffoon, harlequin, jester.
buhardilla *f* skylight; garret.
búho *m* owl; unsociable person; **es un —** he doesn't go anywhere.
buhonero *m* hawker, cheap-jack, peddler.
buitre *m* vulture.
bujía *f* wax candle; candlestick; sparkplug.
bula *f* papal bull.
bulbo *m* bulb; globe.
búlgaro *an* Bulgarian.
bulto *m* bundle; bulk; bale; **a —** wholesale; indiscriminately; **de —** of importance; **escurrir el —** to shirk the consequences, to refuse to face the music.
bulla *f* noise, clatter; **meter —** to make a din.
bullanga *f* tumult, riot.
bullanguero *a* rioting, turbulent.
bullicio *m* noise; bustle (*of a crowd*).
bullicioso *a* rowdy, high-spirited, lively.
bullir *vi* to boil; to bustle, fluster.
buñolero *m* doughnut seller, bun-maker.
buñuelo *m* bun, doughnut: **— de viento** light cream bun.
buque *m* (*large*) vessel, ship; tonnage; **— de vapor** steamship; **— escuela** training ship; **— de guerra** warship.
burbuja *f* bubble.
burdel *m* brothel.
burdo *a* coarse, ordinary.
burgalés *an* of Burgos.
burgués *an* bourgeois, middle-class.
burguesía *f* middle class.
buril *m* graving tool; pen graver.
burla *f* mockery, hoax; jest; **de —** for fun, not seriously; **— pesada** low trick; **— burlando** with one jest or other, easily.
burlador *m* jester; wag; libertine.
burlar *vr* to mock, gibe, ridicule; to frustrate, circumvent, get (around, over), baffle, outwit; to seduce; to deceive.
burlesco *m* burlesque.
burlón *m* wag, jester; scoffer; *a* scoffing, mocking, waggish.
burocracia *f* beaurocracy.
burra *f* she-ass.
burrada *f* blunder, gaffe, howler.
burro *m* ass, donkey; dolt; *Arg* old racing horse; *pl* horse racing.
bursátil *a* Exchange, financial.
busaca *f Col, Ven* bag.
busca *f* search, pursuit; *pl* perquisites.
buscaniguas *m Col, Guat* squib, cracker.
buscapiés *m* snake; firecracker.
buscapleitos *m SA* troublemaker.
buscar *vt* to look for, hunt for; to search; *vr* to bring upon oneself.
buscón *m* seeker, pilferer.
busilis *m* question, knotty point, dark riddle.
búsqueda *f* search, quest.
busto *m* bust.
butaca *f* armchair, easy chair; orchestra seat (*theat*).
butifarra *f* sausage (*esp in Catalonia*).
buzo *m* diver.
buzón *m* conduit; letterbox, mailbox; bung.

C

cabal *a* just; perfect, consummate, complete, exact.
cábala *f* cabal; intrigue; clique.
cabalgadura *f* riding horse, mount; beast of burden.
cabalgar *vi* to ride (on horseback).
cabalgata *f* cavalcade.
caballar *a* equine, of horses.
caballeresco *a* chivalrous, knightly.
caballería *f* a riding beast; cavalry; knighthood; **— andante** knight errantry.
caballeriza *f* stable, stud of horses.
caballerizo *m* stable groom.
caballero *m* knight, horseman; nobleman; gentleman; **— andante** knight errant; **— de industria** sharper, swindler.

caballerosidad *f* generosity, nobility (*of heart or person*).
caballete *m* painter's easel; trestle; ridge; chimney cowl; bridge (*of nose*).
caballo *m* horse; horsepower; queen (*cards*); knight (*chess*); **a —** on horseback.
cabalmente *ad* exactly, quite so, just so.
cabaña *f* hut, hovel, cottage; *Arg, Urug* cattle ranch.
cabecear *vi* to nod, droop; to shake head (*in disapproval*); (*naut*) to pitch.
cabecera *f* bed-head; head; upper end (*of table etc*); bolster or pillow.
cabecilla *m* ringleader, leader, chief.
cabellera *f* hair (*especially of woman*); long hair; tail (*of comet*).
cabello *m* hair; *pl* **— de ángel** sweetmeat in form of fine threads; **tomar la ocasión por los —** to take time by the forelock.
cabelludo *a* hairy, fibrous.
caber *vi* to be contained in, have room for, fit in; to be entitled to partake of; **no— de gozo** to be beside oneself with joy; **no cabe más** the place is full up; **no cabe duda** there is no doubt.
cabestrillo *m* arm sling.
cabestro *m* halter; bell ox.
cabeza *f* head; beginning; leader, chief; upper part; **de —** headlong, decisively, thoroughly; **romperse la —** to rack one's brains.
cabezada *f* blow with the head, nod; halter; **dar —s** to nod drowsily.
cabezudo *a* big-headed; obstinate, pig-headed.
cabida *f* content, capacity; **dar — a** to make room for.
cabildo *m* cathedral chapter; town council.
cabizbajo *a* crestfallen.
cable *m* cable; **— metálico** wire cable; **— submarino** submarine cable.
cabo *m* end, stump; handle; cape, promontory; (*mil*) corporal; **al— de** at the end of; **de — a rabo** from end to end; **llevar a —** to finish, complete, succeed in doing.
Cabo *m* **de Buena Esperanza** Cape of Good Hope.
Cabo *m* **de Hornos** Cape Horn.
cabotaje *m* coastal trade.
cabra *f* goat; *Col, Cub* loaded dice; *Chi* two-wheeled carriage; **loco como una —** as mad as a hatter.
cabrero *m* goatherd; *Arg* (*sl*) quick-tempered person.
cabrestante *m* capstan.
cabria *f* crane, hoist, winch, windlass.
cabrilla *f* small goat; (*sea*) white horses; **hacer —s** to play ducks and drakes.
cabrío *a* pertaining to goats; **macho —** he-goat.
cabriola *f* caper, leap, jump.
cabriolé *m* cabriolet.
cabritilla *f* kid (*leather*).
cabrito *m* kid.
cabrón *m* buck, he-goat; (*vulg*) cuckold.
cabruno *a* goatish; pertaining to goats.
cacahuete *m* peanut; groundnut.
cacahuetero *m* *Mex* peanut-seller.
cacao *m* cacao (tree), cocoa.
cacarear *vi* to cackle, (*cock*) crow; to boast.
cacareo *m* cackling, crowing; boast.
cacarizo *m* *Mex* pock-marked.
cacería *f* hunting, hunt.
cacerola *f* saucepan, casserole dish.
cacique *m* (Indian) chief or prince; political boss.
caciquismo *m* rule or government by local bosses.
cacle *m* *Mex* leather sandal.
caco *m* thief, pickpocket; **más ladrón que —** as big a thief as they make 'em.
cacofonía *f* cacophony; discordant, ugly sound.
cacto *m* cactus.
cacumen *m* height; talent, wit; acumen.
cachaco *m* *Col, Ec, Ven* dandy.
cachalote *m* cachalot whale.
cachar *vt* *Arg* to pull someone's leg; to catch; to chip (*china etc*).
cacharpari *m* *Per* farewell supper.
cacharrería *f* pot shop.
cacharro *m* coarse earthen pot; pots (and pans); **¡qué —!** what junk!
cachaza *f* tardiness; phlegm; coolness; *f* *SA* rum.
cache *a* *SA* coarse, unpolished.
cachemira *f* cashmere.
cachetada *f* slap.
cachete *m* slap; plump cheek.
cachimba *f* *SA* pipe (*for smoking*).
cachiporra *f* club, cudgel.
cachivaches *m pl* kitchenware; broken crockery.
cacho *m* piece, slice.
cachorro *m* puppy; cub, whelp.
cachúa *f* *Per, Ec, Bol* Indian dance.
cada *a* each; every; **— uno** each one.
cadalso *m* scaffold (*for execution*).
cadáver *n* corpse, (dead) body.
cadena *f* chain; **— perpetua** hard labor for life.
cadencia *f* cadence, rhythm.
cadera *f* hip.
cadete *m* cadet; (officer) cadet.
caducar *vi* to dote; to lapse, fall due; to become superannuated, out of date.
caduco *a* senile, decrepit; lapsed (*contracts*).
caer *vi* to fall; to fall off; to happen: **— en la cuenta** to understand, notice; **— bien** to fit, suit; **— en gracia** to make a good impression, to please; *vr* **— de su peso** to be self-evident.
café *m* coffee; café.

cafetal *m* coffee plantation.
cafetera *f* coffeepot, percolator.
cafetero *m* coffee tree.
cáfila *f* horde, band (*of gypsies*).
cafre *m* Kaffir; *PR* unsophisticated.
caída *f* fall; ruin; — **de sol** sunset.
caimán *m* alligator.
caimiento *m* depression, decay; fall.
caja *f* box, case, chest; coffin; stock (*of rifle*); (*mil*) drum; cash; — **de ahorros** savings bank; **libro de** — cash book; — **baja** lower case (*print*); — **del cuerpo** bust; **despedir con —s destempladas** to send (*somebody*) packing.
cajero *m* cashier.
cajetilla *f* packet (of cigarettes).
cajista *m* compositor (*print*).
cajón *m* chest; drawer; *Arg, Par, Urug* coffin; — **de sastre** miscellany, jumble, medley.
cal *f* lime.
cala *f* small bay, cove; (*ship*) hold.
calabaza *f* pumpkin; squash; gourd; fool; **dar —s** *vt* to flunk (*in examinations*); to jilt, turn down.
calabozo *m* dungeon; jail, calaboose.
calado *a* soaked; smart, 'all there'; *m* drawn work in line; open work in metal; (*ship*) draft. *see* **calar.**
calafatear *vt* to calk.
calaíta *f* turquoise.
calamar *m* squid.
calambre *m* cramp; contraction of muscles.
calamidad *f* calamity, misfortune, unfortunate, unhappy (event, happening *etc*).
calamina *f* calamine.
calamita *f* loadstone.
calamitoso *a* calamitous, miserable.
calamorro *m Chi* rough shoe.
calandria *f* bunting (*kind of lark*); mangle, rolling press.
calaña *f* character, sort.
calañés *a* **sombrero** — hat with upturned brim.
calapé *m SA* turtle roasted in its shell.
calar *vt* to penetrate; to drench, soak through; to tumble to (*an idea*); to fix (*bayonet*).
calato *a Per* naked.
calavera *f* skull; *m* rake, wastrel, gay dog.
calaverada *f* escapade.
calcañar *m* heel-bone; heel.
calcar *vt* to trace, copy; to base (*on*).
calce *m* wedge.
calceta *f* (*knee-length*) stocking; **hacer** — to knit.
calcetín *m* sock, half-hose.
calcina *f* mortar, cement.
calcinar *vt* to calcine.
calcio *m* calcium.
calco *m* counter-drawing, tracing; copy.
calcular *vt* to calculate; to make calculations; to estimate, reckon.
cálculo *m* calculation, computation; (*bladder, liver*) stone.
calcha *f Chi* fetlock of horse; *Chi, Arg* old, ugly woman.
calda *f* heating (*of water*); *pl* hot thermal baths.
caldear *vt* to heat; to weld.
caldera *f* boiler, kettle, cauldron.
calderada *f* a cauldronful.
calderería *f* ironmongery, tinker's.
calderilla *f* copper coin; small (loose) change.
caldero *m* small cauldron, pan, copper.
calderón *m* large kettle; (*mus*) pause.
caldo *m* broth; wine, oil, vinegar; *m Mex* juice of sugar cane.
calefacción *f* heating.
calefón *m Arg* immersion heater, geyser.
calembé *m Cub* bathing trunks.
calendario *m* almanac, calendar.
calentador *m* heater; warming pan.
calentano *m SA* lowlander.
calentar (ie) *vt* to warm, heat; *vr* to grow hot; to grow heated (*argument*).
calentura *f* fever; temperature.
calenturiento *a* feverish.
calera *f* limekiln.
calero *a* calcareous; *m* lime-burner.
calesa *f* Spanish chaise.
calesero *m* driver of a chaise.
calesín *m* light chaise.
calesita *f Arg, Par* merry-go-round.
caleta *f* small bay, inlet, creek.
caletre *m* judgment, acumen.
calibrar *vt* to gauge; to measure the caliber.
calibre *m* caliber, diameter; quality.
calicanto *m* allspice.
calidad *f* quality; condition; rank; *pl* (*moral*) qualities; gifts; **en — de** as, representing, in (his) office as.
cálido *a* (*climate*) hot.
caliente *a* (*object*) hot, warm; (*argument*) heated; fiery; *Arg* sexually excited.
califa *m* caliph.
calificación *f* qualification, estimate; standard (*in examination*).
calificado *a* competent, skilled; important, declared, rated.
calificar *vt* to qualify; to authorize; to mark (*examination papers*); *vr* to prove nobility of descent.
caligrafía *f* calligraphy, handwriting.
cáliz *m* chalice.
calizo *a* calcareous, limy.
calma *f* calm; ease of mind, composure; dullness.
calmante *a m* sedative.
calmar *vt* to calm, appease, soothe, quieten.
calmoso *a* tranquil, slow.
calmudo *a SA* easy-going, slow.
caló *m* gypsy cant, slang.
calofrío *m* chilliness; shivering.

calor *m* heat; warmth; **al — de** encouraged by.
calórico *m* caloric, heat.
calorífero *m* heating apparatus.
calpamulo *a Mex* half-breed.
calumnia *f* calumny, slander.
calumniador *m* slanderer.
calumnioso *a* slanderous, slandering.
caluroso *a* warm, hot; eager: fervent.
caluyo *m Bol* Indian clog-dance.
calva *f* bald head.
calvario *m* calvary; suffering; **estaciones del —** Stations of the Cross.
calvicie *f* baldness.
calvo *a* bald, hairless; barren.
calza *f* breeches; stocking; wedge.
calzada *f* causeway, road.
calzado *a* shod; *m* footwear.
calzador *m* shoe-horn.
calzar *vt* to put on (*shoes*).
calzón *m* breeches; **— corto** knee-breeches.
calzoncillos *m pl* pants, drawers; briefs.
callado *a* silent, discreet, quiet.
callana *f SA* flat, earthen bowl.
callar *vi* to be silent; *vt* to quieten; to omit; to conceal; **quien calla otorga** silence gives consent.
calle *f* street, road (*in town*).
calleja *f* narrow street, side street.
callejear *vi* to go about the streets; to loiter, lounge, hang about.
callejero *a* street; common, coarse.
callejón *m* narrow street, alley, lane; **— sin salida** blind alley, cul-de-sac.
callejuela *f* alley-way.
callista *m* chiropodist.
callo *m* corn, callosity; *pl* tripe.
calloso *a* callous, horny.
cama *f* bed; couch; layer, stratum; **guardar —** to stay in bed, be bed-ridden.
camada *f* litter, brood.
camafeo *m* cameo.
camaleón *m* chameleon.
camandulear *vi* to act hypocritically, in an underhand manner; to trick.
camandulero *m* hypocrite, trickster.
cámara *f* hall, chamber, cabin (*of ship*); **— de comercio** Chamber of Commerce; **— de representantes** house of representatives.
camarada *m* comrade, companion, friend.
camarera *f* lady's maid; waitress; stewardess.
camarero *m* chamberlain, valet de chambre; steward; waiter.
camarico *m SA* offering; *Chi* love affair.
camarilla *f* cabal, clique; small room.
camarín *m* dressing room.
camarista *m* member of congress; *f* maid of honor.
camarón *m* prawn.
camarote *m* berth; cabin.
camastrear *vi Chi* to dissemble.
camastro *m* wretched bed, pallet.
camastrón *m* cunning fellow, sly one.
cambar *vt Arg, Ven* to bend, curve.
cambiable *a* exchangeable.
cambiante *m* variety of colors; exchange agent.
cambiar *vt* to change, exchange, barter.
cambio *m* change; exchange; **libre —** free trade; **en —** instead; on the other hand.
cambista *m* money changer; broker; banker; *Arg* (*rl*) switchman.
cambray *m* cambric.
cambrón *m* buckthorn.
cambrona *f Arg* cambric.
cambucho *m Chi* paper cone; waste-basket; hut, bowl.
cambullón *m Per* imposition, swindle; *Col, Mex* secondhand shop.
camelar *vt* to flirt, deceive, trick.
camelia *f* camellia.
camello *m* camel.
camilla *f* stretcher, litter.
caminante *m* traveler; walker.
caminar *vi* to go, walk, proceed.
caminata *f* march, walk, excursion, walking trip.
camino *m* road; way; highway; **— de herradura** bridle path; **— de Santiago** Milky Way; **ponerse en —** to set out.
camión *m* truck, lorry.
camisa *f* shirt; chemise.
camisería *f* shirt shop, shirtmaker's.
camiseta *f* vest.
camisón *m Col, Chi, Ven* costume; *SA* nightgown, nightshirt.
camorra *f* dispute, wrangle, set-to.
camorrista *mf* noisy, quarrelsome person.
camote *m SA* sweet potato; infatuation; lover, mistress; lie, fib.
campal *a* pitched (*battle*).
campamento *m* camp; encampment.
campana *f* bell; cup, cloche, cone.
campanada *f* sound, stroke (of a bell).
campanario *m* belfry, steeple, church tower.
campaneo *m* ringing of bells.
campanilla *f* small bell; bell-flower; uvula.
campanillazo *m* violent ringing (*of a bell*), clanging.
campante *a* excelling.
campanudo bell-shaped; pompous, high-flown, bombastic.
campánula *f* bell-flower.
campaña *f* (*mil*) campaign; plain, level country.
campañol *m* fieldmouse.
campar *vi* to excel, surpass; to camp.
campechana *f Cub, Mex* drink; *Ven* hammock; harlot.

campechano *a* frank, open, genial, hearty, well-disposed; liberal.
campeche *m* Campeachy wood.
campeón *m* champion; defender.
campeonato *m* championship.
campesino *a* rural, rustic; *m* peasant, countryman, farmer.
campestre *a* rustic, country; (*of flowers*) wild.
campiña *f* flat arable land, landscape, countryside.
campista *m SA* owner of or partner in mine.
campo *m* country, field; range, scope; **— de fútbol** football field; **— de tenis** tennis court; **— santo** cemetery; **ir a — travieso** to cut across the fields.
camueso *m* pippin tree; dolt, fool.
can *m* dog; trigger; corbel.
cana *f* gray hair; **peinar —s** to be old.
canaca *f Chi* owner of brothel.
Canadá *m* Canada.
canadiense *an* Canadian.
canal *m* channel; canal; **— de la Mancha** English Channel; *f* gutter, drain pipe; **abrir en —** to slit (*pig*) open.
canalizar *vt* to canalize.
canalón *m* wide gutter.
canalla *f* rabble, mob; *m* rotter, scoundrel.
canapé *m* couch, sofa, settee; canapé.
Canarias, las Islas *f pl* the Canary Islands.
canario *m* canary; Canary Islander.
canasta *f* basket, hamper; canasta.
canastilla *f* small basket; layette; *Arg, PR* trousseau.
canastillo *m* small low basket; flowerpot.
canasto *m* large basket.
cancel *m* wooden screen.
cancelación *f* cancellation.
cancelar *vt* to cancel, annul.
cancelario *m* chancellor (*of university*).
cáncer *m* cancer.
Cancerbero *m* Cerberus; surly doorkeeper; incorruptible, implacable guard.
canciller *m* chancellor; *Arg* Minister for Foreign Affairs.
cancillería *f* chancellor's office; high court; *Arg* Ministry of Foreign Affairs.
canción *f* song, tune, lyric; **— de cuna** lullaby.
cancionero *m* songbook.
canco *m Chi* stewpot, flowerpot.
cancha *f SA* roasted corn or broad beans; clear ground; **— de fútbol** football ground.
candado *m* padlock.
candeal *a* very white; **trigo —** white wheat; **pan —** white (*ie superior*) bread.
candela *f* candle; fire; chestnut blossom.
candelabro *m* candelabrum.
candelaria *f* Candlemas.
candelejón *a Col, Chi, Per* candid; silly.
candelero *m* candlestick.
candente *a* incandescent; white-hot, glowing; **cuestión —** burning question.
candidato *m* candidate; applicant, competitor; pretender.
candidez *f* candor, ingenuousness.
cándido *a* candid; simple; white.
candil *m* oil lamp; lamp.
candileja *f* oil container in lamp; small lamp; *pl* footlights.
candinga *f SA* folly; devil.
candombe *m SA* Negro dance.
candor *m* candor, sincerity, frankness.
canela *f* cinnamon.
canelo *m* cinnamon tree.
canelón *m* gargoyle, gutter; cinnamon sweetmeat.
caney *m Cub, Ven* log cabin.
cangallar *vt Chi, Per* to steal, cheat.
cangrejo *m* crab.
canguro *m* kangaroo.
caníbal *m* cannibal, man-eater.
canícula *f* dog-star.
canicular *a* very hot, midsummer.
canijo *a* weak.
canilla *f* shinbone; tap, plug; spigot; bobbin.
canillera *f Col* awe, dread; *pl* (*sport*) pads.
canillita *m SA* newsboy.
canino *a* canine.
canje *m* exchange.
canjear *vt* to exchange.
cano *a* gray-haired; hoary.
canoa *f* canoe.
canoi *m SA* fishing basket.
canon *m* rule, precept; noun; model; *pl* canonical law.
canonesa *f* canoness.
canonjía *f* canonry.
canónico *a* canonic, canonical.
canónigo *m* canon, prebendary.
canonización *f* canonization.
canonizar *vt* to canonize.
canoro *m* melodious, musical.
canoso *a* gray-haired.
cansado *a* tired, fatigued; tedious, boring; well-worn.
cansancio *m* weariness.
cansar *vt* to tire; to weary; to bore; *vr* to become tired, weary.
cantaletear *vt SA* to nag, harp on.
cantante *mf* singer.
cantar *vt* to sing; to chant, to divulge (*secret*), 'squeal'; *vi* to sing out; to squeak; to creak; *m* song; **cantar de los —es** Song of Songs; **— de gesta** medieval heroic poem.
cántara *f* large pitcher; liquid measure (*about 4-5 gallons*).
cántaro *m* (*wine, water*) pitcher; **llover a —s** to rain cats and dogs.
cantatriz *f* singer.
cantera *f* quarry.

cantería *f* quarrying.
cantero *m* stone cutter, quarryman, mason; flower bud; **— de pan** crust.
cántico *m* canticle; song, chant.
cantidad *f* quantity; amount.
cantiga *f* lyric, song.
cantimplora *f* (*mil*) water bottle.
cantil *m* steep rock.
cantina *f* cellar; canteen; railway buffet; *SA* bar; *Arg* cheap restaurant.
cantinela *f* ballad.
cantinero *m* butler; canteen-keeper.
canto *m* song; stone; end; edge; **— rodado** boulder; **de —** on (its) edge, side; right-side up.
cantor *m* singer.
cantorral *m* stony ground.
canturrear *vi* to hum (*song*).
caña *f* cane, reed; walking stick; glass (*of beer*); **— de azúcar** sugar cane; **— de pescar** fishing rod.
cañada *f* glen, narrow valley.
cañamazo *m* coarse canvas, burlap.
cañamiel *f* sugar cane.
cáñamo *m* hemp; *SA* hempcord; **— en rama** raw, undressed hemp.
cañaveral *m* plantation of reed-grass; cane-brake.
cañería *f* water *or* gas conduit; pipe, piping, guttering.
caño *m* sewer; pipe; conduit; narrow branch of river or sea.
cañón *m* cannon, gun; quill.
cañonazo *m* cannonshot, report (of gunshot).
cañonear *vt* to cannonade, bombard, shell.
cañonera *f* tent; gun port.
cañonero *m* gun boat.
caoba *f* mahogany.
caos *m* chaos, confusion.
capa *f* cloak, mantle, cape; layer, stratum, seam; pretense; **so — de** under pretense of; **andar (ir) de — caída** to be dejected, off color, down in the mouth.
capacidad *f* capacity; authority; talent, competence.
capacitación *f* training.
capacho *m* basket; hamper.
capar *vt* to geld, castrate.
caparazón *m* caparison; carcass of a fowl.
capataz *m* overseer; foreman; steward; (*denoting contempt*) chief.
capaz *a* capacious; able, competent.
capcioso *a* captious.
capea *f* (*amateur*) village bullfight.
capeador *m* (*amateur, young*) bullfighter.
capear *vt* to fry (*meat, fish*) in egg batter.
capellán *m* chaplain; **— castrense** army chaplain.
caperuza *f* hood, cap ending in a point; **caperucita roja** Little Red Riding Hood.
capi *m Chi* pod, capsule; *SA* corn.
capilar *a* capillary.
capilla *f* chapel; hood, cowl; paged proofs; **— ardiente** lying-in-state; **estar en —** to be in the condemned cell; to be on hot bricks.
capirotazo *m* flip (*with fingers*); rap, tap.
capirote *m* doctor's hood; cover of the head; (*for hawk*) hood.
capitación *f* poll tax; capitation.
capital *a* capital, principal; **pena —** capital punishment; death sentence: *m* capital; fortune; capital stock; *f* capital city.
capitalista *m* capitalist.
capitalizar *vt* to capitalize.
capitán *m* captain.
capitana *f* admiral's ship, admiral's wife.
capitanear *vt* to head, lead.
capitanía *f* captaincy.
capitel *m* (*of a pillar*) capital, cornice.
capitolino *a* capitoline.
capitolio *m* capitol; imposing building.
capitoné *m Arg* quilted rug.
capitulación *f* capitulation; stipulation; *pl* articles of marriage.
capitular *vi* to capitulate; *a* (*cathedral*) chapter.
capítulo *m* chapter.
capó *m* (*aut*) bonnet, hood.
capón *m* eunuch; capon.
caporal *m* head; chief; head man in a farm.
capota *f* bonnet; (*aut*) hood, top.
capote *m* (*mil, bullfighter's*) short cloak; **dar — a** to sweep the board (*at cards*); **decir para su —** to keep something to oneself.
capricho *m* caprice, whim, sudden desire.
caprichoso *a* capricious, whimsical, fanciful, unreliable.
cápsula *f* capsule; metal cap (*on bottles*); cartridge.
captar *vt* to captivate; to win, obtain (*sympathy etc*).
captura *f* capture; seizing.
capturar *vt* to capture, seize, arrest.
capucha *f* hood, cowl.
Capuchino *a m* Franciscan friar; *Arg, Urug* Capuchino coffee.
capullo *m* bud; cocoon; acorn cup.
capuz *m* long cloak with hood.
cara *f* face, countenance; appearance, look; **— de Pascua** smiling face; **— de viernes** sullen face; **— y cruz** heads and tails; **dar en —** to reproach.
carabela *f* caravel.
carabina *f* carbine; rifle, fowling-piece; **— de Ambrosio** ineffective or non-existent object; white elephant.
carabinero *m* carabineer, revenue police; frontier officer.
caracol *m* snail; **escalera de —** spiral staircase.
caracolear *vi* to caracole, twist about, twirl.

carácter *m* character; disposition; condition; type, letter; handwriting.
característica *f* characteristic, typical trait, feature, attribute.
característico *a* characteristic, typical.
caracterizar *vt* to characterize; to impart character to; to distinguish.
caracú *m Bol, RP* marrow.
caramanchel *m Arg, Chi* eating house, canteen.
caramanchelero *m SA* hawker, peddler.
caramba *excl* good gracious!; good heavens!
carámbano *m* icicle.
carambola *f* (*billiards*) cannon; **hacer —s** to play billiards.
caramelo *m* caramel; burnt sugar; sweet, toffee, sweetmeat.
caramillo *m* flageolet; high-tuned flute.
carapacho *m* shell.
caraqueño *an* (*inhabitant*) of Caracas.
carátula *f* (*theat*) pasteboard mask; small company of actors; face (*of clock*); front page (*of book*).
caravana *f* caravan.
caray *excl* goodness!
carbón *m* charcoal; coal; **— de piedra** coal, pit coal.
carbonada *f* stew of meat, rice, pumpkin, corn and fruit.
carbonato *m* carbonate.
carbonero *a* coal; *m* coalman, coal merchant.
carbonizar *vt* to carbonize.
carbono *m* carbon.
carbunclo *m* carbuncle (*precious stone*); anthrax.
carburador *m* carburetor.
carcaj *m* quiver (*of arrows*).
carcajada *f* burst of laughter.
carcamal *m* decrepit old person.
carcamán *m Cub* unimportant foreigner; *Per* presumptuous; *Arg* Italian.
cárcel *f* prison, jail.
carcelero *m* jailer, warder.
carcoma *f* dry rot; death-watch beetle; worry.
carcomer *vt* to gnaw, eat away; to corrode.
carcomido *a* worm-eaten, rotten.
cardar *vt* (*wool*) to card, comb.
cardenal *m* cardinal; weal, bruise.
cardenalato *m* cardinalate.
cardenillo *m* verdigris.
cárdeno *a* livid, discolored.
cardíaco *a* cardiac, heart-; suffering from weak heart.
cardillo *m* golden thistle.
cardinal *a* cardinal, fundamental.
cardo *m* thistle.
carear *vt* to confront (*the accused with the witnesses*).
carecer *vi* to be in need of; to lack, not to have.
carena *f* careening.
carenar *vt* to careen.
carencia *f* lack; need, want, absence.
careo *m* confrontation.
carestía *f* scarcity, want, shortage; dearness, cost.
careta *f* pasteboard mask, faceguard; deceitful appearance.
carey *m* tortoiseshell.
carga *f* load, burden, charge, responsibility; cargo; charge (*of firearms, cavalry etc*).
cargadero *m* (un)loading place, wharf.
cargada *f Arg* heavy joke.
cargado *a* loaded, strong (*of tea, coffee*); emphatic; **— de espaldas** round-shouldered.
cargador *m* freighter; loader.
cargamento *m* cargo; freight.
cargar *vt* to load, ship; to stoke (*furnace*); to charge, attack; to increase (*prices*); to charge (*an account*).
cargazón *f* cargo; freight of ship; thick, heavy weather; heaviness (*in head*).
cargo *m* the act of loading; burden; cargo; charge; post, office, dignity; **— de conciencia** remorse, compunction; **hacerse — de** to be responsible for; to take into consideration, understand, realize.
carguero *m Arg, Col, Par* cargo ship; freight train.
cargosear *vt Arg* to pester, bother.
cari *m SA* blackberry; *Arg, Chi* light brown color.
cariaco *m Cub* popular dance; *Ec* beverage.
cariacontecido *a* sad-looking, perplexed.
cariarse *vr* to rot, putrefy, decay (*of teeth*).
caribe *an* Caribbean, Carib.
Caribe, el Mar *m* Caribbean Sea.
caricatura *f* caricature, cartoon.
caricia *f* caress, stroke, pat, hug.
caridad *f* charity; charitableness; alms.
caries *f* caries, rot; bone decay.
carilampiño *a Chi, Per* beardless.
carimbo *m Bol* branding iron.
cariño *m* fondness, tenderness, affection, love.
cariñoso *a* loving, affectionate, tender, kind.
caritativo *a* charitable, benevolent.
cariucho *m Ec* Indian dish.
cariz *m* aspect (*of sky*); appearance, prospect; **tener mal —** to scowl.
carlanga *f Mex* rag, tatter.
Carlista *m* Carlist.
Carlos *m* Charles.
Carlota *f* Charlotte.
carmelita *an* Carmelite.
carmen *m* country house, garden.
carmesí *a* crimson.
carmín *a* carmine; *m* cochineal.
carnada *f* bait; allurement.
carnal *a* carnal, sensual, fleshy; **primo —** full cousin.

carnaval *m* carnival; week before Lent.
carnaza *f* fleshy side of hide or skin.
carne *f* flesh; meat; **ser uña y— con** to be as thick as thieves, be intimate, hand in glove with; **echar —s** to put on flesh; **en —s** naked.
carneada *f SA* butchering.
carnear *vt SA* to kill, slaughter.
carnerada *f* flock of sheep.
carnero *m* sheep; mutton; *Arg* person lacking willpower; strikebreaker.
carnestolendas *f pl* three meat days before Ash Wednesday.
carnicería *f* butcher's shop; carnage, butchery.
carnicero *a* carnivorous; *m* butcher.
carnívoro *a* carnivorous.
carnosidad *f* carnosity, fatness, fleshiness.
carnoso *a* fleshy, carnous; fleshy (*of fruit*).
caro *a* dear, costly; beloved; *ad* dearly, at a high price.
Carolina *f* Caroline.
carozo *m Bol, Mex, RP* pip, stone (*of fruit*).
carpa *f* carp; canvas tent.
carpeta *f* table cover; portfolio.
carpidor *m SA* hoe.
carpintería *f* carpentry; carpenter's shop.
carpintero *m* carpenter, joiner; **pájaro —** woodpecker.
carraca *f* carrack, small freighter; ratchet.
carrada *f RP* cartload, large quantity.
carral *m* (*wine*) butt, pipe.
carrao *m Ven* bird, resembling crane; *Col, Cub* heavy, coarse shoes.
carraspera *f* (*in throat*) hoarseness, huskiness, frog.
carrera *f* running; race; road; course; career, profession; **a la —** hurriedly.
carreta *f* crude country cart.
carretada *f* cartload.
carrete *m* spool, bobbin, reel; (*film*) roll.
carretear *vt* to cart; to drive a cart.
carretel *m* spool; reel; bobbin.
carretela *f Chi* coach, bus.
carretera *f* highroad, main road.
carretería *f* cartwright's shop, cartwright's trade.
carretero *m* carrier, wagoner, drayman, carter; cartwright.
carretilla *f* small cart; wheelbarrow; go-cart.
carril *m* rut; rail; track; cartway.
carrilano *m Chi* railway worker; bandit.
carrillera *f* chinstrap.
carrillo *m* cheek.
carrindango *m Arg* dilapidated car.
carrizo *m* common reed.
carro *m* cart; chariot; two-wheeled vehicle; *SA* car, automobile; (*astr*) Big Dipper; **— fúnebre** hearse.
carrocería *f* coachbuilding business, coachwork.
carrocín *m* chaise, curricle.
carroña *f* carrion, putrid flesh.
carroza *f* coach, carriage.
carruaje *m* carriage (*any wheeled vehicle*).
carta *f* letter; missive, epistle, note; despatch; map; chart; card; **— blanca** carte blanche; **— de aviso** letter of advice; **— de crédito** letter of credit; **— de marear** sea chart; **— de pago** acknowledgment of receipt; **—** (*or* **patente**) **de sanidad** bill of health.
cartabón *m* size pattern.
cartapacio *m* satchel, portfolio.
cartearse *vr* to correspond by letter.
cartel *m* poster; placard; **se prohibe fijar —es** post no bills.
cartelera *f* billboard.
cartera *f* portfolio, writing case; notebook; pocketbook; handbag; bills in hand; (*Ministerial*) portfolio.
cartero *m* postman, mailman.
cartilla *f* primer; elementary treatise.
cartógrafo *m* cartographer.
cartón *m* pasteboard; cardboard; (*paint*) cartoon.
cartuchera *f* cartridge box, pouch; *Arg* pencil box.
cartucho *m* cartridge.
cartujo *m* Carthusian monk.
cartulario *m* archives; archivist.
cartulina *f* thin pasteboard, cardboard.
casa *f* house; home; private dwelling; firm; **— consistorial** town hall; **— de campo** country seat; **— de vecindad** tenement house; **— de huéspedes** lodging house; **— solariega** ancestral family home; **— de empeños** pawnbrokers' shop; **poner —** to set up house; **echar la — por la ventana** to have a grand spread, entertain lavishly.
casaca *f* dress coat; **volver —** to turn one's coat (*ie allegiance*).
casadero *a* marriageable.
casal *m* manor, country house; *RP* couple (*male and female*), brace.
casamata *f* casemate.
casamentero *m* matchmaker.
casamiento *m* marriage; match; wedding.
casar *m* hamlet, village.
casar *vt* to marry; to match (*colors*); to blend; *vr* to get married, wed.
casca *f* skin of dressed grape; oak bark (*used for tanning*).
cascabel *m* hawk-bell, jingle; **serpiente de —** rattlesnake.
cascada *f* cascade waterfall.
cascajal *m* gravel pit.
cascajo *m* gravel; copper coin.
cascanueces *m* nutcracker; nutcrackers.
cascar *vt* to crack, burst, crunch; (*fam*) to lick.
cáscara *f* peel, husk, rind; (egg)shell.

cascarón *m* eggshell.
cascarrabias *mf* irritable person.
cascarria *f Arg* dirt, muck; sheep dung.
cascarriento *a Arg* dirty, filthy.
cascarudo *a* thick-shelled.
casco *m* potsherd; cask (*wine*); helmet; hull (*of ship*); skull; **ligero de —s** feather-brained.
cascote *m* rubbish, refuse.
caserío *m* hamlet; cluster of houses (*in country*).
casero *a* domestic, homely; home-loving, homespun, home-bred; **pan —** homemade bread; **traje —** indoor (*i.e. old*) suit; *m* landlord, caretaker.
casi *ad* almost, nearly.
casilla *f* small house; lodge; box office; (*on forms*) blank; (*chess-board etc*) square; **salirse de sus —s** to lose temper, patience.
casillero *m* pigeonhole, small locker.
casino *m* club, clubhouse; casino.
caso *m* case, event, circumstance; example; opportunity; **en todo —** at any rate; **no hacer al —** to be irrelevant; **hacer — de** to notice, pay attention to; **— de apuros** emergency.
caspa *f* scurf, dandruff.
casquete *m* helmet; cap; wig.
casquijo *m* gravel.
casquillo *m* cap, socket; *SA* cartridge case; horseshoe.
casquivano *a* inconsiderate; not reliable, feather-brained.
casta *f* caste, lineage, breed.
castaña *f* chestnut; (*of hair*) chignon; *Arg* blow, punch; **— pilonga** dried chestnut.
castañar *m* chestnut grove.
castañera *f* (*hot*) chestnut vendor.
castañeta *f* castanet; *see* **castañuela.**
castañetear *vi* to rattle (*castanets*); to chatter (*teeth*).
castaño *m* chestnut tree; **— de Indias** horse chestnut; *a* auburn, nutbrown.
castañuela *f* castanet.
castellano *an* Castilian; *m* the lord of a castle; Castilian (*Spanish*).
castidad *f* chastity, purity.
castigar *vt* to punish; to mortify (*the flesh*).
Castilla *f* Castile.
castillo *m* castle, fort.
castigo *m* punishment, penance.
castizo *a* pure, authentic, typical; **música española —a** (very) (genuine) Spanish music.
casto *a* chaste, pure, continent.
castor *m* beaver.
castración *f* castration.
castrado *m* eunuch.
castrar *vt* to castrate.
castrense *a* military, army.
casual *a* casual; fortuitous.
casualidad *f* accident, hazard, chance; **por —** by accident, as it happens, **—ed.**
casualmente *ad* casually, accidentally.
casucha *f* hovel.
casulla *f* chasuble.
cata *f* testing, trial, sampling.
catacumbas *f pl* catacombs.
cataclismo *m* cataclysm, catastrophe.
catador *m* taster (*of wines etc*), sampler, connoisseur.
catadura *f* tasting, proof; appearance, aspect.
catalán *a* Catalonian; *m* Catalan.
catalejo *m* telescope.
cataléptico *a* cataleptic, subject to fits.
catálogo *m* catalogue.
Cataluña *f* Catalonia.
cataplasma *f* poultice; cataplasm.
catar *vt* to taste, try; to look; to bear in mind.
catarata *f* cataract, waterfall.
catarro *f* catarrh; (*head*) cold.
catastro *m* census of real property.
catástrofe *f* catastrophe.
cataviento *m* weathercock.
cateador *m SA* prospector; hammer.
catear *vt* to search for; to procure, solicit.
catecismo *m* catechism.
cátedra *f* university chair (*i.e. professorship*); university lectureship; course of study.
catedral *f* cathedral.
catedrático *m* (university) professor.
categoría *f* category, class; **persona de —** person of some importance.
categórico *a* categorical, absolute, definitive.
catequista *m* catechist.
catequizar *vt* to catechize; to question closely; to try to convince.
caterva *f* great number of; crowd; swarm.
catilinaria *f* severe censure, philippic.
catinga *f SA* foul smell.
catire *a SA* blond, light-haired: half-breed.
catolicismo *m* catholicism.
católico *a* catholic; universal; *m* Catholic.
catorce *a* fourteen.
catre *m* cot, camp bed; **— de tijera** folding bed, camp bed.
cauce *m* (*river*) bed; drain, trench.
caución *f* precaution; security, guarantee.
caucionar *vt* to give (go) bail.
caucho *m* indiarubber.
caudal *a* abundant; large; *m* estate, property; riches; abundance, plenty.
caudaloso *a* abundant, full-flowing (*rivers, springs etc*); propertied, rich, wealthy.
caudillaje *m* tyranny.
caudillo *m* head, chief, leader.
causa *f* cause; motive; lawsuit, process, trial; **a — de** because of.

causar *vt* to cause; to make; to give rise to, bring about.
cáustico *a* caustic, bitter.
cautela *f* care, caution, prudence; cunning.
cauteloso *a* cautious, wary.
cauterio *m* cautery.
cauterizar *vt* to cauterize.
cautivar *vt* to make prisoner; to captivate, charm.
cautiverio *m* captivity.
cautivo *m* captive, prisoner.
cauto *a* prudent, cautious.
cavar *vt* to dig; to excavate.
caverna *f* cavern, cave, lair.
cavernícola *m* rabid reactionary (*in politics*).
cavernoso *a* cavernous.
cavidad *f* cavity, excavation.
cavilación *f* hesitation, pondering.
cavilar *vt* to ponder on, wonder (about, whether); to quibble.
caviloso *a* captious, doubtful, undecided, finicky.
cayado *m* (*shepherd*) crook; (*bishop*) crozier.
cayo *m* key, rocky islet, shoal.
cayuco *m SA* fishing boat.
caz *m* irrigation channel.
caza *f* chase, hunting; game; — **mayor** big game; — **menor** small game; **partida de** — hunting party.
cazador *m* hunter; chaser.
cazar *vt* to hunt, chase; to pursue, catch; to 'win', 'get'.
cazatorpedero *m* (*naval*) destroyer.
cazo *m* ladle; gluepot.
cazuela *f* earthen pan, stewpan; part of old theater reserved for women; pit.
cazurro *a* sulky; vicious.
ceba *f* fattening of animals.
cebada *f* barley; — **perlada** pearl barley.
cebadal *m* field of barley.
cebadera *f* nosebag.
cebado *a SA* wild, untamed.
cebar *vt* to fatten up (*animals*), feed (*furnace*); to nourish (*an emotion*); *vr* — **en** to batten on, to fasten on.
cebellina *f* sable; sable fur.
cebo *m* fodder; bait; allurement, incentive.
cebolla *f* onion; bulb.
cebollita *m Arg* child.
cebolludo *a* bulbous.
cebra *f* zebra.
ceca *f* mint (*money*); **de — en Meca** from pillar to post.
cecear *vi* to lisp; to pronounce the *s* as c.
ceceo *m* lisping; (Castilian pronunciation).
cecina *f* salt hung beef, jerked beef.
cedazo *m* sieve, strainer.
ceder *vt* to give (up) (way) (in), cede, yield.
cedro *m* cedar; cedar wood.
cédula *f* scrip; schedule; certificate; warrant; — **personal** identity card.
céfiro *m* zephyr; gentle breeze.
cegar (ie) *vt* to blind; to block (*well, window*); *vi* to grow blind.
ceguedad *f* blindness, unreasonableness.
ceguera *f* (*physical*) blindness; soreness of the eye.
ceiba *f* silk-cotton tree; sea moss.
Ceilán *m* Ceylon.
ceja *f* eyebrow; cloud cap; ridge; **hasta las —s** up to the eyebrows (*extremely bored etc*).
cejar *vi* to yield, give way; to give up, relax.
cejijunto *a* beetle-browed.
celada *f* helm; ambush, trap.
celador *m* curator; warden; school prefect.
celaje *m* skylight; *pl* fleecy clouds colored red (*by the sun*).
celar *vt* to watch over; to be careful, watch jealously; to conceal.
celda *f* cell; room.
celebración *f* celebration (*of marriage*); holding (*of meetings etc*), acclamation.
celebrante *m* officiating priest.
celebrar *vt* to praise, applaud; to celebrate (*mass etc*); to hold (*meeting etc*); to be glad of.
célebre *a* celebrated, famous.
celebridad *f* celebrity; notoriety.
celeridad *f* celerity, velocity, speed.
celeste *a* celestial, heavenly; **azul** — sky-blue.
celestial *a* celestial, heavenly.
celestina *f* procuress; go-between.
celibato *m* celibacy; bachelor.
célibe *a* bachelor, single; celibate.
célico *a* heavenly.
celo *m* zeal, interest; *pl* jealousy.
celosía *f* Venetian blind, lattice window.
celoso *a* jealous; zealous, careful.
celta *mf* Celt, Celtic.
céltico *a* Celtic.
célula *f* cell, cellule.
celular *a* cellular.
celuloide *m* celluloid.
celulosa *f* cellulose.
cementar *vt* to cement.
cementerio *m* churchyard, cemetery.
cemento *m* cement, mortar.
cena *f* supper, dinner.
cenáculo *m* cenacle; literary, artistic gathering.
cenador *m* arbor, bower; veranda (*around interior court of house*).
cenaduría *f SA* eating house.
cenagal *m* quagmire, swamp.
cenagoso *a* marshy, boggy.
cenar *vt* to sup, have supper; to dine.
cenceño *a* slender, thin.
cencerro *m* cow-bell.
cendal *m* sendal; fine silk *or* linen cloth; gossamer.
cenefa *f* fringe, border, valance.
cenicero *m* ashtray.
Cenicienta *f* Cinderella.
ceniciento *a* ash-colored.

cenit *m* zenith.
ceniza *f* ash, ashes; **miércoles de —** Ash Wednesday.
cenizoso *a* ashen, ashy, covered with ashes.
cenote *m Mex* deep underground reservoir.
censar *vt Arg* to take a census.
censo *m* census; annual pension, rental.
censor *m* censor, critic.
censura *f* censure, blame, reproach; examination, censorship.
censurable *a* censurable, deserving blame.
censurar *vt* to censure, blame; to criticize.
centauro *m* centaur.
centavo *m* cent, one hundredth.
centella *f* lightning; flash, spark.
centellear *vt* to sparkle, flash, glitter.
centelleo *m* scintillation, flashing.
centena *f* hundred.
centenar *m* hundred; **a —es (by) (in)** hundreds.
centenario *a* centennial; *m* centenary.
centeno *m* common rye.
centésimo *m* hundredth part of, centesimal.
centígrado *a* centigrade.
centímetro *m* centimeter.
céntimo *m* centime, cent.
centinela *f* sentry; sentinel.
centón *m* patchwork quilt; cento, literary composition.
central *a* central, centric; head (*office*).
centralismo *m* centralized system of government; centralism.
centralización *f* centralization.
centralizar *vt* to centralize.
centrar *vt* to center.
céntrico *a* central; **calle —a** principal, main street, main thoroughfare.
centrífugo *a* centrifugal.
centrípeto *a* centripetal.
centro *m* center; middle point; club.
centroamericano *an* Central American.
centuplicar *vt* to centuplicate.
centuria *f* century.
ceñido *a* close-fitting; very close (to).
ceñidor *m* belt, girdle.
ceñir (i) *vt* to fit closely; to clasp; to surround, encircle; *vr* to confine oneself to; **— espada** to gird on, to wear a sword.
ceño *m* frown, knitted brows, look of disapproval, displeasure.
ceñudo *a* frowning; grim.
cepa *f* stub; vinestock, root; stock, origin, source; **de buena —** on good authority, of good stock.
cepillar *vt* to brush, plane.
cepillo *m* brush; plane; **— para ropa** clothes brush.
cepo *m* bough, branch (*of tree*); stocks (*punishment*); poorbox.
cera *f* wax, beeswax; wax candle.
cerámica *f* ceramics; ceramic art.
cerámico *a* **arte —** the art of pottery.
cerbatana *f* blowpipe; popgun.
cerca *ad* near, close by; **— de** close to, near to; *f* enclosure, fence.
cercado *m* fenced enclosure, paddock, enclosure.
cercanía *f* proximity; *pl* neighborhood, vicinity.
cercano *a* near, neighboring.
cercar *vt* to fence in, enclose; to invest (a town).
cercén; a cercén *ad* at the root; **cortar ——** to slice off, cut clean off.
cercenar *vt* to pare, lop off; to reduce, lessen.
cerciorarse *vr* to assure; **— de** to verify, make quite sure (of, about).
cerco *m* enclosure; investment; blockade; **poner — a** to invest, besiege; **saltar el —** to change one's political allegiance.
cerda *f* horsehair, (hog-, badger-) bristle; sow.
Cerdeña *f* Sardinia.
cerdo *m* hog, pig, swine.
cerdoso *a* bristly.
cereal *a* cereal; *m pl* cereals.
cerebral *a* cerebral, brain.
cerebro *m* brain, mind, talent.
ceremonia *f* ceremony, formality; display.
ceremonial *m* ceremonial, formalities.
ceremonioso *a* ceremonious, formal.
cerería *f* wax-chandler's shop.
cerero *m* wax-chandler.
cereza *f* cherry.
cerezo *m* cherry tree; cherry wood.
cerilla *f* wax match, match; wax taper.
cerner (ie) *vt* to sift; *vi* to fecundate (*blossom of vine, olive tree, wheat*); *vr* to hover (*of hawk etc*).
cernícalo *m* sparrowhawk.
cernido *m* sifting; sifted flour.
cero *m* zero, naught.
cerote *m* shoemaker's wax.
cerquillo *m* tonsure.
cerrado *a* closed; obscure; concealed; reserved; secretive; dense; obstinate; incomprehensible (*speech*); **(andaluz) —** out and out, thoroughgoing (Andalusian); **barba —a** heavy beard; **a ojos —s** blindly, on trust.
cerradura *f* lock, the act of closing; **— de muelle** spring lock.
cerraja *f* common sowthistle; lock, bolt.
cerrajería *f* locksmith's trade; locksmith's shop.
cerrajero *m* locksmith.
cerrar (ie) *vt* to close, shut up; to end; to lock; **— una carta** to seal a letter; **— una cuenta** to close an account.
cerrazón *f Arg, Urug, Par* mist, fog.
cerrero *a* wild; *SA* rude, rough;

Ven bitter; **caballo —** unbroken horse.
cerril *a* unbroken, wild; rough, mountainous.
cerro *m* hill, ridge; backbone (*of animal*); **por los —s de Úbeda** wide of the mark, in the air, off the point.
cerrojo *m* bolt, latch.
certamen *m* literary competition; exhibition.
certero *a* sure; well-aimed; certain.
certeza *f* certitude, assurance; precise knowledge.
certidumbre *f* certainty.
certificación *f* affidavit; certificate.
certificado *m* certificate, testimonial.
certificar *vt* to certify, attest;**— una carta** to register a letter.
cerusa *f* ceruse, white-lead.
cerval *a* pertaining to a deer, cervine; **miedo —** excessive timidity.
cervato *m* fawn.
cervatillo *m* young deer.
cervecería *f* brewery; bar.
cervecero *m* brewer: beer seller.
cerveza *f* beer, ale; **— tipo Pilsen, — blanca** lager; **— negra** brown ale.
cerviz *f* neck, nape; cervix; **doblar la —** to submit, humble oneself, bow one's head.
cesación *f* discontinuance, cessation.
cesante *m* unemployed, retired or dismissed public officer; *a* ceasing.
cesantía *f* (white-collar) unemployment; dismissal.
cesar *vi* to cease; to give up; to discontinue, stop; **sin—** unendingly, without (stop, ceasing, end).
César *m* Caesar.
cese *m* dismissal, stoppage, cessation; stoppage.
cesión *f* cession; concession; **— de bienes** surrender of property.
cesionario *m* grantee, transferee.
césped *m* sod, grass, turf; lawn.
cesta *f* (*hand*) basket; pannier; racket (*for 'pelota'*).
cestero *m* basketmaker .
cesto *m* wastepaper basket; large basket; **coger agua en —** to labor in vain.
cesura *f* caesura.
cetrería *f* falconry.
cetrero *m* falconer.
cetrino *a* lemon-colored; jaundiced.
cetro *m* scepter.
cía *f* hip bone.
cianuro *m* cyanide; **— de potasio** potassium cyanide.
ciar *vi* to give way; to back water, go astern.
ciática *f* sciatica.
cicatería *f* stinginess, niggardliness.
cicatero *a* niggardly, stingy.
cicatriz *f* scar, cicatrice.
Cicerón *m* Cicero.
ciclismo *m* cycling, sport of cycling.
ciclo *m* cycle; **— primario** primary education stage.
ciclón *m* hurricane, cyclone.
cicuta *f* hemlock.
ciego *an* blind; blocked up; **a ciegas** blindly, unwittingly.
cielo *m* heaven, paradise; sky; ceiling; cover (*of a bed*); **a — raso** under the stars; **se ha venido el — abajo** the very heavens have burst.
ciempiés *m* centipede; poor literary work.
cien *a see* **ciento.**
ciénaga *f* marsh, miry place, swamp.
ciencia *f* science; knowledge; **a — cierta** with knowledge, for a certainty; **gaya —** troubadour's art, poetry.
cieno *m* mud, slime; bog.
científico *a* scientific.
ciento *m* one hundred; **tres por —** three per cent.
cierne (*used only in*) **en cierne** in blossom, in the beginning, in its infancy.
cierre *m* act of closing, closing; closure; snap, catch; (*industry*) lockout; **— de cremallera** (**— relámpago** *Arg, Urug, Par*) zip fastener, zipper.
cierto *a* sure, positive, true; certain **por —** certainly, of course.
ciervo *m* deer, stag.
cierzo *m* cold north wind.
cifra *f* figure, number; cipher monogram.
cifrar *vt* to write in cipher; **— (su ambición) en** to concentrate (ambition) on, in.
cigarra *f* cicada, grasshopper.
cigarral *m* (*in Toledo*) pleasure orchard, garden.
cigarrera *f* woman cigarette-maker; cigar case.
cigarrería *f SA* tobacconist's, cigar store.
cigarrero *m* cigar (maker, seller).
cigarrillo *m* cigarette.
cigarro *m* cigar; cigarette.
cigüeña *f* white stork, crane.
cilicio *m* hairshirt.
cilindrar *vt* to roll; to calender, bore.
cilíndrico *a* cylindrical.
cilindro *m* cylinder, roller.
cilla *f* granary; tithe.
cima *f* summit, top, peak; completion; (*met*) pinnacle, crown, apex, sum; **dar — a** to finish successfully, to top off, put the finishing touch to.
cimarrón *m* maroon; runaway slave; *a SA* wild, untamed.
címbalo *m* cymbal; small bell.
cimbel *m* decoy pigeon.
cimborrio *m* dome, cupola.
cimbrar, cimbrear *vi* to vibrate; *vt* to brandish, shake, switch (*a cane etc*).
cimbreo *m* vibrating; brandishing.
cimentar *vt* to lay the foundations; to found; to strengthen.
cimento *see* **cemento.**

cimera crest (*of helmet*).
cimiento *m* foundation; bed; groundwork, basis; **abrir los —s** to lay the foundations.
cimitarra *f* scimitar.
cinc *m* zinc.
cincel *m* chisel; burin.
cincelar *vt* to engrave, chisel, cut.
cinco *an* five; **las —** five o'clock.
cincha *f* girth, cinch; belt.
cinchar *vt* to girth, to encircle; to poll; *Arg* to work hard.
cincho *m* belly-band; iron hoop.
cincuenta *an* fifty.
cine *m* cinema, movies.
cinematográfico *a* cinematographic.
cinerario *a* cinerary.
cingalés *a* Sinhalese, of Ceylon.
cíngulo *m* girdle.
cínico *a* cynic; cynical; impudent, barefaced; *m* cynic.
cínife *m* mosquito.
cinismo *m* cynicism; absence of shame, barefacedness; ribaldry.
cinta *f* ribbon, tape, sash, film; **— métrica** tape measure.
cintajo *m* showy piece of ribbon; tawdry ornament.
cintarazo *m* blow (*with flat of sword*).
cintilla *f* narrow tape.
cintillo *m* hatband.
cinto *m* waist; belt.
cintura *f* waist; **meter en —** to dominate, to bring to reason.
cinturón *m* wide belt, strap.
cipote *a Col* dull, stupid; *Guat* chubby.
ciprés *m* cypress.
circo *m* circus, amphitheater.
circuir *vt* to surround, encircle.
circuito *m* circuit, circumference.
circulación *f* circulation; traffic; currency.
circulante *a* circulating.
circular *f* circular letter; *a* circular, circulating; *vi* to move (on, to, about); to circulate; (*of traffic*) to pass (along), cross.
círculo *m* circle; club.
circuncidar *vt* to circumcise; to curtail, modify.
circuncisión *f* circumcision.
circunciso *a* circumcised.
circundar *vt* to surround, compass.
circunferencia *f* circumference.
circunflejo *a* circumflex (accent).
circunlocución *f* periphrasis, circumlocution.
circunloquio *m* circumlocution.
circunnavegación *f* circumnavigation.
circunnavegar *vt* to circumnavigate.
circunscribir *vt* to encircle, circumscribe, limit.
circunscripción *f* circumscription.
circunspección *f* circumspection, decorousness, prudence, care.
circunspecto *a* circumspect, cautious, careful, tactful.
circunstancia *f* circumstance; condition; **poesía de —s** occasional poem.
circunstanciado *a* full and complete, minutely detailed.
circunstante *a* present, surrounding; **—s** *m pl* bystanders.
circunvalar *vt* to surround (*with wall, siege works*).
circunvecino *a* neighboring, adjacent, contiguous.
cirio *m* (long) wax candle; species of cactus.
cirro *m* cirrus clouds.
ciruela *f* plum, prune; **— pasa** prune; **— damascena** damson.
ciruelo *m* plum tree; silly man.
cirugía *f* surgery.
cirujano *m* surgeon.
cisco *m* coal dust, slack; **meter —** to kick up a row.
cisma *m* schism; discord.
cismático *a* schismatic.
cisne *m* swan; *Arg* powderpuff; **canto del —** swan song, last work; **pollo de —** cygnet.
cisterna *f* cistern, water or rain tank.
cisura *f* incision; fissure.
cita *f* appointment, rendezvous, meeting; summons; quotation, authority.
citación *f* summons; quotation, citation.
citar *vt* to quote; to summon; to make an arrangement; to arrange to meet; **el citado** the said, abovementioned.
cítara *f* zithern.
citerior *a* on the near side, nearer.
cítrico *a* citric.
ciudad *f* city, town.
ciudadanía *f* citizenship; freedom of a city.
ciudadano *a* urban, civic; *m* citizen, townsman, city dweller.
ciudadela *f* citadel, fortress, keep.
cívico *a* civic, municipal; *Arg* beer measure.
civil *a* civil, private; polite; **derecho —** civil law, common law.
civilidad *f* civility, politeness, urbanity.
civilista *m SA* opponent of militarism.
civilización *f* civilization, culture.
civilizar *vt* to civilize.
civismo *m* patriotism; public spirit.
cizalla *f* metal cutters, shears; metal shavings.
cizaña *f* darnel; discord; **meter —** to sow discord.
cizañar *vt* to sow discord.
clac *m* opera hat; *see* **claque.**
clamar *vt* to call for; to clamor, wail.
clamor *m* clamor, outcry; toll, tolling (*of bells*).
clamorear *vt* to pray anxiously; to implore.
clamoreo *m* insistent clamor; importunate request.

clamoroso *a* noisy, loud, piteous.
clandestino *a* clandestine, secret, undercover.
claque *m* claque (*hired applauders in theater*).
clara *f* white of egg; (*weather*) bright interval.
claraboya *f* skylight; bull's eye; window.
clarear *vi* to grow light, dawn; to be transparent.
clarete *m* claret.
claridad *f* clearness, brightness; splendor; distinctness, lucidity.
claridoso *a SA* blunt, plain-talking.
clarificación *f* clarification; refining.
clarificar *vt* to clarify; to refine (*sugar*).
clarín *m* bugle; clarion.
clarinero *m* bugler.
clarinete *m* clarinet; clarinet player.
clarión *m* white chalk, crayon.
claro *a* clear, light, pale; manifest, evident, frank, visible; **azul —** light blue; **poner (sacar) en —** to clear up, understand; *m* gap, lacuna; interval, blank, light spot; glade; break (*in clouds*); *ad* manifestly; **a las claras** evidently, clearly; **pasar la noche de — en —** not to have a wink of sleep; *excl* **— que sí (no)** of course (not); **— está** evidently, naturally: of course.
claroscuro *m* chiaroscuro.
clase *f* class; kind, kin; order; rank; quality; classroom, lecture.
clásico *a* classic, classical; principal, notable.
clasificación *f* classification.
clasificar *vt* to classify, arrange.
claudicar *vi* to limp; to act in a disorderly way.
claustro *m* cloister; monastic state; teaching body, faculty (*of a university*).
cláusula *f* clause, period, sentence.
clausura *f* closure; religious retreat; interior of a convent; adjournment or closing scenes (*of meeting*).
clava *f* club, cudgel; scupper.
clavar *vt* to nail; to drive in; to nail down; to pierce; to overcharge, 'sting';**— los ojos** to stare, fix one's eyes.
clave *f* key, clef (*music*); code; clavichord; clue; keystone.
clavel *m*, **clavellina** *f* carnation, pink.
clavero *m* clove tree; treasurer, keeper of the keys.
clavicordio *m* clavichord.
clavícula *f* collarbone.
clavija *f* (*axle*) pin, peg (*stringed instruments*); (*el*) plug; **apretar las —s** (*fig*) to put on the screws.
clavillo *m* clove.
clavo *m* nail, spike; (*on feet*) corn; surgical lint; clove; *Arg* disagreeable thing or situation; **dar en el —** to hit the nail on the head.
clemencia *f* clemency, mercy.
clemente *a* clement, merciful.
clerecía *f* clergy, body or office of clergy.
clerical *a* clerical, of the clergy.
clérigo *m* clergyman, priest, clerk, cleric.
clero *m* clergy.
cliente *m* client, customer.
clientela *f* patronage; clientele.
clima *m* climate, atmosphere.
clínica *m* clinic, nursing home, (*doctor's*) surgery, dispensary.
clisé *m* cliché; (*film*) exposure.
cloaca *f* sewer; (*fowls*) large intestine.
clocar *see* **cloquear.**
cloque *m* grappling iron, harpoon.
cloquear *vi* to cluck, cackle.
clorhídrico *a* hydrochloric.
cloroformizar *vt* to chloroform.
cloroformo *m* chloroform.
club *m* club, political association, social institution.
clueco *a* broody; *f* brooding hen.
cluniacense *a m* Cluniac, monk of Cluny.
coa *f SA* kind of hoe.
coacción *f* coaction; compulsion.
coactivo *a* coercive.
coadjutor *m* coadjutor, assistant; curate.
coadyuvante *a m* assistant, helper.
coadyuvar *vt* to help, assist.
coagular *vtr* to coagulate, congeal, set.
coágulo *m* clot; coagulated blood.
coalición *f* coalition, union, group(ing).
coartada *f* alibi.
coartar *vt* to limit, restrict, restrain.
coba *f* **dar —** to flatter, play up to, 'butter up'.
cobalto *m* cobalt.
cobarde *a* coward, timid; *m* coward.
cobardía *f* cowardice.
cobayo *m* guinea pig.
cobertera *f* cover, saucepan lid.
cobertizo *m* shed, shelter (*usually lacking side walls*); lean-to.
cobertor *m* blanket, bed cover, quilt.
cobertura *f* covering; wrapper.
cobija *f* blanket; *Mex* shawl, bedclothes.
cobijar *vt* to cover, protect; *vi* to take shelter.
cobra *f* cobra.
cobrador *m* (*debts*) collector; (*bus*) conductor; (*bank*) teller; (*dog*) retriever.
cobranza *f* recovery, collection (*of debts*).
cobrar *vt* to recover, collect (amounts due); to recuperate, obtain; to charge; *Arg* to get a beating; **— ánimo** to gain courage, to pick up spirits;**— fuerzas** to gather strength.
cobre *m* copper; copper coin.
cobrizo *a* of copper, coppery.
cobro *m see* **cobranza.**
coca *f* coca, coca leaves.

cocacho *m Arg, Ec, Per* blow on head.
cocada *f Bol, Col* almond paste; coconut sweet.
cocaína *f* cocaine.
cocazo *m Arg* knock on the head.
cocción *f* boiling, cooking.
cocear *vi* to kick, kick out, resist.
cocer *vt* to cook, boil, to bake.
cocido *m* (*Spanish*) stew.
cocimiento *m* (*the act of*) cooking, boiling; decoction.
cocina *f* kitchen; cookery.
cocinar *vt* to cook; *vi* to do the cooking.
cocinero *m* cook; chef.
coco *m* coconut tree; coconut; bogeyman; **agua de—** coconut milk.
cocodrilo *m* crocodile.
cocol *m Mex* bread roll.
cocolía *f Mex* spite, dislike.
cocoliche *m Arg* jargon used by foreigners, especially Italians.
cocotal *m* coconut grove.
cocotero *m* coconut tree.
coche *m* car, carriage, coach; **— de alquiler** hackney cab; **— de punto** cab, taxi (*from the rank*); **— cama** sleeping car, coach.
cochera *f* coach house; garage; **puerta —** main door, carriage entrance.
cochero *m* coachman.
cochinada *f* herd of swine; dirty trick.
cochinería *f* dirtiness, filth, foulness.
cochinilla *f* cochineal; woodlouse.
cochino *a* filthy; *m* pig, swine.
codal *m* carpenter's square; vine shoot.
codazo *m* nudge, shove with elbow.
codear *vti* to elbow (out).
codelincuente *m* accomplice, partner in crime; accessory.
codera *f* elbow patch.
códice *m* old MS, codex.
codicia *f* covetousness, cupidity, greed.
codiciar *vt* to covet, look greedily at, long to have.
codicioso *a m* grasping, avaricious, greedy (*person*).
codicil *m* codicil.
código *m* code, digest.
codillo *m* elbow- *or* shoulder-joint (*in animals*); knee; breech, foot rule.
codo *m* elbow; cubit; angle; **levantar el —** (*fam*) to booze; **comerse los codos de hambre** to be famished; **hablar por los codos** to talk one's head off, prattle, gossip.
codorniz *f* quail.
coeducación *f* coeducation.
coeficiente *m* coefficient.
coerción *f* coercion, restraint.
coercitivo *a* coercive.
coetáneo *a* contemporary.
coexistencia *f* coexistence.
coexistir *vi* to coexist.
cofia *f* woman's indoor cap, hairnet cowl; coif.
cofrade *m* fellow member.
cofradía *f* confraternity, brotherhood, guild.
cofre *m* trunk, coffer.
cogedero *a* (*of fruit*) ripe for picking; *n* handle.
cogedor *m* dustpan, coal shovel.
coger *vt* to take, catch; to soak up: to gather; to contain; *Arg, Par, Urug* to have sexual intercourse.
cogida *f* yield, harvest, catch (*of fish*); goring (*in bullfight*).
cogido *m* tuck, fold.
cognado *an* cognate.
cogollo *m* shoot (*of plant*): heart (*of lettuce*), top.
cogote *m* nape, scruff (*of neck*).
cogulla *f* cowl; monk's habit.
cohabitar *vi* to cohabit, live together.
cohechar *vt* to bribe, suborn, corrupt.
cohecho *m* bribery.
coheredero *m* co-heir, joint heir.
coherente *a* coherent, consistent.
cohesión *f* cohesion.
cohete *m* rocket, sky rocket.
cohetero *m* firework-maker.
cohibición *f* prohibition, restraint.
cohibir *vt* to restrain.
cohombrillo *m* gherkin.
cohombro *m* cucumber.
cohonestar *vt* to palliate, gloss over (*an action*).
coila *f Chi* fraud, lie.
coima *f* bribe; mistress.
coime *m* croupier.
coimero *m* person who takes a bribe; croupier.
coincidencia *f* coincidence.
coincidir *vi* to coincide, fall in (*with*), concur.
coito *m* coition, copulation.
cojear *vi* to limp, hobble, halt; (*of furniture*) to be rickety.
cojera *f* lameness, limping.
cojín *m* cushion, saddle pad.
cojinete *m* small cushion, pad; (*mech*) bearing.
cojo *m* lame person.
cojuelo *a* lame, hobbling.
cok *m* coke.
col *f* cabbage.
cola *f* tail; cue; queue; extremity; (*dress*) train; glue; **hacer (la) —** to queue.
colaborador *m* collaborator, contributor (*writer*).
colaborar *vt* to collaborate, work together; to contribute.
colación *f* conferment (*of degrees etc*); collation; light lunch or meal; **sacar a —** to bring up (*subject, question*).
colactáneo *a* **hermanos —s** foster brothers.
colada *f* wash; **todo saldrá en la —** it will all come out in the wash.
coladera *f* strainer, colander.

colador *m* strainer, colander; conferrer (*of degrees etc*).
coladura *f* blunder.
colapso *m* collapse, breakdown.
colar *vt* to strain, filter; to wash (*clothes*) with lye; to pass (*counterfeit money, inferior goods etc*); *vr* to slip in (slyly); to get in on the sly, gatecrash; to put one's foot in it.
colateral *a* collateral.
colcha *f* quilt, coverlet.
colchón *m* mattress; — **de muelles** spring mattress; — **de pluma** feather bed.
colchoneta *f* long cushion; coverlet.
coleada *f Ven* act of overthrowing bull by twisting tail.
colear *vi* to wag tail.
colección *f* collection.
colecta *f* collection (*of money for a purpose*); collect (*prayer*).
colectar *vt* to collect (*taxes etc*).
colectividad *f* collectivity, sum total, general body (*of people*).
colectivo *a* collective, joint; *m Arg* small bus.
colector *m* collector (*of taxes etc*).
colega *m* colleague.
colegial *a* collegiate; *m* collegian, college student, schoolboy.
colegiala *f* girl student.
colegio *m* school; college, seminary, high school; *Arg* private school.
colegir *vt* to infer, draw conclusions.
cólera *f* anger; *m* cholera.
colérico *a* angry, choleric, testy.
coleta *f* pigtail (*worn by bullfighters*); postscript; **cortarse la** — to give up bullfighting; to throw up, retire from (*career*).
coletazo *m* lash (*with tail*).
coleto *m* buff jacket; body.
colgadero *m* hanger, peg, hook.
colgadizo *m* shed, lean-to, shelter.
colgadura *f* hanging, tapestry, bunting, drapes.
colgante *a* hanging; *m* pendant, hanging ornament.
colgar *vt* to hang, suspend; to fix (*blame*); to adorn with hangings; to give a present;— **los hábitos** to leave the priesthood, abandon (past) career.
colibrí *m* hummingbird.
cólico *m* stomach pains, colic, griping.
coliflor *f* cauliflower.
coligarse *vt* to unite, form an association or confederation.
colilla *f* cigar stub, cigarette end.
colina *f* hill, hillock, slope.
colindante *a* bordering, adjacent.
colindar *vi* to adjoin, to run (along, beside) (*of property*).
coliseo *m* theater, playhouse, coliseum.
colisión *f* collision, clash.
colmado *a* abundant, full; *m* grocery, restaurant.
colmar *vt* to fill up, heap up, satisfy completely, fill to the brim; — **de favores** to heap favors upon.
colmena *f* beehive.
colmenar *m* apiary.
colmenero *a* (*of bears*) fond of honey; *m* beekeeper.
colmillo *m* eye tooth, canine tooth; fang; tusk.
colmo *m* plenty; fill; full measure; complement; top, highest pitch; **es el** — that's the limit, the last straw.
colocación *f* location, site; placing, arranging, place; employment, job, appointment.
colocar *vt* to place, arrange, fix, settle, put, locate; to employ; *vr* to get a job.
colodra *f* wooden pail; horn (*for drinking*); wine measure.
colofón *m* colophon, tailpiece.
colombiano *an* Colombian, from Colombia.
colombino *a* connected with Christopher Columbus.
colon *m* colon; part of the intestines.
Colón *m* Columbus.
colonia *f* colony; dependency; assembly, reunion; narrow silk ribbon; **agua de** — eau-de-Cologne.
coloniaje *m SA* colonial period.
colonización *f* colonization.
colonizador *m* colonist.
colonizar *vt* to colonize.
colono *m* colonist, colonizer; planter, farmer.
coloquio *f* conversation, talk; literary dialogue.
color *m* color, hue; paint; pretense; red; — **quebrado** faded hue; **so — de** under pretext of; *pl* (national) flag; **mudar de** — to change color, lose color.
colorado *a* red; colored; **ponerse** — to blush.
colorar *vt* to dye, paint, color.
colorear *vt* to touch up favorably, paint in favorable colors (*a lie etc*); grow red.
colorete *m* rouge.
colorido *m* color; coloring.
colorinche *m Arg* mixture of garish colors.
colosal *a* colossal.
coloso *m* colossus.
columbrar *vt* to discern, perceive dimly, see afar off; to guess, conjecture.
columna *f* column, support; (*archit*) — **salomónica** twisted (spiral) column.
columpiar *vt* to swing.
columpio *m* (*child's*) swing.
collado *m* hillock, fell; col.
collar *m* necklace; metal collar, dog collar.
collera *f* horse collar, harness collar.
coma *f* comma; (*med*) coma.
comadre *f* midwife; gossip; godmother.
comadrear *vi* to gossip.

comadreja *f* weasel.
comadreo *m* gossip, gossiping.
comadrona *f* midwife.
comal *m* *CA, Mex* earthenware griddle.
comandancia *f* command; the office of a commander.
comandante *m* commander; (*army*) major.
comandar *vt* to command, govern, be in charge.
comandita *f* silent partnership.
comanditario *m* (silent) (sleeping) partner.
comarca *f* region, country, territory, district, area.
comarcano *a* near, neighboring, local.
comarcar *vt* to plant in line; *vi* to be on the borders of.
comba *f* warp (*of wood*); curvature, bulge; skipping, skipping rope.
combar *vt* to bend; *vr* to bulge, jut out; warp.
combate *m* fight, struggle, engagement.
combatiente *m* fighter, combatant.
combatir *vti* to fight, combat; to contend; to dash.
combinación *f* combination; union; arrangement, plan, set-up.
combinar *vt* to combine, unite, put together.
combo *a* crooked, warped.
combustión *f* combustion, burning.
comedero *a* fit to eat, for eating; *m* manger, eating trough, food box.
comedia *f* play, comedy; **es una —** it is a complete pretense.
comediante *m* actor, comedian, player, hypocrite; **— de la legua** strolling player.
comediar *vt* to divide into equal shares.
comedido *a* obliging, courteous, restrained.
comedirse *vr* to be thoughtful, restrained (*in speech etc*); *SA* to be obliging.
comedor *m* dining room; dining-room suite.
comendador *m* commander (*of Military Order*).
comendadora *f* Mother Superior of Convent (*belonging to Military Orders*).
comensal *m* member of a household; (fellow) guest.
comentador *m* commentator.
comentado *a* talked about; **fué muy comentada (su acción) . . .** was the subject of much talk.
comentar *vt* to comment, expound, explain, gloss; to write a commentary on.
comentario *m* commentary; comments, remarks.
comentarista *mf* commentator.
comento *m* comment, explanation.
comenzar (ie) *vt* to commence, begin.
comer *m* eating; *vt* to eat (on, up), dine, feed (upon); to spend; *vr* to itch; take (*in chess*).
comercial *a* commercial, mercantile.
comerciante *m* merchant, trader.
comerciar *vt* to trade, traffic, deal; to do business (with).
comercio *m* trade, business; commerce, intercourse; *SA* shop, store.
comestible *a* eatable; *m pl* provisions, victuals; **tienda de —s** grocer's.
cometa *m* comet; *f* (*child's*) kite.
cometer *vt* to commit, entrust; to perpetrate, make; to commission.
cometido *m* charge, trust, commission, job, stint.
comezón *m* itching (*longing*), desire.
cómico *a* comical, ludicrous, comic; *m* comedian, strolling player.
comida *f* food; meal; dinner.
comidilla *f* hobby; talk, gossip.
comienzo *m* beginning, commencement.
comilón *a* greedy, gluttonous; *n* glutton.
comilona *f* big meal.
comillas *f pl* quotation marks; inverted commas.
comino *m* cumin seed; **no vale un —** it's not worth two pins.
comisar *vt* to confiscate.
comisario *m* commissary; **— de policía** police inspector.
comisión *f* commission, ministry, trust.
comisionado *m* chosen head, envoy *etc*; *a* deputy, proxy.
comisionista *m* broker, commission merchant.
comité *m* committee, assembly.
comitiva *f* retinue, suite, followers, following.
como *ad* as, so, like, as though; **¿cómo?** how? in what way?; **¡cómo!** *excl* why!; **— que** *cj* so that, inasmuch as, since, if.
cómoda *f* chest of drawers.
comodidad *f* comfort, ease; convenience.
comodín *m* joker (*in cards*).
cómodo *a* useful, handy, comfortable; *m* utility, convenience.
comodón *a* comfort-loving, easy-going.
compacto *a* compact, dense, solid.
compadecer *vt* to pity, be sorry for, sympathize with, feel sympathy for.
compadre *m* godfather; acquaintance, pal, friend.
compaginar *vt* to put in order; range; to compare, check, collate.
compañerismo *m* fellowship, companionship.
compañero *m* companion, partner, playmate, fellow; **— de clase** schoolmate.
compañía *f* company, society; troop, partnership; **— de Jesús** Jesuit Order.

comparación *f* comparison, conferring.
comparar *vt* to compare, confer; to confront.
comparativo *a* comparative.
comparecer *vi* to appear (*before a judge, tribunal*).
comparsa *m* masquerade, group (*on stage*); extra, supernumerary; company (*of actors*).
compartimiento *m* compartment; division, department.
compartir *vt* to divide in parts, share.
compás *m* pair of compasses; time, measure; (*mus*) beat; **llevar el —** to beat time.
compasado *a* grave, deliberate, steady.
compasión *f* compassion, pity.
compasivo *a* merciful, tender-hearted, compassionate.
compatibilidad *f* compatibility.
compatible *a* compatible, fit, suitable, in keeping with.
compatriota *m* fellow countryman.
compeler *vt* to force, compel.
compendiar *vt* to sum up; to abridge, summarize.
compendio *m* summary; handbook, manual.
compensación *f* compensation.
compensar *vti* to compensate, indemnify; to make up for, make amends.
competencia *f* competence, aptitude; competition, rivalry.
competente *a* competent; adequate, suitable, apt.
competer *vi* (*defective*) **le compite** it is his due, it is owing to him.
competición *f* competition.
competir (i) *vi* to vie, strive, compete with; to rival.
compilar *vt* to compile, collect.
compinche *m* (*fam*) pal, chum, crony.
complacencia *f* complaisance, gratification, satisfaction.
complacer *vt* to please, be pleasing (to); *vr* to be pleased, delighted, be gracious (enough) to, take pleasure in.
complaciente *a* accommodating, amenable, understanding.
complejo *a* complex, complicated, intricate; *m* complex.
complementario *a* complementary.
completar *vt* to fill up; to complete, finish off; to accomplish.
completo *a* complete; full up; **por —** absolutely; *m Arg* breakfast (*rolls, coffee*).
complexión *f* temperament; constitution.
complicación *f* complication.
complicar *vt* to complicate, make intricate, make difficult.
cómplice *m* accomplice, accessory.
complicidad *f* complicity; aiding and abetting.
complot *m* plot, conspiracy.
componenda *f* compromise, deal.
componer *vt* to compose, mix; to devise; to heal, put right; to mend; to reconcile; to calm (down); **— el semblante** to compose one's features; *vr* to make up (*face*), dress up; **componérselas** to make it up.
comportamiento *m* behavior, conduct.
comportar *vt* to suffer; *vr* to behave, act.
composición *f* composition; adjustment; composure; compromise.
compositor *m* composer; (*printing*) compositor.
compostelano *an* native (of, to) Santiago de Compostela.
compostura *f* composure; mending; neatness; modesty; (*cosmetics*) make-up.
compra *f* purchase; **ir de —s** to go shopping.
comprador *m* buyer, purchaser.
comprar *vt* to buy, purchase.
compraventa *f* commercial transaction; *Arg* **negocio de —** second-hand shop.
comprender *vt* to understand, comprehend; to comprise, contain, consist of.
comprensibilidad *f* comprehensiveness.
comprensión *f* comprehension, understanding.
comprensivo *a* comprehensive, understanding.
compresa *f* compress, poultice.
compresibilidad *f* compressibility, compressible power.
compresión *f* compression.
comprimir *vt* to press, squeeze; to compress, condense; to repress, restrain.
comprobación *f* comprobation, proof, verification.
comprobante *m* voucher, proof.
comprobar (ue) *vt* to prove, verify, check.
comprometer *vt* to expose, endanger, jeopardize; to involve, concern; *vr* to engage oneself, commit oneself, undertake (to), accept responsibility (for doing).
compromiso *m* engagement, date, appointment, nuisance, awkward situation.
compuerta *f* half-door, hatch; sluice gate, floodgate.
compuesto *a* compound; composite, complex, made up; mended; **bien —** nicely got up; *m* compound.
compulsar *vt* to compare; to make an authentic copy.
compulsión *f* compulsion.
compunción *f* compunction, pricking of conscience.
computador *m* computer.
computar *vt* to compute, reckon (up).
cómputo *m* computation, reckoning.

comulgar *vt* to administer Holy Communion; *vi* to receive the sacrament, to communicate.
común *a* common, public, ordinary; frequent, current; customary; vulgar, low, general; **por lo —** generally; *m* community; water closet.
comuna *f Arg, Chi* town council.
comunal *a* belonging to the community, public.
comunero *m* commoner; joint tenant of land; rebel (*16th century*).
comunicación *f* communication, notice; union; intercourse.
comunicado *m* (*official*) announcement; (*mil*) dispatch.
comunicar *vt* to communicate, report, make known, impart; inform; *vr* to adjoin, be united.
comunicativo *a* communicative, unreserved, expansive, approachable.
comunidad *f* community; corporation.
comunión *f* communion.
comunismo *m* communism.
comunista *an* communist.
comúnmente *ad* commonly, usually.
con *prep* with, by; **— tal que** provided that;**— que** and so, why, then; **— todo eso** nevertheless.
conato *m* endeavor, effort; attempt; sign; **— de robo** attempted robbery.
concavidad *f* concavity, hollow.
cóncavo *a* concave, hollow.
concebir (i) *vt* to conceive; to entertain (*an idea, notion of*); to understand; to breed (*affection*).
conceder *vt* to grant, allow, bestow, give; to admit.
concejal *m* alderman, councillor, member of a council.
concejo *m* municipal council; **casa del —** town hall, civic center.
concentración *f* concentration.
concentrar *vt* to concentrate.
concepción *f* conception; idea.
conceptista *a* witty, ingenious; *m* wit; ingenious punster.
concepto *m* concept, notion; conceit, witticism.
conceptuar *vi* to be of opinion, judge.
conceptuoso *a* sententious; (*of style*) conceited.
concerniente *a* relating to, concerning.
concernir (ie) *vi* to apply to, refer to, concern.
concertar (ie) *vt* to contrive, arrange; to settle, bring together, harmonize; to covenant; to tune (*instrument*); *vi* to accord, come to an agreement; *vr* to go hand in hand.
concertista *mf* (*mus*) conductor; performer.
concesión *f* concession, grant.
concesionario *m* concessionaire; grantee.
conciencia *f* conscience, conscientiousness; **ancho de —** easy-going, not very scrupulous; **en —** in good earnest.
concienzudo *a* conscientious, scrupulous, thorough.
concierto *m* agreement, contract; good order; harmony; concert.
conciliábulo *m* secret conference.
conciliación *f* conciliation, reconciliation, reconciling.
conciliador *a* pacific, peace-making, soothing; *m* peacemaker, arbitrator.
conciliar *vt* to conciliate, to win (*friendship or affection*); to reconcile; to induce (*sleep*).
conciliatorio *a* conciliatory, harmonizing.
concilio *m* council, meeting.
concisión *f* conciseness, brevity.
conciso *a* concise, brief.
concitar *vt* to incite, stir up (*passions etc*).
conciudadano *m* fellow citizen.
conclave *or* **cónclave** *m* conclave (*of cardinals*).
concluir *vt* to finish, end, conclude; to draw a conclusion, deduce.
conclusión *f* conclusion, end; **en —** finally.
concluyente *a* conclusive, convincing, decisive.
concomitante *a* concomitant, accompanying.
concordancia *f* concordance; conformity, agreement; concord.
concordar (ue) *vi* to be in accord, agree; *vt* to harmonize.
concordato *m* concordat.
concordia *f* concord, harmony, union.
concretar *vt* to reduce to fact, sum up; *vr* to confine oneself to; to keep close to the point.
concreto *a* concrete, definable, exact; real; **en —** exactly, definite(ly), in fact, in reality.
concubina *f* concubine, mistress.
concupiscencia *f* greed, lust.
concurrencia *f* concurrence, competition (*in trade*); attendance, spectators.
concurrido *a* well-attended, thronged, popular.
concurrir *vi* to concur; to meet, be present, attend, swarm.
concurso *m* concourse, assembly, crowd; competition; cooperation.
concusión *f* concussion; exaction.
concha *f* shell, shellfish; tortoise-shell; **— del apuntador** prompter's box.
conchabar *vt* to unite, join; *SA* to hire.
condado *m* earldom, county.
conde *m* count, earl.
condecoración *f* decoration; insignia, badge, medal.
condecorar *vt* to decorate, confer (*honor etc*).

condena *f* sentence; term (*of imprisonment*).
condenación *f* sentence, condemnation; damnation.
condenar *vt* to sentence, condemn, pronounce judgment; to stop up (*window, passage etc*).
condenado *a* condemned, damned; *m* damned soul.
condensar *vt* to make thicker; to condense; to abbreviate; *vr* to be condensed; to gather.
condescendencia *f* condescension, compliance, agreement.
condescender *vi* to yield; to condescend.
condescendiente *a* condescending, compliant.
condestable *m* constable (*ancient military title*).
condición *f* condition, state; specification; situation; rank, footing; *pl* nature.
condicionado *a* conditioned.
condicional *a* conditional.
condimentar *vt* to dress, season (*food*).
condimento *m* condiment, seasoning.
condiscípulo *m* schoolfellow, classmate.
condolerse (ue) *vr* to deplore, condole (with), sympathize in sorrow.
condominio *m* joint ownership.
condonar *vt* to condone, pardon.
cóndor *m* condor.
conducción *f* conduction; carriage, transport.
conducente *a* conducive.
conducir *vt* to lead, guide, drive (*car etc*), direct; *vr* to behave, act.
conducta *f* conduct, manners, behavior; management; conveyance; leading, driving (*of animals*).
conducto *m* conduit, sewer; **por — de** by means of.
conductor *m* conductor, guide; (*vehicle*) driver, chauffeur.
condueño *m* joint owner.
conduerma *f Ven* drowsiness.
conectar *vt* to connect (*pipes etc*).
conejera *f* rabbit warren.
conejo *m* rabbit; **— de Indias** guinea pig.
conexión *f* connection, union.
confabular *vi* to confer, confabulate; *vr* to plot.
confección *f* make, making, manufacture; handwork; ready-made article.
confeccionar *vt* to make, prepare, complete; to make up.
confederación *f* confederacy; league, union.
confederarse *vr* to join in league together.
conferencia *f* lecture; conference, interview; long distance call (*phone*).
conferenciante *m* lecturer.
conferenciar *vi* to confer, meet for discussion, have an interview.
conferencista *mf* lecturer.
conferir (ie) *vt* to grant, confer, award; to deliberate.
confesar *vt* to confess, admit, own.
confesión *f* confession, avowal.
confesionario *m* confessionary, confession box.
confesor *m* confessor.
confiado *a* vain, confident, trusting confiding.
confianza *f* confidence, trust, faith; familiarity; openness; **de mucha —** trustworthy, intimate, close.
confiar *vt* to trust, entrust; *vi* to have confidence, be faithful; **— en** to rely on.
confidencia *f* (*confided*) secret; confidence, trust.
confidencial *a* confidential.
confidente *a* trustworthy, faithful; *m* confidant, confident, trustworthy servant.
configuración *f* configuration, shape, relief.
configurar *vi* to give shape, form; to configurate.
confín *m* limit, border; *pl* boundaries.
confinar *vt* to border upon; to confine; to banish.
confirmación *f* confirmation, proof; confirmation (*by bishop*).
confirmar *vt* to confirm, corroborate, ratify.
confiscación *f* confiscation.
confiscar *vt* to confiscate.
confite *m* sweet, candy.
confitería *f* confectionery; candyshop.
confitero *m* confectioner; candymaker.
confitura *f* jam, fruit jelly; stewed fruit.
conflagración *f* conflagration.
conflicto *m* conflict; struggle; desperate situation; **— laboral** labor dispute.
confluencia *f* confluence, meeting.
confluente *a* confluent; *m* junction (*of rivers*).
confluir *vi* to flow together; to join.
conformación *f* conformation; form.
conformar *vi* to conform; to alter the shape of; to adjust to fit; *vr* to submit to, agree, resign oneself, accept.
conforme *a* alike; in conformity with; resigned; ready to (accept), (agree).
conforme *ad* according to; **— amanezca** as day breaks.
conformidad *f* conformity; agreement; patience.
confortable *a SA* comfortable.
confortante *a* comforting; *m* consoler, tonic; mitten.
confortar *vt* to console; to comfort; to give spirit.
confraternidad *f* confraternity, brotherhood.
confrontación *f* confrontation, comparison.

confrontar *vt* to collate, confront; to be adjoining.
confundir *vt* to confound; to confuse; to mix up; *vr* to be mistaken, make a mistake.
confusión *f* confusion; disorder; perturbation, bewilderment.
confuso *a* confused, confounded; obscure, jumbled, indistinct, vague.
confutación *f* confutation, disproof.
confutar *vt* to confute, disprove.
congelación *f* freezing, congealing.
congelar *vtr* to congeal, freeze, set, solidify, jell.
congénito *a* congenital.
congestión *f* congestion.
congestionarse *vr* to be congested; *vi* to congest.
conglomeración *f* conglomeration, heterogeneous mixture.
conglomerar *vt* to conglomerate.
congoja *f* anguish, affliction; dismay, anxiety.
congojoso *a* heart-rending.
congraciarse *vr* to ingratiate oneself, win the favor of.
congratulación *f* congratulation.
congratular *vt* to congratulate; *vr* to rejoice, be (rather) pleased at.
congregación *f* congregation; religious brotherhood.
congregar *vt* to congregate, assemble, gather together.
congresal *mf SA* delegate, member of congress.
congresista *mf* delegate, member of congress.
congreso *m* congress; (*Spain*) =House of Commons, *US* House of Representatives.
congruencia *f* fitness, appropriateness.
congruente *a* congruent, suitable.
congruo *a* congruous, suitable.
cónico *a* conic, conical.
conífero *a* coniferous.
conjetura *f* conjecture, guess, guesswork.
conjeturar *vt* to conjecture, foretell.
conjugar *vt* to conjugate; to put together.
conjunción *f* conjunction; set of circumstances, joint appearance.
conjuntamente *a* conjointly.
conjunto *a* united; *m* ensemble, group, the(—) as a whole, the whole; assembly, united body; twinset; **en** — as a whole, altogether.
conjura *f* conspiracy, plot.
conjuración *f* conspiracy, plot.
conjurar *vi* to plot, conspire; to conjure up; to entreat.
conjuro *m* conjuration; entreaty.
conllevar *vt* to bear (*with*), suffer (*patiently*).
conmemoración *f* commemoration; remembrance.
conmemorar *vt* to commemorate.
conmensurable *a* conmensurable, worthy of comparison (*with*).
conmigo *prep pn* with me.
conminar *vt* to threaten, warn.
conmiseración *f* commiseration, sympathy.
conmoción *f* commotion, tumult.
conmovedor *a* touching, moving.
conmover (ue) *vt* to touch, move, affect (*emotionally*).
conmutador *m* commuter, electric switch.
conmutar *vt* to commute, exchange, switch (*over*), barter.
connaturalizarse *vr* to get used to, grow accustomed to, acclimatize oneself, acclimate oneself.
connivencia *f* connivance,complicity.
connotación *f* meaning.
connotar *vt* to imply.
cono *m* cone.
conocedor *m* connoisseur, expert;— **de** familiar with, expert in.
conocer *vt* to know (*people, language, lore*); be acquainted with; (*law*) try.
conocido *a* known; *m* acquaintance.
conocimiento *m* knowledge; skill; bill of lading; **perder el** — to lose consciousness; **con** — **de causa** with one's eyes open, alive to the situation.
conque *cj* so then, then.
conquista *f* conquest, winning.
conquistador *m* conqueror, adventurer, (*hist*) conquistador.
conquistar *vt* to conquer, win over.
consabido *a* aforesaid, before-mentioned; well-known.
consagración *f* devotion, steadiness; hallowing influence; consecration.
consagrar *vt* to consecrate, dedicate; *vr* to devote oneself; to be hallowed (*eg by usage*).
consanguíneo *a* kindred, related by blood.
consanguinidad *f* consanguinity.
consciente *a* conscious, aware, intentional.
consecución *f* attainment.
consecuencia *f* consequence, result; importance; **por** — therefore.
consecuente *a* following, consequent; *m* proposition dependent on the antecedent, effect.
consecutivo *a* consecutive; resultant.
conseguir *vt* to get, achieve, attain, obtain.
conseja *f* fable, story, tale.
consejero *m* counselor, adviser.
consejo *m* advice, opinion; council; — **de ministros** cabinet; **presidente del** — Prime Minister (*Spain*).
consenso *m* consensus.
consentido *a* spoiled, pampered.
consentimiento *m* consent, agreement.
consentir (ie) *vt* to permit, allow; to spoil (*a child*); *vr* to crumple up, break down.
conserje *m* doorman, caretaker, attendant, concierge, janitor.

conserva *f* preserve, jam; canned (*meat etc*); **sardinas en —** canned sardines.
conservación *f* preservation; maintenance.
conservador *m* curator; preserver; *a* conservative.
conservar *vt* to preserve, maintain, keep, take care of.
conservatorio *m* conservatory, greenhouse; **— de música** music academy.
considerable *a* considerable, significant, great, imposing, large.
consideración *f* consideration, regard; due respect; reflection; **en — de** out of respect for.
considerado *a* prudent, considerate, respected.
considerar *vt* to consider, think over; to have regard for, to treat with respect.
consigna *f* watchword, password; luggage office.
consignación *f* consignment, deposit.
consignar *vt* to consign, deposit; to dispatch; to entrust; to state explicitly.
consigo *pn* with (*himself*), (*herself*), (*themselves*), (*oneself*), (*yourself*).
consiguiente *a* dependent, resultant, consequential; **por —** as a result, consequently.
consistencia *f* solidity, firmness, consistence, consistency.
consistente *a* firm, consistent.
consistir *vi* to consist (*in*), be composed of; to be the reason for.
consistorio *m* consistory; municipality.
consocio *m* partner, associate, fellow member.
consolación *f* consolation, comfort.
consolar (ue) *vt* to console, soothe, comfort.
consolidación *f* consolidation.
consolidar *vt* to consolidate, strengthen.
consonancia *f* consonance; conformity, harmony, agreement.
consonante *f* (*letter*) consonant; rhyming word; *a* concordant, consistent.
consorcio *m* partnership.
consorte *mf* consort, companion; husband, wife.
conspicuo *a* conspicuous.
conspiración *f* conspiracy, pilot.
conspirador *m* conspirator.
conspirar *vi* to plot, combine; to conspire.
constancia *f* steadiness, stout-heartedness, constancy; written evidence.
constante *a* constant, reliable, steady; consisting (*of*).
Constantinopla *f* Constantinople.
constar *vi* to be evident; to be composed of, consist of; **consta que** let it be noted that; **hacer —** to reveal.
constatar *vt* to verify, confirm.
constelación *f* constellation.
constelado *a* starry; spangled.
consternación *f* consternation, panic.
consternar *vt* to cause fright, amazement.
constipación *f* cold, chill.
constipado *m* cold (*in head*).
constitución *f* nature, constitution; essence and qualities of a thing; fundamental law.
constitucional *a* constitutional; legal.
constituir *vt* to constitute; to establish; *vr* **— en** to set up as.
constitutivo *a* constitutive, essential.
constituyente *a* establishing; forming; constituent.
constreñir (i) *vt* to constrain, compel.
construcción *f* construction, building.
constructor *m* builder.
construir *vt* to construct, build; to construe.
consuelo *m* consolation, comfort; relief.
consuetudinario *a* customary; **derecho —** common law.
cónsul *m* consul.
consulado *m* consulate.
consulta *f* consultation; conference; **horas de —** consulting hours.
consultar *vt* to consult; to consider; to take advice.
consultivo *a* advisory.
consultor *m* counsel, counselor.
consultorio *m* — information bureau; doctor's office.
consumación *f* consummation; final satisfaction; competition.
consumado *a* consummate, perfect, accomplished; *m* consommé.
consumar *vt* to finish, complete, consummate.
consumición *f* (*in café*) 'plate', portion, bill.
consumido *a* very thin, wasted.
consumidor *m* consumer.
consumir *vt* to consume; to spend, waste; *vr* to wear out, waste away.
consumo *m* consumption (*of food etc*) waste; *pl* excise tax.
consunción *f* consumption, TB, phthisis.
contabilidad *f* book keeping, accountancy.
contacto *m* contact, touch.
contado *a* rare, scarce; **por de —** of course; **al —** for cash, ready money; **de —** immediately.
contador *m* purser, book keeper; desk; (*gas etc*) meter.
contaduría *f* accountant's office; accountancy, book keeping; box office.
contagiar *vt* to infect; to communicate (*disease*); *vr* to become infected.

contagio *m* contagion; infection; corruption.
contagioso *a* contagious, infectious.
contaminar *vt* to contaminate, infect; to vitiate.
contante *a* **dinero**— ready cash.
contar *vt* to count; to reckon on; to narrate; — **con** to depend on, rely upon.
contemplación *f* contemplation, meditation.
contemplar *vt* to gaze at; to please; to meditate, think over, plan.
contemporáneo *a* contemporaneous; *m* contemporary.
contemporizar *vi* to temporize.
contención *f* contention, strife.
contencioso *a* contentious, disputable; litigious.
contender *vt* to contend, dispute.
contendiente *m* contestant, litigant, wrangler.
contener *vt* to contain, comprise, hold; to refrain, stop, detain; to restrain; to restrict; *vr* to constrain oneself, hold back.
contenido *m* contents.
contentadizo *a* **bien** — easy to please; **mal**— difficult to please.
contentar *vt* to satisfy, content, please; *vr* to be pleased, delighted; to be satisfied (*with*), happy (*with*).
contento *a* contented, pleased, glad; *m* contentment, satisfaction, happiness.
conterráneo *m* fellow countryman.
contertuliano *m* fellow clubman, member of same group.
contestable *a* disputable.
contestación *f* answer, reply.
contestar *vt* to answer, reply.
contexto *m* context.
contextura *f* frame, framework; texture.
contienda *f* contest, strife, conflict.
contigo *prep pn* with thee, with you.
contigüidad *f* nearness, contiguity.
contiguo *a* contiguous, adjoining, next (*door etc*).
continencia *f* continence.
continente *a* continent; chaste; *m* continent; appearance, countenance.
contingencia *f* contingency, emergency.
contingente *a* contingent; *m* quota, contingent.
continuación *f* continuation, sequel; **a**— to be continued.
continuar *vt* to continue, go ahead, go on; to carry on.
continuidad *f* continuity.
continuo *a* continuous; incessant, endless; uninterrupted; **acto** — immediately afterward, without a break.
contonearse *vr* to strut, swagger; waddle.
contoneo *m* strut, swagger; waddle.
contorno *m* environs; outline; **en los —s** around about, in the neighborhood.
contorsión *f* contortion.
contra *prep* against; **en**— against, in opposition; *f* counter; opposition; windowsill.
contraalmirante *m* rear-admiral.
contraataque *m* counterattack.
contrabajo *m* contra bass; (*mus*) deep bass; double bass.
contrabandista *m* smuggler.
contrabando *m* contraband; smuggling; smuggled goods.
contrabarrera *f* inner barrier (*in bull ring*); second row of seats.
contracambio *m* barter; re-exchange.
contracarril *m* guard rail.
contracción *f* contraction; shrinkage, reduction; abridgment.
contracifra *f* key to cipher, code.
contracorriente *f* crosscurrent; backwash.
contradanza *f* quadrille.
contradecir *vt* to contradict, gainsay.
contradicción *f* contradiction.
contradictorio *a* contradictory.
contradique *m* counter-dike.
contraer *vt* to reduce, contract; (*illness*) to get, catch; acquire; — **matrimonio** to (be) get married, to marry; *vr* to confine oneself; to reduce; to shrink.
contrafuerte *m* buttress; extra strap (*on harness*); reinforcement; counterfort.
contrahacer *vt* to counterfeit, feign; to pirate (*literary works*); to impersonate.
contrahecho *a* deformed, misshapen; spurious.
contralor *m* controller, inspector.
contramaestre *m* overseer.
contramandar *vt* to countermand.
contramarcha *f* countermarch.
contraorden *f* countermand.
contraparte *f* counterpart; counterpoint.
contrapelo *a* **a**— against the grain.
contrapesar *vt* to counterbalance.
contrapeso *m* counterpoise, counterweight; check, deterrent.
contraponer *vt* to oppose.
contraproducente *a* which defeats its own purpose.
contrapunto *m* counterpoint.
contrariar *vt* to oppose, run counter to; to put out, vex.
contrariedad *f* contrariety, obstacle; disappointment.
contrario *a* contrary, unfavorable, adverse; **al** — on the other hand, on the contrary; **llevar la contraria a** to contradict; *m* opponent, antagonist.
contrarrestar *vt* to oppose, arrest, check.
contrarevolución *f* counter-revolution.
contrasalida *f* reentry ticket.

contrasentido *m* contradiction in terms; absurd deduction.
contraseña *f* countersign; watchword; counterfoil, ticket.
contrastar *vt* to contrast; *vi* to be different.
contraste *m* contrast, opposition.
contrata *f* contract, written agreement.
contratante *f* contracting party.
contratar *vt* to contract, agree, make a contract; to hire.
contratiempo *m* (*mus*) syncopation; mishap, contretemps.
contratista *m* contractor.
contrato *m* pact, agreement, contract; **— de compraventa** contract of bargain and sale.
contravención *f* contravention, violation.
contraveneno *m* antidote.
contravenir *vt* to contravene, transgress, break (*law*).
contraventana *f* shutter.
contraventor *m* transgressor.
contrayente *m* contracting party.
contrecho *a* crippled; *m* cripple.
contribución *f* contribution; tax.
contribuir *vi* to contribute; to supply, furnish.
contribuyente *m* taxpayer; contributor.
contrición *f* contrition, repentance.
contrincante *m* competitor, rival.
contristar *vt* to afflict, grieve.
contrito *a* contrite; repentant.
control *m* control.
controversia *f* controversy, dispute.
controvertir (ie) *vt* to dispute, argue against.
contubernio *m* cohabitation, concubinage; (*fig*) infamous alliance.
contumacia *f* contumacy, persistence in error; contempt of court.
contumaz *a* contumacious, perverse, obstinate.
contumelia *f* contumely, abusiveness.
contundente *a* forceful, powerful (*argument*).
conturbar *vt* to perturb, trouble.
contusión *f* contusion, bruise.
conuco *m Col, Cub, Ven* small plot of land.
convalecer *vi* to convalesce.
convaleciente *a* convalescent.
convecino *a* neighboring; *m* neighbor.
convencer *vt* to convince; *vr* to be assured, make certain, (sure); to be satisfied.
convencimiento *m* assurance, conviction; persuasion.
convención *f* agreement, convention; treaty; pact.
convencional *a* conventional.
convenido *a* agreed (upon).
conveniencia *f* convenience; utility, profit; desirability.
conveniente *a* convenient; agreeable; appropriate; desirable; expedient.
convenio *m* agreement, pact.
convenir *vi* to agree, suit; to contract; to convene.
conventillero *m* gossip.
conventillo *m Arg, Bol, Chi* slum; tenement.
convento *m* convent, nunnery; religious house or community.
convergencia *f* convergence, common direction.
converger or **convergir (i)** *vi* to converge, come together.
conversación *f* conversation, chat, colloquy, talk.
conversar *vi* to talk, converse.
conversión *f* conversion.
converso *m* convert.
convertible *a* convertible.
convertir (ie) *vt* to convert, transform, change; *vr* to be converted.
convexidad *f* convexity.
convicción *f* conviction, certainty.
convicto *a* guilty, convicted.
convidado *m* (*invited*) guest.
convidar *vt* to invite (*to meal*); to induce; *vi* to lend to.
convincente *a* convincing, telling.
convite *m* invitation (*to food, drink*); banquet.
convivencia *f* living together, (*ability etc*) to live together.
convocación *f* convocation, calling.
convocar *vt* to summon, convoke, call together.
convocatoria *f* decree of convocation, notice, summons.
convoy *m* convoy, escort; procession; *SA* (*rl*) train.
convoyar *vt* to convoy, escort.
convulsión *f* convulsion; agitation.
convulso *a* convulsed.
conyugal *a* conjugal.
cónyuge *mf* consort, wife, husband.
coñac *m* cognac, brandy.
cooperación *f* cooperation.
cooperador *m* cooperator, collaborator.
cooperar *vi* to cooperate, work (*for*) (*together*).
coordenadas *f pl* (*math*) coordinates.
coordinar *vt* to coordinate.
copa *f* wine glass, cup; foliage; crown (*of hat*); (*cards*) hearts.
copar *vt* to corner (*supply*); to surprise.
copartícipe *m* co-partner, associate.
copero *m* cupbearer.
copete *m* aigret, toupee; forelock; tail (*of peacock*); **de alto —** of quality (*persons*).
copetín *m Arg* cocktail, aperitif.
copia *f* abundance; copy, imitation.
copiar *vt* to copy, imitate; **— del natural** to copy from life.
copioso *a* copious, abundant, ample.
copista *m* copyist.
copita *f* (*sherry*) glass; **tomar una —** to have a drink.
copla *f* song, ballad; stanza, verse, couplet.

coplero *m* second-rate poet.
copo *m* tuft; (snow)flake; (*of tree*) top; small bundle, skein.
coposo *a* tufted, massy, leafy.
copto *an* Copt, Coptic.
copudo *a* bushy-topped (*tree*).
cópula *f* joining; connection, coupling; sexual intercourse.
coque *m* coke.
coqueta *f* flirt, coquette.
coquetear *vi* to flirt.
coquetería *f* flirtation, coquetry.
coraje *m* courage, dash; passion, temper, fury.
corajudo *a* passionate; ill-tempered, angry.
coral *a* choral; *m* coral.
corambre *f* (*pile of*) hides.
coraza *f* cuirass; armor plate, ship's armor.
corazón *m* heart; courage; core; spirit; **con el — en la mano** openly, frankly; **no le cabe el — en el pecho** he is very jumpy, he is on tenterhooks.
corazonada *f* presentiment, hunch.
corbata *f* (neck)tie; cravat.
corbeta *f* corvette.
corcel *m* steed, charger.
corcova *f* hump; *m* leap, bound, curvet (*of horse*).
corcovado *a* hunchbacked; *m* hunchback.
corchea *f* quaver.
corchete *m* hook, clasp; hook-and-eye; square bracket; constable, bailiff.
corcho *m* cork, corkbark.
cordaje *m* rigging, cordage; set of (*guitar*) strings.
cordel *m* cord; **a —** in a straight line; **mozo de —** porter.
cordelero *m* ropemaker.
cordero *m* yearling lamb; (*tanned*) lambskin.
cordial *a* hearty, cordial; *m* cordial, refreshing drink.
cordialidad *f* warmth, heartiness, friendliness.
cordillera *f* mountain range, cordillera.
cordobán *m* dressed goatskin; Cordovan leather.
cordobés *am* of Cordova.
cordón *m* yarn, string, cord; (*mil*) cordon.
cordura *f* wisdom; saneness, sanity; sense.
coreografía *f* choreography.
coreógrafo *m* choreographer.
coriáceo *a* coriaceous, hard as leather, tough.
corista *mf* street singer; chorus singer; chorus girl.
cornada *f* horn thrust, goring.
cornamenta *f* horns, antlers.
cornamusa *f* cornemuse, bagpipes.
corneja *f* crow.
córneo *a* horny, callous.
corneta *f* horn, bugle; **— de llaves** trumpet, cornet.
cornisa *f* cornice.
cornucopia *f* cornucopia, horn of plenty.
cornudo *a* horned.
coro *m* choir; chorus.
corolario *m* corollary, inference.
corona *f* crown, diadem; top of head, tonsure; arm (*of capstan*); royalty, sovereignty.
coronación *f* coronation.
coronamiento *m* crowning; apex, tip.
coronar *vt* to crown; to achieve; *vr* to be covered; *Arg* to be unfaithful (*to wife etc*).
coronel *m* colonel.
coronilla *f* top of the head; **estar hasta la —** to be fed up.
corpiño *m* vest, bodice.
corporación *f* corporation, body; community; guild.
corporal *a* bodily, corporeal, corporal.
corpóreo *a* corporeal, embodied.
corpulencia *f* corpulence.
Corpus *m* Corpus Christi (*procession and day*).
corpúsculo *m* corpuscle.
corral *m* yard; poultry yard; (*arch*) playhouse.
corralón *m* large yard.
correa *f* leather belt, strap, leash; **tener —** to give, extend; not to resist.
corrección *f* correction; good manners, correctness; reprehension; **casa de —** reformatory.
correcto *a* correct, right, just.
corredera *f* track, slide, rail; racetrack.
corredizo *a* easy to untie, smooth-running.
corredor *m* runner; broker; corridor; racehorse.
corregible *a* corrigible, manageable, subject to correction.
corregidor *m* (High) Sheriff; corregidor, magistrate.
corregidora *f* wife of corregidor; *a* bossy (*woman*).
corregimiento *m* office and jurisdiction of a corregidor.
corregir (i) *vt* to correct; to amend, straighten; to admonish.
correlación *f* correlation.
correo *m* courier; mail, post; post-office messenger.
correr *vi* to run, flow, pass, race, be current; **—la** (*fam*) to be a night bird; **a todo —** at high speed.
correría *f* raid; excursion, trip.
correspondencia *f* correspondence, letter-writing.
corresponder *vti* to answer, correspond; to communicate; to respond; to concern; to live up to; to be appropriate.
correspondiente *a* suitable, appropriate; corresponding.
corresponsal *m* correspondent.
corretaje *m* brokerage.

correvedile *m* gossip, idle chatterer; scandalmonger.
corrida *f* course, race; — **de toros** bullfight; **de** — in haste, one after the other.
corrido *a* experienced; ashamed; **de** — fluently, easily.
corriente *a* usual; present, current; fluent, instant; **moneda** — currency; — **y moliente** honest-to-goodness, genuine; **estar al** — to be au fait; *f* running stream; current; draft.
corrillo *m* knot of people talking.
corro *m* group, knot of people.
corroboración *f* corroboration.
corroborar *vt* to corroborate; to fortify, strengthen.
corroer *vt* to corrode.
corromper *vt* to vitiate, taint, corrupt, deprave.
corrosivo *a* corrosive.
corrupción *f* corruption; perversion; depravity.
corruptor *a* corrupting; *m* corrupter.
corsario *m* privateer; corsair.
corsé *m* corset, stays, girdle.
corsetero *m* corsetier, corsetmaker.
corso *an* Corsican; *m* cruise, privateering.
cortabolsas *m* pickpocket.
cortado *a* cut; abrupt; exact; abashed, ashamed; off (*of milk*); *m* *Arg* coffee with little milk.
cortador *m* cutter, tailor.
cortadura *f* cut, gash; cutting (*railway, newspaper*); *pl* cuttings, peelings.
cortante *a* cutting, keen-edged, sharp; *m* meat chopper.
cortapapel *m* paper cutter, paper knife.
cortapisa *f* obstacle, restriction, impediment; grace, elegance (*of speech*).
cortaplumas *m* penknife.
cortar *vt* to cut (*out, off, up*), break; to hew; to sever; to cut short; *Arg* to take a short cut; to **cut** (*cards*); *vr* to chap (*of skin*); to curdle, go off (*of milk etc*).
cortaviento *m* windscreen, windshield.
corte *m* edge (*sword*), felling (*trees*); length (*cloth*); sectional view; cut (*style*); *f* court, king's residence; royal household; **hacer la** — to pay court.
cortedad *f* briefness; poverty (*speech etc*), meanness, dullness; shyness, diffidence.
cortejar *vt* to court, woo.
cortejo *m* homage; courtship; accompaniment; beau, escort.
cortés *a* courteous, civil, polite.
cortesanía *f* courteousness, gallantry.
cortesano *a* obliging; *m* courtier; *f* courtesan.
cortesía *f* courtesy, civility, politeness.
corteza *f* bark (*tree*); peel, skin (*fruit etc*); crust (*bread*); rough exterior (*person*).
cortijo *m* farmhouse, farm estate, country house.
cortina *f* curtain.
corto *a* short, brief, narrow; abrupt, curt; shy, backward; — **de vista** shortsighted.
coruscar *vi* to glitter, shine.
corveta *f* curvet, prancing (*of horse*).
corvo *a* bent, crooked; *m* hook.
corzo *m* fallow deer.
cosa *f* thing; fact; business; — **de** about; **como si tal** — as if nothing had happened.
coscorrón *m* whack (*on head*).
cosecha *f* harvest, vintage, crop; reaping, harvest time; **de su propia** — off his own bat.
cosechar *vt* to gather (*harvest*), reap.
coser *vt* to sew, seam; **es cosa de** — **y cantar** as easy as wink.
cosmético *am* cosmetic.
cosmografía *f* cosmography.
cosmopolita *m* cosmopolitan.
coso *m* enclosure (*for bullring*).
cosquillas *f pl* tickling; **hacer** — to tickle; **tener** — to be ticklish.
cosquilloso *a* ticklish; squeamish.
costa *f* cost, charge; coast; **a** — **de** at the expense of; **a toda** — at all costs; *pl* costs (*in lawsuit*).
costado *m* side, flank; **por los cuatro** —s thoroughbred, thorough-going.
costal *m* bag, sack.
costalar *vi Arg* to fall on one's side or back.
costanera *f* slope; *Arg* promenade.
costanero *a* coastal, belonging to the coast; **comercio** — coasting trade.
costar (ue) *vi* to cost, be worth; to pain, grieve.
costarricense *a* Costa Rican.
costarriqueño *an* Costa Rican.
coste *m* cost, expense; cost price; **a precio de** — at cost; — **de vida** cost of living; **de gran** — of great price, value.
costear *vt* to pay the cost of; to cost.
costeño *a* coastal.
costilla *f* rib; chop, cutlet; (*fam*) better half, wife.
costo *m* price, cost, value.
costoso *a* expensive, costly.
costra *f* crust, coat; daub; scab; ship's biscuit.
costumbre *f* custom, habit, practice, wont; *pl* habits, manners.
costumbrismo *m* description of customs, social habits *etc*.
costura *f* sewing, seam; needlework.
costurera *f* seamstress, dressmaker.
costurero *m* sewing table, sewing case, sewing room.
cota *f* coat of arms, coat of mail; quota.
cotejar *vt* to confront, compare (*texts*).
cotejo *m* collation (*of texts*).
cotidiano *a* daily.
cotillón *m* cotillion.

cotización *f* (*com*) quotation, current price.
cotizar *vt* to quote (*on Stock Exchange*).
coto *m* estate, preserves; fence, boundary; landmark; **poner — a** to put a stop to.
cotona *f SA* undershirt.
cotonada *f* calico print.
cotorra *f* parrot; talkative woman, chatterbox.
cotorrear *vi* to chatter, gossip.
cototo *m Arg, Chi* bump, bruise.
covachuela *f* small cave; ministry.
covadera *f Chi, Per* guano bed.
coyote *m* Mexican wolf.
coyunda *f* yokestrap; submission.
coyuntura *f* joint, conjuncture; opportunity, situation.
coz *f* (*mule etc*) kick; (*firearms*) recoil; **dar coces** to kick.
cráneo *m* skull.
crapuloso *a* drunken, dissolute.
craso *a* greasy, oily, fat; gross, crass.
cráter *m* crater.
creación *f* creation; the universe.
creador *m* creator, maker.
crear *vt* to create, invent, make.
crecer *vi* to grow, wax strong, increase.
creces *f pl* increase, advantage, augmentation; **con—** amply, in good measure.
crecido *a* grown up; swollen (*rivers*); increase (*knitting*).
creciente *a* crescent, growing; *f* swell, freshet (*rivers*); *m* crescent (*moon*).
crecimiento *m* growth; increase.
credencial *a* giving power, giving authority; *f* credential; *f pl* credentials.
crédito *m* belief; credit; good standing; credence, belief; **a —** on credit; **créditos activos** assets; **créditos pasivos** liabilities.
credo *m* creed, belief.
credulidad *f* credulity.
crédulo *a* credulous, gullible.
creencia *f* belief; creed.
creer *vt* to believe, assume, think; **¡ya lo creo!** of course! I should think so!
creíble *a* credible, likely.
creído *a RP* vain.
crema *f* cream; cold cream; diaeresis.
cremación *f* cremation.
cremallera *f* toothed bar, racket, ratchet; cog; zip fastener, zipper.
cremar *vt* to cremate.
crepitación *f* crepitation, crackling.
crepitar *vi* to crackle, crepitate.
crepuscular *a* crepuscular, twilight, evening.
crepúsculo *m* twilight; dawn.
crespo *a* crisp, curly; involved (*style*).
crespón *m* crape.
cresta *f* cock's comb; tuft; crest, summit.
creta *f* chalk.
cretense *a* Cretan.
cretino *m* cretin; idiot.
cretona *f* linen cloth; calico.
creyente *m* believer, faithful.
cría *f* suckling, breeding; young (*of animals*); (*fam*) baby.
criada *f* maid, maidservant.
criadero *m* nursery, hatchery; hotbed.
criado *a* brought up, bred; *m* servant, valet, waiter.
criador *m* breeder, rearer.
crianza *f* nursing; breeding; **mala —** ill manners.
criar *vt* to create; to breed, nurse, suckle, rear.
criatura *f* creature, baby.
criba *f* cribble, sieve, riddle.
cribar *vt* to sift, pass through a sieve.
crimen *m* crime, guilt, offense.
criminal *a* criminal; *m* criminal, offender.
criminalidad *f* criminality.
crin *f* (*animals*) hair; mane; filament.
crío *m* baby, child (*in arms*).
criollo *m* creole, Spaniard born in the Americas; *a* indigenous.
cripta *f* crypt.
crisálida *f* chrysalis, pupa.
crisis *f* crisis, critical point.
crisma *mf* chrism, sacramental oil; (*fam*) head, nut (*fam*).
crisol *m* crucible; test.
crispar *vt* to contract convulsively (*muscles*), to twitch.
cristal *m* crystal; pane (*of glass*); mirror.
cristalino *a* crystalline, limpid, clear.
cristalizar *vt* to crystallize.
cristianar *vt* to baptize; to go to church.
cristiandad *f* Christendom.
cristianismo *m* Christianity.
cristianizar *vt* to Christianize.
cristiano *an* Christian; **hablar —** to talk Spanish; (*fig*) person, soul.
Cristo *m* Christ; crucifix.
criterio *m* judgment, criterion, point of view.
crítica *f* criticism; critical article.
criticar *vt* to criticize, censure, find fault with.
crítico *a* critical; *m* critic.
cromo *m* chromium; chromo; colored plate, reproduction.
crónica *f* chronicle; news *or* gossip column.
crónico *a* chronic.
cronista *m* chronicler.
cronología *f* chronology.
croqueta *f* croquette, meatball.
croquis *m* sketch, rough draft, outline.
cruce *m* crossing; crossroads.
crucero *m* cruiser; (*archit*) crossing; wayside Cross.
crucificar *vt* to crucify; to torture.
crucifijo *m* crucifix.
crudeza *f* coarseness, crudeness; rawness; cruelty.

crudo *a* raw, coarse; (*of water*) hard; unfinished; creamy, yellowish (*color*).
cruel *a* cruel, ruthless, merciless; harsh, grievous.
crueldad *f* cruelty; harshness.
cruento *a* bloody (*war etc*), implacable.
crujía *f* passage; ward; corridor; **pasar —s** to experience great hardships.
crujido *m* creaking; rustling; crunching.
crujir *vi* to creak, crackle; to rustle; to crunch, crack.
crustáceo *m* crustacean.
cruz *f* cross; **cara o —** heads or tails; (*fig*) sorrows; **— de Mayo** (*equiv of*) Maypole; **— gamada** swastika.
cruzada *f* crusade; crossroads.
cruzado *a* cross-bred; *m* crusader; old Spanish coin; *pl* shading; **palabras cruzadas** crossword puzzle.
cruzamiento *m* crossing.
cruzar *vt* to pass, cross, go across; to cross-breed; *vr* **— de brazos** to be idle.
cuadernillo *m* quire (*paper*).
cuaderno *m* notebook, exercise book, copybook.
cuadra *f* large hall; stable; barracks; ward; *SA* block of buildings.
cuadrado *a* square; at attention; square-built (*man*); *m* square (*number*); *Arg* ill-mannered person.
cuadrangular *a* quadrangular, four-sided.
cuadrante *m* quadrant; sundial.
cuadrar *vt* to square; to square with, fit in with; *vr* (*mil*) to salute, stand to attention.
cuadrilátero *m* four-sided figure; *SA* boxing ring.
cuadrilla *f* troop, gang; group (*bullfighters*); quadrille.
cuadrillero *f* chief, gang leader.
cuadro *m* square; flowerbed; (*theat*) scene; (*lit*) descriptive picture; picture, painting, frame.
cuádruplo *a* quadruple, fourfold.
cuajada *f Arg* yoghourt.
cuajar *vt* to coagulate, curdle; to over-adorn; *vi* to fit, be suitable, be acceptable.
cuajo *m* rennet; coagulation.
cual *pn* which; **el —** which; **cada —** each one; **— padre, tal hijo** like father, like son.
cualidad *f* quality.
cualquier, a *a pn* any, anybody; *m* **un —** somebody or other, any old person.
cuan *see* **cuanto.**
cuando *ad* when; if; although; in case; **de — en —** now and then; **— quiera** whenever; **— mucho** at most.
cuantía *f* amount; **de poca —** of little account.
cuantioso *a* copious, sizable (*amount*).
cuanto *a* so much, so many; as soon as, as much; **¿cuánto?** how much?; **¿cuántos?** how many?; **tanto ... cuánto** as much ... as; **en —** as soon as; **en — a** as for, concerning; (*excl*) how much, what a lot ....
cuáquero *m* Quaker; member of Society of Friends.
cuarenta *an* forty.
cuarentena *f* quarantine.
cuaresma *f* Lent, Lent sermons.
cuarta *f* set of four (*cards*); (*mus*) fourth; guide mule.
cuartear *vt* to divide in four parts; to cut in pieces; (*horses*) to zigzag uphill; *Mex* to whip; to crack.
cuartel *m* barracks, quarters; district, quarter; **— general** headquarters; (*mil*) **sin —** no mercy shown, no prisoners taken.
cuartelada *f* barracks revolt.
cuarteta *f* quatrain.
cuarteto *m* (*mus*) quartet.
cuartilla *f* (*measure*) quarter; sheet of (note)paper.
cuartillo *m* coin, quarter (*dry measure*), pint.
cuarto *m* quarter; room; sentinel watch; farthing, small coin; quarto; **no tiene un —** he hasn't a cent.
cuarzo *m* quartz.
cuasi *ad* almost.
cuate *mf Mex* twin.
cuatrero *m* cattle thief.
cuatro *an* four.
cuba *f* vat, cask; (*fig*) drunkard.
cubano *an* Cuban.
cubero *m* cooper, caskmaker.
cubicar *vt* to cube; to find the volume of a cube.
cúbico *a* cubic, cubical.
cubierta *f* cover, envelope; book jacket; (*ship*) deck; (*aut*) hood, top; outer tire.
cubierto *m* (*at table*) cover, place; *a* **— de** sheltered from; *a* covered.
cubo *m* cube; bucket, pail; hub (*of wheel*).
cubrecama *m* eiderdown, quilt.
cubrir *vt* to cover, load, envelop; to hide; **— los gastos** to cover expenses; **— una vacante** to fill a vacancy; *vr* to be covered; to guard oneself; to put on one's hat.
cucaña *f* greasy pole; a gift (*ie easily obtained*).
cucaracha *f* cockroach.
cuclillas *ad* **en —** crouching, squatting.
cuclillo *m* cuckoo.
cuco *a* dainty, cozy; coy, shy, arch.
cuchara *f* spoon, dipper; trowel.
cucharada *f* spoonful.
cucharilla *f* small spoon, teaspoon, coffeespoon.
cucharón *m* ladle, dipper.
cuchichear *vi* to talk together in whispers, whisper.
cuchicheo *m* whispering, chattering, 'clacking'.

cuchilla *f* cleaver, large knife; blade (*of knife*); sword.
cuchillada *f* gash, knife wound; *pl* slashing (*in clothes*).
cuchillería *f* cutlery; cutler's shop.
cuchillero *m* cutler.
cuchillo *m* knife; gusset, gore (*dressmaking*); — **de monte** hunting knife.
cuchipanda *f* (*fam*) lively dinner party; feed, spread, spree.
cuchitril *m* cubbyhole, den.
cuchufleta *f* joke, smart remark.
cuello *m* neck, throat, collar; **voz en** — shouting, bawling.
cuenca *f* hollow, basin (*of river*); socket (*of eye*); wooden bowl; workings (*of mine*); — **hullera** coalfield.
cuenta *f* account; computation, bill; care; bead; **a** — on account; **por la** — according to all appearances; — **corriente** current account; **tener en** — to take into consideration; **caer en** — to realize; **trabajar por su** — to work for oneself.
cuento *m* tale, story, narrative; ferule; **venir a** — to come in opportunely, to fit the occasion; **sin** — endless(ly).
cuerda *f* cord, string, rope; chord, voice (*in singing*); **dar** — **a** to wind (*watch etc*); to give free play to; **apretar la** — to put on the screws.
cuerdo *a* sane; prudent, wise; sensible.
cuerno *m* horn; tip (*of crescent moon*); antenna (*of insect*); huntsman's horn.
cuero *m* leather, hide; skin, raw hide; wineskin; — **cabelludo** scalp; *pl* **en** —**s** naked; **sacarle el cuero** to gossip about sombody.
cuerpo *m* body, matter; figure; bodice; corpse; corporation; **vino de mucho** — strong-bodied wine; **a** — without an overcoat; **en** — half-clothed; in a body; **tomar** — to increase, grow apace; **luchar** — **a** — to fight hand to hand.
cuervo *m* raven, crow.
cuesta *f* hill, grade, slope; — **arriba** uphill; — **abajo** downhill; **a** —**s** on one's shoulders or back.
cuestión *f* question, matter, point; dispute, quarrel; inquiry; problem (*in mathematics*).
cuestionar *vt* to discuss a question.
cuestionario *m* series of questions, questionnaire.
cueva *f* cave, grotto; cellar.
cuidado *m* care, heed; attention; apprehension; **estar de** — to be critically ill; **ser de** — to be a handful; to need watching; *excl* look out!
cuidadoso *a* careful, watchful, painstaking, neat.
cuidar *vt* to take care of, look after (*esp ill-health*); to heed; *vr* to take good care of oneself; — **de** to mind.
cuita *f* grief, affliction, sorrow.
cuitado *a* wretched, unfortunate.
culada *f* blow (*with a butt end*).
culata *f* haunch (*of animal*); (*gun, rifle*) butt end.
culatazo *m* recoil (*of gun*); blow (*with butt end*).
culebra *f* snake, serpent; — **de cascabel** rattlesnake.
culebrear *vi* to wriggle.
culinario *a* culinary.
culminación *f* culmination, climax.
culo *m* anus, backside; —**s de vaso** fake jewels.
culpa *f* fault, guilt, offense.
culpabilidad *f* guilt.
culpable *a* culpable, to blame, blamable; guilty.
culpado *a* guilty, blameworthy.
culpar *vt* to blame, put the blame on; to reproach.
culteranismo *m* Gongorism, an affected literary style full of conceits.
cultismo *m* learned word.
cultivable *a* arable.
cultivador *m* tiller; cultivator, farmer.
cultivar *vt* to till; to cultivate; to keep up.
cultivo *m* cultivation, tillage, farming.
culto *m* cult, worship; **libertad de**—**s** freedom of worship; *a* well-bred; educated, cultivated, affected, learned.
cultura *f* culture, cultivation; breeding, education, good manners.
cumbre *f* summit, top, peak; height (*of ambition etc*).
cumpleaños *m* birthday.
cumplido *a* full, complete; fulfilled, satisfied; courteous; *m* compliment, ceremony.
cumplimentar *vt* to compliment, congratulate.
cumplimiento *m* compliment; formality; fulfillment.
cumplir *vt* to fulfill, accomplish, perform, comply; to be a duty to; to reach (*of age*); to finish (*military service*); — **con** to do (*one's duty*); *vr* to be realized; — **años** to celebrate one's birthday.
cumular *vt* to accumulate.
cúmulo *m* heap, pile, mass (*of things*); cumulus clouds.
cuna *f* cradle; foundlings' home; lineage; source, origin, birth.
cundir *vi* to spread (*of news, water*); to propagate.
cuneta *f* gutter, ditch, culvert.
cuña *f* wedge; paving stone.
cuñado, -da *mf* brother-, sister-in-law.
cuñete *m* keg, small barrel.
cuño *m* silversmith's mark; a die.
cuota *f* quota, share; (*amount of*) subscription, membership fee.
cupé *m* cab, coupé.
cupo *m* part assigned, share; Mex capacity.

cupón *m* coupon, counterfoil, detachable ticket.
cúpula *f* dome, cupola; (*acorn*) cup; ship's gun turret.
cura *m* parish priest, curate; *f* cure, remedy; priesthood, parish, curacy; **la primera** — first aid.
curable *a* curable, remediable.
curaca *m SA* governor.
curación *f* cure, treatment, healing.
curado *a* cured, salted; tanned; *Chi, Per, Urug* drunk.
curador *m* curator, overseer; guardian.
curandero *m* quack, medicine man, charlatan.
curar *vt* to heal, cure, treat; to cure (*fish etc*).
curativo *a* healing, curative.
curato *m* parish.
cureña *f* gun carriage; **a — rasa** without a parapet; (*fig*) unprotected.
curia *f* ecclesiastical tribunal; **la — romana** Papal jurisdiction and power.
curiosear *vi* to pry, meddle, be a busybody.
curiosidad *f* curiosity, inquisitiveness; cleanliness; rarity.
curioso *a* curious, inquisitive, prying; clean; rare, old, strange.
curro (*fam*) handsome, dashing, swell.
cursante *m* student attending a course.
cursar *vt* to frequent, attend, follow a course of study (*eg* — **leyes** *to study law*); to pass on (*orders etc*).
cursi *a* common; ridiculous, affected, tawdry, mawkish, genteel, pretentious, commonplace.
cursilería *f* affected gentility, vulgar pretension.
cursillo *m* course of lectures.
cursivo *a* running (*of handwriting*); cursive script.
curso *m* course, progress; direction; route.
curtido *a* tanned; weather-beaten; expert, experienced; well-versed in; *m* tanning.
curtidor *m* (*skin*) tanner.
curtir *vt* to tan (*skin, leather*); (*fig*) to harden, toughen.
curucurú *m SA* disease caused by snake bite.
curva *f* curved line, curve, bend.
curvatura *f* curvature; bend.
curvo *a* curved, bent.
cuscurro *m* crust (*of loaf*).
cúspide *f* apex, summit, top.
custodia *f* custody, guardianship; custodia, holy vessel in which Sacrament is exposed.
custodiar *vt* to take care of, keep safe.
custodio *a* **angel** — guardian angel; *m* guard, custodian.
cutáneo *a* of the skin; cutaneous.
cutir *vt* to strike (*blow*).
cutis *f* (*human*) skin.
cuyo *pn* whose, of which.

CH

chabacano *a* clumsy, lacking good taste, vulgar; *Mex* variety of apricot.
chacal *m* jackal.
chacanear *vt Chi* to spur hard.
chacona *f* chaconne (*ancient Spanish dance*).
chacota *f* joking, loud merrymaking, high jinks.
chacotear *vi* to trifle, make merry.
chacra *f SA* farm, ranch.
chaguela *f SA* nose ring; *Mex* slipper.
chajuán *m Col* hot, sultry weather.
chal *m* shawl.
chalán *m* hawker; horse dealer.
chalanear *vt Per* to break horses.
chalanería *f* astuteness of (*gypsy*) horse dealers.
chaleco *m* waistcoat, vest.
chalupa *f* sloop, canoe, shallop.
chamaco *m Mex* boy, youth.
chamagoso *a Mex* dirty, vulgar.
chamarasca *f* brushwood.
chambelán *m* chamberlain.
chambergo *m* slouch hat.
chambón *a* clumsy; *m* bungler.
champú *m SA* shampoo.
chamuchina *f SA* rabble.
chamuscar *vt* to scorch, singe.
chancear *vi* to joke, jest.
chancero *a* merry, full of funny remarks, always joking; *m* jester.
chancillería *f* chancery.
chancleta *f* low-heeled slipper, house slipper.
chanclo *m* galosh, rubber shoe; clog, sabot, wooden overshoe.
chancho *a SA* dirty, unclean.
chanchullo *m* low trick, underhand trick.
changador *m SA* porter.
chantaje *m* blackmail.
chantre *m* precentor.
chanza *f* jest, joke.
chapa *f* plate, metal sheet; tally (*cloakroom, identity etc*); veneer; rouge; *SA* lock.
chapado *a* **muy — a la antigua** old-world, in the antique style.
chaparro *m* evergreen oak.
chaparrón *m* heavy shower.
chapear *vt* to veneer, inlay; to plate.
chapecar *vt Chi* to braid, plait.
chapetón *m SA* Spaniard.
chapín *m* woman's cork-soled clog.
chapitel *m* (*on column*) capital; (*on tower*) pinnacle.
chapón *m* inkstain.
chapotear *vi* to splash, to paddle (*in water*).
chapoteo *m* splash.
chapucero *m* botcher, clumsy workman; old iron dealer
chapurrar *vt* to speak brokenly (*a language*)
chapuza *m* clumsy work, odd job.
chapuzar *vt* to dive, plunge, duck.

chaqueta *f* jacket, sack coat.
charada *f* charade.
charamusca *f Mex* twisted candy; *Per* brushwood.
charanguero *m* hawker, peddler.
charca *f* pool, basin; mere; artificial pond.
charco *m* pool, puddle.
charla *f* chat; (*empty*) talk, gossip; informal talk.
charlar *vi* to babble, have a gossip, chat.
charlatán *a* talkative; *m* prater; quack.
charlatanería *f* garrulity; humbug.
charol *m* varnish; patent leather; **darse—** to swank, show off.
charola *f SA* painted metal tray.
charretera *f* epaulet; shoulder-yoke; buckle.
charro *a* rustic, coarse; *Mex* peasant horseman; *Sp* of Salamanca.
chas *m* crack! (*of whip, wood*).
chascarrillo *m* spicy anecdote.
chasco *m* disappointment, frustration.
chasconear *vt Chi* to entangle, involve.
chasquear *vt* to crack (*a whip*); to play a waggish trick; to disappoint; *SA vr* to be disappointed.
chasquido *m* crack of a whip, cracking, snapping (*of wood*).
chata *f SA* barge.
chato *a* pug, snub-nosed, flat-nosed; squat; *m SA* darling; glass; (*fam*) *f* pretty girl.
chaval *m* lad.
chavala *f* lass.
chaya *f Chi* joke, trick.
checoeslovaco *an* Czechoslovakian.
Checoeslovaquia *f* Czechoslovakia.
chelín *m* shilling.
cheque *m* check, order on bank.
chicle *m* chewing gum; chicle.
chico *a* little, small, short; wee; tiny; *m* little boy, little fellow; young man.
chicoría *f see* **achicoria.**
chicote *m* tubby lad; end of cable; cigar stub; *SA* whip.
chicha *f SA* alcoholic drink; **no es ni — ni limonada** it's neither fish nor flesh (*ie characterless*).
chicharra *f see* **cigarra.**
chicharrón *m* fried piece of fat; (*fig*) cinder, frazzle.
chichear *vi* to hiss (*an actor etc*).
chichería *f Chi* tavern where *chicha* is sold.
chichón *m* bruise, bump.
chichonera *f* child's round (*straw*) hat.
chifladura *f* craziness, madness.
chiflado *a* crazy, cracked, potty.
chiflar *vi* to whistle; *vr* to become insane.
chile *m* red pepper; *see* **ají.**
chileno *an* Chilean.
chillar *vi* to cry, yell, scream, screech.
chillido *m* scream, shriek, shrill cry.
chillón *a* noisy, yelling; (*of colors*) glaring, loud; *m* screamer, shrieker; nail, spike.
chimbador *m Per* expert in river crossing.
chimenea *f* chimney, fireplace.
chimpancé *m* chimpanzee.
china *f* china, porcelain; pebble, small stone; *SA* Indian girl, servant girl.
chinaca *f Mex* beggars, poor people.
chinche *f* bedbug, bug; drawing pin, thumbtack.
chinchilla *f* chinchilla.
chincual *m Mex* measles.
chinchona *f SA* quinine.
chiné *a* with colored spots.
chinela *f* slipper.
chinesco *a* Chinese; **sombras —as** magic lantern, peep show.
chinga *f SA* skunk; *Ven* drunkenness.
chingana *f SA* low music hall, den.
chino *an* Chinese; the Chinese language.
chinquero *m* sty, pigpen.
chipichipi *m Mex* drizzle.
Chipre, Isla de *f* Cyprus.
chiprio *an* of Cyprus, Cypriot.
chiquear *vt Cub, Mex* to over-indulge.
chiquero *m* pigsty; bull pen.
chiquillada *f* childish prank.
chiquillo *m* lad, boy, urchin, brat, small child; 'baby'.
chiquito *a* small, little.
chirapa *f Bol* rag, tatter; *Per* rain during sunshine.
chiribital *m Col* untilled land.
chiribitil *m* small dark room.
chirimía *f* flageolet.
chiripa *f* fluke, pure luck.
chirle *a* insipid, tasteless.
chirlo *m* face wound, slash, long cut, scar.
chirriar *vi* to sizzle; to creak, screech, (*eg of hinges*).
chirrido *m* creak, croak, screech.
chirrión *m* wagon, cart.
chirusa *f Arg* stupid girl.
¡chis! *excl* hush!
chisgarabís *m* meddler, busybody.
chisguete *m* (*fam*) splash; gulp (*of wine*).
chisme *m* gossip, idle rumor; gadget, 'thing'; *pl* odds and ends.
chismoso *m* gossipmonger.
chispa *f* spark, sparkle; small diamond; drop, splash, speck; wit.
chispazo *m* spark, ember.
chispeante *a* sparkling.
chispear *vi* to sparkle; to drizzle slightly.
chisporrotear *vi* to emit sparks, sparkle; splutter.
chisporroteo *m* sparkle, scintillation; splutter.
chistar *vi* to mumble, utter a sound; **no chista** he doesn't say a word.

chiste *m* joke, witticism; **caer en el —** to get the point (joke).
chistera *f* basket; top hat (*XIXth century style*).
chistoso *a* witty, droll, funny.
chita *f* bone of foot; **a la — callando** (*or* **a la chiticallando**) noiselessly.
¡chito! *excl* silence! hush!
chivar *vt SA* to vex, annoy; cheat.
chivato *m* kid.
chivo *m* he-goat, kid; tantrum; **barba de —** goatee (*beard*).
chocante *a* striking, provoking, shocking.
chocar *vi* to collide, run against; to fight; shock, surprise; *vt* to clink (*glasses*); to shock.
chocarrería *f* jest, coarse joke, ribaldry.
chocarrero *a* scurrilous.
choclo *m* clog, low shoe; CA corncob.
chocolate *m* chocolate.
chócolo *m Col* clog, overshoe.
chocha *f* woodcock.
chochear *vi* to reach dotage, grow feeble, drivel.
chochera, chochez *f* dotage.
chocho *a* feeble, doting, decrepit.
cholo *m SA* half-breed, mestizo.
chopo *m* black poplar.
choque *m* shock, collision, clash.
choricero *m* sausage maker; (*fam*) native of Extremadura.
chorizo *m* highly-spiced red sausage.
chorlito *m* gray plover, curlew; **cabeza de —** featherbrain.
chorrear *vi* to spout, drain off, drip.
chorrillo *m* drip-drop, continual flow.
chorro *m* jet, spout; **a —s** copiously; **hablar —** to spout words.
choto *m* calf, sucking kid.
choza *f* hut, hovel, thatched cottage; cabin.
chubasco *m* shower, squall, rainstorm.
chucua *f Col* quagmire, bog.
chuchería *f* knick-knack, gewgaw, small toy; titbit.
chucho *m* dog, doggie.
chueco *a SA* bow-legged, knock-kneed; crooked, bent.
chufa *f* tiger-nut (*used to make* **horchata de chufa**).
chufleta *f* taunting word, mockery.
chuleta *f* chop, cutlet.
chulo *a* common, vulgar, flashy; villainous; unprincipled; *Mex* pretty, charming, nice; *m* (*Madrid*) low type, street-corner type.
chunga *f* jest, fun.
chupa *f* waistcoat, jacket.
chupado *a* (*fam*) thin, drawn.
chupar *vt* to sip, suck, suck up; to eat away.
chupón *a* sucking; *m* sapling.
churrasco *m SA* braised meat.
churrigueresco *a* Spanish florid rococo style.
churro *m* fritter, doughnut.
churumbela *f* reed instrument resembling a flageolet.
chuscada *f* joke, jest, humorous saying or doing.
chusco *a* odd, droll, humorous.
chusma *f* rabble, mob.
chuspa *f SA* pouch, bag.
chuzo *m* long stick ending in point; pike; **llover a —s** to rain torrents.

D

dable *a* practicable, possible, feasible.
dactilografía *f* typewriting.
dactilógrafo *m* typewriter; typist.
dádiva *f* gift, donation.
dadivoso *a* liberal, bountiful.
dado *m* die; block; **—s cargados** loaded dice; *cj* **— que** granted that, assuming that.
dador *m* giver, bearer; drawer (*of bill of exchange*).
daga *f* dagger, short sword.
daguerrotipo *m* daguerreotype.
dama *f* dame, lady, woman; **primera —** leading lady; *pl* checkers; **tablero de —** checkerboard.
damajuana *f* demijohn.
damasco *m* damask (*silk stuff*); damask (*kind of apricot*).
damisela *f* damsel, fine young lady.
damnificar *vt* to damage, injure.
danés *a* Danish; *m* Dane; Great Dane.
danza *f* old formal dance, dancing; fishy business; confusion.
danzar *vi* to dance.
dañar *vt* to damage, hurt, injure, spoil.
dañino *a* hurtful, damaging, injurious; destructive (*animal*).
daño damage, harm, injury; (*law*) **daños y perjuicios** damages.
dañoso *a* hurtful, noxious.
dar *vt* to apply, give, cause, grant, yield; **— gracias** to thank; **— un salto** to jump; **— en** to tend to; to discover; fall into; **— con** to bump into, find; **— a** to look onto; **— contra** to strike against.
dardo *m* light lance, dart; dace.
dársena *f* dock, wharf, inner harbor.
data *f* datum, item.
datar *vt* to date; *vi* to date from.
dátil *m* date (*fruit*).
datilado *a* date-colored, -shaped.
dato *m* datum, premise, detail, fact.
de *prep* of, from, by, with; **— día** by day; **— balde** free, for nothing.
de antemano *ad* in advance.
debajo *ad* beneath, below, underneath; *prep* **— de** under.
debate *m* debate, discussion.
debatir *vt* to debate, discuss.
debe *m* debit.
deber *vt* to owe; must, ought; **— de** to be likely to; *m* duty, obligation.
debidamente *ad* duly; in the proper manner; worthily, adequately.

débil *a* weak, feeble; powerless.
debilidad *f* weakness, debility; infirmity.
debilitar *vt* to weaken, enfeeble, debilitate.
débito *m* debt, debit.
debutar *vi* to make one's debut.
década *f* decade.
decadencia *f* decline, decay, decadence.
decadente *a* decaying, declining; over-refined.
decaer *vi* to decay, decline, fall.
decaimiento *m* decay, loss of strength.
decálogo *m* the Ten Commandments, decalogue.
decano *a* senior, dean; *m* dean.
decantar *vt* to decant; to cry up; to descant.
decapitación *f* beheading, having (*one's*) head cut off.
decapitar *vt* to behead.
decena *f* half a score, ten.
decencia *f* decency; honesty; propriety; cleanliness.
decenio *m* ten-year period.
decente *a* decent, clean; honest; genteel; reasonable (*price etc*).
decepción *f* deception, delusion, disappointment.
decidir *vt* to decide, determine; *vr* to decide, make up one's mind.
décima *f* strophe of ten eight-syllabled lines; tenth of a lottery ticket.
decir *vt* to tell, say, speak, state, utter; es — that is to say; **el qué dirán** other people's opinion, public opinion; — **para sí** to say to oneself; *m* a saying; language.
decisión *f* decision, verdict; firmness, resolution.
decisivo *a* decisive, conclusive.
declamación *f* declamation; recitation, pompous discourse.
declamar *vt* to recite, harangue.
declaración *f* declaration, statement, avowal; — **jurada** affidavit.
declarar *vt* to declare, state; to explain; to profess; *Arg, Per, Urug* to propose; *vr* to proclaim.
declaratorio *a* explanatory.
declinación *f* fall, decline; declination; declension.
declinar *vi* to decline, diminish; to fall, decay, sink.
declive *m* declivity, slope, gradient, incline.
decolorar *vt* to discolor, take color out of.
decomisar *vt* to confiscate, seize.
decoración *f* decoration; stage set, staging.
decorado *m* ornamentation, adornment, trimming.
decorar *vt* to decorate; to bestow an honor on; to learn by rote, repeat.
decorativo *a* decorative, ornamental.
decoro *m* decorum, decency; prudence; circumspection; honor.
decoroso *a* decorous, decent, seemly.
decrecer *vi* to decrease, grow less, shorter.
decreciente *a* diminishing.
decrépito *a* worn out with age, decrepit, tumbledown.
decrepitud *f* decrepitude, dotage.
decretar *vt* to decree, resolve; (*law*) to adjudge.
decreto *m* decree, order.
decuplicar *vt* to multiply by ten, increase tenfold.
décuplo *a* tenfold.
decurso *m* course.
dechado *m* sample, pattern; sampler; model, perfect example.
dedal *m* thimble; fingerstall.
dédalo *m* maze, labyrinth.
dedicación *f* dedication, consecration.
dedicar *vt* to dedicate, devote, consecrate; *vr* to devote oneself; to apply oneself.
dedicatoria *f* dedication.
dedil *m* fingerstall.
dedillo *m* **saber al** — to know perfectly, have at one's fingertips.
dedo *m* finger; — **pulgar** (*or* **gordo**) thumb; — **índice, del corazón, anular, meñique** fore-, middle, ring-, little finger; —**s de los pies** toes; **señalar con el** — to point scorn at, mock at.
deducción *f* deduction, inference.
deducible *a* deductible.
deducir *vt* to deduce, infer; to subtract, deduct.
defección *f* disloyalty, treachery; defection.
defecto *m* defect, fault; failing, weakness.
defectuoso *a* imperfect, defective.
defender (ie) *vt* to protect, guard, defend; to forbid; *vr* to put up a defense.
defensa *f* defense; support; *m* (*football*) full-back.
defensiva *f* defensive; **a la** — on the defensive.
defensivo *a* defensive.
defensor *m* supporter; counsel for the defense; upholder.
deferencia *f* deference, respect, regard.
deferente *a* deferential, willing to accept another's (*opinion etc*).
deferir (ie) *vt* to assent, yield, defer (*to*); to refer.
deficiencia *f* deficiency, imperfection, flaw, lack.
deficiente *a* deficient, faulty, inadequate.
déficit *m* deficit, shortage.
definición *f* definition, exactness.
definir *vt* to determine, make clear, define, decide.
definitivo *a* definitive, final.
deflación *f* deflation.

deformación *f* deformation, disfiguration.
deformar *vt* to deform, distort.
deforme *a* disfigured, deformed, hideous.
deformidad *f* deformity.
defraudación *f* fraud, cheating.
defraudador *m* cheat; defaulter.
defraudar *vt* to cheat, to defraud; to frustrate; to disappoint (*hopes etc*).
defuera *ad* outwardly; out; **por —** on the outside, outwardly.
defunción *f* death, demise.
degeneración *f* degeneration, degeneracy.
degenerar *vi* to degenerate, sink, decay.
deglutir *vt* to swallow.
degollación *f* slaying, slaughter (*by cutting the throat*).
degolladero *m* slaughterhouse; gibbet.
degollar (ue) *vt* to kill (*animals*); to cut the throat, butcher.
degollina *f* slaughter.
degradación *f* (*mil*) demotion; degradation, baseness; dishonorable discharge.
degradar *vt* to demote, degrade; to revile; *vr* to demean oneself.
degüello *m* slaughtering, butchery.
degustación *f* partaking, enjoyment (*of liquid refreshment*).
dehesa *f* pasture.
deidad *f* deity, divine being.
deificar *vt* to deify; to praise excessively.
dejación *f* abandonment, relinquishing.
dejadez *f* languor, apathy.
dejado *a* negligent, slovenly, untidy; apathetic, indolent; **— de la mano de Dios** godforsaken.
dejar *vt* to leave, allow, let; to fail, omit; **— de** to cease, stop; **le dejó por loco** he took him for an idiot.
dejo *m* abandonment; relish; accent, intonation, flavor (*of speech*); aftertaste.
del = **de** + **el.**
delación *f* delation, denunciation, informing.
delantal *m* apron, pinafore.
delante *ad* **— de** before, in front of, in the presence of.
delantera *f* forepart; front part of theater; **tomar la —** to overtake, get ahead (of), take the lead.
delantero *m* (*sport*) forward.
delatar *vt* to denounce, inform, betray.
delator *m* informer, accuser.
delectación *f* pleasure, delight.
delegación *f* delegation, proxy.
delegado *m* delegate, representative, proxy.
delegar *vt* to depute, delegate, assign.
deleitar *vt* to please, delight; *vr* to delight in.
deleite *m* delight, pleasure.
deleitoso *a* agreeable, delightful, pleasurable.
deletéreo *a* deleterious, deadly, harmful.
deletrear *vt* to spell (*out*); to decipher.
deletreo *m* spelling.
deleznable *a* brittle, fragile, frail; slippery.
delfín *m* dolphin; dauphin.
delgadez *f* thinness, slenderness, slimness.
delgado *a* thin, slender, lean.
deliberación *f* deliberation, reflection, consideration.
deliberar *vti* to deliberate, reflect think over, ponder on.
delicadeza *f* delicacy; weakness; refinement, nicety; scrupulousness.
delicado *a* delicate, weak, tender; touchy, nice, fastidious.
delicia *f* delight; pleasure, joy.
delicioso *a* delightful, delicious.
delimitar *vt* to delimit.
delincuencia *f* delinquency.
delincuente *m* offender, delinquent; guilty person.
delineación *f* sketch, draft, drawing.
delinear *vt* to sketch, delineate, design.
delinquir *vi* to break the law.
deliquio *m* swoon, faint.
delirante *a* delirious; enthusiastic.
delirar *vi* to be delirious, rave; to talk wildly.
delirio *m* delirium, madness, craze.
delito *m* guilt, fault, offense, misdemeanor, crime.
delta *m* & *f* delta.
demacrar *vtr* to waste away; *vr* become emaciated.
demagogo *m* demagogue, rabble-rouser.
demanda *f* claim, demand, pretension, search; **en — de** requiring, requesting, in search of.
demandador *m* claimant, solicitor.
demandante *f* claimant, plaintiff, applicant.
demandar *vt* to solicit, ask for; to sue, claim; to request.
demarcación *f* demarcation; limit.
demarcar *vt* to mark out limits.
demás *a* the rest, the others; remaining; **por lo —** as for the rest; **estar —** to be superfluous, to be useless.
demasía *f* excess; outburst; insolence; iniquity.
demasiado *ad* too, too much; *a* excessive.
demencia *f* insanity; madness.
demente *a* demented, insane, distracted.
demérito *m* demerit.
demisión *f* resignation, submission.
demitir *vt* to resign; to give up.
democracia *f* democracy.
demócrata *m* democrat.

democrático *a* democratic, popular.
demoler (ue) *vt* to demolish, raze, tear down.
demolición *f* demolition; overthrow, destruction.
demonio *m* demon, fiend, devil; *excl* the deuce!
demora *f* delay; putting off; **sin —** without delay.
demorar *vi* to delay; to stay, put off; *vt* to retard, postpone.
demostración *f* demonstration; exhibition, show; example; proof.
demostrar (ue) *vt* to demonstrate, manifest, show; to prove, make evident.
demostrativo *a* demonstrative.
demudación *f* change, transformation (*of features*).
demudar *vi* to change, alter (*features*).
denegación *f* denial, refusal.
denegar (ie) *vt* to deny; to refuse.
dengue *m* fastidiousness, affection; a fever.
denigración *f* defamation, slander.
denigrar *vt* to defame, revile, calumniate, smirch.
denodado *a* bold, intrepid, daring.
denominación *f* denomination, title, name.
denominar *vt* to name, denominate, nominate.
denostar (ue) *vt* to abuse, curse at.
denotación *f* designation.
denotar *vt* to denote, mean, indicate.
densidad *f* density; compactness; consistence.
denso *a* compact; thick; close.
dentado *a* serrated, furnished with teeth.
dentadura *f* the teeth, set of teeth; **— postiza** denture.
dental *a* dental, pertaining to the teeth.
dentellada *f* bite, snap.
dentera *f* **dar —** to set one's teeth on edge; to tantalize.
dentición *f* dentition, teething.
dentífrico *m* toothpaste, -powder, dentifrice.
dentista *m* dentist.
dentro *ad* inside, within; **por —** inside, on the inside.
denudar *vt* to denude.
denuedo *m* boldness, intrepidity, dash.
denuesto *m* insult, indignity, curse.
denuncia *f* denunciation, betrayal; accusation; (*law*) **presentar una —** to make a charge.
denunciar *vt* to denounce, betray, accuse; to give notice.
deparar *vt* to offer, afford, present.
departamento *m* department; section, compartment.
departir *vi* to converse, chat.
dependencia *f* dependence, dependency; appendage; subordination; branch (*office*).
depender *vi* to depend; to result from; to turn upon; to rely upon; to be subordinate to.
dependiente *a* dependent, hanging; *m* clerk, (shop) assistant, employee.
depilar *vt* to depilate.
deplorable *a* deplorable, regrettable; wretched.
deplorar *vt* to deplore, bewail, lament.
deponer *vt* to depose, testify; to lay aside, down.
deportación *f* banishment, transportation.
deportar *vt* to banish, exile.
deporte *m* sport, recreation, pastime.
deportista *mf* sportsman, -woman; *a* sports, sporting.
deposición *f* deposition, declaration; testimony.
depositante *m* depositor.
depositar *vt* to deposit; to entrust; (*chem*) to settle, precipitate.
depositario *m* guardian; depository.
depósito *m* deposit; trust; storehouse; **— de agua** tank, reservoir.
depravación *f* depravity.
depravar *vt* to deprave, vitiate.
deprecación *f* prayer, entreaty, supplication.
deprecar *vt* to pray, implore, entreat.
depreciación *f* depreciation.
depreciar *vt* to depreciate, undervalue; **— la moneda** to debase the coinage.
depredación *f* depredation.
depredar *vt* to rob, pillage.
depresión *f* depression, lowering.
deprimido *a* downcast, low-spirited, depressed, out of sorts.
deprimir *vt* to belittle, humiliate, lower.
depuración *f* depuration; purification.
depurado *a* refined, pure, superfine, highly-wrought.
depurar *vt* to depurate, purify, filter.
derecha *f* right hand; the right-hand side; **a la —** to the right; **a tuertas o a —s** rightly or wrongly; *pl* Right Wing in politics.
derechamente *ad* straight; justly, rightly.
derechista *an* rightist.
derecho *m* law, right, power, justice; *pl* dues, fees, duties; *a* right, sound, upright; *ad* straight; **— de gentes** common law, the law of nations.
derechura *f* straightness; **en —** in a straight line, as the crow flies.
deriva *f* drift; deflection; **hielo a la —** drift ice.
derivación *f* derivation; draining away of water.
derivado *m* by-product.
derivar *vi* to derive; to descend from; to originate from; (*naut*) to drift.

derogación *f* repeal, abrogation, revocation.
derogar *vt* to derogate, repeal, abrogate.
derogatorio *a* derogatory.
derramado *a* spendthrift; spilled.
derramamiento *m* pouring; shedding, spilling.
derramar *vt* to pour out, shed, spill; *vr* to run over, overflow.
derrame *m* overflow, shedding; discharge (*of wound*).
derredor *m* circuit, the place or places around; **en —** around.
derretido *a* molten (*metal*), melted.
derretir (i) *vt* to melt, smelt, fuse, dissolve.
derribar *vt* to pull down; to overthrow, fell, knock down, demolish.
derribo *m* knocking down, demolition.
derrocamiento *m* overthrow.
derrocar *vt* to overthrow; to demolish, hurl from position, place.
derrochar *vt* to squander, waste, dissipate.
derroche *m* dissipation, squandering; extravagant display.
derrota *f* defeat, rout; route, course.
derrotar *vt* to rout, defeat; to destroy, tear.
derrotero *m* ship's course, route; well-worn track, way; established way of life.
derrotismo *m* defeatism.
derrotista *mf* defeatist.
derruir *vt* to raze, ruin.
derrumbadero *m* precipice.
derrumbamiento *m* landslide; collapse (*of a structure*).
derrumbar *vti* to precipitate, tumble down; *vr* to collapse.
derviche *m* dervish.
desabotonar *vt* to unbutton; to blossom.
desabrido *a* insipid, tasteless; harsh, unpleasant.
desabrigo *m* lack of shelter; nudity.
desabrimiento *m* insipidity, tastelessness; asperity, roughness (*of manner*).
desabrochar *vt* to unbutton, unclasp; to disclose.
desacatado *a* inconsiderate, disrespectful.
desacato *m* disrespect, irreverence, disregard; incivility.
desacertado *a* mistaken.
desacertar (ie) *vt* to make mistakes, err, blunder.
desacierto *m* error, mistake.
desacomodado *a* lacking accommodation; without employment.
desacomodar *vt* to molest; to deprive of comfort; to discharge (*from job*).
desacomodo *m* discharge.
desaconsejado *a* ill-advised.
desaconsejar *vt* to dissuade.
desacoplar *vt* to uncouple.
desacordado *a* ill-considered, discordant.
desacorde *a* incongruous, discordant.
desacostumbrar *vt* to give up a habit.
desacreditar *vt* to discredit.
desacuerdo *m* disagreement; error; forgetfulness; **en —** at loggerheads.
desafección *f* disaffection.
desafecto *a* showing indifference; disaffected, hostile.
desafiar *vt* to challenge, defy.
desafilar *vt* to blunt.
desafinar *vt* to be out of tune; to (be) (sing) flat.
desafío *m* challenge, duel; rivalry, contest.
desaforado *a* disorderly, lawless; earsplitting (*cries*); outrageous.
desafortunado *ad* unfortunate.
desafuero *m* violence against law; outrage.
desagradable *a* disagreeable, unpleasant, nasty.
desagradar *vti* to displease, offend; to be displeasing, give offense.
desagradecido *a* ungrateful.
desagrado *m* displeasure.
desagraviar *vt* to make amends, give satisfaction for.
desagravio *m* satisfaction (*for injury*); apology, compensation, requital, return, amends.
desaguadero *m* drain, outlet; sink.
desaguar *vt* to drain, empty; *vi* to flow; *vr* to empty.
desagüe *m* drain, outlet, waste.
desaguisado *m* offense, injury, affront.
desahijar *vt* to wean.
desahogado *a* unencumbered; well-to-do; free and easy, forward, unembarrassed; brazen.
desahogar *vt* to alleviate, relieve (*from distress*); *vr* to relieve one's mind, unbosom oneself, let oneself go.
desahogo *m* alleviation, easing; comfortable circumstances; unburdening, release.
desahuciado *a* hopeless (*of a patient*); evicted (*of tenant*); discarded, rejected.
desahuciar *vt* to abandon as hopeless; to eject (*a tenant*), put in the street; to discard or reject (*hopeless, impracticable*).
desahucio *m* dispossession (*of tenant*); final, hopeless diagnosis; verdict.
desairado *a* inelegant, graceless; slighted; rejected, frustrated, dashed.
desairar *vt* to slight, rebuff, not to accept, snub, reject.
desaire *m* rebuff, snub, slight.
desajustar *vt* to put out of joint; *vr* to be out of order.
desajuste *m* disagreement, lack of proportion, discrepancy, unevenness.
desalar *vt* to cut the wings; to be in

great haste; to take the salt from something.
desalentador *a* dispiriting.
desalentar *vt* to discourage, damp (*spirits*); *vr* to lose heart.
desaliento *m* discouragement, dismay, dejection.
desalinear *vt* to disarrange, break (*the lines*).
desaliño *m* untidiness, negligence (*in dress*), slovenliness.
desalmado *a* soulless, inhuman, merciless; *m* bloodthirsty ruffian.
desalojado *a* empty, unoccupied, free.
desalojamiento *m* displacement, dislodging.
desalojar *vr* to dislodge, eject, evict.
desalquilado *a* vacant; not rented.
desalquilar *vt* to give up rented premises.
desamarrar *vt* to let loose, untie; to unmoor (*a ship*).
desamor *m* disaffection, antipathy, hatred.
desamortización *f* redemption from mortmain, entail, debt.
desamortizar *vt* to free, redeem (*debt, mortgage*).
desamparado *a* forsaken, abandoned; **niño —** waif.
desamparar *vt* to abandon, forsake, leave without protection; to dismantle (*ship*).
desamparo *m* abandonment; desertion; helplessness; dereliction.
desamueblar *vt* to strip (*of furniture*).
desandar *vt* to retrace (*one's steps*); **— lo andado** to start again.
desanimado *a* discouraged; dull, upset; listless, lifeless, flat.
desanimar *vt* to discourage; *vr* to become discouraged.
desánimo *m* discouragement, hopelessness.
desanudar *vt* to untie, unravel.
desapacible *a* disagreeable (*weather, mood*).
desaparecer *vi* to disappear; to fade away, vanish.
desaparejar *vr* to unharness, unhitch; to dismantle.
desaparición *f* disappearance.
desapego *m* disinterestedness, indifference, coolness.
desapercibido *a* unprepared, unawares; unsuspecting; **coger —** to catch napping.
desapiadado *a* merciless, pitiless.
desaplicación *f* lack of application, slackness, shiftlessness.
desaplicado *a* neglectful, unindustrious, inattentive.
desapolillar *vt* to clear (*of moths etc*).
desapretar (ie) *vr* to slacken, release, loose; to ease.
desapreciar *vt* to depreciate, underestimate.
desaprisionar *vt* to set free, at liberty.
desaprobar (ue) *vt* to disapprove, condemn, censure.
desaprovechado *a* backward, unenterprising, slow in profiting (*from*); unprofitable; unutilized.
desaprovechamiento *m* negligence, inapplication, shiftlessness; waste, failure (*to use etc*).
desaprovechar *vt* to waste, not to take advantage of (*an opportunity*), to make no good use of.
desapucho *m Per* absurdity, nonsense.
desarbolar *vt* (*ship*) to unmast.
desarmado *a* unarmed, defenseless.
desarmar *vt* to disarm; to dismantle, take to pieces.
desarme *m* disarmament.
desarraigar *vt* to uproot, root out; to extirpate.
desarraigo *m* uprooting, eradication.
desarreglado *a* disarranged; immoderate; untidy.
desarreglar *vt* to upset, disorder.
desarreglo *m* disarrangement, disorder, license, confusion, untidiness.
desarrollar *vt* to develop, promote, unfold, evolve, increase.
desarrollo *m* development, unfolding, expansion, spread, increase; **plan de—** development plan.
desarrugar *vt* to take out wrinkles; to smooth, uncrease.
desarticular *vt* to disarticulate, dislocate.
desaseado *a* unclean, dirty, slovenly, filthy.
desaseo *m* uncleanliness, slovenliness, scruffiness.
desasimiento *m* loosening; disinterestedness.
desasir *vt* to loosen; *vr* to get rid of, give up, break loose (*from*).
desasosegar (ie) *vt* to disturb, make uneasy.
desasosiego *m* uneasiness, disquiet, restlessness, jumpiness.
desastrado *a* wretched; slovenly, ragged.
desastre *m* disaster, misfortune, horror.
desastroso *a* disastrous, unfortunate.
desatado *a* unbound; easy; unloosed.
desatar *vt* to let loose, loosen, untie; to unravel; (*storm*) to break out.
desatención *f* disregard; lack of attention, discourtesy.
desatender (ie) *vt* to disregard, slight; to pay no attention to, ignore.
desatentado *a* unmindful, inconsiderate; careless, heedless.
desatento *a* careless, inattentive; uncivil.
desatinado *a* bewildered; foolish; wild, pointless, blundering, wide of the mark.
desatinar *vt* to bewilder; *vr* to lose

control of oneself; to be quite wrong (*in word, action*).
desatino *m* tactlessness; blunder, nonsense, mistake, stupid (*action, statement*).
desautorizado *a* unauthorized; discredited.
desautorizar *vt* to deprive of authority.
desavenencia *f* disagreement, misunderstanding, quarrel.
desavenir *vt* to make hostile, sow discord among; *vr* to be at loggerheads with.
desaventajado *a* disadvantageous; detrimental.
desayunar *vi* to breakfast.
desayuno *m* breakfast.
desazón *f* insipidity; uneasiness, restlessness, disquiet; malaise; vexation.
desazonado *a* unseasoned; uneasy, perturbed, out of humor.
desazonar *vt* to render tasteless; to vex.
desbandada *f* disbandment, rout (*of troops*), wild dispersal; **a la —** in disorder, helter-skelter.
desbandarse *vr* to disband, break up, disperse; to desert the colors (*troops*).
desbarajustar *vt* to mix up things; to confuse, upset.
desbarajuste *m* disorder, confusion.
desbaratar *vt* to spoil, ruin, defeat, disperse, destroy; (*plans etc*) to frustrate, thwart.
desbarrar *vi* to talk nonsense.
desbastar *vt* to smooth, trim, take the rough off, rough-hew.
desbaste *m* smoothing, paring, trimming; polishing.
desbocado *a* runaway (*horse*); indecent (*in speech*), foul-mouthed.
desbocarse *vr* (*horse*) to run away; to use abusive or indecent language.
desbordamiento *m* overflowing, inundation.
desbordar *vir* to overflow, overlap.
desbravador *m* breaker-in (*of animals*).
desbrozar *vt* to clean, clear (*up, away*) rubbish (*esp from land*).
descabalamiento *m* reduction, diminution.
descabalar *vt* to make less complete, impair.
descabalgar *vi* to dismount, alight.
descabellado *a* disheveled; preposterous, absurd, harebrained.
descabellar *vt* to dishevel, rumple; to kill (*bull at end of bullfight*).
descabezar *vt* to behead; to cut the top off, lop off; **— un sueño** to have forty winks.
descaecimiento *m* decay, decline, weakness.
descalabrado *a* wounded in the head, injured; **salir —** to come out with one's head in a sling; to lose heavily.
descalabro *m* accident, disappointment, misfortune.
descalificar *vt* to disqualify.
descalzar *vt* to take off; to unshoe (*horse*).
descalzo *a* barefoot, discalced (*Carmelites*).
descaminado *a* misguided, ill-advised, off the track.
descaminar *vt* to misguide, mislead; *vr* to go astray.
descamisado *a* shirtless, tattered; *m* urchin.
descampado *a* clear; **en —** in the open air.
descampar *vti* to clear; to stop raining.
descansado *a* rested; quiet, restful.
descansar *vi* to rest, be at rest, peace; to trust, depend on.
descanso *m* repose, rest, relaxation; break (*half-time*); interval; (*on stairs*) landing.
descañonar *vt* to pluck; to shave close.
descarado *a* barefaced, impudent, cheeky, brazen.
descararse *vr* to behave insolently.
descarga *f* unloading; volley, report, discharge (*of firearms, electricity*); relief (*of conscience*).
descargadero *m* wharf, unloading place.
descargar *vt* to unload; to ease, relieve; to discharge; to exonerate, acquit; **— a golpes** to attack.
descargo *m* exoneration, discharge, acquittal; receipt, release; **en su —** in exculpation, to free (*him*) from blame, responsibility *etc*.
descargue *m* unloading.
descarnado *a* bony, fleshless; scraggy.
descarnar *vtr* to emaciate; to scrape (*hides*).
descaro *m* impudence, barefacedness, cheek; assurance.
descarriar *vt* to mislead, misguide, lead astray; *vr* to go astray.
descarrilamiento *m* derailment.
descarrilar *vt* to derail; *vtr* to get off the track, go off the rails.
descarrío *m* deviation; going astray.
descartar *vt* to discard, dismiss (*possibility etc*).
descartado *a* out of the question, discarded.
descascarar *vt* to peel, shell.
descastado *a* unnatural, showing no family affection.
descastarse *vr* to separate from the family; lose caste.
descendencia *f* descent, offspring; ancestry, line.
descender (ie) *vi* to descend, go down; to proceed from; *vt* to let down, take down.
descendiente *an* descendant.

descendimiento *m* descent, declivity, lowering; deposition (*of Christ*).
descenso *m* descent.
descentralizar *vt* to decentralize.
descerrajar *vt* to take off the lock(s) of; to discharge (*firearms*).
descerrojar *vt* to unbolt.
descifrar *vt* to decipher, decode, make out; to interpret, translate.
descoco *m* boldness, barefacedness, sauciness.
descolgar (ue) *vt* to take down; *vi* to come down; *vr* to let oneself down; *Arg* to drop in.
descolorir *vt* to bleach, discolor.
descollar (ue) *vi* to excel, be prominent, stand out, surpass.
descomedido *a* rude; disproportionate, immoderate.
descomedirse (i) *vr* to be ruffled, rude; to overstep.
descompasado *a* extravagant, unharmonious.
descomponer *vt* to derange, unsettle, set at odds; *vr* to decompose, become putrid; to be put out, lose one's temper, be disconcerted.
descomposición *f* derangement; corruption, mortification, decomposition.
descompostura *f* perturbation; immodesty.
descompuesto *a* rude, insolent; out of order.
descomulgar *vt* to excommunicate.
descomunal *a* monstrous, outsize, abnormal.
desconcertado *a* put out, disconcerted, upset.
desconcertar (ie) *vt* to disconcert, thwart, unsettle, put out.
desconcierto *m* confusion, disorder, uneasiness.
desconectar *vt* to disconnect.
desconfiado *a* suspicious, distrustful.
desconfianza *f* mistrust, diffidence, uncertainty.
desconfiar *vt* to distrust, suspect, doubt, mistrust.
desconformidad *f* disagreement, dissent.
descongelar *vt* to defrost, melt.
descongestionar *vt* to disperse, clear (*crowd, traffic*).
desconocer *vt* to disown; to fail to recognize; to be ignorant of, ignore.
desconocido *a* unknown; *m* stranger.
desconocimiento *m* ingratitude; ignorance, unawareness.
desconsiderado *a* thoughtless, inconsiderate.
desconsolar (ue) *vt* to afflict.
desconsuelo *m* affliction, disconsolateness, unconsolable (*grief etc*).
descontar (ue) *vt* to discount, abate, make allowances for.
descontento *a* dissatisfied; hard to please; *m* dissatisfaction, unhappiness.
descorazonante *a* disheartening.
descorazonar *vt* to discourage, dishearten, take the heart out of.
descorchar *vt* to uncork (*bottle*).
descorrer *vt* to draw (*curtains*).
descortés *a* unmannerly, impolite, rude.
descortezar *vt* (*bark, skin*) to strip off.
descoser *vt* to unstitch, unseam, rip.
descosido *m* tear, rip (*esp of seam*); *a* loose-tongued, indiscreet.
descote *m* low-cut (*dress*), décolletage.
descoyuntar *vt* to disarticulate the joints; to disjoint, derange, upset; *vr* — **de risa** to split one's sides.
descrecimiento *m* decrease, diminution.
descrédito *m* discredit, disrepute.
descreído *m* unbeliever, infidel.
describir *vt* to describe; to define.
descripción *f* description, account.
descuajar *vt* to liquefy; to eradicate; to clear; to dishearten.
descubierto *a* discovered; bareheaded; **al** — openly.
descubrimiento *m* discovery, revelation.
descubrir *vt* to discover, uncover, expose, divulge; *vr* to take off one's hat.
descuento *m* discount; allowance.
descuidado *a* careless, forgetful, thoughtless.
descuidar *vt* to overlook, neglect.
descuido *m* oversight, negligence, lack of (*care, thoughtfulness, prevision*); omission.
desde *prep* from, since; — **aquí** hence; — **entonces** from that time; — **luego** of course.
desdecir *vi* to belie; *vr* to deny (*a promise etc*), go back on one's word, retract.
desdén *m* disdain, contempt, slight; **con** — askance.
desdentado *a* toothless.
desdeñar *vt* to disdain, scorn.
desdicha *f* misfortune, ill-luck, unhappiness.
desdichado *a* unhappy, unfortunate, wretched.
desdoblar *vt* to unfold, spread openly; to split, divide.
desdorar *vt* to tarnish.
desdoro *m* blemish, stain, stigma.
deseable *a* desirable.
desear *vt* to wish, desire, long for.
desecar *vt* to drain; to dry, desiccate.
desechar *vt* to exclude, reject, cast aside, away; to renounce, refuse.
desecho *m* reject, rubbish.
desembalar *vt* to unpack, open up (*bales*).
desembarazado *a* free, unrestrained, easy (*manners*).
desembarazar *vt* to free, clear, disencumber.
desembarazo *m* freedom, ease, abandon.

desembarcar *vi* to land, go ashore; *vi* to unload.
desembargar *vt* to free from embargo; to clear away impediments.
desembocadura *f* (*of river*) mouth.
desembocar *vi* to flow out (*rivers*); to lead to, come out into (*streets*).
desembolsar *vt* to disburse, expend, pay out.
desembolso *m* disbursement, expenditure.
desemejante *a* dissimilar, disparate.
desemejanza *f* disparity, unlikeness.
desempacar *vt* to unpack.
desempañar *vt* to clean (*glass*).
desempatar *vi* to break a draw.
desempeñar *vt* to redeem (*a pawned thing*); to fulfill; to discharge (*an office*); to play a part in.
desempeño *m* fulfillment; discharge, execution.
desempleo *m* unemployment.
desempolvar *vt* to dust.
desencadenar *vt* to unchain; *vr* to free oneself, to burst (*storm*).
desencajado *a* (*features*) twisted, tortured.
desencajar *vt* to disjoint; to put out of gear; *vr* to get out of sorts.
desencantar *vt* to disillusion.
desencanto *m* disillusion, disappointment.
desencarcelar *vt* to set at liberty.
desenfadado *a* free; unabashed, unembarrassed; ample.
desenfado *m* ease, nonchalance, sangfroid, unconcern; relaxation.
desenfrenado *a* unbridled, licentious, riotous, wild.
desenfrenar *vt* to lose control, give free rein to (*passions*).
desenfreno *m* licentiousness, abandon, wildness, lack of restraint, unbridled (*liberty, license etc*).
desenganchar *vt* to unhook, unfasten.
desengañar *vt* to disabuse, undeceive, disillusion.
desengaño *m* disillusion(ment); discovery (*of an error*).
desenlace *m* issue, end, conclusion, outcome, denouement.
desenmarañar *vr* to unravel, disentangle.
desenmascarar *vt* to unmask.
desenredar *vt* to disentangle, put in order.
desenredo *m* denouement (*of play etc*).
desenroscar *vt* unscrew, open (*jar*).
desentenderse (ie) *vr* to overlook, pretend not to notice, ignore; not to mind.
desenterrar (ie) *vt* to disinter, dig up, unearth.
desentonar *vi* to be out of (*tune, keeping, taste*).
desentrañar *vt* to disembowel; to get to the bottom of (*question, problem*).
desenvainar *vt* to unsheathe (*sword*).
desenvoltura *f* ease, grace, assurance; boldness, slickness.
desenvolver (ue) *vt* to unfold, develop, decipher.
deseo *m* wish, desire, longing.
deseoso *a* desirous; eager.
desequilibrado *a* unbalanced, unstable.
deserción *f* desertion.
desertar *vi* to desert; to separate.
deservir *vt* to ill-serve.
desesperación *f* despair, desperation, fury.
desesperar *vi* to despair, lose hope.
desestimar *vr* to underestimate, discount, disregard.
desfachatez *f* effrontery, impudence, cheek.
desfalcar *vt* to defalcate, embezzle.
desfallecer *vi* to faint, pine away.
desfavorable *a* unfavorable.
desfigurar *vt* to disfigure; to disguise, alter.
desfiladero *m* defile, gully.
desfilar *vi* to march off by files, pass in review, file past.
desfile *m* march, parade, procession, review.
desgaire *m* untidiness; slovenliness; scornful mien.
desgajar *vt* to tear off, break off.
desgana *f* lack of appetite, distaste, disinclination.
desganarse *vr* to lose appetite.
desgarbado *a* ungraceful, inelegant.
desgarrar *vi* to tear (*to pieces*), rend, claw, slit (*cloth*).
desgarro *m* tear; effrontery, wantonness.
desgastar *vt* to waste, wear away, corrode.
desgaste *m* waste, attrition, wear and tear.
desgracia *f* misfortune, sorrow; **caer en —** to fall into disgrace.
desgraciado *a* unfortunate, luckless, wretched.
desgraciar *vt* to spoil; *Arg* to wound, kill; *vr* to come to naught.
desgranar *vt* to thrash (*grain*).
desgreñar *vt* to dishevel the hair.
deshabitado *a* uninhabited, unoccupied.
deshabitar *vt* to move out, depopulate.
deshacer *vt* to undo, destroy, dissolve, take to pieces; *vr* to outdo oneself, strive; *vr* **— de** to get rid of.
deshecho *a* undone; worn out; cut to pieces, in pieces.
deshelar (ie) *vi* to thaw, melt.
desheredar *vt* to disinherit.
deshielo *m* thaw.
deshilar *vt* to draw threads out of cloth; to make lint.
deshilvanado *a* disjointed, incoherent.
deshinchar *vt* to reduce a swelling; to deflate.

deshojar *vt* to strip off leaves, deflower.
deshonesto *a* dishonest, unchaste, lewd, unseemly.
deshonor *m* dishonor, disgrace.
deshonra *f* dishonor, discredit; ruin; rape, seduction; infamy, obloquy.
deshonrar *vt* to dishonor, sully; seduce.
deshonroso *a* dishonorable.
deshora *ad* **a —** inconveniently, unseasonably.
desidia *f* laziness, indolence.
desierto *m* desert, wilderness.
designar *vt* to purpose; to designate, name, describe.
designio *m* purpose, design, intention.
desigual *a* unequal; uneven; changeable.
desilusión *f* disillusion.
desilusionar *vt* to disillusion; *vr* to have one's eyes opened, be disappointed.
desinfección *f* disinfection.
desinflar *vr* to deflate.
desinterés *m* disinterestedness, indifference, impartiality.
desistir *vi* to desist; to give up.
desjarretar *vr* to hamstring.
desleal *a* disloyal; faithless, unfair.
deslealtad *f* disloyalty.
desleír *vt* to dissolve, dilute.
deslenguado *a* foul-mouthed; *m* scandalmonger.
desligar *vt* to untie, loosen; to free from an obligation.
deslindar *vt* to set boundaries; to explain, define.
deslinde *m* demarcation.
desliz *m* slip, false step, weakness.
deslizar *vt* to slide; *vr* to evade, slip (*in, out, along*).
deslucido *a* inelegant; discomforted, discredited, shown up.
deslucir *vt* to tarnish, sully; to obscure.
deslumbramiento *m* dazzling, glare; confusion.
deslumbrar *vt* to dazzle, amaze; to fascinate.
desmán *m* excess; misbehavior, incident, misdemeanor.
desmanchar *vt* to remove spots.
desmandarse *vr* to go beyond the limit; to transgress, to be impertinent.
desmantelar *vt* to dismantle.
desmayado *a* wan, limp, pale, faint, spiritless.
desmayar *vi* to be discouraged; *vr* to faint.
desmayo *m* fainting fit, swoon.
desmedido *a* excessive, extravagant.
desmedirse (i) *vr* to overstep the mark, act tactlessly.
desmejorar *vt* to spoil, make worse.
desmembrar *vt* to dismember, divide.
desmentir (ie) *vt* to give the lie to, contradict; to counterfeit; *vr* to recant.
desmenuzamiento *m* crumbling, fragmentation, reduction to small pieces.
desmenuzar *vt* to pull to pieces, examine minutely.
desmerecer *vi* to become of less value; lose merit; be unworthy of.
desmesurado *a* immense, excessive.
desmontable *a* adjustable; prefabricated.
desmontar *vt* to clear; to take apart, to pieces; to dismount.
desmoralizar *vt* to demoralize.
desmoronar *vt* to erode; *vr* to crumble, wear away.
desnaturalizar *vt* to denaturalize; to pervert (*facts*).
desnivel *m* difference in level, unevenness; slope.
desnivelar *vt* to put out of level, make uneven.
desnudar *vt* to strip, denude; *vr* to undress, strip.
desnudo *a* naked, nude, bare, destitute; *m* nude.
desnutrido *a* underfed.
desobedecer *vt* to disobey, transgress.
desobediencia *f* disobedience.
desocupación *f* want of occupation; idleness; unemployment; leisure.
desocupado *a* unemployed, free, vacant.
desocupar *vt* to vacate, quit; *vr* to disengage oneself.
desoír *vt* to disregard; not to heed, not to hear.
desolación *f* desolation.
desolar (ue) *vt* to lay waste, desolate.
desollar *vt* to skin, fleece; **— a uno vivo** to skin someone alive.
desorden *m* disorder, mess.
desordenar *vt* to disarrange, disorder, disturb.
desorganizar *vt* to disorganize; to decompose.
desorientar *vt* to mislead, confuse, lead astray.
despabilado *a* vigilant, lively, alert; wide-awake.
despabilar *vt* to snuff a candle; to enliven; **— el ingenio** to sharpen the wits; *vr* to rouse oneself, wake up.
despacio *a* slowly, little by little; *SA* in a low voice.
despachar *vt* to dispatch; to make haste, hasten.
despacho *m* dispatch; expedition; office; official letter; **— de localidades** box office; **— de bebidas** *Arg* bar.
despancar *vi SA* to husk corn.
desparpajo *m* pertness, facility (*of expression*); *CA* disorder, disturbance.
desparramar *vt* to spill, spread, scatter.

desparramo *m Arg, Cub, Chi* spreading, scattering; *Chi* disorder.
despavorido *a* terrified, aghast.
despectivo *a* contemptuous, deprecatory.
despecho *m* spite; hatred; **a — de** despite.
despedazar *vt* to tear into pieces, rend, mangle.
despedida *f* farewell, leave, parting; dismissal.
despedir (i) *vt* to discharge, dismiss; to emit; *vr* to take leave, say goodbye.
despegar *vt* to separate; to unglue; ito take off (*airplane*).
despego *m* indifference; asperity.
despejado *a* smart, bright, clear.
despejar *vt* to clear away; to remove difficulties; *vr* to brighten up.
despejo *m* clearance, clearing away (*of obstacles*); vivacity, sprightliness.
despellejar *vt* to skin.
despensa *f* pantry, larder.
despeñadero *a* steep; *m* precipice.
despeñar *vt* to hurl down (*a precipice*); *vr* to throw oneself headlong (*into, after*).
desperdiciar *vt* to waste, squander, not to use, let slip.
desperdicio *m* waste, refuse.
desperezar *vr* to stretch oneself.
desperfecto *m* fault, weakness, imperfection.
despertador *m* alarm bell, alarm clock; awakener.
despertar (ie) *vr* to awake, awaken; excite (*appetite*); *vi* to awaken.
despezuñarse *vr SA* to rush, speed; long for.
despichar *vt Col, Chi* to squash, smash.
despido *m* dismissal, layoff.
despierto *a* awake; lively.
despilfarrar *vt* to spend wildly, throw (*money*) about, squander.
despilfarro *m* waste, squandering; mismanagement.
despistar *vt* to sidetrack, put off (*scent, trail etc*).
desplante *m* arrogance, cheek.
desplazamiento *m* displacement.
desplegar *vt* to unfold; to display, show, explain; **con banderas desplegadas** with banners flying.
desplomarse *vr* to get out of plumb; to collapse.
despoblación *f* depopulation.
despoblar (ue) *vt* to unpeople, depopulate.
despojar *vt* to despoil, plunder; *vr* to undress, relinquish.
despojo *m* spoils; remains, despoliation; *pl* debris.
desposado *m* newly-married, betrothed.
desposar *vt* to marry; *vr* to be betrothed.
desposeer *vt* to dispossess; to strip, take away from.
despostar *vt SA* to cut up (*a carcass*).
déspota *m* despot, tyrant.
despreciar *vt* to despise, treat with contempt; to neglect.
desprecio *m* contempt, disregard, disdain.
desprender *vt* to unfasten, detach, untie, separate; *vr* to fall away; to abandon (*one's possessions*); to be able to be inferred.
desprendido *a* disinterested; loose, loosened.
desprendimiento *m* disinterestedness; landslide.
despreocupado *a* broadminded, unprejudiced.
despreocupar *vt* to disabuse; *vr* to be disabused; to be set right.
desprestigiar *vt* to disparage, defame.
desprevenido *a* unprepared, improvident.
desproporción *f* disproportion.
despropósito *m* absurdity; nonsense.
desprovisto *a* unprovided, unprepared.
después *ad* after, afterward; then.
despuntar *vt* to take off the point, to blunt; *vi* to dawn; to sprout.
desquiciar *vt* to unhinge, disjoint; cause greater perturbation.
desquicio *m Arg* disorder, mess.
desquitar *vi* to take revenge for; to requite, retaliate, get even with.
desquite *m* revenge, retaliation.
desratizar *vt SA* to rid of vermin.
destacamento *m* (*mil*) detachment.
destajo *m* piecework; **hablar a —** to talk a lot of nonsense.
destapar *vt* to uncover, take the (*top, lid etc*) off; **—le los sesos** to blow his brains out.
destartalado *a* tumbledown.
destazar *vt* to slaughter; cut up (*carcass*).
destello *m* spark, sparkle, scintillation.
destemplanza *f* distemper; disorder; want of moderation.
destemplar *vt* to alter, disconcert; *vr* to be put out, lose temper.
desteñir (i) *vt* to discolor.
desterrar (ie) *vt* to exile, banish.
destierro *m* exile, banishment.
destilación *f* distillation.
destilar *vt* to distill; to drop.
destinar *vt* to destine, assign.
destinatario *m* addressee.
destino *m* destiny; destination; employment; **con — a** consigned to, bound for.
destitución *f* dismissal, loss of post.
destituir *vt* to dismiss; to deprive.
destornillador *m* screwdriver.
destornillar *vt* to unscrew.
destreza *f* skill, dexterity, adroitness.
destripar *vt* to disembowel; to smash, crush.
destronar *vt* to dethrone.

destrozar *vt* to cut to pieces, shatter, destroy.
destrozo *m* destruction, havoc, massacre.
destrucción *f* destruction, ruin.
destruir *vt* to destroy, overthrow, lay waste.
desuello *m* flaying, fleecing.
desunión *f* separation, discord.
desunir *vt* to separate, sever, divide.
desusado *a* out of use, obsolete.
desvalido *vt* destitute, helpless; unprotected.
desvalijar *vt* to rob, steal.
desván *m* garret, attic.
desvanecer *vt* to attenuate; *vi* to vanish; *vr* to fade away.
desvanecimiento *m* giddiness, haughtiness, pride.
desvariar *vi* to rage, be delirious.
desvarío *m* raving, delirium.
desvelar *vi* to keep awake.
desvelo *m* wakefulness, watchfulness.
desvencijado *a* rickety, broken down.
desventaja *f* disadvantage.
desventajoso *a* disadvantageous, detrimental.
desventura *f* misery; misfortune.
desventurado *a* unhappy, unlucky.
desvergonzado *a* shameless, impudent.
desvergüenza *f* effrontery, impudence.
desviación *f* deviation; variation (*of compass*).
desviar *vt* to divert, shift, dissuade, lead off; *vr* to deviate, swerve.
desvío *m* deviation; aversion.
desvirtuar *vt* to debilitate, emasculate.
desvivirse *vr* to nearly kill oneself, put oneself out (greatly) (*to do something*).
detallar *vt* to detail, enumerate.
detalle *m* detail.
detallista *m* retailer.
detener *vt* to detain, stop; to arrest.
detenido *a* careful, prolonged.
deteriorar *vt* to deteriorate, spoil, damage.
deterioro *m* deterioration, worsening.
determinación *f* determination, decision.
determinar *vt* to determine, specify; to assign; to decide.
detestable *a* detestable, hateful.
detestar *vt* to hate, detest.
detonar *vt* to detonate, explode.
detracción *f* detraction, lessening.
detractar *vt* to detract, defame.
detrás *prep ad* behind; at the back of.
detrimento *m* detriment, damage.
deuda *f* debt; indebtedness; — **exterior** foreign debt.
deudo *m* relative, kindred, parent.
deudor *a* indebted; *m* debtor.
devaluación *f* devaluation.
devanar *vt* to wind (*thread*); *vr* — **los sesos** to rack one's brains.
devaneo *m* raving, frenzy; dissipation; flirtation; (amorous) dallying.
devastar *vt* to devastate, lay waste.
devengar *vt* to earn, give a return (*as interest, profit etc*).
devoción *f* devotion, piety.
devolución *f* restitution, devolution.
devolver (ue) *vt* to give back, refund, return.
devorar *vt* to devour.
devoto *a* devout, pious.
día *m* day; daylight; — **festivo** holiday; — **laborable** working day; **al** — up-to-date; **de** — in the daytime; **de — en —** from day to day; **al otro** — on the next day; **cada tercer** — every other day; **a tres —s vista** at three days' sight; **hoy (en)—** the present day.
diablo *m* devil, cunning person.
diablura *f* devilry, mischief.
diabólico *a* diabolical, devilish.
diácono *m* deacon.
diadema *f* diadem, crown.
diáfano *a* transparent; diaphonous.
diagnóstico *m* diagnosis.
dialecto *m* dialect.
diálogo *m* dialogue, colloquy.
diamante *m* diamond; — **en bruto** rough (*uncut*) diamond.
diámetro *m* diameter.
diana *f* (*mil*) reveille.
diario *a* daily; *m* daily newspaper.
dibujar *vt* to draw, sketch; *vr* to show, be (etched, revealed, traced).
dibujo *m* drawing, sketch, plan, design.
dicción *f* diction, word, speech.
diccionario *m* dictionary.
diciembre *m* December.
dictado *m* dictation; *pl* dictates.
dictador *m* dictator.
dictamen *m* opinion, report; judgment.
dictaminar *vi* to give a verdict, judgment, decision.
dictar *vi* to dictate; to prescribe; to prompt.
dicha *f* happiness, good fortune.
dicharachero *a* fond of using slang.
dicharacho *m* vulgar expression.
dicho *a* said; *m* saying; proverb, saw.
dichoso *a* happy, lucky, blessed, fortunate.
diente *m* tooth, fang; **—s postizos** false teeth; **hablar entre —s** to mutter; **hincar el** — to bite into; to harry (*a person*).
diestra *f* right hand.
diestro *a* right, skillful, dexterous; *m* matador; **a — y siniestro** right and left, at random, wildly.
dieta *f* diet (*also assembly*).
diez *an* ten.
diezmar *vt* to decimate; to tithe.
diezmo *m* tithe.
difamar *vt* to defame, libel.

diferencia *f* difference.
diferenciar *vt* to differentiate, establish a difference, make a distinction between.
diferente *a* different, unlike.
diferir (ie) *vi* to differ, be different; *vt* to defer, postpone.
difícil *a* difficult, hard; not easy.
dificultad *f* difficulty, obstacle, trouble.
dificultar *vt* to make difficult, impede, obstruct.
difundir *vt* to spread, diffuse.
difunto *a* late, deceased, defunct; *m* corpse; **Día de los —s** All Souls' Day.
difuso *a* diffuse, prolix, difficult, wordy.
digerir (ie) *vt* to digest.
digestión *f* digestion.
dignarse *vt* to condescend, deign.
dignidad *f* dignity, high office, noble bearing.
digno *f* worthy, deserving, suitable.
digresión *f* digression.
dije *m* charm, trinket.
dilación *f* delay; tardiness.
dilapidar *vt* to delapidate, squander.
dilatación *f* expansion, enlargement.
dilatado *a* dilated; prolix; extensive.
dilatar *vt* to expand, widen, enlarge; to put off, delay.
dilema *m* dilemma.
diligencia *f* diligence, industry; briskness; stagecoach.
diligente *a* diligent, industrious, earnest.
dilucidar *vt* to elucidate, explain, make clear.
dilución *f* dilution.
diluir *vt* to dilute.
diluvio *m* deluge, flood; inundation.
dimanar *vi* to spring from, issue from, flow.
dimensión *f* dimension, size.
diminución *f* diminution; **ir en —** to taper (off).
diminuto *a* very small, minute.
dimisión *f* resignation (*from office etc*).
dimitir *vt* to resign, relinquish.
Dinamarca *f* Denmark.
dinamarqués *an* Dane, Danish.
dinamita *f* dynamite.
dínamo *m* dynamo.
dinástico *a* dynastic.
dineral *m* pile of money, fortune.
dinero *m* money, currency; coin; **— contante y sonante** ready cash.
dintel *m* lintel.
Dios *m* God.
diosa *f* goddess, deity.
diploma *m* diploma, title; credential.
diplomacia *f* diplomacy.
diplomado *an* graduate.
diplomar *vt* to confer an academic degree on; *vr* to graduate.
diplomático *a* diplomatic; *m* diplomatist, diplomat.
diputación *f* deputation.
diputado *m* representative, delegate; **— a Cortes** member of Parliament, congressman.
dique *m* dike, mole, jetty; dry dock.
dirección *f* direction, way; management; address (*letters*).
directo *a* straight, direct.
director *m* director; manager; (*mus*) conductor.
dirigente *m* leader, director.
dirigir *vt* to direct, drive (*car*); to guide, conduct (*orchestra*); to address (*a letter*); *vr* to apply to; go toward.
dirimir *vt* to dissolve, annul.
discernimiento *m* discernment, insight.
discernir (ie) *vt* to judge, discern.
disciplina *f* discipline, training; *pl* studies; scourge.
disciplinar *vt* to discipline, train, correct.
discípulo *m* disciple; pupil.
disco *m* disc; record.
díscolo *a* ungovernable, rebellious.
discordancia *f* disagreement.
discordia *f* discord, discordance.
discreción *f* discretion; sagacity, prudence; **a —** at will, ad lib.
discrecional *a* optional; **parada —** request stop, flag stop.
discrepancia *f* discrepancy, difference, disagreement (*with*).
discreto *a* discreet, prudent; (*quite*) creditable, tolerable, reasonable; mild, inoffensive.
discriminación *f* discrimination.
discriminar *vt* to discriminate.
disculpa *f* excuse; exculpation.
disculpable *a* pardonable.
disculpar *vt* to excuse, exculpate.
discurrir *vi* to walk about, roam; to be intelligent; to conjecture; to talk about, on; to speak (well *etc*); *vt* to contrive.
discurso *m* speech, lecture; reasoning; mind; space (*of time*).
discusión *f* discussion, argument.
discutible *a* debatable.
discutir *vt* to discuss, debate, argue.
disecar *vt* to dissect.
diseminar *vt* to disseminate, spread.
disentir *vi* to dissent.
diseño *m* sketch, design, pattern.
disertar *vt* to discourse, to hold forth (*speech*); to lecture.
disfavor *m* disregard, snub, disfavor.
disforme *a* disproportionate, monstrous.
disfraz *m* mask, disguise.
disfrazar *vt* to disguise, conceal, mask.
disfrutar *vt* to enjoy (*health*); to have the benefit of (*income*); profit by.
disfrute *m* enjoyment.
disgregación *f* disintegration.
disgustar *vt* to displease; to cause distaste, disgust; to upset; *vr* to be offended at.

disgusto *m* displeasure; grief, disagreeable shock; offense.
disidente *an* dissident.
disimulación *f* simulation, dissimulation; hypocrisy; **con —** cautiously, unobserved.
disimular *vt* to conceal, dissemble; to condone, overlook, cover up, connive at; to disguise.
disipación *f* dissipation, scattering; waste, loss; licentiousness.
disipar *vt* to dissipate, squander, scatter; to waste, cast away.
dislocar *vt* to dislocate, sprain.
disminuir *vti* to diminish, decrease.
disociar *vt* to dissociate; to separate.
disolución *f* dissolution, dissipation.
disoluto *a* dissolute, lewd.
disolver *vt* to dissolve; to separate (*matrimony*); to melt.
dispar *a* unlike.
disparada *f Arg, Mex* hasty start, sudden run.
disparar *vt* to shoot, let off, let fly.
disparatado *a* wide of the mark, absurd, foolish, crazy.
disparatar *vi* to talk nonsense.
disparate *m* nonsense, absurdity, crazy idea, notion.
disparejo *a* uneven, rough.
dispensar *vt* to grant, deal out; to excuse.
dispensario *m* clinic.
dispersar *vt* to disperse, rout, scatter.
dispersión *f* dispersion.
displicencia *f* displeasure, ill will, ungraciousness.
disponer *vt* to dispose; to prepare; *vr* to get ready.
disponible *a* available, expendable, ready.
disposición *f* disposition, inclination; regulation; disposal.
dispuesto *a* ready, willing, prepared; laid out.
disputa *f* dispute, quarrel.
disputar *vti* to dispute, wrangle, quarrel; to contend for.
distanciar *vt* to set at a distance; to outdistance; *vr* to draw apart.
distante *a* distant, far.
distar *vi* to be distant, far (from).
distinción *f* distinction, privilege; rank; clarity.
distinguir *vt* to distinguish, differentiate; to esteem; *vr* to excel; to be notable; to be visible.
distintivo *m* characteristic; *Arg* badge.
distinto *a* distinct, different.
distracción *f* diversion, distraction.
distraer *vtr* to amuse; to be distracted; to be absent-minded.
distribuir *vt* to deal out, distribute, share out, divide.
distrito *m* district, ward; canton.
disturbio *m* disturbance, outbreak.
disuadir *vt* to dissuade, deter.
diurno *a* diurnal.
divagar *vi* to ramble, wander, stray.
divergencia *f* divergence; diversity.
divergente *a* dissenting.
diversidad *f* diversity; variety.
diversión *f* amusement; feint.
diverso *a* diverse, different; *pl* various, many, sundry.
divertir (ie) *vtr* to amuse, entertain, enjoy.
dividir *vt* to cut; to divide; to separate.
divino *a* divine, heavenly.
divisa *f* device; badge (*esp on bulls*); *pl* currency.
divisar *vt* to make out (in distance), perceive.
división *f* division, separation.
divorciar *vtr* to divorce.
divorcio *m* divorce, disunion.
divulgar *vt* to reveal, broadcast, spread (*news*).
dobladillo *m* hem.
dobladura *f* crease, pleat, fold.
doblar *vt* to double, to fold, bend; *vi* to toll; *vr* to stoop; to yield.
doble *a* double, twice; strong.
doblegar *vt* to bend, twist; to dissuade.
doblez *f* fold, pleat; insincerity, duplicity.
doce *an* twelve.
docena *f* dozen.
docente *a* educational, teaching.
dócil *a* docile, tractable.
docilidad *f* docility, tractableness.
docto *a* learned.
doctor *m* doctor, physician.
doctrinar *vr* to instruct.
documento *m* document, deed.
dogal *m* halter; (*hangman's*) noose.
doler *vi* to feel pain; to hurt; *vr* to repent, feel sorry.
doliente *a* aching; *m* pallbearer.
dolo *m* fraud, deceit.
dolor *m* pain, anguish, ache, sorrow.
dolorido *a* doleful.
doloroso *a* painful; sorrowful.
domar *vt* to tame, break (*horses, etc.*); to master.
doméstico *a* domestic, tame; *m* servant.
domicilio *m* residence, domicile, home; **servicio a —** all goods delivered.
dominación *f* sway, domination.
dominante *a* dominant, domineering, prevailing.
dominar *vt* to rule over; to master, govern; to overlook, command (*a landscape, view*).
domingo *m* Sunday; **— de Resurrección** Easter Sunday.
dominio *m* domain, dominion, sway; territory.
don *m* (*with Christian name*) Sir (*but usually not translatable*); gift, donation; natural ability.
donación *f* donation.
donaire *m* elegance; witticism.
donar *vt* to donate.

donativo *m* gift, donation.
doncel *m* king's page.
doncella *f* waiting maid; virgin, maid.
donde *ad* where.
doña *f* (*used before Christian name*) Dame, Mistress, Mme., Lady (*but usually not translatable*).
doquier *ad* wherever.
dorada *f* goldfish.
dorar *vt* to gild; to palliate.
dormir (ue) *vi* to sleep; **— a pierna suelta** to be fast asleep.
dormitar *vi* to doze, sleep fitfully.
dormitorio *m* bedroom; dormitory.
dorso *m* back, spine.
dos *an* two; **de — en —** by couples.
dosis *f* dose, quantity.
dotar *vt* to endow; to portion.
dote *mf* dowry, portion; *pl* talent, endowments.
draga *f* dredge.
dragón *m* dragon; dragoon.
dragonear *vi SA* to pretend, play a part.
drama *m* drama, play.
dramaturgo *m* playwright.
drenaje *m* drainage.
droga *f* drug, medicine.
droguería *f* chemist's, drugstore; apothecary's.
dromedario *m* dromedary.
ducado *m* duchy; ducat.
ducha *f* douche; shower bath.
ducho *a* experienced, skillful, knowing.
duda *f* doubt, misgiving, doubtfulness; **sin —** certainly.
dudoso *a* doubtful, uncertain.
duela *f* stave.
duelo *m* sorrow, affliction, mourning; duel.
duende *m* fairy, elf, ghost, goblin.
dueño *m* owner, proprietor; master, landlord.
dulce *a* sweet; mild, soft, benign; fresh (*water*); *m* sweets, candy, toffee, taffy; **— de membrillo** quince jelly.
dulcería *f* sweet shop, candy store.
dulzaina *f* flageolet.
dulzura *f* sweetness; gentleness.
duna *f* downs, dune.
dundo *a CA, Col* stupid, silly.
duplicar *vt* to duplicate, double.
duplicidad *f* duplicity, double-dealing, cheating.
duplo *an* double.
duque *m* duke.
duración *f* duration, length; continuance.
duradero *a* lasting, durable.
durante *prep* during.
durar *vi* to last, endure; to wear well.
durazno *m Arg, Chi* peach, peach tree.
dureza *f* hardness; toughness, harshness.
durmiente *a* sleeping; *m* crosstie, sleeper (*railway*).
duro *a* hard, harsh; solid; **a duras penas** with great difficulty; *m* five-peseta piece; crown.

E

e *cj* and (*used instead of* y *before words beginning with* i *or* hi).
¡ea! *excl* here!, look!, get on there!
ebanista *m* cabinetmaker.
ébano *m* ebony.
ebrio *a* inebriated, intoxicated.
ebullición *f* ebullition.
eclesiástico *a* ecclesiastic; *m* priest.
eclipse *m* eclipse.
eclisa *f* fishplate; coupling.
eco *m* echo.
economía *f* economy; thrift, saving.
económico *a* economical.
ecuador *m* equator; **E—** Ecuador.
ecuatoriano *an* (*inhabitant*) of Ecuador.
ecuestre *a* equestrian.
echar *vt* to cast, pour, throw; to eject, throw (*out, away, off*), expel; to turn (*a key*); to lay, put (*blame*); **— a correr** to start off running; **— de menos** to miss; **— a pique** to sink; **— en cara** to reproach; **— mano de** to utilize; **— raíces** to take root; *vr* to lie down, stretch oneself.
echona *f Arg, Chi* sickle.
edad *f* age; **— media** the Middle Ages; **mayor de —** majority.
edecán *m* aide-de-camp.
edición *f* edition, issue.
edicto *m* edict, proclamation.
edificación *f* building, construction.
edificar *vt* to build; to edify.
edificio *m* building, fabric; structure.
editar *vt* to publish; to issue, edit.
editor *m* editor; publisher.
editorial *a* editorial; leading (*article*); **casa —** publishing house.
Eduardo *m* Edward.
educación *f* good breeding, politeness; upbringing, education.
educar *vt* to educate, bring up, train.
efectivamente *ad* really, in fact; actually.
efectivo *a* effective; *m* **en —** in coin, in bank notes.
efecto *m* effect, consequence; *pl* assets, securities; **en —** in fact, actually.
efectuar *vt* to effect, bring about.
efervescente *a* effervescent.
eficacia *f* efficiency, efficacy.
eficaz *a* efficient, efficacious, powerful, effective.
eficiencia *f* efficiency.
eficiente *a* efficient.
efigie *f* effigy, image.
efímero *a* ephemeral; short-lived.
efusión *f* effusion.
égida *f* egis, protection.
egipcio *an* Egyptian.
Egipto *m* Egypt.
égloga *f* eclogue.

egoísmo *m* egoism, egotism; selfishness.
egoísta *a* selfish, egoistic; *m* egoist.
egregio *a* eminent, distinguished.
egresado *m SA* graduate.
egresar *vt SA* to leave; to graduate.
eie *m* axis, axle, shaft.
ejecución *f* performance, fulfillment, execution.
ejecutar *vt* to perform, fulfill; to execute; *Arg* to play (*musical instrument*).
ejecutivo *a* executive.
ejecutoria *f* writ; letters patent, pedigree.
ejemplar *a* exemplary; *m* copy (*of book*); exemplar, model; example.
ejemplo *m* example, instance; **por —** for example; **dar —** to set an example.
ejercer *vt* to exercise, exert; to practice.
ejercicio *m* exercise, training.
ejercitar *vt* to exercise; to train, practice; *vr* to take exercise, to practice, train.
ejército *m* army; **— permanente** standing army.
ejido *m* common land.
ejotes *m pl Mex, CA* string beans.
el *def art m* the.
él *pn* he.
elaborar *vt* to work out, build up, elaborate.
elasticidad *f* elasticity.
elástico *an* elastic.
elección *f* election; selection, choice.
electorado *m* electorate.
electricidad *f* electricity.
eléctrico *a* electric, electrical.
electrizar *vt* to electrify; to enthuse.
electrónico *a* electronic.
elefante *m* elephant.
elegancia *f* elegance.
elegante *a* elegant, graceful, stylish.
elegía *f* elegy.
elegible *f* eligible.
elegir (i) *vt* to elect, choose, pick.
elemental *a* elementary, fundamental.
elemento *m* element.
Elena *f* Helen.
elenco *m* catalogue, index; *SA* cast of characters.
elevación *f* elevation, height; exaltation.
elevado *a* high, lofty.
elevador *m* lift, elevator.
elevar *vt* to raise, lift, to exalt; *vr* to ascend.
eliminar *vt* to eliminate, remove.
elíseos *a* **campos —** Elysian fields; Champs Elysées.
elocución *f* elocution.
elocuencia *f* eloquence.
elogiar *vt* to praise, extol.
elogio *m* eulogy, praise.
elote *m Mex* ear of green corn.
eludir *vt* to avoid, elude, slip away from.
ella *pn* she.
ello *pn* it.
emanar *vi* to proceed from, emanate, originate.
emancipar *vt* emancipate, free.
embadurnar *vt* to bedaub, clutter up.
embajada *f* embassy; message.
embajador *m* ambassador.
embalaje *m* packing, baling.
embalar *vt* to pack; to bundle up.
embalsar *vt* to dam (up).
embarazada *a* pregnant.
embarazar *vt* to embarrass, obstruct.
embarazo *m* embarrassment, hindrance, encumbrance; pregnancy.
embarcación *f* boat, craft.
embarcadero *m* wharf; pier, landing stage, quay.
embarcador *m* shipper, loader.
embarcar *vt* to ship; *vr* to go on board; *Arg* to plunge into (*business, subject*).
embargar *vt* to embargo, seize; restrain; to stifle (*speech, voice*).
embarque *m* shipment.
embarrar *vt Arg* to cover with mud, mess up.
embastar *vt* to baste, stitch.
embate *m* surge (*of sea*); sudden attack; *pl* blows (*of fortune*).
embaucar *vt* to deceive, trick.
embaular *vt* to pack (*in trunk*).
embebecerse *vr* to be struck with amazement.
embeber *vt* to imbibe; to contain; *vr* to shrink; to be enraptured, soaked (*in a subject*).
embeleco *m* fraud, deceit, humbug; trifle.
embelesar *vt* to fascinate, charm, capture.
embeleso *m* delight; entrancement.
embellecer *vt* to embellish, beautify.
embestida *f* assault, charge, violent attack.
embestir *vt* to assail, rush against, charge (*of bull*).
emblema *m* emblem.
embobado *a* spellbound, agape.
embocadura *f* mouth (*river*); mouthpiece.
embochinchar *vi SA* to make a row.
embolsar *vt* to pocket, emburse, put into a purse.
emborrachar *vt* to intoxicate; *vr* to get drunk.
emboscada *f* ambush; ambuscade.
emboscar *vt* to ambush; *vr* to lie in ambush.
embotar *vt* to blunt, dull, deaden.
embotellamiento *m* bottleneck, traffic jam.
embotellar *vt* to bottle.
embozado *a* (*face*) half-covered (*with cloak*), muffled, disguised, masked.
embozo *m* muffler, mask, disguise, turned-down clothes (*on bed*).
embragar *vt* to sling; to couple.

embravecer *vt* to enrage; *vr* to become enraged (*of sea*).
embrazar *vt* to clasp, grasp.
embriagado *a* intoxicated, drunk; enraptured.
embriagar *vt* to intoxicate; *vr* to get tipsy.
embriaguez *f* intoxication, drunkenness.
embrión *m* embryo; germ.
embrollar *vt* to embroil, perplex, confuse.
embrollo *m* entanglement; tangle, labyrinth; perplexing plot.
embromar *vt* to make fun of, tease.
embrujar *vt* to bewitch.
embrutecer *vt* to stupefy; *vr* to grow stupid, coarse.
embrutecimiento *m* stupefying, coarsening.
embudo *m* funnel (*for liquids*).
embullar *vi Col, CR, Cub* to stir; make noise.
embuste *m* artful lie, trick, lying tale.
embustero *m* liar; impostor.
embutido *m* (*any sort of*) sausage.
embutir *vt* to inlay; to stuff (*foods*).
emergencia *f* unexpected happening, emergency.
emético *m* emetic.
emigración *f* emigration.
emigrar *vi* to emigrate.
Emilia *f* Emily.
eminencia *f* eminence; elevation; distinguished personage.
eminente *a* eminent; illustrious; distinguished.
emisario *m* emissary; spy.
emisión *f* emission, issue; broadcast.
emisora *f* emitter; broadcasting station.
emitir *vt* to issue (*bonds*); to emit, send out (*smoke*).
emoción *f* emotion, excitement, interest, thrill.
emocionante *a* moving, touching.
empacar *vt* to pack (up), bale.
empacón *a Arg, Per* obstinate, stubborn.
empachar *vt* to cram; to embarrass; to cause indigestion.
empacho *m* bashfulness; indigestion; **sin** — unceremoniously, without ceremony.
empadronar *vt* to register, take the census of.
empalagar *vt* to cloy, surfeit; to weary.
empalizada *f* stockade.
empalmar *vt* to couple; to branch; to join (*rl*).
empalme *m* junction, connection.
empanada *f* meat or fish pie.
empañar *vt* to tarnish, blur, take the luster off.
empapar *vt* to imbibe; to soak, drench.
empapelar *vt* to paper, wrap in paper, wrap up.
empaque *m* packing; mien, (*dignified*) presence, style; *Chi, Per* impudence.
empaquetar *vt* to pack up; to bale.
emparamado *a SA* frozen to death.
emparedado *m* recluse; sandwich; *a* immured.
emparejar *vt* to level; to reach; to match.
empastar *vt* to bind (*books*); to paste.
empatar *vt* to tie, be equal; to draw (*football etc*).
empate *m* tie (*speaking of votes*), draw.
empecinado *a SA* stubborn.
empecinarse *vr SA* to persist, be stubborn.
empedernir *vt* to harden; *vr* to become insensible, hard-hearted.
empedrado *m* pavement, paving.
empedrar (ie) *vt* to pave (*with stones*).
empellón *m* hard push, shove.
empeñar *vt* to pawn, pledge; *vr* to engage oneself; to bind oneself; to insist, be insistent.
empeño *m* pawn, pledge; insistence, determination; **con** — repeatedly.
empeorar *vt* to spoil; impair; *vr* to grow worse, deteriorate.
empequeñecer *vt* to belittle.
emperador *m* emperor.
emperatriz *f* empress.
emperifollarse *vr* to dress up.
empero *cj* notwithstanding, however; but.
empezar (ie) *vt* to begin, commence.
empinado *a* steep, high.
empinar *vt* to raise; — **el codo** to bend the elbow, drink; *vr* to stand on tiptoe.
empingorotado *a* stuck-up, haughty.
empírico *a* empiric; empirical; *m* quack.
emplasto *m* plaster.
emplazamiento *m* summons.
emplazar *vt* to call upon to appear, to summon.
empleado *m* employee; clerk; office-holder.
emplear *vt* to employ; to give employment; to use, spend.
empleo *m* job, employment, use, occupation.
emplumar *vt Ec, Ven* to send someone into exile; *Col, Chi, Per* to flee, escape.
empobrecer *vt* to impoverish; *vi* to grow poor.
empobrecimiento *m* impoverishment.
empollar *vt* to hatch; *vr* (*fam*) to study hard.
emponchado *a SA* poncho-wearing; suspicious.
emponzoñar *vt* to poison, corrupt.
emporcar *vt* to soil, dirty.
emporio *m* mart, market.
empotrar *vr* to embed (*in wall*).

emprender *vt* to undertake, begin, start.
empresa *f* enterprise, venture, company, firm.
empresario *m* promoter, impresario.
empréstito *m* loan; — **público** public loan, government loan.
empujar *vt* to push, shove.
empuje *m* pressure, power; (*engine*) thrust; push.
empujón *m* push, shove.
empuntarlas *vi Col* to run away.
empuñadura *f* hilt.
empuñar *vt* to grasp, clutch.
emulación *f* emulation; rivalry.
emular *vt* to rival, emulate.
émulo *m* rival, competitor.
en *prep* in, into, for, at.
enaguas *f pl* petticoat; underskirt.
enajenable *a* alienable.
enajenación *f* alienation, insanity.
enajenar *vt* to alienate; to give up; to sell; *vr* to be lost (*in wonder etc*).
enaltecer *vt* to extol.
enamorado *a* in love, enamored, lovesick; *m* lover.
enamorar *vt* to win the love of, make someonel ove you; *vr* to fall in love.
enano *m* dwarf.
enarbolar *vt* to hoist, hang out (*flags*).
enardecer *vt* to inflame, fire with; *vr* to become impassioned.
enardecimiento *m* ardor, passion.
encabestrar *vt* to halter.
encabezamiento *m* heading, headline, billhead; tax roll.
encabezar *vt* to put a heading to; to make a taxroll; to head.
encabritarse *vr* to rear up (*like goats*).
encabullar *vt Cub, PR, Ven* to tie with sisal.
encadenamiento *m* sequence, connection.
encadenar *vt* to chain, bind, link together.
encajar *vt* to fit in; to force one thing into another; to gear.
encaje *m* fitting; socket, groove; lace.
encajonar *vt* to pack (*in box*), encase.
encalambrarse *vr Col, Chi, Mex, PR* to become numb.
encalamocar *vi Col, Ven* to become stupefied.
encalar *vt* to whitewash, lime.
encallar *vi* to run aground.
encallecer *vt* to develop corns; *vr* to become callous; to harden.
encaminar *vt* to set forward; to direct, guide; *vr* to follow the road to; to go; to be intended for.
encamotarse *vr SA* to fall in love.
encandilar *vt* to dazzle, bewilder; *vr* to be dazzled.
encanecer *vi* to become gray-haired.
encantador *a* charming, delightful, pleasant; *m* enchanter, sorcerer.
encantar *vt* to enchant, charm, bewitch; to please, make happy.
encanto *m* enchantment, spell, charm, delightfulness; delight, pleasure.
encapotar *vt* to cloak; to muffle; *vr* to become cloudy, cloud over (*of sky*).
encapricharse *vr* to be infatuated; to become obstinate.
encaramar *vt* to raise; *vr* to ascend, go up; to climb.
encarar *vt* to face; to look at.
encarcelar *vt* to incarcerate, put in prison.
encarecer *vt* to extol, praise to the skies; to pray; to raise the price; to stress (*difficulty etc*).
encarecimiento *m* price increase; exaggeration, warmth, praise, earnestness.
encargado *m* agent, responsible person, person in charge.
encargar *vt* to commission; to entrust; to warn; to order (*goods*); to recommend; *vr* to take upon oneself.
encargo *m* commission; office; order (*of goods*); errand.
encariñar *vt* to become fond of.
encarnación *f* incarnation.
encarnado *a* carnation-colored, red, flesh-colored; ingrowing (*nail*).
encarnar *vt* to incarnate; to embody.
encarnizado *a* cruel, pitiless, relentless, bloody.
encarnizarse *vr* to become cruel.
encarrilar *vt* to put on the right track, set right.
encarrujado *a Mex* rugged, rough.
encasillado *m* set of pigeonholes; list of (*favored*) candidates.
encasquillar *vt SA* to shoe horses.
encastar *vt* to improve by crossbreeding.
encastillar *vt* to fortify with castles; *vr* to stick to an opinion with obstinacy.
encausar *vt* to prosecute.
encauzar *vt* to direct (*into a channel*), canalize.
encenagarse *vr* to wallow in mire.
enceguecerse *vr SA* to become blind; to become blind with rage.
encendedor *m* lighter.
encender (ie) *vt* to light; to set fire to; to inflame.
encendido *a* bright, inflamed; *m* ignition.
encerado *a* waxy; *m* oilcloth; blackboard; sticking plaster.
encerar *vt* to wax; to cere.
encerrar (ie) *vt* to shut up; to confine, lock up; to contain, hold; *vr* to live in seclusion, to withdraw (*into*).
encía *f* gum (*of teeth*).
encíclica *f* encyclical.
enciclopedia *f* encyclopedia.
encierro *m* seclusion, confinement; prison; corralling of bulls (*before bullfight*).

encima *ad* above, over; **— de** on, upon; **por —** superficially.
encina *f* evergreen oak.
encinta *a* pregnant.
enclavar *vt* to nail; to embed.
enclenque *a* frail, sickly, weak.
encoger *vt* to shrink, contract; *vr* to shrug (*shoulders*); to be disheartened.
encogido *a* bashful, timid; shrunk.
encogimiento *m* shrinkage; bashfulness, timidity.
encojar *vti* to cripple, make lame, grow lame.
encolado *m Chi, Mex* dandy, dude.
encolar *vt* to glue.
encolerizar *vt* to provoke, rile, irritate; *vr* to grow angry, rave.
encomendar (ie) *vt* to commend; *vr* to commend oneself, entrust oneself.
encomiar *vt* to eulogize, extol.
encomienda *f* commission; recommendation; commandery; *SA* parcel post.
encomio *m* praise, eulogy.
enconado *a* bitter (*enmity*).
enconar *vt* to inflame, fester, cause irritation; *vr* to rankle.
encono *m* revengefulness, spitefulness, rancor, bitterness.
encontrado *a* opposite, opposed, contrary, conflicting.
encontrar (ue) *vt* to meet, come upon, encounter; to find; *vr* to feel, be.
encopetado *a* haughty, high and mighty, proud.
encorralar *vt* to corral (*cattle*).
encorvar *vt* to bend, curve.
encrespar *vt* to crisp, curl; *vr* to become rough (*the sea*).
encrucijada *f* crossroads.
encuadernación *f* bookbinding.
encuadernador *m* bookbinder.
encuadernar *vt* to bind (*books*); **sin —** unbound.
encubiertamente *ad* in a secret manner, fraudulently.
encubrir *vt* to conceal, cloak, mask, hide.
encuentro *m* collision, knock; unexpected meeting, encounter; **salir al — de** to go out to meet.
encuerar *vt Cub, Mex* to undress, strip.
encumbrado *a* high, lofty, overweening.
encumbrar *vt* to raise, elevate; *vr* to soar; to grow (*over*) proud.
encurtir *vt* to pickle.
enchapar *vt* to veneer.
encharcado *a* still, stagnant.
enchilada *f Guat, Mex* rolled pancake of corn meal with various fillings.
enchilar *vt CR, Hond, Mex* to season with chili.
enchivarse *vr Col, Ec* to fly into violent passion.
enchuecar *vt Chi, Mex* to bend, curve.
enchufar *vt* to plug in.
enchufe *m* plug, coupling; (*fam*) job, connection.
ende *ad* **por —** therefore.
endeble *a* weak, frail, feeble.
endecha *f* dirge.
endémico *a* endemic.
endemoniado *a* fiendish, devilish; possessed (*by the devil*).
endentar *vt* to mesh, engage; to gear; to provide with indentations.
enderezar *vt* to straighten, make straight; to set up, right; to erect; to direct, indite; *vr* to rise, straighten up.
endeudarse *vr* to run into debt.
endiablado *a* devilish, perverse; *SA* difficult, risky.
endilgar *vt* (*fam*) to dispatch, administer, indite (*letter, sermon*).
endiosar *vt* to deify.
endomingarse *vt* to dress up (*in Sunday best*).
endosar *vt* to endorse; to shift.
endrogarse *vr Chi, Mex, Per* to get into debt.
endulzar *vt* to sugar, sweeten; to soften.
endurecer *vt* to harden, toughen.
endurecido *a* hard(y); callous; inured.
endurecimiento *m* hardening.
enemiga *f* enmity.
enemigo *m* enemy, foe; *a* inimical, hostile.
enemistad *f* enmity, hatred.
enemistar *vt* to make enemies of, rouse enmity of.
energía *f* energy, vigor, power.
enérgico *a* energetic, active, lively.
enero *m* January.
enfadar *vt* to vex, offend, anger; *vr* to get angry, be cross, annoyed.
enfado *m* vexation, huff, irritation.
enfadoso *a* vexatious, irksome, distasteful.
enfardelar *vt* to pack, bale.
énfasis *f* emphasis.
enfático *a* emphatic.
enfermar *vi* to fall ill.
enfermedad *f* illness, disease.
enfermera *f* nurse.
enfermería *f* sanatorium; sickbay; nurses' home.
enfermizo *a* sickly, delicate; morbid.
enfermo *a* ill; *n* patient.
enflaquecer *vi* to grow thin, weaken.
enfocar *vt* to focus; to size up; to approach (*problem*).
enfrascar *vt* to bottle; *vr* to entangle oneself; to get very involved, tied up, in, with.
enfrenar *vt* to bridle, restrain.
enfrentar *vt* to face, confront.
enfrente *ad* opposite, facing, straight ahead.
enfriamiento *m* cooling; cold.
enfriar *vt* to cool, to refresh; *vr* to cool.
enfurecer *vt* to infuriate; *vr* to grow angry.

engalanar *vt* to adorn, bedeck.
enganchar *vt* to harness (*horses*); hitch, couple, connect; to engage; to hook, ensnare; to enlist (*in army*).
enganche *m* hooking; enlisting (*in army*); engaging (*workmen*).
engañar *vt* to deceive, cheat, swindle, dupe.
engaño *m* deceit, imposture, trick, illusion.
engañoso *a* deceitful; deceptive; insidious.
engarce *m* connection; mounting (*of jewels*).
engarzar *vt* to connect; to mount, set.
engastar *vt* to set (*precious stones*), enchase.
engaste *m* setting, mounting.
engatusar *vt* to cajole, wheedle, trick.
engendrar *vt* to engender, beget, conceive; to produce.
englobar *vt* to include, lump together.
engolfarse *vr* to become absorbed.
engolosinar *vt* to allure, entice.
engomar *vt* to glue, gum.
engordar *vt* to fatten; *vi* to grow fat.
engorroso *a* cumbersome, bothersome, annoying, deadly.
engranaje *m* gear, gearing, mesh; **palanca de —** clutch.
engranar *vi* to put into gear; to engage; *vr Arg* to get angry; to stall (*engine*).
engrandecer *vt* to aggrandize; to magnify.
engrasar *vt* to grease, oil.
engreído *a* proud, conceited, self-satisfied.
engreírse *vr* to become vain, be conceited.
engrosar *vt* to swell, augment, expand.
engullir *vt* to gobble, guzzle, devour.
enhebrar *vt* to thread.
enhiesto *a* erect, upright, sheer.
enhorabuena *f* congratulations; **dar la —** to congratulate; *ad* well and good.
enhorquetar *vi Arg, Cub, PR* to ride astride.
enigma *m* enigma, riddle, puzzle.
enjabonar *vt* to soap, lather.
enjaezar *vt* to harness.
enjalbegar *vt* to whitewash.
enjambre *m* swarm, cluster.
enjaular *vt* to cage, pen (in), confine.
enjuagadientes *m* gargle, mouthwash.
enjuagar *vt* to rinse.
enjuague *m* rinse, rinsing, gargling.
enjugar *vt* to wipe; to dry.
enjuiciar *vt* to indict, proceed (against), prosecute.
enjuto *a* dry, dried-up; lean, spare.
enlace *m* bond, ties; affinity, connection, junction; link, union, wedding.
enladrillar *vt* to pave with brick.
enlatar *vt* to can; *SA* roof with tin.
enlazar *vt* to tie, link, connect; *vi* to meet; *vr* to marry.
enlodar *vt* to cover with mud; to splatter, bemire; to stain.
enloquecer *vt* to drive mad, distract, madden; *vr* to become insane, go mad.
enlosar *vt* to flag, tile, pave.
enlutar *vt* to put on mourning; to darken.
enmaderar *vt* to roof with timber; to wainscot.
enmarañar *vt* to entangle, enmesh, snarl; to puzzle, confound.
enmascarar *vt* to mask, disguise; *vr* to masquerade.
enmendar (ie) *vt* to amend; to correct, set right; to repair; *vr* to turn over a new leaf.
enmienda *f* amendment; compensation.
enmohecerse *vr* to get moldy, (mildewed, rusty).
enmonarse *vr Chi, Per* to get drunk.
enmudecer *vi* to become dumb; *vr* to grow silent, be hushed.
ennegrecer *vt* to blacken, darken.
ennoblecer *vt* to ennoble.
enojadizo *a* peevish, testy, crabbed; huffy.
enojar *vt* to annoy, vex, put out; *vr* to become angry; to get ruffled.
enojo *m* annoyance, vexation; trouble; anger, rage.
enojoso *a* troublesome, provoking, annoying.
enorgullecerse *vr* to be proud, swell with pride.
enorme *a* enormous, huge, vast; wicked.
enormidad *f* enormity; monstrous thing; frightful deed.
enramada *f* bower, arbor.
enrarecer *vt* to rarefy; to dilute; *vr* to grow thin.
enredadera *f* vine, creeper, climbing plant.
enredar *vt* to tangle, embroil, enmesh, ensnare, confuse, involve.
enredo *m* tangle; maze; entanglement, pickle; liaison; plot (*of play*).
enredoso *a* entangled; *nm Mex* meddler.
enrejado *m* railing, frame, trellis.
enrejar *vt* to fence in; to fix the plowshare.
enrevesado *a* rebellious, frisky; complicated, intricate, tangled.
Enrique *m* Henry, Harry.
enriquecer *vt* to enrich; *vr* to grow, get rich.
enrojecer *vt* to redden; *vr* to blush.
enrollar *vt* to roll, coil, wind.
enronquecerse *vr* to become hoarse.
enroscar *vt* to twine, wreathe, twirl, wrap around.
enrostrar *vt SA* to upbraid.
ensaimada *f equiv* sugared tea cake.
ensalada *f* (*green*) salad.

ensaladilla *f* salad.
ensalmar *vt* to set; to enchant by spells.
ensalmo *m* charm, spell; **por —** by magic.
ensalzar *vt* to praise, extol.
ensambladura *f* joinery.
ensamblar *vt* to join; to dovetail.
ensanchamiento *m* enlargement, expansion; stretch.
ensanchar *vt* to widen, extend, expand.
ensanche *m* widening; extension, enlargement; outskirts of town; (*sew*) room to let out.
ensangrentar *vt* to stain with blood.
ensañar *vt* to enrage; *vr* to be furious, give vent to rage, wreak one's anger; to pursue fiercely.
ensartar *vt* to string, thread, file; *vr* *Arg* to make a bad bargain.
ensayar *vt* to test, attempt, try; to prove, assay; to rehearse.
ensayista *m* essay writer, essayist.
ensayo *m* examination, test; probation, trial; assay; essay; rehearsal; **— general** dress rehearsal.
ensenada *f* small bay, cove, inlet.
enseña *f* ensign, standard.
enseñanza *f* teaching, education, instruction; **primera —** primary, elementary education; **segunda —** secondary education; **— superior** higher education.
enseñar *vt* to teach; to show.
enseñorearse *vr* to take possession.
enseres *m pl* chattels, implements.
ensillar *vt* to saddle.
ensimismarse *vr* to be absorbed, wrapped up.
ensoberbecerse *vr* to become proud, puffed up; to get on one's high horse.
ensoparse *vr* to get drenched, wet through.
ensordecer *vt* to deafen, stun.
ensortijado *a* curled up, twisted; ringleted, (thickly) curly.
ensuciar *vt* to soil, befoul, defile; *vr* to foul oneself.
ensueño *m* dream, reverie; illusion, fantasy.
entablado *m* floor boarding.
entablar *vt* to cover with boards; to initiate; to strike up (*conversation*); to bring (*an action*); to put on a splint; to place (*chessmen*).
entallar *vt* to carve, engrave; *vi* to fit close to body.
entapizado *m* *Arg* carpet, rug.
ente *m* entity, being; (*fam*) guy.
enteco *a* weak, flaccid.
entelerido *a* shaking with cold; *SA* weak, frail.
entender (ie) *vt* to understand; to know; to be aware; **dar a —** to imply; **a mi —** in my opinion; *vr* to be agreed, get along (*well*) together.
entendido *a* learned, wise, well-informed; **darse por —** to take a hint.
entendimiento *m* intellect; comprehension, understanding; judgment.
enterado *a* **estar —** to be informed, in the know, aware.
enteramente *ad* entirely, quite, totally.
enterar *vt* to inform, acquaint, advise, make known; *vr* to be informed, get to know, find out.
entereza *f* entirety; integrity; constancy, fortitude.
enternecer *vt* to make tender; *vr* to be moved.
entero *a* flawless, entire; unassailable, incorruptible; whole, complete; robust; just; *m SA* payment.
enterrador *m* gravedigger.
enterrar (ie) *vt* to inter, lay in earth, bury.
entibar *vi* to rest, lean upon; *vt* (*min*) to prop.
entibiar *vt* to take the chill off; to moderate.
entidad *f* entity, being; worth, consideration, value; organization, firm; **de —** of consequence.
entierro *m* burial, funeral, interment.
entoldado *m* (group of) tents.
entonado *a* in tune; haughty, stiff and starchy.
entonación *f* intonation; blowing of organ bellows.
entonar *vt* to sing (*in tune*); to intone; to blow organ bellows.
entonces *ad* then, at that time; therefore; **en aquel —** in those days, at that time.
entornar *vt* to half-close, to leave ajar; to roll (*eyes*).
entorpecer *vt* to blur, clog, make stupid; to numb; to obstruct.
entorpecimiento *m* torpor, languidness, stupefaction.
entrada *f* ingress, entrance, entry, door; ticket; approach; entry; revenue; **derechos de —** import duties; **prohibida la —** no admittance; *pl* temples.
entrador *a SA* agressive.
entrambos *a pl* both.
entrante *a* incoming; next.
entraña *f* entrail; *pl* entrails, bowels; innermost parts; affections; depths; **sin —** hard-hearted.
entrañable *a* affectionate; dearly loved; inseparable.
entrado *pp* **— en años** stricken in years.
entrar *vi* to come in, get into, go in; to enter; to fit into; to begin; to penetrate, make an entry; to get at (*an enemy*).
entre *prep* between, among, amongst; **— manos** in hand; **— tanto** meanwhile.
entreabrir *vt* to half-open, leave ajar.
entreacto *m* intermission, entr'acte.
entrecejo *m* frown; space between the eyebrows.

entredicho *m* ban, prohibition; *Arg* misunderstanding; quarrel.
entrega *f* delivery; surrender; issue, part, installment (*of book*); **novela por —s** serial.
entregar *vt* to deliver, hand over, surrender, yield, give up; *vr* to give oneself up; to surrender; **— a** to devote oneself to, abandon oneself to.
entrelazar *vt* to entwine, interlace.
entremés *m* interlude, farce; side dish, hors d'œuvre.
entremeterse *vr* to intrude, meddle, poke, interfere with.
entremetido *a* pushing; *m* intruder; busybody, meddler.
entremezclar *vt* to intermingle.
entrenador *m* trainer.
entrenarse *vr* to get into training.
entreoír *vt* to hear indistinctly.
entresacar *vt* to select, cull, make choice between; to sift, winnow.
entresuelo *m* entresol, mezzanine.
entretanto *ad* meanwhile.
entretecho *m Chi, RP* attic.
entretejer *vt* to interweave, twist, plait.
entretener *vt* to entertain, keep occupied, beguile, while away, amuse; to keep someone too long; to maintain; to put off.
entretenido *a* amusing, diverting.
entretenimiento *m* recreation, amusement, entertainment; upkeep, maintenance, preservation.
entrever *vt* to have a glimpse of, discern.
entreverar *vt* to insert, mingle.
entrevista *f* interview; conference.
entrevistar *vt* to interview.
entristecer *vt* to sadden; to cause affliction; *vr* to grow sad, grieve.
entrometer *vtr* to meddle.
entroncar *vi* to be connected; *SA* (*rl*) to connect.
entronizar *vt* to enthrone, exalt.
entronque *m* relationship; *SA* (*rl*) connection.
entuerto *m* wrong, injustice.
entumecer *vt* to benumb; *vr* to swell, be bloated, puffed up.
entumecido *a* numbed, swollen.
entumirse *vr* to get numb.
enturbiar *vt* to trouble, make muddy; to obscure.
entusiasmar *vt* to enrapture, captivate; *vr* to be enthusiastic, get excited about.
entusiasmo *m* enthusiasm, eagerness, keenness.
entusiasta *m* fan, eager follower.
enumerar *vt* to enumerate, count up.
enunciación *f* utterance, enunciation, declaration.
enunciar *vt* to state, express.
envainar *vt* to sheathe (*sword*).
envalentonar *vt* to encourage, embolden, fill with Dutch courage; to incite.
envanecer *vt* to puff up; *vr* to grow vain *or* bumptious.
envasar *vt* to bottle, pack, sack.
envase *m* filling, bottling; packing case, cask, vessel; container, bag.
envejecer *vt* to make old; *vr* to grow old.
envenenar *vt* to poison.
envergadura *f* spread (*of wings*); span; breadth (*of vision*); (*important*) connections, results, ramifications.
envés *m* wrong side; flat, back (*of hand, sword*).
enviado *m* envoy, nuncio.
enviar *vt* to send; to convey; to remit; **— a paseo** to send someone about his business, send packing.
envidia *f* grudge, envy; spite.
envidiar *vt* to begrudge; to envy; to covet.
envilecer *vt* to debase, disgrace; *vr* to grovel.
envío *m* remittance; sending; consignment, shipment.
enviudar *vi* to become a widow or widower.
envoltura *f* wrapper, swaddling clothes; cover(ings), wrapping(s).
envolver (ue) *vt* to do up, wrap up, tie up; to cover; to involve, imply, include.
enyesar *vt* (*bandage*) to plaster.
enyugar *vt* to yoke.
enzarzar *vt* to entangle; to sow discord; *vr* to get tied up; to squabble.
épica *f* epic poetry.
épico *a* epic, heroic.
epidemia *f* epidemic.
epidémico *a* epidemical, epidemic.
epidérmico *a* epidermic.
epifanía *f* Epiphany, Twelfth Night.
epígrafe *m* title; epigraph; headline; motto.
epílogo *m* epilogue; summing up.
episcopado *m* bishopric, episcopate.
episodio *m* episode, incident; installment.
epístola *f* letter; epistle.
epistolar *a* epistolary, concerned with letter writing.
epitafio *m* epitaph; inscription.
epitalamio *m* bridal song, epithalamium.
epíteto *m* epithet.
epítome *m* epitome; summary, résumé; compendium.
época *f* epoch, era, season, period, time(s).
epopeya *f* epic (*poem*).
equidad *f* equity; fairness, justice.
equilibrar *vt* to balance, poise.
equilibrio *m* balance, poise, equilibrium.
equilibrista *m* tightrope dancer, tumbler.
equinoccio *m* equinox.
equipaje *m* luggage, baggage, traps, bags.
equipar *vt* to equip, rig out, furnish.

equipo *m* outfit, equipment; team; shift (*of workers*).
equis *f* the letter 'X'.
equitación *f* horsemanship, riding.
equitativo *a* equitable, fair, honest.
equivalente *a* equivalent, worth; *m* equal amount.
equivaler *vi* to be equal, be equivalent; to amount to.
equivocación *f* mistake, error, slip, blunder; misunderstanding.
equivocarse *vr* to be mistaken; to misunderstand; to be wrong.
equívoco *a* ambiguous, uncertain, compromising, questionable, with double meaning.
era *f* era, epoch; vegetable patch; threshing floor.
erario *m* exchequer.
eremita *m* hermit, recluse.
erguir *vt* to erect, stiffen, stand erect.
erial *m* waste land, untilled land, common.
erigir *vt* to erect, build, set up; *vr* to rise up.
erizar *vt* to bristle; *vr* to set on end.
erizo *m* hedgehog; sea urchin.
ermita *f* hermitage, chapel.
ermitaño *m* hermit, anchorite.
erogación *f* expense, payment.
erosión *f* erosion.
erótico *a* erotic.
erradicar *vt* to eradicate.
errado *a* mistaken, amiss, erroneous, wide (*of mark*).
errante *a* wandering, vagabond, strolling, nomadic, errant.
errar *vi* to roam, wander about; to miss; to err, sin, go astray.
errata *f* misprint.
erróneo *a* inaccurate, mistaken, false.
error *m* error, mistake, fault, miscalculation; fallacy.
eructar *vi* to belch.
erudición *f* learning, scholarship, lore.
erudito *a* erudite; *m* scholar.
erupción *f* eruption, outbreak; rash.
esbeltez *f* slenderness, willowyness, elegance.
esbelto *a* tall, slim and well shaped.
esbirro *m* myrmidon (*of the law*).
esbozo *m* sketch; rough draft.
escabeche *m* pickle; pickled fish.
escabel *m* footstool.
escabroso *a* rugged, slippery, dangerous; thorny, unpleasant (*subject*).
escabullirse *vr* to scamper off, sneak off, slink off, slip away.
escala *f* ladder, scale; **hacer—** to call (*at seaport*).
escalafón *m* list, roll; establishment; grade list (*of professors etc*); wage scale.
escalar *vt* to climb, escalate.
escaldado *a* scalded; cautious, wary.
escalera *f* staircase, stair; ladder; **— de caracol** spiral staircase.
escalinata *f* stone staircase, terraced steps.
escalofrío *m* chill; shivering, shivers.
escalón *m* step (*of stair*); stage, grade, degree.
escalonar *vt* to draw up; to form in echelon.
escalpelo *m* scalpel, surgeon's knife.
escama *f* (*fish*) scale; suspicion.
escamado *a* 'once bitten, twice shy'; wary, shy; put out, upset.
escamotar *vt* to juggle, conjure, palm.
escamoteo *m* sleight of hand, trick(ery).
escampar *vi* to stop raining, clear up.
escanciar *vt* to pour, serve (*wine*).
escandalizar *vt* to scandalize, cause an uproar.
escándalo *m* scandal, row, rowdiness.
escandaloso *a* scandalous, shameful; disorderly.
Escandinavia *f* Scandinavia.
escandinavo *an* Scandinavian.
escaño *m* bench, settle.
escapada *f* escape, flight; *Arg* short visit.
escapar *vi* to escape, get away; *vr* to make a getaway, slip off, fly; **se me escapó** I overlooked that; it was a slip of the tongue.
escaparate *m* cupboard; showcase, shop window.
escape *m* flight, evasion, escape; lever, escapement (*watch*); release; **a —** speedily, at speed; **no hay —** there is no way out.
escarabajo *m* beetle.
escaramuza *f* skirmish.
escarapela *f* cockade, badge.
escarapelar *vt Col, CR, Ven* to peel, shell; *Col* to rumple; *vr* to get goose pimples.
escarbar *vt* to scrape, scratch (*earth*).
escarcela *f* game pouch.
escarceos *mpl SA* prancing.
escarcha *f* white frost, rime.
escarlata *a f* scarlet.
escarlatina *f* scarlet fever.
escarmentar (ie) *vi* to learn by hard experience; *vt* to punish as example, teach (*a lesson to*).
escarmiento *m* warning, punishment.
escarnecer *vt* to scoff, jeer, sneer.
escarnio *m* scorn, derision, mockery.
escarola *f* endive.
escarpado *a* steep, rugged, craggy.
escasear *vi* to be scarce, fall short, be wanting; *vi* to be sparing.
escasez *f* lack, want, shortage, scarcity; poverty.
escaso *a* scarce, rare; spare, meager; scanty.
escatimar *vt* to pinch, skimp; to haggle; to reduce, lessen; to be sparing (*of praise etc*).
escena *f* scene, stage scenery; view, sight; **director de—** producer.
escenario *m* the stage, boards; scene (*of action*).
escenógrafo *m* scenographer.

escepticismo *m* doubt, skepticism.
escéptico *a* skeptic, skeptical.
escisión *f* division, separation.
esclarecer *vt* to explain, make clear; to ennoble.
esclarecido *a* illustrious, eminent, conspicuous.
esclavitud *f* slavery, servitude, thr lldom.
esclavizar *vt* to enslave.
esclavo *m* slave, drudge.
esclusa *f* lock, floodgate, sluice.
escoba *f* broom; **mango (palo) de —** broomstick.
escocer *vi* to smart, sting; *vr* to smart.
escocés *an* Scotch, Scottish, Scot(s).
Escocia *f* Scotland.
escoger *vt* to choose, elect, pick out, select.
escogido *a* choice, fine, selected.
escogimiento *m* selection, choice.
escolar *a* **vida —** life at school; *m* student, pupil.
escolástico *a* scholastic.
escolta *f* escort, safeguard, convoy; **— real** Royal Guard.
escoltar *vt* to escort, convoy.
escollar *vi Arg* to run aground; *Arg, Chi* to fail, fall through.
escollera *f* breakwater, jetty.
escollo *m* rock, reef; obstacle; stumbling block.
escombrar *vt* to clear of rubbish.
escombro *m* rubbish; *pl* debris, dust, ruins, litter.
esconder *vt* to hide, conceal, stow away; *vr* to lurk, hide.
escondite *m* hiding place; game of hide-and-seek.
escondrijo *m* hiding place, lair, (*secret*) haunt; (*private*) store.
escopeta *f* shotgun, fowling piece.
escoplo *m* chisel.
escoria *f* refuse, dross, scum; slag, clinker.
escorpión *m* scorpion.
escote *m* low neck, décolletage; share.
escotilla *f* hatchway.
escotillón *m* trapdoor.
escozor *m* itching pain, burning.
escribano *m* registrar, magistrate's clerk; **— del número** notary public.
escribiente *m* amanuensis, clerk.
escribir *vt* to write; **máquina de —** typewriter.
escrito *m* writing, manuscript; legal document; *a* written; **poner por —** to commit to writing.
escritor *m* writer, author.
escritora *f* authoress.
escritorio *m* writing desk, bureau; office.
escritura *f* deed, document; writing; **— de venta** deed of sale; **sagrada —** the Scriptures, Holy Writ.
escrúpulo *m* scruple; squeamishness; hesitation.
escrupuloso *a* scrupulous; nice, careful.
escrutar *vt* to scrutinize; to count (*votes*).
escrutinio *m* scrutiny, ballot.
escuadra *f* carpenter's square; squad; fleet.
escuadrilla *f* **— aérea** squadron, flight.
escuadrón *m* squadron.
escuálido *a* weak, languid; squalid.
escuchar *vt* to listen to, heed, mind; to hear.
escudar *vt* to shield.
escudero *m* squire, footman.
escudilla *f* bowl, porringer.
escudo *m* shield, buckler; coat-of-arms; protection, defense; coin.
escudriñar *vt* to search, scan; to rummage; to scrutinize, examine carefully.
escuela *f* school, schoolhouse; doctrine.
escueto *a* bare, clean, reduced to bare bones; solitary.
esculcar *vt SA* search, inspect.
esculpir *vt* to carve, engrave.
escultor *m* sculptor.
escultura *f* sculpture.
escupidera *f* spittoon.
escupir *vti* to spit, spit out.
escurridizo *a* slippery, hard to hold; **lazo —** slip knot.
escurrir *vt* to drain; to wring (*wet clothes*); *vr* to slip out; **— el bulto** to pass the buck, dodge the consequences.
ese *a* that; *pn* **ése** that one.
esencia *f* essence; perfume.
esencial *a* essential, substantial, necessary.
esfera *f* sphere, globe, circle.
esférico *a* spherical, globular.
esfinge *f* sphinx.
esforzado *a* strong, valiant, vigorous, active, energetic.
esforzar (ue) *vt* to encourage, stimulate; make an effort to, try to; *vr* to endeavor.
esfuerzo *m* effort, exertion.
esfumar *vt* to tone, shade.
esgrima *f* fencing.
esgrimir *vt* to fence, wield (*as an arm*).
esguince *m* swerve, sidestep (*of body*); sprained muscle.
eslabón *m* link (*of chain*); steel (*for striking fire*).
eslabonar *vt* to link, connect.
eslingar *vt* to sling, hoist (up).
esmaltar *vt* to enamel; to embellish, adorn.
esmalte *m* enamel.
esmerado *a* careful, painstaking, refined, exquisite, delicate.
esmeralda *f* emerald.
esmerarse *vr* to take (*be at*) great care (*pains, trouble*).
esmero *m* great care, niceness, refinement, delicacy.
eso *pn* that; **a — de** about (*time*); **— es** that's it.

esotérico *a* esoteric, private, abstruse, specialized.
espabilar *vt* to snuff.
espaciar *vt* to put space in between; to distance; *vr* to dilate; to cheer up; to take one's ease.
espacio *m* space, room; slowness; interval.
espacioso *a* roomy, spacious, ample; slow.
espada *f* sword, rapier; *m* swordsman, blade.
espadachín *m* bully, roisterer.
espadín *m* ceremonial sword.
espalda *f* back, shoulders; **a —s** on the back; **a —s de** behind the back of.
espaldar *m* back (*of seat*), backplate (*armor*).
espaldarazo *m* accolade.
espantable *a* frightful.
espantadizo *a* shy, timid, fearful.
espantajo *m* scarecrow.
espantapájaros *m* scarecrow.
espantar *vt* to frighten, scare; *vr* to be frightened, be afraid.
espanto *m* fright, dread, consternation, wonder.
espantoso *a* frightful, horrible.
España *f* Spain.
español *an* Spaniard, Spanish.
esparadrapo *m* court plaster, sticking plaster, adhesive tape.
esparcido *a* scattered.
esparcimiento *m* merriment, joy, recreation; scattering.
esparcir *vt* to scatter, spread; *vr* to spread oneself; make merry.
espárrago *m* asparagus.
esparto *m* esparto grass.
espasmo *m* spasm.
especia *f* spice; condiment.
especial *a* special.
especializarse *vr* to specialize.
especie *f* kind, species, class; incident; news.
especiería *f* grocery; spices.
especiero *m* spicer; grocer.
especificar *vt* to specify, itemize, detail.
especioso *a* specious, deceptive; apparent.
espectáculo *m* spectacle, show, sight.
espectador *m* spectator, looker-on.
espectro *m* specter, ghost, phantom.
especular *vt* to speculate; to contemplate.
especulativo *a* speculative.
espejismo *m* mirage, illusion; self-reflection.
espejo *m* looking-glass, mirror.
espeluznante *a* revolting, disgusting, terrifying.
espera *f* expectation; expectancy; wait; **en — de** hoping for, waiting for.
esperanza *f* hope.
esperanzar *vt* to give hope(s) to, buoy up (*with hope*).
esperar *vt* to hope, expect, wait for.
esperpento *m* ugly person or thing.
espesar *vt* to thicken.
espeso *a* thick, dense.
espesor *m* thickness, density.
espesura *f* closeness; thicket.
espetar *vt* to spit, run through; to spit out at.
espetón *m* skewer, spit.
espía *mf* spy.
espiar *vt* to spy, watch.
espiga *f* ear (*of corn*); spike.
espigado *a* grown, matured.
espigar *vi* to ear, glean, pick up the (*stray*) ears, grains.
espigón *m* (*bee*) sting, (*sharp*) point.
espina *f* thorn; fishbone; spine (*book*).
espinaca *f* spinach.
espinar *vt* to prick; *m* thorn brake.
espinazo *m* backbone.
espino *m* hawthorn.
espinoso *a* thorny, prickly; knotty, intricate, arduous, ticklish.
espionaje *m* spying, espionage.
espiral *a* spiral, helical; *f* spiral line.
espirar *vi* to expire, breathe.
espiritista *mf* spiritualist.
espíritu *m* ghost, spirit, soul; genius; liquor.
espiritual *a* spiritual.
espirituoso *a* spirituous.
espita *f* tap, faucet, stopcock, spigot, bung.
esplendente *a* resplendent, glittering.
esplendidez *f* splendor, largesse, splendidness, liberality.
esplendor *m* brilliance, magnificence, glory, radiance.
espliego *m* lavender.
esplín *m* spleen.
espolear *vt* to spur; to incite.
espoleta *f* fuse (*of bomb*).
espolio *m* despoiling.
espolón *m* cock's spur; buttress; ridge.
espolvorear *vt* to powder.
esponja *f* sponge.
esponjarse *vr* to swell (*with water, pride, vanity*).
esponjoso *a* spongy.
esponsales *m pl* betrothal, nuptials.
espontaneidad *f* spontaneity.
espontáneo *a* spontaneous.
esporádico *a* sporadic.
esportillo *m* pannier, basket.
esposa *f* wife, spouse; *pl* manacle, fetters, handcuffs.
esposar *vt* to handcuff.
esposo *m* husband, consort.
espuela *f* spur; incitement.
espulgar *vt* to delouse; to scrutinize.
espuma *f* froth, foam, (*soap*) lather.
espumar *vt* to skim.
espumoso *a* frothy, foaming.
espurio *a* spurious, false; bastard.
esquela *f* note, billet; memorial notice (*newspapers*); *in memoriam* card.
esqueleto *m* skeleton; *SA* form, application form; *Arg* sketch, outline.

esquema *m* scheme, sketch, plan.
esquife *m* small boat, skiff.
esquila *f* sheep bell; shearing.
esquilar *vt* to shear, fleece, crop.
esquilmar *vt* to impoverish (*land*).
esquimal *an* Eskimo.
esquina *f* corner, angle, edge.
esquirol *m* blackleg.
esquivar *vt* to shun, avoid, elude.
esquivez *f* shyness, coldness, coyness, mistrust, misgiving.
esquivo *a* evasive, shy, elusive.
estabilidad *f* stability, permanence, firmness.
estable *a* stable, firm, durable, permanent.
establecer *vt* to establish, found, set up, lay down; *vr* to settle.
establecimiento *m* establishment, settlement.
establo *m* stable.
estaca *f* stake, pole, cudgel, beam; grafting twig; (*fam*) stalk (*in tobacco*).
estacada *f* stockade, fencing, paling.
estación *f* condition (*of life*); season; (*rl*) station.
estacionar *vt* (*aut*) to park.
estacionario *a* stationary, fixed.
estada *f* stay, sojourn.
estadia *f* stay, detention; (*com, naut*) demurrage.
estadio *m* stadium, training ground (*horses, athletes*); measure of about ⅛ mile.
estadista *m* statesman, man of affairs.
estadística *f* statistics (*science*); *pl*—**s** statistics (*figures*).
estado *m* state, class, condition, place, rank; plight; — **satélite** satellite state; — **de sitio** martial law; — **mayor** (*mil*) general staff.
Estados *m pl* **Unidos de América** United States of America.
estafa *f* swindle, theft.
estafar *vt* to swindle, trick (*out of*).
estafeta *f* branch post office; courier, dispatch rider.
estallar *vi* to explode, burst, break out.
estallido *m* burst, crashing, crack (*of whip, gun*).
estambre *m* woolen yarn.
estameña *f* serge.
estampa *f* print, engraving.
estampado *m* calico, cotton print.
estampar *vt* to print; imprint (*a kiss*); to stamp.
estampida *f* stampede.
estampilla *f* rubber stamp; *SA* postage stamp.
estampillado *m SA* postage.
estampido *m* report (*of gun*), crack, crash(ing).
estancar *vt* to stem, staunch; *vr* to be stagnant, be held up, be stopped, come to a stop (*usually of water*).
estancia *f* sojourn, stay; dwelling, living room; stanza; farm, ranch.
estanciero *m* farmer, ranch owner.
estanco *m* monopoly (*especially in stamps and tobacco*); tobacconist's, tobacco kiosk.
estandarte *m* standard, colors (*of regiment*).
estanque *m* pool, pond; basin, (*ornamental*) lake.
estanquero *m* shopkeeper (*in estanco*), tobacconist.
estanquillo *m* tobacconist's, cigar store; *SA* small store.
estante *m* shelf, bookcase, whatnot.
estantería *f* shelving, shelves.
estaño *m* tin.
estar *vi* to be; to stay, stand; **estarse quieto** to stand still.
estatal *a* pertaining to the state.
estático *a* static.
estatua *f* statue.
estatuir *vt* to establish; to arrange; to enact.
estatura *f* stature, height.
estatuto *m* statute, law; *pl* by-laws.
este *a* this; *pn* **éste** this one.
este *m* east.
estela *f* wake (*of ship*); followers.
estenografía *f* stenography, shorthand.
estepa *f* steppe, waste, (*bare*) uplands.
estera *f* mat, matting.
estercolar *vi* to manure, spread dung.
estereofónico *a* stereophonic.
estereotipia *f* stereotype; printing works.
estéril *a* sterile, barren; fruitless.
esterlina *a* **libra** pound sterling.
estertor *m* death rattle, snort.
estética *m* aesthetics.
estético *a* aesthetic.
estibador *m* stevedore.
estiércol *m* dung, excrement, manure.
estigma *m* stigma; mark.
estigmatizar *vt* to stigmatize.
estilar *vtr* to be accustomed; *vr* to be in fashion, to be worn.
estilo *m* style; use, manner.
estima *f* esteem, appreciation.
estimación *f* esteem, regard, estimate, valuation.
estimar *vt* to esteem, like, hold in (*high*) respect; respect; to appraise, judge, think.
estimulante *a* stimulating.
estimular *vt* to encourage, incite, stimulate.
estímulo *m* encouragement, stimulus.
estío *m* summer.
estipendio *m* stipend, pay.
estiptiquez *m Arg, Col* niggardliness.
estipulación *f* stipulation, promise, bargain, condition.
estipular *vt* to stipulate, contract, lay down (*as condition*).
estirado *a* stretched; stiff(-necked), starched, unbending, strait-laced.
estirar *vt* to stretch (*out*), to pull out

(*elastic*), to crane (*one's neck*).
estirón *m* tug, stiff pull; **dar un—** to shoot up (*in growth*).
estirpe *f* stock, family, blood.
estival *a* summer, summery.
estocada *f* stab.
estofa *f* stuff, materials; quality; **de baja—** low class.
estofado *m* stew, stewed meat.
estofar *vt* to stew; to quilt.
estoico *a* stoic, stoical.
estólido *a* stolid, stupid.
estómago *m* stomach.
estopa *f* tow, hemp, yarn.
estoque *m* rapier, sword(stick), poniard.
estorbar *vt* to obstruct, be in the way, hinder, molest.
estorbo *m* obstacle, hindrance, obstruction, stumbling block.
estornudar *vi* to sneeze.
estrafalario *a* eccentric, odd, queer, untidy (*in dress*).
estragar *vt* to ruin, spoil, corrupt (*manners*).
estrago *m* ravage, havoc, destruction; **hacer —s** to wreak havoc, make inroads (*into emotions etc*); to cause (*huge*) losses.
estrangular *vti* to strangle, choke.
estraperlista *m* profiteer; black-market dealer.
estraperlo *m* black market.
estratagema *f* stratagem, trick.
estrategia *f* strategy.
estrechar *vt* to compress, tighten; to confine; *vi* to become (make) (more) intimate (close) with; **— la mano** to shake hands.
estrechez *f* narrowness, closeness; intimacy; (*often pl*) penury, straitened circumstances.
estrecho *a* narrow, tight; close; intimate; *m* strait(s)
estregar *vt* to rub (*eyes*); scrape, scour.
estrella *f* star; fate, lot.
estrellado *a* starry; shattered, splashed; (*of eggs*) fried; smashed, splattered.
estrellar *vt* to shatter; *vr* to dash, break against; to spend oneself against.
estremecer *vi* to shake, shudder, quiver; *vr* to tremble, shiver.
estremecimiento *m* shaking, trembling, apprehension, shudder.
estrenar *vt* to try on, do, wear (for first time); to have a first performance.
estreno *m* beginning, première, first night (*theat*), début; first performance.
estreñimiento *m* constipation.
estreñir (i) *vt* to bind, restrain; *vr* to be costive.
estrépito *m* noise, din, row, racket.
estrepitoso *a* noisy, strident, rowdy, obstreperous.
estría *f* fluting, groove (*on column*).
estribar *vi* to rest (upon), depend on, be supported by.
estribo *m* stirrup; counterfort, buttress.
estribor *m* starboard.
estricto *a* strict, accurate.
estridente *a* jarring, raucous, strident.
estro *m* (*poet*) inspiration.
estrofa *f* strophe, stanza.
estropajo *m* mop, swab, bundle of rags; panscrubber.
estropear *vt* to spoil; to maim, mutilate, damage, ruin (*clothes etc*).
estructura *f* structure.
estruendo *m* clangor, clashing, clattering.
estrujar *vi* to crush, squeeze, jam.
estuario *m* estuary.
estuco *m* stucco; plaster.
estuche *m* case, sheath (*jewels, dagger*).
estudiantado *m SA* student body, students collectively.
estudiante *m* scholar, student, undergraduate.
estudiantina *f* student wake *or* band (*with guitars*).
estudiar *vt* to study; contemplate; *vi* to attend classes; to read (*for degree*).
estudio *m* study; contemplation; studio; reading room.
estudioso *a* studious.
estufa *f* stove; heater.
estulticia *f* foolishness.
estupefacto *a* stupefied, astonished, set back, put out.
estupendo *a* stupendous, marvelous, tremendous, terrific; (*fam*) fabulous, smashing.
estupidez *f* stupidity.
estúpido *a* stupid, dull, slow.
estupor *m* amazement, stupor.
estupro *m* rape.
etapa *f* station, stage, halting place, relay.
éter *m* ether.
eternidad *f* eternity.
eterno *a* eternal, endless.
ética *f* ethics.
etimología *f* etymology.
etíope *an* Ethiopian.
Etiopía *f* Ethiopia; Abyssinia.
etiqueta *f* etiquette, ceremony; ticket, label; **baile de —** formal dance; **de—** de rigueur, formal dress.
eufemismo *m* euphemism.
europeo *an* European.
Eva *f* Eve.
evacuación *f* evacuation.
evacuar *vt* to evacuate, leave; to empty; to clear; to perform, transact (*business*).
evadir *vt* to evade, elude; *vr* to evade, escape, break (away, out).
evangélico *a* evangelical, Protestant.
evangelio *m* gospel.
evaporación *f* evaporation.
evaporar *vt* to evaporate, vaporize; *vr* to evaporate.

evasión *f* evasion, escape, (*fam*) getaway; **— de impuestos** tax evasion.
evasiva *f* evasion, dodge.
evasivo *a* evasive, elusive.
evento *m* event, issue, happening; contingency.
eventual *a* eventual, contingent, uncertain.
evidencia *f* evidence; obviousness; proof.
evidenciar *vt* to show, prove, make evident, reveal.
evidente *a* clear, manifest, obvious, evident.
evitar *vt* to avoid, shun, elude, shirk.
evocar *vt* to evoke.
evolución *f* evolution, development.
exacerbar *vt* to irritate, exacerbate, aggravate.
exactitud *f* accuracy, exactness.
exacto *a* exact, accurate, just; *ad* (*quite*) right.
exageración *f* exaggeration.
exagerar *vt* to exaggerate, overstate.
exaltado *m* hothead, extremist.
exaltar *vt* to exalt, extol; *vr* to work oneself up.
examen *m* examination.
examinar *vt* to examine, inspect, scan, look into.
exangüe *a* bloodless.
exasperar *vt* to exasperate, irritate.
excavar *vt* to excavate, dig.
excedente *m* surplus.
exceder *vt* to exceed, surpass; *vr* to exceed.
excelencia *f* excellence, excellency.
excelente *a* excellent.
excelso *a* sublime, lofty, elevated.
excentricidad *f* eccentricity.
excéntrico *a* eccentric, odd; outlying.
excepción *f* exception, exclusion.
excepcional *a* exceptional, unique, unusual.
excepcionalmente *ad* exceptionally.
excepto *ad* except, excepting, save for.
exceptuar *vt* to except, leave out.
excesivo *a* excessive, too much, immoderate.
exceso *m* excess, excessiveness, exuberance.
excitación *f* stimulation, agitation, intoxication.
excitado *a* worked-up, affected, transported, disturbed.
excitar *vt* to excite, urge, rouse, thrill, galvanize, stimulate.
exclamación *f* exclamation.
exclamar *vi* to exclaim, cry out, shout.
exclaustrado *m* secularized monk.
excluir *vt* to exclude, debar, shut out, eject.
exclusión *f* exclusion, shutting out, rejection.
exclusiva *f* exclusive right, monopoly.
exclusive *ad* exclusively.
exclusivo *a* exclusive.
excomulgar *vt* to excommunicate.
excomunión *f* excommunication.
excoriar *vt* to flay, excoriate.
excursión *f* excursion, trip.
excusa *f* excuse, apology.
excusado *a* exempted; superfluous, unnecessary, useless; *m* toilet.
excusar *vt* to excuse; to avoid, shun; *vr* to apologize, send apologies.
execrable *a* accursed, hateful.
execrar *vt* to execrate, curse.
exención *f* exemption, franchise.
exento *a* exempt, free, clear.
exequias *f pl* obsequies, funeral rites.
exfoliador *m* *Chi* writing pad.
exhalación *f* effluvium; shooting star.
exhalar *vt* to exhale, emit, utter, breathe.
exhausto *a* exhausted, empty.
exhibir *vt* to exhibit, show, display.
exhortación *f* exhortation, admonition.
exhortar *vt* to exhort, warn, charge.
exigencia *f* exigency, demand, requirement, exaction.
exigente *a* particular, exacting.
exigir *vt* to demand, exact, require, insist on.
exiguo *a* slender, scanty, small, exiguous.
eximio *a* famous, eminent, (*very*) distinguished.
eximir *vt* to exempt, free from (*burden*), excuse, clear (of, from).
existencia *f* existence; *pl* stocks, supplies.
existir *vi* to exist, be.
éxito *m* success; issue, result; **tener —** to be successful.
exonerar *vt* to free from, exonerate, acquit.
exorbitante *a* exorbitant, excessive.
exorcizar *vt* to exorcize, adjure.
exótico *a* exotic, foreign.
expansión *f* expansion.
expatriar *vt* to expatriate, exile.
expectativa *f* expectation, hope; **estar a la —** to be on the look-out for, ready for, waiting for.
expedición *f* expedition; dispatch, haste.
expediente *m* expedient, device, way; file, dossier; minute, draft; documentation.
expedir (i) *vt* to dispatch, forward, send.
expedito *a* speedy, expeditious, prompt; clear, free.
expendedor *m* dealer, seller.
expendio *m* *Arg, Mex, Per* retail selling; *Mex* tobacconist's, cigar store.
expensas *f pl* expenses, costs; **a — de** at the expense of.
experiencia *f* experience, experiment, trial.

experimentado *a* experienced, expert, proficient, practiced.
experimentar *vt* to experience, experiment, feel, undergo.
experimento *m* experiment, trial, experience.
experto *an* experienced; expert.
expiación *f* atonement.
expiar *vt* to expiate, atone for, purify.
expirar *vi* to die, expire, pass away.
explanar *vt* to level, grade (*land*); to expound, unfold.
explicación *f* explanation.
explayar *vt* to dilate, enlarge; *vr* to dwell (*upon*), expatiate, spread oneself (*in speech etc*); to unburden oneself; to disport oneself; have lovely time (*in country particularly*).
explicar *vt* to explain.
explícito *a* explicit.
explorador *m* (boy) scout; explorer.
explorar *vt* to explore, investigate.
explosión *f* explosion, outburst, blast.
explosivo *a* explosive.
explotación *f* working; exploitation.
explotar *vt* to work, exploit, develop, utilize, put to (full) use.
expoliación *f* spoliation, plunder(ing).
exponer *vt* to expose, exhibit, show; to state, disclose, unfold, explain; to stake, risk; *vr* to risk, lay oneself open to.
exportación *f* exportation; export.
exportar *vt* to export.
exposición *f* exposition, statement, claim; exhibition, show (*of pictures etc*).
expósito *m* foundling.
exprés *a* **café —** espresso coffee.
expresar *vt* to express, utter.
expresión *f* expression, utterance; pressing out.
expreso *a* express, clear; *m* special messenger, courier.
exprimir *vt* to squeeze (out).
expuesto *a* liable; exposed; dangerous.
expugnar *vt* to take by storm.
expulsar *vt* to expel, eject.
expulsión *f* expulsion, ejection.
expurgar *vt* to expurgate, expunge.
exquisitez *f* exquisiteness.
exquisito *a* exquisite, refined, delicate; nice.
extasiado *a* delighted; in ecstasy.
éxtasis *f* ecstasy, transport, bliss, heaven.
extender (ie) *vt* to extend, spread, stretch; to draw up (*document*); *vr* to become general, widespread; to dilate (upon); to open up (*as vista etc*).
extendido *a* spread out, unfolded, open, extensive; general, widespread.
extensión *f* extension, expanse, extent; magnitude; spaciousness; range, sweep, scope.
extensivo *a* extensive, ample.
extenso *a* spacious, broad, widespread.
extenuado *a* weak, emaciated, feeble.
extenuar *vt* to debilitate, wear away, mitigate; *vr* to languish, decay, become worn out.
exterior *a* exterior, outer; *m* aspect, outward semblance.
exterminar *vt* to exterminate, destroy.
exterminio *m* extermination, banishment.
externo *a* external, outward; *m* day student.
extinguir *vt* to put out, extinguish; to smother; to quench; *vr* to fade out.
extirpación *f* extirpation, eradication, removal.
extirpar *vt* to extirpate, root out, destroy.
extra *a* extra; *mf* (theat) extra.
extracción *f* extraction, drawing (*of lottery tickets*); taking out (*of roots, in maths*); mining.
extracto *m* summary, abstract.
extraer *vt* to extract, remove, pull out; to pull up; to mine; to export.
extralimitarse *vr* to overdo it.
extranjero *a* outlandish, foreign; *m* alien, foreigner; stranger; **en el —** abroad.
extrañar *vt* deport, banish; *SA* to miss, feel lack of; **me extraña** I am surprised; *vr* to become strangers, to fall out (*of friends*).
extrañeza *f* wonderment, surprise; oddity, strangeness.
extraño *a* strange, queer, rare, outlandish, odd; *m* stranger.
extraordinario *a* extraordinary, out-of-the-way; unusual; extra, supplementary; *m* supplementary course (*at meals*).
extravagancia *f* extravagance; irregularity, freak, antic.
extravagante *a* extravagant; queer, odd, eccentric; *m* a queer fellow, an eccentric.
extraviado *a* mislaid, missing, lost, stray; of unsound mind.
extraviar *vt* to mislead; to mislay, lose; *vr* to get lost, miscarry, go astray.
extravío *m* deviation; misconduct; misplacement; loss; wandering, distraction.
extremar *vt* to carry to extremes, go to great length(s); to outdo.
extremaunción *f* extreme unction.
extremeño *an* (*inhabitant*) of Extremadura.
extremidad *f* extremity; brink, border, margin edge; *pl* **—es** utmost ends.
extremo *a* extreme, utmost, farthest; red-hot; ultra; terminal; *m* extreme, end, edge; great care.
extrínseco *a* extrinsic; extraneous; outlying.

exuberancia *f* exuberance; **con —** abundantly, exuberantly.
exuberante *a* exuberant, luxurious, rampant.
exvoto *m* votive offering.

F

fábrica *f* fabric; make, fabrication; factory, workshop.
fabricación *f* make, manufacture, preparation; invention.
fabricante *m* manufacturer, constructor, maker.
fabricar *vt* to make, manufacture, prepare, put together.
fábula *f* myth, tale, fable; rumor, invention.
fabuloso *a* fabulous, legendary.
faca *f* jackknife.
facción *f* party, side; *pl* features (*of face*).
faccioso *a* rebellious; *m* rebel, traitor.
faceto *a SA* lively, joyful.
fácil *a* easy, simple; ready; compliant, free-and-easy.
facilidad *f* ease, facility; compliance; **—es crediticias** credit facilities.
facilitar *vt* to smooth, facilitate; to supply, obtain; to lend (*money*).
facineroso *a* wicked; criminal; *m* habitual criminal.
facón *m Arg* gaucho's knife.
factible *a* workable, feasible.
factoría *f* factory; trading house, entrepôt.
factura *f* invoice; make.
facturar *vt* to list, register, invoice.
facultad *f* ability, power, authority; faculty; **— de Filosofía y Letras** Faculty of Arts.
facultativo *a* optional; *m* physician.
facha *f* (*fam*) face; look; sight.
fachada *f* front, frontage, frontispiece, façade.
fachoso *a Chi, Mex* vain.
faena *f* task, chore, duty; trick.
faenero *m Chi* farm laborer.
faisán *m* pheasant.
faja *f* band, bandage; sash, belt, girdle; newspaper wrapper.
fajar *vt* to swathe; to gird, wrap; *Cub, Chi, Per* to beat, hit; *vr Cub* to fight.
falange *f* phalanx; Fascist Party in Spain.
falaz *a* fallacious, deceitful, deceptive.
falda *f* skirt; lap; slope; brisket; **perro de —s** lapdog.
faldero *m* lapdog.
faldillas *f pl* skirts; coattails.
falencia *f Arg, Chi, Hon* bankruptcy.
falibilidad *f* fallibility.
falsario *m* forger, counterfeiter.
falseador *m* forger, falsifier.
falsear *vt* to falsify, counterfeit, forge; to weaken.
falsedad *f* falsehood, untruth; spuriousness; treacherousness.
falsete *m* spigot; falsetto voice.
falsificación *f* forgery.
falsificar *vt* to counterfeit, falsify, forge.
falso *a* false, lying; mock; counterfeit; feint; erroneous, incorrect, wrong.
falta *f* lack, need, shortage, deficiency; fault, misdemeanor; shortcoming, (*law*) default; **sin—** without fail; **me hace mucha —** I need it badly.
faltar *vi* to be missing, not to be present; to miss; to fail, not to fulfill; to sin (*against*); **me falta** I need it, I haven't (got).
falto *a* wanting, deficient, in need of.
faltriquera *f* fob, watch pocket.
falla *f* failure, fault; slide; (*geol*) fault; bonfire (*on eve of Saint's day*).
fallar *vi* to pass judgment; to be wanting; to misfire, fail (*to work, go off*); **me falla** it fails me, lets me down.
fallecer *vi* to die, depart, pass away.
fallecimiento *m* death, demise.
fallo *m* award, ruling, sentence.
fama *f* renown, fame; glory, honor, reputation; **de mala—** of ill repute.
famélico *a* starving, hungry.
familia *f* family, ménage, household.
familiar *a* familiar, domestic, intimate; homely, simple; *m SA* relative.
familiaridad *f* familiarity, kinship, intimacy, close terms.
familiarizar *vt* to familiarize; *vr* to become intimately acquainted (*with*); to get conversant (*with*).
famoso *a* famous, noted; proverbial, 'good old'.
fanal *m* lighthouse; lantern.
fanático *a* fanatical, bigoted, rabid; *m* fanatic, bigot.
fanatismo *m* fanaticism.
fanega *f* measure for grains (1·60 *bushels*); **— de tierra** land measure (*about* 1·59 *acres*).
fanfarrón *a* blustering, bragging; *m* blusterer, swaggerer, swashbuckler, boaster, bully.
fango *m* mire, mud, slime.
fangoso *a* muddy, marshy, slimy, slushy.
fantasía *f* fantasy; fancy, imagination; whim, caprice.
fantasma *m* phantom, specter, ghost, shadow; *f* scarecrow.
fantástico *a* fantastic; fanciful; imaginary; unreal; weird, odd, strange.
fantoche *m* marionette, puppet.
farándula *f* strolling band (*of actors*); confusion, pack of lies.
fardo *m* bale, pack, bundle, load, burden.

farfullar *vt* to babble, gabble, jabber.
fariseo *m* pharisee, hypocrite.
farmacéutico *a* pharmaceutical; *m* pharmacist, chemist.
farmacia *f* chemist's shop, pharmacy, druggist's.
faro *m* lighthouse; (*aut*) headlight.
farol *m* lantern; street lamp, light; signal light; conceit, self-importance; **darso** — to show off.
farolillo *m* paper lantern, Japanese lantern.
farra *f SA* spree, revelry; **irse de** — to go on a spree.
farrago *or* **fárrago** *m* medley.
farsa *f* farce; trick; sham; invention; light comedy.
farsante *m* humbug; **es un** — he's no good.
fascinación *f* fascination, glamour; witchcraft.
fascinador *a* bewitching, captivating.
fascinar *vt* to fascinate, allure, charm; to bewitch.
fase *f* aspect, view, phase; *pl* phases (*of moon*).
fastidiar *vt* to annoy, offend, put out, bother; *vr* to be weary, bored, fed up.
fastidio *m* weariness; disgust, bother; squeamishness, fastidiousness.
fastidioso *a* annoying, provoking, irksome; squeamish.
fasto *a* happy; *m* pageantry, pomp; *m pl* annals.
fastuoso *a* pompous; gaudy; ostentatious, splendid, lavish.
fatal *a* deadly, death-dealing, fatal; ominous; accursed; mortal.
fatalidad *f* fatality; mischance, awful fate.
fatídico *a* oracular.
fatiga *f* fatigue, weariness; hardship, anguish, sweat.
fatigar *vt* to tire, fatigue, exhaust, weary; *vr* to be weary, tired out.
fatigoso *a* tedious, tiresome, trying, wearisome.
fatuidad *f* fatuity, silliness; empty vanity.
fatuo *a* fatuous, foppish, conceited; addlepated.
fauno *m* faun.
fausto *a* happy, successful, of good omen; *m* splendor, luxury, display.
favor *m* favor, grace, kindness, help, assistance; good turn; token; **a — de** on behalf of, under cover of, by reason of, in favor of.
favorable *a* favorable; propitious.
favorecer *vt* to favor, countenance, prosper, smile on; to suit.
favoritismo *m* favoritism.
favorito *a* beloved; favored; *m* favorite, pet, darling.
faz *f* aspect, face; front
fe *f* faith, belief, testimony; **buena —** earnestness, sincerity; **mala —** insincerity; **— de erratas** errata; **de buena —** in good faith; **dar —** to attest, prove; **a —** in good earnest.
fealdad *f* ugliness, deformity, unsightliness.
febrero *m* February.
febril *a* feverish, restless.
fecundar *vt* to fecundate.
fecundidad *f* fecundity, fruitfulness.
fecundizar *vt* to fecundate, fertilize.
fecundo *a* prolific, fertile, rich, teeming, fruitful.
fecha *f* date.
fechar *vi* to date.
fechoría *f* misdeed, villainy.
federación *f* federation.
féferes *m pl SA* household goods, tools.
fehaciente *a* valid, authentic, reliable.
felicidad *f* happiness, felicity, bliss, joyousness; **—es** congratulations, happy birthday.
felicitación *f* congratulation.
felicitar *vt* to congratulate, compliment.
feligrés *m* parishioner.
Felipe *m* Philip.
feliz *a* happy, lucky, fortunate, blessed.
felón *m* traitor; felon.
felonía *f* felony; perfidy, treachery.
felpa *f* plush; pile.
felpilla *f* chenille.
felpo *m* rug, doormat.
felpudo *a* plush; *m* doormat.
femenino *a* feminine, female.
fementido *a* false, faithless, perfidious.
fenecer *vi* to die, perish, pass away, depart this life.
fenecimiento *m* finish, end, termination, close.
fenicio *an* Phoenician.
fénix *a* unique, rare; *m* phoenix.
fenómeno *m* phenomenon, rarity, freak.
feo *a* ugly, plain, hideous, ill-favored, unsightly.
feracidad *f* fruitfulness, fertility.
feraz *a* fertile, productive.
féretro *m* hearse, bier, coffin.
feria *f* fair, market; holiday.
feriado *a* **día —** (*public*) holiday.
fermentación *f* fermentation.
fermentar *vi* to ferment, effervesce.
fermento *m* ferment, leaven; fermentation.
ferocidad *f* wildness, fierceness, savageness.
feroz *a* ferocious, wild, savage, fierce.
férreo *a* (*made of*) iron; harsh, stern, rigid.
ferretería *f* hardware, ironmongery; hardware store.
ferrocarril *m* railway, railroad; **— subterráneo** underground railway; **— aéreo** elevated railway.
ferrolano *an* (*native*) of El Ferrol.
ferrovía *f* railway.
ferroviario *a* railway; **compañía —a**

railway company; **obreros —s** railway employees.
fértil *a* rich, fertile; plentiful; lush.
fertilidad *f* fertility, fruitfulness, plenty, richness.
fertilizar *vt* to fertilize, enrich.
férula *f* rod, ferrule; splint.
férvido *a* fervid, ardent.
ferviente *a* fervent, ardent.
fervor *m* warmth, eagerness, enthusiasm, zeal; earnestness.
fervoroso *a* fervent; devout, zealous.
festejar *vt* to regale, feast; to woo, court; to make much of.
festejo *m* feast, entertainment; courtship, wooing.
festín *m* banquet, feast, entertainment, (*fam*) spread.
festinar *vi SA* to hurry, rush.
festividad *f* merrymaking, gaiety, holiday; riotousness; joviality.
festivo *a* festive, gay, jovial, merry; **día** — holiday.
festón *m* garland.
fétido *a* fetid, stinking, rank, malodorous.
feudo *m* fief, manor; feud.
fiado *a* on trust, reliable; **comprar al** — to buy on credit.
fiador *m* bondsman, guarantor; fastener; **salir** — to go surety (for somebody).
fiambre *m* cold meat, cold dish; hoary joke (*fam*) chestnut.
fiambrera *f* lunch basket.
fiambrería *f* shop where cold meats *etc* are sold.
fianza *f* surety, warrant, guarantee, security; **dar** — to give bail.
fiar *vt* to trust, entrust; to go surety for; to give credit; *vi* to rely on, reckon on; **es de** — he is reliable; *vr* to trust, depend.
fiasco *m* failure, flop.
fibra *f* fiber, filament; nerve.
ficción *m* fiction; fable; invention, tale.
ficticio *a* fictitious, made-up, imaginary.
ficha *f* chip; marker; card, index card.
fichero *m* card index, list, filing cabinet.
fidedigno *a* trustworthy, creditable.
fideicomiso *m* trust, responsibility.
fidelidad *f* fidelity, allegiance, loyalty; faithfulness, constancy.
fideos *m pl* vermicelli.
fiebre *f* fever, fever heat.
fiel *a* faithful, staunch, true, loyal; accurate; *pl* **—es** (*church*) congregation, the faithful; needle (*of a pair of scales*).
fieltro *m* felt, felt hat.
fiera *f* wild beast; termagant.
fiereza *f* ferocity, fierceness; ugliness.
fiero *a* cruel, fiery, savage, fierce; ugly.
fierro *m* iron.
fiesta *f* feast; merriment, merrymaking, gay time; holiday, festival; **media** — half-holiday.
fifiriche *a CR, Mex* thin, frail, weak.
figón *m* cheap eating house.
figura *f* figure, form, shape; mien, aspect; image.
figurar *vt* to figure, form, shape; *vi* — **entre** to come under (*category etc*); to be conspicuous; *vr* to imagine, fancy, suppose.
figurín *m* lay figure, model.
fija *f Arg* racing tip; **en** — without doubt, sure.
fijar *vt* to fix, fasten, affix, stick; to fix (*attention etc*); to set, fix (*date etc*); *vr* to settle; to rivet attention (*on*), look hard at.
fijo *a* fixed, steady, immobile, steadfast; determined; **precio** — controlled price.
fila *f* string, row, file; rank; **en** — in a row; abreast.
filantropía *f* philanthropy.
filántropo *m* philanthropist.
filatelia *f* philately, stamp collecting.
filete *m* fillet, ribbon; (*sew*) border; (*beef etc*) fillet.
filiación *f* filiation; connection; personal description.
filial *a* filial.
filigrana *f* filigree, watermark; spun wire work; delicacy.
Filipinas, las Islas *f pl* the Philippines.
filo *m* cutting edge (*of a knife*); dividing line.
filología *f* philology.
filomela *f* nightingale.
filón *m* lode, seam, vein (*of mine*).
filoso *a SA* sharp.
filosofía *f* philosophy; — **moral** ethics.
filósofo *m* philosopher.
filoxera *f* phylloxera.
filtrar *vt* to filter; *vi* to percolate.
filtro *m* filter.
fin *m* end; object, aim; **por** — at last; *pl* **a** — **de** (at) (about) the end of; — **de semana** weekend.
final *a* final, last; ultimate; *m* end; (*mus*) finale; *f* (*sport etc*) finals.
finalizar *vt* to finish.
financiar *vt SA* to finance.
financista *m SA* financier.
finanzas *fpl SA* finance.
finca *f* estate, (*private*) land.
fineza *f* fineness, delicacy; kindness.
fingir *vt* to feign, pretend.
finlandés *an* Finnish, Finn.
Finlandia *f* Finland.
fino *a* fine; slender.
firma *f* signature; **buena** — house or person of good standing (*commercially*).
firme *a* firm; solid, steady.
firmeza *f* firmness, strength, steadiness.
fiscal *a* fiscal; *m* attorney general.
fisco *m* exchequer.
fisgar *vt* to pry, peep; to nose into.

física *f* physics, natural philosophy.
físico *a* physical, bodily; *m* physician; bodily aspect.
fisonomía *f* physiognomy.
flaco *a* meager; thin; weak.
flagelar *vt* to scourge.
flagrante *a* flagrant.
flamante *a* brand new, the latest.
flamenco *a* **cante—** Andalusian folk-song (*esp of gypsies*); *m* flamingo.
flanco *m* flank, side.
flaquear *vi* to slacken; to give in; to dismay.
flaqueza *f* meagerness; weakness; frailty.
flauta *f* flute.
fleco *m* fringe, flounce.
flecha *f* arrow; spire.
flechar *vt* to dart; to 'get' (*inspire with sudden love*).
flechero *m* archer, bowman; shot.
flema *f* phlegm.
fletamento *m* charter(ing) (*of vessels*).
fletar *vt* to freight, charter; *vti Chi, Guat* to rub, scrub; *Cub, Mex* to leave quickly; *Arg* to gatecrash.
flete *m* freight; **falso—** dead freight.
flexible *a* flexible, willowy.
flojo *a* lax, weak, slack.
flor *f* blossom, flower; flour; **— y nata** the fine flower, the cream.
florecer *vi* to flourish, flower, blossom.
floreciente *a* flourishing, prosperous; blossoming.
florería *f SA* florist's shop.
florero *m* flowerpot; vase; florist.
floresta *f* glade; anthology, collection.
florido *a* florid; full of flowers, in bloom.
flota *f* fleet.
flotación *f* flotation; **línea de —** waterline.
flotante *a* floating.
flotar *vi* to float.
flote *m* floating; **a—** afloat.
flotilla *f* fleet.
fluctuación *f* fluctuation, oscillation.
fluctuar *vi* to fluctuate.
fluidez *f* fluidity; fluency.
fluido *a* fluid; *m* fluid.
fluir *vi* to flow; to run.
flujo *m* flow; flux.
fluvial *a* fluvial, river.
foca *f* seal, sealion.
foco *m* focus, center, core, cynosure; *SA* light bulb.
fofo *a* spongy, soft.
fogaje *m Arg, Mex* skin rash; *SA* sultry weather.
fogarata *f SA* bonfire, blaze.
fogata *f* bonfire, blaze.
fogón *m* hearth; stove, cooking range.
fogonero *m* stoker, fireman.
fogosidad *f* vivacity, fire, spirit, dash.
fogoso *a* fiery, impetuous, spirited.
follaje *m* foliage, leaves.
folletín *m* newspaper serial.
folleto *m* pamphlet, booklet.
follisca *f Col, Ven* dispute, quarrel.
fomentar *vt* to foment, promote.
fomento *m* fomentation; encouragement, promotion; **Ministro de —** Minister of Production.
fonda *f* inn, hostelry.
fondeadero *m* anchoring ground, anchorage.
fondear *vi* to cast anchor.
fondo *m* bottom, depth; disposition; background; capital; **— de amortización** sinking fund; **fondos vitalicios** life annuities; **a —** perfectly, very well, thoroughly; **en el—** at bottom.
fonógrafo *m* record player, phonograph.
fontanería *f* hydraulic engineering; plumbing.
fontanero *m* plumber.
forajido *m* highwayman, bandit, outlaw.
forastero *m* stranger, outsider, visitor (*from away*); **guía de —s** official guidebook.
forcejear *vi* to struggle, grapple with, wrestle (*to be free*).
forcejo *m* striving, struggling, violent effort(s).
forja *f* forge, smelting furnace.
forjar *vt* to forge; to frame, shape; to counterfeit, concoct.
forma *f* form, shape; **de — que** so that.
formación *f* formation, shape.
formal *a* formal, regular; steady, dependable (*person*); sincere; courteous, conventional, stiff (*in manners*); definite (*promise*); official; explicit.
formalidad *f* formality, solemnity; requirement, practice, convention(s), seriousness.
formalizar *vt* to draw up, set down, regularize.
formar *vt* to form, shape.
formato *m* format.
formidable *a* formidable, tremendous.
formón *m* chisel.
fórmula *f* formula; recipe; prescription.
formulario *m SA* form, blank.
fornido *a* robust, stout, sturdy.
foro *m* forum, bar; (*theat*) backstage, backdrop.
forraje *m* forage, fodder.
forrajear *vt* to forage.
forrar *vt* to line (*clothes*); to put a cover on (*book etc*).
forro *m* lining, backing, sheathing; (*book*) jacket.
fortalecer *vt* to strengthen; to support, encourage.
fortaleza *f* fortitude, courage, resolution, endurance; fortress, stronghold.
fortín *m* blockhouse.
fortuito *a* fortuitous, accidental.

fortuna *f* fortune; good luck; chance, fate; **probar —** to take a chance.
forzar (ue) *vt* to force, compel; to break in (*door*); to overpower; to ravish.
forzoso *a* forcible, needful; inescapable, obligatory.
forzudo *a* strong, vigorous, stout.
fosa *f* grave.
fosforescencia *f* phosphorescence.
fósforo *m* phosphorus; match.
fósil *a m* fossil.
foso *m* pit; moat, ditch.
foto *f* photo(graph).
fotografiar *vt* to photograph.
fotógrafo *m* photographer.
fotostática *f* photostat.
frac *m* dress coat; swallow-tail coat.
fracasar *vi* to fail, fall through.
fracaso *m* failure, frustration; (*fam*) washout.
fracción *f* fraction.
fraccionar *vt* to divide in fractions; to break into pieces.
fractura *f* breach, fracture.
fragancia *f* fragrance, perfume.
fragata *f* frigate.
frágil *a* breakable, brittle, fragile.
fragilidad *f* fragility, frailty.
fragmento *m* fragment, piece.
fragor *m* noise, crash, tumult.
fragoroso *a* noisy, rowdy.
fragoso *a* craggy; trackless, impenetrable; noisy.
fragua *f* forge.
fraguar *vt* to contrive; to forge.
fraile *m* friar, monk.
frambuesa *f* raspberry.
francés *an* French; Frenchman.
Francia *f* France.
Francisca *f* Frances.
Francisco *m* Francis.
franco *a* frank, generous, open, free; **puerto —** free port; **— a bordo** free on board; **— de porte** post-paid; *m* franc.
franela *f* flannel.
franja *f* band, trimming, braid, fringe.
franquear *vt* to frank (*letters*); to enfranchise; to open up, make free offer of; *vr* to unburden oneself, tell one's hidden thoughts.
franqueo *m* postage, franking.
franqueza *f* frankness, freedom, sincerity; **con toda —** quite frankly, to be quite honest.
frasco *m* bottle, flask.
frase *f* phrase, sentence; **— hecha** stock phrase.
fraseología *f* phraseology; wording.
fraternal *a* brotherly.
fraude *m* fraud, imposture.
fraudulento *a* fraudulent.
fray *m* Friar, Brother.
frazada *f* blanket.
frecuencia *f* frequency.
fregar *vt* to scrub, scour, wash; *SA* annoy, tease.
fregona *f* kitchenmaid.
freír *vt* to fry.
frejol *m* (*black*) bean, kidney bean.
frenesí *m* frenzy; madness.
frenético *a* frantic, furious.
freno *m* bridle; brake; curb, control; restriction.
frente *f* forehead; face; *m* (*mil*) front; (*pol*) front, party; **— por —, en —** directly opposite; **de —** front first or forward; (*mil*) abreast.
fresa *f* strawberry.
fresco *a* fresh, cool; fresh, impudent; *m* cool temperature; **al —** out of doors, in the cool; **tomar el —** to take (a stroll) (the air); **agua —a** fresh, cold water.
frescura *f* coolness, calm, freshness, openness.
fresno *m* ash tree.
friable *a* brittle.
frialdad *f* coldness, indifference, coolness.
fricción *f* friction; rubbing; shampoo.
frigidez *f* frigidity.
frigorífico *a* refrigerating; *m* refrigerator.
frijol *m* kidney bean.
frío *a m* cold; **hace —** it is cold; **tengo —** I am cold.
friolera *f* trifle, bagatelle, mere nothing.
frisar *vi* to frizzle; **— con en** to be (around, about, near) (*of age*).
friso *m* wainscot, dado.
frito *a* fried.
frívolo *a* light, frivolous, empty (headed).
frondio *a* *Col* peevish; *Mex* dirty, untidy.
frondoso *a* leafy, luxuriant (*foliage*).
frontera *f* frontier, border, limit.
frontispicio *m* frontispiece; front; title page.
frontón *m* court (*of pelota, handball, fives etc*).
frotar *vt* to rub.
frote *m* rubbing, friction.
fructífero *a* fruitful; successful, profitable.
fructificar *vi* to fructify, give fruit; to profit.
fructuoso *a* fruitful, useful.
frugal *a* frugal, sparse, economical, thrifty.
fruición *f* enjoyment, relish.
fruncir *vt* (*sew*) to gather; to contract, reduce; (*eyes*) to pucker; **— las cejas** to frown, knit the brows.
frustrar *vt* to frustrate, balk, thwart; *vr* to fail, miscarry.
fruta *f* fruit, result, product.
fruto *m* fruit; produce, profit, results; **dar —** to yield fruit.
fuego *m* fire, heat, vigor; **hacer —** to fire (*on*); **pegar — a** to set fire to; *pl* **—s artificiales** fireworks.
fuente *f* source, spring (*of water*), fountain; dish.
fuera *ad* out of, outside, without

— **de sí** beside oneself; — **de** besides, beyond, in addition to.
fuero *m* charter (*of laws*); jurisdiction, power.
fuerte *a* strong, stout, powerful; *m* fortification.
fuerza *f* strength, force; **a — de** by dint of; **a la —** against the will, willy-nilly.
fuetazo *m SA* stroke with a whip.
fuete *m SA* whip.
fuga *f* flight, escape; leak.
fugacidad *f* brevity, fleetingness.
fugarse *vr* to run away.
fugaz *a* fugitive; brief, passing; **estrella —** shooting star.
fugitivo *a* fugitive, brief, transitory.
fulano *m* So-and-So; — **de Tal** Mr. So-and-So.
fulgor *m* brilliancy, glow.
fulminante *a* crushing.
fulminar *vt* to fulminate; to storm at; to boil over at.
fullero *m* sharper, cheat (*at cards*).
fumador *m* smoker.
fumar *vt* to smoke.
fumigar *vt* to fumigate.
función *f* performance, show; function, ceremony; duty, function.
funcional *a* functional.
funcionar *vi* to operate, work, perform; **no funciona** out of order, not working.
funcionario *m* public official.
funda *f* cover, case, wrapper, sheath.
fundación *f* foundation; establishment; endowed institution; erection.
fundamental *a* fundamental, essential.
fundamentar *vt* to substantiate; to base.
fundamento *m* foundation, ground; principle.
fundar *vt* to found, establish; to endow; to base.
fundición *f* melting, fusion; foundry.
fundido *a SA* ruined.
fundir *vt* to melt, smelt (*metals*); *vr* to fuse; to join.
fúnebre *a* funereal, melancholy, lugubrious.
funesto *a* untoward, lamentable, unfortunate.
furgón *m* (*rl*) luggage van, baggage car.
furia *f* fury, anger; zeal.
furibundo *a* furious, wild.
furioso *a* furious, frantic, violent.
furor *m* rage, anger, frenzy, passion.
furris *a Mex, Ven* bad, contemptible.
furrusca *f Col* quarrel, brawl.
furtivo *a* furtive, sly, clandestine.
fusil *m* rifle, musket, gun.
fusilar *vt* to execute, shoot (*by musketry*).
fusión *f* liquefaction, melting; union, fusion.
fustán *m SA* petticoat.
fuste *m* tree (*of saddle*); shaft (*of lance*).
fustigar *vt* to whip, castigate.
fútbol *m* football.
futbolista *m* footballer.
fútil *a* futile.
futilidad *f* futility, weakness.
futre *m SA* fop, dandy.
futuro *a* future, coming; *m* future, future tense.

G

gabacho *m* (*fam*) Frenchman, Frenchified Spanish.
gabán *m* overcoat.
gabinete *m* cabinet; private parlor; study; — **de lectura** reading room.
gaceta *f* gazette.
gacetilla *f* gossip column, scraps of gossip.
gachas *f pl* porridge, slops.
gacho *a* drooping; **orejas gachas** ears down, crestfallen.
gachupín *m Mex* Spaniard.
gafas *f pl* spectacles, glasses.
gago *m Per, PR, Ven* stammerer.
gaguear *vi SA* to stutter.
gaita *f* flageolet; — **gallega** bagpipe.
gaje *m* wages, pay; *pl* perquisites, fees.
gajo *m* branch (*of tree*); section (*of orange*); prong (*of fork*).
gala *f* gala; wit, elegance; full dress; *pl* finery, regalia; **hacer — de** to display proudly, show off.
galán *m* courtier, escort, lover; **primer —** (*theat*) lead; *a* gallant, flattering.
galante *a* gallant, polished, cavalier.
galantear *vt* to court, woo, flirt with.
galanteo *m* courtesy; courtship, wooing.
galantería *f* politeness, courtesy; grace; compliment, fine words.
galardón *m* reward, guerdon.
galardonar *vt* to reward.
galeote *m* galley slave.
galera *f* galley; van, heavy coach.
galería *f* gallery; corridor.
galés *an* Welsh, Welshman.
Gales, País de *m* Wales.
galgo *m* greyhound.
galimatías *m* gibberish.
galón *m* (*mil*) braid, stripe, galloon; gallon (*measure*); band.
galopar *vi* to gallop.
galope *m* gallop; **a —** in haste, hurriedly; **a — tendido** at full gallop.
galopín *m* scoundrel; kitchen boy.
galpón *m Arg* shed.
galucha *f CA, Col, Ven* gallop, haste.
galuchar *vi Col, CA, Ven* to gallop.
galvanizar *vt* to galvanize.
gallardete *m* pennant.

gallardía *f* gallantry, bravery; elegance, graceful deportment.
gallardo *a* elegant, brisk, spirited.
gallego *an* Galician.
galleta *f* biscuit.
gallina *f* hen; — **de Guinea** guinea hen; — **ciega** blind man's buff.
gallinaza *f* buzzard.
gallinero *m* poultry yard, poultry dealer.
gallo *m* cock, rooster.
gallote *a CR, Mex* forward, free.
gamo *m* fallow deer, buck.
gamuza *f* chamois; chamois leather.
gana *f* desire, mind, inclination; mood; **de buena** — right willingly; **sin** — unwillingly; **tener —s** to have an appetite, be hungry; **tener —s de** to want to, feel like.
ganadería *f* cattle ranch; cattle raising; cattle, stock.
ganado *m* cattle, livestock; — **lanar** sheep; — **de cerda** swine.
ganancia *f* gain, profit; *pl* **—s y pérdidas** profit and loss.
ganapán *m* porter; carrier.
ganar *vt* to win, gain, profit by; to earn; to win over, convince; to beat (*in competition etc*).
gancho *m* hook, crook; *m SA* hairpin.
gandido *a SA* gluttonous.
gandul *m* idler, loafer.
ganga *f* windfall, bargain; (*min*) gangue.
gangrena *f* gangrene.
gansa *f* goose.
gansada *f* stupid action, senseless thing.
ganso *m* gander; wag, ass; lazybones.
ganzúa *f* false key. skeleton key.
gañán *m* day laborer, farmhand.
gapuchín *m Mex* Spanish settler.
garabato *m* scribble, scrawl; grapnel, hook.
garante *a m* guarantor.
garantía *f* warranty; bail.
garantizar *vt* to guarantee, answer for; to assure.
garapiñado *a* **almendras —as** sugared almonds, pralines.
garbanzo *m* chickpea.
garbo *m* gracefulness, grace, jauntiness, dash.
garboso *a* graceful, gallant, dashing.
garfa *f* claw.
garfio *m* hook, gaff.
garganta *f* throat; gorge, ravine.
gargantilla *f* necklace.
gárgara *f* gargle.
gárgola *f* gargoyle.
garita *f* sentry box; cubbyhole.
garito *m* gambling den.
garlopa *f* plane, jackplane.
garoso *a Col, Ven* greedy.
garra *f* claw, talon, clutch.
garrafa *f* carafe.
garrafón *m* large carafe, demijohn.
garrapata *f* cattle tick.
garrido *a* handsome, graceful.
garrote *m* bludgeon, club; garrote.
garrucha *f* pulley, sheave.
garrulería *f* chatter, babble.
gárrulo *a* prattling, garrulous.
garza *f* heron.
garzo *a* blue-eyed.
gas *m* gas; fume.
gasa *f* gauze, chiffon.
gaseoso *a* gaseous; *f* mineral water.
gasolina *f* petrol, gasoline.
gasómetro *m* gasometer.
gastado *a* worn, used; blasé.
gastador *m* spendthrift.
gastar *vt* to spend; waste, use, consume; to sport (*clothes etc*); *vr* to wear out.
gasto *m* expense, cost(s); waste; *pl* (*com*) charges, costs.
gata *f* cat, she-cat; **a gatas** crawling, on all fours.
gatear *vi* to go on all fours; *vt* to steal.
gatillo *m* trigger; catch.
gato *m* cat, tomcat; **dar — por liebre** to sell mutton as lamb.
gatuno *a* catlike, feline.
gauchada *f Arg* favor; *SA* artifice.
gaucho *m* cowboy, herdsman (*in Argentine*).
gaveta *f* (money) till, drawer.
gavilán *m* sparrowhawk; nib (*of pen*).
gavilla *f* sheaf (*of corn*); gang.
gaviota *f* seagull.
gayo *a* gay, showy.
gazapera *f* warren; den.
gazapo *m* rabbit; blunder.
gazmoño *a* prudish, hypocritical; *m* prig.
gaznate *m* windpipe, throttle.
gelatinoso *a* gelatinous.
gélido *a* frigid.
gema *f* gem.
gemelo *m* twin; *pl* binoculars, opera glasses; cufflinks.
gemido *m* moan, lamentation, groan.
gemir (i) *vi* to groan, grieve.
genealogía *f* genealogy, lineage.
generación *f* generation; growth.
general *a m* general; **en** — generally.
generalidad *f* generality.
generalización *f* generalization.
generalizar *vt* to generalize; *vr* to spread, become general, common.
generar *vt* to generate.
genérico *a* generic.
género *m* genus, kind; gender (*grammar*); stuff, cloth; *pl* goods merchandise; dry goods.
generosidad *f* generosity.
generoso *a* noble, liberal, strong.
génesis *m* Genesis; *f* origin.
genial *a* inspired, brilliant, superb.
genio *m* genius; character, temper(ament), humor, gift.
gente *f* people, crowd; — **menuda** youngsters.
gentil *a* graceful, genteel; Gentile.
gentileza *f* grace, courtesy, charm, breeding, gentility; urbanity.

gentilhombre *m* gentleman.
gentilicio *a* national, tribal; hereditary.
gentío *m* crowd, crush (*of people*).
genuflexión *f* genuflexion, bowing the knee.
genuino *a* genuine, pure.
geografía *f* geography.
geógrafo *m* geographer.
geología *f* geology.
geometría *f* geometry.
gerencia *f* management.
gerente *m* manager, executive.
germen *m* germ, bed, source.
germinar *vi* to bud, germinate.
gesticulación *f* gesticulation.
gesta *f* feats, achievements; ballad, romance.
gestión *f* management, conduct, negotiation.
gestionar *vt* to manage, deal, arrange.
gesto *m* gesture; face.
gestor *m* promoter.
giboso *a* crook-, hump-backed.
gigante *a m* giant.
gijonés *an* (*inhabitant*) of Gijón.
gimnasio *m* gymnasium.
gimnástica *f* gymnastics.
ginebra *f* gin; **G—** Geneva.
gira *f* tour, excursion.
girado *m* drawee.
girador *m* drawer.
giralda *f* vane, weathercock.
girar *vi* to revolve, gyrate, spin; *vt* to draw (*bills of exchange*); **— a cargo de** to draw on.
girasol *m* sunflower.
giro *m* turn, course, rotation; course, tendency, trend; draft, exchange; **— postal** postal order.
gis *m* crayon.
gitano *an* gypsy.
glacial *a* ice-cold, frigid.
glándula *f* gland.
glasé *m* glacé, glacé silk.
glauco *a* sea-green.
glicerina *f* glycerine.
globo *m* globe, sphere, Earth; **en —** in bulk, in the lump.
gloria *f* glory, renown; bliss, seventh heaven; splendor.
gloriarse *vr* to glory in, boast.
glorieta *f* (*aut*) roundabout, traffic circle.
glorificación *f* glorification.
glorificar *vt* to glorify, worship, laud.
glorioso *a* glorious.
glosa *f* gloss, commentary.
glosar *vt* to annotate, provide commentary on, comment; to audit accounts.
glosario *m* glossary.
glotón *a* gluttonous; *m* glutton.
glotonería *f* gluttony.
glutinoso *a* glutinous, viscous, sticky.
gobernación *f* government; **Ministerio de la G—** Ministry of the Interior
gobernador *m* governor.
gobernante *a* governing; *m* ruler.
gobernar *vt* to rule, govern; to regulate, control; to steer.
gobierno *m* government, cabinet; rule, control, direction, management.
goce *m* enjoyment (*of*).
godo *an* Goth; *SA* (*pej*) Spaniard.
gofio *m SA* roasted corn.
gol *m* goal.
gola *f* throat, gullet.
goleta *f* schooner.
golfo *m* bay, gulf, abyss; street arab, urchin.
golilla *f* ruff, gorget; law officer; necktie.
golondrina *f* swallow.
golosina *f* delicacy, titbit, fancy dish; sweet tooth.
goloso *a* sweet-toothed.
golpe *m* stroke, blow, clash; **de un —** all at once, in one fell swoop; **— de estado** coup d'état.
golpear *vt* to strike, beat, hammer on, knock.
gollete *m* throttle, neck.
goma *f* gum, mucilage; rubber, eraser; **— elástica** indiarubber.
gonce *m* hinge.
góndola *f* gondola.
gongorino *a* euphuistic.
gordo *a* fat, fleshy; *m* suet, lard.
gorgojo *m* mite, grub.
gorguera *f* ruff.
gorila *m* gorilla.
gorjear *vi* to sing, trill, warble.
gorjeo *m* warble, song (*of birds*).
gorra *f* cap, bonnet; **(ir) de —** without paying, on the cheap; **— en mano** cap in hand; **— de visera** peaked cap.
gorrión *m* sparrow.
gorro *m* cap; **— de dormir** nightcap.
gorrón *m* (*mech*) pillow, swing block; sponger, toady.
gota *f* drop; (*med*) gout.
gotear *vi* to drop, drip, leak.
gotera *f* dripping, leak; gutter.
gotero *m Arg, Mex, PR* dropper.
gótico *a* Gothic.
gotoso *a* gouty.
gozar *vt* to enjoy, have delight in; *vr* to rejoice.
gozne *m* hinge.
gozo *m* joy, delight, happiness, bliss.
gozoso *a* overjoyed, delighted, cheerful, content.
grabación *f* (*action*) engraving; recording.
grabado *a* engraved; etched, stamped; *m* engraving, print; **— en madera** woodcut.
grabador *m* engraver, etcher.
grabar *vt* to engrave, carve; to impress (*on mind*); to record (*on tape*); **— en hueco** to emboss.
gracejada *f CA, Mex* clownish joke.
gracejo *m* wittiness, drollness.
gracia *f* grace(fulness); kindness,

grant; elegance, wit, skill; pardon, mercy, gift; joke, wittiness; charm; **caer en** — to please; **tener** — to be funny; **dar— a** to amuse; *pl* thanks; **dar las —s** to thank, express one's thanks.
grácil *a* thin, slender.
gracioso *a* graceful; witty, funny; entertaining; charming, delightful; *m* (*theat*) fool, jester, clown, funny man.
grada *f* step (*staircase*); terrace (*in amphitheater*).
gradación *f* gradation.
gradería *f* steps, terrace; rows of seats, tiers of seats.
grado *m* grade, degree, rank, class; **de** — willingly.
graduación *f* graduation; classification, estimate.
gradual *a* gradual.
graduar *vt* to gauge, measure; to graduate; *vr* to take a degree.
gráfico *a* graphic, vivid.
gragea *f* small colored candy.
grajo *m* jackdaw, jay.
grama *f SA* grass.
gramática *f* grammar; — **parda** horse-sense.
gramo *m* gram.
gramófono *m* gramophone, phonograph.
gran *a see* **grande.**
Gran Bretaña *f* Great Britain.
grana *f* scarlet color.
granada *f* pomegranate; hand grenade, shell.
granadino *an* (*inhabitant*) of Granada.
granado *a* select, choice, notable.
granar *vi* to seed.
granate *m* garnet.
grande *a* large, big; great, grand; *m* grandee.
grandeza *f* greatness, grandeur, grandness.
grandioso *a* grand, magnificent, overwhelming.
granel *m* heap; **a** — in a heap, in bulk.
granero *m* granary barn.
granito *m* granite.
granizada *f* hailstorm.
granizar *vi* to hail.
granizo *m* hail; hailstorm; **piedra de** — hailstone.
granja *f* grange, farm, farmhouse.
granjear *vt* to earn; to profit; *vr* to get, obtain, win over.
granjería *f* advantage, profit (*in a bad sense*).
grano *m* grain, seed, corn; pimple, spot (*on face*); *pl* cereals; **ir al** — to come to the point.
granoso *a* granular.
granuja *m* rogue, lazy dog; waif, urchin.
grapa *f* clamp, clutch.
grasa *f* grease, fat.
grasiento *a* greasy, oily, filthy.
gratificación *f* gratuity, reward, tip.
gratificar *vt* to reward, gratify, satisfy.
gratis *ad* gratis, free.
gratitud *f* gratitude, gratefulness.
grato *a* agreeable, pleasant, acceptable.
gratuito *a* gratuitous, unnecessary, uncalled-for.
grava *f* gravel.
gravamen *m* charge, obligation; tax, burden; lien.
gravar *vt* to tax, burden; to oppress.
grave *a* grave, serious, dangerous; heavy; important.
gravedad *f* gravity; circumspection, sobriety, seriousness.
grávido *a* pregnant (*with meaning*).
gravitación *f* gravitation.
gravitar *vt* to gravitate, weigh down.
gravoso *a* hard, grievous; onerous.
graznar *vi* to croak, caw.
graznido *m* croak, croaking, cawing.
Grecia *f* Greece.
greco *an* Greek, Grecian.
greda *f* clay, marl, chalk.
gredoso *a* clayey, marly.
gregario *a* gregarious.
Gregorio *m* Gregory.
gregüescos *m pl* wide breeches.
gremio *m* guild, trade union, fraternity, body.
greña *f* matted hair, mop (*of hair*).
greñudo *a* dishevelled.
gresca *f* wrangle, quarrel.
grey *f* herd, flock; congregation (*of parish*).
grial *m* grail.
griego *an* Greek; Grecian.
grieta *f* crevice, fissure, crack, chink.
grietarse *vr* to crack, split; to become chapped (*of hands*).
grifo *m* griffin; (*water*) tap, faucet; *a* curly, kinky.
grillo *m* cricket; *pl* fetters, irons.
grima *f* displeasure; *SA* sadness.
gringo *m SA* North American, foreigner.
gripe *f* influenza.
gris *a m* gray.
grita *f* clamor, shouting, uproar.
gritar *vi* to shout, shriek, call out, bawl.
gritería *f* shouting, clamor.
grito *m* shout, cry, howl; **hablar a gritos** to shout.
Groenlandia *f* Greenland.
grosella *f* red currant; — **blanca** gooseberry.
grosería *f* rudeness, ill-manners, coarseness.
grosero *a* gross, coarse; rude, uncivil; insensitive.
grosor *m* thickness.
grotesco *a* grotesque, farcical, ridiculous.
grúa *f* crane, derrick.
gruesa *f* gross.
grueso *a* thick, fat, stout, large; *m* thickness; main body (*of army etc*).

grulla *f* (*orni*) crane.
grullo *n* *Arg, Cub, Mex, Ven* one-dollar coin; *Arg* stallion.
grumete *m* cabin boy.
grumo *m* clot, cluster.
gruñido *m* grunt, growl.
gruñir *vi* to grunt; to grumble; to creak.
grupa *f* crupper, rump (*of horse*).
grupo *m* group, clump.
gruta *f* cavern; grotto.
guaca *f* *Bol, Per* Indian grave, buried treasure.
guáchara *f* *Cub, PR* lie, fib.
guacho *m* *SA* orphan; *Arg, Chi* wild plant, tree; bastard.
guadamecí *m* printed embossed leather.
guadaña *f* scythe.
guadañar *vt* to scythe, mow.
guádua *f* *Col, Ec, Ven* bamboo cane.
guagua *f* *SA* baby; *Cub* bus, streetcar; **de —** free, gratis.
guaina *m* *Arg, Bol, Chi* boy, youth.
guajalote *m* *Mex* turkey.
gualdo *a* yellow.
gualdrapa *f* horse-trappings, sumpter cloth.
guangocho *a* *Mex* broad, loose.
guano *m* guano, dung, fertilizer.
guantada *f* slap.
guante *m* glove.
guapo *a* neat, spruce, beautiful, handsome, bonny; gallant; *m* gallant, beau; bully.
guaraca *f* *SA* sling. whip.
guarache *m* *Mex* sandal, tire patch.
guarapo *m* *SA* juice of the sugar cane.
guarapón *m* *Arg, Chi, Per* wide-brimmed hat.
guarda *m* keeper; *Arg* bus conductor; **— de coto** gamekeeper; *f* custody, guard.
guardabosque *m* gamekeeper.
guardacostas *m* coastguard; revenue cutter.
guardado *a* guarded, cautious; put away, hidden.
guardapolvo *m* dust cover; *Arg* overall.
guardar *vt* to keep, guard, preserve, watch over; **— silencio** to maintain silence; *vr* to abstain from, avoid.
guardarropa *m* wardrobe; cloakroom.
guardavía *m* signalman.
guardia *f* guard, watch; protection; *m* policeman; guardsman; **estar de —** to be on duty; **estar en —** to be on one's guard.
guardián *m* guardian, watchman.
guardilla *f* garret, attic.
guarecer *vt* to shelter; *vr* to shelter from, take (refuge, cover).
guaricha *f* *Col, Ec, Ven* female, woman.
guarida *f* den, haunt, lair; refuge, shelter.
guarismo *m* (*math*) figure, cipher.
guarnecer *vt* to garnish, furbish, bind, face, adorn; to garrison.
guarnición *f* garniture, trimming, edging, piping, setting (*of jewels*); garrison; *pl* harness, traces.
guarro *a* filthy; *m* hog.
guasa *f* jest, irony, facetiousness.
guasanga *f* *SA* noisy revelry.
guasanguero *a* *SA* jolly, merry.
guasca *f* *SA* cord, thong, whip.
guasería *f* *Arg, Chi* dullness, rudeness.
guaso *a* *Chi* rustic; *Arg, Chi, Cub, Ec* coarse, uncouth.
guasón *m* wag, leg-puller; *a* waggish, facetious.
guasquear *vt* *SA* to whip, scourge.
guatemalteco *an* Guatemalan.
guateque *m* party; *SA* country dance.
guayaba *f* guava.
guayaca *f* *Arg, Bol, Chi* bag, sack.
Guayana *f* Guiana.
guayapil *m* *SA* loose Indian dress.
guayaquileño *an* (*inhabitant*) of Guayaquil.
gubernativo *a* governmental.
guedeja *f* shock, hank (*of hair*), forelock, mane.
guerra *f* war, warfare; **— a muerte** war without quarter; **— fría** cold war; **dar —** to annoy, plague, bother.
guerrear *vi* to wage war.
guerrero *a* martial; *m* warrior, soldier.
guerrilla *f* guerrilla.
guerrillero *m* guerrilla.
guía *f* guidebook, guide sign; (*telephone*) directory; *mf* guide, leader.
guiar *vt* to lead, guide; counsel; *vr* to be led.
guija *f* pebble.
guijarro *m* pebble, cobblestone.
guijo *m* road gravel.
guillotina *f* guillotine.
guinda *f* mazard berry.
guindal *m* mazard tree.
guindar *vt* to hang up.
guindilla *f* red pepper.
guindo *m* mazard tree.
guinea *f* guinea (*coin*).
guiñapo *m* rag, tatter.
guiñar *vt* to wink.
guión *m* standard, gonfalon; hyphen; synopsis (*of lecture, film*).
guirnalda *f* garland, wreath.
guisa *f* wise; manner; **a — de** in the manner of.
guisado *m* stew.
guisante *m* pea; **— de olor** sweet-pea.
guisar *vt* to cook; to arrange.
guiso *m* cooked dish, stew, concoction, preparation.
guita *f* twine.
guitarra *f* guitar.
guito *a* *SA* treacherous, vicious.
gula *f* gluttony.
gusano *m* caterpillar, worm; **— de seda** silkworm.

gustar *vt* to taste; to please; **— de** to like. be fond of.
gusto *m* taste, flavor; pleasure; **dar — a** to satisfy, gratify.
gustoso *a* tasty, palatable; willing, well-disposed, with pleasure.
gutural *a* guttural.

H

¡ha! *excl* ah! alas!
haba *f* bean, broad bean.
Habana, la *f* Havana.
habano *m* (Havana) cigar.
habar *m* beanfield.
haber *vt* to have, possess, own; to hold; **— menester** to be in need of; **— de** to have to; **dos años ha** two years ago; **habérselas con** to have a bone to pick with, have to do with; **habidos y por haber** present and future; *m* property, estate, credit.
habichuela *f* string bean, kidney bean, butter bean.
hábil *a* able, clever, intelligent, skillful, agile, handy.
habilidad *f* ability, capacity, dexterity, knack.
habilidoso *a* accomplished, adroit, ingenious.
habilitación *f* qualification; fitting-out, equipping, outfit(ting), arrangement, preparation.
habilitado *m* paymaster; *a* qualified, competent, authorized.
habilitar *vt* to qualify; to equip, to fit out; to enable.
hábilmente *ad* ably, smartly, neatly, cleverly.
habitación *f* abode, dwelling; room.
habitante *m* inhabitant, resident, native (*of*).
habitar *vt* to inhabit, dwell, reside.
hábito *m* habit (*of monk etc*); robes, dress, garment; custom; **— de Santiago** order of Saint James; **colgar los —s** to leave the priesthood, throw up career.
habitual *a* habitual, customary, common, frequent.
habituar *vt* to accustom, inure; *vr* to get accustomed to, get used to.
habla *f* speech, dialect, local speech; conversation, talk; **perder el —** to lose one's speech; **al —** speaking (*beginning of telephone conversation*), within hailing distance.
hablador *m* gabbler, talker, chatterbox.
habladuría *f* gossip, slanderous talk.
hablantín *m* gabbler, talker.
hablar *vi* to speak, talk, harangue; *vt* to say, to give expression to; **— alto** to talk loudly, raise the voice; **— por —** to talk for talking's sake; **— a tontas y a locas** to talk without rhyme or reason; **— por los codos** to talk nineteen to the dozen, to talk one's head off; **— entre dientes** to mutter.
hablilla *f* rumor, whisper, scrap of gossip.
hacedero *a* feasible, practicable.
hacedor *m* manager, steward; **H—** Maker, God.
hacendado *m* landowner, proprietor, man of property.
hacendar *vt* to deal in real estate.
hacendero *a* industrious, hard-working.
hacendoso *a* diligent, spry, zealous, hard-working, bustling.
hacer *vt* to make, produce, build, compose, create, practice, cause, to prepare (*meal*); make (*bed*); to convince; to amount to; **hace calor** it is warm; **hace tiempo** long ago; *vi* to matter, mean; **no hace al caso** it doesn't meet the case; **— de** to act as; **— por** to try to; *vr* to become, develop; **— su agosto** to reap one's harvest; **— agua** to leak; **— alarde de** to boast of, display; **— bancarrota** to fail, become bankrupt; **— la barba** to shave; **— caso de** to notice, pay attention to; **— chacota** to ridicule; **— hablar** to force to speak; **— hacer** to have made (done *etc*); **— que hacemos** to pretend to be busy; **— juego** to match, suit; **— memoria** to remember, to try to remember; **— (un) papel** to cut a figure; **— perder los estribos** to break (*his*) self-control; **— presente** to remind; **— saber** to impart (*knowledge*), bring to one's knowledge; **hacerse a la vela** to set sail; **— la vista gorda** to close one's eyes to.
hacia *prep* toward, to; **— adelante** forward; **— atrás** back, backward.
hacienda *f* estate, property, fortune; finance; farm, plantation, ranch; *Arg* cattle; **Ministro de H—** Chancellor of the Exchequer (*Spain*); **— pública** treasury, finances.
hacina *f* stack, rick; heap.
hacinamiento *m* heaping, heap, hoard(ing up), piling up.
hacha *f* ax, hatchet; torch, flambeau; **paje de —** link boy.
hachazo *m* blow of an ax.
hache *f* name of the letter H.
hada *f* fairy.
hado *m* fate, destiny.
halagar *vt* to cajole, flatter, wheedle.
halago *m* cajolery, flattery, adulation, allurement, blandishment.
halagüeño *a* attractive, alluring; hopeful; flattering, complimentary; auspicious.
halar *vt* (*naut*) to haul, pull on.
halcón *m* hawk.
halconero *m* falconer.
hálito *m* breath, vapor.
hallado *a* found; **bien —** welcome; **mal —** uneasy.
hallar *vt* to find, come across, find

out, to discover, to meet with; *vr* to happen to be, be, feel (*health*).
hallazgo *m* find, discovery, good luck.
hamaca *f* hammock.
hambre *f* hunger, appetite, longing, desire; famine.
hambrear *vt* to hunger, starve.
hambriento *a* hungry, starved, ravenous.
hampa *f* fraternity of rogues.
hampón *m* rowdy, bully.
haragán *m* lounger, idler; *a* idle, indolent.
haraganear *vi* to loiter, loaf around.
harapiento *a* ragged, in rags and tatters.
harapo *m* rag, tatter.
haraposo *a* ragged.
harina *f* flour, meal; powder, dust.
harinero *m* dealer in flour.
harmonía *f see* **armonía** .
hartar *vt* to stuff, gorge, fill up; *vr* to satiate, glut, satisfy.
harto *a* full, satisfied, fed-up (*with*); enough, quite, amply.
hartura *f* satiety; plethora.
hasta *prep* till, until; up to; **— no más** to the limit, utmost; **— luego** so long, bye-bye; *cj* even.
hastiar *vt* to bore, cloy, revolt.
hastío *m* loathing, disgust.
hatillo *m* small bundle; **coger el —** to pack up one's traps.
hato *m* herd (*cattle*), flock (*sheep*); *SA* farm, estate; apparel.
haxo *m Col* coca.
haya *f* beech tree.
Haya, la *f* The Hague.
haz *m* bundle, faggot; sheaf; *f* face (*of earth etc*); right side (*of cloth etc*); *pl* fasces.
hazaña *f* heroic feat, exploit; *pl* prowess.
hazmerreír *m* guy, laughing stock.
he *ad* **—me aquí** here I am; **—le aquí** here he comes; etc.
hebdomadario *a m* weekly.
hebilla *f* buckle, clasp (*on shoe*).
hebra *f* filament, strand, thread; length (*of cotton*); needleful.
hebreo *an* Hebrew.
hectárea *f* hectare.
hechicería *f* sorcery, witchcraft; fascination.
hechicero *m* sorcerer, wizard, enchanter; *a* fascinating, irresistible.
hechizar *vt* to bewitch.
hechizo *m* spell, enchantment; trance; *a* artificial.
hecho *a* made, done; ready-made; **de —** in fact, de facto; **— y derecho** roundly, completely, in fact and in theory; *m* act, fact, deed, event.
hechura *f* turn, make; build, form; handiwork; tailoring, cut.
hediondez *f* stench.
hediondo *a* foul-smelling, fetid; *m* polecat, skunk.
hedor *m* stink, stench.
helada *f* frost.
heladera *f* refrigerator.
heladería *f* ice-cream shop.
helado *a* icy, glacial, freezing, frozen, frostbitten; *m* ice cream.
helar (ie) *vi* to freeze; to discourage.
helecho *m* bracken, fern.
hélice *f* helix; screw, propeller.
hembra *f* female; nut, screw, brace.
hemisferio *m* hemisphere.
hemorragia *f* hemorrhage.
henchir (i) *vt* to stuff, cram, bloat, fill up.
hender (ie) *vt* to split, slit, cleave.
hendido *a* slit, split, cloven, forked.
hendidura *f* cleft, chink, gape, fissure.
heno *m* hay.
heráldica *f* heraldry.
heraldo *m* herald.
herbáceo *a* herbaceous, grassy.
herbívoro *a* grass-eating, herbivorous.
hercúleo *a* herculean.
heredad *f* domain, estate, property, farm.
heredar *vt* to come into, inherit.
heredero *m* heir, successor, inheritor.
hereditario *a* hereditary, entailed.
hereje *m* heretic.
herejía *f* heresy, hideous error.
herencia *f* inheritance, heritage, estate; heirloom, legacy.
herida *f* wound, stab, hurt, gash.
herido *a* wounded, hurt; *m* wounded man, victim; **los —s** the wounded.
herir (ie) *vt* to wound, hurt; to strike; to offend (*senses etc*).
hermana *f* sister.
hermandad *f* brotherhood, fraternity; guild; friendship; **santa —** (*ancient*) police force.
hermano *m* brother; **— de leche** foster-brother.
hermético *a* hermetical; airtight.
hermosear *vt* to adorn, embellish, beautify.
hermoso *a* handsome, comely, neat, fine, beautiful.
hermosura *f* loveliness, comeliness, beauty; a beauty.
Herodes *m* Herod; (*fam*) **de — a Pilatos** from pillar to post.
héroe *m* hero.
heroico *a* heroic, splendid, shining.
heroína *f* heroine; heroin.
heroísmo *m* gallantry, heroism.
herrador *m* farrier.
herradura *f* horseshoe; **camino de —** bridle track; **mostrar las —s** to bolt, kick over the traces.
herramienta *f* tool, instrument.
herrar *vt* to shoe (*horses*); to brand (*cattle*).
herrería *f* blacksmith's shop, forge; ironworks.
herrero *m* blacksmith, smith.

herrumbre *f* rust.
hervidero *m* boiling spring; bubbling, gushing; throng, bustling crowd.
hervir (ie) *vti* to boil, seethe, effervesce; to surge; — **a fuego lento** to simmer.
hervor *m* boiling, effervescence, swirling, seething, ebullition.
heterodoxo *a* unsound; *m* unorthodox, unbeliever.
hez *f* scum, lees, dregs, sediment.
hidalgo *m* nobleman, gentleman, man of breeding.
hidalguía *f* nobility, true lineage, nobleness; generosity, fine instincts.
hidráulico *a* hydraulic.
hidroavión *m* flying boat, seaplane.
hidrofobia *f* rabies.
hidrógeno *m* hydrogen.
hiedra *f* ivy.
hiel *f* gall, bile; bitterness.
hielo *m* ice; frost; **banco de** — ice field.
hiena *f* hyena.
hierba *f* grass, herb, weed; **mala** — weed; — **de San Benito** herb bennet; — **de San Juan** St. John's wort; — **de Santiago** ragwort, pansy; *pl* —**s** greens.
hierbabuena *f* mint, peppermint.
hierro *m* iron; tool; brand; — **dulce** wrought iron; — **colado** cast iron; — **laminado** sheet iron; — **viejo** scrap iron.
hígado *m* liver.
higiene *f* hygiene, cleanliness.
higiénico *a* hygienic, sanitary.
higo *m* fig; — **chumbo** prickly pear; **de —s a brevas** once in a blue moon.
higuera *f* fig tree.
hija *f* daughter; — **mía** my dear girl.
hijastro *m* stepson.
hijo *m* son; child; native; — **adoptivo** adopted child; — **del agua** foundling; **cada — de vecino** every mother's son.
hilacha *f* shred, frayed part.
hilandero *m* spinner.
hilar *vt* to spin; — **delgado** to be very particular.
hilaza *f* yarn, thread.
hilera *f* range, row, line; wire-drawer.
hilo *m* thread, edge (*of sword etc*); yarn; wire; **perder el** — to lose the thread (*of lecture etc*).
hilván *m* basting stitch; *SA* hem.
himeneo *m* marriage, wedlock.
himno *m* hymn; — **nacional** national anthem.
hincapié *m* insistence; **hacer** — to dwell on, emphasize.
hincar *vt* to drive, thrust; — **la rodilla** to bend the knee; — **el diente** to bite, dig, get one's teeth into.
hinchado *a* puffed, swollen; windy, verbose.
hinchar *vt* to distend, bloat, swell; *vr* to swell out, be puffed up.
hinchazón *m* inflation, swelling, puffiness; vanity.
hinojo *m* fennel; knee; **de —s** on bended knees.
hípico *a* horse, of horses, equine; **concurso** — horse race.
hipil *m SA* loose garment worn by Indians.
hipnotismo *m* hypnotism, mesmerism.
hipo *m* hiccough; longing; hatred.
hipocondría *f* hypochondria, melancholy, spleen, the blues.
hipocresía *f* hypocrisy, cant, humbug.
hipócrita *a* hypocritical, false, dissembling; *m* hypocrite.
hipódromo *m* racecourse; circus.
hipoteca *f* mortgage, hypothecation.
hipotecar *vt* to mortgage.
hipótesis *f* hypothesis, supposition.
hipotético *a* hypothetical, imaginary.
hirsuto *a* shaggy, hairy, bristly.
hispalense *an* of Seville.
hispánico *a* Hispanic, of Spain.
hispanismo *m* Spanish idiom.
hispanista *m* devotee of Spanish studies; Spanish scholar.
hispano *a* (*poet*) Spanish.
hispanoamericano *an* South American.
hispanófilo *an* hispanophile; fond of things Spanish.
histeria *f* hysteria.
histerismo *m* hysteria.
historia *f* history; tale, story; past; *pl* **¡déjese Vd. de —s!** come to the point!
historiador *m* historian.
historiar *vt* to relate; to record.
histórico *a* historical, with an interesting past.
historieta *f* tale, anecdote.
histrión *m* actor, player; juggler.
hito *m* landmark, guidepost; **mirar de — en —** to stare straight at, to look intently at.
hocico *m* snout, muzzle; **meter el — en** to poke one's nose into.
hogar *m* fireplace, hearth; home, roof, shelter; **sin** — homeless, stray.
hogaza *f* large loaf of bread.
hoguera *f* fire, bonfire; pyre, stake.
hoja *f* leaf; petal; sheet; sheaf; blade; shutter; — **de lata** tin; — **de estaño** tinfoil; **la — del lunes** Monday newspaper; **volver la** — to reform; to change the subject.
hojalata *f* tinplate.
hojaldre *f* puff pastry.
hojarasca *f* fallen leaves; trumpery, balderdash.
hojear *vt* to skim, scan, run through (*book etc*).
¡hola! *excl* hallo!
Holanda *f* Holland, the Netherlands.
holanda *f* fine linen.
holandés *an* Dutch(man); **a la holandesa** half-binding.

holgado *a* loose, easy; roomy, ample; at leisure; comfortably off.
holganza *f* ease, quiet, leisure, diversion, recreation.
holgar *vi* to rest, be at leisure; to be idle; *vr* to sport, play, dally, idle.
holgazán *m* idler, loafer, lounger.
holgazanería *f* laziness, indolence, idleness.
holgorio *m* spree, merrymaking, lark, sport.
holgura *f* ease; frolicking; amplitude, width, fullness; looseness, laxity.
hollar *vt* to trample, tread (*down, upon, underfoot*); to degrade, spurn.
hollín *m* soot.
hombre *m* man; mankind; ombre; **— de bien** honest man; **— de estado** statesman; **— de negocios** business man; **muy —** a real man; *excl* good heavens!
hombrera *f SA* shoulder padding.
hombro *m* shoulder; **llevar a —** to shoulder, carry on one's back; **encogerse de —s** to shrug one's shoulders.
hombruno *a* manly, virile.
homenaje *m* homage; testimonial; allegiance.
homicida *mf* homicide, murderer.
homicidio *m* manslaughter, homicide.
homogéneo *a* homogeneous.
honda *f* sling.
hondable *a* soundable.
hondo *a* profound, deep; low; heartfelt, sincere.
hondonada *f* glen, gully, ravine; deep.
hondura *f* depth.
hondureño *an* Honduran.
honestidad *f* chastity, purity, honor, modesty; decency, decorousness.
honesto *a* decent, decorous; modest, chaste, pure; fair, honest.
hongo *m* mushroom, fungus; bowler hat.
honor *m* honor; reputation; chastity; dignity; *pl* rank, status; privileges, ceremony.
honorable *a* honorable, worshipful, revered, dignified; distinguished.
honorario *a* honorary, unpaid; *m* fees, salary; *pl* terms.
honra *f* honor, reverence; reputation, fame, glory; purity, chastity; favor; *pl* obsequies.
honradamente *ad* decently, honorably, as in duty bound, faithfully.
honradez *f* faithfulness, uprightness, integrity; dutifulness; square dealing.
honrado *a* honest; just, fair, decent, upright, honorable; dutiful; conscientious.
honrar *vt* to honor, esteem; to revere; to do honor or credit (to); to honor (*check*); *vr* to regard as a privilege.
honrilla *f* punctiliousness; **por la negra —** for form's sake.
honroso *a* bringing honor, praiseworthy.
hora *f* hour; time; season; **¿qué — es?** what time is it?; **última —** stop-press (*news*); **— menguada** fatal moment; **—s** prayerbook; **por —s** by the hour; **altas —s** small hours.
horadar *vt* to perforate, penetrate, bore through.
horario *a* hour; *m* hour hand; timetable.
horca *f* gallows, gibbet; fork, pitchfork; string of onions, garlic.
horcajada *f* **a —s** astride, straddling.
horchata *f* orgeat, iced drink; **— de chufas** tiger-nut drink.
horda *f* horde, gang.
horgueta *f SA* forked branch; *Arg* fork (*in road*).
horizonte *m* horizon.
horma *f* model, mold; hat-maker's block; last (*of shoe*).
hormiga *f* ant; **— blanca** termite.
hormigón *m* concrete; **— armado** reinforced concrete.
hormiguear *vi* to itch; to swarm.
hormigueo *m* itching, tingling.
hormiguero *m* anthill; swarm of people.
hornear *vt SA* to bake.
hornero *m* baker.
hornilla *f* kitchen grate.
hornillo *m* portable furnace, range, stove, oven.
horno *m* oven, kiln, furnace; **alto —** blast furnace; **— de ladrillo** brick kiln.
horquilla *f* pitchfork; hairpin; fork (*of bicycle*).
horrendo *a* horrible, fearful, dire, dreadful.
hórreo *m* barn, granary (*usu on stone posts*).
horrible *a* frightful, dreadful, ghastly.
hórrido *a* horrid, hideous, horrible.
horripilante *a* harrowing, hair-raising, ghastly.
horripilar *vt* to frighten, horrify, scare out of one's wits; give the creeps (to).
horror *m* horror, fright; grimness, hideousness; abhorrence.
horrorizado *a* aghast.
horrorizar *vt* to horrify, frighten, terrify.
horroroso *a* frightful, awful; horrifying.
hortalizas *f pl* vegetables, greens.
hortelano *m* market gardener, truck farmer.
hortera *m* shop boy, grocer's assistant.
horticultura *f* horticulture, gardening, cultivation of gardens.
hosco *a* frowning, dark, gloomy; crabbed, sullen.
hospedaje *m* lodging.

hospedar *vt* to give lodging, quarter; to board, lodge; *vr* to put up, stay, stop at.
hospedería *f* hostelry; guest house; home, hospice.
hospedero *m* host, innkeeper.
hospicio *m* orphanage, children's home.
hospital *m* hospital, infirmary; **— de campaña** field hospital, dressing station; **— de sangre** emergency hospital.
hospitalario *a* hospitable; *m* Knight Templar.
hospitalidad *f* hospitality; period of stay in hospital; hospitalization.
hospitalización *f* hospitalization.
hospitalizar *vt* to admit to hospital, hospitalize.
hosquedad *f* gloom, darkness; sullenness.
hostal *m* inn, hostel.
hostelero *m* innkeeper; victualer.
hostería *f* inn, eating house, hostelry.
hostia *f* host; oblate, wafer.
hostigar *vt* to scourge; to harass, vex; to persecute.
hostil *a* hostile, antagonistic, adverse.
hostilidad *f* hostility, antagonism, enmity.
hotelero *m* hotel proprietor.
hoy *ad* today; **— día** nowadays; **de— en adelante** from now on, henceforth; **de — a mañana** when you least expect it.
hoya *f* pit, cavity; dale, vale; grave; bed (*of a river*).
hoyada *f* dale.
hoyo *m* hole, cavity; dent, groove; mark; crater.
hoyuela *f* dimple; socket (*of collarbone*).
hoyuelo *m* dimple.
hoz *f* sickle, reaper's hook; narrow pass, defile, gorge.
huaca *f Bol, Per* ancient Indian tomb.
huasca *f Per* whip, lash.
huayno *m Per* Indian dance.
hucha *f* moneybox, toy bank; bin; chest.
huchear *vt* to whoop, shout, call out.
hueco *m* gap, hole; depression, emptiness, loneliness; lacuna; vacancy; notch; *a* hollow; blank; vacant; inflated (*voice*).
huelga *f* rest, leisure; strike; **declararse en —** to strike, down tools.
huelgo *m* windage; room, space clearance.
huelguista *m* man on strike, striker
huella *f* trace; track, footprint imprint, trail; trace, vestige; *pl* **—s digitales** fingerprints.
huemul *m Arg, Chi* Andes deer.
huérfano *a* fatherless, motherless; *m* orphan boy, waif.
huero *a* empty; addled; sterile.
huerta *f* vegetable garden; **la — de Valencia** irrigated land in province of Valencia.
huerto *m* orchard.
hueso *m* bone; pit, pip; (*fruit*) stone.
huésped *m* inmate, lodger, guest; host, landlord; *pl* **casa de —es** boarding house.
hueste *f* host (*army*).
huesudo *a* bony, raw-boned.
huevo *m* egg; **— pasado por agua** soft-boiled egg; **— revuelto** scrambled egg; **— estrellado** fried *or* poached egg; **— batido** beaten egg.
Hugo *m* Hugh.
hugonote *an* Huguenot.
huída *f* flight, escape, getaway.
huincha *f SA* tape, ribbon.
huiliento *a Chi* ragged.
huir *vt* to shun; *vtr* to flee, escape, make off, decamp, elope, run away.
hule *m* oilcloth; indiarubber.
hulla *f* soft coal.
hullera *f* coalpit, colliery.
hullero *a* **industria —a** coal industry; **cuenca —a** coalfield.
humanidad *f* mortal man, humankind; humanity, kindliness; *pl* the Humanities, Classics.
humanismo *m* humanism.
humanista *m* humanist, classical scholar.
humanizarse *vr* to become human; to grow more like one's fellows.
humano *a* human; humane; **el género —** mankind; **ser —** human being.
humareda *f* smoke; smokiness; clouds of smoke.
humeante *a* smoky, fuming.
humear *vi* to reek with smoke; to smoke, be smoky.
humedad *f* humidity, dampness; moisture.
humedecer *vt* to moisten, damp, wet; to soak.
húmedo *a* damp, moist; watery.
humildad *f* humility, meekness, lowliness; obscurity.
humilde *a* humble, meek; poor, plain, of low degree; down-trodden.
humillación *f* humiliation; submission; humbling; lowering of pride; insult.
humillante *a* humiliating, degrading.
humillar *vt* to lower, make humble, degrade, take down a peg, humiliate; *vr* to debase oneself, to be prostrate.
humita *f Arg, Chi, Per* cake of corn and sugar.
humo *m* smoke; vapor, fume; vanity, presumption; **echar —** to smoke (*of chimney etc*).
humor *m* humor, temper; temperament, disposition; **buen —** good spirits, joviality; **mal —** crossness, moodiness; **de buen —** in fine fettle, gay; **de mal —** cross, crusty.
humorada *f* practical joke.

humorístico *a* funny; **diario —** comic paper.
hundimiento *m* sinking; downfall, collapse, caving in.
hundido *a* sunken.
hundir *vt* to sink, thrust (into), crush, swamp; to ruin, dash, pull down; *vr* to sink, collapse, cave in, subside; to sag.
húngaro *an* Hungarian; gypsy.
Hungría *f* Hungary.
huracán *m* hurricane.
huraño *a* shy, elusive, diffident; unsociable, bearish.
hurgar *vt* to stir up, rake, poke; **—se las narices** to pick one's nose.
hurgonear *vt* to poke (*fire*).
hurón *a* shy, unaffectionate, disdainful; *m* ferret.
hurtadillas *ad* **a—** stealthily, on the sly; on tiptoe.
hurtar *vt* to steal, pilfer, make off with.
hurto *m* robbery, thieving, theft, stealing.
húsar *m* Hussar.
husmear *vt* to scent, sniff out, get wind of, ferret out.
huso *m* spindle; (*her*) lozenge.
huyente *a* **frente —** receding forehead.

I

ibérico *a* Iberian.
ibero *m* Iberian.
ibicenco *an* (*inhabitant*) of Ibiza.
icho *m* *Per* Andes grass.
ida *f* going, outgoing, departure; **de — y vuelta** return, round-trip (*ticket*).
idea *f* idea; plan, intention, scheme; plot, fancy.
ideal *a* ideal, imaginary, abstract, unreal; *m* ideal.
idealista *a* idealistic; *mf* idealist.
idealizar *vt* to idealize.
idear *vt* to imagine, conceive, devise, plan; to contrive, project.
ídem *pr* ditto, the same.
idéntico *a* identical.
identidad *f* identity, sameness.
identificación *f* identification.
ideología *f* ideology.
idilio *m* idyll.
idioma *m* language, speech, tongue, idiom.
idiota *a* silly, daft, idiotic; *mf* idiot, oaf, loony.
idiotez *f* idiocy, feeble-mindedness, stupidity.
idiotismo *m* imbecility, foolishness; idiom, locution, turn of speech.
idólatra *a* idolatrous, heathen, pagan; *mf* idolater, idolatress.
idolatrar *vt* to idolize.
idolatría *f* idolatry, heathenism, worship of idols.
idoneidad *f* capacity, fitness, suitability, aptitude.
idóneo *a* apt; capable; proper, likely, suitable, appropriate, fit.
iglesia *f* church, temple.
ignición *f* ignition, kindling, firing.
ignominia *f* shame, dishonor, disgrace, ignominy.
ignominioso *a* discreditable, shameful, ignominious.
ignorado *a* unknown, undiscovered.
ignorancia *f* ignorance, illiteracy.
ignorante *a* ignorant, untutored, unlettered; blind.
ignorar *vt* not to know, be unaware of.
ignoto *a* hidden, unknown.
igual *a* the same, like, similar, equal; level, uniform, flat; constant, unchanging; **sin—** matchless, peerless; **me es—** I don't mind.
igualar *vt* to equalize; to make equal; to pair; to make even, flatten; to balance up, make amends; *vi* to be equal (*to*).
igualdad *f* equality; evenness, smoothness; parity.
igualmente *a* similarly; likewise; the same to you; also, too.
ijar *m* flank (*of animals*).
ilegal *a* illegal, unlawful; false; contraband.
ilegalmente *ad* on false pretenses, unlawfully.
ilegítimo *a* illegitimate; unlawful; out of wedlock.
ileso *a* unharmed, unscarred.
ilícito *a* illicit.
ilimitado *a* boundless, limitless, unconfined; vast, immense.
ilógico *a* illogical, irrational.
iluminación *f* illumination, lighting.
iluminado *a* lit up; colored, illuminated.
iluminar *vt* to illuminate, kindle, set alight, light up; to adorn with engravings.
ilusión *f* illusion, daydream; (delightful) anticipation, dream; **con una gran —** with great pleasure, thrill.
ilusionado *vt* **estar —** to be looking forward to (*pleasure etc*), be buoyed up by.
ilusionista *m* juggler, conjurer.
iluso *a* deluded; *m* daydreamer, wishful thinker.
ilusorio *a* illusory, deceptive; unsubstantial, unreal.
ilustración *f* illustration: edification, enlightenment, learning; engraving.
ilustrado *a* cultured, well-read, polished, educated; **déspota —** enlightened despot.
ilustrar *vt* to illustrate, explain, interpret, elucidate; *vr* to become illustrious, to acquire learning.
ilustre *a* illustrious, distinguished, brilliant, eminent, splendid, lofty.
imagen *f* reflection, counterpart, image; statue, effigy; conception, idea; spectrum.

imaginación *f* imagination, fancy; fantasy, dream.
imaginar *vt* to imagine; to fancy; *vr* to suppose, assume.
imaginario *a* imaginary, fanciful, unsubstantiated, airy.
imaginativo *a* imaginative, fanciful, creative, fertile.
imaginero *m* sculptor of religious statues.
imán *m* loadstone, magnet.
imbécil *a* silly, foolish, half-witted, idiotic; *mf* simpleton, dolt; fool, idiot.
imbecilidad *f* imbecility, feeble-mindedness, stupidity.
imberbe *a* beardless; immature.
imbuir *vt* to imbue, inspire, fill.
imitación *f* imitation, counterfeit, copy.
imitado *a* mock, pretended, copy of.
imitar *vt* to imitate, copy, mimic, counterfeit, ape.
impaciencia *f* restlessness, haste, impatience.
impaciente *a* restless, fidgety, impatient.
impago *a Arg. Chi* unpaid.
impalpable *a* intangible, impalpable.
impar *a* odd, uneven.
imparcial *a* impartial, dispassionate.
imparcialidad *f* dispassionateness, impartiality, fairness; indifference; lack of prejudice.
impartir *vt* to bestow, grant, impart.
impasible *a* unfeeling, unimpassioned; undisturbed, unmoved, serene, calm, unruffled.
impavidez *f* intrepidity, dauntlessness; fearlessness.
impávido *a* intrepid, fearless, undaunted.
impecable *a* sinless, faultless.
impedimento *m* impediment, obstruction, encumbrance.
impedir (i) *vt* to obstruct, thwart, hinder, obviate, stay, impede, stand in the way of.
impeler *vt* to impel, push, drive, spur on, urge on.
impenetrabilidad *f* imperviousness, proof.
impenetrable *a* impervious; fathomless, bottomless, impenetrable.
impenitente *a* obdurate, unrepentant.
impensado *a* out of the blue, random, unplanned; unexpected.
imperante *a* ruling, prevailing.
imperar *vi* to rule, reign, command, be in force, be the order of the day.
imperativo *a m* imperative.
imperceptible *a* imperceptible, not discernible, faint.
imperdible *a* sure, safe; *m* safety pin.
imperdonable *a* unforgivable, inexcusable.
imperecedero *a* imperishable, deathless.
imperfección *f* imperfection, defect, flaw, fault, blemish; inadequacy, weakness.
imperfecto *a* imperfect, faulty, unfinished, incomplete.
imperial *a* imperial, of emperors, of empire; *f* top, roof, outside (*of vehicle*).
impericia *f* unskillfulness, lack of skill.
imperio *m* empire; command, sway; arrogance; the purple.
imperioso *a* arrogant, haughty, overbearing.
imperito *a* unskilled, without training.
impermeable *a* impervious, waterproof; *m* mackintosh, raincoat.
impermutable *a* not interchangeable.
impersonalidad *f* lack of personal touch.
impertérrito *a* intrepid, unafraid, unshakable.
impertinencia *f* impertinence, nonsense, irrelevancy.
impertinente *a* impertinent, obnoxious, out of place, inappropriate; *m pl* lorgnette.
imperturbable *a* stolid, imperturbable, unshakable.
ímpetu *m* impetus, impulse, fit, violence, momentum.
impetuosidad *f* impetuousness, heedlessness.
impetuoso *a* impetuous, wild, headlong, headstrong, willful.
impiedad *f* godlessness, ungodliness, lack of piety.
impío *a* impious, godless, wicked, blasphemous.
implacable *a* relentless, unforgiving, remorseless, unyielding.
implantar *vt* to implant, introduce.
implicar *vti* to involve, implicate, to contradict, oppose.
implícito *a* implicit.
implorar *vt* to implore, entreat, beseech, beg.
impolítico *a* impolite; impolitic.
imponente *a* impressive; grandiose, stately.
imponer *vt* to lay down, enforce, impose; to levy (*taxes*); to make an impression, be imposing; *vr* to ride roughshod (over), get one's own way; to be necessary.
importación *f* importation, import(ing).
importancia *f* consequence, import, significance, importance; solemnity; scope; **de gran —** of great moment; **darse —** to be pompous; **dar — a** to value.
importante *a* important, urgent, weighty; serious.
importar *vt* to import, be of (some) importance; *vi* to signify, matter; *vr* to amount (to), to come (to).
importe *m* amount, total.

importunar *vt* to pester, solicit, importune.
importuno *a* importunate, troublesome, pressing, obtrusive.
imposibilidad *f* impossibility; hopelessness.
imposibilitar *vt* to incapacitate, disable; to prevent, cut out, cut short, make impossible.
imposible *a* impossible, unfeasible, hopeless; **es —** there isn't a chance, it can't be done.
imposición *f* charge, duty, imposition; infliction; **— de manos** laying-on of hands.
impositivo *a Arg* pertaining to income tax; domineering.
impostor *m* impostor.
impostura *f* imposture, fraud, deceit; sham.
impotencia *f* impotence, inability, powerlessness.
impotente *a* impotent, feeble, powerless.
impracticable *a* impracticable: impassable; not working.
imprecar *vt* to curse.
impregnar *vt* to impregnate; *vr* to be pervaded, steeped; to be fraught (with).
imprenta *f* printing (office), press; imprint; **libertad de —** freedom of the press.
imprescindible *a* indispensable, essential.
impresión *f* impression, stamp, imprint; issue, printing; effect; image.
impresionable *a* impressionable, sensitive, highly-strung, easily influenced.
impresionar *vt* to impress, make an impression (on); to influence; to fix, imprint.
impreso *m* printed matter, pamphlet, leaflet.
impresor *m* printer.
imprevisión *f* improvidence, lack of forethought.
imprevisor *a* improvident, lacking in forethought, easy-going.
imprevisto *a* unlooked-for, unforeseen.
imprimir *vt* to print, stamp; to fix.
improbabilidad *f* unlikelihood.
improbable *a* improbable, unlikely; **es —** it isn't likely.
ímprobo *a* dishonest; hard, laborious, thankless.
improcedente *a* unfounded, without (legal) foundation.
improductivo *a* unproductive, unfruitful, fruitless.
improperio *m* insult, taunt, curse, oath.
impropiedad *f* impropriety, unsuitability, infelicity, malapropism.
impropio *a* improper; uncalled-for, out-of-place, inept, unsuitable, unfit; unbecoming.
improvidencia *f* lack of foresight; unpreparedness, carelessness, improvidence, wastefulness.
improvisación *f* impromptu, addition, improvisation.
improvisado *a* improvised, extempore, temporary.
improvisar *vt* to improvise, extemporize.
improviso *a* unexpected; **de —** all of a sudden, unawares.
improvisto *a* unforeseen; **a la —a** unexpectedly.
imprudencia *f* imprudence, indiscretion, heedlessness.
imprudente *a* imprudent, indiscreet, unwise, rash.
impúdico *a* immodest, lewd, unchaste, shameless.
impudor *m* shamelessness, cynicism, immodesty.
impuesto *m* tax, duty; **fijación de—s** rating of taxes.
impugnar *vt* to confute, oppose, contradict, impugn.
impulsar *vt* to rush, drive, impel.
impulsión *f* impulse, impetus, momentum.
impulso *m* urge, impulse; force, pressure, push, beat.
impune *a* unpunished, with impunity.
impunidad *f* impunity; **con —** scot-free.
impureza *f* adulteration, grit, impurity; uncleanness, unchastity.
impuro *a* unclean, impure, foul.
imputable *a* attributable.
imputación *f* imputation, accusation; entry (*book-keeping*).
imputar *vt* to impute, attribute, tax (with), ascribe.
inacabable *a* endless, unending.
inaccessible *a* unapproachable, out-of-the-way, lost.
inacción *f* inactivity, inertia; lack of movement.
inaceptable *a* unacceptable.
inactividad *f* lethargy, stillness, lifelessness.
inactivo *a* inactive, dormant, inert.
inadaptado *a* unsuited; unsettled.
inadecuado *a* inadequate; unsuitable, out-of-place.
inadmisible *a* unacceptable, out of the question.
inadvertencia *f* inadvertence, carelessness, oversight.
inadvertido *a* inadvertent; unobserved, unnoticed.
inagotable *a* inexhaustible, endless, never-failing.
inaguantable *a* unbearable, past endurance.
inajenable *a* inalienable, untransferable.
inalterable *a* stable, unchangeable, fast.
inamovible *a* immovable.
inanición *f* starvation, exhaustion.
inanimado *a* inanimate, lifeless.

inapreciable *a* inestimable, priceless, without price.
inasequible *a* unattainable.
inaudito *a* unheard-of, unspeakable, outrageous.
inauguración *f* inauguration, opening.
inaugurar *vt* to inaugurate, open.
incalculable *a* untold, unnumbered, inestimable.
incandescente *a* incandescent.
incansable *a* indefatigable, tireless.
incapacidad *f* incapacity, inability, incompetence.
incapacitar *vt* to disable, make incapable (unable); to disqualify.
incapaz *a* incapable, inefficient, unable, unfit.
incautación *f* appropriation, legal seizure.
incautarse *vr* to attach (*property*); to take possession of, seize.
incauto *a* careless, unwary, thoughtless, imprudent.
incendiar *vt* to set fire to, commit arson.
incendiario *m* incendiary; firebrand.
incendio *m* fire; conflagration, arson.
incensario *m* incensory, thurible.
incentivo *m* incentive, stimulus, encouragement.
incertidumbre *f* uncertainty, doubt.
incesante *a* incessant, uninterrupted, continual.
incidencia *f* incidence.
incidental *a* incidental, by the way, subsidiary.
incidente *a* casual; *m* incident, event.
incidir *vi* to fall into (*error etc*); *Arg* to have an effect on.
incienso *m* incense; eulogy.
incierto *a* uncertain, doubtful, unsteady.
incineración *f* incineration.
incinerar *vt* to cremate.
incipiente *a* incipient, embryonic, nascent; coming on (*of illness*).
incisión *f* cut, incision; gash.
incisivo *a* incisive, keen, sharp, clipped.
incitación *f* incitement, encouragement.
incitante *a* stimulating, exciting, persuasive, provocative.
incitar *vt* to incite, excite, spur on, instigate, goad.
incivil *a* impolite.
incivilidad *f* incivility, rudeness.
inclemencia *f* inclemency, rigor, harshness; hard weather.
inclemente *a* inclement, unmerciful.
inclinación *f* inclination, fondness, liking, preference, bent, tendency; bow (*of head*); fall (*in music*); pitch; gradient, slope.
inclinado *a* inclined, well-disposed.
inclinar *vt* to incline, bend, tilt, influence, induce; *vr* to lean, sway, to be inclined (well disposed to); to stoop, bow (down).
ínclito *a* renowned, illustrious.
incluir *vt* to include; enclose, comprise, contain.
inclusa *f* foundling home.
inclusión *f* inclusion.
inclusive *ad* inclusively, in addition.
incluso *ad* besides, as well, too.
incobrable *a* irrecoverable, irretrievable; (*com*) uncollectable.
incógnito *a* unknown; **de —** incognito.
incoherente *a* incoherent.
incoloro *a* colorless.
incólume *a* sound, unharmed, untouched.
incombustible *a* incombustible, fireproof.
incomodar *vt* to vex, trouble, disturb, inconvenience; *vr* to be put out, annoyed, ruffled, take umbrage, take offense.
incomodidad *f* inconvenience, uncomfortableness, trouble, pains; vexation.
incómodo *a* uncomfortable, troublesome, inconvenient, cumbersome.
incomparable *a* matchless.
incompatible *a* incompatible, uncongenial, unacceptable, repugnant.
incompetencia *f* incompetency.
incompetente *a* incompetent, incapable, unqualified.
incompleto *a* incomplete, not full, unfinished.
incomprensible *a* incomprehensible.
incomunicado *a* isolated, cut off; solitary (*confinement*).
inconcebible *a* inconceivable.
inconcluso *a* unfinished, incomplete, inadequate, unsatisfactory.
inconcuso *a* uncontrovertible, indubitable.
incondicional *a* unconditional, unqualified, out and out.
inconexo *a* incoherent, broken.
inconfundible *a* unmistakable.
incongruente *a* incongruous, beside the mark.
inconmensurable *a* incommensurable, unbounded.
inconmovible *a* firm, unyielding, inexorable.
inconsciente *a* unconscious, unwitting, ignorant.
inconsecuencia *f* inconsistency, inconsequence, irresponsibility.
inconsecuente *a* inconsistent, irresponsible, unreasonable.
inconsiderado *a* inconsiderate, thoughtless.
inconsistente *a* changeable, unsteady.
inconstancia *f* inconstancy, unsteadiness, fickleness.
inconstante *a* unsteady, changeable, variable.
incontestable *a* incontestable, indisputable.

incontinencia *f* incontinence, lewdness.
incontinente *ad* instantly, straight away; *a* incontinent.
incontrastable *a* irresistible, insurmountable.
inconveniencia *f* inconvenience, trouble, impropriety.
inconveniente *a* inconvenient, inopportune, unfortunate; unbecoming; *m* difficulty, obstacle, objection; **no veo —** I see no reason why (not).
incorporación *f* incorporation.
incorporar *vt* to incorporate; *vr* to join; to sit up (*in bed*).
incorrección *f* inaccuracy; lack of correctness.
incorrecto *a* inaccurate, incorrect.
incorregible *a* incorrigible.
incorruptible *a* incorruptible.
incredulidad *f* incredulity.
incrédulo *a* incredulous, disbelieving; *m* unbeliever.
increíble *a* incredible, unbelievable.
incremento *m* increase, increment.
increpar *vt* to rebuke, reproach, scold.
incruento *a* bloodless (*battle*).
incrustar *vt* to encrust, enchase, inlay.
incubar *vt* to hatch, brood.
inculcar *vt* to inculcate, teach, impress on.
inculpar *vt* to accuse, blame, throw the blame on.
inculto *a* untilled; uneducated, uncultured, coarse.
incuria *f* carelessness, neglect, thoughtlessness, fecklessness.
incurrir *vi* to incur, become liable, fall into (*error etc*).
indagación *f* investigation, inquiry, search.
indagar *vt* to inquire, examine into.
indebido *a* illegal, unauthorized.
indecente *a* indecent, obscene, shameful, scandalous.
indecible *a* unspeakable, unutterable.
indeciso *a* irresolute, uncertain, hesitant.
indeclinable *a* unavoidable; undeclinable; (*gram*) indeclinable.
indefectible *a* unfailing, infallible, without fail.
indefenso *a* defenseless.
indefinido *a* indefinite, vague, undefined.
indeleble *a* indelible.
indemne *a* unharmed, undamaged.
indemnizar *vt* to indemnify, compensate, make good.
independiente *a* independent, separate, free.
indeseable *a* undesirable.
indeterminado *a* indeterminate, indistinct, uncertain.
indiano *an* Indian; resident of America; emigrant returned rich from America.
indicación *f* indication, hint, sign, token, direction.
indicar *vt* to point out; to hint, indicate, show.
índice *m* index; forefinger; table of contents.
indicio *m* sign; trace; circumstantial evidence.
indiferencia *f* indifference, unconcern, listlessness.
indiferente *a* indifferent, inattentive, lukewarm, impartial.
indígena *mf* native; *a* indigenous, native.
indigencia *f* penury, poverty.
indigestión *f* indigestion.
indigesto *a* indigestible, disordered, undigested, heavy.
indignación *f* anger.
indignado *a* indignant, offended, hurt.
indignar *vt* to anger, provoke, revolt.
indignidad *f* indignity, insult.
indigno *a* unworthy, undeserving; mean, low, unsuitable, disgraceful.
indio *an* Indian.
indirecta *f* innuendo, half-statement, hint, hit (*at*).
indirecto *a* indirect.
indiscreción *f* indiscretion, tactlessness, rashness.
indiscreto *a* indiscreet, foolish, injudicious, unwise, imprudent.
indiscutible *a* unquestionable, indisputable.
indispensable *a* indispensable, necessary, essential.
indisponer *vt* to disable; to prejudice; *vr* to fall ill, fall out (with).
indisposición *f* ailment, indisposition.
indistinto *a* vague, not clear, indistinct.
individual *a* individual, characteristic.
individuo *m* individual, person, fellow.
indiviso *a* undivided.
indocto *a* unlearned, uneducated.
índole *f* inclination, nature, character, disposition.
indolencia *f* indolence.
indomable *a* indomitable, unmanageable, untamable.
indómito *a* rebellious, wild, unconquerable, unbroken, untamed.
indubitable *a* indubitable, undoubted, unquestionable.
inducir *vt* to induce; to persuade.
indudable *a* undoubted, quite definite.
indulgencia *f* forbearance, indulgence, grace.
indultar *vt* to free, pardon.
indulto *m* pardon, forgiveness, amnesty.
indumentaria *f* clothing, dress.
industria *f* industry, trade; diligence.
industrial *a* industrial; *m* industrialist.

industrioso *a* industrious, skillful.
inédito *a* unpublished, unknown, inedited.
inefable *a* ineffable, unspeakable.
ineficaz *a* inefficient, ineffectual, ineffective.
ineludible *a* unavoidable, inescapable, inevitable.
ineptitud *f* ineptitude; incapacity; inability.
inepto *a* inept, useless, incompetent; foolish.
inequívoco *a* unmistakable.
inercia *f* inertia, inertness.
inerme *a* defenseless.
inerte *a* inert, dull.
Inés *f* Agnes, Inez.
inesperado *a* unexpected.
inevitable *a* inevitable, unavoidable.
inexactitud *f* inaccuracy.
inexperiencia *f* inexperience.
inexplicable *a* inexplicable.
inexpugnable *a* impregnable; stubborn.
infalible *a* infallible.
infamar *vt* to defame, libel.
infame *a* infamous, vile, despicable, hateful, damnable.
infamia *f* dishonor, disgrace, baseness.
infancia *f* infancy.
infante *m* infant; King's son (*in Spain, except the heir*); foot soldier.
infantería *f* infantry.
infantil *a* infantile, childish, childlike.
infatigable *a* indefatigable, tireless.
infausto *a* unhappy; ill-omened, luckless.
infección *f* infection, contagion.
infeccioso *a* infectious, contagious.
infectar *vt* to infect, corrupt, pervert.
infelicidad *f* unhappiness, misery.
infeliz *a* wretched, unhappy, luckless.
inferior *a* subordinate, inferior, lower.
inferir (ie) *vt* to infer, deduce; to inflict (*wound*).
infestar *vt* to infest, to infect.
inficionar *vt* to infect, contaminate, corrupt.
infidelidad *f* infidelity, unfaithfulness, faithlessness, disbelief.
infiel *a* disloyal, unfaithful; *m* infidel.
infierno *m* hell.
ínfimo *a* lowest, meanest, least, worst.
infinidad *f* infinity, endless number.
infinito *a* infinite, endless, unbounded, immense.
inflación *f* inflation; swelling.
inflamable *a* inflammable.
inflamado *a* inflamed, sore.
inflamar *vt* to inflame; to set on fire.
inflar *vt* to inflate, blow up, distend; to inspire.
inflexible *a* inflexible, unbending.
infligir *vt* to inflict.
influencia *f* influence.
influir *vt* to influence, prevail upon.
influjo *m* influence, power; influx.
influyente *a* influential, persuasive.
información *f* information, account, report.
informal *a* informal, without ceremony, unconventional, incorrect, rude, offhand.
informalidad *f* informality, unconventionality, roughness, rudeness.
informante *m* informant.
informar *vt* to report, inform, instruct.
informe *a* shapeless, irregular; *m* report, account, statement, White Paper, advice.
infortunio *m* misfortune.
infracción *f* breach (*of laws etc*).
infranqueable *a* unscalable, insurmountable.
infringir *vt* to infringe, break (*the law*).
infructuoso *a* fruitless, vain.
ínfulas *f pl* conceit.
infundado *a* baseless, groundless.
infundir *vt* to infuse, instill in.
infusión *f* infusion.
ingeniar *vt* to devise; *vr* to contrive, act skillfully.
ingeniería *f* engineering.
ingeniero *m* engineer; **— de caminos canales y puertos** civil engineer; **— agrónomo** agricultural engineer.
ingenio *m* talent, wit, skill, knack, gift for improvisation; talented or witty person; engine; sugar plantation.
ingenioso *a* ingenious, skilful, inventive, with a gift for improvisation.
ingénito *a* inborn, innate.
ingente *a* huge, prodigious, unwieldy.
ingenuidad *f* candor, frankness, innocence.
ingenuo *a* candid, naïve.
ingerencia *f* interference, insertion.
ingerir (ie) *vt* to insert, introduce; to graft; *SA* to swallow, take in; *vr* to work one's way into.
Inglaterra *f* England.
ingle *f* groin.
inglés *an* English; Englishman.
ingratitud *f* ungratefulness, ingratitude.
ingrato *a* ungrateful, harsh, unpleasant.
ingrediente *m* ingredient.
ingresar *vt* to enter (*school, army, etc.*), be admitted to.
ingreso *m* entrance, ingress; intake, admission, entry; **derechos de —** entrance fee; *pl* receipts, takings.
inhábil *a* unable, incapable, unfit; disqualified.
inhabilitación *f* disqualification, disability.
inhabitable *a* uninhabitable.
inhalar *vt* to inhale.
inherente *a* inherent.
inhibir *vt* to inhibit.

inhospitalario *a* inhospitable.
inhumano *a* inhuman, savage.
inhumar *vt* to bury.
inicial *a* initial, first.
iniciar *vt* to initiate, begin, start.
inicuo *a* iniquitous, wicked.
injerto *m* graft, grafting.
injuria *f* insult, offense, injury, curse, hard words.
injuriar *vt* to insult, offend.
injurioso *a* outrageous, insulting.
injusticia *f* injustice.
injusto *a* unjust.
inmarcesible *a* unfading.
inmediación *f* continuity; *pl* environs, outskirts.
inmediato *a* contiguous, adjoining, next, immediate.
inmejorable *a* unsurpassable, unequalled.
inmemorial *a* immemorial.
inmenso *a* immense, huge, vast, countless.
inmerecido *a* undeserved.
inmigración *f* immigration.
inminente *a* imminent.
inmiscuir *vt* to mix; *vr* to interfere in, get mixed up in, get involved in.
inmoderado *a* immoderate.
inmolar *vt* to immolate, sacrifice.
inmoral *a* immoral.
inmortalizar *vt* to immortalize.
inmotivado *a* unwarranted, ungrounded, unreasonable.
inmóvil *a* fixed, motionless, constant.
inmuebles *mpl* immovables, real estate.
inmundicia *f* filth, refuse, garbage, nastiness.
inmunidad *f* immunity, exemption.
inmutar *vr* to fall, contract, change.
innato *a* innate, inborn.
innecesario *a* unnecessary.
innoble *a* ignoble.
innocuo *a* harmless.
innovación *f* innovation.
innovar *vt* to innovate.
inobediente *a* disobedient.
inocencia *f* innocence, simplicity.
inocente *a* innocent, guileless, harmless; *SA* **día de los—s** 28th December, Fools' Day.
inocular *vt* to inoculate.
inofensivo *a* inoffensive.
inolvidable *a* unforgettable.
inoportuno *a* inopportune.
inopia *f* indigence, penury, scarcity.
inopinado *a* unexpected, unforeseen.
inoxidable *a* non-rust.
inquebrantable *a* inviolable, unyielding.
inquietar *vt* to trouble, upset; *vr* to worry, fret.
inquieto *a* restless, unquiet, anxious, worried.
inquietud *f* restlessness, disquiet, uneasiness.
inquilino *m* tenant, lodger.
inquina *f* spitefulness, rancor, bitter feelings.
inquirir *vt* to inquire, look into; to investigate.
insaciable *a* insatiable, greedy.
insalubre *a* unhealthy.
inscribir *vt* to inscribe, register.
inscripción *f* inscription, registration, register.
insecticida *f* insecticide.
insecto *m* insect.
inseguridad *f* insecurity.
inseguro *a* insecure.
insensatez *f* nonsense, stupidity, foolish (action *etc*).
insensato *a* stupid, fatuous, wild, nonsensical.
insensibilidad *f* insensibility, insensitiveness.
insensible *a* senseless, unconscious; insensitive.
insepulto *a* unburied.
insertar *vt* to insert.
insidioso *a* insidious, sly.
insigne *a* notable, celebrated, noted.
insignia *f* decoration; insignia.
insignificante *a* insignificant.
insinuar *vt* to insinuate; *vr* to ingratiate oneself (*into, with*).
insípido *a* insipid, tasteless, flat.
insistencia *f* persistence, repetition.
insistir *vi* to insist, emphasize.
insolación *f* sunstroke.
insolencia *f* insolence, effrontery, cheek(iness).
insolente *a* insolent, impudent.
insólito *a* unwonted, singular, unusual.
insoluble *a* insoluble; (*color*) fast.
insolvencia *f* insolvency.
insomnio *m* insomnia.
insondable *a* unfathomable, inscrutable.
insoportable *a* unbearable.
inspección *f* inspection, survey.
inspeccionar *vt* to inspect.
inspector *m* inspector.
inspiración *f* inspiration; inhalation.
inspirar *vt* to inspire; to suggest, induce.
instalar *vt* to install, set up; *vr* to settle.
instancia *f* urgency; petition, suit, instance; **juez de primera —** Stipendiary Magistrate (*approx*); **a —s de** at the (*strong*) request of.
instantáneo *a* instantaneous; *f* snapshot.
instante *m* instant, moment; **al —** immediately, straight away; *a* pressing.
instar *vt* to urge on, press, spur.
instigar *vt* to instigate, incite, set on.
instinto *m* instinct.
institución *f* institution.
instituir *vt* to institute, set up.
instituto *m* institute, secondary school.
instrucción *f* instruction; teaching; knowledge; **Ministerio de I— Pública** Ministry of Education.
instructivo *a* enlightening.

instruir *vt* to instruct, teach; (*mil*) to drill.
instrumento *m* instrument, tool.
insubordinarse *vr* to rebel, be insubordinate.
insuficiencia *f* insufficiency.
insuficiente *a* insufficient.
insufrible *a* intolerable, unbearable.
insular *a* insular.
insulsez *f* flatness, staleness, insipidity.
insultar *vt* to insult.
insulto *m* insult, outrage.
insuperable *a* insuperable.
insurgente *m* insurgent, rebel.
insurrección *f* insurrection.
insustituíble *a* indispensable.
intacto *a* intact, untouched, whole.
intachable *a* blameless.
integrar *vt* to integrate; *vi* to be made up of, form part of.
integridad *f* integrity, honesty; wholeness.
íntegro *a* entire, integral, whole, complete; honest.
intelecto *m* intellect, understanding.
intelectual *an* intellectual.
inteligencia *f* intelligence, intellect.
inteligente *a* intelligent, clever, skillful.
intemperancia *f* intemperance.
intemperie *f* bad weather; **a la —** out-doors.
intempestivo *a* inopportune, unseasonable, ill-timed.
intención *f* intention, meaning; **con —** meaningfully, pointedly.
intencionado *a* pointed, barbed (*remark etc*).
intendencia *f* administration (*of estate, position etc*); *SA* mayoralty.
intenso *a* intense.
intentar *vt* to try, attempt.
intento *m* purpose; attempt; **de —** purposely.
intercalar *vt* to intercalate, interleave.
intercambio *m* exchange, interchange.
interceder *vi* to intercede.
intercesión *f* intercession.
interdicto *m* prohibition, interdiction.
interés *m* interest, profit, concern; **de —** interesting.
interesado *m* interested party.
interesar *vt* to interest; *vr* to take an interest in.
interestatal *a SA* interstate.
interfecto *m* (*law*) murdered person.
interino *a* temporary, provisional, substitute.
interior *a* interior; *m* inside.
interjección *f* interjection.
intermediario *m* middleman, mediator.
intermedio *a* intermediate; *m* interval.
intermitente *a* intêrmittent.
internar *vt* to intern; *vr* to penetrate inland, up-country; go deeper into.
interno *a* internal, interior, living-in; *m* boarder.
interpelar *vt* to question, interpellate.
interponer *vtr* to interpose, put between.
interposición *f* interposition, meddling, mediation.
interpretación *f* interpretation, explanation, elucidation, understanding.
interpretar *vt* to interpret, explain.
intérprete *m* interpreter.
interrogar *vt* to interrogate, question.
interrumpir *vt* to interrupt, break off, stop, cut short.
interrupción *f* interruption.
intersección *f* intersection.
intersticio *m* interstice, crack.
intervalo *m* interval.
intervenir *vi* to happen; to come between; to intervene; *vt* to audit; to control, regulate.
interventor *m* comptroller, inspector, auditor.
intestino *m* intestine.
intimar *vt* to intimate; *vt* to become intimate.
intimidad *f* intimacy, close friendship; **en la —** in private (life).
intimidar *vt* to intimidate.
íntimo *a* innermost; intimate, private.
intitular *vt* to entitle, give (title, name) to (*book, etc.*).
intolerable *a* intolerable.
intoxicar *vt* to poison.
intransigente *a* intransigent.
intransitable *a* impassable.
intratable *a* intractable, unapproachable, difficult, unsociable.
intrepidez *f* boldness, fearlessness, hardiness.
intrépido *a* intrepid, dauntless.
intriga *f* intrigue; plot (*of play, etc.*).
intrigar *vi* to scheme, plot.
intrincado *a* intricate, labyrinthine, pathless.
intrínseco *a* intrinsic.
introducción *f* introduction.
introducir *vt* to introduce, insert; *vr* to push oneself in; to get in(to).
intruso *m* intruder; *a* intrusive.
intuición *f* intuition.
inundación *f* flood, inundation.
inundar *vt* to flood, inundate, deluge.
inusitado *a* unusual, obsolete.
inútil *a* useless.
inutilidad *f* uselessness.
inutilizar *vt* to spoil, render (make) useless, disable, put out of action.
invadir *vt* to invade.
inválido *a* useless, cripple; null, void; *m* disabled soldier.
invariable *a* invariable.
invasión *f* invasion.
invasor *m* invader.
invención *f* invention, contrivance (*invented*), (*imaginative*) power.

inventar *vt* to invent, find out, contrive.
inventariar *vt* to inventory, make list of.
inventiva *f* inventiveness.
inventor *m* inventor.
invernadero *m* hot house.
invernar *vi* to hibernate.
inverosímil *a* unlikely, improbable, unlikely to be true.
inversa *ad* **a la** — on the contrary.
inversión *f* inversion; investment.
inversionista *mf* investor.
invertir (ie) *vt* to invert; to invest.
investigación *f* investigation.
investigar *vt* to investigate, look into.
inveterado *a* inveterate, deep-seated.
invicto *a* unconquered, undefeated, unbowed (*head*), unconquerable
invierno *m* winter.
inviolable *a* inviolable; inviolate.
invitar *vt* to invite; to bring on.
invocar *vt* to invoke, implore, call upon, on.
involucrar *vt* to mingle, upset, confuse.
inyección *f* injection.
inyectado: **—s en sangre** bloodshot (*eyes*).
inyectar *vt* to inject.
iodo, yodo *m* iodine.
ipil *m* *CA* kind of outer garment.
ir *vi* to go, walk; to suit, to fit, be convenient; to match, suit; **— a caballo** to ride; **— a gatas** to crawl; **— a pie** to walk, go on foot; **— en coche** to ride; **— por tren** to go by train; **— por agua** to go for water; *vr* to go away; to grow.
ira *f* anger, wrath, ire.
iracundo *a* angry, enraged, irate.
iris *m* iris; **arco** — rainbow.
Irlanda *f* Ireland.
irlandés *an* Irish.
ironía *f* irony.
irónico *a* ironical.
irracional *a* irrational.
irreemplazable *a* irreplaceable.
irreflexión *f* rashness.
irrefragable *a* irrefutable, undeniable.
irremediable *a* irremediable, incurable.
irresoluto *a* irresolute, hesitant.
irrespetuoso *a* disrespectful.
irresponsable *a* irresponsible.
irrigar *vt* to irrigate, water.
irrisorio *a* ridiculous; non-existent.
irritable *a* irritable.
irrompible *a* unbreakable.
irrupción *f* irruption; raid; rash.
Isabel *f* Elizabeth, Isabel.
isla *f* island.
islandés *a* Icelandic; *m* Icelander.
isleño *an* islander.
islote *m* small island, islet.
israelí *an* Israeli.
israelita *an* Israelite, Jew(ish).
istmo *m* isthmus.
Italia *f* Italy.
italiano *an* Italian.
itinerario *m* itinerary, route; program, timetable, guide.
izar *vt* to hoist (*flag*).
izquierdo *a* left-handed; *f* left hand; the Left (*pol*).

J

jabalí *m* wild boar.
jabón *m* soap; *Arg* fright.
jabonar *vt* to soap, lather; to reprimand, give a drubbing to.
jaca *f* pony, cob.
jacal *m* *Mex* Indian hut, wigwam.
jácara *f* a gay dance and song.
jacarandoso *a* merry, noisily gay, hilarious.
jacinto *m* hyacinth.
jactancia *f* boastfulness, arrogance.
jactarse *vr* to boast, be proud of.
jadeante *a* panting.
jadear *vi* to pant.
jadeo *m* panting.
jaez *m* harness, trappings; sort, kind.
jaguar *m* jaguar.
jagüey *m* *SA* large pool or basin.
Jaime *m* James.
jalbegue *m* whitewash.
jalea *f* jelly.
jalear *vt* to set on (*dogs*); to urge on, encourage.
jaleo *m* noise; row; a dance.
jamás *ad* never; ever; **nunca —** never again, absolutely never.
jamelgo *m* sorry nag.
jamón *m* ham.
jámparo *m* *Col* small boat or canoe.
Japón *m* Japan.
japonés *an* Japanese.
jaque *m* check; **— mate** checkmate (*chess*).
jaqueca *f* headache, migraine.
jarabe *m* syrup.
jarano *m* Mexican sombrero
jarcia *f* shrouds, cordage (*of a ship*); accouterments.
jardín *m* garden.
jardinería *f* gardening.
jardinero *m* gardener.
jaripeo *m* *Mex* rodeo.
jarra *f* earthen jar; **brazos en —** arms akimbo.
jarro *m* jug; pitcher.
jarrón *m* vase.
jaspe *m* jasper.
jaspeado *a* marbled, mottled.
jaspear *vt* to vein, marble.
jaula *f* birdcage; cage (*for wild animals*); madman's cell.
jauría *f* pack of hounds.
jazmín *m* jessamine.
jefe *m* chief, leader, head; **— político** governor.
jején *m* gnat; *SA* midget.
jengibre *m* ginger.
jerarquía *f* hierarchy.
jerárquico *a* hierarchical.
jerez *m* sherry.

jerga *f* jargon; straw mattress.
jericoplear *vt Guat, Hond* to disturb, to annoy.
jerigonza *f* jargon, slang.
jeringa *f* syringe.
jeringar *vt* to inject; to annoy.
jeroglífico *m* hieroglyph.
jesuita *m* Jesuit; hypocrite.
jeta *f* thick lips; face.
jíbaro *m PR* rustic, peasant.
jícara *m* cup (*for chocolate*).
jilguero *m* linnet.
jinete *m* horseman, rider.
jipijapa *m* straw hat, Panama.
jira *f* outing; excursion; strip, shred (*of cloth*).
jirafa *f* giraffe.
jirón *m* rag, tatter.
jocosidad *f* waggery.
jocoso *a* waggish, jocular.
jocoyote *m SA* youngest child, pet.
jofaina *f* basin.
Jorge *m* George.
jornada *f* one-day's march or work; journey, stage; expedition; act (*of play*).
jornal *m* a day's work *or* wage; wages, pay.
jornalero *m* journeyman, day laborer, worker.
joroba *f* hump.
jorobado *an* hump-backed, hunchback.
José *m* Joseph.
jota *f* iota, jot; Spanish dance and song; **no saber ni —** not to know a thing.
joven *a* young; *m* young man, youth; *f* lass, girl.
jovial *a* Jovian; jovial, blithe, cheery.
jovialidad *f* joviality.
joya *f* jewel, gem.
joyería *f* jewelry; jeweler's shop.
joyero *m* jeweler, jewel casket.
Juana *f* Jane, Jean, Joan.
juanete *m* bunion; prominent cheekbones.
juanillo *m Chi, Per* gratuity, tip.
juay *m Mex* knife.
jubilación *f* pensioning, pension, retirement (*from job*).
jubilar *vt* to pension off, superannuate.
jubileo *m* jubilee.
júbilo *m* jubilation, merriment.
jubón *m* (leather) jacket, waist (*woman's dress*), bodice.
judaísmo *m* Judaism.
judía *f* bean, kidney bean.
judicatura *f* judicature.
judicial *a* judicial, legal.
judío *an* Jewish, Jew.
juego *m* play, game; set (*of articles*); movement (*of watches*); **— de palabras** pun; **hacer —** to match (*colors, clothes etc*); **— limpio** fair play.
juerga *f* spree.
jueves *m* Thursday.
juez *m* judge, magistrate; expert; **— de primera instancia** judge in a court of first instance.
jugada *f* move (*in a game*); evil, ill-turn, bad trick.
jugador *m* player, gambler.
jugar (ue) *vt* to play, gamble; **— limpio** to play fair; *vr* to risk.
jugarreta *f* foul play; dirty trick.
juglar *m* juggler, tumbler; minstrel, ballad singer.
jugo *m* juice; substance, pith.
jugoso *a* juicy, meaty, full of matter.
juguete *m* toy, plaything.
juguetear *vi* to gambol; to toy with.
juguetón *a* playful.
juicio *m* judgment; sense, opinion; **a mi —** in my opinion; **estar en su —** to be in one's senses.
juicioso *a* sensible, discreet, judicious, wise.
julepear *vt Arg* to alarm, scare; *Mex* to torment, annoy.
Julieta *f* Juliet.
julio *m* July.
jumento *m* donkey, ass; mount.
junco *m* rush; **— de Indias** rattan.
jungla *f* jungle.
junio *m* June.
junquillo *m* jonquil.
junta *f* meeting, junta, council; assembly; board, committee; junction.
juntamente *ad* together; conjointly.
juntar *vt* to join, unite, collect, gather, heap together; *vr* to gather together; *Arg* to live together.
junto *a* united; together; *ad* near; **— a** next to.
juntura *f* joint.
jurado *m* jury.
juramentar *vt* to interrogate somebody on oath.
juramento *m* oath, curse; **— falso** perjury.
jurar *vi* to swear; *vt* to declare on oath.
jurídico *a* juridical, legal, lawful.
jurisconsulto *m* jurist, authority on legal matters.
jurisdicción *f* jurisdiction, authority.
jurisprudencia *f* jurisprudence, law.
jurista *m* jurist, lawyer.
justa *f* joust.
justamente *ad* just, exactly.
justicia *f* justice, fairness.
justiciero *a* just.
justificación *f* justification, defense, support.
justificar *vt* to justify; *vr* to vindicate oneself.
justo *a* just, right, exact; righteous; close (fitting); *ad* tightly.
juvenil *a* juvenile, youthful.
juventud *f* youth; young people.
juzgado *m* court of justice; **— de primera instancia,** court of first instance; *a* judged; sentenced.
juzgar *vt* to judge, deliver judgment; to give an opinion; to think.

K

kilo *m* kilo(gram).
kilogramo *m* kilogram.
kilolitro *m* kiloliter.
kilometraje *m* number of kilometers.
kilométrico *a* kilometric; *m* (*Spain*) long-distance railway ticket.
kilómetro *m* kilometer.
kiosco *m* kiosk.

L

laberinto *m* labyrinth, maze.
labial *a* labial.
labio *m* lip, brim (*of cup*).
labor *f* task, labor, work, needlework; **es una — muy fina** it is fine work.
laborable *a* working (*day*).
laborar *vt* to till (*soil*); to work.
laboreo *m* working, exploitation.
laborioso *a* assiduous; laborious, wearisome.
laborista *a inv* labor.
labrado *a* wrought, hewn, worked.
labrador *m* husbandman; tiller; farmer.
labrantío *a* arable.
labranza *f* husbandry, plowing.
labrar *vt* to work, plow; to carve, dress (*stone*), to carve out (*career etc*).
labriego *m* farmhand.
laca *f* lacquer.
lacayo *m* footman, lackey, servant.
lacerar *vt* to tear (*flesh*); to hurt.
lacio *a* lank, straight (*hair*); languid.
lacónico *a* laconic; brief.
lacra *f* defect, blemish; *SA* ulcer.
lacrar *vt* to seal.
lacre *m* sealing wax.
lacrimoso *a* tearful, lachrymose.
lácteo *a* milky; **via —a** milky way.
ladear *vt* to tilt, tip, turn; to skirt (*hill*); *vr* to incline to one side.
ladera *f* slope, hillside.
ladino *a* cunning, crafty; *m* Ladin, Ladino.
lado *m* side, edge, direction; **al —** nearby, aside, next door.
ladrar *vi* to bark.
ladrido *m* barking.
ladrillo *m* tile, brick.
ladrón *m* thief, robber.
lagar *m* wine press.
lagarto *m* lizard.
lago *m* lake.
lágrima *f* tear; drop.
laguna *f* pond, lagoon; lacuna, gap.
laico *a* lay, civil; *m* layman.
laja *f Arg* slate.
lama *f* slime; seaweed; *m* lama.
lamentable *a* lamentable; deplorable.
lamentación *f* wail.
lamentar *vt* to deplore, regret; to mourn, wail; *vr* to cry.
lamento *m* wail, moan.
lamer *vt* to lick.
lamida *f* lick.
lámina *f* plate; sheet; engraving; full-page illustration.
laminar *vt* to roll metal.
lámpara *f* lamp; stain (*of oil*).
lampiño *a* beardless, immature.
lamuso *a Cub, PR* impudent, barefaced.
lana *f* wool; woolen cloth.
lanar *a* woolly; **ganado —** sheep.
lance *m* cast; episode; incident; chance; **de —** secondhand; **— de honor** affair of honor, duel.
lancero *m* lancer.
lanceta *f* lancet.
lancha *f* gig; launch; lighter; **— de socorro** lifeboat.
lanchero *m* bargee; boatman.
landó *m* landau.
lanero *m* wool dealer.
langosta *f* locust; lobster.
langostín *m* crawfish.
languidecer *vi* to languish.
languidez *f* languor; unresponsiveness; weariness; indolence.
lánguido *a* languid; feeble; lazy; weak, spineless.
lanilla *f* thin flannel; nap (*of cloth*).
lanudo *a* woolly; fleecy.
lanza *f* lance; spear; spike; shaft; **— en ristre** on the qui vive, ready for action.
lanzada *f* stroke with a lance; lance wound.
lanzadera *f* shuttle.
lanzallamas *m SA* flamethrower.
lanzamiento *m* throwing; launching.
lanzar *vt* to throw; to hurl; to launch; to throw up, be sick; *vr* to launch oneself, throw oneself.
lapa *f* slime (*on stagnant water*), scum.
lapicero *m* pencil holder, pencil.
lápida *f* tablet; tombstone; polished stone; **— mortuoria** gravestone.
lapidar *vt* to stone (*to death*).
lapidario *a* lapidary, pungent (*phrase*).
lápiz *m* pencil; graphite.
lapón *m* Laplander.
lapso *m* lapse; slip.
largar *vt* to let go; to give (*sigh, slap*); *vr* to clear off, go away, betake oneself off.
largo *a* long, protracted, liberal; *m* length; **a la —a** in the long run; **a lo —** along, all through, from end to end; **pasar de —** to pass (*by, on the other side, off the coast*).
larguera *f* length.
largueza *f* liberality, largesse, bounty.
lárice *m* larch tree.
laringe *f* larynx.
larva *f* mask; grub, larva.
lascivo *a* lascivious, lewd.
lasitud *f* lassitude.
lástima *f* sympathy, pity, compassion; **¡qué —!** what a pity

(shame)!; **da —** it is (pitiful, a pity), it rouses pity.
lastimadura *f* sore, hurt, wound.
lastimar *vt* to hurt, wound; to injure, offend; *vr* to complain; to injure oneself (*seriously*), be hurt.
lastimero *a* doleful, pitiful.
lastrar *vt* to ballast.
lastre *m* ballast; weight.
lata *f* tin plate; tin can; nuisance; **dar la —** to annoy, bore; **en —** tinned, canned
latear *vi Arg* to talk too much.
latente *a* latent, hidden.
lateral *a* lateral, side (*door etc*).
latido *m* pulsation, beating, throb.
latifundio *m* large estate.
latigazo *m* whiplash, stroke (*with whip*); crack (*of whip*).
látigo *m* whip.
latín *m* Latin language.
latinidad *f* Latin.
latinajo *m* Latin tag or quotation.
latino *a* Latin; **vela —** a lateen sail.
latir *vi* to palpitate, beat, throb.
latitud *f* breadth, width, latitude; freedom.
lato *a* extensive, diffuse; free, easy.
latón *m* brass.
latoso *a* annoying, boring.
latrocinio *m* robbery, stealing.
laucha *f SA* mouse.
laúd *m* lute.
laudable *a* praiseworthy.
laudo *m* award.
laureado *a* decorated, honored.
laurel *m* laurel; *pl* honors.
lava *f* lava.
lavabo *m* washstand; lavabo.
lavadero *m* washing place.
lavado *m* washing, wash.
lavamanos *m* washstand.
lavandera *f* washerwoman, laundress.
lavandería *f SA* laundry.
lavar *vt* to wash, cleanse; *vr* **— las manos de** to wash one's hands of.
lavativa *f* enema.
laxante *an* softening, laxative.
laxitud *f* laxity.
laya *f* manner, kind, quality.
lazada *f* knot, bow.
lazar *vt* to lasso.
lazarillo *m* guide (*for blind people*).
lazo *m* loop, snare; bow, tie; lasso; slipknot; bond, ties, connection.
leal *a* loyal, faithful.
lealtad *f* loyalty, sincerity, devotion.
lebrel *m* greyhound.
lección *f* lesson, reading; example.
lector *m* reader, lecturer.
lectura *f* reading.
lechada *f* grout; *SA* whitewash.
leche *f* milk; **— crema** custard.
lechera *f* milkmaid; *a* milch.
lechería *f* dairy.
lecho *m* couch, bed; layer, stratum; bottom (*of river*).
lechón *m* sucking pig.
lechoso *a* milky.
lechuga *f* lettuce.
lechuza *f* barn owl.
leer *vti* to read.
legación *f* legation.
legado *m* legacy; legate, ambassador.
legajo *m* file, bundle of documents, docket, dossier.
legal *a* lawful, legal; faithful.
legalidad *f* legality, lawfulness.
legalizar *vt* to legalize.
légamo *m* slime, filthy mud, ooze.
legar *vt* to bequeath; to transmit.
legatario *m* legatee.
legendario *a* legendary.
legión *f* legion.
legionario *m* legionary, legionnaire.
legislación *f* legislation, law.
legislar *vt* to legislate, enact laws.
legitimar *vt* to legalize, render legitimate.
legítimo *a* legitimate, authentic, genuine.
lego *a* lay; ignorant, uneducated; *m* layman.
legua *f* league (*about 3 miles*).
leguleyo *m* petty lawyer, scrivener.
legumbre *f* vegetable.
leído *a* well-read.
lejanía *f* distance; **en la —** far off.
lejano *a* distant, far, remote.
lejía *f* lye.
lejos *ad* far, far off; **a lo —** in the distance; **de —** from a distance.
lelo *a* slow-witted, dull.
lema *m* motto, device.
lencería *f* store of linen goods; draper's shop.
lengua *f* tongue; language, (*bell*) clapper; (*of land*) strip; **no morderse la —** not to mince words.
lenguado *m* sole (*fish*).
lenguaje *m* language, style, speech.
lengüeta *f* needle (of a balance); (*carp*) tongue; (*mech*) feather, wedge; epiglottis; tongue (*of shoe*).
lenidad *f* lenity, mildness (*of treatment*).
lenitivo *a m* lenitive.
lente *f or m* magnifying glass; lens; *pl* spectacles, glasses.
lenteja *f* lentil.
lentitud *f* slowness: tardiness.
lento *a* slow, tardy, heavy.
leña *f* firewood; kindling; **llevar — al monte** to carry coals to Newcastle.
leñador *m* woodman; woodcutter.
leño *m* log.
león *m* lion; Leo; **— marino** sealion.
leonés *an* (*inhabitant*) of León.
leonino *a* leonine.
leopardo *m* leopard.
Leopoldo *m* Leopold.
Lepe *m* **sabe más que —** he knows more than old Nick.
lépero *a Mex* low, base.
lepra *f* leprosy.
leproso *a* leprous; *m* leper.
lerdo *a* slow to understand, dull, dense.
lesión *f* damage, injury.

lesivo *a* harmful, injurious.
letal *a* mortal, lethal, deadly.
letanía *f* litany; rigmarole.
letargo *m* lethargy.
letra *f* letter (*of alphabet*); handwriting; character (*print*); — **de cambio** bill of exchange; **a la** — literally; *pl* letters, learning; **en** — **de molde** in print.
letrado *a* learned; *m* lawyer, man of letters.
letrero *m* sign, label; letterhead; notice, (*some*) lettering.
letrina *f* latrine, water closet.
leva *f* levy; weighing anchor; **mar de** — swell.
levadizo *a* liftable; **puente** — drawbridge.
levadura *f* ferment; yeast.
levantamiento *m* raising; uprising, revolt.
levantar *vt* to raise, lift up, erect, stir up; to draw up, complete (*forms*); — **acta** to write (up) minutes; — **un plano** to draw a plan; — **la mesa** to clear the table; *vr* to rise.
levante *m* Levant; Mediterranean regions of Spain; east wind.
levar *vt* to weigh anchor.
leve *a* light, slight, trifling.
levedad *f* lightness, inconsequence.
levita *f* frockcoat; *m* Levite.
léxico *m* vocabulary, dictionary.
ley *f* law; statute; act; **de buena** — sterling, reliable.
leyenda *f* legend, story; device, inscription, lettering.
liar *vt* to tie; to bundle; to roll (*cigarettes*); to set at loggerheads; *vr* to get mixed up (*with*).
libar *vt* to suck, taste; to make libations.
libelo *m* libel.
libélula *f* dragonfly.
liberal *a* liberal, generous.
liberalidad *f* liberality, openhandedness.
libertad *f* freedom, liberty; — **de comercio** free trade; — **de cultos** freedom of worship; — **de prensa** freedom of the press.
libertar *vt* to free, set at liberty, liberate.
libertino *an* libertine, loose liver.
liberto *m* freed slave.
libra *f* pound (*weight*); pound (*coin*); — **esterlina** pound sterling.
librador *m* drawer (*of bill of exchange*).
libramiento *m* order of payment, delivery.
libranza *f* draft, bill of exchange.
librar *vt* to deliver, free; to issue; to pass (*sentence*); to engage (*in battle*); to draw (*bills*); *vr* — **de** to get rid of.
libre *a* free; vacant, disengaged; — **a bordo** free on board; — **de derechos** duty free; — **cambio** free trade.
librea *f* livery, uniform.
librería *f* bookshop.
librero *m* bookseller.
libreta *f* passbook; notebook; one pound loaf.
libro *m* book; — **diario** journal; — **mayor** ledger; — **talonario** check book.
licencia *f* license, permission; leave, furlough; — **absoluta** discharge, demobilization.
licenciado *m* holder of university license, bachelor, B.A.; lawyer.
licenciar *vt* to license; to allow; to discharge.
licensioso *a* licentious.
liceo *m* lyceum, club.
licitador *m* bidder (*at auction*).
licitar *vt* to bid at auction; *see* **pujar**.
lícito *a* lawful, permitted, permissible.
licor *m* liquid, liquor, spirits.
licuar *vt* to liquefy.
lid *f* contest; fight, battle.
líder *m* leader.
lidia *f* combat; bullfight.
lidiar *vi* to contend, fight.
liebre *f* hare.
lienzo *m* canvas, picture, linen cloth; length (*of battlements*).
liga *f* league; garter; alloy.
ligadura *f* binding; ligature.
ligamento *m* ligament; tie.
ligar *vt* to bind, tie; to alloy.
ligereza *f* lightness, agility; swiftness; levity; off-handedness.
ligero *a* light; swift, fast; slight; — **de cascos** featherbrained; *f* **a la** —**a** superficially, quickly.
lija *f* sandpaper; dogfish.
lila *f* lilac.
lima *f* file; lime (tree).
limar *vt* to file, polish.
limeño *an* (*inhabitant*) of Lima.
limitación *f* limitation; qualification.
limitar *vt* to limit, restrict; to qualify; *vi* to border on.
límite *m* limit; end; boundary.
limítrofe *a* **terreno** — land along the boundary; **naciones** —**s** neighboring countries.
limón *m* lemon.
limosna *f* alms, charity.
limosnero *m* beggar.
limpiabotas *m* bootblack, shoeshine.
limpiar *vt* to clean; to clear a place; *Arg* to steal.
limpieza *f* cleanliness, purity; neatness (*of action*); the act of cleaning; **Sección de** — Sanitation Department.
limpio *a* clean; neat; free, clear; **poner en** — to make a fair copy of, make clear; **sacar en** — to deduce, conclude, make out (*of statements, arguments etc*).
linaje *m* lineage, kin; sort.
linajudo *a* blue-blooded.
linaza *f* linseed.
lince *a* sharp-sighted; *m* lynx.
lindar *vi* to border on.
lindante *a* adjoining, contiguous.

linde *m* boundary (*stone or mark*).
lindero *a* bordering upon; *m* boundary.
lindo *a* pretty, genteel; *Arg, Par, Urug* good, excellent; **de lo —** perfectly, neatly.
línea *f* line, lineage; boundary; **en — directa** as the crow flies.
lineamiento *m* lineament; **-s** general outline.
lingote *m* ingot.
lingüista *m* linguist.
lingüística *f* linguistics.
linimento *m* liniment; embrocation.
lino *m* linen; flax.
lintel *m* lintel.
linterna *f* lantern; **— sorda** dark lantern; **— mágica** magic lantern.
lío *m* bundle; mess; **¡qué —!** What a mess (problem, jam)!; **armar un —** to make trouble.
lioso *a Arg* troublemaking, gossiping.
liquidación *f* liquidation; liquefaction; sale.
liquidar *vt* to liquefy; to liquidate.
líquido *a* liquid; net.
lira *f* lyre.
lírico *a* lyric(al); *Arg, Par, Urug* Utopian.
lirio *m* lily.
lisiado *a* injured; crippled.
lisiar *vt* to injure, lame, cripple.
liso *a* smooth, flat; **— y llano** plain and simple.
lisonja *f* compliment, flattering remark.
lisonjear *vt* to flatter.
lisonjero *a* flattering; promising, complimentary.
lista *f* list; roll; **— de platos** bill of fare; **pasar —** to call the roll; **— de correos** poste-restante.
listado *a* striped.
listo *a* ready; clever, smart.
listón *m* ribbon; beam.
litera *f* litter; berth.
literato *m* man of letters; literary man, writer.
litigar *vti* to litigate; to contend.
litigio *m* litigation; lawsuit.
litografía *f* lithography.
litoral *m* littoral; shore; *a* coastal.
litro *m* liter (1¾ *pints*).
liudo *a Col, Chi* leavened, fermented.
liviano *a* light, slight; lewd; venial.
lívido *a* livid.
loa *f* praise; panegyric; prologue (*to play*).
loable *a* laudable.
loar *vt* to praise, extol.
lobato *m* wolfcub.
lobo *m* wolf; lobe (*of ear*); **— marino** seal.
lóbrego *a* murky, lugubrious, gloomy.
lóbulo *m* lobe.
loca *f Arg, Urug* fast woman, prostitute.
locación *f* lease.
local *a* local; *m* premises, site.
localidad *f* locality; place, seat (*in theater*).
localizar *vt* to localize; to place.
loción *f* lotion.
loco *a* insane; *m* madman; **— de atar** raving lunatic; **— rematado** quite mad, completely crazy.
locomoción *f* locomotion.
locomotora *f* locomotive; railway engine.
locro *m SA* kind of stew.
locuaz *a* talkative, garrulous.
locución *f* locution, phrase, idiom.
locura *f* madness, craziness; lunacy.
lodo *m* mud.
lógica *f* logic.
lógico *a* logical; *m* logician.
logogrifo *m* riddle, puzzle.
lograr *vt* to obtain, manage, succeed, achieve, attain.
logro *m* success; gain, profit; attainment; usury.
loma *f* hillock, knoll, down.
lombriz *f* earthworm; **— solitaria** tapeworm.
lomo *m* loin; back (*of animal, book*).
lona *f* canvas; duck canvas.
londinense *an* (*inhabitant*) of London.
longaniza *f* pork sausage.
longitud *f* length; longitude.
lonja *f* exchange (*for corn etc*); slice, strip.
loro *m*, *SA* **lora** *f* parrot.
losa *f* flagstone; tombstone.
lote *m* lot, part, portion; *SA* remnant; plot of ground.
lotería *f* lottery, raffle.
loza *f* porcelain, china, crockery.
lozanía *f* vigor; freshness, bloom; luxuriance.
lozano *a* sprightly; luxuriant, vigorous.
lubricar *vt* to lubricate.
lucero *m* star, morning star.
lucidez *f* brilliancy, clarity.
lucido *a* brilliant, splendid, magnificent.
lúcido *a* clear, lucid; perspicuous.
luciente *a* shining, bright.
luciérnaga *f* glowworm, firefly.
lucimiento *m* splendor; success.
lucir *vi* to shine, glow; *vt* to display; *vr* to do well, show to advantage, show off, display oneself.
lucrarse *vr* to profit by, earn money by, get rich.
lucro *m* gain, lucre.
luctuoso *a* sad, mournful.
lucha *f* struggle, fight; strife; wrestle.
luchar *vi* to struggle, wrestle.
luego *ad* presently; *cj* then; **desde —** at once; of course, naturally; **hasta —** so long.
lugar *m* place, spot; room; space; time; opportunity; town; **hacer —** to make room; **en — de** instead of; **en su —** in its (stead, place), instead of it; **dar — a** to occasion, cause.

lugareño *m* villager, rustic.
lúgubre *a* gloomy, dismal.
luirse *vr SA* to wear away.
Luis *m* Louis.
lujo *m* luxury.
lujoso *a* showy, luxurious, lavish.
lujuria *f* lust, lewdness.
lumbre *f* fire; light; **sacar —** to strike a light.
lumbrera *f* luminary, shining light; skylight.
luminoso *a* luminous, dazzling; **idea —a** brilliant idea.
luna *f* moon; mirror; **— de miel** honeymoon.
lunar *a* lunar; *m* mole, beauty spot; flaw; **— postizo** patch.
lunes *m* Monday.
luneta *f* orchestra seat; spectacle lens.
lunfardo *m Arg* thief, pimp.
lusitano *an* Lusitanian, Portuguese.
lustrar *vt* to polish, gloss; to expiate.
lustre *m* gloss; luster, glaze; brilliancy.
lustro *m* five years, lustrum.
lustroso *a* shining, glossy.
luterano *an* Lutheran.
luto *m* mourning; **estar de —** to be in mourning.
luz *f* light, daylight; knowledge; *pl* culture, enlightenment; obviously; **entre dos luces** in the twilight; **dar a —** to give birth to; to publish.
Luzbel *m* Lucifer.

LL

llaga *f* ulcer, sore, wound.
llama *f* flame; llama.
llamada *f* call; notice; index mark.
llamamiento *m* summons, call-up.
llamar *vt* to call, cite; to name, denominate; to attract; *vr* to be called.
llamarada *f* blaze, flash.
llamativo *a* striking, showy.
llamear *vi* to flame, blaze up.
llanero *mf SA* plains dweller.
llaneza *f* plainness, simplicity, directness; homeliness.
llano *a* plain, level; homely, untutored, unaffected, simple; evident, clear; *m* plain, flat stretch (*of land*).
llanta *f* tire.
llanto *m* weeping; flood of tears.
llanura *f* plain, prairie; flatness.
llave *f* key; tap, wrench; clef (*mus*); **— maestra** master-key; **echar la —** to lock.
llavero *m* key ring
llavín *m* latch key.
llegada *f* arrival.
llegar *vi* to arrive; to come, come to; to amount to, suffice; *vr* to bring together; **— a las manos** to come to blows; **— a saber** to find out.
llena *f* flood.
llenar *vt* to fill, fill up; to fulfill; to satisfy.
lleno *a* full, replenished; *m* plenty, completeness, glut; (*theat*) full house.
lleulle *a Chi* incompetent.
llevadero *a* tolerable, bearable.
llevar *vt* to carry, take, take away; to produce; to lead; to endure; **— a cabo** to carry through; **— al crédito** to credit, place to the credit; **— los libros** to keep books, accounts; *vr* **— un chasco** to be disappointed; **— bien** to get along well together.
llorar *vi* to weep, cry.
lloro *m* weeping, cry.
llorón *m* cry-baby; **sauce —** weeping willow.
lloroso *a* tearful.
llover (ue) *vi* to rain; **— a cántaros** to rain bucketfuls.
llovizna *f* drizzle.
lloviznar *vi* to drizzle.
lluvia *f* rain.
lluvioso *a* rainy, wet.

M

macaco *a Cub, Chi* ugly; *n Mex* hobgoblin.
macana *f Mex* ancient wooden weapon; *Col* palm tree; *Arg* blunder.
macerar *vt* to soak; to mortify (*the flesh*).
maceta *f* flowerpot.
macilento *a* lean, extenuated, drawn.
macizo *a* massive, solid.
macuache *a Mex* ignorant; *n* illiterate Indian.
mácula *f* stain, blemish.
machacar *vt* to pound, grind; *vi* to harp on (*a subject*).
machete *m* cutlass; machete.
macho *a* male; *m* he-mule; male; male animal; sledge hammer; **— cabrío** he-goat.
madeja *f* skein; lock, shock (*hair*).
madera *f* wood; lumber, timber; **— brava** hard wood; **— de deriva** driftwood.
madero *m* log, beam.
madrastra *f* stepmother.
madre *f* mother; origin; bed (*of river*); **— política** mother-in-law.
madreselva *f* honeysuckle.
madriguera *f* burrow, den, lair.
madrileño *an* (*inhabitant*) of Madrid.
madrina *f* godmother; patroness.
madrugada *f* dawn, early morning (*before dawn*).
madrugar *vi* to rise early, get up with the dawn; **quien madruga, Dios le ayuda** the early bird catches the worm.
madurar *vti* to ripen, mature; to think over.
madurez *f* maturity, ripeness.
maduro *a* ripe, mellow; perfect.

maestra *f* schoolmistress.
maestría *f* mastery, skill.
maestro *a* principal, main, master; *m* master; (*elementary*) teacher.
magancear *vi Col, Chi* to loiter, idle.
magia *f* magic.
magistrado *m* magistrate.
magistral *a* masterly; prescribed.
magistratura *f* judicature.
magnánimo *a* magnanimous, big-hearted.
magnate *m* magnate.
magnético *a* magnetic.
magnetizar *vt* to magnetize.
magnífico *a* magnificent, splendid; stately.
magnitud *f* size, magnitude.
mago *m* magician; **los reyes—s** Magi, the Wise Men of the East.
magra *f* slice of ham.
magro *a* lean, thin.
magullar *vt* to bruise, mangle.
maitines *m pl* matins.
maíz *m* maize, corn.
majada *f* shepherd's cot, sheepfold.
majadero *a* silly; *m* clown, bore; pestle.
majar *vt* to hammer, pound; to bother, be tiresome.
majestad *f* majesty.
majestuoso *a* majestic.
maja *a f* fashionable flirt (*of lower classes*).
majo *a m* dandy, poppycock (*of lower classes*).
mal *a apocopation of* **malo**; *m* evil, harm; illness; *ad* ill, badly; **echar a —** to despise; **llevar a —** to complain (*of*); **de— en peor** from bad to worse; **del — el menor** the lesser of the evils.
malaconsejado *a* easily led (*astray*), ill thought out, imprudent.
malagueño *an* from, of Málaga.
malbaratar *vt* to sell cheap; to squander.
malcontento *a* malcontent, hard to please.
malcriado *a* ill-bred.
maldad *f* wickedness, mischievousness, evil(ness).
maldecir *vt* to damn, curse; to swear at.
maldiciente *m* defamer, slanderer, foul mouth.
maldición *f* curse.
maldito *a* accursed, blessed; condemned; (*fam*) no one, not a scrap.
malear *vt* to pervert; to injure.
malecón *m* embankment, breakwater, wharf.
maledicencia *f* slander(ing).
maleficiar *vt* to harm; to bewitch.
malestar *m* uneasiness, discomfort; disquiet.
maleta *f* handbag, briefcase, valise; portmanteau; **hacer la —** to pack up, to be on.
malevolencia *f* ill-will.
malévolo *a* malignant.
maleza *f* patch of weed; thicket; scrub, bramble patch.
malgastar *vt* to squander.
malhechor *m* malefactor.
malhumorado *a* ill-tempered, disgruntled, surly.
malicia *f* malice, cunning, slyness.
malicioso *a* malicious, cunning, sly.
malignidad *f* evil, malice; malignancy.
maligno *a* malignant.
malintencionado *a* impertinent; pointed; nasty.
malo *a* bad, evil, harmful, wicked; ill; naughty.
maloca *f SA* invasion of Indian lands.
malogrado *a* unfortunate, ill-starred, unlucky.
malograr *vt* to waste, miss; *vr* to fail, be frustrated; to come to naught.
malogro *m* frustration, failure, miscarriage.
malón *m SA* attack by Indians.
malsano *a* unhealthy, insanitary.
malsonante *a* evil-sounding, unpleasant, distasteful.
maltratar *vt* to abuse, ill-treat.
maltrato *m* unkindness; ill-treatment.
malva *f* mallow, marshmallow.
malvado *a* wicked; *m* scoundrel.
malla *f* net, network, mesh; (*coat of*) mail; stockinette.
Mallorca *f* Majorca.
mallorquín *an* Majorcan, from Majorca.
mamá *f* mother, mamma.
mamandurria *f SA* sinecure.
mamar *vt* to suck.
mamarracho *m* grotesque figure; daub, mess; **¡qué —!** what a sight!
mampara *f* screen; shelter.
mampostería *f* (*stone*) masonry.
mampuesto *m* parapet.
maná *m* manna.
manada *f* herd, flock; handful.
manantial *m* source, spring.
manar *vi* to spring, ooze, flow.
mancebo *m* youth; shop boy.
mancilla *f* stain.
mancillar *vt* to spot, blemish.
manco *a* one-armed, armless; maimed; *m* one-handed person.
mancomunado *ad* conjoint, combined.
mancomunidad *f* fellowship, association; commonwealth.
mancha *f* spot; stain, blot.
manchar *vt* to stain, tarnish, blot.
manchego *an* (*inhabitant*) of La Mancha.
mandadero *m* messenger.
mandado *m* errand, message, order, request.
mandamás *m* boss, head man.
mandamiento *m* order; (*Scripture*) commandment; writ.

mandar *vt* to command, give orders; to send.
mandatario *m* agent, attorney; ruler.
mandato *m* mandate; order.
mandíbula *f* jaw; — **inferior** lower jaw.
mando *m* command, power of command.
mandón *a* bossy, overweening.
manejable *a* manageable.
manejar *vt* to handle, manipulate; to govern.
manejo *m* handling, conduct; intrigue.
manera *f* manner, style; way, mode; **sobre** — excessively, very particularly.
manga *f* sleeve; hose; wide-meshed net; waterspout; breadth of ship's beam; — **de riego** hosepipe.
manganear *vt SA* to lasso.
manganeo *m SA* rodeo.
mangle *m* mangrove tree.
mango *m* handle, (*broom*) stick, haft; mango, mango tree.
manguera *f* hose; ventilation shaft.
manguito *m* muff.
maní *m SA* peanut.
manía *f* mania, obsession; whim.
maniatar *vt* to manacle, handcuff.
manicomio *m* lunatic asylum.
manifestación *f* (*public*) demonstration, procession, declaration.
manifestar *vt* to manifest, show, tell, declare; to expose, report.
manifiesto *a* clear, manifest, apparent, obvious; *m* manifesto.
maniobrar *vi* to handle (*esp a ship*); to maneuver troops.
manipulador *m* manipulator; telegraph key.
maniquí *m* puppet, dressmaker's dummy, model; manikin.
manirroto *a* wasteful; *m* spendthrift.
manjar *m* food, delicacy, titbit.
mano *f* hand; forefoot; player, turn (*at cards*); quire of paper; **a** — by, at, on, hand; **a la** — near by; **de —s a boca** in a trice, hastily; **de segunda** — secondhand; **coger con las —s en la masa** to catch red-handed; **venir a las —s** to come to blows; — **de obra** hand, workman.
manojo *m* bundle, handful.
manosear *vt* to dirty, mess up, spoil (*by handling*).
manotazo *m* slap.
mansión *f* mansion; sojourn.
manso *a* tame; meek; suave, mild.
manta *f* traveling rug, blanket; wrap, shawl; plaid, poncho.
mantear *vt* to toss in a blanket.
manteca *f* lard; butter.
mantecado *m* ice cream.
mantel *m* table cloth.
mantener *vt* to hold, keep up, maintain, support; *vr* to feed on; to earn one's living.
mantenimiento *m* subsistence, maintenance.
mantequera *f* butterchurn; butter woman; butter dish.
mantequilla *f* butter.
mantilla *f* headshawl, mantilla.
manto *m* cloak; robe; manteau.
mantón *m* — **de Manila** large embroidered shawl.
manual *a* handy, manual; *m* manual, compendium.
manubrio *m* handle, crank, winch; barrel organ.
Manuel *m* Emmanuel.
manufactura *f* manufacture; factory.
manuscrito *m* manuscript.
manutención *f* support, maintenance.
manzana *f* apple; block (*of houses*).
manzanilla *f* camomile; type of dry sherry.
manzano *m* apple tree.
maña *f* skill, dexterity; craftiness; *pl* manner, habits.
mañana *ad* tomorrow; *f* morning; — **por la** — tomorrow morning; **pasado**— the day after tomorrow.
maño *m Arg, Chi* brother, sister.
mañoco *m Ven* Indian corn meal.
mañoso *a* skillful, cunning, cautious.
mapa *m* map, chart.
máquina *f* machine; (*fig*) grandiose schemes; imposing building; — **de vapor** steam engine; — **de coser** sewing machine; — **de escribir** typewriter; — **quitanieve** snow plow.
maquinación *f* machination, plotting, contrivance.
maquinal *a* mechanical; without thinking.
maquinaria *f* machinery; engineering.
maquinista *m* machinist; mechanic; engineer; (*rl*) driver, engineer.
mar *m* (*or f*) sea; **alta** — high sea; — **de fondo** swell.
Mar del Norte *m* North Sea.
maraña *f* jungle; intricate plot; snarl.
maravedí *m* old Spanish coin (*farthing*).
maravilla *f* wonder, marvel; **a las mil—s** wondrously, perfectly.
maravillar *vt* to astound; *vr* to marvel, wonder.
maravilloso *a* marvelous.
marbete *m* stamp, label; sticker.
marca *f* mark; make, brand; frontier district; — **de fábrica** trademark; **de— mayor** first-class quality.
marcar *vt* to mark, brand; to observe, respect; — **el compás** to beat time.
marcial *a* warlike; martial.
marco *m* frame; weight (*about half a pound*); (*German*) mark.
marcha *f* march, course, running, progress; **cambio de** — change of gear.

marchante *m* dealer.
marchar *vi* to go, move, progress, function, work, march; *vr* to go (*off, away*), leave.
marchitar *vt* to wither, fade, reduce.
marchito *a* faded, shrunk, withered.
marea *f* tide; **— alta** high tide.
marear *vt* to navigate a ship; to sicken, nauseate, make dizzy or ill; *vr* to be seasick; to be damaged (*at sea*).
marejada *f* surf, swell.
marea *m* seasickness, nausea, sickliness.
marfil *m* ivory.
margarina *f* margarine.
margarita *f* common daisy; pearl; **M—** Margaret.
María *f* Mary.
Mariana *f* Marion.
margen *f* margin, edge; motive, room (*for complaint etc*); *m* bank (*river*).
marido *m* husband.
marina *f* navy, marine; seamanship; seascape.
marinero *m* seaman, sailor; *a* seaworthy.
marino *a* of, from the sea, nautical; **azul—** navy blue; *m* mariner, sailor.
mariposa *f* butterfly.
mariscal *m* marshal.
marisco *m* shellfish.
marisma *f* marsh, marshy tract.
marítimo *a* maritime, marine, sea.
marmita *f* kettle, stew pan, stew pot.
mármol *m* marble.
marmóreo *a* of marble; stony.
maroma *f* rope, cable.
marqués, a *m* marquis; *f* marchioness.
marquesina *f* marquee.
marquetería *f* cabinetwork; marquetry.
marrano *m* pig, hog.
marrar *vi* to miss, err, fail.
marro *m Mex* maul.
marrón *a* brown (*cloth, shoes etc*).
marroquí *an* Moroccan.
martes *m* Tuesday.
martillar *vt* to hammer.
martillo *m* hammer.
martín *m* **— pescador** kingfisher.
martinete *m* drop-hammer.
mártir *m* martyr.
martirio *m* martyrdom.
marzo *m* March.
más *ad* more; plus; besides; **a lo —** at most; **por — que** however much; **— bien** rather; **estar de —** to be de trop, be unnecessary, redundant; **sin — ni —** without more ado.
mas *cj* but.
masa *f* mass,· volume; dough; mortar; **con las manos en la —** (*caught*) in the act, at work.
masaje *m* massage.
mascada *f Mex* silk handkerchief.
mascar *vt* to masticate, chew.
máscara *f* mask.
mascarada *f* masquerade, masque, masked ball.
masculino *a* masculine.
mascullar *v* to mumble, grind out (*words*).
masón *m* Freemason.
masonería *f* Freemasonry.
masticar *vt* to chew, masticate.
mástil *m* mast (*ship*).
mastín *m* mastiff, bulldog.
mata *f* bush; root; copse; **— de pelos** head (*shock*) of hair.
matadero *m* slaughterhouse.
matador *m* bullfighter who does the final killing of bull, matador.
matanza *f* butchery, slaughter, pig-killing; salted pigmeat.
matar *vt* to kill, slaughter; to put out (*light*); to ruin; to cancel (*stamps*); *vr* to wear oneself out.
matasellos *m* stamp canceler.
mate *a* dull (*speaking of colors*); *m* checkmate; yerba mate; **dar —** to checkmate.
matemáticas *f pl* mathematics.
matemático *a* mathematical; *m* mathematician.
materia *f* matter, substance, stuff; substance (*in school*); **— prima** raw material.
material *a* material; *m* material.
maternal *a* maternal, motherly.
matero *m SA* maté drinker.
matinal *a* early morning.
materno *a* motherly, on the mother's side, mother.
Matilde *f* Matilda.
matiz *m* hue, shade, blend; *pl* tones.
matón *m* bully.
matorral *m* thicket, bramble patch, copse.
matrícula *f* matriculation; list; entrance (*registration*) fees; license.
matricular *vt* to matriculate; *vr* to be put on a list; to enter (*a university*), register (*as student*).
matrimonial *a* **cama—** double bed.
matrimonio *m* matrimony; marriage; married couple.
matriz *a* chief; principal; *f* womb; origin; mold, die, matrix.
matrona *f* matron; neighbor; midwife.
maturrango *m SA* bad horseman.
matutino *a* early, early morning.
maullar *vt* to mew (*of cats*).
máxima *f* maxim.
máxime *ad* especially, principally.
máximo *a* greatest; *m* maximum.
maya *f* daisy; May Queen; the Maya language; *mf* Maya.
mayo *m* May; Mayflower.
mayor *a* older, elder; major, larger; *pl* elders and betters; **al por —** wholesale.
mayoral *m* chief shepherd; coachman; overseer.

mayorazgo *m* primogeniture; son and heir, entailed estate.
mayordomo *m* butler, majordomo.
mayoría *f* coming-of-age, majority; greater part.
mayorista *a* wholesale; *m* wholesaler.
mayúscula *f* capital (*letter*).
maza *f* mace, hammer, war club.
mazacote *m SA* mixture; doughv food.
mazapán *m* marzipan, almond paste.
mazmorra *f* dungeon.
mazo *m* mallet; bunch.
meandro *m* meander, zigzag course.
mecánica *f* mechanics.
mecánico *a* mechanical; *m* engineer; mechanic; machinist.
mecanógrafo *m* typist.
mecedora *f* rocking chair.
mecer *vt* to rock; *vr* to swing.
mecha *f* wick; fuse; hank (*of hair*); roll of lint.
mechero *m* gas burner; cigarette lighter.
mechón *m* shock of hair.
medalla *f* medal.
médano *m* sandbank, dune.
media *f* stocking; (*math*) mean.
mediación *f* mediation, intervention.
mediados *prep* **a— de** in, about the middle of (*time, date*).
mediano *a* middling, moderate; mediocre.
mediante *prep* by means of.
mediar *vi* to mediate; to intervene; to be half-way (*between*); to lie between.
medicación *f* (*med*) treatment.
medicina *f* medicine; remedy.
medicinar *vt* to administer medicines.
médico *m* physician, doctor.
medida *f* measure; rule; moderation; **a — que** in proportion, as . . . as.
medio *a* half, medium, middle; *m* middle, midst; a mean; way, means; **por —** by means; *pl* means, circumstances; **a medias** half, incompletely.
mediocridad *f* mediocrity.
mediodía *m* noon; south.
medir (i) *vt* to measure; to scan (*verse*).
meditar *vt* to think, muse; to consider.
mediterráneo *a* Mediterranean.
medrar *vi* to thrive; to grow.
medro *m* progress; gain.
medroso *a* timid; fearsome.
médula *or* **medula** *f* marrow.
mejicano *an* Mexican.
Méjico *m* Mexico.
mejilla *f* cheek.
mejor *a, ad* better; rather, preferably; **a lo—** likely as not.
mejora *f* improvement.
mejorar *vt* to improve, better; *vr* to get better.
mejoría *f* improvement.
meladura *f SA* treacle.
melaza *f* molasses.
melena *f* mane; long, loose hair.
melindroso *a* finicky, namby-pamby.
melocotón *m* peach.
melocotonero *m* peach tree.
melodía *f* melody.
melodrama *m* melodrama.
melón *m* melon, canteloupe; **— de agua** watermelon.
meloso *a* honey-sweet.
mella *f* notch, dent; **hacer —** to impress, make an impression.
mellar *vt* to jag, dint, indent.
mellizo *an* twin.
membrillo *m* quince; quince tree; **carne de—** quince jelly.
memorable *a* memorable.
memorándum *m* notebook, memorandum.
memoria *f* memory; recollection; remembrance; dissertation; report, memoir; **de—** by heart.
memorial *f* petition; notebook.
mencionar *vt* to mention, name.
mendigar *vti* to beg (*alms*).
mendigo *m* beggar, mendicant.
mendrugo *m* hard crust (*of bread*).
menear *vt* to shake, stir, wag (*tail*), wave, agitate; run (*business etc*); *vr* to get going.
menester *m* trade, occupation; need, want; **ser —** to be necessary; *pl* bodily needs.
menestral *m* mechanic, artisan.
mengua *f* diminution; discredit, shame.
menguado *m* coward, wretch; decrease (*knitting*).
menguante *a* diminishing; *f* waning moon; wane; decrease.
menguar *vti* to diminish, decrease, reduce, wane.
menina *f* lady-in-waiting to Queen or Infanta.
menor *a* lesser, younger; *m* a minor; **— edad** minority; **al por—** retail.
Menorca *f* Minorca.
menos *a, ad* fewer, less; except; minus; **a—** unless; **por lo—** at least; **echar de —** to miss; **venir a —** to come down in the world.
menoscabar *vt* to impair; to declaim.
menoscabo *m* deterioration, detriment.
menospreciar *vt* to underrate, despise, scorn.
menosprecio *m* undervaluation, scorn.
mensaje *m* message.
mensajero *m* messenger; *a* **paloma mensajera** carrier pigeon.
menso *a SA* silly.
mensual *a* monthly.
mensualidad *f* monthly pay, installment.
menta *f* peppermint.
mentar (**ie**) *vt* to mention, refer to, name.
mente *f* mind, understanding.

mentecato *a* stupid, foolish; *m* dolt, ass.
mentidero *m* village pump; place where gossips assemble.
mentir (ie) *vt* to lie.
mentira *f* lie, untruth.
mentiroso *a* lying; *m* liar.
menudear *vi* to happen frequently; to rain; to sell by retail.
menudencia *f* trifle; *pl* minute detail, trivialities; odds and ends.
menudo *a* minute, tiny; **a —** frequently.
meñique *a m* little (finger).
meollo *m* marrow; brains.
mercader *m* merchant, tradesman, shopkeeper.
mercado *m* market, marketplace; **— de frutos** produce market.
mercancía *f* goods, wares.
mercantil *a* mercantile.
mercar *vt* to buy.
merced *f* favor; grace, mercy; **a — de** at the discretion of; **hacer — de** to grant, discount, make a gift of.
mercería *f SA* flower girl.
mercurio *m* mercury, quicksilver.
merecer *vt* to merit, deserve.
merecimiento *m* desert; worthiness.
merendar (ie) *vt* to lunch, supper; to have (a picnic, afternoon tea).
meridiano *a* noon; *m* meridian.
meridional *a* southern.
merienda *f* light lunch, snack, picnic, afternoon tea.
mérito *m* merit, worth.
merluza *f* hake.
merma *f* waste, reduction, wearing (away, down), decrease.
mermar *vi* to go down, diminish, eat away, wear away; *vt* to lessen, reduce.
mermelada *f* marmalade.
mero *a* mere, only; pure.
merodear *vt* to maraud, harass.
mes *m* month.
mesa *f* table, plateau;**— presidencial** chair, tribunal, high table.
meseta *f* tableland, plateau; staircase landing.
mesilla *f* **— de noche** bedside table.
mesnada *f* troop of soldiers (*arch*).
mesón *m* hostelry, inn.
mesonero *m* innkeeper.
mestizo *a* hybrid; *m* half-breed (*white and Indian*).
mesura *f* gravity, solemnity, dignity, moderation, circumspection.
meta *f* limit, goal, aim.
metafísica *f* metaphysics.
metáfora *f* metaphor, figure of speech.
metal *m* metal; brass (*in orchestra*); **— de voz** timbre (*voice*); **— blanco** nickel.
metálico *a* metallic; *m* coin, cash.
meteoro *m* meteor.
meteorólogo *m* meteorologist.
meter *vt* to insert, put in, introduce; to place; to put on; *vr* **—en** to poke one's nose into; to get involved in; **— con** to quarrel with, go for (*somebody*).
metódico *a* methodical.
método *m* method, system; manner.
métrico *a* metric, metrical.
metro *m* meter; measuring rod or tape; underground, subway.
metrópoli *f* metropolis.
mexicano *an* Mexican.
mezcla *f* mixture, blend.
mezclar *vt* to mix, mingle, blend; *vr* to meddle; to mix.
mezcolanza *f* mixture, hotchpotch.
mezquino *a* wretched, mean; petty; miserly.
mezquita *f* mosque.
mi *a* my; *m* (*mus*) mi.
mí *pn* me, myself.
miaja *f* crumb.
mico *m* monkey.
microbio *m* microbe.
micrófono *m* microphone.
miedo *m* fear, dread, apprehension; **tener —** to be afraid.
miedoso *a* fearful, nervous; cowardly.
miel *f* honey; **luna de—** honeymoon.
miembro *m* limb; member.
mientes *f pl* **parar — en** to pay attention to.
mientras *ad* while; **— tanto** meanwhile.
miércoles *m* Wednesday.
mies *f* ripe wheat; *pl* fields of grain.
miga *f* crumb, substance, marrow; *pl* **hacer buenas migas con** to get on well with.
migaja *f* crumbly part (*of bread*), crumbs.
Miguel *m* Michael.
mil *an* a thousand; *pl* **—es de** masses of.
milagro *m* miracle; **vivir de —** to manage to live.
milagroso *a* miraculous.
milano *m* (*orni*) kite.
milicia *f* warfare; militia.
militar *a* military; martial; *vi* to serve as soldier; **— en su favor** to stand in good stead, lend weight to, support.
milla *f* mile.
millar *m* a thousand.
millón *m* million.
mimar *vt* to spoil, pet.
mimbre *m* osier.
mimo *m* petting; mime, buffoon.
mina *f* mine, deposit, subterranean passage.
minar *vt* to mine, undermine; to sap; to eat into.
mineral *a* mineral; *m* mineral ore.
minería *f* mining.
minero *a* mining; *m* miner.
miniatura *f* miniature; illuminated capital letter; tiny, delicate work of art.
mínima *f* (*mus*) minim.
mínimo *a* least, slightest.
ministerio *m* ministry, cabinet;

— de Estado Foreign Office, *US* State Department; **— de Gobernación** Ministry of the Interior.
ministro *m* minister, diplomatic agent; sheriff; Protestant clergyman.
minoría *f* minority.
minucioso *a* minute; particular.
minúscula *a* **letra —** small letter.
minuta *f* minute; agenda; list, entry, memorandum.
minuto *a m* minute.
miope *a* shortsighted.
miopía *f* shortsightedness.
mira *f* design; vigilance; sight; **con — a** with a view to.
mirada *f* look; glance.
mirador *m* turret, look-out; balcony.
miramiento *m* attention; circumspection, caution.
mirar *vt* to look at, gaze upon, let the eyes dwell upon, behold; to look (*to*), see (*to*).
mirlo *m* blackbird.
mirón *m* bystander, onlooker.
mirra *f* myrrh.
mirto *m* myrtle.
misa *f* mass; **— del gallo** Midnight Mass (*Christmas Eve*); **— mayor** High Mass; **no saber de la — la media** not to know what one is talking about.
miscelánea *f* miscellany.
miserable *a* miserable; wretched, poverty-stricken; miserly.
miseria *f* wretchedness, poverty; filth, dirt; miserliness, trifle.
misericordia *f* clemency, mercy; compassion.
misión *f* mission; embassy.
mismo *a* same, very, selfsame, like; **yo —** myself; **por lo —** for that reason.
misterio *m* mystery; mystery play; Passion play.
misticismo *m* mysticism.
mita *f SA* enforced service of Indians; tax paid by Indians of Peru.
mitad *f* half; middle; **cara —** (*fam*) better half.
mitayo *m SA* Indian engaged in forced labor.
mitigar *vt* to alleviate, soften, lessen.
mito *m* myth.
mitote *m SA* Indian dance; *Mex* riot, uproar.
mitotero *a SA* fastidious; jolly.
mitra *f* miter.
mixto *a* mixed, compound; **tren —** passenger and freight train.
mobiliario *m* furniture, set of furniture.
mocedad *f* youth; youthful exploit.
moción *f* motion; proposition.
moco *m* mucus; candle grease; **llorar a — tendido** to weep copiously.
mocoso *a* sniveling; sniffy, superior.
mochila *f* bag; haversack, knapsack.
mocho *a* cut off; mutilated, maimed.
mochuelo *m* owl.
moda *f* fashion, mode, style; **de —** fashionable, in fashion.
modelo *m* model, pattern.
moderado *a* moderate; mild; conservative.
moderar *vt* to soften, moderate; *vr* to calm down.
modestia *f* modesty; simplicity, unaffectedness.
modesto *a* modest, unpretentious, unassuming.
módico *a* moderate (*price*).
modificar *vt* to modify, alter.
modismo *m* idiom.
modista *f* dressmaker.
modo *m* mode, manner, way; mood; mode (*mus*); **de — que** so that; **de todos —s** in any case.
modorra *f* drowsiness; heavy slumber.
mofa *f* mock, mockery.
mofar *vt* to mock; *vr* to jeer at.
mohino *a* peevish, cross.
moho *m* moss; mold, mildew, rust.
mohoso *a* moldy, musty, mildewed.
mojar *vt* to wet, damp; to dip (*food into sauce etc*).
mojicón *m* punch, blow.
mojigato *a* hypocritical, prudish.
mojón *m* landmark, boundary mark, milestone.
molde *m* mold.
moldura *f* molding.
mole *f* mass; *Mex* meat dish with chili sauce.
moler (ue) *vt* to grind, pound; to bore; to beat, belabor.
molestar *vt* to annoy, bother, vex, be (a nuisance, in the way).
molestia *f* trouble, bother, inconvenience, nuisance.
molesto *a* troublesome, annoying.
molinero *m* miller.
molino *m* mill.
mollera *f* crown (*of head*); **cerrado de —** slow witted, not too bright.
momentáneo *a* momentary.
momento *m* moment; importance; momentum.
momia *f* mummy.
monacillo *or* **monaguillo** *m* acolyte, altar boy.
monarca *m* monarch.
monarquía *f* monarchy.
mondar *vt* to peel; to clean; to prune; to strip clean.
moneda *f* money; coin; **— corriente** currency; **— sonante** hard cash; **papel —** paper money; **casa de —** mint.
monja *f* nun.
monje *m* friar, religious, monk.
mono *a* pretty; *m* monkey.
monopolizar *vt* to monopolize.
monstruo *m* monster, freak.
monstruoso *a* monstrous, grotesque, frightful.
monta *f* amount; worth; **de poca —** practically worthless.

montacargas *m* windlass; lift; dumbwaiter.
montaje *m* mounting, assembly, assembling.
montante *m* amount.
montaña *f* mountain; — **rusa** switchback railway (*in fairs*).
montañés *a* highland, mountain-bred; of the province of Santander.
montar *vi* to mount; *vt* to ride; to set up (*machinery*); to come to, result in.
monte *m* mountain; wooded hill; thicket, forest; — **de piedad** public pawnshop.
montera *f* hunting cap, cloth cap.
montevideano *an* (*inhabitant*) of Montevideo.
montón *m* heap; lot; mass.
montonera *f* *SA* group of mounted revolutionaries.
montura *f* mount, horse; saddle and trappings.
moño *m* chignon, bun, topknot.
mora *f* default (*law*); mulberry, blackberry.
morada *f* mansion, residence, dwelling.
morado *a* dark purple.
moral *a* moral; *f* morals; *m* blackberry bush, mulberry tree.
moraleja *f* moral (*of story*); lesson.
morar *vi* to reside, dwell.
morboso *a* morbid.
morcilla *f* sausage, black pudding.
mordaz *a* biting, sarcastic; keen.
mordaza *f* gag, muzzle.
mordelón *m* *Mex* official who takes bribes.
morder (ue) *vt* to bite, gnaw; to eat up, corrode.
mordisco *m* bite, snap.
moreno *a* brown; dark-haired, swarthy.
morera *f* mulberry tree.
morería *f* Arab quarter.
moribundo *a* moribund, dying.
morir (ue) *vi* to die; to fade; to reach a terminus (*of bus route*).
moro *an* Moor(ish), Mohammedan.
moroso *a* tardy, slow, deliberate.
morral *m* haversack; gamebag; nosebag.
morriña *f* homesickness, blues, nostalgic longing (for).
mortaja *f* shroud.
mortandad *f* mortality; massacre, slaughter.
mortecino *a* dying; pale, wan, wasted.
mortero *m* mortar.
mortífero *a* deadly, death-dealing.
mortificar *vt* to torment; to mortify, humiliate.
mosca *f* fly.
moscada *a* **nuez** — nutmeg.
moscardón *m* hornet.
moscorrofio *m* *Col, Hond* ugly person.
moscovita *an* Muscovite.
mosquete *m* musket.
mosquetero *m* musketeer.
mosquitero *m* mosquito net.
mosquito *m* mosquito; gnat.
mostaza *f* mustard.
mosto *m* grape juice.
mostrador *m* counter (*in shop*).
mostrar (ue) *vt* to show, prove, demonstrate.
mostrenco *a* vagrant; *m* stray (*animal*).
mote *m* motto; nickname.
motín *m* riot, mutiny.
motivar *vt* to cause, give rise to; to assign a motive.
motivo *m* reason, cause; theme; **con — de** owing to, on the occasion of, under pretext of.
motor *m* motor.
movedizo *a* shifting, moving, unsteady.
mover (ue) *vt* to move, shake, promote.
móvil *a* movable; *m* motive.
movilidad *f* mobility.
movilizar *vt* to mobilize.
movimiento *m* movement, motion.
mozo *m* young man; porter, waiter.
mucama *f* *Arg, Chi* servant.
muchacho *m* boy, lad.
muchedumbre *f* crowd.
mucho *a, ad* much, plenty; a great deal.
muda *f* change, change of clothes.
mudanza *f* removal; change; fickleness.
mudar *vt* to change; to molt; *vr* to move (*to another house*); to change (*clothes*).
mudéjar *m* Mohammedan (*subject to Christian rule*).
mudo *a* dumb, silent
mueble *m* piece of furniture.
mueca *f* grimace.
muela *f* tooth, grinder.
muelle *a* tender, soft, springy; relaxing; *m* (*steel*) spring; pier, wharf.
muerte *f* death.
muerto *an* dead; a dead person.
muestra *f* specimen, sample, sign, indication.
muestrario *m* collection of samples, display window.
mugir *vi* to moo, bellow.
mugre *f* dirt, filth.
mujer *f* woman, wife.
mujerengo *a* *CA, Arg* effeminate.
mula *f* mule; she-mule; shoe used by Popes.
muladar *m* rubbish heap.
muleta *f* crutch; red cloth (*bullfighting*).
muletilla *f* tag (*in speech*), stock phrase.
mulo *m* mule.
multa *f* fine.
multar *vt* to fine.
multiplicar *vt* to multiply.
multitud *f* crowd; multitude.

mullido *a* soft, downy, yielding (*as bed, cushion*).
mundo *m* world; the earth; **todo el —** everybody.
munición *f* munition; provisions.
municipio *m* township.
muñeca *f* puppet, doll; wrist.
muñón *m* stump (*of amputated limb*).
muralla *f* rampart; wall.
murciano *an* (*inhabitant*) of Murcia.
murciélago *m* (*zool*) bat.
murmullo *m* ripple, rustle; murmur.
murmuración *f* gossip, undercurrent of protest, dissatisfaction.
murmurar *vi* to ripple, rustle, whisper; to backbite, speak ill of.
muro *m* wall.
músculo *m* muscle.
museo *m* museum, (*art*) gallery.
musgo *m* moss.
músico, a *a* musical; *m* musician; *f* music.
muslo *m* thigh.
mustio *a* withered; bored; parched, tired.
mutación *f* mutation; change (*of scene in theater*).
mutilar *vt* to mutilate; to cripple.
mutuamente *ad* mutually.
mutuo *a* mutual, reciprocal.
muy *ad* very, most; much.

N

nabo *m* turnip; rape.
naborí *m SA* free Indian servant.
naboría *f SA* allotment of Indians.
nácar *m* nacre, mother-of-pearl.
nacer *vi* to be born; to shoot; *vr* to sprout.
nacido *a* born; *m* pimple.
nacimiento *m* birth; origin; nativity scene, crib; **control de —** birth control.
nación *f* nation, country.
nacionalizar *vt* to nationalize.
nada *f* nothing; naught; *pn* nothing, not anything; **de —** not at all.
nadador *m* swimmer.
nadar *vi* to swim.
nadie *pn* nobody.
nado *ad* **a —** swimming, afloat.
nafta *f* naphta; *SA* gasoline.
naipe *m* playing card.
nalga *f* rump, buttock.
nana *f Mex* child's nurse.
naranja *f* orange; **mi media —** (*fam*) my better half.
naranjada *f* orangeade.
naranjado *a* orange-colored.
naranjo *m* orange tree.
narciso *m* daffodil.
narcótico *an* narcotic.
narcotizar *vt* to narcotize.
nardo *m* spikenard.
narigudo *a* with a large nose.
nariz *f* nostril; *sing* & *pl* nose.
narración *f* account, narration, story, narrative.
narrador *m* narrator, teller.
narrar *vt* to narrate, recite, tell.
narrativa *f* narrative; history.
nata *f* cream; skin (*on coffee etc*).
natación *f* swimming.
natal *a* natal, native; **día —** birthday.
natalicio *m* birthday.
natatorio *a* (*to do with*) swimming.
natillas *f pl* custard.
natividad *f* nativity; Christmas.
nativo *a* native, indigenous.
nato *a* born, inborn, inherent, natural.
natural *a* natural; plain; *m* nature, temper; **pintado del —** painted from life.
naturaleza *f* nature; disposition; **— muerta** still life.
naturalidad *f* plainness; naturalness; ingenuousness.
naturalización *f* naturalization.
naturalizar *vt* to naturalize; *vr* to get used to; to be naturalized.
naturalmente *ad* of course; plainly, naturally.
naufragar *vi* to be shipwrecked; to come to naught, fall through.
naufragio *m* shipwreck.
náufrago *m* shipwrecked person.
náusea *f* nausea.
nauseabundo *a* nauseous, nasty.
náutico *a* nautical, sea.
nava *f* high valley, hollow.
navaja *f* (*clasp*) knife; razor.
navajazo *m* gash or slash (*with knife*).
navarro *an* Navarrese, of Navarre.
nave *f* ship, vessel; nave, aisle (*of church*).
navegación *f* navigation; sailing; voyage.
navegante *m* navigator; traveler by sea.
navegar *vi* to navigate, steer, sail.
Navidad *f* Nativity; Christmas Day.
navío *m* ship; **— de transporte** transport.
náyade *f* naiad.
nazareno *m* Nazarene; penitent.
neblina *f* mist, thin fog, haze.
nebulosa *f* nebula.
nebuloso *a* hazy, foggy, misty; nebulous, vague.
necedad *f* foolishness, ignorance; nonsense.
necesario *a* necessary; requisite.
neceser *m* toilet case.
necesidad *f* necessity; want, need.
necesitado *a* necessitous, needy; in need of.
necesitar *vt* to necessitate; to want, be in need of.
necio *a* ignorant, silly; *m* fool.
necrología *f* necrology, obituary notice.
necrológico *a* necrological.
nefando *a* nefarious, heinous.
nefasto *a* ominous; sad, unlucky.
negable *a* deniable.

negación *f* negation, refusal, denial.
negar (ie) *vt* to deny; to refuse, hinder; *vr* to refuse, decline.
negativa *f* refusal, negative.
negativo *an* negative.
negligencia *f* negligence, neglect, carelessness.
negligente *a* negligent; easy.
negociable *a* negotiable.
negociación *f* negotiation; business; business house.
negociado *m* business; section of a public office.
negociante *m* trader, merchant.
negociar *vt* to negotiate; to trade; to arrange.
negocio *m* business; trade; employment; *SA* shop, store; — **redondo** profitable business.
negrero *m* slavetrader.
negro *a* black; *m* Negro.
negrura *f* blackness.
nemoroso *a* woody, wooded.
nene, a *m f* baby, child.
nenúfar *m* white water-lily.
neófito *m* neophyte, novice, beginner.
neológico *a* neological.
neoyorquino *an* (*inhabitant*) of New York.
nepotismo *m* nepotism.
Neptuno *m* Neptune, the sea.
nervadura *f* nervure, rib (*in vaulting*).
nervio *m* nerve, tendon; vigor, strength.
nervioso *a* nervous; active, vigorous, strong.
nervosidad *f* strength, vigor.
nervudo *a* vigorous, sinewy.
neto *a* neat; clear; genuine; unmistakable; **producto** — net produce; **peso** — net weight.
neumático *a* pneumatic; *m* rubber tire.
neumonía *f* pneumonia.
neurálgico *a* neuralgic.
neurastenia *f* nervous prostration.
neurasténico *a* high-strung, excitable.
neutralizar *vt* to neutralize, counter.
neutro *a* neuter, neutral.
nevada *f* snowfall.
nevar (ie) *vi* to snow.
nevasca *f* snowfall, snowstorm.
nevera *f* icehouse, icebox, refrigerator.
neviscar *vi* to snow gently.
nevoso *a* snowy.
nexo *m* nexus; connection, tie.
ni *cj* neither, nor.
nicaragüense, nicaragüeño *an* (*inhabitant*) of Nicaragua.
nicho *m* niche; burial niche (*chamber*).
nido *m* nest; home, haunt.
niebla *f* fog, mist, haze.
nieto *m* grandson; *f* grand-daughter.
nieve *f* snow.
nigromancia *f* necromancy.
nigromante *m* magician, conjurer.
nihilismo *m* nihilism.
Nilo, el *m* the Nile.
nimbo *m* halo, nimbus.
nimiedad *f* excessive (exact) detail, prolixity, attention to (insistence on) detail.
nimio *a* prolix, detailed, careful, painstaking.
ningún *a* **de — modo** not at all, by no means, certainly not.
ninguno *a pn* no, none; nobody, not any.
niña *f* girl; pupil, apple (*of eye*).
niñera *f* nursemaid.
niñería *f* childish action, object, thought; gewgaw.
niñez *f* infancy, childhood.
niño *m* child, infant; *a* childish; — **expósito** foundling; **desde** — from childhood.
niquelar *vt* to nickel-plate.
nitidez *f* brightness, polish, brilliance, clarity.
nítido *a* bright, shining, polished, clear-cut.
nitrato *m* nitrate.
nitroglicerina *f* nitro-glycerine.
nivel *m* level, standard; water level, **sobre el — del mar** above sea level; **paso a** — level crossing, grade crossing.
nivelar *vt* to level, flatten; to grade (*road*).
níveo *a* snowy, snow-white.
no *ad* not, no; — **bien** no sooner; — **sea que** unless.
noble *a* noble; generous; *m* nobleman.
nobleza *f* nobility, nobleness; **la — obliga** noblesse oblige.
noción *f* notion, idea; *pl* rudiments.
nocivo *a* injurious, noxious, harmful.
nocturno *a* nocturnal, night.
noche *f* night; — **toledana** restless night; **de** — in the night time, at *or* by night; **quedarse a buenas noches** to be left in the dark.
nochebuena *f* Christmas Eve.
nodriza *f* wet-nurse.
Noé *m* Noah.
nogal *m* walnut tree, walnut (*wood*).
nogueral *m* walnut grove.
nómada *an* nomad(ic).
nombradía *f* renown, fame.
nombramiento *m* appointment; nomination.
nombrar *vt* to name, mention, appoint, nominate.
nombre *m* name; reputation; noun; — **de pila** Christian name.
nomenclatura *f* nomenclature.
nomeolvides *m* forget-me-not.
nómina *f* payroll; list.
nominal *a* nominal.
nómino *m* nominee.
non *a* odd, uneven (*number*); *pl* **pares y—es** odds or evens.
nonada *f* trifle, nothing at all.
nono *a* ninth.
nopal *m* prickly pear.
norabuena *f* congratulations.

nordeste *a m* north-east.
noria *f* waterwheel; **dar vueltas a la —** to go round and round (*a question etc*).
norma *f* standard; rule; model.
normal *a* normal; **escuela —** training college.
normalidad *f* normality.
normalizar *vt* to standardize; *vr* to become normal, settle down.
normando *an* Norman.
noroeste *an* north-west.
norte *m* north; polestar; guide.
norteamericano *an* North American, American.
Noruega *f* Norway.
noruego *an* Norwegian.
nos *pn* us; we (*authoritatively*).
nosotros *pn* we, us; (*fem*) **nosotras.**
nostalgia *f* nostalgia; homesickness.
nota *f* notes, mark (*in examination*); remark, sign; bill (*in café*); letter; renown.
notabilidad *f* notability; notable thing or person.
notable *a* remarkable; notable, noticeable, well worth seeing; praiseworthy, special; credit (*in examinations*).
notación *f* notation.
notar *vt* to note, observe, remark, take notice of, criticize; **es de—** it is worth noticing.
notarial *a* notarial.
notario *m* notary public, commissioner for oaths.
noticia *f* news; item of news; tidings; (*com*) advice; *pl* news.
noticiar *vt* to give notice of, inform.
noticiario *m* news bulletin, newscast.
notificación *f* notification.
notificar *vt* to notify, inform, advise.
notoriedad *f* notoriety; **de —** well-known.
notorio *a* notorious, well-known, quite evident, an open secret.
novato *m* novice, tyro, beginner.
novedad *f* novelty; latest news or fashion; **sin —** all quiet, no change.
novel *a* newly elected (arrived *etc*); green.
novela *f* novel.
novelero *a* fond of novelties, changeable, fickle.
novelesco *a* exalted, sentimental, romantic.
noveno *a* ninth.
novia *f* bride; fiancée, sweetheart, girlfriend.
noviazgo *m* betrothal, engagement (*period*), courtship.
novicio *m* (*eccl*) novice; apprentice.
noviembre *m* November.
novilla *f* heifer.
novillada *f* drove of young bulls; bullfight (*with young bulls and bullfighters*).
novillero *m* stable for cattle; herdsman; bullfighter (*at novilladas*).
novillo *m* young bull; **hacer —s** to play truant.
novio *m* bridegroom; fiancé; boyfriend, suitor.
nubarrón *m* dark heavy cloud.
nube *f* cloud; crowd (*of*); **por las nubes** (*prices*) skyhigh; (*praise*) to the skies.
nublado *a* overcast, cloudy; *m* clouded sky.
nuca *f* nape.
núcleo *m* kernel; nucleus, center.
nudillo *m* knuckle.
nudo *a* naked, nude; *m* knot; tangle; tie, bond; **— en la garganta** lump in one's throat; **— corredizo** slip knot.
nudoso *a* knotty, knotted.
nuera *f* daughter-in-law.
nuestro *pn* our, ours.
nueva *f* tidings.
Nueva Escocia *f* Nova Scotia.
Nueva Gales del Sur *f* New South Wales.
Nueva York *f* New York.
Nueva Zelanda *f* New Zealand.
nuevecito *a* brand new.
nuevo *a* new; fresh; **de —** again, recently; *m* novice.
nuez *f* walnut, nut; Adam's apple; **— moscada** nutmeg.
nulidad *f* nullity; a nobody; incompetence.
nulo *a* null, void.
numen *m* divinity; inspiration.
numeración *f* numbering.
numeral *a* numeral.
numerar *vt* to number, enumerate.
numerario *m* cash, specie.
numérico *a* numerical.
número *m* number, figure; quantity; **sin—** numberless; **de—** full member (*of Academy etc*).
numeroso *a* numerous, rhythmical.
nunca *ad* never; **— jamás** never again.
nuncio *m* messenger; nuncio.
nupcias *f pl* wedding.
nutria *f* otter.
nutrición *f* nutrition, nourishment.
nutrido *a* plenty, abundant, quite large, heavy (*volley*); packed with.
nutrir *vt* to nourish, feed; to encourage.
nutritivo *a* nourishing.

Ñ

ña *f SA* landlady.
ñame *m* yam.
ñandutí *m Arg Par* hand-made cloth.
ñango *a Mex* foreign; silly, stupid.
ñaña *f Chi* children's nurse.
ñaño *m Col* spoiled child; *Per* close friend; *Chi* elder brother or sister.
ñato *a SA* flat-nosed.
ño *m SA* landlord, owner, boss.
ñoñería *f* dotage.
ñoño *a* timid; dotard, feeble-minded.

O

o *cj* or, either.
oasis *m* oasis.
obcecación *f* obfuscation; blindness.
obcecar *vt* to blind; *vr* to be obfuscated.
obedecer *vt* to obey, yield, to respond.
obediencia *f* obedience, submission.
obediente *a* obedient, submissive, compliant.
obelisco *m* obelisk.
obertura *f* (*mus*) overture.
obesidad *f* corpulence, obesity.
obeso *a* fat, corpulent.
óbice *m* obstacle.
obispado *m* bishopric.
obispo *m* bishop.
objeción *f* objection.
objetivo *a m* objective.
objeto *m* object; purpose; end.
oblación *f* offering (*in church*).
oblea *f* wafer (*for communion*).
oblicuidad *f* obliquity, bias.
oblicuo *a* oblique, glancing, slanting.
obligación *f* obligation, duty; debenture.
obligar *vt* to force, constrain; compel; *vr* to bind oneself.
óbolo *m* obol, mite.
obra *f* work; fabric; book; **mano de —** labor; **— de romanos** herculean task.
obrar *vt* to act, work.
obrero *m* workman; day laborer.
obsceno *a* lewd, obscene.
obscuras *ad* **a —** in the dark.
obscurecer *vt* to darken, dim; *vi* to become dark, grow dark.
obscuridad *f* darkness; obscurity.
obscuro *a* dark; obscure; little known.
obsequiar *vt* to make presents; to present with; to entertain.
obsequio *m* present, gift; offering; obsequiousness; **en — de** in honor of, out of respect for.
obsequioso *a* obliging; obsequious.
observación *f* observation, remark, comment.
observador *m* observer.
observancia *f* observance.
observante *a* observant, obedient.
observar *vt* to observe; to notice, remark; to follow, obey.
observatorio *m* observatory.
obsesión *f* obsession, mania.
obstáculo *m* obstacle, obstruction.
obstante *a* **no —** notwithstanding, nevertheless.
obstar *vi* to oppose, hinder, prevent.
obstinación *f* obstinacy.
obstinado *a* obstinate, headstrong.
obstinarse *vr* to be obdurate, persist in.
obstrucción *f* obstruction.
obstruir *vt* to obstruct, block, hinder.
obtener *vt* to obtain, get.
obturar *vt* to plug, stop up.
obtuso *a* obtuse, blunt.
obviar *vt* to obviate, avoid, make unnecessary.
obvio *a* obvious, evident.
oca *f* goose.
ocasión *f* opportunity, moment, occasion; **de —** secondhand.
ocasionar *vt* to cause, bring about, excite, arouse.
ocaso *m* west; setting; decadence.
occidente *m* west.
océano *m* ocean.
ochenta *an* eighty.
ocho *an* eight.
ocio *m* leisure; idleness; diversion.
ociosidad *f* idleness, leisure.
ocioso *a* idle, useless.
ocre *m* ochre.
octubre *m* October.
ocular *a* ocular; **testigo —** eyewitness.
oculista *m* oculist.
ocultar *vt* to conceal, hide, mask, withhold.
oculto *a* occult, secret, hidden, clandestine.
ocupación *f* occupation, pursuit, business.
ocupado *a* engaged, busy.
ocupar *vt* to occupy; to employ, keep busy; to fill a place; *vr* to busy oneself with, fill up one's time with.
ocurrencia *f* incident; idea, notion; witty sally.
ocurrente *a* apposite, witty, bright.
ocurrir *vi* to happen, occur; to be struck by (*idea*).
ocurso *m* *Mex* petition, claim.
odiar *vt* to hate, detest.
odio *m* hate.
odiosidad *f* odium.
odioso *a* hateful, odious, detestable.
odorífero *a* oderiferous, fragrant.
odre *m* wineskin.
oeste *m* west.
ofender *vt* to insult, injure; to offend.
ofensa *f* insult, offense.
ofensiva *f* offensive.
ofensivo *a* offensive, rude, disgusting, aggressive.
oferta *f* offer; tender; **— y demanda** supply and demand.
oficial *a* official; *m* (*mil*) officer; workman; clerk, (civil) servant.
oficialidad *f* officers, office staff.
oficiar *vi* to officiate.
oficina *f* office; workshop.
oficio *m* trade; occupation, business, office, employ; (*relig*) office, service; **Santo O—** Inquisition; **de —** by trade.
oficiosidad *f* officiousness; alacrity.
oficioso *a* officious, diligent, meddling.
ofrecer *vt* to offer, promise, show; *vr* to present itself; to propose; to volunteer.
ofrecimiento *m* offer, offering.
ofrenda *f* offering, oblation.
ofrendar *vt* to present offerings.

ofuscar *vt* to confuse, darken; dazzle.
oída *f* hearing; **de (por) oídas** by hearsay.
oído *m* (*sense of*) hearing, ear; **tocar de —** to play by ear; **tener buen —** to have a good ear.
oidor *m* listener; judge.
oír *vti* to hear, listen.
ojal *m* buttonhole.
¡ojalá! *excl* would to heaven!, heaven grant!; I wish; I hope so.
ojeada *f* look, glance; glimpse.
ojear *vt* to stare at, eye; to beat (*for game*).
ojera *f* dark ring under the eye.
ojeriza *f* envy, spite, grudge.
ojiva *f* pointed arch, ogive.
ojival *a* ogival, gothic.
ojo *m* eye; keyhole; span (*of a bridge*); care; **a ojos vistas** publicly; **hacer del —** to wink; **en un abrir y cerrar de —s** in the twinkling of an eye.
ojota *f SA* Indian woman's sandal.
ola *f* wave.
olaje *m* surge.
oleada *f* big wave; surge, swell.
oleaje *m* = **olaje**
óleo *m* holy oil; **cuadro al —** oil painting.
oleoso *a* oily.
oler (hue) *vti* to smell.
olfatear *vt* to scent out, sniff out, catch scent of.
olfato *m* (*sense of*) smell.
oliente *a* **mal —** evil-smelling.
oligarquía *f* oligarchy.
oliva *f* olive; **aceite de —** olive oil.
olivar *m* olive grove.
olivo *m* olive tree.
olmeda, o *f m* elm grove.
olmo *m* elm tree.
olor *m* odor, scent, smell; **mal —** stink.
oloroso *m* odoriferous, fragrant, scented.
olvidadizo *a* forgetful, absent-minded.
olvidar *vt* to forget.
olvido *m* forgetfulness; oblivion; omission, something forgotten.
olla *f* stewpot, pan.
ombligo *m* navel.
ominoso *a* ominous, foreboding.
omisión *f* omission; neglect.
omiso *a* remiss; **hacer caso — de** to overlook, count as absent.
omitir *vt* to omit, drop.
omnibus *m* bus; **tren —** local train.
omnipotencia *f* omnipotence.
omnipotente *a* almighty.
once *an* eleven.
onda *f* wave, ripple.
ondear *vi* to undulate, wave; to scallop (*dress*).
ondulación *f* waving; **— permanente** permanent waving.
ondulante *a* undulating, wavy.
oneroso *a* burdensome, onerous.
onza *f* (*weight, zool*) ounce; doubloon.
opaco *a* opaque, dark.
ópalo *m* opal
opción *f* option, choice.
ópera *f* opera; **— bufa** comic opera.
operación *f* operation; transaction; **operaciones de banco** banking business.
operador *m* operator; prospector.
operar *vt* to operate, cause, set going.
operario *m* workman, working man.
opimo *a* rich, abundant.
opinar *vi* to hold an opinion; to estimate, opine, consider.
opinión *f* opinion, view, estimate.
oponer *vt* to oppose; to resist; to face; to contrast.
oportunidad *f* opportunity, set of circumstances.
oportuno *a* opportune, fitting, happy, pat.
oposición *f* opposition, resistance; *pl* examination.
opositor *m* competitor, contender.
opresión *f* oppression; pressure.
oprimir *vt* to oppress; to press, squeeze; to overwhelm.
oprobio *m* ignominy, stigma.
optar *vr* **— por** to choose, decide (on) (for).
optativo *a* optional; *an* (*gram*) optative.
óptico *a* optic; *m* optician.
óptimo *a* best.
opuesto *a* opposed, adverse, opposite.
opulencia *f* wealth, opulence, affluence.
opúsculo *m* pamphlet; booklet.
oquedad *f* cavity, hollow (*of eyeball etc*).
ora *cj* now; whether, either.
oración *f* oration, speech, prayer; sentence.
oráculo *m* oracle.
orador *m* orator, speaker.
orar *vti* to harangue; to pray.
orbe *m* orb, sphere; the earth.
órbita *f* orbit.
Órcadas, las *f pl* the Orkneys.
orden *m* order, method, régime; *f* command, order; order (*of knights etc*).
ordenación *f* disposition, ordering, arrangement; array.
ordenado *a* methodical, tidy.
ordenanza *f* ordinance; decree; *m* (*mil*) orderly.
ordenar *vt* to order, classify, arrange; to put in order; *vr* to be ordained (*priest*).
ordeñar *vt* to milk.
ordinario *a* ordinary; common, rough.
oreja *f* ear; handle, flange.
orejera *f* earflap.
orfandad *f* homelessness; orphanage.

orfebre *m* goldsmith; silversmith.
orfeón *m* choir.
organillo *m* barrel organ, hurdy-gurdy.
organista *m* organist.
órgano *m* organ; medium.
organización *m* organization; arrangement.
orgía *f* orgy, revel.
orgullo *m* pride, presumption; haughtiness.
orgulloso *a* proud, lofty, arrogant, haughty.
oriental *a* oriental.
orientar *vt* to orientate, guide, direct; *vr* to find one's bearings, make one's way.
oriente *m* Orient, east; **Extremo, (Lejano)** — Far East; — **Medio** Middle East; **Próximo**— Near East.
orífice *m* goldsmith.
orificio *m* aperture, hole, orifice.
origen *m* origin; source, cause.
original *a* original; novel, odd; *m* original.
originar *vt* to originate, start, found.
originario *a* primary; native of.
orilla *f* border, edge, brink; —**del mar** sea shore.
orillar *vi* to border; *vt* to avoid difficulties, set aside.
orín *m* iron rust.
oriundo *a* — **de** native of, coming from.
orla *f* border, fringe.
orlar *vt* to border, work a (fringe) (border) on.
ornamentar *vt* to ornament, adorn.
ornamento *m* ornament; accomplishment.
ornato *m* embellishment, decoration.
oro *m* gold; wealth; — **batido** gold leaf; — **en barras** gold ingots, bullion; **de** — golden, (of) gold; *pl* diamonds (*cards*).
oropel *m* glitter; tinsel.
orquesta *f* orchestra.
ortiga *f* nettle.
ortodoxo *a* orthodox.
ortografía *f* orthography, spelling.
ortología *f* science of pronunciation.
oruga *f* caterpillar.
orujo *m* skin and stones (*of olives, grapes, after pressing*).
orzuelo *m* sty (*on eye*); snare (*for birds*).
osa *f* she-bear;— **mayor** the Dipper, Great Bear.
osadía *f* daring; boldness, audacity.
osar *vi* to dare, venture.
osario *m* charnel house.
oscilar *vi* to oscillate, swing, sway, vibrate.
ósculo *m* ceremonial kiss; — **de paz** kiss of peace.
oscuro — *see* **obscuro, obscuridad.**
oso *m* bear; — **blanco** polar bear; **hacer el**— to play the fool.
ostensible *a* ostensible, apparent.
ostentación *f* ostentation, show.
ostentar *vti* to exhibit, show, bear; to boast.
ostentoso *a* ostentatious.
ostra *f* oyster.
ostracismo *m* ostracism.
osuno *a* bear-like, bearish.
otear *vt* to observe, make out, examine.
otero *m* hillock, knoll.
otoñal *a* autumnal.
otoño *m* autumn.
otorgamiento *m* granting; grant; execution (*of a legal document*).
otorgar *vt* to grant; to agree, consent; to execute; — **poder** to grant power of attorney; **quien calla otorga** silence gives consent.
otro *a* other; another.
otrosí *ad* besides, moreover; also.
ovación *f* ovation; enthusiastic reception.
óvalo *m* oval.
ovar *vi* to lay eggs.
oveja *f* sheep; ewe.
ovejuno *a* ovine, sheep.
overol(es) *m Mex* overalls.
ovetense *an* (*inhabitant*) of Oviedo.
ovillo *m* ball of yarn; tangle; **por el hilo se saca el** — a nod's as good as a wink.
oxidar *vti* to oxidize, rust.
oyente *m* hearer; casual visitor (*at lecture, class etc*); (*radio*) listener.

P

pabellón *m* pavilion; banner (*national*) flag.
pábilo *m* wick.
Pablo *m* Paul.
pábulo *m* food (*for thought etc*).
paca *f* bale.
pacer *vt* to graze.
paciencia *f* patience; forbearance; — **y barajar** wait and see.
paciente *a* patient, (long-)suffering.
pacienzudo *a* patient, persevering.
pacificar *vt* to pacify, to appease.
pacificación *f* pacification; settlement (*of disturbances*).
pacificar *vt* to pacify, appease; *vr* to grow calm.
pacífico *a* peaceful, pacific.
Pacífico, el Océano *m* the Pacific Ocean.
pacotilla *f* (*com*) venture; **de**— paltry wares, trash.
pactar *vt* to covenant, pact, stipulate.
pacto *m* covenant, pact.
pachorrudo *a* sluggish.
padecer *vt* to suffer.
padecimiento *m* suffering.
padrastro *m* stepfather.
padre *m* father; — **nuestro** Lord's Prayer; *pl* parents.
padrinazgo *m* title or charge of a godfather, best man.

padrino *m* godfather; second (*in duel*); patron; sponsor.
padrón *m* poll, census; pattern; blot (*of ill-repute*).
paella *f* Valencian dish (*rice, chicken, shellfish etc*).
paga *f* payment; satisfaction; wages, fee.
pagadero *a* payable.
pagado *a* paid; **— de sí mismo** self-satisfied.
pagador *m* paymaster.
pagaduría *f* paymaster's office.
pagano *an* pagan, heathen.
pagar *vt* to pay; to atone; *vr* to be pleased with, conceited about.
pagaré *m* promissory note; IOU.
página *f* page (*of book*).
paginar *vt* to paginate.
pago *m* payment, requital; **en —** in payment.
paila *f* kettle, cauldron; boiler.
país *m* country, state; region, territory.
paisaje *m* landscape, countryside.
paisano *m* countryman; fellow countryman; civilian.
Países Bajos, los *m pl* the Low Countries, the Netherlands.
paja *f* straw; chaff; padding (*in writing*).
pajar *m* barn, straw loft, rick.
pájaro *m* bird; **— carpintero** woodpecker.
paje *m* page, valet; servant.
pajizo *a* straw, straw-colored.
pala *f* shovel; blade, leaf (*of oar, table etc*).
palabra *f* word; speech; **pedir (tener) la —** to ask (have) permission to speak (*in debate etc*); **de —** by word of mouth.
palaciego *a* palace; *m* courtier.
palacio *m* palace.
paladar *m* palate; taste.
paladear *vt* to taste with pleasure, enjoy the taste of.
paladín *m* paladin, champion.
palafrén *m* palfrey.
palanca *f* lever; joystick; crowbar, bar; brake.
palangana *f* washstand.
palco *m* box (*in theater*).
palenque *m* palisade; arena, ring (*for fighting*).
paleta *f* fire shovel; trowel; palette.
paleto *m* country bumpkin.
paletó *m* overcoat.
paliar *vt* to palliate, extenuate; to excuse, gloss over.
palidecer *vi* to become pale.
palidez *f* paleness, pallor.
pálido *a* pale, pallid.
palillo *m* toothpick; drumstick; pin (*billiards*).
palinodia *f* palinode, (public) recantation.
palio *m* cloak; canopy.
palique *m* chit-chat.
paliza *f* bastinado; beating (up).
palizada *f* palisade, stockade.
palma *f* palm (*hand*); palm tree.
palmada *f* hand claps, applause; **dar —s** to applaud.
palmario *a* obvious, patent.
palmatoria *f* candlestick.
palmera *f* palm tree.
palmesano *an* (*inhabitant*) of Palma.
palmo *m* span; measure (8 *inches*); **— a —** inch by inch.
palmotear *vt* to applaud, clapping hands.
palmoteo *m* hand-clapping.
palo *m* stick; log; suit (*cards*); **— mayor** mainmast; **— de Campeche** Campeachy wood.
paloma *f* dove; pigeon.
palomar *m* dovecot.
palomilla *f* moth.
palpable *ad* evident, palpable, obvious.
palpar *vt* to touch, feel, grope.
palpitante *a* palpitating, vibrating.
palpitar *vi* to throb, palpitate, beat, quiver.
palta *f SA* avocado.
paludismo *m* malaria.
palurdo *a* rustic; rude; *m* clod, hick.
palustre *a* marshy; *m* trowel.
pallador *m SA* minstrel, roving singer.
pampa *SA f* plain.
pámpano *m* young vine branch.
pampeano *a SA* of *or* from pampas.
pampero *m SA* person living on pampas.
pan *m* bread; loaf; **— de jabón** cake of soap.
pana *f* velveteen, corduroy.
panacea *f* panacea.
panadería *f* bakery; baker's shop.
panadero *m* baker.
panal *m* honeycomb.
Panamá *m* Panama.
panameño *an* (*inhabitant*) of Panama, Panamanian.
pancarta *f* placard.
pandearse *vr* to bulge, sag.
pandereta *f* tambourine.
pandero *m* tambourine; kite.
pandilla *f* gang, set, league.
panegírico *m* panegyric.
panegirista *m* panegyrist.
pánico *a* panic; *m* panic, fright.
panocha *f* ear of corn; *Mex* brown sugar.
panoplia *f* panoply.
panorama *m* panorama.
panque *m SA* pancake; small cake.
pantalón *m* (*more used in pl*) trousers, pants.
pantalla *f* screen; lampshade; (*film*) screen.
pantano *m* morass, marsh; reservoir, dam.
panteísmo *m* pantheism.
pantera *f* panther.
pantomima *f* pantomime; dumb show.
pantorrilla *f* calf, leg.

panza *f* paunch, belly (*of vase etc*).
panzudo *a* stout, big-bellied.
pañal *m* swaddling cloth; *pl* **estar en—** to be in its beginnings (*infancy*).
pañero *m* draper.
paño *m* cloth, (woolen *or* woven) stuff; rag; **— burdo** shoddy cloth; **— de manos** towel; *pl* clothes; **—s menores** underclothes.
pañuelo *m* handkerchief, kerchief.
papa *m* Pope; *SA* potato; *pl* mushy food.
papá *m* daddy, papa.
papacho *m Mex* cuddle, caress.
papada *f* double chin.
papagayo *m* parrot; tailor's dummy, dandy.
papalote, papelote *m SA* kite.
papamoscas *m* flycatcher; ninny, gaper.
papanatas *m* simpleton.
paparrucha *f* silliness; fake.
papel *m* paper; document; role, (*actor's*) part; **— moneda** paper money; **— de seda** tissue paper; **— de lija** sandpaper; **hacer un —** to play a part.
papeleo *m* paperwork; red tape.
papelera *f* paper case, writing desk.
papelería *f* stationery.
papeleta *f* card, ticket, index card.
papera *f* goiter.
papiro *m* papyrus.
papo *m* double chin.
paquete *m* packet, parcel.
par *a* equal; **de — en —** wide open; even; *m* pair, couple; peer; **pares y nones** odds or evens.
para *prep* for, to, toward; in order to; **¿— qué?** what for?, why?
parabién *m* congratulation.
parábola *f* parable; parabola.
parabrisa *m* windscreen, windshield.
paraca *f SA* wind from Pacific.
paracaídas *m* parachute.
parada *f* (*bus*) stop; suspension; parade; parry; stakes, bet; **— en seco** dead stop; **— discrecional** request (flag) stop.
paradero *m* halting place, halt; whereabouts.
paradoja *f* paradox.
parador *m* roadhouse, hostel.
paráfrasis *f* paraphrase.
parágrafo *m* paragraph; *see* **párrafo.**
paraguas *m* umbrella.
paraguayo *an* Paraguayan.
paraíso *m* paradise; garden of Eden; (*theat*) gallery.
paraje *m* spot, place; condition.
paralelo *a* parallel.
paralelogramo *m* parallelogram.
paralítico *an* paralytic.
paralizar *vt* to paralyze; to stop.
paramento *m* ornament, hanging.
paramera *f* moors, moorland.
páramo *m* moor, waste.
parangón *m* paragon, model; comparison.
paraninfo *m* Great Hall (*for University ceremonies*); paranymph.
parapetar *vi* to raise a parapet; *vr* to defend oneself from behind a parapet, to entrench oneself.
parapeto *m* parapet, breastwork.
parar *vt* to stop, check; to stake, bet; *vi* to come to; to become; *SA* to get up; **— mientes (en)** to consider carefully; **sin —** constantly, continually.
pararrayos *m* lightning rod, conductor.
parasismo *m* fit, paroxysm.
parásito *a* parasitic; *m* parasite.
parasol *m* parasol, sunshade.
parca *f* fate, death.
parcela *f* parcel of land, lot, plot.
parcial *a* partial; one-sided, partisan.
parcialidad *f* partiality; party.
parco *a* sparing; parsimonious, sober.
parche *m* plaster; drumhead; patch.
pardo *a* brown, dark, gray-brown; *m* (*poet*) leopard.
parear *vt* to couple, match.
parecer *m* opinion; look.
parecer *vi* to appear, turn up; to seem; *vr* to resemble, look like; **el buen —** appearance's sake; **al —** apparently.
parecido *a* like, resembling; *m* resemblance, likeness.
pared *f* (*interior*) wall.
pareja *f* couple, brace, pair, partner.
parejo *a* even; similar.
parentela *f* parentage, relations; kindred.
parentesco *m* relationship.
paréntesis *m* parenthesis.
paria *m* pariah, outcast.
paridad *f* equality, parity.
pariente *m* relation, kinsman.
parihuela *f* stretcher.
parir *vti* to give birth.
parla *f* talk, gossip.
parlador *a* talkative; *m* chatterer.
parlamentar *vi* to converse; (*mil*) to parley, to treat.
parlamentario *a* parliamentary; *m* flag of truce.
parlamento *m* parliament; parley.
parlanchín *a* talkative; *m* talkative person.
parlar *vt* to talk, chatter.
Parnaso *m* Parnassus.
paro *m* suspension; strike, unemployment.
parodiar *vt* to parody.
parpadear *vi* to blink.
párpado *m* eyelid.
parque *m* park; garden; paddock.
parquedad *f* parsimony, care.
parra *f* grape vine.
párrafo *m* paragraph.
parranda *f* spree.
parricida *m* parricide.
parrilla *f* broiler, grill, gridiron.
párroco *m* parish priest.
parroquia *f* parish.

parroquiano *a* parochial; *m* parishioner; customer.
parsimonia *f* temperance, moderation.
parte *f* part, portion, lot, section; communiqué; place; side, party; **dar** — to notify; **de mi** — for my part; **de** — **de** from; **por todas** —**s** on all sides.
partera *f* midwife.
partición *f* partition, distribution.
participante *m* participant, sharer.
participar *vi* to share, participate; *vt* to inform, notify, tell.
partícipe *m* partner, participant.
particular *a* special, peculiar, particular; **casa** — private house; particular; private individual, person.
partida *f* departure; (*robber*) band, party; item (*of account*); parcel, lot; game; (*birth etc*) certificate; — **de caza** hunting party.
partidario *an* partisan, follower, believer in.
partido *m* (*pol*) party; profit; (*sport*) game; **sacar** — **de** to profit by; derive benefit from; *a* divided, split.
partir *vt* to divide, cleave, cut; *vi* to leave, depart.
partitura *f* (*mus*) score.
parto *m* childbirth.
parva light breakfast; heap of unthreshed grain.
parvada *f* *SA* flock (*of birds*).
parvo *a* small, little.
párvulo *a* very small; *m* child; **escuela de**—**s** infant school.
pasa *f* dried grape, raisin.
pasada *f* passage, turn; bad turn.
pasadera *f* stepping stone.
pasadero *a* tolerable, bearable, tolerably good.
pasadizo *m* corridor, passage, alley.
pasado *a* last, past; stale;— **mañana** day after tomorrow; *m* the past.
pasaje *m* passage, way.
pasajero *a* transient, provisional; *m* passenger.
pasamano *m* banister.
pasaporte *m* passport.
pasar *vti* to pass, move; to pierce; to cross; to pass, to go by; to spend (*time*); to endure; to surpass; to go bad; — **por alto** to overlook; — **de largo** to pass by; — **de** to exceed, be more than; —**se de** to do without.
pasarela *f* gangplank.
pasatiempo *m* pastime.
pascana *f* *SA* inn.
pascua *f* (*relig*) feast; — **de Resurrección** Easter; Passover.
pase *m* permit, (*free*) pass; pass, stroke.
paseante *m* good for nothing, lazy dog.
pasear *vi* to walk, take a walk; *vt* to take for a walk (ride).
paseo *m* walk; stroll, turn, promenade; **mandar a** — to send packing.
pasiego *an* native of highlands of Santander.
pasibilidad *f* passiveness.
pasillo *m* corridor; short step.
pasión *f* passion.
pasito *m* short step; *ad* softly, gently, slowly.
pasivo *a* passive; *m* (*com*) liabilities.
pasmar *vt* to astound, stun; *vi* to wonder; *vr* to be completely amazed.
pasmo *m* astonishment; spasm.
pasmoso *a* wonderful, extraordinary, amazing.
paso *m* step, pace; passage; — **a** — step by step;— **a nivel** level crossing, grade crossing; **de** — in passing; **marcar el** — to mark time; **apretar el** — to hurry, step it out.
pasta *f* paste, dough (*also fam*); pulp; cardboard.
pastar *vi* to graze.
pastel *m* pie; cake.
pastelería *f* pastry; cake shop, confectioner's.
pastelero *m* pastrycook, confectioner.
pastilla *f* cake (*soap etc*), tablet, lozenge.
pasto *m* pasture, food; *SA* grass; **a** — abundantly; **de** — of daily use, ordinary; — **de las llamas** fuel to the flames.
pastor *m* shepherd; Protestant clergyman.
pastorear *vt* to pasture.
pastoreo *m* tending of flocks.
pastoso *a* pasty; doughy.
pastura *f* pasture; feed.
pata *f* foot, leg (*animals, furniture*); — **de palo** wooden leg; **meter la** — to put one's foot in it.
patada *f* kick.
patalear *vi* to kick repeatedly, stamp both feet (*in disapproval*).
pataleo *m* kicking, stamping.
pataleta *f* convulsion; fainting fit.
patán *m* rustic, churl, rough brute.
patanería *f* rudeness, churlishness.
patata *f* potato.
patatús *m* swoon, fainting fit.
patear *vi* to kick, stamp.
patente *a* manifest, obvious; *f* patent, warrant; — **de invención** patent.
patentizar *vt* to reveal, make clear, evident.
patético *a* pathetic, touching.
patíbulo *m* gibbet, gallows.
patillas *f pl* sideboards, sideburns.
patín *m* skate; — **de ruedas** roller skates.
patinar *vi* to skate; to skid, slip.
patio *m* yard, court, quadrangle, inner square (*of a house*).
pato *m* drake, duck.
patología *f* pathology.
patraña *f* fake, story, fib, lie.
patria *f* native country, home country; motherland.

patriarca *m* patriarch.
Patricio *m* Patrick.
patrimonio *m* inheritance; heritage, possession(s).
patriota *mf* patriot.
patriotero *a* exaggerated (*ill-judged*) patriot.
patrocinar *vt* to patronize, guarantee, support, back.
patrocinio *m* patronage, protection; **bajo el — de** under the auspices of.
patrón *m* patron; standard, pattern; host, owner, captain, skipper; **— de oro** gold standard.
patronato *m* patronage, guardianship; association; board of trustees, governing body.
patrulla *m* patrol.
Paula *f* Pauline.
paulatinamente *a* little by little, gradually.
pausa *f* pause, rest.
pausado *a* slow, deliberate, quiet.
pauta *f* guide, standard; guide-lines; main lines (of approach, to follow).
pava *f* turkey-hen; **pelar la—** to flirt.
pavesa *f* embers; snuff (*of candle*).
pavimentar *vt* to pave.
pavimento *m* pavement, road surface.
pavo *m* turkey; **— real** peacock.
pavón *m* peacock.
pavonear *vi* to strut, act like a peacock.
pavor *m* fright, dread, horror.
pavoroso *a* awful, terrible, fearful.
pavura *f* great fright, horror.
payaso *m* clown, buffoon.
payés *an* Catalonian peasant or farmer.
payo *m* clown, fool; villager.
paz *f* peace, rest, quiet; **en —** quits; **gente de —** friend.
peaje *m* road toll.
peana *f* pedestal.
peatón *m* pedestrian; rural postman.
peca *f* freckle.
pecado *m* sin; guilt, transgression; **— capital** deadly sin.
pecador *m* sinner.
pecaminoso *a* sinful.
pecar *vi* to sin; to offend; **— de** to be too (*kind etc*).
pécora *f* head of sheep.
pecoso *a* freckly.
pecuario *a* pertaining to cattle.
peculiar *a* peculiar, special, restricted (*to*).
peculiaridad *f* peculiarity, individual characteristic.
peculio *m* private purse, fortune.
pecunia *f* specie, cash.
pecuniario *a* pecuniary.
pechar *vt* to pay taxes.
pechera *f* shirtfront.
pecho *m* chest, breast; gradient; **tomar a —** to take seriously (*to heart*).
pechuga *f* breast (*of fowls*).
pedagogía *f* pedagogy.
pedal *m* pedal, treadle.
pedante *m* pedant.
pedantería *f* pedantry.
pedantesco *a* pedantic.
pedazo *m* piece, bit, fragment.
pedernal *m* flint.
pedestal *m* pedestal, base.
pedestre *an* pedestrian.
pedido *m* order,demand.
pedigüeño *a* importunate (*beggar*).
pedimento *m* petition.
pedir (i) *vt* to ask, beg, request, demand; **— cuenta** to bring to account; **a — de boca** just as one would wish.
pedrada *f* blow with a stone.
pedrea *f* lapidation, stone-fight.
pedregal *m* stony land.
pedregoso *a* stony, rocky.
pedrería *f* jewelry.
pedrisco *m* hailstorm; heaps of pebbles.
Pedro *m* Peter.
pega *f* cementing, jointing; deceit.
pegadizo *a* sticky, adhesive; contagious.
pegador *m* **— de carteles** billposter.
pegajoso *a* sticky, viscous; catching, contagious; difficult to shake off; catchy (*music*).
pegar *vt* to glue, fasten, paste; post (*bills*); to beat, hit, slap; **— fuego a** to set fire to; *vi* to be understandable, catchy; to stick.
peinado *m* coiffure.
peinador *m* dressing gown.
peinar *vt* to comb; **— canas** to be old.
peine *m* comb; rack.
peineta *f* ornamental comb.
pelado *a* bare, treeless, barren.
peladura *f* plucking (*feathers*).
pelagatos *m* tramp.
pelar *vt* to cut the hair short; to skin, peel, shell; to pluck (*feathers*); **— la pava** to flirt with, make love to.
peldaño *m* step (*staircase*).
pelea *f* flight, battle, quarrel.
pelear *vi* to fight, contend, quarrel.
pelele *m* dummy, stuffed shirt.
peletería *f* furrier.
peliagudo *a* downy; ticklish (*situation*).
pelícano *m* pelican.
película *f* film.
peligrar *vi* to be in danger.
peligro *m* peril, danger, risk.
peligroso *a* dangerous, perilous.
pelirrojo *a* red-haired.
pelirrubio *a* blond.
pelma *m* bore, tiresome person.
pelmazo *m* slow person.
pelo *m* hair, down; coat (*animals*); **a —** to the purpose; **montar a —** to ride bareback; **de— en pecho** virile, brave; **a contra—** against the grain.
pelota *f* (*inflated*) ball; *SA* punt made of leather; **en —** naked, without a stitch on; **juego de—** ball game.
pelotear *vt* to audit accounts; to throw up balls.

pelotera *f* wrangle, dispute.
pelotón *m* platoon, squad.
peltre *m* pewter.
peluca *f* wig.
peluquería *f* hairdresser's, barber's shop, barbershop.
peluquero *m* hairdresser, barber.
pelleja *f* skin, hide.
pellejo *m* skin; wine skin; **salvar el—** to save one's skin (*life*).
pellizcar *vt* to pinch, nip.
pena *f* penalty; pain (*mental, emotional*); sorrow, grief; **valer la —** to be worthwhile.
penacho *m* aigret; panache.
penal *a* penal.
penalidad *f* suffering, hardship; penalty.
penar *vi* to suffer; to be suffering, grieve.
penco *m* nag, horse; *SA* boor.
pendejo *m* *SA* fool.
pendencia *f* quarrel, dispute, feud.
pendenciero *a* quarrelsome, easily roused (*to quarrel*).
pender *vi* to hang; to be pending; to depend.
pendiente *a* pending, hanging; *m* earring; *f* slope, incline.
péndola *f* pendulum; quill.
pendón *m* banner, pennon.
péndulo *m* pendulum.
penetración *f* penetration, acuteness.
penetrante *a* penetrating, keen, piercing.
penetrar *vt* to penetrate, break into; to comprehend; to permeate.
penetrativo *a* piercing.
península *f* peninsula.
peninsular *a* peninsular.
penique *m* penny.
penitencia *f* penance, penitence.
penitencial *a* penitential.
penitenciaría *f* prison.
penitente *a* penitent, contrite.
penoso *a* painful; laborious.
pensado *a* deliberate; **tener —** to have thought.
pensador *m* thinker.
pensamiento *m* thought, idea, mind.
pensar (ie) *vt* **— en** to think (of) (over); to reflect; to fancy.
pensativo *a* thoughtful, pensive.
pensión *f* pension, board and lodgings, boarding house.
pensionista *m* boarder.
pentecostés *m* Pentecost, Whitsuntide.
penúltimo *a* penultimate, next to the last, last but one.
penumbra *f* penumbra, shade.
penuria *f* penury, indigence.
peña *f* rock, peak; group, circle (*of friends*).
peñascal *m* rocky hill.
peñasco *m* cliff, boulder.
peón *m* day laborer; spinning top; pawn (*chess*).
peonza *f* whipping top.
peor *a ad* worse, worst.
pepino *m* cucumber; **no importar un—** not to care a hang.
pepita *f* pip (*apple etc*).
pepitoria *f* medley, hash (*of things*).
pequeñez *f* smallness.
pequeño *a* small, little.
pera *f* pear.
peral *m* pear tree, pear orchard.
percal *m* percale, muslin, calico.
percance *m* misfortune, mishap.
percatarse *vr* to be aware of, notice.
percepción *f* perception; collection.
perceptible *a* noticeable.
percibir *vt* to perceive; to collect.
percusión *f* percussion.
percha *f* perch; clothes rack, hanger.
perchero *m* clothes rack.
perder (ie) *vt* to lose; to ruin; **— de vista** to lose sight of; to spoil; *vr* to go astray, get lost; to be spoiled (*fruit etc*).
perdición *f* perdition; ruin, loss.
pérdida *f* loss, waste, damage, shrinkage; *pl* **—s y ganancias** profit and loss.
perdido *a* lost; misguided, profligate.
perdidoso *m* loser.
perdigón *m* young partridge; buckshot.
perdiz *f* partridge.
perdón *m* pardon, grace, forgiveness; **con—** by your leave.
perdonar *vt* to pardon, forgive; to excuse.
perdurar *vi* to last, endure.
perecedero *a* perishable.
perecer *vi* to perish, to succumb.
peregrinación *f* pilgrimage.
peregrinar *vi* to make a pilgrimage; to wander.
peregrino *a* strange, rare; *m* pilgrim.
perejil *m* parsley.
perenne *a* perennial, perpetual.
perentorio *a* peremptory, urgent.
pereza *f* laziness; tardiness; sloth.
perezoso *a* lazy, idle; *m* (*zool*) sloth.
perfección *f* perfection; **a la —** perfectly.
perfeccionar *vt* to perfect, improve.
perfecto *a* perfect, complete.
perfidia *f* perfidy, treachery.
pérfido *a* perfidious.
perfil *m* profile, outline.
perfilar *vt* to profile, draw (sketch) outline of.
perforación *f* perforation, drilling.
perforador *m* driller, borer.
perforar *vt* to drill, perforate.
perfumador *m* perfumer; perfuming vessel.
perfumar *vt* to perfume.
perfume *m* perfume, fragrance.
perfumería *f* perfumery.
pergamino *m* parchment, vellum.
pergeñar *vt* to prepare, elaborate.
pergeño *m* appearance, looks.
pericia *f* skill, expertness.
periferia *f* periphery.

perifollo *m* chervil; cheap excessive ornament.
perilla *f* goatee, imperial; **de —** to the purpose; **venir de—** to come pat.
periódico *a* periodical; *m* journal, newspaper.
periodismo *m* journalism.
periodista *mf* journalist.
periodístico *a* journalistic.
período *m* period, era; sentence.
peripecia *f* incident; *pl* ups and downs. episodes.
perito *m* expert; appraiser.
perjudicar *vt* to damage; to prejudice; to count against, be a disadvantage.
perjuicio *m* damage, injury, prejudice.
perjurar *vi* to commit perjury.
perjurio *m* perjury.
perla *f* pearl; **de—s** perfectly, pat.
permanecer *vi* to remain, stay; to last.
permanencia *f* sojourn, stay, remaining.
permanente *a* permanent, lasting.
permisión *f* permission; (*mil*) leave.
permiso *m* leave, permit; **con su —** by your leave.
permitido *a* permissible, allowable, possible, allowed.
permitir *vt* to permit, allow, let.
permuta *f* barter.
permutación *f* barter, exchange.
permutar *vt* to exchange, interchange; to permute.
pernicioso *a* pernicious, harmful.
pernil *m* ham, shoulder.
perno *m* bolt.
pernoctar *vt* to stay overnight.
pero *cj* but, except.
perogrullada *f* platitude, self-evident statement.
perol *m* kettle, copper pan.
peroración *f* peroration, discourse.
perorar *vi* to declaim (*a speech*), orate.
peróxido *m* peroxide.
perpendicular *a* perpendicular, upright.
perpetración *f* perpetration.
perpetrar *vt* to perpetrate, commit.
perpetuar *vt* to perpetuate.
perpetuidad *f* perpetuity.
perpetuo *a* perpetual.
perplejidad *f* perplexity, hesitation.
perplejo *a* perplexed, uncertain, confused.
perro *m* dog; **— cobrador** retriever; **— de ajeo** setter; **— dogo** bulldog.
persecución *f* persecution; pursuit.
perseguidor *m* persecutor; pursuer.
perseguir (i) *vt* to persecute, importune; to pursue.
perseverante *a* perseverant, constant, steady.
perseverar *vi* to persevere; to insist; to persist.
persiana *f* (*Venetian*) (window)blinds.
persignarse *vr* to cross oneself.
persistente *a* persistent.
persistir *vi* to persist, persevere.
persona *f* person; individual.
personaje *m* personage; (*theat*) character.
personal *a* personal.
personalidad *f* personality; distinguished person.
personarse *vt* to appear in person, turn up.
personificar *vt* to personify.
perspectiva *f* perspective, prospect, outlook.
perspicacia *f* sagacity, acumen, perspicacity.
persuadir *vt* to persuade, convince.
persuasión *f* persuasion, opinion.
pertenecer *vi* to belong; to concern.
pertenencia *f* ownership, belonging, tenure.
perteneciente *a* belonging, appertaining.
pértiga *f* staff, pole, rod; **a la—** pole jump.
pertiguero *m* verger.
pertinacia *f* obstinacy, doggedness.
pertinaz *a* pertinacious, stubborn, insistent, persistent.
pertinente *a* relevant, appropriate; pertaining.
pertrechar *vtr* to supply, equip.
pertrechos *m pl* (*mil*) stores; tools.
perturbador *m* disturber.
perturbar *vt* to perturb, unsettle, confuse, agitate.
Perú *m* Peru.
peruano *an* Peruvian.
perversión *f* perversion, depravity.
perverso *a* wicked, perverted, contrary.
pervertir (ie) *vt* to pervert, deprave; *vr* to become depraved.
pesa *f* weight; *pl* **—s y medidas** weights and measures.
pesadez *f* gravity; heaviness; fatigue.
pesadilla *f* nightmare.
pesado *a* heavy, weighty, cumbersome; boring, tiresome; profound (*sleep*).
pesadumbre *f* grief, sorrow; heaviness.
pésame *m* condolence; **dar el —** to express (send) one's sorrow (*to bereaved relatives*).
pesantez *f* gravity.
pesar *m* regret, sorrow; *vt* to weigh; *vi* to be weighty; to be sorry, regret; **a — de** despite, in spite of; **a— mío** in spite of myself; **mal que le pese** like it or not.
pesaroso *a* sorrowful, regretful.
pesca *f* fishing, angling.
pescado *m* fish (*caught*).
pescar *vt* to fish, to angle, to catch.
pescuezo *m* neck.
pesebre *m* manger, crib.
peseta *f* Spanish coin, peseta.
pesimista *m* pessimist.
pésimo *a* very bad, the worst, abominable.

peso *m* weight; scales; burden, load; sound judgment; silver coin; — **bruto** gross weight; — **neto** net weight.
pesquería *f* fishery.
pesquisa *f* inquiry, investigation, search.
pestaña *f* eyelash.
pestañear *vi* to wink, blink.
peste *f* plague, pest, epidemic.
pestífero *a* pestiferous, noxious.
pestilencia *f* pestilence, plague.
pestilencial *f* pestiferous, plaguey, infectious.
pestilente *a* pestilent, pestiferous.
pestillo *m* doorlatch, bolt (*on door*).
petaca *f* cigar case, tobacco pouch.
pétalo *m* petal.
petardista *m* cheat, impostor, swindler.
petardo *m* bomb; fraud.
petate *m* sleeping mat; **liar el** — to pack up one's traps.
petición *f* petition, request; — **de manos** betrothal; **a — de** on (at) the request of.
peticionario *m* petitioner.
petimetre *m* dandy, beau.
peto *m* breastplate; stomacher.
pétreo *a* stony, rocky.
petrificar *vt* to petrify.
petróleo *m* petroleum, mineral oil.
petrolero *m* oil tanker.
petulancia *f* petulance, pertness.
petulante *a* petulant, pert, cheeky.
pez *m* fish; *f* pitch, tar.
pezón *m* stalk; nipple.
piadoso *a* pious, godly, good.
piafar *vi* to paw (*of horses*).
piano *m* pianoforte;— **de cola** grand; — **vertical** upright.
piar *vi* to peep, chirp; to whine.
piara *f* herd (*swine*), drove (*horses*).
pica *f* pike; (*print*) pica.
picacho *m* peak, summit.
picadillo *m* minced meat.
picado *a* bitten, stung, hurt, piqued; **carne —a** minced meat; **tabaco —** loose tobacco.
picador *m* horsebreaker; picador (*bullfights*).
picadura *f* puncture, pricking; bite (*of insects*); cut (*tobacco*).
picaflor *m* humming bird.
picana *f SA* fool.
picanear *vt SA* to goad.
picante *a* pricking; hot, highly seasoned; *m* piquancy.
picapedrero *m* stone cutter.
picar *vt* to prick, sting, bite; to mince; to goad, pique; to burn; *vr* to itch; to be offended, stung (*to anger, rivalry etc*).
picardía *f* knavery, roguery, mischief.
picaresco *a* knavish, roguish, picaresque.
pícaro *m* rogue; *a* naughty, mischievous, sly.
pico *m* beak, bill; pickax; peak; — **de oro** golden-mouthed (*eloquent*) orator; **callar el** — to hold one's tongue.
picota *f* gibbet.
picotear *vt* to strike with the beak.
pictórico *a* pictorial.
pichana *f Arg, Chi* broom.
pichón *m* pigeon.
pie *m* foot, support, base; bottom (*of page*); (*theat*) cue; **a** — on foot; (**de**) (**en**) — standing; **al — de la letra** verbatim, exactly; **ni —s ni cabeza** neither head nor tail.
piedad *f* piety, mercifulness, charity.
piedra *f* stone; gravel; — **fina** precious stone; — **angular** cornerstone; — **de toque** touchstone; — **rodada** boulder.
piel *f* hide, skin, pelt, fur.
piélago *m* (open) sea.
pienso *m* feed (*for animals*).
pierna *f* leg; **a — suelta** at ease; soundly.
pieza *f* piece, portion; room; play; game (*bird*); **de una** — in one piece.
pigmeo *m* dwarf, pygmy.
pila *f* pile, heap; sink; font; (*el*) battery; **nombre de** — Christian name.
pilar *m* pillar, column; *vt* to hull.
píldora *f* pill.
pileta *f Arg* swimming pool.
pilmama *f SA* child's nurse.
pilón *m* mortar (*for pounding*); basin (*of fountain*).
pilongo *m* dried chestnut.
piloto *m* pilot; sailing master; *Arg* raincoat.
pillaje *m* plunder; pillage.
pillar *vt* to catch, take hold of; to plunder.
pillería *f* lowdown trick.
pillo *m* rascal, rogue, petty thief, urchin.
pilluelo *m* urchin, guttersnipe.
pimentón *m* red pepper.
pimienta *f* pepper.
pimiento *m* red pepper; capsicum.
pimpollar *m* nursery (*of plants*).
pimpollo *m* sucker; young blood; bud.
pináculo *m* pinnacle.
pinar *m* pine wood.
pincel *m* (*painter's*) brush.
pincelada *f* brush stroke.
pinchar *vt* to prick, puncture.
pinchazo *m* (*tire*) puncture, flat; (*med*) injection.
pinche *m* minion.
pingüe *a* abundant, rich (*profits etc*), fat.
pino *m* pine tree; — **alerce** larch; — **marítimo** cluster pine.
pinocho *m* pine cone.
pinol *m SA* cereal meal.
pinta *f* spot, mark; appearance; pint; (*fam*) face, mug; **¡qué —!** what a sight!
pintar *vt* to paint; to stain; to

describe; *vr* to paint one's face, make up.
pintiparado *a* exactly like, the very image (*of*).
pintor *m* painter; — **de brocha gorda** house painter; dauber, rough and ready.
pintoresco *a* picturesque, exotic.
pintura *f* painting; picture; — **a la aguada** watercolor; — **al óleo** oil painting.
pinzas *f pl* nippers, tweezers; claws; forceps; (clothes)pegs.
piña *f* pine cone; pineapple.
piñata *f* decoration at ball.
piñón *m* gear wheel; cog wheel; pine kernel.
pío *a* pious, merciful; piebald.
piojo *m* louse.
pipa *f* cask, butt; pipe.
pique *m* resentment; **irse a** — to founder, go to the bottom; **echar a** — to sink.
piqueta *f* pickax.
piquete *m* prick, sting.
piragua *f* canoe, pirogue.
pirámide *f* pyramid.
pirata *m* pirate, corsair.
piratería *f* piracy.
pirenaico *a* Pyrenean.
Pirineos, los *m pl* the Pyrenees.
piropo *m* compliment, flattering phrase.
pirueta *f* pirouette.
pirotecnia *f* pyrotechnics, art of firework-making.
pisada *f* footstep, imprint (*of foot*).
pisapapeles *m* paperweight.
pisar *vt* to tread, trample on, step on.
pisaverde *m* dandy, fop.
piscina *f* swimming pool, baths.
piso *m* floor, pavement, story; flat, apartment; — **resbaladizo** slippery underfoot; — **principal** first floor.
pisonear *vt* to ram (*earth*) down.
pisotear *vt* to trample on, tread on.
pisotón *m* hard step, stamp of the foot.
pista *f* trail, scent, track; (*race, dance*) track, floor, course; **seguir la — de** to follow, pursue, go after.
pisto *m* mixture of egg, peppers, tomatoes, fried together.
pistola *f* pistol.
pistón *m* piston, embolus.
pitada *f* puff (*of cigar etc*).
pitanza *f* pittance; stipend.
pitar *vi* to blow a whistle; *SA* to smoke; whistle at; (*fam*) to work, go, function.
pitillo *m* cigarette.
pito *m* pipe, whistle, fife; **no me importa un** — I don't care a straw.
pitonisa *f* fortuneteller.
pizarra *f* slate; blackboard.
pizca *f* whit, bit, jot; **no sabe ni** — he hasn't an inkling.
pizpireta *f* smart little piece (*woman*).
placa *f* plate; insignia.
placentero *a* merry, pleasant, pleasing.
placer *vt* to please; *m* pleasure; will.
placidez *f* placidity, contentment.
plácido *a* placid, calm, easy-going.
plaga *f* plague, pest, scourge; drug (*on market*).
plagar *vt* to plague, infest.
plagiar *vt* to plagiarize.
plagiario *m* plagiarist.
plagio *m* plagiarism, (unauthorized) copy.
plan *m* plan, scheme, project, drawing; — **de desarrollo** development plan.
plana *f* trowel; page (*of newspaper*).
plancha *f* plate, sheet; iron (*for clothes*).
planchar *vt* (*clothes*) to iron, press.
planchear *vt* to plate, sheathe.
planear *vt* to plan.
planicie *f* plain.
plano *a* plain; level; smooth, even; *m* plan, map, chart; plane; flat (*of sword*); **en el primer** — in the foreground.
planta *f* plant; sole (*foot*); plant, site; *Arg* tree; — **baja** ground floor; **buena** — fine presence.
plantación *f* plantation; planting.
plantar *vt* to plant; to set up; to leave in the lurch, to dumbfound; to jilt.
planteamiento *m* planning.
plantear *vt* to plan; to establish, state, explain (*problem*).
plantel *m* training school, nursery.
plantilla *f* model, pattern; insole.
plantío *m* plantation.
planto *m* plaint.
plantón *m* graft, shoot; doorkeeper, sentry; **dar un** — to keep someone waiting.
plañidero *a* moaning, plaintive, wailing.
plañir *vi* to whimper, whine; to bewail.
plasta *f* soft substance (*dough, mud etc*); sloppy piece of work.
plástica *f* plastics, the art of molding.
plástico *a* plastic, yielding; (*of style*) formal, enhancing the beauty of form.
plata *f* silver; money; (*her*) argent; **como una** — like a new pin.
plataforma *f* platform, upper floor, terrace; standing place at ends of tramcars; (*pol*) stand, viewpoint.
plátano *m* plantain tree; banana (*tree and fruit*); plane tree.
platea *f* orchestra seat.
plateado *a* silver, silvery; plated.
plateresco *a* Plateresque.
platería *f* silversmith's art, trade *or* shop.
platero *m* silversmith; — **de oro** goldsmith.
plática *f* talk, homily, address; chat, conversation.

platicar *vt* to talk, chat.
platillo *m* saucer; scale, pan (*of balance*); stew; cymbal.
platino *m* platinum.
plato *m* plate; dish; course (*at meals*); **nada entre dos—s** much ado about nothing; *Arg* **¡qué —!** what fun!
Platón *m* Plato.
platónico *a* Platonic; pure, disinterested.
plausible *a* praiseworthy, laudable; plausible.
playa *f* beach, sandy shore.
playera *f* sandshoe, sandal.
plaza *f* main square; market; town; **ir a la —** to go to market to buy; fortified place; room, space; **sentar —** to enlist; **— de toros** bullring.
plazo *m* term; time limit; **a —s** by installment.
pleamar *f* high tide.
plebe *f* common people, plebs.
plebeyo *an* plebeian; of low degree; commoner.
plebiscito *m* plebiscite, general vote.
plectro *m* plectrum; (*poet*) inspiration.
plegadizo *a* pliable, folding.
plegadura *f* fold, pleat, crease.
plegar (ie) *vt* to fold, crease, tuck, pucker, pleat; *vr* to give way, crumple up.
plegaria *f* prayer.
pleitear *vt* to litigate, contend.
pleitista *m* pettifogger.
pleito *m* lawsuit, contention; proceedings; dispute; case.
plenilunio *m* full moon.
plenipotenciario *a m* plenipotentiary.
plenitud *f* fullness, wholeness, completion; fulfillment.
pleno *a* full, complete.
plétora *f* plethora; over-fullness.
pleuresía *f* pleurisy.
pliego *m* sheet (*paper*); sheaf, wad (*of papers*); document in envelope; **— de condiciones** tender; **—s de cordel** ballad sheets, broadsheets.
pliegue *m* pleat, fold, gather.
plinto *m* plinth, base of column; skirting board, baseboard.
plomada *f* plumb; plummet; sounding lead; sinker.
plomero *m* plumber, leadworker.
plomizo *a* leaden.
plomo *m* lead; **a —** true plumb; **caer a —** to drop flat; **andar con pies de —** to proceed very gingerly.
pluma *f* feather, plume; quill; pen, nib; **— de agua** measure of running water; **— estilográfica** fountain pen.
plumaje *m* plumage, crest of feathers.
plumazo *m* feather quilt, eiderdown.
plúmbeo *a* leaden.
plumero *m* feather duster; penholder, pencil box; panache, plume.
plumón *m* down; feather bed.
plural *a m* plural.
plus *m* (*mil*) extra pay.
pluvial *a* rainy; **capa —** cope.
población *f* population; city, town.
poblado *a* populated; thick (*beard*); *m* village; settlement.
poblador *m* settler.
poblar *vt* to people; to colonize; *vr* to put forth leaves.
pobre *a* poor; needy; wretched; paltry; *m* pauper; **—s de solemnidad** the utterly poor, the poverty-stricken.
pobreza *f* poverty, indigence, want; meagerness; lack of spirit.
pocilga *f* pigsty.
pócima *f* potion, brew.
poción *f* potion, drink.
poco *a* little, small, limited, scanty; *pl* few; *ad* little, only slightly, shortly; **— a —** gradually, softly; **tener en —** to think little of.
pocho *m Mex* person of Mexican descent born in US.
podadera *f* pruning hook.
podar *vt* to prune, lop off, trim.
podenco *m* hound.
poder *vi* to be able; to be capable of; to have authority to; to afford; **no — más** to be exhausted; **no — menos** to be obliged (to); **no — ver a** not to be able to stand (*someone*); *m* might; power, power of attorney; proxy.
poderío *m* power, might; jurisdiction; worldly wealth.
poderoso *a* powerful, potent; mighty; weighty.
podredumbre *f* corruption, decay, putrid matter.
podrido *a* rotten.
podrir *vi see* **pudrir.**
poema *m* poem (*usu long, serious*).
poesía *f* poetry, poem, lyric.
poeta *m* poet.
poética *f* poetry, the poetic art; poetics.
poético *a* poetic.
poetisa *f* poetess.
polaco *an* Pole, Polish, Polish language.
polaina *f* leggings, spats.
polaridad *f* polarity.
polea *f* pulley.
polémica *f* polemics, controversy (*politics*).
polen *m* pollen.
policía *f* police; cleanliness; *m* policeman.
policíaco *a* **novela —a** detective story, thriller.
poligamia *f* polygamy.
poligloto *a* polyglot; *nf* Polyglot Bible.
polilla *f* moth; bookworm.
pólipo *m* octopus; polyp; polypus.
polisón *m SA* fool.
política *f* politics; policy; civility.
político *a* political; in-law; *m* politician.
póliza *f* policy; scrip; draft; ticket.

polizón *m* idler, tramp, vagrant; stowaway.
polizonte *m* (*sl*) policeman.
polo *m* pole; polo; Andalusian song; — **de desarrollo** development center, pole, area.
Polonia *f* Poland.
poltrón *a* sluggish, cowardly, lazy; *m* poltroon.
polvareda *f* cloud of dust.
polvera *f* powder box, compact.
polvo *m* dust, powder, pinch of snuff; *pl* face powder; — **de la madre Celestina** magic formula, secret recipe.
pólvora *f* gunpowder.
polvoriento *a* dusty, dust laden.
polvorín *m* powder magazine; powder flask.
polla *f* young hen; chicken; (*fam*) lass.
pollada *f* covey, hatch.
pollera *f* chicken coop; child's play-pen; petticoat; *SA* skirt.
pollino *m* donkey, ass.
pollito *m* youth, young lad.
pollo *m* chicken; (*fam*) lad, boy, youth.
poma *f* apple; scent bottle.
pomar *m* apple orchard.
pomelo *m* grapefruit.
pomo *m* flask; pommel.
pompa *f* pomp, splendor, pageantry; bubble; pump.
pomposo *a* majestic, ostentatious, pompous; inflated, swollen.
pómulo *m* cheekbone.
ponche *m* punch.
poncho *m* (*mil*) overcoat; *SA* cloak, blanket.
ponderación *f* consideration, appreciation, praise; gravity.
ponderar *vt* to weigh, consider; to exaggerate; to praise.
ponderoso *a* weighty, ponderous; grave, solemn; cautious.
ponente *m* referee, judge.
poner *vt* to put, place; to set; to bet; to lay (*eggs*); to contribute; to assume; to call; to add; — **por escrito** to put in writing; *vr* to set about; to put on; to become; to get; — **enfermo** to fall ill; — **de pie** to get up; — **colorado** to blush.
pongo *m Bol, Per* Indian servant.
poniente *m* west; west wind.
pontificado *m* papacy, pontificate.
pontifical *a* papal.
pontífice *m* pontiff; the Pope; archbishop, bishop.
pontón *m* pontoon; lighter.
ponzoña *f* poison, venom.
ponzoñoso *a* poisonous, toxic.
popa *f* (*naut*) stern; **a** — aft; **viento en** — sailing along merrily, flourishingly.
popote *m SA* drinking straw.
populacho *m* mob, rabble, common herd.
popular *a* popular, of the people; **canción** — folksong.
popularizarse *vt* to become the rage; to spread.
populoso *a* populous.
poquedad *f* paucity, littleness; poverty.
poquísimo *a* diminutive (*amount*), tiny (*fragment*), negligible.
poquito *m* a little bit.
por *prep* by; through; for; during; in; around; about; as; per; on behalf of; **5** — **ciento** 5 per cent; — **qué** why; — **más que** however much; — **tanto** therefore; **ir** — **leña** to fetch firewood; **carta** — **escribir** unwritten letter; — **supuesto** of course.
por si acaso *cj* just in case.
porcelana *f* porcelain, china.
porcentaje *m* percentage.
porción *f* part, dose, share, lot.
porche *m* roof, portico.
pordiosero *m* beggar, mendicant.
porfía *f* insistence, stubbornness, obstinacy.
porfiado *a* stubborn, persistent.
porfiar *vt* to contend; to persist.
pórfido *m* porphyry.
pormenor *m* detail; **al** — retail.
poro *m* pore.
pororó *m SA* toasted corn.
poroto *m SA* bean; runt.
porque *cj* because.
por qué *m* motive; reason; *cj* why?
porquería *f* filth; dirty remark or joke; rubbish.
porquero *m* swineherd.
porra *f* club, bludgeon; truncheon; (*games*) last man in.
porrazo *m* blow, whack.
porro *m* leek.
porrón *m* earthenware jug; glass flask (*for drinking wine*); *a* (*fam*) slow, sluggish.
portada *f* title page, frontispiece; porch, doorway; façade.
portador *m* bearer, holder; porter; **bono al** — bearer bond.
portal *m* porch; vestibule, gateway, doorway.
portalón *m* (*naut*) gangway.
portamonedas *m* pocketbook, purse.
portaplumas *m* penholder.
portar *vt* to carry; *vr* to behave, act.
portátil *a* portable, pocket-size.
portavoz *m* voice, representative; megaphone.
portazgo *m* toll.
portazo *m* **dar un** — to slam a door (*in someone's face*).
porte *m* cost of carriage; portage; behavior, bearing; burden, tonnage; postage; — **franco** post-free.
portear *vt* to convey for a price.
portento *m* wonder, prodigy; omen.
portentoso *a* prodigious, marvelous.
porteño *an* of Buenos Aires.

portería *f* porter's lodge; goal, goalnet, goalposts.
portero *m* porter; doorman, janitor, commissionaire; goalkeeper.
portezuela (*carriage*) door.
pórtico *m* portico, porch, lobby.
portilla *f* porthole.
portillo *m* opening; way out, way in, passage; breach; pass.
portón *m* large gate.
portugués *an* Portuguese.
porvenir *m* future.
pos *ad* **en — de** after, in pursuit of.
posa *f* passing bell; pause for response during funeral.
posada *f* inn, lodging house, tavern.
posadera *f* hostess; *pl* buttocks.
posadero *m* innkeeper.
posar *vi* to rest; to perch, alight, be poised; to lodge; to lay down; *vr* to settle.
posdata *f* postscript.
poseedor *m* owner, holder.
poseer *vt* to own; to master, be master of.
poseído *a* crazed, possessed; **estar — de** to be thoroughly convinced of.
posesión *f* possession, tenure, holding.
posesionarse *vr* to take possession of.
posibilidad *f* possibility.
posibilitar *vt* to facilitate.
posible *a* likely, feasible; **lo —** all in one's power; *pl* means.
posición *f* position; attitude; standing; situation.
positivo *a* sure, certain, positive.
poso *m* sediment, lees, dregs.
posponer *vt* to postpone, delay, put off; to subordinate.
posta *f* relay, post station; bet, wager.
postal *a* postal; *f* postcard.
postdata *f* postscript.
poste *m* pillar; **oler el —** to smell a rat.
postergación *f* postponement, disparagement.
postergar *vt* to leave behind, postpone, shelve; to pass over (*in promotion scale*); to deny legitimate hopes, pretensions.
posteridad *f* the coming generations; fame after death, posterity.
posterior *a* later, posterior; hind, rear.
posterioridad *f* posteriority; **con —** later, subsequently.
postigo *m* shutter, postern, wicket.
postillón *m* driver, postilion.
postín *m* (*fam*) swank; **de —** showy, luxurious.
postizo *a* artificial, false; *m* switch, hairpiece.
postración *f* prostration, dejection.
postrado *a* prostrate, prone.
postrar *vt* to prostrate; *vr* to kneel down; to be exhausted.
postre *m* dessert; **a la —** at long last.
postremo *a* last, ultimate, final.
postrero *a* last, hindermost.
postrimerías *f pl* last moments (*of life, day etc*).
postrimero *a* ultimate.
postulado *m* axiom.
póstumo *a* posthumous.
postura *f* position, attitude; bid; stake.
potable *a* drinkable.
potaje *m* stewed vegetables; soup; medley.
pote *m* jug, jar; **— gallego** (*vegetable*) broth.
potencia *f* power; ability; great power, strength; faculty.
potencial *a* potential, virtual.
potentado *m* sovereign, ruler, power.
potente *a* potent, strong, capable; powerful (*engine*).
potestad *f* power, dominion, might; (*math*) power; *pl* angelic powers.
potestativo *a* facultative, optional; in the hands (power) of.
potranca *f* young mare.
potrillo *m SA* colt.
potro *m* colt, young horse; rack (*for torture*).
poyo *m* stone seat; hillock.
pozo *m* well; deep spot, pool; pit, shaft; hold (*ship*).
práctica *f* practice, exercise, use, habit; method; experience; **prácticas restrictivas** restrictive practices.
practicable *a* feasible; (*theat*) **puerta —** door which opens.
practicante *a* practicing; *m* doctor's assistant; first-aid worker.
practicar *vt* to perform, do, exercise.
práctico *a* practical; *m* pilot; expert.
pradera *f* meadow, field; grassland, prairie.
prado *m* field, meadow, pasture; lawn.
pragmática *f* decree, pragmatic.
preámbulo *m* exordium; preface, preamble.
prebenda *f* canonry, prebend.
precario *a* uncertain, precarious.
precaución *f* vigilance, precaution, forethought, care.
precautelar *vt* to forewarn.
precaver *vt* to provide against, warn against, obviate; *vr* to be on one's guard, take heed, act circumstantially.
precavido *a* cautious, wary, circumspect, prudent.
precedencia *f* precedence, priority; origin, source.
preceder *vt* to precede, to go ahead of.
preceptivo *a* didactic.
precepto *m* precept, rule; order.
preceptor *m* teacher, master; prefect.
preceptuar *vt* to give orders, lay down precepts.
preces *f pl* prayers, supplications.
preciado *a* prized, valued, esteemed, precious.

preciar *vt* to value, appraise; *vr* to boast; to take pride in, pride oneself on.
precio *m* price; value; cost;— **fijo** net price; — **de tasa** official (*controlled*) price.
preciosidad *f* worth; **¡qué —!** how lovely!
precioso *a* precious; pretty, beautiful; affected.
precipicio *m* chasm, precipice.
precipitación *f* hurry, rush, haste; precipitation.
precipitado *a* hasty, hurried, precipitate.
precipitar *vt* to hurl from above; to accelerate, to hasten; *vr* to hurry, rush headlong.
precipitoso *a* steep, hasty.
precisamente *ad* exactly; necessarily; just.
precisar *vt* to fix, set; to force, oblige; to make clear; to be necessary.
precisión *f* preciseness, accuracy; necessity; **en la — de** under the necessity of.
preciso *a* accurate; precise, exact; essential, requisite, necessary; **es —** it is necessary.
preclaro *a* famous, illustrious.
precocidad *f* precocity.
precolombino *a* pre-Columbian.
preconizar *vt* to commend publicly, eulogize.
precoz *a* forward, precocious; premature.
precursor *m* harbinger, herald, forerunner.
predecesor *m* predecessor, antecedent.
predecir *vt* to foretell, predict.
predestinado *a* predestined; foredoomed.
predestinar *vt* to foredoom, to predestinate.
prédica *f* sermon.
predicación *f* preaching.
predicador *m* preacher.
predicar *vt* to preach; to predicate.
predicción *f* forecast.
predilección *f* special affection, preference, liking.
predilecto *a* favorite, special, chosen.
predisponer *vt* to predispose.
predominar *vt* to be in control of; to overrule; to predominate; to overlook, have a commanding view of.
predominio *m* mastery, control, command.
preeminencia *f* pre-eminence, authority.
preeminente *a* pre-eminent, most distinguished.
prefacio *m* prologue, preface.
prefecto *m* prefect; chairman.
preferencia *f* choice; priority; **de —** reserved.
preferir (ie) *vt* to prefer, choose; to have rather; to be ahead.
pregón *m* cry; banns; proclamation.
pregonar *vt* to proclaim; to cry (*wares*); to bring to public notice.
pregonero *m* town crier; auctioneer.
pregunta *f* question, query; (*fam*) **estar a la cuarta —** to be on the rocks.
preguntar *vt* to question, ask, inquire; to interrogate.
preguntón *a* inquisitive.
prejuicio *m* bias, prejudice.
prejuzgar *vt* to prejudge.
prelado *m* prelate.
preliminar *a* preliminary; fundamental.
preludio *m* prelude; overture.
prematuro *a* premature, untimely.
premeditar *vt* to premeditate.
premiar *vt* to reward, recompense, requite.
premio *m* reward, prize; premium.
premiosidad *f* sluggishness, difficulty (*of speech etc*).
premioso *a* urgent; close, strict, tight, rigid; tongue-tied, close-lipped; stumbling, difficult (*in speech*).
premisa *f* premise.
premura *f* urgency, haste.
prenda *f* pawn, security, pledge; jewel; garment; adornment; pretty thing; beloved (one).
prendado *pl* gifts, charm, talents, appeal; forfeits; *a* (*with* **ser**) gifted; (*with* **estar**) enraptured.
prendedero *m* hook, brooch.
prendedor *m* safety pin, brooch.
prender *vt* to seize, grasp, catch; to arrest, imprison; *vi* to take (*fire, root*).
prendero *m* pawnbroker; second-hand dealer.
prendimiento *m* arrest.
prensa *f* press, vise, clamp; journalism, daily press; — **de lagar** wine press.
prensar *vt* to press (*grapes etc*).
preñado *a* pregnant; replete, charged with.
preñez *f* pregnancy; fullness; peril; confusion.
preocupación *f* preoccupation, prejudice, bias, worry, responsibility.
preocupar *vt* to preoccupy, concern; *vr* to worry, take great interest, care.
preparado *a* ready; manufactured (*not natural*).
preparar *vt* to prepare; *vr* to get ready.
preparativo *m pl* preparations.
preponderar *vi* to be preponderant, prevail, overpower.
preposición *f* preposition.
prerrogativa *f* prerogative, privilege.
presa *f* capture, prey, prize; morsel; dam, dike; talon, claw; **tribunal de —** prize court; **hacer —** to capture.

presagiar *vt* to forebode.
presagio *m* omen.
presbítero *m* priest, presbyter.
presciencia *f* prescience, foreknowledge.
prescindir *vi* to do without, omit, dispense (*with*).
prescindible *a* dispensable.
prescribir *vt* to prescribe.
prescripción *f* prescription.
presea *f* gem.
presencia *f* presence; build, physique.
presencial *a* **testigo** — eyewitness.
presenciar *vt* to attend, be present at; to witness.
presentación *f* show, exhibition; introduction.
presentar *vt* to display, exhibit; to introduce (*persons*); offer (*as candidate*); to present; *vr* to appear, offer oneself.
presente *a* present, current (*month or year*); *m* gift; *f* the present document; **mejorando lo** — present company excepted; **hacer** — to remind, recall.
presentimiento *m* foreboding, misgiving.
presentir (ie) *vt* to forebode, have a feeling, presentiment.
preservación *f* preservation, conservation.
preservar *vt* to preserve, guard, keep.
preservativo *m* preventive, preservative.
presidencia *f* presidency, president's chair, the chair.
presidencial *a* presidential.
presidente *m* president; chairman.
presidiar *vt* to garrison.
presidiario *m* convict.
presidio *m* hard labor; garrison, fortress; penitentiary.
presidir *vt* to preside, act as chairman.
presilla *f* loop, eye, hole, noose; *SA* (*mil*) stripe.
presión *f* pressure; **botón de** — push button.
preso *a* imprisoned; *m* prisoner; **llevar** — to carry off.
prestado *a* **pedir** — to borrow.
prestamista *m* moneylender, pawnbroker.
préstamo *m* loan.
prestar *vt* to lend, loan; to give (*an air*); — **atención** to pay attention; *vr* to offer; to lend oneself; **se presta a** it gives rise to.
presteza *f* haste, promptitude; alacrity.
prestidigitador *m* juggler, conjurer.
prestigio *m* prestige, fame, reputation, name; spell; sleight of hand.
prestigioso *a* eminent, famous.
presto *a* swift; *ad* quickly, prompt.
presumible *a* presumable.
presumido *a* conceited, vain.
presumir *vti* to presume, conjecture; to boast; *Arg* to flirt.
presunción *f* presumption; presumptuousness.
presuntivo *a* presumptive, supposed.
presunto *a* presumed; presumptive; **heredero** — heir apparent.
presuntuoso *a* presumptuous, vain, conceited.
presupuesto *m* pretext; understanding; budget.
presuroso *a* hasty, speedy, hurried.
pretender *vt* to pretend, claim; to try, endeavor; to have aspirations to (*win, possess etc*).
pretendiente *m* suitor, office seeker, claimant.
pretensión *f* pretension, claim.
pretextar *vt* to pretext; to allege as pretext.
pretexto *m* pretext, cover, excuse.
pretil *m* railing, parapet; breastwork.
pretina *f* girdle, waistband.
prevalecer *vi* to prevail, surpass.
prevalerse *vr* to avail oneself of, make use of.
prevaricar *vi* to prevaricate.
prevención *f* prevention, forethought; warning; prejudice.
prevenido *a* ready, prepared, cautious, forewarned.
prevenir *vt* to warn, forestall, notify; to prepare, provide; to hinder.
preventivo *a* preventive.
prever *vt* to foresee.
previamente *ad* previously, earlier, in good time.
previo *a* previous, advance, prior.
previsión *f* foresight.
prez *f* honor, glory.
prieto *a* very black; mean; compressed.
prima *f* cousin (*female*); premium.
primario *a* (*geol*) primary; chief, primary; elementary.
primavera *f* spring; primrose.
primaveral *a* springlike, spring.
primero *a* first; **de** — **a** first class quality, very well; *ad* rather.
primicia *f* first fruit.
primitivo *a* primitive, original.
primo *m* cousin; simpleton, ass; — **hermano** first cousin; *a* first; prime; **materia prima** raw material.
primogénito *a* first-born, eldest (*son*).
primor *m* beauty, exquisiteness, loveliness.
primordial *a* primordial, original, fundamental.
primoroso *a* exquisite, curious, lovely, neat, fine.
princesa *f* princess.
principado *m* principality.
principal *a* principal; first; *m* capital, stock.
príncipe *m* prince; — **de Asturias** *Span equiv of* Prince of Wales.
principiante *m* beginner, tyro.
principiar *vt* to begin, start.

principio *m* beginning, start, origin; principle, motive; entrée; **al —** at the beginning; **en —** in principle.
prior *m* prior.
prioridad *f* priority, precedence.
prisa *f* haste, promptness; **llevar (tener) —** to be in a hurry.
prisco *m Arg* kind of peach.
prisión *f* prison, jail; seizure; *pl* chains, fetters.
prisionero *m* prisoner.
prisma *m* prism.
prismático *a* prismatic.
prístino *a* pristine, pure, unspoiled.
privación *f* privation, deprivation, want.
privado *a* private, secret; *m* favorite.
privanza *f* favor (*at Court*), protection.
privar *vt* to deprive, dispossess.
privativo *a* peculiar, restricted to, exclusive.
privilegiado *a* distinguished, outstanding, (*extremely*) gifted.
privilegiar *vt* to distinguish, grant privileges.
privilegio *m* privilege, concession, faculty.
pro *m or f* profit; advantage; **en —** for the benefit of; **hombre de —** substantial citizen.
proa *f* prow, bows; steerage.
probabilidad *f* probability.
probable *a* probable, likely.
probación *f* proof, trial.
probanza *f* proof, evidence.
probar (ue) *vt* to prove, test, examine; to justify; to taste (*wine*); to try on (*clothes*); **— fortuna** to try one's luck.
probidad *f* probity, integrity.
problema *m* problem.
probo *a* honest, upright.
procacidad *f* impudence, insolence.
procaz *a* bold, impudent.
procedencia *f* origin, source.
procedente *a* **— de** originating in; coming from.
proceder *vi* to proceed, to go on; to proceed from; *m* conduct, behavior.
procedimiento *m* process, method, manner, custom, procedure.
proceloso *a* tempestuous.
prócer *a* lofty; *m* distinguished citizen, Senator.
procesado *an* accused, prosecuted.
procesar *vt* to prosecute, indict, try.
procesión *f* (*relig*) procession.
proceso *m* progress; proceedings; trial.
proclama *f* proclamation; banns.
proclamar *vt* to proclaim, promulgate.
proclividad *f* proclivity, propensity, inclination.
procrear *vt* to breed, procreate, generate.
procuración *f* diligence; procuration; proxy.
procurador *m* procurer; solicitor, attorney.
procurar *vt* to procure; to try; to get.
prodigalidad *f* prodigality, lavishness.
prodigar *vt* to lavish, squander.
prodigio *m* prodigy, monster.
prodigioso *a* prodigious, marvelous, portentous.
pródigo *a* prodigal, wasteful, bountiful.
producción *f* production; produce.
producir *vt* to produce, bring forth; to cause.
productivo *a* productive, profitable.
producto *m* product, production; produce; growth.
proemio *m* preface, prologue.
proeza *f* valorous deed, prowess.
profanar *vt* to profane, desecrate, defile.
profanidad *f* profanity.
profano *a* profane, secular; unlettered; *m* layman, uninitiated.
profecía *f* prophecy.
proferir (ie) *vt* to utter, express, mouth.
profesar *vt* to practice (*profession*), profess; to take religious vows.
profesión *f* profession; declaration.
profesional *an* professional.
profesionista *m SA* professional.
profesor *m* professor.
profesorado *m* faculty, senate, teaching staff; *SA* training college.
profeta *m* prophet.
profetizar *vt* to foretell, prophesy.
prófugo *an* fugitive (*from justice*).
profundidad *f* profundity, depth.
profundizar *vt* to deepen; to penetrate, go deep.
profundo *a* deep, profound.
profusión *f* profusion.
progenie *f* progeny, descendants.
progenitor *m* progenitor, ancestor, begetter.
programa *m* program.
progresar *vi* to progress, advance.
progresión *f* progression.
progreso *m* progress, growth.
prohibición *f* prohibition, ban.
prohibir *vt* to forbid, prohibit.
prohijar *vt* to adopt (*a child*); to foster, support.
prójimo *m* neighbor, fellow creature.
prole *f* offspring, children, tribe, progeny.
proletariado *m* proletariat.
proletario *an* proletarian, pleb.
prolífico *a* prolific, abundant.
prolijidad *f* prolixity, tediousness, minute detail.
prolijo *a* prolix, long-winded, repetitious.
prólogo *m* prologue, preface, introduction.
prolongación *f* extension, lengthening, renewal.

prolongar *vt* to lengthen, protract, extend.
promediar *vt* to divide into two; to average; *vi* to mediate.
promedio *m* average; middle.
promesa *f* promise.
promesante *mf Arg* pilgrim.
prometedor *a* promising, auspicious.
prometer *vt* to promise, offer.
prometido *a* betrothed.
prominencia *f* prominence, knoll.
prominente *a* prominent.
promiscuo *a* promiscuous, ambiguous.
promisión *f* promise; **tierra de —** promised land.
promoción *f* promotion, preferment; (*mil*) grade, rank; (*acad*) year, generation.
promontorio *m* promontory, headland.
promotor *m* promoter, furtherer.
promover (ue) *vt* to promote, forward, raise, cause, stir up.
promulgar *vt* to promulgate, issue, publish.
pronosticar *vt* to prognosticate, foretell, promise, predict.
pronóstico *m* prognostication, foreboding, prediction.
prontitud *f* promptitude, quickness, dispatch.
pronto *a* quick, ready, prompt; **por lo —** for the time being; *ad* quickly.
prontuario *m* memorandum.
pronunciación *f* pronunciation, accent.
pronunciamiento *m* (*mil*) revolt, uprising, rebellion.
pronunciar *vt* to pronounce, utter; *vr* to revolt, to declare oneself.
propagación *f* spread(ing), dissemination.
propaganda *f* propaganda.
propagar *vt* to propagate, spread, diffuse.
propalar *vt* to disclose, reveal, betray, noise abroad.
propasarse *vr* to overstep, exceed, go beyond.
propensión *f* propensity, tendency.
propenso *a* given to, apt to, inclined.
propiamente *ad* properly; **— dicho** properly speaking, more exactly.
propiciar *vt* to propitiate, conciliate.
propicio *a* propitious, favorable.
propiedad *f* property, ownership; character(istic); propriety.
propietario *m* owner, landlord.
propina *f* gratuity, fee, tip; **de —** in addition, as an extra.
propinar *vt* (*fam*) to treat, give a drink to.
propincuo *a* contiguous, close by.
propio *a* proper, convenient; peculiar, characteristic; *m* messenger.
proponer *vt* to propose, suggest; to plan, aim.
proporcionado *a* proportionate, adequate.
proporcionar *vt* to supply, provide, get for; to make.
proposición *f* proposition, proposal, offer.
propósito *m* purpose, aim, intent; **a —** apropos, by the way; suitable; **de —** on purpose.
propuesta *f* proposal, offer.
propuesto *a* proposed.
propugnar *vt* to defend, protect.
prorratear *vt* to apportion.
prórroga *f* prorogation; extension.
prorrogar *vt* to extend; to prorogue, adjourn.
prorrumpir *vi* to burst out, break out.
prosa *f* prose.
prosador *m* prosewriter, writer of prose.
prosaico *a* prosaic, dull, uninspired.
prosapia *f* lineage.
proscribir *vt* to proscribe, banish.
proscripción *f* exile, banishment; prohibition.
prosecución *f* prosecution.
proseguir (i) *vt* to go on, proceed, continue, follow, pursue.
prosélito *m* proselyte.
prosista *m* prose writer.
prospecto *m* prospectus; prospect.
prosperar *vi* to prosper; thrive; *vt* to favor.
prosperidad *f* prosperity, success.
próspero *a* prosperous, fair.
prosternarse *vr* to bend, prostrate oneself.
prostituir *vt* to prostitute, debase.
protagonista *m* protagonist.
protagonizar *vi SA* (*theat*) to take the leading part.
protección *f* protection, favor.
proteccionismo *m* protectionism.
protector *m* protector, defender.
proteger *vt* to protect, shield, shelter.
protesta *f* protestation; protest.
protestante *an* Protestant; protesting.
protestar *vt* to protest; to assure; **— una letra** to protest a draft.
protesto *m* protest (*of a bill*).
protocolo *m* protocol; procedure.
prototipo *m* prototype, model.
protuberancia *f* protuberance.
provecto *a* advanced (*years*), mature (*knowledge etc*).
provecho *m* profit, advantage, use(fulness); **de —** useful, suitable.
provechoso *a* profitable, useful.
proveedor *m* supplier, provider.
proveer *vt* to provide, supply with, furnish.
proveniente *a* coming from.
provenir *vi* to proceed from, originate in.
provenzal *an* Provençal.
proverbio *m* proverb, saw.
providencia *f* Providence; foresight.
providente *a* provident, careful.
próvido *a* provident.

provincia *f* province.
provinciano *an* provincial.
provisión *f* provision, store, stock; writ; condition.
provisto *a* supplied, stocked.
provocación *f* provocation.
provocar *vt* to provoke, rouse, cause, badger.
provocativo *a* provoking, provocative.
proximidad *f* nearness, vicinity.
próximo *a* next, close to.
proyección *f* projection.
proyectar *vt* to scheme, plan; to jut.
proyectil *m* missile, projectile.
proyecto *m* plan, scheme, project.
proyector *m* projector; **— eléctrico** searchlight.
prudencia *f* prudence, wisdom.
prudente *a* prudent, circumspect.
prueba *f* proof, test, trial; sample; assay; sign, mark; **a —** on trial, to the test; **a — de** proof against; **poner a —** to test.
prurito *m* itch, hankering, yearning, aspiration.
Prusia *f* Prussia.
prusiano *an* Prussian.
psicoanálisis *m* psychoanalysis.
psicoanalítico *a* psychoanalytic(al).
psicología *f* psychology.
psicológico *a* psychological.
psicólogo *m* psychologist.
psicópata *mf* psychopath.
psiquiatra *mf* psychiatrist.
psiquiatría *f* psychiatry.
psiquiátrico *a* psychiatric.
púa *f* prickle, graft, tooth (*of comb*); quill (*of hedgehog*); plectrum.
pubertad *f* adolescence.
publicación *f* publication.
publicar *vt* to publish, proclaim, make known.
publicidad *f* publicity; **dar —** to publicize, advertise.
público *a m* public.
puchero *m* stew; dish made of boiled meat and vegetables; **hacer —s** to pout, look rueful.
púdico *a* modest, chaste, virtuous.
pudiente *an* well-to-do, rich (*person*).
pudín *m* pudding.
pudor *m* modesty.
pudoroso *a* modest, shy, delicate.
pudrir *vt* to rot; *vr* to rot, putrefy, disintegrate, decay.
pueblo *m* town; common people; nation, the people.
puente *m* bridge; deck (*ship*); **— colgante** suspension bridge; **— levadizo** drawbridge.
puerco *a* nasty, dirty, foul; *m* hog; **— espín** porcupine.
pueril *a* childish, puerile.
puerilidad *f* childish (*action, statement etc*), bagatelle.
puerta *f* door, gate; **— accesoria** side door; **— cochera** carriage door; **— franca** open house.
puerto *m* harbor, port; (*mountain*) pass; refuge; **— habilitado** port of entry; **— libre** free port; **— de depósito** bond port.
puertorriqueno *an* Puerto Rican.
pues *cj* then; because; well, since; yes.
puesta *f* setting (*of sun*); stake.
puesto *a* put; *m* place, spot, position, post, job; stall; **— que** although, since.
pugilista *m* pugilist, boxer.
pugna *f* conflict, struggle, rivalry, contest.
pugnacidad *f* pugnacity.
pugnar *vi* to struggle to, contend, be (*in rivalry, in conflict*).
pujante *a* strong, pushing, powerful.
pujanza *f* strength, power, puissance.
pujar *vt* to push; to outbid, bid.
pujido *m SA* grunt.
pulcritud *f* neatness, seemliness, loveliness.
pulcro *a* lovely, refined, seemly, proper.
pulga *f* flea; **tener malas —s** to be cross-grained.
pulgada *f* inch.
pulgar *m* thumb.
pulido *a* neat, polished, nice, shiny.
pulimentar *vt* to polish, burnish.
pulir *vt* to burnish, polish; to embellish, beautify; *vr* to polish oneself up.
pulla *f* repartee; stinging remark.
pulmón *m* lung.
pulmonía *f* pneumonia.
pulpa *f* pulp, flesh.
pulpería *f SA* grocer's shop.
pulpero *m SA* grocer.
púlpito *m* pulpit.
pulpo *m* cuttlefish, octopus.
pulque *m SA* pulque, fermented juice of the agave.
pulquería *f SA* shop where pulque is sold.
pulsación *f* pulsation, beating.
pulsar *vt* to feel the pulse; to finger (*stringed instrument*); to sound out (*an affair*).
pulsera *f* bangle, bracelet; **reloj de —** wrist watch.
pulso *m* pulse; pulsation; circumspection, care, steadiness (*of handling*); **a —** by the strength of one's arm; **con mucho —** gingerly.
pulular *vi* to swarm, teem.
pulverizar *vt* to grind, pulverize.
puma *m* puma, cougar.
puna *f SA* bleak waste.
punción *f* puncture (*of skin etc*).
pundonor *m* point of honor.
pungente *a* pungent.
pungista *m Arg, Urug* pickpocket.
punición *f* punishment.
punitivo *a* punitive.
punta *f* end, extremity; tip; point; tinge; suggestion; **andar en —s** to be at loggerheads.
puntal *m* support; stay, prop.
puntapié *m* kick.

puntear *vt* to sew; to play (*guitar*); (*art*) to stipple; *Arg* to dig.
puntería *f* aim (*with rifle etc*).
puntiagudo *a* sharp (*pointed*).
puntilla *f* tack; joiner's nail; lace; **andar de —s** on tiptoe.
punto *m* point; place, spot; mark, point; detail ,aspect; end, object; **— final** full stop; **— y coma** semicolon; **al —** immediately; **a — fijo** without a doubt; **en —** on the dot, exactly; **hasta cierto —** to some extent;**— menos** practically, almost; **estar a —** to be about, ready; **obra de punto** knitted wear, knitting; **— de apoyo** fulcrum; **en su —** just right, perfect; **— de vista** point of view.
puntual *a* punctual, exact; accurate, reliable.
puntualidad *f* preciseness, punctuality.
puntualizar *vt* to finish, perfect, draw up, enumerate; to fix in one's mind.
punzada *f* prick; stitch (*in side*).
punzar *vt* to puncture, perforate.
punzón *m* punch; countersink; bodkin.
puñado *m* handful, bunch, fistful.
puñal *m* dagger.
puñalada *f* stab.
puñetazo *m* blow (*with fists*).
puño *m* fist; cuff; handle, hilt, head; **por sus —s** by his own efforts.
pupila *f* pupil (*of the eye*).
pupilaje *m* wardship; boarding house.
pupilo *m* ward; boarder.
pupitre *m* (*writing*) desk.
puré *m* purée; **— de patatas** mashed potatoes.
pureza *f* purity.
purgante *a* purgative; *m* purge, cathartic.
purgar *vt* to purge; to expiate; *vr* to take a purge.
purgatorio *m* purgatory.
puridad *f* purity; **en —** without beating about the bush.
purificar *vt* to purify, cleanse, refine.
puritano *an* puritan.
puro *a* pure, chaste; unalloyed; **cayó de — viejo** it fell down out of sheer old age; *m* cigar.
púrpura *f* purple.
purpúreo *a* purple.
pusilánime *a* faint-hearted.
puta *f* whore.
putativo *a* presumed, reputed.
putrefacción *f* corruption.
pútrido *a* rotten, decayed.
puya *f* goad.

Q

que *rel pn* which, that, who, whom; **lo —** what; *cj* that, to; for, because, since.
qué *inter pn* what?, which?; *excl pn* how!, what (a)!
quebrada *f* ravine, gully.
quebradero *m* **— de cabeza** worry, headache.
quebradizo *a* fragile, brittle.
quebrado *a* broken; uneven (*ground*); bankrupt; *m* fraction.
quebradura *f* rupture, hernia; slit, gap.
quebrantar *vt* to break, smash, crush; to violate, transgress; to weaken, run down; to annul.
quebranto *m* breaking; affliction.
quebrar (ie) *vt* to break; to interrupt; to bend; *vi* to fail, to become bankrupt.
queda *f* curfew.
quedar *vi* to remain, be left, be, stay; to linger; *vr* to remain, stay; **— con** to retain, keep.
quedito *ad SA* softly, gently.
quedo *a* quiet, soft, gentle.
quehacer *m* occupation, job, chore.
queja *f* complaint, plaint, querulousness.
quejarse *vr* to moan, whine, grumble, complain.
quejido *m* moan, whimper, plaint, complaint.
quejoso *a* complaining, querulous, plaintive.
quejumbroso *a* whining, complaining.
quemadura *f* burn, scald.
quemar *vt* to burn, scald, scorch; to parch; *vr* to burn, be consumed by fire.
quemazón *f* burn(ing), combustion, excessive heat; *Arg* mirage on pampas.
quena *f SA* kind of Indian flute.
querella *f* quarrel, dispute, jangle, squabble, complaint.
querellante *m* complainant, plaintiff.
querelloso *a* quarrelsome, plaintive.
querencia *f* affection, fondness; favorite spot.
querer (ie) *vt* to want, wish, intend, desire; to cherish, love; **— decir** to mean; **sin —** unintentionally; *m* love, will.
querido *a* dear, darling, beloved; *m* lover; *f* lady love, mistress.
querubín *m* cherub.
queso *m* cheese; **— de bola** Dutch cheese; **— de nata** cream cheese.
¡quiá! *excl* what nonsense!, pooh!
quicio *m* hinge; **sacar de —** to exasperate, unhinge, put out.
quiebra *f* fracture; failure, loss, crash, slump, bankruptcy.
quiebro *m* twist; trill; catch (*in voice*).
quien *rel pn* who, whom.
quién *inter pn* who?
quienquiera *rel pn* whoever, whosoever, whichever.
quieto *a* still, quiet; steady, orderly; unperturbed.

quietud *f* quiet, quietude, hush, still, calm.
quijada *f* jawbone, chap.
quijo *m SA* silver or gold ore.
Quijote, Don *m* Don Quixote.
quijotesco *a* Quixotic.
quilate *m* carat; *pl* **de muchos —s** very perfect, of great value.
quilco *m Chi* large basket.
quilombo *m Arg* cabin, shack; *Arg, Chi* brothel.
quilla *f* keel.
quimera *f* chimera, illusion, fancy.
quimérico *a* chimerical, unreal, fantastic.
química *f* chemistry.
químico *a* chemical; *m* chemist.
quincalla *f* hardware, ironmongery.
quincallería *f* hardware trade, ironmonger's, hardware shop.
quince *an* fifteen, fifteenth.
quincena *f* fortnight.
quincenal *a* fortnightly, bi-weekly.
quingos *m pl SA* zigzag.
quinina *f* quinine.
quinqué *m* oil lamp.
quinquenal *a* quinquennial, five-yearly.
quinta *f* cottage, villa, manor, country seat; draft, recruitment (*of soldiers by lot*); series of five (*cards*).
quintaesencia *f* quintessence, essence, pith.
quintal *m* hundredweight.
quiosco *m* kiosk, pavilion.
quiquiriquí *m* cock-a-doodle-do.
quirúrgico *a* surgical.
quisquemenil *m SA* short cloak.
quisquilloso *a* peevish, touchy; particular, faddy, fastidious.
quisto *a* **bien —** generally beloved; **mal —** disliked.
quita *f* discharge, release; **de — y pon** adjustable, detachable.
¡quita! *excl* God forbid!
quitapesares *m* consolation.
quitar *vt* to take (*away, off, out*); to deprive, strip, rob; to move; to subtract; *vr* to move away, withdraw; to doff, take off; **— la vida** to commit suicide.
quitasol *m* parasol, sunshade.
quite *m* hindrance; parry; removal (*of bull when a fighter is in danger*).
quiteño *an* (*inhabitant*) of Quito.
quizá(s) *ad* perhaps, perchance, maybe.

R

rabadilla *f* rump.
rábano *m* radish; **— picante** horseradish.
rabí *m* rabbi, rabbin.
rabia *f* rabies; fury, exasperation.
rabiar *vi* to be rabid,rage; **— por** to be itching to.
rabieta *f* tantrum.
rabioso *a* rabid; mad, raging, furious.
rabo *m* tail; end; **con el — entre las piernas** crestfallen, with tail between one's legs; **de cabo a —** out-and-out.
rabona *f* **hacerse la —** to play hooky, miss school.
racimo *m* cluster, bunch.
raciocinar *vi* to reason.
raciocinio *m* reasoning.
ración *f* ration, mess, allowance; pittance; share.
racional *a* reasonable; rational.
racionamiento *m* rationing; distribution of rations; **cartilla de —** ration card.
racionar *vt* to ration.
racha *f* gust (*of wind*); burst, flurry.
rada *f* roadstead.
radiador *m* radiator.
radiactividad *f* radioactivity.
radiante *a* radiant; ablaze, beaming, brilliant.
radiar *vt* to radiate, broadcast.
radical *a* radical, fundamental, essential.
radicar *vtr* to take root.
radio *m* radius, scope, circuit; radium; *f* radio (*set*).
radiodifusión *f* broadcasting.
radioyente *m* listener (*to radio*).
raer *vt* to erase, scrape, rub off; to raze.
Rafael *m* Raphael.
ráfaga *f* gust, gale (*wind*); beam (*light*).
raído *a* worn, rubbed off.
raíz *f* root, origin, base, foundation; **echar raíces** to settle.
raja *f* rent, crack, split; slice; rasher (*bacon*).
rajar *vt* to split, rend, crack; *vr* to throw in the sponge, give up.
rajarse *vr* to split, cleave; *Mex, CA* to back out; *Arg* to be mistaken; *PR* to get drunk.
ralea *f* breed, stock, race, ilk.
ralo *a* sparse, thin.
ralladura *f* **—s** gratings, peelings.
rama *f* branch, twig; department (*of studies etc*); **en —** raw; **tabaco en —** leaf tobacco; **andarse por las —s** to beat about the bush.
ramaje *m* foliage; spread (*of branches*).
ramal *m* branch; branch line; strand, offshoot.
rambla *f* dry ravine; avenue.
ramera *f* harlot, strumpet.
ramificación *f* ramification, branching off.
ramificarse *vr* to branch out, spread out.
ramillete *m* bouquet, posy, nosegay; centerpiece; bunch.
ramo *m* bough, branch; bouquet; cluster; branch (*of business*); department (*of knowledge*).
rampa *f* incline, gradient, ramp.
ramplón *a* coarse, common, rude.
rana *f* frog.

rancio *a* rancid, rank; very old, ancient.
ranchería *f* camp; settlement; stock farm; group of ranches.
ranchero *m* steward; stockfarmer, ranch owner.
rancho *m* mess; hut, ranch, stock farm; **hacer — aparte** to form an independent group.
rango *m* rank, status, dignity.
ranura *f* groove; slot.
rapacidad *f* rapacity, greed.
rapar *vt* to shave (off), shear, crop.
rapaz *m* lad, young boy; *a* ravenous, thieving.
rape *m* **al —** close-cropped.
rapé *m* snuff.
rapidez *f* speed, rapidity, ease.
rápido *a* fleet-footed, speedy, fast, rapid; **tren —** express train.
rapingancho *m Col, Per* cheese omelette.
rapiña *f* rapine; plunder; **ave de —** bird of prey.
raposa *f* vixen.
raposo *m* fox.
raptar *vt* to snatch away; to abduct.
rapto *m* ecstasy, swoon, transport, rapture; rape, ravishment, abduction.
raqueta *f* racket.
raquítico *a* rickety; spineless, woebegone, sorry.
raquitismo *m* rickets.
rareza *f* uncommonness, queerness, oddity; rarity, strangeness; scarcity.
raro *a* rare; odd, out-of-the-way, uncommon; queer, eccentric; **rara vez** seldom.
ras *m* level.
rascacielos *m* skyscraper.
rascar *vt* to rasp, scrape, scratch (*head*); to scour; to strum (*guitar*).
rasgadura *f* tear, rip.
rasgar *vt* to rend, rip, slit, tear.
rasgo *m* dash, stroke, flourish; trait, characteristic; (*heroic*) gesture.
rasguño *m* scratch; sketch.
raso *a* open, free, flat, clear; **al —** on the open ground; *m* satin.
raspadura *f* erasure; scraping, scrape; **—s** raspings, shavings, peelings.
raspar *vt* to erase; to graze, scratch, scrape.
rastra *f* sled; harrow; reaping machine; string (*onions etc*); trace.
rastracueros *m SA* rich dealer in hides.
rastrear *vt* to track, trace; to rake, harrow; *vr* to sweep, drag.
rastrero *a* creeping, sneaking; low-flying.
rastrillar *vt* to rake.
rastrillo *m* rake.
rastro *m* track, scent, trace; harrow; vestige, relic; slaughterhouse; **el —** (*Madrid*) rag market, secondhand market.
rastrojo *m* stubble.
rasurar *vt* to shave.
rata *f* rat.
rataplán *m* rub-a-dub (*sound of drum*).
ratería *f* larceny, pilfering.
ratero *m* pickpocket, petty thief.
ratificación *f* ratification, confirmation.
ratificar *vt* to ratify, sanction.
rato *m* while, spell, moment; **de — en —** occasionally, at odd moments; **—s perdidos** spare time; **a —s** spasmodically.
ratón *m* mouse; **— campestre** fieldmouse.
ratonera *f* mousehole; mousetrap.
raudal *m* stream, rapids; plenty.
raya *f* stripe; dash, line, stroke; boundary, limit; parting (*in hair*); **pasar de la —** to go beyond the pale; *m* rayfish.
rayador *m SA* paymaster; umpire.
rayar *vt* to draw lines; to streak, stripe, score; to scratch; to underline; to cross out; *vi* to border on; to come to.
rayo *m* beam, ray; flash (*lightning*); (thunder)bolt; spoke (*wheel*); **como un —** swift as lightning; **— de sol** sunbeam; **—s X** X-rays.
raza *f* race; breed, strain; **de —** thoroughbred.
razón *f* sense, reason; right; ratio, rate; justice; **Vd tiene —** you are right; **— social** name (*of firm*); **perder la —** to lose one's wits.
razonable *a* reasonable, fair; just; sensible.
razonamiento *m* reasoning.
razonar *vi* to reason, converse, discourse.
re- *prefix used to suggest emphasis and repetition*: eg **rebueno** very good.
reacción *f* reaction; **a —** jet (*plane*).
reaccionar *vi* to react.
reacio *a* stubborn, allergic, contrary.
reactor *m* reactor; jet plane.
real *a* real, genuine; royal, kingly, magnificent; *m* camp; fairground; real (*coin, not now in use*).
realce *m* splendor; highlight; raised ornament, prominence; **dar — a** to enhance.
realeza *f* royalty.
realidad *f* reality; sincerity; **en —** really, in fact.
realismo *m* realism.
realizable *a* achievable; salable; convertible (*into cash*).
realización *f* achievement; sale; conversion (*into cash*).
realizar *vt* to perform; to sell; to carry through, bring into being; *vr* to come true.
realmente *ad* really, truly.
realzar *vt* to enhance, heighten; to raise; to emboss.
reanimar *vt* to cheer up; to revive, restore, quicken.
reanudar *vt* to resume.

reaparición *f* re-emergence, return, recurrence.
reata *f* rope, lasso.
rebaja *f* abatement; rebate, reduction (*in price*).
rebajar *vt* to diminish, lessen; to knock off, rebate; to make a reduction; to lower, debase; *vt* to demean oneself.
rebanada *f* slice.
rebanar *vt* to slice.
rebaño *m* herd, flock.
rebasar *vt* to exceed, overtake.
rebatir *vt* to refute; to repel.
rebato *m* sortie; **tocar a**— to sound the alarm.
rebeca *f* cardigan; **R**— Rebecca.
rebelarse *vr* to rebel, revolt.
rebelde *a* rebellious; undisciplined (*child*); *m* insurgent, rebel.
rebeldía *f* sedition, rebelliousness; default, defiance (*of law*).
rebelión *f* rebellion, revolt, insurrection.
rebenque *m SA* riding whip.
rebosante *a* brimming.
rebosar *vi* to overflow, spill over; to abound.
rebotar *vi* to rebound.
rebozar *vtr* to muffle oneself up.
rebozo *m* muffler; **sin**— openly.
rebusca *f* research; gleaming.
rebuscado *a* elaborate, recherché.
rebuscar *vt* to ransack.
rebuznar *vi* to bray.
recadero *m* errand boy, messenger.
recado *m* message; greeting, regards; *SA* saddle with trappings; **mandar**— to send word.
recaer *vi* to relapse; to behove.
recaída *f* relapse.
recalcar *vt* to cram, squeeze; *vi* to list, heel over; *vr* to harp (on), overemphasize.
recalcitrante *a* recalcitrant.
recalcitrar *vi* to wince.
recalentar (ie) *vt* to heat up, warm up (*food*).
recámara *f* dressing room; breech (*gun*).
recambio *m* **piezas de**— spare parts.
recapacitar *vi* to think over
recapitular *vt* to recapitulate, sum up, run over (*points etc*), resume.
recargado *a* heavy, excessive; heavily flavored; ornate.
recargar *vt* to overload, cram, overwork.
recargo *m* overload; surcharge, additional charge.
recatado *a* circumspect, shy, retiring.
recatar *vt* to conceal; *vr* to behave modestly.
recato *m* shyness, bashfulness, modesty.
recaudador *m* tax collector.
recelar *vt* to distrust, be suspicious, fear.
recelo *m* misgiving, suspicion.
receloso *a* apprehensive.
recepción *f* reception; admission; at home.
receptáculo *m* receptacle, sac, pocket.
receptor *m* receiver; radio set.
receso *m* recess, withdrawal.
receta *f* prescription; recipe.
recetar *vt* to prescribe medicines.
recibimiento *m* reception, receipt; welcome; hall, vestibule.
recibir *vt* to receive; to admit; to welcome.
recibo *m* receipt; acquittance; **acusar — de** to acknowledge receipt.
recién *ad* just, recently; — **nacido** newborn; — **llegado** newcomer.
reciente *a* recent, fresh; modern; just out.
recientemente *ad* recently, lately.
recinto *m* precinct; enclosure, bounds.
recio *a* stout, strong; coarse, rude; severe; *ad* strongly, loud.
recipiente *m* container, vessel.
recíproco *a* mutual; interchangeable.
recitar *vt* to recite, declaim.
reclamación *f* claim, complaint.
reclamar *vt* to claim, to demand; to complain (*against*).
reclamo *m* decoy bird; inducement, allurement; slogan.
reclinar *vtr* to lean (back).
reclusión *f* seclusion; retirement.
recluso *a* secluded; imprisoned; *m* prisoner.
recluta *f* levy; *m* conscript, recruit.
recobrar *vt* to recover, retrieve; — **el ánimo** to pluck up courage.
recodo *m* turning, bend (*road*); angle; elbow.
recoger *vt* to gather (in), collect; to pick up, receive; to call (*for*), fetch; to lock up; *vr* to take shelter; to retire; to retire from the world.
recogido *a* retired, secluded; *m* tuck, fold.
recogimiento *m* concentration, seclusion; abstraction from worldly thoughts.
recolección *f* gathering, harvesting; collection, crop; compilation.
recomendación *f* recommendation; **carta de**— letter of introduction.
recomendar (ie) *vt* to recommend.
recompensa *f* reward, return; amends, satisfaction.
recompensar *vt* to recompense, reward
reconciliar *vt* to reconcile, put to rights; to receive brief confession of; *vr* to cleanse oneself (*of minor sins*).
reconciliación *f* reconciliation.
recóndito *a* recondite, secret, hidden.
reconocer *vt* to own, admit, acknowledge; to scrutinize, inspect; to recognize; to reconnoiter.
reconocimiento *m* acknowledg-

ment, recognition; gratitude; survey; inspection.
reconquista *f* reconquest (*of Spain from the Arabs*).
reconstruir *vt* to rebuild, reconstruct.
reconvenir *vt* to upbraid, reprimand.
recopilación *f* collection; summary; digest.
recopilador *m* collector, compiler.
recopilar *vt* to compile.
recordar (ue) *vt* to recall to mind, remind; to remember.
recorrer *vt* to examine, peruse, survey, run over; to traverse, go over; to repair.
recorrido *m* run, sweep, range, tour, course, trip.
recortado *a* notched; cut out, silhouetted.
recortar *vt* to shorten; to chip, shear, cut out.
recorte *m* clipping, cutting; **un — de periódico** press cutting.
recostar (ue) *vt* to lean against.
recoveco *m* winding, turning, innermost recesses.
recreación *f* recreation, pastime.
recrear *vt* to amuse, delight; *vr* to disport, play, pass the glad hours.
recreativo *a* amusing.
recreo *m* recreation, play, amusement; interval, recess; sport.
recriminar *vt* to recriminate.
recrudecer *vi* to break out again, get worse.
rectamente *ad* rightly, justly; honestly; in a straight line.
rectangular *a* right-angled.
rectificación *f* rectification, correction.
rectificar *vt* to rectify, set right, amend.
rectitud *f* honesty; uprightness; rectitude, justness.
recto *a* right, straight; upright; conscientious; faithful.
rector *m* rector; curate; superior; Vice-Chancellor (*of University*).
recua *f* drove, train, pack of mules.
recuento *m* recount.
recuerdo *m* recollection, remembrance; memory; token, souvenir, keepsake; record, monument; *pl* kind regards.
recular *vi* to fall back, recoil, recede.
recuperable *a* recoverable.
recuperación *f* recuperation, rescue, recovery.
recuperar *vt* to regain, retrieve, recover; *vr* to retrieve oneself.
recurrir *vi* to resort to; to revert.
recurso *m* resource, resort; petition, plea; *pl* means; **sin —** without appeal.
recusación *f* refusal; (*law*) challenge (*competence of judge etc*).
recusar *vt* to decline; (*law*) to recuse.
rechazar *vt* to refuse, reject, repulse, hurl back.
rechazo *m* repulse, recoil, rebuff.
rechifla *f* hooting, hissing.
rechiflar *vt* to hiss, whistle at, ridicule.
rechinar *vi* to grate, creak; to gnash.
rechoncho *a* chubby.
red *f* net; snare; luggage rack; network; **— ferroviaria** railway system; **caer en la —** to fall into the trap; **tender la —** to lay a trap.
redacción *f* editing, wording, style, writing; editorial (office, staff *etc*).
redactar *vt* to edit; compose, write, draw up.
redactor *m* editor, journalist.
redada *f* catch (*of fish*).
redención *f* redemption, ransom, salvation.
redentor *m* redeemer, redemptor.
redicho *a* emphatically said.
redil *m* sheepfold.
redimir *vt* to redeem, recover, save; to pay off, clear (*of debt*).
rédito *m* revenue, interest, proceeds, yield.
redivivo *a* redivivus, resurrected.
redoblar *vt* to redouble, to rivet; to roll (*a drum*).
redoble *m* redoubling; roll (*of drum*).
redoma *f* phial, vial, flask.
redomado *a* artful, skillful, sly; out-and-out, thorough-paced.
redonda *f* neighborhood; **a la —** round about, all around.
redondamente *ad* plainly, roundly.
redondear *vt* to round (out, off), perfect.
redondel *m* arena, (bull)ring.
redondo *a* round; **en —** all around.
reducción *f* reduction, decrease; shrinkage.
reducido *a* reduced, small, limited.
reducir *vt* to reduce, decrease, abridge, confine.
reducto *m* redoubt.
redundancia *f* redundance, superfluity.
redundar *vi* to be redundant; to redound.
reedificar *vt* to rebuild.
reembolsar *vt* to reimburse, refund, pay back.
reembolso *m* reimbursement; **contra —** cash on delivery.
reemplazar *vt* to replace, supersede, act as substitute.
reemplazo *m* replacement, substitution, substitute.
refacción *f* refection, repast; *SA* spare part; financing, loan.
refajo *m* (flannel) underskirt.
refección *f* repast.
referencia *f* reference; recital, account.
referéndum *m* referendum.
referente *a* referring, concerning, relating (*to*).
referir (ie) *vt* to refer; to make reference (*to*); to submit; to retail, rehearse, tell.

refinado *a* refined, exquisite, pure.
refinamiento *m* refining, refinement, delicacy (*of taste*), elegance.
refinar *vt* to refine, purify.
refinería *f* refinery.
reflector *m* searchlight.
reflejar *vi* to reflect.
reflejo *a* reflex, reflected; *m* reflection.
reflexión *f* reflection, meditation, consideration.
reflexionar *vt* to think (*over*); to reflect.
reflexivo *a m* reflexive.
reflujo *m* ebb(ing).
reforma *f* reform, reformation, alteration.
reformar *vt* to reform, change, improve; *vr* to mend one's ways.
reformatorio *an* reformatory.
reforzado *a* strengthened, reinforced, bound (*of clothes*).
reforzar (ue) *vt* to strengthen; to encourage.
refractario *a* refractory, recalcitrant, unyielding.
refrán *m* proverb, saying.
refregar *vt* to rub, fray; to reprove.
refrenar *vt* to restrain, check; to rein.
refrendar *vt* to check; to authenticate.
refrescante *a* refreshing.
refrescar *vt* to freshen; *vi* to cool, cool off; to get cool.
refresco *m* refreshment, snack, light meal.
refriega *f* affray, skirmish, scuffle.
refrigerar *vt* to cool, refrigerate.
refrigerio *m* refrigeration.
refuerzo *m* reinforcement, binding, strengthening.
refugiado *m* refugee.
refugiar *vt* to shelter; *vr* to take refuge.
refugio *m* refuge; air-raid shelter; mountain hut.
refulgencia *f* splendor, bright glow.
refundición *f* recasting, adaptation.
refundir *vt* to rearrange, recast, adapt (*a play*); to include; to refund.
refunfuñar *vi* to mumble, mutter (*in one's beard*), snort.
refutación *f* refutation, disproof.
refutar *vt* to refute, disprove, deny.
regadera *f* watering can; sprinkler; *SA* shower.
regadío *a* irrigated; *m* irrigated land.
regalado *a* dainty, delightful.
regalar *vt* to present; to regale; to make presents.
regalía *f* royal rights; *pl* perquisites.
regaliz *m* licorice.
regalo *m* present, gift; comfort, ease.
regañar *vt* to scold, chide; *vi* to growl, snarl.
regaño *m* reprimand, scolding, harsh words.
regañón *a* shrewish, captious.
regar (ie) *vt* to sprinkle; to water (*plants*); irrigate.
regatear *vt* to bargain, haggle; to evade.
regateo *m* haggling, bargaining.
regazo *m* lap; **en el — de la familia** in the bosom of the family.
regencia *f* regency.
regeneración *f* regeneration.
regenerar *vt* to regenerate, revive.
regentar *vt* to govern, manage.
regente *m* regent; director.
regicidio *m* regicide.
regidor *m* alderman.
régimen *m* regime; rule; diet; system.
regimiento *m* regiment.
regio *a* regal, royal; stately.
región *f* region, district; country.
regionalismo *m* regionalism; regional autonomy.
regir (i) *vt* to rule, govern; to control, manage; to be (laid down, in force, followed).
registrador *m* registrar.
registrar *vt* to record, register; to inspect, search, go through.
registro *m* registration; record, search.
regla *f* rule, norm, precept; ruler; **en —** in order.
reglamentar *vt* to regulate, set in order, establish rules for; to issue by-laws.
reglamentario *a* customary, necessary, set, as laid down.
reglamento *m* regulations; by-laws, constitution (*of a society*).
reglar *vt* to rule (*lines*); to regulate.
regocijar *vt* to rejoice, gladden, enliven.
regocijo *m* joy, gladness, mirth, rejoicing.
regodeo *m* (*fam*) spree, carousal, beano.
regresar *vi* to return.
regreso *m* return.
reguero *m* trickle, rivulet; **— de pólvora** trail of powder.
regulador *m* governor, regulator.
regular *a* regular; middling (*fam*), fair, normal, moderate; ordinary, not bad; **por lo —** normally; *vt* to regulate, adjust.
regularidad *f* regularity.
regularizar *vt* to regularize.
rehabilitar *vt* to rehabilitate, restore, repair.
rehacer *vt* to remake, renovate, revive; *vr* to build up again, get back again.
rehén *m* hostage.
rehuir *vti* to shun, avoid.
rehusar *vt* to refuse, decline.
reimprimir *vt* to reprint.
reina *f* queen.
reinado *m* reign.
reinar *vt* to reign, govern; to prevail.
reincidir *vi* to relapse into error, backslide.

reino *m* kingdom, reign.
reintegrar *vt* to reimburse; to make up, restore.
reír *vi* to laugh; *vr* — **de** to laugh at, mock.
reiterar *vt* to reiterate, repeat.
reivindicar *vt* to regain possession.
reja *f* railing, rail; grating, grille, lattice; plowshare.
rejilla *f* luggage rack.
rejonear *vt* (*taur*) to jab (*bull*) with a lance.
rejuvenecer *vi* to rejuvenate.
relación *f* proportion; relation, connection; account, story; (*law*) brief; (*mil*) return.
relacionar *vt* to connect; to report; *vr* to join forces with, ally oneself with, get to know.
relajación *f* slackening, looseness; delivery to civil authority.
relajado *a* dissolute, dissipated, loose.
relajar *vt* to loosen, slacken; *vr* to be corrupted.
relajo *m* *Mex* disorder, commotion; *SA* baseness.
relamer *vr* to smack one's lips, relish.
relamido *a* affected, prim and proper.
relámpago *m* lightning.
relampaguear *vi* to lighten, flash, sparkle.
relatar *vt* to report, narrate.
relativo *a* relative, comparative.
relato *m* account, narrative, report.
relente *m* night dew.
relevante *a* notable, outstanding, striking.
relevar *vt* to relieve (*of*), release; to bring into relief; to acquit.
relevo *m* (*mil*) relief.
relicario *m* shrine; locket.
relieve *m* relief; raised work; **bajo** — bas-relief.
religión *f* religion, faith, creed.
religiosidad *f* religiousness.
religioso *a* religious, pious.
relinchar *vi* to neigh, whinny.
reliquia *f* remains; vestige, holy relic.
reloj *m* clock; watch; — **de bolsillo** watch; — **de sol** sundial; — **despertador** alarm clock.
relojero *m* watchmaker.
reluciente *a* shining, glittering, brilliant.
relucir *vi* to glow, shine, glitter.
relumbrante *a* dazzling, brilliant.
relumbrar *vi* to shine, sparkle.
rellano *m* landing (*of stairs*).
rellenar *vt* to fill; to refill; to cram; to stuff (*a fowl*).
relleno *m* stuffing (*of fowl etc*), padding.
remachar *vt* to rivet, knock farther in; to reaffirm, clinch (*statement, matters etc*).
remache *m* clinching; rivet.
remanente *m* remainder; residue; leftover.
remanso *m* backwater, eddy, quiet corner.
remar *vi* to paddle, row.
rematado *a* finished off, completed, rounded off, topped off, ended; **loco** — stark raving mad.
rematar *vt* to put an end to, complete, finish, finish off; to knock down (*at auction*).
remate *m* end, finish, conclusion; final (*touch etc*); finial, pinnacle, topmost (*stone etc*); **loco de** — quite mad.
remedar *vt* to ape, copy, imitate, mimic.
remediar *vt* to remedy, help.
remedio *m* remedy, cure; **sin** — without fail.
remedo *m* imitation.
remembranza *f* remembrance, recollection.
remendar *vt* to mend, patch, darn.
remendón *m* botcher, cobbler
remesa *f* remittance; shipment.
remiendo *m* repair; amendment, patch, darn.
remilgado *a* affected, nice, fastidious, mincing.
remilgo *m* squeamishness, prudery, airs (and graces), simperings.
reminiscencia *f* reminiscence, memory.
remirado *a* cautious, precise, pernickety.
remisión *f* remission; pardon, forgiveness.
remiso *a* unwilling, remiss, careless.
remitir *vt* to send, forward; to pardon, remit.
remo *m* oar.
remoción *f* removal, stirring-up.
remojar *vt* to soak, steep.
remolacha *f* beet.
remolcar *vt* to tow, take in tow.
remolinar *vtr* to whirl, spin around, swirl (*of skirt*).
remolino *m* whirlwind; eddy, vortex.
remolque *m* towage, towing; **dar** — to give a tow to.
remontar *vt* to repair, remount; to go up (*a river*).
rémora *f* hindrance; sucking-fish.
remorder *vt* to trouble (*conscience etc*).
remordimiento *m* remorse.
remoto *a* remote; unlikely.
remover (ue) *vt* to take away, remove; to stir (*up*).
remozar *vt* to refurbish; *vr* to spruce oneself up.
remuneración *f* remuneration.
remunerar *vt* to remunerate, reward.
renacer *vi* to be born again, spring up.
renaciente *a* renascent.
renacimiento *m* renaissance; regeneration.
rencilla *f* discord, feud blood,

bickering, spite(fulness), antipathy.
renco *m* lame.
rencor *m* rancor, bitterness, venom, malevolence.
rencoroso *a* malicious, spiteful, relentless, fell.
rendición *f* surrendering, yielding; surrender.
rendido *a* devoted, overcome; worn out, exhausted.
rendimiento *m* yield, income, return; submission; fatigue.
rendir (i) *vt* to conquer, subdue; to surrender, give up; to return, produce; to vomit; — **gracias** to render thanks; — **la bandera** to strike one's colors.
renegado *m* renegade.
renegar (ie) *vi* to curse, swear; to deny, disown.
renglón *m* line (*printed*); line of business; item; **a — seguido** right afterward.
reniego *m* blasphemy, curse.
renombrado *a* celebrated, renowned.
renombre *m* renown.
renovable *a* renewable.
renovación *f* renewal, renovation.
renovar (ue) *vt* to renew, refresh.
renquear *vi* to limp.
renta *f* income, rent, revenue, return.
rentabilidad *f* profitability.
rentar *vt* to rent, rent at.
rentero *m* lessee.
rentista *m f* rentier; financier.
renuevo *m* sprout, bud; renewal.
renuncia *f* renunciation; resignation.
renunciar *vt* to resign, renounce, waive, abandon.
renuncio *m* mistake, slip; revoke (*at cards*).
reñido *a* at variance, at odds, contrary, opposed, conflicting.
reñir (i) *vi* to quarrel, wrangle; *vt* to reprimand, revile, reprove, scold, berate.
reo *m* offender, culprit, criminal.
reojo *m* **mirar de —** to look askance at, look with jaundiced eye at.
reorganizar *vt* to reorganize.
reparación *f* reparation, repair; amends.
reparar *vt* to repair; to remark, notice; to compensate, atone for.
reparo *m* remark; warning, doubt, notice; objection; parry; **poner —s** to object, raise an objection.
reparón *a* faultfinding.
repartición *f* sharing, distribution.
repartidor *m* distributor.
repartir *vt* to distribute, apportion, allot; to divide.
reparto *m* distribution, allocation, sharing-out; (*theat*) cast; delivery (*of letters*).
repasar *vt* to glance over, peruse; to mend (*clothes*); to review, revise, go over.
repaso *m* final inspection, revision.
repatriar *vt* to repatriate.
repelente *a* repellent.
repeler *vt* to repulse.
repelo *m* twist, turn; *SA* rag.
repente *m* sudden impulse; **de —** suddenly, of a sudden.
repentino *a* sudden, unexpected, abrupt.
repercusión *f* repercussion.
repercutir *vi* to reflect, rebound, re-echo.
repertorio *m* repertory.
repetición *f* repetition.
repetir (i) *vt* to repeat, echo; to demand one's rights.
repicar *vt* to chime; to mince, chop up fine.
repique *m* chime, peal.
repiqueteo *m* chiming, pealing.
repisa *f* bracket, console; shelf, (*fire*) mantelpiece.
replegar *vt* to fold again; *vr* to fall back (*troops*).
repleto *a* replete, quite full.
réplica *f* retort, sharp reply; repetition.
replicar *vt* to answer (back), reply; to argue.
repliegue *m* doubling, folding, fold.
repoblación *f* resettlement, repopulation; — **forestal** reafforestation.
repollo *m* cabbage.
reponer *vt* to replace; to reinstate; *vr* to get better (*in health*); to get on one's feet again.
reportar *vt* to afford, bring, offer, provide.
reportarse *vr* to refrain, forbear, compose oneself.
reportero *m* reporter.
reposado *a* quiet, peaceful, at rest.
reposar *vt* to repose, rest.
reposición *f* replacement; recovery.
reposo *m* rest, repose, peace.
repostero *m* pastry cook, confectioner.
reprender *vt* to reprimand, reprove.
reprensión *f* reprimand, reprehension.
represa *f* dam, sluice.
represalia *f* reprisal.
representación *f* representation; statement, performance; image.
representar *vt* to represent, state; to perform, act; to take the form of.
representante *m* representative.
representativo *a* representative.
represión *f* repression, check.
reprimenda *f* reprimand.
reprimir *vi* to repress, check, contain, hold back.
reprobar *vt* to reprove; to reprobate; to fail (*exam*).
réprobo *an* reprobate.
reprochar *vt* to reproach, impute.
reproducción *f* reproduction.
reproducir *vt* to reproduce.
reptil *a m* reptile.
república *f* republic.
republicano *an* republican.

repudiación *f* rejection, disavowal, disowning.
repudiar *vt* to repudiate, disclaim.
repudio *m* divorce, denial.
repuesto *a* recovered; *m* store, stock; sideboard, dresser; **de** — spare; **pieza de** — spare part.
repugnancia *f* reluctance, loathing; opposition, contradiction.
repugnante *a* repugnant, repellent.
repugnar *vt* to loathe; to be reluctant; be repugnant.
repujar *vt* to emboss (*leather, metal etc*).
repulsa *f* refusal.
repulgar *vt* to hem, put a hem on.
repulido *a* spruce, neat, spick and span.
repulsivo *a* repulsive.
repuntar *vt* to turn (*of tide*).
reputación *f* reputation, name.
reputar *vt* to repute, estimate, prize.
requebrar *vt* to woo, court, flatter.
requemado *a* burned; tanned.
requerimiento *m* intimation, injunction.
requerir (ie) *vt* to request, to require; to intimate (*law*); to examine, look to; to need; to make (*love, advances*).
requesón *m* curd, cream cheese.
requiebro *m* flattery, endearment.
requisar *vt* to inspect.
requisito *m* requirement, necessity.
res *f* head of cattle, beast.
resabio *m* (*nasty*) aftertaste; viciousness; **con sus—s de** smacking of.
resabioso *a SA* bad-tempered.
resaca *f* surge, undercurrent, undertow.
resalado *a* lively, vivacious, bonny.
resaltar *vi* to jut out, project; to be (very) evident; **hacer** — to emphasize, throw into (high) relief.
resarcimiento *m* compensation.
resarcir *vt* to indemnify, recoup.
resbaladizo *a* slippery.
resbalar *vi* to slide, slip.
resbaloso *a* slippery.
rescatar *vi* to ransom, recover; *SA* to buy ore.
rescate *m* ransom; barter.
rescindir *vt* to rescind; to annul.
rescisión *f* rescission, cancellation.
rescoldo *m* embers; scruple.
resecar *vt* to desiccate.
reseco *a* too dry, dry as a bone.
resentido *a* resentful, chagrined, sore, irked; feeling the effects of.
resentimiento *m* resentment, grudge; weakening, impairment.
resentirse (ie) *vr* to resent; to be weakened, suffer from (feel) the effects of.
reseña *f* summary; review (*of book*).
reseñar *vt* to review, give an account of.
reserva *f* reservation; reserve; **fondo de**— reserve fund; **sin**— freely.
reservado *a* reserved, circumspect, private.
reservar *vt* to reserve; to keep back.
resfriado *m* a cold.
resfriarse *vr* to catch cold.
resguardar *vt* to protect, shield; *vr* to guard against.
resguardo *m* guard; protection security; voucher; — **de aduana** custom-house officers.
residencia *f* residence; dwelling.
residente *m* resident.
residir *vi* to reside; to rest on.
residuo *m* remainder, rest, residue.
resignación *f* resignation.
resignarse *vr* to resign, submit.
resistencia *f* resistance, endurance.
resistente *a* solid, tough, durable, hard-wearing, resistant.
resistir *vi* to resist; *vt* to (with)stand, endure, hold (up); *vr* to refuse, struggle against, find it hard to.
resma *f* ream (*of paper*).
resolución *f* resolution; courage.
resoluto *a* bold, resolute.
resolver (ue) *vt* to resolve, solve, dissolve; *vr* to decide, determine.
resollar *vt* to breathe heavily.
resonancia *f* resonance; echo.
resonar (ue) *vi* to resound, echo, ring (out).
resoplar *vi* to snort, breathe heavily.
resoplido *m* snorting, blowing.
resorte *m* spring; resource, means.
respaldar *vt* to back, guarantee, endorse.
respaldo *m* back (*of seat*); backing, support; *SA* protection.
respecto *m* proportion; — **a** as regards; concerning.
respetable *a* respectable; considerable, quite fair.
respetar *vt* to respect; to honor.
respeto *m* respect, regard, attention, reverence.
respetuoso *a* respectful.
respingar *vi* to obey unwillingly; to kick against.
respingo *m* kick, start.
respiración *f* breathing.
respirar *vti* to breathe.
respiro *m* respite.
resplandecer *vi* to glow, shine; to gleam; to excel.
resplandeciente *a* brilliant, resplendent.
resplandor *m* brightness, glow, radiance; splendor.
responder *vt* to answer; *vi* to be responsible for.
respondón *a* saucy.
responsabilidad *f* responsibility.
responsable *a* responsible.
responso *m* responses.
respuesta *f* answer.
resquebrajar *vt* to crack, split.
resquemo(r) *m* pungency, smart, heartburn.
resquicio *m* crevice, chink.
restablecer *vt* to re-establish, re-

store; *vr* to recover, recuperate, get better.
restallar *vi* to crack (*of whip*); to crackle.
restante *m* (*math*) remainder.
restañar *vt* to staunch, stop blood; to re-tin.
restaño *m* cloth of gold (*or* silver).
restar *vt* (*math*) to subtract; to deprive of, take away.
restauración *f* restoration.
restaurante *m* restaurant.
restaurar *vt* to restore; to renew.
restitución *f* restitution, return.
restituir *vt* to give back, restore, return.
resto *m* remainder, rest, balance; *pl* remains.
restregar *vt* to rub, scrub.
restricción *f* restriction.
restrictivo *a* restrictive.
restringir *vt* to restrict, constrain, confine.
resucitar *vt* to revive.
resuelto *a* determined, resolute, audacious.
resuello *m* breath, (*heavy*) breathing, wheezing.
resulta *f* result; **de —s** as a consequence.
resultado *m* result, effect; product.
resultar *vi* to result; to (turn out to) be.
resumen *m* summary, résumé; **en —** briefly, in short.
resumido *a* summed up; *f pl* **en —as cuentas** all in all, to sum up, to recapitulate.
resumir *vt* to resume, sum up; *vr* to be contained (*in*).
retablo *m* altarpiece, retable, reredos.
retaguardia *f* rearguard; **a la —** behind, in the rear.
retahila *f* string (*of curses etc*).
retal *m* remnant.
retama *f* (*bot*) broom.
retar *vt* to challenge, defy, dare.
retardar *vt* to delay, retard, slacken.
retardo *m* delay, protraction.
retazo *m* piece, remnant, cutting.
retemblar (ie) *vi* to shake, quiver, shudder.
retén *m* reserve; reserve corps.
retener *vt* to retain, keep back.
retentivo *a* retentive; *f* memory.
retina *f* retina.
retintín *m* tinkling, jingle; inflection of voice.
retinto *a* dark.
retirada *f* withdrawal, retreat.
retirado *a* isolated, quiet, secluded, distant; *m* retired officer.
retirar *vt* to withdraw, lay aside; to retire; *vi* to retreat.
retiro *m* retirement, seclusion; (*eccl*) retreat.
reto *m* challenge.
retobado *a SA* ill-tempered; obstinate, unruly; *Arg, Per* cunning, wily.
retobar *vt Arg, Chi* to cover with hides.
retocar *vt* to retouch, touch up.
retoño *m* sprout, sucker, shoot.
retorcer (ue) *vt* to twist, contort.
retorcimiento *m* twisting, contortion, writhing.
retórica *f* rhetoric, grammar, stylistics; specious arguments.
retornar *vi* to return; *vt* to give back, return.
retorno *m* return; requital; barter.
retozar *vi* to gambol, romp; *vt* to tickle, bubble (*of an emotion*).
retozo *m* gambol, frolic; **— de la risa** suppressed laughter.
retozón *a* frolicsome.
retractación *f* recantation.
retractar *vtr* to withdraw, disavow, retract.
retraer *vt* to keep from, dissuade; *vr* to keep away from, shun.
retraimiento *m* seclusion, refuge, retirement.
retrasar *vt* to defer, put off, postpone; to fall (be) behind; *vr* to be late.
retraso *m* delay, backwardness; **con 20 minutos de —** 20 minutes late.
retratar *vt* to portray, make a portrait of; *vr* to have a photograph taken.
retrato *m* portrait, likeness, picture.
retreta *f* (*mil*) retreat, tattoo.
retrete *m* alcove; closet, toilet.
retribución *f* reward, recompense.
retribuir *vt* to recompense.
retroceder *vi* to fall (go) back, to recede from.
retroceso *m* retrocession.
retrógrado *a* retrogressive, reactionary.
retruécano *m* pun; play on words.
retumbante *a* sonorous, resonant, bombastic.
retumbar *vi* to resound.
reuma *f* rheumatism.
reumatismo *m* rheumatism.
reunión *f* reunion, meeting, gathering, group.
reunir *vt* to unite, gather, collect, get together; to possess.
reválida *f* final examination (*before university entrance*).
revalidación *f* confirmation.
revalidar *vt* to ratify, confirm, to have confirmed.
revancha *f* revenge.
revelación *f* revelation; disclosure, discovery.
revelador *a* revealing; *m* developer.
revelar *vt* to reveal, disclose; to develop (*phot*).
revendedor *m* hawker; retailer; (ticket) speculator.
revenimiento *m* landslide.
reventar (ie) *vi* to break, explode, burst (*out*), to flatten, overwhelm; to long for; *vt* to smash, demolish, shatter, blast; to ride to death (*a horse*); **— de risa** to burst with laughter.

reventón *a* **ojos reventones** protruding eyes.
reverberación *f* reverberation, reflection.
reverberar *vi* to reverberate; to reflect (*light*).
reverbero *m* reflector; street lamp.
reverdecer *vi* to grow green again, renew, revive.
reverencia *f* reverence; bow.
reverenciar *vt* to revere; to venerate.
reverendo *a* reverend.
reverente *a* reverential.
reversión *f* reversion, return.
reverso *m* reverse (*of coin*); back side.
revés *m* back, wrong side; slap (*with back of hand*); **al** — wrong side out, on the contrary.
revestir (i) *vt* to clothe; to cover.
revisar *vt* to revise, review, check.
revisor *m* reviser; corrector; ticket collector, conductor.
revista *f* review; inspection.
revivir *vi* to revive, resuscitate.
revocación *f* abrogation.
revocar *vt* to revoke, abrogate, repeal.
revolcar *vt* to knock down; *vr* to wallow, to roll about (*in*).
revolotear *vi* to flutter around.
revoloteo *m* fluttering, hovering.
revoltoso *a* turbulent, unruly, wild.
revolucionar *vt* to revolutionize.
revolucionario *an* revolutionary.
revólver *m* pistol.
revolver *vt* to turn (up, over, upside down); to stir; *vi* to turn around.
revuelta *f* revolt; disturbance, tumult, revolution; turn.
revuelto *a* restless, intricate, turbid; untidy, mixed-up, jumbled.
revulsión *f* revulsion.
rey *m* king; *pl* Epiphany, Twelfth Night.
reyerta *f* wrangle, brawl.
rezagado *a* left behind, late; *m* laggard, straggler.
rezagar *vt* to leave behind; *vi* to lag.
rezar *vt* to pray, say prayers; to say (*of inscriptions etc*).
rezo *m* prayer.
rezongar *vi* to grumble.
rezongón *a* grumbling; *m* grumbler, growler.
rezumarse *vr* to ooze, exude.
ría *f* estuary.
ribera *f* (*river*) bank; shore.
ribete *m* braid, binding, piping; addition; touch of, hint.
ribetear *vt* (*sew*) to bind.
Ricardo *m* Richard.
ricino *m* castor-oil plant.
rico *a* rich, wealthy; delicious (*of food etc*); sweet (*of babies etc*).
ridiculez *f* ridicule; ridiculous action, eccentricity.
ridiculizar *vt* to ridicule, mock at, deride.
ridículo *a* ridiculous, laughable, ludicrous, absurd; **hacer el** — to make a fool of.
riego *m* irrigation.
riel *m* rail; ingot.
rienda *f* reins; government; **a — suelta** at full speed, unchecked.
riente *a* smiling.
riesgo *m* risk, danger; **correr** — to run (be) a risk.
rifar *vt* to raffle.
rifle *m* rifle.
rigidez *f* stiffness, sternness; inflexibility.
rígido *a* rigid, stiff, inflexible.
rigor *m* severity, strictness, harshness, intensity, rigor, stiffness; **en** — actually, strictly speaking; **de** — essential, de rigueur.
riguroso *a* severe, rigorous, strict, scrupulous.
rijoso *a* quarrelsome.
rima *f* heap, pile; rhyme; verse.
rimar *vt* to rhyme, make verses; to be in keeping with.
rimbombante *a* high-sounding, bombastic.
Rin, el *m* the Rhine.
rincón *m* corner, nook.
rinconera *f* corner table.
riña *f* quarrel, fight, dispute.
riñón *m* kidney.
río *m* river; **a — revuelto** in troubled waters.
ripio *m* rubble, rubbish; verbiage.
riqueza *f* wealth, riches, richness.
risa *f* laughter, laugh.
risco *m* crag, cliff.
risible *a* laughable, ludicrous.
risotada *f* horse laugh, bray.
risueño *a* smiling, agreeable.
ristra *f* string (*of onions*).
ristre *m* **con lanza en** — with lance leveled (*for the charge*).
ritmo *m* rhythm.
rito *m* rite, ceremony.
ritual *m* ritual; ceremonial; *a* customary.
rival *an* rival.
rivalidad *f* rivalry, emulation.
rivalizar *vi* to rival, compete, vie with.
rizado *a* curled, frizzled.
rizar *vt* to curl, crimp, ruffle; to ripple (*of water*).
rizo *a* curled; *m* curl, ringlet; *pl* (*naut*) reef points.
robar *vt* to rob, plunder, steal.
Roberto *m* Robert.
roble *m* oak tree.
robledo *m* oak grove.
robo *m* robbery, theft.
robustecer *vt* to strengthen, bolster (up).
robusto *a* robust, hale, vigorous.
roca *f* rock; cliff.
roce *m* friction; rubbing, attrition; (*social*) intercourse.
rociada *f* sprinkling, shower.
rociar *vt* to sprinkle, spray.

rocín *m* nag.
rocío *m* dew; sprinkling.
rocoso *a* rocky.
rochela *f Col, Ven* disorder, great noise.
rodada *f* rut, wheeltrack.
rodado *a* (*horse*) dappled; **canto —** boulder.
rodaja *f* small wheel; rowel; slice (*of bread*).
rodar *vi* to roll, turn, revolve, wheel.
rodear *vt* to surround, encircle; to invest; *SA* to round up cattle; make a detour.
rodela *f* buckler.
rodeo *m* turn; winding, roundabout way; subterfuge; circumlocution, evasions.
Rodesia *f* Rhodesia.
rodezno *m* turbine; cogwheel.
rodilla *f* knee; **de—s** on one's knees; **a media—** on one knee.
rodillo *m* roller; inking roller.
roedor *m* rodent; remorse.
roer *vt* to gnaw.
rogar (ue) *vt* to pray, beg, entreat.
rogativa *f* rogation.
rojizo *a* reddish, ruddy.
rojo *a m* red.
Rolando *m* Roland.
rollizo *a* plump, round, sturdy.
rollo *m* roll.
romance *a* Romance; *m* Romance language; ballad.
romancero *m* corpus of ballads.
romanesco *a* romanesque, Roman (*archit etc*).
romería *f* pilgrimage; excursion, picnic.
romero *m* pilgrim; rosemary.
romo *a* blunt, obtuse.
rompecabezas *m* puzzle, riddle; catapult.
rompedero *a* breakable, brittle.
rompeolas *m* breakwater, mole.
romper *vt* to break, tear, smash, crush; to burst open (*flowers etc*).
rompiente *m* breaker, surf.
rompimiento *m* break; rupture; violation, infraction.
ron *m* rum.
roncadora *f Arg, Bol, Ec* spur with large wheel.
roncar *vi* to snore.
ronco *a* hoarse, harsh, raucous.
roncha *f SA* bump, swelling; round slice.
ronda *f* beat, round; night patrol, serenading; party; round (*of drinks*).
rondalla *f* old wive's tale, story.
rondar *vt* to go the rounds, patrol (*the streets*); to haunt; to serenade.
rondón *ad* **de —** unexpectedly, abruptly.
ronquedad *f* hoarseness, huskiness.
ronquera *f* hoarseness.
ronquido *m* snore.
ronronear *vi* to purr.
ronzal *m* (*horse*) halter.
roña *f* scab; filth.
ropa *f* clothes, inner clothing, underclothes, costume; **— blanca** linen; **— hecha** ready-made clothing; **a quema—** point blank.
ropaje *m* apparel, clothing, robe; (*art*) drapery.
ropavejero *m* old-clothes dealer.
ropero *m* wardrobe; dealer in clothes.
roque *m* rook, castle (*chess*).
roquedal *m* rocky, boulder-strewn place.
rosa *f* rose; rose color.
rosado *a* rosy, flushed.
rosal *m* rose bush.
rosario *m* rosary.
rosca *f* screw thread; screw and nut; ring; ringshaped cake (*for parties, birthdays, etc*).
rosetón *m* rose window.
rostro *m* human face, beak; rostrum.
rotación *f* rotation.
rotar *vi* to rotate.
roto *a* broken, torn, destroyed, spoiled.
rotonda *f* rotunda.
rotoso *a Arg, Chi* ragged, torn.
rotular *vt* to label, stamp.
rótulo *m* label, sign; heading.
rotundo *a* rotund; plain, definite, categorical.
rotura *f* breakage; breach.
roturar *vt* to break up the ground, plow (*for the first time*).
rozadura *f* friction, attrition, abrasion.
rozar *vt* to clear the ground, grub up; to chafe; to graze, brush against, rub against; *vr* to rub shoulders (*with*).
rubí *m* ruby.
rubicundo *a* reddish.
rubio *a* fair (*hair*), blond.
rubor *m* bashfulness; blush.
ruborizarse *vr* to blush, color up, flush.
rúbrica *f* flourish (*in signature*).
rubricar *vt* to sign, indorse (*with a rúbrica*).
ruca *f Arg, Chi* Indian hut, cabin.
rucio *a* dapple, silver gray; *m* donkey.
ruco *a CA* old, worthless.
rudeza *f* roughness, crudeness, crudity.
rudimento *m* rudiment.
rudo *a* rough; coarse, unlettered, simple; hard.
rueca *f* distaff, spinning wheel.
rueda *f* wheel, circle; (*crowd of*) people; slice.
ruedo *m* edge (*of a round thing*); bottom (*of skirt*); arena (*bull ring*).
ruego *m* prayer, request, entreaty.
rufián *m* ruffian; pimp; go-between.
rugido *m* roar.
rugir *vi* to roar, bellow, howl.
rugoso *a* creased, wrinkled, corrugated.
ruido *m* noise, uproar, outcry; rumor.

ruidoso *a* noisy.
ruin *a* mean, base, low; wretched, puny; heartless.
ruina *f* ruin, fall; ruination.
ruindad *f* meanness, malice, baseness.
ruinoso *a* ruinous.
ruiseñor *m* nightingale.
ruma *f Arg, Chi, Ec* heap, pile.
rumbatela *f Cub, Mex* feast, repast.
rumbeador *m Arg* guide.
rumbo *m* course, direction; route; **con — a** bound for, on a course for.
rumboso *a* splendid, liberal, grand.
rumiante *a m* ruminant.
rumor *m* rumor; hearsay, murmur.
rumoroso *a* murmurous.
ruptura *f* break, rupture.
rural *a* rural, rustic.
Rusia *f* Russia.
ruso *an* Russian.
rústico *a* rustic, unmannerly; **en rústica** in paper covers, unbound.
ruta *f* route, course, way.
rutilar *vt* to twinkle, sparkle.
rutina *f* routine, habit, rut.
rutinario *a* routine.

S

sábado *m* Saturday.
sábana *f* (*linen*) sheet.
sabana *f* plain, savanna.
sabandija *f* vermin, nasty creature.
sabanero *m SA* herdsman of the savannas.
sabañón *m* chilblain.
sabara *f Ven* very light fog.
sabelotodo *m* knowall.
saber *vt* to know, know how; **— nadar** to be able to swim; *vi* to taste, savor; **— a** to taste of; **a —** to wit; *m* learning, knowledge.
sabiamente *ad* wisely, cunningly, skillfully.
sabiduría *f* wisdom, learning.
sabiendas *a* **a —** knowingly.
sabio *a* wise, learned, cunning; *m* learned man, scholar; wise person.
sablazo *m* blow, wound (*with saber*); touch (*for money*).
sable *m* saber; sable.
sabor *m* taste, smack, flavor.
saborear *vt* to flavor, savor; to roll on the tongue; *vr* to relish, enjoy.
sabotaje *m* sabotage.
sabroso *a* delightful, savory, tasty.
sabueso *m* foxhound, bloodhound.
sacabocado *m* ticket punch.
sacacorchos *m* corkscrew.
sacar *vt* to take (out), draw (out); to make out, understand; *SA* to take off; **— a luz** to publish, to make, take (*copy etc*); to start, begin (*a game*); **— a bailar** to invite to dance; to drag in (*mention of*); **— en claro, — en limpio** to get clear, understand; **— de quicio** to jolt, upset.
sacerdote *m* priest.
saciar *vt* to satiate, satisfy.
saciedad *f* satiety.
saco *m* sack, bag; pillage; **— de noche** valise; *SA* coat, jacket.
sacramento *m* sacrament.
sacrificar *vt* to sacrifice.
sacrificio *m* sacrifice.
sacrílego *a* sacrilegious.
sacristán *m* sexton, sacristan.
sacristía *f* sacristy.
sacro *a* holy, sacred.
sacudida *f* shake, jerk, jolt.
sacudidor *m* duster.
sacudir *vt* to shake, jolt; to beat, drub; *vr* to shake off.
sádico *a* sadistic.
saeta *f* arrow; hand (*of a clock*); song.
saetero *m* bowman, archer.
sagacidad *f* sagacity; cleverness, intelligence.
sagaz *a* far-seeing, sagacious, wise.
sagitario *m* archer; Sagittarius.
sagrado *a* sacred, holy; *m* sanctuary, asylum.
Sahara, el *m* the Sahara.
sahumar *vt* to fumigate, smoke (*food*); to perfume.
sai *m SA* monkey.
sainete *m* farcical short play.
sajuriana *f Chi, Per* ancient popular dance.
sal *f* salt; wit.
sala *f* parlor, drawing room, room.
salado *a* salty, witty.
salamanqués *an* (*inhabitant*) of Salamanca.
salar *vt* to salt; to season.
salario *m* salary, pay, wages.
salazón *f* salted meat.
salchicha *f* sausage.
salchichón *m* (*large*) sausage.
saldado *a* balanced, paid (*of accounts*).
saldar *vt* to settle, balance.
saldo *m* settlement, balance; (*bargain*) sale.
salero *m* salt cellar; gracefulness, liveliness.
salida *f* departure, outlet, issue, exit, way out; loophole, excuse.
saliente *a* salient, projecting.
salina *f* salt (mine, pit, lagoons).
salino *a* saline.
salir *vi* to go out; to set out, leave, depart; to come (out) (off) (*of a stain*); to appear, be published; **— por (uno)** to stand security for; *vr* **— con la suya** to get one's own way.
saliva *f* spittle, saliva.
salmo *m* psalm.
salmón *m* salmon.
salmuera *f* brine.
salobre *a* brackish, briny.
salón *m* drawing room, lounge; (*large*) hall.
salpicar *vt* to splash, spatter.
salpullido *m* rash.

salsa *f* sauce, dressing.
saltamontes *m* grasshopper.
saltar *vt* to jump, spring, skip, hop; to burst, crack, fly off; — **a la vista** to be clear as a pikestaff.
saltarín *a* dancing; restless.
salteador *m* highwayman.
saltear *vt* to rob on the highway; to assault.
saltimbanqui *m* mountebank, quack.
salto *m* spring, jump, leap; skip; — **de agua** waterfall; — **mortal** somersault; **a —s** dodging *or* leaping here and there; **de un** — at one bound.
saltón *a* **ojos —es** pop eyes; *m* grasshopper.
salubre *a* salubrious, healthy.
salud *f* health; public weal; salvation.
saludable *a* wholesome, salutary, healthy.
saludar *vt* to salute, greet, pay one's compliments to, say how do you do to.
saludo *m* greeting, bow, salutation.
salvación *f* salvation.
salvadoreño *an* (*inhabitant*) of San Salvador.
salvaguardia *f* security; safe conduct.
salvajada *f* piece of savagery.
salvaje *a* savage; wild; *mf* savage.
salvar *vt* to save; to salve; to jump over (*an obstacle*).
salvavidas *m* lifebelt; lifeguard; **bote** — lifeboat.
salvedad *f* excuse, reservation.
salvo *a* safe; **sano y** — safe and sound; *ad* save, except(ing).
salvoconducto *m* passport; safe conduct.
sambenito *m* penitential garment, (*outer*) hair shirt.
samuro *m Col, Ven* turkey buzzard.
san *a* (*abbrev of*) **santo.**
sanable *a* curable.
sanar *vt* to heal; *vi* to recover, get better; to heal.
sanatorio *m* sanatorium.
sancionar *vt* to sanction, permit, ratify.
sanco *m Arg, Chi* kind of porridge.
sancochar *vt* to parboil.
sandalia *f*, **sandalla** *f* sandal.
sandez *f* simplicity; absurdity, inane statement, stupid remark, silly talk.
sandía *f* watermelon.
sandío *a* silly, foolish.
saneado *a* drained, freed, clear, cleared up.
saneamiento *m* guarantee, indemnification; drainage.
sanear *vt* to give guarantee (*bail*); to drain.
sangrar *vt* to bleed.
sangre *f* blood; kindred; **a — fría** in cold blood; **mala** — bad blood, viciousness.
sangría *f* bleeding; drainage; drink of red wine and fruit.
sangriento *a* bloody, gory; bloodthirsty.
sanguijuela *f* leech.
sanguinario *a* bloody, cruel.
sanguíneo *a* of a blood color; sanguine.
sanidad *f* health, soundness.
sanitario *a* sanitary.
sano *a* sane, wholesome; honest; healthy, sound; whole.
santabárbara *f* (*naut*) magazine.
santanderino *an* (*inhabitant*) of Santander.
santiagués *an* (*inhabitant*) of Santiago de Compostela.
santiamén *m* **en un** — before you could say Jack Robinson, in a twinkling.
santidad *f* sanctity; godliness; holiness; the Pope.
santificar *vt* to sanctify, hallow; *vr* to justify, whitewash oneself.
santiguar *vt* to bless; *vr* to cross oneself.
santo *a* holy, saint, blessed; **todo el — día** all day long; *m* saint; — **y seña** countersign, password.
santón *m* dervish.
santuario *m* sanctuary.
saña *f* rage, fury, fierce hatred.
sañudo *a* furious, malignant, implacable, bitter.
sapiencia *f* wisdom.
sapo *f* toad; *Arg, Chi* children's play.
saque *m* drive (*at tennis etc*), first kick, turn *etc* (*of a game*).
saquear *vt* to plunder, sack, ransack, foray.
saqueo *m* sack, plunder(ing).
sarampión *m* measles.
sarape *m CA, Mex* poncho, shawl, blanket.
saraviado *a Col, Ven* spotted, piebald.
sarcasmo *m* sarcasm.
sardina *f* sardine.
sardo *an* Sardinian.
sardónico *a* sardonic.
sargento *m* sergeant.
sarna *f* itch, mange.
sarracina *f* scuffle, fight.
sarta *f* string (*of beads, pearls, lies*).
sartén *f* frying pan.
sastre *m* tailor.
satélite *m* satellite, crony, henchman.
sátira *f* satire.
satirizar *vt* to satirize, lampoon.
sátiro *m* satyr.
satisfacción *f* satisfaction, atonement.
satisfacer *vt* to satisfy, meet.
satisfecho *a* satisfied, conceited, pleased.
saturar *vt* to saturate, soak; to fill.
saturnino *a* saturnine; melancholy.
sauce *m* willow; — **llorón** weeping willow.

saúco *m* alder tree.
savia *f* sap.
saya *f* (*outer*) skirt, (*arch*) mantle.
sayal *m* sackcloth, serge.
sayo *m* loose garment.
sayón *m* executioner.
sazón *f* season, ripeness; **a la —** at that time; **fuera de—** out of season.
sazonado *a* seasoned, mellow, flavored.
sazonar *vt* to season, flavor; to ripen.
se *pn* himself, herself, itself, themselves, oneself; him, her (*in dative*); **— dice** it is said, they say.
sebo *m* tallow, candlefat.
secano *m* unirrigated arable land.
secante *a* drying; *m* blotting paper; *f* secant.
secar *vt* to dry, desiccate, parch, drain.
sección *f* section.
secesión *f* secession.
seco *a* dry, arid, bare, plain, curt; **a secas** plainly, simply; **en —** high and dry, (*stopped*) short; **a palo —** under bare poles.
secretaría *f* (*secretary's*) office, secretariat.
secretario *m* secretary;**— particular** private secretary.
secretearse *vr* to whisper to each other.
secreto *a m* secret; **— a voces** open secret; **en—** secretly, in private.
secta *m* sect.
secuaz *m* follower, disciple, adherent.
secuela *f* result, consequence.
secuestrar *vt* to sequestrate.
secuestro *m* sequestration; abduction.
secundar *vt* to second, support, favor.
secundario *a* secondary, unimportant.
sed *f* thirst; eagerness.
seda *f* silk;**— cruda** hard silk;**— en rama** raw silk; **— floja** floss silk; **como una —** soft, like silk; easy-going, easily.
sedal *m* fishing line.
sedativo *a m* sedative.
sede *f* **Santa S—** Holy See.
sedentario *a* sedentary.
sedería *f* silk shop; silk goods.
sedición *f* sedition.
sedicioso *a* seditious.
sediento *a* thirsty; anxious, dying (*to*).
sedimentar *vti* to settle (*of dregs*).
sedimento *m* dregs, lees, sediment; base.
seducción *f* seduction, thrill, attraction.
seducir *vt* to seduce, lead astray; to charm, delight.
seductor *m* seducer; charmer.
segador *m* reaper, mower, harvester.
segar *vt* to mow, harvest, reap; to cut (off) (down).
seglar *a* secular, lay; *m* layman.
segregar *vt* to segregate, separate.
seguida *f* continuation; **de —** successively, without interruption; **en —** without delay, immediately, at once.
seguido *a* one after the other, straight (*ahead*).
seguimiento *m* pursuit, chase; endeavor.
seguir (i) *vt* to follow, proceed, continue; to dog, shadow; to carry (out) (on).
según *prep* according to, as; **— y conforme** it depends.
segundo *a m* second; **de —a mano** (at) secondhand; **— a intención** double meaning.
segundón *m* younger son.
seguridad *f* security, certainty, confidence; surety bond.
seguro *a* sure, secure, safe, certain, fast; *m* assurance, insurance; ratchet; **— sobre la vida** life insurance; **póliza de —** insurance policy; **a buen —** certainly; **de —** assuredly; **sobre—** on firm ground, without danger.
selección *f* choice, selection.
selecto *a* select, choice.
selva *f* jungle, forest.
selvático *a* wild, rustic.
sellar *vt* to seal, stamp.
sello *m* seal; stamp; **— de correo** postage stamp.
semana *f* week; **día entre —** mid-week, working day.
semanal *a* weekly.
semanario *m* weekly (*paper*).
semblante *m* countenance, expression, face; appearance; **mudar de—** to change color.
semblanza *f* portrait, sketch (*usually in words*).
sembrado *m* sown ground.
sembrador *m* sower.
sembrar *vt* to sow, plant, scatter.
semejante *a* similar, resembling, like; *m* likeness, fellow creature.
semejanza *f* similarity, resemblance, likeness; **a— de** as, like.
semejar *vi* to resemble, be like.
sementar (ie) *vt* to sow, seed.
semestre *m* half-year, semester.
semi- *pref* semi . . . , half-.
semilla *f* seed.
seminario *m* seminary, seminar.
sempiterno *a* everlasting, eternal.
Sena, el *m* the Seine.
senado *m* senate.
senador *m* senator.
sencillez *f* simplicity, candor, artlessness.
sencillo *a* single, simple, unadorned, plain.
senda *f* path, footpath.
sendero *m* path.
sendos *a pl* each one; **recibieron — golpes** each one received a blow.
senectud *f* old age.

senil *a* senile, aged.
seno *m* chest, bosom, lap.
sensación *f* sensation, feeling.
sensatez *f* good sense; prudence.
sensato *a* sensible, wise, judicious.
sensible *a* sensitive, perceptible; painful, grievous.
sensitivo *a* sensitive.
sensual *a* sensual, sensuous.
sentada *f* sitting; **de una —** at one sitting.
sentadillas: a — side-saddle.
sentar (ie) *vi* to suit, become; *vt* to establish (*as a fact*); *vr* to sit down; **dar por sentado** to take for granted.
sentencia *f* sentence; judgment.
sentenciar *vt* to pass judgment, condemn.
sentido *a* (*deeply*) felt, sensitive; touchy; *m* sense, feeling, meaning; direction, course; understanding; **— común** common sense; **perder el —** to lose consciousness; **valer un —** to be worth a fortune.
sentimiento *m* sentiment, feeling, emotion; grief, concern.
sentir *vt* to feel, hear, perceive; to be sorry for, regret; *vr* to be moved; *m* feeling, opinion.
seña *f* sign, token, signal; password; trace; *pl* address; **—s personales** personal description; **por más —** in further support (*detail*), into the bargain.
señal *f* sign, mark, indication.
señalar *vt* to point out; to mark, stamp; to fix (on); *vr* to distinguish oneself, itself.
señero *a* solitary, isolated; unique.
señor *m* mister, sir, gentleman; owner, master.
señora *f* mistress, lady, woman.
señorear *vt* to master, lord (over); to tower over, excel.
señoría *f* (over)lordship.
señorío *m* dominion, seigneury; imperiousness, command; domain, self-control, graveness.
señorita *f* miss, young lady.
señorito *m* young (man, gentleman); (young) master; young gentleman (*of leisure*).
señuelo *m* lure, decoy.
seo *m* cathedral.
separación *f* separation; dismissal.
separar *vt* to separate; to detach, sever; to discharge; *vr* to part.
sepelio *m* interment.
septentrión *m* north.
septiembre *m* September.
sepulcro *m* grave, tomb, sepulcher.
sepultar *vt* to bury, inter; to hide.
sepultura *f* interment; **dar —** to inter.
sepulturero *m* gravedigger, sexton.
sequedad *f* dryness; surliness; sterility.
sequía *f* drought.
séquito *m* retinue, train, following.
ser *vi* to be, exist, belong to; *m* being, essence.
serenarse *vr* to clear up, grow clear.
serenata *f* serenade.
serenidad *f* serenity, calmness, peace; coolness (of mind).
sereno *a* serene, quiet, placid, clear; **al —** under the stars; *m* night watchman.
serie *f* series, suite, succession.
seriedad *f* seriousness, gravity, earnestness, sobriety.
serio *a* serious, grave, earnest, sober.
sermón *m* sermon, homily.
serpentear *vi* to meander.
serpiente *f* serpent, snake; **— de cascabel** rattlesnake.
serranía *f* ridge of mountains.
serrano *an* mountaineer, mountain-bred.
serrar *vt* to saw.
serrín *m* sawdust.
serrucho *m* hand-saw.
servicial *a* obliging, serviceable, accommodating.
servicio *m* service; favor, good turn, use(fulness); (*tea*) set; **hacer un flaco —** to do an ill turn.
servido *a* pleased, served.
servidor *m* servant; **— de Vd** at your service.
servidumbre *f* servitude; servants of a household.
servil *a* servile; abject, menial.
servilleta *f* serviette, napkin.
servir (i) *vi* to serve, be useful; *vt* to wait, attend; *vr* to deign; **— de** to serve as, act as; **sírvase** please.
sesenta *an* sixty.
sesgado *a* oblique, slanting.
sesgar *vt* to slant, bevel.
sesgo *m* bias, bevel, slope; turn, direction.
sesión *f* session, sitting; **levantar la —** to adjourn a meeting.
seso *m* brain, talent; **calentarse, devanarse los —s** to rack one's brains.
sestear *vi* to take a siesta.
sesudo *a* prudent, weighty, intelligent, judicious.
seta *f* mushroom.
setenta *an* seventy.
seto *m* hedge, fence.
seudónimo *m* pseudonym.
severidad *f* severity, harshness, sternness.
severo *a* severe, stern, strict, hard, exact(ing).
sevillano *an* (*inhabitant*) of Sevilla.
sexo *m* sex; **bello —** fair sex.
sexual *a* sexual.
si *cj* if; in case; **— bien** although; **un — es no es** something and nothing.
sí *ad* yes; **dar el —** to say yes, agree to marry.
s *pn* himself, herself, itself (*reflexive after preposition*); **de por —** of its own account;

sibarita *m* epicure, voluptuary.
Sicilia *f* Sicily.
sicoanálisis *m* psychoanalysis.
sicoanalítico *a* psychoanalytic(al).
sicológico *a* psychological.
sicómoro *m* sycamore.
sicópata *mf* psychopath.
siderurgia *f* siderurgy, iron and steel industry.
siderúrgico *a* of *or* pertaining to steel industry.
sidra *f* cider.
siega *f* mowing, reaping, harvest.
siembra *f* sowing.
siempre *ad* always; **— que** provided, whenever; **para —** forever; **— jamás** for ever and ever.
siempreviva *f* evergreen.
sien *f* (*anat*) temple.
sierpe *f* serpent, snake.
sierra *f* saw; mountain range.
siervo *m* serf.
siesta *f* afternoon nap.
siete *an* seven; **hablar más que —** to speak ten to the dozen.
sifón *m* syphon.
sigilo *m* secret reserve; **— confesional** secrecy of the confessional.
sigiloso *a* reserved, secretive, privy.
sigla *f* abbreviation.
siglo *m* century.
signatario *an* signatory.
significación *f* meaning.
significado *m* meaning.
significar *vt* to signify, mean; to indicate.
signo *m* sign, mark; nod; (*mus*) character, notation.
siguiente *a* following, next.
sílaba *f* syllable.
silbar *vi* to whistle; *vt* to hiss, catcall.
silbato *m* whistle; chink.
silbido *m* whistling, hiss; **— de oídos** ringing in the ears.
silbo *m* whistle.
silencio *m* silence.
silencioso *a* silent, still.
sílfide *f* sylph.
silueta *f* silhouette, outline, profile.
silvestre *a* rustic; wild (*flowers*); uncultivated.
silla *f* chair; saddle; **— (plegadiza) (de tijera)** folding chair; **— poltrona** armchair; **— de columpio** rocking chair.
sillar *m* building block.
sillería *f* (*eccles*) stalls.
sillón *m* armchair, easy chair.
sima *f* abyss.
simbólico *a* symbolical.
símbolo *m* symbol, emblem.
simetría *f* symmetry; harmony.
simiente *f* seed.
símil *a* alike, like; *m* simile.
similar *a* similar.
similitud similitude, resemblance.
simio *m* ape.
simón *m* hack(ney carriage).
simpa *f* *Arg, Per* braid, plait.
simpatía *f* fellow-feeling, sympathy, friendliness, warmth, amiability, toleration.
simpático *a* congenial, agreeable, pleasant, nice, amiable, friendly.
simpatizar *vi* to get along well together, like, feel fellow-feeling.
simple *a* simple, single; silly; ingenuous.
simpleza *f* silliness, foolishness, absurdity, simpleness, simplicity.
simplicidad *f* simplicity, artlessness.
simplificar *vt* to simplify.
simplón *m* simpleton.
simulacro *m* sham, hollow mockery, superficial copy.
simular *vt* to simulate, feign.
simultáneo *a* simultaneous.
sin *prep* without; **— embargo** yet, however, nevertheless.
sinagoga *f* synagogue.
sinapismo *m* poultice; nuisance, bore.
sincerar *vt* to explain; *vr* to justify oneself.
sinceridad *f* sincerity, frankness.
sincero *a* sincere, true.
síncope *f* faint(ing fit).
sindicato *m* syndicate; trade union.
singular *a* singular, single; extraordinary, unique, peculiar, odd.
singularidad *f* strangeness, oddity, originality.
singularizar *vt* to single out; *vr* to distinguish oneself.
siniestra *f* left hand.
siniestro *a* sinister; *m* disaster, shipwreck, (*insurance*) accident, claim.
sinnúmero *m* endless number.
sino *cj* but, only except; *m* destiny.
sinónimo *a* synonymous; *m* synonym.
sinopsis *f* synopsis.
sinrazón *f* wrong, injustice; excess.
sinsabor *m* displeasure, unpleasantness, gall.
síntesis *f* synthesis.
sintetizar *vt* to synthesize, reduce, compress.
síntoma *m* symptom.
sinuosidad *f* sinuousness, twists and turns.
sinvergüenza *a* brazen, shameless; *m* scoundrel.
siquiatra *mf* psychiatrist.
siquiatría *f* psychiatry.
siquiátrico *a* psychiatric.
siquiera *cj* although, even; scarcely; **ni —** not even.
sirena *f* mermaid.
sirviente *m* servant, waiter.
sisa *f* petty theft.
sisal *m* sisal hemp.
sisar *vt* to pinch, pilfer, lift; to give short weight.
sisear *vt* to hiss.
sistema *m* system.
sistemático *a* systematic.
sitiar *vt* to besiege; to surround.
sitio *m* place, room; seat, site; siege.
sito *a* situated, located, lying (*in*).

situación *f* situation, position, state.
situado *a* situated, placed.
situar *vt* to place, locate, site; *vr* to station oneself.
so *prep* under, below; — **capa de** under the cloak of; — **pena** under penalty.
soata *f Ven* kind of squash.
sobaco *m* armpit.
sobado *a* dog-eared.
sobar *vt* to knead; to pummel.
soberanía *f* sovereignty; suzerainty.
soberano *an* sovereign, mighty.
soberbia *f* pride; anger, haughtiness, presumption, sumptuousness.
soberbio *a* proud; superb; passionate.
sobornar *vt* to bribe, suborn, corrupt.
soborno *m* bribery, subornation; *Arg, Bol, Chi* overload.
sobra *f* surplus, excess; *pl* the remains, leavings; **de** — over, extra, too well.
sobrado *a* excessive, superabundant.
sobrante *m* residue, surplus.
sobrar *vi* to be more than enough, be de trop.
sobre *prep* on, upon, above; *m* envelope.
sobrecama *f* bedspread.
sobrecargar *vt* to surcharge; to overload.
sobrecejo *f* frown.
sobrecoger *vt* to take by surprise, catch out; *vr* to be overawed, abashed.
sobreexcitar *vt* to over-excite.
sobrehumano *a* superhuman.
sobrellevar *vt* to bear, carry, endure.
sobremanera *ad* exceeding(ly), excessive(ly).
sobremesa *f* after-dinner conversations; **de** — over coffee.
sobrenadar *vi* to float, swim.
sobrenatural *a* supernatural.
sobrentender (ie) *vt* to take something for granted.
sobrepasar *vt* to surpass; to exceed, excel.
sobreponer *vt* to superpose; *vr* to rise above, be superior to, overcome.
sobrepujar *vt* to excel, surpass.
sobresaliente *a* projecting; excelling; *m* (*exam*) distinction.
sobresalir *vi* to excel, stand out; to project, overhang.
sobresaltar *vt* to startle.
sobresalto *m* startled surprise.
sobrescrito *m* address, superscription.
sobretodo *m* overcoat, greatcoat.
sobrevenir *vi* to happen, take place, come upon, follow, fall (out).
sobreviviente *a* surviving; *mf* survivor.
sobriedad *f* sobriety, frugality, soberness, restraint, forbearance.
sobrino *m* nephew.
sobrio *a* sober, temperate, restrained.
socaliña *f* cunning.
socapar *vt Bol, Ec, Mex* to hide, conceal.
socarrón *a* cunning, shrewd, sly, canny, crafty.
socavar *vt* to excavate, undermine.
socavón *m* cave, cavern.
sociable *a* sociable.
social *a* social, companionable.
socialista *an* socialist.
sociedad *f* society, company, corporation.
socio *m* associate, shareholder; partner, member (*of society*).
sociología *f* sociology.
sociológico *a* sociological.
sociólogo *m* sociologist.
socorrer *vt* to aid, help, assist, succor.
socorrido *a* handy, ready to hand.
socorro *m* help, support, assistance, relief.
socucho *m SA* small room, den.
soez *a* vile, mean, coarse.
Sofía *f* Sophia.
sofisma *m* sophism.
sofista *m* quibbler.
sofocar *vt* to stifle, smother, choke.
sofoco *m* **tener un** — to be choked with (*emotion etc*).
soga *f* rope, halter.
sojuzgar *vt* to subdue, subjugate.
sol *m* sun, day(light); **tomar el** — to stand (be) in the sun, sunbathe; **de** — **a** — from dawn to dusk.
solana *f* sun terrace.
solapa *f* lapel.
solapado *a* underhand, cunning.
solar *m* ground, plot, lot (*of ground*), ancestral home (*or site of such home*).
solariego *a* home, traditional, ancestral, family.
solaz *m* enjoyment, comfort, consolation.
solazar *vt* to comfort, solace; to amuse; *vr* to enjoy oneself, beguile the time.
soldada *f* pay.
soldado *m* soldier; — **raso** private; — **bisoño** raw recruit.
soldadura *f* soldering; solder.
soldar *vt* to solder, weld.
soledad *f* solitude, loneliness, seclusion.
solemne *a* solemn.
solemnidad *f* solemnity; **pobres de** — the under-privileged, the down and out.
solemnizar *vt* to solemnize.
soler *vi* to be wont; *eg* **suele ocurrir** it usually happens.
solevantar *vt* to perturb, raise up, uplift.
solicitación *f* solicitation, application.
solicitar *vt* to solicit, search; to apply (*for post*); to importune, worry.
solícito *a* diligent, solicitous, apprehensive, anxious to help.

solicitud *f* solicitude, importunity; application (*for post*).
solidaridad *f* solidarity.
solidario *a* in sympathy, agreement (*with*).
solidez *f* solidity, strength, firmness.
sólido *a* solid, compact.
solio *m* canopied throne.
solitario *a* lonely, solitary, single, isolated; *m* recluse, hermit.
soliviantar *vt* to stir up, instigate.
soliviar *vt* to raise, prop up.
sólo *ad* only, solely.
solo *a* sole, only, single.
solomillo *m* sirloin.
soltar *vt* to let (loose) (off) (free) (fly); to unfasten, cast off; *vr* to come (off) (loose), break (loose) (free).
soltero *a* unmarried, single; *m* bachelor.
solterón *m* old bachelor; **—a** *f* old maid.
soltura *f* fluency, easiness, ease, skill.
soluble *a* soluble.
solución *f* solution, outcome, break.
solvente *a* solvent, soluble.
sollozar *vi* to sob.
sollozo *m* sob.
somatar *vt Mex, Hond* to misspend, squander.
sombra *f* shade, shadow, ghost; sign, suspicion; **buena —** good luck; **hacer —** to (out)shadow, shade, put in the shade.
sombrerería *f* manufacture of hats; hatter's shop.
sombrero *m* hat; **— de copa** top hat; **— hongo** bowler hat.
sombrilla *f* parasol, sunshade.
sombrío *a* gloomy, shady, sullen.
somero *a* shallow, superficial.
someter *vt* to submit, subject.
somnolencia *f* sleepiness.
son *m* sound, report; **sin ton ni —** without rhyme or reason.
sonaja *f* rattle.
sonámbulo *m* sleepwalker.
sonante *a* sounding; **moneda —** cash, specie.
sonar *vi* to sound, ring; **— a** to seem like; *vr* to blow one's nose.
sonda *f* (*naut*) sounding, lead.
sondear *vt* (*naut*) to sound, take soundings; to sound out (*opinions*), fathom.
soneto *m* sonnet.
sonido *m* sound; report, rumor.
sonoro *a* sonorous, musical, resounding.
sonreír *vi* to smile.
sonrisa *f* smile.
sonrojo *m* blush.
sonrosado *a* rosy.
sonsacar *vt* to wheedle, win round, draw out; to pilfer, entice.
sonsonete *m* singsong, monotony (*of voice*).
soñar *vi* to dream.
soñoliento *a* sleepy, drowsy, placid, dull.
sopa *f* soup; **hecho una —** soaked to the skin.
sopapo *m* slap.
soplar *vtir* to blow, fan; to lift, win; to whisper, suggest, prompt.
soplo *m* blowing, puff of wind; breath.
soplón *m* sneak, informer, telltale.
soponcio *m* faint, swoon.
sopor *m* lethargic sleep, drowsiness.
soportable *a* bearable, tolerable.
soportal *m* portico, arcade.
soportar *vt* to bear, endure, resist.
soporte *m* stand, bracket.
sorber *vt* to sip, suck, absorb, imbibe, swallow.
sorbete *m* sherbet; *SA* ice-cream cone.
sorbo *m* sip, swallow, draft, drink.
sordera *f* deafness.
sórdido *a* sordid, indecent, nasty.
sordina *f* (*mus*) mute; **a la —** on the quiet.
sordo *an* deaf; muffled, dull (*sound*).
sordomudo *an* deaf and dumb.
sorna *f* irony, double meaning, knavery, guile; slowness.
soroche *m SA* mountain sickness.
sorprender *vt* to surprise, astonish, catch unawares.
sorpresa *f* surprise.
sortear *vt* to draw lots, raffle, choose.
sorteo *m* draw (*of lots, tickets etc*), raffle.
sortija *f* (*finger*) ring; hoop; ringlet (*of hair*).
sortilegio *m* sorcery.
sosegado *a* tranquil, composed, calm.
sosegar (ie) *vt* to appease, to quiet, lull, calm (down).
sosiego *m* quiet, calmness, peace.
soslayo *m* slanting; **de —** sideways, obliquely.
soso *a* tasteless, insipid, silly, flat, dull.
sospecha *f* suspicion, mistrust.
sospechar *vi* to suspect, mistrust, conjecture.
sospechoso *a* suspicious, mistrustful.
sostén *m* support, buttress, prop; brassiere.
sostener *vt* to maintain, support, hold (up); *vr* to keep alive, earn one's living.
sostenido *a* sustained, supported; *m* (*mus*) sharp.
sota *f* jack, knave (*cards*).
sotana *f* cassock.
sótano *m* cellar, basement.
sotavento *m* leeward; **a —** under the lee.
soterrar (ie) *vt* to bury, hide.
soto *m* thicket, grove; dingle, dell.
soviético *a* Soviet.
suave *a* smooth, soft, gentle.
suavidad *f* smoothness, ease, gentleness.
suavizar *vt* to soften, mitigate, smooth (down).

subalterno *a* inferior, subordinate.
subarrendar (ie) *vt* to sublet.
subasta *f* auction sale; **sacar a —** to auction (off).
subdesarrollado *a* underdeveloped.
súbdito *m* subject (*of a king*).
subdividir *vt* to subdivide.
subida *f* ascent, climb, rise; rise (*of price*).
subido *a* raised; high (*price*); high, loud (*color*); special, notable (*value*).
subir *vi* to ascend, climb, go up, come up; to amount to; to rise (*river, price*); to intensify; *vt* to raise, lift up, put up; **— a caballo** to mount, get on.
súbito *a* sudden.
sublevación *f* revolt, rising, insurrection.
sublevar *vt* to bring out (*in revolt*); to disgust, nauseate; *vr* to rise; to rebel.
sublime *a* sublime, lofty.
submarino *a m* submarine.
subordinar *vt* to subordinate, subject.
subrayar *vt* to underline, emphasize, underscore.
subsanar *vt* to exculpate; to make up (*losses etc*), repair.
subscribir *vt* to subscribe; to undersign.
subsecretario *m* under-secretary, assistant secretary.
subsidio *m* subsidy, (*family*) allowance.
subsistencia *f* subsistence, living.
subsistir *vi* to last; to exist, live on.
substancia *f* substance, body.
substanciar *vt* to abridge, substantiate, back up.
substituir *vt* to replace, substitute.
substraer *vt* to subtract, draw off, remove; *vr* to keep away from, elude, withdraw.
subteniente *m* second lieutenant.
subterfugio *m* subterfuge.
subterráneo *a* underground, subterranean.
suburbio *m* suburb, outskirt.
subvención *f* subsidy, grant.
subyugar *vt* to subdue, overcome.
suceder *vi* to happen, occur; to follow, inherit.
sucedido *m* event.
sucesión *f* series; succession, heirs.
sucesivo *a* next, consecutive; **en lo —** henceforth.
suceso *m* happening, event, incident.
suciedad *f* filthiness, dirtiness.
sucinto *a* brief, succinct, concise.
sucio *a* dirty, unclean, foul.
suculento *a* juicy.
sucumbir *vi* to perish, succumb, yield.
sucursal *a* ancillary; *m* branch (*shop, bank etc*).
sud *m* south.
sudamericano *an* South American.
sudar *vi* to sweat, perspire; **— tinta** to sweat blood.
sudario *m* winding sheet.
sudor *m* sweat, perspiration.
sudoroso *a* sweaty, sweating.
Suecia *f* Sweden.
sueco *a* Swedish; *n* Swede.
suegro *m* father-in-law.
suela *f* sole (*of shoe*).
sueldo *m* salary, pay, stipend.
suelo *m* ground, floor, flooring.
suelto *a* loose, free, easy, fluent, blank (*verse*); odd; small change; odd article (*in newspaper*), offprint.
sueño *m* dream, sleep; **tener —** to be sleepy; **entre —s** half-asleep, half-awake.
suero *m* serum.
suerte *f* luck, chance, hazard, fate; sort, kind; trick, action; **de — que** so that; **echar —s** to cast lots.
suéter *m* sweater.
suficiencia *f* capacity; **aire de —** arrogance, self conceit.
suficiente *a* sufficient, enough; competent.
sufragar *vt* to defray, meet (*expenses*); to favor.
sufragio *m* suffrage, vote.
sufrido *a* long-suffering, patient; hard-wearing, practical.
sufrimiento *m* suffering, sufferance.
sufrir *vt* to endure, bear, tolerate.
sugerir (ie) *vt* to suggest, inspire.
sugestión *f* suggestion, hint.
sugestionar *vt* to influence, direct.
suicida *m f* suicide.
suicidio *m* suicide, self-murder.
Suiza *f* Switzerland.
suizo *an* Swiss.
sujeción *f* subordination, subjection.
sujetar *vt* to subdue, subject, fasten, hold down; *vr* to submit.
sujeto *a* subject, liable; *m* subject, topic; individual, person, fellow.
suma *f* amount, addition, sum; **— y sigue** carried forward; **en—** in short, briefly.
sumaca *f SA* smack, coasting vessel.
sumamente *ad* extremely, notably, especially.
sumar *vt* to add (up); to amount to.
sumario *a* brief, cursory; *m* summary, précis, abstract.
sumergir *vt* to submerge.
sumersión *f* submersion, immersion.
sumidero *m* sink; sewer, drain.
suministrar *vt* to distribute, supply, provide, furnish.
suministro *m* supply, rations.
sumir *vt* to depress; *vr* to fall into, be sunk.
sumisión *f* submission, compliance.
sumiso *a* resigned, humble(d), patient.
sumo *a* highest, great, special; **a lo—** at most.
suntuoso *a* sumptuous, gorgeous, ostentatious.

supeditar *vt* to subdue, subject, override.
superabundar *vi* to be overflowing, superabundant.
superar *vt* to overcome, excel, surpass, to be beyond, exceed.
superávit *m* surplus.
superchería *f* fraud, swindle.
superficial *a* superficial.
superficie *f* surface; area.
superfluo *a* superfluous, unnecessary.
superintendente *m* superintendent.
superior *a* superior, beyond, upper, better; *m* head, superior.
supersticioso *a* superstitious.
supervivencia *f* survival.
suplantar *vt* to supplant; to forge.
suplemento *m* supplement, addition.
suplente *am* substitute; alternate.
súplica *f* supplication, request.
suplicar *vt* to pray, beg, request, implore; — **de** to appeal against (*sentence*).
suplicio *m* torture.
suplir *vt* to provide, afford; to act as substitute.
suponer *vt* to suppose.
suposición *f* supposition, authority, assumption.
supremo *a* supreme, paramount.
supresión *f* suppression, omission.
suprimir *vt* to suppress, omit, cut out.
supuesto *a* supposed, suppositious; *m* supposition; **por** — of course; — **que** since, granting that.
sur *m* south.
suramericano *an* South American.
surcar *vt* to furrow, cut in.
surco *m* furrow, groove; line, wrinkle.
surgir *vi* to come (out) (forth), spurt, sprout, arise out (of), spring (from) (up).
surtido *m* assortment, stock (*of shop*), variety.
surtidor *m* fountain, spout, jet (*of water*).
surtir *vt* to supply, provide, furnish; — **efecto** to produce effect.
surumbiar *vt Arg* to punish, beat.
susceptible *a* susceptible, open (to).
suscitar *vt* to (a)rouse, cause, stir up.
susodicho *a* above-mentioned.
suspender *vt* to suspend, hang (up); to amaze, suspend, adjourn; — **pagos** to stop payment.
suspensión *f* suspension; suspense, pause; — **de pagos** suspension of payments.
suspicacia *f* suspiciousness, wariness.
suspicaz *a* mistrustful, wary, circumspect.
suspirar *vi* to sigh; — **por** to long for.
suspiro *m* sigh.
sustancia *f* body, solidity, sustenance, substance.
sustentar *vt* to sustain, bear up; to assert, maintain, nourish (*hopes, arguments etc*).
sustento *m* food, maintenance, support.
susto *m* fright, scare; **llevar un** — to have a scare.
susurrar *vi* to whisper, murmur, rustle; *vr* to be noised abroad.
susurro *m* hum(ming), whisper.
sute *a Col, Ven* sickly, thin.
sutil *a* keen, subtle, flimsy.
sutileza *f* fineness, cunning, skill, penetration, acumen.
suyo *pn* his, hers, its, theirs, yours.

T

taba *f* knucklebone; jack.
tabaco *m* tobacco; — **en rama** leaf tobacco; — **en polvo** snuff; — **rubio** American tobacco.
taberna *f* tavern, public house, wine shop, bar room.
tabernero *m* publican, licensee.
tabique *m* partition wall, boarding.
tabla *f* board, slab, plate, plank; list; block; —**s** the stage, boards; lumber.
tablado *m* stage; flooring; scaffold; platform, dais.
tablero *m* board, panel; checker board; gaming table; counter; — **de cocina** dresser, kitchen table.
tablilla *f* tablet, slab; noticeboard.
tablón *m* plank, beam; — **de avisos** bulletin board; —**es** lumber.
tabular *a* tabular; *vt* to tabulate.
taburete *m* stool; bench.
tacaño *a* mean, close, stingy, miserly.
tácito *a* silent, implied, wordless, implicit.
taciturno *a* silent, reserved.
taco *m* cue; plug, bung, stopper; oath, swear word, curse.
tacón *m* heel (*shoe*).
taconazo *m* stamp (*of heel*); **dar** —**s** to stamp (*heels*).
taconeo *m* tap-dancing.
táctica *f* tactics.
tacto *m* feel, touch; tact, finesse.
tacha *f* blemish, flaw, fault; **poner** — to object.
tachable *a* exceptionable, blameworthy.
tachar *vt* to tax, censure, blame; to obliterate, efface, cross out.
tachigual *m Mex* cheap cotton cloth.
tachuela *f* tack, small nail.
tafetán *m* taffeta; thin silk; — **inglés** court plaster.
tafilete *m* morocco leather.
tahona *f* bakehouse.
tahur *m* gambler, sharper.
taimado *a* crafty, sly.
taita *an Ven* name of head of family; *Arg, Chi* child's name for father.
taja *f* incision.
tajada *f* slice, chop.
tajadura *f* cut, notch.

tajar *vt* to hack, slice, cut; to cleave, hew, split; to trim.
tajo *m* cut, incision, notch; cliff, gully; cutting; face (*mining*).
Tajo, el *m* the Tagus.
tal *a ad* such, so, as; equal; **un —** so-and-so; such and such; **— cual** more or less, some sort of; **— para cual** tit for tat; **con — que** provided that; **¿qué —?** how?, how are things?, what sort of?
tala *f* felling (*trees*), devastation, desolation.
talabartero *m* saddler, beltmaker.
taladrar *vt* to bore, pierce, drill.
taladro *m* brace and bit.
tálamo *m* bridal chamber, bed.
talante *m* manner, bearing, address; countenance, mien; frame of mind.
talar *vt* to fell (*trees*), deforest, lay waste.
talco *m* tinsel, talc, french chalk.
talego -a *mf* bag, sack.
taleguilla *f* satchel, small bag.
talento *m* talent, ability; intelligence; **tiene mucho —** he's very able.
talión *m* retaliation, requital.
talismán *m* talisman, charm, amulet.
talmente *ad* similarly.
talón *m* heel; check, counterfoil, voucher.
talonario *a* **libro —** receipt book.
talud *m* talus; slope, ramp, incline.
talla *f* height, size; cut; intaglio; wood carving; prisoner's ransom.
tallado *a* carved, engraved; **bien —** well-shaped.
tallar *vt* to carve; to engrave.
tallarín *m* noodle.
talle *m* figure, waist, bodice; **tomar por el —** to put one's arm around.
taller *m* workshop, workroom; laboratory; studio; cruet.
tallo *m* stalk, stem; shoot.
tamal *m Mex* tamale; *SA* intrigue.
tamaño *a* this big, so big; *m* dimensions, size.
tambalear *vi* to stagger, reel.
tambero *m Per* innkeeper; *Arg* tame, gentle (*cattle*)
también *ad* also, too
tambo *m SA* roadside inn.
tambocha *f Col* a poisonous ant.
tambor *m* drum; drummer.
tameme *m Chi, Mex, Per* Indian porter, carrier.
Támesis, el *m* the Thames.
tamiz *m* strainer, sieve; sifting cloth; riddle.
tamo *m* chaff, dust, fluff.
tampoco *ad* nor, neither.
tan *ad abbrev of* **tanto; — siquiera** even.
tanda *f* turn, task; shift, relay; gang (*of workers*).
tangible *a* tangible, manifest.
tanque *m* tank; pool, pond.
tantear *vt* to try, reckon, measure, to gauge; to feel around; to sound, fathom.
tanteo *m* computation, reckoning; score (*games*).
tanto *a ad* so much, as much; **por lo —** therefore; **otro —** as much again; *m* point (*in games*); **un — por ciento** a percentage.
tañer *vt* to play, strike up (on) (*musical instrument*).
tapa *f* lid, top, cover.
tapaboca *m* muffler.
tapadera *f* stopper; covering.
tápalo *m Mex* woman's shawl.
tapar *vt* to cover, hide, conceal; to disguise; to stop up, block up.
taparrabo *m* loincloth.
tapayagua *f Hond, Mex* drizzle.
tapete *m* small carpet, rug; **— verde** card table, green baize.
tapia *f* (*mud*) wall.
tapiar *vt* to wall up.
tapicería *f* upholstery; tapestry.
tapiz *m* tapestry, hanging.
tapizar *vt* to drape, hang (*with tapestry*).
tapón *m* stopper, cork, bung; **— de espita** spigot.
taquigrafía *f* shorthand.
taquígrafo *m* stenographer, shorthand typist.
taquilla *f* box office, booking office, counter (*in post office*); ticket office; letter file.
tara *f* tare; tally stick.
tarabita *f SA* main cable of rope bridge
tarantín *m CA, Cub* rubbish.
tararear *vti* to hum (*a tune*)
tarascón *m SA* wound with teeth, bite.
tardanza *f* delay, tardiness, slowness.
tardar *vi* to tarry, delay, be late; **— una hora en llegar** to take an hour to get there; **a más —** at the latest.
tarde *ad* late; *f* afternoon, evening; **de — en —** occasionally.
tardío *a* tardy, slow, late (*fruit etc*).
tardo *a* slow, sluggish, tardy, backward.
tarea *f* task, job, work.
tarifa *f* tariff, fare; price list, rate.
tarima *f* bench, dais, platform.
tarjeta *f* card; label; **— postal** postcard.
tarraconense *an* (*inhabitant*) of Tarragona.
tarro *m* earthenware jar.
tartamudear *vi* to stammer, stutter.
tartamudo *m* stammerer, stutterer.
tartana *f* (*covered*) two-wheeled carriage; buggy
tártaro *m* tartar; cream of tartar.
tarraya *f Col, Ven, PR* casting net.
tarugo *a SA* foolish; *m* wooden plug.
tasa *f* measure; estimate, valuation; appraisement; **precio de —** official price.
tasación *f* appraisement; price-fixing.

tasador *m* valuer; price-control inspector.
tasajear *vi SA* to jerk; slash, cut.
tasajo *m* (*hung, jerked, salt*) beef.
tasar *vt* to value, appraise; to regulate prices.
tasca *f* tavern, wineshop, dive.
tatarabuelo *m* great-great-grandfather.
tatuaje *m* tattooing.
taurino *a* **el arte —** the art of bull fighting.
tauromaquia *f* the art of bull fighting.
taxista *m* taxi driver.
taza *f* cup; bowl, basin (*of fountain*).
tazón *m* basin.
té *m* tea; tea party.
tea *f* torch, (*burning*) brand.
teatral *a* scenic, theatrical.
teatro *m* theatre, stage, playhouse; scene (*of event*); dramatic works; **el — de Lope** Lope's plays; **el — español** Spanish drama.
tecali *m Mex* transparent marble.
tecla *f* key (*piano*), note, stop.
teclado *m* keyboard.
técnica *f* technique.
técnico *a* technical; *n* technician.
tecnológico *a* technological.
techado *m* roofing, ceiling.
techo *m* roof, ceiling; dwelling, shelter.
techumbre *f* lofty roof.
tedio *m* loathing; boredom, tediousness.
tedioso *a* irksome, wearisome.
teja *f* (roof)tile; **sombrero de —** shovel hat; **de —s abajo** in this world, here below.
tejado *m* tiled roof; shed.
tejamaní *or* **tejamanil** *m Mex, Cub, Per* shingle, wood roof covering.
tejer *vt* to weave, wind, wreathe, plait, knit.
tejido *m* tissue, weaving; fabric; web.
tejón *m* badger; gold bar.
tela *f* fabric, stuff, cloth; cobweb; **— de araña** spider's web.
telar *m* loom, frame.
telaraña *f* cobweb, spider's web.
telefonear *vt* to telephone, ring up.
teléfono *m* telephone.
telegrafía *f* telegraphy; **— sin hilos** wireless telegraphy.
telegrafiar *vt* to wire, telegraph, cable.
telégrafo *m* telegraph; **— óptico** semaphore.
telegrama *m* telegram, dispatch, wire.
telele *m CA, Mex* swoon, fainting fit.
telescopio *m* telescope.
telón *m* curtain (*theat*).
tema *m* theme, subject, topic; strain, motif.
temario *m* agenda.
temblar (ie) *vi* to tremble, quiver, shiver, quake.
temblón *a* **álamo —** aspen.
temblor *m* tremor, trembling; **— de tierra** earthquake.
tembloroso *a* shaking, shivering.
temer *vt* to fear, dread, apprehend.
temerario *a* rash, reckless, hasty, imprudent, foolhardy.
temeridad *f* rashness, boldness, bold move.
temeroso *a* timid, fearful, nervous, apprehensive, timorous.
temible *a* awful, dreadful, terrible.
temor *m* dread, apprehension; fear, fright.
témpano *m* tympanum; iceberg; thick slice, slab.
temperamento *m* nature, constitution, temperament.
temperatura *f* temperature.
tempestad *f* storm, tempest; **— en un vaso de agua** storm in a teacup.
tempestuoso *a* rough, stormy, boisterous, high (*wind*).
templado *a* temperate, moderate; sober; tepid; in tune; modified, subdued.
templador *m* tuner; (sword) temperer; tuning hammer.
templanza *f* temperance, abstemiousness, moderation; mildness.
templar *vt* to temper; to allay, assuage; to moderate, modify, to tune; to trim (*sails*); *vr* to cool down; to be restrained.
templario *m* Knight Templar.
temple *m* temper (*metal*); disposition; spirit.
templo *m* temple, church, shrine.
temporada *f* season; spell; time spent; **pasar una —** to stay.
temporal *a* temporary; worldly; *m* gale, storm.
temporizar *vi* to temporize.
temprano *a* early; premature; *ad* early, betimes.
tenacidad *f* tenacity, doggedness; **con —** doggedly.
tenacillas *f pl* tongs, pincers, tweezers.
tenaz *a* tenacious, stubborn, obstinate.
tenaza *f* claw (*crab*); *pl* tongs, curling tongs; forceps; pliers.
tendedero *m* clothesline.
tendedor *m* rack, clothes horse.
tendencia *f* tendency, inclination, bent; liability (*to*); trend.
tendencioso *a* biased, tendentious.
tender *m* tender (*rl*).
tender (ie) *vt* to extend, stretch; to lead, conduce (*to*); to fling out (*nets*); *vi* to have a tendency (*to*); to aim (*at*); *vr* to stretch out, lie (*full length*).
tendero *m* shopkeeper, tradesman.
tendido *a* prostrate, stretched out; *m* row of seats; **— (eléctrico)** grid.
tendón *m* sinew; **— de Aquiles** Achilles' heel.
tenebroso *a* dark, gloomy; blind; cavernous, murky.

tenedor *m* holder; fork; ball boy (*games*); — **de libros** book-keeper.
teneduría *f* keeping; — **de libros** book-keeping.
tenencia *f* tenancy, occupancy, tenure; lieutenancy.
tener *vt* to have, hold; to own, possess; to keep; — **razón** to be right; — **gana** to have a mind to; — **que** to have to; — **hambre** to be hungry; — **miedo** to be afraid; — **sueño** to be sleepy; *vr* — **en pie** to remain on foot; — **de pie** to be standing.
tenería *f* tannery.
teniente *m* owner, tenant, holder; deputy; lieutenant; — **coronel** lieutenant-colonel; — **de navío** commander.
tenis *m* tennis; tennis court.
tenor *m* tenor, condition; (*mus*) tenor; **a** — **de** in compliance with.
tenorio *m* Don Juan, ladykiller.
tensión *f* tension, strain, tightness; voltage.
tenso *a* taut, stiff; tense.
tentación *f* temptation; attempt.
tentáculo *m* tentacle, feeler.
tentador *a* tempting, alluring; tentative; *m* tempter, Satan.
tentar (ie) *vt* to tempt; to try, essay, attempt; to feel, touch, pat, grope (*about*); to search, probe.
tentativa *f* attempt, trial, experiment.
tentempié *m* (*fam*) snack, bite.
tenue *a* thin, slender; faint, dim, slight; negligible.
tenuidad *f* feebleness; slenderness (*of hope, clue* etc).
teñir (i) *vt* to dye, tincture, tinge.
teocali *m Mex* teocalli (*temple*).
teología *f* theology, divinity.
teólogo *m* theologian, divine.
teoría *f* theory, speculation.
teóricamente *ad* theoretically, in theory.
teórico *a* theoretical; not real.
tequila *f Mex* a drink like gin.
tercera *f* (*mus*) third; procuress, bawd.
tercería *f* mediation, arbitration; third party rights.
tercero *a* third; *m* mediator; go-between, procurer; referee.
tercerón *an SA* mulatto.
terceto *m* (*poet*) tercet, triplet; (*mus*) trio.
terciado *a* crosswise, slanting; **azúcar** — brown sugar.
terciar *vt* to sling (*diagonally*), to divide into three parts; to join in conversation.
tercio *m* bale, bundle; good or bad turn; regiment; third part; **los —s** Foreign Legionaries (*Morocco*).
terciopelo *m* velvet.
terco *a* stubborn, obdurate, pig-headed, obstinate.
Teresa *f* Theresa.
tergiversación *f* distortion, perversion.
tergiversar *vt* to misrepresent, distort.
termas *f pl* hot springs.
terminación *f* end, ending, termination.
terminante *a* conclusive, definitive, final.
terminar *vt* to end, stop, complete, finish; *vi* to be over, come to an end; be over and done with.
término *m* end, completion; boundary, limit; district; term; expression; **primer** — foreground; — **medio** compromise, mean; average.
termómetro *m* thermometer; thermostat.
termos *m* thermos flask, vacuum flask.
ternera *f* calf, heifer; veal.
ternero *m* calf, bullock.
terneza *f* affection, fondness; endearments, words of love, fond phrases, loving things.
ternura *f* tenderness, affection, sweetness, sensitiveness.
terquedad *f* obstinacy, pig-headedness, stubbornness.
Terranova *f* Newfoundland.
terraplén *m* rampart, mound, bank.
terraza *f* terrace; two-handled jar.
terremoto *m* earthquake.
terreno *a* earthly, worldly; *m* plot, piece of ground, land, soil, terrain; **preparar el** — to pave the way.
terrestre *a* earthbound, earthly, terrestrial.
terrible *a* terrible, frightful, awful.
territorial *a* territorial.
territorio *m* territory, land; domain.
terrón *m* lump, mound; — **de azúcar** sugar lump.
terror *m* terror, fright, dread.
terruño *m* (*esp Galicia*) the old country, homeland, bit of earth.
terso *a* smooth, glossy.
tersura *f* smoothness; cleanliness; terseness.
tertulia *f* gathering, evening party; reunion, circle, group; café set.
tesis *f* thesis, dissertation; theme.
tesón *m* tenacity.
tesorería *f* treasury.
tesorero *m* treasurer, purser; canon in charge of relics.
tesoro *m* treasure, riches; exchequer.
testa *f* head.
testador *m* testator.
testamentario *m* executor (*of will*), administrator.
testamento *m* will; testament.
testar *vt* to will, make a testament; to erase, efface, blot out.
testarudo *a* willful, stubborn, headstrong.
testificar *vt* to witness, vouch, attest.
testigo *m* witness.

testimonio *m* warrant, attestation; **falso —** false accusation.
teta *f* breast, nipple; udder.
tetera *f* teapot; kettle.
tétrico *a* gloomy, sullen, somber, hair-raising.
textil *a* textile.
texto *m* text; authority.
textura *f* weaving; texture; fabric.
tez *f* complexion, skin.
ti *pn* you, thee (*after preposition*).
tía *f* aunt; goodwife, dame.
tibia *f* shinbone; flute.
tibieza *f* tepidity; lack of enthusiasm, lukewarmness.
tibio *a* tepid, lukewarm.
tibor *m* jar; *SA* chamberpot.
tiburón *m* shark.
tictac *m* pit-a-pat; ticking (*of clock*).
tiempo *m* time, epoch, season; opportunity, occasion; weather; **a —** timely; **de — en —** occasionally; **a — que** just as; **a su —** in (his) own good time; **con —** betimes, in good time, early.
tienda *f* shop; tent; awning.
tienta *f* probe; **andar a —s** to grope along.
tiento *m* feeling, touching, groping about; trial shot; preliminary flourish (*mus*); blind man's stick.
tierno *a* tender, soft; pathetic; delicate; **pan —** fresh bread.
tierra *f* ground; earth; land, soil; country; **perder —** to lose one's footing.
tieso *a* taut, stiff, straight, rigid; starchy, poker-backed.
tiesto *m* flowerpot.
tifo *m* typhus; **— asiático** cholera; **— de oriente** bubonic plague.
tifón *m* typhoon.
tifus *m* typhus.
tigre *m* tiger.
tijera *f* sawhorse; **silla de —** folding chair; **—s** scissors, shears.
tila *f* lime tree, lime flower; infusion of lime flowers.
tildar *vt* to cross out.
tilde *f* jot, sign over the letter **n.**
tiliche *m CA, Arg, Chi* drunk.
tilichero *m SA* pedlar.
tilín *m* —, — ting-a-ling; **tener —** to be attractive, make an appeal.
tilingo *a Arg, Mex* silly, foolish.
tilo *m* linden tree, lime tree.
timar *vt* to cheat, swindle, trick.
timbrar *vt* to seal, stamp.
timbre *m* signet, seal; stamp; timbre, tone; glorious deed.
timidez *f* timidity, bashfulness, shyness.
tímido *a* timid, shame-faced, bashful, shy; fearful, afraid.
timo *m* cheat, hoax, swindle.
timón *m* helm; beam (*of plow*).
timonel *m* coxswain, helmsman.
tímpano *m* eardrum; kettledrum; (*archit*) tympanum.
tina *f* earthen jar; vat; bathtub.
tinaja *f* large water jar.
tinerfeño *an* (*inhabitant*) of Tenerife.
tinglado *m* shed, roof; **conocer el —** to know the ropes.
tiniebla *f* darkness; **—s** the dark, the black night (*of ignorance*); outer darkness.
tino *m* tact; prudence; finesse; steady aim; knack, way; cunning hand; **sacar de —** to confound, exasperate.
tinta *f* ink; **de buena —** on good authority.
tinte *m* dyeing; paint, stain, dye; **— fijo** fast dye.
tintero *m* inkstand, inkpot; **me quedó en el —** I left that out, I completely forgot it.
tintirintín *m* bray (*of trumpet*), bugle call, trumpet blast.
tinto *a* dyed; **vino —** red wine.
tintorería *f* dry cleaner's, dyer's.
tintura *f* tincture. dye; smattering.
tío *m* uncle; (*fam*) fellow; **el — Paco** old Joe.
tiovivo *m* merry-go-round, roundabout.
típico *a* characteristic; genuine, representative.
tiple *f* soprano; chorus girl; *m* treble.
tipo *m* type, standard, model; letterpress type; person, chap; **un buen —** a good sort; (*exchange*) rate.
tipografía *f* typography, printing.
tipógrafo *m* printer.
tira *f* strip, band.
tirabuzón *m* corkscrew; ringlet, (*corkscrew*) curl.
tirada *f* cast, throw, stretch (*of time*); edition, printing; **de una —** at one time, at a stretch.
tirado *a* dirt cheap, given away.
tirador *m* marksman; drawer; handle, button, bell-pull.
tiranía *f* tyranny, cruelty.
tirano *m* tyrant; *a* tyrannical.
tirante *m* brace; stretcher, strut, tie-beam; shoestrap; **—s** braces, suspenders.
tirantez *f* tension, enseness, tightness.
tirar *vt* to draw; to dart, throw, hurl, fling; to cast off; to print; to squander **— al blanco** to shoot at a target; *vi* to draw, burn; to incline, tend; *vr* to fling oneself, make a dash (for).
tiritar *vi* to shiver.
tiro *m* shot; fling, cast, throw; team; draft (*of chimney*); shaft (*mine*); **de —s largos** in full dress; **de un —** at one fell swoop; **caballo de —** draft horse.
tiroteo *m* shooting, firing.
tísico *a* consumptive.
tisis *f* phthisis, consumption.
titánico *a* Titanic, gigantic, colossal.
títere *m* puppet, marionette; **—s** Punch and Judy show, puppet show.

titiritero *m* puppet master; Punch and Judy showman; juggler.
titilar *vi* to twinkle, wink, glitter.
titubear *vi* to falter, shilly-shally, hesitate; to totter, reel, stagger.
titular *a* titular, nominal; *f* headline; *vt* to title.
título *m* title; caption, headline; privilege, right, legal title; diploma; pretext; **—s** securities.
tiza *f* chalk.
tiznado *a* grimy, soot-begrimed, smudgy; CA, *Arg, Chi* drunk.
tiznar *vt* to smut, smudge, smear.
tizne *m* soot.
tizón *m* firebrand.
toalla *f* towel; **— sin fin** roller towel.
tobillo *m* ankle.
toca *f* bonnet, headdress, coif, hood.
tocado *a* touched; of unsound mind; *m* toilet, headdress.
tocador *m* dressing table; **juego de —** perfume and toilet set.
tocante *a* **— a** respecting, concerning, as for.
tocar *vt* to touch; to feel (*with hands*); to move; to play (*instruments*); to appertain, belong; to knock, ring (*bell*); to win (*lottery*); to be obliged to; to fall to one's lot; to call (*at a port*); **me toca de cerca** it strikes home, it concerns me intimately.
tocino *m* bacon; salt pork; **— del cielo** sweetmeat made of syrup and eggs.
todavía *ad* nevertheless, yet, still, even.
todo *a* all; every one; complete, total, whole; **— un hombre** quite a man; *m* whole, entirety; **con —** anyway, nevertheless, all the same.
todopoderoso *a* almighty; *m* Almighty God.
toga *f* toga; judge's robe; academic gown.
toldo *m* tent, awning; sunblind.
toledano *an* (*inhabitant*) of Toledo; **noche —a** sleepless night.
tolerable *a* bearable; allowable.
tolerancia *f* broadmindedness; permission.
tolerar *vt* to allow, tolerate; to bear, put up with, brook, suffer.
toma *f* hold; capture, conquest; dose; tap (*of water main*); outlet; wall socket; **más vale un — que dos te daré** a bird in the hand is worth two in the bush.
tomar *vt* to take, seize, grasp, get; to drink; to assume; to capture; **— té** to have tea; **— las de Villadiego** to take to one's heels.
Tomás *m* Thomas.
tomate *m* tomato.
tomillo *m* thyme.
tomo *m* volume, tome; importance.
ton *m* **sin — ni son** without rhyme or reason.
tonada *f* tune, song.
tonadilla *f* tune, lilt, air.
tonel *m* barrel, pipe, cask.
tonelada *f* ton (20 *cwt*).
tonelaje *m* tonnage.
tonelero *m* cooper, hooper.
tónico *a m* tonic; *f* tone, tonic.
tono *m* pitch, tone; key, scale; tune; manner, style; **darse —** to put on airs; **de buen —** smart, correct, fashionable, tasteful.
tonsura *f* tonsure; fleecing.
tontería *f* foolishness, stupidity; foolish thing (*to do*).
tonto *a* silly; *m* fool, silly man; dunce; blockhead; **a tontas y a locas** without rhyme or reason.
topar *vi* to run into, collide; to knock; to come upon, meet accidentally; *vr* **— con** to meet, come upon.
tope *m* butt; buffer; apex; **hasta los —s** to the top, absolutely packed.
topetón *m* collision.
tópico *a* topical; *m* subject, topic.
topil *m Mex* constable, policeman.
topo *m* mole.
topocho *a Ven* plump.
topografía *f* topography.
toque *m* touch; touching; ringing (*bells*); beat (*drum*); touchstone; trial, proof; point; **— de difuntos** passing bell.
toquilla *f* headdress; kerchief.
torbellino *m* whirlwind; swirl, rush.
torcedura *f* wrench, strain.
torcer (ue) *vt* to twist, wind, screw up, bend; to spin; to incline; *vr* to sprain, twist; to curve, wind.
torcido *a* twisted; crooked, bent, curved, awry.
tordo *a* dapple (*color*); *m* thrush.
torear *vti* to fight a bull.
toreo *m* (*the art of*) bullfighting.
torero *m* bullfighter.
tormenta *f* storm, tempest.
tormento *m* torture, torment; pang, anguish.
tormentoso *a* stormy, turbulent.
tornada *f* envoi; return.
tornar *vti* to turn, restore, return; to alter, change; *vr* to change, become.
tornasol *m* sunflower; shot silk.
tornasolado *a* (*silk*) shot, chatoyant.
tornear *vt* to turn (*with a lathe*).
tornero *m* turner.
torneo *m* tilt, tournament, joust.
tornera *f* portress (*in nunnery*).
tornillo *m* screw; vise; **apretar los —s** to put pressure on; **le falta un —** he has a screw loose.
torniquete *m* turnstile; torniquet.
torno *m* lathe; winch, potter's wheel; **en —** round about.
toro *m* bull; Taurus; **ir a los —s** to go to the bullfight.
toronja *f* grapefruit.
torpe *a* heavy, cloddish, clumsy; unhappy; dull; torpid; unchaste.
torpedo *m* torpedo.
torpeza *f* crassness, dullness; lewdness; clumsiness, awkwardness.

torre *f* tower, turret, keep; castle, rook (*chess*).
torrente *m* torrent, rush.
tórrido *a* torrid.
torta *f* pie, shortcake; (*fam*) slap; **—s y pan pintado** a mere trifle.
tortícolis *m* stiff neck.
tortilla *f* omelet(te); thin oven-cake.
tórtola *f* turtledove.
tortuga *f* turtle, tortoise.
tortuoso *a* winding, sinuous.
tortura *f* torture, torment, rack; torsion.
torturar *vt* to torment; *vr* to fret.
torvo *a* grim, stern, fierce.
tos *f* cough; **— ferina** whooping cough.
tosco *a* rough, coarse; boorish, uncouth.
toser *vi* to cough.
tostada *f* toast.
tostado *a* crisp, toasted; sunburned.
tostar (ue) *vt* to roast, toast; to scorch, burn; to tan.
tostón *m* buttered toast; small coin.
total *a* total, utter, entire; *m* total, whole, sum total.
totalmente *a* wholly, altogether, quite.
tozudo *a* obstinate.
traba *f* hobble; obstacle; bond, tie; clasp, brace.
trabajador *a* hardworking; *m* workman.
trabajar *vt* to toil, work; to till the soil.
trabajo *m* work, job, occupation; toil, sweat, labor, hardship; **—s forzados** hard labor, penal servitude.
trabajoso *a* painful, difficult; hard; uphill, laborious.
trabalenguas *m* tongue twister.
trabar *vt* to join, unite, connect, clasp; to begin (*friendship*); **—se la lengua** to stammer.
trabazón *f* connection, bracing, bond.
trabe *f* beam.
trabuco *m* blunderbuss.
tracala *f Mex, Per* scheme, trick.
tracalada *f SA* multitude.
tracalero *a Mex* tricky, artful.
tracción *f* traction, cartage.
tractor *m* tractor.
tradición *f* tradition.
traducción *f* translation, rendering.
traducir *vt* to translate, interpret.
traductor *m* translator.
traer *vt* to carry, bring, fetch; to draw, attract; to bring over; to bind.
traficar *vi* to deal, trade; to journey.
tráfico *m* trade, business; traffic.
tragaluz *m* skylight, bull's-eye.
tragar *vt* to gulp (down), swallow; **— el anzuelo** to be taken in.
tragedia *f* tragedy.
trágico *a* tragic.
trago *m* drink, draft, mouthful, gulp; **a —s** in stages.
tragón *m* glutton.
traición *f* perfidy; treason; disloyalty; treachery; **reo de —** state criminal.
traicionar *vt* to betray.
traidor *a* treacherous, perfidious, false; *m* traitor.
traje *m* dress, suit, costume; apparel, attire; **— de montar** riding habit; **— de etiqueta** evening dress; **— de luces** bullfighter's costume.
trajín *m* coming and going, rushing about.
trajinante *m* carrier.
trajinar *vt* to carry (*goods*); *vi* to dash to and fro; to be forever on the go.
trama *f* weft; plot (*of play, novel*); intrigue; fraud.
tramar *vt* to plot, scheme; to weave.
trámite *m* business transaction; step; procedure; *pl* stages, levels, procedure (*of administration*).
tramo *m* stretch, space, (*archit*) span; flight (*of stairs*).
tramoya *f* trick, artifice.
tramoyista *m* stage carpenter, scene shifter; trickster.
trampa *f* trap, spring, snare; trapdoor; foul play; **caer en la —** to fall into the trap.
trampear *vt* to obtain money under false pretenses.
trampista *m* swindler.
tramposo *a* deceitful, tricky.
tranca *f* (*on door*) bar, crossbar; truncheon.
trancar *vt* to bar; *vi* to stride along.
trance *m* predicament; emergency, critical hour, peril; **a todo —** anyway, at any risk, at all costs.
tranco *m* stride; **a —s** striding along, shambling along.
tranquilidad *f* calm, ease, quietude.
tranquilizar *vt* to appease, calm down, reassure.
tranquilo *a* placid, calm, quiet, untroubled, still.
transacción *f* transaction, arrangement.
transar *vt SA* to compromise, adjust, settle.
transatlántico *a* transatlantic; *m* liner.
transbordo *m* transshipment; transfer; change (*trains*).
transcripción *f* transcription, copy.
transcurrir *vi* to elapse.
transcurso *m* (*of time*) course, passage, passing.
transeúnte *a* transient; *m* passer-by.
transferir (ie) *vt* to transfer, make over, carry over.
transfigurar *vt* to transform, transfigure; *vr* to be transfigured.
transformación *f* transformation; metamorphosis; change.
transformador *m* (*el*) transformer.

transformar *vt* to change; to transform; *vr* to change, assume (*forms*), turn into.
tránsfuga *m* deserter; runaway.
transfusión *f* transfusion.
transgredir *vt* to transgress.
transgresión *f* transgression; sin; infringement (*of rules*).
transido *a* perished (with cold, hunger); — **de dolor** grief-stricken.
transigir *vt* to compromise; to compound; to accommodate (*differences*).
transitar *vi* to travel; to pass by.
tránsito *m* transit, transition; journey, course, way; removal.
transitorio *a* transitory, ephemeral.
transmisión *f* transmission.
transmitir *vt* to transmit, convey, forward.
transparencia *f* transparency.
transparente *a* transparent, limpid, crystalline; obvious.
transpirar *vi* to transpire, perspire.
transponer *vt* to transpose, remove; *vr* to set (*the sun*).
transportado *a* rapt; in ecstasy.
transportar *vt* to carry, shift, transport, convey; to enrapture; *vr* to be carried away.
transporte *m* transportation; conveyance, hauling, carriage; rapture, transport.
transverberación *f* (*mystic*) transfixing.
transversal *a* transversal, cross.
tranvía *m* tram(way), streetcar.
trapacería *f* fraud, cheating.
trapense *an* Trappist.
trapero *m* ragdealer, rag-and-bone man.
trapiche *m* sugar mill, olive press.
trapisonda *f* scuffle; snare.
trapo *m* rag, duster; **a todo** — with might and main, all-out; **poner como un trapo** to wipe the floor with.
traqueteo *m* tossing, jolting, rattling.
trarilongo *m Chi* Indian headband.
tras *prep* after; behind; beyond; besides; **día — día** day in, day out.
trascendencia *f* consequence, significance.
trascendental *a* transcendental, far-reaching, momentous.
trascender *vi* to extend itself; to be pervasive; to leak out, become known.
trasegar (ie) *vt* to upset; to rummage; to decant (*wine*).
trasero *a* hind, rear, back; *m* backside, bottom, buttocks.
trasgo *m* hobgoblin, bogeyman.
trashumante *a* nomadic (*flocks of sheep*).
trasladar *vt* to transfer, remove; to translate; *vr* to change place, pass, repair (*from one place to another*).
traslado *m* transfer; copy.
traslapar *vt* to overlap.
trasluz *m* reflected light, glow; **al** — through, athwart.
trasnochador *m* night owl, nightbird.
trasnochar *vi* to sit up all night; to make merry at night.
traspapelar *vt* to mislay (*papers*).
traspasar *vt* to pierce through; to trespass; to transfer.
traspaso *m* transfer, conveyance (*of property*).
traspié *m* stumble; lapse.
trasplantar *vt* to transplant; *vr* to migrate.
traspunte *m* (*theat*) prompter.
trasquilar *vt* to shear, clip.
traste *m* (*mus*) fret; **dar al — con** to spoil, waste.
trastienda *f* back, inner shop.
trasto *m* piece of furniture; piece of lumber; **—s** implements, bits and pieces.
trastornado *a* upset; out of one's senses, crazy.
trastornar *vt* to disturb; to upset, overthrow; to confuse, derange.
trastorno *m* disorder, upset, disturbance; upheaval.
trasunto *m* copy, image.
tratable *a* amenable, approachable.
tratado *m* treaty; treatise.
tratamiento *m* treatment; title, address, style.
tratar *vt* to handle, treat; to trade; deal (in); to deal (with); to meet; — **de** to try, to address as; — **con** to deal with; **¿de qué se trata?** what is it all about?
trato *m* treatment; behavior, manners; pact; dealings, converse, relationship; **mal** — ill usage.
través *m* inclination; reverse; **al** — aslant, across; **dar al** — to be stranded.
travesaño *m* bolster; crossbar; (*rl*) sleeper.
travesía *f* crossroad; sea voyage, passage, crossing.
travesura *f* prank; mischief; mischievousness, naughtiness.
traviesa *f* crosstie; rafter; (*rl*) tie, sleeper.
travieso *a* restless; impish, mischievous; wanton.
trayecto *m* space; tract; road.
trayectoria *f* trajectory, flight.
traza *f* sketch, outline; aspect; trace, smell.
trazado *m* layout, plan.
trazar *vt* to draw, sketch; to lay out, plan out.
trazo *m* drawing, tracing; outline.
trébol *m* clover, trefoil, shamrock.
trecho *m* span, space; **a —s** by (at) intervals.
tregua *f* truce; respite.
treinta *an* thirty.
tremendo *a* tremendous, awful; huge, imposing.
trémulo *a* tremulous.

tren *m* outfit, train; suite, following; — **expreso** express train; — **de recreo** excursion train; — **de mercancías** goods train; freight train; — **de correo** mail train.
trenza *f* braid, lock (*hair*); —**s** tresses.
trenzar *vt* to braid, weave, twist; *vi* to caper, interweave feet in dancing.
trepadora *f* climbing plant, creeper.
trepar *vi* to climb, swarm up.
trepidación *f* trepidation.
trepidar *vi* to shake, quake, tremble.
tresillo *m* ombre (*card game*); three-piece suite.
treta *f* trick, feint, wile, ruse.
triangular *a* three-cornered.
triángulo *m* triangle.
tribu *f* tribe.
tribuna *f* tribune, rostrum, pulpit; box, gallery.
tribunal *m* bar, judgment seat, court of justice.
tributar *vt* to pay taxes; — **homenaje** to pay homage.
tributo *m* contribution, tribute, tax; (*praise*) tribute.
tricornio *m* three-cornered hat.
trifulca *f* squabble, row.
trigal *m* wheatfield.
trigo *m* wheat; *pl* crops.
trigonometría *f* trigonometry.
trigueño *a* dark, brownish, nut-brown, chestnut.
trilladera *f* harrow.
trillado *a* hackneyed; **camino** — beaten track.
trilladora *f* threshing machine.
trillar *vt* to thresh.
trimestre *m* quarter; term (*school*).
trinar *vi* to warble, trill.
trincar *vt* to bind, make fast; to drink (*to health*).
trinchar *vt* to carve.
trinche *m* *SA* fork.
trinchera *f* entrenchment; trench.
trineo *m* sleigh, sled.
trinidad *f* trinity.
trino *m* trill, warble.
trinquete *m* foremast; catch, racket; **a cada** — at every step.
tripa *f* belly, gut; *pl* intestines, bowels; **hacer de —s corazón** to pluck up one's courage.
triple *a* triple.
trípode *m* tripod, trivet.
tripulación *f* ship's crew.
tripular *vt* to man.
triscar *vi* to hurry, hustle, make merry; to set (*a saw*).
triste *a* sad, sorrowful, gloomy.
tristeza *f* sadness, melancholy, grief, pain.
triturar *vt* to grind, pulverize, mash.
triunfar *vi* to conquer, be victorious, win.
triunfo *m* triumph, victory; trump (*at cards*).
trivial *a* trivial, ordinary, unimportant, mean, trite.
triza *f* bit, small piece, mite, shred.
trocar *vt* to barter, exchange; to change, to equivocate; *vr* to change, change places with.
trocha *f* cross-path, short cut, track.
troche *ad* **a — y moche** regardless, pell mell, without rhyme or reason.
trofeo *m* trophy, spoils (*of war*).
troj(e) *f* granary, barn (*for storing fruit*), straw- or earth-covered heap (*of potatoes, turnips, olives*).
tromba *f* water spout.
trombón *m* trombone.
trompa *f* proboscis; (*mus*) horn; trunk (*elephant*); (*child's*) top.
trompada *f* blow with fist; bump, collision.
trompeta *f* bugle, trumpet; *m* bugler.
trompetazo *m* bugle (blast, call).
trompo *m* spinning top.
trompón *m* narcissus; **a** — helter-skelter.
tronar (ue) *vi* to thunder.
tronco *m* trunk (*of tree, animal*); stem, stalk; team (*of horses*); **dormir como un** — to sleep like a log.
tronchar *vt* to chop off, lop off, break off; *vr* — **de risa** to burst with laughing.
tronera *f* embrasure; porthole, dormer; *m* harum-scarum.
tronido *m* thunder, sudden noise.
trono *m* throne; the royal rights.
tropa *f* troops, soldiers, crowd; — **ligera** skirmishing troops.
tropel *m* rush, heap, jumble; **de, en** — in disorder, pell-mell, higgledy-piggledy, in a mass, in a crowd.
tropelía *f* arbitrary action; vexation, outrage.
tropezar (ie) *vi* to stumble, strike (upon) (on); to meet by accident.
tropezón *m* slip, trip, stumbling; obstacle, snag.
trópico *m* tropic.
tropiezo *m* obstacle, stumbling block, hitch, embarrassment, fault.
trotar *vi* to trot.
trote *m* trot; **al** — at the double.
trova *f* ballad.
trovador *m* troubadour, minstrel.
trovar *vt* to versify, make (rhymes, verses).
Troya *f* Troy.
trozo *m* piece, fragment, length, section.
truco *m* trick, gadget, thing.
truculencia *f* truculence; cruelty.
truculento *a* truculent; cruel, fierce.
trucha *f* trout.
trueno *m* thunder.
trueque *m* exchange, barter.
trufa *f* truffle; fraud, deceit.
truhán *m* scoundrel, knave; jester.
truncar *vt* to truncate, cut short, mutilate.
tu *a* your, thy.
tú *pn* you, thou.

tubérculo *m* tuber; tubercle.
tubería *f* pipes, piping, set of tubes.
tubo *m* pipe, tube.
tuco *a Bol, Ec, PR* armless.
tuerca *f* nut, female screw.
tuerto *m* wrong; one-eyed person; **a tuertas o a derechas** rightly or wrongly, appropriately or no.
tuétano *m* marrow.
tufo *m* fume, vapor; offensive smell; presumption, snobbishness.
tugurio *m* hut, cottage, hovel.
tul *m* tulle.
tulipán *m* tulip.
tullido *a* lamed, hurt, crippled.
tumba *f* grave, tomb.
tumbado *a* prone, lying down.
tumbar *vt* to fell, floor, throw down; *vr* to lie down, fling down (*into chair etc*), drop.
tumbo *m* fall, somersault.
tumido *a* swollen, frostbitten.
tumor *m* tumor.
tumulto *m* tumult, row, uproar; mob.
tuna *f* prickly pear.
tunante *m* rascal, rogue, (*fam*) loafer.
tunda *f* shearing of cloth; beating (up).
tundir *vt* to shear (*cloth*).
túnel *m* tunnel.
túnica *f* tunic.
tuno *m* rascal, rogue, truant.
tupé *m* toupee; cheek, impertinence.
tupido *a* dense, thick, overgrown, choked.
turba *f* rabble; peat, turf.
turbación *f* confusion, disturbance.
turbar *vt* to disturb, trouble.
turbina *f* turbine.
turbio *a* turbid, troubled, obscure.
turbión *m* squall, shower.
turbulencia *f* turbulence.
turbulento *a* turbulent, disorderly; muddy, troubled.
turco *an* Turk, Turkish.
turnar *vi* to alternate, take turns.
turno *m* turn; **por —** by turns.
turquesa *f* turquoise.
Turquía *f* Turkey.
turrón *m* nougat, almond sweetmeat.
tusa *f Bol, Col, Ven* corncob; *CA, Cub* corn husks.
tutear *vt* to address familiarly, using *tú* form.
tutela *f* guardianship, protection.
tutelar *a* tutelary.
tutor *m* tutor, guardian.
tuyo *a* your; *pn* yours.

U

u *cj* or (*used instead of* **o** *before* o *or* ho).
ubérrimo *a* teeming, abounding, luxuriant.
ubicación *f* location, position.
ubicar *vir* to lie, be situated.
ubicuidad *f* ubiquity.
ubicuo *a* ubiquitous.
ubre *f* udder.
ufanarse *vr* to boast, pride oneself.
ufano *a* conceited, arrogant, contented.
ujier *m* usher; doorkeeper; janitor.
úlcera *f* ulcer.
ulpo *m Per, Chi* gruel made of toasted maize.
ulterior *a* further, farther.
ulteriormente *ad* further, in time to come.
ultimar *vt* to finish, put finishing touches to, finish (off).
último *a* last, latest, ultimate, most recent; **por —** finally; **a —s de** toward the end of.
ultrajar *vt* to insult, outrage.
ultraje *m* outrage, insult.
ultramarino *a* ultramarine; *p* foreign produce, groceries.
ultratumba *ad* beyond the grave.
ulular *vi* to howl, hoot (*of owl*).
umbral *m* threshold; lintel.
umbrío *a* shady; umbrageous.
un, una *art* a, an; a, one.
unánime *a* unanimous.
unanimidad *f* unanimity.
unción *f* unction.
uncir *vt* to yoke.
undoso *a* wavy, undulating.
undulación *f* undulation, wave motion.
ungir *vt* to anoint, consecrate.
ungüento *m* unguent, ointment.
único *a* only, unique, single.
unidad *f* unity, agreement, unit.
unificar *vt* to unite, unify.
uniformar *vt* to uniform, make (alike, uniform).
uniforme *a* uniform, regular; *m* uniform.
uniformidad *f* uniformity, regularity.
unigénito *a* only-begotten.
unión *f* union, conjunction.
Unión Soviética *f* Soviet Union.
Unión Sudafricana *f* Union of South Africa.
unir *vt* to unite, join, connect, bring together; *vr* to join (up) (with), share.
unísono *a* unison; **al —** together, with one voice.
universal *a* universal.
universidad *f* university.
universitario *a* of university; *mf* student.
universo *m* universe.
un(o) *an pn* one.
untar *vt* to anoint, smear, oil, grease; **— las manos** to grease the palms.
unto *m* grease, ointment, fat (*of animals*).
untuoso *a* unctuous, oily, greasy.
untura *f* liniment, ointment.
uña *f* (*finger etc*) nail; **hincar la —** to sting, overcharge; **ser — y carne** to be inseparable, fast friends.

uranio *m* uranium.
urbanidad *f* urbanity, civility, culture.
urbano *a* urban, urbane, courteous, polished.
urdimbre *f* warp, warping chain; web (*of plot*).
urdir *vt* to warp, plot, scheme, weave.
urgencia *f* urgency, exigence.
urgente *a* urgent, pressing, convincing.
urgir *vi* to be urgent, be of the utmost importance.
urna *f* urn; ballot box.
urraca *f* magpie.
uruguayo *an* Uruguayan.
usado *a* used, accustomed; worn (out, thin), secondhand.
usanza *f* usage, custom.
usar *vt* to use, wear; *vi* to be wont, be accustomed; to be worn.
usía *f* lordship.
uso *m* usage, use, custom, fashion, enjoyment, loan, usufruct, wear and tear; **al** — fashionable, like others; **estar en buen** — to be full of good wear.
usted *pn* you.
usual *a* usual, customary, normal, general.
usufructo *m* usufruct, enjoyment.
usura *f* usury.
usurario *a* usurious.
usurero *m* usurer, moneylender.
usurpación *f* usurpation.
usurpar *vt* to usurp.
utensilio *m* utensil, implement; *pl* tools.
útil *a* useful; *m pl* tools.
utilidad *f* utility, usefulness, profit.
utilizar *vt* to utilize, make use of.
utópico *a* Utopian.
uva *f* grape; — **pasa** raisin; — **espín** gooseberry.

V

vaca *f* cow, beef.
vacación *f* vacation; *pl* holidays, vacations.
vacante *a* vacant, disengaged, unoccupied; *f* vacancy (*ie job*).
vacar *vi* to be vacant, vacate, give up.
vaciado *m* cast (*in mold*).
vaciar *vt* to empty, cast (pour) out.
vaciedad *f* emptiness, banality, commonplace.
vacilación *f* hesitation, vacillation.
vacilante *a* hesitating, irresolute, unstable.
vacilar *vi* to hesitate, waver, vacillate.
vacío *a* empty, void; vain; untenanted; *m* vacuum, empty space; hollowness, blank, lacuna; **ir de** — to travel empty.
vacunar *vt* to vaccinate.
vacuno *a* bovine, vaccine.
vacuo *a* empty, hollow, vacant; *m* vacuum.
vadear *vi* to wade across, ford.
vado *m* (*river*) ford; resource; **dar** — to expedite.
vagabundo *a* vagabond, vagrant; *m* tramp.
vagancia *f* vagrancy.
vagar *vi* to loiter about, roam; to be idle.
vagido *m* cry (*of newborn child*).
vago *a* vague, errant, roving; *m* vagabond; loafer.
vagón *m* wagon.
vaguedad *f* vagueness, ambiguity.
vahido *m* dizziness, fainting spell.
vaho *m* fume, effluvium, hot smell (*of animals*).
vaina *f* scabbard, sheath; pod.
vainilla *f* vanilla.
vaivén *m* sway, oscillation, vibration, coming and going.
vajilla *f* dish, pot ware, pots, dinner service.
vale *m* bond, I O U.
valedero *a* valid.
valenciano *an* (*inhabitant*) of Valencia.
valentía *f* valor, courage, bravery.
valentón *m* bully, swaggerer.
valer *vti* to be worth, cost, be the same as, amount to; to defend; — **la pena** to be worth while; to be the (cause of, reason for, explanation); *vr* to make use of, take advantage of; **más vale tarde que nunca** better late than never.
valeroso *a* courageous.
valía *f* price, value, worth; influence.
validar *vt* to validate.
validez *f* validity, soundness.
valido *a* accepted; — **de** under cover of, backed (up) by; *m* favorite.
válido *a* valid.
valiente *a* spirited, courageous, valiant, gallant.
valija *f* mailbag; valise, bag.
valimiento *m* value, support, benefit; good graces.
valioso *a* expensive, costly, valuable, wealthy.
valor *m* price, worth, value; valor, courage; validity; *pl* (*com*) bonds, stocks.
valoración *f* valuation.
valorar *vt* to value, appraise.
valsar *vi* to waltz.
valuación *f* valuation, appraisal.
valuar *vt* to appraise, value, set price to.
válvula *f* valve; — **de escape** safety valve; — **de seguridad** safety valve.
valla *f* fence, hurdle, stockade, barrier, impediment.
valladar *m* obstacle.
vallado *m* enclosure.
vallar *vt* to fence.
valle *m* valley, dale; — **de lágrimas** vale of tears.

vallesoletano *an* (*inhabitant*) of Valladolid.
vampiro *m* vampire; ghoul; bat.
vanagloria *f* vaingloriousness; conceit.
vándalo *m* vandal.
vanguardia *f* vanguard.
vanidad *f* vanity, levity, conceit, shallowness, uselessness.
vanidoso *a* vain, showy.
vano *a* shallow, vain, useless, futile; arrogant; *m* opening (*in wall*).
vapor *m* steam, vapor, fume, mist; steamship, boat.
vaporoso *a* vaporous.
vapul(e)ar *vt* to beat (*with sticks*).
vaquero *m* cowboy, herdsman.
vaqueta *f* leather.
vara *f* rod, twig, stock, wand; measure (2·78 *ft*), yard; **— de pescar** fishing rod.
varada *f* running aground.
varadero *m* shipyard, repair dock.
varar *vi* to be stranded; to ground.
varear *vt* to beat (*fruit trees*).
variable *a* variable, changeable.
variación *f* variation, change.
variante *f* variant.
variar *vt* to change, shift; to deviate (*magnetic needle*).
variedad *f* variety.
varilla *f* rod; curtain rod; **— mágica** magician's wand.
varillero *m SA* peddler.
vario *a* different, inconstant, variable, variegated; *pl* several, various.
varón *a m* male; man.
varonil *a* manly, male, vigorous.
vasco *an* Basque.
vascuence *m* Basque language.
vasija *f* jar.
vaso *m* glass, tumbler, vessel.
vástago *m* sucker, shoot; offspring, scion.
vasto *a* huge, extensive, immense, vast.
vate *m* poet, bard.
vaticinar *vt* to divine, predict.
vaticinio *m* prediction.
vaya *f* scoff, jest; *excl* go!, come!, indeed!
vecinal *a* **camino —** country road, side road.
vecindad *f* neighborhood, vicinity.
vecindario *m* local inhabitants.
vecino *a* neighboring, near; *m* neighbor; resident.
veda *f* close season (*for hunting*).
vedado *m* enclosed (*private*) land.
vedar *vt* to forbid, prohibit, close to.
veedor *m* busybody; overseer.
vega *f* open plain (*cultivated*).
vegetal *a* vegetable; *m* plant.
vegetar *vi* to vegetate, live.
vehemencia *f* vehemence, impetuosity, power, force.
vehemente *a* impetuous, vehement.
vehículo *m* vehicle.
veinte *an* twenty.
vejación *f* vexation, oppression.
vejar *vt* to vex, oppress, censure.
vejez *f* old age.
vejiga *f* bladder; blister.
vela *f* candle; sail; wakefulness, vigil; **hacerse a la—** to set sail; **en—** without sleeping, without going to bed.
velado *a* hidden, veiled.
velador *m* watchman; keeper; candlestick; lamp stand.
velar *vi* to keep awake; to watch, be vigilant; *vt* to watch; to veil, cover.
veleidad *f* velleity, fickleness, inconstancy.
veleidoso *a* fickle, inconstant.
velero *a* swift-sailing; *m* glider.
veleta *f* weathercock; pennant; *m* unstable person, fickle person.
velís *m SA* valise.
velo *m* veil; cloak, pretense; **correr (echar) el — sobre** to draw a veil over, cover up; **tomar el —** to take the veil.
velocidad *f* speed, rapidity, swiftness.
veloz *a* swift, fast, nimble.
vello *m* down, nap.
vellocino *m* fleece; **— de oro** golden fleece.
vellón *m* fleece, wool; copper and silver alloy; **real de —** five-cents coin.
velloso *a* hairy.
velludo *a* downy; hirsute, hairy; *m* shag.
vena *f* vein; seam; lode (*mine*); inspiration.
venablo *m* javelin, dart.
venado *m* stag; venison.
venal *a* venal, mercenary; relating to the veins.
venalidad *f* venality.
vencedor *m* victor, conqueror; (*in race etc*) winner; vanquisher.
vencer *vt* to conquer, vanquish, overpower; *vi* to fall due; **— un plazo** expire (*a term*), become due.
vencido *a* overcome, conquered; due (*of bill*).
vencimiento *m* maturity (*of bill*).
venda *f* bandage.
vendaje *m Col, CR, Ec, Per* gratuity, tip.
vendar *vt* to bandage; to blind.
vendaval *m* strong wind, gale.
vendedor *m* seller, vendor, huckster, salesman.
vender *vt* to sell; to betray one's friends (*for money*); **— al por mayor** to sell wholesale; **— al pormenor** to sell retail; **— a plazo** to sell on credit; **— al contado** to sell for cash; *vr* to give oneself away.
vendido *a* sold; betrayed.
vendimia *f* vintage, grape harvest.
vendimiar *vt* to harvest (*grapes*).
veneno *m* poison, venom.
venenoso *a* poisonous.
venera *f* scallop shell; spring (*of water*).

venerable *a* venerable.
veneración *f* worship.
venerar *vt* to venerate, worship, honor.
venero *m* spring (*of water*); lode, seam (*of metal*).
venezolano *an* Venezuelan.
venganza *f* revenge; vengeance.
vengar *vt* to avenge; *vr* to take vengeance.
vengativo *a* vindictive, revengeful.
venia *f* leave, permission; bow.
venial *a* venial, pardonable.
venida *f* arrival.
venidero *a* coming; future.
venir *vi* to come; to become, fit; to determine; — **en ello** to agree to it; — **al caso** to be relevant; — **a parar** to come to; — **a menos** to come down in the world; — **a las manos** to come to blows; **venirse abajo** to come (*tumbling*) down, collapse.
venta *f* sale; inn; — **pública** public auction.
ventaja *f* advantage, profit, gain.
ventajoso *a* advantageous, profitable, lucrative.
ventana *f* window.
ventarrón *m* gale, strong wind.
ventear *vt* to scent; *vi* to blow (*the wind*).
ventero *m* innkeeper.
ventilación *f* ventilation.
ventilar *vt* to ventilate, examine.
ventisca *f* snowdrift, blizzard.
ventisquero *m* snowstorm; glacier.
ventosear *vir* to break wind.
ventoso *a* windy.
ventrílocuo *m* ventriloquist.
ventriloquía *f* ventriloquism.
ventura *f* happiness; luck; **por** — by chance; **probar** — to try one's luck.
venturoso *a* happy, successful.
ver *vti* to see; to inspect, look into; to consider; to visit.
vera *f* border, edge (*of road*).
veracidad *f* veracity, truthfulness.
veranear *vi* to spend the summer holidays.
veraneo *m* summer holidays; **lugar de** — (*summer*) holiday resort.
veraniego *a* of summer.
veranillo *m* — **de San Martín** Indian summer.
verano *m* summer.
veras *f pl* reality, truth; **de** — in truth, really.
veraz *a* truthful.
verbena *f* verbena; wake, fair (*on eve of local saint's day*).
verbigracia *f* for example, eg.
verbo *m* the Word; verb.
verboso *a* verbose.
verdad *f* truth; **en** — truly; **la pura** — the honest truth.
verdadero *a* true, real, sincere, genuine.
verde *a* green; unripe; immodest; — **limón** bright green; **viejo** — gay old dog, amorous old gentleman.
verdor *m* verdure, greenness, freshness.
verdugo *m* hangman, executioner.
verdulero *m* greengrocer; *f* vegetable woman; fishwife.
verdura *f* verdure, greenness; vegetables.
vereda *f* footpath, by-path.
veredicto *m* verdict.
vergonzoso *a* shy, bashful; shameful, disgraceful.
vergüenza *f* shame; modesty, shyness; shamefulness; **perder la** — to lose all shame; **tener** — to be ashamed, have a sense of what is proper, have self-respect.
verídico *a* truthful; **es** — it's a fact.
verificar *vt* to verify, prove, substantiate; to carry out; *vr* to take place.
verja *f* grate, grating, iron railing.
verosímil *a* likely, probable, credible.
verruga *f* wart.
versado *a* — **en** conversant with, familiar with, experienced.
versar *vi* to turn around; — **sobre** to deal with, discuss; *vr* to become (be) conversant.
versátil *a* inconstant, versatile; fickle.
versículo *m* verse (*in Bible*).
versificar *vi* to make verses, versify.
versión *f* version, translation.
verso *m* verse, line (*poet*), stanza.
vértebra *f* vertebra.
vertedero *m* dump, tip.
verter (ie) *vt* to pour, spill, empty, dump; to translate; *vi* to run (*of liquids*).
vertical *a* vertical.
vértice *m* vertex; apex.
vertiente *m or f* slope, watershed, side (*of mountain*).
vértigo *m* giddiness.
vertiginoso *a* giddy, dizzy.
vesícula *f* vesicle.
vespertino *a* vespertine, evening.
vestíbulo *m* vestibule; hall.
vestido *m* dress; clothes; costume; — **de corte** court dress; — **de etiqueta** full dress; — **de noche** evening dress.
vestidura *f* (*eccles*) vestment; robe.
vestigio *m* trace, vestige, remains; relic.
vestiglo *m* horrid monster.
vestimenta *f* garments; *pl* ecclesiastical robes.
vestir (i) *vt* to clothe, dress; to cloak, palliate; *vi* to dress; *vr* to dress oneself.
vestuario *m* wardrobe, clothing; outfit; vestry.
veta *f* lode (*mine*); vein (*wood*).
vetado *a* streaked, veined, grained.
veterano *an* veteran.
veterinaria *f* veterinary science.
veto *m* veto.
vetustez *f* venerable antiquity.
vez *f* turn; time; **a la** — at the same

time; **uno a la** — one at a time; **en — de** instead of; **de una —** at once; **de una — para siempre** once for all; **a veces** sometimes; **hacer las veces de** to act as substitute for; **dos veces** twice.
vía *f* way, road, track; passage; **— férrea** railway; **— ancha** broad gauge; **— estrecha** narrow gauge; **en — recta** straight along.
viable *a* feasible.
viajante *m* traveling salesman.
viajar *vi* to travel, journey.
viaje *m* travel, trip, journey.
viajero *m* traveler.
vianda *f* food, meal, meat.
viandante *m* traveler, wanderer, tramp.
viático *m* viaticum, host.
víbora *f* viper.
vibración *f* vibration, shaking.
vibrar *vt* to vibrate; to shake, to oscillate.
vicario *a* vicarious; *m* priest-in-charge.
Vicente *m* Vincent.
viciado *a* contaminated, foul, perverted.
viciar *vt* to vitiate, spoil; to adulterate; to make void; to pervert, corrupt.
vicio *m* vice, depravity; defect, blemish.
vicioso *a* vicious, defective; abundant.
vicisitud *f* vicissitude.
víctima *f* victim.
victoria *f* victory.
victorioso *a* victorious, triumphant.
vichoso *a Arg, Chi* weak, disabled.
vid *f* vine.
vida *f* life; livelihood, liveliness; **de por —** for life; **en la —** never.
vidente *m* seer.
vidriar *vt* to glaze.
vidriera *f* showcase, show window.
vidriero *m* glass-blower, glazier.
vidrio *m* glass.
vidrioso *a* vitreous; brittle; touchy.
viejo *a* old, antique; *m* old man.
vienés *an* Viennese.
viento *m* wind; *pl* **—s generales** trade winds; **— en popa** favorable wind, (*to sail*) merrily along.
vientre *m* belly, abdomen, stomach.
viernes *m* Friday; **cara de —** face of misery, glum face.
viga *f* beam, girder, joist.
vigente *a* in force (*of law*).
vigía *f* watchtower; *m* watch, lookout.
vigilancia *f* vigilance, watchfulness.
vigilar *vt* to watch, watch over, oversee.
vigilia *f* vigil, wakeful nights, wakefulness; fast; (*mil*) watch, guard.
vigor *m* strength, energy, force.
vigoroso *a* vigorous, active.
vigués *an* (*inhabitant*) of Vigo.
vigueta *f* small beam.
vihuela *f* lute.
vil *a* vile, mean, low; infamous, abject, contemptible.
vileza *f* vileness, meanness, lowness.
vilipendiar *vt* to revile.
vilo en — *ad* suspended, in the air, in suspense.
vilote *m Arg, Chi* cowardly, timid.
villa *f* town; villa.
Villadiego *m* **tomar las de —** to take to one's heels.
villancico *m* Christmas carol.
villanía *f* villainy, lowness.
villano *a* rustic, common; villainous; *m* villain; commoner.
villorrio *m* hamlet.
vinagre *m* vinegar.
vincular *vt* to entail; to perpetuate.
vínculo *m* tie, bond.
vincha *f SA* ribbon, handkerchief for head or hair.
vindicar *vt* to vindicate, clear.
vino *m* wine; **— tinto** red wine.
viña *f* vineyard.
viñedo *m* vineyard.
viñeta *f* vignette.
violar *vt* to violate, infringe.
violencia *f* violence, intensity.
violentar *vt* to enforce, violate, force open; *vr* to force oneself, do violence to oneself.
violento *a* violent, forced, strained, excessive.
violeta *f* violet; **erudición a la —** superficial learning.
violín *m* violin.
violón *m* bass-viol, double bass.
virar *vi* to tack, veer.
virgen *a* virgin, pure, chaste, spotless; *f* virgin, maid.
viril *a* virile, manly.
virilidad *f* virility, manliness.
virreinato *m* viceroyship.
virrey *m* viceroy.
virtualmente *ad* virtually.
virtud *f* virtue; power; force, courage; goodness; **en — de** in (by) virtue of.
virtuoso *a* virtuous, just.
viruela *f* pock; smallpox.
virulencia *f* virulence, acrimony.
virulento *a* virulent, malignant.
viruta *f* (*wood*) shaving.
visado *m* visa.
visaje *m* grimace, smirk.
víscera *f* viscus; viscera.
viscoso *a* slimy; glutinous, viscid.
visera *f* peak (*of cap*), eyeshade.
visible *a* visible, evident.
visión *f* sight, vision.
visita *f* visit, call; guest, visitor.
visitar *vt* to visit; to call upon.
vislumbrar *vt* to catch a glimpse of, make out dimly, conjecture.
vislumbre *f* glimpse, surmise, appearance.
viso *m* prospect, outlook.
víspera *f* eve, day before; *pl* vespers
vista *f* sight, view, prospect, vista eye; aspect; apparition; **a la —**

on sight (*bills*), on demand; **a tres días —** at three days' sight; **a primera —** at first view; **conocer de —** to know by sight; **hacer la — gorda** to shut one's eyes to; **en — de** in view of.
visto *a* seen; evident; *cj* whereas; **— bueno** correct, approved; **— que** seeing that.
vistoso *a* showy, beautiful, loud.
vital *a* vital, lively.
vitalicio *a* lasting for life, during life; **pensión —a** life pension, annuity.
vitela *f* vellum, parchment.
vítreo *a* of glass; vitreous.
vitrina *f* show *or* display case.
vitualla *f* victuals; food.
vituperar *vt* to blame, vituperate, curse.
vituperio *m* blame, reproach, insult, curse.
viudez *f* widowhood.
viudo, a *m* widower; *f* widow.
vivac *m* bivouac.
vivacidad *f* lifeliness, gaiety, brilliance.
vivaracho *a* lively, frisky, sprightly.
vivaz *a* vivacious, lively, alive, quick.
víveres *m pl* victuals; provisions, food.
vivero *m* (*plant*) nursery; fishpond.
viveza *f* liveliness, vivacity; energy, vehemence, impetuosity; quickness, penetration; sharpness.
vivienda *f* residence; dwelling house; lodgings.
vivificar *vt* to vivify, comfort, enliven.
vivir *vi* to live, exist; (*mil*) **¿quién vive?** who goes there?; *m* life, existence.
vivo *a* live, alive, living, quick.
vizcaíno *an* of, from, Basque provinces.
Vizcaya, el Golfo de *m* the Bay of Biscay.
vizconde *m* viscount.
vocablo *m* word, diction, term.
vocación *f* vocation, calling.
vocal *a* vocal; *m* alderman; voting member; *f* vowel.
vocalizar *vt* to articulate.
voceador *m* town crier.
vocear *vt* to cry out; *vi* to scream.
vocería *f* shouting, hullabaloo.
vocero *m* spokesman.
vociferar *vi* to vociferate, bawl, shout.
vocinglero *a* loquacious, chattering.
volante *a* flying; *m* shuttlecock; balance wheel, (*aut*) steering wheel.
volar *vi* to fly; to explode; *vt* to blow up.
volátil *a* volatile; flying.
volcán *m* volcano.
volcánico *a* volcanic.
volcar (ue) *vt* to overturn, upset; to turn upside down; to capsize; to pour out (*over*).
volición *f* volition, will.
voltear *vt* to whirl, upset; *SA* to turn around.
voltereta *f* somersault, tumble.
voltio *m* volt.
voluble *a* voluble, fickle, versatile.
volumen *m* volume, bulk.
voluminoso *a* voluminous, bulky.
voluntad *f* will, purpose, determination, desire.
voluntario *a* voluntary, willing; *m* volunteer.
voluntarioso *a* willful, headstrong.
voluptuoso *a* voluptuous.
volver (ue) *vt* to turn (up, over, down), return; to give (up, back); to change, translate; to vomit; *vi* to come back; to deviate, turn; **— a** to do again; **— por** to stand up for; **— en sí** to come round, come to one's senses; *vr* to become, turn.
vomitar *vt* to vomit.
vómito *m* vomit.
voraz *a* voracious, greedy, ravenous.
vórtice *m* vortex, whirlpool.
vos *pn* you.
vosotros *pn* you.
votación *f* voting, balloting.
votar *vi* to vote; to vow.
voto *m* vow; vote; oath.
voz *f* voice; word; expression; vote, suffrage; **a media —** in a whisper; **a — en cuello** shouting.
vuelco *m* overturning, spill, somersault.
vuelo *m* flight: soaring; projection; **al —** flying; **falda de mucho —** full skirt; **coger al —** to catch on the wing.
vuelta *f* turn, turning; revolution; regress, return; back(side); rotation; change; requital, repetition; walk, stroll; (*money*) change; **a la —** on (my) return, (*business*) carried forward; turn over; **a — de correo** by return post; **dar una —** to take a walk; **dar vueltas a** to consider further, turn over (in one's mind); **no tiene — de hoja** there's no answering that.
vuelto *a* turned, returned; **folio —** back of the page.
vuestro *a pn* your, yours.
vulcanizar *vt* to vulcanize.
vulgar *a* vulgar, common, ordinary.
vulgaridad *f* vulgarity, commonness.
vulgarizar *vt* to vulgarize, spread, popularize; *vr* to become vulgar.
vulgo *m* multitude, the masses.
vulnerable *a* vulnerable.
vulnerar *vt* to damage, injure.

X

xenofobia *f* xenophobia.
xilófono *m* xylophone.
xilografía *f* xylography, wood engraving.

Y

y *cj* and.
ya *ad* already, now, immediately, finally; — **lo creo** I do believe it.
yacaré *m Arg* alligator.
yacer *vi* to lie, to lie down (*in grave*).
yacimiento *m* (*ore*) deposit, layer, bed.
yaguré *m SA* skunk.
yanqui *an* Yankee.
yantar *vt* to take a repast.
yaraví *m SA* an Indian song.
yate *m* yacht.
yegua *f* mare.
yema *f* bud; yolk (*of egg*); tip (*of finger*).
yerba *f* herb, grass, weed.
yermo *a* barren, childless; *m* desert, waste.
yerno *m* son-in-law.
yerro *m* error, mistake, fault; — **de imprenta** erratum.
yerto *a* rigid, stiff, motionless.
yesca *f* tinder; *pl* tinderbox.
yeso *m* gypsum; plaster; — **mate** plaster of Paris.
yeta *f SA* bad luck; misfortune.
yo *pn* I; — **mismo** myself.
yodo *m* iodine.
yugo *m* yoke, oppression; **sacudir el** — to throw off the yoke.
yugoeslavo *an* Yugoslavian.
Yugoeslavia *f* Yugoslavia.
yunque *m* anvil.
yunta *f* yoke (*of oxen*); pair.
yuntero *m* plowboy.
yute *m* jute (*fiber*).
yuxtaponer *vt* to place side by side.
yuxtaposición *f* juxtaposition.
yuyo *m Arg, Chi* wild weed.

Z

zacate *m SA* grass; hay.
zafacoca *f SA* squabble, row.
zafado *a SA* impudent.
zafar *vt* to clear (*from encumbrances*), to lighten (*a ship*); *vr* to escape, slip off, decamp, sheer off.
zafio *a* coarse, ignorant, lacking manners.
zafir(o) *m* sapphire.
zafra *f* sugar-cane harvest.
zaga *f* rear (part); **a la** — behind, at the last.
zagal *m* shepherd, swain, country youth; coach-boy.
zagala *f* shepherdess, country lass.
zaguán *m* entrance, vestibule, main corridor (*of inn*).
zaherir (ie) *vt* to censure, reproach, decry, fling into (his) face, scourge.
zahorí *m* wizard, impostor.
zaino *a* treacherous, nasty (*beast etc*), chestnut (*horse*).
zalamear *vt Chi* to flatter.
zalamería *f* wheedling, cajolery.
zalamero *m* wheedler, flatterer.
zamarra *f* sheepskin jacket.
zambaigo *m Mex* Indian and Mexican half-breed.
zambo *a* knockkneed.
zambra *f* (*Moorish*) (*artistic*) feast, festival; merry-making; noisy stir.
zambullir *vi* to dive, duck, plunge in.
zampar *vt* to stuff (away, in), eat gluttonously.
zampoña *f* rustic flute.
zanahoria *f* carrot.
zanca *f* shank, long leg (eg *of crane*).
zancada *f* long stride.
zancadilla *f* trip (*up*), hook; trap.
zanco *m* stilt.
zancudo *a* long-shanked; *m SA* mosquito; *f pl* wading birds.
zángano *m* drone, sluggard, lazy dog.
zanja *f* ditch, conduit, (*foundation*) trench.
zanjar *vt* to open *or* cut ditches, trenches; to compromise, clear away (*difficulties*).
zapa *f* spade.
zapador *m* (*mil*) sapper.
zapapico *m* pickax, mattock.
zapar *vt* to sap, drive a mine (*under*).
zapata *f* buskin, half-boot.
zapatear *vt* to tap-dance; to beat time with the feet.
zapatería *f* shoemaker's trade, shop.
zapatero *m* shoemaker.
zapatilla *f* slipper.
zapato *m* shoe.
zar *m* czar.
zarabanda *f* saraband.
zaragate *m SA* contemptible person.
zaragozano *an* (*inhabitant*) of Saragossa.
zaramullo *m Per, Ven* busybody.
zaranda *f* screen, sieve.
zarandear *vt* to sift, winnow; *vr* to move to and fro.
zaraza *f* printed cotton cloth; chintz.
zarcillo *m* earring.
zarco *a* light blue (*eyes*).
zarina *f* czarina.
zarpa *f* paw; **echar la** — to grip, grasp.
zarpar *vi* to weigh anchor.
zarrapastroso *a* slovenly.
zarza *f* bramble, blackberry bush.
zarzal *m* bramble patch.
zarzamora *f* blackberry.
zarzuela *f* comic opera, musical comedy.
zeta *f* name of letter z.
zigzag *m* zigzag.
zinc *m* zinc.
zoca *f* square.
zócala *m* socle, pediment, plinth, base; beading; skirting board, baseboard.
zoclo *m* clog, overshoe.
zona *f* zone; — **templada** temperate zone.
zoología *f* zoology.
zoólogo *m* zoologist.

zoológico *a* zoological.
zopenco *m* blockhead.
zopilote *m SA* buzzard.
zoquete *m* block, chunk; blockhead.
zorra *f* vixen; prostitute.
zorrillo *m* skunk.
zorro *a* cunning, foxy; *m* fox.
zote *m* blockhead, dunce.
zozobra *f* uncertainty, anguish, suspense, perplexity; foundering (*of ship*).
zozobrar *vi* to founder, sink; to worry, be harassed; to hang (in suspense, in the balance).
zueco *m* wooden clog, overshoe.
zumba *f* cattle bell.
zumbar *vi* to buzz, hum (*ie in ears*).
zumbido *m* buzzing sound, humming, ringing (*in ears*); whizz, ping (*of bullet*).
zumbón *a* waggish; *m* wag, funny man.
zumo *m* juice, sap.
zurcir *vt* to darn, sew up, draw (*skillfully*) together.
zurdo *a* left-handed.
zurra *f* spanking, belting.
zurrar *vt* to dress leather; to spank, flog, whip, beat up; to hatch, concoct (*story, lie*).
zurriago *m* whip.
zurrir *vt* to clatter, rattle.
zurrón *m* leather bag; gamebag.
zutano *m* so-and-so.

English - Spanish

A

a [ə] *indef art* un, una.
aback [ə'bæk] *ad* de improviso; detrás, atrás; **to take —** desconcertar.
abandon [ə'bændən] *n* descaro; naturalidad, facilidad.
abandon [ə'bændən] *vt* abandonar; renunciar, evacuar; soltar; *vr* entregarse, confiarse.
abandoned [ə'bændənd] *a* desmantelado, arrinconado, ruinoso, desamparado; abandonado.
abandonment [ə'bændənmənt] *n* abandono, dejación.
abash [ə'bæʃ] *vt* desconcertar, confundir, sonrojar, desalentar.
abashed [ə'bæʃt] *a* corrido, cortado; *vi* **to be —** sobrecogerse.
abate [ə'beit] *vti* disminuir, rebajar; apaciguar, moderar; (*tempest*) amainar.
abatement [ə'beitmənt] *n* disminución, diminución, reducción, rebaja.
abattoir ['æbətwɑ:] *n* matadero.
abbess ['æbis] *n* abadesa.
abbey ['æbi] *n* monasterio, abadía.
abbot ['æbət] *n* abad, prior.
abbreviate [ə'bri:vieit] *vt* abreviar, compendiar, condensar, reducir.
abbreviation [ə,bri:vi'eiʃən] *n* abreviatura, contracción; resumen, compendio.
ABC ['eibi:'si:] *n* abecedario.
abdicate ['æbdikeit] *vt* abdicar, renunciar.
abdication [,æbdi'keiʃən] *n* abdicación; renuncia, abandono.
abdomen ['æbdəmen] *n* abdomen; vientre.
abdominal [æb'dɔminl] *a* abdominal.
abduct [æb'dʌkt] *vt* raptar, arrebatar.
abduction [æb'dʌkʃən] *n* rapto, robo; secuestro; plagio.
aberration [,æbə'reiʃən] *n* aberración; extravío; locura parcial.
abet [ə'bet] *vt* sostener, inducir, excitar, alentar, apoyar, ser cómplice.
abettor [ə'betə] *n* instigador, cómplice.
abeyance [ə'beiəns] *n* expectativa; **in —** en suspenso, vacante; **estate in —** tierras mostrencas.
abhor [əb'hɔ:] *vt* detestar, abominar, aborrecer, sentir horror a.
abhorrence [əb'hɔrəns] *n* horror, aborrecimiento, aversión, abominación, asco.
abhorrent [əb'hɔrənt] *a* repugnante; ajeno, contrario, incompatible.
abide [ə'baid] *vti* habitar, morar, quedar; sostener; atenerse; aguantar; resistir; **to — by** atenerse a mantener, contar con, regirse.
abiding [ə'baidiŋ] *a* constante permanente; **law- —** observante de la ley, que respeta las leyes.
ability [ə'biliti] *n* capacidad, facultad, habilidad; arte, talento, maña; potencia; **artistic —** disposición, aptitud (artística).
abject ['æbdʒekt] *a* abyecto, vil, bajo, rastrero, ruin, servil; **— poverty** pobreza de solemnidad.
abjection [æb'dʒekʃən] *n* abyección, vileza, bajeza; humillación, envilecimiento.
abjure [əb'dʒuə] *vt* abjurar, renunciar; *vi* renegar.
ablaze [ə'bleiz] *a* en llamas, ardiendo; radiante, brillante.
able ['eibl] *a* capaz, hábil, talentudo, competente; apto, diestro; **—-bodied** robusto, vigoroso; recio; **to be —** poder, saber (*nadar etc*); **he is very —** tiene mucho talento.
ablution [ə'blu:ʃən] *n* ablución, baño.
abnegate ['æbnigeit] *vt* renunciar, rehusar; renegar de.
abnegation [,æbni'geiʃən] *n* abnegación; renuncia, sacrificio.
abnormal [æb'nɔ:məl] *a* anormal; deforme.
abnormality [,æbnɔ:'mæliti] *n* anormalidad, anomalía.
aboard [ə'bɔ:d] *ad* a bordo; **to go —** embarcarse, ir a bordo.
abode [ə'boud] *n* morada, domicilio, mansión.
abolish [ə'bɔliʃ] *vt* abolir, derogar, suprimir.
abolition [,æbə'liʃən] *n* abolición, abrogación, aniquilamiento; **total —** abolición total.
abominable [ə'bɔminəbl] *a* abominable, detestable; pésimo (*gusto*); odioso, asqueroso.
abominate [ə'bɔmineit] *vt* abominar, detestar, odiar.
abomination [ə,bɔmi'neiʃən] *n* abominación, aversión, asco; impureza.
aboriginal [,æbə'ridʒənl] *a* aborigen, primitivo.
aborigines [,æbə'ridʒəni:z] *n pl* aborígenes.
abort [ə'bɔ:t] *vti* abortar.
abortion [ə'bɔ:ʃən] *n* aborto.
abortive [ə'bɔ:tiv] *a* abortivo, malogrado, fracasado.

abound [ə'baund] *vi* abundar, rebosar.
abounding [ə'baundiŋ] *a* abundante.
about [ə'baut] *prep ad* (*time*) a eso de, hacia, sobre, unas (*cinco horas*); (*place*) cerca, de, por, en torno; **round** — en los contornos, alrededor, a la redonda, en las cercanías; **round** — (*circumstantially*) en torno, acerca de, sobre; — (*close*) junto a, cerca de; **all** — por todas partes; **to be** — **to** estar a punto de, estar para (por); **right** — **turn** media vuelta a la derecha; **to come** — ocurrir, resultar; **to bring** — ocasionar; **what's it all —?** ¿de qué se trata?
above [ə'bʌv] *a* anterior, supradicho; *prep* sobre, encima, superior a; — **zero** sobre cero; — **all** ante todo, más que nada; *ad* arriba, en lo alto; **over and** — además, por encima; — **-mentioned** susodicho.
abrasion [ə'breiʒən] *n* desgaste, roce, rozadura, refregón.
abrasive [ə'breisiv] *a* abrasivo.
abreast [ə'brest] *ad* (*mil*) de frente; en fila, de lado; **four** — a cuatro de frente; **to keep** — **of** (*ideas*) mantenerse (al tanto, al día, a la altura).
abridge [ə'bridʒ] *vt* abreviar, acortar, reducir, substanciar.
abridgement [ə'bridʒmənt] *n* abreviación, compendio, resumen, extracto, contracción, merma, menoscabo.
abroad [ə'brɔ:d] *ad* en el extranjero, fuera; **to go** — ir al extranjero; **to noise** — propalar, trascender (*un secreto*).
abrogate ['æbrougeit] *vt* abrogar, abolir, derogar.
abrogation [,æbrou'geiʃən] *n* abrogación, anulación.
abrupt [ə'brʌpt] *a* abrupto, brusco; rudo; súbito, precipitado; cortado, corto, repentino; (*manners*) rudo, tosco.
abruption [ə'brʌpʃən] *n* ruptura, separación; brusquedad.
abruptly [ə'brʌptli] *ad* bruscamente, de rondón.
abruptness [ə'brʌptnis] *n* brusquedad; aspereza, escabrosidad; precipitación; descortesía.
abscess ['æbsis] *n* absceso.
abscond [əb'skɔnd] *vi* desaparecer, ocultarse; llevarse, escaparse, zafarse.
absence ['æbsəns] *n* ausencia; carencia, falta; — **of mind** distracción.
absent [æb'sent] *vr* ausentarse, separarse, mantenerse alejado de.
absent ['æbsənt] *a* ausente; que falta; —**minded** distraído, olvidadizo; **to count as** — hacer caso omiso de.
absentee [,æbsən'ti:] *n* (*legal*) ausente.
absinth(e) ['æbsinθ] *n* ajenjo.
absolute ['æbsəlu:t] *a* absoluto, acabado, completo; despótico, arbitrario; (*denial*) categórico; rotundo, cabal; (*knave*) redomado.
absoluteness ['æbsəlu:tnis] *n* decisión, firmeza, integridad.
absolution [,æbsə'lu:ʃən] *n* absolución, remisión.
absolutism ['æbsəlu:tizəm] *n* absolutismo, arbitrariedad.
absolve [əb'zɔlv] *vt* absolver, descargar (*la conciencia*); perdonar (*los pecados*).
absorb [əb'zɔ:b] *vt* (*soak*) absorber, empapar; (*suck*) sorber, chupar, tragar; consumir; (*in enthusiasm etc*) enfrascarse, embeberse, ensimismarse.
absorbed [əb'zɔ:bd] *a* absorto, perdido; (*water*) absorbido.
absorbent [əb'zɔ:bənt] *a* absorbente.
absorbing [əb'zɔ:biŋ] *a* intenso, fascinador, seductor.
absorption [əb'zɔ:pʃən] *n* absorción, sorbo; preocupación, embeleso.
abstain [əb'stein] *vi* abstenerse, guardarse; privarse de.
abstainer [əb'steinə] *n* abstemio total.
abstemious [əb'sti:miəs] *a* sobrio, moderado, abstemio.
abstemiousness [əb'sti:miəsnis] *n* sobriedad, templanza.
abstention [əb'stenʃən] *n* abstención.
abstinence ['æbstinəns] *n* abstinencia, sobriedad; **day of** — día de vigilia, ayuno.
abstract ['æbstrækt] *a* abstracto, ideal, ilusorio; recóndito; *n* extracto, resumen, sumario; [æb'strækt] *vt* hurtar; *vi* sacar de, desprenderse, hacer caso omiso de; *vr* abstraerse.
abstraction [æb'strækʃən] *n* abstracción; retraimiento; recogimiento.
abstracted [æb'stræktid] *a* preocupado, abstraído, sustraído; (*fam*) en babia.
abstruse [æb'stru:s] *a* abstruso, obscuro, esotérico; recóndito.
absurd [əb'sə:d] *a* absurdo, ridículo, disparatado, necio.
absurdity [əb'sə:diti] *n* absurdo, simpleza, sandez, contrasentido, tontería.
abundance [ə'bʌndəns] *n* abundancia, plenitud; regalo.
abundant [ə'bʌndənt] *a* abundante; (*water*) caudaloso, copioso; (*many, close*) nutrido; (*land*) feraz.
abundantly [ə'bʌndəntli] *ad* a pasto, con exuberancia.
abuse [ə'bju:z] *vt* ultrajar, insultar, denostar, engañar; abusar de; maltratar.
abuse [ə'bju:s] *n* abuso, ultraje, mal trato; (*curses*) denuestos, improperios.
abusive [ə'bju:siv] *a* insultante, ofensivo, abusivo.
abusiveness [ə'bju:sivnis] *n* grosería.

abysmal [ə'bizməl] *a* abismal; insondable; sin fondo; — **ignorance** una profunda ignorancia.
abyss [ə'bis] *n* abismo, sima, precipicio.
Abyssinian [,æbi'siniən] *an* abisinio.
academic [,ækə'demik] *a* académico, universitario; *n* académico.
academy [ə'kædəmi] *n* academia; — **of music** conservatorio.
accede [æk'si:d] *vi* acceder, consentir, admitir; subir (*al trono*).
accelerate [æk'seləreit] *vt* acelerar; apresurar, precipitar.
acceleration [æk,selə'reiʃən] *n* aceleración; diligencia.
accent [æk'sent] *vt* acentuar; (*strongly*) recalcar.
accent ['æksənt] *n* acento, pronunciación; **trace of** — dejo.
accentuate [æk'sentjueit] *vt* acentuar; cargar.
accentuation [æk,sentju'eiʃən] *n* acentuación, modulación.
accept [ək'sept] *vt* aceptar, recibir, acoger.
acceptable [ək'septəbl] *a* aceptable, grato; **to be** — ser grato.
acceptance [ək'septəns] *n* aceptación; acogida, aprobación.
acceptation [,æksep'teiʃən] *n* acepción, sentido (*de palabra*).
access ['ækses] *n* acceso, entrada; (*med*) ataque, arrebato; **to gain** — lograr acceso.
accessible [æk'sesəbl] *a* accesible, abordable.
accession [æk'seʃən] *n* acrecentamiento; (*to throne*) subida; accesión; refuerzo; asentimiento; — **catalogue** registro de entrada.
accessory [æk'sesəri] *a* accesorio; secundario; *n* cómplice; — **(after) (before) the fact** (encubridor) (instigador).
accident ['æksidənt] *n* accidente; equivocación; caso; (*chance*) lance, azar; (*street*) atropello; (*mistake*) casualidad, accidente, error.
accidental [,æksi'dentl] *a* accidental, fortuito, contingente, inesperado; subordinado, poco esencial, equivocado.
accidentally [,æksi'dentəli] *ad* casualmente, por casualidad.
acclaim [ə'kleim] *vt* aclamar; *n* aplauso, renombre.
acclamation [,æklə'meiʃən] *n* aclamación, celebración, aplausos.
acclimatize [ə'klaimətaiz], **acclimate** ['æklimeit] *vti* aclimatar(se).
accolade ['ækəleid] *n* espaldarazo.
accommodate [ə'kɔmədeit] *vt* acomodar, complacer; ajustar, conformar, acostumbrarse; instalar; componer; alojar.
accommodating [ə'kɔmədeitiŋ] *a* complaciente; acomodadizo, servicial.
accommodation [ə,kɔmə'deiʃən] *n* acomodo; avenencia, arreglo; hospedaje; servicio; *pl* comodidades; — **bill** pagaré de favor; **to come to an** — llegar a un acomodo.
accompaniment [ə'kʌmpənimənt] *n* acompañamiento.
accompanist [ə'kʌmpənist] *n* acompañante.
accompany [ə'kʌmpəni] *vt* acompañar, escoltar.
accomplice [ə'kʌmplis] *n* cómplice.
accomplish [ə'kʌmpliʃ] *vt* efectuar, llevar a cabo, cumplir, conseguir, ejecutar, lograr.
accomplished [ə'kʌmpliʃt] *a* cabal, perfecto, habilidoso; consumado, redomado (*bribón*); distinguido, dotado.
accomplishment [ə'kʌmpliʃmənt] *n* logro, cumplimiento, éxito; *pl* prendas, méritos, dotes.
accord [ə'kɔ:d] *vt* conceder, otorgar; *vi* concordar, concertar, hacer juego con; avenirse con.
accord [ə'kɔ:d] *n* acuerdo, concierto, avenimiento, todos a uno, en común; **(with) (of) one** — de común acuerdo; acomodo, buena inteligencia; **of one's own** — espontáneamente, de su propio impulso.
accordance [ə'kɔ:dəns] *n* conformidad; convenio; **in — with** según, conforme, de acuerdo con.
according [ə'kɔ:diŋ] *a* conforme; — **to** según, de acuerdo con.
accordingly [ə'kɔ:diŋli] *ad* en consecuencia, por consiguiente.
accordion [ə'kɔ:diən] *n* acordeón.
accost [ə'kɔst] *vt* acercarse, dirigirse, (*a uno*) abordar.
account [ə'kaunt] *n* relación, informe; cuenta (*bank*); referencia, partida; importancia; **on** — a cuenta; **on — of** a cuenta de; **current** — cuenta corriente; **to keep an** — tener cuenta abierta; **of little** — de poca monta; **of its own** — de por sí; *vt* considerar, estimar; tener por, juzgar, contar; *vi* explicar, dar cuenta de, justificar; **to — for** responder de; **to keep —s** llevar los libros; **on no** — de ninguna manera; **by all accounts** a decir de todos; **on that** — por eso; **to settle an** — liquidar una cuenta; **to give a good — of oneself** defenderse bien.
accountable [ə'kauntəbl] *a* responsable.
accountancy [ə'kauntənsi] *n* contabilidad, contaduría.
accountant [ə'kauntənt] *n* contador, perito en contabilidad, perito mercantil, tenedor de libros, contable.
accounted [ə'kauntid] *a* reputado por, considerado, tomado en cuenta.
accouterment [ə'ku:tərmənt] *n* equipo, vestido; *pl* adornos, pertrechos.
accredit [ə'kredit] *vt* acreditar, autorizar; creer.

accredited [ə'kreditid] *a* abonado, admitido.
accretion [ə'kriːʃən] *n* aumento; acrecentamiento.
accrue [ə'kruː] *vt* aumentar; resultar; **accrued interest** intereses acumulados.
accumulate [ə'kjuːmjuleit] *vt* acumular, amontonar, reunir, juntar.
accumulation [əˌkjuːmju'leiʃən] *n* acumulación; acervo.
accumulative [ə'kjuːmjulətiv] *a* acumulativo.
accuracy ['ækjurəsi] *n* precisión, exactitud.
accurate ['ækjurit] *a* preciso, exacto, fiel, puntual, perfecto, esmerado.
accurately ['ækjuritli] *ad* con precisión, puntualmente; **to speak —** puntualizar.
accurse [ə'kəːs] *vt* maldecir, execrar.
accursed [ə'kəːst] *a* maldito, fatal; perseguido, perverso.
accusation [ˌækju'zeiʃən] *n* acusación, delación, denuncia; **to bring an —** presentar una denuncia.
accusative [ə'kjuːzətiv] *n* acusativo.
accuse [ə'kjuːz] *vt* acusar; imputar; delatar; inculpar, tachar.
accuser [ə'kjuːzə] *n* acusador, delator.
accustom [ə'kʌstəm] *vi* acostumbrar, habituar; soler.
accustomed [ə'kʌstəmd] *a* acostumbrado; avezado (*to dangers*); corriente; **to be — to** estar acostumbrado a; **to grow — to** connaturalizarse, acostumbrarse a.
ace [eis] *n* as; **within an — of** a dos dedos de.
acetic [ə'siːtik] *a* acético.
ache [eik] *n* dolor; **ear—** dolor de oído; **head—** dolor de cabeza; **heart—** pena; **tooth —** dolor de muelas; *vi* doler; estar afligido; **my foot aches** me duele el pie.
achievable [ə'tʃiːvəbl] *a* hacedero, realizable, factible.
achieve [ə'tʃiːv] *vt* llevar a cabo, ejecutar, conseguir, lograr.
achievement [ə'tʃiːvmənt] *n* hazaña, proeza, empresa; obra, ejecución, realización, logro; consumación; acierto.
aching ['eikiŋ] *a* doloroso, (*heart*) herido; (*tooth*) que duele; *n* dolencia, pena, desasosiego.
acid ['æsid] *an* ácido, agrio; (*test*) definitivo; (*look*) agrio, de vinagre.
acidity [ə'siditi] *n* acidez; acedía.
acknowledge [ək'nɔlidʒ] *vt* reconocer, agradecer (*favour*), admitir; **— receipt** avisar, acusar (*recibo*).
acknowledged [ək'nɔlidʒd] *a* reconocido, incontestable.
acknowledgment [ək'nɔlidʒmənt] *n* reconocimiento, confesión; agradecimiento; acuse de recibo.
acme ['ækmi] *n* colmo, cima, auge; apogeo; (*of perfection*) suma.
acolyte ['ækəlait] *n* acólito.
acorn ['eikɔːn] *n* bellota; **— cup** capullo.
acoustic [ə'kuːstik] *a* acústico.
acquaint [ə'kweint] *vt* informar, dar (parte) (aviso), avisar, enterar, instruir.
acquaintance [ə'kweintəns] *n* conocimiento, familiaridad; (*pers*) conocido.
acquainted [ə'kweintid] *a* enterado, impuesto; **to be — with** conocer, estar enterado de; **to become —** relacionarse, conocerse.
acquiesce [ˌækwi'es] *vi* consentir, allanarse, acceder, conformarse.
acquiescence [ˌækwi'esns] *n* consentimiento, sumisión, conformidad.
acquiescent [ˌækwi'esnt] *a* condescendiente, sumiso, acomodadizo.
acquire [ə'kwaiə] *vt* adquirir; obtener, venir a tener, alcanzar; contraer.
acquisition [ˌækwi'ziʃən] *n* adquisición; obtención; beneficio.
acquisitive [ə'kwizitiv] *a* adquisitivo; ahorrativo.
acquit [ə'kwit] *vt* libertar, absolver, relevar, exonerar; desempeñar; cumplir; **to — oneself (well)** salir (bien) (airoso), defenderse.
acquittal [ə'kwitl] *n* (*of criminal*) absolución, descargo.
acquittance [ə'kwitəns] *n* descargo, quita.
acre ['eikə] *n* acre; *pl* terrenos; **God's —** camposanto.
acreage ['eikridʒ] *n* superficie en acres, extensión.
acrid ['ækrid] *a* (*dispute*) acre, agrio; (*remark*) mordaz; (*smell*) pungente.
acrimonious [ˌækri'mouniəs] *a* áspero, agrio; mordaz; **— dispute** discusión enconada.
acrimony ['ækriməni] *n* virulencia, amargura, aspereza.
acrobat ['ækrəbæt] *n* acróbata, volteador.
across [ə'krɔs] *ad* de, (a) (al) través; de una parte a otra, en cruz; *prep* al través de, contra, por medio de; **— country** a campo traviesa; **to run (come) —** tropezar con, dar con.
act [ækt] *n* acción, obra; (*theat*) acto, jornada; **in the —** con las manos en la masa; (*Bible*) **Acts** Los Hechos; *vi* obrar, hacer, funcionar, andar, actuar; portarse, conducirse, comportarse; representar; **to — the fool** hacer el tonto; **to — as** hacer de, servir de; **to — on** obrar (con arreglo a) (según).
acting ['æktiŋ] *a* interino, suplente; *n* acción; representación; (*theat*) declamación, trabajo.
action ['ækʃən] *n* acción, obra, hecho, gesto; suerte; movimiento; (*mil*) pelea, combate; (*mech*) marcha (*de un reloj*); **to put out of —** inutili-

zar; **to bring an — against** llevar a los tribunales.

active ['æktiv] *a* activo, diligente, listo, agudo, enérgico, nervioso, esforzado, vigoroso; (*volcano*) en erupción; (*mil*) **— service** en servicio activo.

activity [æk'tiviti] *n* actividad, diligencia, expedición, movimiento.

actor ['æktə] *n* actor, comediante, cómico.

actress ['æktris] *n* actriz.

actual ['æktjuəl] *a* efectivo, real.

actuality [æktju'æliti] *n* realidad, realismo.

actually ['æktjuəli] *ad* realmente, en efecto, de hecho, verdaderamente, a decir la verdad.

actuary ['æktjuəri] *n* escribano, secretario, registrador, actuario.

actuate ['æktjueit] *vt* mover, excitar, animar.

acumen [ə'kju:men] *n* agudeza, ingenio, cacumen; penetración, sutileza, perspicacia.

acute [ə'kju:t] *a* agudo, penetrante, vivo, sutil; (*med*) agudo, crítico.

acutely [ə'kju:tli] *ad* vivamente; agudamente.

acuteness [ə'kju:tnis] *n* vivacidad, sutileza, agudeza, penetración, aprehensión; violencia.

adage ['ædidʒ] *n* adagio, proverbio.

Adam ['ædəm] *m* Adán; **—'s apple** nuez.

adamant ['ædəmənt] *a* firme, inquebrantable; *n* diamante.

adapt [ə'dæpt] *vt* adaptar, ajustar, acomodar; (*theat*) arreglar, refundir; *vr* amoldarse, acomodarse, habituarse.

adaptability [ə,dæptə'biliti] *n* adaptabilidad, facilidad (*para*).

adaptable [ə'dæptəbl] *a* adaptable, ajustable; fácil.

adaptation [,ædæp'teiʃən] *n* adaptación, ajuste; (*theat*) arreglo, refundición.

add [æd] *vt* añadir, agregar, aumentar, unir, contribuir, poner; **to — up** sumar.

adder ['ædə] *n* víbora, culebra.

addict [ə'dikt] *vt* darse a; aplicarse; destinar; *n* ['ædikt] devoto, adicto.

addicted [ə'diktid] *a* dado a, aficionado a.

addiction [ə'dikʃən] *n* tendencia; entrega; apego, adicción.

addition [ə'diʃən] *n* (*math*) suma; adición; **in —** inclusive; **in — to** fuera de, además.

additional [ə'diʃənl] *a* adicional, accesorio.

addle ['ædl] *vt* podrir, enhuerar; **addled** (*eggs*) hueros; **—pated** fatuo, chalado.

address [ə'dres] *n* (*house etc*) señas, dirección; (*scroll*) memorial; (*talk*) plática; (*appearance*) talante; (*skill*) destreza; tratamiento; *pl* **to pay —** to cortejar, obsequiar; *vt* dirigir; hablar, arengar, enderezar (*remarks*); **to — as** tratar de.

addressee [,ædres'i:] *n* destinatario.

addresser [ə'dresə] *n* remitente.

adduce [ə'dju:s] *vt* aducir, alegar; llevar.

adept ['ædept] *n* adepto, maestro, *a* consumado, hábil.

adequate ['ædikwit] *a* adecuado, proporcionado, competente, bastante, necesario; regular.

adequately ['ædikwitli] *ad* adecuadamente, debidamente.

adhere [əd'hiə] *vi* adherir(se), pegar(se), allegar(se).

adherence [əd'hiərens] *n* adherencia, adhesión.

adherent [əd'hiərent] *an* adherente, partidario, secuaz; *a* pegajoso.

adhesion [əd'hi:ʒən] *n* adhesión, adherencia, apego.

adhesive [əd'hi:siv] *a* adhesivo, pegadizo; **— tape** cinta adhesiva.

adhesiveness [əd'hi:sivnis] *n* adherencia, calidad adhesiva, viscosidad.

adieu [ə'dju:] *excl* ¡adiós!; *n* adiós.

adjacent [ə'dʒeisənt] *a* adyacente, al lado, contiguo, afín; (*land*) comarcano.

adjective ['ædʒiktiv] *n* adjetivo.

adjoin [ə'dʒɔin] *vti* lindar, colindar; unir, comunicarse.

adjoining [ə'dʒɔiniŋ] *a* contiguo, inmediato, al lado, (co)lindante; **to be —** confrontar, estar (contiguo, limítrofe) con.

adjourn [ə'dʒə:n] *vt* aplazar, diferir, prorrogar; clausurar, levantar, suspender (*sesiones*).

adjournment [ə'dʒə:nmənt] *n* aplazamiento; clausura.

adjudge [ə'dʒʌdʒ] *vt* adjudicar; decretar; conceder (*premio*); *vi* dictar sentencia.

adjudicate [ə'dʒu:dikeit] *vt* decidir judicialmente, adjudicar.

adjunct ['ædʒʌŋkt] *an* adjunto, auxiliar.

adjunction [æ'dʒʌŋkʃən] *n* adición.

adjure [ə'dʒuə] *vt* implorar, conjurar, exorcizar, imprecar.

adjust [ə'dʒʌst] *vt* ajustar; arreglar, regular, conformar, componer, graduar, habituar.

adjustable [ə'dʒʌstəbl] *a* ajustable, desmontable, de quita y pon, móvil, adaptable.

adjustment [ə'dʒʌstmənt] *n* ajuste, transacción, avenencia, arreglo.

adjutant ['ædʒutənt] *n* ayudante.

administer [əd'ministə] *vt* administrar; (*supply*) suministrar; (*laws*) regir; (*Communion*) comulgar; (*sermon*) endilgar; (*a beating*) propinar.

administration [əd'ministreiʃən] *n* administración, dirección; manejo;

(*of house*) gobierno; (*of estate*) intendencia.
administrator [əd.minis'treitə] *n* administrador; (*of will*) albacea, testamentario.
admirable ['ædmərəbl] *a* admirable, notable.
admiral ['ædmərəl] *n* almirante; **—'s flagship** capitana; **rear —** contraalmirante; **—'s wife** capitana.
admiralty ['ædmərəlti] *n* almirantazgo, ministerio de Marina.
admiration [.ædmə'reiʃən] *n* admiración, sorpresa, pasmo.
admire [əd'maiə] *vt* admirar; *vi* maravillarse.
admirer [əd'maiərə] *n* pretendiente; amante, aficionado, apasionado.
admissible [əd'misəbl] *a* admisible, lícito.
admission [əd'miʃən] *n* acceso, entrada, admisión, ingreso, recepción; asentimiento; **no —** se prohibe la entrada, prohibida la entrada; **on his own —** de su propia palabra.
admit [əd'mit] *vt* admitir, recibir; reconocer, aceptar, confesar, conceder; dar entrada a; dar lugar a; **to be admitted to** (*Academy etc*) ingresar en.
admittance [əd'mitəns] *n* entrada, acceso.
admonish [əd'mɔniʃ] *vt* amonestar, advertir, reprender; reñir.
admonition [.ædmə'niʃən] *n* consejo, exhortación, amonestación, advertencia.
ado [ə'du:] *n*; **without more —** sin más ni más; **much — about nothing** mucho ruido y pocas nueces.
adobe [ə'doubi] *n* adobe.
adolescence [.ædə'lesns] *n* adolescencia, pubertad.
adolescent [.ædə'lesnt] *n* adolescente.
adopt [ə'dɔpt] *vt* adoptar, prohijar, ahijar; aceptar, tomar; arrogarse; **adopted son** hijo adoptivo.
adopted [ə'dɔptid] *a* adoptivo.
adoption [ə'dɔpʃən] *n* adopción; afiliación.
adoptive [ə'dɔptiv] *a* fingido, adoptivo.
adorable [ə'dɔ:rəbl] *a* adorable, precioso.
adoration [.ædɔ:'reiʃən] *n* adoración, culto, veneración.
adore [ə'dɔ:] *vt* adorar, reverenciar, idolatrar.
adorn [ə'dɔ:n] *vt* adornar, ornamentar, hermosear, decorar, esmaltar, embellecer, acicalar, engalanar; *vr* pulirse, acicalarse; **adorned** ataviado.
adornment [ə'dɔ:nmənt] *n* adorno, prenda (*de vestir*), ornamento; (*pers*) atavío, gala, afeites.
Adriatic [.eidri'ætik] *n* (Mar) Adriático.
adrift [ə'drift] *ad* a merced de las olas, al garete.
adroit [ə'drɔit] *a* hábil, diestro, mañoso, listo.
adroitness [ə'drɔitnis] *n* destreza, habilidad, maña.
adulation [.ædju'leiʃən] *n* adulación, lisonja, halago.
adult ['ædʌlt] *an* adulto, mayor.
adulterate [ə'dʌltəreit] *vt* adulterar; falsificar.
adulteration [ə.dʌltə'reiʃən] *n* adulteración, falsificación, impureza.
adulterer [ə'dʌltərə] *n* adúltero.
adulterous [ə'dʌltərəs] *a* adúltero.
adultery [ə'dʌltəri] *n* adulterio.
advance [əd'vɑ:ns] *vti* avanzar; adelantar; anticipar (*fondos*); fomentar, promover (*causa*); ascender (*grado*); alegar, insinuar (*intención*); **to make —s** requerir (*de amores*); *n* avance; (*payment*) adelanto, anticipo, préstamo; mejora; insinuación; (*love*) requerimiento(s); **in —** por adelantado; al frente; previa; alza (*precio*).
advanced [əd'vɑ:nst] *a* avanzado, adelantado; (*studies*) superiores; (*ideas*) avanzado; (*years*) provecto.
advancement [əd'vɑ:nsmənt] *n* adelanto; progreso; adelantamiento; **— of learning** progreso de la ciencia.
advancing [əd'vɑ:nsiŋ] *a* (*years*) con el paso de los años.
advantage [əd'vɑ:ntidʒ] *n* ventaja; beneficio, provecho; superioridad; valimiento; *vt* **to take — of** sacar ventaja, aprovechar(se); mejorar; **to take — of** valerse de, embaucar; **to have the —** llevar ventaja; **to show to —** quedar bien, resaltar, lucirse.
advantageous [.ædvən'teidʒəs] *a* ventajoso; útil, beneficioso, aventajado.
advent ['ædvənt] *n* llegada, venida; (*eccl*) adviento; advenimiento (*de Cristo*).
adventitious [.ædven'tiʃəs] *a* casual, adventicio, fortuito.
adventure [əd'ventʃə] *n* aventura, contingencia; lance, azar; *vi* arriesgarse, lanzarse, adventurarse.
adventurer [əd'ventʃərə] *n* aventurero; caballero de industria; (*in New World*) conquistador.
adventurous [əd'ventʃərəs] *a* aventurado; arrojado, emprendedor, arriesgado.
adventuresome [əd'ventʃəsəm] *a* aventurado, audaz, osado, intrépido.
adverb ['ædvə:b] *n* adverbio.
adversary ['ædvəsəri] *n* adversario, contrario, rival.
adverse ['ædvə:s] *a* adverso, contrario (*viento*); hostil, opuesto, funesto, desgraciado; desfavorable.
adversity [əd'və:siti] *n* adversidad; infortunio, desgracia, calamidad.
advert [əd'və:t] *vi* hacer referencia a, referirse a.

advertence [əd'və:təns] *n* aviso, advertencia.
advertise ['ædvətaiz] *vt* anunciar, poner un anuncio; dar publicidad; publicar; **to — for** pedir por medio de anuncios.
advertisement [əd'və:tismənt] *n* anuncio, aviso.
advertiser ['ædvətaizə] *n* publicista, anunciador.
advertising ['ædvətaiziŋ] *n* publicidad; proclamación.
advice [əd'vais] *n* aviso; consejo; dictamen, opinión; **a piece of —** un buen consejo; advertencia; (*com*) aviso, informe, noticia; **to take —** consultar.
advisability [əd,vaizə'biliti] *n* conveniencia, cordura.
advisable [əd'vaizəbl] *a* conveniente, prudente.
advise [əd'vaiz] *vti* aconsejar, dar consejo; advertir, notificar; consultar, enterar.
advised [əd'vaizd] *a* advertido, aconsejado; deliberado.
advisedly [əd'vaizidli] *ad* deliberadamente; adrede.
adviser [əd'vaizə] *n* consejero.
advisory [əd'vaizəri] *a* consultivo.
advocate ['ædvəkit] *n* abogado, defensor, jurisconsulto; *vt* ['ædvəkeit] abogar; interceder, propugnar.
aegis ['i:dʒis] *n* égida; **under the — of** bajo el patrocinio de.
aerate ['eiəreit] *vt* ventilar, orear; **aerated water** agua gaseosa.
aerial ['ɛəriəl] *a* aéreo; *n* antena.
aeronautics [,ɛərə'nɔ:tiks] *n* aeronáutica.
aesthetics [i:s'θetiks] *n* estética.
afar [ə'fɑ:] *ad* de lejos; a lo lejos, remoto; en la lontananza.
affability [,æfə'biliti] *n* afabilidad, amabilidad, agrado.
affable ['æfəbl] *a* afable, atento, cariñoso, expansivo.
affair [ə'fɛə] *n* negocio, ocupación, asunto; lance (*de honor*); relación (*de amor*); **painful —** asunto penoso; **— (of state)** asunto; **it's not your —** no es cosa tuya.
affect [ə'fekt] *vt* afectar, conmover, obrar, enternecer; hacer ostentación de.
affectation [,æfek'teiʃən] *n* afectación, dengue, cursilería.
affected [ə'fektid] *a* (*person*) artificioso cursi, remilgado; conmovido, excitado, afectado.
affecting [ə'fektiŋ] *a* patético, tierno, lastimero; relativo a.
affection [ə'fekʃən] *n* afecto, amor; afición, cariño, terneza, ternura; **special —** predilección.
affectionate [ə'fekʃnit] *a* afectuoso, cariñoso, entrañable; **your — nephew** su afectuoso sobrino.
affidavit [,æfi'deivit] *n* declaración jurada, certificación, atestación.
affiliate [ə'filieit] *vt* afiliar, adoptar.
affiliation [ə,fili'eiʃən] *n* afiliación, adopción, legitimación.
affinity [ə'finiti] *n* afinidad, enlace, parentesco; atracción.
affirm [ə'fə:m] *vt* afirmar, aseverar, asentar, sostener.
affirmation [,æfə:'meiʃən] *n* afirmación, aserción, declaración, aseveración.
affirmative [ə'fe:mətiv] *a* afirmativo; *n* afirmativa.
affix [ə'fiks] *vt* fijar, (*stick*) pegar, unir.
afflict [ə'flikt] *vt* afligir, atormentar, aquejar; desazonar, acongojar.
affliction [ə'flikʃən] *n* aflicción, congoja, tribulación, angustia; (*stifling*) ahogo.
affluence ['æfluəns] *n* afluencia; abundancia, opulencia.
affluent ['æfluənt] *n* afluente, tributario; *a* opulento.
afford [ə'fɔ:d] *vt* suministrar, dar; tener (recursos, medios) para; **I cannot — it** es superior a mis recursos; permitirse; parar (*una ocasión*) de, proporcionar, ofrecer; poder.
afforestation [æ,fɔris'teiʃən] *n* repoblación forestal.
affray [ə'frei] *n* querella, disputa, refriega, reyerta, riña.
affront [ə'frʌnt] *n* afrenta; (*blot*) baldón; agravio, ultraje, desaguisado; *vt* afrentar, ultrajar, denostar (*con palabras*).
affronting [ə'frʌntiŋ] *a* provocativo, agresivo.
aflame [ə'fleim] *ad* en llamas; **to be —** arder.
afloat [ə'flout] *ad* a flote, flotante, boyante, a nado.
afoot [ə'fut] *ad* en movimiento; **to set —** poner en marcha, tramar.
aforesaid [ə'fɔ:sed] *a* antedicho, susodicho, consabido, precitado.
afraid [ə'freid] *a* tímido, temeroso, espantado; miedoso; **I am —** tengo miedo; **to be —** temer; **I'm — he won't come** me temo que no venga; **I'm — so** lo siento, asi es.
afresh [ə'freʃ] *ad* de nuevo, otra vez, desde el principio.
Africa ['æfrikə] *n* África.
African ['æfrikən] *an* africano.
after ['ɑ:ftə] *ad* después, (*then*) luego, en seguida; *prep* después de; (*place*) detrás de; **one — the other** seguido; **— all** después de todo, con todo; **soon —** poco después; **— tomorrow** pasado mañana; **day — day** día tras día; **— Murillo** según M.; **—glow** (*in sky*) celajes; **—life** vida futura; **to look —** cuidar de; **to ask —** preguntar por.
afternoon ['ɑ:ftə'nu:n] *n* tarde.
aftertaste ['ɑ:ftəteist] *n* dejo, resabio, (*mal*) sabor de boca.

afterthought ['ɑ:ftəθɔ:t] *n* reflexión.
afterward ['ɑ:ftəwəd] *ad* después; **immediately —** acto (continuo, seguido).
again [ə'gen] *ad* otra vez, de nuevo, nuevamente; **— and —** repetidamente; **as much —** otro tanto; **now and —** de vez en cuando, una que otra vez; **never —** nunca jamás; **to speak —** volver a hablar.
against [ə'genst] *prep* (*en*) contra, enfrente, al lado de, junto a; **over —** justo en frente; **— his coming** para su venida; **— the grain** a contra pelo.
agape [ə'geip] *ad* con la boca abierta, boquiabierto, embobado.
age [eidʒ] *n* edad; época, tiempo; era, período; vejez; **of —** mayor de edad; **Iron A—** Edad de Hierro; **what is his —?** ¿cuántos años tiene?; **coming of —** mayoría; **old —** senectud; *vi* volverse viejo, envejecer.
aged ['eidʒid] *a* viejo, anciano, entrado en años, senil; (*of tree etc*) añoso.
agency ['eidʒənsi] *n* agencia, acción, operación, gestión, intervención; **by his —** por su mediación.
agent ['eidʒənt] *n* agente, comisionado, encargado, apoderado.
agglomeration [ə,glɔmə'reiʃən] *n* aglomeración, montón.
aggrandize [ə'grændaiz] *vt* agrandar, aumentar; enaltecer.
aggrandizement [ə'grændizmənt] *n* engrandecimiento, exaltación.
aggravate ['ægrəveit] *vt* agravar, exasperar, empeorar, molestar, exacerbar.
aggravation [,ægrə'veiʃən] *n* circunstancia agravante; provocación.
aggregate ['ægrigit] *n* **in the —** en conjunto, en total; agregado; ['ægrigeit] *vt* agregar, sumar, ascender a.
aggression [ə'greʃən] *n* ataque, agresión.
aggressive [ə'gresiv] *a* agresivo, belicoso, ofensivo.
aggressor [ə'gresə] *n* agresor.
aggrieve [ə'gri:v] *vt* afligir, apenar; vejar, dañar.
aghast [ə'gɑ:st] *a* espantado, horrorizado.
agile ['ædʒail] *a* ágil, ligero, vivo, hábil.
agility [ə'dʒiliti] *n* agilidad, prontitud, ligereza.
agitate ['ædʒiteit] *vt* agitar, perturbar, inquietar; debatir; (*water*) encrespar; (*tail etc*) menear.
agitation [,ædʒi'teiʃən] *n* agitación, perturbación, excitación, convulsión.
agitator ['ædʒiteitə] *n* agitador, instigador, alborotador.
aglow [ə'glou] *a* encendido, fulgido, fulgente.
ago [ə'gou] *ad* pasado; **long time —** hace mucho tiempo; **long —** tiempo ha, antaño.
agog [ə'gɔg] *a* ansioso, excitado, nerviosísimo, (re)dispuesto.
agonizing ['ægənaiziŋ] *a* desgarrador, angustioso.
agonize ['ægenaiz] *vti* torturar, agonizar.
agony ['ægəni] *n* **death —** agonía; zozobra, angustia, suplicio.
Agnes ['ægnis] *f* Inés.
agrarian [ə'grɛəriən] *a* agrario.
agree [ə'gri:] *vi* acordar, concordar, quedar en, ponerse de acuerdo; hacer juego con; conformarse, consentir, venir en; (*of food*) sentar; **to — with** (*person*) dar la razón a, convenir con; estar de acuerdo con; **to — to marry** dar el sí.
agreeable [ə'griəbl] *a* conveniente, grato, agradable, ameno; conforme, dispuesto; (*view etc*) risueño, deleitoso; simpático.
agreeableness [ə'griəblnis] *n* agrado, afabilidad, amenidad.
agreeably [ə'griəbli] *ad* agradablemente; de conformidad.
agreed [ə'gri:d] *a* **— upon** convenido, (*laid down*) asentado; **to be —** entenderse.
agreement [ə'gri:mənt] *n* acuerdo, convenio, contrato, arreglo; concordia; (*of parts*) concordancia; consentimiento, consonancia; **to come to an —** concertar.
agricultural [,ægri'kʌltʃərəl] *a* agrícola; **— expert** agrónomo.
agriculture ['ægrikʌltʃə] *n* agricultura.
aground [ə'graund] *ad* varado, embarrancado; **to run —** encallar, embarrancarse.
ague ['eigju:] *n* fiebre, escalofrío; calofrío.
ahead [ə'hed] *ad* adelante, enfrente, al frente, a la cabeza; **right —** todo directo; **to be —** ir a la cabeza, llevar (la delantera, la ventaja); **to get — of** tomar la delantera; **to go —** continuar, proceder; **to go — of** preceder.
aid [eid] *n* ayuda, auxilio, socorro; (*support*) refuerzo; **by the — of** al amparo de; **in — of** a beneficio de; **first —** primeros auxilios; **medical —** practicante; *vt* ayudar; **to — and abet** ser cómplice.
aide-de-camp ['eiddə'kɑ̃:ŋ] *n* edecán.
aiding ['eidiŋ] *n* **— and abetting** complicidad.
ail [eil] *vt* afligir, molestar, aquejar; *vi* estar indispuesto.
ailing ['eiliŋ] *a* achacoso, malo, doliente, enclenque, enfermizo.
ailment ['eilmənt] *n* enfermedad, padecimiento, achaque, indisposición, alifafe.
aim [eim] *n* puntería; blanco, fin,

objeto, mira, propósito; **steady —** tino; *vti* hacer puntería, apuntar, aspirar a; picar alto; ir contra; **well —ed** certero; **to miss one's —** errar el tiro; **to take good —** apuntar bien.

aimless ['eimlis] *a* sin objeto, desatinado.

air [ɛə] *n* aire; ambiente, atmósfera, aura; (*appearance*) semblante, continente, porte; (*mus*) aire, tonada, tonadilla; **foul —** aire viciado; **open —** aire libre; **Air Force** Aviación, fuerzas aéreas; **—gun** escopeta de viento; **—hole** respiradero, lumbrera; **— raid** incursión, ataque aéreo; **—tight** hermético; **hanging in mid —** suspendido en vilo; **in the —** indefinido, vago, en proyecto; **in the open —** al aire libre, a la intemperie; **to take the —** tomar el fresco; **to put on airs** darse tono; **airs and graces** remilgos; *vt* (*grievance*) ventilar, publicar.

aircraft ['ɛəkrɑːft] *n* avión; **— carrier** porta(a)viones.

airily ['ɛərili] *ad* ligeramente, como si tal cosa, gentilmente.

airiness ['ɛərinis] *n* vivacidad, ligereza; airosidad.

airing ['ɛəriŋ] *n* paseo, caminata; **to take an —** dar una vuelta; **to give an — to** (*idea*) sacar a colación.

airman ['ɛəmən] *n* aviador.

airplane ['ɛəplein] *n* avión.

airport ['ɛəpɔːt] *n* aeropuerto.

airy ['ɛəri] *a* aéreo, etéreo, imaginario, vaporoso, ventilado; airoso, ligero.

aisle [ail] *n* nave lateral, ala.

ajar [ə'dʒɑː] *a ad* entreabierto, (*puerta*) entornada.

akimbo [ə'kimbou] *a* **arms —** brazos en jarras.

akin [ə'kin] *a* pariente, consanguíneo; semejante, análogo; **— to** muy parecido a.

alabaster ['æləbɑːstə] *n* alabastro.

alacrity [ə'lækriti] *n* presteza, prontitud; alegría.

alarm [ə'lɑːm] *n* alarma; sobresalto, alboroto; *vt* alarmar, inquietar, asustar; **to sound the —** tocar a rebato, dar la alarma.

alarm clock [ə'lɑːmklɔk] *n* despertador.

alarming [ə'lɑːmiŋ] *a* alarmante.

alas [ə'læs] *excl* ¡ay!

albeit [ɔːl'biːit] *cj* bien que, aunque.

Albert ['ælbəːt] *m* Alberto.

album ['ælbəm] *n* álbum.

alchemist ['ælkimist] *n* alquimista.

alchemy ['ælkimi] *n* alquimia.

alcohol ['ælkəhɔl] *n* alcohol.

alcoholic [ˌælkə'hɔlik] *an* alcohólico.

alcove ['ælkouv] *n* alcoba.

alder ['ɔːldə] *n* aliso.

alderman ['ɔːldəmən] *n* regidor, concejal.

ale [eil] *n* cerveza inglesa.

alert [ə'ləːt] *a* vigilante, activo, vivo; **to be on the —** estar sobre aviso.

alertness [ə'ləːtnis] *n* vigilancia, diligencia, viveza.

Alexander [ˌælig'zɑːndə] *m* Alejandro.

Alfred ['ælfrid] *m* Alfredo.

algebra ['ældʒibrə] *n* álgebra.

Algeria [æl'dʒiəriə] *n* Argelia.

Algerian [æl'dʒiəriən] *an* argelino.

Algiers [æl'dʒiəz] *n* Argel.

alias ['eiliæs] *ad* por otro nombre; alias; *n* seudónimo.

alibi ['ælibai] *n* coartada.

Alice ['ælis] *f* Alicia.

alien ['eiliən] *n* extranjero, forastero, *a* de otro; ajeno, extraño; contrario; remoto.

alienate ['eiliəneit] *vt* (*property, mind*) enajenar; desviar, traspasar.

alienation [ˌeiliə'neiʃən] *n* (*mental*) enajenación, desvío, extrañamiento; delirio; (*property*) expropiación.

alight [ə'lait] *vi* (*from coach*) bajar, apearse; (*bird*) posarse; *a* **to set —** iluminar, (*fire*) encender; **the wood is —** arde la madera.

align [ə'lain] *vt* alinear.

alike [ə'laik] *a* semejante, parecido, símil, par; *ad* igualmente; **all —** todos a uno, todos sin distinción.

aliment ['ælimənt] *n* alimento.

alimentary [ˌæli'mentəri] *a* alimenticio; **— canal** tubo digestivo.

alimony ['æliməni] *n* alimentos, pensión alimenticia; asistencias.

alive [ə'laiv] *a* vivo, vivaz; con vida, viviente, activo; **to be — to the situation** con conocimiento de causa, hacerse cargo de, enterado; **— with** rebosante de; plagado de; **while —** en vida; **to keep —** sostener(se), mantener vivo.

all [ɔːl] *a* todo; **— told** en conjunto; **not at —** de nada; de ningún modo; **on — fours** a gatas; *ad* del todo, enteramente; **— but** menos; **I — but fell** por poco me caigo; **— out** a toda velocidad; **— the better** tanto mejor; **— right** está bien; **— at once** de repente; **for — that** con todo; **after —** después de todo; **once for —** de una vez (*para siempre*); **— in —** en resumidas cuentas; **it's — one to me** me es completamente indiferente; *n* todo, totalidad.

allay [ə'lei] *vt* apaciguar, aliviar, templar, aquietar, mitigar.

allaying [ə'leiiŋ] *n* calmante, desahogo, alivio.

allegation [ˌælə'geiʃən] *n* alegato, alegación.

allege [ə'ledʒ] *vt* alegar, sostener.

alleged [ə'ledʒd] *a* supuesto, pretendido.

allegiance [ə'liːdʒəns] *n* obediencia, fidelidad, lealtad; homenaje.

allegoric [ˌælə'gɔrik] *a* alegórico.

allegory ['æligəri] *n* alegoría.

alleviate [ə'li:vieit] *vt* aliviar, aligerar, aplacar.
alleviation [ə,li:vi'eiʃən] *n* alivio, calmante; desahogo.
alley ['æli] *n* callejón, callejuela; (*in park*) paseo; **blind** — callejón sin salida.
alliance [ə'laiəns] *n* alianza, unión, fusión; parentesco.
allied ['ælaid] *a* aliado, confederado, combinado.
alligator ['æligeitə] *n* caimán; — **pear** aguacate.
alliteration [ə,litə'reiʃən] *n* aliteración.
allocate ['æləkeit] *vt* asignar, colocar, señalar, disponer.
allocation [,ælə'keiʃən] *n* asignación, colocación, fijación, disposición, repartición.
allot [ə'lɔt] *vt* adjudicar, asignar, repartir, destinar, fijar.
allotment [ə'lɔtmənt] *n* asignación, repartimiento, porción, reparto; (*land*) parcela.
allow [ə'lau] *vt* permitir, dar permiso, admitir, tolerar, confesar, consentir, dejar, conceder, descontar; **talking not allowed** no se permite hablar.
allowable [ə'lauəbl] *a* permitido, legítimo, tolerable.
allowance [ə'lauəns] *n* permiso; pensión, asignación; (*of food*) ración; concesión, licencia; **to make — for** tomar (en cuenta, en consideración); **family** — subsidio familiar.
alloy ['ælɔi] *n* liga, aleación; [ə'lɔi] *vt* ligar, alear.
All Saints' Day ['ɔ:l'seintsdei] *n* Día de Todos los Santos.
All Souls' Day ['ɔ:l'soulzdei] *n* Día de las Animas, de los Difuntos.
allude [ə'lu:d] *vi* aludir, referirse, hacer referencia a.
allure [ə'ljuə] *vt* seducir, fascinar, atraer.
allurement [ə'ljuəmənt] *n* incentivo, halago, atractivo; anzuelo, aliciente, reclamo.
alluring [ə'ljuəriŋ] *a* halagüeño, atractivo, tentador.
allusion [ə'lu:ʒən] *n* alusión (intencionada), indirecta, referencia; **to catch an** — caer en el chiste.
allusive [ə'lu:siv] *a* alusivo.
ally ['ælai] *n* aliado, confederado.
ally [ə'lai] *vt* aliarse, relacionarse (con), juntar(se); **allied to** relacionado (a, con).
almanack ['ɔ:lmənæk] *n* almanaque.
almighty [ɔ:l'maiti] *a* omnipotente; enorme, muy; — **God** el Todopoderoso.
almond ['ɑ:mənd] *n* almendra; **green** — almendruco; — **paste** mazapán; **sugared** —, — **tree** almendro.
almost ['ɔ:lmoust] *ad* casi, cuasi, punto menos (*que imposible*); — **at any moment** de un momento a otro.
alms [ɑ:ms] *n* limosna, caridad; —**house** hospicio.
aloft [ə'lɔft] *ad* en alto, arriba, en el cielo.
alone [ə'loun] *a* solo, único, a solas, solitario; **to leave** — dejar quieto; **let** — sin mencionar.
along [ə'lɔŋ] *prep* a lo largo de; *ad* en compañía con, hacia adelante; **all** — desde el principio, a lo largo; — **with** junto con; **to get — with** simpatizar con, llevarse con.
aloof [ə'lu:f] *ad* de lejos, a lo lejos; **to stand** — mantenerse (apartado, distanciado, retirado, indiferente).
aloud [ə'laud] *ad* en voz alta, recio, alto.
alphabet ['ælfəbit] *n* alfabeto, abecé; — **card** abecedario.
alpine ['ælpain] *a* alpestre, alpino.
Alps [ælps] *n* los Alpes.
already [ɔ:l'redi] *ad* ya.
also ['ɔ:lsou] *ad* también, igualmente, asimismo, además.
altar ['ɔ:ltə] *n* altar; —**boy** monaguillo; —**cloth** sábana, mantel; —**piece** retablo; **high** — altar mayor; **on the — of** en aras de.
alter ['ɔ:ltə] *vti* alterar, cambiar, mudarse, cambiarse, tornar; (*expression*) demudar.
alterable ['ɔ:ltərəbl] *a* alterable, mudable.
alteration [,ɔ:ltə'reiʃən] *n* alteración; cambio, reforma, reformación; (*expression*) demudación.
altercation [,ɔ:ltə'keiʃən] *n* altercado, disputa.
alternate [ɔ:l'tə:nit] *a* alterno, alternativo; ['ɔ:ltəneit] *vti* alternar, turnarse.
alternating ['ɔ:ltəneitiŋ] *a* — **current** corriente alterna.
alternation [,ɔ:ltə'neiʃən] *n* turno, cambio, vez.
alternative [ɔ:l'tə:nətiv] *adj* alternativo; *n* alternativa.
although [ɔ:l'ðou] *cj* aunque, bien que, (aun) cuando, puesto que, si bien, a pesar de.
altitude ['æltitju:d] *n* elevación; (*person, triangle*) altura; altitud.
altogether [,ɔ:ltə'geðə] *ad* enteramente, completamente, en conjunto, totalmente, del todo, total.
altruistic [,æltru'istik] *an* altruista.
aluminum [ə'luminəm] *n* aluminio.
alumnus [ə'lʌmnəs] *n* graduado.
always ['ɔ:lweiz] *ad* siempre, en todo tiempo.
amalgamate [ə'mælgəmeit] *vt* amalgamar; *vi* amalgamarse.
amalgamation [ə,mælgə'meiʃən] *n* amalgamación, amalgama, mezcla.
amass [ə'mæs] *vt* amontonar, juntar, acumular, amasar.
amateur ['æmətə] *n* aficionado; — **dramatics** función de aficionados.
amateurish ['æmətʃəriʃ] *a* torpe.

amatory ['æmətəri] *a* amatorio.
amaze [ə'meiz] *vt* sorprender, asombrar, confundir, maravillarse, aturdir, suspender; **to be amazed** pasmarse.
amazement [ə'meizmənt] *n* asombro, sorpresa, atolondramiento, pasmo, arrobamiento.
amazing [ə'meiziŋ] *a* sorprendente, asombroso.
Amazon ['æməzən] *n* amazona.
Amazon (River) ['æməzən('rivə)] *n* el (Río de las) Amazonas.
ambassador [æm'bæsədə] *n* embajador.
amber ['æmbə] *n* ámbar, electro; **black** — azabache.
ambidextrous [.æmbi'dekstrəs] *a* ambidextro.
ambiguity [.æmbi'gjuiti] *n* ambigüedad, doble sentido, vaguedad.
ambiguous [æm'bigjuəs] *a* ambiguo, equívoco, promiscuo.
ambition [æm'biʃən] *n* ambición.
ambitious [æm'biʃəs] *a* ambicioso.
amble ['æmbl] *n* paso de andadura; *vi* amblar, llevar un paso tranquilo.
ambulance ['æmbjuləns] *n* ambulancia; hospital de sangre.
ambulatory ['æmbjulətəri] *n* ambulatorio; galería.
ambush ['æmbuʃ] *n* emboscada; **in** — en acecho; *vti* poner celada; emboscarse, acechar; **to lie in** — estar en acecho, en celada.
ameliorate [ə'mi:liəreit] *vt* mejorar, adelantar.
amelioration [ə'mi:liə'reiʃən] *n* mejora, reforma.
amen ['ɑ:'men] *ad* amén, así sea.
amenable [ə'mi:nəbl] *a* responsable; dócil, complaciente, tratable, sujetable.
amend [ə'mend] *vti* enmendar, reparar, rectificar; enmendarse, corregirse, reformar.
amendment [ə'mendmənt] *n* enmienda, mejora, reforma.
amends [ə'mendz] *n* reparación, restitución, recompensa, paga, desagravio; **to make** — igualar, compensar, desagraviar, satisfacer, expiar.
amenity [ə'mi:niti] *n* amenidad, attracción, mejora.
America [ə'merikə] *n* América; Estados Unidos.
American [ə'merikən] *an* americano, norteamericano, hispanoamericano; — **tobacco** tabaco rubio.
amethyst ['æmiθist] *n* amatista.
amiability [.eimiə'biliti] *n* amabilidad, simpatía, bondad.
amiable ['eimiəbl] *a* amable, afable, afectuoso, tierno.
amicable ['æmikəbl] *a* amistoso, amigable, simpático.
amicableness ['æmikəblnis] *n* cariño, amistad, afecto.
amid [ə'mid] *prep* entre, en medio de, rodeado de.
amidships [ə'midʃips] *ad* en medio del navío.
amiss [ə'mis] *ad* mal, fuera de sazón; inoportunamente; impropio, errado; **it is not** — no está de más; **to take** — llevar a mal, tomar a mala parte; **what's —?** ¿qué (le) pasa?
ammonia [ə'mouniə] *n* amoníaco, alcalí volátil.
ammunition [.æmju'niʃən] *n* munición; pertrechos (*of war*).
amnesty ['æmnisti] *n* amnistía, indulto.
among [ə'mʌŋ] *prep* entre, en medio de, de entre.
amongst [ə'mʌŋst] *prep* entre, en medio de.
amorous ['æmərəs] *a* amoroso, enamoradizo, enamorado, tierno; — **old gentleman** viejo verde.
amorphous [ə'mɔ:fəs] *a* amorfo.
amortize [ə'mɔ:taiz] *vt* amortizar.
amount [ə'maunt] *n* monto, monta, cantidad, importe, total, suma; *vi* montar, importar; **to — to** valer, subir a, sumar a, hacer, ascender a, llegar a; significar.
amour [ə'muə] *n* amores, amoríos.
amphibious [æm'fibiəs] *a* anfibio.
amphitheater ['æmfi.θiətə] *n* anfiteatro.
ample ['æmpl] *a* amplio, ancho, vasto, espacioso; (*dress*) holgado; bastante, suficiente; **to be** (*more than*) — bastar (*de sobra*).
ampleness ['æmplnis] *n* abundancia, suficiencia; amplitud, espaciosidad.
amplification [.æmplifi'keiʃən] *n* ampliación, extensión.
amplify ['æmplifai] *vt* ampliar, amplificar, aumentar, hacer más detallado; machacar.
amplitude ['æmplitju:d] *n* amplitud, anchura, holgura, extensión.
amply ['æmpli] *ad* ampliamente, harto, con creces.
amputate ['æmpjuteit] *vt* amputar, cortar; (*slice off*) cercenar.
amputation [.æmpju'teiʃən] *n* amputación.
amuck [ə'mʌk] *ad* **to run** — correr demente, correr a ciegas.
amulet ['æmjulit] *n* amuleto, talismán, higa.
amuse [ə'mju:z] *vt* divertir, entretener, solazar, holgarse, distraerse; **we are not amused** no nos cae en gracia.
amusement [ə'mju:zmənt] *n* diversión, entretenimiento, recreo, pasatiempo.
amusing [ə'mju:ziŋ] *a* divertido, entretenido, gracioso; **how —!** ¡qué divertido!
an [æn, ən] *indef art* un, una.
anachronism [ə'nækrənizəm] *n* anacronismo.

analogous [ə'næləgəs] *a* análogo, semejante, parecido.
analogy [ə'nælədʒi] *n* analogía, afinidad, semejanza; **on the — of** por analogía con.
analysis [ə'næləsis] *n* análisis.
analytic [ˌænə'litik] *a* analítico.
analyze ['ænəlaiz] *vt* analizar.
anarchical [æ'nɑːkikl] *a* anárquico.
anarchist ['ænəkist] *n* anarquista.
anarchy ['ænəki] *n* anarquía, desorden, confusión.
anathema [ə'næθimə] *n* anatema, excomunión.
anatomy [ə'nætəmi] *n* anatomía, disección.
ancestors ['ænsistəz] *n pl* antepasados, ascendientes, progenitores.
ancestral [æn'sestrəl] *a* ancestral, hereditario; **— home** casa solariega.
ancestry ['ænsistri] *n* abolengo, alcurnia, ascendencia, estirpe, linaje, prosapia.
anchor ['æŋkə] *n* ancla; **at —** al ancla; *vti* anclar, echar anclas; **to cast —** dar fondo; **to weigh —** zarpar, levar anclas.
anchorage ['æŋkəridʒ] *n* anclaje, ancladero, fondeadero, (*tying-up*) agarradero; **— dues** derechos de anclaje.
anchorite ['æŋkərait] *n* anacoreta, ermitaño.
anchovy ['æntʃəvi] *n* anchoa, boquerón.
ancient ['einʃənt] *a* antiguo, anciano; (*city*) vetusta; (*historical*) antiguo; (*stock*) rancio; **very —** antiquísimo; **in — days** de antaño.
and [ænd] *cj* y, e; **— yet** sin embargo; **— so forth** etcétera, y así sucesivamente.
Andalusia [ˌændə'luːziə] *n* Andalucía.
Andalusian [ˌændə'luːziən] *an* andaluz.
Andrew ['ændruː] *m* Andrés.
anecdote ['ænikdout] *n* anécdota, chascarrillo, historieta.
anemia [ə'niːmiə] *n* anemia.
anemic [ə'niːmik] *a* anémico.
anesthesia [ˌænis'θiːziə] *n* anestesia.
anemone [ə'neməni] *n* anemone.
anew [ə'njuː] *ad* de nuevo, otra vez, nuevamente.
angel ['eindʒəl] *n* ángel ; **guardian —** ángel custodio.
angelic [æn'dʒelik] *a* angélico, seráfico.
anger ['æŋgə] *n* cólera, furia, enojo, ira, coraje, saña; *vt* provocar, enfurecer, irritar, encolerizar, indignar; **to show —** enfurecerse.
angle ['æŋgl] *n* ángulo; (*in street*) recodo; anzuelo.
angle ['æŋgl] *vt* pescar con caña, echar el anzuelo.
angler ['æŋglə] *n* pescador de caña.
Anglican ['æŋglikən] *an* anglicano.
anglicism ['æŋglisizəm] *n* anglicismo.
angling ['æŋgliŋ] *n* pesca con caña.
angry ['æŋgri] *a* colérico, airado, encolerizado; irritado, enfadado, enojado; **to grow —** enfadarse, ponerse (*furioso etc*); calentarse.
anguish ['æŋgwiʃ] *n* angustia, congoja, ahogo, aflicción, tormento, fatiga, pena, ansia.
angular ['æŋgjulə] *a* angular.
animadversion [ˌænimæd'vəːʃən] *n* animadversión, censura, reparo.
animadvert [ˌænimæd'vəːt] *vt* reprochar, hacer observaciones, censurar, poner reparo(s) a.
animal ['æniməl] *an* animal, bestia; **— spirits** exuberancia vital.
animate ['ænimeit] *vt* animar, vivificar, alentar, dar vida a, alegrar.
animated ['ænimeitid] *a* animado, lleno de vida, vivo, vital; concurrido.
animating ['ænimeitiŋ] *a* vivificante, excitante, divertido.
animation [ˌæni'meiʃən] *n* animación, vivacidad, calor, viveza; concurrencia.
animosity [ˌæni'mɔsiti] *n* animosidad, hostilidad, rencor, inquina, encono.
ankle ['æŋkl] *n* tobillo.
annalist ['ænəlist] *n* cronista, analista.
annals ['ænəlz] *n pl* anales; crónica; fastos.
Anne [æn] *f* Ana.
annex ['æneks] *a* anexo, anejo; *n* aditamento, apéndice; *vt* [ə'neks] anexar, adjuntar, apoderarse de.
annexation [ˌænek'seiʃən] *n* anexión, unión.
annihilate [ə'naiəleit] *vt* aniquilar; anonadar, destruir.
annihilation [əˌnaiə'leiʃən] *n* aniquilación; anonadamiento.
anniversary [ˌæni'vəːsəri] *n* aniversario.
annotate ['ænouteit] *vt* anotar, apuntar, glosar; **annotated edition** edición (comentada, con comentario).
annotation [ˌænou'teiʃən] *n* anotación, nota, apuntación; **musical —** solfa.
announce [ə'nauns] *vt* anunciar, avisar, participar, pregonar, proclamar, publicar; prometer.
announcement [ə'naunsmənt] *n* anuncio, aviso, (*of marriage*) participación; **official —** comunicado.
announcer [ə'naunsə] *n* **radio —** radiolocutor.
annoy [ə'nɔi] *vt* fastidiar, molestar, disgustar, dar guerra a, dar la lata a; (*fam*) jorobar.
annoyance [ə'nɔiəns] *n* molestia, fastidio, aburrimiento, enojo.
annoyed [ə'nɔid] *a* **to be —** incomodarse, enfadarse.
annoying [ə'nɔiiŋ] *a* fastidioso,

importuno, engorroso, molesto, empalagoso.
annual ['ænjuəl] *a* anual; de todos los años.
annually ['ænjuəli] *ad* anualmente, por año.
annuity [ə'nju:iti] *n* renta, pensión vitalicia.
annul [ə'nʌl] *vt* anular, quebrantar, abrogar (*laws*), abolir.
annulment [ə'nʌlmənt] *n* anulación, revocación, cancelación.
annum ['ænəm] *n* **per** — (al) (por) año.
annunciation [əˌnʌnsi'eiʃən] *n* anunciación.
anoint [ə'nɔint] *vt* ungir, consagrar.
anointing [ə'nɔintiŋ], **anointment** [ə'nɔintmənt] *n* unción.
anomalous [ə'nɔmələs] *a* anómalo, irregular, fuera de lo normal.
anomaly [ə'nɔməli] *n* anomalía.
anon [ə'nɔn] *ad* a poco, luego.
anonymity [ˌænə'nimiti] *n* anónimo.
anonymous [ə'nɔniməs] *a* anónimo.
another [ə'nʌðə] *a* otro; distinto; **one** — uno a otro, recíprocamente; **another's** ajeno, de otro.
answer ['ɑ:nsə] *n* respuesta; réplica; contestación; solución; *vt* responder, contestar, replicar; servir, corresponder, convenir; **to** — **back** replicar; **to** — **for** acreditar, abonar, responder de, dar cuenta; **to wait for an** — esperar respuesta; **there's no answering that** no tiene vuelta de hoja.
answerable ['ɑ:nsərəbl] *a* responsable.
ant [ænt] *n* hormiga; —**eater** oso hormiguero.
antagonism [æn'tægənizəm] *n* antagonismo, hostilidad, rivalidad.
antagonist [æn'tægənist] *n* antagonista, contrario, rival.
antagonistic [ænˌtægə'nistik] *a* antagónico, hostil, opuesto.
Antarctic [ænt'ɑ:ktik] *an* antártico.
antecedence [æn'ti:sid'ans] *n* precedencia.
antecedent [ˌænti'si:dənt] *a* antecedente, precedente, previo.
antedate ['ænti'deit] *vt* antedatar.
antelope ['æntiloup] *n* antílope; gacela.
antenna [æn'tenə] *n* cuerno; (*TV*) antena.
anteroom ['æntirum] *n* antecámara, vestíbulo.
anthem ['ænθəm] *n* antífona; **national** — himno nacional.
anthology [æn'θɔlədʒi] *n* antología, florilegio.
Anthony, Antony ['æntəni] *m* Antonio.
anthracite ['ænθrəsait] *n* antracita; carbón de piedra.
anthropology [ˌænθrə'pɔlədʒi] *n* antropología.
anti-aircraft ['ænti'ɛəkrɑ:ft] *a* antiaéreo.
antic ['æntik] *a* extraño, grotesco; *n* bufón; farsa, cabriola; extravagancia, travesura; **to play** —**s** hacer de las suyas.
anticipate [æn'tisipeit] *vt* anticipar, prever, barruntar; adelantar(se).
anticipation [ænˌtisi'peiʃən] *n* anticipación; previsión; interés, anhelo.
anticlerical ['ænti'klerikl] *a* anticlerical.
antidote ['æntidout] *n* antídoto, remedio, contraveneno.
antipathetic [ˌæntipə'θetik] *a* antipático, contrario, opuesto.
antipathy [æn'tipəθi] *n* antipatía, repugnancia, rencilla.
antipode [æn'tipədi] *n* antípoda.
antiquarian [ˌænti'kwɛəriən] *n* anticuario, aficionado de antigüedades.
antiquated ['æntikweitid] *a* anticuado, añejo, arcaico.
antique [æn'ti:k] *a* antiguo; *n pl* antigüedades.
antiquity [æn'tikwiti] *n* antigüedad; **venerable** — vetustez.
antiseptic [ˌænti'septik] *an* antiséptico.
antithesis [æn'tiθisis] *n* antítesis, oposición.
antler ['æntlə] *n* asta, cuerno; *pl* cornamenta.
anvil ['ænvil] *n* yunque; **on the** — en el telar.
anxiety [æŋ'zaiəti] *n* ansiedad, inquietud, quitasueño; (*desire*) ansia, afán, anhelo; zozobra, desvelo.
anxious ['æŋʃəs] *a* inquieto, ansioso, desasosegado, impaciente, deseoso.
any ['eni] *pn, a* & *ad* cualquiera, cualesquiera, alguno, alguna; — **more** más aún; **not** — **more** no más; — **body** alguien, alguno; todo el mundo; — **person** un cualquier; — **of them** cualquiera de ellos; **at** — **rate** de todos modos, pase lo que pase.
anyhow ['enihau] *ad* de todos modos; sin embargo; de cualquier modo.
anything ['eniθiŋ] *pn* algo, alguna cosa; — **but** todo menos.
anyway ['eniwei] *ad* con todo.
anywhere ['eniwɛə] *ad* dondequiera, en cualquier parte.
anywise ['eniwaiz] *ad* de cualquier modo, comoquiera.
apace [ə'peis] *ad* a prisa, a trancos; **to grow** — tomar cuerpo.
apart [ə'pɑ:t] *ad* separadamente, aparte, aislado, apartado; **to set** — separar, segregar; **to tear** — despedazar.
apartment [ə'pɑ:tmənt] *n* piso, cuarto; aposento.
apathetic [ˌæpə'θetik] *a* apático, dejado, indiferente.
apathy ['æpəθi] *n* apatía, dejadez, flema.
ape ['eip] *n* mono, mico; simio; imitador; *vt* imitar, remedar.
aperient [ə'piəriənt] *n* laxante.

apex ['eipeks] *n* cúspide, ápice, cima, tope, coronamiento.
aphorism ['æfərizəm] *n* aforismo.
apiarist ['eipiərist] *n* colmenero.
apiary ['eipiəri] *n* colmenar, abejar.
apiece [ə'pi:s] *ad* por barba, por persona, por cabeza.
aplomb [ə'plɔm] *n* seguridad, aplomo; a plomo.
apocalypse [ə'pɔkəlips] *n* apocalipsis.
apogee ['æpoudʒi:] *n* apogeo, auge.
apologetic [ə.pɔlə'dʒetik] *a* apologético.
apologize [ə'pɔlədʒaiz] *vt* excusarse, presentar excusas; pedir perdón.
apologue ['æpəlɔg] *n* apólogo.
apology [ə'pɔlədʒi] *n* apología, excusa, disculpa, justificación; **to send —** excusarse; **to offer —** disculparse.
apoplectic [.æpə'plektik] *a* apoplético.
apoplexy ['æpəpleksi] *n* apoplegía.
apostasy [ə'pɔstəsi] *n* apostasía.
apostate [ə'pɔstit] *n* apóstata, renegado.
apostle [ə'pɔsl] *n* apóstol, enviado.
apostolic [.æpəs'tɔlik] *a* apostólico; **— See** Santa Sede.
apostrophe [ə'pɔstrəfi] *n* apóstrofe, (*gram*) apóstrofo.
apothecary [ə'pɔθikəri] *n* boticario, farmacéutico; **—'s shop** botica, farmacia.
apotheosis [ə.pɔθi'ousis] *n* apoteosis, deificación.
appall [ə'pɔ:l] *vt* aterrar, espantar.
appalling [ə'pɔ:liŋ] *a* espantoso, aterrador, espantable.
apparatus [.æpə'reitəs] *n* aparato, instrumento, aparejo.
apparel [ə'pærəl] *n* ropa, traje, vestimenta, hato, ropaje; *vt* vestir, adornar.
apparent [ə'pærənt] *a* aparente; obvio, notable, (al) desnudo, evidente, visible, especioso; **heir —** presunto heredero; **to become —** ponerse de manifiesto.
apparently [ə'pærəntli] *ad* al parecer.
apparition [.æpə'riʃən] *n* visión, aparición, fantasma.
appeal [ə'pi:l] *n* simpatía; súplica, petición; prendados; rogación, instancia, apelación; **without —** inapelable, sin recurso; **lack of —** antipatía; **judge of —** juez de alzadas; **Court of A—** Tribunal de apelación.
appeal [ə'pi:l] *vi* apelar; recurrir; **to — against** suplicar de.
appear [ə'piə] *vi* aparecer; asomar, salir; rayar (en); comparecer (*before tribunal etc*); (*in person*) personarse; (*seem*) parecer.
appearance [ə'piərəns] *n* apariencia; traza, facha, pinta; continente, semblante; comparación, aparición; vislumbre; **joint —** conjunción; **—'s sake** el buen parecer; **to keep up —s** salvar las apariencias.
appease [ə'pi:z] *vt* apaciguar, calmar, pacificar, desenojar.
appeasement [ə'pi:zmənt] *n* apaciguamiento, pacificación.
appeaser [ə'pi:zə] *n* aplacador, apaciguador.
append [ə'pend] *vt* añadir, agregar; fijar; colgar.
appendage [ə'pendidʒ] *n* dependencia; accesorio.
appendix [ə'pendiks] *n* apéndice.
appertain [.æpə'tein] *vi* pertenecer; ser de; atañer, competer.
appetite ['æpitait] *n* apetito, hambre, ganas; **to have an —** tener ganas; **lack of —** desgana.
appetizing ['æpitaiziŋ] *a* apetitoso; excitante; apetecible.
applaud [ə'plɔ:d] *vt* aplaudir, dar palmadas, palmotear; celebrar.
applause [ə'plɔ:z] *n* aplauso, elogio, palmadas; aprobación, aclamación.
apple ['æpl] *n* manzana; (*of eye*) pupila, niña; **— tree** manzano; **Adam's —** nuez; **— orchard** manzanar, pomar.
appliance [ə'plaiəns] *n* instrumento, herramienta; aplicación; (*el*) aparato.
applicable ['æplikəbl] *a* aplicable,
applicant ['æplikənt] *n* suplicante, solicitante, pretendiente, candidato.
application [.æpli'keiʃən] *n* (*for post*) solicitud; solicitación; (*industry*) aplicación.
apply [ə'plai] *vti* recurrir, solicitar, dirigirse a; concernir; apropiar, aplicar; (*for post*) solicitar; (*paint etc*) dar; pretender a; **to — oneself to** darse a, ponerse a.
appoint [ə'pɔint] *vt* nombrar, designar; señalar; surtir; **to be appointed to** colocarse; **to be appointed as** ser nombrado.
appointment [ə'pɔintmənt] *n* nombramiento; decreto; cita, compromiso; (*job*) empleo, cargo, colocación; (*at dentist etc*) hora; **to make an —** citar; **to have an —** tener hora.
apportion [ə'pɔ:ʃən] *vt* repartir, distribuir.
apposite ['æpəzit] *a* a propósito, oportuno, ocurrente, atinado, justo.
appraisal [ə'preizəl] *n* valoración, tasa(ción); estimación.
appraise [ə'preiz] *vt* apreciar, valuar, justipreciar, valorizar.
appreciable [ə'pri:ʃəbl] *a* apreciable, notable, sensible.
appreciate [ə'pri:ʃieit] *vt* apreciar, darse cuenta de, encarecer; (*of price*) tener un alza.
appreciation [ə.pri:ʃi'eiʃən] *n* apreciación, aprecio, ponderación; alza de precio; estima.
appreciative [ə'pri:ʃətiv] *a* apreciativo.
apprehend [.æpri'hend] *vt* asir,

aprehender; prender (*criminal*); coger, comprender; recelar, sospechar.

apprehension [ˌæpri'henʃən] *n* aprensión, temor, estremecimiento, recelo.

apprehensive [ˌæpri'hensiv] *a* receloso, temeroso, aprensivo, solícito (*for others*); perspicaz; **to grow —** sobrecogerse.

apprentice [ə'prentis] *n* aprendiz, novicio; *vt* poner de aprendiz.

apprenticeship [ə'prentiʃip] *n* aprendizaje, noviciado; **to serve an —** hacer el aprendizaje.

apprise [ə'praiz] *vt* enseñar, avisar, informar, comunicar, hacer saber.

approach [ə'proutʃ] *n* proximidad, llegada, entrada, paso; **the nearest —** lo más cercano, apropiado; **to make an —** intentar un acercamiento; *vti* llegar a, acercar, acercarse, aproximar; (*age*) frisar, rayar en; arrimar.

approachable [ə'proutʃəbl] *a* accesible; comunicativo; abordable.

approaching [ə'proutʃiŋ] *a* próximo, cercano.

approbation [ˌæprə'beiʃən] *n* aprobación, beneplácito.

appropriate [ə'proupriit] *a* propio, conveniente, adecuado, bueno, pertinente, idóneo, correspondiente; [ə'prouprieit] *vt* apropiar; apropiarse, incautarse de; **to be —** cuadrar, caer bien.

appropriately [ə'proupriitli] *ad* convenientemente, propiamente, de modo adecuado.

appropriateness [ə'proupriitnis] *n* congruencia, indoneidad.

appropriation [əˌproupri'eiʃən] *n* apropiación, incautación; (*financial*) crédito.

approval [ə'pru:vəl] *n* aprobación; **on —** a prueba.

approve [ə'pru:v] *vt* aprobar, autorizar, sancionar; **to — of** estar de acuerdo con, dar el beneplácito.

approximate [ə'prɔksimit] *a* aproximado, cercano; [ə'prɔksimeit] *vti* aproximar, aproximarse.

approximation [əˌprɔksi'meiʃən] *n* aproximación.

appurtenance [ə'pə:tinəns] *n* dependencia, accesorio; pertenencia.

apricot ['eiprikɔt] *n* albaricoque; **— tree** albaricoquero.

April ['eiprəl] *n* abril; **— fool** inocente.

apron ['eiprən] *n* mandil, delantal; **tied to — strings** cosido a las faldas.

apropos ['æprəpou] *ad* a propósito, oportunamente; *a* pertinente.

apt [æpt] *a* apto, idóneo, propenso a; inclinado, propio; listo, hábil; (*remark*) pertinente; **to be — to** estar expuesto a, ser pronto a.

aptitude ['æptitju:d] *n* aptitud, disposición, facilidad.

aptness ['æptnis] *n* idoneidad.

aquatic [ə'kwætik] *a* acuático.

aqueduct ['ækwidʌkt] *n* acueducto.

aquiline ['ækwilain] *a* aquilino; (*nose*) aguileño.

Arab ['ærəb] *an* árabe; **— quarter** morería; (*fam*) **street —** (*Madrid*) chulo, golfo; **— ic** árabe.

Arabia [ə'reibiə] *n* Arabia

Arabian [ə'reibiən] *an* árabe.

arable ['ærəbl] *a* arable; propio para labranza, (*tierra de*) labrantío; **— land** campiña.

Aragonese [ˌærəgə'ni:z] *an* aragonés.

arbiter ['ɑ:bitə] *n* árbitro.

arbitrary ['ɑ:bitrəri] *a* arbitrario; caprichoso; despótico.

arbitrate ['ɑ:bitreit] *vt* decidir como árbitro, arbitrar, terciar.

arbitration [ˌɑ:bi'treiʃən] *n* arbitramento; arbitraje, tercería; **court of —** tribunal de arbitraje.

arbitrator ['ɑ:bitreitə] *n* árbitro; arbitrador; tercero.

arbor ['ɑ:bə] *n* enramada, cenador; glorieta.

arc [ɑ:k] *n* arco.

arcade [ɑ:'keid] *n* arcada, galería, soportal(es).

arch [ɑ:tʃ] *a* astuto, socarrón; consumado, travieso; *n* arco, bóveda; *vti* arquear, abovedar.

archaic [ɑ:'keiik] *a* arcaico, desusado, caído en desuso.

archangel ['ɑ:kˌeindʒəl] *n* arcángel.

archbishop ['ɑ:tʃ'biʃəp] *n* arzobispo, pontífice, metropolitano.

archbishopric [ɑ:tʃ'biʃəprik] *n* arzobispado.

archduke ['ɑ:tʃ'dju:k] *n* archiduque.

arched [ɑ:tʃt] *a* abovedado, arqueado; corvo.

archeological [ˌɑ:kiə'lɔdʒikəl] *a* arqueológico.

archeology [ˌɑ:ki'ɔlədʒi] *n* arqueología.

archer ['ɑ:tʃə] *n* arquero, ballestero, saetero, flechero.

archetype ['ɑ:kitaip] *n* arquetipo, prototipo.

archipelago [ˌɑ:ki'peligou] *n* archipiélago.

architect ['ɑ:kitekt] *n* arquitecto.

architectural [ˌɑ:ki'tektʃərəl] *a* arquitectónico.

architecture ['ɑ:kitektʃə] *n* arquitectura.

archives ['ɑ:kaivz] *n pl* archivos.

archivist ['ɑ:kivist] *n* archivero.

archly ['ɑ:tʃli] *ad* graciosamente, sutilmente, con salero, con socarronería.

archness ['ɑ:tʃnis] *n* travesura; sutileza, gracia picaresca.

archway ['ɑ:tʃwei] *n* portal, bóveda, pasaje abovedado, arcada.

Arctic ['ɑ:ktik] *an* ártico.

ardent ['ɑ:dənt] *a* ardiente, fogoso, vehemente, fervoroso; **— spirits** bebidas espirituosas.

ardor ['ɑ:də] *n* ardor, calor; fogosidad, ahinco; celo; viveza.
arduous ['ɑ:djuəs] *a* arduo, trabajoso, difícil, recio, laborioso.
arduously ['ɑ:djuəsli] *ad* trabajosamente.
area ['ɛəriə] *n* área, ámbito; (*theat etc*) patio, corral.
arena [ə'ri:nə] *n* arena, liza, redondel, (*bullfights*) ruedo.
Argentine ['ɑ:dʒəntain] *n* Argentina.
Argentinian [,ɑ:dʒən'tiniən] *an* argentino.
argue ['ɑ:gju:] *vti* argüir, discurrir, discutir, razonar, sostener, argumentar; **to — against** controvertir.
argument ['ɑ:gjumənt] *n* argumento, discusión; raciocinio, razón, (*of book*) argumento.
arid ['ærid] *a* árido, seco; estéril.
aridity [ə'riditi] *n* aridez, sequedad.
arise [ə'raiz] *vi* elevarse, subir, surgir (*de*); (*in revolt*) sublevarse; (*from bed*) levantarse; (*origin*) proceder de, provenir.
aristocracy [,æris'tɔkrəsi] *n* aristocracia.
aristocrat ['æristəkræt] *n* aristócrata, hidalgo.
aristocratic [,æristə'krætik] *a* aristocrático.
Aristotle ['æristɔtl] *m* Aristóteles.
arithmetic [ə'riθmətik] *n* aritmética.
ark [ɑ:k] *n* arca.
arm [ɑ:m] *n* brazo; (*bot*) rama, gajo; (*sea*) brazo; (*handle*) manga; arma; **with —s folded** los brazos cruzados; **— in —** de bracete, cogidos del brazo; **infant in —s** niño de teta; **call to —s** rebato; **—'s reach** alcance; **at —'s length** a distancia; **up in —s** sublevado; **— chair** silla poltrona, sillón, butaca; **one-armed** manco; *vti* armar, armarse.
armament ['ɑ:məmənt] *n* armamento.
armful ['ɑ:mful] *n* brazada.
armhole [ɑ:mhoul], **armpit** ['ɑ:mpit] *n* sobaco, axila.
armistice ['ɑ:mistis] *n* armisticio.
armless ['ɑ:mlis] *a* manco.
armor ['ɑ:mə] *n* armadura, arnés; **— plating** blindaje; (*ship's*) — coraza; **— ed** (*car*) blindado.
armorial [ɑ:'mɔ:riəl] *a* heráldico.
armory ['ɑ:məri] *n* arsenal; armería.
army ['ɑ:mi] *a* castrense; *n* ejército; (*fig*) multitude.
aroma [ə'roumə] *n* aroma, fragancia.
aromatic [,ærou'mætik] *a* aromático, odorífero.
around [ə'raund] *prep ad* por, alrededor, a la redonda; (*the corner*) a la vuelta de, en los contornos; **to be —** (*age*) frisar con; **to put arm —** tomar por el talle.
arouse [ə'rauz] *vt* despertar, conmover, sacudir, ocasionar, suscitar, atizar.
arraign [ə'rein] *vt* acusar, procesar.
arraignment [ə'reinmənt] *n* acusación, denuncia.
arrange [ə'reindʒ] *vt* arreglar, poner en orden, acomodar, colocar, ordenar, aprestar, aliñar, clasificar, negociar; **to — to meet** citar.
arrangement [ə'reindʒmənt] *n* arreglo, disposición; plan(es); ajuste, combinación, concierto, organización; habilitación; **to come to an —** llegar a un acomodo.
arrant ['ærənt] *a* notorio, redomado.
arras ['ærəs] *n* tapicería.
array [ə'rei] *n* orden de batalla; aparato, pompa; ostentación, riqueza.
arrears [ə'riəz] *n pl* atrasos, sumas por pagar, vencidas.
arrest [ə'rest] *n* detención, arresto, prendimiento, prisión; *vt* arrestar; (*police*) prender, detener; capturar; (*an advance*) contrarrestar, parar; (*attention*) llamar, traer.
arrival [ə'raivəl] *n* llegada, entrada; advenimiento; consecución; **a new —** un recién llegado.
arrive [ə'raiv] *vi* llegar; suceder, ocurrir; conseguir, llevar a cabo.
arrogance ['ærəgəns] *n* arrogancia, soberbia, señorío, entono.
arrogant ['ærəgənt] *a* arrogante, orgulloso, altanero, altivo, valentón.
arrogate ['ærougeit] *vt* arrogarse, usurpar.
arrow ['ærou] *n* flecha, dardo, virote; **— head** punta de flecha.
arsenal ['ɑ:sinl] *n* arsenal, maestranza, armería.
arsenic ['ɑ:snik] *n* arsénico.
arson ['ɑ:sn] *n* incendio provocado.
art [ɑ:t] *n* arte; habilidad, maña, artificio; **fine —s** bellas artes; **Faculty of Arts** Facultad de Filosofía y Letras.
artery ['ɑ:teri] *n* arteria.
artful ['ɑ:tful] *a* astuto, ladino, redomado, tacaño, solapado, mañoso.
artfulness ['ɑ:tfulnis] *n* astucia; habilidad; maña, socarronería.
arthritis [ɑ:'θraitis] *n* artritis.
Arthur ['ɑ:θə] *m* Arturo.
article ['ɑ:tikl] *n* artículo, objeto, cosa; cláusula, estipulación; mercancía; renglón; *pl* **— of marriage** capitulaciones; **small —** menudencias; *vt* pactar; contratar.
articulate [ɑ:'tikjulit] *a* articulado, claro; que sabe hablar; [ɑ:'tikjuleit] *vt* articular; vocalizar.
articulation [ɑ:,tikju'leiʃən] *n* articulación, pronunciación; (*bot*) nudo.
artifice ['ɑ:tifis] *n* artificio, engaño, fraude, ardid; invención, treta; destreza, sutileza.
artificial [,ɑ:ti'fiʃəl] *a* artificial; ficticio; fingido; postizo, afectado.
artillery [ɑ:'tiləri] *n* artillería; **field —** artillería de campaña, de acompañamiento.

artilleryman [ɑ:'tilərimən] *n* artillero.
artisan ['ɑ:tizæn] *n* artesano, oficial, menestral.
artist ['ɑ:tist] *n* artista.
artistic [ɑ:'tistik] *a* artístico.
artless ['ɑ:tlis] *a* sencillo, simple; cándido, ingenuo.
artlessly ['ɑ:tlisli] *ad* sin arte, sencillamente.
artlessness ['ɑ:tlisnis] *n* sencillez, naturalidad, simplicidad.
as [æz] *cj* como; a guisa de, según, ya que, a semejanza de, por; — **(soon)** — tan (pronto) como; — **for** por lo que toca a, tocante a, en cuanto a; **such** — tal como; los que; — **if nothing had happened** como si tal cosa; *ad* conforme, hasta; — **yet** todavía, aún; — **it were** por decirlo así, en cierto modo.
ascend [ə'send] *vti* subir; (*throne*) subir a; elevar(se), escalar.
ascendant [ə'sendənt] *a* ascendente, superior; *n* altura; predominio; (*astr*) ascensión; **to be in the** — ir en aumento.
ascendency [ə'sendənsi] *n* ascendiente, influjo, dominación.
ascension [ə'senʃən] *n* ascensión.
ascent [ə'sent] *n* subida, elevación; (*slope*) cuesta, pendiente.
ascertain [ˌæsə'tein] *vt* cerciorarse, verificar, indagar, averiguar.
ascetic [ə'setik] *a* ascético; *n* asceta.
ascribe [ə'skraib] *vt* asignar, atribuir, imputar; (*blame*) achacar.
ash [æʃ] *n* (*bot*) fresno; (*fire*) ceniza; — **grove** fresnada; — **Wednesday** miércoles de ceniza; —**colored** ceniciento; —**tray** cenicero; *pl* cenizas.
ashamed [ə'ʃeimd] *a* avergonzado, vergonzoso, cortado, corrido; **to be** — tener vergüenza; cortarse.
ashen ['æʃn] *a* ceniciento, cenizoso.
ashes ['æʃiz] *n pl* cenizas.
ashore [ə'ʃɔ:] *ad* a tierra, en tierra; **to go** — desembarcar; **to run** — encallar.
Asia ['eiʃə] *n* Asia.
Asian ['eiʃən] *an* asiático.
aside [ə'said] *ad* a parte, al lado; a un lado; (*theat*) aparte; **to lay** — despreciar, omitir, arrimar, deponer, orillar, retirar; **to set** — anular; dejar de un lado.
ask [ɑ:sk] *vt* (*question*) preguntar, (*favor, for*) pedir, suplicar, solicitar; (*require*) exigir, requerir, (*invite*) convidar; *vi* buscar; **to** — **after** preguntar por.
askance [ə'skɑ:ns] *ad* oblicuamente, de soslayo; **to look** — **at** mirar de reojo.
askew [ə'skju:] *a, ad* de soslayo, desviado, ladeado.
asleep [ə'sli:p] *a* dormido; **to fall** — caer(se) dormido, dormirse; **fast** — hecho un tronco.
asparagus [əs'pærəgəs] *n* espárrago.
aspect ['æspekt] *n* aspecto, apariencia; aire, semblante, faz, cara; exterior, traza, catadura; punto, fase; **northern** — vistas al norte.
aspen ['æspən] *n* tiemblo, álamo temblón.
asperity [æs'periti] *n* aspereza; rudeza; (*of manner*) desabrimiento, acerbidad.
aspersion [æs'pə:ʃən] *n* aspersión, difamación, calumnia; mancha.
asphalt ['æsfælt] *n* asfalto, betún judaico.
aspirant ['æspirənt] *n* aspirante, pretendiente, candidato.
aspirate ['æspireit] *vt* aspirar.
aspiration [ˌæspə'reiʃən] *n* aspiración; anhelo, deseo vehemente, prurito.
aspire [əs'paiə] *vi* aspirar a, pretender.
aspirin ['æsprin] *n* aspirina.
aspiring [əs'paiəriŋ] *a* ambicioso.
ass [æs] *n* asno, burro, jumento; mentecato, primo, ganso; **to make an** — **of oneself** hacer el mentecato.
assail [ə'seil] *vt* atacar, embestir, arremeter, asaltar; (*by doubts*) asaltar.
assailant [ə'seilənt] *n* asaltante, asaltador; (*criminal*) atracador; agresor.
assassin [ə'sæsin] *n* asesino.
assassinate [ə'sæsineit] *vt* asesinar.
assault [ə'sɔ:lt] *n* asalto, ataque; embestida, agresión, arremetida; (*criminal*) atraco; *vt* atacar, asaltar, saltar.
assay [ə'sei] *n* ensayo; (*metals*) ensaye; prueba, toque; — **office** oficina de ensayes; *vt* ensayar; (*metal*) acrisolar; probar, aquilatar.
assemblage [ə'semblidʒ] *n* reunión, agregado, grupo, junta; concurso.
assemble [ə'sembl] *vt* congregar, convocar; reunir; (*mech*) montar; *vi* juntarse.
assembly [ə'sembli] *n* junta, asamblea, colonia, comité; concurso, conjunto; (*mech*) montaje, ensamblaje; — **room** sala de (sesiones, fiestas *etc*).
assent [ə'sent] *n* consentimiento, venia, beneplácito; **royal** — sanción regia; *vi* consentir, dar consentimiento; asentir.
assert [ə'sə:t] *vt* afirmar; aseverar; sostener, defender, sustentar.
assertion [ə'sə:ʃən] *n* aserción, afirmación, aseveración, fe.
assertive [ə'sə:tiv] *a* dogmático; **self-** — confiado.
assess [ə'ses] *vt* imponer (*taxes*); fijar, señalar; apreciar; **to** — **at** fijar en.
assessment [ə'sesmənt] *n* fijación de impuesto, contribución; tributo; avalúo.
assets ['æsets] *n pl* activo, haber;

personal, real — bienes muebles, inmuebles.
assiduity [ˌæsi'djuiti] *n* asiduidad, diligencia, aplicación.
assiduous [ə'sidjuəs] *a* asiduo, constante; aplicado, concienzudo.
assign [ə'sain] *vt* asignar, señalar; adscribir; (*law*) consignar; (*goods*) ceder, traspasar.
assignment [ə'sainmənt] *n* asignación; cesión.
assimilate [ə'simileit] *vt* asimilar; asemejar.
assimilation [əˌsimi'leiʃən] *n* asimilación.
assist [ə'sist] *vt* ayudar, auxiliar, socorrer; acudir, presenciar, estar presente, asistir; remediar.
assistance [ə'sistəns] *n* asistencia, auxilio, apoyo, socorro, favor.
assistant [ə'sistənt] *n* auxiliar, ayudante, asistente; **shop —** dependiente; **doctor's —** practicante; **— teacher** auxiliar, adjunto; **— director** subdirector.
associate [ə'souʃiit] *n* (*com*) socio, individuo; copartícipe, cómplice; [ə'souʃieit] *vt* asociar, juntar; *vi* asociarse, mancomunarse.
association [əˌsousi'eiʃən] *n* asociación, sociedad, mancomunidad, patronato.
assort [ə'sɔ:t] *vt* clasificar; compaginar, hacer juego; **assorted packets** paquetes surtidos.
assortment [ə'sɔ:tmənt] *n* clasificación; surtido, variedad, acopio.
assuage [ə'sweidʒ] *vti* aquietar, apaciguar; suavizar, templar, acallar, atemperar.
assume [ə'sju:m] *vt* tomar, poner; asumir, imaginarse, dar por sentado; creer; arrogarse, atribuir.
assumed [ə'sju:md] *a* sentado; **— virtue** virtud falsa; **— name** nombre ficticio.
assumption [ə'sʌmpʃən] *n* suposición, supuesto; **(Feast of the) —** Asunción.
assurance [ə'ʃuərəns] *n* seguridad, certeza; (*com*) seguro; aplomo, arrojo, ánimo; despejo, desenvoltura.
assure [ə'ʃuə] *vt* asegurar, garantizar; protestar; *vr* cerciorarse de; (*com*) asegurar.
assuredly [ə'ʃuəridli] *ad* seguramente, de seguro.
astern [ə'stə:n] *ad* en popa, a popa; **to go —** ciar; **to drop —** caer para atrás.
asthma ['æsmə] *n* asma.
astonish [ə'stɔniʃ] *vti* sorprender, suspender, maravillar, admirar.
astonished [ə'stɔniʃt] *a* atónito, estupefacto.
astonishing [ə'stɔniʃiŋ] *a* sorprendente.
astonishment [ə'stɔniʃmənt] *n* asombro, sorpresa, embobamiento, pasmo.
astound [ə'staund] *vti* maravillar, pasmar, helar, aturdir.
astray [ə'strei] *ad* fuera de la vía; extraviado, desviado, descarriado; **to go —** (*letters*) extraviarse; (*persons*) errar; **to lead —** extraviar; seducir; levar por mal camino.
astride [ə'straid] *ad* a horcajadas.
astringent [əs'trindʒənt] *a* astringente; áspero, austero.
astrology [əs'trɔlədʒi] *n* astrología.
astronomer [əs'trɔnəmə] *n* astrónomo.
astronomy [əs'trɔnəmi] *n* astronomía.
astute [əs'tju:t] *a* astuto, mañoso, sagaz; (*fam*) largo.
astuteness [əs'tju:tnis] *n* astucia, sutileza; chalanería.
asunder [ə'sʌndə] *ad* en dos, separadamente; **to tear —** despedazar, desgajar.
asylum [ə'sailəm] *n* asilo, refugio, amparo; (*lunatic*) manicomio; (*in church*) sagrado; **to give — to** dar acogida a.
at [æt] *prep* en, a, hacia; sobre, por; **(ambassador) — (the Court)** cerca de.
atavism ['ætəvizəm] *n* atavismo.
atheism ['eiθiizəm] *n* ateísmo.
atheist ['eiθiist] *n* ateo.
Athens ['æθinz] *n* Atenas.
athlete ['æθli:t] *n* atleta.
athletic [æθ'letik] *a* atlético; fuerte, deportista; *n pl* —s atlética.
atlas ['ætləs] *n* atlas.
atmosphere ['ætməsfiə] *n* atmósfera, clima, ambiente, aire.
atoll ['ætɔl] *n* atolón.
atom ['ætəm] *n* átomo.
atomize ['ætəmaiz] *vt* pulverizar.
atone [ə'toun] *vi* expiar, purgar, pagar; compensar, reparar; aplacar.
atonement [ə'tounmənt] *n* expiación, compensación, satisfacción.
atrocious [ə'trouʃəs] *a* atroz, espantoso.
atrocity [ə'trɔsiti] *n* atrocidad, crueldad.
attach [ə'tætʃ] *vt* adherir; ligar, pegar, conectar; (*property*) incautar; atraer, asirse; atribuir; (*importance*) dar.
attaché [ə'tæʃei] *n* agregado (*de embajada*).
attached [ə'tætʃt] *a* **— to** adjunto a; adicto a, aficionado a.
attachment [ə'tætʃmənt] *n* adhesión, apego; aplicación; ligazón, enlace; secuestro.
attack [ə'tæk] *n* ataque, asalto; (*violent*) embestida; arremetida; agresión; **sudden —** arrebato; **— of fever** acceso de fiebre; *vt* atacar, acometer; impugnar; corroer.
attain [ə'tein] *vt* lograr, alcanzar, conseguir.

attainable [ə'teinəbl] *a* asequible, accesible.
attainment [ə'teinmənt] *n* adquisición, logro, obtención; *pl* talentos, conocimientos.
attempt [ə'tempt] *n* ensayo, intento, conato, tentación, empresa; *vt* ensayar, probar, tentar, intentar; **to make — on** (*criminal*) atentar a; **to make — on** (*record*) intentar batir (*el récord*).
attend [ə'tend] *vti* servir, atender; (*sick*) asistir; presenciar, poner atención; concurrir; escuchar; (*lectures*) asistir, ir.
attendance [ə'tendəns] *n* servicio; asistencia; atención; servidumbre, séquito; concurrencia; (*audience*) auditorio, (*in theater*) público; **to dance — on** cortejar; **to be in —** (*med*) asistir.
attendant [ə'tendənt] *n* criado, servidor, asistente; (*cinema*) acomodador.
attended [ə'tendid] *a* **well- —** concurrido.
attention [ə'tenʃən] *n* atención; cuidado; miramiento; esmero cumplido; obsequio; respeto; (*mil*) **at —** cuadrado; **to pay — to** hacer caso de, parar mientes en, prestar atención; **to stand to —** cuadrarse.
attentive [ə'tentiv] *a* solícito; atento (*con*); galante.
attenuate [ə'tenjueit] *vt* atenuar, disminuir.
attenuation [əˌtenju'eiʃən] *n* atenuación.
attest [ə'test] *vt* dar (fe, testimonio); atestiguar; autenticar; deponer, afirmar.
attic ['ætik] *n* guardilla, buhardilla, desván, ático.
attire [ə'taiə] *n* atavío, gala, vestido, vestimenta, traje; *vi* ataviar, adornar, componer.
attitude ['ætitju:d] *n* actitud, posición, ademán.
attorney [ə'tə:ni] *n* procurador, operado; **power of —** poder legal, procura; **by —** por poder; **district —** fiscal.
attract [ə'trækt] *vt* (*magnet*) atraer; ganarse, llamar (*atención*).
attraction [ə'trækʃən] *n* atracción; imán; encanto; atractivo, seducción.
attractive [ə'træktiv] *a* atractivo; halagüeño, atrayente; (*fam*) **to be —** tener tilín.
attractiveness [ə'træktivnis] *n* atractivo, buena sombra, fuerza atractiva.
attributable [ə'tribjutəbl] *a* imputable.
attribute ['ætribju:t] *n* atributo; [ə'tribju:t] *vt* atribuir, imputar; (*blame*) achacar.
attune [ə'tju:n] *vt* templar, afinar (*instrument*); acordar, armonizar.
auburn ['ɔ:bən] *a* castaño rojizo.
auction ['ɔ:kʃən] *n* subasta, pregón, almoneda; **public —** subasta; *vt* subastar, rematar, sacar a subasta.
audacious [ɔ:'deiʃəs] *a* audaz, resuelto, osado, arrojado; descarado.
audacity [ɔ:'dæsiti] *n* audacia, osadía, arrojo, atrevimiento; descaro; demasía.
audible ['ɔ:dibl] *a* audible, perceptible.
audience ['ɔ:diəns] *n* audiencia, auditorio; (*theat*) público.
audit ['ɔ:dit] *n* verificación (de cuentas); *vt* intervenir.
auditor ['ɔ:ditə] *n* auditor, interventor, verificador de cuentas.
auditorium [ˌɔ:di'tɔ:riəm] *n* auditorio, sala de espectáculos; locutorio.
aught [ɔ:t] *n* algo; nada.
augment [ɔ:g'ment] *vti* aumentar; aumentarse, engrosar.
augmentation [ˌɔ:gmen'teiʃən] *n* aumento, acrecentamiento.
augur ['ɔ:gə] *n* augur, agorero; *vi* augurar; conjeturar, pronosticar; prometer.
augury ['ɔ:gjuri] *n* augurio, presagio, agüero.
August ['ɔ:gəst] *n* agosto; [ɔ:'gʌst] *a* augusto.
Augustine [ɔ:'gʌstin] *m* Agustín.
aunt [ɑ:nt] *n* tía.
aura ['ɔ:rə] *n* ambiente, aire.
aurora [ɔ:'rɔ:rə] *n* aurora; albores; comienzo; **— borealis** aurora boreal.
auspice ['ɔ:spis] *n* auspicio; presagio; **under the —s of** bajo el patrocinio de.
auspicious [ɔ:s'piʃəs] *a* favorable; de buen augurio, prometedor, halagüeño, propicio.
austere [ɔs'ti:ə] *a* austero, adusto; acerbo.
austerity [ɔs'teriti] *n* austeridad, rigor; estrechez, época de estrecheces.
Australia [ɔs'treiliə] *n* Australia.
Australian [ɔs'treiliən] *an* australiano.
Austria ['ɔstriə] *n* Austria.
Austrian ['ɔstriən] *an* austríaco.
authentic [ɔ:'θentik] *a* auténtico; legítimo, castizo.
authenticate [ɔ:'θentikeit] *vt* autenticar, refrendar, legalizar.
authenticity [ˌɔ:θen'tisiti] *n* autenticidad.
author ['ɔ:θə] *n* autor, escritor; **—ess** autora, escritora.
authoritative [ɔ:'θɔritətiv] *a* autoritario; autorizado, perentorio.
authority [ɔ:'θɔriti] *n* autoridad, poderío, poder, mando; texto; facultad; preeminencia; **civil —** brazo secular; **on good —** de buena tinta; **to have — to** poder; *pl* autoridades.
authorization [ˌɔ:θərai'zeiʃən] *n* autorización; poder; sanción.
authorize ['ɔ:θəraiz] *vt* autorizar,

conferir, poder, acreditar; sancionar.
authorized ['ɔːθəraizd] *a* habilitado, apoderado; (*translation etc*) autorizado.
autobiography [ˌɔːtoubai'ɔgrəfi] *n* autobiografía.
autocrat ['ɔːtəkræt] *n* autócrata.
autocratic [ˌɔːtə'krætik] *a* autocrático.
autograph ['ɔːtəgrɑːf] *n* autógrafo.
automobile ['ɔːtəməbiːl] *n* automóvil.
autonomy [ɔː'tɔnəmi] *n* autonomía.
autopsy ['ɔːtəpsi] *n* autopsia.
autumn ['ɔːtəm] *n* otoño.
autumnal [ɔː'tʌmnəl] *a* otoñal.
auxiliary [ɔːg'ziljəri] *a* auxiliar.
avail [ə'veil] *n* provecho, ventaja; *vi* aprovecharse de, (pre)valerse; **to — nothing** no servir para nada; **without —** sin prevalecer, sin resultado.
available [ə'veiləbl] *n* asequible, conseguible, válido, disponible, a (*su*) disposición; **not —** que no se puede obtener; **— funds** fondos disponibles.
avalanche ['ævəlɑːnʃ] *n* alud, lurte.
avarice ['ævəris] *n* avaricia, codicia, mezquindad.
avaricious [ˌævə'riʃəs] *a* avariento, codicioso, avaro.
avenge [ə'vendʒ] *vt* vengar, castigar.
avenger [ə'vendʒə] *n* vengador.
avenue ['ævənjuː] *n* avenida, arboleda, alameda; pasadizo; vía, medio.
average ['ævəridʒ] *n* promedio; **on an —** por regla general; **general —** promedio general; *a* promedial, medio, ordinario, regular; *vti* tomar el promedio, promediar, llegar a un promedio.
averse [ə'vəːs] *a* contrario, adverso, opuesto.
aversion [ə'vəːʃən] *n* aversión, repugnancia, desgana, antipatía; (*fam*) hincha.
avert [ə'vəːt] *vt* impedir, alejar, desviar, conjurar.
aviary ['eiviəri] *n* pajarera.
aviation [ˌeivi'eiʃən] *n* aviación.
avidity [ə'viditi] *n* avidez, codicia, ansia.
avoid [ə'vɔid] *vti* evitar, (re)huir; guardarse de, librarse; **not to be able to —** no poder menos de.
avoidable [ə'vɔidəbl] *a* evitable, eludible.
avoidance [ə'vɔidəns] *n* evitación.
avow [ə'vau] *vt* confesar, declarar, manifestar.
avowal [ə'vauəl] *n* confesión; profesión, declaración.
await [ə'weit] *vt* esperar, aguardar.
awake [ə'weik] *vti* despertar(se); excitar; *a* despierto; despabilado, listo; **to stay —** velar.
awaken [ə'weikən] *vt* despertar.
awakening [ə'weikniŋ] *n* despertar.
award [ə'wɔːd] *n* fallo; premio, recompensa, honor; juicio, sentencia, laudo (*of tribunal*); *vti* adjudicar; conferir, conceder (*prize*); otorgar; sentenciar, decretar.
aware [ə'wɛə] *a* vigilante; enterado; consciente; **to be —** estar enterado; **to be — of** percatarse; **as far as I am —** que yo sepa.
awash [ə'wɔʃ] *ad* a flor de agua.
away [ə'wei] *a* ausente; a lo lejos; **to be —** estar fuera; **to go —** alejarse; **— with you!** ¡quita de allí!
awe [ɔː] *n* horror, miedo; respeto; **to stand in — of** tener miedo de.
awesome ['ɔːsəm] *a* aterrador, pavoroso.
awful ['ɔːfəl] *a* horrible, terrible, tremendo, espantoso, pavoroso; malísimo, pésimo.
awfulness ['ɔːfəlnis] *n* terror, temor.
awhile [ə'wail] *ad* durante algún tiempo, un rato.
awkward ['ɔːkwəd] *a* torpe, desmañado, zurdo; (*business*) embarazoso, peliagudo.
awkwardness ['ɔːkwədnis] *n* torpeza, falta de habilidad.
awning ['ɔːniŋ] *n* toldo, tienda.
awry [ə'rai] *a* sesgado, torcido, atravesado; **to look —** mirar de reojo.
ax [æks] *n* hacha; **pick—** zapapico.
axiom ['æksiəm] *n* axioma, postulado.
axis ['æksis] *n* eje.
axle ['æksl] *n* eje; **crank —** eje de codillo.
azure ['æʒə] *n* azul celeste; (*her*) azur.

B

B.A. ['biː'ei] *abbrev* Licenciado en Filosofía y Letras, Bachiller.
babble ['bæbl] *n* charla, charlatanería; murmullo; rumor; *vi* balbucear; hablar por los codos; garlar; (*water*) murmurar.
babbler ['bæblə] *n* charlatán, parlanchín.
babbling ['bæbliŋ] *n* charla, balbuceo.
babe [beib] *n* nene, criatura; (*royal*) infante.
babel ['beibəl] *n* babel, tumulto, baraúnda.
baby ['beibi] *n* nene, crío, criatura, chiquillo; **—'s diaper** pañal.
babyish ['beibiiʃ] *a* infantil.
Bacchus ['bækəs] *m* Baco.
bachelor ['bætʃələ] *n* (*old*) soltero, solterón; (*acad*) bachiller, licenciado.
back [bæk] *ad* atrás, detrás; a espaldas de, trasero; de vuelta; otra vez; (*movement*) hacia atrás; *n* espalda; revés, parte posterior; espaldar; (*of hand*) envés; (*theat*) foro; (*animal, book*) lomo; (*in football*) defensa; (*of seat*) respaldar, respaldo;

— **shop** trastienda; *vti* hacer retroceder; (*of motor car*) dar marcha atrás; respaldar; apoyar; **to — out, down** desdecirse, volver atrás; retroceder; (*books*) aforrar, encuadernar; **to — water** ciar; **to get — again** rehacerse; **backed (up) by** apoyado por; **on one's —** a cuestas; **fall on one's —** caer boca arriba; **to turn one's — to** volverse de espaldas a; **to turn one's — on someone** volverle la espalda a, desairar.

backbite ['bækbait] *vt* calumniar, difamar.

backbiting ['bækbaitiŋ] *n* maledicencia, detracción, murmuración.

backbone ['bækboun] *n* espina (*dorsal*), cerro, columna vertebral; **English to the —** inglés hasta los tuétanos.

backdoor ['bæk'dɔ:] *n* puerta trasera.

background ['bækgraund] *n* fondo, último término.

backing ['bækiŋ] *n* forro; (*influence*) respaldo, apoyo.

backroom ['bæk'rum] *n* cuarto interior, recámara.

backside ['bæksaid] *n* trasero, parte trasera, espalda.

backslide ['bæk'slaid] *vi* (*beliefs etc*) reincidir, volver a las andadas.

backstairs ['bæk'stɛəz] *n* escalera (secreta, excusada).

backward ['bækwəd] *a* atrasado, tardío; (*wit*) corto; tardo; *ad* hacia atrás.

backwardness ['bækwədnis] *n* tardanza; ignorancia, atraso; (*delay*) retraso.

backwater ['bækwɔ:tə] *n* remanso.

backyard ['bæk'jɑ:d] *n* patio interior; corral.

bacon ['beikən] *n* tocino; jamón; **to save one's —** salvar el pellejo.

bad [bæd] *a* mal, malo, nocivo; indispuesto; podrido; **very —** pésimo; **— blood** rencilla, mala sangre; **from — to worse** de mal en peor; **to go —** pasar, (*milk*) cortarse; **with — grace** de mala gana, a regañadientes.

badge [bædʒ] *n* insignia, marca, placa, condecoración; divisa.

badger ['bædʒə] *n* tejón; **— bristle** cerda; *vt* atormentar, provocar, fastidiar.

badly ['bædli] *ad* mal, malamente.

badness ['bædnis] *n* maldad.

baffle ['bæfl] *vt* frustrar; desconcertar; confundir; desbaratar.

bag [bæg] *n* saco, bolsillo, bolsa; talega; (*leather*) zurrón; valija; (*game*) morral; (*small*) taleguilla; *pl* equipaje; *vti* entalegar, meter en un saco; (*clothes*) hacer bolsas; insacular; capturar; **to pack one's bags** liar el petate.

bagatelle [,bægə'tel] *n* fruslería, bagatela, puerilidad, friolera.

baggage ['bægidʒ] *n* equipaje; (*mil*) bagaje; **— car** furgón.

bagpipe ['bægpaip] *n* gaita, cornamusa.

bail [beil] *n* fianza, caución, afianzamiento; **to go —** afianzar, caucionar, responder por; **to give —** sanear.

bailiff ['beilif] *n* alguacil, corchete.

bait [beit] *n* cebo; anzuelo, señuelo, carnada; *vti* cebar, poner cebo; refrigerarse; hostigar, acosar.

bake [beik] *vt* cocer (*en el horno*), hornear.

baker ['beikə] *n* panadero.

bakery ['beikəri] *n* panadería, tahona.

baking ['beikiŋ] *n* hornada; cocimiento; **— tin** tortera.

balance ['bæləns] *n* balanza; cotejo; balance; contrapeso; resto; (*com*) saldo; **— sheet** balance; **— of trade** balanza comercial; **— wheel** volante; **to draw a —** echar un balance; *vt* equilibrar, hacer balance; *vi* balancearse, mecerse; **to — up** igualar, pesar.

balancing ['bælənsiŋ] *n* balanceo, equilibrio.

balcony ['bælkəni] *n* balcón, antepecho, mirador; (*theat*) galería, anfiteatro.

bald [bɔ:ld] *a* calvo; pelado; desnudo, escueto; **— head** calva.

balderdash ['bɔ:ldədæʃ] *n* hojarasca, disparate.

baldness ['bɔ:ldnis] *n* calvicie, calva.

bale [beil] *n* fardo; tercio, balón; *vt* empacar, enfardelar, empaquetar.

Balearic Islands [,bæli'ærik 'ailəndz] *n* las Islas Baleares.

baleful ['beilful] *a* triste, funesto, pernicioso.

balk [bɔ:k] *n* viga; obstáculo; *vt* impedir, desbaratar, frustrar.

ball [bɔ:l] *n* (*solid*) bola, globo, (*inflated*) pelota, balón; (*of wool*) ovillo; (*cannon*) bala; baile; **— bearings** cojinete de bolas; **fancy —** baile de trajes (*de máscaras*).

ballad ['bæləd] *n* romance; balada, canción, copla, trova; **corpus of —s** romancero.

ballast ['bæləst] *n* lastre; *vt* lastrar.

ballet ['bælei] *n* ballet; danza.

balloon [bə'lu:n] *n* globo aerostático.

ballot ['bælət] *n* escrutinio, votación; **—box** urna; *vi* votar, sacar.

balm [bɑ:m] *n* bálsamo; alivio.

balsam ['bɔ:lsəm] *n* bálsamo.

balustrade [,bæləs'treid] *n* balaustrada, barandilla.

bamboo [bæm'bu:] *n* bambú.

ban [bæn] *n* edicto; prohibición, pregón; entredicho; *vt* proscribir.

banality [bə'næliti] *n* vaciedad, vulgaridad.

banana [bə'nɑ:nə] *n* banana, plátano.

band [bænd] *n* (*strip*) faja, cinta; tira; (*robbers*) cuadrilla, pandilla, partida; (*gypsies*) cáfila; (*mus*)

banda; farándula, bandada; franja; unión; *vti* congregar, congregarse; **to — together** (*in league etc*) apandillarse, asociarse.
bandage ['bændidʒ] *n* venda(je); faja.
bandit ['bændit] *n* bandolero, bandido, forajido.
bandy ['bændi] *vti* cambiar; trocar, disputar; *a* **—legged** arqueado, patizambo.
bang [bæŋ] *n* detonación; golpazo, ruido, puñada, golpe, porrazo; *vt* lanzar, cerrar con estrépito; **with a —** (*ie success*) un exitazo.
bangle ['bæŋgl] *n* ajorca, pulsera.
banish ['bæniʃ] *vt* desterrar, exilar, confinar, deportar; (*care*) ahuyentar.
banishment ['bæniʃmənt] *n* destierro, deportación, extrañación, exterminio.
banister ['bænistə] *n* baranda, pasamano.
bank ['bæŋk] *n* banco; casa de banca; (*earth*) terraplén; (*river*) orilla, ribera; (*flowers*) banco; **—note** billete de banco; **—book** libreta; **savings —** caja de ahorro; **to — up** represar, estancar.
banker ['bæŋkə] *n* banquero.
banking ['bæŋkiŋ] *a* bancario; *n* banca; **— house** casa de banca.
bankrupt ['bæŋkrʌpt] *a* insolvente, quebrado; *n* fallido; **to become —** quebrar, hacer bancarrota.
bankruptcy ['bæŋkrʌptsi] *n* bancarrota, quiebra.
banner ['bænə] *n* bandera; estandarte.
banns ['bænz] *n* amonestaciones; proclama, pregón; **to publish the —** amonestar, hacer las proclamas.
banquet ['bæŋkwit] *n* banquete, festín, convite; *vti* banquetear.
banter ['bæntə] *n* burla, chanza; *vt* burlarse, fisgar(se), tomar el pelo de.
baptism ['bæptizəm] *n* (*sacrament*) bautismo; (*action*) bautizo.
baptize [bæp'taiz] *vt* bautizar.
baptismal [bæp'tizməl] *a* bautismal; **— name** nombre de pila.
bar [bɑ:] *n* barra, valla, barrera; tranca; (*mech*) palanca; (*music*) raya; (*hotel*) mostrador; (*law*) tribunal; (*strip*) faja, lista; (*obstacle*) obstáculo, traba; *vt* cerrar el paso, impedir, interrumpir, excluir, estorbar, obstar; **to — up** (*a door*) atrancar.
barb [bɑ:b] *n* púa; pincho; (*bot*) arista, barba; (*arrow*) lengüeta.
Barbara ['bɑ:bərə] *f* Bárbara.
barbarian [bɑ:'bɛəriən] *an* bárbaro.
barbarism ['bɑ:bərizəm] *n* (*lang*) barbarismo; (*savagery*) barbarie; (*enormity etc*) barbaridad.
barbarous ['bɑ:bərəs] *a* bárbaro.
barbed ['bɑ:bd] *a* con púas; erizado; **— wire** alambre de púas.
barber ['bɑ:bə] *n* barbero, peluquero, rapador.
bare ['bɛə] *a* seco, desnudo, llano, descubierto; (*stripped*) pelado; (*essential*) escueto; *vt* descubrir; **to lay —** poner a descubierto; desnudar, revelar.
barebacked ['bɛəbækt] *a* en pelo.
barefaced ['bɛəfeist] *a* descarado, impudente, desvergonzado, cínico.
barefoot ['bɛə'fut] *a* descalzo.
bareheaded ['bɛə'hedid] *a* descubierto.
barely ['bɛəli] *ad* apenas; simplemente, escasamente.
bareness ['bɛənis] *n* desnudez, miseria.
bargain ['bɑ:gin] *n* (*agreement*) ajuste, pacto, convenio; (*cheap*) ganga; estipulación; **— sale** saldo; **into the —** por más señas; *vi* negociar; regatear.
bargaining ['bɑ:giniŋ] *n* regateo.
barge [bɑ:dʒ] *n* barca, bote, lanchón.
bark [bɑ:k] *n* (*tree*) corteza, cáscara; **oak —** casca; (*boat*) barco; (*dog*) ladrido; *vt* quitar la corteza; *vi* ladrar.
barking ['bɑ:kiŋ] *n* ladrido.
barley ['bɑ:li] *n* cebada; **milk —** cebadilla.
barmaid ['bɑ:meid] *n* moza (*de taberna*), camarera.
barn [bɑ:n] *n* granero, pajar; (*fruit*) troj(e); (*in Asturias*) hórreo; patio de granja; **— owl** lechuza.
barnacle ['bɑ:nəkl] *n* lapa; percebe.
barometer [bə'rɔmitə] *n* barómetro.
baron ['bærən] *n* barón.
baronet ['bærənit] *n* barón.
baroque [bə'rouk] *an* barroco.
barrack(s) ['bærək(s)] *n* (*mil*) cuartel; barraca.
barracks revolt ['bærəks ri'voult] *n* cuartelada.
barrage ['bærɑ:ʒ] *n* presa; (*mil*) barrera.
barrel ['bærəl] *n* barril, barrica; **— organ** manubrio, organillo; (*rifle*) cañon; *vt* envasar.
barren ['bærən] *a* (*earth*) estéril, yermo; (*bare*) pelado, calvo.
barrenness ['bærənnis] *n* esterilidad, aridez, pobreza.
barricade [ˌbæri'keid] *n* barricada, barrera, empalizada; *vt* obstruir, cerrar con barricadas; **to — o.s. in** hacerse fuerte.
barrier ['bæriə] *n* valla, barrera; (*in bullring*) contrabarrera; obstáculo.
barrister ['bæristə] *n* abogado.
barter ['bɑ:tə] *n* trueque, tráfico, barata, rescate, cambalache; *vi* traficar; *vt* cambiar, permutar, conmutar.
Bartholomew [bɑ:'θɔləmju:] *m* Bartolomé.
bas-relief ['bæsriˌli:f] *n* bajorrelieve.
base [beis] *n* base; basa, pedestal;

sedimento; (*origin*) raíz; *a* (*music*) bajo; vil, infame; ruín, innoble; *vt* fundar; — (**on**) calcar; *vi* apoyarse.
baseball ['beisbɔ:l] *n* pelota base, béisbol.
baseless ['beislis] *a* infundado.
basement ['beismənt] *n* sótano.
baseness ['beisnis] *n* bajeza, infamia, vileza, ruindad.
bashful ['bæʃful] *a* tímido, vergonzoso, ruboroso, encogido.
bashfulness ['bæʃfulnis] *n* timidez, pudor, cortedad, recato, rubor, apocamiento.
basic ['beisik] *a* básico.
basin [beisn] *n* bacia, aljofaina; (*water*) estanque, represa; (*river*) cuenca, hoya; (*dock*) dársena; (*of fountain*) pilón; **wash** — palangana; **pudding** — molde, tartera.
basis ['beisis] *n* base; cimiento.
bask [bɑ:sk] *vi* tomar el sol.
basket ['bɑ:skit] *n* canasta, esportillo; (*large*) cesto; (*frail*) capacho; espuerta; (*small, low*) canastillo.
basketmaker ['bɑ:skit,meikə] *n* cestero.
Basque [bæsk] *a* vasco, vizcaíno; (*lang*) vascuence.
Basque Provinces ['bæsk 'prɔvinsiz] *n* las Provincias Vascongadas.
bass [beis] *an* (*mus*) bajo; **deep, double** — contrabajo.
bassoon [bə'su:n] *n* fagot; bajón; — **player** bajón.
bastard ['bæstəd] *an* bastardo; espurio.
bastion ['bæstiən] *n* bastión, baluarte.
bat [bæt] *n* (*orn*) murciélago; palo; **off his own** — de su propia cuenta; *vt* moverse, agitarse, pestañear.
batch [bætʃ] *n* (*oven*) hornada; porción; lote, tanda.
bath [bɑ:θ] *n* baño; cuarto de baño; **bird** — bebedero; — **tub** bañadera; **blood** — carnicería.
bathe [beið] *vt* bañar; *vi* bañarse.
bather ['beiðə] *n* bañista.
bathing ['beiðiŋ] *n* baño; — **beach** playa; — **suit** bañador, traje de baño; — **wrap** bata, albornoz.
baton ['bætən] *n* bastón de mando; (*mus*) batuta.
battalion [bə'tæliən] *n* batallón.
batter ['bætə] *n* batido; *vti* apalear, golpear; demoler, cañonear; **to — a breach in** batir en brecha.
battering ram ['bætəriŋræm] *n* ariete.
battery ['bætəri] *n* batería; (*el*) pila, acumulador.
battle ['bætl] *n* batalla, pelea, lid, combate; *vi* batallar, luchar.
battlement ['bætlmənt] *n* muralla; almena, almenaje.
bauble ['bɔ:bl] *n* chuchería, fruslería, baratija.
bawd [bɔ:d] *n* alcahueta, tercera.
bawdy ['bɔ:di] *a* indecente, obsceno.
bawl [bɔ:l] *vi* chillar, gritar, vociferar, dar voces, desgañitarse; *vt* pregonar.
bay [bei] *n* abra, bahía, ensenada; (*small*) anconada; pajar; (*howl*) aullido; — **window** mirador; (*tree*) laurel; **at** — acorralado, en jaque; **to keep at** — mantener a raya; *a* bayo; *vi* aullar.
bayonet ['beiənit] *n* bayoneta; **fixed** — bayoneta calada; — **thrust** bayonetazo.
bazaar [bə'zɑ:] *n* feria, bazar; tómbola.
be [bi:] *vi* ser, existir; estar; (*somewhere*) quedar, encontrarse; (*ill*) encontrarse; **to — hungry** tener hambre; **to — off** hacer la maleta, largarse, marcharse.
beach [bi:tʃ] *n* playa, orilla, costa.
beacon ['bi:kən] *n* (*light*) fanal; (*naut*) boya; antorcha; *vt* iluminar.
bead [bi:d] *n* cuenta; gota; *pl* rosario.
beadle ['bi:dl] *n* bedel.
beagle ['bi:gl] *n* sabueso.
beak [bi:k] *n* pico.
beaker ['bi:kə] *n* vaso; copa.
beam [bi:m] *n* (*wood*) viga, tablón, madero; (*in eye*) estaca; **tie** — tirante; (*light*) rayo, destello; *vi* destellar, dirigir; sonreír.
beaming ['bi:miŋ] *a* radiante, brillante.
bean [bi:n] *n* (*broad*) haba, (*kidney*) habichuela, (*black*) frejol; — **field** habar; **without a** — sin blanca; **he hasn't a** — no tiene un cuarto.
bear [bɛə] *n* oso; (*com*) bajista; **Great B—** Osa mayor; — **cub** osezno; **polar** — oso blanco; **—like** osuno.
bear [bɛə] *vt* (*trouble*) aguantar, sobrellevar, sufrir; (*weight*) cargar, sostener; (*com*) jugar a la baja; (*arms*) ostentar; producir, devengar, dar; *vti* padecer; dar fruto; (*sea*) enfilar el curso; **to — down upon** echarse sobre, vencer, aplastar; **to — on** referirse a; atañer; **to — out** corroborar, confirmar; **to — up** hacer frente a; cobrar ánimo; **to — toward** dirigirse sobre; **to — with** conllevar, aguantar; **to — malice** tener ojeriza.
bearable ['bɛərəbl] *a* soportable, tolerable, pasadero, llevadero.
beard [biəd] *n* barba; *vt* desafiar.
bearded ['biədid] *a* barbudo.
beardless ['biədlis] *a* imberbe, barbilampiño.
bearer ['bɛərə] *n* llevador, portador.
bearing ['bɛəriŋ] *n* situación; relación; conducta; talante, porte, actitud; orientación; **ball** — cojinete de bolas; **to take a** — arrumbar; **to find one's —s** orientarse; **to lose one's —s** desorientarse, desatinar; **to have a — on** atañer, concernir.
beast [bi:st] *n* bestia; res; (*of burden*) acémila; (*wild*) fiera.
beastliness ['bi:stlinis] *n* bestialidad.

beastly ['bi:stli] *a* bestial.
beat [bi:t] *n* (*mus*) compás; (*drum*) toque; (*heart*) latido, impulso; (*police*) ronda; *vt* (*eggs*) batir; (*games*) derrotar, ganar; (*with stick etc*) golpear, vapul(e)ar, zurrar, moler; **to — down** atropellar; **to — time** llevar (marcar) el compás; **to — about the bush** andarse por las ramas, con rodeos; **to — it** (*sl*) largarse; (*for game*) ojear; (*heart*) palpitar, latir; (*a retreat*) emprender la retirada.
beaten [bi:tn] *a* sacudido; (*games*) vencido; **— track** camino (asendereado, trillado).
beating ['bi:tiŋ] *n* (*of heart*) latido, pulsación; **— up** palizada, meneo, tunda; (*cook*) batidura; **without — about the bush** a las claras.
Beatrice ['biətris] *f* Beatriz.
beau [bou] *n* petimetre, guapo, cortejo.
beauteous ['bju:tiəs] *a* bello.
beautiful ['bju:təful] *a* bello, hermoso; guapo; vistoso; venusto.
beautifully ['bju:təfli] *ad* bellamente, bien; (*fam*) estupendamente.
beautify ['bju:tifai] *vt* embellecer, pulir, hermosear, adornar.
beauty ['bju:ti] *n* belleza; hermosura; primor; preciosidad; **— spot** lunar.
beaver ['bi:və] *n* castor.
becalm [bi'kɑ:m] *vt* calmar; *vi* (*sea*) encalmarse.
because [bi'kɔz] *cj* porque; **— of** a causa de.
beckon ['bekən] *vti* llamar por señas; invitar; hacer señas.
become [bi'kʌm] *vt* convenir, sentar, ir bien; *vi* llegar a ser, volverse, convertirse en; ponerse; tornarse; hacerse; **to — bankrupt** hacer bancarrota; **to — the rage** popularizarse.
becoming [bi'kʌmiŋ] *a* que sienta bien; correcto, propio, decoroso; **it is very — (on) (to) you** le favorece mucho.
becomingly [bi'kʌmiŋli] *ad* convenientemente; con gracia.
bed [bed] *n* cama, lecho; (*camp*) catre; **double —** cama matrimonial; (*wretched*) camastro; (*feather*) colchón (*de pluma*); (*ore*) yacimiento; (*river*) cauce, madre; (*mech*) asiento; (*flower*) macizo, arriate; **— and breakfast** pensión; **to put to —** acostar; **to stay in —** (*sickness*) guardar cama; (*pleasure*) quedarse en la cama; **—cover** cobertor; **—spread** sobrecama, cobertura; **—side** cabecera; *vt* acostar, meter en cama; **to go to —** acostarse.
bedding ['bediŋ] *n* ropa, coberturas de cama.
bedeck [bi'dek] *vt* adornar, ornamentar, engalanar.
bedevil [bi'devəl] *vt* endemoniar, atormentar.
bedlam ['bedləm] *n* confusión, gritería, jaleo; belén, casa de orates.
bedridden ['bed.ridn] *a* postrado en cama.
bedroom ['bedrum] *n* dormitorio, alcoba.
bedstead ['bedsted] *n* cuja.
bedtime ['bedtaim] *n* hora de dormir.
bee [bi:] *n* abeja; **—hive** colmena; **bumble—** moscón, abejarrón: abejorro; **—line** línea recta.
beech [bi:tʃ] *n* haya; **— grove** hayal, hayedo.
beef [bi:f] *n* carne de vaca; **dried —** cecina; **jerked —** tasajo.
beer [biə] *n* cerveza; **— shop, — café, — garden** cervecería.
beet [bi:t] *n* remolacha.
beetle ['bi:tl] *n* escarabajo; pisón; (*death-watch*) carcoma; **—browed** cejijunto.
beetling ['bi:tliŋ] *a* salidizo, pendiente.
befall [bi'fɔ:l] *vi* suceder, acaecer, acontecer.
befit [bi'fit] *vt* convenir, cuadrar, ser propio de.
befitting [bi'fitiŋ] *a* propio, conveniente.
before [bi'fɔ:] *prep* (*in presence of*) ante; delante de, enfrente de; *ad* (*place*) delante; (*time*) anteriormente, antes, precedentemente; **as —** como antes, inalterado; **day —** víspera; **— mentioned** consabido.
beforehand [bi'fɔ:hænd] *ad* con anticipación, de antemano.
befriend [bi'frend] *vt* favorecer, proteger.
beg [beg] *vt* pedir, rogar, suplicar; *vi* mendigar.
beget [bi'get] *vt* engendrar, procrear; suscitar.
beggar ['begə] *n* mendigo, pordiosero; *vt* empobrecer; reducir a la mendicidad; apurar, agotar; **to — description** superar a toda calificación.
beggarly ['begəli] *a* indigente, pobre; mezquino.
begging ['begiŋ] *a* mendicante; **to go —** andar mendigando; *n* pordioseo.
begin [bi'gin] *vt* comenzar, empezar, iniciar, abrir, emprender; *vi* empezar; entrar; estrenar; **to — with** para empezar.
beginner [bi'ginə] *n* principiante, aprendiz, neófito, novato.
beginning [bi'giniŋ] *n* principio, comienzo, origen; **at the —** al principio; **in the —** en el principio; **from — to end** de cabo a rabo, de pe a pa.
begotten [bi'gɔtn] *a* engendrado; **only —** unigénito.
begrimed [bi'graimd] *a* ensuciado, enlodado; **soot —** tiznado.
beguile [bi'gail] *vt* engatusar; defraudar; entretener.
behalf [bi'hɑ:f] *n* provecho; **on — of**

en nombre de, a favor de, de parte de.
behave [bi'heiv] *vi* conducirse, manejarse, obrar.
behavior [bi'heivjə] *n* conducta, porte, proceder; (*mech*) marcha.
behead [bi'hed] *vt* decapitar, degollar.
beheading [bi'hediŋ] *n* decapitación, degüello, descabezamiento.
behind [bi'haind] *prep ad* atrás, (por) (hacia) detrás; **left —** rezagado; **to be, fall —** retrasarse; **to be — (time)** retrasarse; **— someone's back** a espaldas de, sin saberlo.
behindhand [bi'haindhænd] *a* atrasado.
behold [bi'hould] *vt* mirar, considerar, contemplar; *excl* hé aquí . . .
behove [bi'houv] *vt* convenir; ser propio; incumbir, tocar.
being ['bi:iŋ] *n* ser, estado, existencia; entidad; **divine —** deidad; **human —** ser humano.
belabor [bi'leibə] *vt* pegar, apalear, moler.
belated [bi'leitid] *a* tardío, atrasado.
belay [bi'lei] *vt* amarrar, rodear.
belch [beltʃ] *n* eructo; *vti* arrojar, vomitar; eructar.
beleaguer [bi'li:gə] *vt* sitiar, bloquear.
belfry ['belfri] *n* campanario, torre.
Belgian ['beldʒən] *an* bélgico; *n* belga.
Belgium ['beldʒəm] *n* Bélgica.
belie [bi'lai] *vt* engañar; desmentir, contradecir.
belief [bi'li:f] *n* creencia, fe; crédito; confianza; parecer.
believable [bi'li:vəbl] *a* creíble, digno de fe.
believe [bi'li:v] *vt* creer, entender, tener por, fiarse de.
believer [bi'li:və] *n* creyente, fiel; **— in** partidario de.
belittle [bi'litl] *vt* empequeñecer, achicar, burlarse (*de*).
bell [bel] *n* (*church*) campana; (*el etc*) timbre; (*hand*) esquila; (*small*) címbalo; (*cow*) cencerro; (*cattle*) zumba; (*passing*) toque de difuntos; (*flower*) campanilla; **—shaped** acampanudo; **—clapper** badajo; **stroke of —** campanada.
bellboy ['belbɔi] *n* botones.
bellhop ['belhɔp] *n* botones.
bellicose ['belikous] *a* belicoso, bélico.
bellied ['belid] *a* **fat-—** barrigudo; **big-—** panzudo.
belligerent [bi'lidʒərənt] *an* beligerante.
bellow ['belou] *vi* mugir, bramar, rugir.
bellowing ['belouiŋ] *n* mugido, bramido.
bellows ['belouz] *n* fuelle.
bellringer ['bel,riŋə] *n* campanero.
belly ['beli] *n* vientre, barriga, panza; tripas; (*bottle*) barriga; **—band** (*horse*) cincha, (*man*) faja; *vi* inflarse.
belong [bi'lɔŋ] *vi* pertenecer; tocar a, competer; **to — to** ser de.
belongings [bi'lɔŋiŋz] *n pl* bienes; bártulos.
beloved [bi'lʌvd] *a* amado, querido, favorito; **well-—** bienquisto.
below [bi'lou] *ad prep* abajo, debajo (de), bajo; **— zero** bajo cero; **here —** de tejas abajo; aquí abajo.
belt [belt] *n* cinto, ceñidor, faja; (*leather*) correa, cinturón; zona; *vt* ceñir, fajar, rodear; (*fam*) zumbar.
belting ['beltiŋ] *n* (*mech*) correa; correaje; (*fam*) zurra.
bench [bentʃ] *n* banco; banca; (*stool*) escabel; (*settle*) escaño; (*law*) tribunal.
bend [bend] *n* curvatura, comba; (*in road*) recodo, vuelta; (*river*) meandro; *vt* inclinar, encorvar, dirigir, encaminar; torcer, doblar, plegar; **to — the elbow** (*fam*) empinar el codo; **to — to one's will** doblegar, sujetar; (*brows*) enarcar, fruncir (*las cejas*).
bended ['bendid] *a* **on — knees** de hinojos.
bending ['bendiŋ] *n* curvatura, doblamiento.
beneath [bi'ni:θ] *ad prep* debajo, bajo, abajo, debajo de; **— regard** indigno de consideración.
Benedict ['benidikt] *m* Benedicto, Benito.
benediction [,beni'dikʃən] *n* bendición; gracia divina.
benefaction [,beni'fækʃən] *n* beneficio, merced.
benefactor ['benifæktə] *n* bienhechor, patrono.
benefice ['benifis] *n* beneficio, prebenda.
beneficent [bi'nefisənt] *a* benéfico, caritativo.
beneficial [,beni'fiʃəl] *a* benéfico; ventajoso, propicio.
benefit ['benifit] *n* beneficio, ventaja, provecho; **to derive — from** sacar partido de; **for the — (of)** en favor, en pro (de); *vti* beneficiar, servir; aprovecharse.
benevolence [bi'nevələns] *n* benevolencia, humanidad; merced.
benevolent [bi'nevələnt] *a* benévolo, caritativo; angélico.
benign [bi'nain] *a* benigno, afable; obsequioso.
benignant [bi'nignənt] *a* propicio, saludable.
bent [bent] *n* inclinación, afición, tendencia, propensión; curvatura; *a* encorvado, torcido; **— upon** resuelto a.
benumb [bi'nʌm] *vt* (*with cold etc*) entumecer, aterir, entorpecer; (*with fear etc*) pasmar.
benzine ['benzi:n] *n* bencina.
bequeath [bi'kwi:ð] *vt* legar, dejar (*herencia*).

bequest [bi'kwest] *n* legado, manda.
berate [bi'reit] *vt* reñir, regañar.
bereave [bi'ri:v] *vt* despojar, privar de, arrebatar; (*death*) arrebatar; acongojar; **—d** *n pl* los afligidos.
bereavement [bi'ri:vmənt] *n* privación, pérdida, despojo; (*death*) pérdida, aflicción; desgracia.
beret ['berei] *n* boina.
Bernard ['bə:nəd] *m* Bernardo.
berry ['beri] *n* baya; grano.
berth [bə:θ] *n* (*bed*) litera, camarote; (*dock*) fondeadero; destino; *vt* proporcionar anclaje, litera; **to give a wide — to** apartarse de, dejar pasar (muy) de largo.
beseech [bi'si:tʃ] *vt* suplicar, rogar, implorar.
beset [bi'set] *vt* (*town*) sitiar, rodear; (*enemy, trouble*) acosar, perseguir.
beside [bi'said] *prep* al lado de; en comparación con; **— oneself** fuera de sí; **to be — oneself (with joy)** no caber en sí (de gozo).
besides [bi'saidz] *ad* además, igualmente; asimismo; *prep* amén de, aparte de, tras, fuera de, por encima de, sobre.
besiege [bi'si:dʒ] *vi* bloquear, poner cerco a, sitiar; (*fig*) asediar, acosar.
besieger [bi'si:dʒə] *n* sitiador.
besieging [bi'si:dʒiŋ] *n* sitio, cerco.
best [best] *a ad* óptimo; muy bueno, superior, mejor, del mejor modo; *n* el mejor, lo mejor; **to do one's —** esmerarse en, hacer cuanto se puede; **— man** padrino; **to make the — of a bad job** poner a mal tiempo buena cara; sacar el mejor partido; **the — in the world** lo mejor del mundo; **at (the) —** en el mejor caso, cuando más; **to get the — of** llevar ventaja, vencer.
bestial ['bestiəl] *a* bestial, brutal.
bestiality [ˌbesti'æliti] *n* bestialidad.
bestir [bi'stə:] *vt* sacudir, remover, menear; *vr* menearse.
bestow [bi'stou] *vt* dar, conceder, otorgar, regalar; **to — an honor on** condecorar, conferir.
bestowal [bi'stouəl] *n* dádiva.
bet [bet] *n* parada, apuesta; *vt* apostar, parar, poner.
betray [bi'trei] *vt* engañar; traicionar, hacer traición; vender; revelar.
betrayal [bi'treiəl] *n* traición, perfidia, denuncia; violación.
betrayer [bi'treiə] *n* traidor.
betroth [bi'trouð] *vt* comprometerse; dar palabra de casamiento.
betrothal [bi'trouðəl] *n* petición de manos, compromiso matrimonial, noviazgo.
betrothed [bi'trouðd] *an* prometido.
better ['betə] *a* superior, mejor; *ad* mejor, más bien; *n* ventaja, mejoría; **— half** (*fam*) costilla; **to get —** (*after illness*) mejorar(se), reponerse, restablecerse, sanar; **— . . . than** más vale . . . que; **so much the —** tanto mejor; **to get the — of** superar a, vencer; **it is — that** más vale que; **— off** (más) acomodado; *vt* mejorar, adelantar.
betterment ['betəmənt] *n* mejora, mejoría.
betting ['betiŋ] *n* apuesta.
between [bi'twi:n] *ad* en medio, de por medio, entre tanto; *prep* entre; en medio de; **— now and then** de aquí a entonces; **to go —** terciar.
bevel ['bevl] *n* sesgo, bisel; *vt* biselar, sesgar.
beverage ['bevəridʒ] *n* brebaje, poción, bebida.
bevy ['bevi] *n* (*birds*) bandada, (*sheep*) manada, (*girls*) pandilla.
bewail [bi'weil] *vt* deplorar, llorar; *vi* plañir.
bewailing [bi'weiliŋ] *n* lamento.
beware [bi'wɛə] *vi* guardarse de, tener cuidado de, recelar; desconfiar de; *excl* ¡atención!; cuidado con.
bewilder [bi'wildə] *vt* desconcertar, encandilar, aturrullar, aturdir, distraer.
bewildered [bi'wildəd] *a* azorado, aturdido, desatinado.
bewilderment [bi'wildəmənt] *n* confusión, azoramiento, desconcierto, anonadamiento.
bewitch [bi'witʃ] *vt* hechizar, maleficiar, fascinar, aojar, embrujar.
bewitching [bi'witʃiŋ] *a* hechicero, fascinador, encantador; *n* hechizo, encanto.
beyond [bi'jɔnd] *prep ad* allá lejos, allende, al lado de, allá; atrás, detrás de, fuera de, superior a, al otro lado; **— doubt** fuera de duda, indiscutible; **— measure** sobremanera; **to be —** superar a; **to go — (what is right)** propasarse.
bias ['baiəs] *n* sesgo, oblicuidad; prejuicio, parcialidad; preocupación; *vt* influir, torcer.
biased ['baiəst] *a* tendencioso; terciado.
bib [bib] *n* babero, babador.
Bible ['baibl] *n* biblia.
biblical ['biblikəl] *a* bíblico.
bibliophile ['biblioufail] *n* bibliófilo.
bicker ['bikə] *vi* querellarse, reñir, disputar.
bickering ['bikəriŋ] *n* querella, rencilla, altercado.
bicycle ['baisikl] *n* bicicleta; **motor —** motocicleta.
bid [bid] *n* oferta, puja, postura; tentativa; *vt* ofrecer, pujar; pedir, rogar; mandar; **to — adieu** despedirse; **to — welcome** dar la bienvenida.
bidding ['bidiŋ] *n* orden, invitación; mandato, deseo; postura.
bide [baid] *vti* sufrir, aguantar; aguardar.
bier [biə] *n* féretro, andas.
big [big] *a* grande, voluminoso,

gordo; (*thick*) grueso; (*swollen*) (*fat*) abultado, hinchado; **—hearted** magnánimo; **—bellied** ventroso, ventrudo; **—boned** huesudo; **to talk —** fanfarronear.
bigamy ['bigəmi] *n* bigamia.
bigness ['bignis] *n* grandeza, tamaño.
bigot ['bigət] *n* fanático, beato.
bigotry ['bigətri] *n* fanatismo, beatería.
bile [bail] *n* bilis, hiel; **black —** atrabilis.
bilge [bildʒ] *n* sentina; *vi* desfondar, hacer agua.
bilingual [bai'liŋgwəl] *a* bilingüe.
bill [bil] *n* (*com*) cuenta, nota; (*invoice*) factura; (*menu*) lista; (*IOU*) pagaré; (*display*) cartel; billete; proyecto (*de ley*); (*bird*) pico; **— board** (*theat*) cartelera; **— of lading** conocimiento de embarque; **bank —** billete de banco; **bills receivable** obligaciones por cobrar; **— of health** patente de sanidad; **—head** encabezamiento; **—poster** pegador de carteles; **post no —s** se prohibe fijar carteles; *vt* cargar en cuenta; anunciar.
billet ['bilit] *n* billete; boleta; (*mil*) acantonamiento; (*letter*) esquela; *vt* alojar.
billiards ['biljədz] *n* billar; (*ball*) bola; (*cue*) taco; (*room*) sala; (*table*) mesa; **to play —** hacer carambolas.
billion ['biljən] *n* billón; mil millones.
billow ['bilou] *n* ola, oleada; *vi* ondular.
billowy ['biloui] *a* ondoso, ondeante.
bin [bin] *n* (*bread etc*) hucha; cofre, arca.
bind [baind] *vt* trincar, atar, ligar; aprisionar; unir, juntar; restriñir; (*tightly*) agarrotar; enlazar, ceñir; (*book*) encuadernar; (*sew*) ribetear, guarnecer; (*in sheaves*) agavillar; *vr* empeñarse, comprometerse a.
binder ['baində] *n* encuadernador.
binding ['baindiŋ] *n* ligamiento, lazo, cinta, tira; ligadura; (*book*) encuadernación; (*sew*) refuerzo; **in half —** holandés.
binocular [bi'nɔkjulə] *a* binocular; **—s** binóculo, gemelos.
biographer [bai'ɔgrəfə] *n* biógrafo.
biographical [ˌbaiə'græfikəl] *a* biográfico; **— sketch** semblanza.
biography [bai'ɔgrəfi] *n* biografía.
biology [bai'ɔlədʒi] *n* biología.
biped ['baiped] *an* bípedo.
birch [bəːtʃ] *n* abedul.
bird [bəːd] *n* pájaro, (*large, domestic*) ave; **— of prey** ave de rapiña; **— cage** jaula; **— call** reclamo; **a — in the hand is worth two in the bush** más vale un toma que dos te daré; **to be a night —** (*fam*) correrla.
birdlime ['bəːdlaim] *n* liga.
birth [bəːθ] *n* nacimiento; origen; cuna; parto; (*litter*) camada; **— certificate** partida de nacimiento; **—day** cumpleaños, natalicio, día natal; **to give — to** parir, dar a luz.
Biscay, the Bay of ['biskei, ðəbei ɔv] *n* el Golfo de Vizcaya.
biscuit ['biskit] *n* galleta; (*sponge*) bizcocho; bollo; **ship's —** costra.
bisect [bai'sekt] *vt* dividir en dos, bisecar.
bishop ['biʃəp] *n* pontífice, obispo; (*chess*) alfil.
bishopric ['biʃəprik] *n* obispado.
bit [bit] *n* pedazo, poco; (*of bread*) cacho; (*jot*) pizca, jota; trozo; (*horse*) bocado; (*mech*) taladro; **— by —** poco a poco; **to take the — between one's teeth** descobarse; **he's a — of ...** es un tanto ...
bitch [bitʃ] *n* perra; ramera.
bite [bait] *n* mordedura; (*dog*) mordisco, picadura; (*sl*) tentempié; *vt* morder; (*fish*) picar; (*spices*) resquemar; corroer; hincar el diente en.
biting ['baitiŋ] *a* mordiente, picante; (*remark etc*) mordaz.
bitten ['bitn] *a* picado; **once — twice shy** escamado.
bitter ['bitə] *a* amargo; (*smell*) acre; (*taste*) amargo, áspero; (*harsh*) duro; amargado, mordaz; cáustico; (*fig*) enconado; sañudo; **— feeling** inquina; *n pl* bítter.
bitterness ['bitənis] *n* amargura, rencor, hiel, inquina, encono; amargor, acritud; mordacidad; angustia.
bitumen ['bitjumin] *n* betún.
bivouac ['bivuæk] *n* vivaque, vivac; *vi* vivaquear.
bi-weekly ['bai'wiːkli] *a* quincenal.
blab [blæb] *vti* divulgar; chismear.
black [blæk] *a* negro; tétrico; **— and blue** lívido, amoratado; **— bread** pan de centeno; **— list** lista negra; **— Maria** coche celular; **— market** estraperlo; **— marketeer** estraperlista; **—out** oscurecimiento; **— pudding** morcilla; *n* el color negro; *vi* dar de negro; ennegrecer; **ivory—** negro de marfil.
blackberry ['blækbəri] *n* zarzamora; **— bush** zarza.
blackboard ['blækbɔːd] *n* encerado, pizarra.
blacken ['blæken] *vt* atizar, ennegrecer; embetunar; denigrar.
blackguard ['blægɑːd] *n* tunante, pillo, canalla.
blacklead ['blæk'led] *n* lápizplomo, grafito.
blackleg ['blækleg] *n* esquirol.
blackmail ['blækmeil] *n* chantaje; *vt* hacer un chantaje.
blackness ['blæknis] *n* negrura; obscuridad.
blacksmith ['blæksmiθ] *n* herrero.
blackthorn ['blækθɔːn] *n* endrino, espino negro.
bladder ['blædə] *n* vejiga.

blade [bleid] *n* (*knife*) hoja, cuchilla; (*oar*) pala; (*grass*) brizna; **a gay —** calavera, tronera.
blame [bleim] *vt* culpar; achacar, vituperar, acusar, reprochar; **to throw (lay) — on** achacar a, echar la culpa a; *n* culpa; vituperio, censura, reproche.
blameless ['bleimlis] *a* intachable, inculpado.
blameworthy ['bleim.wəːði] *a* vituperable, tachable, culpable.
blanch [blɑːntʃ] *vt* blanquear; *vi* desteñirse; palidecer, ponerse blanco.
bland [blænd] *a* suave, complaciente, amable.
blandish ['blændiʃ] *vt* engatusar, lisonjear, halagar.
blandishment ['blændiʃmənt] *n* halago, zalamería.
blank [blæŋk] *a* (*empty*) hueco; (*clean*) en blanco, vacuo; limpio; (*verse*) suelto; turbado; *n* laguna, blanco, vacío; documento, hoja; *SA* esqueleto; **to draw a —** (*fig*) quedarse en albis, no tocar.
blanket ['blæŋkit] *n* manta; frazada; cobertor, cobertura, (*of dust*) capa; *vt* cubrir con manta; **to toss in a —** mantear.
blankly ['blæŋkli] *ad* sin comprender, atontado.
blare [blɛə] *n* trompetazo; *vi* rugir, sonar como trompeta.
blasé ['blɑːzei] *a* gastado.
blaspheme [blæs'fiːm] *vt* blasfemar; maldecir; *vi* decir blasfemias.
blasphemous ['blæsfiməs] *a* blasfemo, impío.
blasphemy ['blæsfimi] *n* blasfemia, reniego.
blast [blɑːst] *n* (*wind*) ráfaga, bocanada; explosión; (*trumpet*) llamada, tintirintín; (*bugle*) trompetazo; **— furnace** alto horno; **in full —** a toda marcha; **— off** disparo; *vt* arruinar, reventar; marchitar, agostar.
blasting ['blɑːstiŋ] *n* voladura, explosión.
blatant ['bleitənt] *a* vocinglero, llamativo; bramante.
blaze [bleiz] *n* llama(rada), hoguera; brillo, ardor, furia; *vt* **to — forth** publicar, proclamar; *vi* **to — up** llamear, flamear; arder.
blazing ['bleiziŋ] *a* resplandeciente, en llamas, sobre excitado.
blazon ['bleizn] *n* blasón; *vt* blasonar; publicar.
bleach [bliːtʃ] *vt* (*in sun*) blanquear; desteñir, descolorir.
bleak [bliːk] *a* pálido; helado, crudo; desamparado; (*prospect*) sombrío; raso, yermo; **— stretch of country** paramera, páramo.
bleakness ['bliːknis] *n* intemperie, destemplanza; palidez, frialdad; lo pelado.
bleat [bliːt] *vi* balar.
bleating ['bliːtiŋ] *n* balido.
bleed [bliːd] *vti* sangrar; echar sangre; desangrar; **to — to death** morir desangrado.
bleeding ['bliːdiŋ] *n* sangría.
blemish ['blemiʃ] *n* mácula, borrón, tacha; imperfección, lunar, defecto; *vt* echar a perder, dañar; infamar; (*glass, honor*) empañar.
blend [blend] *n* mezcla; (*color*) matiz; *vt* mezclar, fundir; casar; (*color*) matizar.
blending ['blendiŋ] *n* mezcla, fusión.
bless [bles] *vt* bendecir; alabar, congratularse; **bless me!** ¡caray!; **God bless** (*of the dead*) que en paz descanse.
blessed ['blesid] *a* bienaventurado; dichoso, feliz, santo; (*iro*) maldito.
blessing ['blesiŋ] *n* bendición; beneficio; bien, merced.
blest [blest] a bendito, beato; **well I'm —!** ¡canario!, ¡vaya!
blight [blait] *n* pulgón, mancha; (*on corn etc*) tizón, roña; *vt* marchitar, agostar, añublar.
blind [blaind] *a* ciego; tenebroso, oscuro; (*passage*) sin salida; (*person*) ignorante; **window —** biombo, persiana; **— alley** callejón sin salida; *n* **Venetian —** celosía; *vt* cegar; deslumbrar.
blinded ['blaindid] *a* ciego, deslumbrado.
blindfold ['blaindfould] *a* a ciegas; *vt* vendar (*los ojos*).
blinding ['blaindiŋ] *a* (*light*) cegador, deslumbrante.
blindly ['blaindli] *ad* ciegamente, a ciegas, a ojos cerrados.
blindness ['blaindnis] *n* ceguedad; (*state of*) ceguera.
blink [bliŋk] *vi* parpadear, pestañear, guiñar; esquivar.
bliss [blis] *n* felicidad, bienaventuranza; gozo, éxtasis; (*relig*) gloria, arrobamiento.
blissful ['blisful] *a* bienaventurado, en gloria.
blissfulness ['blisfulnis] *n* felicidad suprema, bienaventuranza.
blister ['blistə] *n* ampolla, vejiga; (*on lip etc*) pupa; **— plaster** vejigatorio; *vi* ampollarse; *vt* ampollar.
blithe [blaið] *a* alegre, jovial, gozoso.
blithesomeness ['blaiðsəmnis] *n* alegría, júbilo.
blizzard ['blizəd] *n* ventisca.
bloat [blout] *vt* hinchar.
block [blɔk] *n* bloque, trozo; tabla; (*buildings*) manzana; (*flats*) casa de vecindad; **horse —** apeadero; (*hatmaker's*) horma; construcción; (*wood*) viga, leño; (*com*) lote; (*fool*) zoquete, zopenco; *vt* obstruir; bloquear; cerrar; (*window etc*) cegar; (*view*) obscurecer; **to — up** tapar; **to — in** (*sketch*) esbozar.
blockade [blɔ'keid] *n* bloqueo,

cerco; *vt* bloquear, poner cerco a.
blocked [blɔkt] *a* cerrado, obstruído; **— up** ciego, cegado.
blockhead ['blɔkhed] *n* bruto, tonto de capirote, animal, zote.
blond(e) [blɔnd] *an* rubio.
blood [blʌd] *n* sangre; (*fig*) estirpe; **— donor** donante de sangre; **young —** pimpollo; **bad —** encono, hostilidad; **— hound** sabueso; **— letter** sangrador; **in cold —** a sangre fría; **—shed** efusión de sangre; matanza; **—shot** ensangrentado, inyectado de sangre; **—sucker** sanguijuela; **— vessel** vaso sanguíneo.
bloodless ['blʌdlis] *a* exangüe; incruento.
bloodthirsty ['blʌd.θəːsti] *a* sangriento, sanguinario.
bloody ['blʌdi] *a* sangriento, cruento, encarnizado, sanguinario; (*fam*) maldito.
bloom [bluːm] *n* flor, florecimiento; (*on fruit*) vello; belleza, lozanía; *vi* florecer.
blossom ['blɔsəm] *n* floración, flor; *vi* florecer, reventar.
blossoming ['blɔsəmiŋ] *n* floración.
blot [blɔt] *n* mancha, borrón; (*of ill repute*) padrón, bochorno; *vti* manchar, ennegrecer; **to — out** tachar, borrar, testar; (*ink*) secar; obscurecer.
blotch [blɔtʃ] *n* mancha, borrón; *vt* manchar, ennegrecer.
blotting paper ['blɔtiŋ.peipə] *n* (papel) secante.
blouse [blauz] *n* blusa.
blow [blou] *vti* soplar; hinchar; abrir; resoplar; (*organ*) entonar; (*nose*) sonarse; **— up** (*balloon*) inflar, (*bridge*) volar, (*glass*) soplar; (*after exercise*) jadear, bufar; **to — down** echar por tierra; **to — out** apagar, matar de un soplo; **to — out** (*cheeks etc*) hinchar; **to — out one's brains** levantar la tapa de los sesos; *n* golpe; choque, desdicha; (*fist*) puñetazo, (*sword*) sablazo; (*ax*) hachazo; (*butt end*) culatazo; (*on face*) bofetada; **to come to —s** venir (llegar) a las manos.
blower ['blouə] *n* soplador, fuelle; tapadera (*de chimenea*).
blowing ['blouiŋ] *n* resoplido.
blowpipe ['bloupaip] *n* soplete, cerbatana.
bludgeon ['blʌdʒən] *n* clava, garrote, porra.
blue [bluː] *a* azul; (*with cold etc*) cárdeno, amoratado; **out of the —** impensado, de manos a boca; **once in a — moon** de higos a brevas; (*eyes*) garzo; **light —** (*eyes*) zarco; **navy —** azul marino; **— -blooded** linajudo; *n pl* morriña.
bluestocking ['bluː.stɔkiŋ] *n* bachillera, marisabidilla.
bluff [blʌf] *a* burdo, brusco, franco; *n* morro, risco; (*boast*) fanfarronada.
blunder ['blʌndə] *n* desatino, desacierto, yerro; burrada, coladura; *vi* desacertar, desatinar, errar; (*fam*) meter la pata.
blundering ['blʌndəriŋ] *a* desatinado, torpe.
blunt [blʌnt] *a* embotado; brusco, rudo, lerdo, obtuso; *vt* embotar; desafilar; despuntar; adormecer.
bluntly ['blʌntli] *ad* bruscamente, secamente, sin rodeos.
bluntness ['blʌntnis] *n* brusquedad, grosería.
blur [bləː] *n* borrón; *vt* empañar, manchar, hacer borrones; entorpecer; **blurred** (*outlines*) borroso, empañado.
blurt [bləːt] *vt* soltar, espetar (torpemente, tontamente, con aturdimiento).
blush [blʌʃ] *n* rubor, sonrojo; (*with shame*) bochorno; **at first —** al primer vistazo; *vi* ruborizarse, enrojecerse, ponerse colorado.
bluster ['blʌstə] *n* ruido, estrépito; jactancia; *vi* bravear, fanfarrear.
blusterer ['blʌstərə] *n* fanfarrón.
blustering ['blʌstəriŋ] *a* ruidoso, estrépitoso.
boar [bɔː] *n* jabalí.
board [bɔːd] *n* tabla; mesa; (*ship*) bordo; **black—** encerado, pizarra; **notice —** tablilla; **consulting —** junta; (*food*) comida, pupilaje; **— and lodging** pensión (completa); *pl* **—s** escenario, tablas; *vt* entablar; (*warfare*) abordar; hospedar; **to go on —** ir a bordo; **to sweep the —** (*cards*) dar capote.
boarder ['bɔːdə] *n* pupilo, huésped; (*at school*) interno, pensionista, porcionista.
boarding ['bɔːdiŋ] *n* (*floor*) entablado; (*wall*) tabique; pupilaje; **— house** casa de huéspedes, pensión, pupilaje.
boast [boust] *n* jactancia, fanfarronada; alarde, ostentación; *vt* ostentar; **to — of** blasonar de, hacer alarde de; *vi* jactarse, vanagloriarse; cacarear, presumir.
boaster ['boustə] *n* fanfarrón, plantista.
boastful ['boustful] *a* jactancioso, avalentonado, confiado.
boastfulness ['boustfulnis] *n* bravura.
boat [bout] *n* barco, buque; (*small*) barca, bote, lancha; vapor; **life—** lancha de socorro.
boating ['boutiŋ] *n* ir en bote, ir embarcado.
boatswain ['bousn] *n* contramaestre.
bob [bɔb] *n* cabellera, melena; (*fam*) chelín; *vti* menear(se).
bobbin ['bɔbin] *n* carrete, bobina, carrilla; (*lace*) bobillo.
bodice ['bɔdis] *n* cuerpo, talle; corpiño, jubón.
bodied ['bɔdid] *a* corpóreo; **big-—**

corpulento; **full-—** (*wine*) de mucho cuerpo.

bodily ['bɔdili] *a* corporal, corpóreo; tan grande como era, todo.

body ['bɔdi] *n* cuerpo; (*dead*) cadáver; materia; realidad, substancia; individuo; fortaleza, densidad; (*of car*) armazón, carrocería; gremio, corporación; **—guard** guardia de corps; **main —** (*army*) grueso; **united —** conjunto.

bog [bɔg] *n* pantano, fangal, ciénaga.

boggle ['bɔgl] *vi* vacilar, cejar.

boggy ['bɔgi] *a* pantanoso, cenagoso.

bohemian [bou'hi:miən] *a* bohemio.

boil [bɔil] *vt* hervir; *vi* bullir; **to — down** reducir por cocción; **to — over** (*fig*) ponerse fuera de sí, (*milk etc*) irse.

boiler ['bɔilə] *n* caldera; marmita; **steam —** caldera de vapor.

boiling ['bɔiliŋ] *a* herviente; *n* hervor, ebullición.

boisterous ['bɔistərəs] *a* bullicioso, impetuoso, violento, tempestuoso.

bold [bould] *a* atrevido; arrojado, resoluto, intrépido, temerario; gallardo, audaz; **—-faced** descarado, desvergonzado; (*cliff etc*) arriscado.

boldly ['bouldli] *ad* atrevidamente.

boldness ['bouldnis] *n* temeridad, atrevimiento, intrepidez; animosidad, arrojo; descaro, descoco; desenvoltura, osadía.

Bolivia [bə'liviə] *n* Bolivia.

Bolivian [bə'liviən] *an* boliviano.

bolster ['boulstə] *n* travesero, travesaño; *vt* **to — up** estribar, auxiliar; levantar, animar.

bolt [boult] *n* (*arrow*) flecha, dardo; (*door*) pestillo, cerraja, cerrojo; (*carp*) perno; fuga; **thunder—** rayo; *pl* grillos; *ad* **— upright** enhiesto; *vt* echar el cerrojo; *vi* saltar repentinamente, mostrar las herraduras escaparse (*como un rayo*).

bomb [bɔm] *n* bomba; granada, petardo; *vt* bombardear.

bombard [bɔm'bɑ:d] *vt* bombardear.

bombardment [bɔm'bɑ:dmənt] *n* bombardeo.

bombast ['bɔmbæst] *n* ampulosidad.

bombastic [bɔm'bæstik] *a* ampuloso, retumbante, rimbombante.

bomber ['bɔmə] *n* bombardero; **dive —** bombardero en picado.

bombing ['bɔmiŋ] *n* bombardeo, ataque aéreo.

bond [bɔnd] *n* traba, lazo, vínculo; trabazón; (*moral*) obligación; (*money*) fianza; bono; **—s** valores; prisión, cadena; *vt* dar fianza; dejar mercancías en depósito, aduanar.

bondage ['bɔndidʒ] *n* esclavitud, cautiverio.

bone [boun] *n* hueso; (*fish*) raspa, espina; **to have a — to pick (with)** habérselas (con); **to make no —s about** no tener empacho; **to be skin and —s** estar en los huesos; **to set —s** ensalmar; *vt* quitar los huesos; **to — up** (*sl*) empollar; **— of contention** materia de discordia.

bonfire ['bɔn,faiə] *n* hoguera, fogata.

bonnet ['bɔnit] *n* gorro, toca, gorra; (*eccles, acad*) bonete; (*Doctor's*) borla.

bonny ['bɔni] *a* resalado, guapo.

bony ['bouni] *a* huesudo.

book [buk] *n* libro; libreta; **day—** diario; **pocket—** cartera; **check—** libro talonario; **note—** cuaderno; **— jacket** cubierta; **—mark** señal; **—shop** librería; **—stall** puesto de libros; *vt* inscribir; anotar, retener; (*theat*) sacar (tomar) localidades.

bookbinding ['buk,baindiŋ] *n* encuadernación.

bookcase ['bukkeis] *n* librería, estantes.

booking office ['bukiŋ,ɔfis] *n* taquilla, expendeduría, despacho (*de billetes*).

bookish ['bukiʃ] *a* estudioso, aficionado a los libros; pedante; teórico.

book-keeping ['buk,ki:piŋ] *n* tene, duría de libros, contabilidad.

booklet ['buklit] *n* folleto, opúsculo, librete.

bookseller ['buk,selə] *n* librero.

bookshop ['bukʃɔp] *n* librería.

bookworm ['bukwə:m] *n* (*pers*) ratón de biblioteca; polilla.

boom [bu:m] *n* (*ship*) botavara, botalón; (*noise*) estampido; (*com*) auge repentino.

boon [bu:n] *n* dádiva, presente; dicha; favor, merced, recompensa; ventaja, suerte; *a* íntimo, predilecto; jovial, festivo; afortunado.

boorish ['buəriʃ] *a* rústico, tosco, grosero.

boot [bu:t] *n* bota, calzado; ganancia; **—black** limpiabotas; **—laces** cordones; *ad* **to —** además, a mayor abundamiento.

booth [bu:ð] *n* barraca, puesto, gabinete.

booty ['bu:ti] *n* botín, presa.

Bordeaux [bɔ:'dou] *n* Burdeos.

border ['bɔ:də] *a* fronterizo; *n* (*garment, river*) borde, orla, orilla; (*cloth*) cenefa; (*country*) extremidad, frontera; *vi* orillar; **to — on** confinar (*con*), rayar (*en*); **to be on the —s of** comarcar (*con*); *vt* guarnecer, orlar.

borderer ['bɔ:dərə] *n* limítrofe.

bordering ['bɔ:dəriŋ] *a* fronterizo, contiguo, lindante (*con*), vecino.

borderland ['bɔ:dərlænd] *n* frontera.

bore [bɔ:] *n* taladro, barreno; (*pers*) majadero, pelma; *vt* aburrir, cansar, dar la lata a, moler, molestar, incomodar, cargar; **to — through** horadar, taladrar.

bored [bɔ:d] *a* aburrido, mustio; **to be —** estar aburrido, fastidiarse.

boredom ['bɔ:dəm] *n* tedio, cansancio, aburrimiento.

boring ['bɔ:riŋ] *a* pesado, aburrido, cansado.
born [bɔ:n] *a* nacido; **newly —** recién nacido; **— and bred** de pura cepa, hasta los tuétanos.
borough ['bʌrə] *n* burgo, municipio, distrito.
borrow ['bɔrou] *vt* pedir prestado.
borrower ['bɔrouə] *n* él que pide prestado; comodatario.
borrowing ['bɔrouiŋ] *n* empréstito.
bosom ['buzəm] *n* seno, corazón; (*fig*) regazo, pechos; **in the — of** en el seno de.
boss [bɔs] *n* amo; protuberancia, giba; **local political —** cacique; *vt* dominar; (*metal*) repujar.
bossy ['bɔsi] *a* mandón.
botany ['bɔtəni] *n* botánica.
both [bouθ] *a* ambos, uno y otro; **on — sides** por ambos lados; *conj* tanto . . . como.
bother ['bɔðə] *n* molestia, fastidio; *vi* marear, molestar, incomodar; majar; dar guerra a.
bothersome ['bɔðəsəm] *a* engorroso, cargante, fastidioso.
bottle ['bɔtl] *n* botella, frasco; **wine—** (*of glass*) porrón; (*child's*) biberón; **water—** cantimplora; *vt* embotellar.
bottling ['bɔtliŋ] *n* envase.
bottom ['bɔtəm] *n* fondo, cimiento; (*of skirt*) ruedo; (*hulk*) casco, nave; (*anat*) trasero; (*river*) lecho; (*chair*) asiento; (*page*) pie; (*lees*) sedimento; **to go to the —** irse a pique; **at —** en el fondo.
bottomless ['bɔtəmlis] *a* sin fondo, impenetrable, insondable.
bough [bau] *n* rama.
boulder ['bouldə] *n* canto rodado, peña, peñasco, pedrusco; piedra de rodada; **—-strewn place** roquedal.
bounce [bauns] *n* salto, (re)bote, respingo; *vi* (re)botar; saltar; hacer saltar.
bouncing ['baunsiŋ] *a* fuerte, robusto.
bound [baund] *a* sujeto, ligado; **— for** con rumbo a; (*sew*) reforzado; **— in** absorto; *n* (*limit*) confín, término; (*jump*) brinco, corcovo, respingo; **at one —** de un salto; *vt* deslindar; acotar; poner coto a; *vi* saltar; **to be —** apostar.
boundary ['baundəri] *n* límite, confín; linde, término, raya; (*of estate*) aledaño; **— mark** mojón.
bounded ['baundid] *a* limitado, cerrado, confinado.
boundless ['baundlis] *a* ilimitado.
bounteous ['bauntiəs] *a* largo, generoso, bondadoso.
bountiful ['bauntiful] *a* bondadoso, generoso, pródigo, liberal.
bounty ['baunti] *n* liberalidad, munificencia, largueza, merced, subsidio; (*mil*) enganche.
bouquet [bu'kei] *n* ramillete, ramo; (*of wine*) aroma.
bourgeois ['buəʒwɑ:] *an* burgués.
bout [baut] *n* turno; (*fencing etc*) asalto; (*illness*) ataque.
bow [bau] *n* inclinación, saludo; (*ship*) proa; *vti* saludar, hacer una reverencia, inclinarse; (*weigh down*) agobiar, doblar; arquear, inclinar; ceder, someterse.
bow [bou] *n* arco; (*ribbon*) lazo, lazado.
bowel ['bauəl] *n* intestino; **—s** entrañas.
bower ['bauə] *n* enramada, cenador.
bowl [boul] *n* escudilla; taza, bol, tazón; (*game*) bola; **sugar —** azucarero; *vt* tumblar; lanzar la pelota; bolear; *vi* jugar a las bolas.
bowler ['boulə] *n* jugador de bolos; **— (hat)** hongo.
box [bɔks] *n* caja; (*chest*) cofre, arca; (*jewel*) estuche, alhajero; (*theat*) palco; (*coach*) pescante; tribuna; **letter —** buzón: **food—** comedero; **— office** contaduría, taquilla; (*blow*) puñetazo, revés, cachete; (*plant*) boj; (*PO*) apartado de correo; *vt* encajonar; *vi* boxear; abofetear.
boxcar ['bɔkskɑ:] *n* furgón.
boxer ['bɔksə] *n* boxeador.
boxing ['bɔksiŋ] *n* boxeo; pugilato.
boy [bɔi] *n* muchacho, chico, chiquillo; pollo; hijo, mozo; *SA* chino.
boycott ['bɔikət] *n* boicot; *vt* boicotear.
boyhood ['bɔihud] *n* niñez.
boyish ['bɔiiʃ] *a* pueril, juvenil; de chico(s).
brace [breis] *n* abrazadera; tirante; (*mech*) hembra; (*two*) par; **—s** tirantes; *vt* trabar, ligar; reforzar; vigorizar.
bracelet ['breislit] *n* pulsera, brazalete, ajorca.
bracing ['breisiŋ] *a* tónico; *n* trabazón.
bracken ['brækən] *n* helecho.
bracket ['brækit] *n* soporte, repisa, rinconera; (*typ*) paréntesis, corchete.
brag [bræg] *n* jactancia, fanfarronada; *vti* jactarse; alardear de.
braggart ['brægət] *n* fanfarrón, avalentonado, matasiete.
bragging ['brægiŋ] *n* fanfarronería.
braid [breid] *n* fleco, galoncillo, galón; franja; (*mil*) galón, trencilla; (*hair*) trenza; *vt* trenzar; galonear.
brain [brein] *n* cerebro, sesos; **he is —y** es un talento; **— trust** consultorio intelectual; **—wave** idea luminosa; *vt* romper la crisma a, saltar la tapa de los sesos a; **to rack one's —s** devanarse los sesos.
brainless ['breinlis] *a* insensato.
brake [breik] *n* (*bot*) maleza, matorral, soto; (*mech*) freno; *vt* frenar.
bramble ['bræmbl] *n* zarza, maleza; **— patch** breña, breñal, zarzal, matorral, maleza.
bran [bræn] *n* salvado; afrecho.

branch [brɑːntʃ] *n* (*tree, family*) rama, ramal, ramo; brazo; — **office** dependencia, sucursal; — **line** ramal; *vi* ramificar, bifurcar; **to — out** ramificarse.
branching ['brɑːntʃiŋ] *n* — **off** bifurcación, ramificación.
brand [brænd] *n* tizón, (*flaming*) tea; (*for animals*) hierro; (*stigma*) baldón, (*manufacture*) marca; *vt* marcar; infamar, estigmatizar.
brandish ['brændiʃ] *vt* blandir, cimbrear.
brand-new ['brænd'njuː] *a* flamante, nuevecito.
brandy ['brændi] *n* aguardiente, coñac.
brasier ['breiziə] *n* brasero; latonero.
brass [brɑːs] *n* latón, bronce; (*mus*) metal; (*sl*) descaro; — **band** banda, murga.
brassière ['bræsiə] *n* sostén.
brave [breiv] *a* valiente, intrépido, alentado; de pelo en pecho, bizarro, esforzado, animoso; *vt* desafiar, arrostrar.
bravery ['breivəri] *n* valentía, valor, coraje; esplendor, magnificencia.
bravo ['brɑː'vou] *excl* ¡bravo!; *n* matón, chulo.
brawl [brɔːl] *n* querella, reyerta, camorra; *vi* armar querella, alborotar; murmurar.
brawler ['brɔːlə] *n* camorrista.
brawn [brɔːn] *n* carnosidad; músculo, nervio.
brawny ['brɔːni] *a* musculoso, membrudo.
bray [brei] *n* risotada; (*trumpet*) tintirintín; (*ass*) rebuzno; *vi* rebuznar.
brazen ['breizn] *a* de bronce, broncino; (*fig*) desahogado, desvergonzado.
Brazil [brə'zil] *n* el Brasil.
Brazilian [brə'ziliən] *an* brasileño.
breach [briːtʃ] *n* (*mil*) brecha; rompimiento; ruptura, violación; — **of promise** quebranto de promesa, falta de palabra; (*law*) infracción; — **of faith** abuso de confianza; — **of the peace** alteración de orden público; — **of duty** incumplimiento del deber; *vt* hacer brecha en.
bread [bred] *n* pan; **fine white —** pan blanco; (*unleavened*) ázimo; (*new*) tierno; (*old*) duro; **slice of —** rebanada.
breadth [bredθ] *n* anchura, amplitud; (*of ship's beam*) manga; (*vision*) envergadura.
break [breik] *n* ruptura; (*in parag*) aparte; (*holiday*) asueto; (*crack*) grieta; (*geol*) falla; interrupción, blanco, laguna; (*voice*) quiebra; pausa; **—down** avería; **nervous —down** crisis de nervios; **without a —** sin solución de continuidad, acto continuo, sin parar; *vt* estrellar, romper, quebrar, quebrantar; (*heart*) matar a disgustos; (*burst*) saltar, reventar; (*day*) apuntar; **to — off** tranchar; romperse; interrumpir; **to — in** (*door etc*) forzar; (*animals*) domar, amaestrar; **to — into** (*pieces*) fraccionar; *vi* **to — away from** romper con; **to — in upon** entrar de sopetón; **to — off** romper; hacer bancarrota; **to — down** prorrumpir en lágrimas; abatirse; consentir, no resistir más; **to — loose** (*free*) desasirse, soltarse; **to — out** estallar; evadir, salir, (*storm*) des atarse; — (*into cries etc*) prorrumpir en; **to — up** deshacerse, (*school*) cerrarse, (*sitting*) levantar; (*plans*) desbaratar; (*ground*) roturar.
breakable ['breikəbl] *a* frágil, quebradizo, rompedero.
breakage ['breikidʒ] *n* fractura, destrozo.
breaker ['breikə] *n* rompiente, golpe de mar.
breakfast ['brekfəst] *n* desayuno; *vi* desayunarse, tomar el desayuno.
breaking ['breikiŋ] *n* fractura, rompimiento; ruptura.
breakwater ['breik,wɔːtə] *n* rompeolas, malecón.
bream [briːm] *n* besugo.
breast [brest] *n* pecho, seno; teta; (*bird*) pechuga; **—plate** coraza; — **work** parapeto; **to make a clean — of** desahogarse.
breath [breθ] *n* aliento, respiración, soplo; **out of —** sin aliento; — **of air** soplo de aire; **to draw —** respirar; **to waste one's — on** gastar saliva en.
breathe [briːð] *vti* respirar, inspirar, exhalar; tomar aliento; **to — one's last** exhalar el último suspiro, boquear; **to — heavily** resollar; (*tired*) jadear.
breathing ['briːðiŋ] *n* respiración; **heavy —** resuello; — **space** momento de descanso.
breathless ['breθlis] *a* sin aliento, jadeante, falto de aliento.
breech [briːtʃ] *n* codillo, trasero; (*gun*) recámara; *n pl* pantalones; **knee —es** calzón corto; **wide —es** pantalones bombachos.
breed [briːd] *n* casta, raza, progenie; **half- —** mulato; *SA* chino; *vti* criar, procrear, educar; ocasionar; **to — disturbances** meter cizaña.
breeder ['briːdə] *n* criador, ganadero; — **reactor** reactor nuclear.
breeding ['briːdiŋ] *n* crianza; educación, cultura; gentileza; instrucción, maneras; buena educación; (*of animals*) cría; **a man of —** hidalgo; **good —** buena crianza.
breeze [briːz] *n* brisa; (*gentle*) aura, céfiro, viento flojo.
brethren ['breðrin] *n pl* hermanos, cofrades.
breviary ['briːviəri] *n* breviario.
brevity ['breviti] *n* brevedad, concisión; (*time etc*) fugacidad.

brew [bru:] *n* pócima, poción; *vt* hacer (*cerveza*); mezclar; fermentar; (*tea*) infusionar.
brewing ['bru:iŋ] *n* cerveceo; **to be —** estarse incubando, amenazando.
bribe [braib] *n* cohecho; **to take —s** tener manos puercas; *vt* sobornar, cohechar.
bribery ['braibəri] *n* cohecho, soborno.
brick [brik] *n* ladrillo; **ice-cream —** queso helado; **— kiln** horno; **—layer** albañil; *vt* enladrillar; **to be like a cat on hot —s** estar en capilla ardiente, estar en brasas (ascuas).
bridal ['braidl] *a* nupcial; **— chamber (bed)** tálamo; **— song** epitalamio.
bride ['braid] *n* desposada, novia.
bridegroom ['braidgru:m] *n* novio.
bridesmaid ['braidzmeid] *n* madrina de boda.
bridge [bridʒ] *n* puente; (*of nose*) caballete; (*mus*) puentecilla; **draw—** puente levadizo; **— of boats** puente de barcas.
Bridget ['bridʒit] *f* Brígida.
bridle ['braidl] *n* brida, freno; **— path** camino de herradura; *vti* embridar, refrenar; erguirse, sentirse picado.
brief [bri:f] *a* breve, corto, conciso; apresurado; fugitivo; *n* compendio, alegato; (*law*) relación; informe.
briefly ['bri:fli] *ad* en breve, en resumen.
briefness ['bri:fnis] *n* brevedad, cortedad.
brier ['braiə] *n* zarza, rosal silvestre.
brigade [bri'geid] *n* brigada; **fire —** cuerpo de bomberos.
brigand ['brigənd] *n* bandido, bandolero.
bright [brait] *a* brillante, luciente; vivo, agudo, ocurrente; **not too —** (*fam*) cerrado de mollera.
brighten ['braitn] *vt* iluminar, aclarar; pulir, dar lustre; **to — up** (*sky etc*) despejarse; (*conversation*) animarse.
brightness ['braitnis] *n* brillo, esplendor, brillantez, nitidez; (*general*) resplandor; agudeza.
brilliance ['briljəns] *n* lustre, brillantez, esplendor, nitidez, vivacidad.
brilliant ['briljənt] *a* reluciente, brillante; (*idea*) luminoso; relumbrante; ilustre; lúcido; genial; *n* brillante.
brim [brim] *n* labio (*of glass*); ala (*of hat*); borde, extremidad; **to the —** hasta el borde.
brimful ['brim'ful] *a* rebosante, lleno de bote en bote.
brimming ['brimiŋ] *a* rebosante.
brine [brain] *n* salmuera.
bring [briŋ] *vt* traer, llevar; inducir; persuadir; **to — about** ocasionar, originar, provocar; **to — back** devolver; **to — down** abatir; **to — down the house** hacer que se viene abajo el teatro; **to — in** producir, reportar; presentar, traer; **to — into being** realizar; **to — forth** producir, parir, sacar a luz; **to — nearer** arrimar; **to — round** (*from faint*) sacar (*de un desmayo*); **to — out** (*in revolt*) sublevar; sacar a luz, publicar, hacer público; **to — together** avenir, juntar, reunir; **to — to public notice** pregonar; **to — to one's knowledge** hacer saber; **to — up** criar, (*a subject*) sacar a colación; **to — upon oneself** buscarse.
brink [briŋk] *n* borde, extremo, orilla, extremidad.
brisk [brisk] *a* vigoroso, vivaz; animado, gallardo.
briskness ['brisknis] *n* vivacidad, viveza, despejo.
bristle ['brisl] *n* cerdo; *vi* erizar, erizarse, encresparse.
British ['britiʃ] *a* británico.
British Commonwealth ['britiʃ 'kɔmənwelθ] *n* la Mancomunidad Británica.
brittle ['britl] *a* frágil, quebradizo, rompedero; friable, deleznable.
brittleness ['britlnis] *n* fragilidad.
broach [broutʃ] *n* broche, imperdible; *vt* promover (*un asunto*), ensartar; (*barrel*) espitar.
broad [brɔ:d] *a* ancho, amplio; abierto, claro; extenso; **—brimmed** de ala ancha; **— -minded** tolerante.
broadcast ['brɔ:dkɑ:st] *a* al voleo; *n* emisión; *vt* radiar.
broadcasting ['brɔ:dkɑ:stiŋ] *n* radiodifusión; **— station** emisor(a).
broaden ['brɔ:dn] *vti* ensanchar, ampliar.
broadening ['brɔ:dniŋ] *n* ampliación.
broadness ['brɔ:dnis] *n* amplitud, anchura, ancho.
broadsheet ['brɔ:dʃi:t] *n* pliego de cordel.
broadways, broadwise ['brɔ:dweiz, 'brɔ:dwaiz] *ad* a lo ancho.
broil [brɔil] *n* pendencia, camorra; carne a la parrilla; *vt* asar (*a la parilla*).
broke [brouk] *a* quebrado; (*sl*) sin blanca.
broken ['broukn] *a* quebrado, roto; (*voice*) cascada; imperfecto; (*speech*) chapurreado; (*terrain*) desigual, pelado; (*down*) quebrantado, deshecho, estropeado; (*split*) partido; inconexo; **—winded** corto de resuello; **to speak —ly** chapurrear.
broker ['broukə] *n* cambista, corredor, bolsista.
bronchitis [brɔŋ'kaitis] *n* bronquitis.
bronze [brɔnz] *n* bronce; *vt* broncear.
brooch [broutʃ] *n* broche, prendedero.
brood [bru:d] *n* cría, camada, ralea; *vt* empollar, incubar, cobijar.
broody [bru:di] *a* clueco.

brook [bruk] *n* riachuelo, arroyuelo; *vt* sufrir, aguantar, soportar, tolerar.
broom [bru:m] *n* (*bot*) retama; escoba; **—stick** palo de escoba.
broth [brɔθ] *n* caldo.
brothel ['brɔθl] *n* burdel.
brother ['brʌðə] *n* hermano; (*title*) Fray; **—in-law** cuñado; **foster-—** hermano de leche; **half-—** hermanastro.
brotherhood ['brʌðəhud] *n* fraternidad; (*relig*) congregación; hermandad.
brow [brau] *n* ceja, sienes, frente; (*of hill*) cima; **knitted —s** ceño; **to —beat** intimidar, mirar con ceño.
brown [braun] *a* (*skin etc*) moreno, castaño; **gray—** pardo; **— paper** papel de estraza; **— study** ensimismamiento; **— sugar** azúcar terciado; *vti* teñir de moreno, tostar.
brownish ['brauniʃ] *a* que tira a moreno; **dark—** trigueño.
browse [brauz] *vti* pacer, ramonear; **to — (around)** rebuscar.
bruise [bru:z] *n* magulladura, chichón, contusión, abolladura; (*black*) cardenal; *vt* magullar, golpear.
brunt [brʌnt] *n* choque, embate; **to bear the — of** aguantar lo más recio de.
brush [brʌʃ] *n* (*clothes etc*) cepillo; (*paint*) pincel, brocha; **clothes —** cepillo para ropa; **— stroke** pincelada; (*mil*) pelea, escaramuza; (*shrub*) matorral; bosque; *vt* acepillar; **to — against** rozar; **to — up** repasar, refrescar.
brushwood ['brʌʃwud] *n* matorral, chamarasca.
Brussels ['brʌsls] *n* Bruselas.
Brussels sprouts ['brʌsl'sprauts] *n* repollita; col de Bruselas.
brutal ['bru:tl] *a* brutal, bestial, cruel, inhumano.
brutality [bru:'tæliti] *n* brutalidad, bestialidad, grosería.
brutalize ['bru:təlaiz] *vt* embrutecer.
brute [bru:t] *n* bruto, bestia; **rough —** patán.
brutish ['bru:tiʃ] *a* brutal, bestial, sensual.
bubble ['bʌbl] *n* burbuja; pompa; *vi* burbujear; *vt* retozar, hervir.
bubbling ['bʌbliŋ] *n* burbujeo, hervidero.
bubbly ['bʌbli] *a* espumoso.
buccaneer [ˌbʌkə'niə] *n* filibustero.
buck [bʌk] *n* (*goat*) macho cabrío; (*deer*) gamo; macho; (*pers*) petimetre; (*of steer*) salto, corcovo; **—skin** ante; *vi* tirar por las orejas; **to — up** animar, estimular.
bucket ['bʌkit] *n* cubo, caldero; **to rain —fuls** llover a cántaros.
buckle ['bʌkl] *n* hebilla, bucle; *vt* (en)hebillar, abrochar; *vi* (*of wheel*) torcerse, (*of fender*) abollarse; **to — down to** dedicarse (*de lleno, con empeño a*).
buckwheat ['bʌkwi:t] *n* alforfón, trigo sarraceno.
bucolic [bju:'kɔlik] *a* pastoril, bucólico.
bud [bʌd] *n* botón, pimpollo, yema, capullo; *vi* brotar, retoñar, abotonar; **to nip in the —** ahogar en germen.
Buddha ['budə] *m* Buda.
budding ['bʌdiŋ] *a* en cierne.
budge [bʌdʒ] *vi* mover; moverse, menearse, apartarse.
budget ['bʌdʒit] *n* presupuesto; *vi* hacer el presupuesto.
buff [bʌf] *n* piel de ante; **blind man's —** (*game*) gallina ciega.
buffalo ['bʌfəlou] *n* búfalo.
buffer ['bʌfə] *n* almohadilla, muelle; tapón; (*rl*) tope.
buffet ['bufei] *n* (*dining room*) alacena, repostería; (*rl*) cantina; ['bʌfit] (*slap*) bofetada; *vt* abofetear, pegar.
buffeting ['bʌfitiŋ] *n* zurra, tunda.
bug [bʌg] *n* insecto, chinche, pulga; virus, microbio; **big —** señorón.
bugbear ['bʌgbɛə] *n* espantajo, cuco; pelma, molestia.
buggy ['bʌgi] *n* calesa, tartana.
bugle ['bju:gl] *n* corneta; cuerno de caza; (*mil*) trompeta, clarín.
build [bild] *n* hechura, presencia; forma; *vti* edificar, construir, erigir, fabricar; **to — up** robustecer, elaborar; **to — again** rehacer.
builder ['bildə] *n* constructor, arquitecto.
building ['bildiŋ] *n* edificio; obra; construcción.
bulb [bʌlb] *n* (*plant*) cebolla; bulbo; (*light*) bombilla; foco; (*barometer*) cubeta.
bulbous ['bʌlbəs] *a* cebolludo.
Bulgarian [bʌl'gɛəriən] *an* búlgaro.
bulge [bʌldʒ] *n* desplome, pandeo, protuberancia; *vi* combar(se).
bulk [bʌlk] *n* bulto, masa, mole, volumen; **in —** en globo, a granel.
bulkiness ['bʌlkinis] *n* corpulencia, dimensión.
bulky ['bʌlki] *a* voluminoso, abultado, grueso.
bull [bul] *n* toro; **—dog** perro de presa, dogo; (*papal*) bula; (*stocks*) alcista; **young —** novillo.
bullet ['bulit] *n* bala; **—proof** *a* prueba de bala.
bulletin ['bulitin] *n* boletín; **— board** tablón de avisos.
bullfight ['bulfait] *n* corrida de toros; (*amateur*) capea; (*of young bulls*) novillada; **—er** torero; (*killer*) matador; capeador; novillero; **to go to a —** ir a los toros.
bullfighting ['bulfaitiŋ] *n* toreo; **the art of —** el arte taurino, tauromaquia.
bullion ['buliən] *n* oro, plata en barras.
bullock ['bulək] *n* buey, ternero.

bullring ['bulriŋ] *n* redondel, ruedo; plaza de toros.
bull's-eye ['bulzai] *n* claraboya, tragaluz; (*target*) blanco.
bully ['buli] *n* valentón, guapo, camorrista; espadachín, buscarruidos, perdonavidas, matón; *vt* amenazar, fanfarronear, promover riña, amedrentar.
bulrush ['bulrʌʃ] *n* junco.
bulwark ['bʌlwək] *n* baluarte; (*ship*) antepecho.
bumblebee ['bʌmblbi:] *n* abejarrón.
bump [bʌmp] *n* (*swelling*) chichón; tope, golpe, porrazo; *vt* **to — into** dar con, chocar contra.
bumpkin ['bʌmpkin] *n* patán, paleto.
bun [bʌn] *n* bollo, buñuelo; (*hair*) moño; **— maker (seller)** buñolero.
bunch [bʌntʃ] *n* (*grapes*) racimo; (*onions*) ristra; (*flowers*) manojo, ramillete, haz; (*fruit*) cuelga.
bundle ['bʌndl] *n* bulto, lío, paquete, tercio; (*heavy*) fardo; (*large*) balón; (*documents*) legajo, fajo; *vt* empaquetar, liar; **to — out** poner en la puerta, despedir con cajas destempladas.
bung [bʌŋ] *n* tapón, tarugo, buzón, taco, espita; **—hole** boca de tonel.
bungalow ['bʌŋgəlou] *n* casa de un solo piso, chalé.
bungle ['bʌŋgl] *vt* chapucear, echar a perder, estropear.
bungler ['bʌŋglə] *n* chambón, zurdo, chapucero.
bunion ['bʌnjən] *n* juanete.
bunker ['bʌŋkə] *n* carbonera; **to be —ed** estar en un atolladero.
bunting ['bʌntiŋ] *n* lanilla; colgadura; (*orn*) calandria.
buoy [bɔi] *n* boya; *vt* boyar, flotar; **to — up (with hope)** reanimar, esperanzar.
buoyancy ['bɔiənsi] *n* liviandad, acción de flotar.
buoyant ['bɔiənt] *a* boyante, que flota; animado, alegre.
burden ['bə:dn] *n* peso, porte, fardo, carga; aflicción; **beast of —** bestia de carga; (*of song*) estribillo, retornelo; *vt* cargar; oprimir, agobiar.
burdensome ['bə:dnsəm] *a* pesado, oneroso, premioso.
bureau [bjuə'rou] *n* (*writing*) escritorio; (*cupboard*) armario; (*office*) bufete, despacho, oficina.
bureaucracy [bjuə'rɔkrəsi] *n* burocracia.
burglar ['bə:glə] *n* ladrón.
burglary ['bə:gləri] *n* robo de una casa.
burglarize ['bə:gləraiz] **burgle** ['bə:gl] *vt* robar.
Burgos ['bə:gəs] **native of —** *a* burgalés.
burial ['beriəl] *n* entierro, enterramiento.
burlesque [bə:'lesk] *a* burlesco; *n* parodia.
burly ['bə:li] *n* grueso, fornido, cuadrado.
Burma ['bə:mə] *n* Birmania.
Burmese [bə:'mi:z] *an* birmano.
burn [bə:n] *n* quemadura; *vt* (*flames*) quemar, encender; (*spice, sun*) picar, tostar; *vi* arder, consumirse; (*of fire*) tirar; **to — to ashes** reducir a cenizas.
burning ['bə:niŋ] *a* abrasador; vehemente; **— question** cuestión candente, palpitante; *n* quema.
burnish ['bə:niʃ] *vt* bruñir, pulir, dar lustre (a), pulimentar.
burrow ['bʌrou] *n* conejera, madriguera, cueva; *vi* minar, horadar, zapar.
burst ['bə:st] *n* estallido, reventón; *vt* reventar, estallar; prorrumpir; **to — open** (*a door*) echar abajo; **to — open** romper; quebrantar, forzar; **to — out** soltar; **to — into tears** deshacerse en lágrimas; **to — with laughing** reventar de risa; (*with pride*) reventar; **the heavens have —** se ha venido el cielo abajo.
bury ['beri] *vt* enterrar, sepultar.
burying ['beriiŋ] *n* entierro; **— ground** cementerio.
bus [bʌs] *n* autobús.
bush [buʃ] *n* arbusto, mata; matorral; (*fox*) hopo; **to beat about the —** andarse por las ramas; **don't beat about the —** hable sin ambajes.
bushel ['buʃl] *n* fanega.
bushy ['buʃi] *a* espeso, peludo; matoso; copudo.
business ['biznis] *n* negocio; comercio; oficio; ocupación; trabajo; asunto(s); **good —** buen negocio, negocio redondo; **to do — with** comerciar (con); **to send (someone) about his —** enviar (a uno) a paseo.
businesslike ['biznislaik] *a* formal, práctico, sistemático.
bust [bʌst] *n* (*statue*) busto; (*fem*) seno.
bustle ['bʌsl] *n* animación, bullicio; alboroto; (*of dress*) polisón; *vi* bullir, apresurarse, menearse.
bustling ['bʌsliŋ] *a* (*person*) hacendoso; (*crowd*) hervidero.
busy ['bizi] *a* ocupado, activo; **to keep —** mantener(se) ocupado.
busybody ['bizi,bɔdi] *a* entremetido; chismoso; *n* veedor, chisgarabís; **to be a —** curiosear.
but [bʌt] *cj, ad, prep* pero; más, más que; sino (*with negative*); solamente, excepto, menos; **— for** menos, a no ser que; **all — that** todo menos eso.
butcher ['butʃə] *n* carnicero, jifero; *vt* matar.
butchery ['butʃəri] *n* carnicería, matanza; mortandad.
butler ['bʌtlə] *n* mayordomo, despensero.
butt [bʌt] *n* (*wine*) bota, carral, pipa,

tonel; (*cigarette*) colilla; (*cigar*) punta; (*ferrule*) contera; extremo, objeto, blanco, fin.
butter ['bʌtə] *n* mantequilla; **—dish** mantequera; *vt* **to — up** (*fam*) dar coba a.
butterfly ['bʌtəflai] *n* mariposa.
buttery ['bʌtəri] *a* mantecoso; *n* despensa.
buttock(s) ['bʌtək(s)] *n* trasero, asentaderas; (*animal*) ancas.
button ['bʌtn] *n* botón; **— hole** ojal; tirador; *vti* abotonar.
buttress ['bʌtris] *n* estribo, contrafuerte; **flying —** arbotante; apoyo, sostén.
buxom ['bʌksəm] *a* (*f*) rolliza, gorda, jovial.
buy [bai] *vt* comprar; **to — over** sobornar; **to — off** librarse (*de uno*) con dinero.
buyer ['baiə] *n* comprador.
buzz [bʌz] *n* zumbido, susurro; *vi* susurrar, cuchichear.
by [bai] *prep* por, con, cerca de, a; *ad* cerca; **—law** estatuto, reglamento; **—stander** circunstante, mirón; **—path** vereda; **—roads** andurriales; **— the dozen** por docenas; **— Sunday** para el domingo; **— day** de día; **— train** en tren; **— the way** de paso; **—-product** producto secundario.
bye-bye ['bai'bai] hasta luego, abur.
byre ['baiə] *n* establo.

C

cab [kæb] *n* taxi; cabriolé, coche (de alquiler, de punto); **—stand** parada, sitio de coches.
cabal [kə'bæl] *n* cábala; maquinación.
cabbage ['kæbidʒ] *n* col; (*cooked*) repollo; **red —** berza lombarda.
cabin ['kæbin] *n* choza, cabaña; (*naut*) camarote.
cabin boy ['kæbinbɔi] *n* grumete.
cabinet ['kæbinit] *n* gabinete; (*display*) escaparate, vitrina; caja, estuche; consejo de ministros, Gobierno; **—maker** ebanista.
cable ['keibl] *n* cable; (*rope*) maroma; *vt* telegrafiar.
cabman ['kæbmən] *n* cochero.
cackle ['kækl] *n* cacareo; *vi* cacarear, cloquear.
cacophony [kæ'kɔfəni] *n* cacofonía.
cactus ['kæktəs] *n* cacto.
caddy ['kædi] *n* caja de té; (*golf*) cadi.
cadence ['keidəns] *n* cadencia, ritmo.
cadet [kə'det] *a* segundón; *n* cadete, voluntario.
cadre [kɑ:dr] *n* (*mil*) cuadro.
Caesar ['si:zə] *m* César.
café ['kæfei] *n* café; salón de té; restaurante.
cage [keidʒ] *n* jaula, prisión; *vt* enjaular; coger.
cajole [kə'dʒoul] *vt* adular, lisonjear, requebrar, halagar, engatusar.
cake [keik] *n* pastel, bollo, (*ring-shaped*) rosca; (*flat*) tortilla; **sponge —** bizcocho; (*of soap*) pastel, pan, pastilla; **— shop** pastelería; **wedding —** pastel de boda; **to take the —** llevarse la palma.
calaboose [kælə'bu:s] *n* calabozo.
calamitous [kə'læmitəs] *a* calamitoso, desdichado, trágico.
calamity [kə'læmiti] *n* calamidad, adversidad, azote, infortunio.
calcium ['kælsiəm] *n* calcio.
calculate ['kælkjuleit] *vt* calcular, computar, contar; hacer cálculos.
calculation [ˌkælkju'leiʃən] *n* cálculo, cómputo, cuenta; presupuesto.
calendar ['kælində] *n* calendario, almanaque; **— of saints** santoral.
calf [kɑ:f] *n* ternero, becerro; (*of leg*) pantorrilla; **sea —** buey marino; **the golden —** becerro de oro; (*bound*) **in —** en piel.
caliber ['kælibə] *n* calibre; capacidad.
calico ['kælikou] *n* calicó, cretona, percal.
caliph ['kælif] *n* califa.
call [kɔ:l] *n* llamada; visita; (*mil*) **— up** llamamiento; **bugle —** trompetazo, tintirintín; *vt* llamar, convocar; visitar; citar; (*at port*) tocar, hacer escala; (*for article*) recoger; (*by name*) apellidar; (*for attention*) requerer, exigir, pedir; **to — forth** provocar; **to — out** dar voces, gritar; **to — the roll** pasar lista; **to — into question** poner en duda; **to — upon** visitar; invocar; **to — up** evocar, recordar, despertar; (*mil*) levantar; **to — to account** pedir cuentas de; **to — names** tratar de; poner.
caller ['kɔ:lə] *n* visitante, (*f*) visita.
calling ['kɔ:liŋ] *n* vocación, profesión, empleo.
callous ['kæləs] *a* endurecido; insensible, córneo.
callousness ['kæləsnis] *n* callosidad; endurecimiento, salvajismo.
calm [kɑ:m] *a* tranquilo, sosegado, pausado, sereno, apacible, calmado; *n* sosiego, quietud, tranquilidad, calma; *vti* tranquilizar, calmar, pacificar; (*weather*) abonanzarse; componer; (*pain*) aplacar.
calmness ['kɑ:mnis] *n* tranquilidad, serenidad, sosiego.
calumniate [kə'lʌmnieit] *vt* calumniar, denigrar.
calumny ['kæləmni] *n* calumnia, maledicencia.
Calvary ['kælvəri] *n* calvario.
calve ['kɑ:v] *vi* (*of cow*) parir.
camel ['kæməl] *n* camello; **— driver** camellero.
cameo ['kæmiou] *n* camafeo.
camera ['kæmərə] *n* máquina,

aparato (fotográfico); **folding —** cámara plegadiza.
camisole ['kæmisoul] *n* camiseta.
camouflage ['kæmuflɑ:ʒ] *n* camuflaje.
camp [kæmp] *n* campamento, ranchería, real; **— bed** catrecillo; **— chair** silla de campaña; **— stool** silla de tijera; *vti* acampar.
campaign [kæm'pein] *n* campaña.
campaigner [kæm'peinə] *n* veterano; (*for rights etc*) paladín.
campanile [ˌkæmpə'ni:li] *n* campanario.
camphor ['kæmfə] *n* alcanfor.
can [kæn] *n* lata; **tin —** envase de latón; **— opener** abrelatas; *vt* conservar en lata, enlatar.
Canada ['kænədə] *n* el Canadá.
Canadian [kə'neidiən] *an* canadiense.
canal [kə'næl] *n* canal, conducto; **irrigation —** acequia.
canalize ['kænəlaiz] *vt* canalizar.
canary [kə'nεəri] *n* canario; **— seed** alpiste.
Canary Islands [kə'nεəriˌailəndz] *n* las Islas Canarias.
cancel ['kænsəl] *vt* cancelar, borrar, tachar; (*math*) eliminar.
canceling ['kænsəliŋ] *n* cancelación, anulación.
cancer ['kænsə] *n* cáncer.
candelabrum [ˌkændi'lɑ:brəm] *n* candelabro, hachero.
candid ['kændid] *a* cándido, sencillo, franco, abierto, ingenuo, veraz.
candidate ['kændidit] *n* candidato, aspirante; (*examination*) opositor.
candied ['kændid] *a* (*words*) azucarado; **— chestnut** marrón.
candle ['kændl] *n* (*esp relig*) vela; bujía; **— grease** sebo, moco; **—power** bujía; **—stick** bujía, almatoria.
candor ['kændə] *n* candor, candidez, franqueza, sinceridad, sencillez, ingenuosidad.
candy ['kændi] *n* confite; bombón, dulce; azúcar.
cane [kein] *n* bastón; caña, junco; **— brake** cañaveral; **— chair** silla de junco; **— sugar** caña dulce.
canine ['kænain] *a* canino, perruño; **— tooth** colmillo.
canister ['kænistə] *n* canasta, frasco, lata; caja de té.
canker ['kæŋkə] *n* gangrena, úlcera; *vti* roer, corromper.
cannery ['kænəri] *n* fábrica de conservas.
cannibal ['kænibəl] *n* caníbal; antropófago.
cannon ['kænən] *n* cañón; (*billiards*) carambola; **—ball** bala de cañón.
cannonade [ˌkænə'neid] *n* cañoneo.
canny ['kæni] *a* socarrón.
canoe [kə'nu:] *n* canoa, chalupa.
canon ['kænən] *n* canónigo; *f* canonesa; (*mus*) canon.
canonical [kə'nɔnikəl] *a* canónico.
canopy ['kænəpi] *n* dosel, baldaquín; (*eccles*) palio.
cant [kænt] *n* jerigonza; hipocresía; (*slope*) desplome, sesgo, inclinación; *vt* ladear.
cantankerous [kən'tæŋkərəs] *a* criticón; pendenciero.
canteen [kæn'ti:n] *n* cantina; bote; (*cutlery*) juego; (*mil*) cantimplora.
canter ['kæntə] *vi* ir al galope corto; *n* medio galope.
cantonment [kən'tu:nmənt] *n* acantonamiento.
canvas ['kænvəs] *n* lona; (*coarse*) cañamazo; (*paint*) lienzo; *vt* solicitar, pedir (*votos*); *n* investigación.
canvasser ['kænvəsə] *n* vendedor, viajante; agente electoral.
canyon ['kænjən] *n* garganta, desfiladero, cañón.
cap [kæp] *n* (*child's, without peak*) gorro, (*with peak*) gorra; sombrero, bonete; (*woman's indoor*) cofia; (*academic, cardinal's*) birrete; (*cloth, hunting*) montera; (*peaked*) gorra de visera; **— in hand** gorra en mano; (*bottle*) tapa, cápsula, tapón; *vt* tocar, cubrir la cabeza; coronar; dar la última mano; **if the — fits** el que se pica, ajos come.
capability [ˌkeipə'biliti] *n* capacidad, competencia.
capable ['keipəbl] *a* capaz, hábil, susceptible, potente; **to be — of** poder; saber; ser capaz de.
capacity [kə'pæsiti] *n* capacidad, cabida; inteligencia, aptitud, facultad; puesto; porte.
cape [keip] *n* (*geog*) cabo, punta de tierra; capa (*corta*), caperuza.
Cape Horn ['keip'hɔ:n] *n* Cabo de Hornos.
caper ['keipə] *n* cabriola; (*bot*) alcaparra; *vi* hacer cabriolas, trenzar, cabriol(e)ar.
capital ['kæpitl] *a* capital; (*letter*) mayúscula; excelente; *n* (*city*) capital; (*wealth*) capital, fondos; (*archit*) capitel, chapitel; **to make — out of** aprovecharse de.
capitol ['kæpitl] *n* capitolio.
capitulate [kə'pitjuleit] *vi* capitular.
capitulation [kəˌpitju'leiʃən] *n* capitulación.
caprice [kə'pri:s] *n* antojo, capricho, fantasía; desvarío.
capricious [kə'priʃəs] *n* caprichoso, antojadizo.
capsize [kæp'saiz] *vti* volcar(se); zozobrar.
capstan ['kæpstən] *n* cabrestante.
capsule ['kæpsju:l] *n* cápsula.
captain ['kæptin] *n* capitán, patrón.
caption ['kæpʃən] *n* título, rótulo, lema.
captious ['kæpʃəs] *a* capcioso, regañón, delicado, caviloso.
captivate ['kæptiveit] *vt* cautivar, seducir, captar.

captivating ['kæptiveitiŋ] *a* fascinador, encantador.
captivation [,kæpti'veiʃən] *n* fascinación, encanto, seducción.
captive ['kæptiv] *an* cautivo, prisionero, preso.
captivity [kæp'tiviti] *n* cautividad, cautiverio, prisión.
captor ['kæptə] *n* apresador, raptor.
capture ['kæptʃə] *n* captura, toma; botín (*thing captured*); presa; *vt* capturar, prender, apresar, tomar; hacer presa; (*fig*) embelesar.
Capuchin ['kæpjuʃin] *n* capuchino; capucha.
car [kɑ:] *n* (*motor*) coche; (*tram*) tranvía; **dining —** vagón restaurante, carro comedor; **sleeping —** coche-cama; carro, carreta; vagón (*de ferrocarril*).
carabineer [,kærəbi'niə] *n* carabinero.
carafe [kə'rɑ:f] *n* garrafa.
carat ['kærət] *n* quilate.
caravel ['kærəvel] *n* carabela.
carbide ['kɑ:baid] *n* carburo.
carbine ['kɑ:bain] *n* carabina.
carbon ['kɑ:bən] *n* carbón; **— paper** papel carbón.
carbonize ['kɑ:bənaiz] *vt* carbonizar.
carbuncle ['kɑ:bʌŋkl] *n* carbunclo.
carcass ['kɑ:kəs] *n* res muerta; carroña; esqueleto.
card [kɑ:d] *n* (*playing*) naipe; (*visiting*) tarjeta; **index —** ficha, papeleta; **identity —** cédula personal; **— table** tapete verde; **— catalogue** fichero; **post—** tarjeta postal; *vt* cardar.
cardboard ['kɑ:dbɔ:d] *n* cartón, cartulina.
cardigan ['kɑ:digən] *n* suéter, jersé.
cardinal ['kɑ:dinl] *a* cardinal; *n* cardenal.
care [kɛə] *n* (*attention*) aviso, pulso, precaución, detenimiento, cuidado; atención; parquedad; (*trouble*) cuita, ansiedad; (*charge*) cargo, tarea, cuidado; *vi* cuidar de, cuidarse, tener cuidado, poner atención; **not to — a rap** no importar un pepino; **to take great —** preocupar, mirar mucho por; **take care!** ¡ojo!, ¡cuidado!
career [kə'riə] *n* carrera, curso; *vi* lanzarse, correr a carrera tendida.
carefree ['kɛəfri:] *a* despreocupado.
careful ['kɛəful] *a* cuidadoso, esmerado; providente; detenido; (*appearance*) acicalado, cuidado.
carefulness ['kɛəfulnis] *n* cuidado, atención, cautela, ansia, esmero.
careless ['kɛəlis] *a* descuidado, negligente, remiso.
carelessness ['kɛəlisnis] *n* descuido; indiferencia, dejo, negligencia, inadvertencia, improvidencia; incuria, desaliño.
caress [kə'res] *n* caricia; *vt* acariciar; regalar.
caressing [kə'resiŋ] *a* halagüeño.
caretaker ['kɛə,teikə] *n* conserje, guardián.
cargo ['kɑ:gou] *n* carga, cargazón, cargamento.
Caribbean Sea [kæri'bi:ən'si:] *n* el Mar Caribe.
caricature [,kærikə'tjuə] *n* caricatura; *vt* caricaturar, ridiculizar.
Carmelite ['kɑ:milait] *n* carmelita.
carmine ['kɑ:main] *n* carmín.
carnage ['kɑ:nidʒ] *n* carnicería, matanza, estrago.
carnal ['kɑ:nl] *a* carnal, sensual.
carnation [kɑ:'neiʃən] *n* clavel.
carnival ['kɑ:nivəl] *n* carnaval.
carnivorous [kɑ:'nivərəs] *a* carnívoro.
carol ['kærəl] *n* villancico, canción.
carousal [kə'rauzəl] *n* festín, francachela, regodeo; borrachera.
carp [kɑ:p] *n* carpa; *vti* censurar, criticar.
carpenter ['kɑ:pintə] carpintero; **stage —** tramoyista.
carpentry ['kɑ:pintri] *n* carpintería.
carper ['kɑ:pə] *n* reparón, criticón.
carpet ['kɑ:pit] *n* alfombra, tapete; **— sweeper** aspirador (*de polvo*); *vt* alfombrar.
carriage ['kæridʒ] *n* coche, carruaje; transporte, porte, conducción, acarreo; **gun —** cureña; **— door** portezuela; **— entrance** puerta cochera; **two-wheeled —** tartana; **— paid** porte pagado; **good —** buen porte, garbo.
carried ['kærid] *pp* **to be — away** (*by emotion*) arrebatarse, transportarse.
carrier ['kæriə] *n* acarreador, carretero, trajinante, porteador, tractor.
carrion ['kæriən] *n* carroña; *a* podrido.
carrot ['kærət] *n* zanahoria.
carry ['kæri] *vt* llevar; (*goods*) acarrear, trajinar; **to — off** llevar preso; (*prizes etc*) ganar; **to — on** continuar, seguir; **to — out** verificar, llevar a cabo; seguir, cumplir; **to — through** realizar; **to — on one's back** llevar a hombro(s); **to — coals to Newcastle** llevar leña al monte.
cart [kɑ:t] *n* (*country*) carreta, carro, carretilla; *vt* acarrear.
carter ['kɑ:tə] *n* carretero.
Carthusian [kɑ:'θu:ziən] *an* cartujo.
cartoon [kɑ:'tu:n] *n* cartón; (*paint*) caricatura.
cartridge ['kɑ:tridʒ] *n* cartucho.
carve [kɑ:v] *vti* tallar; labrar; grabar; entallar; (*meat*) trinchar; **to — out** (*career*) labrarse.
carver ['kɑ:və] *n* grabador; entallador, escultor.
carving ['kɑ:viŋ] *n* escultura, obra de

talla; trinchar; (*applied to ceilings*) artesón.
cascade [kæs'keid] *n* cascada, catarata.
case [keis] *n* caso; (*box*) caja; (*jewel*) estuche; **show—** vidriera, vitrina; (*cover*) funda, vaina; (*law*) — pleito, causa; **cigarette —** petaca; **in any —** de todos modos; *vt* encerrar, guardar en estuche, encajonar.
casement ['keismənt] *n* (*puerta*) ventana; cubierta.
cash [kæʃ] *n* efectivo, metálico; **ready —** dinero contante; **for —** al contado; **—book** libro de caja; **— register** caja registradora; *vt* pagar, descontar; convertir en efectivo.
cashier [kæ'ʃiə] *n* cajero; *vt* destituir, degradar.
casing ['keisiŋ] *n* cubierta, envoltura, (*inner*) forro.
cask [kɑ:sk] *n* barril, tonel, casco; **—maker** cubero.
casket ['kɑ:skit] *n* estuche, arquilla; cofre, ataúd.
cassock ['kæsək] *n* sotana, balandrán.
cast [kɑ:st] *a* de fundición, fundido; **— iron** hierro colado; *n* lanzamiento, tiro, tirada; (*metal*) fundición, molde; (*features*) estampa; (*theat*) reparto; (*eye*) defecto, tendencia; *vti* tirar, arrojar; vaciar; **to — aside, away** desechar, desperdiciar; **to — off, away** tirar, soltar, disipar; **to — lots** echar suertes; **to — a ballot** votar; (*metals*) fundir.
castanet [kæstə'net] *n* castañuelas, castañetas.
castaway ['kɑ:stəwei] *n* náufrago; abandonado, réprobo.
caste [kɑ:st] *n* casta, clase social; **to lose —** desprestigiarse.
castigate ['kæstigeit] *vt* corregir, fustigar, castigar; (*style*) pulir.
Castille [kæs'ti:l] *n* Castilla.
Castilian [kæs'tiliən] *an* castellano.
casting ['kɑ:stiŋ] *n* cálculo; plan, modelo; (*metals*) fundición, moldaje; (*theat*) reparto, distribución de papeles.
castle ['kɑ:sl] *n* castillo; (*chess*) roque, torre; *vi* (*chess*) enrocar(se).
castor oil ['kɑ:stər'ɔil] *n* aceite de ricino.
casual ['kæʒuəl] *a* casual, fortuito, ocasional; superficial, ligero; (*person*) poco atento, despreocupado.
casually ['kæʒuəli] *ad* por casualidad; (*muy*) por encima.
casualty ['kæʒuəlti] *n* accidente, victima, (*mil*) baja.
cat [kæt] *n* gato, gata; **to rain —s and dogs** llover a cántaros; **—like** gatuño; **— and dog life** una vida de perros y gatos.
cataclysm ['kætəklizəm] *n* cataclismo, hundimiento.
catacombs ['kætəku:mz] *n* las catacumbas.
Catalan ['kætəlæn] *an* catalán.
catalogue ['kætəlɔg] *n* catálogo; *vt* catalogar, fichar; *vi* hacer catálogos.
Catalonia [ˌkætə'louniə] *n* Cataluña.
Catalonian [ˌkætə'louniən] *a* catalán; **— farmer** payés.
catapult ['kætəpʌlt] *n* tirabeque, catapulta.
cataract ['kætərækt] *n* catarata, salto.
catarrh [kə'tɑ:] *n* catarro.
catastrophe [kə'tæstrəfi] *n* catástrofe, cataclismo, desastre; (*theat*) desenlace.
catch [kætʃ] *n* (*mech*) gatillo, cierre; (*in voice*) quiebro; (*of fish*) redada, cogida; *vt* agarrar, asir, atrapar, cazar; (*ball, cold etc*) coger, pescar; (*disease*) contraer; (*scent*) olfatear; **to — out** sobrecoger; **to — red-handed** coger con las manos en la masa.
catching ['kætʃiŋ] *a* contagioso; (*tune*) pegajoso.
catchy ['kætʃi] *a* pegajoso; **to be —** (*mus*) pegar.
catchword ['kætʃwə:d] *n* reclamo, tópico, slogan.
catechism ['kætikizəm] *n* catecismo.
categorical [ˌkæti'gɔrikəl] *a* categórico, rotundo.
category ['kætigəri] *n* categoría, clase, tipo.
cater ['keitə] *vi* proveer, abastecer.
caterpillar ['kætəpilə] *n* oruga.
catgut ['kætgʌt] *n* cuerda.
cathedral [kə'θi:drəl] *a* episcopal; *n* catedral.
Catherine ['kæθərin] *f* Catalina.
catholic ['kæθəlik] *an* católico; **non—** no católico.
catholicism [kə'θɔlisizəm] *n* catolicismo.
cattle ['kætl] *n* ganado, res, cabeza de res, ganadería.
cauldron ['kɔ:ldrən] *n* caldera.
cauliflower ['kɔliflauə] *n* coliflor.
cause [kɔ:z] *n* causa, motivo, origen, fundamento; *vt* causar, obligar, ocasionar, producir, suscitar, dar, producir, dar lugar a, promover, provocar, operar; **to be the — of** valer, originar, motivar; **to — huge losses** hacer estragos; **to — to be made** mandar hacer.
causeway ['kɔ:zwei] *n* calzada; dique; (*sea*) arrecife.
caustic ['kɔ:stik] *a* cáustico, acerado.
cauterize ['kɔ:təraiz] *vt* cauterizar.
caution ['kɔ:ʃən] *n* prudencia, cautela, miramiento, precaución, caución; *vt* prevenir, avisar, amonestar.
cautious ['kɔ:ʃəs] *a* cuidadoso, precavido, disimulado, avisado, cauto, ponderoso.
cautiousness ['kɔ:ʃəsnis] *n* circunspección, prudencia.
cavalcade [ˌkævəl'keid] *n* cabalgata.
cavalier [ˌkævə'liə] *n* caballero; *a*

galante; desenvuelto; descortés, grosero.
cavalry ['kævəlri] *n* caballería.
cave [keiv] *n* cueva, antro, guarida; **— dweller, — man** trogdolita; *vi* **to — in** hundirse.
cavern ['kævən] *n* caverna, antro, gruta.
cavernous ['kævənəs] *a* cavernoso, tenebroso.
caving-in ['keiviŋ'in] *n* hundimiento.
cavity ['kæviti] *n* hoyo; oquedad.
caw [kɔ:] *vi* graznar; **cawing** *n* graznido.
cease [si:s] *vti* cesar, dejar de.
ceaseless ['si:slis] *a* incesante, continuo, sin parar.
cedar ['si:də] *n* cedro.
cede [si:d] *vt* ceder; traspasar.
ceiling ['si:liŋ] *n* techado, techo, cielo raso.
celebrate ['selibreit] *vt* (*mass etc*) celebrar; solemnizar, conmemorar.
celebrated ['selibreitid] *a* insigne, afamado, renombrado.
celebrity [si'lebriti] *n* celebridad, fama.
celebration [ˌseli'breiʃən] *n* (*of marriage*) celebración; conmemoración; fiesta, festejo.
celery ['seləri] *n* apio.
celestial [si'lestiəl] *a* celeste, celestial.
celibacy ['selibəsi] *n* celibato.
cell [sel] *n* (*biol*) célula; (*relig*) celda; (*el*) pila eléctrica; (*fig*) **to be in the condemned —** estar en capilla ardiente.
cellar ['selə] *n* sótano; (*wine*) bodega, cueva.
Celtic ['seltik] *a* celta, céltico.
cement [si'ment] *n* cemento; argamasa; *vti* cementar, pegar con cemento; **to mix —** argamasar.
cemetery ['semitri] *n* cementerio, camposanto.
censor ['sensə] *n* censor; crítico.
censorious [sen'sɔ:riəs] *a* hipercrítico; severo.
censorship ['sensəʃip] *n* censura.
censurable ['senʃərəbl] *a* censurable.
censure ['senʃə] *n* censura; (*severe*) catilinaria; reprensión, crítica; *vt* censurar, criticar, vejar, atildar, tachar; (*harshly*) zaherir.
censurer ['senʃərə] *n* criticón.
census ['sensəs] *n* censo, empadronamiento.
cent [sent] *n* céntimo, centavo; **per —** por ciento.
centenary [sen'ti:nəri] *n* centenario.
centennial [sen'teniəl] *a* centenario.
center ['sentə] *n* centro, núcleo, eje, punto medio; *vti* concentrar, fijar, determinar el centro; **to — upon, around** girar en torno de, versar sobre, estribar en.
centigrade ['sentigreid] *n* centígrado.
centipede ['sentipi:d] *n* ciempiés.
central ['sentrəl] *a* central, céntrico; **— streets** calles céntricas.
centralize ['sentrəlaiz] *vt* centralizar.
century ['sentʃuri] *n* siglo, centuria.
ceramic [si'ræmik] *a* cerámico; *n* **—s** cerámica.
Cerberus ['sə:bərəs] *n* Cancerbero.
cereals ['siəriəlz] *n pl* granos.
ceremonial [ˌseri'mouniəl] *a* ceremonial, ritual; *n* ceremonial.
ceremonious [ˌseri'mouniəs] *a* ceremonioso, cumplimentero.
ceremony ['seriməni] *n* ceremonia, rito, honores; cumplido; función; **without —** informal.
certain ['sə:tn] *a* cierto, seguro, evidente, positivo; **for —** sin falta.
certainly ['sə:tnli] *ad* ciertamente, seguramente, por cierto, claro, a buen seguro, sin falta; **— not** de ningún modo.
certainty ['sə:tnti] *n* certidumbre, seguridad, convicción; **for a —** a ciencia cierta.
certificate [sə'tifikit] *n* certificado, acta; bono, obligación; (*of baptism*) fe de bautismo; (*birth*) partida; (*death*) partida (*de defunción*).
certification [ˌsə:tifi'keiʃən] *n* atestado.
certify ['sə:tifai] *vt* certificar, declarar, afirmar, dar fe.
cessation [se'seiʃən] *n* cesación, paro.
cession ['seʃən] *n* traspaso, cesión.
Ceylon [si'lɔn] *n* Ceilán.
Ceylonese [silɔ'ni:z] *an* cingalés.
chafe [tʃeif] *vti* frotar, calentar; (*against*) rozar, irritar.
chaff [tʃɑ:f] *n* paja, arista; (*fig*) broza; *vt* burlarse de.
chaffinch ['tʃæfintʃ] *n* pinzón.
chagrin ['ʃægrin] *n* resentimiento, desazón, sofoco; *vt* mortificar.
chain [tʃein] *n* cadena; (*events*) serie, eslabonamiento; *pl* prisiones; **guard —** grillo; **— mail** cota de malla; *vt* encadenar; aherrojar.
chair [tʃɛə] *n* silla, asiento; (*University*) cátedra; (*chairman*) presidencia, mesa presidencial; (*easy*) butaca, sillón; **arm—** butaca; **rocking —** mecedora.
chairman ['tʃɛəmən] *n* presidente (*de junta*).
chaise [ʃeiz] *n* silla (volante, de posta); (*light*) calesín, carrocín; **— longue** meridiana.
chalice ['tʃælis] *n* cáliz.
chalk [tʃɔ:k] *n* greda, creta; (*writing*) tiza; (*stucco*) yeso; **french —** talco; **white —** clarión; *vt* enyesar.
challenge ['tʃælindʒ] *n* desafío, reto; (*law*) recusación; *vt* desafiar, retar; requerir; (*mil*) dar el quién vive.
challenger ['tʃælindʒə] *n* provocador; (*in sport*) retador; duelista.
chamber ['tʃeimbə] *n* cámara, cuarto, alcoba; **— of Commerce** Cámara de Comercio; **— music**

música de cámara; **—maid** camarera, doncella, criada.

chamberlain ['tʃeimbəlin] *n* chambelán, camarero; **Lord —** Camarlengo.

chamois ['ʃæmwɑ:] *n* ante, gamuza, piel de ante.

champion ['tʃæmpiən] *n* campeón, paladín, adalid; *vt* abogar por.

championship ['tʃæmpiənʃip] *n* campeonato.

chance [tʃɑ:ns] *a* fortuito, casual; *n* azar, suerte; accidente, lance, oportunidad, coyuntura, casualidad; **by —** casualmente, acaso, por casualidad; **no —** sin esperanza; *vt* suceder por casualidad; **to take a —** probar fortuna, aventurarse; **to — to meet** topar con; **to give (a) —** dar margen a, poner en condiciones de.

chancellor ['tʃɑ:nsələ] *n* canciller; **— of the Exchequer** Ministro de Hacienda; (*university*) Rector.

chandelier [.ʃændi'liə] *n* candelabro, araña.

chandler ['tʃɑ:ndlə] *n* cerero; **ship's —** proveedor de buques.

change [tʃeindʒ] *n* cambio, alteración; vueltas; (*money*) vuelta; (*small money*) suelto, calderilla; (*house, heart*) mudanza; (*trains*) transbordo; (*scene, theat*) mutación; (*expression*) demudación; **no —** sin novedad; *vti* cambiar, trocar, permutar; tornar; (*house, opinion, clothes*) mudar de, variar, volver, reformar; (*of face*) inmutarse, demudarse; **to — places with** trocarse con; **to — the subject** volver la hoja.

changeable ['tʃeindʒəbl] *a* cambiante, variable, inconstante, novelero.

changeableness ['tʃeindʒəblnis] *n* inconstancia, variabilidad, mutabilidad.

changeful ['tʃeindʒful] *a* inconstante, variable.

changeless ['tʃeindʒlis] *a* invariable, inmutable.

channel ['tʃænl] *n* canal; (*groove*) ranura; (*of river*) cauce, madre; (*trench*) zanja; **irrigation —** acequia, caz; conducto; **English —** Canal de la Mancha; **the usual —s** los trámites reglamentarios; *vt* acanalar, encauzar.

chant [tʃɑ:nt] *n* canto llano; (*singsong*) sonsonete; *vti* cantar (*psalmos, himnos, etc*).

chaos ['keiɔs] *n* caos, desorden.

chaotic [kei'ɔtik] *adj* caótico.

chap [tʃæp] *n* grieta, hendidura; (*pers*) tío, mozo, tipo, sujeto, chico; *vti* hender, rajar; (*of skin*) cortarse; (*of hands*) grietarse.

chapel ['tʃæpəl] *n* capilla, ermita, santuario; (*Protest*) templo.

chaperon ['ʃæpəroun] *n* acompañadora, dueña; *vt* acompañar, escudar.

chapfallen ['tʃæp.fɔ:lən] *a* alicaído.

chaplain ['tʃæplin] *n* capellán; **army —** capellán castrense.

chapter ['tʃæptə] *n* capítulo; (*eccl*) capítulo, cabildo.

char [tʃɑ:] *n* tarea, trabajo a jornal; **—woman** asistenta, criada por horas; *vt* carbonizar; *vi* trabajar por días.

character ['kæriktə] *n* carácter, personalidad; (*nature*) índole, genio; propiedad; (*print*) letra; (*theat*) personaje; **man of —** hombre de (mucha) personalidad.

characteristic [.kæriktə'ristik] *a* característico; típico, propio, individual; *n* peculiaridad, rasgo, característica.

characterize ['kæriktəraiz] *vt* caracterizar, representar.

charcoal ['tʃɑ:koul] *n* carbón de leña; **— brazier** cisco.

charge [tʃɑ:dʒ] *n* (*post, duty*) cargo; (*care*) guarda, custodia; (*cost*) coste; (*cavalry, weight, bull*) carga; embestida; ataque; **man in —** encargado; (*task*) cometido, encargo; (*tax*) imposición, impuesto; (*com*) gastos; *vt* cargar, recomendar, exhortar, encargar; acusar, presentar una denuncia; cobrar; **to be in —** mandar, comandar, llevar la batuta.

charger ['tʃɑ:dʒə] *n* corcel.

chariness ['tʃɛərinəs] *n* prudencia, cuidado, parquedad, desgana.

charitable ['tʃæritəbl] *adj* caritativo; **— works** obras pías.

charity ['tʃæriti] *n* caridad; limosna, piedad.

charlatan ['ʃɑ:lətən] *n* charlatán, curandero.

Charles [tʃɑ:lz] *m* Carlos.

charm [tʃɑ:m] *n* encanto, gentileza, gracia, hechizo, atractivo; (*object*) dije, talismán; (*for baby*) higa; *vt* hechizar, encantar, seducir, embelesar.

charmer ['tʃɑ:mə] *n* hechicero; fascinador.

charming ['tʃɑ:miŋ] *adj* encantador, precioso, gracioso; **to be very —** tener ángel.

charnelhouse ['tʃɑ:nlhaus] *n* osario.

chart [tʃɑ:t] *n* mapa, carta de navegar.

charter ['tʃɑ:tə] *n* título, escritura de concesión; (*of town, laws*) fuero; constitución; fletamento; *vt* (*ship*) fletar; estatuir.

chary ['tʃɛəri] *adj* cuidadoso, cauteloso; parco.

chase ['tʃeis] *n* caza, persecución; *vt* cazar, perseguir, dar caza; (*jewel*) engastar; **to — away** ahuyentar, disipar.

chasm ['kæzəm] *n* precipicio, sima; abertura; vacío.

chaste [tʃeist] *adj* casto, puro, virgen, púdico, honesto, continente.

chasten ['tʃeisn] *vt* corregir, castigar.

chastise [tʃæs'taiz] *vt* corregir, castigar.
chastisement ['tʃæstizmənt] *n* castigo, corrección; pena, disciplina.
chastity ['tʃæstiti] *n* castidad, honestidad, honra.
chat [tʃæt] *n* charla, conversación, plática; *vi* charlar, platicar, departir.
chatter ['tʃætə] *n* charla, cháchara, palabreo; *vi* charlar; (*teeth*) rechinar.
chattering ['tʃætəriŋ] *a* gárrulo, clamoroso; *n* (*teeth*) rechino; cotorreo.
chauffeur ['ʃoufə] *n* chófer, conductor.
cheap [tʃi:p] *a* barato; vil, miserable; cursi; **dirt —** tirado; **to feel —** sentir vergüenza; **to hold —** tener en poco.
cheapen ['tʃi:pən] *vt* abaratar; regatear.
cheapjack ['tʃi:pdʒæk] *n* buhonero, baratillero, pacotillero.
cheapness ['tʃi:pnis] *n* baratura, lo barato.
cheat [tʃi:t] *n* fraude, trampa; engaño, engatusamiento; (*person*) timador; trampista, buscón; *vt* (*rob*) timar; defraudar, engañar; (*at school*) hacer trampas.
cheater ['tʃi:tə] *n* timador, petardista, fullero, estafador.
cheating ['tʃi:tiŋ] *n* engaño, timo, defraudación, duplicidad.
check [tʃek] *n* obstáculo; coto, dique, freno, represión; contrapeso, restricción; descalabro; (*receipt*) talón; (*bank*) cheque; **— book** libro de cheques; **double —** contramarca; *vt* reprimir, detener, parar, refrenar; contrarrestar; castigar; confrontar, comprobar, revisar.
checkered ['tʃekəd] *a* variado, pintarrajeado.
checkers ['tʃekəz] *n pl* juego de damas.
checkmate ['tʃek'meit] *vt* (*chess*) dar mate; desconcertar, desbaratar.
checkroom ['tʃekrum] *n* vestuario; consigna
cheek [tʃi:k] *n* mejilla; (*fat*) cachete; **—bone** pómulo; insolencia, descaro, frescura.
cheeky ['tʃi:ki] *a* petulante, descarado, fresco, desvergonzado.
cheer [tʃiə] *n* banquete, festín; vivas; *vti* consolar; alegrarse; alentar, reanimar; vitorear; **— up!** ¡ánimo!; **· eerio!** ¡adiós!
cheerful ['tʃiəful] *a* alegre, jovial, animado.
cheerfulness ['tʃiəfulnis] *n* alegría, buen humor.
cheering ['tʃiəriŋ] *a* animador; *n* gritos, ovaciones.
cheerless ['tʃiə:lis] *a* frío, triste, melancólico.
cheery ['tʃiəri] *a* animado, placentero, animoso.
cheese [tʃi:z] *n* queso; **Dutch —** queso de bola; **cream —** de nata, requesón; **—maker** quesero; **—cloth** estopilla.
chemical ['kemikəl] *a* químico.
chemist ['kemist] *n* químico; farmacéutico; **—'s shop** farmacia.
chemistry ['kemistri] *n* química.
cherish ['tʃeriʃ] *vt* querer, estimar; (*hopes, ideas*) acariciar, abrigar.
cherry ['tʃeri] *n* cereza; **— tree** cerezo.
chess [tʃes] *n* ajedrez; **—board** tablero; **—man** pieza.
chest [tʃest] *n* (*box*) caja, cofre; **— of drawers** cómoda; (*anat*) pecho, seno.
chestnut ['tʃesnʌt] *a* castaño; trigueño; (*horse*) zaino; *n* castaña; **— tree** castaño; **horse —** castaña de Indias; **dried —** pilongo.
chew [tʃu:] *vti* mascar, masticar; **chewing gum** chicle.
chicanery [ʃi'keinəri] *n* trampa, embrollo.
chick [tʃik] *n* pollo; *sl* chica.
chicken ['tʃikin] *n* pollo, pollito; **— coop** pollera; **—pox** viruelas locas.
chicory ['tʃikəri] *n* achicoria.
chide [tʃaid] *vti* regañar, reprender, reñir, refunfuñar.
chiding ['tʃaidiŋ] *n* increpación, reprensión.
chief [tʃi:f] *a* principal, primero, mayor; *n* jefe; caudillo; (*mil*) **— of staff** jefe de estado mayor.
chiefly ['tʃi:fli] *ad* principalmente, ante todo, mayormente.
chieftain ['tʃi:ftən] *n* caudillo, capataz, capitán.
chiffon ['ʃifɔn] *n* gasa.
chignon ['ʃi:njɔ̃:ŋ] *n* castaña, moño.
child [tʃaild] *n* niño; hijo; (*in arms*) crío; (*infant*) párvulo; **— bearing** parto.
childhood ['tʃaildhud] *n* niñez, infancia; **from —** desde niño.
childish ['tʃaildiʃ] *a* pueril, infantil, de niño.
childishness ['tʃaildiʃnis] *n* puerilidad, niñería.
childlike ['tʃaildlaik] *a* de niño, aniñado, pueril.
children ['tʃildrən] *n* prole, hijos.
Chile ['tʃili] *n* Chile.
Chilean ['tʃiliən] *an* chileno.
chill [tʃil] *a* frío, helado, desapacible; *n* escalofrío; constipado; resfriado; *vt* enfriar, helar; *vi* escalofriarse; resfriarse; **to take the — off** entibiar; **to catch a —** resfriarse.
chilliness ['tʃilinis] *n* frialdad escalofrío.
chilly ['tʃili] *a* frío, helado.
chime [tʃaim] *n* armonía, (*bells*) repiqueteo; *vi* sonar, tañer; (*bells*) repicar; concordar.
chimney ['tʃimni] *n* chimenea; **— cowl** caballete; **—piece** delantera de chimenea; **—pot** caperuza de chimenea.

chin [tʃin] *n* barba, barbilla; **double —** papo, papada; **—strap** carrillera.
china ['tʃainə] *n* porcelana, loza.
China ['tʃainə] *n* China.
Chinese ['tʃai'ni:z] *an* chino; **— lantern** farolillo de papel.
chink [tʃiŋk] *n* grieta, hendidura, resquicio, resquebrajo.
chip [tʃip] *n* astilla, (*shaving*) viruta; brizna; (*stone*) lasca; *vt* cortar, desmenuzar; **a — off the old block** de tal palo, tal astilla; **to — in** contribuir con su cuota.
chirp [tʃə:p] *n* gorjeo, chirrido, piada; *vi* gorjear, piar.
chisel ['tʃizl] *n* cincel; formón; *vt* cincelar.
chitchat ['tʃittʃæt] *n* palique; charla.
chivalrous ['ʃivəlrəs] *a* caballeresco.
chivalry ['ʃivəlri] *n* caballería, hidalguía; caballerosidad.
chlorine ['klɔ:ri:n] *n* cloro.
chocolate ['tʃɔkəlit] *n* chocolate.
choice [tʃɔis] *a* selecto, raro, escogido, granado, delicado; *n* elección, alternativa; preferencia, escogimiento, selección; **to have no —** no tener preferencia; **to have no — but to** no tener más alternativa que; **to make a — between** entresacar, elegir.
choiceness ['tfɔisnis] *n* delicadeza, primor.
choir ['kwaiə] *n* coro, orfeón; **—boy** niño de coro; **— singer** corista.
choke [tʃouk] *vt* sofocar, ahogar; estrangular; **to — up** atorar, abstruir; **to — off** poner término a.
choked [tʃoukt] *a* (*vegetation*) tupido; (*emotion*) ahogado; **to be —** (*with emotion*) tener un sofoco.
cholera ['kɔlərə] *n* cólera, tifc asiático.
choleric ['kɔlərik] *a* colérico, enojado, irascible.
choose [tʃu:z] *vt* escoger, elegir, preferir; optar por; (*by lot*) sortear.
chop [tʃɔp] *n* tajada; chuleta; **mutton —** chuleta de cordero; *vt* cortar; tajar, hacer trozos; **to — up finely** repicar; hender, rajar.
chopper ['tʃɔpə] *n* cuchilla (*de carnicero*), cortante.
choppy ['tʃɔpi] *n* agitado, picado.
chord [kɔ:d] *n* acorde, armonía; cuerda; fibra, cuerda sensible.
chore [tʃɔ:] *n* faena, quehacer.
choreography [.kɔri'ɔgrəfi] *n* coreografía.
chorus ['kɔ:rəs] *n* coro; **— girl** tiple, corista.
chosen ['tʃouzn] *a* predilecto, exquisito, escogido.
Christ [kraist] *m* Cristo.
christen ['krisn] *vt* cristianar, bautizar.
christendom ['krisndəm] *n* (*people*) cristiandad.
christening ['krisniŋ] *n* bautismo; (*act of —*) bautizo.
Christian ['kristiən] *an* cristiano.
Christianity [.kristi'æniti] *n* cristianismo.
Christine ['kristi:n] *f* Cristina.
Christmas ['krisməs] *n* Navidad, pascua de navidad; **— present** aguinaldo; **— carol** villancico.
Christopher ['kristəfə] *m* Cristóbal.
chronic ['krɔnik] *a* crónico, inveterado.
chronicle ['krɔnikl] *n* crónica; *vt* narrar, historiar.
chronicler ['krɔniklə] *n* cronista.
chronology [.krə'nɔlədʒi] *n* cronología.
chrysalis ['krisəlis] *n* crisálida, ninfa.
chubby ['tʃʌbi] *n* gordiflón, rechoncho, regordete.
chuck [tʃʌk] *n* (*under chin*) sopapo; *vt* **to — out, away, up** tirar, echar.
chuckle ['tʃʌkl] *vi* reír entre dientes; *n* risita.
chum [tʃʌm] *n* camarada; condiscípulo; compinche.
church [tʃə:tʃ] *n* iglesia.
churchman ['tʃə:tʃmən] *n* sacerdote, eclesiástico.
churchyard ['tʃə:tʃ'jɑ:d] *n* cementerio, patio de la iglesia.
churlish ['tʃə:liʃ] *a* rudo, grosero; ruín.
churn [tʃə:n] *n* mantequera; *vt* batir; agitar, menear.
Cicero ['sisərou] *m* Cicerón.
cider ['saidə] *n* sidra.
cigar [si'gɑ:] *n* cigarro, puro; **choice —** breva; **—case** petaca; **— holder** boquilla; **— store** estanco, tabaquería.
cigarette [.sigə'ret] *n* cigarillo, pitillo; **— butt** colilla; **— paper** papel de fumar.
cinder ['sində] *n* ceniza, rescoldo; (*hot*) ascuas; **to burn to a —** hacer un chicharrón.
Cinderella [.sində'relə] *f* Cenicienta.
cinema ['sinimə] *n* cine.
cinnamon ['sinəmən] *n* (*spice*) canela; (*tree*) canelo.
cipher ['saifə] *n* cifra; (*arith*) cero; **to be a —** ser un cero a la izquierda; *vti* numerar; calcular, escribir en cifra.
circle ['sə:kl] *n* círculo, esfera; (*social*) tertulia, peña; cerco, rueda; *vti* rodear, ceñir, moverse en círculo.
circuit ['sə:kit] *n* circuito, vuelta, radio, derredor.
circuitous [sə:'kju:itəs] *a* tortuoso; desviado, (*road*) que da un (*gran*) rodeo.
circular ['sa:kjulə] *a* circular, redondo; **— saw** sierra circular.
circulate ['sa:kjuleit] *vt* propalar, divulgar, esparcir; *vi* circular.
circulation [.sə:kju'leiʃən] *n* circulación.
circumcise ['sə:kəmsaiz] *vt* circuncidar.
circumference [sə'kʌmfərəns] *n*

circunferencia, ámbito, derredor.
circumlocution [.sə:kəmlə'kju:ʃən] *n* circunlocución, circunloquio, rodeo.
circumnavigate [.sə:kəm'nævigeit] *vi* circunnavegar.
circumscribe ['sə:kəmskraib] *vt* circunscribir, fijar, limitar.
circumspect ['sə:kəmspekt] *a* circunspecto, reservado, precavido, suspicaz, recatado.
circumspection [.sə:kəm'spekʃən] *n* mesura, pulso, miramiento, gravedad.
circumstance ['sə:kəmstəns] *n* circunstancia, detalle; *pl* medios; **set of —s** conjunción, oportunidad; **in easy —s** acomodado, holgado.
circumstantial [.sə:kəm'stænʃəl] *a* accesorio, detallado; — **evidence** prueba de indicios.
circumvent [.sə:kəm'vent] *vt* enredar, engañar, burlar.
circus ['sə:kəs] *m* circo, hipódromo.
cistern ['sistən] *n* cisterna, (*rainwater*) aljibe.
citadel ['sitədl] *n* ciudadela.
citation [sai'teiʃən] *n* emplazamiento, cita; mención.
cite [sait] *vt* citar, aducir; llamar; emplazar.
citizen ['sitizn] *n* ciudadano; vecino.
citizenship ['sitiznʃip] *n* ciudadanía.
city ['siti] *n* ciudad, (*large*) población; — **hall** Ayuntamiento; — **dweller** ciudadano.
civic ['sivik] *a* cívico; — **center** casa consistorial.
civil ['sivl] *n* civil; político; atento, cortés, bien educado; (*lay*) laico; — **servant** oficial.
civilian [si'viljən] *a* (de) paisano; *n* paisano.
civility [si'viliti] *n* cortesía, civilidad, urbanidad, atención.
civilization [.sivilai'zeiʃən] *n* civilización.
civilize ['sivilaiz] *vt* civilizar.
clad [klæd] *a* vestido.
claim [kleim] *n* reclamación, demanda; derecho, exposición, pretención; *vt* reclamar, exigir, demandar; pretender.
claimant ['kleimənt] *n* reclamante; demandante, pretendiente.
clam [klæm] *n* almeja.
clamber ['klæmbə] *vi* trepar, gatear, subir.
clammy ['klæmi] *a* (*hand*) viscoso, húmedo.
clamminess ['klæminis] *n* viscosidad.
clamor ['klæmə] *n* clamor, gritería, vocería, alboroto; *vi* clamar, gritar, vociferar.
clamorous ['klæmərəs] *a* clamoroso, ruidoso, estruendoso.
clamp [klæmp] *n* empalmadura; tenaza, prensa; *vt* fijar, encajar, empalmar.
clan [klæn] *n* tribu, casta, familia, estirpe.
clandestine [klæn'destin] *a* clandestino, furtivo, oculto.
clang [klæŋ] *n* sonido rechinante; estruendo, estrépito; *vi* rechinar, resonar.
clanging ['klæŋiŋ] *n* (*of bells*) campanillazo.
clank [klæŋk] *n* sonido metálico; *vi* sonar secamente.
clap [klæp] *n* golpe, palmada, aplauso; (*of thunder*) trueno; *vti* golpear ligeramente; aplaudir; echar, pegar; (*in jail*) meter.
clapper ['klæpə] *n* (*bell*) badajo, lengua; (*door*) aldaba.
clapping ['klæpiŋ] *n* (*of hands*) palmoteo, aplauso; (*of heels*) zapateo.
clarify ['klærifai] *vt* aclarar, clarificar.
clarinet [.klæri'net] *n* clarinete.
clash [klæʃ] *n* choque, fragor; conflicto; contienda; *vti* batir, golpear; estar en pugna, oponerse, chocar con.
clashing ['klæʃiŋ] *n* (*of weapons*) estruendo.
clasp [klɑ:sp] *n* broche; (*usu on shoes*) hebilla; cierre; gancho; *vt* abrochar; abrazar, ceñir.
class [klɑ:s] *n* clase; orden, rango, estado, categoría, grado; **low — de** baja estofa; **middle —** burgués; **—mate** condiscípulo; **—room** aula; *vt* clasificar.
classic ['klæsik] *a* clásico; *n pl* las humanidades, los clásicos.
classification [.klæsifi'keiʃən] *n* clasificación.
classify ['klæsifai] *vt* clasificar, ordenar.
clatter ['klætə] *n* ruido, alboroto, estrépito; gresca; *vi* hacer ruido, gritar, meter bulla.
clattering ['klætəriŋ] *n* estruendo.
clause [klɔ:z] *n* cláusula, estipulación, artículo.
claw [klɔ:] *n* garra; presa; *pl* pinzas; *vt* gafar, arpar; arañar, rasgar, despedazar.
clay [klei] *n* arcilla, greda; — **pit** barrera.
clean [kli:n] *a* limpio, puro, neto, aseado; (*bare*) escueto; *vt* limpiar, asear; — **-cut** bien definido.
cleaning ['kli:niŋ] *n* limpieza; **dry** — lavado al seco.
cleaning ['kli:niŋ] *a* — **department** sección de sanidad.
cleanliness ['klenlinis] *n* limpieza, pureza, decencia, aseo.
cleanse [klenz] *vt* limpiar, purificar, depurar; mondar.
clear [kliə] *a* claro, justo, evidente, manifiesto; llano; (*water*) limpio, cristalino; (*sky*) sereno, despejado; (*freed*) exento, expedito, saneado; *vti* aclarar, definir; esclarecer; saltar por; **to — up** serenarse; poner en claro, sacar en limpio; **to — off**

largarse; **to — away difficulties** zanjar; **to — of, from** (*dues*) eximir, vindicar; (*debt*) redimir; (*table*) levantar; **to make —** patentizar; **to be —** saltar a la vista; **the coast is —** ya no hay moros en la costa.
clearing ['kliəriŋ] *n* aclaración; (*in wood*) claro; **— house** banco de liquidación.
clearness ['kliənis] *n* claridad, luz, perspicuidad.
clearway ['kliəwei] *n* carretera donde está prohibido pararse.
cleavage ['kli:vidʒ] *n* hendidura, división.
cleave [kli:v] *vt* hender, rajar, partir, abrir; *vi* pegarse, unirse, arrimarse.
clef [klef] *n* llave, clave.
cleft [kleft] *n* hendidura, grieta, resquicio.
clemency ['klemənsi] *n* clemencia, indulgencia, piedad.
clench [klentʃ] *vt* (*fist*) apretar.
clergy ['klə:dʒi] *n* clero; clerecía; **—man** pastor, ministro (*protestante*).
cleric, clerical ['klerik, 'klerikəl] *a* clerical; *n* clérigo.
clerk [klɑ:k] *n* escribiente; dependiente, empleado; oficial, covachuelista; clérigo.
clever ['klevə] *a* inteligente, hábil, listo, experto, aprovechado, avisado.
cleverness ['klevənis] *n* habilidad, maña, talento, ingenio.
click [klik] *n* golpe seco.
cliff [klif] *n* risco, tajo; (*sea*) acantilado; peñasco.
climate ['klaimit] *n* clima.
climax ['klaimæks] *n* culminación; crisis.
climb [klaim] *n* subida; *vti* subir, trepar; encaramarse.
clime [klaim] *n* clima.
clinch [klintʃ] *vt* agarrar; (*bargain etc*) remachar, rematar.
cling [kliŋ] *vi* agarrarse, pegarse, colgarse, adherirse.
clinic ['klinik] *n* clínica.
clink [kliŋk] *n* tintín; choque; *vti* resonar, hacer retintín; (*glasses*) chocar.
clip [klip] *vt* (re)cortar; (*sheep*) trasquilar; (*hedge*) podar; (*tickets*) picar.
clipped [klipt] *a* (*speech*) incisivo.
clipping ['klipiŋ] *n* (*newspaper*) recorte; (*cloth*) retal; (*sheep*) trasquilón.
clique [kli:k] *n* pandilla, peña.
cloak [klouk] *n* capa, manto; excusa, pretexto; *vt* cubrir, encubrir, embozar.
cloakroom ['kloukrum] *n* guardarropa; sala de descanso.
clock [klɔk] *n* reloj; **—face** cuadrante; (*socks*) cuadrado; **hands of —** agujas.
clockwork ['klɔkwə:k] *n* **to go like —** ir como una seda.
clod [klɔd] *n* césped, terrón; (*pers*) gaznápiro, bestia, palurdo.
clog [klɔg] *n* (*footwear*) zoclo, zueco; traba, embarazo; carga; *vti* impedir, entorpecer, embarazar; obstruir, atorar.
cloister ['klɔistə] *n* claustro.
close [klous] *a* cerrado, (*tight*) ajustado, ceñido; denso; (*mean*) tacaño, agarrado; aproximado; **—cropped** al rape; **—lipped** premioso; **— friend** amigo de mucha confianza, íntimo; **— to** cerca de, próximo; **— by** contiguo; **to be — to** aproximar; **to put — together** arrimar; [klouz] *n* fin, clausura, conclusión; *vti* cerrar, terminar, rematar; vedar; **to — one's eyes to** hacer la vista gorda.
closed-circuit television ['klouzd 'sə:kit'teli,viʒən] *n* circuito cerrado de televisión.
closely ['klousli] *ad* estrechamente, de cerca; **to fit —** ceñir.
closeness ['klousnis] *n* estrechez; densidad; tacañería; contigüedad; intimidad.
closure ['klouʒə] *n* clausura, cierre.
cloth [klɔθ] *n* tela; (*woolen*) paño, paños, género; (*fine*) cendal; **table—** mantel.
clothe [klouð] *vt* vestir; **to — with** (*authority*) investir, revestir de; **half-clothed** en paños menores.
clothes [klouðz] *n* vestido, ropa, paños; **bed—** ropa de cama; **suit of —** traje; **— horse** camilla; **— moth** polilla; **— rack** perchero.
clothing ['klouðiŋ] *n* vestidos, ropa; **under—** ropa interior.
cloud [klaud] *n* nube; (*storm*) nubarrón; **— cap** ceja; *pl* (*of smoke*) humareda; (*fleecy*) celaje; *vti* anublarse; (*glass etc*) empañar.
cloudless ['klaudlis] *a* sin nubes, despejado, claro.
cloudy ['klaudi] *a* nebuloso, obscuro, (*liquids*) turbio; **to become —** encapotarse, enturbiarse.
cloven ['klouvn] *a* hendido; **—hoofed** patihendido.
clover ['klouvə] *n* trébol.
clown [klaun] *n* (*circus*) payaso, gracioso, bobo; majadero; patán.
clownish ['klauniʃ] *a* rústico; tosco, grosero.
cloy [klɔi] *vt* empalagar, saciar; obstruir.
club [klʌb] *n* maza, porra; (*cards*) basto; (*society*) club, liceo, círculo; **—foot** pie zambo; *vti* contribuir, reunir; prorratear, escotar; pegar con un garrote.
cluck [klʌk] *vi* cloquear.
clue [klu:] *n* indicio, pista, signo, clave; **I haven't a —** no tengo idea.
clump [klʌmp] *n* grupo, mata, boscaje.
clumsiness ['klʌmzinis] *n* tosquedad, desmaña; torpeza.
clumsy ['klʌmzi] *n* tosco, desmañado, zafio, basto; torpe.
cluster ['klʌstə] *n* (*grapes*) racimo;

(*flowers*) ramo; (*swarm*) enjambre; (*houses in country*) caserío; (*trees*) mata; *vi* agruparse, enracimarse.
clutch [klʌtʃ] *n* (*mech*) embrague; garra; palanca de engranaje; agarro; *vt* asir, empuñar.
coach [koutʃ] *n* carroza, coche; (*heavy*) galera; **—building** carrocería; **—man** cochero; *vt* amaestrar, adiestrar, enseñar, dar clase particular.
coagulate [kou'ægjuleit] *vti* coagular, cuajar; coagularse.
coal [koul] *n* carbón de piedra; **hot —s** brasa; **— bunker, bucket** *etc* carbonera; **— seam** filón; **— industry** industria hullera; **—field** cuenca hullera; **—tar** alquitrán; *vt* proveer de carbón; **to carry —s to Newcastle** llevar leña al monte.
coalman ['koulmən] *n* carbonero.
coarse [kɔ:s] *a* (*cloth*) basto; tosco, burdo; (*vulgar*) callejero, ordinario; **— -grained** grueso; inculto, ramplón; **to grow —** embrutecerse.
coarseness ['kɔ:snis] *n* tosquedad, grosería, crudeza.
coarsening ['kɔ:sniŋ] *n* embrutecimiento.
coast [koust] *n* costa, playa, litoral; **the — is not clear** aun hay moros en la costa; *vi* costear.
coastal ['koustəl] *a* litoral; (*trade*) costanero, costeño,.
coaster ['koustə] *n* piloto práctico, barco costañero.
coastguard ['koustgɑ:d] *n* guardacosta.
coat [kout] *n* (*jacket*) chaqueta, americana; **top—** abrigo; **frock—** levita; **swallowtail —** frac; **— of arms** escudo; (*of paint*) baño; (*animals*) pelo, pelaje; cubierta; *vt* cubrir, revestir; (*with sugar*) confitar; **to turn one's —** volver casaca.
coating ['koutiŋ] *n* cubierta, capa, mano de pintura.
coax [kouks] *vt* halagar, engatusar, conciliar.
coaxing ['kouksiŋ] *a* almibarado; ruegos, halagos, coba.
cobble ['kɔbl] *vt* remendar; *n* **—(stone)** guijarro.
cobbler ['kɔblə] *n* zapatero remendón.
cobweb ['kɔbweb] *n* telaraña.
cock [kɔk] *n* gallo; *vt* (*pistol*) amartillar; (*ears*) erguir, enderezar; **cocked hat** sombrero (apuntado, de tres picos); **weather—** veleta; **hay—** montón; **—sure** segurísimo; **—fight** riña de gallos.
cockle ['kɔkl] *n* cúpula de horno; (*bot*) ballico, cizaña; (*zool*) coquina; **—s of one's heart** entretelas del corazón.
Cockney ['kɔkni] *n* oriundo de Londres; (*cf Madrid* chulo).
cockpit ['kɔkpit] *n* gallera; (*plane*) cabina.
cockroach ['kɔkroutʃ] *n* cucaracha.
cocoa ['koukou] *n* cacao.
coconut ['koukənʌt] *n* coco; **— grove** cocotal.
cocoon [kə'ku:n] *n* capullo.
cod [kɔd] *n* bacalao, abadejo.
coddle ['kɔdl] *vt* criar con mimo, mimar, consentir.
code [koud] *n* código; clave.
coerce [kou'ə:s] *vt* forzar, obligar, ejercer coerción.
coercion [kou'ə:ʃən] *n* coerción, fuerza, violencia.
coffee ['kɔfi] *n* café; **— bean** grano; **— grounds** posos; **—pot** cafetera; **— set** juego de café.
coffer ['kɔfə] *n* cofre, arca.
coffin ['kɔfin] *n* ataúd, féretro.
cog [kɔg] *n* diente de rueda; **—wheel** rueda dentada, rodezno; **—wheel railway** cremallera.
cogitate ['kɔdʒiteit] *vi* pensar, meditar, recapacitar.
cogitation [ˌkɔdʒi'teiʃən] *n* cogitación, meditación.
cognate ['kɔgneit] *a* pariente; afín, análogo; *an* (*gram*) cognado.
coherence [kou'hiərəns] *n* coherencia, adhesión; relación, consecuencia.
cohesion [kou'hi:ʒən] *n* cohesión, conexión, enlace.
coif [kɔif] *n* (*hair*) toca; cofia, escofieta.
coiffure [kwɑ:'fjuə] *n* peinado.
coin [kɔin] *n* moneda, metálico; *vt* acuñar, batir.
coinage ['kɔinidʒ] *n* acuñación; invención; sistema monetario.
coincide [ˌkouin'said] *vi* coincidir, concurrir.
coincidence [kou'insidəns] *n* coincidencia, casualidad.
coiner ['kɔinə] *n* acuñador; monedero falso.
coke [kouk] *n* cok, coque.
cold [kould] *a* frío; indiferente; casto, reservado, seco; **— steel** arma blanca; *n* frío; (*nose*) constipado; (*chill*) resfriado; **to get a —** resfriarse, coger frío; **to be —** (*person*) tener frío, (*weather*) hacer frío, (*thing*) estar (ser) frío.
coldness ['kouldnis] *n* frialdad; indiferencia, despego.
collapse [kə'læps] *n* desplome, hundimiento, derrumbamiento; fracaso, ruina; (*med*) colapso; *vi* derrumbarse, hundirse, venirse abajo, desbaratarse; desmayarse.
collar ['kɔlə] *n* cuello; (*dog*) collar (*horse*) collera; **—bone** asilla, clavícula; *vt* apercollar, coger (*por el cuello*).
colleague ['kɔli:g] *n* colega, compañero.
collect ['kɔlekt] *n* colecta; [kə'lekt] *vt* recoger, coger; reunir, compilar, juntar, cobrar; (*taxes*) colectar, recaudar; (*antiques etc*) coleccionar;

vi reunirse; congregarse; *vr* volver en sí.
collection [kə'lekʃən] *n* colección; (*money*) recaudación, cobro; (*for charity*) colecta; (*laws etc*) compilación, recopilación; (*poems*) floresta; conjunto.
collective [kə'lektiv] *a* colectivo.
collector [kə'lektə] *n* colector, recaudador; (*antiques etc*) coleccionador.
college ['kɔlidʒ] *n* colegio; **training** — escuela normal.
collie ['kɔli] *n* perro de pastor.
collide [kə'laid] *vti* chocar, topar con(tra).
colliery ['kɔljəri] *n* mina de carbón, hullera.
collision [kə'liʒən] *n* choque, colisión, encuentro.
colloquial [kə'loukwiəl] *a* familiar, popular.
colloquialism [kə'loukwiəlizəm] *n* locución familiar.
collusion [kə'lu:ʒən] *n* connivencia, colusión.
Colombia [kə'lɔmbiə] *n* Colombia.
Colombian [kə'lɔmbiən] *an* colombiano.
colonel ['kə:nl] *n* coronel.
colonial [kə'louniəl] *a* colonial.
colonist ['kɔlənist] *n* colono.
colonize ['kɔlənaiz] *vt* colonizar, poblar.
colony ['kɔləni] *n* colonia.
color ['kʌlə] *n* color; **—s** bandera; **with flying —s** con banderas desplegadas; *vt* dar color, pintar; colorar; *vi* **to — up** ruborizarse; **to change —** mudar (de color de semblante); **to take the — out of** decolorar; **to be off —** andar de capa caída.
colored ['kʌləd] *a* (*pencils, races*) de color; (*art*) policromado; (*MSS*) iluminado.
colorful ['kʌləfal] *a* vistoso, vívido, pintoresco.
coloring ['kʌləriŋ] *n* (*dye*) colorante; (*color*) coloración, colorido, colores.
colorless ['kʌləlis] *n* sin color, descolorido; incoloro, pálido.
colossal [kə'lɔsl] *a* titánico, descomunal.
colt [koult] *n* potro.
Columbus [kə'lʌmbəs] *m* Colón.
column ['kɔləm] *n* columna; **(twisted) —** salomónica; **gossip —** crónica.
comb [koum] *n* peine; (*high*) peineta; (*for wool*) carda; (*honey*) panal; *vt* peinar; (*wool*) cardar; rastrillar.
combat ['kɔmbət] *n* combate, lidia, lucha, pelea; **single —** desafío; *vti* combatir, luchar; resistir, impugnar.
combatant ['kɔmbətənt] *an* combatiente.
combination [,kɔmbi'neiʃən] *n* combinación; complot.
combine [kəm'bain] *vti* combinar; unirse, juntarse, combinarse; tramar.
combined [kəm'baind] *a* (*forces etc*) mancomunado.
combustible [kəm'bʌstəbl] *an* combustible.
combustion [kəm'bʌstʃən] *n* combustión; quema, incendio.
come [kʌm] *vi* venir, llegar, aparecer; resultar, suceder; **to — about** suceder, acontecer; **to — across** hallar, tropezar, dar con; atravesar; **to — along** ir con, venir con; **to — apart** deshacerse; **to — back** volver, regresar; **to — by** pasar (cerca de, junto a); alcanzar; **to — down** bajar; desplomarse; **to — down in the world** venir a menos; **to — forward** adelantarse; medrar; **to — in** entrar, introducirse; ocurrir; **— in!** ¡adelante!; **to — into (estate)** heredar; **to — loose** soltarse, aflojarse; **to — of age** llegar a ser mayor de edad; **to — off** soltarse; zafarse; (*stain*) salir; **to — off well** salir airoso, lucirse; **to — out** salir, surgir; (*of stain*) salir; traslucirse, saberse; **to — over to** pasarse a; **to — round** volver en sí; **to — to** importar, montar a, rayar en; **to — to blows** venir a las manos; **to — to grief** salir mal (*parado*); **to — together** converger; reunirse; **to — true** realizarse; **to — under** figurar, caer bajo, entrar en; **to — up** salir; **to — upon** dar con, encontrar, sobrevenir, topar(se con).
comedian [kə'mi:diən] *n* cómico, actor; comediante.
comedy ['kɔmidi] *n* comedia; **musical —** zarzuela.
comely ['kʌmli] *a* donoso, gracioso; apuesto; hermoso, de buen parecer.
comet ['kɔmit] *n* cometa.
comfort ['kʌmfət] *n* comodidad, conveniencia, bienestar; consolación, consuelo; regalo; **—-loving** comodón; *vt* confortar, ayudar, fortalecer, consolar.
comfortable ['kʌmfətəbl] *a* cómodo, conveniente, consolador.
comfortably ['kʌmfətəbli] *a* **— off** holgado, acomodado.
comforter ['kʌmfətə] *n* consolador; coldra.
comforting ['kʌmfətiŋ] *a* consolador.
comfortless ['kʌmfətlis] *a* desolado, triste; inconsolable.
comic, comical ['kɔmik, 'kɔmikəl] *a* cómico, bufo; **— opera** ópera bufa; **— paper** periódico humorístico.
coming ['kʌmiŋ] *n* llegada, arribo; (*of age*) mayoría; advenimiento; *a* que llega, por venir, futuro; (*native*) oriundo de; **— and going** vaivén, trajín, ajetreo.
command [kə'mɑ:nd] *n* mandato, orden; señorío, imperio, predominio; (*power of*) mando; *vti* mandar, ordenar; imponer respeto; imperar.

commandant [ˌkɔmən'dænt] *n* comandante.
commander [kə'mɑːndə] *n* jefe, comandante; (*mil order*) comendador; (*naval*) teniente de navío.
commanding [kə'mɑːndiŋ] *a* imponente, dominante; (*presence*) señorial; (*mil*) comandante.
commandment [kə'mɑːndmənt] *n* mandamiento.
commemorate [kə'meməreit] *vt* celebrar, conmemorar.
commence [kə'mens] *vti* comenzar, empezar, dar principio a.
commencement [kə'mensmənt] *n* comienzo, principio, inauguración.
commend [kə'mend] *vt* recomendar, alabar, encomiar; (*entrust*) confiar.
comment ['kɔment] *n* comento, observación; *pl* comentario; *vt* comentar, glosar.
commentary ['kɔməntəri] *n* comentario, glosa; **to write, make — on** glosar, comentar.
commentator ['kɔmenteitə] *n* comentarista.
commerce ['kɔmə(ː)s] *n* comercio, negocio; trato, comunicación.
commercial [kə'məːʃəl] *a* comercial, mercantil; **— traveler** viajante, agente viajero.
commiserate [kə'mizəreit] *vt* compadecer, apiadarse.
commiseration [kəˌmizə'reiʃən] *n* conmiseración; piedad, compasión.
commission [kə'miʃən] *n* comisión, encargo, cometido; **— merchant** comerciante comisionista; *vt* comisionar, encargar, facultar, autorizar, apoderar.
commissioner [kə'miʃənə] *n* **— for oaths** notario público.
commit [kə'mit] *vt* cometer; confiar; perpetrar; **to — oneself** dar prendas, obligarse; **to — to writing** poner por escrito.
committee [kə'miti] *n* junta, comisión, comité; **standing —** comisión permanente.
commodious [kə'moudiəs] *a* cómodo, conveniente, espacioso, amplio.
commodity [kə'mɔditi] *n* comodidad; interés, ventaja; *pl* géneros; mercaderías, frutos.
common ['kɔmən] *a* (*general*) común, corriente, habitual; ordinario; (*coarse*) callejero, chulo, villano; cursi; **in — with** de común con; **— law** derecho consuetudinario; **—sense** sentido común; **— soldier** soldado raso; **— herd** populacho; **to become —** generalizarse; *n* (*land*) erial.
commoner ['kɔmənə] *n* pechero, villano.
Commons ['kɔmənz] *n* **House of —** Cámara de los Comunes; (*in Spain*) Congreso.
commonwealth ['kɔmənwelθ] *n* comunidad (*de naciones*), mancomunidad, colectividad.
commotion [kə'mouʃən] *n* conmoción, alteración, excitación; escándalo, revuelta.
commune ['kɔmjuːn] *n* comuna.
communicate [kə'mjuːnikeit] *vti* comunicar, poner en comunicación; comunicarse; (*relig*) comulgar; (*disease*) contagiar; hacer saber, participar.
communication [kəˌmjuːni'keiʃən] *n* comunicación; acceso; participación; trato, comercio.
communicative [kə'mjuːnikətiv] *a* comunicativo.
communion [kə'mjuːnjən] *n* comunión.
communiqué [kə'mjuːnikei] *n* parte, comunicatión.
community [kə'mjuːniti] *n* comunidad, sociedad.
compact [kəm'pækt] *a* compacto, sólido, apretado, denso; sucinto, breve; *vt* consolidar, pactar; ['kɔmpækt] *n* pacto; convenio, concierto.
compactness [kəm'pæktnis] *n* solidez; densidad; firmeza.
companion [kəm'pænjən] *n* compañero, camarada.
companionship [kəm'pænjənʃip] *n* compañerismo.
company ['kʌmpəni] *n* compañía; (*social*) visita; (*business*) empresa; asamblea; asociación; **joint-stock —** sociedad anónima; **limited liability —** sociedad de responsabilidad limitida; **to keep — (with)** frecuentar, acompañar.
comparable ['kɔmpərəbl] *a* comparable, conmensurable.
comparative [kəm'pærətiv] *ad* comparativo; relativo.
compare [kəm'pɛə] *vt* comparar, equiparar, paragonar, conferir; (*texts*) cotejar, compaginar.
comparison [kəm'pærisn] *n* comparación, confrontación, paragón; **worthy of —** conmensurable; **beyond —** sin par, sin igual.
compartment [kəm'pɑːtmənt] *n* compartimiento, departamento.
compass ['kʌmpəs] *n* círculo, circuito; (*naut*) brújula; ámbito, alcance; *vt* rodear; obtener, lograr.
compassion [kəm'pæʃən] *n* piedad, compasión, lástima, misericordia.
compassionate [kəm'pæʃənit] *a* compasivo, misericordioso.
compatibility [kəmˌpætə'biliti] *n* compatibilidad.
compel [kəm'pel] *vt* forzar, obligar, compeler.
compendium [kəm'pendiəm] *n* epítome, resumen.
compensate ['kɔmpenseit] *vti* compensar; indemnizar, reparar.
compensation [ˌkɔmpen'seiʃən] *n* compensación; desagravio, desquite, enmienda.

compete [kəm'pi:t] *vi* competir, hacer competencia, concurrir, rivalizar.
competence ['kɔmpitəns] *n* competencia, capacidad; suficiencia.
competent ['kɔmpitənt] *a* competente, capaz; (*qualified*) calificado, habilitado.
competition [,kɔmpi'tiʃən] *n* (*com*) concurrencia; rivalidad, competencia; (*sport etc*) concurso.
competitor [kəm'petitə] *n* competidor, rival, candidato, contrincante; (*exams*) opositor.
compile [kəm'pail] *vt* compilar, recopilar.
complacent [kəm'pleisnt] *a* complaciente, condescendiente.
complain [kəm'plein] *vi* quejarse; **to — of** llevar a mal; **to — against** reclamar.
complaint [kəm'pleint] *n* (*illness*) queja, enfermedad; (*law*) demanda; reclamación; agravio.
complaisance [kəm'pleizəns] *n* complacencia, afabilidad.
complaisant [kəm'pleizənt] *a* complaciente; cortés; condescendiente.
complement ['kɔmplimənt] *n* complemento; *vt* ['kɔmpliment] complementar.
complete [kəm'pli:t] *a* completo, entero, cabal; íntegro, perfecto; consumado; *vt* completar, acabar, llevar a cabo; (*forms*) levantar; rematar; (*years*) cumplir.
completely [kəm'pli:tli] *ad* completamente, perfectamente, enteramente.
completion [kəm'pli:ʃən] *n* terminación, consumación, plenitud.
complex ['kɔmpleks] *a* complejo; complicado; compuesto, múltiple; *n* complejo.
complexion [kəm'plekʃən] *n* tez, cutis; calidad, temperamento, índole.
complexity [kəm'pleksiti] *n* complejidad, enredo.
compliance [kəm'plaiəns] *n* condescendencia, complacencia; facilidad, sumisión; **in — with** de acuerdo con.
compliant [kəm'plaiənt] *a* complaciente, fácil, sumiso; obediente, dócil; obsequioso.
complicate ['kɔmplikeit] *vt* complicar; embrollar.
complicated ['kɔmplikeitid] *a* complicado; (*style*) enrevesado.
complication [,kɔmpli'keiʃən] *n* complicación, enredo.
complicity [kəm'plisiti] *n* connivencia, complicidad.
compliment ['kɔmplimənt] *n* cumplido, cumplimiento; fineza, lisonja; (*to woman*) piropo, requiebro; ['kɔmpliment] *vt* hacer cumplimientos; adular; saludar.
complimentary [,kɔmpli'mentəri] *a* lisonjero, halagüeño; regalado.
comply [kəm'plai] *vi* cumplir, llenar; consentir, condescender; satisfacer.
compose [kəm'pouz] *vt* hacer, componer, redactar; apaciguar, conciliar; ordenar; *vr* reportarse.
composed [kəm'pouzd] *a* sosegado; compuesto; **to be — of** constar de, consistir en.
composer [kəm'pouzə] *n* autor; compositor; (*print*) cajista.
composition [,kɔmpə'ziʃən] *n* composición; ajuste, arreglo.
composure [kəm'pouʒə] *n* serenidad, calma, compostura, presencia de ánimo; composición.
compound ['kɔmpaund] *a* compuesto; *n* mezcla; combinación; [kəm'paund] *vt* combinar; componer, transigir; *vi* avenirse.
comprehend [,kɔmpri'hend] *vt* comprender, penetrar, alcanzar; encerrar.
comprehensible [,kɔmpri'hensəbl] *a* comprensible, inteligible.
comprehension [,kɔmpri'henʃən] *n* entendimiento, comprensión.
comprehensiveness [,kɔmpri'hensivnis] *n* cabida; extensión; comprensión.
compress [kəm'pres] *vt* comprimir; condensar, sintetizar.
compressed [kəm'prest] *a* comprimido, apretado.
comprise [kəm'praiz] *vt* comprender; contener, incluir, abarcar.
compromise ['kɔmprəmaiz] *n* avenimiento, arreglo, término medio, transacción; *vt* transigir, arreglar; arriesgar, componer.
compulsion [kəm'pʌlʃən] *n* compulsión, apremio, coacción.
compulsory [kəm'pʌlsəri] *a* obligatorio.
compunction [kəm'pʌŋkʃən] *n* compunción; remordimiento, cargo de conciencia.
compute [kəm'pju:t] *vt* computar; calcular.
computer [kəm'pju:tə] *n* computadora.
comrade ['kɔmrid] *n* camarada, compañero.
concave ['kɔn'keiv] *a* cóncavo; hueco.
conceal [kən'si:l] *vt* (*materially*) esconder; (*supersensorily*) ocultar; encubrir, tapar, recatar; celar.
concealment [kən'si:lmənt] *n* ocultación; encubrimiento; **place of —** escondite, escondrijo.
concede [kən'si:d] *vt* conceder, admitir.
conceit [kən'si:t] *n* vanidad, amor propio, engreimiento; ínfulas; capricho; idea, concepto.
conceited [kən'si:tid] *a* vano, engreído, afectado, fatuo, presuntuoso; (*of style*) conceptuoso; **to be — about** pagarse de.

conceivable [kən'si:vəbl] *a* concebible.
conceive [kən'si:v] *vti* concebir, engendrar, idear, imaginar.
concentrate ['kɔnsentreit] *vti* concentrar(se); **to** — (*hopes*) **on** cifrar en.
concentration [,kɔnsen'treiʃən] *n* concentración; recogimiento.
concept ['kɔnsept] *n* concepto, idea, noción.
conception [kən'sepʃən] *n* concepción; noción, idea, imagen, sentimiento.
concern [kən'sə:n] *n* asunto, negocio; preocupación; cariño, interés, sentimiento; *vt* tocar, competer, interesar, corresponder; preocupar, inquietar; **that's my** — eso me corresponde a mí.
concerning [kən'sə:niŋ] *prep* respecto a, tocante a, acerca de, en cuanto a.
concert ['kɔnsət] *n* concierto; [kən'sə:t] *vti* concertar, acordar, ajustar.
concession [kən'seʃən] *n* cesión, gracia, privilegio.
conciliate [kən'silieit] *vt* conciliar, ganar, granjear.
conciliation [kən,sili'eiʃən] *n* conciliación.
concise [kən'sais] *a* conciso, sucinto, breve.
conciseness [kən'saisnis] *n* concisión, laconismo, brevedad.
conclude [kən'klu:d] *vti* concluir, determinar, entender, decidir; fenecer, acabar, terminarse; sacar en limpio.
conclusion [kən'klu:ʒən] *n* conclusión, terminación, remate; (*lit*) desenlace; **to draw a** — concluir.
conclusive [kən'klu:siv] *a* final, decisivo, terminante, concluyente.
conclusively [kən'klu:sivli] *ad* de una manera terminante.
conclusiveness [kən'klu:sivnis] *n* determinación.
concoct [kən'kɔkt] *vt* mezclar, confeccionar; urdir, forjar, fraguar.
concoction [kən'kɔkʃən] *n* mezcla; maquinación; guiso.
concord ['kɔŋkɔ:d] *n* concordia, armonía; acuerdo.
concourse ['kɔŋkɔ:s] *n* concurso, concurrencia, muchedumbre.
concrete ['kɔnkri:t] *a* concreto; *n* hormigón; **reinforced** — hormigón armado.
concur [kən'kə:] *vi* concurrir; estar de acuerdo; acordarse, coincidir, conformarse.
concurrence [kən'kʌrəns] *n* coincidencia; acuerdo, aprobación, cooperación.
concurrent [kən'kʌrənt] *a* concurrente; coexistente.
concussion [kən'kʌʃən] *n* concusión: conmoción.
condemn [kən'dem] *vt* condenar, sentenciar; (*conduct*) afear, censurar.
condemned [kən'demd] *a* maldito, condenado.
condemnation [,kɔndem'neiʃən] *n* condenación, perdición.
condense [kən'dens] *vti* condensar, comprimir, condensarse; abreviar; **condensed milk** leche condensada.
condescend [,kɔndi'send] *vi* condescender; dignarse, consentir.
condescendence [,kɔndi'sendəns] *n* condescendencia, complacencia.
condescension [,kɔndi'senʃən] *n* condescendencia.
condiment ['kɔndimənt] *n* condimento, aderezo.
condition [kən'diʃən] *n* condición, circunstancia, estado, suerte, calidad, artículo, provisión, estipulación; *vt* condicionar.
conditional [kən'diʃənl] *a* condicional.
condole [kən'doul] *vti* condolerse; deplorar.
condolence [kən'douləns] *n* pésame.
condone [kən'doun] *vt* condonar, perdonar, disimular.
conducive [kən'dju:siv] *a* conducente, propenso a.
conduct ['kɔndəkt] *n* conducta, proceder; escolta; comportamiento; manejo, gestión; **safe** — salvoconducto; [kən'dʌkt] *vt* conducir, guiar, dirigir; manejarse, comportarse; (*an orchestra*) dirigir.
conductor [kən'dʌktə] *n* conductor: guía; (*music*) director; (*streetcar*) cobrador.
cone [koun] *n* cono; **pine** — piña.
confection [kən'fekʃən] *n* confección; dulce; *vt* confeccionar.
confectioner [kən'fekʃənə] *n* confitero, pastelero, repostero.
confederacy [kən'fedərəsi] *n* confederación; alianza, liga.
confederate [kən'fedərit] *an* confederado, aliado, cómplice.
confer [kən'fə:] *vti* consultar; conferir; platicar, conferenciar; otorgar; (*honor*) condecorar.
conference ['kɔnfərəns] *n* conferencia, consulta; vistas.
confess [kən'fes] *vti* confesar(se); reconocer.
confessed [kən'fest] *a* confesado, declarado; incontestable.
confessedly [kən'fesidli] *ad* manifiestamente.
confession [kən'feʃən] *n* confesión; — **box** confesionario.
confessor [kən'fesə] *n* confesor.
confidant [,kɔnfi'dænt] *n* confidente, (*fam*) compinche.
confide [kən'faid] *vti* confiar(se); fiarse.
confidence ['kɔnfidəns] *n* confianza, fe; seguridad; satisfacción; secreto, confidencia; **to gain** — animarse.
confident ['kɔnfidənt] *a* confiado, seguro; resuelto; de buen ánimo.

confidential [ˌkɔnfi'denʃəl] *a* confidencial.
confine ['kənfain] *n* confín, límite, frontera; [kən'fain] *vti* confinar, limitar, restringir, reducir, limitarse; aprisionar, encerrar, enjaular; *vr* contraerse.
confinement [kən'fainmənt] *n* encierro, clausura, prisión; destierro; (*birth*) parto.
confirm [kən'fəːm] *vt* confirmar, comprobar, corroborar; sancionar; (*status*) revalidar; fortalecer.
confirmation [ˌkɔnfə'meiʃən] *n* confirmación, corroboración, ratificación.
confirmed [kən'fəːmd] *a* comprobado; demostrado; inveterado, consumado.
confiscate ['kɔnfiskeit] *vt* confiscar, (de)comisar.
confiscation [ˌkɔnfis'keiʃən] *n* confiscación, comiso.
conflagration [ˌkɔnflə'greiʃən] *n* conflagración, incendio.
conflict ['kɔnflikt] *n* conflicto, lucha, pugna, choque; contienda; [kən'flikt] *vt* luchar, chocar, estar (en oposición, en desacuerdo con).
conflicting [kən'fliktiŋ] *a* opuesto, contrario, encontrado.
confluence ['kɔnfluəns] *n* confluencia; concurso.
conform [kən'fɔːm] *vti* conformar(se), concordar; ajustarse, acomodarse, amoldarse, allanarse.
conformist [kən'fɔːmist] *n* conformista; **non—** mal avenido; (*relig*) nonconformista.
conformity [kən'fɔːmiti] *n* conformidad, concordancia, consonancia; **in — with** con arreglo a, conforme.
confound [kən'faund] *vt* confundir; turbar, enmarañar, desconcertar, atontar, sacar de tino.
confounded [kən'faundid] *a* detestable, maldito; confuso.
confraternity [ˌkɔnfrə'təːniti] *n* cofradía; confraternidad.
confront [kən'frʌnt] *n* (a), (con)-frontar, enfrentar; (*face up to*) arrostrar; hacer frente a; (*documents*) cotejar, comparar.
confuse [kən'fjuːz] *vt* confundir, (per)turbar, aturrullar, embrollar, desconcertar, trastornar.
confused [kən'fjuːzd] *a* confuso, azorado; revesado; desconcertado.
confusing [kən'fjuːziŋ] *a* confuso, turbador, desconcertante.
confusion [kən'fjuːʒən] *n* confusión, belén; aturdimiento, atolondramiento; azoramiento, trastorno; desorden.
congeal [kən'dʒiːl] *vti* congelar, helar(se), cuajar(se).
congealment [kən'dʒiːlmənt] *n* conelación.
congenial [kən'dʒiːniəl] *a* congenial; natural; simpático.
congenital [kən'dʒenitl] *a* congénito.
congest [kən'dʒest] *vt* amontonar, congestionar.
congestion [kən'dʒestʃən] *n* congestión.
conglomerate [kən'glɔməreit] *vt* conglomerar, redondear.
congratulate [kən'grætjuleit] *vt* felicitar, dar la enhorabuena, congratular.
congratulation [kənˌgrætju'leiʃən] *n* felicitación, enhorabuena, felicidades.
congregate ['kɔŋgrigeit] *vti* reunir(se).
congregation [ˌkɔŋgri'geiʃən] *n* asamblea, concurso, congregación; (*of parish*) grey; (*in church*) fieles.
congress ['kɔŋgres] *n* congreso, asamblea, junta.
congressman ['kɔŋgresmən] *n US* miembro del Congreso de los EE.UU.
conjecture [kən'dʒektʃə] *n* conjetura, suposición, asomo; *vt* conjeturar, brujulear, columbrar, presumir, sospechar, vislumbrar.
conjoin [kən'dʒɔin] *vt* juntar; conectar; unir.
conjugal ['kɔndʒugəl] *a* conyugal.
conjugate ['kɔndʒugeit] *vt* conjugar.
conjunction [kən'dʒʌŋkʃən] *n* conjunción, unión.
conjuncture [kən'dʒʌŋktʃə] *n* coyuntura.
conjure ['kʌndʒə] *vti* hechizar; conjurar; hacer juegos de manos; **to — away** exorcizar; **to — up** conjurar, evocar.
conjurer ['kʌndʒərə] *n* prestidigitador, mago, ilusionista; nigromante.
connect [kə'nekt] *vt* ligar, unir; enganchar, conectar; emparentar, relacionar; (*telephone*) poner en comunicación; (*el*) enchufar; (*train*) empalmar.
connection [kə'nekʃən] *n* conexión, relación; trabazón, enlace; (*rl*) empalme; parentesco; afinidad; **good —** (*sl*) enchufe.
connivance [kə'naivəns] *n* connivencia, consentimiento.
connive [kə'naiv] *vi* consentir, disimular, hacer la vista gorda.
connoisseur [ˌkɔni'səː] *n* perito, conocedor; (*wine*) catador.
conquer ['kɔŋkə] *vt* conquistar, vencer, someter, dominar; (*a weakness*) superar.
conquering ['kɔŋkəriŋ] *a* victorioso, triunfante.
conqueror ['kɔŋkərə] *n* vencedor, conquistador.
conquest ['kɔŋkwest] *n* toma; conquista, triunfo.
conscience ['kɔnʃəns] *n* conciencia;

— **stricken** remordido por la conciencia.
conscientious [ˌkɔnʃi'enʃəs] *a* escrupuloso, concienzudo, recto, cumplidor.
conscientiousness [ˌkɔnʃi'enʃəsnis] *n* escrupulosidad, rectitud, conciencia.
conscious ['kɔnʃəs] *a* consciente.
consciously ['kɔnʃəsli] *ad* a sabiendas.
consciousness ['kɔnʃəsnis] *n* conocimiento, sentido; **to lose** — perder (el sentido, el conocimiento).
conscript ['kɔnskript] *n* conscripto, recluta, quinto; [kən'skript] *vt* reclutar.
conscription [kən'skripʃən] *n* conscripción, reclutamiento.
consecrate ['kɔnsikreit] *vt* consagrar, dedicar; (*a priest*) ungir.
consecration [ˌkɔnsi'kreiʃən] *n* consagración, dedicación.
consecutive [kən'sekjutiv] *a* consecutivo, sucesivo.
consent [kən'sent] *n* (a), (con)sentimiento, acuerdo; aprobación, venia, permiso, beneplácito; *vi* consentir en; avenirse a, otorgar.
consequence ['kɔnsikwəns] *n* consecuencia; importancia, trascendencia; secuela; **as a** — de resultas de.
consequent ['kɔnsikwənt] *a* consiguiente, lógico.
consequential [ˌkɔnsi'kwenʃəl] *a* consiguiente, arrogante.
consequently ['kɔnsikwəntli] *ad* por consiguiente; en consecuencia.
conservation [ˌkɔnsə(:)'veiʃən] *n* preservación, sostenimiento.
conservative [kən'sə:vətiv] *an* conservador, moderado.
conservatory [kən'sə:vətri] *n* conservatorio; (*flowers*) invernadero.
conserve [kən'sə:v] *vt* conservar, cuidar, guardar.
consider [kən'sidə] *vti* considerar, estimar, examinar, meditar; tener por, reconocer; opinar, ser de opinión; consultar; darse cuenta de; **to — carefully** parar mientes en; **to — further** dar (*más*) vueltas a.
considerable [kən'sidərəbl] *a* considerable; grande, importante, notable, respetable; cuantioso.
considerate [kən'sidərit] *a* considerado, circunspecto, discreto, indulgente, fino.
consideration [kənˌsidə'reiʃən] *n* consideración, ponderación, reflexión, deliberación; respeto; **to take into** — tener en cuenta, hacerse cargo de, cargar con.
considering [kən'sidəriŋ] *ad* en atención, visto (*que*).
considered [kən'sidəd] *a* **ill-—** desacordado; **well-—** bien considerado.
consign [kən'sain] *vt* consignar, ceder.
consignment [kən'sainmənt] *n* consignación, envío.
consist [kən'sist] *vi* consistir (*en*); comprender, constar de; componerse de.
consistence [kən'sistəns] *n* consistencia, densidad.
consistency [kən'sistənsi] *n* consistencia; regularidad, consecuencia.
consistent [kən'sistənt] *a* consistente, constante; conforme; compatible, consonante, consecuente, (*texture*) firme, sólido, estable.
consolation [ˌkɔnsə'leiʃən] *n* alivio, consuelo; consolación; solaz, quitapesares.
console ['kɔnsoul] *n* repisa; [kən'soul] *vt* consolar.
consolidate [kən'sɔlideit] *vti* (con)solidar(se).
consort ['kɔnsɔ:t] *n* consorte, cónyuge; compañero; [kən'sɔ:t] *vi* asociarse, acompañar, juntarse con.
conspicuous [kən'spikjuəs] *a* conspicuo, visible, esclarecido, notable; llamativo.
conspiracy [kən'spirəsi] *n* conspiración, conjuración, complot.
conspirator [kən'spirətə] *n* conspirador, conjurado.
conspire [kən'spaiə] *vi* conspirar; conjurar(se), tramar; concurrir.
constable ['kʌnstəbl] *n* policía; (*of castle*) condestable; **special** — policía voluntario.
constancy ['kɔnstənsi] *n* constancia, fidelidad, entereza, insistencia.
constant ['kɔnstənt] *a* constante, inmóvil, igual, firme.
constantly ['kɔnstəntli] *ad* sin parar.
constellation [ˌkɔnstə'leiʃən] *n* constelación.
consternation [ˌkɔnstə(:)'neiʃən] *n* consternación, espanto.
constipate ['kɔnstipeit] *vti* estreñirse; cerrar.
constituent [kən'stitjuənt] *n* elector; poderdante, comitente; (*chemical*) componente; *a* constitutivo; — **parliament** cortes constituyentes.
constitute ['kɔnstitju:t] *vt* constituir; componer; diputar.
constitution [ˌkɔnsti'tju:ʃən] *n* constitución; (*of society*) reglamento; (*person*) temperamento, condición.
constitutional [ˌkɔnsti'tju:ʃənl] *a* constitucional.
constrain [kən'strein] *vt* forzar, obligar; compeler; restringir; constreñir, apretar; *vr* contenerse.
constraint [kən'streint] *n* apremio; fuerza; compulsión, represión.
constrict [kən'strikt] *vt* constreñir, estrechar, apretar.
construct [kən'strʌkt] *vt* construir, edificar, erigir, montar.
construction [kən'strʌkʃən] *n* (*action*) construcción, edificación; (*object*) estructura, obra, edificio; (*impression*) interpretación, sentido.

construe [kən stru:] *vt* interpretar, explicar; traducir.
consul ['kɔnsəl] *n* cónsul.
consular ['kɔnsjulə] *a* consular; — **invoice** factura consular.
consulate ['kɔnsjulit] *n* consulado.
consult [kən'sʌlt] *vti* consultar, considerar, discutir.
consultation [ˌkɔnsəl'teiʃən] *n* consulta.
consulting [kən'sʌltiŋ] *a* — **hours** horas de consulta.
consume [kən'sju:m] *vti* consumir(se); (des)gastar(se), deshacerse; devorar, minar; aniquilar.
consumed [kən'sju:md] *a* **to be** — (*passion*) abrasarse.
consumer [kən'sju:mə] *n* consumidor.
consummate [kən'sʌmit] *a* consumado, cabal, perfecto; ['kɔnsʌmeit] *vt* consumar.
consummation [ˌkɔnsʌ'meiʃən] *n* consumación, perfección, fin.
consumption [kən'sʌmpʃən] *n* consunción; (*disease*) tisis; (*of food*) consumo; (*wear*) desgaste, uso.
contact ['kɔntækt] *n* contacto; acercamiento; (*mech*) engranaje; **to be in — with** estar en relación con.
contagion [kən'teidʒən] *n* contagio, infección; peste.
contagious [kən'teidʒəs] *a* contagioso, infeccioso; (*laughter*) pegajoso.
contain [kən'tein] *vt* contener, incluir, encerrar, abarcar, reprimir; coger; *vr* aguantarse, contenerse.
contained [kən'teind] *a* **to be** — resumirse, caber.
container [kən'teinə] *n* recipiente, envase.
contaminate [kən'tæmineit] *vt* contaminar; manchar, corromper, inficionar, viciar.
contamination [kənˌtæmi'neiʃən] *n* contaminación, mancha.
contemplate ['kɔntempleit] *vti* contemplar; tener en mira, proponerse, proyectar; meditar.
contemplation [ˌkɔntem'pleiʃən] *n* contemplación, meditación; proyecto, expectativa.
contemplative ['kɔntempleitiv] *a* contemplativo.
contemporary [kən'tempərəri] *an* contemporáneo, coetáneo.
contempt [kən'tempt] *n* desdén, desprecio, menosprecio, (*of court*) contumacia.
contemptible [kən'temptəbl] *a* despreciable, vil.
contemptuous [kən'temptjuəs] *adj* desdeñoso, altivo, despectivo.
contend [kən'tend] *vti* afirmar, aseverar, sostener; luchar, disputar, pugnar (*por*).
contender [kən'tendə] *n* opositor, contendiente.
contending [kən'tendiŋ] *a* en lucha, rival, opuesto; — **parties** partes litigantes.
content [kən'tent] *a* contento, satisfecho; *vt* contentar, satisfacer, complacer; ['kɔntent] *n* contento, agrado; *pl* **table of —s** índice.
contented [kən'tentid] *a* contento, satisfecho; tranquilo.
contention [kən'tenʃən] *n* aseveración, opinión, pendencia, disputa.
contentment [kən'tentmənt] *n* contento, satisfacción, agrado, alegría, placidez.
contentious [kən'tenʃəs] *a* contencioso, litigioso; pendenciero, porfiado.
contest ['kɔntest] *n* disputa, desafío; altercado; conflicto, contienda, pugna, lid; concurso; [kən'test] *vti* disputar, litigar.
contestant [kən'testənt] *n* contendiente, concursante.
context ['kɔntekst] *n* contexto, sentido.
contiguous [kən'tigjuəs] *a* contiguo, lindante, inmediato, propincuo.
continent ['kɔntinənt] *a* casto, continente, moderado; *n* continente.
contingency [kən'tindʒənsi] *n* contingencia, caso, casualidad.
continual [kən'tinjuəl] *a* continuo, incesante.
continually [kən'tinjuəli] *ad* sin parar.
continuance [kən'tinjuəns] *n* continuación, permanencia; continuidad.
continuation [kənˌtinju'eiʃən] *n* continuación.
continue [kən'tinju(:)] *vti* continuar, mantener, seguir; perseverar; prolongar; durar, quedar.
continued [kən'tinju(:)d] *a* prolongado, seguido; **to be —** a continuación.
continuous [kən'tinjuəs] *a* continuo.
contort [kən'tɔ:t] *vtr* retorcer(se).
contortion [kən'tɔ:ʃən] *n* retorcimiento, contorsión.
contraband ['kɔntrəbænd] *a* ilegal, prohibido; *n* contrabando.
contract ['kɔntrækt] *n* contrato, concierto, ajuste; (*document*) contrata, escritura; **marriage —** esponsales; [kən'trækt] *vti* contraer, estrechar, apretar; contratar; (*of expression*) inmutarse; (*of muscles*) crispar; (*disease*) contraer, coger; (*promise*) comprometerse (*por contrato*) a; (*brows*) fruncir.
contraction [kən'trækʃən] *n* contracción, abreviatura; encogimiento.
contractor [kən'træktə] *n* contratista.
contradict [ˌkɔntrə'dikt] *vt* contradecir, impugnar; implicar; llevar la contraria a.
contradiction [ˌkɔntrə'dikʃən] *n* contradicción; oposición, contrariedad, repugnancia.

contradictory [ˌkɔntrəˈdiktəri] *a* contradictorio, contrario, opuesto.
contrarily [ˈkɔntrərili] *ad* al contrario.
contrariness [ˈkɔntrərinis] *n* contrariedad, discrepancia.
contrary [ˈkɔntrəri] *a* contrario, encontrado, reñido, antagónico; divergente; **on the —** al contrario, al revés, a la inversa.
contrast [ˈkɔntrɑːst] *n* contraste; contraposición; [kənˈtrɑːst] *vt* contrastar, oponer, hacer (*un*) contraste con; **in —** haciendo contraste; (en, por) contraste.
contravention [ˌkɔntrəˈvenʃən] *n* contravención, infracción.
contravene [ˌkɔntrəˈviːn] *vt* infringir, contravenir.
contribute [kənˈtribju(ː)t] *vti* contribuir, poner, concurrir.
contribution [ˌkɔntriˈbjuːʃən] *n* contribución, aportación; cooperación; cuota, tributo.
contributor [kənˈtribju(ː)tə] *n* (*newspaper*) colaborador; (*money*) contribuyente.
contrite [ˈkɔntrait] *a* contrito, penitente, arrepentido.
contrition [kənˈtriʃən] *n* contrición, compunción.
contrivance [kənˈtraivəns] *n* invención, expediente, maquinación, aparato; (*artful*) maña, artificio, treta.
contrive [kənˈtraiv] *vti* inventar, tratar de, acomodarse, idear, concertar, darse buenas mañas para.
control [kənˈtroul] *n* dominio, manejo, mando; inspección; gobierno, predominio; dirección; freno; **self-—** señorío de sí; *vt* dominar, controlar, dirigir, reprimir, regir, gobernar, predominar; fiscalizar.
controlled [kənˈtrould] *a* **— price** precio de tasa, precio regulado.
controversial [ˌkɔntrəˈvəːʃəl] *a* polémico, contencioso; debatido, discutible.
controversy [ˈkɔntrəvəːsi] *n* controversia, polémica, disputa.
contumacy [ˈkɔntjuməsi] *n* contumacia, rebeldía, terquedad.
convalescence [ˌkɔnvəˈlesns] *n* convalecencia.
convene [kənˈviːn] *vti* convocar, citar, reunir(se).
convenience [kənˈviːniəns] *n* conveniencia, comodidad; **public —** retrete, excusado.
convenient [kənˈviːniənt] *a* conveniente, cómodo, oportuno.
convent [ˈkɔnvənt] *n* convento.
convention [kənˈvenʃən] *n* (*social*) convención, formalidades, conveniencia(s); asamblea; pacto, convenio.
conventional [kənˈvenʃənl] *a* convencional, rutinario, ordinario.
converge [kənˈvəːdʒ] *vti* converger, dirigirse hacia; (*streets*) desembocar.
convergence [kənˈvəːdʒəns] *n* convergencia.
conversant [kənˈvəːsənt] *a* versado (*en*), experimentado, entendido, conocedor; **to become — with** familiarizarse con.
conversation [ˌkɔnvəˈseiʃən] *n* conversación, plática, coloquio.
conversational [ˌkɔnvəˈseiʃənl] *a* de conversación.
converse [ˈkɔnvəːs] *n* plática, trato; *a* opuesto, inverso; [kənˈvəːs] *vi* conversar, platicar, razonar, departir; (*mil*) parlamentar.
conversion [kənˈvəːʃən] *n* conversión; (*into cash*) realización.
conversely [ˈkɔnvəːsli] *ad* recíprocamente, a la inversa.
convert [ˈkɔnvəːt] *n* converso; [kənˈvəːt] *vti* convertir(se), transformar.
convey [kənˈvei] *vt* transportar, conducir, llevar; enviar, transmitir.
conveyance [kənˈveiəns] *n* transporte, vehículo; (*property*) traspaso; conducta.
convict [ˈkɔnvikt] *n* condenado, reo; convicto, preso; [kənˈvikt] *vt* declarar culpable, convencer.
conviction [kənˈvikʃən] *n* convicción; condenación.
convince [kənˈvins] *vt* persuadir, ganar, convencer; **to try to —** catequizar.
convinced [kənˈvinst] *a* **to be thoroughly — of** estar convencido de.
convincing [kənˈvinsiŋ] *a* convincente, urgente.
convivial [kənˈviviəl] *a* sociable, jovial, alegre, festivo.
convocation [ˌkɔnvəˈkeiʃən] *n* convocación; asamblea.
convoke [kənˈvouk] *vt* convocar, citar.
convoy [ˈkɔnvɔi] *n* convoy, escolta; *vt* convoyar, conducir.
convulse [kənˈvʌls] *vt* (*nerves etc*) crispar; convulsar; **to be convulsed with laughter** desternillarse de risa.
convulsion [kənˈvʌlʃən] *n* convulsión, pasmo, espasmo.
convulsive [kənˈvʌlsiv] *a* convulsivo, espasmódico.
coo [kuː] *vi* arrullar.
cook [kuk] *n* cocinero; *vt* cocer, cocinar, guisar; **cooked dish** guiso.
cookery [ˈkukəri] *n* cocina; **— book** libro de cocina.
cooking [ˈkukiŋ] *n* guiso, cocina; **to do the —** cocinar; **— stove** cocina económica.
cool [kuːl] *a* fresco; tibio; *n* fresco, frescura; **in the —** al fresco; *vti* (*weather*) refrescarse; **to — down, to — off** (*of emotions, things etc*) enfriarse; templarse.
cooling [ˈkuːliŋ] *a* refrescante; *n* enfriamiento.

coolness ['ku:lnis] *n* frescura; fresco; serenidad, calma; (*attitude*) frialdad, indiferencia, tibieza.
coop [ku:p] *n* gallinero, caponera; *vt* enjaular, encerrar.
cooperate [kou'ɔpəreit] *vi* cooperar.
cooperation [kou,ɔpə'reiʃən] *n* cooperación, concurso.
cooperative [kou'ɔpərətiv] *an* cooperativo.
copartner ['kou'pɑ:tnə] *n* copartícipe, consocio.
cope [koup] *n* arco, bóveda; (*eccles*) capa pluvial; *vti* cubrir; contender, rivalizar; poder con.
copier ['kɔpiə] *n* copista.
coping stone ['koupiŋstoun] *n* teja cumbrera; (*fig*) coronamiento.
copious ['koupiəs] *a* copioso, abundante, afluente, cuantioso, caudaloso.
copiously ['koupiəsli] *ad* a chorros, copiosamente.
copiousness ['koupiəsnis] *n* copia, profusión; prolijidad.
copper ['kɔpə] *n* cobre; (*coin*) calderilla; (*pan*) caldero; *pl* (*coins*) suelto; **—smith** calderero.
copulate ['kɔpjuleit] *vt* unir, juntar, acoplar; *vi* copularse, ayuntarse.
copy ['kɔpi] *n* copia; (*superficial*) simulacro; (*close*) calco; (*unauthorized*) plagio, imitación, remedo; (*of book*) ejemplar; **rough —** borrador; **a — of** imitado de; *vt* copiar, imitar, calcar; **to make authentic —** compulsar; **to — from life** copiar al natural.
copyreader ['kɔpi,ri:də] *n* redactor (*adjunto*), revisor.
copyright ['kɔpirait] *n* propiedad literaria.
coquet [kɔ'ket] *vi* coquetear; requebrar.
coquetry ['kɔkitri] *n* coquetería.
coral ['kɔrəl] *n* coral; *a* coralino, de coral.
cord [kɔ:d] *n* cuerda; (*shoelace*) cordón; (*carrying*) cordel; **spinal —** médula espinal.
cordial ['kɔ:diəl] *a* cordial, amistoso, sincero; *n* cordial.
cordiality [,kɔ:di'æliti] *n* cordialidad.
core [kɔ:] *n* corazón, interioridad, centro, alma, foco; *vt* despepitar.
cork [kɔ:k] *n* corcho, tapón; *vt* corchar; **—screw** sacacorchos, tirabuzón; **—tree** alcornoque.
corkscrew ['kɔ:kskru:] *a* en espiral, en caracol.
corn [kɔ:n] *n* maíz; grano, cereal; (*on foot*) clavo, callo; **to develop —s on feet** encallecer; **— bread** pan de maíz; **— meal** harina de maíz.
Cornelius [kɔ:'ni:liəs] *m* Cornelio.
corner ['kɔ:nə] *n* (*projecting*) esquina; rincón; ángulo; **—stone** piedra angular; **a quiet —** remanso, escondrijo; *vt* arrinconar, poner en un aprieto; (*supplies*) copar.
cornet ['kɔ:nit] *n* corneta; cornetín.
coronation [,kɔrə'neiʃən] *n* coronación.
coroner ['kɔrənə] *n* médico judicial.
corporal ['kɔ:pərəl] *a* corpóreo; *n* cabo.
corporation [,kɔ:pə'reiʃən] *n* (*town*) cabildo, ayuntamiento; gremio, cuerpo; sociedad anónima, sociedad de responsabilidad limitada.
corporeal [kɔ:'pɔ:riəl] *a* corpóreo, tangible.
corps [kɔ:] *n* cuerpo.
corpse [kɔ:ps] *n* cadáver, difunto, muerto.
corpulence ['kɔ:pjuləns] *n* corpulencia.
corpulent ['kɔ:pjulənt] *a* corpulento, gordo, grueso, repleto.
Corpus Christi ['kɔ:pəs'kristi] *n* día del Corpus, Corpus Christi.
correct [kə'rekt] *a* correcto, exacto, justo; *vt* corregir, rectificar; (*style etc*) castigar, enmendar; censurar; remediar.
correction [kə'rekʃən] *n* corrección, rectificación; enmendación; castigo.
correctness [kə'rektnis] *n* corrección, exactitud.
correspond [,kɔris'pɔnd] *vi* corresponder, convenir; (*letters*) escribirse, cartear(se).
correspondence [,kɔris'pɔndəns] *n* correspondencia; correo; relación.
correspondent [,kɔris'pɔndənt] *a* correspondiente; *n* corresponsal.
corresponding [,kɔris'pɔndiŋ] *a* condigno, conforme, análogo.
corridor ['kɔridɔ:] *n* pasillo, corredor; pasadizo; (*main*) zaguán.
corroborate [kə'rɔbəreit] *vt* corroborar, apoyar.
corrode [kə'roud] *vt* corroer, roer, morder, (car)comer.
corrosive [kə'rousiv] *a* corrosivo; mordaz.
corrugate ['kɔrugeit] *vt* arrugar, acanalar, encarrujar.
corrugation [,kɔru'geiʃən] *n* arruga.
corrupt [kə'rʌpt] *a* corrompido, podrido; viciado, depravado; *vti* corromper, seducir, viciar, pervertir; adulterar; relajarse, podrirse; infectar, emponzoñar; (*manners*) estragar; (*with money*) sobornar.
corrupting [kə'rʌptiŋ] *a* corruptor.
corruption [kə'rʌpʃən] *n* corrupción, putrefacción.
corsair ['kɔ:sɛə] *n* corsario, pirata.
corselet ['kɔ:slit] *n* corselete, (*armor*) peto.
corset ['kɔ:sit] *n* corsé.
Corsica ['kɔ:sikə] *n* Córcega.
Corsican ['kɔ:sikən] *an* corso.
coruscate ['kɔrəskeit] *vi* relucir, brillar.
cosmetics [kɔz'metiks] *n* cosméticos, pinturas; afeites.
cosmonaut ['kɔzmənɔ:t] *n* cosmonauta.
cost [kɔst] *n* precio, costa, coste

costo; **to my —** a mis expensas, por mi daño; **— of living** coste de vida; **at all —s** a todo trance, cueste lo que cueste; *pl* costas, gastos; *vi* costar, valer; **to pay the — of** costear.
costliness ['kɔstlinis] *n* suntuosidad.
costly ['kɔstli] *a* caro, costoso, valioso, suntuoso.
costume ['kɔstju:m] *n* traje, vestido; **bullfighter's —** traje de luces.
cot [kɔt] *n* cabaña, choza; (*shepherd's*) majada; (*bed*) catre.
coterie ['koutəri] *n* corrillo, camarilla.
cottage ['kɔtidʒ] *n* cabaña; (*Val*) barraca; casa de campo; (*thatched*) choza; **— cheese** requesón.
cotton ['kɔtn] *n* algodón; **raw —** algodón en rama; **— plant** algodonero; **— spool** hilo de algodón; **— wool, absorbent —** algodón hidrófilo.
couch [kautʃ] *n* lecho; canapé, meridiana; silla poltrona; *vt* recostar(se); (*speech*) redactar, formular.
cough [kɔf] *n* tos; *vi* toser.
coughing ['kɔfiŋ] *n* **fit of —** golpe de tos.
council ['kaunsl] *n* consejo, concilio, concejo, ayuntamiento; **town —** cabildo.
councilor ['kaunsilə] *n* concejal, consejero.
counsel ['kaunsəl] *n* consejero; consultor; consejo, dictamen; (*for the defense*) defensor; *vt* aconsejar, guiar.
counselor ['kaunsələ] *n* consejero, abogado.
count [kaunt] *n* (*noble*) conde; cuenta; cálculo; valor; atención; *vt* contar, calcular, estimar; (*votes*) escrutar; **—down** cuenta inversa; **to — up** enumerar; **to lose —** (*of ideas etc*) perder el hilo; **to — upon** contar con.
countenance ['kauntinəns] *n* semblante, figura, rostro; corte, apariencia, continente; talante; **out of —** desconcertado, corrido, abochornado; *vt* favorecer, apoyar.
counter ['kauntə] *ad* contra, en oposición; *n* (*shop*) mostrador, taquilla; (*in game*) tablero; ficha; *vt* neutralizar; **to run — to** oponerse, contrariar.
counteract [ˌkauntə'rækt] *vt* contrarrestar, contrariar, frustrar.
counterattack ['kauntərəˌtæk] *n* contraataque.
counterfeit ['kauntəfit] *n* falsificación, imitación; *vt* falsear, imitar, contrahacer; forjar.
countermand [ˌkauntə'mɑ:nd] *vt* revocar; contramandar.
counterpane ['kauntəpein] *n* cubrecama, cobertor.
counterpart ['kauntəpɑ:t] *n* duplicado, imagen, traslado, copia; contraparte.
counterpoise ['kauntəpɔiz] *n* contrapeso; equilibrio.
countersign ['kauntəsain] *n* contraseña, consigna, santo y seña; *vi* visar, refrendar.
countess ['kauntis] *n* condesa.
countless ['kauntlis] *a* innumerable, inmenso, incontable.
country ['kʌntri] *a* del campo, rústico, campestre; agreste; *n* (*native*) patria; (*land*) campo; (*political*) país; (*region*) comarca; (*earth*) tierra; (*farming*) campiña; (*landscape*) paisaje; **— people** campesinos, paisanos; labriegos; **fellow —man** compatriota; **local fellow —man** paisano, (*bumpkin*) pelo de la dehesa, paleto; **— house** (*Andal*) cortijo; alquería, granja; **— road** camino vecinal; *pl* **neighboring —** naciones limítrofes.
county ['kaunti] *n* condado, distrito.
couple ['kʌpl] *n* (*pers*) pareja; (*two*) par; **married —** matrimonio; *vti* parear, acoplar, enganchar, enchufar; casar.
coupling ['kʌpliŋ] *n* acopladura, ajuste, cópula; (*el*) enchufe.
courage ['kʌridʒ] *n* valor, coraje, fortaleza, animosidad, denuedo; *excl* ¡ánimo!
courageous [kə'reidʒəs] *a* valeroso, valiente, bizarro.
course [kɔ:s] *n* (*way, direction*) curso, sentido, carrera, giro; (*naut*) rumbo, derrotero; dirección; **on a — for** con rumbo a; (*racing*) pista; (*meal*) plato, cubierto; (*of lectures*) cursillo; (*water*) corriente; (*time*) tránsito, lapso, marcha, transcurso; **to follow — of study** cursar (*en*); **of —** por cierto, desde luego, por supuesto, ya lo creo, por de contado.
court [kɔ:t] *n* (*royal*) corte; (*law*) tribunal; (*house*) patio; (*tennis*) campo; (*fives*) frontón; **— martial** consejo de guerra; **— plaster** esparadrapo; *vt* cortejar, hacer la corte; requerir de amores; adular; (*woo*) galantear.
courteous ['kə:tiəs] *a* cortés, afable, comedido, formal.
courtesy ['kə:tisi] *n* cortesía, gentileza, finura, cumplido; *vi* hacer una cortesía.
courtier ['kɔ:tiə] *n* cortesano; cortejo.
courtly ['kɔ:tli] *a* elegante, galante, cortés, noble.
courtship ['kɔ:tʃip] *n* corte; cortejo, festejo; noviazgo.
courtyard ['kɔ:tjɑ:d] *n* patio, corral, atrio.
cousin ['kʌzn] *n* primo, prima; **first —** primo carnal, primo hermano.
cove [kouv] *n* abra, ancón, ensenada, cala.
covenant ['kʌvənənt] *n* pacto, convenio, contrato; *vt* empeñar; concertar (*con*).

cover ['kʌvə] *n* cubierta, tapa(dera); (*place at table*) cubierta; (*top*) tapa; (*bed*) cobertor; (*book*) forro; (*shelter*) abrigo, albergue; (*hunt*) guarida; (*case*) funda; (*table*) tapete; **under — (of)** al abrigo (de), so capa de, valido de, en pliego cerrado, disimulado; *vt* cubrir, tapar, abrigar; (*include*) abarcar; (*losses*) compensar; (*expenses*) cubrir; (*distance*) recorrer; (*height*) saltar, montar; **to — up** paliar, disfrazar, correr el velo sobre, disimular; (*mil*) dominar.
covering ['kʌvəriŋ] *n* cubierta, envoltura; vestido; tapadura; **—s** envoltura.
covert ['kʌvət] *a* tapado, oculto, escondido; *n* (*hunt*) guarida; cubierta; refugio; abrigo.
covet ['kʌvit] *vt* codiciar, ambicionar, apetecer.
covetous ['kʌvitəs] *a* codicioso, ávido; sórdido.
covetousness ['kʌvitəsnis] *n* codicia, avaricia; avidez.
cow [kau] *n* vaca; **—lick** mechón; *vt* amilanar.
coward ['kauəd] *n* cobarde, menguado.
cowardice ['kauədis] *n* cobardía; timidez.
cowardly ['kauədli] *a* poltrón, apocado, cobarde, medroso, miedoso.
cower ['kauə] *vi* agacharse; acurrucarse.
cowl [kaul] *n* cogulla, capuz, capucha; (*chimney*) caballete, campaña.
coxswain ['kɔksn] *n* timonel.
coy [kɔi] *a* modesto, recatado, esquivo; cuco.
coyness ['kɔinis] *n* modestia, recato, encogimiento; esquivez.
crab [kræb] *n* cangrejo; (*mech*) cabrestante; **—apple** manzana silvestre.
crabbed ['kræbid] *a* áspero, hosco; bronco, avinagrado, enojadizo, gruñón.
crack [kræk] *a* agrietado; **— -brained** chiflado; **— shot** tiro certero; *n* hendedura, grieta, raja, intersticio; resquebrajo; (*whip, gun*) estallido, estampido, chasquido; (*with whip*) latigazo; rotura; *vt* hender, rajar, resquebrajar, saltar; chasquear, (r)estallar; *vi* crujir; reventar; hendirse, agrietarse; estallar.
cracked [krækt] *a* grietado, hendido; (*person*) chiflado.
crackle ['krækl] *vi* crujir, crepitar, restallar, chasquear.
crackling ['krækliŋ] *n* (*sound*) crepitación, crujido.
cradle ['kreidl] *n* cuna; (*arch*) trompa.
craft [krɑ:ft] *n* oficio, profesión; artificio; (*ship*) bajel, embarcación; **air—** avión; (*guile*) astucia, treta, maña.
craftiness ['krɑ:ftinis] *n* astucia, socarronería, maña.
craftsman ['krɑ:ftsmən] *n* artesano, artífice.
crafty ['krɑ:fti] *n* astuto, ladino, socarrón, taimado, solapado, vulpino.
crag [kræg] *n* despeñadero, risco, peña.
craggy ['krægi] *a* escarpado, rocalloso, arriscado, escabroso.
cram [kræm] *vt* rellenar, embutir, henchir, atiborrar, recargar; *vi* hartarse.
cramp [kræmp] *n* (*body*) calambre; agujetas; grapa, prensa; *vt* encalambrar; engrapar; sujetar.
crane [krein] *n* (*orn*) grulla; (*mech*) grúa; *vt* **to — one's neck** estirarse.
cranium ['kreiniəm] *n* cráneo.
crank [kræŋk] *n* manivela; codo; (*person*) maniático, chiflado, extravagante, lunático.
crape [kreip] *n* crespón.
crash [kræʃ] *n* estallido, estrépito; choque; (*financial*) quiebra; *vti* estallar; quebrantar; (*air*) estrellarse.
crashing ['kræʃiŋ] *n* estampido.
crass [kræs] *a* craso, torpe, tosco.
crater ['kreitə] *n* cráter, hoyo.
crave [kreiv] *vt* implorar, solicitar; ansiar, suspirar (*por*).
craving ['kreiviŋ] *a* insaciable; *n* deseo vehemente, anhelo, sed, reconcomio.
crawl [krɔ:l] *vi* arrastrarse; serpear; (*child*) ir a gatas, gatear.
crawling ['krɔ:liŋ] *a* a gatas.
crayon ['kreiən] *n* lápiz, tiza; dibujo a lápiz.
craze [kreiz] *n* delirio, manía, capricho; *vti* enloquecer(se).
crazed [kreizd] *a* alocado, poseído; demente, trastornado.
craziness ['kreizinis] *n* chifladura; locura; trastorno.
crazy ['kreizi] *a* loco; insensato, demente; chiflado; (*idea*) disparatado, desatinado; **completely —** loco rematado.
creak [kri:k] *n* chirrido; canto; *vi* (*metal*) rechinar; (*wood*) crujir, gruñir; (*axles*) chirriar, cantar.
creaking ['kri:kiŋ] *n* ruido; crujido.
cream [kri:m] *n* crema; nata; (*of society etc*) la flor y nata; **— bun** buñuelo de viento; **whipped —** crema batida; **— cheese** queso de nata, queso crema.
crease [kri:s] *n* pliegue, plegadura; (*untidy*) arruga; *vt* plegar, doblar, hacer pliegues, arrugar.
create [kri(:)'eit] *vt* crear, producir, hacer, criar; ocasionar, originar.
creation [kri(:)'eiʃən] *n* creación; naturaleza.
creative [kri(:)'eitiv] *a* imaginativo.
creator [kri(:)'eitə] *n* creador.
creature ['kri:tʃə] *n* criatura, ser; hechura.

crèche [kreiʃ] *n* (*Christmas*) belén, nacimiento.
credence ['kri:dəns] *n* creencia, fe, crédito.
credentials [kri'denʃəlz] *n pl* credenciales, nombre, nombradía.
credible ['kredəbl] *a* creíble, verosímil.
credit ['kredit] *a* (*balance*) activo; crédito; fe, creencia; (*exams*) notable; **to do — to** honrar; **on —** al fiado, a plazos; *vt* creer, dar fe; dar crédito; (*com*) abonar.
creditable ['kreditəbl] *n* honorable, respetable, honroso; fidedigno; creíble.
credited ['kreditid] *a* acreditado; reputado; (*com*) abonado en cuenta.
creditor ['kreditə] *n* acreedor.
credulity [kri'dju:liti] *n* credulidad.
credulous ['kredjuləs] *a* crédulo; **to be —** comulgar con ruedas de molino.
creed [kri:d] *n* credo; creencia; religión, doctrina.
creek [kri:k] *n* (*coastal*) ensenada, caleta, abra; riachuelo.
creep [kri:p] *vi* arrastrarse; deslizarse, insinuarse; **to — up** trepar; **to give the —s to** horripilar.
creeper ['kri:pə] *n* planta (rastera, trepadora, enredadera).
crescent ['kresnt] *n* creciente; media luna.
crest [krest] *n* (*bird*) cresta, penacho, copete; (*helmet*) cimera; (*hill*) cima.
crestfallen ['krest,fɔ:lən] *a* abatido, alicaído; orejas gachas; con el rabo entre las piernas.
crevice ['krevis] *n* grieta, abertura, resquicio.
crew [kru:] *n* tripulación; banda, horda.
crib [krib] *n* pesebre; artesa; (*Christmas*) nacimiento; (*child's*) camita de niño.
cricket ['krikit] *n* grillo.
crier ['kraiə] *n* pregonero, voceador.
crime [kraim] *n* crimen; delito; (*general*) criminalidad.
criminal ['kriminl] *a* criminal; *n* criminal, reo, delincuente; **state —** reo de traición.
crimson ['krimzn] *a* carmesí.
crinoline ['krinəlin] *n* miriñaque.
cripple ['kripl] *n* cojo, inválido; contrecho; tullido; **to be a —** ser cojo; *vt* mutilar, lisiar; estropear, baldar.
crippled ['kripld] *a* contrecho, tullido; (*naut*) desarbolado; **to be —** estar cojo.
crisis ['kraisis] *n* crisis.
crisp [krisp] *a* crespo, rizado; erizado; (*food*) tostado; (*phrase*) cortado, decidido, vigoroso; mordaz; (*weather*) fresco; **to cook —** achichar; *vt* encrespar, rizar.
crispness ['krispnis] *n* encrespadura; viveza, decisión, concisión.
criss-cross ['kriskrɔs] *a* cruzado; *ad* en cruz.
criterion [krai'tiəriən] *n* criterio, juicio.
critic ['kritik] *n* crítico.
critical ['kritikəl] *a* crítico, difícil; **— article** crítica; **— point** crisis; **— comment** animadversión.
critically ['kritikəli] *ad* **to be — ill** estar de cuidado.
criticism ['kritisizəm] *n* crítica; juicio crítico.
criticize ['kritisaiz] *vt* criticar, censurar, notar.
croak [krouk] *n* (*crow*) graznido; (*frog*) canto; chirrido; *vi* graznar.
crockery ['krɔkəri] *n* loza, cacharros.
crocodile ['krɔkədail] *n* cocodrilo.
crony ['krouni] *n* compinche, amigo íntimo; satélite.
crook [kruk] *n* (*hook*) gancho, garfio; (*shepherd*) cayado; artificio, tramposo; criminal; *vi* encorvarse.
crooked ['krukid] *a* encorvado, combo, torcido, giboso; avieso.
crop [krɔp] *n* (*harvest*) cosecha, recolección, mieses; (*of animal*) buches; *vti* cosechar, recolectar; (*hair*) rapar; (*animal*) esquilar; (*cow*) pacer.
cross [krɔs] *n* cruz; **wayside —** crucero; (*St. Andrew's*) aspa; aflicción; (*biol*) cruzamiento; *a* atravesado; opuesto; de mal humor, enfadado, arisco, picado; mohino; (*direction*) transversal; **—bar** barra, tranca, travesaño; **—bred** cruzado; **—-examination** repreguntas; **—-eyed** bizco; **—-grained** desabrido; **to be (get) —** tener malas pulgas; molestarse; **—road** atajo, trocha, travesía; **—wise** terciado; *vt* atravesar, cruzar, (tras)pasar; (*person*) desbaratar; vejar; intersecarse; **to — out** borrar, rayar; **to —-breed** cruzar.
crossing ['krɔsiŋ] *n* (*roads, trains*) cruce; (*arches*) crucero; (*sea*) travesía; (*mountains*) paso; (*ford*) vado; (*parting of ways*) encrucijada; **level —, grade —** paso a nivel; **pedestrian —** paso para peatones; **street —** bocacalle.
crossness ['krɔsnis] *n* mal humor.
crosswise ['krɔswaiz] *ad* (de, al) través, en cruz; de parte en parte.
crouch [krautʃ] *vi* acurrucarse; acuclillarse; agacharse; rebajarse.
crouching ['krautʃiŋ] *ad* en cuclillas.
crow [krou] *n* corneja; marica; cuervo; (*cock*) canto; **as the — flies** en derechura; *vi* **to —** cacarear.
crowbar ['krouba:] *n* palanca.
crowd [kraud] *n* multitud, gentío, montón, turba: rueda; gente; concurso; tropa; tropel; **—s of** una nube de; **in —s, in a —** a tropel; *vt* amontonar; *vi* amontonarse; **to — together,** agolparse; **to — around** (ar)remolinarse.
crowded ['kraudid] *n* lleno, atestado, apiñado.
crown [kraun] *n* corona; (*flowers*)

guirnalda; (*head*) coronilla; (*hat*) copa; (*prize*) galardón; (*hill*) cima; *vt* coronar.
crucial ['kru:ʃəl] *a* crítico, decisivo, conclusivo; atravesado.
crucifix ['kru:sifiks] *n* crucifijo, Cristo.
crucifixion [,kru:si'fikʃən] *n* crucifixión.
crucify ['kru:sifai] *vt* crucificar; atormentar.
crude [kru:d] *a* crudo, áspero, bruto, tosco, indigesto.
crudity ['kru:diti] *n* rudeza.
cruel ['kruəl] *a* cruel, fiero, duro, feroz; sanguíneo, despiadado, bárbaro.
cruelty ['kruəlti] *n* crueldad, tiranía, barbaridad, ensañamiento, barbarie.
cruise [kru:z] *n* viaje por mar; *vi* cruzar, navegar.
cruiser ['kru:zə] *n* crucero.
crumb [krʌm] *n* migaja, miaja; (*fig*) pizca; *vt* desmenuzar.
crumble ['krʌmbl] *vti* desmigajar(se), desmenuzar(se); (*stone*) desmoronarse, derrumbarse.
crumple ['krʌmpl] *vt* arrugar, manosear, ajar; **to — up** consentirse, deshacerse, desplomarse.
crunch [krʌntʃ] *vt* cascar; *vi* crujir.
crunching ['krʌntʃiŋ] *n* crujido.
crusade [kru:'seid] *n* cruzada.
crusader [kru:'seidə] *n* cruzado.
crush [krʌʃ] *n* choque; aplastamiento; machacadura; (*of people*) gentío, agolpamiento; *vt* aplastar, machacar, moler, quebrantar; (*press*) prensar, estrujar; (*squeeze*) apretar, comprimir; (*overwhelm*) abrumar, trastornar, aniquilar, hundir; (*spoil*) ajar, deslucir.
crushing ['krʌʃiŋ] *a* (*retort, blow etc*) fulminante.
crust [krʌst] *n* costra; capa; (*bread*) corteza, cuscurro; **a — of bread** un mendrugo de pan; un cantero.
crustiness ['krʌstinis] *n* dureza, mal genio, aspereza.
crusty ['krʌsti] *a* costroso; bronco; (*person*) de mal humor, brusco.
crutch [krʌtʃ] *n* muleta, muletilla.
cry [krai] *n* grito; clamor; lamento; (*of horror, pain*) aullido; (*of newborn baby*) vagido; *vt* gritar; exclamar; llorar; lamentar; (*wares*) pregonar; *vi* llorar; **to — out** gritar; **to — down** rebajar, desacreditar; **to — up** encarecer; **to — out loudly** poner el grito en el cielo.
crying ['kraiiŋ] *a* urgente, atroz; llorón; *n* lloro, llanto, plañido; pregoneo.
crypt [kript] *n* cripta.
cryptic ['kriptik] *a* oculto, enigmático.
crystal ['kristl] *n* cristal; **— clear** cristalino, claro.
crystalline ['kristəlain] *a* transparente, cristalino.
crystallize ['kristəlaiz] *vti* cristalizar.
cub [kʌb] *n* cachorro; **bear —** osezno; **wolf —** lobato.
cube [kju:b] *n* cubo; **— root** raíz cúbica; *vt* cubicar.
cuckoo ['kuku:] *n* cuclillo.
cucumber ['kju:kʌmbə] *n* pepino, cohombro; **cool as a —** fresco como una lechuga.
cuddle ['kʌdl] *vt* acariciar, abrazar.
cudgel ['kʌdʒel] *n* garrote, porra, palo; *vt* apalear, aporrear; **to — one's brains** devanarse los sesos.
cue [kju:] *n* cola, extremidad apunte; (*billiards*) taco; (*theat*) pie.
cuff [kʌf] *n* (*shirt*) puño; (*blow*) revés, sopapo, bofetada; **—links** gemelos; *vt* dar una bofetada.
cul-de-sac ['kʌldə'sæk] *n* callejón (sin salida).
cull [kʌl] *vt* escoger, entresacar, coger.
culminate ['kʌlmineit] *vi* culminar; conseguir.
culpable ['kʌlpəbl] *a* culpable, culpado.
culprit ['kʌlprit] *n* culpado, acusado, delincuente.
cult [kʌlt] *n* culto, devoción.
cultivate ['kʌltiveit] *vt* cultivar, lab(o)rar; beneficiar; estudiar.
cultivation [,kʌlti'veiʃən] *n* cultivo, labranza; cultura.
cultivator ['kʌltiveitə] *n* cultivador, labrador; (*mech*) cultivadora.
culture ['kʌltʃə] *n* cultura, civilización; urbanidad; luz.
cultured ['kʌltʃəd] *a* culto, ilustrado.
cumbersome ['kʌmbəsəm] *a* embarazoso, incómodo; abultado.
cumbrous ['kʌmbrəs] *a* engorroso, pesado.
cunning ['kʌniŋ] *a* astuto, mañoso; artero, solapado, socarrón, sabio, bellaco; **— skill** malas artes; *n* astucia, treta, ardid; cautela, sutileza, socaliña.
cup [kʌp] *n* taza; (*for athletics*) copa, trofeo; (*communion*) cáliz; (*of chocolate*) jícara; (*of acorn*) capullo, cúpula; **—bearer** copero; **in one's —s** bebido; **many a slip between — and lip** de la mano a la boca desaparece la sopa.
cupboard ['kʌbəd] *n* armario; alacena; **— love** amor interesado.
Cupid ['kju:pid] *m* Cupido.
cupidity [kju:'piditi] *n* codicia; avidez.
cupola ['kjupələ] *n* cúpula; cimborrio.
curable ['kjuərəbl] *a* curable, sanable.
curate ['kju:rət] *n* coadjutor, cura.
curator [kjuə'reitə] *n* conservador, director (*de museo*).
curb [kə:b] *n* brocal (*de pozo*); (*horse*) freno, brida; (*pavement*) orilla; *vt* refrenar, contener, reprimir, cortar.

curd [kə:d] *n* cuajada, requesón; *pl* cuajada; *vti* cuajar(se).
curdle ['kə:dl] *vr* cortarse, cuajar; (*blood*) helar(se).
cure [kjuə] *n* cura(ción); remedio; **—-all** panacea; *vti* curar(se); recuperarse; (*food*) conservar, ahumar, salar.
curfew ['kə:fju:] *n* (*toque de*) queda.
curiosity [,kjuəri'ɔsiti] *n* curiosidad, rareza.
curious ['kjuəriəs] *a* curioso, preguntón, entremetido; raro, peregrino, delicado, primoroso.
curl [kə:l] *n* rizo, bucle, tirabuzón; (*of wood*) alabeo; *vti* rizar, encrespar, retortijar; **to — up** acurrucarse; **— around** enroscar(se); (*lips*) fruncir.
curled [kə:ld] *a* (*hair*) rizado; **— up** ensortijado.
curlew ['kə:lu:] *n* chorlito.
curling ['kə:liŋ] *n* rizada; torcimiento; **— tongs** tenacillas.
curly ['kə:li] *a* rizado, crespo.
currant ['kʌrənt] *n* pasa de Corinto; grosella.
currency ['kʌrənsi] *n* moneda en circulación, medio circulante; circulación; **paper —** papel moneda; divisas.
current ['kʌrənt] *a* corriente, común, en boga; popular, de actualidad; **— year** el año en curso; *n* (*air, water*) corriente; (*passage*) curso, marcha; **to be —** correr, ser de actualidad.
curry ['kʌri] *vt* curtir, adobar (*el cuero*); zurrar; **to — favor** adular, complacer; *n* cari.
curse [kə:s] *n* maldición, juramento; vituperio, reniego, injuria, improperio; taco; *vti* maldecir, echar maldiciones; renegar, vituperar, execrar, denostar, echar pestes.
cursed ['kə:sid] *a* maldito, condenado, execrable.
cursory ['kə:səri] *a* precipitado, sumario, por encima, de carrera.
curt [kə:t] *a* seco, breve, conciso.
curtail [kə:'teil] *vt* cortar, abreviar, cercenar, restringir, reducir.
curtain ['kə:tn] *n* cortina; (*theat*) telón; **to draw a — over** correr un velo sobre.
curve [kə:v] *n* curva, serpenteo, recodo; *vt* encorvar, torcer(se).
curved [kə:vd] *a* curvo.
cushion ['kuʃən] *n* cojín, almohadilla; (*billiards*) banda; (*mech*) cojinete.
custard ['kʌstəd] *n* natillas, leche crema; (*baked*) flan.
custody ['kʌstədi] *n* custodia, guardia; encierro, cárcel.
custom ['kʌstəm] *n* costumbre, moda, usanza, procedimiento, uso; impuesto; clientela, despacho; *pl* aduana; **—s duties** impuestos de aduana; (*local*) fielato; **—s officer** aduanero.
customary ['kʌstəməri] *a* acostumbrado, usual, común, ritual, reglamentario, habitual.
customer ['kʌstəmə] *n* parroquiano, cliente.
customhouse ['kʌstəmhaus] *n* aduana.
cut [kʌt] *n* (*slice*) corte, tajo, cortadura, tajada; (*wound*) herida, incisión; (*cards*) alce; (*insult*) desaire; (*tailoring*) hechura, corte; **short —** atajo, trocha; *vti* cortar; tallar, cincelar; partir, dividir; (*cards*) alzar, cortar; **to — down** segar; **to — off** cortar; **to — out** recortar; suprimir, imposibilitar, cortar; **to — short** truncar, imposibilitar, interrumpir, atajar; **to — up** cortar; surcar, lastimar; **to — dead** desairar; **to — both ways** ser una arma de dos filos; **to — across fields** ir a campo travieso; **to — a figure** hacer (un) papel; **to — one's way through** abrirse paso; **— off** cortado, recortado, incomunicado, aislado.
cutlass ['kʌtləs] *n* machete, alfanje.
cutlery ['kʌtləri] *n* cuchillería; cubiertos.
cutlet ['kʌtlit] *n* chuleta.
cutter ['kʌtə] *n* cortador; (*naut*) cúter.
cut-throat ['kʌtθrout] *n* asesino.
cutting ['kʌtiŋ] *a* cortante, mordaz, picante; *n* cortadura, incisión; picadura; (*newspaper*) recorte; (*rl*) desmonte; (*cloth*) retazo; (*in rock*) tajo; (*snippets*) cortaduras.
cycling ['saikliŋ] *n* ciclismo.
cyclone ['saikloun] *n* ciclón, huracán.
cylinder ['silində] *n* cilindro.
cymbal ['simbəl] *n* platillo.
cynical ['sinikəl] *a* impasible, frío, indiferente; cínico; desdeñoso.
cynicism ['sinisizəm] *n* cinismo; impudor, descaro; frialdad.
cynosure ['sinəzjuə] *n* foco, blanco.
cypress ['saiprəs] *n* ciprés.
Cypriot ['sipriət] *an* chipriota.
Cyprus ['saiprəs] *n* Isla de Chipre.
Czar [zɑ:] *n* zar.
Czech [tʃek] *an* checo.
Czechoslovakia ['tʃekouslou'vækiə] *n* Checoeslovaquia.

D

dabble ['dæbl] *vti* salpicar, mojar: chapotear, revolcarse; especular; ser aficionado a.
daffodil ['dæfədil] *n* narciso.
dagger ['dægə] *n* puñal; daga.
daily ['deili] *a* diario, cotidiano; *ad* diariamente, todos los días, de un día a otro.
daintiness ['deintinis] *n* delicadeza, elegancia, gracia, golosina; afectación.
dainty ['deinti] *a* delicado; donoso; gracioso; regalado; sabroso; *n* golosina; gollería.

dairy ['dɛəri] *n* lechería.
dais ['deiis] *n* baldaquín, tablado, estrado.
daisy ['deizi] *n* margarita, maya.
dale [deil] *n* cañada, hoya, hoyada, valle.
dally ['dæli] *vi* holgar, entretenerse; perder el tiempo, camelar.
dam [dæm] *n* presa, represa; dique; *vt* represar, embalsar, tapar.
damage ['dæmidʒ] *n* daño; perjuicio, deterioro, menoscabo; avería; pérdida; *pl* (*law*) daños y perjuicios.
damage ['dæmidʒ] *vt* dañar; damnificar; deteriorar; averiarse.
damaging ['dæmidʒiŋ] *a* dañino, dañoso, perjudicial,
damask ['dæməsk] *a* adamascado, damasquino; *n* damasco; *vt* damasquinar.
dame [deim] *n* dama, mujer; tía.
damn [dæm] *vt* condenar, reprobar, maldecir.
damnable ['dæmnəbl] *a* infame.
damnation [dæm'neiʃən] *n* condenación.
damned [dæmd] *a* maldito; condenado; *n pl* los condenados.
damp [dæmp] *a* húmedo; mojado; *n* humedad.
damp(en) ['dæmp(ən)] *vt* humedecer; desanimar, apagar.
dampness ['dæmpnis] *n* humedad.
damsel ['dæmzəl] *n* damisela, doncella.
dance [dɑ:ns] *n* baile; (*old-world*) danza; **formal —** baile de etiqueta; *vi* bailar, danzar; **to — attendance on** no dejar a sol ni a sombra.
dancer ['dɑ:nsə] *n* danzante; (*professional*) bailarín *m*, bailarina *f*.
dancing [dɑ:nsiŋ] *n* baile, danza; **— girl** bailarina.
dandy ['dændi] *n* majo, petimetre, pisaverde.
danger ['deindʒə] *n* peligro, riesgo, trance; **without —** sobre seguro.
dangerous ['deindʒrəs] *a* aventurado; expuesto; peligroso, arriesgado; (*illness*) grave.
dangle ['dæŋgl] *vti* colgar, suspender, guindar; bambolearse.
Danish ['deiniʃ] *a* danés.
dapper ['dæpə] *a* apuesto; gentil, gallardo.
dare [dɛə] *vt* arrostrar, desafiar; retar; *vi* atreverse, osar; **I — say me** figuro.
daring ['dɛəriŋ] *a* atrevido, osado; arriesgado, temerario; *n* osadía, bravura, atrevimiento.
dark [dɑ:k] *a* obscuro, opaco; sombrío, hosco; fúnebre, ciego; **—-haired** moreno; **— lantern** linterna sorda; **the —** tinieblas; **in the —** a ciegas, a oscuras, a tientas; **to be left in the —** quedarse a buenas noches; **to grow —** anochecer, oscurecer; **to keep —** ocultar.
darken ['dɑ:kən] *vt* ennegrecer; obscurecer; manchar, entristecer; enlutar; *vi* obscurecerse.
darkness ['dɑ:knis] *n* obscuridad; hosquedad; **outer —** tinieblas.
darling ['dɑ:liŋ] *a* querido, amado; *n* favorito, predilecto; *SA* (*fam*) chata; **my —** mi bien, amor mío.
darn [dɑ:n] *n* remiendo, zurcido; *vt* zurcir, remendar.
dart [dɑ:t] *n* flecha; dardo; venablo; *vti* lanzar(se).
dash [dæʃ] *n* ataque, arremetida; (*waves*) embate, choque; (*in writing*) guión, raya; (*food*) mezcla, sabor; (*of person*) coraje, garbo; fogosidad; **to make a —** tirarse; *vtr* lanzar(se), arrojar(se); hundir; acometer; **to — to pieces** hacer(se) añicos, estrellarse; estallar; **to — to and fro** trajinar, arremeter.
dashing ['dæʃiŋ] brillante, fogoso; (*person*) garboso; (*fam*) curro; *n* embate; arremetida.
dastardly ['dæstədli] *a* cobarde, tímido.
data ['deitə] *n pl* datos.
date [deit] *n* fecha; (*fruit*) dátil; **—-colored** datilado; **out of —** desusado, pasado de moda; **up to —** al día, al tanto; *vt* datar, poner la fecha, fechar.
daub [dɔ:b] *n* mamarracho; birria; *vt* embadurnar; disfrazar.
daughter ['dɔ:tə] *n* hija; **grand—** nieta; **—-in-law** nuera, hija política; **god—** ahijada.
daunt [dɔ:nt] *vt* acobardar, atemorizar, intimidar, domar.
dauntless ['dɔ:ntlis] *a* intrépido, impávido.
dawdle ['dɔ:dl] *vi* gastar tiempo, pasar el rato.
dawn [dɔ:n] *n* alba, amanecer; **at —** de madrugada; **from — to dusk** de sol a sol; **to get up with the —** madrugar; *vi* amanecer, romper el día, alborear, apuntar.
day [dei] *n* día; (*work*) jornada; **— book** diario; **by —** de día; **the — before** la víspera; **the — before yesterday** anteayer; **the — after tomorrow** pasado mañana; **a — off** un día de asueto; **— in — out** día tras día; **—boy** (*in boarding school*) externo; **— school** externado; **— laborer** jornalero; **every other —** cada tercer día, un día sí y otro no.
daybreak ['deibreik] *n* amanecer, alba; **at —** al amanecer.
daylight ['deilait] *n* sol; **luz del día.**
daytime ['deitaim] *n* día; **in the —** durante el día.
daze [deiz] *n* aturdimiento, trastorno; *vt* ofuscar, aturdir.
dazzle ['dæzl] *vt* deslumbrar, ofuscar.
dazzling ['dæzliŋ] *a* luminoso, relumbrante.
dead [ded] *a* muerto; difunto; (*sound*) sordo; (*matter*) inorgánico;

(*light*) sordo; seguro; — **stop** parada en seco; **in the — of night** en las altas horas; — **certainty** certeza absoluta; — **drunk** perdido; — **end** callejón sin salida; — **shot** tirador certero; —**weight** peso muerto.
deaden ['dedn] *vt* amortiguar; apagar.
deadliness ['dedlinis] *n* lo mortífero.
deadly ['dedli] *a* mortal; letal; fatal; — **sin** pecado capital.
deadness ['dednis] *n* muerte, inercia.
deaf [def] *a* sordo; — **and dumb** sordomudo; **stone** — sordo como una tapia; **to turn a — ear** hacerse el sordo.
deafen ['defn] *vt* ensordecer, aturdir.
deafening ['defniŋ] *a* ensordecedor.
deafness ['defnis] *n* ensordecimiento, sordera.
deal [di:l] *n* cantidad, porción; (*wood*) pino en tablas; negocio, trato; **a great** — mucho; **a good** — bastante; *vti* distribuir; (*cards*) dar; tratar, negociar; **to — in** comerciar; **to — with** tratar de, versar sobre.
dealer ['di:lə] *n* comerciante, expendedor; (*at cards*) mano.
dealings ['di:liŋz] *n* trato; conducta, proceder.
dean [di:n] *n* (*eccles*) dean; (*univ*) decano.
dear ['diə] *a* costoso, caro; querido, predilecto.
dearness ['diənis] *n* cariño; (*cost*) carestía; lo caro.
dearth [də:θ] *n* carestía, escasez.
death [deθ] *n* muerte, fallecimiento, defunción; parca; **the pangs of** — agonía; **war to the** — guerra sin cuartel; —**dealing** *a* fatal, mortífero; — **certificate** partida de defunción.
deathbed ['deθbed] *n* lecho mortuorio, lecho de muerte.
deathless ['deθlis] *a* imperecedero.
debar [di'bɑ:] *vt* excluir, privar, alejar.
debase [di'beis] *vt* rebajar, envilecer, prostituir, pervertir; (*coinage*) depreciar; *vr* humillarse.
debasement [di'beismənt] *n* envilecimiento, adulteración.
debasing [di'beisiŋ] *n* (*of coinage*) alteración.
debate [di'beit] *n* debate; discusión, contienda, controversia; *vti* debatir; contender, disputar; deliberar.
debauch [di'bɔ:tʃ] *n* crápula, orgía; *vt* corromper; relajar, sobornar.
debauchery [di'bɔ:tʃəri] *n* crápula, lujuria, mal vivir.
debilitate [di'biliteit] *vt* debilitar, extenuar, postrar, quebrantar.
debit ['debit] *n* debe, débito, cargo; *vt* cargar.
debonair [ˌdebə'nɛə] *a* gallardo, afable, cortés.
Deborah ['debərə] *f* Débora.
debris ['debri:] *n* escombros, ripio, desecho.
debt [det] *n* deuda.
debtor ['detə] *n* deudor.
debut ['deibu:] *n* estreno; presentación en sociedad.
decade ['dekeid] *n* década.
decadence ['dekədəns] *n* decadencia, ocaso.
decamp [di'kæmp] *vi* huir, escaparse, decampar; (*sl*) zafarse.
decanter [di'kæntə] *n* garrafa, botellón.
decapitate [di'kæpiteit] *vt* decapitar, degollar.
decay [di'kei] *n* decadencia; decaimiento; mengua; podridumbre, putrefacción seca; *vi* decaer, declinar; empeorar, extenuarse, pudrir; venir a menos, degenerar; (*teeth*) cariarse.
decaying [di'keiiŋ] *n* decadencia; decaimiento.
decease [di'si:s] *n* fallecimiento, defunción; *vi* morir, fallecer.
deceit [di'si:t] *n* fraude, engaño; impostura, duplicidad, trampa, camelo.
deceitful [di'si:tful] *a* falso, engañoso; artificioso, solapado.
deceitfulness [di'si:tfulnis] *n* perfidia, engaño, bellaquería.
deceive [di'si:v] *vt* engañar, defraudar, burlar, camelar, embaucar.
December [di'sembə] *n* diciembre.
decency ['di:snsi] *n* decencia; honestidad, pudor, recato.
decent ['di:snt] *a* decente, acomodado, honrado; aseado.
deception [di'sepʃən] *n* decepción, desengaño, desilusión.
deceptive [di'septiv] *a* engañoso, especioso, falaz, ilusorio.
decide [di'said] *vti* decidir, resolver; **to — on** optar por; *vr* decidirse, resolverse.
decided [di'saidid] *a* decidido, resuelto; asegurado; categórico; patente.
decimate ['desimeit] *vt* diezmar.
decipher [di'saifə] *vt* descifrar; aclarar; deletrear.
decision [di'siʒən] *n* decisión, resolución, firmeza.
decisive [di'saisiv] *a* decisivo, crítico, concluyente; —**ly** *ad* de cabeza.
deck [dek] *n* (*ship*) puente; cubierta; plataforma; —**chair** silla de tijera; *vt* adornar(se), ataviar(se).
declaim [di'kleim] *vti* declamar, recitar, perorar, arengar.
declaration [ˌdeklə'reiʃən] *n* declaración, manifestación, manifesto.
declare [di'klɛə] *vt* declarar, manifestar; afirmar, testificar; *vr* pronunciarse.
declared [di'klɛəd] *a* calificado, declarado, abierto.
decline [di'klain] *n* declinación,

decadencia; mengua, menoscabo; *vt* rehusar, rechazar; *vi* excusarse, evitar, negarse.
declivity [di'kliviti] *n* declive, pendiente.
decompose [ˌdi:kəm'pouz] *vt* descomponer, pudrir; *vi* descomponerse.
decorate ['dekəreit] *vt* (con)decorar, adornar, hermosear.
decoration [ˌdekə'reiʃən] *n* (con)-decoración; adorno, ornato, embellecimiento.
decorous ['dekərəs] *a* decoroso, púdico.
decorum [di'kɔ:rəm] *n* decoro, decencia, corrección; pudor.
decoy ['di:kɔi] *n* señuelo; **— pigeon** cimbel, señuelo; *vt* atraer con señuelo, embaucar.
decrease ['di:kri:s] *n* disminución, mengua; merma; (*knit*) menguado; [di:'kri:s] *vti* disminuir, menguar.
decree [di'kri:] *n* decreto, estatuto; pragmática, ley; *vt* decretar, ordenar.
decrepit [di'krepit] *a* decrépito, chocho, caduco.
decry [di'krai] *vt* desacreditar, afear; rebajar; zaherir.
dedicate ['dedikeit] *vt* dedicar, consagrar, aplicar, dar(se) a.
dedication [ˌdedi'keiʃən] *n* (*place*) consagración; (*book*) dedicatoria.
deduce [di'dju:s] *vt* deducir, inferir; sacar; sacar en limpio.
deduct [di'dʌkt] *vt* deducir; descontar; (*math*) restar.
deduction [di'dʌkʃən] *n* deducción, reducción; (*money*) descuento; **absurd —** contrasentido.
deed [di:d] *n* acción; hecho, acto; hazaña; (*valorous*) proeza; (*youthful*) *pl* mocedades; (*law*) escritura; documento.
deem [di:m] *vt* juzgar, creer, estimar.
deep [di:p] *a* profundo, serio; (*sorrow*) hondo; (*thought*) recóndito; (*love*) fuerte; (*music*) grave; (*color*) oscuro; **— -chested** ancho de pecho; **— spot** *n* pozo; hondanada; (*the sea*) **—** piélago, fondo del mar, alta mar; **to go —** *vi* ahondar, profundizar.
deepen ['di:pən] *vt* profundizar; (*voice*) ahuecar.
deeper ['di:pə] *ad* **to go ever — into** *vi* internarse en.
deepness ['di:pnis] *n* profundidad, intensidad.
deer [diə] *n* ciervo, venado.
deface [di'feis] *vt* estropear, afear, mutilar; desfigurar.
defacement [di'feismənt] *n* destrucción, mutilación.
defame [di'feim] *vt* amenguar, difamar, calumniar, infamar, menoscabar.
default [di'fɔ:lt] *n* falta, omisión; culpa; defecto; **by —** por ausencia; en rebeldía; *vt* faltar, no cumplir; *vi* ponerse en mora.
defeat [di'fi:t] *n* derrota; descalabro, anulación; *vt* derrotar, frustrar; vencer; **which —s its own purpose** contraproducente.
defect ['di:fekt] *n* defecto, vicio; imperfección, tacha; [di'fekt] *vi* huir, largarse.
defective [di'fektiv] *a* defectuoso, defectivo, imperfecto; escaso.
defend [di'fend] *vt* defender, vindicar, amparar; *vr* defenderse; (res)-guardar(se).
defendant [di'fendənt] *n* acusado, procesado, demandado.
defender [di'fendə] *n* (*law*) defensor, abogado; protector, campeón; apologista.
defense [di'fens] *n* defensa, apoyo, escudo, sostén; apología.
defenseless [di'fenslis] *a* indefenso, inerme, desamparado.
defensible [di'fensəbl] *a* defendible, sostenible.
defensive [di'fensiv] *n* defensiva; **to be on the —** estar a la defensiva.
defer [di'fə:] *vti* diferir, aplazar, postergar, posponer, postergar; **to — to** deferir, ceder.
deference ['defərəns] *n* deferencia, respeto, consideración.
deferential [ˌdefə'renʃəl] *a* respetuoso.
defiance [di'faiəns] *n* provocación; desafío; reto; (*law*) rebeldía; **in — of** a despecho de; **to bid —** desafiar.
defiant [di'faiənt] *a* provocativo, osado.
deficiency [di'fiʃənsi] *n* deficiencia, insuficiencia, falta.
deficient [di'fiʃənt] *a* deficiente, defectuoso, incompleto.
deficit ['defisit] *n* déficit.
defile ['di:fail] *n* desfiladero, hoz; [di'fail] *vt* manchar, profanar, deshonrar, violar, ensuciar; infectar.
defilement [di'failmənt] *n* corrupción, contaminación, profanación, violación.
define [di'fain] *vt* definir, determinar, delimitar.
definite ['definit] *a* definido, rotundo, terminante; (*promise etc*) formal; categórico; **quite —** indudable.
definition [ˌdefi'niʃən] *n* definición; precisión.
definitive [di'finitiv] *a* categórico, terminante.
deflate [di:'fleit] *vt* desinflar, deshinchar.
deflect [di'flekt] *vti* desviar, separar del camino; *vr* desviarse, apartarse.
deflection [di'flekʃən] *n* desvío; declinación, torcimiento.
deform [di'fɔ:m] *vt* desfigurar, deformar.
deformed [di'fɔ:md] *a* disforme, contrahecho, deforme.
deformity [di'fɔ:miti] *n* deformidad, malformación.

defraud [di'frɔ:d] *vt* defraudar, engañar; frustrar.
defray [di'frei] *vt* costear, sufragar (*los gastos*).
deft [deft] *a* diestro, hábil, mañoso.
deftness ['deftnis] *n* destreza, habilidad, maña.
defy [di'fai] *vt* desafiar, retar.
degenerate [di'dʒenərit] *an* degenerado; [di'dʒenəreit] *vi* degenerar.
degeneration [di,dʒenə'reiʃən] *n* degeneración; empeoramiento.
degradation [,degrə'deiʃən] *n* degradación; descenso.
degrade [di'greid] *vt* degradar, envilecer; hollar; humillar.
degrading [di'greidiŋ] *a* humillante.
degree [di'gri:] *n* (*up or down*) grado, escalón; (*station*) casta, estirpe; (*univ*) licenciatura; doctorado; **of low** — *a* plebeyo.
deign [dein] *vi* dignarse, servirse, condescender.
deity ['di:iti] *n* deidad, divinidad.
deject [di'dʒekt] *vt* abatir, afligir, contristar.
dejected [di'dʒektid] *a* desanimado, abismado, afligido, abatido, triste; **to be** — andar (ir) de capa caída.
dejection [di'dʒekʃən] *n* abatimiento, desaliento; postración.
delay [di'lei] *n* tardanza, retardo, demora; (*rl*) retraso; **without** — en seguida, sin demora; *vt* aplazar, (re)tardar, posponer; *vi* demorarse, tardar(se).
delegate ['deligit] *n* delegado; ['deligeit] *vt* delegar, diputar.
delegation [,deli'geiʃən] *n* delegación.
delete [di'li:t] *vt* borrar, suprimir.
deletion [di'li:ʃən] *n* borradura, supresión.
deliberate [di'libərit] *a* circunspecto; compasado, pausado, lento, deliberado; [di'libəreit] *vti* deliberar, discurrir.
deliberately [di'libəritli] *ad* deliberadamente, a sabiendas, de propósito.
deliberation [di,libə'reiʃən] *n* deliberación, ponderación.
delicacy ['delikəsi] *n* delicadeza, elegancia; (*taste*) refinamiento; (*manner*) esmero; escrupulosidad; (*health*) flaqueza; (*of artistic work*) filigrana; (*food*) bocado de rey, manjar, delicado.
delicate ['delikit] *a* tierno, delicado; (*workmanship*) afiligranado; (*taste*) exquisito; (*feeling*) pudoroso; (*health*) enfermizo, alfeñique; (*sense*) suave, gentil, ligero; (*strength*) deleznable, quebradizo.
delicious [di'liʃəs] *a* delicioso, exquisito; (*food*) rico, sabroso.
delight [di'lait] *n* encanto, placer, delicia; gozo; atractivo; *vt* seducir, encantar, recrear; deleitarse, gozar; complacerse.
delighted [di'laitid] *a* gozoso, complacido, encantado; **to be** — contentarse, tener mucho gusto en.
delightful [di'laitful] *a* delicioso, ameno, deleitoso, encantador, gracioso, regalado, sabroso.
delightfulness [di'laitfulnis] *n* delicia; suavidad; encanto; placer.
delineation [di,lini'eiʃən] *n* trazo, bosquejo, delineamiento.
delinquency [di'liŋkwənsi] *n* delincuencia; delito.
delinquent [di'liŋkwent] *an* delincuente.
delirious [di'liriəs] *a* delirante.
delirium [di'liriəm] *n* delirio, desvarío.
deliver [di'livə] *vt* entregar; (*from bondage*) librar, libertar; (*speech*) recitar, pronunciar; (*blow*) asestar; (*child*) partear; **to be —ed** (*of child*) parir.
deliverance [di'livərəns] *n* liberación; rescate.
deliverer [di'livərə] *n* libertador.
delivery [di'livəri] *n* entrega; (*letters*) reparto; (*from bondage*) liberación, libramiento, rescate; (*birth*) parto, alumbramiento; (*speech*) dicción.
deliveryman [di'livərimæn] *n* mozo de reparto.
delude [di'lu:d] *vt* engañar, alucinar.
deluded [di'lu:did] *a* iluso.
deluge ['delju:dʒ] *n* diluvio; *vt* inundar, diluviar.
delusion [di'lu:ʒən] *n* error, engaño; ilusión.
delve [delv] *vt* cavar; ahondar.
demand [di'mɑ:nd] *n* demanda, reclamación, pedido, solicitud; *vt* pedir, exigir, demandar, reclamar.
demeanor [di'mi:nə] *n* conducta, porte.
demise [di'maiz] *n* fallecimiento, defunción; óbito; *vt* legar, transferir, dar en arriendo.
demobilization ['di:,moubilai'zeiʃən] *n* demobilización; licencia absoluta.
democracy [di'mɔkrəsi] *n* democracia.
democrat ['deməkræt] *n* demócrata.
democratic [,demə'krætik] *a* democrático.
demolish [di'mɔliʃ] *vt* demoler, derribar; arruinar, batir, derrocar; reventar.
demolition [,demə'liʃən] *n* derribo.
demon ['di:mən] *n* demonio, diablo.
demonstrate ['demənstreit] *vt* demostrar, probar, manifestar.
demonstration [,demən'streiʃən] *n* demostración; (*public, in street*) manifestación.
demonstrative [di'mɔnstrətiv] *a* demostrativo, abierto.
demoralize [di'mɔrəlaiz] *vt* desmoralizar, descorazonar.
demure [di'mjuə] *a* recatado, modesto, formal.

den [den] *n* madriguera, caverna; antro; (*fam*) cuchitril; (*hiding place*) escondrijo, rincón.
denial [di'naiəl] *n* denegación, negación; repudio.
Denmark ['denmɑ:k] *n* Dinamarca.
denominate [di'nɔmineit] *vt* calificar, denominar, nombrar.
denomination [di,nɔmi'neiʃən] *n* denominación; categoría, clase; (*eccles*) secta, confesión.
denote [di'nout] *vt* denotar, significar, señalar.
dénouement [dei'nu:mɑ̃:ŋ] *n* desenlace.
denounce [di'nauns] *vt* denunciar, acusar, delatar.
denouncement [di'naunsmənt] *n* denuncia, denunciación.
dense [dens] *a* denso, espeso; compacto, cerrado; (*undergrowth*) tupido; (*person*) lerdo, torpe.
denseness ['densnis] *n* densidad, solidez; espesor; estupidez.
density ['densiti] *n* densidad; espesor.
dent [dent] *n* hoyo; abolladura; *vt* abollar.
dentifrice ['dentifris] *n* dentífrico.
dentist ['dentist] *n* dentista; (*fam*) sacamuelas.
denunciate [di'nʌnsieit] *vt* denunciar, acusar.
deny [di'nai] *vt* negar, refutar, renegar, renunciar, negarse a; desdecirse.
depart [di'pɑ:t] *vi* salir, irse, marcharse; (*soul*) fallecer; (*from truth etc*) desviarse, apartarse; **the departed** los difuntos.
department [di'pɑ:tmənt] *n* departamento; sección; (*of knowledge etc*) rama, ramo; **fire —** cuerpo de bomberos.
departure [di'pɑ:tʃə] *n* salida, partida; el irse, desviación.
depend [di'pend] *vi* depender (de); **to — on** contar con, fiarse de; estribar en.
dependable [di'pendəbl] *a* formal, seguro.
dependence [di'pendəns] *n* dependencia; relación; confianza, seguridad.
dependent [di'pendənt] *a* dependiente; (*fact*) consiguiente; necesitado; pendiente; *n* dependiente, subalterno.
depict [di'pikt] *vt* describir, pintar, representar.
deplete [di'pli:t] *vt* agotar; vaciar; mermar.
deplorable [di'plɔ:rəbl] *a* deplorable, lamentable; **it is —** es de lamentar.
deplore [di'plɔ:] *vt* deplorar, lamentar, llorar, dolerse de.
deploy [di'plɔi] *vt* desplegar.
deport [di'pɔ:t] *vt* deportar, extrañar, desterrar; *vr* conducirse, portarse.
deportation [,di:pɔ:'teiʃən] *n* deportación, destierro.
deportment [di'pɔ:tmənt] *n* porte, conducta, proceder.
depose [di'pouz] *vt* deponer; *vi* dar testimonio.
deposit [di'pɔzit] *n* depósito, sedimento; (*com*) arras, prenda; (*ore*) yacimiento; *vt* depositar; poner (*dinero*); (*chem*) precipitar.
deposition [,di:pə'ziʃən] *n* deposición; testimonio; depósito.
depot ['depou] *n* almacén; muelle; (*rl*) estación.
deprave [di'preiv] *vt* depravar, pervertir; (*taste*) estragar.
depravity [di'præviti] *n* depravación, corrupción, vileza, perversión.
deprecate ['deprikeit] *vt* lamentar; criticar, desaprobar; *vi* oponerse.
depreciate [di'pri:ʃieit] *vt* denigrar; despreciar, rebajar.
depreciation [di,pri:ʃi'eiʃən] *n* depreciación, rebaja.
depress [di'pres] *vt* deprimir, bajar, desanimar; sumir, abismar.
depressed [di'prest] *a* alicaído, deprimido.
depression [di'preʃən] *n* (*mental etc*) abatimiento; depresión; (*hollow*) hueco.
deprivation [,depri'veiʃən] *n* pérdida, privación, carencia.
deprive [di'praiv] *vt* privar (de), quitar (a), destituir.
depth [depθ] *n* profundidad; fondo; (*sound*) gravedad; (*colour*) viveza; (*in fathoms*) braceaje; **—s** abismo; entrañas; **the —s of** lo hondo de; **out of one's —** sin dar pie.
deputy ['depjuti] *n* delegado, suplente, diputado; comisionado.
derail [di'reil] *vi* descarrilar.
derange [di'reindʒ] *vt* desarreglar; (*mind*) trastornar.
derangement [di'reindʒmənt] *n* desarreglo, desconcierto; desbarajuste; trastorno; (*mental*) locura, desvarío.
derelict ['derilikt] *a* abandonado.
deride [di'raid] *vt* ridiculizar, burlarse (de), mofarse (de).
derision [di'riʒən] *n* irrisión; mofa, escarnio.
derisive [di'raisiv] *a* irrisorio, burlesco.
derivation [,deri'veiʃən] *n* derivación, etimología.
derive [di'raiv] *vt* derivar, deducir.
derogatory [di'rɔgətəri] *a* derogatorio.
derrick ['derik] *n* grúa, torre.
descend [di'send] *vi* descender, bajar; declinar; **to — to** rebajarse a; **to — upon** caer sobre; **to — from** descender de.
descendant [di'sendənt] *a* descendente; *n* descendiente, vástago.
descent [di'sent] *n* origen, descenso; (*family*) cuna, abolengo, estirpe; descendencia; posteridad; (*from the*

Cross) descendimiento; (*slope*) pendiente, declive; (*from mountain*) bajada; (*mil*) incursión.
describe [dis'kraib] *vt* describir, pintar, definir.
description [dis'kripʃən] *n* descripción, reseña; género, clase; **personal —** señas personales.
descriptive [dis'kriptiv] *a* descriptivo, narrativo.
desecrate ['desikreit] *vt* profanar.
desert ['dezət] *a* desierto; despoblado; solitario: *n* páramo, yermo, desierto; soledad; merecimiento; [di'zə:t] *vti* desertar; abandonar, dejar, desamparar; **to get one's —s** llevar su merecido.
deserted [di'zə:tid] *a* abandonado, desierto, solitario, inhabitado, despoblado.
deserter [di'zə:tə] *n* desertor, tránsfuga.
desertion [di'zə:ʃən] *n* abandono; (*mil*) deserción.
deserve [di'zə:v] *vt* merecer, ser digno de; incurrir (en).
deserving [di'zə:viŋ] *a* digno, benemérito, meritorio.
design [di'zain] *n* designio, proyecto, plan, dibujo; trazo, patrón; mira, propósito; *vt* dibujar; proponerse, idear; delinear; *vi* tener un designio.
designate ['dezigneit] *vt* designar, nombrar.
designedly [di'zainidli] *ad* adrede, de propósito, con intención.
designing [di'zainiŋ] *a* insidioso, intrigante; *n* dibujo.
desirability [di,zaiərə'biliti] *n* conveniencia.
desirable [di'zaiərəbl] *a* deseable; conveniente, apetecible.
desire [di'zaiə] *n* deseo; antojo, afán, comezón, aspiración, hambre; voluntad; *vt* desear, anhelar, ambicionar; suspirar por; suplicar, rogar.
desirous [di'zaiərəs] *a* deseoso.
desist [di'zist] *vi* desistir de, dejar de, cesar de.
desk [desk] *n* (*school*) pupitre; (*writing*) escritorio, papelera; (*lawyer's*) bufete; (*cashier*) caja.
desolate ['desəlit] *a* desolado, solitario, despoblado; ['desəleit] *vt* talar, devastar.
desolation [,desə'leiʃən] *n* desconsuelo, tristeza; devastación, tala; desolación, páramo.
despair [dis'pɛə] *n* desesperación; *vti* desesperar(se).
despairing[dis'pɛəriŋ] *a* desesperado, desesperante.
despatch [dis'pætʃ] *n* (*speed*) prisa, expedición; (*message*) mensaje, billete, pliego; (*mil*) parte; *vt* mandar, enviar, despachar, expedir; (*letter etc*) endilgar.
desperado [,despə'rɑ:dou] *n* desalmado, bandido.
desperate ['despərit] *a* desesperado; furioso, arrojado, temerario, desesperado.
desperation [,despə'reiʃən] *n* desesperación; furor, rabia.
despicable [dis'pikəbl] *a* despreciable, vil, ruin, infame.
despicableness [dis'pikəblnis] *n* bajeza, vileza, ruindad.
despise [dis'paiz] *vt* despreciar, echar a mal, menospreciar.
despite [dis'pait] *prep* a pesar de, no obstante.
despondency [dis'pɔndənsi] *n* desaliento, desabrimiento, abatimiento.
despondent [dis'pɔndənt] *a* desanimado, desalentado; **to be —** andar de capa caída.
despot ['despɔt] *n* déspota, tirano.
despotic [des'pɔtik] *a* despótico, tiránico.
despotism ['despətizəm] *n* absolutismo; tiranía.
dessert [di'zə:t] *n* postre; dulce; fruta.
destination [,desti'neiʃən] *n* destino, paradero, meta.
destine ['destin] *vt* destinar, designar, predestinar.
destiny ['destini] *n* suerte, destino, sino, hado.
destitute ['destitju:t] *a* desamparado, desprovisto, necesitado, desvalido.
destitution [,desti'tju:ʃən] *n* desamparo, abandono, miseria.
destroy [dis'trɔi] *vt* destruir, romper; destrozar, arrasar, devastar; exterminar, extirpar; acabar con.
destroyed [dis'trɔid] *a* roto; desecho, destruido; minado, consumido.
destroyer [dis'trɔiə] *n* destructor; (*naut*) destróyer, destructor.
destruction [dis'trʌkʃən] *n* destrucción, demolición; desbarate, mortandad; estrago.
destructive [dis'trʌktiv] *a* destructor, ruinoso; (*animals*) dañino.
desultory ['desəltəri] *a* pasajero, mudable, inconstante, irregular, discontinuo.
detach [di'tætʃ] *vt* separar, desprender, despegar.
detachable [di'tætʃəbl] *a* de quita y pon, desmontable, separable.
detachment [di'tætʃmənt] *n* separación, desprendimiento; (*mil*) destacamento; objetividad.
detail ['di:teil] *n* detalle; punto, pormenor; **the smallest —** prolijidad, ápice; **excessive —** nimiedad; (*mil*) destacamento; *vt* detallar, especificar.
detailed [di:teild] *a* nimio.
detain [di'tein] *vt* detener, arrestar.
detect [di'tekt] *vt* descubrir, averiguar, echar de ver.
detection [di'tekʃən] *n* descubrimiento.
detective [di'tektiv] *n* policía, detective; *a* **— story** novela policíaca.

deter [di'tə:] *vt* desviar, disuadir, impedir; desanimar.
deteriorate [di'tiəriəreit] *vt* empeorar, deteriorar; *vi* empeorarse, deteriorarse.
deterioration [di,tiəriə'reiʃən] *n* deterioro, menoscabo, desperfecto.
determinate [di'tə:minit] *a* determinado, positivo, decidido, resuelto.
determination [di,tə:mi'neiʃən] *n* determinación, voluntad, resolución, empeño.
determine [di'tə:min] *vt* determinar, fijar, decidir, cerciorarse, señalar; *vi* resolver(se), determinarse, decidirse.
determined [di'tə:mind] *a* determinado, resuelto, decidido.
deterrent [di'terənt] *n* contrapeso.
detest [di'test] *vt* detestar, aborrecer, execrar, odiar.
detestable [di'testəbl] *a* detestable, aborrecible, odioso.
detestation [,di:tes'teiʃən] *n* horror, abominación.
dethrone [di:'θroun] *vt* destronar.
detonate ['detəneit] *vi* detonar, estallar.
detour ['di:tuə] *n* vuelta, desviación, rodeo.
detract [di'trækt] *vt* quitar; disminuir; denigrar, maldecir; *vi* menguar.
detraction [di'trækʃən] *n* detracción; calumnia.
detriment ['detrimənt] *n* detrimento, daño, perjuicio, menoscabo.
detrimental [,detri'mentl] *a* perjudicial, desventajoso, nocivo.
devastate ['devəsteit] *vt* devastar, asolar.
devastation [,devəs'teiʃən] *n* asolación, tala.
develop [di'veləp] *vt* desarrollar, explotar, fomentar, descubrir, echar; (*phot*) revelar; *vir* hacerse; desarrollarse.
development [di'veləpmənt] *n* desarrollo, evolución, fomento.
deviate ['di:vieit] *vi* desviarse, disentir, volver, variar.
deviation [,di:vi'eiʃən] *n* desviación, divergencia; desvío.
device [di'vais] *n* invención; expediente, recurso, ingenio, ardid; leyenda, lema, mote; dispositivo.
devil ['devl] *n* el diablo, demonio.
devilish ['devliʃ] *a* diabólico; endiablado.
devilry ['devlri] *n* diablura.
devious ['di:viəs] *a* extraviado, descarriado; tortuoso.
devise [di'vaiz] *vt* trazar, proyectar, idear, inventar.
devoid [di'vɔid] *a* libre, exento, vacío, privado.
devote [di'vout] *vt* dedicar, consagrar; *vr* entregarse, consagrarse.
devoted [di'voutid] *a* devoto; apasionado; rendido; consagrado, destinado; adicto, fiel; (*epist*) **your — servant** suyo afmo.
devotee [,devou'ti:] *n* devoto, beato; aficionado.
devotion [di'vouʃən] *n* devoción; fervor, celo, lealtad, consagración, afecto; *pl* rezo, preces.
devotional [di'vouʃənl] *a* piadoso, devoto.
devour [di'vauə] *vt* devorar, engullir, tragar, consumir.
devout [di'vaut] *a* devoto, fervoroso, piadoso; **— lady** beata.
devoutness [di'vautnis] *n* piedad, devoción.
dew [dju:] *n* rocío, relente.
dexterity [deks'teriti] *n* destreza, habilidad; acierto, tino.
dexterous ['dekstrəs] *a* diestro, hábil, ducho.
diabolic [,daiə'bɔlik] *a* diabólico.
diadem ['daiədem] *n* diadema; corona.
diagnose ['daiəgnouz] *vt* diagnosticar.
diagonal [dai'ægənl] *n* diagonal.
diagram ['daiəgræm] *n* mapa; dibujo, plan, esquema.
dial ['daiəl] *n* esfera; **sun—** reloj de sol, cuadrante; **to —** (*tel*) *vt* marcar, llamar, telefonear.
dialect ['daiəlekt] *n* dialecto, habla.
dialogue ['daiəlɔg] *n* diálogo; (*lit*) coloquio; **to speak in —** dialogar.
diameter [dai'æmitə] *n* diámetro.
diamond ['daiəmənd] *n* diamante.
diaphanous [dai'æfənəs] *a* transparente, diáfano, terso.
diary ['daiəri] *n* diario, memorándum; (*business*) dietario; libro de efemérides.
dice [dais] *n pl* dados; **—box** cubilete de dados.
dickens ['dikinz] *pr n* **who the —?** ¿qué diablo —?; **why the —?** ¿por qué diablos?
dictate ['dikteit] *n* precepto, dictado, máxima; [dik'teit] *vti* dictar, mandar.
dictation [dik'teiʃən] *n* dictado.
dictator [dik'teitə] *n* dictador.
dictatorship [dik'teitəʃip] *n* dictadura.
diction ['dikʃən] *n* estilo, lenguaje, dicción, expresión.
dictionary ['dikʃənri] *n* diccionario, léxico.
dictum ['diktəm] *n* dicho, aforismo.
didactic [dai'dæktik] *a* didáctico, preceptivo.
die [dai] *n* (*print*) cuño; matriz; *vi* morir, fallecer; **to — down** extinguirse; **to be dying to** tener muchas ganas de, anhelar; **the — is cast** la suerte está echada.
diehard ['daihɑ:d] *a* cerrado, hasta no más, acérrimo, por los cuatro costados.
diet ['daiət] *n* dieta, alimento, régimen.

differ ['difə] *vi* diferenciar, diferir, ser distinto, ser otro; (*of opinion*) no estar de acuerdo, no estar conforme, discrepar.
difference ['difrəns] *n* diferencia, desemejanza, disensión; **it makes no —** es igual, igual da.
different ['difrənt] *a* diferente, vario, diverso, distinto; **to be —** *vi* contrastar.
difficult ['difikəlt] *a* difícil, árduo; intratable; (*speech*) premioso; (*problem*) enrevesado, peliagudo; (*situation*) apurado, penoso.
difficulty ['difikəlti] *n* dificultad; obstáculo, inconveniente; apuro; (*speech*) premiosidad; **to get into difficulties** atollarse.
diffidence ['difidəns] *n* cortedad, vergüenza, modestia.
diffident ['difidənt] *a* tímido, apocado, huraño.
diffuse [di'fju:s] *a* difundido, difuso; prolijo; [di'fju:z] *vt* difundir, propagar; verter; propagar.
diffusion [di'fju:ʒən] *n* difusión, prolijidad; propagación, esparcimiento, diseminación.
dig [dig] *vt* cavar, ahondar, escarbar; **to — up** excavar; *vi* **to — deeper** profundizar.
digest ['daidʒəst] *n* recopilación; [dai'dʒest] *vt* digerir, rumiar; ordenar, clasificar; asimilar.
digestible [di'dʒestəbl] *a* digerible.
digestion [di'dʒestʃən] *n* digestión, asimilación.
digital computer ['didʒitlkəm'pjutə] *n* computador digital.
dignified ['dignifaid] *a* grave, serio, honorable.
dignify ['dignifai] *vt* dignificar, exaltar, honrar.
dignitary ['dignitəri] *n* dignatario, dignidad.
dignity ['digniti] *n* dignidad, mesura, nobleza; (*office*) cargo; (*rank*) rango.
digress [dai'gres] *vi* divagar.
digression [dai'greʃən] *n* digresión.
dike [daik] *n* dique, malecón, presa.
dilapidated [di'læpideitid] *a* en ruina, arrumbado, derruido.
dilapidation [di,læpi'deiʃən] *n* dilapidación.
dilate [dai'leit] *vt* dilatar, extender, amplificar; **to — upon** *vi* explayarse.
dilated [dai'leitid] *a* hinchado; dilatado.
dilatory ['dilətəri] *a* tardo, lento; pesado, dilatorio.
dilemma [dai'lemə] *n* dilema, apuro.
diligence [dilidʒəns] *n* industria, diligencia, aplicación; cuidado, solicitud.
diligent ['dilidʒənt] *a* diligente, aplicado, activo, hacendoso, laborioso, solícito, servicial.
dilute [dai'lu:t] *vt* diluir, aguar; enrarecer.
dim [dim] *a* obscuro, opaco, tenue; confuso; empañado; pobre; (*memories*) vago; *vt* obscurecer; empañar.
dime [daim] *n* 10 centavos de dólar.
dimension [di'menʃən] *n* medida; **—s** tamaño.
diminish [di'miniʃ] *vt* amenguar, achicar, disminuir, mermar, rebajar, *vi* declinar, disminuirse.
diminution [,dimi'nju:ʃən] *n* rebaja, merma.
diminutive [di'minjutiv] *a* diminuto, pequeño, diminutivo; **— amount** poquísimo.
diminutiveness [di'minjutivnis] *n* pequeñez.
dimness ['dimnis] *n* ofuscamiento, deslustre; obscuridad.
dimple ['dimpl] *n* hoyuelo; *vti* formar hoyuelos; (*sea*) ondear.
din [din] *n* ruido, estrépito; baraúnda; *vt* clamorear, asordar; **to make a —** *vi* meter bulla; **to — it in** machacarlo.
dine [dain] *vi* comer, cenar.
dinginess ['dindʒinis] *n* obscuridad, suciedad; deslustre.
dingy ['dindʒi] *a* empañado, sucio; deslustrado; borroso, obscuro.
dining car ['dainiŋka:] *n* coche comedor.
dining room ['dainiŋrum] *n* comedor.
dinner ['dinə] *n* comida, cena; banquete; **after —** (*conversations etc*) (*charlas*) de sobremesa; **— jacket** smoking; **— wagon** carrito de comedor.
dint [dint] *n* mella, abolladura; **by — of** a fuerza de; *vt* mellar.
diocese ['daiəsis] *n* diócesis.
dioxide [dai'ɔksaid] *n* bióxido.
dip [dip] *n* (*in sea*) inmersión, baño; (*candle*) bujía; (*in ground*) inclinación, hoyo; *vt* mojar, bañar, chapuzar, sumergir; (*food, into sauce etc*) mojar; (*flag*) saludar; (*into book*) hojear; *vi* bajar; inclinarse.
diploma [di'ploumə] *n* diploma, título.
diplomacy [di'plouməsi] *n* diplomacia, cautela; tacto.
diplomatic [,diplə'mætik] *a* diplomático.
diplomatist [di'ploumətist] *n* diplomático.
dire ['daiə] *a* espantoso, horrible, cruel, funesto.
direct [dai'rekt] *a* directo, derecho; (*road*) seguido; (*answer*) claro, franco; *ad* derecho, sin vacilar; *vt* dirigir, apuntar; encaminar; regir, sugestionar; encargar; orientar; (*into channel*) encauzar.
direction [di'rekʃən] *n* curso, rumbo; (*order*) dirección; gobierno, mandato; (*guidance*) indicación; señas; (*flow, tendency*) sesgo; sentido; **from this —** de este lado; **a common —** convergencia; *pl* instrucciones.

directly [di'rektli] *ad* directamente, inmediatamente, en seguida.
directness [dai'rektnis] *n* llaneza, franqueza; derechura.
director [di'rektə] *n* director, administrador; **board of —s** consejo de administración.
directory [di'rektəri] *n* guía (de forasteros, de teléfonos).
dirge [də:dʒ] *n* canto fúnebre; endecha, plegaria.
dirt [də:t] *n* (*filth*) cieno, lodo; mugre; (*earth*) barro; miseria, porquería; (*rubbish*) basura; — **cheap** *a* regalado, tirado; — **road** camino de barro.
dirtiness ['də:tinis] *n* suciedad; desaseo; cochinería, inmundicia; vileza.
dirty ['də:ti] *a* sucio, inmundo, asqueroso, indecente; — **joke, remark** porquería; — **trick** cochinada; *vt* ensuciar, enlodar, manosear.
disability [.disə'biliti] *n* inhabilitación, incapacidad.
disable [dis'eibl] *vt* imposibilitar, incapacitar, inutilizar; indisponer.
disabled [dis'eibld] *a* incapacitado, baldado, mutilado.
disadvantage [.disəd'vɑ:ntidʒ] *n* desventaja; detrimento, menoscabo.
disagree [.disə'gri:] *vi* discrepar, no estar de acuerdo; diferir, disentir; (*of food*) sentar(le) mal (a uno).
disagreeable [.disə'gri:əbl] *a* desagradable, repugnante; ingrato, antipático.
disagreement [.disə'gri:mənt] *n* desacuerdo, discordia, discordancia, discrepancia.
disappear [.disə'piə] *vi* desaparecer.
disappearance [.disə'piərəns] *n* desaparición.
disappoint [.disə'pɔint] *vt* chasquear; frustrar; desilusionar, decepcionar.
disappointing [.disə'pɔintiŋ] *a* desengañador, pobre, triste, decepcionante.
disappointment [.disə'pɔintmənt] *n* desilusión, desengaño, decepción.
disarm [dis'ɑ:m] *vt* desarmar.
disarray ['disə'rei] *n* desarreglo, desorden; desaliño.
disaster [di'zɑ:stə] *n* desastre, siniestro; catástrofe, calamidad; (*unforseen*) azar.
disastrous [di'zɑ:strəs] *a* desastroso, funesto; fulminante, calamitoso.
disavow ['disə'vau] *vt* repudiar, desautorizar, retractar.
disband [dis'bænd] *vt* licenciar, despedir; *vi* desbandarse.
disbelief ['disbə'li:f] *n* incredulidad, escepticismo.
disbelieve ['disbə'li:v] *vt* no creer, no dar fe (en); *vi* ser escéptico.
disbelieving ['disbə'li:viŋ] *a* incrédulo.
disc [disk] *n* disco; plato, tejo; (*identity*) placa.
discard [dis'kɑ:d] *vt* despedir, renunciar; descartar, desechar.
discern [di'sə:n] *vt* percibir, columbrar, discernir, distinguir, entrever.
discernible [di'sə:nəbl] *a* discernible, perceptible, sensible.
discerning [di'sə:niŋ] *a* sagaz, entendido, perspicaz.
discernment [di'sə:nmənt] *n* discernimiento, penetración; caletre.
discharge [dis'tʃɑ:dʒ] *vt* descargar; relevar, absolver, (*mil*) licenciar; (*from hospital*) dar de alta; separar; (*from job*) despedir, desacomodar; (*duty*) cumplir, desempeñar, actuar de; (*wound*) despedir; *a* — **certificate** alta; **—ed civil servant** cesante; *n* (*gun*) descarga; quita; (*water*) desagüe; (*army*) licencia absoluta; (*from job*) despido, despedida, (*of wound*) derrame; (*duty*) desempeño.
disciple [di'saipl] *n* discípulo, alumno, apóstol.
discipline ['disiplin] *n* disciplina, enseñanza; orden, castigo; *vt* disciplinar, educar, corregir.
disclaim [dis'kleim] *vt* rechazar, negar, desconocer, repudiar, recusar.
disclose [dis'klouz] *vt* descubrir, desabrochar, revelar, exponer, propalar, publicar.
disclosure [dis'klouʒə] *n* descubrimiento, revelación, publicación.
discomfort [dis'kʌmfət] *n* incomodidad; malestar; *vt* incomodar, molestar.
disconcert [.diskən'sə:t] *vt* desconcertar, confundir, descomponer.
disconcerted [.diskən'sə:tid] *a* **to be —** alterarse.
disconnect ['diskə'nekt] *vt* desconectar; desunir, disociar.
disconsolate [dis'kɔnsəlit] *a* desconsolado, inconsolable, cabizbajo.
discontent ['diskən'tent] *vt* descontentar, desagradar; *n* descontento, desagrado; disgusto, malestar.
discontented ['diskən'tentid] *a* descontento, descontentadizo; malcontento.
discontentedness ['diskən'tentidnis] *n* descontento.
discontinue ['diskən'tinju:] *vt* interrumpir, cesar, suspender.
discord ['diskɔ:d] *n* discordia, rencilla, disensión; desacuerdo; **to sow —** sembrar la discordia.
discordant [dis'kɔ:dənt] *a* incóngruo, discordante; — **sound** cacofonía.
discothèque ['diskoutek] *n* discoteca, sala de baile.
discount ['diskaunt] *n* descuento, rebaja; *vt* [dis'kaunt] descontar, rebajar; (*story etc*) desconfiar de.
discourage [dis'kʌridʒ] *vt* desanimar, disuadir.
discouragement [dis'kʌridʒmənt] *n* desánimo, desaliento, desmayo.
discourse ['diskɔ:s] *n* discurso,

plática; (*pompous*) declamación; raciocinio; [dis'kɔ:s] *vti* discurrir, hablar, pronunciar, razonar.
discourteous [dis'kə:tiəs] *a* descortés, grosero; poco fino.
discourtesy [dis'kə:tisi] *n* descortesía, grosería, falta de atención.
discover [dis'kʌvə] *vt* descubrir, hallar, revelar.
discoverer [dis'kʌvərə] *n* descubridor, explorador, conquistador.
discovery [dis'kʌvəri] *n* descubrimiento, hallazgo, revelación; (*of truth*) averiguación.
discredit [dis'kredit] *n* descrédito; mengua, deshonra; *vt* dudar, desacreditar, difamar.
discreditable [dis'kreditəbl] *a* vergonzoso, ignominioso.
discreet [dis'kri:t] *a* discreto, circunspecto; sano, sesudo.
discrepancy [dis'krepənsi] *n* discrepancia, desajuste; desacuerdo.
discretion [dis'kreʃən] *n* discreción, prudencia, reserva, circunspección; **at the — of** a merced de.
discriminate [dis'krimineit] *vt* diferenciar, distinguir, discriminar.
discriminating [dis'krimineitiŋ] *a* fino, penetrante, distintivo, diferencial.
discrimination [dis,krimi'neiʃən] *n* discernimiento, distinción; discriminación.
discursive [dis'kə:siv] *a* razonador; amplio, difuso.
discuss [dis'kʌs] *vt* discutir, ventilar, debatir; versar (sobre).
discussion [dis'kʌʃən] *n* discusión; argumento, consultorio.
disdain [dis'dein] *n* desdén, menosprecio; desprecio; altivez; *vt* desdeñar, despreciar.
disdainful [dis'deinful] *a* desdeñoso, altanero, despreciativo.
disease [di'zi:z] *n* enfermedad; mal, achaque.
diseased [di'zi:zd] *a* enfermo; mórbido.
disembark ['disim'bɑ:k] *vt* desembarcar.
disembarkation [,disembɑ:'keiʃən] *n* desembarco.
disengage ['disin'geidʒ] *vt* desunir, desenganchar; *vi* soltarse, librarse, romper el contacto con.
disengaged ['disin'geidʒd] *a* desocupado, suelto.
disentangle ['disin'tæŋgl] *vt* desenredar, desligar.
disfavor [dis'feivə] *n* disfavor, desaprobación.
disfigure [dis'figə] *vt* desfigurar, afear.
disgrace [dis'greis] *n* ignominia, desvergüenza, afrenta; oprobio; baldón, mancha; *vt* deshonrar, envilecer.
disgraceful [dis'greisful] *a* vergonzoso, ignominioso, indigno.
disgruntled [dis'grʌntld] *a* malhumorado.
disguise [dis'gaiz] *n* máscara, disfraz; (*theat*) embozo; *vt* disfrazar, tapar, enmascarar; disimular.
disgust [dis'gʌst] *n* sinsabor, disgusto, hastío; aversión, desgana; *vt* repugnar, enfadar, hastiar.
disgusted [dis'gʌstid] *a* asqueado, disgustado, furioso.
disgusting [dis'gʌstiŋ] *a* repugnante, asqueroso, ofensivo.
dish [diʃ] *n* plato, fuente; (*portion*) consumición; (*cold*) fiambre; **—cloth** estropajo; **— water** agua de lavar los platos; **fruit —** compotera; **—es** vajilla; *vt* servir.
disharmony ['dis'hɑ:məni] *n* discordancia, desarmonía.
dishearten [dis'hɑ:tn] *vt* desanimar, descorazonar, abatir.
disheartening [dis'hɑ:tniŋ] *a* descorazonante.
disheveled [di'ʃevld] *a* greñudo, desmelenado.
dishonest [dis'ɔnist] *a* fraudulento, engañoso, falso, malo.
dishonesty [dis'ɔnisti] *n* engaño, falsedad, dolo, fraude.
dishonor [dis'ɔnə] *n* deshonor; ignominia; mancha; *vt* deshonrar, afrentar, profanar.
dishonorable [dis'ɔnərəbl] *a* malo, engañoso; malvado; deshonroso; que deshonra.
dishpan ['diʃpæn] *n* vasija, jofaina para lavar los platos.
disillusion [,disi'lu:ʒən] *n* desengaño; *vt* desengañar.
disinclination [,disinkli'neiʃən] *n* aversión; desgana, desamor.
disincline [,disin'klain] *vt* malquistar, indisponer; **to be disinclined to** estar poco dispuesto a.
disinfect [,disin'fekt] *vt* desinfectar, descontagiar.
disinherit ['disin'herit] *vt* desheredar.
disintegrate [dis'intigreit] *vt* disgregar, despedazar; *vi* desmoronarse.
disintegration [dis,inti'greiʃən] *n* disolución, pulverización.
disinterested [dis'intristid] *a* desinteresado; imparcial.
disinterestedness [dis'intristidnis] *n* desinterés; garbo; imparcialidad; desapego.
disjoint [dis'dʒɔint] *vt* desarticular, descoyuntar, dislocar.
disk [disk] *n see* **disc.**
dislike [dis'laik] *n* aversión, antipatía, repugnancia; *vt* no gustar de; **I — him** no me gusta; me es antipático; me repugna.
disliked [dis'laikt] *a* malquisto.
dislocate ['disləkeit] *vt* dislocar, descoyuntar.
dislodge [dis'lɔdʒ] *vt* desalojar; quitar, descolgar, desanidar.
disloyal ['dis'lɔiəl] *a* desleal, infiel, pérfido, alevoso.

disloyalty ['dis'lɔiəlti] *n* deslealtad, traición, perfidia.
dismal ['dizməl] *a* triste, lúgubre, lóbrego.
dismantle [dis'mæntl] *vt* desmantelar, desguarnecer; (*mech*) desmontar.
dismay [dis'mei] *n* espanto, desaliento, pavor, consternación, congoja; *vt* aterrar, desanimar, aplanar, espantar; **to be filled with —** estar apurado; desesperarse.
dismiss [dis'mis] *vt* despedir, remover, deponer, destituir, echar, despachar; licenciar.
dismissal [dis'misəl] *n* destitución, deposición, separación; (*from job*) despedida.
dismissed [dis'mist] *a* echado, despedido.
dismount [dis'maunt] *vi* apearse, bajar; *vt* desmantelar, desmontar; desarmar.
disobedient [,disə'bi:diənt] *a* desobediente, rebelde, insumiso, desmandado.
disobey ['disə'bei] *vt* desobedecer; no cumplir.
disorder [dis'ɔ:də] *n* desorden, descompostura, desarreglo, trastorno, barullo, confusión; (*illness*) indisposición, destemplanza; **in —** (en) (de) tropel; (*mental*) enajenación, enfermedad.
disorderly [dis'ɔ:dəli] *a* desordenado, desaforado, turbulento, escandaloso.
disorganization [dis,ɔ:gənai'zeiʃən] *n* desorganización, confusión.
disorganize [dis'ɔ:gənaiz] *vt* desorganizar.
disown [dis'oun] *vt* repudiar; (re)-negar, renunciar.
disparage [dis'pæridʒ] *vt* rebajar, menospreciar, desacreditar.
disparagement [dis'pæridʒmənt] *n* detracción, menosprecio, postergación.
disparity [dis'pæriti] *n* desigualdad, desemejanza.
dispassionate [dis'pæʃnit] *a* imparcial.
dispatch [dis'pætʃ] *n* prisa, prontitud; pliego, billete, mensaje; *vt* consignar, expedir, mandar; despachar; acabar con.
dispel [dis'pel] *vt* disipar; dispersar.
dispensary [dis'pensəri] *n* dispensario, clínica.
dispensation [,dispen'seiʃən] *n* dispensa; exención.
dispense [dis'pens] *vt* distribuir, repartir, administrar; **to — with** hacer caso omiso de, prescindir de.
dispersal [dis'pə:səl] *n* dispersión, esparcimiento, difusión.
disperse [dis'pə:s] *vt* desparramar, disgregar; *vi* dispersar; disipar(se).
dispirit [dis'pirit] *vt* desanimar, oprimir.
dispiritedness [dis'piritidnis] *n* desánimo.
displace [dis'pleis] *vt* desalojar; remover, quitar; desplazar.
displacement [dis'pleismənt] *n* desalojamiento, remoción; (*ship*) desplazamiento; coladura; (*geol*) quiebra, falla.
display [dis'plei] *n* ostentación; fausto; exposición, exhibición; (*extravagant*) derroche; *a* **— case** vitrina; **— window** escaparate; *vt* lucir, ostentar, exhibir, presentar; (*proudly*) hacer alarde de, hacer gala de.
displease [dis'pli:z] *vt* desagradar, ofender, enojar, disgustar; **to be displeasing** desagradar, no gustar.
displeased [dis'pli:zd] *a* desagradado, molesto; **she is — with it** no le gusta nada.
displeasure [dis'pleʒə] *n* disgusto, pena, desagrado, sinsabor.
disport [dis'pɔ:t] *vr* divertirse, explayarse, recrearse.
disposal [dis'pouzəl] *n* disposición, arreglo; distribución, reparto; venta; **I am at your —** estoy a su disposición.
dispose [dis'pouz] *vt* distribuir, disponer; dirigir, colocar, arreglar; **to — of** desprenderse de; vender, enajenar.
disposed [dis'pouzd] *a* **to be well — toward** simpatizar con; **to be — to** inclinarse a.
disposition [,dispə'ziʃən] *n* disposición, método, arreglo, fondo; carácter, índole, naturaleza, genio; tendencia.
dispossess ['dispə'zes] *vt* desposeer, privar (*de*); (*of house etc*) desahuciar.
disproportionate [,disprə'pɔ:ʃnit] *a* desigual, desmesurado.
disproportionately [,disprə'pɔ:ʃnitli] *ad* sobremanera; desmesuradamente.
disprove [dis'pru:v] *vt* refutar.
disputable [dis'pju:təbl] *a* contencioso, controvertible.
dispute [dis'pju:t] *n* pleito, litigio: riña, querella; disputa, contienda; debate; *vt* disputar; argumentar, discutir; litigiar; pelear.
disqualified [dis'kwɔlifaid] *a* inhábil, incapacitado.
disqualify [dis'kwɔlifai] *vt* inhabilitar, incapacitar; (*games*) descalificar.
disquiet [dis'kwaiət] *n* inquietud, malestar; *vt* (per)turbar, malestar, ocupar.
disregard ['disri'gɑ:d] *n* desprecio; desatención, desaire; **with complete — (for)** sin poner la menor atención (a); *vt* desatender, descuidar; prescindir de; omitir.
disrepair ['disri'pɛə] *n* **in —** en malas condiciones; sin remendar.
disreputable [dis'repjutəbl] *a* despreciable, mal reputado, infame.

disrepute ['disri'pju:t] *n* descrédito, ignominia; **in —** mal considerado.
disrespect ['disris'pekt] *n* incivilidad, falta de atención, falta de respeto; *vt* desairar.
disrespectful [,disris'pektful] *a* irreverente, poco atento, descortés, irrespetuoso.
disrupt [dis'rʌpt] *vt* quebrantar, romper, hacer pedadazos; partir, separar.
dissatisfaction ['dis,sætis'fækʃən] *n* descontento; (*audible*) murmuración.
dissatisfy ['dis'sætisfai] *vt* desagradar, descontentar, no satisfacer.
dissect [di'sekt] *vt* anatomizar; disecar, analizar; **—ing knife** escalpelo.
dissemble [di'sembl] *vti* disimular, fingir; *vi* ser hipócrita.
dissembler [di'semblə] *n* hipócrita, embustero.
disseminate [di'semineit] *vt* diseminar, propagar, sembrar, propalar.
dissension [di'senʃən] *n* disensión; discordia; oposición.
dissent [di'sent] *n* disentimiento; *vi* disentir, diferir, no estar conforme.
dissertation [,disə'teiʃən] *n* tesis, memoria; discurso.
disservice ['dis'sə:vis] *n* **to do a — (to)** perjudicar.
dissimilar ['di'similə] *a* diferente, desigual, distinto.
dissimilarity [,disimi'læriti] *n* desemejanza, disparidad, diferencia.
dissimulation [di,simju'leiʃən] *n* disimulo.
dissipate ['disipeit] *vt* disipar, desperdiciar, desparramar; (*fortune*) malgastar; esparcirse, evaporarse, desaparecer.
dissipated ['disipeitid] *a* disoluto, pródigo; perdido; crapuloso, libertino.
dissipation [,disi'peiʃən] *n* evaporación; (*life*) vida relajada, libertinaje.
dissolute ['disəlu:t] *a* disoluto, crapuloso, licencioso, libertino.
dissoluteness ['disəlu:tnis] *n* relajación, liviandad, crápula.
dissolution [,disə'lu:ʃən] *n* disolución; descomposición; muerte.
dissolve [di'zɔlv] *vt* deshacer, derretir, disolver; (*marriage etc*) anular, abrogar; *vi* disolverse, derretirse, evaporarse, deshacerse; **to — into tears** deshacerse en lágrimas.
dissuade [di'sweid] *vt* disuadir, desaconsejar, retraer, apartar.
distaff ['distɑ:f] *n* rueca.
distance ['distəns] *n* distancia, lejanía; **in the —** a lo lejos, en la lontananza; **from a —** de lejos; **to keep one's —** mantenerse a distancia; **what's the — from A to B?** ¿cuánto hay de A a B?; **the — between** intervalo, espacio.
distant ['distənt] *a* distante, lejano, apartado; (*character*) huraño, esquivo, frío; (*relative*) lejano.
distaste ['dis'teist] *n* aversión, tedio, disgusto.
distasteful [dis'teistful] *a* desagradable, poco grato, ingrato, enfadoso, malsonante.
distemper [dis'tempə] *n* enfermedad; mal humor; (*painting*) templa, temple; *vt* pintar al temple; destemplar.
distill [dis'til] *vt* destilar, alambicar; *vi* gotear, destilar.
distillation [,disti'leiʃən] *n* destilación, gasificación.
distillery [dis'tiləri] *n* destilería, destilatorio.
distinct [dis'tiŋkt] *a* distinto, diferente; (*voice etc*) preciso, claro; (*tendency etc*) fuerte; **a — advantage** una gran ventaja.
distinction [dis'tiŋkʃən] *n* distinción, honor, fama, brillo; discernimiento; (*in examination*) sobresaliente.
distinctive [dis'tiŋktiv] *a* característico, distintivo.
distinctness [dis'tiŋktnis] *n* claridad, nitidez.
distinguish [dis'tiŋgwiʃ] *vt* discernir, percibir, distinguir; señalar, clasificar; honrar; *vi* caracterizar; *vr* singularizarse.
distinguished [dis'tiŋgwiʃt] *a* eminente, preclaro, ilustre, honorable; **very —** preeminente, eximio; **— personage** eminencia; **— citizen** prócer.
distort [dis'tɔ:t] *vt* torcer, desfigurar, tergiversar, deformar.
distortion [dis'tɔ:ʃən] *n* contorsión, tergiversación, desviamiento.
distract [dis'trækt] *vt* distraer, enloquecer, confundir.
distracted [dis'træktid] *a* distraído, demente, apurado, frenético.
distraction [dis'trækʃən] *n* distracción, perturbación; alboroto; locura, extravío, diversión, recreo; **to —** con locura.
distraught [dis'trɔ:t] *a* frenético, demente, loco, desesperado.
distress [dis'tres] *n* miseria; zozobra, apuro, pena, angustia; **in —** (*ship*) en peligro; (*person*) desamparado; *vt* afligir, desolar, poner en un aprieto, angustiar, acongojar.
distressing [dis'tresiŋ] *a* aflictivo, congojoso; lastimoso, que da pena.
distribute [dis'tribju:t] *vt* distribuir, repartir, suministrar.
distribution [,distri'bju:ʃən] *n* distribución, repartición, suministro.
district ['distrikt] *n* distrito, cantón, región, término, comarca, territorio; (*of town*) barrio.
distrust [dis'trʌst] *n* desconfianza, recelo; *vt* desconfiar, sospechar.
distrustful [dis'trʌstful] *a* desconfiado, receloso; (*fam*) escamado.

disturb [dis'tə:b] *vt* perturbar, estorbar, revolver, incomodar, alterar, excitar, interrumpir.
disturbance [dis'tə:bəns] *n* disturbio, tumulto, barullo, alboroto; (*of mind*) confusión, trastorno.
disunite ['disju'nait] *vt* enajenar, disolver, desunir; *vi* separarse.
disuse ['dis'ju:s] *n* desuso; **to fall into —** caducar; pasar de moda.
ditch [ditʃ] *n* zanja, foso; (*irrigation*) acequia; (*roadside*) cuneta.
divan [di'væn] *n* diván, sofá, otomana; cama turca; sala de consejo.
dive [daiv] *n* buceo; (*sl*) garito, tasca; *a* **— bombing** bombardeo en picado; *vi* zabullirse, bucear.
diver ['daivə] *n* buzo.
diverge [dai'və:dʒ] *vi* divergir, desviarse.
divergence [dai'və:dʒəns] *n* divergencia.
divers ['daivə:z] *a* varios, diversos, distintos, unos cuantos.
diverse [dai'və:s] *a* diferente, diverso, multiforme.
diversify [dai'və:sifai] *vt* variar, cambiar.
diversion [dai'və:ʃən] *n* diversión, holganza, entretenimiento, cambio, ocio; deporte; (*of traffic*) desviación.
diversity [dai'və:siti] *n* diversidad, variedad, diferencia.
divert [dai'və:t] *vt* desviar, apartar, divertir; (*mind etc*) distraer, entretener.
divest [dai'vest] *vt* despojar, desnudar.
divide [di'vaid] *vti* dividir, compartir; deslindar; separarse; (*equally*) comediar; (*share*) repartir.
dividend ['dividend] *n* dividendo.
divine [di'vain] *a* divino, sublime; *n* teólogo; *vt* adivinar, vaticinar.
diviner [di'vainə] *n* agorero, vate.
diving ['daiviŋ] *n* buceo.
divinity [di'viniti] *n* divinidad; (*study*) teología.
division [di'viʒən] *n* división, (re)partición, distribución; (*section*) ramo; (*between rooms*) tabique; (*opinion, vote*) votación, escisión; (*mil*) división.
divorce [di'vɔ:s] *n* divorcio, separación, repudio; *vt* divorciar.
divulge [dai'vʌldʒ] *vt* divulgar, propalar, publicar; (*fam*) cantar.
dizziness ['dizinis] *n* aturdimiento, desvanecimiento, vértigo, mareo.
dizzy ['dizi] *a* mareado, desvanecido; **to make —** marear.
do [du:] *vti* hacer, obrar, ejecutar, practicar, despachar; (*duty*) cumplir con; (*for first time*) estrenar; **to — well** lucir; **to have to — with** habérselas con, tener que ver con; **to — away with** suprimir; **to — with** componérselas; **to — without** prescindir de, pasar sin; **to say how — you — to** saludar a; **how — you —?** ¿cómo está Vd?; **that will —** eso sirve, eso basta; **that won't —** eso no sirve, no cuenta, no conviene; **now I've done it** metí la pata; **well done!** bien!; **well done** (*food*) bien asado; *n* (*sl*) cuchipanda.
docile ['dousail] *a* dócil, sumiso.
docility [dou'siliti] *n* docilidad, obediencia.
dock [dɔk] *n* dársena, dique; (*in court*) banquillo; **dry —** astillero, dique seco; *vt* cortar, reducir, cercenar; poner en dique.
doctor ['dɔktə] *n* doctor, médico, facultativo; *vt* recetar; curar.
doctrine ['dɔktrin] *n* doctrina.
document ['dɔkjumənt] *n* documento, expediente; **the present —** el presente.
doddering ['dɔdəriŋ] *a* chocho, decrépito.
dodge [dɔdʒ] *n* evasiva; (*fam*) truco; *vt* evadir; regatear; *vi* tergiversar; **to — the consequences** escurrir el bulto; **to be dodging about** andar a saltos.
doe [dou] *n* gama, corza.
doer ['du:ə] *n* hacedor, agente.
doeskin ['douskin] *n* ante.
dog [dɔg] *n* perro; **good —!** ¡cuz, cuz!; **— star** sirio, can, canícula; **— days** canícula; **— Latin** latín macarrónico; **— watch** guardia de cuartillo; **— in the manger** perro del hortelano; **— rose** rosa silvestre, zarzarrosa; **—-eared** (*of book*) sobado, muy usado; **gay —** calavera; **gay old —** viejo verde; **lazy —** pasante, zángano; **every — has his day** a cada puerco su San Martín; *vt* seguir, perseguir.
dogged ['dɔgid] *a* terco, tenaz; **—ly** *ad* con tenacidad.
doggedness ['dɔgidnis] *n* tenacidad.
doggerel ['dɔgərəl] *n* coplas de ciego, versos de almanaque.
dogma ['dɔgmə] *n* dogma, axioma.
dogmatic [dɔg'mætik] *a* dogmático.
doing ['du:iŋ] *participle* **to be up and —** ser activo; **—s** *n pl* hechos, actividades, acciones; aventuras.
doleful ['doulful] *a* lastimero, triste, adusto, lúgubre.
doll [dɔl] *n* muñeca; *vt* **to — up** ataviar, endomingar.
dollar ['dɔlə] *n* dólar.
dolorous ['dɔlərəs] *a* lamentable, doloroso, plañidero.
dolphin ['dɔlfin] *n* delfín.
dolt [doult] *n* bobo, burro, camueso, imbécil, mentecato, zopenco.
domain [də'mein] *n* dominio, imperio, territorio, señorío, heredad, finca.
dome [doum] *n* cúpula, cimborrio.
domestic [də'mestik] *a* doméstico, casero; (*animals*) manso, del corral; (*strife etc*) intestino, nacional; *n* criado.

domesticate [də'mestikeit] *vt* amansar, desembravecer.
domicile ['dɔmisail] *n* domicilio.
domiciled ['dɔmisaild] *a* residente.
dominate ['dɔmineit] *vt* mandar, dominar.
domineer [ˌdɔmi'niə] *vi* dominar, señorear.
domineering [ˌdɔmi'niəriŋ] *a* mandón.
Dominican [də'minikən] *an* dominicano.
dominion [də'minjən] *n* poder, autoridad, imperio, potestad, dominio, señorío, soberanía.
domino ['dɔminou] *n* dominó; disfraz, máscara; **to play—es** jugar |al dominó.
don [dɔn] *n* caballero, hidalgo español; profesor, académico, catedrático; *vt* vestirse, ponerse.
donate [dou'neit] *vt* dar, contribuir.
donation [dou'neiʃən] *n* donación, dádiva.
donkey ['dɔŋki] *n* asno, burro, borrico, rucio; **— ride** borricada.
donor ['dounə] *n* donador.
doom [du:m] *n* condena, juicio; suerte, hado, sino; ruina; **the crack of —** el juicio final.
doomed ['du:md] *a* condenado.
doomsday ['du:mzdei] *n* día del juicio.
door [dɔ:] *n* puerta, entrada; (*carriage*) portezuela; (*main*) puerta cochera; (*on stage*) puerta practicable; **trap —** trampa; **—handle (knob)** picaporte, aldaba; **back —** puerta trasera; **to lay at someone's —** echar la culpa a; **behind —s** a puerta cerrada; **to be at death's —** estar a dos dedos de la muerte.
doorman ['dɔ:mæn] *n* portero, conserje.
dormant ['dɔ:mənt] *a* durmiente, inactivo, latente.
doorway ['dɔ:wei] *n* portal.
dormitory ['dɔ:mitri] *n* dormitorio.
dose [dous] *n* porción, dosis; trago; *vt* dosificar; administrar una dosis.
dossier ['dɔsiei] *n* expediente, documentación, legajo.
dot [dɔt] *n* punto; **on the —** en punto; *vt* puntear.
dotage ['doutidʒ] *n* chochera, chochez; **to be in one's —** chochear, ser chocho.
dote [dout] *vi* chochear; **to — upon** estar loco por.
double ['dʌbl] *n* doble; (*theat*) contrafigura; *a* doble, falso; duplicado; **— bass** violón; **— check** contramarca; **— intent** sorna; **— meaning** segunda intención; **at the —** al trote; **— dealing** doblez, fraude; **— -faced** hipócrita; *vti* duplicar, doblar.
doubt [daut] *n* duda; reparo, incertidumbre, escepticismo; **no —** no cabe duda; **without —** sin duda alguna; *vt* dudar, desconfiar; temer.
doubtful ['dautful] *a* dudoso, problemático; incierto, caviloso; ambiguo.
doubtless ['dautlis] *a* indudable; *ad* probablemente; sin duda.
dough [dou] *n* masa, pasta, amasijo; (*sl*) dinero, pasta.
dove [dʌv] *n* paloma; **—cot(e)** palomar.
down [daun] *n* plumón, pelo, vello; (*on lips*) bozo; *n pl* **ups and —s** vaivenes, altibajos; *prep* & *ad* abajo, hacia abajo; **—stream** río abajo; *a* pendiente, descendente; **to come — in the world** venir a menos; **(to be) — in the mouth** (estar) cariacontecido; *vt* derribar, echar por tierra; **to — tools** declararse en huelga.
downcast ['daunkɑ:st] *a* deprimido, alicaído.
downfall ['daunfɔ:l] *n* caída, ruina, hundimiento.
downhearted ['daun'hɑ:tid] *n* alicaído, abatido, desanimado.
downhill ['daun'hil] *ad* cuesta abajo; *n* pendiente, declive.
downpour ['daunpɔ:] *n* aguacero, lluvia torrencial.
downright ['daunrait] *a* categórico; llano; extremo; *ad* absolutamente.
downstairs ['daun'stɛəz] *ad* abajo.
downward ['daunwəd] *a* inclinado, pendiente; **—s** *ad* hacia abajo; **face —** boca abajo, de bruces.
dowry ['dauri] *n* dote, arras.
doze [douz] *vi* dormitar.
dozen [dʌzn] *n* docena; **to talk twenty to the —** hablar más que siete; **baker's —** docena de fraile.
drab [dræb] *a* pardusco; gris; monótono; *n* burra; ramera.
draft [drɑ:ft] *n* expediente; plano, dibujo, delineación; (*rough*) borrador; (*recruitment*) quinta; (*finance*); giro, libranza; corriente (*de aire*); tiro (*de chimenea*); trazo, boceto; (*ship*) calado; (*liquid*) trago, sorbo, pócima; brebaje; tracción; **—horse** caballo de tiro; *vt* trazar, diseñar; destacar, expedir.
draftsman ['drɑ:ftsmən] *n* dibujante.
drag [dræg] *n* draga; traba, obstáculo; *vt* (*rivers etc*) dragar; arrastrar; *vi* arrastrarse, rastrearse; **to — into** (*conversation*) sacar a colación; **to — behind** ir a la zaga.
dragon ['drægən] *n* dragón.
dragonfly ['drægənflai] *n* libélula.
dragoon [drə'gu:n] *n* dragón; *vt* intimidar.
drain [drein] *n* desagüe, albañal; (*gutter*) alcantarilla; (*channel*) zanja; *vt* desaguar; apurar, desecar, escurrir; (*land*) avenar; **to — (grief) to dregs** apurar el cáliz del dolor; **to — off** agotar, chorrear, desangrar.
drainage ['dreinidʒ] *n* desagüe, desecación; saneamiento; (*water*)

derivación; sistema de desaguaderos; desecamiento.
drake [dreik] *n* pato; **to play ducks and —s** hacer cabrillas.
drama ['drɑ:mə] *n* drama; **Spanish —** el teatro español.
dramatist ['dræmətist] *n* dramaturgo.
dramatize [ˌdræmɑtaiz] *vt* [dramatizar.
drape [dreip] *vt* tapizar, vestir, colgar; *n pl* cortinas, colgaduras.
draper ['dreipə] *n* pañero; **—'s** pañería.
drapery ['dreipəri] *n* pañería.
drastic ['dræstik] *a* severo, duro, enérgico.
draw [drɔ:] *n* tirada; (*lottery*) sorteo; (*games*) empate; *vt* tirar; atraer; dibujar; (*outline*) perfilar; (*sword*) desenvainar; (*game*) empatar; (*money*) cobrar; librar, girar; (*curtain*) descorrer; (*bow*) tender; (*fowl*) destripar; **to — along** arrastrar; **to — out** sacar; **to — up** (*terms etc*) levantar, extender, formalizar; **to — off** substraer; **to — out** (*person*) sonsacar; **to — together** (*sew*) zurcir; **to — a veil over** correr el velo sobre; (*lots*) echar (*suertes*); (*bills*) librar; *vi* (*of fire*) tirar; (*games*) empatar; **to — back** retirarse; **to — up to** arrimar(se) a; **to — near** acercarse a.
drawback ['drɔ:bæk] *n* desventaja, inconveniente.
drawbridge ['drɔ:bridʒ] *n* puente levadizo.
drawer ['drɔ:ə] *n* (*com*) girador, tirador; (*furniture*) gaveta, cajón; *pl* calzoncillos; pantalones (*de mujer*); **chest of —s** cómoda.
drawing ['drɔ:iŋ] *n* dibujo, plan; (*lottery tickets etc*) extracción; saca; **— board** tablero de dibujo; **— pin** chinche; **— room** salón.
drawl [drɔ:l] *n* voz lánguida; *vi* arrastrar las palabras.
drawn [drɔ:n] *a* estirado; apenado; (*fam*) chupado; **— thread** obra de calado; (*sports*) empatado; **long- — out** (*cry*) sostenido, alargado.
dread [dred] *a* horrible, pavoroso, tremendo, temible; *n* asombro, miedo, pavor, terror; *vt* temer, tener miedo a.
dreadful ['dredful] *a* terrible, temible, horroroso, horrendo, aterrador, horripilante; **penny —** cuento de miedo.
dream [dri:m] *n* (*sleep*) sueño; imaginación; (*fancy*) ensueño; quimera; *vti* soñar, fantasear.
dreamer ['dri:mə] *n* soñador, visionario; **day—** iluso.
dreamy ['dri:mi] *a* soñador, fantástico.
dreary ['driəri] *a* triste, lúgubre, monótono; pesado.
dregs [dregz] *n* poso, sedimento, hez (*pl* heces); solada; (*wine*) madre; escoria, desperdicio; (*people*) canalla, gentuza; **to drink to the —** apurar.
drench [drentʃ] *vt* mojar, empapar, calar, recalar.
drenching ['drentʃiŋ] *n* **to get a —** mojarse, empaparse; **a — shower** un chaparrón.
dress [dres] *n* vestido(s); traje, arreos; **evening —** traje de etiqueta; **in full —** de gala, de tiros largos; *vt* ataviar, componer, vestir, adornar; (*wounds*) vendar; (*food*) adobar, aliñar; *vr* **to — up** atusarse, endomingarse, componerse; *a* **— rehearsal,** ensayo general; **— circle** (*theat*) anfiteatro; **in — clothes** de smoking, de etiqueta.
dresser ['dresə] *n* aparador, armario, tocador.
dressing ['dresiŋ] *n* adorno; (*food*) salsa, adobo; (*for wounds*) hila, vendaje; **— case** neceser; **— gown** bata; **— table** tocador.
dressmaker ['dresˌmeikə] *n* costurera, modista.
dressmaking ['dresˌmeikiŋ] *n* costurería, corte de ropa.
dried [draid] *a* seco; secado; paso; pilongo; **— up** enjuto.
drift [drift] *n* rumbo; (*conversation*) giro; impulso; (*in meaning*) móvil, significado; **— ice** hielo a deriva; **snow—** ventisca, ventisquero; **—wood** madera de deriva; *vi* impeler, amontonar; (*mar*) derrotar, derivar; dejarse(llevar, arrastrar), ir a la deriva.
drill [dril] *n* surco; ejercicio; taladro; (*cloth*) dril; *vt* (*bore*) taladrar, barrenar, horadar; (*mil*) instruir; *vi* ejercer; (*mil*) hacer el ejercicio.
drink [driŋk] *n* bebida; (*mouthful*) trago; (*sip*) sorbo; (*refreshing*) cordial; **to have a —** tomar una copita; *vti* beber; (*healths*) trincar, brindar (a); (*fam*) empinar; ser bebedor; (ab)sorber, embeber.
drinkable ['driŋkəbl] *a* potable.
drip [drip] *a* **— spout** chorrera; *n* gota, gotera; *vti* gotear, manar; caer gota a gota.
drive [draiv] *n* paseo en coche; (*tennis etc*) saque; ímpetu, viveza, urgencia, pujanza; *vt* impeler, impulsar, empujar, inducir, guiar; (*car*) conducir, SA manejar; (*stake etc*) hincar; *vi* ir en coche; **to — on** acuciar; **to — away** disipar, ahuyentar; **to — back** rechazar; **to — out** expulsar; **to — mad** volver loco.
driver ['draivə] *n* cochero, carretero; (*car*) conductor, chófer; (*train*) maquinista.
drizzle ['drizl] *n* llovizna, calabobos, rocío; *vi* lloviznar; (*slightly*) chispear.
droll [droul] *a* gracioso, raro, chistoso, chusco.
dromedary ['drɔmidəri] *n* dromedario.
droop [dru:p] *n* caída; *vi* entriste-

cerse, desanimarse; cabecear; consumirse, marchitarse.

drop [drɔp] *n* gota, lágrima; chispa; caída, pendiente; **— curtain** telón de boca; **— by —** gota a gota; *vti* gotear; renunciar a, desistir de; derribar; bajar, (*venom*) destilar; caer, dejar caer; **to — flat** caer a plomo; **to — into** (*chair etc*) tumbarse; **to — off** quedar dormido; dispersarse; **to — a hint** soltar una indirecta; **to — a subject** cambiar de asunto; **to — a line** escribir, poner dos letras.

dropsy ['drɔpsi] *n* hidropesía.

dross [drɔs] *n* excoria, basura, granzas.

drought [draut] *n* sequía, seca.

drove [drouv] *n* (*sheep*) rebaño; (*beasts*) manada, arria; (*horses*) piara; (*mules*) recua; gentío.

drown [draun] *vt* ahogar, inundar; (*sorrow*) anegar; sofocar; *vi* ahogarse.

drowsiness ['drauzinis] *n* somnolencia, modorra, letargo, pesadez.

drowsy ['drauzi] *a* soñoliento; **to grow —** amodorrarse.

drudgery ['drʌdʒəri] *n* trabajo penoso, faena, perrera, trabajo reventador.

drug [drʌg] *n* droga; (*on market*) plaga; **—store** farmacia; *vt* mezclar drogas; narcotizar.

druggist ['drʌgist] *n* droguista, farmacéutico.

drum [drʌm] *n* (*mil*) tambor, atabal; (*com*) bidón, cuñete; (*ear*) tímpano; zambomba; *a* **—head** parche; *vt* redoblar; **to — in, into** machacar, insistir.

drummer ['drʌmə] *n* (*mil*) tambor; tamborilero.

drunk [drʌŋk] *a* borracho, embriagado; **— as a lord** borracho como una cuba; **to get —** emborracharse.

drunken ['drʌŋkən] *a* borracho, ebrio.

drunkenness ['drʌŋkənnis] *n* borrachera; (*often spiritual etc*) embriaguez.

dry [drai] *a* seco; (*as a bone*) reseco; enjuto; ávido; **—shod** a pie enjuto; *vt* secar, desecar; (*tears*) enjugar; *vi* secarse.

dryness ['drainis] *n* sequedad, aridez.

dubious ['dju:biəs] *a* incierto, dudoso, irresoluto, problemático.

duchess ['dʌtʃis] *n* duquesa.

duchy ['dʌtʃi] *n* ducado.

duck [dʌk] *n* ánade, pato; **to play —s and drakes** hacer cabrillas; *vt* (*in water*) chapuzar; (*head*) agacharse; *vi* zambullir.

due [dju:] *a* debido, vencido, cumplido; propio, oportuno, legítimo, justo, conveniente; **it is — to him** se debe a él; **— respect** consideración; **to fall —** correr, vencer; *n* deuda, obligación; *pl* derechos.

duel ['djuəl] *n* duelo, lance de honor; **to challenge to a —** desafío; **to engage in a —** batirse.

dueling ['djuəliŋ] *n* duelo, desafío.

duke [dju:k] *n* duque.

dukedom [dju:kdəm] *n* ducado.

dull [dʌl] *a* obtuso; (*person*) lelo, lerdo; (*speech etc*) aburrido, pesado; (*surface*) mate; (*view*) opaco; (*style*) prosaico; (*sound*) apagado, sordo; (*taste*) soso; (*point*) embotado; (*light*) apagado; (*brain*) flojo, tardo; (*color*) bajo, obscuro; [(*hearing*) duro; (*pain*) sordo; (*wit*) lerdo, estúpido; *vt* embotar; apagar, mitigar; empañar.

dullness ['dʌlnis] *n* estupidez, cortedad; embotamiento; depresión; torpeza; prosaísmo; pesadez.

duly ['dju:li] *ad* debidamente, a su tiempo.

dumb [dʌm] *a* mudo, callado; **deaf and —** sordomudo; **—waiter** montacargas; **— show** pantomima; **to strike —** pasmar, asombrar.

dumbfound [dʌm'faund] *vt* plantar, aturdir.

dumbness ['dʌmnis] *n* mutismo, mudez.

dummy ['dʌmi] *a* postizo, fingido; *n* testaferro; (*tailor*)'*s* papagayo; (*baby's*) chupete; (*dressmaker's*) maniquí.

dump [dʌmp] *n* escorial; vertedero; *pl* modorra, morriña; *vt* descargar de golpe, vaciar.

dun [dʌn] *a* pardo, castaño, obscuro; *n* acreedor importuno; *vti* importunar, apremiar.

dunce [dʌns] *n* bobo, tonto, zote.

dune [dju:n] *n* duna.

dung [dʌŋ] *n* estiércol; *vti* estercolar.

dungeon ['dʌndʒən] *n* calabozo, mazmorra.

dupe [dju:p] *n* primo, simple, simplón; *vt* engañar, embaucar.

duped [dju:pt] *a* engañado; **to be —** tragar el anzuelo.

duplicate ['dju:plikit] *n* duplicado, copia; ['dju:plikeit] *vt* duplicar, copiar.

duplicity [dju(:)'plisiti] *n* doblez, engaño, segunda intención.

durability [,djuərə'biliti] *n* durabilidad.

durable ['djuərəbl] *a* durable, resistente, duradero.

duration [djuə'reiʃən] *n* duración.

duress [djuə'res] *n* compulsión, obligación; encierro.

during ['djuəriŋ] *prep* durante, por.

dusk [dʌsk] *n* crepúsculo, anochecer.

dusky ['dʌski] *a* moreno, oscuro.

dust [dʌst] *n* polvo; (*rubbish*) basura; harina; escombros; (*human*) restos mortales, cenizas; *a* **— cover** guardapolvo; **—pan** basurero, cogedor; **to knock the — out of** sacudir el polvo a; *vt* sacudir el polvo.

duster ['dʌstə] *n* trapo; (*feather*)

plumero; guardapolvo; (*blackboard*) borrador.
dusty ['dʌsti] *a* polvoriento, polvoroso.
Dutch [dʌtʃ] *an* holandés; — **cheese** requesón; **to go** — compartir los gastos.
dutiful ['dju:tiful] *a* obediente, sumiso, respetuoso, honrado.
duty ['dju:ti] *n* deber, obligación; faena; función; imposición; (*on goods*) carga; (*mil*) deber, servicio; *pl* derechos; — **bound** honradamente; **to be on** — estar (de servicio, de guardia).
dwarf [dwɔ:f] *n* enano; *vt* empequeñecer, achicar.
dwell [dwel] *vi* morar, permanecer, habitar, residir; anidar; **to — (on, upon)** explayarse, hacer hincapié (sobre), espaciarse (en, sobre); ensimismarse en.
dweller ['dwelə] *n* habitante, morador.
dwelling ['dweliŋ] *n* habitación, domicilio, vivienda, morada; techo.
dwindle ['dwindl] *vi* disminuirse, consumirse, mermar, menguar.
dye [dai] *a* —**works** tintorería; *n* tinte, color; **fast** — tinte fijo; *vt* teñir.
dyed [daid] *a* tinto, teñido.
dying ['daiiŋ] *a* (*light etc*) mortecino, moribundo; agonizante; (*person*) agonizante; (*with thirst*) sediento.
dynasty ['dinəsti] *n* dinastía.

E

each [i:tʃ] *pn a* cada, cada uno, todo; **one** — sendos.
eager ['i:gə] *a* deseoso, ávido, vehemente, impaciente.
eagerness ['i:gənis] *n* anhelo, vehemencia, sed, fervor, entusiasmo, afán.
eagle ['i:gl] *n* águila; — **-eyed** lince.
ear [iə] *n* (*organ*) oreja; (*sense*) oído; **inner** — oído; — **of corn** mazorca; — **muff** ojera; — **drum** tímpano; —**ring** pendiente, zarcillo; arete; **to have a good** — tener buen oído; **to play by** — tocar de oído; **to turn a deaf** — hacerse el sordo; —**ache** dolor de oídos.
earl [ə:l] *n* conde.
earliness ['ə:linis] *n* lo temprano; precocidad; presteza, prontitud, anticipación.
early ['ə:li] *a* temprano; precoz; (*morning*) matutino; adelantado; (*fruit*) temprano; *ad* temprano, con tiempo; — **in the morning** de madrugada; **as — as possible** lo más pronto posible.
earn [ə:n] *vt* ganar, obtener, merecer; lucrarse; (*praise*) granjear; (*one's living*) mantenerse, sostenerse.
earnest ['ə:nist] *a* serio, formal; cuidadoso, diligente; *n* arras, prenda, señal; seriedad; **not in** — de broma.
earnestness ['ə:nistnis] *n* buena fe, formalidad, seriedad, encarecimiento, diligencia.
earnings ['ə:niŋz] *n* paga, estipendio; (*com*) ganancias, ingresos.
earsplitting ['iəsplitiŋ] *a* ensordecedor, desaforado.
earth [ə:θ] *n* tierra, globo; (*fox*) madriguera; (*radio*) tierra.
earthenware ['ə:θənwɛə] *n* loza de barro, cacharros.
earthly ['ə:θli] *a* terrestre, mundano, terrenal.
earthquake ['ə:θkweik] *n* temblor de tierra, terremoto.
earthwork ['ə:θwə:k] *n* terraplén.
earthworm ['ə:θwə:m] *n* gusano de tierra.
earthy ['ə:θi] *a* térreo, terroso; grosero.
ease [i:z] *n* quietud, ocio, comodidad, holgura; libertad; soltura, rapidez; tranquilidad, regalo; **at** — a pierna suelta, a sus anchas, descansadamente; **ill at** — incómodo; *vt* aliviar, aligerar, suavizar, descargar; **to take one's** — ponerse cómodo.
easel ['i:zl] *n* caballete.
easiness ['i:zinis] *n* facilidad, soltura; holgura, bienestar; desembarazo.
east [i:st] este, oriente; **Near E—** Próximo Oriente; **Middle E—** Medio Oriente; **Far E—** Extremo *or* Lejano Oriente; — **wind** (*Spain*) Levante.
Easter ['i:stə] *n* pascua (de resurrección, florida).
eastern ['i:stən] *a* del este, oriental.
easy ['i:zi] *a* fácil, cómodo, complaciente, negligente; despacio: suelto, lato, como seda; — **to please** contentadizo; — **as wink** burla burlando; cosa de coser y cantar; —**going** plácido, lento; imprevisor; como una seda, ancho de conciencia; — **chair** butaca, sillón.
eat [i:t] *vti* comer; roer; **to — away** carcomer; (*income etc*) mermar; **to — into** minar; **to — up** comer, morder.
eatable ['i:təbl] *n* comestible; *a* comestible.
eating ['i:tiŋ] *n* comida; **fit for** — comestible; — **house** hostería, bodegón.
eaves ['i:vz] *n* alero.
eavesdrop ['i:vzdrɔp] *vi* fisgonear.
ebb [eb] *n* reflujo; bajamar; *vi* bajar.
ebony ['ebəni] *n* ébano.
eccentric [ik'sentrik] *a* excéntrico, estrafalario, raro, extravagante.
echo ['ekou] *n* eco; *vti* resonar, repercutir, repetir.
eclipse [i'klips] *n* eclipse; *vt* eclipsar, superar.
economic [ˌi:kə'nɔmik] *a* económico; *n* —**s** económica.
economical [ˌi:kə'nɔmikəl] *a* económico, frugal.

economize [i'kɔnəmaiz] *vt* economizar.
economy [i'kɔnəmi] *n* economía; *pl* ahorros.
ecstasy ['ekstəsi] *n* éxtasis, exaltación, arrobamiento, rapto; **in —** trasportado.
Ecuador [,ekwə'dɔ:] *n* el Ecuador.
Ecuadorian [,ekwə'dɔ:riən] *an* ecuatoriano.
eddy ['edi] *n* remolino, remanso; *vi* arremolinar, remansarse.
edge [edʒ] *n* filo, borde; (*river*) orilla; (*sword*) hilo, corte; (*table, book*) canto; lado, extremidad; extremo, esquina; **on its —** de canto; **to set one's teeth on —** dar dentera; *vt* afilar; (*sew*) ribetear; guarnecer; *vi* **to — along** avanzar de lado.
edging ['edʒiŋ] *n* (*dress*) guarnición; orla.
edict ['i:dikt] *n* edicto, auto.
edifice ['edifis] *n* edificio.
edify ['edifai] *vt* edificar, ilustrar.
Edinburgh ['edinbərə] *n* Edimburgo.
edit ['edit] *vt* redactar, dirigir (*un periódico*).
editing ['editiŋ] *n* redacción.
edition [i'diʃən] *n* edición, tirada.
editor ['editə] *n* editor; (*newspaper*) director, redactor.
editorial [,edi'tɔ:riəl] *n* (*office etc*) redacción; (*article*) artículo de fondo, comentario político.
Edmund ['edmənd] *m* Edmundo.
educate ['edjukeit] *vt* instruir, educar.
educated ['edjukeitid] *a* ilustrado, culto.
education [,edju'keiʃən] *n* educación; enseñanza; cultura; **Ministry of E—** Ministerio (de Instrucción Pública, de Educación); **higher —** enseñanza superior; **secondary —** segunda enseñanza; **elementary —** primera enseñanza.
educational [,edju'keiʃənl] *a* educativo, pedagógico, instructivo.
educator ['edjukeitə] *n* educador, institutor.
Edward ['edwəd] *m* Eduardo.
eel [i:l] anguila; **conger —** congrio.
eerie ['iəri] *a* misterioso, tétrico.
efface [i'feis] *vt* borrar, tachar, testar.
effect [i'fekt] *n* efecto, impresión, consecuente; fuerza; resultado; *vt* efectuar, ejecutar, llevar a cabo; **to take —** salir bien, producir su efecto; **to feel the — of** estar resentido de.
effective [i'fektiv] *a* efectivo, real, eficaz; de mucho efecto.
effectual [i'fektjuəl] *a* eficaz.
effeminate [i'feminit] *a* afeminado; **— man** marica; [i'femineit] *vti* afeminar, afeminarse.
effervescent [,efə'vesnt] *a* efervescente.
effete [i'fi:t] *a* usado, gastado.
efficacious [,efi'keiʃəs] *a* eficaz.
efficacy ['efikəsi] *n* eficacia.
efficient [i'fiʃənt] *a* capaz, eficaz, competente.
efficiency [i'fiʃənsi] *n* eficiencia, habilidad.
effigy ['efidʒi] *n* efigie, imagen.
effort ['efət] *n* esfuerzo, empeño, gestión, conato; (*violent*) forcejeo; **to make an —** esforzarse; **by one's own —s** por sus puños.
effrontery [i'frʌntəri] *n* descaro, atrevimiento, insolencia, desgarro.
effusive [i'fju:siv] *a* expansivo, efusivo, empalagoso.
egg [eg] *n* huevo; (*beaten*) batido; (*fried*) frito; (*boiled*) hervido; pasado por agua; (*scrambled*) revuelto; (*poached*) escalfado; **—shell** cáscara; *vt* **to — on** instigar, provocar.
egotist ['egoutist] *n* egotista.
egoism ['egouizəm] *n* egoísmo.
egoist ['egouist] *n* egoísta.
egoistic [,egou'istik] *a* egoísta.
Egypt ['i:dʒipt] *n* Egipto.
Egyptian [i'dʒipʃən] *an* egipcio.
eight [eit] *an* ocho.
eighteen ['ei'ti:n] *an* diez y ocho.
eighteenth ['ei'ti:nθ] *an* decimoctavo, diez y ocho.
eighth [eitθ] *an* octavo.
eighty ['eiti] *an* ochenta.
Eire ['ɛərə] *n* Estado libre de Irlanda.
either ['aiðə] *cj* o, sea; en todo caso; tampoco; *pn* uno u otro.
ejaculation [i,dʒækju'leiʃən] *n* exclamación; ejaculación, emisión.
eject [i'dʒekt] *vt* arrojar, expulsar, excluir, vomitar.
eke [i:k] *vt* **to — out** suplir las deficiencias de . . . con.
elaborate [i'læbərit] *a* detallado, complicado, primoroso, rebuscado, esmerado; [i'læbəreit] *vt* elaborar, labrar.
elapse [i'læps] *vi* pasar, transcurrir, andar.
elastic [i'læstik] *a* elástico.
elasticity [,i:læs'tisiti] *n* elasticidad.
elation [i'leiʃən] *n* gozo, júbilo, regocijo.
elbow ['elbou] *n* codo, (*fig*) recodo; *vti* codear, dar codazos, formar recodos.
elder ['eldə] *a* mayor; *n* (*tree*) saúco; *pl* **—s and betters** mayores.
elderly ['eldəli] *a* de cierta edad, mayor.
eldest ['eldist] *a* el mayor; **— son** primogénito.
Eleanor ['elinə] *f* Leonor.
elect [i'lekt] *vt* elegir, escoger.
election [i'lekʃən] *n* elección.
elector [i'lektə] *n* elector.
electoral [i'lektərəl] *a* electoral.
electric [i'lektrik] *a* eléctrico.
electrical [i'lektrikl] *a* eléctrico.
electrician [ilek'triʃən] *n* electricista.
electricity [ilek'trisiti] *n* electricidad.
electrify [i'lektrifai] *vt* electrizar; entusiasmar.

elegance ['eligəns] *n* elegancia, refinamiento, gala, gracia, donaire; (*of speech*) gracia, donosura.
elegant ['eligənt] *a* elegante, gallardo, apuesto, garboso.
elegy ['elidʒi] *n* elegía.
element ['elimənt] *n* elemento; (*chem*) cuerpo simple; *pl* principios. nociones.
elemental [,eli'mentl] *a* elemental, primordial.
elementary [,eli'mentəri] *a* elemental; (*education*) primario.
elephant ['elifənt] *n* elefante; **white —** carabina de Ambrosio.
elevate ['eliveit] *vt* elevar, exaltar; (*in rank*) encumbrar; (*the Host*) alzar.
elevated ['eliveitid] *a* excelso, levantado, encumbrado.
elevation [,eli'veiʃən] *n* eminencia, altura; altitud; elevación; exaltación; (*archit*) alzado.
elevator ['eliveitə] *n* ascensor, montacargas.
eleven [i'levn] *an* once.
eleventh [i'levnθ] *an* undécimo.
elf [elf] *n* duende, trasgo, enano.
elicit [i'lisit] *vt* sacar, sonsacar.
eligible ['elidʒəbl] *a* elegible.
eliminate [i'limineit] *vt* eliminar, quitar, suprimir.
elite [ei'li:t] *n* la flor (y nata), lo mejor.
Elizabeth [i'lizəbəθ] *f* Isabel.
elm [elm] *n* olmo.
elocution [,ele'kju:ʃən] *n* elocución, declamación.
elope [i'loup] *vi* fugarse; escaparse, huirse.
elopement [i'loupmənt] *n* rapto, fuga.
eloquence ['eləkwəns] *n* elocuencia.
eloquent ['eləkwənt] *a* elocuente.
else [els] *pn* otro; *ad* (ade)más; **or —** en otro caso.
elsewhere ['els'wɛə] *ad* en (cualquier) otra parte.
elucidate [i'lu:sideit] *vt* aclarar, ilustrar, delucidar.
elude [i'lu:d] *vt* eludir, evitar, substraerse.
elusive [i'lu:siv] *a* evasivo, fugaz, esquivo, huraño.
emaciate [i'meiʃieit] *vti* extenuar, adelgazar; **to become emaciated** demacrarse.
emanate ['eməneit] *vi* emanar, proceder.
emancipate [i'mænsipeit] *vt* emancipar, libertar.
embalm [im'bɑ:m] *vt* embalsamar.
embankment [im'bæŋkmənt] *n* (*sea*) malecón; (*rl*) terraplén; (*water*) presa, dique; (*London*) ría.
embargo [im'bɑ:gou] *n* embargo; traba.
embark [im'bɑ:k] *vti* embarcar(se), lanzarse.
embarkation [,embɑ:'keiʃən] *n* embarque.
embarrass [im'bærəs] *vt* turbar, desconcertar, avergonzar, poner en aprieto.
embarrassment [im'bærəsmənt] *n* (per)turbación, perplejidad; compromiso, embarazo, aprieto, apuro; estorbo.
embassy ['embəsi] *n* embajada.
embellish [im'beliʃ] *vt* embellecer, hermosear, esmaltar, guarnecer.
embellishment [im'beliʃmənt] *n* enbellecimiento, ornato.
ember ['embə] *n* ascua, rescoldo, chispazo.
embezzle [im'bezl] *vt* apropiarse, desfalcar.
embitter [im'bitə] *vt* agriar, irritar, amargar.
embittered [im'bitəd] *a* amargado, avinagrado.
emblem ['embləm] *n* emblema, símbolo.
embodiment [im'bɔdimənt] *n* personificación, encarnación.
embody [im'bɔdi] *vt* incorporar.
embolden [im'bouldən] *vt* envalentonar.
emboss [em'bɔs] *vt* relevar, repujar; damasquinar.
embossed [im'bɔst] *a* labrado, repujado; **— leather** guadamecí.
embrace [im'breis] *n* abrazo; *vti* abrazar; (*with vision etc*) abarcar; (*tightly*) ceñir; (*contain*) encerrar, aceptar.
embroider [im'brɔidə] *vt* bordar, recamar.
embroidery [im'brɔidəri] *n* bordado.
embroil [im'brɔil] *vt* embrollar, confundir, enredar.
embryo ['embriou] *n* embrión.
embryonic [,embri'ɔnik] *a* incipiente, embrionario.
emerald ['emərəld] *n* esmeralda.
emerge [i'mə:dʒ] *vi* surgir, brotar, aparecer; **to — with credit** salir airoso.
emergency [i'mə:dʒənsi] *n* aprieto, necesidad urgente, contingencia, trance, apuro.
emigrant ['emigrənt] *a* emigrante; *n* emigrado.
emigrate ['emigreit] *vi* emigrar.
emigration [,emi'greiʃən] *n* emigración.
Emily ['emili] *f* Emilia.
eminence ['eminəns] *n* eminencia; (*geog*) altura; encumbramiento.
eminent ['eminənt] *a* eminente, ilustre, distinguido, esclarecido, eximio, prestigioso.
emit [i'mit] *vt* emitir, exhalar; (*sparks*) arrojar, despedir.
Emmanuel [i'mænjuəl] *m* Manuel.
emolument [i'mɔljumənt] *n* emolumento, gaje.
emotion [i'mouʃən] *n* emoción, sentimiento; (*strong*) alteración.
emperor ['empərə] *n* emperador.

emphasis ['emfəsis] *n* énfasis, fuerza, intensidad.
emphasize ['emfəsaiz] *vt* recalcar, acentuar, subrayar, hacer resaltar, hacer hincapié en, insistir en.
emphatic [im'fætik] *a* enfático, cargado, enérgico, categórico.
emphatically [im'fætikəli] *ad* enfáticamente, categóricamente; a pies juntillas.
empire ['empaiə] *a* imperial; *n* imperio.
employ [im'plɔi] *n* empleo; *vt* emplear, ocupar, colocar; servirse, valerse de.
employee [ˌemplɔi'i:] *n* dependiente; (*rl*) obrero; empleado.
employer [im'plɔiə] *n* amo, patrón.
employment [im'plɔimənt] *n* empleo, ocupación, cargo; acomodo, plaza.
empress ['empris] *n* emperatriz.
emptiness ['emptinis] *n* vacío, vaciedad, hueco.
empty ['empti] *a* vacío, vacuo; frívolo, hueco; desocupado, vacante; *vt* vaciar, desaguar, verter, descargar.
emulate ['emjuleit] *vt* emular, rivalizar.
emulation [ˌemju'leiʃən] *n* emulación, rivalidad, envidia.
enable [i'neibl] *vt* habilitar, poner en capacidad, facilitar, permitir.
enact [i'nækt] *vt* decretar, ejecutar; (*laws*) legislar; (*scene*) realizar, desempeñar, desarrollar.
enactment [i'nækt mənt] *n* ley, estatuto, promulgación.
enamel [i'næml] *n* esmalte; *vt* esmaltar.
enamor [i'næmə] *vt* enamorar, amartelar.
encamp [in'kæmp] *vti* acampar.
encampment [in'kæmpmənt] *n* campamento.
encase [in'keis] *vt* encajar, encerrar.
enchant [in'tʃɑ:nt] *vt* encantar; (*by spells*) ensalmar, hechizar; deleitar, fascinar.
enchanter [in'tʃɑ:ntə] *n* hechicero.
enchanting [in'tʃɑ:ntiŋ] *a* encantador, delicioso.
enchantment [in'tʃɑ:ntmənt] *n* encanto, encantamiento, embeleso, hechizo; hechicería, ensalmo.
enchantress [in'tʃɑ:ntris] *n* bruja, encantadora.
encircle [in'sə:kl] *vt* cercar, rodear; (*waist*) ceñir.
enclose [in'klouz] *vt* cerrar, cercar, encerrar, circunscribir.
enclosed [in'klouzd] *a* (*in letter*) adjunto; (*land*) vedado.
enclosure [in'klouʒə] *n* cerca; (*fenced*) cercado, anexo, coto, recinto; (*fence*) barrera, valla(do), tapia.
encompass [in'kʌmpəs] *vt* rodear, encerrar, abarcar.
encore [ɔŋ'kɔ:] *n* repetición; *excl* ¡bis!, ¡que se repita!
encounter [in'kauntə] *n* encuentro, choque, pelea, refriega; *vti* encontrar, acometer; tropezar con.
encourage [in'kʌridʒ] *vt* animar, alentar, esforzar, fortalecer, nutrir, reforzar.
encouragement [in'kʌridʒmənt] *n* estímulo, incentivo, incitación.
encroach [in'kroutʃ] *vt* usurpar, pasar los límites.
encumber [in'kʌmbə] *vt* estorbar, embarazar, sobrecargar.
encumbrance [in'kʌmbrəns] *n* impedimento, estorbo, traba.
encyclical [en'siklikəl] *n* encíclica.
end [end] *n* extremo, fin, cabo, remate; fenecimiento; (*of play*) desenlace; (*cigarette*) colilla; (*street*) bocacalle; (*upper — of table, bed*) cabecera; **at the — of** al cabo de; **in the —** en definitiva; **toward the — of** a últimos de; **from — to —** de cabo a rabo; **to come to an —** terminar(se); **to make an — of** acabar con; *vti* **to — in, by** acabar, terminar, terminarse, cerrar.
endanger [in'deindʒə] *vt* poner en peligro, comprometer.
endearing [in'diəriŋ] *a* almibarado; cariñoso.
endearment [in'diəmənt] *n* requiebro, ternura, encariñamiento.
endeavor [in'devə] *n* esfuerzo, empeño, seguimiento; *vi* esforzarse, tratar de, pretender, procurar.
ending ['endiŋ] *n* fin, conclusión; (*book*) desenlace.
endless ['endlis] *a* sin fin, infinito, eterno, continuo, inagotable, inacabable; **an — number** un sinnúmero.
endorse [in'dɔ:s] *vt* endosar, respaldar, rubricar.
endow [in'dau] *vt* dotar, fundar.
endowment [in'daumənt] *n* dotación; dote, talento; prendas.
endurance [in'djuərəns] *n* paciencia, duración, fortaleza, sufrimiento; **past all —** inaguantable.
endure [in'djuə] *vti* soportar, resistir, aguantar, (sobre)llevar; continuar, durar.
enduring [in'djuəriŋ] *a* constante; sufrido.
enemy ['enimi] *n* enemigo, adversario.
energetic [ˌenə'dʒetik] *a* enérgico, esforzado.
energy ['enədʒi] *n* energía, vigor, viveza, nervio.
enfeeble [in'fi:bl] *vt* debilitar.
enforce [in'fɔ:s] *vt* hacer cumplir, obligar, imponer, poner en vigor.
enforcement [in'fɔ:smənt] *n* compulsión, ejecución, coacción.
enfranchise [in'fræntʃaiz] *vt* franquear, emancipar.
engage [in'geidʒ] *vti* (*hire*) ajustar, emplear, comprometer; (*battle*) librar; (*to marry*) comprometerse; emplear; (*mech*) engranar; em-

peñarse, dar palabra; (*conversation*) entretener, ocupar.
engaged [in'geidʒd] *a* (*person, telephone*) ocupado; (*woman*) prometida.
engagement [in'geidʒmənt] *n* compromiso; combate; (*of maid*) ajuste; (*period of betrothal*) noviazgo; empeño; contrato; (*to meet*) cita, compromiso.
engaging [in'geidʒiŋ] *a* atractivo, agradable, amable, simpático.
engine ['endʒin] *n* máquina; ingenio; (*rl*) locomotora; **—driver** maquinista.
engineer [ˌendʒi'niə] *n* ingeniero; mecánico; (*rl*) maquinista; *vt* gestionar.
engineering [ˌendʒi'niəriŋ] *n* ingeniería.
England ['iŋglənd] *n* Inglaterra.
English ['iŋgliʃ] *a* inglés; **—man** inglés; **the — Channel** el Canal de la Mancha.
engrave [in'greiv] *vt* grabar, burilar, esculpir, entallar.
engraver [in'greivə] *n* grabador.
engraving [in'greiviŋ] *n* grabado, estampa.
engross [in'grous] *vt* (*law* & *com*) poner en limpio; absorber, monopolizar.
enhance [in'hɑːns] *vt* encarecer, mejorar, realzar.
enigmatic [ˌenig'mætik] *a* enigmático.
enjoy [in'dʒɔi] *vt* saborear, divertirse, pasarlo bien, gozar de, lograr; (*taste*) paladear.
enjoyable [in'dʒɔiəbl] *a* agradable, divertido.
enjoyment [in'dʒɔimənt] *n* gozo; gusto, placer; goce; fruición; (*use*) usufructo.
enlarge [in'lɑːdʒ] *vti* ensanchar, agrandar, aumentar; **to — upon** explayar; engrosar.
enlargement [in'lɑːdʒmənt] *n* aumento; (*film*) ampliación; (*broad*) ensanche; expansión.
enlighten [in'laitn] *vt* iluminar, ilustrar, instruir.
enlightenment [in'laitnmənt] *n* ilustración, entendimiento, luces.
enlist [in'list] *vti* enganchar, alistarse, sentar plaza.
enliven [in'laivn] *vt* animar, alegrar, avispar, regocijar, vivificar.
enmity ['enmiti] *n* enemistad, hostilidad.
ennoble [i'noubl] *vt* ennoblecer.
enquire [in'kwaiə] *vi* averiguar, preguntar (por), indagar, inquirir.
enormity [i'nɔːmiti] *n* enormidad; atrocidad.
enormous [i'nɔːməs] *a* enorme, colosal, descomunal; atroz.
enough [i'nʌf] *ad* bastante, harto; **to be more than —** sobrar.
enrage [in'reidʒ] *vt* exasperar, ensañar; enfurecer; **to become enraged** (*sea*) embravecerse.
enrapture [in'ræptʃə] *vt* transportar, arrobar, enajenar.
enraptured [in'ræptʃəd] *a* **to be —** estar prendado, embebido.
enrich [in'ritʃ] *vt* enriquecer, fertilizar, fecundar; abonar.
enroll [in'roul] *vt* alistar; (*in school etc*) matricular; (*mil*) sentar plaza.
enshrine [in'ʃrain] *vti* guardar como reliquia, grabar, consagrar.
ensign ['ensain] *n* bandera, enseña; (*mil*) alférez, abanderado.
enslave [in'sleiv] *vt* esclavizar.
ensue [in'sjuː] *vi* seguir(se), sobrevenir.
ensuing [in'sjuːiŋ] *a* resultante, siguiente.
ensure [in'ʃuə] *vt* asegurar(se), hacer (que).
entail [in'teil] *n* vinculación, herencia; *vt* vincular, legar.
entangle [in'tæŋgl] *vt* enmarañar, embrollar; **to be entangled in** enfrascarse en.
entanglement [in'tæŋglmənt] *n* embrollo, enredo.
enter ['entə] *vti* entrar, introducir(se); anotar; (*school*) ingresar; (*university*) matricularse; (*theat*) salir; **to — upon** emprender, empezar.
enterprise ['entəpraiz] *n* empresa.
enterprising ['entəpraiziŋ] *a* aprovechado; emprendedor.
entertain [ˌentə'tein] *vt* entretener, divertir, hospedar, tomar en consideración, agasajar; (*idea*) concebir.
entertaining [ˌentə'teiniŋ] *a* divertido, distraído, entretenido.
entertainment [ˌentə'teinmənt] *n* entretenimiento; diversión; hospitalidad; agasajo, convite; función.
enthusiasm [in'θjuːziæzəm] *n* entusiasmo, fervor, ánimo.
enthusiast [in'θjuːziæst] *n* entusiasta, fanático, aficionado.
enthusiastic [inˌθjuːzi'æstik] *a* lleno de entusiasmo, animoso, delirante.
entice [in'tais] *vt* atraer, seducir, tentar.
entire [in'taiə] *a* entero, perfecto, total, cabal, íntegro.
entirety [in'taiərəti] *n* todo; **in its —** completamente, enteramente.
entitle [in'taitl] *vt* intitular, dar derecho.
entrails ['entreilz] *n pl* entrañas.
entrance ['entrəns] *n* entrada; (*river*) embocadura; ingreso; **— fee** cuota; *vi* [in'trɑːns] extasiar, hechizar.
entreat [in'triːt] *vti* suplicar, rogar, implorar.
entreaty [in'triːti] *n* súplica, petición, ruego, conjuro.
entrust [in'trʌst] *vt* confiar, cometer, encargar, fiar; *vr* encomendarse.
entry ['entri] *n* entrada, ingreso; (*fee*) derecho de ingreso; (*in book*) partida, minuta; **to make an —** entrar; **no —** prohibida la entrada.

enumerate [i'nju:mэreit] *vt* enumerar, puntualizar, detallar.
enunciate [i'nʌnsieit] *vt* enunciar, pronunciar.
enunciation [i,nʌnsi'eiʃэn] *n* enunciación; articulación.
envelop [in'velэp] *vt* envolver, poner bajo sobre, cubrir.
envelope ['envэloup] *n* sobre; envoltura.
enviable ['enviэbl] *a* envidiable.
envious ['enviэs] *a* envidioso.
environs [in'vaiэrэnz] *n pl* alrededores, contornos, inmediaciones.
envisage [en'vizidʒ] *vt* concebir, imaginarse, enfocar.
envoy ['envɔi] *n* enviado, mensajero.
envy ['envi] *n* ojeriza, envidia, codicia; *vt* envidiar, codiciar.
ephemeral [i'femэrэl] *a* transitorio, efímero.
epic ['epik] *a* épico; *n* — **poetry** la épica, epopeya.
epicure ['epikjuэ] *an* epicúreo.
epidemic [,epi'demik] *n* epidemia.
Epiphany [i'pifэni] *n* epifanía, noche de Reyes, los Reyes.
episode ['episoud] *n* episodio, lance; *pl* peripecias.
epistle [i'pisl] *n* epístola, carta, misiva.
epitaph ['epitɑ:f] *n* epitafio.
epithet ['epiθet] *n* epíteto.
epitome [i'pitэmi] *n* epítome, breviario, compendio.
epitomize [i'pitэmaiz] *vt* compendiar, extractar; resumir.
epoch ['i:pɔk] *n* época, edad, tiempo.
equable ['ekwэbl] *a* igual, uniforme; plácido.
equal ['i:kwэl] *a* igual, equivalente; justo; **to be — to** igualarse a, ser a propósito para, empatar, saber cumplir.
equality [i:'kwɔliti] *n* igualdad, uniformidad.
equanimity [,i:kwэ'nimiti] *n* ecuanimidad, serenidad.
equator [i'kweitэ] *n* ecuador.
equestrian [i'kwestriэn] *a* ecuestre.
equilibrium [,i:kwi'libriэm] *n* equilibrio.
equip [i'kwip] *vt* aprestar, aparejar, pertrechar.
equipage ['ekwipidʒ] *n* equipaje, tren.
equipment [i'kwipmэnt] *n* equipo, apresto, arreos, material.
equipping [i'kwipiŋ] *n* habilitación.
equitable ['ekwitэbl] *a* justo, equitativo.
equity ['ekwiti] *n* equidad, imparcialidad.
equivalent [i'kwivэlэnt] *n* equivalente.
equivocal [i'kwivэkэl] *a* equívoco, ambiguo.
era ['iэrэ] *n* era, época, período.
eradicate [i'rædikeit] *vt* extirpar, desarraigar.
erase [i'reiz] *vt* borrar, rayar, tachar.
eraser [i'reizэ] *n* borrador, goma.
erect [i'rekt] *a* derecho, erguido, enhiesto; *vti* erigir, erguir, levantar, enderezar; (*mech*) montar.
erection [i'rekʃэn] *n* erección, elevación, construcción; (*mech*) montaje.
ermine ['э:min] *n* armiño.
Ernest ['э:nist] *m* Ernesto.
erode [i'roud] *vi* (des)gastarse.
erosion [i'rouʒэn] *n* erosión, desgaste.
err [э:] *vi* errar, engañarse, equivocarse, no dar en el blanco; pecar de.
errand ['эrэnd] *n* recado, mensaje, encargo.
errant ['erэnt] *a* errante.
erratic [i'rætik] *a* errático, excéntrico.
erring ['э:riŋ] *a* errado; descarriado, extraviado.
erroneous [i'rouniэs] *a* erróneo, falso, errado.
error ['erэ] *n* error, yerro; equivocación, desacierto; desatino; **hideous** — herejía.
erudite ['erudait] *a* erudito, instruído.
escapade [,eskэ'peid] *n* escapada, calaverada, travesura.
escape [is'keip] *n* fuga, escape, huida; (*liquid*) derrame; *vti* escapar(se), evadirse, huir de, rehuir; (*gas*) desprenderse; **to — notice** pasar inadvertido.
escort ['eskɔ:t] *n* escolta; pareja; [is'kɔ:t] *vt* escoltar, convoyar, acompañar, resguardar.
eskimo ['eskimou] *an* esquimal.
esoteric [,esou'terik] *a* esotérico, oculto.
especial [is'peʃэl] *a* especial, particular.
especially [is'peʃэli] *ad* especialmente, sobre todo, máxime, suma mente.
espionage [,espiэ'nɑ:ʒ] *n* espionaje.
esquire [is'kwaiэ] *n* caballero, escudero, señor.
essay ['esei] *n* ensayo, composición; [e'sei] *vt* ensayar, intentar.
essayist ['eseiist] *n* ensayista.
essence ['esэns] *n* esencia, quintaesencia, constitución, médula.
essential [i'senʃэl] *a* esencial, constitutivo, radical, de rigor, imprescindible, indispensable, preciso, capital.
establish [is'tæbliʃ] *vt* establecer, fundar, acreditar, plantear; (*argument*) sentar; verificar.
establishment [is'tæbliʃmэnt] *n* establecimiento; fundación; (*staff*) escalafón.
estate [is'teit] *n* (*land*) finca, (*property*) hacienda, bienes, herencia, (*hunting*) coto; **real** — bienes raíces.
esteem [is'ti:m] *n* estima, consideración, acatamiento, aprecio; *vt* honrar, estimar, apreciar, tener (en, por).
Esther ['estэ] *f* Ester.

esthetics *see* **aesthetics.**
estimable ['estimabl] *a* apreciable, estimable.
estimate ['estimeit] *vt* estimar, valuar, apreciar, calcular, calificar, reputar, opinar.
estimate ['estimit] *n* (*com*) tasa, cálculo, presupuesto, cómputo; opinión, apreciación, estimación, calificación, graduación.
estimation [,esti'meiʃən] *n* estimación, estima, valuación, presupuesto.
estranged [is'treindʒd] *a* **to become** — estrañarse, malquistarse.
estrangement [is'treindʒmənt] *n* estrañamiento, desvío.
estuary ['estjuəri] *n* estuario; abra; (*Galicia*) ría.
etch [etʃ] *vt* grabar al agua fuerte.
etching ['etʃiŋ] *n* grabado.
eternal [i'tə:nl] *a* eterno, sempiterno, perpetuo.
eternity [i'tə:niti] *n* eternidad.
ether ['i:θə] *n* éter.
ethereal [i'θiəriəl] *a* etéreo; sutil, vaporoso.
ethic ['eθik] *a* ético, moral.
ethics ['eθiks] *n* la moral, ética, filosofía moral.
Ethiopia [i:θi'oupiə] *n* Etiopía.
Ethiopian [,i:θi'oupiən] *an* etíope.
etiquette ['etiket] *n* etiqueta, ceremonia.
etymology [,eti'mɔlədʒi] *n* etimología.
eulogize ['ju:lədʒaiz] *vt* elogiar, encomiar, preconizar, loar.
eulogy ['ju:lədʒi] *n* encomio, elogio, incienso.
eunuch ['ju:nək] *n* eunuco, capón, castrado.
euphuistic [,ju:fju(:)'istik] *a* gongorino, alambicado, culterano.
Europe ['juərəp] *n* Europa.
European [,juərə'piən] *an* europeo.
evacuate [i'vækjueit] *vt* evacuar, vaciar; hacer del cuerpo.
evade [i'veid] *vti* escapar, rehuir, esquivar, burlar, evadir.
evaluate [i'væljueit] *vt* avaluar.
evaporate [i'væpəreit] *vti* evaporar(se), disipar.
evasion [i'veiʒən] *n* evasión, subterfugio; escape, rodeo.
evasive [i'veiziv] *a* evasivo, esquivo.
eve [i:v] *n* víspera, tarde; **on the — of** la víspera de.
Eve [i:v] *f* Eva.
even ['i:vən] *a* unido, igual, plano; liso; sereno; (*number*) redondo; *ad* aun, hasta, todavía, tan siquiera; **not —** ni siquiera; *vt* igualar, aplanar, nivelar; **to get — with** desquitarse.
evening ['i:vniŋ] *a* crepuscular, vespertino; (*theat*) de la noche; *n* tarde, noche, atardecer, anochecer.
evenness ['i:vənnis] *n* igualdad, serenidad.
event [i'vent] *n* acontecimiento, suceso, caso; **at all —s** en todo caso, sea lo que fuera; **in the — of** en caso de.
eventful [i'ventful] *a* memorable.
eventual [i'ventʃuəl] *a* eventual, final, fortuito.
ever ['evə] *ad* siempre, jamás; en cualquier grado; **for —** para siempre; **for — and —** por siempre jamás; **— since** desde entonces; **as —** como siempre.
evergreen ['evəgri:n] *a* vivaz; *n* siempreviva.
everlasting [,evə'lɑ:stiŋ] *a* perpetuo, sempiterno, perenne.
every ['evri] *a* cada, todo; **— day** todos los días, cada día; **—body** todo el mundo; **— mother's son** cada hijo de vecino; **— other day** cada dos días, cada tercer día.
everyone ['evriwʌn] *n* todo el mundo, todos, cada uno.
everything ['evriθiŋ] *n* todo.
everywhere ['evriwɛə] *ad* por todas partes.
evermore ['evə'mɔ:] *ad* eternamente, siempre jamás.
evidence ['evidəns] *n* prueba(s); evidencia; **a piece of —** una prueba; (*law*) **to give —** dar testimonio, deponer; *vt* evidenciar, probar, mostrar.
evident ['evidənt] *a* evidente, aparente, visible; palmario; **quite —** notorio; **to be —** constar, resaltar; **to make —** demostrar.
evidently ['evidəntli] *ad* a las claras; por lo visto.
evil ['i:vl] *a* malo, maligno, perverso; **— -smelling** maloliente; **— -sounding** malsonante; **— eye** aojo; *n* mal, malignidad, maldad; **—doer** malhechor.
evoke [i'vouk] *vt* evocar.
evolution [,i:və'lu:ʃən] *n* evolución, desenvolvimiento.
evolve [i'vɔlv] *vti* desenvolver, desarrollar; hacer evolución.
ewe [ju:] *n* oveja.
exacerbate [eks'æsəbeit] *vt* exacerbar.
exact [ig'zækt] *a* exacto, preciso; concreto, cortado, cabal; *vt* exigir, imponer.
exacting [ig'zæktiŋ] *a* severo, exigente.
exactly [ig'zæktli] *ad* en punto, al pie de la letra, en concreto; **more —** propiamente dicho.
exactness [ig'zæktnis] *n* precisión, exactitud, definición, cuidado.
exaggerate [ig'zædʒəreit] *vt* exagerar; ponderar.
exaggeration [ig,zædʒə'reiʃən] *n* exageración, encarecimiento; **beyond all —** sobre todo encarecimiento, hasta no más.
exalt [ig'zɔ:lt] *vt* elevar, exaltar, ensalzar.

exaltation [ˌegzɔːl'teiʃən] *n* exaltación, elevación.
examination [igˌzæmi'neiʃən] *n* examen, verificación; (*for public post*) oposiciones; indagación; registro.
examine [ig'zæmin] *vt* examinar, verificar, probar, requerir; (*question*) ventilar; (*carefully*) escudriñar, indagar.
examiner [ig'zæminə] *n* examinador; inspector.
example [ig'zɑːmpl] *n* ejemplo, modelo, dechado; caso, lección, demostración; **for —** por ejemplo, verbigracia.
exasperate [ig'zæspereit] *vt* exasperar, irritar, sacar (de tino, de quicio).
exasperation [igˌzæspə'reiʃən] *n* exasperación, irritación, rabia.
excavate ['ekskəveit] *vt* cavar, excavar.
exceed [ik'siːd] *vt* exceder, pasar; (*expectations etc*) superar; propasarse; rebasar.
exceeding [ik'siːdiŋ] *n* excedente, extremo; *ad* en extremo.
exceedingly [ik'siːdiŋli] *ad* sobremanera, sumamente.
excel [ik'sel] *vti* sobresalir, superar, sobrepasar, señorear, resplandecer.
excellence ['eksələns] *n* excelencia, superioridad; (*title*) alteza.
excellent ['eksələnt] *a* excelente, precioso, admirable.
except [ik'sept] *vti* exceptuar, excluir, omitir; hacer caso omiso de; *prep* excepto, a menos que, salvo, menos, fuera de.
excepting [ik'septiŋ] *prep* excepto, a excepción de, salvo.
exception [ik'sepʃən] *n* excepción; **to take — to** objetar, desaprobar, resentirse de.
exceptional [ik'sepʃənl] *a* excepcional.
excess [ik'ses] *n* (*quantity*) exceso, sobrante, sobra; (*action*) desmán, desafuero; **— of care** nimiedad; **to be in —** sobrar.
excessive [ik'sesiv] *a* excesivo; **— detail** nimiedad; exorbitante, sobrado, recargado, violento.
exchange [iks'tʃeindʒ] *n* cambio; intercambio; (*financial*) bolsa; (*barter*) trueque; (*corn etc*) lonja; (*prisoners, documents*) canje; (*telephone*) oficina de teléfonos; *vt* cambiar; (*prisoners etc*) canjear; conmutar.
exchequer [iks'tʃekə] *n* hacienda.
excitable [ik'saitəbl] *a* neurasténico, entusiasta.
excite [ik'sait] *vt* excitar, provocar, incitar, ocasionar, sobreexcitar; **to get excited (about)** alborotarse, acalorarse, entusiasmarse; agitarse.
excitement [ik'saitmənt] *n* emoción, conmoción, excitación.
exciting [ik'saitiŋ] *a* estimulante, provocativo, conmovedor, apasionante, apasionado, incitante.
exclaim [iks'kleim] *vi* exclamar, gritar.
exclamation [ˌeksklə'meiʃən] *n* exclamación, grito; **— mark** punto de admiración.
exclude [iks'kluːd] *vt* excluir, exceptuar.
exclusion [iks'kluːʒən] *n* exclusión, excepción, eliminación.
exclusive [iks'kluːsiv] *a* exclusivo, privativo; **— rights** la exclusiva.
excommunicate [ˌekskə'mjuːnikeit] *vt* excomulgar, anatematizar.
excruciating [iks'kruːʃieitiŋ] *a* agudísimo; atroz.
excursion [iks'kəːʃən] *n* excursión, gira; (*on foot*) caminata; día de campo.
excuse [iks'kjuːs] *n* excusa, disculpa; salvedad, pretexto, salida; [iks'kjuːz] *vt* excusar, disculpar; dispensar; disimular; perdonar, eximir.
execute ['eksikjuːt] *vt* ejecutar; llevar a cabo, cumplir; (*theat*) trabajar, desempeñar; (*hang etc*) ajusticiar; (*document*) otorgar.
execution [ˌeksi'kjuːʃən] *n* ejecución, ejercicio; (*of document*) otorgamiento; (*death*) suplicio.
executioner [ˌeksi'kjuːʃnə] *n* verdugo.
executive [ig'zekjutiv] *a* ejecutivo; *n* gerente.
exemplary [ig'zempləri] *a* ejemplar.
exempt [ig'zempt] *a* exento, excusado, libre; *vt* exceptuar, excusar, libertar, dispensar.
exemption [ig'zempʃən] *n* exención; (*from taxes*) franquicia; inmunidad.
exercise ['eksəsaiz] *n* ejercicio; práctica, ensayo; *vti* ejercitar(se); hacer ejercicios; practicar; atarear, preocupar.
exert [ig'zəːt] *vt* esforzar(se); (*influence*) ejercer.
exertion [ig'zəːʃən] *n* esfuerzo.
exhaust [ig'zɔːst] *n* escape; *vt* agotar, gastar, fatigar, postrar; vaciar.
exhausted [ig'zɔːstid] *a* rendido, agotado, apurado; **to be —** no poder más.
exhaustion [ig'zɔːstʃən] *n* agotamiento; evacuación; postración.
exhaustive [ig'zɔːstiv] *a* agotador; minucioso, exhaustivo.
exhibit [ig'zibit] *vt* exhibir, mostrar, exponer; presentar, ofrecer.
exhibition [ˌeksi'biʃən] *n* exhibición; (*art*) exposición; demostración; **to make an — of oneself** ponerse en ridículo.
exhilarate [ig'zilərreit] *vt* regocijarse, alborozar, exaltar, excitar.
exhilaration [igˌzilə'reiʃən] *n* alegría, alborozo, excitación, acción *or* efecto vivificador(a).

exigence ['eksidʒəns] *n* exigencia, necesidad, demanda.
exile ['eksail] *n* (*state*) destierro; (*person*) desterrado; *vt* desterrar, proscribir, expatriar.
exist [ig'zist] *vi* existir.
existence [ig'zistəns] *n* existencia, vivir, ser.
existing [ig'zistiŋ] *a* existente.
exit ['eksit] *n* salida; partida; (*theat*) hace(n) mutis, va(n)se.
exonerate [ig'zɔnəreit] *vt* exonerar, disculpar, exculpar, aliviar.
exorbitant [ig'zɔ:bitənt] *a* exorbitante, excesivo, desproporcionado.
exorcize ['eksɔ:saiz] *vt* exorcizar, conjurar.
exotic [ig'zɔtik] *a* exótico, pintoresco.
expand [iks'pænd] *vti* extender, ensanchar; engrosar, (*of metals*) dilatarse.
expanse [iks'pæns] *n* extensión, envergadura.
expansion [iks'pænʃən] *n* expansión; (*metals*) dilatación; (*town etc*) ensanche; desarrollo.
expansive [iks'pænsiv] *a* expansivo, expresivo.
expect [iks'pekt] *vt* esperar; contar con; suponer.
expectation [.ekspek'teiʃən] *n* expectativa, esperanza.
expedience [iks'pi:diəns] *n* conveniencia, oportunidad, aptitud, propiedad.
expedient [iks'pi:diənt] *a* oportuno, conveniente, prudente; *n* expediente; medio, recurso.
expedition [.ekspi'diʃən] *n* expedición; prisa.
expel [iks'pel] *vt* arrojar, despedir, expulsar, echar.
expenditure [iks'penditʃə] *n* gasto, desembolso.
expense [iks'pens] *n* gasto, expensas; desembolso; **at any —** a toda costa.
expensive [iks'pensiv] *a* costoso, caro, dispendioso.
experience [iks'piəriəns] *n* experiencia, práctica; experimento; tentativa; aventura; *vt* experimentar, sentir.
experienced [iks'piəriənst] *a* experimentado, práctico, experto, adiestrado, versado, curtido.
experiment [iks'perimənt] *n* experimento, ensayo; [iks'periment] *vt* experimentar, hacer experimentos.
experimental [iks'perimentl] *a* experimental, tentativo.
expert ['ekspə:t] *a* experto, perito, hábil, autorizado; *n* experto, perito, trujimán.
expertness ['ekspə:tnis] *n* destreza, maña, habilidad.
expire [iks'paiə] *vti* expirar, fallecer; expeler; (*com*) vencer, cumplir(se).
explain [iks'plein] *vt* explicar, exponer, interpretar, ilustrar; *vr* sincerarse.
explanation [.ekspla'neiʃən] *n* explicación, aclaración, interpretación.
explanatory [iks'plænətəri] *a* explicativo.
explicit [iks'plisit] *a* explícito, formal, categórico.
explode [iks'ploud] *vti* volar, hacer saltar; reventar, desbaratar; estallar; hacer explosión; (*with anger*) reventar.
exploit ['eksplɔit] *n* hazaña; proeza; **youthful —** mocedad; [iks'plɔit] *vt* explotar.
exploration [.eksplɔ:'reiʃən] *n* exploración.
explore [iks'plɔ:] *vt* explorar; buscar, sondar.
explorer [iks'plɔ:rə] *n* explorador.
explosion [iks'plouʒən] *n* explosión, disparo, detonación.
explosive [iks'plouziv] *an* explosivo.
export ['ekspɔ:t] *n* exportación; *vt* exportar.
expose [iks'pouz] *vt* exponer, exhibir, manifestar; divulgar.
exposure [iks'pouʒə] *n* divulgación; escándalo; **north —** orientación al norte; (*phot*) exposición.
expound [iks'paund] *vt* exponer, manifestar; explicar, comentar, ampliar, desarrollar.
express [iks'pres] *a* expreso; formal, terminante, categórico; rápido; de encargo; **— train** tren expreso; **— company** compañía de transportes; *vt* expresar, manifestar; expedir por expreso; detonar; explicarse; **to — one's sorrow** (*on bereavement*) dar el pésame.
expression [iks'preʃən] *n* expresión, manifestación; semblante; (*word*) término, vocablo.
expressive [iks'presiv] *a* expresivo, vivo; (*eyes*) parleros.
expressly [iks'presli] *ad* expresamente, terminantemente; de propósito.
expulsion [iks'pʌlʃən] *n* expulsión.
expurgate ['ekspə:geit] *vt* (ex)purgar.
exquisite [eks'kwizit] *a* exquisito, excelente, esmerado, primoroso, rico; elegante.
exquisiteness [eks'kwizitnis] *n* excelencia, primor, perfección, delicadeza.
extempore [eks'tempəri] *a* improvisado; *ad* sin preparación; **to speak —** improvisar.
extend [iks'tend] *vt* extender, ensanchar, ampliar, prolongar; tender; (*offer*) ofrecer, otorgar; (*pull out*) estirar; *vi* extenderse; estirarse.
extension [iks'tenʃən] *n* extensión, prolongación, ensanche, ampliación; (*building*) anexo; (*com*) prórroga.
extensive [iks'tensiv] *a* extenso, vasto; extensivo, extendido, dilatado.
extent [iks'tent] *n* extensión, alcance,

amplitud, capacidad; **to some —** hasta cierto punto.
extenuate [eks'tenjueit] *vt* disminuir, minorar, atenuar, paliar.
extenuation [eks.tenju'eiʃən] *n* atenuación.
exterior [eks'tiəriə] *a* exterior, externo; *n* **rough —** corteza.
exterminate [eks'tə:mineit] *vt* exterminar, extirpar.
extermination [eks.tə:mi'neiʃən] *n* exterminio.
external [eks'tə:nl] *a* externo; **— trade** comercio exterior.
extinct [iks'tiŋkt] *a* (*volcano*) extinto; extinguido, abolido.
extinction [iks'tiŋkʃən] *n* extinción, abolición, aniquilación.
extinguish [iks'tiŋgwiʃ] *vt* extinguir, apagar; matar; suprimir.
extirpate ['ekstə:peit] *vt* extirpar, desarraigar.
extol [iks'tɔl] *vt* exaltar, celebrar, encarecer, encomiar, ensalzar.
extort [iks'tɔ:t] *vt* arrancar, arrebatar.
extortion [iks'tɔ:ʃən] *n* extorsión, exacción.
extra ['ekstrə] *a* suplementario, extraordinario; (*as spare*) de repuesto; *ad* de sobra; *n* exceso; (*on bill*) recargo, extra; (*in theat*) comparsa, extra.
extract ['ekstrækt] *n* extracto; resumen; [iks'trækt] *vt* extraer; (*teeth*) sacar; arrancar.
extraneous [eks'treiniəs] *a* extraño, extrínseco, exótico, ajeno.
extraordinary [iks'trɔ:dnri] *a* extraordinario, pasmoso, raro, prodigioso.
extravagance [iks'trævəgəns] *n* extravagancia; prodigalidad, derroche.
extravagant [iks'trævəgənt] *a* extravagante, exorbitante; disparatado, pródigo, manirroto.
Extremaduran [.ekstrəmə'dju:rən] *an* extremeño.
extreme [iks'tri:m] *a* extremo, sumo; riguroso; *n* extremo, extremidad.
extremely [iks'tri:mli] *ad* sumamente; (*bored etc*) hasta las cejas; hasta no más.
extremist [iks'tri:mist] *n* exaltado.
extremity [iks'tremiti] *n* extremidad, cabo, punta; (*trouble*) apuro; medida extrema.
extricate ['ekstrikeit] *vti* desembarazar(se), zafar(se), librar(se).
exuberance [ig'zu:bərəns] *n* exuberancia.
exuberant [ig'zu:bərənt] *a* exuberante, superfluo.
exude [ig'zju:d] *vt* (*juice etc*) rezumarse; transpirar.
exult [ig'zʌlt] *vi* regocijarse, exultar.
eye [ai] *n* ojo; **—ball** globo del ojo; (*sew*) corcheta; (*bot*) yema; (*mech*) ojal; mirada; **—brow** ceja; **—glass** anteojo; **—lash** pestaña; **—lid** párpado; **one-eyed** tuerto; **—shade** visera; **— socket** cuenca; **—tooth** colmillo; **evil —** mal de ojo; **to cry one's —s out** llorar (a mares, a moco tendido); **to keep an — on** vigilar; **to give black — to** poner el ojo como un tomate; **up to one's —s in** hasta las cejas; **with one's —s open** con conocimiento de causa; **blue-eyed** zarco; *vt* mirar (*detenidamente*), ojear.
eyesight ['aisait] *n* vista.
eyewitness ['ai.witnis] *n* testigo presencial.

F

fable ['feibl] *n* fábula, conseja, argumento, apólogo.
fabric ['fæbrik] *n* tejido, género, paño, fábrica; textura; edificio.
fabulous ['fæbjuləs] *a* fabuloso.
façade [fə'sɑ:d] *n* portada, fachada.
face [feis] *n* cara, semblante, rostro; superficie; frente; (*fam*) facha; (*vulg*) pinta; (*of earth*) faz; **smiling —** cara de Pascua(s); **sullen, gloomy —, — of misery** cara de viernes; (*mining*) tajo; **— to —** cara a cara; **— upward** boca arriba; **— downward** boca abajo, de bruces; **— guard** (*fencing etc*) careta; (*cheeky*) descaro, desfachatez; (*grimace*) mueca; **— value** valor nominal; **to shut the door in someone's —** darle con la puerta en las narices; *vt* afrontar, enfrentar, arrostrar, hacer (cara a, frente a); (*sew*) guarnecer, revestir; *vi* dar a; **to — up to** arrostrar, enfrentar, dar el pecho; **to — the music** pagar el pato, arrostrar las consecuencias; **not to — the music** escurrir el bulto.
facetious [fə'si:ʃəs] *a* chistoso, gracioso.
facetiousness [fə'si:ʃəsnis] *n* chiste, gracia.
facile ['fæsail] *a* fácil, vivo, ágil; obediente.
facilitate [fə'siliteit] *vt* facilitar, allanar, posibilitar; conseguir.
facing ['feisiŋ] *n* revestimiento, cubierta; *ad* en frente; frente a.
fact [fækt] *n* hecho, realidad, dato; **in —** en realidad, de hecho; **the — of the matter** la pura verdad.
faction ['fækʃən] *n* facción, pandilla, bando.
factory ['fæktəri] *n* fábrica, taller; factoría, manufactura.
faculty ['fækəlti] *n* facultad, potencia, poder, privilegio; (*univ*) facultad, profesorado.
fad [fæd] *n* capricho; chifladura; novedad.
fade [feid] *vi* marchitar(se), desteñirse, desmejorarse; **to — away,**

— **out** morir; extinguirse, ajarse.
faded ['feidid] *a* (*plants*) seco, marchito, mustio; (*color*) descolorido, pálido.
fading [feidiŋ] *a* que palidece, mortecino, decadente; *n* desparecimiento, decadencia.
fail [feil] *n* (*exam*) suspenso; **without —** sin falta; sin remedio; *vt* abandonar, faltar a; (*exam*) suspender; *vi* abortar, frustrarse, no lograr; fracasar; (*fin*) hacer bancarrota; (*exam*) salir mal; dar calabazas; **to —** to dejar de.
failing ['feiliŋ] *n* debilidad, falta, defecto.
failure ['feiljə] *n* fracaso, quiebra, malogro, falla; (*exam*) suspenso.
faint [feint] *a* imperceptible, tenue; débil; *n* deliquio, soponcio, desmayo; **— -hearted** pusilánime; *vi* desanimarse, desvanecerse, desmayarse.
faintness ['feintnis] *n* debilidad, desfallecimiento, desaliento.
fair [fɛə] *a* claro, limpio; bello, hermoso; honesto, honrado, justo; (*colour*) blondo, rubio; próspero; razonable; regular; **— play** juego limpio; **to make a — copy of** poner en limpio; *n* feria; **—ground** real.
fairness ['fɛənis] *n* lo rubio; hermosura; equidad, justicia, imparcialidad; **in all —** para ser justo.
fairy ['fɛəri] *n* hada; **— tale** cuento de hadas.
fairyland ['fɛərilænd] *n* país de las hadas.
faith [feiθ] *n* fe, lealtad; religión; crédito; **as an article of —** a pies juntillas; **to break —** faltar a la palabra.
faithful ['feiθful] *a* fiel, sincero; leal; recto; legal; puntual; **to be —** confiar, ser leal.
faithfully ['feiθfuli] *ad* honradamente; **yours —** quedo de Vd su servidor.
faithfulness ['feiθfulnis] *n* lealtad, fidelidad, honradez.
faithless ['feiθlis] *a* desleal, infiel, fementido.
faithlessness ['feiθlisnis] *n* deslealtad, perfidia, infidelidad.
fake [feik] *a* falso, postizo.
falcon ['fɔ:lkən] *n* halcón.
fall [fɔ:l] *n* caída; (*in ground*) bajada, declive, desnivel, descenso; (*morals*) desliz; (*water*) salto, cascada; (*ruin*) decadencia, degradación; (*price*) baja; (*music*) cadencia; inclinación; otoño; *vi* caer, bajar; disminuir, rendirse; corresponderle; echar por tierra; (*of face*) inmutarse; **to — asleep** dormirse; **to — in love** enamorarse; **to — to** (*one's lot*) tocar; **to — away** enflaquecer, desfallecer; **to — back** retroceder, hacerse atrás; **to — back on** recurrir a; **to — down** caerse; (*rock, picture etc*) desplomarse, desprenderse; **to — headlong** caer de bruces; **to — ill** indisponerse; **to — in** (*with idea*) coincidir (*con*); **to — into** dar en, sumirse (en), incurrir; **to — into** (*error*) incidir; **to — out** (*with*) extrañarse (*con*), indisponerse (*con*); **to — on** acometer; echarse sobre, asaltar; **to — short** escasear; **to — through** (*plans*) fracasar, naufragar, malograrse.
fallacy ['fæləsi] *n* engaño, falacia, error.
fallen ['fɔ:lən] *a* caído, arruinado, degradado.
falling ['fɔ:liŋ] *n* caída, deserción; **— in** desplome; **— star** estrella fugaz.
fallow ['fælou] *a* (*color*) flavo, leonado; (*land*) en barbecho; *n* barbecho; **— deer** gamo.
false [fɔls] *a* falso, fementido, traidor, pérfido, ilegal, hipócrita, postizo.
falsehood ['fɔlshud] *n* falsedad, embuste; (*lie*) mentira.
falsify ['fɔlsifai] *vt* falsificar, falsear, forjar.
falter ['fɔltə] *vi* temblar, vacilar, titubear; (*speech*) balbucir.
fame [feim] *n* fama, renombre, honra, gloria, prestigio, nombradía; (*after death*) posteridad.
familiar [fə'miliə] *a* conocido, íntimo; presumido, fresco; **— with** conocedor de.
familiarity [fə,mili'æriti] *n* familiaridad, confianza, intimidad; llaneza; conocimiento; (*fam*) frescura.
familiarize [fə'miliəraiz] *vt* familiarizar(se), acostumbrarse.
family ['fæmili] *a* familiar, casero; *n* familia, linaje, estirpe.
famine ['fæmin] *n* hambre, carestía.
famish ['fæmiʃ] *vi* morir de hambre; **to be —ed** comerse los codos de hambre.
famous ['feiməs] *a* famoso, célebre, celebrado, eximio, prestigioso, preclaro.
fan [fæn] *n* abanico; (*fam*) aficionado, entusiasta; *vt* abanicar, ventilar, aventar, soplar.
fanatic [fə'nætik] *an* fanático.
fanaticism [fə'nætisizəm] *n* fanatismo.
fancied ['fænsid] *a* imaginario, imaginado.
fanciful ['fænsiful] *a* fantástico, bizarro, caprichoso, imaginario, imaginativo.
fancy ['fænsi] *n* fantasía; imaginación, quimera; idea, ilusión; (*fam*) magín; *vi* imaginarse, creer; figurarse, antojarse, encapricharse por; **to take a — to** prenderse de; **— dress** disfraz.
fang [fæŋ] *n* colmillo, diente.
fantastic [fæn'tæstik] *a* fantástico, quimérico, ilusorio.
fantasy ['fæntəzi] *n* fantasía, ensueño, imaginación.
far [fɑ:] *a* lejano, distante; **— reach-**

ing trascendente, remoto; — **away** (*fig*) distraído; —**-fetched** forzado, traído por los pelos; —**-seeing** perspicaz; *ad* (*a lo*) lejos; en alto grado; **by** — (con, por) mucho; **from** — desde lejos; — **from** lejos de.
farce [fɑ:s] *n* farsa, sainete, entremés.
farcical ['fɑ:sikəl] *a* burlesco, bufo, ridículo.
fare [fɛə] *n* (*price*) pasaje, precio (*del billete*); (*scale of*) —**s** tarifa; vianda, comida; **bill of** — lista de platos; *vi* pasarlo, suceder, acontecer.
farewell [fɛə'wel] *a* de despedida; *n* adiós; **to bid** — despedirse (*de*).
farm [fɑ:m] *n* granja; (*Andal*) cortijo; *SA* hato; —**hand** gañán, peón, labrador; —**house** alquería, granja, casa; —**yard** corral; *vt* cultivar, labrar la tierra, dar en arriendo.
farmer ['fɑ:mə] *n* labrador, cultivador, colono, hacendado, agricultor.
farther ['fɑ:ðə] *ad* más lejos, más allá; además.
farthing ['fɑ:ðiŋ] *n* (*equiv*) maravedí, cuarto, cuartillo.
fascinate ['fæsineit] *vt* fascinar, encantar, embelesar.
fascinating ['fæsineitiŋ] *a* hechicero.
fascination [ˌfæsi'neiʃən] *n* encanto, fascinación, hechicería.
fascist ['fæʃist] *an* fascista; (*Spanish*) falangista.
fashion ['fæʃən] *n* manera, forma, moda; buen tono; uso; **to be in** — estar de moda; **out of** — pasado de moda; *vt* formar, dar forma, ajustar; forjar; modelar.
fashionable ['fæʃnəbl] *a* a la moda, de buen tono, al uso; **to be** — estar de boga.
fast [fɑ:st] *n* vigilia; — **day** día de abstinencia; *a* firme; (*pace etc*) apretado, rápido, veloz; (*dye etc*) fijo, insoluble, inalterable; constante, duradero; ligero; (*watch*) adelantado; **to be** — **friends** ser uña y carne; **to make** — trincar, sujetar, asegurar; *vi* ayunar.
fasten ['fɑ:sn] *vt* fijar, afirmar, asegurar; pegar; atarugar; **to** — **down** sujetar; amarrar; **to** — **on** (*like leech*) cebarse en; *vi* agarrarse, asirse, cerrarse.
fastener ['fɑ:snə] *n* fiador; asegurador; cerrojo; **zip** — cremallera.
fastening ['fɑ:sniŋ] *n* unión, ligazón, cierre.
fastidious [fæs'tidiəs] *a* delicado; quisquilloso; exigente; descontentadizo, melindroso.
fastness ['fɑ:stnis] *n* firmeza; plaza fuerte; velocidad.
fat [fæt] *a* gordo, grasiento; grueso; lerdo; opulento, lucrativo; (*money etc*) pingüe; **to get** — engordar, echar carnes; *n* grasa; sebo; (*animal*) unto.
fatal ['feitl] *a* fatal, funesto, mortal; — **moment** hora menguada.
fatality [fə'tæliti] *n* fatalidad; desgracia; sino.
fate [feit] *n* hado, destino, suerte; **awful** — fatalidad.
father ['fɑ:ðə] *n* padre; —**-in-law** suegro; *vt* prohijar, reconocer; **to** — **upon** achacar, imputar.
fatherland ['fɑ:ðəlænd] *n* (madre) patria.
fathom ['fæðəm] *n* braza, toesa, brazada; *vt* sondar, sondear, tantear.
fathomless ['fæðəmlis] *a* sin fondo, insondable; impenetrable.
fatigue [fə'ti:g] *n* fatiga, cansancio: pesadez; (*mil*) faena; *vt* fatigar, rendir, reventar.
fatness ['fætnis] *n* grasa, carnosidad; (*land*) fecundidad.
fatten ['fætn] *vt* engordar; (*land*) abonar; **to** — **up** (*animals*) cebar.
fatty ['fæti] *a* untoso, grasiento, graso.
fatuous ['fætjuəs] *a* fatuo, necio, insensato, majadero.
faucet ['fɔ:sit] *n* grifo.
fault [fɔlt] *n* falta; culpa; desliz, tropiezo; (*geol*) falla; (*blot*) defecto, lunar, imperfección; **to find** — **with** tachar, criticar.
faultless ['fɔltlis] *a* perfecto, sin tacha, acabado, impecable.
faulty ['fɔlti] *a* defectuoso, deficiente, imperfecto.
favor ['feivə] *n* favor, servicio, gracia; honra; protección; (*at Court*) privanza; **popular** — aura popular; (*token*) prenda; *vt* favorecer; sufragar, secundar.
favorable ['feivərəbl] *a* conveniente, favorable, propicio.
favored ['feivəd] *a* favorito; **well-**— bien parecido.
favorite ['feivərit] *n* favorito, predilecto, preferido, valido.
fawn [fɔ:n] *a* color de cervato; *n* cervato; *vt* **to** — **on** acariciar, adular, lisonjear.
fawning ['fɔ:niŋ] *n* adulación, lisonja(s).
fear [fiə] *n* miedo, recelo, aprensión, espanto, (*great*) pavor; — **of God** temor de Dios; **for** — por miedo; *vt* temer; *vi* tener miedo.
fearful ['fiəful] *a* (*thing etc*) pavoroso, terrífico, horrendo, miedoso, horrible; (*person*) miedoso, temeroso, aprensivo, espantadizo, tímido.
fearless ['fiəlis] *a* intrépido, atrevido, impávido, audaz.
fearlessness ['fiəlisnis] *n* intrepidez, impavidez.
fearsome ['fiəsəm] *a* medroso; (*thing*) espantoso.
feasible ['fi:zəbl] *a* factible, posible, dable, hacedero.
feast [fi:st] *n* fiesta, festín; (*relig*)

pascua; banquete; *vti* festejar, agasajar, comer opíparamente.

feasting ['fi:stiŋ] *n* banquete, fiesta.

feat [fi:t] *n* hazaña, hecho, proeza.

feather ['feðə] *n* pluma; — **-brained** casquivano, ligero de casco(s); **—brain** *n* badulaque, cabeza de chorlito; — **duster** plumero; *vt* adornar con plumas, emplumar.

feature ['fi:tʃə] *n* (*of face*) facción; (*of character*) rasgo, característica; *pl* semblante.

February ['februəri] *n* febrero.

fed [fed] *v* **to be — up** estar hasta la coronilla; fastidiarse; estar harto (*de*).

federal ['fedərəl] *a* federal, federalista.

federation [,fedə'reiʃən] *n* federación.

fee [fi:] *n* honorarios; gratificación; derechos; **membership** — cuota; **entrance —s** matrícula; *vt* pagar, retener.

feeble ['fi:bl] *a* débil, lánguido, endeble; impotente, flojo; (*from age*) chocho.

feebleminded ['fi:bl'maindid] *a* fioño, idiota, imbécil.

feebleness ['fi:blnis] *n* debilidad, tenuidad.

feed [fi:d] *n* comida; (*sl*) cuchipanda; (*for animals*) pienso; *vt* alimentar, dar de comer a; (*furnace*) cebar; *vi* mantenerse; (*pasture*) pacer; **to — upon** comer.

feeding ['fi:diŋ] *n* alimento, forraje, alimentación; — **bottle** biberón.

feel [fi:l] *n* tacto, tocamiento; sensación; *vt* sentir, tocar, palpar, percibir; experimentar; **to — for** (con)dolerse de; buscar a tientas; **to — around** tantear, tentar; *vi* (*ill*) encontrarse, hallarse; **to — like** tener ganas de.

feeling ['fi:liŋ] *a* sensible, patético; *n* (*emotion*) sentimiento; (*senses*) sensación; sensibilidad; **to have a —** presentir; **to hurt one's —s** tocar en lo vivo, herir el amor propio.

feign [fein] *vti* fingir, simular, disimular.

felicity [fi'lisiti] *n* felicidad, bienaventuranza, dicha.

fell [fel] *a* cruel; *n* (*hide*) piel; (*moor*) páramo; *vt* derribar; (*trees*) talar; tumbar, tronchar; (*cattle*) acogotar.

fellow ['felou] *n* compañero, compadre; camarada; individuo; **young** — chico; **old** — tío; (*fam*) tipo; — **guest** comensal; — **member** consocio; (*of special group*) contertuliano; — **creature** semejante, prójimo; — **partner** consocio; **to have a — feeling for** simpatizar con.

fellowship ['felouʃip] *n* compañerismo, confraternidad, (*grant*) beca, colegiatura.

felt [felt] *a* **deeply** — sentido; *n* fieltro; — **hat** fieltro.

female ['fi:meil] *a* femenino, propio de la hembra; *n* mujer, hembra.

feminine ['feminin] *a* femenino, femenil, mujeril.

fen [fen] *n* pantano, marjal.

fence [fens] *n* cerca, valla, defensa; estacada; seto; *vti* defender, encerrar, cercar; esgrimir; **to sit on the** — estar a ver venir.

fencing ['fensiŋ] *n* (*sport*) esgrima; valladar.

fend [fend] *vt* parar golpes; **to — for oneself** defenderse.

fender [fendə] (*aut*) alero, guardabarros.

Ferdinand ['fə:dinənd] *m* Fernando.

ferment ['fə:ment] *n* fermento; levadura; agitado; [fə'ment] *vti* fermentar, revenirse.

fermentation [,fə:men'teiʃən] *n* fermentación.

fern [fə:n] *n* helecho.

ferocious [fə'rouʃəs] *a* feroz, fiero, salvaje.

ferocity [fə'rɔsiti] *n* ferocidad, fiereza, ensañamiento.

ferret ['ferit] *n* hurón: *vt* huronear, indagar; **to — out** husmear.

ferry ['feri] *n* pasaje, embarcadero; **—boat** barca; (*large*) barcaza, balsa; *vti* pasar; **to — across** cruzar (un río).

fertile ['fə:tail] *a* fértil; feraz; (*brain*) imaginativo.

fertility [fə:'tiliti] *n* fertilidad, abundancia.

fertilize ['fə:tilaiz] *vt* fertilizar, fecundizar; (*manure*) abonar.

fertilizer ['fə:tilaizə] *n* abono.

fervent ['fə:vənt] *a* fervoroso, fogoso, ardiente.

fervor ['fə:və] *n* fervor, ardor, calor, celo, devoción.

fester ['festə] *vi* ulcerar(se); enconar(se).

festival ['festivəl] *n* fiesta, festividad.

festive ['festiv] *a* festivo, regocijado, de fiesta.

festivity [fes'tiviti] *n* fiesta, regocijo, alborozo.

fetch [fetʃ] *vt* ir a traer, recoger, ir por; venderse por.

fetid ['fetid] *a* hediondo, fétido.

fetter ['fetə] *n pl* grillos, cadenas, prisiones, esposas; *vt* encadenar, trabar.

feud [fju:d] *n* feudo; riña, enemistad, pendencia, rencilla.

feudal ['fju:dl] *a* feudal.

feudalism ['fju:dəlizəm] *n* feudalismo.

fever ['fi:və] *n* fiebre; calentura, dengue; **typhoid** — tifoidea; — (*of excitement*) sobreexcitación.

feverish ['fi:vəriʃ] *a* febril, calenturiento; ardiente.

few [fju:] *a* pocos; **quite a** — bastantes; **the** — los menos; **—er** menos.

fewness ['fju:nis] *n* corto número.

fiancé [fi'ɑ:nsei] *n* novio; **—e** *f* novia, prometida.
fiber ['faibə] *n* fibra, hebra.
fickle ['fikl] *a* voluble, inconstante, novelero, veleidoso, antojadizo.
fickleness ['fiklnis] *n* inconstancia, volubilidad, mudanza.
fiction ['fikʃən] *n* fábula, ficción; embuste.
fictitious [fik'tiʃəs] *a* imaginario, falso; contrahecho.
fiddle ['fidl] *n* violín; *vi* jugar; enredar; *vt* engañar, estafar.
fidelity [fi'deliti] *n* fidelidad, lealtad.
fidget ['fidʒit] *vti* molestar, inquietar, afanarse; **don't —!** ¡estáte quieto!
fidgety ['fidʒiti] *a* inquieto, agitado, impaciente.
field [fi:ld] *n* campo, campaña; (*meadow*) prado, pradera; **ice—** banco de hielo; **wheat—** trigal; **sports —** campo de deportes; **— mouse** ratón, campañol; *vt* recoger (*la pelota*).
fiend [fi:nd] *n* demonio, diablo; arpía.
fierce [fiəs] *a* feroz, torvo, acérrimo, furioso, fogoso.
fierceness ['fiəsnis] *n* ferocidad, fiereza.
fiery ['faiəri] *a* fogoso, ardiente, caliente, vehemente, furibundo, brioso, fiero.
fifteen [fif'ti:n] *an* quince.
fifteenth [fif'ti:nθ] *an* décimoquinto, (el) quince.
fifth [fifθ] *an* quinto; (*mus*) quinta; (*of month*) el cinco.
fifty ['fifti] *an* cincuenta; **about —** una cincuentena, unos cincuenta.
fig [fig] *n* higo; **early —** breva; **—tree** higuera; **to be not worth a —** no valer un bledo; (*fig*) **— leaf** hoja de parra.
fight [fait] *n* pelea, lucha, combate; *vti* luchar, batirse, combatir; **to — with bare fists** luchar a brazo partido; **to — to** pugnar por, batallar.
fighter ['faitə] *n* combatiente, guerrero, luchador.
fighting ['faitiŋ] *a* aguerrido, guerrero; **— cock** gallo de pelea; *n* combate, riña, disputa.
figure ['figə] *n* forma, figura, cuerpo; tipo, talla; **lay —** figurín; *vt* figurar, dar forma, representar; **to cut a —** hacer papel.
file [fail] *n* (*mech*) lima; (*papers*) carpeta; expediente, legajo; (*mil*) fila; *vt* limar; archivar, legajar; (*mil*) desfilar; ensartar.
filial ['filiəl] *a* filial.
fill [fil] *n* terraplén; abundancia, hartura; colmo; *vt* llenar; saturar; hartar; **to — in, up** terraplenar, llenar un hueco; colmar; (*form*) llenar, cubrir; (*with emotion*) imbuir; (*to brim*) colmar; **to — a vacancy** cubrir una vacante.
filling ['filiŋ] *n* envase; relleno; (*dental*) empaste; **gold —** orificación.
film [film] *n* película; cinta; (*of dirt*) capa; *vi* (*cinema*) rodar; **to — over** empañar.
filth [filθ] *n* suciedad; basura, inmundicia, roña, mugre; miseria; cochinería, porquería.
filthiness ['filθinis] *n* porquería, asquerosidad.
filthy ['filθi] *a* sucio, inmundo, grasiento, cochino, guarro; **what a — mess!** ¡qué porqueıía!, ¡qué asco!
fin [fin] *n* aleta.
final ['fainl] *a* final, decisivo, definitivo, terminante; **— exam** (*before University*) reválida.
finally ['fainəli] *ad* en fin, finalmente, en conclusión, en definitiva, por último, ya.
finance [fai'næns] *n* hacienda; fondos, finanzas; *vt* financiar.
financial [fai'nænʃəl] *a* financiero, bancario, rentístico; bursátil.
find [faind] *n* hallazgo; *vt* encontrar, hallar, descubrir, dar con; (*supply*) abastecer, surtir; **to — out** hallar, llegar a saber, enterarse; **I found out** supe; averigüé.
fine [fain] *a* bello, primoroso, hermoso; fino, refinado, escogido, elegante; **— work** (*sew*) labor fina; tenue, sútil; agudo; **— arts** bellas artes; *n* multa; *vt* multar.
fineness ['fainnis] *n* elegancia, delicadeza, fineza, sutileza; (*of thread, sand etc*) grosor, grueso.
finery ['fainəri] *n* adorno(s), galas.
finesse [fi'nes] *n* tino, tacto.
finger ['fiŋgə] *n* dedo; **fore —** dedo índice; **middle —** dedo del corazón; **ring —** dedo anular; **little —** dedo meñique; **—nail** uña; **—prints** huellas (dactilares, digitales); **—stall** dedil, dedal; **light-fingered** ligero de manos; **to have at one's —tips** saber al dedillo; *vt* (*instrument*) pulsar, tañer; (*to mark, spoil*) manosear.
finish ['finiʃ] *n* fin, final; remate; brillo; colmo; *vt* acabar, completar, rematar; (*mil service*) cumplir; **to — off** rematar; ultimar, completar; acabar con; (*vulg*) despachar; dar la última mano a.
finished ['finiʃt] *a* acabado; **— off** rematado; (*fam*) matado, muerto.
Finland ['finlənd] *n* Finlandia.
Finnish ['finiʃ] *an* finlandés.
fir [fə:] *n* abeto, pino.
fire ['faiə] *n* fuego; incendio; (*in house*) lumbre; ardor, viveza; (*shot*) descarga, tiro; **—arm** arma de fuego; **—brand** tizón, paveza; **—eater** matamoros; **—engine** bomba de incendios; **— escape** escala de incendios; **—place** hogar, chimenea; **—proof** incombustible, a prueba de incendio; **—proof curtain** telón de incendios; **—screen** pantalla; **—wood** leña; **to set on —** inflamar, incendiar;

to set — to pegar fuego a; *vt* abrasar, quemar, enardecer; tirar; **to — on** disparar sobre, hacer fuego sobre; (*fig*) enfadarse, descargar.
fireman ['faiəmən] *n* bombero; (*rl*) fogonero.
fireworks ['faiəwə:ks] *n pl* fuegos artificiales; **the art of making —** pirotécnica; **maker of —** cohetero.
firing ['faiəriŋ] *n* incendio, fuego; ignición; **— on** disparo; **— party** pelotón de ejecución, piquete.
firm [fə:m] *a* firme, fuerte, seguro, estable, sólido; consistente; tenaz; *n* casa de comercio; empresa; entidad.
firmament ['fə:məmənt] *n* firmamento.
firmness ['fə:mnis] *n* firmeza, constancia, decisión; solidez.
first [fə:st] *a* primero; original; **— night performance** estreno; **— kick, turn** (*in games*) saque; **— fruit** primicia; **— class** (*quality*) de primera (clase); sobresaliente; **— cousin** primo hermano; *ad* en primer lugar; **— and foremost** principalmente; **— hand** de primera mano.
fish [fiʃ] *n* pez; (*caught*) pescado; **flying —** pez volador; **neither — nor fowl** ni es chicha ni limonada; **— hook** hamo; *vt* pescar.
fisher ['fiʃə] *n* pescador.
fisherman ['fiʃəmən] *n* pescador.
fishing ['fiʃiŋ] *n* pesca; **— rod** caña de pescar; **— tackle** aparejo de pescar.
fissure ['fiʃə] *n* grieta, hendidura, raja, resquebrajo.
fist [fist] *n* puño; **—ful** puñado; **with —s** a bofetadas.
fit [fit] *a* conveniente, propio, apto, bueno, adecuado, apropiado, compatible; **— to eat** comestible; **— to drink** potable; **to be —** (*physically*) estar fuerte, en buenas condiciones; *n* (*illness etc*) ataque, acceso; (*clothes*) ajuste; (*box etc*) encaje; (*sudden desire*) arranque; ímpetu; (*fainting*) desmayo, síncope; **by fits and starts** a tontas y a locas; **subject to —s** epiléptico; *vt* ajustar, acomodar, adaptar; disponer; entallar (*un vestido*); *vi* cuajar: convenir, venir bien; ser a propósito; **to — in(to)** caber; **to — in with** cuadrar; **to — into** entrar en; **to — closely** ceñir, entallar; **to — perfectly** venir como anillo al dedo; **to — out** (*ship*) armar.
fitful ['fitful] *a* caprichoso
fitness ['fitnis] *n* conveniencia, idoneidad; propiedad; condición.
fitting ['fitiŋ] *n* ajuste, entalladura; **— on** (*clothes*) prueba; **— out** habilitación; *pl* guarniciones.
five [faiv] *an* cinco.
fix [fiks] *n* (*sl*) lío; **to be in a —** hallarse en un (apuro, aprieto); *vt* colocar; estampar; (*attention, date etc*) fijar; señalar; (*eyes*) clavar; (*blame*) colgar; (*price*) tasar; (*in one's mind*) precisar, puntualizar; (*bayonet*) calar; (*color etc*) imprimir; **to — on** señalar, determinar; **to — up** componer, arreglar; **to — up** (*with*) citarse, arreglarlo (*con*).
fixed [fikst] *a* fijo, inmutable; asentado.
fixture ['fikstʃə] *n* instalación, accesorio fijo; (*sport*) partido.
flabby ['flæbi] *a* flojo, lacio, blanducho.
flag [flæg] *n* bandera, estandarte; (*small*) banderín; (*national*) pabellón, colores; **—stone** losa baldosa; **— staff** asta de bandera; **to lower the —** arriar la bandera; *vi* flaquear.
flagrant ['fleigrənt] *a* notorio, flagrante, público.
flake [fleik] *n* cascajo, hojuela; (*snow*) copo; (*scale*) escama.
flame [fleim] *n* llama; fuego; *vi* llamear, flamear, encenderse, inflamarse.
flaming ['fleimiŋ] *a* llameante; (*color*) llamativo, chillón.
flange [flændʒ] *n* pestaña; reborde, brida, oreja.
flank [flæŋk] *n* (*mil*) flanco; costado; (*animal*) ijar, ijada; *vt* orillar; (*mil*) flanquear: *vi* lindar con.
flannel ['flænl] *n* franela.
flap [flæp] *n* falda, faldilla; (*mech*) lengüeta; *vt* batir, agitar; **to — wings** aletear.
flare [flɛə] *n* llamarada, destello; (*sew*) ensanche, vuelo; **—up** arrebato de cólera; *vi* resplandecer, fulgurar; **to — up** encolerizarse.
flash [flæʃ] *n* (*lightning*) relámpago; (*flame*) llamarada; (*of wit*) rasgo de ingenio; (*light*) ráfaga, destello; (*gun*) fogonazo; *vti* relampaguear, destellar, centellear, fulgurar.
flashing ['flæʃiŋ] *n* centelleo; *a* centellador, brillante, chispeante.
flashlight ['flæʃlait] *n* lamparilla eléctrica.
flask [flɑ:sk] *n* frasco, redoma, pomo.
flat [flæt] *a* llano, raso, liso; igual; insípido, soso; monótono; *ad* **to sing —** desafinar; *n* (*land*) llano, llanura; (*of hand*) palma; (*mus*) bemol; (*sword*) plano; (*dwelling*) piso, cuarto.
flatness ['flætnis] *n* llanura; insipidez; insulsez.
flatten ['flætn] *vt* aplastar, apisonar; aplanar, nivelar; igualar; achatar, deprimir; (*fam*) reventar; *vi* aplanarse.
flatter ['flætə] *vt* lisonjear, adular, requebrar, dar coba a.
flattering ['flætəriŋ] *a* lisonjero, halagüeño; galán; **— phrase** piropo.
flattery ['flætəri] *n* (*often pl*) adulación, halago, lisonja, piropo.
flaunt [flɔ:nt] *vt* hacer alarde ostentar, lucir.
flavor ['fleivə] *n* sabor olor; (*speech*)

dejo; *vt* saborear, sazonar, condimentar.
flaw [flɔ:] *n* tacha, imperfección; deficiencia; (*complexion*) lunar; grieta; (*in argument*) falla.
flax [flæks] *n* lino.
flay [flei] *vt* desollar, excoriar.
flea [fli:] *n* pulga.
flee [fli:] *vt* huir de, esquivar; *vi* huir, fugarse.
fleece [fli:s] *n* vellón; **Golden —** vellocino de oro; *vt* esquilar, despojar.
fleecy ['fli:si] *a* lanoso, lanudo; (*clouds*) aborregadas.
fleet [fli:t] *a* veloz, ligero; **— -footed** rápido; *n* flota; armada, flotilla.
fleeting ['fli:tiŋ] *a* efímero, fugaz, pasajero.
fleetness ['fli:tnis] *n* rapidez, velocidad, ligereza.
flesh [fleʃ] *n* carne; (*fruit*) pulpa; **—pot** olla; **—colored** encarnado; **in the —** en persona.
fleshy ['fleʃi] *a* carnal; (*fruit*) carnoso.
flex [fleks] *n* flexible; *vt* doblar.
flexibility [ˌfleksi'biliti] *n* flexibilidad; docilidad.
flexible ['fleksəbl] *a* flexible, dúctil, plástico.
flicker ['flikə] *n* parpadeo; *vi* vacilar, fluctuar, aletear.
flight [flait] *n* (*bird, plane*) vuelo; (*escape*) huida, fuga; (*bullet etc*) trayecto; (*arrows, etc*) descarga; (*of planes*) escuadrilla; (*of birds*) bandada; (*of fancy*) ilusión, exaltación.
flimsy ['flimzi] *a* endeble, sutil, baladí, frívolo.
flinch [flintʃ] *vi* vacilar, retroceder, acobardarse, titubear.
fling [fliŋ] *n* tiro; brinco; bravata; *vt* lanzar, arrojar, botar; **to — away** tirar; **to — out** (*nets etc*) tender; (*into face*) zaherir; **to — oneself** tirarse, arrojarse; **to — oneself down** tumbarse; **to have a —** correrla.
flint [flint] *n* pedernal.
flippant ['flipənt] *a* poco serio, ligero, petulante.
flirt [flə:t] *n* coqueta; (*lower class*) maja; *vi* coquetear; camelar, pelar la pava; burlarse.
flit [flit] *vi* revolotear, mariposear.
float [flout] *n* cosa que (flota, balsa-boya;) (*fishing*) corcho, bote; carromato; *vt* mantener a flote; poner en circulación; *vi* (*person*) hacer la plancha, flotar.
floating ['floutiŋ] *a* flotante.
flock [flɔk] *n* (*sheep*) rebaño, hato; (*birds*) bandada; (*relig*) grey; *vi* congregarse, juntarse.
floe [flou] *n* masa de hielo flotante, témpano.
flog [flɔg] *vt* azotar, vapulear, zurrar.
flood [flʌd] *n* inundación, diluvio, riada, avenida; (*fig*) plétora; **— tide** pleamar; **—gates** compuertas; *vt* inundar.
flooding ['flʌdiŋ] *n* inundación.
floor [flɔ:] *n* piso, suelo, pavimento; fondo; **ground—** planta baja; **first —** piso principal; (*dance etc*) pista; *vt* tumbar; derrotar, aplanar.
flooring ['flɔ:riŋ] *n* piso, suelo; tablado, entarimado.
Florence ['flɔrəns] *f* Florencia.
florid ['flɔrid] *a* florido; (*color*) bermejo, colorado, vivo; (*skin*) encarnado.
florist ['flɔrist] *n* florista.
flotsam ['flɔtsəm] *n* pecio(s); resto, deshecho.
flounce [flauns] *n* volante, fleco; *vi* brincar (*de impaciencia*).
flour ['flauə] *n* harina.
flourish ['flʌriʃ] *n* boato, gallardía; trompeteo; prosperidad, vigor; (*writing*) rasgo, rúbrica; *vt* blandir, menear, vibrar; *vi* florecer, prosperar; preludiar; (*writing*) rasguear.
flourishing ['flʌriʃiŋ] *a* floreciente.
flout [flaut] *vti* burlarse de; ridiculizar; despreciar.
flow [flou] *n* curso, corriente; flujo; caudal; copia; *vi* fluir, correr; dimanar, proceder; **to — into** desaguar, desembocar; **to — together** confluir.
flower ['flauə] *n* flor; **—bed** cuadro, arriate; **—pot** tiesto, maceta; canastillo; *vi* florecer, *SA* florear.
flowery ['flauəri] *a* florido.
flowing ['flouiŋ] *a* corriente; (*hair*) suelto; fácil; fluido; **full —** caudaloso.
fluctuate ['flʌktjueit] *vi* fluctuar; balancearse.
fluctuation [ˌflʌktju'eiʃən] *n* vaivén, incertidumbre, variación.
fluency ['flu:ənsi] *n* fluidez; (*speech*) soltura, facilidad; afluencia.
fluent ['flu:ənt] *a* corriente, abundante; copioso; (*language*) fluido, suelto, fácil.
fluff [flʌf] *n* pelusa, lanilla.
fluid ['flu:id] *an* fluido, líquido.
flurry ['flʌri] *n* conmoción; barullo; (*snow*) ráfaga, racha; *vt* agitar, aturrullar.
flush [flʌʃ] *a* ras, nivelado; adinerado; *n* (*water*) flujo; (*shame*) sonrojo, rubor; abundancia, copia; *vt* inundar; *vi* brotar; ruborizarse, sonrojarse; (*with triumph*) engreírse.
fluster ['flʌstə] *vt* bullir; embriagar, aturdir.
flute [flu:t] *n* flauta; acanaladura; (*archit*) estría.
flutter ['flʌtə] *n* batir de alas; agitación; *vt* menear, agitar; *vi* mover sin ton ni son; agitarse; **to — around** revolotear.
fly [flai] *n* mosca; pliegue, bragueta; **—leaf** anteportada; **—wheel** rueda volante; (*theat*) bambalina; *vi* escaparse, huir; volar, saltar; precipitarse; **to — into passion** montar en cólera; **to — off** desprenderse; **to let —** descargar.

flying ['flaiiŋ] *a* volante, volador; veloz; **— boat** hidroavión; **— buttress** arbotante; **with — colors** (*mil*) con banderas desplegadas; *n* volar, vuelo.
foam [foum] *n* espuma; *vi* hacer, echar espuma.
focus ['foukəs] *n* foco, centro; *vt* enfocar, concentrar.
fodder ['fɔdə] *n* forraje.
foe [fou] *n* enemigo, adversario.
fog [fɔg] *n* (*sea*) bruma; (*land*) niebla; (*thin*) neblina; (*heavy*) cerrazón.
foggy ['fɔgi] *a* brumoso, nebuloso; (*sea*) abrumado.
foil [fɔil] *n* oropel; florete; *vt* frustrar, deshacer, chasquear.
fold [fould] *n* pliegue, doblez; (*sheep etc*) majada; corral, redil; *vt* arrugar, plegar; envolver; doblar; enlazar; **to — one's arms** cruzar los brazos.
folding ['fouldiŋ] *a* plegable; plegadizo; **— bed** catre de tijera; **— chair** silla de tijera; *n* pliegue.
foliage ['fouliidʒ] *n* follaje, copa.
folk [fouk] *n* gente, gentes; raza, pueblo; **—song** canción popular.
follow ['fɔlou] *vt* seguir, acompañar; seguir la pista a; perseguir; (*profession*) ejercer; acatar; copiar; *vi* resultar, sobrevenir, suceder; **to — suit** (*cards*) asistir.
follower ['fɔlouə] *n* compañero, partidario, discípulo; secuaz; (*eager*) entusiasta; **—s** comitiva; estela; **camp —** vivandera.
following ['fɔlouiŋ] *n* séquito.
folly [fɔli] *n* necedad, tontería, insensatez; disparate; locura.
foment [fou'mənt] *vt* fomentar; nutrir; provocar.
fond [fɔnd] *a* aficionado, muy dado a, tierno, cariñoso; **to be — of** querer; ser amigo de; **I am — of coffee** me gusta el café.
fondle ['fɔndl] *vt* acariciar, arrullar.
fondness ['fɔndnis] *n* ternura, terneza, inclinación, afición, afecto, pasión, apego.
food [fu:d] *n* alimento; pasto; (*mushy*) papas; (*for thought*) pábulo; comida, víveres, provisiones.
fool [fu:l] *n* necio, tonto, loco, imbécil, idiota; (*theat*) gracioso; **to play the —** hacer el tonto; *vt* engañar, hacer (el bobo, el ridículo); **to make a — of oneself** ponerse en ridículo; **April F—s' Day** día de inocentes.
foolhardy ['fu:lha:di] *a* temerario.
foolish ['fu:liʃ] *a* tonto, necio, imbécil; (*action*) indiscreto; (*remark*) inepto, disparatado.
foolishness ['fu:liʃnis] *n* simpleza, necedad, idiotismo, tontería; (*act*) bobería, insensatez.
foot [fut] *n* (*human*) pie; (*animal*) pata; (*mil*) infantería; **— rule** regla de un pie; **to put one's — in it** meter la pata, colarse; **on, by —** a pie, en marcha; **to trample under—** pisotear, atropellar; **— bridge** pasadera; **—fall, —step** pisada, paso; **—hill** falda; **—hold** asidero; **—loose** andariego; **—mark** huella; **—pad** salteador de caminos; **—sore** los pies doloridos; **—stool** escabel, tarima, banquete; **—wear** calzado.
football ['futbɔ:l] *n* balón; (*game*) fútbol.
footballer ['futbɔ:lə] *n* futbolista.
footing ['futiŋ] *n* pie; entrada; condición; **on equal —** igualmente, con igualdad; **to lose one's —** perder tierra.
footlights ['futlaits] *n pl* candilejas.
footnote ['futnout] *n* nota.
footpath ['futpa:θ] *n* vereda, senda, sendero.
footprint ['futprint] *n* huella, pisada.
for [fɔ:] *prep* por, para, a causa de; *cj* porque, por cuanto, pues; **as —** tocante a; **— cash** al contado; **— oneself** por su cuenta.
forage ['fɔridʒ] *n* forraje; *vi* forrajear.
foray ['fɔrei] *n* incursión.
forbear [fə'bɛə] *vti* abstenerse de, no mencionar; sufrir con pacienca, reportarse; no poder menos de.
forbearance [fɔ:'bɛərəns] *n* indulgencia, paciencia, sobriedad.
forbid [fə'bid] *vt* prohibir; **to — entry** vedar, negar; **God —** no quiera Dios.
forbidden [fə'bidn] *a* prohibido, ilícito.
forbidding [fə'bidiŋ] *a* repugnante.
force [fɔ:s] *n* fuerza, vigor; impulso, vehemencia; validez; **motive —** fuerza motriz; **to be in —** regir, imperar, estar vigente; *vt* precisar, forzar, obligar, hacer; violentar; **to join —s with** relacionarse con.
forceful ['fɔ:sful] *a* contundente, potente.
forcible ['fɔ:səbl] *a* violento; enérgico, recio; fuerte; **— entry** entrada a viva fuerza.
ford [fɔ:d] *n* vado; *vt* vadear, pasar a vado.
forebear ['fɔ:bɛə] *n* antepasado.
foreboding [fɔ:'boudiŋ] *n* presentimiento, presagio, amago.
forecast ['fɔ:ka:st] *n* pronóstico; predicción, previsión; *vt* prever; proyectar.
forefather ['fɔ:fa:ðə] *n* antepasado antecesor.
for(e)go [fɔ:'gou] *vt* renunciar a, ceder.
foreground ['fɔ:graund] *n* primer término.
forehead ['fɔrid] *n* frente, sienes.
foreign ['fɔrin] *a* extranjero, extraño, ajeno; advenedizo; **— trade** comercio exterior; **F— Office** Ministerio (de Estado, de Asuntos Exteriores).
foreigner ['fɔrinə] *n* extranjero; forastero.
forelock ['fɔ:lɔk] *n* copete, guedeja.

foreman ['fɔːmən] *n* capataz; mayoral, encargado.
foremost ['fɔːmoust] *a* delantero, principal.
forenoon ['fɔːnuːn] *n* mañana.
foresee [fɔː'siː] *vt* prever, barruntar.
foresight ['fɔːsait] *n* previsión, sagacidad; **lack of —** improvidencia, imprevisión.
forest ['fɔrist] *n* bosque; (*tropical*) selva.
forestall [fɔː'stɔːl] *vt* anticipar; prevenir; acaparar.
foretell [fɔː'tel] *vt* predecir, pronosticar; conjeturar.
forethought ['fɔːθɔːt] *n* prevención, premeditación; precaución; presciencia; **lack of —** imprevisión; **lacking in —** imprevisor.
forever [fər'evə] *ad* para siempre; **— and ever** por siempre jamás.
forewarn [fɔː'wɔːn] *vt* prevenir, intimar; avisar, precautelar.
foreword ['fɔːwəːd] *n* advertencia.
forfeit ['fɔːfit] *n* multa; (*games*) prenda; *vt* perder.
forge [fɔːdʒ] *n* fragua; *vt* forjar, fraguar; (*fig*) falsificar, contrahacer; tramar.
forgery ['fɔːdʒəri] *n* falsificación.
forget [fə'get] *vt* olvidar; *vi* olvidarse, distraerse; **to — oneself** perder los estribos.
forgetful [fə'getful] *a* olvidadizo, descuidado.
forgetfulness [fə'getfulnis] *n* olvido, negligencia; mala memoria.
forgive [fə'giv] *vt* perdonar, remitir, dispensar.
forgiveness [fə'givnis] *n* perdón, remisión, indulto.
fork [fɔːk] *n* (*table*) tenedor; (*garden*) horquilla; (*road*) bifurcación; (*river*) confluencia.
forlorn [fə'lɔːn] *a* abandonado, desamparado, olvidado.
form [fɔːm] *n* forma, figura; talle; manera; formalidad; estilo; sombra, (*seat*) banco; documento, hoja; *SA* esqueleto; (*school*) grado, clase; *vti* formar, componer, dar forma; formarse; **to — an association** coligarse.
formal ['fɔːməl] *a* formal, en regla; (*style*) plástico; (*dance*) de etiqueta; ceremonioso, afectado.
formality [fɔː'mæliti] *n* formalidad, requisito.
formation [fɔː'meiʃən] *n* formación; desarrollo.
former ['fɔːmə] *a* primero; anterior, precedente; *pn* aquél.
formerly ['fɔːməli] *ad* antes, en otro tiempo, anteriormente, antaño.
formidable ['fɔːmidəbl] *a* tremendo, imponente, dificilísimo; temible.
formula ['fɔːmjulə] *n* fórmula.
formulate ['fɔːmjuleit] *vt* formular; plantear.
forsake [fə'seik] *vt* abandonar, desamparar, renegar de.
forswear [fɔː'swɛə] *vt* abjurar, desdecirse.
fort [fɔːt] *n* fuerte, fortín.
forth [fɔːθ] *ad* en adelante, hacia adelante; fuera; **and so —** y así de lo demás, así sucesivamente.
forthcoming [fɔːθ'kʌmiŋ] *a* venidero, próximo.
forthwith ['fɔːθ'wiθ] *ad* en el acto, sin dilación.
fortification [,fɔːtifi'keiʃən] *n* fortificación.
fortify ['fɔːtifai] *vt* fortificar; corroborar; reforzar.
fortitude ['fɔːtitjuːd] *n* fortaleza, valor, entereza, firmeza.
fortnight ['fɔːtnait] *n* quincena.
fortnightly ['fɔːtnaitli] *a* quincenal, cada dos semanas.
fortress ['fɔːtris] *n* fortaleza, plaza fuerte, alcázar.
fortuitous [fɔː'tjuːitəs] *a* fortuito, accidental, inesperado.
fortunate ['fɔːtʃənit] *a* afortunado, feliz, venturoso.
fortune ['fɔːtʃən] *n* fortuna; bienandanza; suerte; **to cost a —** valer un sentido; **—teller** pitonisa, adivino.
forty ['fɔːti] *an* cuarenta.
forward ['fɔːwəd] *n* (*sport*) delantero; *a* delantero; precoz; atrevido, audaz; (*fam*) desahogado, descarado, impertinente; *ad* adelante; **to be —** tener mucho copete; **to go —** adelantarse, avanzar; *vt* (*enterprise*) promover; (*scheme etc*) favorecer; adelantar; expedir, encaminar; (*letter*) remitir, expedir.
forwardness ['fɔːwədnis] *n* progreso; premura; descaro.
foster ['fɔstə] *a* **— brother** hermano de leche; *vt* criar, alimentar; mimar; promover, fomentar.
foul [faul] *a* sucio, indecente; (*air*) viciado; asqueroso, puerco; **— play** juego sucio, trampa; **— -smelling** hediondo; *vt* ensuciar, deshonrar; manchar; *vi* ensuciarse.
foulness ['faulnis] *n* suciedad, impureza, asquerosidad, cochinería.
found [faund] *vt* fundar, establecer, basar, cimentar; originar.
foundation [faun'deiʃən] *n* fundamento; raíz; fundación; base, cimiento; **to lay the —s** asentar los cimientos; **— stone** primera piedra.
founder ['faundə] *n* fundador.
foundling ['faundliŋ] *n* (niño) expósito; hijo del agua; inclusero; **—s' home** casa de expósitos.
fount [faunt] *n* fuente, manantial.
fountain ['fauntin] *n* surtidor, fuente; **— pen** pluma estilográfica.
four [fɔː] *an* cuatro; **set of —** (*cards*) cuarta; **— -sided** cuadrangular; **on all —s** a gatas.
fourteen ['fɔːti'ːn] *an* catorce.

fourth [fɔːθ] *an* cuarto; (*mus*) cuarta.
fowl [faul] *n* ave de corral; volatería.
fox [fɔks] *n* raposo, zorro; **—hound** sabueso; **—glove** digital.
fraction ['frækʃən] *n* (*math*) fracción; fragmento.
fractious ['frækʃəs] *a* arisco; rebelón; de mal humor; vidrioso.
fracture ['fræktʃə] *n* quebradura, rotura; (*bone*) fractura; *vt* quebrar, romper, fracturar.
fragile ['frædʒail] *a* frágil, quebradizo, deleznable.
fragment ['frægmənt] *n* fragmento, retazo, trozo.
fragrance ['freigrəns] *n* fragancia, aroma, perfume.
fragrant ['freigrənt] *a* fragante, perfumado, aromático, odorífero.
frail [freil] *a* frágil, endeble, delicado.
frailty ['freilti] *n* fragilidad; debilidad, flaqueza.
frame [freim] *n* forma; (*picture*) marco; (*embroidery*) bastidor; estructura; contextura, enrejado; **— of mind** talante; *vt* formar; enmarcar; ajustar, arreglar; inventar.
framework ['freimwəːk] *n* armazón, armadura.
France ['frɑːns] *n* Francia.
Frances ['frɑːnsis] *f* Francisca.
Francis ['frɑːnsis] *m* Francisco.
frank [fræŋk] *a* franco, liberal, campechano; *vt* franquear.
frankly ['fræŋkli] *ad* con franqueza, en verdad, francamente, con el corazón en la mano; **quite —** con toda franqueza.
frankness ['fræŋknis] *n* franqueza, candor, sinceridad; ingenuidad.
frantic ['fræntik] *a* frenético, furioso.
fraternal [frə'təːnl] *a* fraterno, fraternal.
fraternize ['frætənaiz] *vi* fraternizar.
fraud [frɔːd] *n* fraude, engaño, impostura, trama, petardo, supercheria.
fraught [frɔːt] *a* cargado, preñado; **to be — with** impregnarse de.
fray [frei] *n* querella ruidosa, trifulca; *vt* raer; desgastar.
freak [friːk] *n* capricho, fantasía, extravagancia; fenómeno, aborto.
freckle ['frekl] *n* peca.
Frederick ['fredrik] *m* Federico.
free [friː] *a* libre, desocupado; suelto; horro, franco; expedito; limpio, despejado; (*country etc*) independiente, autónomo; (*of tax etc*) exento; liberal; desatado; (*no payment*) gratis, de balde; **— and easy** fácil, desahogado; **— hand drawing** dibujo a mano alzada; **— trade** libre cambio; **—will** albedrío; *vt* libertar, librar, poner en libertad; (*from burden*) eximir; quitar, desembarazar; **to be — with one's money** ser manirroto; **to make — with** no gastar cumplidos.
freed [friːd] *a* libertado, liberado, saneado.
freedom ['friːdəm] *n* libertad, latitud; soltura; (*conversation etc*) franqueza; licencia; (*of manners etc*) desenfado, frescura; **— of worship, press** libertad de cultos, prensa.
freemason ['friːˌmeisn] *n* francmasón.
freethinker ['friː'θiŋkə] *n* libre pensador.
freeze [friːz] *vt* helar, congelar; *vi* helarse, congelarse; **to — to death** morir de frío.
freezing ['friːziŋ] *a* congelado, helado; **— point** punto de congelación.
freight [freit] *n* carga; flete; **— car** furgón.
French [frentʃ] *a* francés; **—man** francés; gabacho; **— bean** judía verde; **— fried potatoes** papar fritas en trozos.
frenzy ['frenzi] *n* frenesí, furor, manía.
frequent ['friːkwənt] *a* frecuente, común, habitual; [fri'kwent] *vt* frecuentar.
frequented [friː'kwentid] *a* concurrido; trillado, asendereado.
fresh [freʃ] *a* fresco, nuevo, reciente; (*bread*) tierno; (*water*) dulce; (*air*) puro; *n* riada.
freshen ['freʃn] *vt* refrescar; *vi* refrescarse.
freshness ['freʃnis] *n* frescura, verdor.
fret [fret] *vt* rozar, irritar, molestar; inquietarse, torturarse, apurarse.
fretful ['fretful] *a* mohino, displicente.
friar ['fraiə] *n* fraile, monje; **— (John *etc*)** Fray (Juan).
friction ['frikʃən] *n* roce, frote, refregón, rozadura.
Friday ['fraidi] *n* viernes; **Good —** viernes santo.
friend [frend] *n* amigo, allegado, compañero; **—!** (*response*) gente de paz; **boy—** novio; **girl—** novia; **to have a — at court** tener el padre alcalde.
friendliness ['frendlinis] *n* amistad, cordialidad, amabilidad, simpatía.
friendly ['frendli] *a* amigable, amistoso, simpático, amable.
friendship ['frendʃip] *n* amistad, hermandad; (*close*) intimidad.
fright [frait] *n* susto, espanto, temor, pavor, terror; **she looks a —** ¡qué facha!
frighten ['fraitn] *vt* espantar, asustar, aterrorizar, sobresaltar; **to — away** ahuyentar.
frightful ['fraitful] *a* espantoso, terrible, horroroso, aterrador, horrible, monstruoso; **— deed** enormidad; **how —!** ¡qué barbaridad!

frigid ['fridʒid] *a* frígido, frío, helado.
frigidity [fri'dʒiditi] *n* frialdad, frigidez.
fringe [frindʒ] *n* orla, franja; cenefa, borde; (*with tassels*) fleco; (*hair*) flequillo; *vt* franjear, orillar, orlar.
frisky ['friski] *a* juguetón, vivaracho, enrevesado.
fritter ['fritə] *n* buñuelo, churro; fragmento; *vt* hacer pedazos; disipar.
frivolity [fri'vɔliti] *n* frivolidad, ligereza.
frivolous ['frivələs] *a* frívolo, trivial, liviano.
frock [frɔk] *n* vestido; **— coat** levita.
frog [frɔg] *n* rana; (*horse's foot*) horquilla; (*in throat*) carraspera; **the big — in the little pond** en tierra de ciegos el tuerto es rey.
frolic ['frɔlik] *n* gira; retozo; *vi* retozar, juguetear.
frolicsome ['frɔliksəm] *a* juguetón, alegre, travieso.
from [frɔm] *ad* hacia atrás; **to and —** hacia adelante y hacia atrás; *prep* de, desde, para, de parte de.
front [frʌnt] *n* (*pol* & *mil*) frente; (*theat*) delantera; (*shirt*) pechera; (*house*) fachada; **in — of** delante de; **— view** vista de frente; *vt* hacer frente a.
frontier ['frʌntiə] *n* frontera; **— district** marco; **— guard (officer)** carabinero.
frontispiece ['frʌntispi:s] *n* frontispicio; (*book*) portada; fachada.
frost [frɔst] *n* helada; (*hoar*) escarcha; **—bitten** tumido, helado; *vt* **to — over** deslustrar; **—bite** congelación(es).
frosty ['frɔsti] *a* glacial, escarchado.
frothy ['frɔθi] *a* espumoso, frívolo.
froward ['frouwəd] *a* obstinado, contumaz, díscolo.
frown [fraun] *n* ceño; entrecejo; *vt* mirar con ceño; *vi* fruncir el ceño, arrugar la frente.
frowning ['frauniŋ] *a* hosco, torvo; *n* ceño.
frugal ['fru:gəl] *a* frugal, económico; sobrio.
frugality [fru:'gæliti] *n* frugalidad, sobriedad, parsimonia.
fruit [fru:t] *n* (*product*) fruto; (*from trees*) fruta, fruto; (*from work*) provecho, resultado; (*stewed*) compota; **to yield —** dar frutos; **to give —** fructificar; *vi* producir fruta; dar fruto.
fruitful ['fru:tful] *a* fructífero, fértil, fecundo; fructuoso, productivo.
fruitless ['fru:tlis] *a* infructuoso, estéril, inútil; improvidente.
frustrate [frʌs'treit] *vt* frustrar, burlar, defraudar.
fry [frai] *n* **small —** morralla; gentecilla; *vt* freír.
frying pan ['fraiiŋ,pæn] *n* sartén.
fuel [fjuəl] *n* combustible; (*of flames*) pasto, pábulo.
fugitive ['fju:dʒitiv] *a* fugitivo, fugaz; *n* prófugo, tránsfuga.
fulfill [ful'fil] *n* cumplir, desempeñar, llenar; verificar; **to — orders** ejecutar (pedidos, órdenes).
fulfillment [ful'filmənt] *n* cumplimiento, ejecución; plenitud.
full [ful] *a* lleno, completo, cabal, amplio, harto, pleno, plenario; (*river*) caudaloso; (*skirt*) de mucho vuelo; (*vehicle*) completo; (*satisfied*) harto; (*detailed*) extenso, detallado; (*mature*) maduro; (*member*) de número; **— house** está lleno; **— up (with people)** de bote en bote; **the place is —** no cabe(n) más; **— dress** uniforme de gala; **—grown** crecido; **— length** de tamaño natural, tan largo como es; **— moon** plenilunio; **— powers** plenos poderes; *ad* del todo.
fullness ['fulnis] *n* plenitud; amplitud; preñez; holgura.
fully ['fuli] *ad* por entero, del todo, de lleno.
fulsome ['fulsəm] *a* grosero, ramplón, repugnante; (*praises*) fastidioso.
fumble ['fʌmbl] *vi* revolver torpemente; ir a tientas; manosear.
fume [fju:m] *n* vaho, humo; *vi* humear; refunfuñar, rabiar.
fumigate ['fju:migeit] *vt* fumigar.
fuming ['fju:miŋ] *a* humeante; (*fam*) **to be —** reventar, echar chispas.
fun [fʌn] *n* diversión, buen humor, gracia; **in —** de broma; **to be —** ser divertido; **to make — of** burlarse de.
function ['fʌŋkʃən] *n* función; desempeño; *vi* marchar, andar, funcionar; (*sl*) pitar.
fund [fʌnd] *n* fondo, capital; **sinking —** fondo de amortización.
fundamental [,fʌndə'mentl] *a* fundamental; radical; preliminar; *n* principio fundamental.
funeral ['fju:nərəl] *a* funeral, fúnebre; *n* entierro, funerales; duelo.
fungus ['fʌŋgəs] *n* hongo; fungo.
funnel ['fʌnl] *n* (*filtering etc*) embudo; (*ship*) chimenea.
funny ['fʌni] *a* cómico, divertido, gracioso, chistoso, humorístico; curioso; **— man** zumbón, burlón.
fur [fə:] *n* piel; **— coat** abrigo de pieles.
furious ['fjuəriəs] *a* furioso, furibundo, frenético, sañudo, airado; **to be —** ensañarse, enfurecerse.
furnace ['fə:nis] *n* horno; **blast —** alto horno.
furnish ['fə:niʃ] *vt* suministrar, equipar, surtir, proveer; (*furniture*) amueblar; (*opportunity*) proporcionar, deparar.
furnishing(s) ['fə:niʃiŋz] *n* menaje, avíos; **set of —** mobiliario.
furniture ['fə:nitʃə] *n* muebles,

mueblaje; (*unwieldy*) armatoste.
furrow ['fʌrou] *n* surco; **first —** besana; (*face etc*) arruga; *vt* surcar, abrir surcos.
further ['fə:ðə] *a* ulterior, adicional; *ad* además; aún; más allá; **in — support** por más señas; *vt* promover, adelantar, fomentar; servir.
furtherance ['fə:ðərəns] *n* fomento, promoción, apoyo.
furthermore ['fə:ðə'mɔ:] *ad* además, por añadidura.
furtive ['fə:tiv] *a* furtivo, oculto.
fury ['fjuəri] *n* rabia, furor, saña, berrinche; (*elements*) braveza.
furze [fə:z] *n* jaramago, aliaga, aulaga.
fuse [fju:z] *n* fusible, mecha; (*el*) cortacircuitos; (*explosive*) espoleta; *vti* fundir; fundirse.
fusillade [ˌfju:zi'leid] *n* descarga cerrada.
fusion ['fju:zən] *n* fusión, fundición; unión.
fuss [fʌs] *n* alboroto, ruido, desasosiego, remilgos.
fussy ['fʌsi] *a* fastidioso; remilgado, exigente.
futile ['fju:tail] *a* vano, fútil, frívolo.
futility [fju:'tiliti] *n* futileza, futilidad.
future ['fju:tʃə] *a* futuro, por venir; *n* futuro, porvenir; **for, in the —** en adelante.

G

gabble ['gæbl] *n* algarabía, charla; *vi* charlar, farfullar.
gad [gæd] *vi* corretear; **—fly** tábano.
gag [gæg] *n* mordaza; (*joke*) broma; *vt* amordazar, hacer callar; (*theat*) meter morcillas.
gage [geidʒ] *n* caución, prenda; (*fruit*) **green—** ciruela claudia; **to throw down the —** desafiar, retar.
gaiety ['geiiti] *n* alegría, gozo, vivacidad, festividad.
gain [gein] *n* ganancia, ventaja; logro; beneficio; *vt* ganar, conseguir, cobrar; vencer; *vi* crecer, medrar.
gainsay [gein'sei] *vt* contradecir, desdecir, negar.
gait [geit] *n* porte, andar(es), paso; **at a good —** a buen paso.
gale [geil] *n* ventarrón, viento fresco, ráfaga, temporal; (*southerly*) vendaval.
gall [gɔ:l] *n* bilis, hiel; sinsabor; amargura; *vt* irritar, rozar, atormentar, hostigar.
gallant ['gælənt] *a* valiente, intrépido, valeroso, garboso, galano, majo; *n* galán, guapo.
gallantry ['gæləntri] *n* bravura, valentía, bizarría, heroísmo; galanteo, cortesanía.
gallery ['gæləri] *n* galería; corredor, tribuna; (*theat*) paraíso.
galley ['gæli] *n* galera; **— proof** galerada; **— slave** galeote.
gallon ['gælən] *n* galón.
gallop ['gæləp] *n* galope; **at a —** a uña de caballo; **at full —** a galope tendido, a rienda suelta; *vi* galopar.
gallows ['gælouz] *n* horca, patíbulo.
galvanize ['gælvənaiz] *vt* galvanizar; excitar.
gamble ['gæmbl] *vi* jugar(se).
gambler ['gæmblə] *n* jugador, tahur.
gambling ['gæmbliŋ] *n* juego; **— table** tablero.
gambol ['gæmbəl] *n* cabriola, retozo, travesura; *vi* hacer cabriolas, retozar.
game [geim] *a* valiente; cojo; *n* juego; partido; partida; deporte; caza; **big —** caza mayor; **small —** caza menor; (*bird*) pieza; **— of chance** juego de azar; **—keeper** guardabosque, guarda de coto: **— pouch** escarcela, morral; **to make — of** tomar el pelo a.
gamester ['geimstə] *n* tahur, jugador.
gamut ['gæmət] *n* gama.
gang [gæŋ] *n* tropa, pandilla, banda; horda; (*workmen*) tanda; (*oxen*) yunta, huebra.
gangrene ['gæŋgri:n] *n* gangrena; *vt* grangrenar.
gangster ['gæŋstə] *n* atracador, bandolero.
gangway ['gæŋwei] *n* pasamano; (*naut*) portalón, pasillo.
gap [gæp] *n* portillo, brecha; quebradura; vacío, hueco, claro; **—toothed** mellado.
gape [geip] *n* boqueada; hendidura; *vi* bostezar; embobarse.
gaping ['geipiŋ] *a* boquiabierto; *n* bostezo.
garage ['gærɑ:ʒ] *n* garaje, cochera.
garb [gɑ:b] *n* vestido, vestidura, traje.
garbage ['gɑ:bidʒ] *n* basura, inmundicia(s); **— can** basurero; **— man** *n* basurero.
garden ['gɑ:dn] *n* jardín; (*orchard and kitchen*) huerto; (*large area, kitchen and orchard*) huerta; **nursery —** criadero.
gardener ['gɑ:dnə] *n* jardinero; (*market*) hortelano; (*landscape*) plantista.
gardening ['gɑ:dniŋ] *n* jardinería, horticultura.
gargle ['gɑ:gl] *n* gárgara; enjuagadientes; *vi* hacer gárgaras, gargarizar.
garish ['gɛəriʃ] *a* brillante, deslumbrador, llamativo.
garland ['gɑ:lənd] *n* guirnalda; *vt* enguirnaldar.
garlic ['gɑ:lik] *n* ajo; **clove of —** diente de ajo.
garment ['gɑ:mənt] *n* prenda, vestido, traje.
garret ['gærit] *n* buhardilla, desván, zaquizamí.

garrison ['gærisən] *n* guarnición; presidio; *vt* acantonar, presidiar, guarnecer; **to be on — duty** estar de guarnición.
garrulity [gə'ru:liti] *n* locuacidad, garrulería.
garrulous ['gæruləs] *a* gárrulo, locuaz, boquirroto.
garter ['gɑ:tə] *n* liga; **Order of the G—** orden de la Jarretera.
gas [gæs] *n* gas; gasolina; **— stove** estufa de gas; **— jet** mechero de gas.
gash [gæʃ] *n* herida, incisión, cortadura; (*knife*) cuchillada, chirlo; *vt* dar cuchilladas a.
gasoline ['gæsəli:n] *n* gasolina.
gasp [gɑ:sp] *n* suspiro, agonía; **last —** boqueada; *vi* boquear; jadear.
gate [geit] *n* puerta; (*iron*) **garden —** verja; (*wooden*) barrera; **—way** portal; **to —crash** colarse.
gather ['gæðə] *n* pliegue; *vt* coger, amontonar; (*crops*) cosechar; (*meaning*) colegir, inferir; (*strength*) cobrar, tomar fuerzas; (*money*) recaudar; (*sew*) fruncir; *vi* **to — together** reunirse, congregarse, condensarse.
gathering ['gæðəriŋ] *n* reunión, tertulia; (*lit*) cenáculo; **— in** (*harvest*) (re)colección, cosecha; **— together** (*people*) afluencia.
gaudy ['gɔ:di] *a* chillón, brillante, lucido, suntuoso.
gauge [geidʒ] *n* regla de medir, medida; calibrador; *vt* medir, computar, aforar, avaluar.
gaunt [gɔ:nt] *a* descarnado, flaco.
gauntlet ['gɔ:ntlit] *n* manopla, guantelete; **to throw down the —** arrojar el guante.
gay [gei] *a* (*person*) alegre, gozoso, de buen humor; (*event*) festivo; (*clothes*) alegre, guapo.
gaze [geiz] *n* mirada; *vi* **to — on, at** mirar (fijamente) contemplar.
gazette [gə'zet] *n* gaceta, diario; **official —** boletín oficial.
gear [giə] *n* (*mech*) engranaje, rueda dentada; mecanismo; (*clothes*) atavíos; (*kit*) aperos, aparejo; **to put into —** engranar; **in —** en juego, encajado; *vt* aparejar.
gem [dʒem] *n* joya, piedra preciosa.
general ['dʒenərəl] *a* general, común, usual, de uso, de costumbre; ordinario; extendido; **in —** por lo común, por regla general; **to become —** extenderse, generalizarse; *n* general, jefe.
generality [ˌdʒenə'ræliti] *n* generalidad.
generalize ['dʒenərəlaiz] *vt* generalizar.
generally ['dʒenərəli] *ad* generalmente, en general, por lo general, por lo común.
generate ['dʒenəreit] *vt* producir; (*el*) generar.
generation [ˌdʒenə'reiʃən] *n* generación, raza; casta; **the coming —** la posteridad.
generator ['dʒenəreitə] *n* generador, dínamo.
generosity [ˌdʒenə'rɔsiti] *n* liberalidad, largueza, bizarría, caballerosidad.
generous ['dʒenərəs] *a* generoso, magnánimo, liberal, pródigo, holgado, amplio, abundante.
Geneva [dʒi'ni:və] *n* Ginebra.
genial ['dʒi:niəl] *a* genial, afable, campechano, cordial.
genius ['dʒi:niəs] *n* genio, numen.
Genoa ['dʒənouə] *n* Génova.
Genoese [ˌdʒenou'i:z] *an* genovés.
genteel [dʒen'ti:l] *a* elegante, apuesto, gentil, decente; **over —** cursi.
gentle ['dʒentl] *a* benigno, dulce, manso, blando, apacible, tranquilo, pausado.
gentleman ['dʒentlmən] *n* caballero, señor; (*of lineage*) hidalgo; (*court*) gentilhombre; **young —** señorito.
gentlemanly ['dʒentlmənli] *a* caballeroso, civil.
gentleness ['dʒentlnis] *n* blandura, dulzura, suavidad; nobleza.
gentlewoman ['dʒentlwumən] *n* dama, dama de honor.
gently ['dʒentli] *ad* suavemente, despacio, qued(it)o.
gentry ['dʒentri] *n* clase acomodada, la baja nobleza.
genuine ['dʒenjuin] *a* genuino, auténtico, legítimo, verdadero; típico; (*language*) corriente y moliente.
genuineness ['dʒenjuinnis] *n* pureza, legitimidad, autenticidad.
Geoffrey ['dʒefri] *m* Geofredo.
geographer [dʒi'ɔgrəfə] *n* geógrafo.
geographical [dʒiə'græfikəl] *a* geográfico.
geography [dʒi'ɔgrəfi] *n* geografía.
geology [dʒi'ɔlədʒi] *n* geología.
geometry [dʒi'ɔmitri] *n* geometría.
geometric [dʒiə'metrik] *a* geométrico.
geranium [dʒi'reiniəm] *n* geranio.
George [dʒɔ:dʒ] *m* Jorge.
germ [dʒə:m] *n* germen, renuevo, embrión, yema; microbio.
German ['dʒə:mən] *an* alemán, tudesco.
Germany ['dʒə:məni] *n* Alemania.
germinate ['dʒə:mineit] *vi* germinar, apimpollarse.
Gertrude ['gə:tru:d] *f* Gertrudis.
gesticulate [dʒes'tikjuleit] *vi* gesticular, accionar, hacer gestos.
gesticulation [dʒesˌtikju'leiʃən] *n* gesticulación.
gesture ['dʒestʃə] *n* gesto, acción; (*heroic*) rasgo; (*movement*) ademán; (*facial*) mueca.
get [get] *vt* (ob)tener, recibir, conseguir, adquirir, llevar, hacer que, procurar, agenciar, contraer; (*for*

someone) proporcionar; (*what you are after*) (*fam*) cazar, flechar; **to — at** (*enemy*) entrar; **to — on** (*vehicle*) subir a; **to — ready** preparar, aprestar; (*in emergency*) improvisar; *vi* (*ill etc*) ponerse; meterse; **to — on** medrar, montar; **to — along well with** avenirse con, llevarse bien con, entenderse con, hacer buenas migas con; **to — away** escapar(se); **to — about** (*news etc*) divulgarse, (*person*) viajar; **to — dark** oscurecer; **to — along** adelantar, medrar, ir tirando; **to — better** mejorar; **to — clear (of)** salir bien, librarse de; **to — down** bajar; **to — even with** desquitarse; **to — in** entrar, (*by stealth*) colarse; **to — into** introducirse, meterse; **to — into passion** montar en cólera; **to — out** salir, sacar; **to — out of the way** apartarse; **to — out of order** descomponerse; **to — over** (*an illness*) reponerse, (*an obstacle*) salvar, (*fear*) sobreponerse a; (*surprise*) no poder menos de; **to — the better of** llevar ventaja a; **to — through (with)** conectar; despachar; acabar con; aprobar; **to — up** ponerse de pie, (*from bed*) levantarse; **to — to know** enterarse de; **to — used to** acostumbrarse a; **to — a job** colocarse; **to — going** menearse.

getting ['getiŋ] *n* adquisición.

ghastliness ['gɑːstlinis] *n* aspecto cadavérico.

ghastly ['gɑːstli] *a* lívido, cadavérico, horrible, horripilante.

ghost [goust] *n* (*departed spirit*) sombra; alma; espíritu; (*visible*) fantasma, espectro, aparecido; **not the — of a** (*doubt*) ni asomo de (*duda*).

giant ['dʒaiənt] *an* gigante.

gibbet ['dʒibit] *n* horca, patíbulo.

gibe [dʒaib] *n* escarnio, burla; *vt* escarnecer, mofarse (de), burlar.

giddiness ['gidinis] *n* (*med*) vértigo, vahido; devaneo; vaivén.

giddy ['gidi] *a* vertiginoso, atolondrado, veleidoso; aturdido; casquivano.

gift [gift] *n* (*object*) don; (*Christmas*) — aguinaldo, regalo, presente; (*charitable etc*) donativo; (*mental etc*) genio, don, ingenio, gracia; **—s** cualidades, dotes; prendas; **to make a — of** hacer merced de; **a —** (*fam*) tirado; **it's a gift** (*fam*) es una cucaña; **I wouldn't take it as a —** no lo quiero ni regalado; *vt* dotar, dar.

gifted ['giftid] *a* prendado, talentoso.

gigantic [dʒai'gæntik] *a* gigantesco, titánico, colosal.

giggle ['gigl] *n* falsa risa; retozo de risa; *vi* reírse.

Gilbert ['gilbət] *m* Gilberto.

gild [gild] *vt* dorar, dar brillo a; **to — the pill** dorar la píldora.

gilt [gilt] *a* áureo; **— -edged stock** valores de toda confianza; *n* dorado.

gin [dʒin] *n* ginebra; (*mech*) trampa.

ginger ['dʒindʒə] *n* jengibre.

gingerly ['dʒindʒəli] *ad* con mucho pulso, cautelosamente.

gingham ['giŋəm] *n* guinga.

giraffe [dʒi'ræf] *n* jirafa.

gird [gəːd] *vt* **to — on** (*sword etc*) ceñir; **to — oneself** arremangarse los faldones.

girdle ['gəːdl] *n* cinto, ceñidor; faja; corsé; *vt* ceñir, rodear.

girl [gəːl] *n* niña, chica, moza, muchacha; (*servant*) muchacha, criada, doncella; *SA* china.

girlish ['gəːliʃ] *a* juvenil.

girth [gəːθ] *n* cincha, pretina; grueso, corpulencia; *vt* cinchar, ceñir.

gist [dʒist] *n* substancia, quid; busilis.

give [giv] *vt* dar, otorgar, conceder; (*as gift*) regalar; (*aid*) prestar; (*blow*) pegar, arrear; (*hopes*) esperanzar; (*lecture*) explicar; (*sigh, slap*) largar; (*slap*) (*fam*) propinar; (*word*) empeñar; **— and take** toma y daca; *vi* tener correa; **to — away** dar, enajenar; **to — back** (de)volver; **to — comfort (to)** confortar; **to — forth** publicar, divulgar; proferir; **to — in (to)** ceder (a), darse por vencido; **to — off** echar, despedir; **to — out** revelar; agotarse, fallar; repartir; **to — over, up** cesar, entregar, renunciar, ceder; **to — rise to** prestarse a; **to — up** ceder, vacar, entregar, cejar, dimitir, devolver; **to — up hope** (*med*) desahuciar; **to — way** plegar; ceder, resignarse.

given ['givn] *a* **— to** propenso a, dado a; **— away** tirado; **— name** nombre de pila, nombre de bautismo.

giver ['givə] *n* donador, dador.

glacier ['glæsiə] *n* ventisquero.

glad [glæd] *a* contento, alegre; **to be —** alegrarse.

gladden ['glædn] *vt* dar gusto a, alegrar, regocijar, dar gusto a.

glade [gleid] *n* claro (del bosque).

gladly ['glædli] *ad* de buena gana, gustosamente, alegremente.

gladness ['glædnis] *n* alegría, gozo, contentamiento.

glamour ['glæmə] *n* fascinación, hechizo.

glance [glɑːns] *n* mirada; (*at, off*) ojeada, vistazo; **at first —** a primera vista; *vi* **to — at** lanzar miradas a, echar la mirada sobre; **to — back** (*bullet*) rebotar; **to — around** echar una mirada atrás; **to — off** resbalar, desviarse.

glancing ['glɑːnsiŋ] *a* (*blow etc*) oblicuo; de soslayo.

glare [glɛə] *n* resplandor; fulgor, brillantez; *vti* deslumbrar, relumbrar; echar fuego por los ojos.

glaring ['glɛəriŋ] *a* deslumbrador, brillante; notorio, manifiesto, chillón.

glass [glɑːs] *n* (*material*) vidrio, cristal; (*window*) cristal; (*mirror*) espejo; (*binoculars*) gemelos; (*beer*) caña; (*wine*) vaso, copa; *pl* gafas, lentes; (*horn-rimmed*) quevedos; **cut —** cristal tallado; **magnifying —** lente de aumento; **plate —** luna, cristal de espejo; **powdered —** polvo de vidrio; **spy—** catalejo; **stained —** vidrio de color; **— case** vidriera, escaparate; **— shop** cristalería; **— window** vidriera; **—ful** copa, vaso; **—ware** cristalería, vajilla de cristal.

glassy ['glɑːsi] *a* de vidrio, cristalino; frío, vidrioso.

gleam [gliːm] *n* fulgor; destello, brillo, centelleo; *vi* lucir, brillar, resplandecer.

gleaming ['gliːmiŋ] *a* brillante, deslumbrante, nítido.

glean [gliːn] *vti* espigar, recoger, arrebañar.

gleaning ['gliːniŋ] *n* rebusca.

glee [gliː] *n* alegría, gozo, júbilo.

glen [glen] *n* cañada, cañón, hondonada.

glib [glib] *a* voluble, locuaz, pronto, prevenido.

glibness ['glibnis] *n* volubilidad, fluidez, facilidad.

glide [glaid] *vi* deslizarse, resbalar suavemente; **to — away** escurrirse.

glider ['glaidə] *n* deslizador, planeador, velero.

glimmer ['glimə] *n* vislumbre, claror; (*fam*) pizca; **last — of day** las postrimerías; *vt* vislumbrar; *vi* rielar; (*daylight*) alborear.

glimpse [glimps] *n* ojeada, vistazo, vislumbre; **to catch a — of** vislumbrar; *vt* vislumbrar.

glint [glint] *n* destello, reflejo; *vi* reflejar, brillar.

glisten ['glisn] *vi* brillar, relucir, resplandecer.

glitter ['glitə] *n* brillo, esplendor; *vi* relucir, centellear, coruscar, titilar.

glittering ['glitəriŋ] *n* brillo, resplandor; *a* reluciente, brillante.

gloat [glout] *vi* gozar (*con el daño ajeno*).

globe [gloub] *n* globo, esfera, tierra, bulbo.

gloom [gluːm] *n* obscuridad, tenebrosidad; tristeza, hosquedad.

gloomy ['gluːmi] *a* obscuro, tenebroso, sombrío; hosco, lóbrego, tétrico.

glorify ['glɔːrifai] *vt* glorificar, exaltar.

glorious ['glɔːriəs] *a* glorioso, soberbio, ilustre, espléndido.

glory ['glɔːri] *n* gloria, esplendor; fama, honor; honra; *vi* **to — in** gloriarse, jactarse; **to be in one's —** estar en sus glorias.

gloss [glɔs] *n* lustre, viso; (*on text*) glosa; *vti* glosar, comentar, apostilar; **to — over** *vt* cohonestar, paliar; **to put a — on** sacar brillo a.

glossy ['glɔsi] *a* lustroso; terso, especioso.

glove [glʌv] *n* guante; **to be hand in — with** ser uña y carne con; **to put —s on** calzarse los guantes.

glow [glou] *n* (*light*) brillo, trasluz, fulgor, resplandor, refulgencia; (*red, pink*) arrebol; (*warm*) calor; **—worm** luciérnaga, gusanillo de luz; *vi* brillar, relucir.

glowing ['glouiŋ] *n* resplandeciente; caluroso, entusiasta.

glue [gluː] *n* engrudo, cola; *vt* encolar, engrudar, pegar, fijar.

glum [glʌm] *a* malhumorado; **— face** cara de viernes.

glutton ['glʌtn] *n* glotón, comilón.

gluttony ['glʌtəni] *n* glotonería, gula.

gnarled [nɑːld] *a* nudoso.

gnash [næʃ] *vti* rechinar (*los dientes*).

gnashing ['næʃiŋ] *n* rechinamiento, crujir (*de dientes*).

gnat [næt] *n* cínife, jején.

gnaw [nɔː] *vti* roer, carcomer, morder; **—ing** roedor.

go [gou] *n* energía; giro; **it's no —** es inútil; *vi* (*person*) ir, marchar, andar; encaminarse; (*machine etc*) andar, funcionar; (*fam*) pitar; **to — about** intentar; rodear, ponerse a; **to — across** cruzar, pasar; **to — after** *vt* seguir la pista de; **to — astray** extraviarse; **to — away** marcharse, irse; largarse; **to — ahead** continuar, seguir, no parar; **to — back** retroceder, volverse atrás; **to — back on** dedecirse; **to — by** pasar por (*alto*); atenerse a; **to — for** (*fam*) meterse con; **to — off** marcharse, largar, (*of gun*) dispararse; **to — out** salir; **to — out to meet** salir al encuentro de; **to — out of fashion** pasar de moda; **to — over** (*work etc*) *vt* repasar, (*ground*) recorrer, atravesar, (*to enemy*) pasarse a; **to — through** (*forest etc*) atravesar, (*search*) escudriñar, (*pain*) sufrir, (*town*) pasar por, (*pockets etc*) registrar; **to — with** acompañar; (*clothes*) hacer juego con; **to — to, toward** concurrir, contribuir; **to — well with** harmonizar con; convenir (*a*), sentar bien (*a*); **to — without** pasarse (de, sin); **to — without saying** sobreentenderse; **who goes there?** ¿quién vive?; **on the —** vivaracho; **to be forever on the —** trajinar; **to let —** soltar, dejar ir; **—-ahead** *a* emprendedor.

goad [goud] *n* aguijón; garrocha, puya; *vt* picar, excitar, incitar.

goal [goul] *n* blanco, objetivo, término; (*sport*) meta, portería; (*scored*) gol, tanto; **—keeper** portero; **—net** poste, portería.

goat [gout] *n* cabra, chivo; **he-—** cabrón.

goatee [gou'tːi] *n* barba de chivo.

gobble ['gɔbl] *vti* engullir, tragar; (*turkey*) gluglutear.

go-between ['goubiˌtwiːn] *n* trotaconventos, alcahuete; medianero.

goblet ['gɔblit] *n* copa.
God [gɔd] *n* Dios.
godchild ['gɔdtʃaild] *n* ahijado.
goddess ['gɔdis] *n* diosa.
godfather ['gɔd,fɑ:ðə] *n* padrino.
godforsaken ['gɔdfə,seikn] *a* dejado de la mano de Dios.
Godfrey ['gɔdfri] *m* Godofredo.
godliness ['gɔdlinis] *n* piedad, santidad, devoción.
godmother ['gɔd,mʌðə] *n* madrina; **fairy —** hada madrina.
goggle ['gɔgl] *vi* abrir los ojos desmesuradamente; *a* **— eyes** ojos saltones.
going ['gouiŋ] *n* paso, andadura, marcha, ida; salida; **—s-on** alboroto.
goiter ['goitə] *n* bocio, papera.
gold [gould] *n* oro; **— -bearing** aurífero; **—beater** batihoja; **— standard** patrón de oro; **to be as good as —** ser más bueno que el pan.
gold dust ['goulddʌst] *n* oro en polvo.
golden ['gouldən] *a* de oro, dorado, áureo, amarillento.
goldfinch ['gouldfintʃ] *n* jilguero amarillo.
goldfish ['gouldfiʃ] *n* carpa dorada.
gold mine ['gouldmain] *n* mina de oro.
goldsmith ['gouldsmiθ] *n* orfebre, orífice, platero.
good [gud] *a* bueno; conveniente, adecuado; bondadoso, amable; hábil; piadoso; **a — turn** un favor; **in — time** a tiempo, previamente; **all in — time** paciencia; **to hold —** valer, subsistir; **to make —** indemnizar; cumplir; salir bien, llevar a cabo; **he's no —** es un farsante; **a — while** un buen rato; **— for nothing** inútil, farsante; **—will** buena voluntad, clientela; **— -looking** bien parecido, guapo; **— -natured** bueno, bonachón, amable; **— old** famoso; **— standing** crédito; *n* bien, provecho; *pl* (*com*) géneros, mercancías; (*in shop*) surtido; (*train*) mercancías; **—s and chattels** bienes muebles, bártulos; **for — and all** de una vez para siempre; **to have a — time** passar un buen rato, divertirse.
good-bye ['gud'bai] *excl* adiós, hasta la vista; **to say — to** despedirse de.
good day [gud'dei] *excl* buenos días.
goodness ['gudnis] *n* bondad, virtud; favor; **—!** (*excl*) ¡caramba!; **— gracious!** ¡Dios mío!
goodnight ['gud'nait] *n* buenas noches.
goodwill ['gud'wil] *n* benevolencia, buena voluntad; (*business*) clientela.
goose [gu:s] *n* oca, ganso, ánade; **—flesh** carne de gallina.
gooseberry ['guzbəri] *n* grosella (blanca), uva espín.
gore [gɔ:] *n* (*from horns*) cornada; (*dressmaking*) cuchillo; (*blood*) sangre; *vt* cornear, coger.
gorge [gɔ:dʒ] *n* garganta, cañada, hoz, abra, barranco; *vti* engullir, tragar, atiborrar, hartarse.
gorgeous ['gɔ:dʒəs] *a* espléndido, magnifico, suntuoso.
goring ['gɔ:riŋ] *n* (*bullfight*) cogida, cornada.
gory ['gɔ:ri] *a* ensangrentado, sangriento.
gospel ['gɔspəl] *n* evangelio.
gossamer ['gɔsəmə] *a* ligero, sutil, delgado; *n* telaraña; cendal, gasa.
gossip ['gɔsip] *n* (*talk*) charla, murmuración, habladuría, chisme; (*person*) correvedile, chismoso, comadre; **scraps of —** hablilla(s), gacetilla; **— column** gacetilla; *vi* charlar, chismear, comadrear.
Gothic ['gɔθik] *a* gótico; ojival.
gout [gaut] *n* gota; (*in feet*) podagra.
govern ['gʌvən] *vt* gobernar, regir, comandar, regentar; moderar.
governess ['gʌvənis] *n* institutriz, aya.
governing ['gʌvəniŋ] *a* gobernante, director.
government ['gʌvnmənt] *n* gobierno, dirección; manejo.
governor ['gʌvənə] *n* gobernador; tutor; (*of province*) adelantado; gobernador civil; (*mech*) regulador.
gown [gaun] *n* (*evening*) traje de noche, vestido; (*academic*) toga.
grab [græb] *vt* asir, coger, agarrar; (*snatch away*) arrebatar, posesionarse de; *n* gancho.
grace [greis] *n* gracia, bondad; elegancia; (*of address*) galantería; (*speech*) cortapisa; (*relig*) indulgencia; **good —s** valimiento; *vt* adornar, agraciar, favorecer.
Grace [greis] *f* Engracia.
graceful ['greisful] *a* gracioso, gentil, garrido, elegante.
gracefully ['greisfuli] *ad* con gracia.
gracefulness ['greisfulnis] *n* donaire, garbo; sandunga; gracia.
gracious ['greiʃəs] *a* benigno, benévolo, afable.
gradation [grə'deiʃən] *n* gradación, graduación.
grade [greid] *n* grado, escalón; (*mil*) promoción; (*of road*) inclinación, desnivel; (*school*) grado, año, clase; *vt* graduar; (*land*) explanar.
graded ['greidid] *a* graduado; **— list** (*professors etc*) escalafón.
gradient ['greidiənt] *n* desnivel, pendiente, declive, rampa, inclinación.
gradual ['grædjuəl] *a* gradual.
gradually ['grædjuəli] *ad* por grados, poco a poco, con el tiempo; paulatinamente.
graduate [grædjuit] *n* licenciado, graduado; ['grædjueit] *vi* graduarse.
graft [grɑ:ft] *n* injerto, plantón;

(*hacer*) chanchullos; *vti* injertar, ingerir, insertar.
grain [grein] *n* grano; (*in wood*) veta; **against the —** a contrapelo; *vt* granular, granear.
grammar ['græmə] *n* gramática, retórica.
grammatical [grə'mætikəl] *a* gramático.
granary ['grænəri] *n* granero; (*Galicia and Asturias*) hórreo.
grand [grænd] *a* grande, sublime; **— piano** piano de cola.
grandee [græn'di:] *n* grande (de España); ricohombre.
grandeur ['grændjə] *n* grandeza, magnificencia, majestad.
grandchild ['græn,tʃaild] *n* nieto; **great-great-—** tataranieto; **great-—** biznieto.
grandfather ['grænd,fɑ:ðə] *n* abuelo; **great-—** bisabuelo; **great-great-—** tatarabuelo.
grandmother ['græn,mʌðə] *n* abuela.
grandson ['grænsʌn] *n* nieto.
grange ['greindʒ] *n* granja, cortijo, alquería.
granite ['grænit] *n* granito.
grant [grɑ:nt] *n* concesión, privilegio; (*acad*) beca; (*state*) subvención; *vt* hacer merced de, conceder, otorgar; admitir, importar.
grape [greip] *n* uva; **— juice** mosto; **— vine** vid, parra.
grapefruit ['greipfru:t] *n* toronja, pomelo.
graphic ['græfik] *a* gráfico, pintoresco, a lo vivo.
grapple ['græpl] *vti* agarrar, amarrar, aferrarse; **—** (*with*) forcejear.
grappling ['græpliŋ] *n* **— iron** cloque, rezón.
grasp [grɑ:sp] *n* apretón; (*fig*) dominio; *vt* agarrar; (*in fist*) empuñar; (*meaning*) comprender; prender; (*by the hand*) estrechar, asir; *vi* echar la zarpa.
grasping ['grɑ:spiŋ] *a* avaro, codicioso; ávido.
grass [grɑ:s] *n* hierba, césped; **— -eating** herbívoro.
grasshopper ['grɑ:s,hɔpə] *n* saltamontes, saltón, langosta.
grassland ['grɑ:slænd] *n* pradera.
grassy ['grɑ:si] *a* herboso, verde, herbáceo.
grate [greit] *n* reja, verja; (*cooking*) parrilla; *vti* rallar, raspar, cortar.
grateful ['greitful] *a* reconocido, agradecido; **to be — for** agradecer; reconocer.
gratefulness [greitfulnis] *n* gratitud, agradecimiento.
gratification [,grætifi'keiʃən] *n* satisfacción, complacencia; recompensa.
gratify ['grætifai] *vt* satisfacer, agradar, complacer, dar gusto a.
gratifying ['grætifaiiŋ] *a* grato, agradable.
grating ['greitiŋ] *a* (*sound*) rechinante, discordante; ofensivo, áspero; *n* verja, reja; **—s** (*cheese etc*) ralladuras.
gratis ['grɑ:tis] *ad* gratis, gratuito, de balde, de gorra.
gratitude ['grætitju:d] *n* gratitud, agradecimiento, reconocimiento.
gratuitous [grə'tju:itəs] *a* gratuito.
gratuity [grə'tju:iti] *n* gratificación, propina.
grave [greiv] *a* grave, serio, compasado, ponderoso; *n* tumba, hoya, sepulcro; **— stone** lápida mortuaria; **beyond the —** ultratumba; **— digger** sepulturero, enterrador.
gravel ['grævəl] *n* grava, cascajo, casquijo.
graveness ['greivnis] *n* gravedad, señorío, compostura.
graveyard ['greivjɑ:d] *n* camposanto, cementerio.
gravitate ['græviteit] *vi* gravitar.
gravity ['græviti] *n* gravedad, pesantez, mesura, seriedad; **specific —** peso específico.
gravy ['greivi] *n* salsa, jugo.
gray [grei] *a* gris, pardo; **— hair** cana(s).
graze [greiz] *n* roce; *vt* rozar; (*skin*) raspar; *vi* pacer, pastar.
grease [gri:s] *n* grasa; (*filthy*) mugre; *vt* engrasar; untar; **to — the palms of** untar las manos a.
greasy ['gri:si] *a* grasiento; graso; untuoso.
great [greit] *a* grande, grueso, eminente, sumo; **— hall** (*univ etc*) paraninfo; **— age** edad avanzada.
Great Britain ['greit 'britn] *n* Gran Bretaña.
greatcoat ['greit'kout] *n* sobretodo.
greatness ['greitnis] *n* grandeza, amplitud; nobleza.
Grecian ['gri:ʃən] *a* greco.
greed(iness) ['gri:d(inis)] *n* voracidad; codicia, concupiscencia, rapacidad.
greedily ['gri:dili] *ad* **to look — at, upon** codiciar.
greedy ['gri:di] *a* comilón; voraz, glotón, codicioso, insaciable.
Greece [gri:s] *n* Grecia.
Greek [gri:k] *an* griego.
green [gri:n] *n* lo verde, verdura, pradera; **—s** verdura(s), hierbas, hortalizas; *a* verde, fresco; **sea—** glauco; **bright —** verde limón, verdegay; **—** (*sl*) novel; **—house** conservatorio, invernadero.
greengrocer ['gri:n,grousə] *n* verdulero.
Greenland ['gri:nlənd] *n* Groenlandia.
greenness ['gri:nnis] *n* verdor, verdura.
greet [gri:t] *vti* saludar, felicitar, dar la bienvenida a.
greeting ['gri:tiŋ] *n* salutación,

saludo, recado; **—s** (*in letters*) un abrazo, saludos (cariñosos); (*Christmas*) felicitaciones navideñas.
gregarious [gri'gɛəriəs] *a* gregario.
Gregory ['gregəri] *m* Gregorio.
grenade [gri'neid] *n* granada, bomba.
greyhound ['greihaund] *n* lebrel, galgo.
grid [grid] *n* rejilla; (*el*) tendido eléctrico.
grief [gri:f] *n* pena, dolor, pesadumbre, tristeza, sentimiento.
grievance ['gri:vəns] *n* agravio, perjuicio, ofensa.
grieve [gri:v] *vt* agraviar, oprimir; lastimar; contristar, penar; *vi* afligirse, entristecerse, gemir, apenarse; **it —s me to say ...** me cuesta decir ...
grievous ['gri:vəs] *a* gravoso, cruel, sensible, aflictivo, penoso.
grievousness ['gri:vəsnis] *n* aflicción, pena, calamidad; enormidad.
grill [gril] *vt* asar en parrillas, sollamar.
grille [gril] *n* reja, verja.
grim [grim] *a* torvo, ceñudo; odioso, horroroso.
grimace [gri'meis] *n* mueca, visaje, mohín; *vi* hacer muecas.
grime [graim] *n* tizne, mugre.
grimly ['grimli] *a* espantoso, horrible; firme; *ad* horriblemente, ásperamente.
grimness ['grimnis] *n* horror; tesón.
grimy ['graimi] *a* tiznado, mugriento, sucio.
grin [grin] *n* (*unpleasant*) mueca, visaje; sonrisa; *vi* sonreírse.
grind [graind] *vt* moler, triturar, dar vueltas; **to — out** (*words*) mascullar; **to — down** agobiar; *vi* rozar, frotar.
grindstone ['graindstoun] *n* piedra de afilar, asperón.
grip [grip] *n* apretón; (*hold*) asidero, puño; (*bag*) maletín; *vti* agarrar, empuñar; (*by emotion*) poseer.
grit [grit] *n* arena, cascajo; impureza; firmeza, ánimo, entereza.
groan [groun] *n* gemido, gruñido; *vi* gemir, gruñir, suspirar.
grocer ['grousə] *n* especiero, tendero (de ultramarinos, de comestibles).
grocery ['grousəri] *n* tienda de comestibles; *pl* ultramarinos.
groin [grɔin] *n* ingle.
groom [gru:m] *n* novio; mozo de caballos, lacayo; **head —** caballerizo; *vt* cuidar (*los caballos*); acicalar.
groove [gru:v] *n* muesca, acanaladura; surco; (*wood*) ranura, hoyo; (*stone*) estría; *vt* acanalar.
grope [group] *vi* andar a tientas, palpar, tentar.
groping ['groupiŋ] *n* tiento; **—ly** *ad* a tientas.
gross [grous] *a* grueso; (*ignorance*) craso; denso; (*weight*) bruto; descortés, pesado; *n* gruesa; **by the —** por gruesas.
grossness ['grousnis] *n* grosería, tosquedad.
grotesque [grou'tesk] *a* grotesco, monstruoso.
grotto ['grɔtou] *n* gruta, antro, covacha.
ground [graund] *n* (*earth*) tierra; (*land*) terreno; (*floor*) piso, suelo; (*plot*) solar, heredad; (*reason*) motivo, pie, fundamento; **back—** fondo; **fore—** primer termino; **stony —** pedregal, cantorral; *pl* heces, sedimento; terrenos; **to fall to the —** venirse abajo; malograrse; *vti* funda(menta)r, cimentar; (*sea*) embarrancar, encallar.
groundless ['graundlis] *a* infundado, gratuito.
groundwork ['graundwə:k] *n* fundamento, base.
group [gru:p] *n* grupo; (*people*) reunión, corro; (*friends*) peña, tertulia; (*bullfighters*) cuadrilla; (*houses*) caserío; (*stage*) comparsa; (*artistic*) conjunto; *vt* agrupar.
grove [grouv] *n* arboleda, boscaje; enramada, soto; (*orange*) naranjal, huerto; (*maples*) arcedo; (*myrtles*) arrayanal; (*oaks*) robledo; (*pines*) pinar.
grovel ['grɔvl] *vi* arrastrarse; envilecerse.
grow [grou] *vt* cultivar; *vi* crecer, brotar; desarrollarse; hacerse, llegar a; **to — green** (re)verdecer.
growl [graul] *n* gruñido; *vi* gruñir; regañar.
grown-up [groun'ʌp] *an* (persona) mayor.
growth [grouθ] *n* crecimiento, desarrollo, aumento, progreso; generación; vegetación.
grudge [grʌdʒ] *n* rencor, resentimiento; ojeriza, envidia, mala gana; *vt* envidiar, codiciar; regatear.
gruel ['gruəl] *n* (*oats*) avenate; (*corn*) atole; (*mush*) gachas.
gruesome ['gru:səm] *a* horrendo, horripilante, horrible.
gruff [grʌf] *a* brusco, áspero, de mal humor, ceñudo.
gruffness ['grʌfnis] *n* rudeza, brusquedad, aspereza.
grumble ['grʌmbl] *n* regaño; queja; *vi* quejarse; refunfuñar, murmurar.
grumbling ['grʌmbliŋ] *n* murmuración, queja, descontento.
grunt [grʌnt] *n* gruñido; *vi* gruñir, refunfuñar.
guarantee [.gærən'ti:] *n* abono; fianza; seguridad; *vt* garantizar, dar fianza, asegurar, patrocinar.
guarantor [.gærən'tɔ:] *n* fiador.
guard [gɑ:d] *n* guarda, guardia; (*mil*) vigilia; (*sword*) cazoleta; **—sman** guardia; dragón; **—rail** contracarril; **to be on one's —** estar prevenido; **rear—** retaguardia;

vti preservar(se), guardar, vigilar; (res)guardarse.

guarded ['gɑ:did] *a* circunspecto, cauteloso, precavido.

guardian ['gɑ:diən] *a* tutelar; **— angel** ángel custodio; ángel de la guarda; *n* guardián, custodio, tutor.

guardianship ['gɑ:diənʃip] *n* tutela, protección.

guerrilla [gə'rilə] *n* guerrilla; (*man*) guerrillero.

guess [ges] *n* conjetura; sospecha; *vti* adivinar, columbrar, conjeturar; (*accurately*) atinar; brujulear.

guest [gest] *n* huésped, convidado; **to have —**(s) tener visita(s); **—house** hospedería.

guidance ['gaidəns] *n* conducta, guía, gobierno.

guide [gaid] *n* guía, conductor; **—lines** pauta; **— book** guía; **— post** hito; *vt* guiar, orientar, conducir, dirigir; gobernar.

guile [gail] *n* dolo, engaño, artificio, sorna.

guileless ['gaillis] *a* inocente, sencillo, cándido.

guillotine [ˌgilə'ti:n] *n* guillotina; *vt* guillotinar.

guilt [gilt] *n* delito, crimen, culpa; delincuencia; culpabilidad.

guiltless ['giltlis] *a* inocente, libre de culpa.

guilty ['gilti] *a* culpable, delincuente, convicto; **not —** inculpable; **to plead —** confesarse culpable.

guinea ['gini] *n* guinea (21 *chelines*); **—fowl** pintada, gallina de guinea; **—pig** conej(ill)o de Indias.

guise [gaiz] *n* modo, manera; pretexto; forma; **under the — of** so capa de.

guitar [gi'tɑ:] *n* guitarra; **— player** guitarrista.

gulf [gʌlf] *n* golfo; abismo, sima; **G— Stream** Corriente del Golfo.

gullible ['gʌlibl] *a* bobo, crédulo, fácil de engañar.

gully ['gʌli] *n* barranca, quebrada, tajo, hondonada.

gulp [gʌlp] *n* trago; (*fam*) chisguete; *vt* tragar, engullir.

gum [gʌm] *n* goma; (*of teeth*) encía; **chewing —** chicle; *vt* engomar.

gun [gʌn] *n* arma de fuego, fusil; (*hunting*) escopeta; cañón; **machine-—** ametralladora; **— barrel** cañón; **— carriage** cureña.

gunboat ['gʌnbout] *n* cañonero, lancha cañonera.

gunner ['gʌnə] *n* artillero.

gunpowder ['gʌnpaudə] *n* pólvora.

gunshot ['gʌnʃɔt] *n* tiro; (*distance*) alcance; **— wound** escopetazo; trabucazo.

gurgle ['gə:gl] *n* gorgoteo; *vi* murmurar, gorgotear.

gush [gʌʃ] *n* chorro, borbotón; (*water from spring*) buey de agua; efusión; *vi* brotar, manar, borbotar, borbollar.

gust [gʌst] *n* ráfaga, racha, bocanada de viento, borrasca; (*of temper*) arrebato.

gusty ['gʌsti] *a* tempestuoso, borrascoso.

gutter ['gʌtə] *n* (*house*) gotera, canal; canalón; (*street*) arroyo; *vti* acanalar.

guy [gai] *n* hazmerreír, adefesio; tío, tipo.

guzzle [gʌzl] *vti* tragar, engullir; (*fam*) (*drink*) soplar.

gymnasium [dʒim'neiziəm] *n* gimnasio.

gymnastics [dʒim'næstiks] *n* gimnasia.

gypsy ['dʒipsi] *n* gitano, húngaro; **— cant** caló.

gyrate [dʒai'reit] *vi* girar, dar vueltas, remolin(e)ar(se).

H

habit ['hæbit] *n* prática, costumbre, rutina, hábito; (*dress*) hábito, vestido; **riding —** traje de montar; **monk's —** cogulla; *pl* costumbres, mañas; **bad —s** malas costumbres; **to form the —** contraer la costumbre; soler.

habitable ['hæbitəbl] *a* habitable.

habitation [ˌhæbi'teiʃən] *n* morada, habitación.

habitual [hə'bitjuəl] *a* habitual, acostumbrado.

habitué [hə'bitjuei] *n* asiduo; aficionado, parroquiano; (*of tertulia*) contertulio.

hack [hæk] *n* brecha, corte, machetazo, cuchillada; (*nag*) cuártago, rocín; *vti* **to — (at)** tajar, picar, cortar.

hacking ['hækiŋ] *a* **— cough** tos seca; *n* montar.

hackney ['hækni] *n* caballo de alquiler; **— carriage** coche de alquiler, simón.

hackneyed ['hæknid] *a* trillado, muy usado.

haggard ['hægəd] *n* macilento, ojeroso, trasnochado; zahareño.

haggle ['hægl] *vi* regatear.

hail [heil] *n* granizo; llamada; *vti* saludar, llamar; granizar.

hair [hεə] *n* pelo, cabello; (*long, loose*) melena, cabellera; (*down*) vello; hebra; **—brush** cepillo de cabeza; **— shirt** cilicio, (*outer*) sambenito; **—less** calvo; **— -raising** horripilante; **to a —** al pelo; **—cut** corte de pelo; **—pin** horquilla; **—splitting** quisquilloso, puntilloso; **—'s-breadth escape** escape por un pelo.

hairdresser ['hεəˌdresə] *n* peluquero; **—'s** peluquería.

hairy ['hεəri] *n* cabelludo, peludo, velloso, velludo, hirsuto.

hake [heik] *n* merluza.

hale [heil] *a* robusto, sano.

half [hɑːf] *a* medio; casi; *ad* a medias; **to go halves** ir a medias; — **-awake,** — **-asleep** entre sueños; **better** — cara mitad, costilla; — **-baked** a medio cocer; — **-hearted** flojo, desanimado; — **length** de medio cuerpo; — **-open(ed)** entreabierto, entornado; — **price** a mitad de precio; —**way** a medio camino, no del todo; — **and** — mitad y mitad; — **-witted** imbécil; **to** — **open** entreabrir; **to** — **close** entornar; **to be** —**way between** mediar entre; *n* mitad.

hall [hɔːl] *n* salón; **entrance** — recibimiento, vestíbulo; **lecture** — aula; sala; **great** — paraninfo.

hallow ['hælou] *vt* consagrar, bendecir, sanctificar.

hallucination [həˌluːsi'neiʃən] *n* alucinación, error, ilusión.

halo ['heilou] *n* halo, nimbo.

halt [hɔlt] *a* cojo, lisiado; *n* alto (*place*); paradero; (*rl*) apeadero; parada; *vti* detenerse, hacer alto; parar.

halve [hɑːv] *vt* dividir en dos, partir por mitad.

ham ['hæm] *n* jamón, pernil.

hamlet ['hæmlit] *n* aldea, caserío, villorio.

hammer ['hæmə] *n* martillo, maza; (*for stones*) almadana; **sledge**— macho; **tuning** — templador; (*gun*) rastrillo; *vt* amartillar, forjar, golpear.

hammering ['hæməriŋ] *n* martilleo, martillazo.

hammock ['hæmək] *n* hamaca.

hamper ['hæmpə] *n* canasto, cesta, canasta, capacho; *vt* embarazar, estorbar.

hand [hænd] *n* mano; (*meas. of horse*) palmo; (*worker*) mano de obra, obrero; (*clock*) aguja, manecilla; (*writing*) letra; (*cards*) mano, juego; —**bag** bolsa, saco de noche; —**basin** (al)jofaina; —**book** manual; —**made** hecho a mano; —**writing** letra, carácter; —**shake** apretón de manos; —**guard** (*sword*) cazoleta; **at** — a mano, al lado; **by** — a mano; **in** — entre manos; **on** — entre manos; presente, disponible; **on the one** — por una parte; **on the other** — al contrario, en cambio; por otra parte; **to have a** — **in** tener parte en, participar en; — **to** — (*fighting*) cuerpo a cuerpo; **to lend a** — echar una mano, arrimar el hombro; — **to mouth existence** vida (arrastrada, precaria); **to go** — **in** — concertarse; ir de mano con; **to be** — **in glove with** ser uña y carne con; **second**— de segunda mano, de lance; *vt* dar la mano a; alargar, pasar; **to** — **over** entregar; transmitir; **to** — **out** (*slap etc*) (*fam*) propinar, largar; **to** — **in** entregar.

handcuff ['hændkʌf] *n* esposas; *vt* maniatar.

handful ['hændful] *n* puñado, manojo; **to be a** — ser de cuidado.

handicap ['hændikæp] *n* obstáculo; compensación.

handkerchief ['hæŋkətʃif] *n* pañuelo.

handle ['hændl] *n* mango, asa; agarradero, cogedero, tirador; *vt* manejar; manosear; trazar; dirigir; (*subject*) tratar; (*ship etc*) maniobrar.

handling ['hændliŋ] *n* manejo, dirección; (*subject*) tratamiento, trato; manoseo.

handsome ['hænsəm] *a* hermoso, guapo, bello; garrido; generoso; distinguido.

handwork ['hændwəːk] *n* obra a mano, trabajo a mano.

handy ['hændi] *a* hábil; cómodo, manual; a mano, a propósito.

hang [hæŋ] *n* (*dress*) caída; **not to care a** — no importar un pepino; *vt* colgar, suspender; (*man*) ahorcar; (*flag*) enarbolar; *vi* (*of things*) colgar; pender; (*men*) ser ahorcado; (*in suspense*) zozobrar; **to** — **about streets** callejear; rondar; **to** — **on to** pegarse a, agarrarse a.

hanging ['hæŋiŋ] *a* pendiente, dependiente, suspendido, en vilo; *n* colgadura(s), tapicería; tapiz.

hangman ['hæŋmən] *n* verdugo.

hanker ['hæŋkə] *vt* **to** — **after** ansiar, anhelar, ambicionar.

Hannah ['hænə] *f* Ana.

haphazard ['hæp'hæzəd] *a* fortuito, sin ton ni son.

happen ['hæpən] *vi* suceder, ocurrir, acontecer, caer; **as if nothing had** —**ed** como si tal cosa; **as it happens** da la casualidad.

happening ['hæpniŋ] *n* suceso, acontecimiento.

happiness ['hæpinis] *n* felicidad, ventura, gozo.

happy ['hæpi] *a* dichoso, alegre, bienaventurado, feliz, afortunado, oportuno; **to make** — encantar, alegrar; **to be** — alegrarse; — **-go-lucky** atolondrado; — **birthday** felicidades.

harass ['hærəs] *vt* acosar, vejar; (*mil*) hostigar, merodear; apretar; incomodar; **to be** —**ed** zozobrar.

harbinger ['hɑːbindʒə] *n* precursor.

harbor ['hɑːbə] *n* puerto, asilo; albergue; *vt* abrigar, amparar; (*hopes etc*) acariciar, abrigar.

hard [hɑːd] *a* duro, firme; (*stiff*) tieso; difícil, penoso; riguroso, severo; áspero, ímprobo, rudo; (*water*) cruda, gorda; — **of hearing** duro de oído; — **-hearted** sin entrañas; — **-fisted** agarrado; — **-headed** terco, duro de mollera; perspicaz; — **set** rígido; — **-working** aplicado, trabajador, hacendoso; — **-wearing** resistente, duradero, sufrido; — **weather** inclemencia; — **words** in-

jurias; — **to please** mal contentadizo; — **to hold** escurridizo; *ad* **to drink** — beber de firme; **to look — at** mirar (de hito en hito, de cerca, detenidamente); **to be — up** estar a la cuarta pregunta; *ad* difícilmente, con (ahinco, empeño), duro.
harden ['hɑ:dn] *vt* endurecer; curtir; templar; *vi* endurecerse.
hardiness ['hɑ:dinis] *n* intrepidez, vigor, ánimo.
hardly ['hɑ:dli] *ad* difícilmente, no del todo; duramente; apenas.
hardness ['hɑ:dnis] *n* dureza; rigor, penuria.
hardship ['hɑ:dʃip] *n* penalidad, fatiga; **to experience great —s** pasar crujías, estar en apuros.
hardy ['hɑ:di] *a* fuerte, bravo, robusto, endurecido, resistente.
hardware ['hɑ:dwɛə] *n* ferretería.
hare [hɛə] *n* liebre; **— -brained** descabellado.
haricot ['hærikou] *n* judía, habichuela.
harlot ['hɑ:lət] *n* puta, ramera, prostituta.
harm [hɑ:m] *n* mal, daño, ofensa; *vt* hacer daño, dañar, maleficiar.
harmful ['hɑ:mful] *a* dañoso, nocivo, deletéreo, malo.
harmless ['hɑ:mlis] *a* inofensivo.
harmonious [hɑ:'mouniəs] *a* armonioso, sonoro, inocente.
harmonize ['hɑ:mənaiz] *vti* poner de acuerdo, acordar, armonizar, concertar, concordar; (*color*) entonar.
harmony ['hɑ:məni] *n* armonía, acuerdo, concierto, consonancia, concordia.
harness ['hɑ:nis] *n* arnés, arreos, guarniciones; *vt* enjaezar.
harp [hɑ:p] *n* arpa; *vi* tocar el arpa, porfiar; **to — on** (*a subject*) machacar, recalcar(se).
harpoon [hɑ:'pu:n] *n* arpón; cloque; *vt* arponear.
harpsichord ['hɑ:psikɔ:d] *n* clavicordio.
harrow ['hærou] *n* traílla; *vt* atormentar, perturbar, conmover.
harrowing ['hærouiŋ] *a* lastimoso, lacerante, conmovedor.
harry ['hæri] *vt* devastar, asolar, perseguir, atormentar, molestar.
Harry ['hæri] *m* Enrique.
harsh [hɑ:ʃ] *a* áspero, (*taste*) agrio, acerbo; duro, ingrato, cruel, sacudido; — **words** regaño; (*colors*) chillón.
harshness ['hɑ:ʃnis] *n* aspereza, rigor, severidad; (*weather*) inclemencia.
hart [hɑ:t] *n* ciervo.
harvest ['hɑ:vist] *n* cosecha, siega, agosto; (*grapes*) vendimia; *vt* cosechar, segar; (*grapes*) vendimiar.
harvester ['hɑ:vistə] *n* segador, cosechero; máquina segadora.
harvesting ['hɑ:vistiŋ] *n* recolección.
haste [heist] *n* prisa, premura, diligencia, precipitación, impaciencia; **to make —** apresurarse, darse prisa.
hasten ['heisn] *vt* apresurar, abreviar, activar.
hastily ['heistili] *ad* apresuradamente, de prisa, de manos a boca.
hasty ['heisti] *a* premuroso, inconsiderado, precipitado, apresurado, temerario, precipitoso.
hat [hæt] *n* sombrero; **three-cornered —** tricornio, sombrero de tres picos; **to put on one's —** cubrirse.
hatch [hætʃ] *n* (*chickens*) pollada; (*door*) portezuela; cuartel; *vti* incubar, empollar; tramar.
hatchet ['hætʃit] *n* hacha, destral.
hate [heit] *n* odio, aversión; *vt* odiar, detestar, aborrecer; **I — (doing) it** me repugna.
hateful ['heitful] *a* odioso, aborrecible, infame; — **thing** abominación.
hatred ['heitrid] *n* odio, enemistad; (*fierce*) saña; (*bitter*) inquina.
haughtiness ['hɔ:tinis] *n* altanería, soberbia, altivez, ínfulas, orgullo.
haughty ['hɔ:ti] *a* altivo, arrogante, imperioso, orgulloso, entonado, empingorotado, encopetado.
haul [hɔ:l] *n* (es)tirón; arrastre; hala; *vt* tirar, arrastar; (*naut*) halar; (*goods*) acarrear; **to — down** arriar.
haunch [hɔ:ntʃ] *n* anca, cadera, grupa.
haunt [hɔ:nt] *n* sitio preferido, guarida, nido, escondrijo, querencia; *vt* rondar, frecuentar; obsesionar.
haunted ['hɔ:ntid] *a* encantado.
Havana [hə'vænə] *n* La Habana.
have [hæv] *vt* tener, poseer; obtener; (*drink*) tomar; pasar; **to —** (*made etc*) mandar hacer, hacer que; **to — to** tener que, haber de; **to — out** (*with*) decir(le) cuatro verdades, pedir(le) cuentas a, arreglárselas con; despachar.
haven ['heivn] *n* puerto, asilo, abrigo, refugio.
haversack ['hævəsæk] *n* mochila, morral.
havoc ['hævək] *n* ruina, estrago(s), destrozo(s).
hawk [hɔ:k] *n* halcón; **sparrow—** gavilán; **— -nosed** de nariz aguileña.
hawker ['hɔ:kə] *n* vendedor ambulante, buhonero; revendedor.
hawthorn ['hɔ:θɔ:n] *n* espino, acerolo.
hay [hei] *n* heno; **—stack** almiar; **—fork** horca; **to make — while the sun shines** cuando pasan rábanos, comprarlos.
hazard ['hæzəd] *n* acaso, azar; riesgo; *vti* arriesgar, aventurarse.
hazardous ['hæzədəs] *a* arriesgado, peligroso; azaroso, aventurado.
haze [heiz] *n* bruma, niebla, neblina.

hazel [heizl] *a* garzo; *n* avellano; **— plantation** avellaneda.
haziness ['heizinis] *n* vaguedad; (*poet*) calígine; obscuridad.
hazy ['heizi] *a* brumoso; confuso, borroso; elemental.
he [hi:] *pn* él.
head [hed] *a* principal; *n* cabeza, (*fam*) crisma; (*tree*) copa; (*bed, table*) cabecera; (*stick*) puño; jefe; cabo; (*of cattle*) res; (*of hair*) mata; (*of water*) salto; (*of column*) capitel; **—s and tails** cara y cruz; **per —** por barba; **from — to foot** de pies a cabeza; **neither — nor tail** ni pies ni cabeza; **to fall — over heels** caer patas arriba; (*in love*) enamorarse perdidamente; **to bring to a —** ultimar, provocar; **to fall — first** caer de cabeza; *vt* encabezar; mandar.
headache ['hedeik] *n* dolor de cabeza; (*fig*) quebradero de cabeza.
headdress ['heddres] *n* tocado, peinado; sombrero.
heading ['hediŋ] *n* encabezamiento, título, epígrafe.
headland ['hedlənd] *n* cabo, promontorio.
headline ['hedlain] *n* epígrafe, encabezamiento, título.
headlong ['hedlɔŋ] *a* precipitado, despeñado; **to fall —** caer de cabeza.
headquarters ['hed'kwɔ:təz] *n* cuartel general; oficina principal.
headstrong ['hedstrɔŋ] *a* obstinado, testarudo, aferrado, voluntarioso, impetuoso.
heal [hi:l] *vt* curar, componer, sanar; *vi* curarse.
healing ['hi:liŋ] *a* sanativo; *n* curación.
health [helθ] *n* salud; **— officer** médico de sanidad.
healthy ['helθi] *a* (*person*) sano, robusto; saludable, bueno.
heap [hi:p] *n* montón, tropel, hacina, cúmulo; **in a —** a granel; *vt* amontonar, apilar; **to — up** colmar; **to — favors upon** colmar de favores.
hear [hiə] *vti* oír, sentir, hacer caso; oír decir.
hearer ['hiərə] *n* oyente.
hearing ['hiəriŋ] *n* oído; presencia, alcance del oído; **hard of —** corto de oído.
hearsay ['hiəsei] *n* rumor, dicho, voz pública; **by —** de oídas.
hearse [hə:s] *n* carro fúnebre, féretro.
heart [hɑ:t] *n* corazón; (*cards*) copas; (*lettuce*) cogollo; (*of country*) riñón; **at —** en el fondo; **to one's —'s content** a pedir de boca, a gusto; **by —** de memoria; **to take to —** tomar a pechos; **to have one's — in one's mouth** tener el alma en un hilo; **—ache** aflicción, congoja; **—beat** latido; **— failure** colapso cardíaco; **— of hearts** entretelas del corazón; **big-hearted** magnánimo; **weak of —** cardíaco.
heartbroken ['hɑ:t.broukən] *a* acongojado, afligido, angustiado.
heartburn ['hɑ:tbə:n] *n* acidez del estómago, acedía,
hearten ['hɑ:tn] *vt* animar, estimular, alentar.
heartfelt ['hɑ:tfelt] *a* sincero, hondo.
hearth [hɑ:θ] *n* hogar; horno.
heartiness ['hɑ:tinis] *n* sinceridad, cordialidad; campechanía.
heartless ['hɑ:tlis] *a* cruel, ruin, desalmado.
heartrending ['hɑ:t.rendiŋ] *a* congojoso, desgarrador.
hearty ['hɑ:ti] *a* sincero, cordial; robusto, campechano.
heat [hi:t] *n* calor; ardor, fuego, acaloramiento; temperatura; vivacidad; **—stroke** insolación; *vt* **to — (up)** (re)calentar; *vi* acalorarse.
heater ['hi:tə] *n* calentador, calorífero.
heath [hi:θ] *n* brezo, brezal, matorral.
heathen ['hi:ðən] *an* pagano, idólatra.
heather ['heðə] *n* brezo.
heating ['hi:tiŋ] *n* calefacción.
heave [hi:v] *n* esfuerzo; levantamiento, (*sickness*) nausea, basca; *vt* cargar, alzar, levantar; (*sigh*) exhalar; *vi* suspirar, jadear.
heaven ['hevn] *n* cielo; paraíso; **seventh —** gloria, éxtasis; **good —s!** ¡hombre!; **the —s have burst** se ha venido el cielo abajo.
heavenly ['hevnli] *a* celeste, angélico.
heavily ['hevili] *ad* pesadamente; **to breathe —** resoplar.
heaviness ['hevinis] *n* pesadez, peso; pesadumbre; modorra; torpeza; opresión.
heaving ['hi:viŋ] *n* palpitación; jadeo; (*sea*) oleada.
heavy ['hevi] *a* pesado, fuerte, denso; (*footed, mental*) lento, torpe, lerdo; (*color*) recargado; indigesto; (*silence*) opresivo; nutrido; **to make heavier** agravar; **— weather** cargazón.
Hebrew ['hi:bru:] *an* hebreo, judío.
hedge [hedʒ] *n* seto, valla; *vt* cercar con seto; *vi* evitar contestar.
hedgehog ['hedʒhɔg] *n* erizo.
heed [hi:d] *n* cuidado, guardia, atención; **to take —** precaverse; **to pay no — to** desoír; *vti* atender, escuchar, prestar atención a, hacer caso de.
heedful ['hi:dful] *a* cuidadoso, atento, vigilante.
heedless ['hi:dlis] *a* distraído, atolondrado; desatento.
heedlessness ['hi:dlisnis] *n* impetuosidad, imprudencia; descuido, olvido.
heel [hi:l] *n* talón; calcañal; (*of boot*) tacón; **Achilles' —** tendón; **to take to one's —s, to show a clean pair of —s** tomar las de Villadiego; **to be down at —** andar de capa caída;

vi **to — over** zozobrar, recalcar.
heifer ['hefə] *n* ternera, vaquilla.
height [hait] *n* (*above sea*) altura; (*altitude*) altitud; (*person*) estatura, talla; (*position*) elevación; (*horses*) alzada; (*ambition etc*) cumbre; (*a hill*) eminencia, cerro; extremo; **what is your —?** ¿cuánto mide Vd?
heighten ['haitn] *vt* realzar, poner en relieve; (*colors*) avivar, perfeccionar.
heir [εə] *n* heredero, sucesor; **—s** sucesión; **— apparent** heredero presunto.
heirloom ['εəlu:m] *n* herencia; cosa heredada.
held [held] *a* tenido; **to be — up** estancarse; estar parado.
Helen ['helin] *f* Elena.
hell [hel] *n* infierno, abismo; (*poet*) averno.
hello ['he'lou] *interj* hola, buenos días, adiós.
helm [helm] *n* timón; yelmo; **to be at the —** timonear.
helmet ['helmit] *n* casco, yelmo.
helmsman ['helmzmən] *n* timonero, timonel.
help [help] *n* ayuda, socorro; apoyo, auxilio, favor; (*domestic*) servidumbre; **there is no — for it** no hay remedio; *vt* servir, ayudar, auxiliar; socorrer; remediar; **he cannot — it** no lo puede remediar, no puede menos de.
helper ['helpə] *n* ayudante, asistente.
helpful ['helpful] *a* útil, saludable, servicial.
helpless ['helplis] *a* desvalido, abandonado, irremediable; desmañado.
helter-skelter ['heltə'skeltə] *ad* a trochemoche, a trompón, atropelladamente.
hem [hem] *n* dobladillo, borde, orla; *vt* bastillar, dobladillar, repulgar.
hemisphere ['hemisfiə] *n* hemisferio.
hen [hen] *n* gallina.
hence [hens] *ad* de aquí, por ende; por tanto, luego.
henceforth ['hens'fɔ:θ] *ad* de aquí, (hoy) en adelante, en lo sucesivo.
henchman ['hentʃmən] *n* satélite.
Hendaye ['ɔŋdai] *n* Hendaya.
Henrietta [henri'etə] *f* Enriqueta.
Henry ['henri] *m* Enrique.
her [hə:] *pn*; *dir obj* la; *indir obj* le; *after prep* ella; *poss* su.
herald ['herəld] *n* heraldo, precursor; *vt* anunciar.
heraldry ['herəldri] *n* heráldica, blasón.
herb [hə:b] *n* hierba.
herculean [,hə:kju'li:ən] *a* hercúleo; **— task** obra de romanos.
herd [hə:d] *n* rebaño; tropa; banda; (*turkeys, wolves etc*) manada; (*swine*) piara; **— instinct** instinto gregario; *vt* acorralar; *vi* vivir en rebaño, ir en manadas.
herdsman ['hə:dzmən] *n* (*sheep*) pastor; (*cattle*) vaquero.
here [hiə] *ad* aquí, acá; ¡presente! **— and there** acá y allá; **— I am** heme aquí.
hereabouts ['hiərə,bauts] *ad* cerca de aquí, por aquí.
hereafter ['hiər'ɑ:ftə] *ad* en lo futuro; *n* posteridad.
hereditary [hi'reditəri] *a* hereditario.
heresy ['herəsi] *n* herejía.
heretic ['herətik] *n* hereje.
heritage ['heritidʒ] *n* herencia, patrimonio.
hermit ['hə:mit] *n* ermitaño, solitario, eremita.
hermitage ['hə:mitidʒ] *n* ermita; rábida.
hero ['hiərou] *n* héroe.
heroic [hi'rouik] *a* heroico, épico.
heroine ['herouin] *n* heroína.
heroism ['herouizəm] *n* heroísmo, heroicidad.
herring ['heriŋ] *n* arenque.
hers [hə:z] *poss* (el) suyo, (la) suya, (los) suyos, (las) suyas.
herself [hə:'self] *pron* ella misma.
hesitant ['hezitənt] *a* indeciso, vacilante, irresoluto; (*speech*) tardo.
hesitate ['heziteit] *vi* vacilar, dudar.
hesitation [,hezi'teiʃən] *n* vacilación, duda; escrúpulo; balbuceo.
hew [hju:] *vt* tajar, hachear, desbastar; (*down*) abatir.
hewn ['hju:n] *a* labrado, desbastado; **rough—** basto.
hidden ['hidn] *a* ignoto; escondido; guardado; oculto.
hide [haid] *n* piel, cuero.
hide [haid] *vt* (*from view*) esconder; (*from knowledge*) ocultar, encubrir, tapar, velar; sepultar; *vi* ocultarse, esconderse; **— and seek** escondite.
hideous ['hidiəs] *a* horroroso, horrible, espantoso.
hideousness ['hidiəsnis] *n* fealdad, deformidad, horror.
hiding ['haidiŋ] *n* **a good —** zurra, paliza; **in —** escondido, a escondite; **— place** escondite, escondrijo.
high [hai] *a* alto; (*raised*) elevado; (*color, price*) subido; (*wind*) tempestuoso; (*meat*) pasado, podrido; (*music*) agudo; **—hat** (*sl*) (en)copetado; **—born** linajudo; **—-handed** arbitrario; **—road** camino real, carretera; **— -sounding** altisonante; **— -spirited** bullicioso, bizarro; **— tide** pleamar; **— and mighty** encopetado; **— table** mesa presidencial; **— and dry** en seco, varado; **to be —** (*of meat*) oliscar; *ad* **— and low** por todas partes.
highland ['hailənd] *n* altiplanicie; *pl* montañas; *a* montañoso.
highly ['haili] *ad* sumamente, en

sumo grado, altamente; — **-strung** impresionable.
highness ['hainis] *n* altura; (*rank*) alteza.
highway ['haiwei] *n* carretera, camino real; **—man** salteador, bandido, bandolero, forajido.
hill [hil] *n* cerro, colina; (*rocky*) peñascal; (*wooded*) monte; (*slope*) cuesta; **up —** cuesta arriba; **down—** cuesta abajo.
hillock ['hilək] *n* otero, altillo.
hillside ['hilsaid] *n* ladera.
hilltop ['hiltɔp] *n* cumbre.
hilly ['hili] *a* montañoso; quebrado.
hilt [hilt] *n* empuñadura, guarnición, puño; **up to the —** hasta las cachas.
him [him] *pn* le, lo; *after prep* él.
himself [him'self] *pn* él mismo.
hind [haind] *a* trasero, posterior; *n* cierva.
hinder ['hində] *vt* impedir, obstruir, estorbar, negar.
hindrance ['hindrəns] *n* obstáculo, impedimento, estorbo, quite, rémora.
hindquarters ['haind,kwɔ:təz] *n* cuarto trasero; (*horse*) ancas.
hinge [hindʒ] *n* gozne, bisagra; *vi* (de)pender.
hint [hint] *n* indirecta, indicación, insinuación, sugestión; **with a — of** con asomo de, con (sus) ribetes de; **to take a —** darse por entendido; *vti* apuntar, insinuar, aludir.
hip [hip] *n* cadera.
hire ['haiə] *n* alquiler, arriendo; jornal; *vt* alquilar, arrendar, contratar; (*servant*) ajustar; **to — out** aquilarse, ponerse a servir a otro.
his [hiz] *a* su; *pn* suyo.
Hispanic [his'pænik] *a* hispánico.
hiss [his] *n* silbido; *vti* silbar; rechiflar; (*theat*) chichear.
hissing ['hisiŋ] *n* silba, siseo.
historian [his'tɔ:riən] *n* historiador.
historical [his'tɔ:rikl] *a* histórico.
history ['histəri] *n* historia, narrativa.
hit [hit] *n* golpe, choque; **a — (at)** una indirecta; acierto; éxito; *vt* pegar, golpear; (*aim*) atinar, acertar; chocar; **to — the mark** dar en el blanco, dar en el clavo; **to — it off with** hacer buenas migas con.
hither ['hiðə] *ad* **— and thither** de aquí para allá.
hitherto ['hiðə'tu:] *adv* hasta aquí.
hive [haiv] *n* colmena; *vt* enjambrar.
hoar [hɔ:] *a* blanco, cano; **—frost** escarcha.
hoard [hɔ:d] *n* montón, tesoro; repuesto; *vt* **to — up** atesorar, amontonar, almacenar; recoger.
hoarding ['hɔ:diŋ] *n* **— up** hacinamiento; almacenamiento; (*wooden*) valla, cartelera.
hoarse [hɔ:s] *a* ronco, bronco.
hoarseness ['hɔ:snis] *n* ronquera, ronquedad.
hoary ['hɔ:ri] *a* blanco, blanquecino; **— joke** castaño.
hoax [houks] *n* mistificación, mentira; burla, timo; *vt* mistificar, engañar.
hobble ['hɔbl] *n* manea, traba; *vi* cojear; **to — along** renquear.
hobby ['hɔbi] *n* pasatiempo, tema, manía, afición.
hobgoblin ['hɔb,gɔblin] *n* trasgo, estantigua; enano.
hoe [hou] *n* azada, azadón, sacho; *vt* cavar, azadonar, sachar.
hog [hɔg] *n* puerco, marrano; (*fig*) guarro.
hogshead ['hɔgzhed] *n* pipa, barril.
hoist [hɔist] *n* cabría, grúa, montacargas; *vt* **to — up** levantar, elevar, eslingar.
hold [hould] *n* (*on object*) asidero; mango, asa; (*holding*) presa, agarro; (*influence*) dominio; (*ship*) bodega; **to lay — of** agarrar, adueñarse de; *vt* tener, coger, agarrar; tener cabida para; **to — back** contener, refrenar, reprimir; **to — down** sujetar; **to — fast** asegurar(se); **to — forth** perorar; **to — in high respect** estimar; **to — one's tongue** callarse (*el pico*); **to — out** proponer; mantenerse firme; **to — out against** resistir; **to — over** tener suspendido; aplazar; **to — to a course** singular; **to — up** levantar; apoyar; atracar; parar; saltear; mantener, sostener; **to — with** convenir con, estar de acuerdo con; **to — within** encerrar.
holder ['houldə] *n* poseedor, dueño; (*cigarette*) boquilla; mango, estuche.
holding ['houldiŋ] *n* posesión, pertenencia.
hole [houl] *n* hueco, agujero, orificio, boquerón; (*in clothes*) roto, descosido; (*in stocking*) carrera, punto; **button—** presilla; **filthy —** zaquizamí.
holiday ['hɔlədi] *n* día de fiesta, día festivo, festividad; (*short*) asueto; **half —** media fiesta; *pl* vacaciones; **summer —** veraneo; **to spend the summer —** veranear.
holidaymaker ['hɔlədi,meikə] *n* excursionista, turista, veraneante.
holiness ['houlinis] *n* santidad.
Holland ['hɔlənd] *n* Holanda, Países Bajos.
hollow ['hɔlou] *a* hueco; vacío; **— -eyed** ojos hundidos; *n* concavidad, hueco; (*eye*) oquedad; (*in hills*) nava.
holly [hɔli] *n* acebo.
holy ['houli] *a* santo, pío, sagrado; **— water** agua bendita.
homage ['hɔmidʒ] *n* homenaje, culto.
home [houm] *n* hogar, casa; hospedería; nido; (*ancestral, family*) morada, solar; casa solariega; (*for children*) hospicio; (*for aged*) asilo; **— address** domicilio; *a* doméstico; solariego; natal; indígena; **— country** patria; **—-loving** casero;

—made casero; **— office** oficina matriz, sede; **— thrust** estocada certera; **at —** *ad* en casa, en su casa; **to strike —** dar en el blanco; herir en lo vivo.
homecoming ['houm,kʌmiŋ] *n* vuelta, regreso al hogar.
homeland ['houmlənd] *n* patria, tierra, patria chica; (*Galicia*) terruño.
homeless ['houmlis] *a* destituído, sin techo, sin hogar.
homeliness ['houmlinis] *n* sencillez, llaneza.
homely ['houmli] *a* familiar, hogareño, casero, llano, grosero; feo.
Homer ['houmə] *m* Homero.
homesick ['houmsik] *a* nostálgico.
homesickness ['houmsiknis] *n* nostalgia; añoranza; (*Galicia*) morriña.
homeward ['houmwəd] *ad* hacia la casa; de regreso.
homily ['hɔmili] *n* sermón, páltica.
honest ['ɔnist] *a* honrado, sincero; (*morals*) honesto; leal, íntegro, bueno, equitativo; **— man** hombre de bien.
honesty ['ɔnisti] *n* honradez, lealtad, sinceridad, rectitud.
honey ['hʌni] *n* miel; **to make —** (*bees*) melar; **—ed** (*words*) azucarado, almibarado.
honeycomb ['hʌnikoum] *n* panal.
honeymoon ['hʌnimu:n] *n* viaje de novios, luna de miel.
honor ['ɔnə] *n* honor; (*reputation*) honra; fama, dignidad, gloria; (*purity*) honestidad, pudor, castidad; (*position*) dignidad, cargo; (*award*) lauro; *vt* honrar, venerar; enaltecer; condecorar; (*check*) pagar; **maid of —** camarista; dama; **in — of** en obsequio de; **affair of —** lance de honor; **bringing —** honroso.
honorable ['ɔnərəbl] *a* honorable; ilustre; honrado; honorífico.
hood [hud] *n* capucha, caperuza, toca; (*doctor's, hawk's*) capirote; (*aut*) cubierta; **Little Red Riding —** Caperucita Roja.
hoodwink ['hudwiŋk] *vt* vendar los ojos, engañar.
hoof [hu:f] *n* casco; (*cloven*) pezuña.
hook [huk] *n* gancho, garfio; (*for hanging*) colgadero; (*clothes*) prendedero; (*reaping*) hoz; (*writing*) garabato; (*games*) zancadilla; **— and eye** corchete; **by — or by crook** a tuertas o a derechas; **on his own —** por su propia cuenta; *vt* enganchar, engatusar, pescar.
hooked ['hukt] *a* encorvado; **— nose** aguileño.
hooky ['huki] *n* **to play —** hacer novillos.
hoop [hu:p] *n* (*child's*) aro; círculo, anillo, sortija.
hoot [hu:t] *n* grita, rechifla; *vi* gritar; (*owl*) ulular.
hop [hɔp] *n* brinco, salto; (*bot*) lúpulo; *vi* danzar, brincar, saltar.
hope [houp] *n* esperanza, expectativa; *vt* **to — for** esperar; *vi* **to give —** dar esperanzas, confiar.
hopeful ['houpful] *a* esperanzado, confiado; optimista; halagüeño.
hopeless ['houplis] *a* desesperado, imposible; perdido; (*illness*) desahuciado.
hopelessness ['houplisnis] *n* (*sensation*) desesperación; (*situation*) imposibilidad.
hoping ['houpiŋ] *a* **— for** en espera de.
Horace ['hɔrəs] *m* Horacio.
horde [hɔ:d] *n* horda, cáfila; (*gypsies*) aduar.
horizon [hə'raizn] *n* horizonte.
horizontal [,hɔri'zɔntl] *a* horizontal.
horn [hɔ:n] *n* cuerno, asta; trompa, corneta; (*fog, car*) bocina; (*drinking*) colodra; (*shoe*) calzador; **— -shaped** corniforme; **— thrust** (*gore*) cornada; **—s of a dilemma** términos de un dilema.
horned [hɔ:nd] *a* cornudo.
hornet ['hɔ:nit] *n* avispa, moscardón.
horny [hɔ:ni] *a* córneo; calloso.
horrible ['hɔribl] *a* horrible, horroroso, espantoso.
horrid ['hɔrid] *a* horroroso, hórrido.
horrify ['hɔrifai] *vt* horrorizar, horripilar.
horror ['hɔrə] *n* horror, espanto, pavor; detestación, repugnancia.
horse [hɔ:s] *n* caballo, caballería; **to be on high —** ensoberbecerse; **—fly** tábano; **— hair** cerda; **— laugh** risotada; **— racing** concurso(s) hípico(s); **— sense** gramática parda; **—power** caballo de fuerza; **—shoe** herradura; **clothes—** tendedor; *pl* **white —s** cabrillas.
horseback ['hɔ:sbæk] *n* lomo de caballo; **on —** a caballo.
horseman ['hɔ:smən] *n* jinete, caballero.
hose [houz] *n* calceta; (*men's*) **half—** calcetín; manguera, manga de riego.
hospice ['hɔspis] *n* hospicio, hospedería.
hospitable [hɔs'pitəbl] *a* hospitalario, acogedor.
hospital ['hɔspitl] *n* hospital; **field —** hospital de campaña; **emergency —** hospital de sangre.
hospitality [,hɔspi'tæliti] *n* hospitalidad, agasajo.
host [houst] *n* (*inn*) hospedero, patrón, mesonero; (*meal*) anfitrión; (*army*) hueste; (*house*) huésped; (*relig*) hostia; **to elevate the —** alzar la hostia.
hostage ['hɔstidʒ] *n* rehén.
hostelry ['hɔstəlri] *n* hotel, parador, hostería; pensión.
hostess ['houstis] *n* patrona, huéspeda, ama, señora.

hostile ['hɔstail] *a* hostil, enemigo.
hostility [hɔs'tiliti] *n* hostilidad.
hot [hɔt] *a* (*climate*) cálido; (*sun*) ardiente; (*substance*) caliente; (*day*) caluroso; (*dispute*) acalorado; (*mustard etc*) picante; **to be —** tener calor.
hotbed ['hɔtbed] *n* criadero, vivero.
hotel [hou'tel] *n* hotel.
hothead ['hɔthed] *n* exaltado, fanático.
hot-house ['hɔthaus] *n* invernadero.
hound [haund] *n* sabueso, podenco; *vt* **to — down** acosar, perseguir.
hour ['auə] *n* hora; **critical —** trance; **by the —** por horas; **the small —s** las altas horas.
hourly ['auəli] *ad* de hora en hora, de un momento a otro, a cada hora.
house [haus] *n* casa, habitación; (*business*) empresa, casa de comercio; **boarding —** pensión, casa de huéspedes; **public —** taberna; **— of Representatives** Congreso, Cámara de Representantes; **a full —** (*theat*) un lleno completo; **— coat** bata; [hauz] *vti* albergar, almacenar, residir.
household ['haushould] *n* casa, familia; **royal —** Corte; **— Cavalry** Escolta Real.
householder ['haushouldə] *n* jefe de familia, dueño, inquilino.
housekeeper ['haus,ki:pə] *n* ama de llaves.
housekeeping ['haus,ki:piŋ] *n* manejo de la casa.
housewife ['hauswaif] *n* ama de casa, ama de gobierno; la mujer casada.
housetop ['haustɔp] *n* tejado, azotea.
housework ['hauswə:k] *n* faenas, quehaceres (*de la casa*).
housing ['hauziŋ] *n* alojamiento, vivienda.
hovel ['hɔvəl] *n* cobertizo, cabaña, choza, casucha, tugurio.
hover ['hɔvə] *vi* revolotear; (*hawk etc*) cerner(se).
how [hau] *ad* como; **— dull** (*etc*)**!** ¡qué aburrido!; **— are things?** ¿qué tal?; **— much?** ¿cuánto?; **— many?** ¿cuántos?; **to say — do you do to** saludar a; **the — and the why** el como y el por qué.
however [hau'evə] *cj* sin embargo, no obstante, con todo; *ad* de cualquier modo, cualquiera que.
howl [haul] *n* grito, aullido, bramido; alarido; *vi* aullar, gritar, ulular, rugir, mugir.
howling ['hauliŋ] *n* (*wind*) bramido, silbido, aullido.
hub [hʌb] *n* eje; cubo.
hubbub ['hʌbʌb] *n* gritería, alboroto, batahola.
Hubert ['hju:bət] *m* Huberto.
huddle ['hʌdl] *n* tropel, montón; *vti* mezclar(se), amontonar(se), arracimar(se).
hue [hju:] *n* color, matiz, tinte; **— and cry** alarida.
hug [hʌg] *n* abrazo; *vt* abrazar, acariciar.
huge [hju:dʒ] *a* enorme, inmenso, tremendo, ingente.
hugeness ['hju:dʒnis] *n* enormidad, grandeza.
Hugh [hju:] *m* Hugo.
hulk [hʌlk] *n* casco de navío; armatoste.
hull [hʌl] *n* (*ship*) casco; cáscara, corteza.
hullabaloo [,hʌləbə'lu:] *n* zaragata, vocería, gritería.
hum [hʌm] *n* zumbido, murmullo; *vi* zumbar, susurrar; *vti* (*tune*) canturrear, tararear.
human ['hju:mən] *a* humano; **— being** ser humano; **to become —** humanizarse.
humane [hju:'mein] *a* humanitario, compasivo.
humanity [hju:'mæniti] *n* humanidad; *pl* humanidades.
humble ['hʌmbl] *a* humilde, modesto; sumiso; **to make —** humillar; **to eat — pie** achicarse; *vt* abatir, humillar; **to — oneself** doblar la cerviz.
humbled ['hʌmbld] *a* sumiso.
humbug ['hʌmbʌg] *n* charlatán; farsante; hipocresía; impostura; embuste.
humid ['hju:mid] *a* húmedo.
humidity ['hju:miditi] *n* humedad.
humiliate [hju:'milieit] *vt* humillar, abatir, mortificar.
humiliation [hju:,mili'eiʃən] *n* humillación, degradación.
humility [hju:'militi] *n* humildad, sumisión.
humming ['hʌmiŋ] *n* zumbido, susurro; (*of song*) canturreo.
humor ['hju:mə] *n* humor; índole; genio; sal, agudeza; *vt* complacer, dar gusto, mimar.
humorist ['hju:mərist] *n* humorista, chancero.
humorous ['hju:mərəs] *a* festivo, jocoso, divertido, chistoso.
hump [hʌmp] *n* (*camel*) joroba; giba; **— -backed** jorobado, giboso.
hundred ['hʌndrid] *an* cien(to); **in —s** a centenares.
hundredth ['hʌndrədθ] *an* centésimo.
Hungarian [hʌŋ'gɛəriən] *an* húngaro.
Hungary ['hʌŋgəri] *n* Hungría.
hunger ['hʌŋgə] *n* hambre; *vi* tener hambre; **to — for** ansiar.
hungry ['hʌŋgri] *a* hambriento, famélico, con hambre; **I am —** tengo hambre.
hunt [hʌnt] *n* caza, cacería; *vt* cazar, perseguir; **to — for** buscar, ir en busca de; ansiar; *vi* cazar, ir de caza.
hunter ['hʌntə] *n* cazador.
hunting ['hʌntiŋ] *n* caza; cacería; **— party** partida de caza.

hurdle ['hə:dl] *n* zarzo, encañado; valla.
hurdy-gurdy ['hə:di,gə:di] *n* organillo, manubrio.
hurl [hə:l] *n* tiro; *vt* lanzar; (*from above*) precipitar, (*from position*) derrocar; **to — away** tirar; **to — back** rechazar; **to — oneself on** abalanzarse sobre, precipitarse sobre, arrojarse a.
hurrah [hu'rɑ:] *excl* ¡bravo!, ¡viva!
hurricane ['hʌriken] *n* huracán.
hurried ['hʌrid] *a* precipitado, atropellado, presuroso.
hurriedly ['hʌridli] *ad* de prisa, precipitadamente, a la carrera.
hurry ['hʌri] *n* prisa, priesa, precipitación; *vt* apurar, apresurar, urgir; *vi* apretar el paso, apresurarse, darse prisa, apurarse; **to be in a —** llevar (tener) prisa; **there's no — about it** no corre prisa.
hurt [hə:t] *n* daño, herida; **to get —** lastimarse; *a* (*morally*) picado, indignado, herido; (*physically*) tullido, lastimado, herido; *vt* herir, hacer (daño, mal) a, dañar.
hurtful ['hə:tful] *a* nocivo, pernicioso, dañino.
husband ['hʌzbənd] *n* marido, esposo, consorte, cónyuge; *vt* medir, economizar.
husbandry ['hʌzbəndri] *n* agricultura, economía doméstica; frugalidad.
hush [hʌʃ] *n* quietud, silencio; *vti* sosegar, hacer callar, callarse; **—!** *excl* ¡chist!, ¡chito!, ¡chitón!
hushed [hʌʃt] *a* callado, silencioso; **to be —** enmudecerse, callarse.
husk [hʌsk] *n* vaina, cáscara; (*pod*) vainilla.
huskiness ['hʌskinis] *n* carraspera, ronquedad.
husky ['hʌski] *a* cascarudo; ronco; fuerte, forzudo; *n* **— (dog)** perro de trineo.
hustle ['hʌsl] *n* actividad; *vt* empujar; mezclar; *vi* apresurarse, menearse, andar a empellones.
hut [hʌt] *n* cobertizo; choza, cabaña, borda; tugurio.
hyacinth ['haiəsinθ] *n* jacinto.
hybrid ['haibrid] *a* híbrido.
hydrant ['haidrənt] *n* boca de riego.
hydrogen ['haidridʒən] *n* hidrógeno.
hyena [hai'i:nə] *n* hiena.
hygiene ['haidʒi:n] *n* higiene.
hymn [him] *n* himno.
hyperbole [hai'pə:bəli] *n* hipérbole.
hypocrisy [hi'pɔkrisi] *n* hipocresía, disimulación, gazmoñería.
hypocrite ['hipəkrit] *n* hipócrita, mojigato, camandulero, comediante; (*relig*) beata.
hypocritical [,hipə'kritikəl] *a* mojigato, gazmoño.
hypothesis [hai'pɔθisis] *n* hipótesis, suposición.
hysteria [his'tiəriə] *n* histeria, histerismo.
hysterical [his'terikəl] *a* histérico.

I

I [ai] *pn* yo.
Iberian [ai'biəriən] *an* ibérico.
Iberian Peninsula [ai'biəriən pi'ninsjulə] *n* Península Ibérica.
ice [ais] *n* hielo; **—box** nevera; **—cream** helado, mantecado; **—field** banca de hielo; **— merchant's** nevería; *vt* helar, congelar; **to break the —** romper el hielo.
iceberg ['aisbə:g] *n* témpano.
Iceland ['aislənd] *n* Islandia.
Icelandic [ais'lændik] *an* islandés.
icicle ['aisikl] *n* carámbano.
icy ['aisi] *a* helado, glacial, álgido.
idea [ai'diə] *n* idea, noción, ocurrencia; imagen; plan.
ideal [ai'diəl] *a* ideal, utópico; *n* modelo, ideal.
idealism [ai'diəlizəm] *n* idealismo.
idealist [ai'diəlist] *n* idealista.
identification [ai'dentifi'keiʃən] *n* identificación; **— tag, disc** disco de identidad.
identify [ai'dentifai] *vt* identificar.
identity [ai'dentiti] *n* identidad; **— card** cédula personal.
identical [ai'dentikəl] *n* idéntico, igual.
idiocy ['idiəsi] *n* idiotez, imbecilidad, necedad.
idiom ['idiəm] *n* idioma; modismo, idiotismo, locución, giro.
idiot ['idiət] *n* idiota, imbécil, cretino.
idle ['aidl] *a* ocioso, perezoso, desocupado; fútil; haragán; **— fellow** zángano, majadero; **to be —** cruzarse de brazos, estar ocioso, vagar; *vt* holgazanear, holgar, gastar.
idleness ['aidlnis] *n* ociosidad, pereza, desocupación, holgazanería.
idler ['aidlə] *n* holgazán, polizón, zángano.
idol ['aidl] *n* ídolo.
idolatry [ai'dɔlətri] *n* idolatría.
idolize ['aidəlaiz] *vt* idolatrar, adorar.
idyll [idl] *n* idilio.
if [if] *cj* si, con tal que, como que, como si.
Ignatius [ig'neiʃəs] *m* Ignacio.
ignite [ig'nait] *vt* encender, poner fuego a, inflamar; *vr* inflamarse.
ignoble [ig'noubl] *a* innoble; afrentoso, indigno; plebeyo.
ignominious [ignə'miniəs] *a* ignominioso, afrentoso.
ignominy ['ignəmini] *n* ignominia, oprobio, infamia.
ignorance ['ignərəns] *n* ignorancia; desconocimiento.
ignorant ['ignərənt] *a* ignorante, lego; necio; **— of** inconsciente de.
ignore [ig'nɔ:] *vt* hacer caso omiso: desconocer; (*a person*) desairar.

ill [il] *n* mal, desgracia; *a* malo, enfermo; **to fall —** ponerse enfermo; **to make —** marear; *ad* mal, malamente; **— -bred** mal criado; **— breeding** mala crianza; **— -mannered** grosero; **— manners** grosería; **— -omened** infausto; **— -starred** malogrado; **— -tempered** malhumorado, de mal genio; **— -timed** intempestivo.

illegal [i'li:gəl] *a* ilegal, indebido.

illegible [i'ledʒibl] *a* ilegible, borroso.

illegitimate [ili'dʒitimit] *a* ilegítimo, bastardo.

illicit [i'lisit] *a* ilícito.

illiteracy [i'litərəsi] *n* ignorancia; analfabetismo.

illiterate [i'litərit] *a* indocto, iliterato, analfabeto.

illness ['ilnis] *n* enfermedad, indisposición.

illogical [i'lɔdʒikl] *a* ilógico, descabellado.

illtreat ['il'tri:t] *vt* maltratar.

illumination [i,lu:mi'neiʃən] *n* iluminación; (*lighting*) alumbrado.

illumine [i'lu:min] *vt* ilustrar; alumbrar.

illusion [i'lu:ʒən] *n* ilusión, ensueño; engaño, quimera, espejismo.

illusive [i'lu:siv] *a* ilusorio, engañoso.

illustrate ['iləstreit] *vt* explicar, ilustrar, (a)clarar.

illustration [ilə'streiʃən] *n* ilustración; (*moral*) ejemplo; (*in book*) lámina.

illustrious [i'lʌstriəs] *a* célebre, ilustre, glorioso, ínclito, preclaro.

image ['imidʒ] *n* imagen, figura, impresión, representación, trasunto; **the very — of** pintiparado.

imaginary [i'mædʒinəri] *a* imaginario, ficticio, hipotético; fantástico; ideal.

imagination [i,mædʒi'neiʃən] *n* imaginación, inventiva.

imaginative [i'mædʒinətiv] *a* imaginativo; **— power** invención.

imagine [i'mædʒin] *vt* imaginar, imaginarse, figurarse, suponer.

imbecile ['imbəsi:l] *n* imbécil, idiota.

imbecility [,imbi'siliti] *n* imbecilidad, debilidad, idiotismo.

imbibe [im'baib] *vt* (ab)sorber, (em)beber.

imbue [im'bju:] *vt* imbuir, inspirar; calar.

imitate ['imiteit] *vt* imitar, copiar, remedar, contrahacer.

imitation [,imi'teiʃən] *n* imitación, copia, traslado.

imitator ['imiteitə] *n* imitador, remedador.

immaculate [i'mækjulit] *a* inmaculado, puro, depurado.

immaterial [,imə'tiəriəl] *a* inmaterial, de poca importancia.

immature [,imə'tjuə] *a* inmaturo, verde, prematuro; (*youth*) lampiño, imberbe, impúbero.

immaturity [,imə'tjuriti] *n* inmadurez; falta de sazón.

immediate [i'mi:diət] *a* inmediato, urgente; cercano.

immediately [i'mi:diətli] *ad* inmediatamente, en seguida, al instante.

immense [i'mens] *a* inmenso, ilimitado, infinito, vasto.

immerse [i'mə:s] *vt* sumergir, zambullir.

immigration [,imi'greiʃən] *n* inmigración.

imminent ['iminənt] *a* inminente.

immobile [i'moubail] *a* fijo, inmóvil.

immobility [,imou'biliti] *n* inmovilidad.

immoderate [i'mɔdərit] *a* inmoderado, excesivo, desmesurado.

immodesty [i'mɔdisti] *n* impudor; deshonestidad.

immoral [i'mɔrəl] *vt* inmoral, depravado, pervertido.

immorality [,imə'ræliti] *n* inmoralidad.

immortal [i'mɔ:tl] *a* inmortal.

immortality [,imɔ:'tæliti] *n* inmortalidad.

immortalize [i'mɔ:təlaiz] *vt* inmortalizar.

immovable [i'mu:vəbl] *a* inmóvil, inmovible, fijo, firme.

immunity [i'mju:niti] *n* inmunidad, privilegio, exención.

immutable [i'mju:təbl] *a* inmutable, invariable, inconmutable.

imp [imp] *n* demonio, diablillo, duende.

impact ['impækt] *n* choque, golpe.

impair [im'pɛə] *vt* perjudicar, disminuir, lastimar, deteriorar.

impalpable [im'pælpəbl] *a* impalpable.

impart [im'pɑ:t] *vt* comunicar, conceder, hacer saber; prestar.

impartial [im'pɑ:ʃəl] *a* imparcial, indiferente.

impartiality ['im,pɑ:ʃi'æliti] *n* imparcialidad, desinterés.

impassable [im'pɑ:səbl] *a* impracticable, intransitable.

impasse ['impɑ:s] *n* callejón sin salida.

impassibility ['im,pɑ:sə'biliti] *n* insensibilidad.

impassioned [im'pæʃnd] *a* apasionado.

impassive [im'pæsiv] *a* impasible, insensible.

impatience [im'peiʃəns] *n* impaciencia, desasosiego.

impatient [im'peiʃənt] *a* impaciente, mal sufrido.

impede [im'pi:d] *vt* impedir, estorbar; dificultar.

impediment [im'pedimənt] *n* im-

pedimento, obstáculo, embarazo, cortapisa.
impel [im'pel] *vt* impeler, empujar, obligar, incitar.
impending [im'pendiŋ] *a* inminente, próximo; **to be —** amenazar.
impenetrable [im'penitrəbl] *a* impenetrable; (*forest*) fragoso.
imperceptible [ˌimpə'septəbl] *a* imperceptible.
imperfect [im'pə:fikt] *a* imperfecto, defectuoso, manco.
imperfection [ˌimpə'fekʃən] *n* imperfección, deficiencia, tacha.
imperial [im'piəriəl] *a* imperial.
imperil [im'peril] *vt* poner en peligro.
imperious [im'piəriəs] *a* imperioso, perentorio; **—ly** *ad* imperativamente.
imperiousness [im'piəriəsnis] *n* señorío; arrogancia.
imperishable [im'periʃəbl] *a* imperecedero.
impersonate [im'pə:səneit] *vt* personificar, contrahacer; representar.
impertinence [im'pə:tinəns] *n* impertinencia, descaro; (*fam*) frescura.
impertinent [im'pə:tinənt] *a* impertinente, malintencionado; desvergonzado; (*fam*) fresco; **to be (very) —** tener (mucho) copete.
impervious [im'pə:viəs] *a* impenetrable.
impetuosity [imˌpetju'ɔsiti] *n* impetuosidad, viveza, ímpetu.
impetuous [im'petjuəs] *a* impetuoso, arrebatado, fogoso.
impetus ['impitəs] *n* ímpetu, impulsión.
impious ['impiəs] *a* impío, sacrílego.
impish ['impiʃ] *a* travieso.
implacable [im'plækəbl] *a* sañudo, cruento.
implement ['implimənt] *n* herramienta, utensilio; **—s** enseres, trastos; ['impliment] *vt* cumplir, llevar a cabo.
implicate ['implikeit] *vt* comprometer, embarazar.
implication ['impli'keiʃən] *n* implicación; deducción; insinuación.
implicit [im'plisit] *a* implícito, tácito; ciego.
implore [im'plɔ:] *vt* implorar, suplicar, deprecar.
imply [im'plai] *vt* implicar, significar, envolver, connotar, dar a entender; sobreentender.
impolite [ˌimpə'lait] *a* descortés, mal educado, poco fino.
import ['impɔ:t] *n* importancia; significado; (*com*) importación; [im'pɔ:t] *vt* importar; significar; convenir.
importance [im'pɔ:təns] *n* importancia, peso, consecuencia; **of —** de bulto; **of some —** de categoría; **to be of some —** importar; **of little —** de poca monta, de poco fuste.
important [im'pɔ:tənt] *a* importante; calificado, de categoría.
importation [ˌimpɔ:'teiʃən] *n* importación.
importunate [im'pɔ:tjunit] *a* importuno, insistente; porfiado; urgente; **— request** exigencia.
importune [ˌimpɔ:'tju:n] *vt* importunar, perseguir, solicitar; marear.
impose [im'pouz] *vt* imponer, cargar; **to — on** embaucar; molestar.
imposing [im'pouziŋ] *a* considerable, importante; imponente; **to be —** imponer.
imposition [ˌimpə'ziʃən] *n* imposición.
impossibility [imˌpɔsə'biliti] *n* imposibilidad.
impossible [im'pɔsəbl] *a* imposible.
impostor [im'pɔstə] *n* impostor, engañador, embustero.
impotence ['impətəns] *n* impotencia.
impotent ['impətənt] *a* impotente.
impoverish [im'pɔvəriʃ] *vt* empobrecer; (*land*) esquilmar.
impoverishment [im'pɔvəriʃmənt] *n* empobrecimiento.
impracticable [im'præktikəbl] *a* impracticable, imposible.
impregnable [im'pregnəbl] *a* invulnerable, inexpugnable.
impregnate ['impregneit] *vt* impregnar; imbuir.
impress ['impres] *n* huella, impresión; [im'pres] *vt* **to — on** imprimir, inculcar, hacer mella; **to — on mind** grabar.
impression [im'preʃən] *n* impresión; **to make an —** hacer mella, imponer; **to make an — on** impresionar.
impressive [im'presiv] *a* impresionante, conmovedor; imponente.
imprint ['imprint] *n* imprenta, impresión; huella; (*foot*) pisada; pie de imprenta; [im'print] *vt* imprimir, grabar; impresionar; (*kiss*) estampar.
imprison [im'prizn] *vt* encarcelar.
imprisonment [im'priznmənt] *n* encarcelamiento, prisión; **term of —** condena.
improbable [im'prɔbəbl] *a* improbable, inverosímil.
impromptu [im'prɔmptju:] *a* repentino; **— addition** improvisación.
improper [im'prɔpə] *a* impropio, inconveniente; indecoroso.
impropriety [ˌimprə'praiəti] *n* inconveniencia; indecoro.
improve [im'pru:v] *vt* mejorar, perfeccionar; reformar, aventajar, beneficiar; (*by cross-breeding*) encastar; *vi* mejorarse, ganar, avanzar, hacer progresos.
improvement [im'pru:vmənt] *n* mejora, progreso; alivio; reforma.
improvident [im'prɔvidənt] *a* impróvido, imprevisor, desprevenido.
improvise ['imprəvaiz] *vt* improvisar, repentizar.
improviser ['imprəvaizə] *n* repentista, improvisador.
imprudence [im'pru:dəns] *n* im-

prudencia, indiscreción, descuido.
imprudent [im'pru:dənt] *a* imprudente, indiscreto, incauto, temerario.
impudence ['impjudəns] *n* desvergüenza, descaro, procacidad, cinismo; desenvoltura.
impudent ['impjudənt] *a* impudente, descarado, insolente; cínico; fresco.
impugn [im'pju:n] *vt* impugnar, atacar, poner (en duda, en tela de juicio).
impulse ['impʌls] *n* impulsión, ímpetu; impulso, arranque: corazonada.
impulsive [im'pʌlsiv] *a* impulsivo.
impunity [im'pju:niti] *n* impunidad.
impure [im'pjuə] *a* impuro, sucio; adulterado; deshonesto.
impurity [im'pjuəriti] *n* impureza; adulteración; torpeza.
impute [im'pju:t] *vt* imputar, reprochar, achacar.
in [in] *ad* adentro, entre; *prep* en, a, para, por, sobre; — **the afternoon** por la tarde; — **the night** de noche; **to know the —s and outs of a question** conocer los recovecos de una cuestión.
inability [.inə'biliti] *n* incapacidad, impotencia.
inaccessible [.inæk'sesəbl] *a* inaccessible, inabordable.
inaccuracy [in'ækjurəsi] *n* inexactitud; descuido.
inaccurate [in'ækjurit] *a* inexacto, impreciso, erróneo.
inactive [in'æktiv] *a* inactivo, ocioso.
inadequate [in'ædikwit] *a* inadecuado, insuficiente, inconcluso, deficiente.
inadvertence [.inəd'və:təns] *n* inadvertencia.
inalienable [in'eiliənəbl] *a* inajenable.
inane [i'nein] *a* vano, vacío, soso; — **remark** sandez.
inappropriate [.inə'proupriit] *a* impertinente, impropio.
inasmuch [inəz'mʌtʃ] *ad* como (quiera) que, en vista de; (por, en) cuanto.
inattention [.inə'tenʃən] *n* desatención, negligencia, distracción.
inattentive [.inə'tentiv] *a* desatento, indiferente, distraído.
inaudible [in'ɔ:dəbl] *a* bajo, inaudible.
inaugurate [i'nɔ:gjureit] *vt* inaugurar; estrenar, iniciar.
inauspicious [.inɔ:s'piʃəs] *a* infeliz, poco propicio; nefasto; desfavorable.
inborn ['in'bɔ:n] *a* innato, ingénito.
incapable [in'keipəbl] *a* incapaz, inhábil, incompetente; **to be, make** — incapacitar.
incapability [in.keipə'biliti] *n* incapacidad, impotencia.
incapacitate [.inkə'pæsiteit] *vt* incapacitar, debilitar, imposibilitar.
incapacity [.inkə'pæsiti] *n* ineptitud, insuficiencia.
incautious [in'kɔ:ʃəs] *a* indiscreto, negligente, descuidado.
incense ['insens] *n* perfume, incienso; [in'sens] *vt* incensar; irritar, exasperar.
incentive [in'sentiv] *n* incentivo, cebo, estímulo.
incessant [in'sesnt] *a* incesante, continuo.
incest ['insest] *n* incesto.
inch [intʃ] *n* pulgada; — **by** — palmo a palmo.
incidence ['insidəns] *n* incidencia; gravamen; carga.
incident ['insidənt] *n* acontecimiento, episodio, suceso, lance; *a* incidente.
incidental [.insi'dentl] *a* accidental, incidental.
incipient [in'sipiənt] *a* incipiente, principiante.
incision [in'siʒən] *n* incisión, tajo, corte.
incisive [in'saisiv] *a* incisivo, mordaz.
incite [in'sait] *vt* incitar, instigar, estimular, espolear, concitar.
incivility [.insi'viliti] *n* incivilidad, desacato, descortesía.
inclemency [in'klemənsi] *n* inclemencia, rigor; (*weather*) intemperie.
inclination [.inkli'neiʃən] *n* inclinación, predilección, tendencia, gana(s); (*land*) declive; reverencia.
incline ['inklain] *n* rampa, talud, declive, pendiente; [in'klain] *vt* inclinar; (*to one side*) ladear; *vir* ladearse; inclinarse, estar dispuesto a; **to — toward** tirar a.
inclined [in'klaind] *a* dispuesto, propenso, afecto; ladeado; **to be** — inclinarse.
include [in'klu:d] *vt* incluir, comprender, abrazar, envolver.
included [in'klu:did] *a* **everything** — todo comprendido.
inclusive [in'klu:siv] *a* inclusivo.
incoherence [.inkou'hiərəns] *n* incoherencia.
income ['inkʌm] *n* ingreso(s), renta(s); **person living on** — rentista; — **tax** impuesto sobre la renta.
incomparable [in'kɔmpərəbl] *a* incomparable, sin igual.
incompatible [.inkəm'pætəbl] *a* incompatible.
incompetence [in'kɔmpitəns] *n* incompetencia, insuficiencia, incapacidad.
incompetent [in'kɔmpitənt] *a* incompetente, incapaz, insuficiente; — **person** nulidad.
incomplete [.inkəm'pli:t] *a* incompleto, imperfecto, inconcluso; —**ly** *ad* a medias.
incomprehensible [in.kɔmpri'hensəbl] *a* incomprensible.

inconceivable [,inkən'si:vəbl] *a* inconcebible.
incongruous [in'koŋgruəs] *a* incongruo, absurdo, incongruente.
inconsiderable [,inkən'sidərəbl] *a* insignificante.
inconsiderate [,inkən'sidərit] *a* desconsiderado.
inconsistency [,inkən'sistənsi] *n* inconsecuencia, incompatibilidad, inconsistencia.
inconsistent [,inkən'sistənt] *a* inconsecuente, inconsistente, incompatible, contradictorio, disparatado.
inconstancy [in'kɔnstənsi] *n* inconstancia, veleidad, mudanza, vaivén.
inconstant [in'kɔnstənt] *a* inconstante, mudable, vario.
inconvenience [,inkən'vi:niəns] *n* incomodidad, inconveniencia; molestia; *vt* causar inconveniencias, molestar, incomodar.
inconvenient [,inkən'vi:niənt] *a* inconveniente, incómodo, molesto, inoportuno.
incorporate [in'kɔ:pəreit] *a* incorporado; *vti* incorporar, incorporarse, asociarse, reunir(se).
incorrect [,inkə'rekt] *a* incorrecto, informal; falso, erróneo.
incorrectness [,inkə'rektnis] *n* incorrección, inexactitud.
incorruptible [,inkə'rʌptəbl] *a* incorruptible, incorrupto, probo.
increase ['inkri:s] *n* aumento; (*knitting*) crecido; ganancia; [in'kri:s] *vt* aumentar; acrecer; (*prices*) cargar; tomar cuerpo.
increasing [in'kri:siŋ] *part* **to go on —** ir en aumento; **—ly** *ad* con creces.
incredible [in'kredəbl] *a* increíble.
incredulous [in'kredjuləs] *adj* incrédulo.
incriminate [in'krimineit] *vt* incriminar.
incubate ['inkjubeit] *vt* incubar; madurar.
inculcate ['inkʌlkeit] *vt* inculcar.
incur [in'kə:] *vt* incurrir en; atraerse; contraer.
incurable [in'kjuərəbl] *an* incurable.
incursion [in'kə:ʃən] *n* correría.
indebted [in'detid] *a* endeudado; reconocido.
indecency [in'di:sinsi] *n* indecencia, indecoro, grosería.
indecent [in'di:snt] *n* indecente, obsceno, grosero.
indecision [,indi'siʒən] *n* indecisión, irresolución.
indecorous [in'dekərəs] *a* indecoroso.
indeed [in'di:d] *ad* en verdad, verdaderamente, de veras.
indefatigable [,indi'fætigəbl] *a* infatigable.
indefensible [,indi'fensəbl] *a* indefensible.
indefinite [in'definit] *a* indefinido, indeterminado.
indefinable [,indi'fainəbl] *a* indefinible.
indelible [in'deləbl] *a* indeleble.
indelicate [in'delikit] *a* grosero, indecoroso.
indemnify [in'demnifai] *vt* indemnizar, resarcir, compensar.
indemnity [in'demniti] *n* resarcimiento, indemnidad.
independence [,indi'pendəns] *n* independencia; holgura.
independent [,indi'pendənt] *a* independiente; libre, (*money*) acomodado, adinerado; **to form an — group** hacer rancho aparte.
indescribable [,indis'kraibəbl] *a* indescriptible.
indeterminate [,indi'tə:minit] *a* indeterminado.
indetermination [,indi'tə:mineiʃən] *n* irresolución, indecisión.
index ['indeks] *n* índice.
India ['indiə] *n* la India.
indiarubber ['indiə'rʌbə] *n* goma elástica, caucho.
Indian ['indiən] *an* indio.
indicate ['indikeit] *vt* indicar, denotar, significar, señalar; intimar.
indication [,indi'keiʃən] *n* indicación, indicio; señal; asomo.
indicative [in'dikətiv] *a* indicativo.
indictment [in'daitmənt] *n* acusación, sumario, proceso.
indifference [in'difrəns] *n* indiferencia; imparcialidad, despego; apatía, desvío.
indifferent [in'difrənt] *a* indiferente, imparcial, igual.
indigenous [in'didʒinəs] *a* indígena; *n* natural.
indigestible [,indi'dʒestəbl] *a* indigesto.
indigestion [,indi'dʒestʃən] *n* indigestión, empacho, ahito.
indignant [in'dignənt] *a* indignado.
indignation [,indig'neiʃən] *n* indignación, ira.
indignity [in'digniti] *n* indignidad, afrenta; baldón, oprobio.
indigo ['indigou] *n* añil, índigo.
indirect [,indi'rekt] *a* indirecto, extraviado, desleal, tortuoso.
indiscreet [,indis'kri:t] *a* indiscreto, imprudente, malaconsejado.
indiscretion [,indis'kreʃən] *n* indiscreción, imprudencia.
indiscriminate [,indis'kriminit] *a* confuso, indistinto.
indispensable [,indis'pensəbl] *a* indispensable, imprescindible, forzoso.
indispose [,indis'pouz] *vt* indisponer(se).
indisposition [,indispə'ziʃən] *n* indisposición, destemplanza, achaque.
indisputable [,indis'pju:təbl] *a* indiscutible, indisputable, incontestable.
indistinct [,indis'tiŋkt] *a* indistinto, confuso, vago.
indistinctness [,indis'tiŋktnis] *n*

confusión, falta de claridad, incertidumbre.
individual [,indi'vidjuəl] *a* individual; (*private*) particular; único, singular; *n* individuo, sujeto, tío.
indolence ['indələns] *n* indolencia, holgazanería, abandono, descuido, dejadez.
indolent ['indələnt] *a* indolente, haragán, dejado, desmañado.
indoor ['indɔ:] *a* interior; **— suit** traje casero; **—s** *ad* en casa, dentro (de casa).
induce [in'dju:s] *vt* inducir, persuadir, convidar, inclinar, inspirar, (*sleep etc*) conciliar.
inducement [in'dju:smənt] *n* móvil, aliciente, reclamo, estímulo.
induction [in'dʌkʃən] *n* inducción; ingreso.
inductive [in'dʌktiv] *a* inductivo.
indulge [in'dʌldʒ] *vt* consentir; condescender, gratificar, entregarse a; acariciar; seguir(le).
indulgence [in'dʌldʒəns] *n* (*self*) abandono; (*others*) mimo; (*relig*) indulgencia.
indulgent [in'dʌldʒənt] *a* indulgente, complaciente.
industrial [in'dʌstriəl] *a* industrial.
industrious [in'dʌstriəs] *a* laborioso, industrioso, aprovechado, hacendoso.
industry ['indəstri] *n* industria; actividad, diligencia, aplicación.
ineffable [in'efəbl] *a* inefable.
ineffective [,ini'fektiv] *a* ineficaz, inútil.
inefficacy [in'efikəsi] *n* insuficiencia, ineficacia.
inefficient [,ini'fiʃənt] *a* ineficaz, incapaz.
inept [i'nept] *a* inepto.
inequality [,ini'kwɔliti] *n* desigualdad, diferencia, disparidad; aspereza.
inert [i'nə:t] *a* inerte, inactivo.
inertia [i'nə:ʃə] *n* inercia, inacción; desgana.
inescapable [,inis'keipəbl] *a* forzoso.
inestimable [in'estiməbl] *a* incalculable.
inevitable [in'evitəbl] *a* inevitable.
inexcusable [,iniks'kju:zəbl] *a* inexcusable, imperdonable.
inexhaustible [,inig'zɔ:stəbl] *a* inagotable.
inexorable [in'eksərəbl] *a* implacable.
inexpensive [,iniks'pensiv] *a* barato, módico.
inexperienced [,iniks'piəriənst] *a* inexperto, novel.
inexplicable [in'eksplikəbl] *a* inexplicable.
inexpressible [,iniks'presəbl] *a* indecible, inefable.
inexpressive [,iniks'presiv] *a* insignificante, inexpresivo.
Inez ['i:nez] *f* Inés.
infallibility [in,fælə'biliti] *n* infalibilidad.
infallible [in'fæləbl] *a* infalible, cierto, indefectible.
infamous ['infəməs] *a* infame, indigno, vil, odioso.
infamy ['infəmi] *n* infamia, deshonra, baldón.
infancy ['infənsi] *n* infancia, minoridad; **to be in one's —** estar en pañales.
infant ['infənt] *n* niño, nene, crío, criatura, infante; **— school** escuela de párvulos.
infantile ['infəntail] *a* infantil; pueril; **— paralysis** polio.
infantry ['infəntri] *n* infantería.
infatuate [in'fætjueit] *vt* cegar, atontar, tener (ciego, atontado).
infatuated [in'fætjueitid] *a* encaprichado; **to be —** encapricharse.
infatuation [in,fætju'eiʃən] *n* infatuación, apasionamiento, encaprichamiento.
infect [in'fekt] *vt* infectar, contagiar, contaminar, inficionar, pegar.
infected [in'fektid] *a* **to become —** contagiarse.
infection [in'fekʃən] *n* infección, afección, contagio.
infectious [in'fekʃəs] *a* infeccioso, pestilencial, infecto, contagioso.
infer [in'fə:] *vt* concluir, deducir, inferir.
inference ['infərəns] *n* conclusión, inferencia, consecuencia.
inferior [in'fiəriə] *an* inferior, subalterno.
inferiority [in,fiəri'ɔriti] *n* inferioridad.
infernal [in'fə:nl] *a* infernal.
infest [in'fest] *vt* infestar, plagar; atormentar.
infidel ['infidəl] *n* infiel, pagano.
infinite ['infinit] *an* infinito.
infinity [in'finiti] *n* infinidad; inmensidad.
infirm [in'fə:m] *a* débil, achacoso, enfermizo; inestable, poco firme.
infirmary [in'fə:məri] *n* enfermería, hospital.
infirmity [in'fə:miti] *n* debilidad, dolencia, achaque, flaqueza.
inflame [in'fleim] *vt* encender, inflamar, acalorar, enardecer; *vi* inflamarse.
inflamed [in'fleimd] *a* encendido; enardecido, acalorado; (*swollen*) inflamado, infectado.
inflammable [in'flæməbl] *a* inflamable.
inflammation [,inflə'meiʃən] *n* inflamación.
inflate [in'fleit] *vt* inflar, hinchar.
inflation [in'fleiʃən] *n* hinchazón, inflación; (*com*) inflación.
inflect [in'flekt] *vt* doblar; (*gram*) declinar; (*tone*) modular.
inflection [in'flekʃən] *n* inflexión;

acento, (*voice*) modulación; (*speech*) dejo.
inflexible [in'fleksəbl] *a* rígido, terco, tieso.
inflict [in'flikt] *vt* infligir, imponer.
infliction [in'flikʃən] *n* imposición; pena.
influence ['influens] *n* influjo, ascendiente; influencia; (*fam*) enchufe; *vt* influir, inclinar, sugestionar.
influenced ['influənsd] *a* **easily —** impresionable.
influential [ˌinflu'enʃəl] *a* influyente.
influenza [ˌinflu'enzə] *n* influenza, dengue, gripe.
influx ['inflʌks] *n* afluencia, entrada.
inform [in'fɔ:m] *vti* informar, comunicar, notificar; instruir; **to — against** denunciar.
informal [in'fɔ:məl] *a* informal; corriente; (*dance etc*) de confianza.
informality [ˌinfɔ:'mæliti] *n* informalidad.
informant [in'fɔ:mənt] *n* informante, acusador, denunciador.
information [ˌinfə'meiʃən] *n* información, aviso, noticia(s), datos.
informed [in'fɔ:md] *a* **well —** entendido; **to be —** estar enterado.
informer [in'fɔ:mə] *n* denunciador; soplón.
infraction [in'frækʃən] *n* (*of rules*) rompimiento, infracción.
infrequent [in'fri:kwənt] *a* infrecuente, raro, contado.
infringe [in'frindʒ] *vt* infringir, violar, quebrantar.
infringement [in'frindʒmənt] *n* infracción, transgresión.
infuriate [in'fjuərieit] *vt* enfurecer.
infuse [in'fju:z] *vt* infundir, inspirar.
ingenious [in'dʒi:niəs] *a* ingenioso, discreto, inventivo, artificioso; (*of style*) conceptista.
ingenuity [ˌindʒi'nju(:)iti] *n* ingeniosidad, inventiva; maña industria.
ingenuous [in'dʒenjuəs] *a* ingenuo, sincero, natural, simple.
ingenuousness [in'dʒenjuəsnis] *n* naturalidad, candidez.
ingrain [in'grein] *vt* impregnar, arraigar.
ingratiate [in'greiʃieit] *vr* congraciarse, insinuarse.
ingratitude [in'grætitju:d] *n* ingratitud.
ingredient [in'gri:diənt] *n* ingrediente; **—s** (*seasoning*) adobo.
inhabit [in'hæbit] *vt* habitar.
inhabitant [in'hæbitənt] *n* habitante, vecino.
inhale [in'heil] *vt* respirar, aspirar.
inharmonious [ˌinhɑ:'mouniəs] *a* discordante; destemplado.
inherent [in'hiərənt] *a* inherente, natural, intrínseco.
inherit [in'herit] *vt* heredar.
inheritance [in'heritəns] *n* herencia, patrimonio, abolengo.
inhibit [in'hibit] *vt* inhibir, detener.
inhospitable [ˌinhɔs'pitəbl] *a* inhospitalario.
inhuman [in'hju:mən] *a* inhumano, atroz, despiadado.
inhumanity [ˌinhju:'mæniti] *n* inhumanidad, barbarie.
inimical [i'nimikəl] *a* enemigo, hostil.
inimitable [i'nimitəbl] *a* inimitable
iniquitous [i'nikwitəs] *a* inicuo malvado.
iniquity [i'nikwiti] *n* iniquidad maldad.
initial [i'niʃəl] *an* inicial.
initiate [i'niʃieit] *vt* iniciar, comenzar; (*conversation etc*) entablar.
initiative [i'niʃiətiv] *n* iniciativa.
inject [in'dʒekt] *vt* inyectar, introducir.
injudicious [ˌindʒu:'diʃəs] *a* indiscreto, imprudente.
injunction [in'dʒʌŋkʃən] *n* requerimiento, precepto.
injure ['indʒə] *vt* dañar, lastimar; perjudicar, ofender; descalabrar.
injurious [in'dʒuəriəs] *a* nocivo, dañoso, pernicioso.
injury ['indʒəri] *n* daño, herida, lesión; perjuicio, deterioro; ofensa, injuria, afrenta.
injustice [in'dʒʌstis] *n* injusticia, entuerto.
ink [iŋk] *n* tinta; **—stain** chapón; **—pot** tintero.
inkling ['iŋkliŋ] *n* insinuación, atisbo; **he hasn't an —** no sabe ni pizca, no tiene idea.
inkstand ['iŋkstænd] *n* tintero.
inkwell ['iŋkwel] *n* tintero.
inky [iŋki] *a* parecido a la tinta; sombrío.
inland ['inlænd] *n* interior; *ad* tierra adentro.
inlet ['inlət] *n* entrada, vía; (*sea*) abra, ensenada; (*Galicia*) ría.
inmate ['inmeit] *n* inquilino, huésped; (*asylum*) interno.
inmost ['inmoust] *a* íntimo, recóndito.
inn [in] *n* posada, mesón, fonda; (*poor*) venta.
innate [i'neit] *a* innato, natural, ingénito.
inner ['inə] *a* interior.
innkeeper ['inki:pə] *n* posadero, ventero, hospedero, fondista.
innocence ['inəsns] *n* inocencia, ingenuosidad, candor.
innocent ['inəsnt] *a* inocente, simple, libre.
innovation [ˌinou'veiʃən] *n* innovación, novedad.
innuendo [ˌinju:'endou] *n* indirecta.
innumerable [i'nju:mərəbl] *a* innumerable.
inoculate [i'nɔkjuleit] *vt* inocular, inficionar; imbuir.
inoffensive [ˌinə'fensiv] *a* inofensivo, discreto.

inopportune [in'ɔpətju:n] *a* inoportuno, inconveniente, intempestivo.
inordinate [i'nɔ:dinit] *a* desmesurado, excesivo.
inquest ['inkwest] *n* indagación, pesquisa; sumario.
inquire [in'kwaiə] *vi* inquirir, preguntar, informarse, examinar, enterarse, indagar.
inquiry [in'kwaiəri] *n* pregunta, examen, indagación, encuesta.
Inquisition [ˌinkwi'ziʃən] *n* Santo Oficio.
inquisitive [in'kwizitiv] *a* curioso, preguntón.
inquisitor [in'kwizitə] *n* inquisidor.
inroad ['inroud] *n* incursión, irrupción; **to make —s into** hacer estragos en.
insane [in'sein] *a* insano, loco, insensato, frenético.
insanitary [in'sænitəri] *a* malsano.
insanity [in'sæniti] *n* locura, demencia.
insatiable [in'seiʃəbl] *a* insaciable.
inscribe [in'skraib] *vt* inscribir, grabar.
inscription [in'skripʃən] *n* inscripción, leyenda, letrero.
inscrutable [in'skru:təbl] *a* insondable.
insect ['insekt] *n* insecto.
insecticide [in'sektisaid] *n* insecticida.
insecurity [ˌinsi'kjuəriti] *n* inseguridad, incertidumbre.
insensible [in'sensəbl] *a* insensible; sordo; (*from blow*) inconsciente.
insensitive [in'sensitiv] *a* insensible, grosero.
insensitiveness [in'sensitivnis] *n* insensibilidad.
inseparable [in'sepərəbl] *a* entrañable; **to be —** ser uña y carne.
insert [in'sə:t] *vt* insertar, introducir, intercalar.
insertion [in'sə:ʃən] *n* inserción, introducción.
inside ['in'said] *a* interior; *ad* en el interior, adentro; **— out** al revés; *n* interior; *pl* entrañas.
insidious [in'sidiəs] *a* insidioso, engañoso, solapado.
insight ['insait] *n* conocimiento, perspicacia, penetración, intuición.
insignificance [ˌinsig'nifikəns] *n* insignificancia, bagatela.
insignificant [ˌinsig'nifikənt] *a* insignificante, despreciable.
insincere [ˌinsin'siə] *a* disimulado, falso, hipócrita.
insincerity [ˌinsin'seriti] *n* falta de sinceridad.
insinuate [in'sinjueit] *vt* i nsinuar, sugerir; *vr* insinuarse.
insinuation [inˌsinju'eiʃən] *n* insinuación; pulla.
insipid [in'sipid] *a* insipido, desabrido.
insipidity [ˌinsi'piditi] *n* insipidez, insulsez.
insist [in'sist] *vi* insistir en, porfiar, afirmar, exigir.
insistence [in'sistəns] *n* insistencia.
insistent [in'sistənt] *a* pertinaz, porfiado; **to be —** empeñarse en.
insolence ['insələns] *n* insolencia, procacidad, descaro.
insolent ['insələnt] *a* insolente, atrevido, descomedido.
insoluble [in'sɔljubl] *a* insoluble.
insolvable [in'sɔlvəbl] indisoluble, inexplicable.
insomnia [in'sɔmniə] *n* insomnio.
inspect [in'spekt] *vt* examinar, inspeccionar, registrar.
inspection [in'spekʃən] *n* inspección, vigilancia, reconocimiento; (*final*) repaso.
inspector [in'spektə] *n* inspector, interventor; (*police*) comisario; (*ticket*) revisor; (*price control*) tasador.
inspiration [ˌinspə'reiʃən] *n* inspiración, numen; (*poet*) estro.
inspire [in'spaiə] *vt* inspirar, animar, imbuir, sugerir.
inspired [in'spaiəd] *a* genial.
install [in'stɔ:l] *vt* instalar; (*mech*) montar.
installation [ˌinsti'leiʃən] *n* instalación.
installment [in'stɔ:lmənt] *n* entrega; **by —** a plazos.
instance ['instəns] *n* ejemplo, caso, circunstancia; (*law*) instancia; *vt* poner (por caso, por ejemplo).
instant ['instənt] *a* urgente, presente, perentorio; *n* momento, instante, punto; **the 5th inst.** el 5 del corriente.
instantaneous [ˌinstən'teiniəs] *a* instantáneo.
instantly ['instəntli] *adv* inmediatamente, al punto.
instead [in'sted] *prep* en lugar de, en cambio, en vez de.
instigate ['instigeit] *vt* instigar, incitar, soliviantar, fomentar.
instigation [ˌinsti'geiʃən] *n* instigación.
instill [in'stil] *vt* instilar, inculcar, infundir.
instinct [in'stiŋkt] *a* animado, impulsado, movido por; ['instiŋkt] *n* instinto.
instinctive [in'stiŋktiv] *a* instintivo, espontáneo.
institute ['institju:t] *n* instituto, precepto; *vt* instituir, establecer; entablar, iniciar.
institution [ˌinsti'tju:ʃən] *n* institución; (*endowed*) fundación.
instruct [in'strʌkt] *vt* instruir; (a)doctrinar; enterar.
instruction [in'strʌkʃən] *n* instrucción, enseñanza; doctrina.
instrument ['instrumənt] *n* instrumento, herramienta; agente.

instrumental [ˌinstru'mentl] *a* instrumental.
insubordinate [ˌinsə'bɔːdənit] *a* **to be —** insubordinarse.
insufferable [in'sʌfərəbl] *a* intolerable, insoportable, inaguantable.
insufficient [ˌinsə'fiʃənt] *a* insuficiente, incapaz.
insufficiency [ˌinsə'fiʃənsi] *n* insuficiencia.
insular ['insjələ] *a* insular, isleño.
insulate ['insjuleit] *vt* aislar.
insult ['insʌlt] *n* insulto, ofensa, indignidad, humillación, agravio, atropello, ultraje; [in'sʌlt] *vt* insultar, ofender, atropellar, denostar.
insuperable [in'suːpərəbl] *a* insuperable.
insurance [in'ʃɔːrəns] *n* (*com*) seguro; garantía; seguridad; **fire —** seguro de incendio.
insure [in'ʃɔː] *vt* asegurar; garantizar, abonar.
insurer [in'ʃɔːrə] *n* asegurador.
insurgent [in'səːdʒənt] *n* insurgente, rebelde.
insurrection [ˌinsə'rekʃən] *n* insurrección, sublevación, motín.
intact [in'tækt] *a* intacto, íntegro.
intangible [in'tændʒəbl] *a* impalpable.
integral ['intigrəl] *a* íntegro, integral.
integrate ['intigreit] *vt* integrar.
integrity [in'tegriti] *n* integridad, probidad, limpieza.
intellect ['intilekt] *n* inteligencia, intelecto, entendimiento, talento.
intellectual [ˌinti'lektjuəl] *an* intelectual.
intelligence [in'telidʒəns] *n* sagacidad, talento, inteligencia; noticia, acuerdo; **piece of —** aviso, noticia.
intelligent [in'telidʒənt] *a* inteligente, sesudo, hábil, talentoso.
intemperate [in'tempərit] *a* inmoderado, intemperante, desenfrenado, bebedor.
intend [in'tend] *vt* querer, pensar, tener intención, proponerse.
intended [in'tendid] *a* **to be — for** encaminarse a, destinarse (par)a.
intense [in'tens] *a* intenso, vehemente, fuerte; extremado, reconcentrado.
intensify [in'tensifai] *vt* intensificar; *vi* subir, crecer.
intensity [in'tensiti] *n* intensidad, energía, rigor, violencia; tensión.
intensive [in'tensiv] *a* intensivo; entero, completo.
intent [in'tent] *a* asiduo, dedicado, atento, preocupado; *n* intento, designio, propósito; **to all —s and purposes** para todos los fines y efectos.
intention [in'tenʃən] *n* intención, idea, ánimo, mira.
intentional [in'tenʃənl] *a* intencional, premeditado, querido.
intentionally [in'tenʃnəli] *ad* deliberadamente, aposta, adrede, queriéndolo.
inter [in'təː] *vt* enterrar, dar sepultura a.
intercede [ˌintə'siːd] *vt* interceder, abogar por, mediar.
intercept [ˌintə'sept] *vt* interceptar, atajar, captar.
interchange ['intə'tʃeindʒ] *n* intercambio, correspondencia; [ˌintə'tʃeindʒ] *vt* cambiar, permutar; (*prisoners*) canjear.
interchangeable [ˌintə'tʃeindʒəbl] *a* mutuo, recíproco; **not —** impermutable.
intercourse ['intəkɔːs] *n* comunicación, comercio, tráfico; (*social*) trato, roce, relaciones; **sexual —** trato sexual.
interest ['intrist] *n* interés, beneficio, ganancia; emoción; **to take an — (in)** interesarse (en, por); **to take a great —** preocuparse; **to take no —** desinteresarse, hacerse el sueco; *vt* interesar.
interested ['intristid] *a* **— in** (*sport etc*) aficionado a; **— party** interesado; **are you —?** ¿le interesa?
interesting ['intristiŋ] *a* interesante; de (mucho) interés.
interfere [ˌintə'fiə] *vi* (entre)meterse, inmiscuirse, mezclarse; estorbar; **to — in other people's business** meterse en camisa de once varas.
interference [ˌintə'fiərəns] *n* intervención, ingerencia; obstáculo.
interfering [ˌintə'fiəriŋ] *a* entrometido.
interim ['intərim] *a* interino; **in the —** entretanto.
interior [in'tiəriə] *an* interior; (*of country*) tierra adentro.
interloper ['intəloupə] *n* entrometido, intruso.
interlude ['intəluːd] *n* intermedio, intervalo, entremés; rato, descanso.
intermediate [ˌintə'miːdiət] *a* intermedio.
interment [in'təːmənt] *n* entierro, sepelio, sepultura.
intermission [ˌintə'miʃən] *n* pausa, tregua, intermitencia; (*theat*) descanso, entreacto.
intermittent [ˌintə'mitənt] *a* intermitente, entrecortado.
internal [in'təːnl] *a* interno.
international [ˌintə'næʃnəl] *a* internacional.
interplay ['intəplei] *n* acción recíproca; cruce, interacción.
interpose [ˌintə'pouz] *vti* interponer(se).
interpret [in'təːprit] *vt* interpretar, descifrar; ilustrar.
interpretation [inˌtəːpri'teiʃən] *n* interpretación, traducción, exposición.
interpreter [in'təːpritə] *n* intérprete, trujamán.

interrogate [in'terəgeit] *vti* interrogar, preguntar; *vt* (*witness*) articular.
interrogation [in,terə'geiʃən] *n* interrogación.
interrupt [,intə'rʌpt] *vti* interrumpir, quebrar, (entre)cortar.
interruption [,intə'rʌpʃən] *n* interrupción, suspensión; solución de continuidad.
intersect [,intə(:)'sekt] *vti* (entre)cortarse, intersectar, cruzar(se).
intersperse [,intə(:)'spə:s] *vt* esparcir, entremezclar, salpicar.
interval ['intəvəl] *n* intervalo, espacio; (*theat*) descanso; (*school*) recreo; **at —s** a trechos; **bright —** clara.
intervene [,intə(:)'vi:n] *vi* intervenir, meter baza; sobrevenir, acontecer.
intervening [,intə(:)'vi:niŋ] *a* mediante, de en medio, interpuesto.
intervention [,intə'venʃən] *n* intervención.
interview ['intəvju:] *n* entrevista, conferencia; *vti* ver, consultar con, entrevistarse con.
intimacy ['intiməsi] *n* intimidad, familiaridad, confianza.
intimate ['intimit] *a* íntimo, entrañable, estrecho, de mucha confianza.
intimate ['intimeit] *vt* intimar, anunciar; (*law*) requerir.
intimation [,inti'meiʃən] *n* intimación, aviso; (*hint*) indirecta, pulla; (*law*) requerimiento.
intimidate [in'timideit] *vt* intimidar, amedrentar, acobardar.
into ['intu] *prep* en, entre, adentro.
intolerable [in'tɔlərəbl] *a* insufrible, insoportable, inaguantable.
intonation [,intou'neiʃən] *n* entonación, dejo.
intoxicate [in'tɔksikeit] *vt* embriagar, excitar; envenenar.
intoxication [in,tɔksi'keiʃən] *n* embriaguez, excitación; borrachera; arrebato.
intractable [in'træktəbl] *a* intratable, huraño.
intransigent [in'trænsidʒənt] *a* intransigente.
intrepid [in'trepid] *a* intrépido, impertérrito, arrojado, impávido.
intrepidity [,intri'piditi] *n* denuedo, osadía.
intricacy ['intrikəsi] *n* complicación, embarazo, enredo.
intricate ['intrikit] *a* complicado, enredado, revuelto.
intrigue [in'tri:g] *n* intriga, trama; **love —** galanteo, lío; (*theat*) enredo; *vti* intrigar, tramar; despertar la curiosidad de.
intrinsic [in'trinsik] *a* intrínseco, real.
introduce [,intrə'dju:s] *vt* (*objects*) introducir, meter; ingerir; (*people*) presentar.
introduction [,intrə'dʌkʃən] *n* introducción; (*people*) presentación; (*book*) prólogo; **letter of —** recomendación.
introductory [,intrə'dʌktəri] *a* preliminar.
intrude [in'tru:d] *vi* entremeterse, mezclarse.
intruder [in'tru:də] *n* intruso, entrometido.
intrusion [in'tru:ʒən] *n* intrusión, entremetimiento.
intuition [,intju(:)'iʃən] *n* intuición.
intuitive [in'tju(:)itiv] *a* intuitivo.
inundate ['inʌndeit] *vt* inundar, abrumar.
inundation [,inʌn'deiʃən] *n* inundación, desbordamiento.
invade [in'veid] *vt* invadir, usurpar.
invader [in'veidə] *n* invasor, usurpador.
invalid ['invəlid] *an* inválido, enfermo.
invalid [in'vælid] *a* inválido, nulo.
invalidate [in'vælideit] *vt* invalidar, anular.
invaluable [in'væljuəbl] *a* precioso, inestimable, imprescindible.
invariable [in'vɛəriəbl] *a* invariable, fijo, constante.
invasion [in'veiʒən] *n* invasión, usurpación.
invective [in'vektiv] *n* vituperio.
inveigle [in'vi:gl] *vt* seducir, engatusar, engañar.
invent [in'vent] *vt* inventar, crear, componer, tramar.
invention [in'venʃən] *n* invención, ficción; embuste; (*powers of —*) inventiva, ingeniosidad.
inventive [in'ventiv] *a* inventivo, ingenioso; **— power** invención; **— gift (skill)** inventiva.
inventor [in'ventə] *n* inventor, autor.
invert [in'və:t] *vt* invertir, volver (al revés), trastrocar.
invest [in'vest] *vt* (*money*) invertir; (*siege*) poner cerco a; **to — with** revestir, investir; condecorar.
investigate [in'vestigeit] *vt* investigar, explorar, buscar, examinar; *vi* inquerir, ahondar.
investigation [in,vesti'geiʃən] *n* investigación, indagación, pesquisa.
investment [in'vestmənt] *n* (*siege*) cerco, sitio; (*com*) inversión, empleo.
investor [in'vestə] *n* inversionista.
inveterate [in'vetərit] *a* inveterado, encarnizado, arraigado.
invidious [in'vidiəs] *a* odioso, aborrecible.
invigorate [in'vigəreit] *vt* fortificar, fortalecer.
invincible [in'vinsəbl] *a* invencible.
inviolate [in'vaiəlit] *a* intacto, íntegro; inviolado.
invisible [in'vizəbl] *a* invisible.
invitation [,invi'teiʃən] *n* invitación; (*to food*) convite.
invite [in'vait] *vt* invitar; (*to food, drink*) convidar; (*to dance*) sacar a

bailar; atraer, pedir, requerir.
inviting [in'vaitiŋ] *a* atractivo, apetecible, acogedor.
invoice ['invɔis] *n* factura; *vt* facturar.
invoke [in'vouk] *vt* invocar, implorar, rogar; (*law*) traer a la vista.
involuntary [in'vɔləntəri] *a* involuntario, sin querer.
involve [in'vɔlv] *vt* envolver, traer consigo; implicar.
involved [in'vɔlvd] *a* complicado; **to get —** meterse, inmiscuirse, enfrascarse; **to be — in** estar comprometido.
inward ['inwəd] *a* interno, interior; oculto; *adv* hacia dentro, (*buses*) al centro.
irate [ai'reit] *a* encolerizado, de bastante malhumor.
ire ['aiə] *n* cólera, ira.
Ireland ['aiələnd] *n* Irlanda.
iris ['aiəris] *n* iris; arco iris; (*bot*) flor de lis.
Irish ['aiəriʃ] *a* irlandés; **— coffee** café irlandés, bebida irlandesa a base de café y whisky.
irk [irk] *vt* molestar, fastidiar.
irksome ['ə:ksəm] *a* molesto, fastidioso, penoso, tedioso, enfadoso.
iron ['aiən] *a* férreo; **— ore** mineral de hierro; **—work** obra de hierro, herrería; *n* hierro; **corrugated —** hierro encarrujado; **(flat) —** plancha; **—s** grillos; *vt* planchar; aplanchar; aherrojar; **to strike while the — is hot** a hierro caliente, batir de repente.
ironic(al) [ai'rɔnik(əl)] *a* irónico.
irony ['aiərəni] *n* ironía, sorna, guasa.
irreconcilable [i,rekən'sailəbl] *a* incompatible, intransigente.
irregular [i'regjulə] *a* irregular; anormal.
irregularity [i,regju'læriti] *n* irregularidad, anomalía; extravaganza; desigualdad.
irrelevant [i'relivənt] *a* fuera de propósito; desatinado, ajeno, traído por los pelos; **to be —** no hacer al caso.
irreligious [,iri'lidʒəs] *a* profano, impío.
irreparable [i'repərəbl] *a* irreparable.
irresistible [,iri'zistəbl] *a* irresistible, hechicero.
irresolute [i'rezəlu:t] *a* irresoluto, vacilante.
irresponsible [,iris'pɔnsəbl] *a* irresponsable, inconsecuente.
irreverence [i'revərəns] *n* desacato.
irreverent [i'revərənt] *a* irreverente, irrespetuoso.
irrigate ['irigeit] *vt* regar.
irrigation [,iri'geiʃən] *n* riego; (*med*) irrigación; **— channel** reguera, acequia.
irritable ['iritəbl] *a* irritable, irascible, nervioso.
irritate ['iriteit] *vt* irritar, molestar, exasperar, exacerbar, azuzar; poner (furioso *etc*).
irritation [,iri'teiʃən] *n* irritación, ataque de nervios.
irruption [i'rʌpʃən] *n* irrupción.
island ['ailənd] *n* isla.
islander ['ailəndə] *n* isleño.
isle [ail] *n* isleta; (*barren*) islote.
isolate ['aisəleit] *vt* aislar, apartar.
isolated ['aisəleitid] *a* aislado; incomunicado, solitario.
isolation [,aisə'leiʃən] *n* aislamiento.
issue ['isju:] *n* resultado, salida, conclusión; decisión; (*children*) prole; (*bonds*) emisión; (*happy*) éxito; (*newspaper*) número; (*of book, magazine*) impresión, tirada, entrega; (*of blood*) pérdida de sangre; **point at —** punto en cuestión; **to avoid the —** esquivar la pregunta; *vt* publicar; (*edict etc*) promulgar; (*bonds*) emitir; *vi* (*ooze*) manar; salir, brotar, terminarse.
isthmus ['isməs] *n* istmo.
Italian [i'tæljən] *an* italiano.
Italy ['itəli] *n* Italia.
itch [itʃ] *n* sarna; (*to write etc*) comezón, prurito; *vi* picar; sentir comezón, antojarse, comerse.
itching ['itʃiŋ] *n* picor; comezón; **to be — to** rabiar por; **an — desire** comezón.
item ['aitəm] *ad* ítem; *n* partida, artículo.
itinerant [i'tinərənt] *a* ambulante, viandante, peripatético.
itinerary [ai'tinərəri] *n* itinerario.
its [its] *poss a* su.
ivory ['aivəri] *n* marfil.
ivy ['aivi] *n* hiedra.

J

jackal ['dʒækɔ:l] *n* chacal.
jackass ['dʒækæs] *n* asno; bestia, imbécil.
jackdaw ['dʒækdɔ:] *n* grajo.
jacket ['dʒækit] *n* (*lounge*) americana; (*dinner*) smoking; chaqueta, jubón; calesera; (*book*) cubierta.
jade [dʒeid] *n* (*nag*) rocín; (*min*) nefrita; *vt* cansar; *vi* desalentarse.
jagged ['dʒægid] *a* aserrado; mellado.
jail [dʒeil] *n* calabozo, prisión; **—bird** presidiario.
jailer ['dʒeilə] *n* carcelero; (*arch*) alcaide.
jam [dʒæm] *n* confitura, conserva, compota; (*traffic*) congestión, aglomeración (de tráfico); *sl* lío; **what a —!** ¡qué lío!; *vt* apretar, oprimr, estrujar, entallar
Jamaica [dʒə'meikə] *n* Jamaica.
Jamaican [dʒə'meikən] *an* jamaicano.
James [dʒeimz] *m* Jaime.
Jane [dʒein] *f* Juana.
janitor ['dʒænitə] *n* portero; (*university*) bedel.

January ['dʒænjuəri] *n* enero.
Japan [dʒə'pæn] *n* el Japón.
Japanese [ˌdʒæpə'niːz] *an* japonés.
jar [dʒɑː] *n* cántaro; vasija; (*with spout and handle*) botijo; (*two-handled*) jarra, terraza; (*jam etc*) pote; choque, sacudida; chirrido; *vti* sacudir, hacer vibrar; agitar, trepidar, vibrar, chocar.
jarring ['dʒɑːriŋ] *a* discordante, estridente.
jasmin ['dʒæsmin] *n* jazmín.
jaundice ['dʒɔːndis] *n* ictericia.
jaundiced ['dʒɔːndist] *a* cetrino; **to look at with — eye** mirar de reojo.
jaunt [dʒɔːnt] *vti* corretear, ir y venir; *n* excursión, paseo; **to go for a —** ir de excursión.
jauntiness ['dʒɔːntinis] *n* garbo, soltura.
jaunty ['dʒɔːnti] *a* gentil, gracioso, ligero, garboso.
jaw [dʒɔː] *n* quijada; mandíbula; maxilar.
jealous ['dʒeləs] *a* celoso, envidioso, suspicaz.
jealousy ['dʒeləsi] *n* celos; desconfianza.
jeer [dʒiə] *n* befa, escarnio, injurias; *vt* mofar(se), escarnecer; **to — at** burlarse de; mofarse de.
jelly ['dʒeli] *n* jalea, gelatina, jaletina.
jeopardize ['dʒepədaiz] *vt* exponer, comprometer, poner en peligro.
jeopardy ['dʒepədi] *n* riesgo, peligro.
jerk [dʒəːk] *n* sacudida, tirón; brinco, respingo; *vt* arrojar, dar un tirón, sacudir; (*beef*) atasajar.
jerky ['dʒəːki] *a* espasmódico.
Jerome [dʒə'roum] *m* Jerónimo.
jest [dʒest] *n* chanza, burlaguasa; *vi* chancearse, reírse.
jester ['dʒestə] *n* burlón, chancero, bufón; (*theat*) gracioso.
Jesuit ['dʒezjuit] *n* Jesuita; **— Order** Compañía de Jesús.
Jesus ['dʒiːzəz] *m* Jesús.
jet [dʒet] *n* (*jewel*) azabache; (*liquid*) surtidor, chorro; (*gas*) boquilla; *vt* arrojar; **— plane** reactor, avión (a chorro, a reacción).
jetty ['dʒeti] *n* muelle, malecón, rompeolas.
Jew [dzuː] *n* judío.
jewel ['dʒuːəl] *n* joya, alhaja, presea; prenda.
jewelry ['dʒuːəlri] *n* joyas, alhajas, pedrería; **— store** joyería.
jiffy ['dʒifi] *n* (*fam*) instante.
jilt [dʒilt] *n* coqueta; *vti* plantar, dar calabazas a.
jingle ['dʒiŋgl] *n* retintín, cascabel; *vti* hacer retintín, rimar.
job [dʒɔb] *n* trabajo, puesto, empleo; (*household*) quehacer; (*duty*) ocupación; enchufe; **odd —** (*paid*) chapuza; **to get a —** colocarse.
jocose [dʒə'kous] *a* jocoso, festivo, burlesco.
jocular ['dʒɔkjulə] *a* guasón, burlesco.
jocund ['dʒɔkənd] *a* alegre, festivo, jovial.
jog [dʒɔg] *n* golpecito; trote (corto); *vti* sacudir, empujar; andar despacio; **to be jogging along** ir tirando.
John [dʒɔn] *m* Juan.
join [dʒɔin] *vt* juntar, unir, acoplar; reunir, trabar, aunar; (*metals*) fundir; (*rl*) empalmar; **to — forces with** relacionarse con; **to — up with** unirse con; (*mil*) **to — up** alistarse.
joiner ['dʒɔinə] *n* carpintero, ebanista.
joinery ['dʒɔinəri] *n* carpintería.
joining ['dʒɔiniŋ] *n* unión, juntura, cópula.
joint [dʒɔint] *n* juntura; unión; (*bot*) nudo; coyuntura, articulación; *a* unido, combinado, junto, asociado, colectivo; copartícipe; **— owner** condueño; **— stock company** compañía por acciones; *vi* unirse por articulaciones.
jointed ['dʒɔintid] *a* articulado; **not —** inarticuado.
joke [dʒouk] *n* chanza; (*pun*) chiste, gracia; —(*coarse*) chocarrería; (*practical*) broma, humorada; (*gone too far*) broma pesada; (*hoary*) fiambre.
joker ['dʒoukə] *n* (*practical*) bromista.
jolly ['dʒɔli] *a* alegre, divertido.
jolt [dʒoult] *n* traqueteo, sacudida; *vti* traquetear, sacudir; sacar de quicio, dar sacudidas.
jolting ['dʒoultiŋ] *n* traqueteo.
Jonah ['dʒounə] *m* Jonás.
Joseph ['dʒouzif] *m* José.
jostle ['dʒɔsl] *vt* dar empellones, empujar.
jot [dʒɔt] *n* jota, pizca, tilde; **to — down** tomar nota de, apuntar.
journal ['dʒəːnl] *n* periódico, diario.
journalist ['dʒəːnəlist] *n* periodista, redactor.
journalistic [ˌdʒəːnə'listik] *a* periodístico.
journey ['dʒəːni] *n* viaje; tránsito, camino; **—man** jornalero; *vi* viajar; ir de viaje, recorrer.
joust [dʒaust] *n* justa, torneo; *vi* ajustar.
jovial ['dʒouviəl] *a* jovial, festivo.
joviality [ˌdʒouvi'æliti] *n* festividad; regocijo.
joy [dʒɔi] *n* alegría, delicia, regocijo, gozo, gusto.
joyful ['dʒɔiful] *a* gozoso, regocijado, alegre.
joyfulness ['dʒɔifulnis] *n* gozo, júbilo.
joyousness ['dʒɔiəsnis] *n* felicidad, alegría.
joystick ['dʒɔistik] palanca.
jubilant ['dʒuːbilənt] *a* alborozado.
jubilation [ˌdʒuːbi'leiʃən] *n* júbilo, regocijo.
jubilee ['dʒuːbiliː] *n* jubileo.
judge [dʒʌdʒ] *n* juez; (*arch*) oidor;

conocedor; *vt* juzgar; medir; *vi* estimar; conceptuar, opinar.

judgment ['dʒʌdʒmənt] *n* juicio, dictamen, entendimiento, opinión, sentencia; discernimiento; **Day of —** Día del Juicio; **to the best of one's —** según el leal saber y entender de uno.

judicial [dʒu:'diʃəl] *a* judicial, penal.

judicious [dʒu(:)'diʃəs] *a* juicioso, cuerdo, sesudo, sensato; fino.

jug [dʒʌg] *n* cántara, (*larger*) cántaro; (*earthenware*) botija, botijo; jarro; (*sl*) bote, cárcel.

juggle ['dʒʌgl] *n* juego de manos, escamoteo; *vi* escamotear, hacer juegos de manos.

juggler ['dʒʌglə] *n* juglar, titiritero, jugador de manos, ilusionista, histrión.

Jugoslav ['ju:gou'slæv] *an* yugoeslavo.

Jugoslavia ['ju:gou'slæviə] yugoeslavia.

juice [dʒu:s] *n* jugo, zumo; **gastric —** jugo gástrico; **orange —** zumo de naranja.

juicy ['dʒu:si] *a* jugoso, suculento.

Julian ['dʒu:liən] *m* Julián.

July [dʒu(:)'lai] *n* julio.

jumble ['dʒʌmbl] *n* mezcla, revoltijo, enredo; cajón de sastre; tropel; *vt* revolver, enredar, confundir.

jumbled ['dʒʌmbld] *a* confuso, atropellado, embarullado.

jump [dʒʌmp] *n* salto, brinco; *vt* saltar, brincar, dar unsalto, dar saltos (brincos).

jumpy ['dʒʌmpi] *a* **he is very —** no le cabe el corazón en el pecho; **to be —** estar en ascuas.

junction ['dʒʌŋkʃən] *n* unión, trabadura; (*of rivers*) confluente; (*rl*) empalme.

June [dʒu:n] *n* junio.

jungle ['dʒʌŋgl] *n* selva; (*Cub*) manigua.

junior ['dʒu:njə] *a* más joven *n* menor.

jurisdiction [ˌdʒuəris'dikʃən] *n* jurisdicción, fuero; poderío.

jurisprudence [ˌdʒuəris'pru:dəns] *n* jurisprudencia.

jury ['dʒuəri] *n* jurado; los jurados; **—box** tribuna.

just [dʒʌst] *a* justo, justiciero, razonable, exacto, cabal, honrado, fiel; *ad* justamente, precisamente, ahora mismo, de nuevo, apenas; **to have —** acabar de; **— out** reciente.

justice ['dʒʌstis] *n* justicia, equidad; **to do oneself —** quedar bien; **to do full — to** hacer los debidos honores a.

justifiable [ˌdʒʌsti'faiəbl] *a* justificable, legítimo.

justification [ˌdʒʌstifi'keiʃən] *n* justificación.

justify ['dʒʌstifai] *vt* justificar, probar, vindicar; **to — oneself** sincerarse, santificarse; (*selection, appointment etc*) acreditarse.

justness ['dʒʌstnis] *n* justicia, exactitud, precisión, rectitud.

jut [dʒʌt] *vi* **to — out** proyectar, sobresalir; combarse.

juvenile ['dʒu:vənail] *a* juvenil, joven; **J— Court** Tribunal de Menores.

K

Kate, Katharine [keit, 'kæθərin] *f* Catalina.

keel [ki:l] *n* quilla; *vt* surcar el mar, dar carena.

keen [ki:n] *a* (*point*) agudo, penetrante; ladino; sutil; mordaz, incisivo; **— -edged** cortante, afilado; **—witted** lince, agudo.

keenness ['ki:nnis] *n* agudeza, perspicacia; aspereza; entusiasmo.

keep [ki:p] *n* (*fort*) alcázar, guardia, torre; (*food*) manutención, pensión, lo que come; *vt* guardar, tener, mantener; quedarse con, preservar; (*house*) llevar; celebrar; retener; *vi* quedar, conservarse, guardarse; **to — away** mantener(se) a distancia; **to — back** retener, reservar, suprimir; **to — up** mantener, mantenerse firme, no cejar; **to — someone waiting** dar (a uno) un plantón; **to — accounts** llevar los libros; **to — someone (too long)** entretener; **to — up appearances** salvar las apariencias; **to — to one's bed** guardar cama; **to — at bay** mantener a raya; **to — time** marcar el compás.

keeper ['ki:pə] *n* guardián, conservador; (*of turkeys*) pavero; (*of books*) tenedor; (*game*) guardabosque.

keeping ['ki:piŋ] *n* custodia, guarda, cuidado, conservación; armonía; **to be in — with** rimar con; **in — with** de acuerdo con.

kerchief ['kə:tʃif] *n* pañuelo, toquilla.

kernel ['kə:nl] *n* almendra; (*pip*) pepita; meollo; (*dried coconut*) copra.

kerosene ['kerəsi:n] *n* keroseno.

kettle ['ketl] *n* caldera; (*large*) caldero, tetera, palma.

kettledrum ['ketldrʌm] *n* timbal.

key [ki:] *n* llave; (*— to cipher, code*) contracifra; (*piano*) tecla; (*mech*) cuña; (*mus*) clave; tono; **master —** llave maestra, ganzúa; **—hole** ojo.

keystone ['ki:stoun] *n* clave, llave; piedra angular.

kick [kik] n patada, puntapié; respingo, protesta; (*of animal*) coz; *vti* dar (coces, puntapiés), cocear; (*repeatedly*) patalear; **to — against the pricks** dar coces contra el aguijón; respingar; **to — over the traces** mostrar las herraduras.

kicking ['kikiŋ] *n* pataleo.

kid [kid] *n* cabrit(ill)o; (*leather*) cabritilla; niño, niña.
kidnap ['kidnæp] *vt* secuestrar.
kidnapper ['kidnæpə] *n* ladrón de niños, secuestrador.
kidney ['kidni] *n* riñón, lomo; índole; — **bean** judia verde, habichuela, alubia.
kill [kil] *vt* matar, destruir, neutralizar; (*by blow on neck*) acogotar; (*at one blow*) birlar; despachar; **to — two birds with one stone** matar dos pájaros de un tiro.
killer ['kilə] *n* matador; asesino.
kiln [kiln] *n* horno.
kilogram ['kiləgræm] *n* kilogramo.
kilometer ['kilə,mi:tə] *n* kilómetro.
kin [kin] *a* pariente, emparentado, aliado, análogo, afín, allegado; *n* parentesco, vínculo; parientes; **next of —** pariente próximo.
kind [kaind] *a* amable, cariñoso, bondadoso; propicio; **very —** angélico; **— -hearted** benévolo, bondadoso; *n* género, especie, clase, suerte; (*com*) **in —** en especie.
kindle ['kindl] *vt* encender, iluminar, inflamar; *vi* prender, arder, encenderse, inflamarse.
kindliness ['kaindlinis] *n* benevolencia, bondad, humanidad.
kindling ['kindliŋ] *n* ignición; **— wood** leña.
kindly ['kaindli] *ad* bondadosamente; *a* benévolo; **— accept** dígnese aceptar.
kindness ['kaindnis] *n* bondad, benevolencia, amabilidad, gracia.
kindred ['kindrid] *a* consanguíneo; congenial; *n* parentela, afinidad.
king [kiŋ] *n* rey; **the three —s** los reyes magos; **—'s son, daughter** (*Spain*) Infante, Infanta; **—cup** botón de oro.
kingdom ['kiŋdəm] *n* reino.
kingly ['kiŋli] *a* real, regio; *ad* regiamente.
kingship ['kiŋʃip] *n* majestad.
kinship ['kinʃip] *n* parentela, familiaridad.
kinsman ['kinzmən] *n* pariente, allegado.
kiosk ['kiɔsk] *n* quiosco.
kiss [kis] *n* beso; (*of peace, ceremonial*) ósculo; **to cover with —es** besuquear; *vt* besar; **to — the ground** morder el polvo.
kit [kit] *n* cubo, caja de herramientas; avíos.
kitchen ['kitʃin] *n* cocina; **— garden** huerta; **—maid** fregona; **— range** cocina económica.
kite [kait] *n* (*bird*) milano; (*paper*) cometa, birlocha.
kitten ['kitn] *n* gatito.
knack [næk] *n* maña, habilidad, ingenio, tino, acierto.
knapsack ['næpsæk] *n* mochila.
knarled [nɑ:ld] *a* nudoso, torcido.
knave [neiv] *n* pícaro, bribón, bellaco; (*cards*) sota.
knead [ni:d] *vt* amasar.
kneading ['ni:diŋ] *n* amasadura, amasijo; **— trough** artesa.
knee [ni:] *n* rodilla; (*arch*) hinojo; (*mech*) codillo; **on one's —s** de rodillas; **— breeches** calzón corto.
kneel [ni:l] *vi* arrodillarse, hincar la rodilla, ponerse (de rodillas, (*arch*) de hinojos).
knell [nel] *n* tañido fúnebre, clamoreo; *vt* doblar.
knickers ['nikəz] *n pl* bragas.
knickknack ['niknæk] *n* chuchería, baratija, fruslería.
knife [naif] *n* cuchillo; (*large*) cuchilla; (*hunting*) cuchillo de monte; (*jack*) navaja; (*pocket*) cortaplumas.
knight [nait] *n* caballero; (*chess*) caballo; **K— Templar** hospitalario, templario; *vt* armar caballero.
knight-errant ['nait'erənt] *n* caballero andante.
knight-errantry ['nait'erəntri] *n* caballería andante.
knightly ['naitli] *a* caballeresco, de caballero.
knit [nit] *vti* hacer (punto, calceta), anudar, ligar; entretejer; (*brows*) fruncir (*las cejas*).
knitted ['nitid] *a* (*garment*) de punto; **— brows** ceño.
knitting ['nitiŋ] *n* calceta, punto; obra de punto.
knob [nɔb] *n* prominencia, nudo, botón; (*door*) tirador, perilla.
knock [nɔk] *n* golpe; (*on door*) aldabazo; **—kneed** zambo, befo; *vti* golpear, llamar a la puerta; **to — off** *vt* rebajar; **to — down** derribar, abatir, (*by vehicle*) atropellar, (*at auction*) rematar; **to — farther in** remachar.
knocker ['nɔkə] *n* llamador, golpeador, (*door*) aldaba.
knoll [noul] *n* loma, otero, prominencia; *vti* doblar, tocar a muerto.
knot [nɔt] *n* nudo; atadura; (*of ribbons*) moño; (*of people*) corro, corrillo; **running —** lazo escurridizo; **slip —** lazo; *vti* anudar, echar nudos, atar.
knotty ['nɔti] *a* nudoso, duro, difícil, espinoso; **— point** busilis.
know [nou] *vt* (*facts*) saber; (*people, language*) conocer; **to — how** saber; **to — by sight** conocer de vista; **to be in the —** estar enterado; **to get to —** llegar a saber, enterarse de; (*people*) relacionarse con; **to — better than to** guardarse de; **for all I —** que yo sepa; a mi juicio.
knowing ['nouiŋ] *a* instruido; astuto; diestro; avisado, entendido; *n* conocimiento, inteligencia.
knowledge ['nɔlidʒ] *n* conocimiento(s), saber, instrucción; **with —** a ciencia cierta; **to the best of my —** según mi leal saber y entender.

known [noun] *a* conocido; **well-** — de notoriedad, notorio; (*already*) consabido; **little** — obscuro; **to make** — publicar, comunicar; **to become** — llegarse a saber, trascender.
knuckle ['nʌkl] *n* nudillo, artejo; **—bones** taba; *vi* **to** — **under** someterse, doblarse.

L

label ['leibl] *n* rótulo, etiqueta, letrero; tarjeta; *vt* rotular, marcar.
labor ['leibə] *n* trabajo, labor, obra; (*workmen*) mano de obra; (*med*) dolores de parto; **hard** — trabajos forzados; — **party** partido laborista; *vt* trabajar, elaborar, fabricar; *vi* afanarse, esforzarse, torcejear.
laboratory [lə'bɔrətəri] *n* laboratorio, taller.
laborer ['leibərə] *n* trabajador; jornalero, bracero; (*farm*) gañán, peón.
laborious [lə'bɔriəs] *a* laborioso, penoso, ímprobo; asiduo.
labyrinth ['læbərinθ] *n* laberinto, embrollo, dédalo.
lace [leis] *n* encaje; (*for tying*) cordón; **shoe—** cordón; *vt* hacer encaje; bordar; **to** — **up** atar.
lack [læk] *n* necesidad, escasez, falta, carencia; ausencia; — **of spirit** pobreza; — **of movement** inacción; — **of taste, tact** *etc* desacierto; — **of enthusiasm** tibieza; *vt* tener necesidad de; *vi* carecer, faltar.
lacking ['lækiŋ] *a* falto de, defectivo en.
laconic [lə'kɔnik] *a* lacónico, breve, conciso.
lacquer ['lækə] *n* laca, barniz; *vt* barnizar.
lad [læd] *n* joven, muchacho, chiquillo, rapaz, chaval, pollo.
ladder ['lædə] *n* escala, escalera; (*in stockings*) carrera; **rope** — escala de cuerda.
laden ['leidn] *pp* cargado, colmado.
ladle ['leidl] *n* cucharón, cazo.
lady ['leidi] *n* dama, señora; **fine young** — damisela; — **-in-waiting** (*Spanish Royal Household*) menina; **—killer** tenorio; **—ship** señoría.
ladylike ['leidilaik] *a* delicado, elegante.
lag [læg] *n* retraso; *vt* **to** — **behind** rezagarse, quedarse atrás.
laggard ['lægəd] *an* rezagado, holgazán, perezoso.
lair [lɛə] *n* guarida, madriguera; escondrijo, cubil.
laity ['leiiti] *n* la gente lega, los seglares.
lake [leik] *a* lacustre; *n* lago; (*ornamental*) estanque.
lamb [læm] *n* cordero, borrego.
lame [leim] *a* cojo, cojuelo; tullido; (*excuse etc*) débil; *vt* estropear, lisiar; **to walk** — cojear.
lameness [leimnis] *n* cojera.
lament [lə'ment] *n* queja, lamento; llanto; *vti* deplorar, lamentarse, quejarse, sentir.
lamentable ['læməntəbl] *a* deplorable, lamentable, lastimero; funesto.
lamentation [ˌlæmen'teiʃən] *n* lamentación, duelo, lamento.
lamp [læmp] *n* lámpara; (*heating*) quemador; **oil** — candil; **street** — farol; — **glass** tubo de lámpara; **—shade** pantalla.
lance [lɑ:ns] *n* lanza; (*med*) lanceta; *vt* lancear, atravesar, cortar.
land [lænd] *n* (*earth, country*) tierra; (*ground*) terreno(s); (*nation*) país; (*area, region*) comarca; (*on boundary*) terreno limítrofe; *vti* desembarcar; tomar tierra; (*aircraft*) aterrizar; *vt* (*slap etc*) propinar, arrear.
landing ['lændiŋ] *n* desembarco; (*aircraft*) aterrizaje; (*stairs*) descanso; (*dock*) desembarcadero.
landlady ['lænˌleidi] *f* señora, patrona, casera.
landlord ['lænlɔ:d] *n* propietario, huésped, dueño, patrón, casero.
landmark ['lændmɑ:k] *n* (*stone etc*) mojón, hito, coto.
landowner ['lændˌounə] *n* propietario, terrateniente, hacendado.
landscape ['lænskeip] *n* paisaje, campiña, vista.
landslide ['lændslaid] *n* (*mining*) revenimiento; desprendimiento de tierra.
lane [lein] *n* (*town*) callejuela, callejón; (*country*) camino vecinal, senda.
language ['læŋgwidʒ] *n* lengua, idioma; lenguaje.
languid ['læŋgwid] *a* lánguido, débil, lacio.
languidness ['læŋgwidnis] *n* entorpecimiento, desmayo.
languish ['læŋgwiʃ] *vi* languidecer, extenuarse, consumirse.
languor ['læŋgə] *n* dejadez, languidez.
lank [læŋk] *a* flaco, descarnado, delgado; (*hair*) lacio.
lantern ['læntən] *n* linterna; (*big*) farola; (*paper*) farolillo; (*magic*) linterna mágica; (*dark*) linterna sorda.
lap [læp] *n* falda, seno, regazo; etapa, trecho; **—dog** perro faldero; *vti* sobreponer, plegar; envolver; lamer.
lapel [lə'pel] *n* solapa.
lapse [læps] *n* (*of time*) lapso, transcurso; traspié, falta; *vi* pasar, transcurrir; caducar, (re)caer en.
larceny ['lɑ:sni] *n* (*petty*) hurto; ratería.
larch [lɑ:tʃ] *n* alerce.

lard [lɑ:d] *n* manteca (*de cerdo*); *vt* mechar.
larder ['lɑ:də] *n* despensa, repostería.
large [lɑ:dʒ] *a* grande, grueso, amplio; (*number*) nutrido; extenso; (*clothes*) holgado; **— -headed** cabezudo; **— -hearted** desprendido.
largeness ['lɑ:dʒnis] *n* extensión, amplitud, generosidad.
lark [lɑ:k] *n* alondra; (*fam*) holgorio.
lasciviousness [lə'siviəsnis] *n* lascivia, incontinencia.
lash [læʃ] *n* látigo; (*with whip*) latigazo; (*with tail*) coletazo; azote; *vti* azotar; amarrar, (*with tail*) dar coletazos.
lass [læs] *n* chavala, moza, doncella, muchacha; (*fam*) polla; **bonny —** moza garrida; **country —** zagala.
lasso [læ'su:] *n* lazo; *vt* lazar.
last [lɑ:st] *a* último, postrero; supremo; pasado; (*gasp*) postrero, último; (*Monday*) pasado; (*one*) último; **— night** anoche; **— but one** penúltimo; **— man in** (*games*) porra; **at —** en fin, finalmente; *ad* **at the —** a la zaga, al fin; **at long —** a la postre; **to the —** hasta lo último; (*mil*) **— post** retreta; **on one's — legs** a no poder más; **— moments** (*of life*) postrimerías; *n* horma; *vi* (per)durar; **to — out** subsistir; sostenerse.
lasting ['lɑ:stiŋ] *a* duradero, durable.
lastly ['lɑ:stli] *ad* (en, por) fin; finalmente, por último.
latch [lætʃ] *n* aldaba, aldabilla, picaporte, cerrojo; **—key** llavín.
late [leit] *a* (*flowers etc*) tardío; (*train*) retrasado; **— king** el difunto rey; tardo, lento; reciente; (*hours*) altas horas; **to be —** llegar (tarde, retrasado), retrasarse, llevar un retraso de (10 *mins*); **of —, lately** recientemente, de poco tiempo acá, últimamente; **too —** demasiado tarde.
latecomer ['leitkʌmə] *n* persona que llega tarde.
lately ['leitli] *ad* ha poco, recientemente.
lateness ['leitnis] *n* lo tarde, lo tardío; (*of hour*) lo avanzado.
latent ['leitənt] *a* oculto, latente, secreto.
later ['leitə] *ad* con posterioridad, más tarde, posteriormente.
lateral ['lætərəl] *a* lateral, ladero.
latest ['leitist] *ad* **at the —** a más tardar.
lather ['lɑ:ðə] *n* espuma de jabón; *vt* enjabonar; hacer espuma.
Latin ['lætin] *a n* latino; *n* (*language*) latín.
latitude ['lætitju:d] *n* latitud, extensión; **in the — of** en las alturas de.
latter ['lætə] *a* último, éste, posterior; **the — part** la segunda parte.
laudable ['lɔ:dəbl] *a* loable.
laudatory ['lɔ:dətəri] *a* laudatorio.
laugh [lɑ:f] *n* risa; *vi* reír; **to — at** reírse de, ridiculizar; **to — out loud** reír a carcajadas; **to — up one's sleeve** reírse por dentro.
laughable ['lɑ:fəbl] *a* risible, divertido.
laughing ['lɑ:fiŋ] *a* risueño; **— gas** gas hilarante; **—stock** hazmerreír.
laughter ['lɑ:ftə] *n* risa, carcajada.
launch [lɔ:ntʃ] *n* botadura, lanzamiento; lancha; *vt* lanzar, botar al agua; *vi* arrojarse, lanzarse, acometer.
launderette [lɔ:n'dret] *n* lavandería.
laundress ['lɔ:ndris] *n* lavandera.
laundry ['lɔ:ndri] *n* lavadero, lavandería; ropa lavada.
lavatory ['lævətəri] *n* lavatorio, lavadero, (*wc*) retrete.
lavender ['lævində] *n* espliego, alhucema.
lavish ['læviʃ] *a* lujoso; fastuoso, manirroto, pródigo; *vt* prodigar.
lavishness ['læviʃnis] *n* prodigalidad, despilfarro, derroche.
law [lɔ:] *n* ley; (*study*) derecho; (*fundamental*) constitución; **canon —** derecho canónico; (*civil*) civil; (*commercial*) mercantil; (*criminal*) penal; **— student** estudiante de derecho; **beyond the —** fuera de la ley; *pl* **the — of** las leyes de; **according to the —** según la ley; **— officer** policía; golilla; **to go to —** poner pleito; **to take the — into one's own hands** tomarse la justicia por su mano; **— -abiding** observante de la ley.
lawful ['lɔ:ful] *a* legal, legítimo, lícito.
lawless ['lɔ:lis] *a* desordenado, ilegal, desaforado.
lawlessness ['lɔ:lisnis] *n* licencia, ilegalidad.
lawn [lɔ:n] *n* césped; (*sew*) linón.
Lawrence ['lɔrəns] *m* Lorenzo.
lawsuit ['lɔ:su:t] *n* pleito, acción.
lawyer ['lɔ:jə] *n* abogado, letrado; (*petty*) **—** leguleyo; **—'s office** bufete; **to set up as —** abrir bufete.
laxity ['læksiti] *n* holgura; (*morals*) relajamiento.
lay [lei] *a* seglar, laico, profano; *vt* poner, colocar, (ex)tender; echar, acabar con; (*eggs, table*) poner; (*fears etc*) sosegar, aquietar; achacar; (*bet*) apostar; (*gun*) apuntar; *vi* **to — about one** dar palos de ciego; **to — aside** poner a un lado, desechar; arrinconar; guardar; **to — bare** revelar: **to — before** exponer (ante los ojos); **to — down** posar; (*grain*) acostar, (*arms*) deponer; dictar, sentar, establecer, imponer; (*in earth*) enterrar; **to —** (*oneself*) **open** exponer(se), descubrir(se); **to — out** trazar; (*corpse*), amortajar; (*money*) invertir, gastar.
layer ['leiə] *n* capa, yacimiento.
laziness ['leizinis] *n* pereza.

lazy ['leizi] *a* perezoso, descuidado, lánguido; — **dog** paseante.
lead [led] *n* plomo; (*naut*) sonda, plomada.
lead [li:d] *n* primer lugar, primacía; (*theat*) protagonista, primer actor; (*cards*) mano; *vt* llevar, guiar; (*procession etc*) ir a la cabeza; encauzar, inducir; (*expedition*) capitanear; *vi* llevar la delantera; tender; (*cards*) ser mano; **to — into error** inducir a error; **to — to** salir a; **to take the —** adelantarse, tomar la delantera.
leader ['li:də] *n* guía; jefe; cabecilla, adalid; caudillo; líder; (*newspaper*) editorial, artículo de fondo; (*gang*) cuadrillero.
leadership ['li:dəʃip] *n* dirección; jefatura, mando.
leading ['li:diŋ] *a* principal, capital, primero; conducta; conducción.
leaf [li:f] *n* hoja; (*tobacco*) en rama; (*table*) pala; (*door*) ala, batiente; (*gold*) oro batido; **to turn over a new —** enmendarse, volver la hoja.
leaflet ['li:flit] *n* hojilla, hojuela, folleto, circular.
leafy ['li:fi] *a* coposo, frondoso.
league [li:g] *n* liga; confederación; legua; *vi* ligarse, confederarse.
leak [li:k] *n* gotera, escape; *vi* gotear, hacer agua, rezumar; **to — out** trascender.
leaky ['li:ki] *a* roto, averiado; **it is —** hace agua.
lean [li:n] *a* flaco, magro, enjuto; *n* carne magra; **—to** colgadizo, cobertizo; *vti* inclinar(se), apoyar(se); **to — back** reclinarse; **to — against** arrimar(se) a.
leaning ['li:niŋ] *n* inclinación, disposición, propensión.
leanness ['li:nnis] *n* flaqueza, magrura.
leap [li:p] *n* salto, brinco; corcovo; **— year** año bisiesto; *pl* **by —s and bounds** a pasos agigantados; *vti* saltar, brincar; (*heart*) latir; **to — over** salvar.
learn [lə:n] *vti* aprender; darse cuenta; enterarse de, averiguar.
learned ['lə:nid] *a* docto, erudito; versado en; sabio; (*style*) culto.
learner ['lə:nə] *n* escolar, estudiante; aprendiz; principiante.
learning ['lə:niŋ] *n* saber; **superficial —** erudición a la violeta.
lease [li:s] *n* arriendo, arrendamiento; *vt* arrendar, dar en arriendo.
least [li:st] *a* el menor, ínfimo; *ad* lo menos; **at —** por lo menos; **when you — expect it** cuando menos se piensa; de hoy a mañana; **not in the —** de ningún modo, ni con mucho.
leather ['leðə] *n* cuero; **Spanish —** cordobán.
leave [li:v] *n* permiso, licencia; **by your —** con perdón, con su permiso; **without so much as a by your —** de buenas a primeras; *vt* dejar, abandonar; irse, salir; (*money etc*) legar; **to — out** omitir; **to — the priesthood** colgar los hábitos.
leaving ['li:viŋ] *n* salida, partida; despedida; *pl* sobras, desperdicios.
Lebanon ['lebənən] *n* el Líbano.
lecture ['lektʃə] *n* (*speech*) conferencia, discurso; reprimenda; **— hall** aula, salón; *vt* dar (una) conferencia; sermonear, regañar.
lecturer ['lektʃərə] *n* conferenciante.
led [led] *pp* **to be —** guiarse; **easily — astray** malaconsejado.
ledge [ledʒ] *n* borde, capa; saliente; **window —** alféizar.
leer [liə] *n* mirada (maliciosa, lasciva); *vi* mirar (con malicia, con lascivia).
lees [li:z] *n pl* sedimento, heces; (*wine*) poso.
left [left] *a* izquierdo; **— -handed** zurdo; **— hand** siniestra; **to be —** quedar; **— behind** rezagado; **on the —** a la izquierda; **— out** omitido; olvidado.
leftover ['left'ouvə] *n* resto, sobrante; *pl* sobras.
leg [leg] *n* pierna; pantorrilla; (*animals, furniture*) pata; **long —** zanca; **on one's last —s** a la cuarta pregunta; **to pull one's —** tomarle el pelo.
legacy ['legəsi] *n* legado, herencia.
legal ['li:gəl] *a* legal, legítimo, judicial, constitucional.
legality [li(:)'gæliti] *n* legalidad.
legend ['ledʒənd] *n* leyenda, fábula; (*notice*) letrero.
legion ['li:dʒən] *n* legión, multitud.
legislate ['ledʒisleit] *vi* hacer leyes, legislar.
legislation [ˌledʒis'leiʃən] *n* legislación.
legislator ['ledʒisleitə] *n* legislador.
legislature ['ledʒisleitʃə] *n* legislatura, cuerpo legislativo.
legitimacy [li'dʒitiməsi] *n* legitimidad.
legitimate [li'dʒitimit] *a* legítimo.
leisure ['leʒə] *n* ocio, holganza, desocupación, comodidad; **at —** holgado, a gusto; **to be at —** holgar, estar (libre, desocupado); **— time** ratos de ocio, ratos perdidos.
lemon ['lemən] *n* limón; **—colored** cetrino.
lemonade [ˌlemə'neid] *n* limonada.
lend [lend] *vt* prestar; **— at interest** prestar a rédito; **to — a hand** echar una mano; **to — oneself** prestarse.
lending ['lendiŋ] *n* empréstito, préstamo.
length [leŋθ] *n* longitud, extensión; (*time*) espacio, duración; (*of cloth*) corte; **to go to great —s** extremar; **at —** a la larga; **full —** de cuerpo entero.

lengthen ['leŋθən] *vt* alargar, extender, estirar.
lengthy ['leŋθi] *a* difuso, prolongado, extenso.
leniency ['li:niənsi] *n* clemencia, lenidad.
lenient ['li:niənt] *a* clemente, benigno.
lens [lenz] *n* lente; (*spectacles*) luneta.
lent [lent] *n* cuaresma.
lentil ['lentil] *n* lenteja.
Leopold ['liəpould] *m* Leopoldo.
leper ['lepə] *n* leproso, lazarino.
leprosy ['leprəsi] *n* lepra.
less [les] *a, ad* menor, menos; **to grow —** decrecer.
lessen ['lesn] *vt* disiminuir, mermar; *vi* disminuirse; aminorar; (*wind*) amainar.
lesson ['lesn] *n* lección; enseñanza; reprimenda; (*moral*) moraleja; **to teach a — to** aleccionar.
lest [lest] *cj* no sea que; para que no.
let [let] *n* estorbo; *vt* dejar; (*rooms etc*) alquilar; **to — into** dejar entrar; enterar; **to — fly, free, loose** soltar, desencadenar; **to — off** (*gun*) disparar; perdonar; **to — out** (*rope*) aflojar, soltar, (*slap*) largar; **to — know** hacer saber, advertir, hacer presente.
lethargy ['leθədʒi] *n* inactividad, estupor.
letter ['letə] *n* carta; letra; carácter; **small —** minúscula; **— -writing** correspondencia, epistolería; **— perfect** al pie de la letra; **—box** buzón.
letting ['letiŋ] *n* arrendamiento.
lettuce ['letis] *n* lechuga.
leukemia [lu'ki:miə] *n* leucemia.
level ['levl] *a* igual, plano, lleno, liso; *n* nivel; **above sea —** sobre el nivel del mar; **— crossing** paso a nivel; *vt* nivelar, allanar, explanar; arrasar; **to — at** (*gun*) apuntar.
leveling ['levliŋ] *n* nivelación, aplanamiento; (*site*) desmonte.
levity ['leviti] *n* ligereza, liviandad.
levy ['levi] *n* leva, enganche; exacción de tributos; *vt* reclutar; imponer, exigir (tributos).
lewdness ['lu:dnis] *n* lujuria, incontinencia.
liability [,laiə'biliti] *n* responsabilidad, compromiso; *pl* (*com*) pasivo; tendencia.
liable ['laiəbl] *a* responsable; expuesto; propenso a; **to become —** incurrir en.
liaison [li(:)'eizɔ̃:ŋ] *n* enredo.
liar ['laiə] *n* embustero, mentiroso.
libel ['laibəl] *n* libelo, difamación; *vt* difamar, calumniar, infamar.
liberal ['libərəl] *a* liberal, generoso, largo, desprendido.
liberality [,libə'ræliti] *n* liberalidad, esplendidez.
liberate ['libəreit] *vt* libertar, librar, redimir
libertine ['libə(:)ti:n] *n* burlador, libertino.
liberty ['libəti] *n* libertad; libre albedrío; licencia, desembarazo.
librarian [lai'brεəriən] *n* bibliotecario.
library ['laibrəri] *n* biblioteca.
Libya ['libjə] *n* Libia.
Libyan ['libjən] *an* libio.
license ['laisəns] *n* licencia, permiso; título, diploma; libertinaje, desenfreno; *vt* autorizar, conceder (un permiso, una licencia).
licentious [lai'senʃəs] *a* licencioso, desahogado.
lick [lik] *vt* lamer; pegar, (*fam*) cascar.
licorice ['likəris] *n* regaliz.
lid [lid] *n* tapa, tapador.
lie [lai] *n* mentira, embuste, falsedad; **white —** mentirilla; (*of land etc*) caída; *vi* mentir; (*be situated*) ubicar; **to — about** estar esparcido, desparramado, tumbado; **to — against** arrimarse a; **to — between** mediar; **to — down** echarse, acostarse, tenderse; **to — in wait for** acechar; **to — low** agacharse; **to — on** pesar sobre; (*in grave*) yacer; **to give the — to** dar el mentis, desmentir, contradecir.
lieutenant [lu'tenənt] *n* teniente; **second —** alférez; **— colonel** teniente coronel.
life [laif] *n* vida; vivacidad; vivir, conducta; **for —** vitalicio, de por vida; **painted from —** pintado del natural; **—belt** salvavidas; **—boat** lancha de socorro, bote salvavidas.
lifeless ['laiflis] *a* sin vida, inanimado, desanimado, exánime.
lifelike ['laiflaik] *a* muy parecido; natural.
lifelong ['laiflɔŋ] *a* de toda la vida.
lifesize ['laif'saiz] *a* de tamaño natural.
lift [lift] *n* elevación, alzamiento; (*mech*) ascensor, montacargas; *vt* levantar, elevar, subir; (*coll*) sisar.
light [lait] *n* luz, claridad; **signal —** farol; (*met*) **shining —** lumbrera; iluminar;*vt* encender; *vi* encenderse; **to — on** posarse.
light [lait] *a* (*color*) claro; (*weight*) ligero, leve; delgado, sutil; fácil, frívolo; brillante; **— -headed** ligero de cascos.
lighten ['laitn] *vt* (*weight*) aligerar; aclarar, iluminar, alumbrar; *vi* relampaguear.
lighter ['laitə] *n* encendedor; (*cigarette*) mechero; (*boat*) lancha, barcaza, pontón.
light-hearted ['lait'hɑ:tid] *a* alegre, festivo.
lighthouse ['laithaus] *n* faro.
lightness ['laitnis] *n* ligereza, levedad.
lighting ['laitiŋ] *n* (*street*) alumbrado (público).
lightning ['laitniŋ] *n* relámpago,

rayo; — **conductor,** — **rod** pararrayos.
lightweight ['lait'weit] *n* peso ligero; *a* de peso ligero.
like [laik] *a* semejante, parecido; igual; *n* semejante, igual; *ad* como, del mismo modo; a semejanza de; — **father** — **son** cual padre tal hijo; *vti* gustar, gustar de, estimar, apreciar, simpatizar con; **what I** — de mi agrado; — **it or not** mal que le pese; **to be** — semejar a, parecerse a.
likely ['laikli] *a, ad* probable, posible, idóneo, verosímil, dable, a propósito; — **as not** a lo mejor; **to be** — **to** deber de: **it isn't** — es improbable; **not** —! claro que no!
likeness ['laiknis] *n* semejanza, parecido, retrato, semejante; **to be a good** — estar parecido; **family** — aire de familia.
likewise ['laikwaiz] *ad* también, del mismo modo, igualmente.
liking ['laikiŋ] *n* gusto, grado, inclinación, afición.
lily ['lili] *n* lirio; **water**— nenúfar.
limb [lim] *n* miembro; (*tree*) rama.
lime [laim] *n* cal, liga; (*bot*) lima.
limit ['limit] *n* límite; (*end*) término; —**s** frontera; **that's the** — es el colmo; **to the** — hasta no más; *vt* limitar, circunscribir.
limitation [ˌlimi'teiʃən] *n* limitación, restricción.
limited ['limitid] *a* limitado, poco; escaso; de responsabilidad limitada.
limp [limp] *a* flojo, lacio; *n* cojera; *vi* cojear, claudicar.
limpid ['limpid] *a* límpido, cristalino, transparente.
limping ['limpiŋ] *n* cojera; *a* cojo.
line [lain] *n* línea, fila; raya, cuerda; ramo; (*print*) renglón; (*poetry*) verso; (*writing*) raya; (*on face*) surco; (*mil*) **behind the** —**s** a la retaguardia; *vt* alinear, revestir; (*clothes*) forrar; **to** — **up** alinear.
lineage ['liniidʒ] *n* raza, linaje, abolengo; genealogía; (*gentlemanly*) hidalguía.
linen ['linin] *n* lino, lienzo; ropa blanca.
liner ['lainə] *n* transatlántico.
linger ['liŋgə] *vi* tardar, demorarse, ir despacio.
lingering ['liŋgəriŋ] *a* prolongado, dilatado, moroso.
lining ['lainiŋ] *n* (a)forro.
link [liŋk] *n* eslabón; enlace; *vt* enlazar, eslabonar; **to** — **together** encadenar.
linnet ['linit] *n* jilguero.
lint [lint] *n* hilas, clavo, gasa.
lintel ['lintl] *n* dintel, lintel; (*house*) umbral.
lion ['laiən] *n* león.
lip [lip] *n* labio; (*of cup etc*) borde; pico.
lipstick ['lipstik] *n* pintalabios, lápiz labial.
liquid ['likwid] *an* líquido; límpido.
liquidate ['likwideit] *vt* saldar, pagar (cuentas).
liquor ['likə] *n* licor.
Lisbon ['lizbən] *n* Lisboa.
lisp [lisp] *n* balbucencia, ceceo; *vti* balbucir, cecear.
list [list] *n* lista; tabla; borde; fichero; minuta; (*students*) matrícula; (*ship*) banda, inclinación; (*salary, promotion*) escalafón; *vi* recalcar; *vt* facturar.
listen ['lisn] *vi* escuchar; oír; **to** — **to reason** atender a razones.
listener ['lisnə] *n* (*radio*) oyente.
listless ['listlis] *a* desatento, negligente; desanimado.
listlessness ['listlisnis] *n* desatención. indiferencia, apatía, abulia.
liter ['li:tə] *n* litro.
literal ['litərəl] *a* literal, al pie de la letra.
literary ['litərəri] *a* literario.
literature ['litəritʃə] *n* literatura; bellas letras; **light** — literatura amena.
lithe [laið] *a* delgado, flexible, ágil; mimbreante.
litigant ['litigənt] *n* litigante, contendiente.
litigation [ˌliti'geiʃən] *n* litigio, pleito, proceso.
litter ['litə] *n* litera; (*bier*) andas, camilla; (*enclosed*) palanquín; (*animal*) cría; (*paper etc*) desorden, basura, desperdicios; (*animal bedding*) cama de paja.
little ['litl] *a* poco, pequeño, chico; escaso, limitado; *ad* poco, escasamente.
littleness ['litlnis] *n* poquedad, pequeñez; mezquindad.
live [laiv] *a* vivo, ardiente, brillante; (*el*) cargado; — **coal** ascua, brasa; [liv] *vi* vivir, subsistir, morar, habitar; **to** — **on** subsistir; **to** — **up to** corresponder; **to manage to** — vivir de milagro, vivir al día.
livelihood ['laivlihud] *n* mantenimiento, subsistencia, vida.
liveliness ['laivlinis] *n* vivacidad, brío, salero, vida, prontitud.
lively ['laivli] *a* vivo, vivaz, fogoso, animado, despabilado, brioso, enérgico, resalado; **to make** — animar (*with drink*), refocilar.
liver ['livə] *n* hígado.
livery ['livəri] *n* librea, uniforme.
livid ['livid] *a* lívido, amoratado, cárdeno, pálido.
living ['liviŋ] *a* viviente, vivo; *n* **to earn one's** — sostenerse; (*eccles*) beneficio; — **together** convivencia; **to purchase a** — beneficiar; — **in** *a* interno.
load [loud] *n* carga; peso; fardo; *vt* cargar, cubrir.
loading ['loudiŋ] *n* carga, cargamento; — **place** cargadero.
loaf [louf] *n* pan; (*small*) bollo; *vi*

bribonear, haraganear, zanganear.
loafer ['loufə] *n* desocupado, holgazán, vago, gandul.
loan [loun] *n* préstamo; (*fin*) (em)préstito; uso; *vt* prestar.
loathe [louð] *vt* detestar, cobrar aversión a, aborrecer, repugnar(se).
loathing ['louðiŋ] *n* disgusto, asco, repugnancia, hastío.
loathsome ['louðsəm] *a* repugnante, aborrecible, asqueroso.
lobby ['lɔbi] *n* pasillo, corredor; pórtico, antecámara.
lobe [loub] *n* lóbulo; (*of ear*) lobo.
lobster ['lɔbstə] *n* langosta.
local ['loukəl] *a* local; del barrio; **— inhabitants** vecindario.
locality [lou'kæliti] *n* localidad.
locate [lou'keit] *vt* colocar, situar; ubicar; dar con.
located [lou'keitid] *a* sito.
location [lou'keiʃən] *n* situación, ubicación.
lock [lɔk] *n* cerradura, cerraja; (*canal*) esclusa; **love—** tirabuzón; (*hair*) trenza, mecha, guedeja; bucle; **under — and key** bajo llave; *vti* cerrar con llave, echar la llave a; **to — up** recoger; encerrar(se).
locket ['lɔkit] *n* medallón, relicario.
lockout ['lɔkaut] *n* cierre (*de fábrica*).
locomotive [,loukə'moutiv] *n* locomotora.
locust ['loukəst] *n* langosta, saltamontes; cigarra.
lodge [lɔdʒ] *n* casa de guarda, pabellón; *vt* alojar, albergar, acomodar; (*complaint*) presentar; *vi* habitar, fijarse, posar.
lodger ['lɔdʒə] *n* huésped, inquilino.
lodging ['lɔdʒiŋ] *n* hospedaje, habitación, vivienda; acomodo; pensión; **— house** casa de huéspedes; posada, pensión.
loftiness ['lɔftinis] *n* altura, elevación; magnificencia; (*pride*) altivez.
lofty ['lɔfti] *a* elevado, alto, excelso, ilustre, encumbrado.
log [lɔg] *n* leño, tronco; (*naut*) **—book** cuaderno de bitácora; **to sleep like a —** dormir como un tronco.
loggerheads ['lɔgəhedz] *ad* **at —** en desacuerdo; **to be at —** andar de puntas.
logic ['lɔdʒik] *n* lógica.
logical ['lɔdʒikəl] *a* lógico.
loin [lɔin] *n* lomo, ijar; (*of beef*) filete, solomillo; **—cloth** taparrabo.
loiter ['lɔitə] *vi* holgazanear, mangonear, hacer tiempo, vagar.
loll [lɔl] *vi* recostarse, apoyarse, tenderse; (*tongue*) colgar, sacar.
London ['lʌndən] *n* Londres; *a* londinense.
Londoner ['lʌndənə] *n* londinense.
lone [loun] *a* solo, solitario.
loneliness ['lounlinis] *n* soledad, aislamiento, hueco.
lonely ['lounli] *a* solitario.
lonesome ['lounsəm] *a* solitario, desierto.
long [lɔŋ] *a* largo, extendido, extenso; lento, tardo, pausado; **in the — run** a la larga, al fin y al cabo; **so —** (*fam*) hasta luego; **— -winded** prolijo; **— -suffering** sufrido; *ad* largo tiempo, largo rato; **as — as** mientras; **before —** en breve, sin tardar (mucho); **—-lived** duradero; *vi* tener nostalgia; **to — for** suspirar por; apetecer; antojarse; **to — to have** codiciar.
longing ['lɔŋiŋ] *n* deseo ardiente, ansia, antojo, anhelo, hambre.
longitude ['lɔŋgitju:d] *n* longitud.
long-standing [,lɔŋ'stændiŋ] *a* establecido.
longways ['lɔŋweiz] *ad* a lo largo.
look [luk] *n* mirada; (*appearance*) aire, aspecto, parecer; (*fam*) facha, pinta, traza; (*of disapproval*) ceño; (*of inspection*) ojeada, vistazo; *vti* mirar; contemplar; aparentar; **to — well** tener buena cara; **to — alive** (*fam*) darse prisa; **to — at** mirar; **to — intently at** mirar de hito en hito; **to — after** cuidar de, requerir; mirar por, atender; **to — down on** dominar; despreciar; **to — for** buscar; **to — on** estimar, considerar; **to — on to** mirar a, dar a; **to — into** examinar, inquirir; **to — out of** asomarse a; **to — over** mirar por encima; revisar, repasar, hojear; **to — like** parecerse a; **— here!** ¡oiga!; **— out!** ¡cuidado!, ¡atención!
looker-on ['lukər'ɔn] *n* mirón.
looking ['lukiŋ] *a* **good- —** guapo; bien parecido, gallardo.
looking glass ['lukiŋglɑ:s] *n* espejo, cristal.
look-out ['luk'aut] *n* (*man*) vigía; (*tower*) vigía, mirador, atalaya; **to keep a sharp —** avizorar; **to be on the —** estar (a la expectativa, a la mira).
loom [lu:m] *n* telar; *vi* mostrarse, aparecer, amenazar.
loop [lu:p] *n* lazo, ojal, lazada; (*road*) vuelta; (*av*) rizo; *vt* asegurar, formar festones, curvas; hacer el rizo.
loophole ['lu:phoul] *n* aspillera; tronera, salida, escapatoria.
loose [lu:s] *a* suelto, flojo, holgado; relajado; **— -fitting** ancho; **— -living** incontinente, relajado; remiso, descuidado; *vt* aflojar, soltar, desatar; **to break —** desatarse, zafarse; estallar; **to work —** aflojarse, desprenderse.
loosen ['lu:sn] *vti* soltar, desprender, deshacerse.
looseness ['lu:snis] *n* relajación, holgura, soltura, flojedad.
loot [lu:t] *n* botín; *vti* saquear, pillar.
lop [lɔp] *vt* descabezar, cortar; (*trees*) podar; **to — off** cercenar, truncar.

loquacious [lou'kweiʃəs] *a* locuaz, hablador.
lord [lɔ:d] *n* señor; lord; **L— Chamberlain** camarero mayor; **L—'s Prayer** padre nuestro; *vi* **to — it over** señorear.
lordship ['lɔ:dʃip] *n* señoría; (*power or estate*) señorío.
lorry ['lɔri] *n* camión, tractor.
lose [lu:z] *vt* extraviar, perder, malograr, desperdiciar; **to — sight of** perder de vista; **to — patience, temper** salirse de sus casillas; **to — self-control** perder los estribos; **to — oneself** (*in thoughts*) abismarse.
loss [lɔs] *n* pérdida; (*article etc*) extravío; disipación; daño; (*reputation*) menoscabo; (*bank*) quiebra; perdición; **profit and —** pérdidas y ganancias; **at a —** perplejo, indeciso; perdiendo.
lost [lɔst] *ad* extraviado; descarriado; malogrado; desperdiciado; inaccesible, ignoto; **to get —** perderse, extraviarse; **to be —** (*in wonder etc*) enajenarse; **— to insensible** a.
lot [lɔt] *n* suerte; (*auction*) lote; porción; (*ground*) solar; **a — of, —s of** la mar de, una gran cantidad de, mucho; muchos; **to cast —s** echar suertes; **it fell to his —** le tocó.
lottery ['lɔtəri] *n* lotería, rifa.
loud [laud] *a* alto, recio; ruidoso, estrepitoso; (*colors*) subido, chillón; (*taste*) chabacano; **—speaker** *n* altavoz.
loudly ['laudli] *ad* en voz alta, reciamente, recio.
loudness ['laudnis] *n* ruido, sonoridad, chabacanería.
Louis ['lu:i] *m* Luis.
Louise [lu:'i:z] *f* Luisa.
lounge [laundʒ] *n* salón; **— suit** traje; *vi* holgazanear; ponerse cómodo, recostarse.
lovable ['lʌvəbl] *a* amable, encantador.
love [lʌv] *n* amor, pasión, devoción, galanteo; **— of** afición a, cariño por; **lady —** querida, novia, dama; **— at first sight** flechazo; **— affair** relaciones amorosas, (*fam*) plan; **for — or money** por las buenas o las malas; **— token** prenda de amor; **to make — to** galantear, requerir (de amores), enamorar, pelar la pava; **to be in —** estar enamorado de, (*madly*) beber los vientos por; *vt* amar, querer; tener afición a, entusiasmarse, deleitarse.
loveliness ['lʌvlinis] *n* amabilidad; belleza, primor, hermosura, pulcritud.
lovely ['lʌvli] *a* primoroso, bello, hermoso; venusto; pulcro; atractivo; **how —!** ¡qué preciosidad!
lover ['lʌvə] *n* amante; enamorado; querido; **— of** aficionado a, amigo de.
lovesick ['lʌvsik] *a* enamorado.
loving ['lʌviŋ] *a* tierno, cariñoso, afectuoso; **—ly** *ad* con amor.
low [lou] *a* bajo; hondo; común, innoble, rastrero; despreciable, ruin; (*spirited*) deprimido, abatido, amilanado; humilde, sumiso; **— spirits** abatimiento; **— type** chulo; **— trick** mala pasada; *ad* bajo, en voz baja, quedo; *n* mugido; *vt* mugir, berrear.
lower ['louə] *a* inferior; **in —ed tones** bajo; **—ed** (*ears*) agachadas; *vt* bajar, rebajar, menguar; deprimir; humillar, abatir; (*sky*) encapotarse.
lowering ['lauəriŋ] *a* sombrío, amenazante; (*sky*) encapotado; *n* depresión; (*of pride*) humillación.
lowing ['louiŋ] *n* mugido; (*calf*) berreo.
lowland ['loulənd] *n* tierra baja.
lowliness ['loulinis] *n* humildad; ruindad.
lowly ['louli] *a* humilde, sumiso, vil, mezquino.
loyal ['lɔiəl] *a* leal, fiel.
loyalty ['lɔiəlti] *n* lealtad, fidelidad.
lucid ['lu:sid] *a* luminoso, claro; lúcido, límpido.
lucidity [lu:'siditi] *n* perspicuidad; lucidez, esplendor.
luck [lʌk] *n* fortuna, azar; suerte; **good —** buena sombra, dicha; **to be in —** tener suerte; **to try one's —** probar (ventura, fortuna).
luckless ['lʌklis] *a* infeliz, infausto, desdichado.
lucky ['lʌki] *a* feliz, dichoso, afortunado.
lucrative ['lu:krətiv] *a* lucrativo, ventajoso.
Lucy ['lu:si] *f* Lucía.
ludicrous ['lu:dikrəs] *a* burlesco, ridículo, cómico, risible.
luggage ['lʌgidʒ] *n* equipaje; **— rack** red, rejilla.
lugubrious [lu:'gu:briəs] *a* fúnebre, lóbrego.
lukewarm ['lu:kwɔ:m] *a* tibio; templado; indiferente.
lull [lʌl] *vt* arrullar, adormecer; calmar, sosegar; **to be —ed** apaciguarse, arrullarse.
lumber ['lʌmbə] *n* tablas; tablones; madera de construcción; (*fig*) **piece of —** trasto; **—yard** depósito de maderas.
luminous ['lu:minəs] *a* luminoso; perspicuo, claro.
lump [lʌmp] *n* bulto, masa; (*swollen*) hinchazón; (*in throat*) nudo; (*sugar*) terrón.
lunatic ['lu:nətik] *a* lunático; loco; *n* loco; **raving —** loco de atar.
lunch [lʌntʃ] *n* almuerzo; (*light*) colación; (*open-air*) merienda; **— basket** fiambrera; *vi* almorzar.
luncheon ['lʌntʃən] *n* almuerzo; *vi* almorzar.
lung [lʌŋ] *n* pulmón; *pl* bofes; **at the top of one's —s** a voz en cuello.
lurch [lə:tʃ] *n* sacudida, vaivén; embarazo; (*naut*) bandazo; **to leave**

in the — dejar en las astas del toro; *vi* tambalearse; (*naut*) guiñar.
lure [ljuə] *n* señuelo, cebo; *vt* tentar, inducir.
lurid ['ljuərid] *a* lívido, espeluznante, hórrido.
lurk [lə:k] *vi* ocultarse, acechar.
luscious ['lʌʃəs] *a* sabroso, delicioso, meloso.
lush [lʌʃ] *a* lozano, jugoso.
lust [lʌst] *n* codicia, lujuria; concupiscencia; *vi* codiciar.
lustful ['lʌstful] *a* lujurioso, voluptuoso, salaz, carnal.
luster ['lʌstə] *n* reflejo, lustre, brillo;esplendor; **take the — off** empañar.
lusty ['lʌsti] *a* robusto, vigoroso, lozano, fornido.
lute [lu:t] *n* laúd; (*ant*) vihuela.
Lutheran ['lu:θərən] *an* luterano.
Luxembourg ['lʌksəmbə:g] *n* Luxemburgo.
luxuriance [lʌg'zjuəriəns] *n* exuberancia, superabundancia, lozanía, demasía.
luxuriant [lʌg'zjuəriənt] *a* exuberante, lozano, ubérrimo; (*foliage*) frondoso.
luxurious [lʌg'zjuəriəs] *a* lujoso; suntuoso; exuberante; (*fam*) de postín; dado al lujo.
luxury ['lʌkʃəri] *n* lujo, fausto; molicie.
lying ['laiiŋ] *a* falso, mentiroso; *n* mentira; **— tale** embuste; **— down, back** tumbado, echado; (*situated*) sit(uad)o.
lyre ['laiə] *n* lira.
lyric ['lirik] *a* lírico; *n* poesía, lírica, cantiga, canción.

M

macaroni [,mækə'rouni] *n* macarrones.
mace [meis] *n* maza, porra; (*spice*) macis.
machination [,mæki'neiʃən] *n* maquinación, conjura(ción).
machine [mə'ʃi:n] *n* máquina, artefacto; aparato; **— gun** ametralladora; **— -made** hecho a máquina.
machinery [mə'ʃi:nəri] *n* mecanismo, maquinaria.
mackerel ['mækrəl] *n* escombro, caballa; **— sky** cielo aborregado.
mackintosh ['mækintɔʃ] *n* impermeable.
mad [mæd] *a* loco, furioso; rabioso; demente, maniático; **quite —** loco rematado; **to go —** enloquecer(se).
madam ['mædəm] *n* señora.
madden ['mædn] *vt* enloquecer.
madhouse ['mædhaus] *n* manicomio, casa de orates.
made [meid] *part* **— up** fabricado, hecho, inventado; (*face*) maquillado; (*story*) ficticio, (*clothes*) confeccionado; **I had it — up** lo hice hacer; **to be — up of** consistir en; integrarse de.
madman ['mædmən] *n* loco, maniático, insensato.
madness ['mædnis] *n* locura, demencia; delirio, furor, furia.
Madonna [mə'dɔnə] *n* la Virgen.
Madrid [mə'drid] **of —** *a* madrileño; matritense.
magazine [,mægə'zi:n] *n* (*store*) almacén; (*gunpowder*) polvorín; (*naut*) santabárbara; (*periodical*) revista.
magic ['mædʒik] *n* magia; **— lantern** sombras chinescas; **by —** por ensalmo; *a* mágico.
magical ['mædʒikəl] *a* mágico, encantador.
magician [mə'dʒiʃən] *n* mago, brujo, nigromante, prestidigitador.
magistrate ['mædʒistrit] *n* magistrado, juez.
magnanimous [mæg'næniməs] *a* magnánimo, generoso.
magnet ['mægnit] *n* imán.
magnetic [mæg'netik] *a* magnético.
magnificence [mæg'nifisns] *n* esplendor, suntuosidad, grandeza.
magnificent [mæg'nifisnt] *a* magnífico, soberbio, real, regio, rumboso.
magnify ['mægnifai] *vt* amplificar, aumentar; magnificar, engrandecer.
magnifying glass ['mægnifaiiŋ,glɑ:s] *n* lente de aumento, lupa.
magnitude ['mægnitju:d] *n* magnitud, grandeza; importancia, extensión.
magpie ['mægpai] *n* urraca, picaza, marica.
mahogany [mə'hɔgəni] *n* caoba.
Mahommedan [mə'hɔmədən] *an* mahometano.
maid [meid] *n* doncella, virgen; (*servant*) muchacha, criada; sirvienta; **— of honor** camarista; **lady's —** camarera; **old —** soltera, solterona.
maiden ['meidn] *n* doncella, virgen; soltera; **— name** apellido de soltera; *a* virginal; primero, inicial.
mail [meil] *n* correo; **—bag** valija; **— coach** coche correo; **— train** (tren) correo; **chain —** cota de malla; **air —** correo aéreo; **—man** cartero; *vt* echar al correo.
maim [meim] *vt* estropear, lisiar, mutilar.
maimed ['meimd] *a* manco, lisiado.
main [mein] *a* principal, primero, mayor, maestro; **— mast** palo mayor; **— road** carretera; **— street** calle mayor.
mainland ['meinlənd] *n* tierra firme.
maintain [mən'tein] *vt* guardar, mantener, conservar; sostener; (*argument*) alegar.
maintenance ['meintinəns] *n* mantenimiento, conservación, sostén; entretenimiento.

maize [meiz] *n* maíz.
majestic [mə'dʒestik] *a* majestuoso, augusto; pomposo.
majesty ['mædʒisti] *n* majestad, soberanía.
major ['meidʒə] *a* mayor, principal; *n* comandante.
Majorca [mə'jɔ:kə] *n* Mallorca.
Majorcan [mə'jɔ:kən] *an* mallorquín.
majority [mə'dʒɔriti] *n* mayoría, mayor edad; mayor parte.
make [meik] *n* (*clothes*) hechura, confección; **— of** (*articles*) marca, (*making*) fábrica, fabricación; *vt* hacer, producir; elaborar; causar; inclinar a, completar; (*speech*) pronunciar; (*copy*) sacar; (*rhymes*) trovar; *vi* **to — believe** fingir, aparentar; **to — clear** patentizar, poner en limpio, dejar establecido; **to — for** dirigirse, encaminarse a; **to — good** subsanar, resarcir; cumplir, salir airoso de; **to — known** comunicar; **to — little of** sacar poco en claro; hacer poco caso de; **to — much of** festejar, apreciar; **to — merry** divertirse, (*at night*) trasnochar; **to — most of** sacar el mayor partido de; **to — off** huir, largarse; **to — off with** llevarse, hurtar, quedarse con; **to — one's way** abrirse paso, salir bien, medrar; **to — out** distinguir, columbrar, vislumbrar, otear; sacar (en limpio, en claro), descifrar; **to — over** traspasar, transferir; **to — up** (*face*) componer, pintar, (*number*) completar, (*loss*) subsanar, (*level*) ajustar, (*mind*) decidirse, (*lies*) fabricar, (*parcel*) empaquetar; **to — it up** componérselas, hacer las paces; **to — up to** congraciarse con.
maker ['meikə] *n* hacedor, creador, artífice.
makeshift ['meikʃift] *n* expediente, recurso, improvisación, substituto.
make-up ['meikʌp] *n* compostura, modo de ser; (*face*) maquillaje.
making ['meikiŋ] *n* creación, forma, composición, trabajo, confección; **the —s of** puntos y collares de.
malady ['mælədi] *n* enfermedad, dolencia.
Malayan [mə'leiən] *an* malayo.
malcontent ['mælkən,tent] *an* descontento, malcontento.
male [meil] *an* macho; masculino; varón.
malevolence [mə'levələns] *n* malevolencia, rencor, inquina.
malice ['mælis] *n* malicia, malignidad, ruindad.
malicious [mə'liʃəs] *a* malicioso, maligno, rencoroso, pícaro.
malign [mə'lain] *a* maligno, dañino; *vt* difamar, calumniar.
malignant [mə'lignənt] *a* malvado, maligno, sañudo, virulento.
Malta ['mɔ:ltə] *n* Malta.
Maltese [mɔ:l'ti:z] *an* maltés.
maltreat [mæl'tri:t] *vt* maltratar.
mammal ['mæməl] *n* mamífero.
man [mæn] *n* hombre; **a real —** muy hombre; **— of the world** hombre de mundo; **to a —** todos a uno; *vt* equipar, tripular.
manacle ['mænəkl] *n pl* esposas; *vt* maniatar.
manage ['mænidʒ] *vt* manejar, conducir, regir; (*house etc*) regentar, administrar; **to — to** lograr; procurar; gestionar; *vi* ingeniarse (para), componérselas; **to — to live** vivir de milagro.
manageable ['mænidʒəbl] *a* manejable, dócil, tratable.
management ['mænidʒmənt] *n* manejo; dirección, administración; gerencia.
manager ['mænidʒə] *n* director, administrador, jefe, gerente.
mandate ['mændeit] *n* mandato, orden.
maneuver [mə'nu:və] *n* maniobra; evolución, manejo; *vti* maniobrar.
mane [mein] *n* crin, guedeja, melena.
manful ['mænful] *a* valiente, viril, esforzado.
mange [meindʒ] *n* sarna, roña.
manger ['meindʒə] *n* pesebre, comedero; **dog in the —** perro del hortelano.
mangle ['mæŋgl] *n* calandria; *vt* mutilar, despedazar, desgarrar; alisar.
mangy ['meindʒi] *a* sarnoso.
manhood ['mænhud] *n* virilidad, hombradía; valentía; edad viril.
mania ['meiniə] *n* manía, obsesión.
maniac ['meiniæk] *n* maníaco.
manifest ['mænifest] *a* manifiesto, patente, notorio; *vt* manifestar, demostrar, patentizar.
manifestation [,mænifes'teiʃən] *n* **public —** demostración; manifestación, alarde.
manifold ['mænifould] *a* numeroso, múltiple; *n* múltiple.
manipulate [mə'nipjuleit] *vt* manipular, manejar.
mankind [mæn'kaind] *n* el género humano, el hombre, los hombres.
manliness ['mænlinis] *n* valentía, fuerza, hombradía, bravura.
manly ['mænli] *a* vigoroso, valiente, hombruno, viril.
mannequin ['manikin] *n* maniquí.
manner ['mænə] *n* manera, método, procedimiento; hábito; género; aire; *pl* modales, trato; **good —s** corrección, buen tono, finura, buena educación; **in a —** en cierto modo, hasta cierto punto.
mannerly ['mænəli] *a* cortés, atento.
manor ['mænə] *n* casa solariega, quinta, solar.
mansion ['mænʃən] *n* mansión, residencia, morada; castillo.

mantelpiece ['mæntlpi:s] *n* cornisa, repisa (de chimenea).
mantle ['mæntl] *n* manto, capa, saya; manguito incandescente; *vti* cubrir.
manual ['mænjuəl] *an* manual.
manufacture [,mænju'fæktʃə] *n* fabricación; confección; (*ie not natural*) preparado; producto; *vt* fabricar, labrar.
manufacturer [,mænju'fæktʃərə] *n* fabricante.
manure [mə'njuə] *n* abono, estiércol; *vt* abonar, estercolar.
manuscript ['mænjuskript] *n* manuscrito, códice.
many ['meni] *a pu* varios, muchos; — **-colored** multicolor, abigarrado; *n* gran número.
map [mæp] *n* mapa, carta, plano.
maple ['meipl] *n* arce, meple.
mar [mɑ:] *vt* echar a perder, desfigurar; frustrar, malear.
marble ['mɑ:bl] *a* marmóreo, jaspeado; *n* mármol.
march [mɑ:tʃ] *n* marzo; marcha; *vti* hacer marchar, marchar; lindar.
mare [mɛə] *n* yegua.
Margaret ['mɑ:grit] *f* Margarita.
margin ['mɑ:dʒin] *n* borde; (*on page*) margen; extremidad; (*com*) reserva, sobrante.
marine [mə'ri:n] *a* marino; *n* soldado de marina; **merchant** — marina mercante.
mariner ['mærinə] *n* marinero.
Marion ['mæriən] *f* Mariana.
marionette [,mæriə'nət] *n* fantocha, títere.
mark [mɑ:k] *n* (*stain etc*) tacha, borrón; (*sign*) señal, indicio; amago; indicación, huella; (*target*) blanco, nivel; marca; (*of boundary etc*) mojón; distinción; (*money*) marco; (*games*) tanto; (*examination*) nota, calificación; (*silversmith*) cuño; **beside the** — incongruente; **to hit the** — atinar, dar en el blanco; **to make one's** — firmar con una cruz; señalarse; *vt* señalar, rotular; observar; marcar; **to — out** trazar; (*examination*) calificar; **to — time** marcar el paso.
Mark [mɑ:k] *m* Marcos.
market ['mɑ:kit] *n* mercado; **to go to** — (*ie shopping*) ir a la plaza; **—place** mercado, plaza; **black** — estraperlo; **black —eer** estraperlista.
marksman ['mɑ:ksmən] *n* (buen) tirador.
marmalade ['mɑ:məleid] *n* conserva de naranja, mermelada.
marquis ['mɑ:kwis] *n* marqués.
marriage ['mæridʒ] *n* (*state*) matrimonio; (*action*) enlace, casamiento; (*poet*) himeneo; (*ceremony*) boda, bendición.
marriageable ['mæridʒəbl] *a* núbil, casadero.
marry ['mæri] *vt* casar; *vi* contraer matrimonio; casarse, enlazarse (con).
Marseilles [mɑ:'seilz] *n* Marsella.
marsh [mɑ:ʃ] *n* pantano, ciénaga, marjal; marisma.
marshal ['mɑ:ʃəl] *n* mariscal; bastonera.
marshy ['mɑ:ʃi] *a* pantanoso, cenagoso; — **tract** marisma.
Martha ['mɑ:θə] *f* Marta.
martial ['mɑ:ʃəl] *a* marcial, bélico; **court** — consejo de guerra.
Martinmas ['mɑ:tinməs] *n* día de San Martín.
martyr ['mɑ:tə] *n* mártir.
martyrdom ['mɑ:tədəm] *n* martirio.
marvel ['mɑ:vəl] *n* maravilla, portento; *vi* maravillarse, asombrarse, pasmarse.
marvelous ['mɑ:viləs] *a* maravilloso, portentoso; estupendo, prodigioso.
Mary ['mɛəri] *f* María.
marzipan [,mɑ:zi'pæn] *n* mazapán.
masculine ['mɑ:skjulin] *a* masculino, varonil.
mask [mɑ:sk] *n* máscara; embozo; (*plays*) carátula; disfraz; capa, color, pretexto; *vt* enmascarar, ocultar, encubrir; disfrazar; *vi* disfrazarse.
masked ['mɑ:skt] *a* en disfraz; — **ball** baile de máscaras.
mason ['meisn] *n* albañil, masón.
masonry ['meisnri] *n* albañilería, mampostería; masonería.
masquerade [,mæskə'reid] *n* mascarada, comparsa; *vi* enmascararse, disfrazarse de.
mass [mæs] *n* misa; **high** — misa (mayor, solemne, cantada); **midnight** — misa del gallo; **to go to** — oír misa; masa, montón, mole, cúmulo; **—es of** miles de, montones de; *vt* juntar(se) en masas.
massacre ['mæsəkə] *n* carnicería, matanza, mortandad; *vi* destrozar.
massage ['mæsɑ:ʒ] *n* masaje; *vt* sobar.
massive ['mæsiv] *a* macizo, sólido; abultado; coposo.
mass meeting ['mæs'mi:tiŋ] *n* mitín popular.
mast [mɑ:st] *n* palo, mástil; **at half** — a media asta.
master ['mɑ:stə] *n* maestro; (*owner*) amo, dueño; (*ship*) capitán, patrón; (*young* —) el señorito; jefe; — **of ceremonies** maestro de ceremonias; **school—** maestro, preceptor; (*debate*) águila; diestro, perito; — **key** llave maestra; **to be — of** dominar, poseer; *vt* dominar, domar, conocer bien, poseer; sobreponerse a.
masterful ['mɑ:stəful] *a* imperioso, arbitrario, dominante.
masterly ['mɑ:stəli] *a* magistral, imperioso.
masterpiece ['mɑ:stəpi:s] *n* obra maestra.
mastery ['mɑ:stəri] *n* (*power*) dominio, poder, predominio; (*skill*)

maestría, destreza; superioridad.
masticate ['mæstikeit] *vt* mascar.
mastiff ['mæstif] *n* mastín, alano.
mat [mæt] *n* estera, felpudo, tapete; *vi* (*hair*) desgreñar, enmarañarse.
match [mætʃ] *n* (*wax*) cerilla, fósforo; matrimonio; (*game*) partida; pareja, competidor; **a good —** buena pareja; *vt* igualar, emparejar, (*colors*) casar, competir; equiparar; corresponder; *vi* hacer juego.
matchless ['mætʃlis] *a* incomparable, sin par.
mate [meit] *n* pareja, cónyuge; compañero, compinche; **school—, class—** compañero de clase, condiscípulo; (*naut*) oficial; *vt* aparear; igualar; casar; (*chess*) dar mate.
material [mə'tiəriəl] *a* material; considerable; *n* material, materia, materiales; (*sewing*) avío (de coser); (*cloth*) género, tela; **raw —** materia prima.
mathematical [ˌmæθi'mætikl] *a* matemático.
mathematics [ˌmæθi'mætiks] *n* matemática(s).
Matilda [mə'tildə] *f* Matilde.
matins ['mætinz] *n* maitines.
matriculation [məˌtrikju'leiʃən] *n* matriculación, matrícula.
matrimony ['mætriməni] *n* matrimonio.
matron ['meitrən] *n* matrona, mujer casada; directora.
Matthew ['mæθju:] *m* Mateo.
matter ['mætə] *n* cuestión; consecuencia; (*med*) pus; materia, substancia, asunto; **it's a — of ...,** se trata de **...; what is the —?** ¿qué pasa?; *vi* importar, convenir; hacer; **it doesn't —** no importa; **it doesn't — a bit** no tiene la menor importancia.
matter-of-fact ['mætərəv'fækt] *a* práctico, sin imaginación.
matting ['mætiŋ] *n* esterado.
mattress ['mætris] *n* colchón.
mature [mə'tjuə] *a* maduro; (*knowledge*) provecto, sentado, juicioso; *vti* madurar; (*bills*) vencer.
maturity [mə'tjuəriti] *n* madurez; sazón.
maul [mɔ:l] *vt* aporrear, maltratar; manosear.
Maurice ['mɔris] *m* Mauricio.
maxim ['mæksim] *n* máxima, apotogema, sentencia; axioma.
maximum ['mæksiməm] *n* máximo.
May [mei] *n* mayo; (*bot*) espino blanco.
maybe ['meibi:] *ad* quizá(s), tal vez.
maypole ['meipoul] *n* cruz de mayo.
mayor [mɛə] *n* alcalde, corregidor.
maze [meiz] *n* laberinto; enredo; perplejidad.
me [mi:] *pn* me; (*after prep*) mí.
meadow ['medou] *n* pradera, prado.
meager ['mi:gə] *a* escaso, deficiente, mezquino; flaco, magro.
meagerness ['mi:gənis] *n* pobreza, escasez; flaqueza.
meal [mi:l] *n* comida; (*light*) refresco, colación; (*flour*) harina.
mean [mi:n] *a* agarrado, tacaño; humilde, basto; ruin, indigno, menguado, despreciable; trivial, mediocre, mezquino; *n* término medio; *pl* (*funds*) recursos, medios, bienes, fondos; medio, recurso, resorte; **by all —** positivamente; no faltaba más; por todos los medios; **by no —** de ninguna manera, de ningún modo; **by — of** por conducto (medio) de; **to live on one's —** vivir de sus rentas; *vt* querer decir, significar; dar a entender; pretender, intentar; hacer; *vi* tener intención.
meanest ['mi:nist] *a* ínfimo.
meander [mi'ændə] *n* meandro; *vi* serpear, serpentear.
meaning ['mi:niŋ] *n* (*words etc*) sentido, significación, significado, conotación; (*purpose*) intención; voluntad, designio; **double —** equívoco.
meanness ['mi:nnis] *n* mezquindad, ruindad; miseria; humildad; infamia; cortedad.
meantime ['mi:n'taim] *ad* entretanto.
meanwhile ['mi:n'wail] *ad* mientras tanto, entretanto.
measles ['mi:zlz] *n* sarampión.
measure ['meʒə] *n* medida; (*wine*) colodra; capacidad, cuantía; (*mus*) compás; **in good —** con creces; **in abundant —** a fanegadas; *vt* medir, tomar medidas, graduar; **to — one's height** caer cuan largo se es.
measurement ['meʒəmənt] *n* medida, medición.
meat [mi:t] *n* vianda, carne; (*cold*) fiambre; (*canned*) conserva; **minced —** picadillo; **— chopper** cortante; **— ball** albóndiga, croqueta.
mechanic [mi'kænik] *n* mecánico, artesano, menestral.
mechanical [mi'kænikl] *a* mecánico.
mechanics [mi'kæniks] *n* mecánica.
mechanism ['mekənizəm] *n* mecanismo.
medal ['medl] *n* medalla, condecoración.
medallion [mi'dæljən] *n* medallón.
meddle ['medl] *vi* curiosear, mezclarse, entremeterse.
meddlesome ['medlsəm] *a* curioso, importuno, oficioso.
mediation [ˌmi:di'eiʃən] *n* tercería, interposición, intercesión.
mediator ['mi:dieitə] *n* tercero, mediador.
medical ['medikəl] *a* médico.
medicine ['medsin] *n* medicina; medicamento; **— man** curandero.
mediocre ['mi:dioukə] *a* mediano, vulgar.
mediocrity [ˌmi:di'ɔkriti] *n* mediocridad, medianía.

meditate ['mediteit] *vi* pensar; meditar; proyectar, tramar; **to — on** contemplar.
meditation [,medi'teiʃən] *n* meditación, contemplación.
Mediterranean [,meditə'reiniən] *an* mediterráneo; **— regions** (*Spain*) levante.
medium ['mi:djəm] *a* mediano, regular; corriente; *n* medio, órgano, manera; intermediario.
medley ['medli] *n* mezcla, mescolanza, potaje, baturrillo, cajón de sastre, fárrago.
meek [mi:k] *a* dulce, manso, dócil.
meekness ['mi:knis] *n* benignidad, mansedumbre, humildad.
meet [mi:t] *vt* encontrar, hallar, chocar, tocar; (*danger*) afrontar; (*debts etc*) satisfacer, honrar, saldar, sufragar; (*person*) conocer; (*arguments etc*) refutar, combatir; **to arrange to —** citar; **to — the eye** saltar a la vista; *vi* juntarse, reunirse, encontrarse, concurrir; (*rivers*) confluir; **to go to —** ir (salir) al encuentro de.
meeting ['mi:tiŋ] *n* (*unexpected*) encuentro; (*many people*) reunión, asamblea; (*arranged*) entrevista, cita; (*rivers etc*) confluencia; (*political*) mitin.
megaphone ['megəfoun] *n* bocina, altavoz, portavoz.
melancholic [,melən'kɔlik] *a* melancólico, fúnebre.
melancholy ['melənkəli] *a* lúgubre, desconsolado, deprimente; *n* melancolía.
mellow ['melou] *a* maduro, sazonado, blando, madurado, dulce, jugoso; *vti* madurar.
mellowness ['melounis] *n* madurez, dulzura, suavidad.
melodious [mi'loudiəs] *a* melodioso, armonioso.
melody ['melədi] *n* melodía, aire; copla.
melon ['melən] *n* melón; **water —** sandía, melón de agua.
melt [melt] *vti* (*ice*) derretir; fundir; deshacer(se), enternecerse, desvanecer.
member ['membə] *n* miembro; (*of guild*) cofrade; (*tertulia*) tertuliano; (*society*) socio, individuo; **voting —** socio vocal; **full —** (*of Academy etc*) socio de número; **— of Parliament** diputado; **—ship fee** cuota.
memoir ['memwɑ:] *n* memoria, informe, reseña.
memorable ['memərəbl] *a* memorable.
memorandum [,memə'rændəm] *n* nota, memorándum, prontuario.
memorial [mi'mɔ:riəl] *a* conmemorativo; *n* memorial.
memorize ['meməraiz] *vt* aprender de memoria.
memory ['meməri] *n* (*faculty*) memoria, retentiva; recuerdo; conmemoración; **from —** de memoria.
menace ['menəs] *n* amenaza; *vt* amenazar.
mend [mend] *vt* arreglar, componer; (*socks etc*) remendar; mejorar; *vi* reformarse, restablecerse; **to — one's ways** reformarse; **he's on the —** está restableciéndose.
mending ['mendiŋ] *n* adobo, composición.
menial ['mi:niəl] *a* doméstico, servil.
mental ['mentl] *a* mental, intelectual.
mention ['menʃən] *n* mención, alusión; *vt* hacer mención, mencionar, mentar, nombrar.
menu ['menju:] *n* lista (de platos), carta, menú.
mercantile ['mə:kəntail] *a* mercantil, mercante.
mercenary ['mə:sinəri] *a* venal, mercenario.
merchandise ['mə:tʃəndaiz] *n* mercancía(s), géneros.
merchant ['mə:tʃənt] *n* comerciante, negociante, mercader.
merciful ['mə:siful] *a* misericordioso, compasivo, piadoso, clemente.
mercifulness ['mə:sifulnis] *n* piedad, misericordia, compasión.
merciless ['mə:silis] *a* despiadado, cruel, inhumano, desalmado, fiero.
mercury ['mə:kjuri] *n* azogue.
mercy ['mə:si] *n* misericordia, gracia; piedad, compasión; **no — shown** (*war*) sin cuartel.
mere [miə] *a* solo, sencillo, mero; *n* charca.
merge [mə:dʒ] *vt* sumergir; fundir; *vi* sumergirse, absorberse, perderse, hundirse.
meridian [mə'ridiən] *n* meridiano.
merino [mə'ri:nou] *n* merino.
merit ['merit] *n* mérito, excelencia; *vt* merecer.
meritorious [,meri'tɔ:riəs] *a* meritorio, benemérito.
mermaid ['mə:meid] *n* sirena (del mar).
merrily ['merili] *ad* alegremente; (*to sail*) **— along** viento en popa.
merriment ['merimənt] *n* alegría, gozo; fiesta, festividad; alborozo.
merriness ['merinis] *n* contento, alegría.
merry ['meri] *a* alegre, divertido, festivo, bullicioso, gozoso, chancero; **—making** alborozo, zambra; holgorio; festividad; fiesta; **to be —** echar una cana al aire; **—maker** bromista.
merry-go-round ['merigou,raund] *n* tiovivo, caballitos.
mesh [meʃ] *n* malla; trampa; (*mech*) engranaje.
mesmerize ['mezməraiz] *vt* magnetizar, hipnotizar.
mess [mes] *n* (*mil*) ración, rancho; lío, confusión; desorden; mama-

rracho, revoltijo; **what a —!** ¡qué birria!, ¡qué lío!; **to get into a —** liarse; **to — up** manosear, ensuciar; desbaratar.
message ['mesidʒ] *n* mensaje, comunicación; recado, aviso, nota.
messenger ['mesindʒə] *n* mensajero, recadero, mandadero.
messiah [mi'saiə] *n* mesías.
metal ['metl] *n* metal; **— fatigue** fatiga del metal.
metallic [mi'tælik] *a* metálico.
metamorphosis [,metə'mɔ:fəsis] *n* metamorfosis.
metaphor ['metəfə] *n* metáfora, tropo.
meteor ['mi:tiə] *n* meteoro.
meter ['mi:tə] *n* **gas —** contador (de gas).
method ['meθəd] *n* método, procedimiento, práctica; orden.
methodical [mi'θɔdikəl] *a* metódico, ordenado.
meticulous [mi'tikjuləs] *a* meticuloso, minucioso.
metropolis [mi'trɔpəlis] *n* metrópoli.
metropolitan [,metrə'pɔlitən] *a* metropolitano.
mettle ['metl] *n* temple, brío, bizarría.
mettlesome ['metlsəm] *a* brioso, fogoso, vivo ardiente.
Mexican ['meksikən] *an* mexicano.
Mexico ['meksikou] *n* México.
Michael ['maikl] *m* Miguel.
Michaelmas ['miklməs] *n* día de San Miguel.
microbe ['maikroub] *n* microbio.
microphone ['maikrəfoun] *n* micrófono.
microscope ['maikroskoup] *n* microscopio.
mid [mid] *a* medio, del medio.
midday ['middei] *n* mediodía.
middle ['midl] *n* punto medio, centro; (*of month*) mediados; **the M— Ages** la edad media; **— -aged** de edad madura; **—class** *n* burguesía; *a* burgués; **M— East** Oriente medio.
middleman ['midlmæn] *n* intermediario; agente de negocios.
midnight ['midnait] *n* medianoche; **— mass** misa del gallo.
midst [midst] *n* punto medio; medio; **in the — of** en medio de, entre.
midsummer ['mid'sʌmə] *n* canícula.
midway ['mid'wei] *n* medio (mitad) del camino; *ad* a medio camino.
midwife ['midwaif] *n* comadrona, matrona, comadre, partera.
mien [mi:n] *n* semblante, porte, empaque, figura.
might [mait] *n* poder, fuerza; **with — and main** a todo trapo, a más no poder; *v aux* es posible, podría (*etc*).
mighty ['maiti] *a* poderoso, vigoroso, soberbio.
migrate [mai'greit] *vi* emigrar, trasplantarse.
migration [mai'greiʃən] *n* migración.
mild [maild] *a* benigno, suave, dulce, manso; tierno; discreto; moderado.
mildness ['maildnis] *n* dulzura, benignidad, templanza; (*treatment*) lenidad.
mile [mail] *n* milla; **— stone** mojón.
mileage ['mailidʒ] *n* kilometraje.
military ['militəri] *a* militar, castrense; guerrero, marcial; *n* tropa(s), militares.
militia [mi'liʃə] *n* milicia.
milk [milk] *n* leche; **—maid** lechera; *vt* ordenar; apurar.
milkman ['milkmən] *n* lechero.
milky ['milki] *a* lechoso, dulce; **M— Way** vía láctea; camino de Santiago.
mill [mil] *n* molino, fábrica; **— dam** esclusa, represa; **— pond** alberca; *vt* moler, desmenuzar.
millennium [mi'leniəm] *n* milenio.
miller ['milə] *n* molinero.
milliner ['milinə] *n* modista de sombreros.
millinery ['milinəri] *n* sombrerería.
million ['miljən] *n* millón.
millionaire [,miljə'nεə] *n* millionario.
mime [maim] *n* mimo, bufón; pantomima; *vt* remedar.
mimic ['mimik] *a* mímico, imitativo; *n* mimo, remedador; *vt* remedar, imitar, contrahacer.
mince [mins] *vt* desmenuzar, hacer picadillo, (re)picar; **he doesn't — words** no se muerde la lengua.
mincing ['minsiŋ] *a* minucioso, afectado, remilgado.
mind [maind] *n* entendimiento, inteligencia, espíritu; (*fam*) magín; mente; parecer; deseo; propensión; afición; **to call to —** recordar; **to go out of one's —** volverse loco; **to give someone a piece of one's —** decirle cuantas son cinco; **to bear in —** tener presente; **to put in — of** recordar; **to change one's —** cambiar de opinión; **presence of —** presencia de ánimo; **to make up one's —** decidirse; *vt* tratar de, cuidar de, atender a, velar, ocuparse; *vi* tener deseo; escuchar; atender, acordarse; **I don't —** me es igual; lo mismo me da; **to — one's p's and q's** poner los puntos sobre los íes.
minded ['maindid] *a* dispuesto, inclinado; **evil-—** perverso.
mindful ['maindful] *a* atento, cuidadoso.
mine [main] *n* mina; *pn* mío; *vti* cavar, socavar, minar, destruir, zapar; (*metals*) extraer.
miner ['mainə] *n* minero.
mineral ['minərəl] *an* mineral.
mingle ['mingl] *vt* mezclar; incorporar(se); confundir; *vi* mezclarse en, entremeterse.
mini ['mini] *a* mini.
miniature ['minətʃə] *n* miniatura.
minimum ['minimәm] *n* mínimo.

mining ['mainiŋ] *n* (*coal etc*) extracción.
minion ['minjən] *n* privado, valido.
minister ['ministə] *n* ministro; **Prime M—** primer ministro; *vi* administrar, servir; (*eccl*) oficiar, celebrar.
ministry ['ministri] *n* ministerio; comisión, sacerdocio, clero.
minor ['mainə] *n* menor (de edad).
minority [mai'nɔriti] *n* menor edad; minoría.
minstrel ['minstrəl] *n* trovador, cantor, juglar.
mint [mint] *n* casa de moneda; (*bot*) menta, ceca, hierbabuena; *vt* (a)cuñar.
minus ['mainəs] *ad* menos.
minute [mai'nju:t] *a* minucioso, nimio, escrupuloso, menudo; **— detail(s)** menudencia(s); ['minit] *n* expediente; minuta; (*time*) minuto; **— book** libro de minutas; *pl* actas.
minuteness [mai'nju:tnis] *n* minuciosidad; primor.
miracle ['mirəkl] *n* milagro; portento, prodigio; (*theat*) auto.
miraculous [mi'rækjuləs] *a* milagroso.
mire ['maiə] *n* fango, lodo.
mirror ['mirə] *n* espejo, cristal; *vt* reflejar.
mirth [mə:θ] *n* alegría, alborozo, jovialidad.
miry ['maiəri] *a* fangoso, cenagoso, lodoso.
misadventure ['misəd'ventʃə] *n* revés, infortunio.
misapprehend ['mis,æpri'hend] *vt* entender mal.
misapprehension ['mis,æpri'henʃən] *n* error, engaño, equivocación, aprensión.
misbehave ['misbi'heiv] *vi* conducirse mal, portarse mal.
misbehavior ['misbi'heivjə] *n* mala conducta, desmán.
miscalculate ['mis'kælkjuleit] *vt* calcular mal.
miscalculation ['mis,kælkju'leiʃən] *n* error, desacierto.
miscarry [mis'kæri] *vi* (*plans*) encallar, salir mal, fracasar; (*birth*) abortar; (*letters*) extraviarse.
miscellaneous [,misi'leiniəs] *a* misceláneo, diverso.
miscellany [mi'seləni] *n* miscelánea, mesa revuelta, cajón de sastre.
mischance [mis'tʃɑ:ns] *n* contratiempo; desventura, fatalidad, percance.
mischief ['mistʃif] *n* daño, mal; diablura, picardía; travesura.
mischievous ['mistʃivəs] *a* dañino; malicioso; pícaro, travieso; chismoso.
misconduct [mis'kɔndəkt] *n* mala conducta; ['miskən'dʌkt] *vti* dirigir mal, portarse mal.
misdeed ['mis'di:d] *n* delito, fechoría.
misdemeanor [,misdi'mi:nə] *n* delito; mala conducta; calaverada.
misdirect ['misdi'rekt] *vt* extraviar, dirigir mal.
miser ['maizə] *n* avaro, tacaño, roñoso.
miserable ['mizərəbl] *a* miserable, desgraciado, calamitoso; menguado, mísero, lastimoso.
miserliness ['maizəlinis] *n* miseria.
miserly ['maizəli] *a* avariento, tacaño, transido, miserable, mezquino, agarrado.
misery ['mizəri] *n* desdicha, infortunio, miseria; desgracia; aflicción, infelicidad.
misfit ['misfit] *n* traje (*etc*) que no cae bien; (*person*) inadaptado.
misfortune [mis'fɔ:tʃən] *n* infortunio, calamidad, desventura, desgracia, contratiempo.
misgiving [mis'giviŋ] *n* sospecha, esquivez; duda; temor, aprehensión, presentimiento, recelo.
misgovernment ['mis'gʌvənmənt] *n* desgobierno, mala administración.
misguidance ['mis'gaidəns] *n* extravío, mala dirección.
misguided ['mis'gaidid] *a* perdido, desatinado.
mishap ['mishæp] *n* accidente, contratiempo, desgracia.
misinterpret ['misin'tə:prit] *vt* interpretar mal.
misjudge ['mis'dʒʌdʒ] *vt* juzgar erradamente, juzgar mal.
mislaid [mis'leid] *a* extraviado.
mislay [mis'lei] *vt* extraviar; (*papers etc*) traspapelar.
mislead [mis'li:d] *vt* extraviar, seducir, despistar, pervertir.
mismanagement ['mis'mænidʒmənt] *n* mala administración, desbarajuste, desconcierto.
misplace ['mis'pleis] *vt* colocar mal, traspapelar.
misprint ['misprint] *n* mala impresión, error de imprenta.
misrepresent ['mis,repri'zent] *vt* desfigurar, desnaturalizar.
miss [mis] *n* extravío, malogro, fracaso; señorita; *vti* (*fire*) fallar, perder; (*aim*) errar; echar de menos, faltar (a); (*occasion*) malograr; **to — out** omitir, pasar por alto.
missal ['misəl] *n* misal.
misshapen ['mis'ʃeipən] *a* deforme, disforme, contrahecho.
missile ['misail] *n* proyectil.
missing ['misiŋ] *a* que falta, perdido, ausente, extraviado; **to be —** faltar, no constar.
mission ['miʃən] *n* misión.
missionary ['miʃnəri] *n* misionero.
missive ['misiv] *n* carta, misiva.
mist [mist] *n* niebla, neblina; vapor, vaho.
mistake [mis'teik] *n* equivocación, error; **to make a —** equivocarse, confundirse.

mistaken [mis'teikən] *a* erróneo, errado; **to be —** equivocarse, confundirse.
mister ['mistə] *n* señor.
mistletoe ['misltou] *n* muérdago.
mistress ['mistris] *n* (*address*) dueña, señora; querida, concubina; (*school*) maestra, profesora.
mistrust ['mis'trʌst] *n* desconfianza; esquivez, recelo; *vt* desconfiar de, recelar.
mistrustful ['mis'trʌstful] *a* desconfiado, sospechoso; escamado.
misty ['misti] *a* nebuloso, brumoso.
misunderstand ['misʌndə'stænd] *vt* entender mal; *vi* equivocarse.
misunderstanding ['misʌndə'stændiŋ] *n* error, engaño, mala interpretación, equivocación; desavenencia.
misuse ['mis'ju:s] *n* abuso; ['mis'ju:z] *vt* abusar de, maltratar.
mite [mait] *n* óbolo; triza, blanca, pizca.
mitigate ['mitigeit] *vt* mitigar, ablandar, moderar, suavizar.
mitigation [,miti'geiʃən] *n* mitigación, alivio.
miter ['maitə] *n* mitra.
mitten ['mitn] *n* mitón.
mix [miks] *vt* mezclar; (*salad*) aderezar; confundir; combinar; *vi* inmiscuirse, meterse, entremeterse.
mixed [mikst] *a* mixto, mezclado; **to get — up in** inmiscuirse en; liarse.
mixture ['mikstʃə] *n* mezcla; mezcolanza; (*heterogeneous*) conglomeración.
mix-up ['miks'ʌp] *n* confusión.
moan [moun] *n* gemido, lamento, queja; *vi* gemir, quejarse, lamentarse; *vt* lamentar, deplorar.
moat [mout] *n* foso, fonsado.
mob [mɔb] *n* populacho, turba; canalla, chusma; *vt* atropellar, promover alborotos.
mobile ['moubail] *a* móvil; movedizo, inestable.
mobility [mou'biliti] *n* movilidad.
mobilization [,moubilai'zeiʃən] *n* movilización.
mobilize ['moubilaiz] *vt* movilizar.
mock [mɔk] *a* imitado, falso, postizo; *n* burla; *vt* (*at*) mofar(se de), escarnecer, ridiculizar, burlar, remedar; señalar con el dedo; burlarse de, reírse de.
mockery ['mɔkəri] *n* burla, chifleta, mofa; **hollow —** simulacro; **subject of —** ludibrio; (*representation of*) remedo.
model ['mɔdl] *n* modelo; parangón, tipo, prototipo; (*block*) horma; (*figure*) figurín; **— of perfection** dechado; *vt* modelar, formar, bosquejar.
moderate ['mɔdərit] *a* moderado; (*price*) módico; arreglado, comedido, regular, suave; ['mɔdəreit] *vti* moderar(se), entibiar, morigerar, templar, reprimir, serenarse.
moderation [,mɔdə'reiʃən] *n* moderación, mesura; frugalidad.
modern ['mɔdən] *a* moderno, reciente, actual; (*languages*) vivas.
modernize ['mɔdənaiz] *vt* modernizar.
modest ['mɔdist] *a* (*moral*) modesto, recatado, pudoroso, honesto; moderado, decente, regular.
modesty ['mɔdisti] *n* modestia, pudor, compostura, discreción, humildad.
modify ['mɔdifai] *vt* modificar, templar, moderar; circuncidar.
modulate ['mɔdjuleit] *vt* modular; (*voice*) entonar.
Mohammedan [mou'hæmidən] *an* mahometano; (*subject to Christian rule, Spain*) morisco.
moist [mɔist] *a* húmedo, mojado.
moisten ['mɔisn] *vt* humedecer, mojar.
moistness ['mɔistnis] *n* humedad.
moisture ['mɔistʃə] *n* humedad.
mold [mould] *n* molde, matriz; forma, horma; (*earth*) tierra vegetal; (*rotting*) moho, verdín, mancha de orín.
molder ['mouldə] *vi* reducirse a polvo, desmoronarse; consumirse.
molding ['mouldiŋ] *n* moldura; **the art of —** la plástica, artesanía.
moldy ['mouldi] *a* mohoso, enmohecido.
mole [moul] *n* (*animal*) topo; (*on skin*) lunar, mancha; (*harbor*) muelle, rompeolas, malecón.
molest [mə'lest] *vt* molestar, vejar, estorbar; incomodar, acosar, perseguir.
mollify ['mɔlifai] *vt* ablandar, suavizar.
molten ['moultən] *a* fundido, derretido.
moment ['moumənt] *n* momento, rato, ocasión; **of great —** de gran importancia.
momentarily ['mouməntərili] *ad* momentáneamente.
momentary ['mouməntəri] *a* momentáneo.
momentous [mou'mentəs] *a* trascendente, grave.
momentum [mou'mentəm] *n* impulsión, momento, ímpetu.
monarch ['mɔnək] *n* monarca, rey.
monarchist ['mɔnəkist] *a* realista, monárquico; *n* monárquico.
monarchy ['mɔnəki] *n* monarquía.
monastery ['mɔnəstəri] *n* monasterio.
monastic [mə'næstik] *a* monástico, monacal.
Monday ['mʌndi] *n* lunes.
money ['mʌni] *n* dinero, plata; (*coin*) moneda; fondos; **—box** hucha, alcancía; **— lender** prestamista; **— order** giro.
mongrel ['mʌŋgrəl] *an* mestizo, cruzado.
monk [mʌŋk] *n* monje, religioso.

monkey ['mʌŋki] *n* mono, mico.
monkish ['mʌŋkiʃ] *a* monacal, monástico.
monogram ['mɔnəgræm] *n* monograma.
monologue ['mɔnəlɔg] *n* monólogo, soliloquio.
monopolize [mə'nɔpəlaiz] *vt* monopolizar, acaparar, abarcar.
monopoly [mə'nɔpəli] *n* monopolio, exclusiva.
monosyllable ['mɔnə,siləbl] *n* monosílabo.
monotonous [mə'nɔtnəs] *a* monótono.
monotony [mə'nɔtni] *n* monotonía; (*of voice*) sonsonete.
monster ['mɔnstə] *n* monstruo, aborto, prodigio; **foul** — vestigio.
monstrosity [mɔns'trɔsiti] *n* monstruosidad.
monstrous ['mɔnstrəs] *a* monstruoso; prodigioso; horrendo, disforme; inaguantable; — **thing** enormidad.
month [mʌnθ] *n* mes.
monthly ['mʌnθli] *a ad* mensual(mente).
monument ['mɔnjumənt] *n* monumento; recuerdo.
monumental [,mɔnju'mentl] *a* monumental.
mood [mu:d] *n* modo; estado de ánimo, humor; genio; **(not) to be in the** — (no) tener ganas.
moodiness ['mu:dinis] *n* mal humor, capricho, cavilación.
moody ['mu:di] *a* triste, caprichoso, malhumorado, taciturno.
moon [mu:n] *n* luna; **full** — plenilunio.
moonlight ['mu:nlait] *n* luz de la luna.
moor [muə] *n* páramo, paramera, marjal; (*pers*) moro; *vti* anclar, amarrar.
Moorish ['muəriʃ] *a* moro, moruno.
moorland ['muələnd] *n* páramo, paramera; **waste** — breñas, breñal.
mop [mɔp] *n* estropajo; *vti* lavar, limpiar, fregar; (*mil*) **to** — **up** liquidar.
mope [moup] *vi* estar cabizbajo.
moral ['mɔrəl] *a* moral, virtuoso; *n* moral; (*of story*) moraleja; moralidad; *pl* costumbres, honestidad.
moralist ['mɔrəlist] *n* moralista.
morality [mə'ræliti] *n* moralidad.
moralize ['mɔrəlaiz] *vi* moralizar.
morass [mə'ræs] *n* ciénaga, aguazal, marisma.
morbid ['mɔ:bid] *a* mórbido, malsano, enfermizo.
morbidness ['mɔ:bidnis] *n* estado (mórbido, morboso).
mordant ['mɔ:dənt] *a* mordaz, cáustico, acre.
more [mɔ:] *ad* más; *a* más; — **or less** tal cual.
moreover [mɔ:'rouvə] *ad* además, por otra parte, sobre (que).
morning ['mɔ:niŋ] *n* mañana; **early** — madrugada; *a* (*early*) matutino; — **coat** levita.
Moroccan [mə'rɔkən] *an* marroquín.
Morocco [mə'rɔkou] *n* Marruecos.
morose [mə'rous] *a* malhumorado, triste, arisco.
moroseness [mə'rousnis] *n* aspereza de genio, acrimonia.
morphia ['mɔ:fiə] *n* morfina.
morsel ['mɔ:səl] *n* bocado; pedazo; presa; **dainty** — bocado de rey.
mortal ['mɔ:tl] *an* mortal; — **man** humanidad.
mortality [mɔ:'tæliti] *n* mortalidad; (*slaughter*) mortandad.
mortar ['mɔ:tə] *n* mezcla, argamasa; (*cannon*) mortero; (*apothecary's*) almirez, pilón.
mortgage ['mɔ:gidʒ] *n* hipoteca; *vt* hipotecar.
mortify ['mɔ:tifai] *vt* mortificar; abochornar; (*flesh*) macerar, castigar; domar; *vi* gangrenarse; humillar.
mortuary ['mɔ:tjuəri] *a* mortuorio; *n* osario, cementerio.
mosaic [mə'zeiik] *an* mosaico.
Moscow ['mɔskou] *n* Moscú.
mosque [mɔsk] *n* mezquita.
mosquito [məs'ki:tou] *n* mosquito, cínife; — **net** mosquitero.
moss [mɔs] *n* musgo, moho.
most [moust] *a ad* lo más, la mayor parte, muy, sumamente; *n* la mayor parte; la mayoría de; **at** — a lo sumo; **to make the** — **of** sacar todo el partido posible de.
mostly ['moustli] *ad* más frecuentemente, en su mayor parte, mayormente.
motel [mou'tel] *n* motel.
moth [mɔθ] *n* polilla, mariposa nocturna.
moth-eaten ['mɔθ,i:tn] *a* apolillado; **to get** — apolillarse.
mother ['mʌðə] *a* materno, nativo; *n* madre; — **-in-law** suegra, madre política; — **Superior** Madre Superiora, prelada; **step**— madrasta.
motherhood ['mʌðəhud] *n* maternidad.
motherly ['mʌðəli] *a* materno.
mother-of-pearl ['mʌðərəv'pə:l] *n* madreperla.
mother tongue ['mʌðə'tʌŋ] *n* lengua materna.
motif [mou'ti:f] *n* motivo, tema.
motion ['mouʃən] *n* movimiento, moción; ademán; **in** — en marcha; *vi* hacer señas.
motionless ['mouʃənlis] *a* inmóvil, sin mover.
motive ['moutiv] *a* motor; — **power** fuerza motriz; *n* motivo; principio; razón; causa; margen; móvil; pie.
motor ['moutə] *n* motor; — **car** automóvil; —**cycle** motocicleta; —**way** autopista.
mottle ['mɔtl] *vt* motear; **mottled** *a* veteado, jaspeado.

motto ['mɔtou] *n* divisa, lema, epígrafe.
mound [maund] *n* montículo, terrón, terraplén; baluarte.
mount [maunt] *n* monte, caballería, cabalgadura, montura; *vt* montar; armar; (*jewels*) engastar; (*horse*) subir a; elevarse; *vi* subir; ascender a.
mountain ['mauntin] *n* montaña; **— range** cordillera, sierra; **—bred** montañés; **—goat** cabra montès; **— lion** puma.
mountaineer [,maunti'niə] *n* montañés; alpinista.
mountainous ['mauntinəs] *a* montañoso.
mounting ['mauntiŋ] *n* subida; (*picture*) montaje; (*jewels*) engaste.
mourn [mɔ:n] *vt* deplorar, lamentar, llorar; *vi* llorar, afligirse, estar de luto.
mournful ['mɔ:nful] *a* triste, lúgubre, lastimero.
mournfulness ['mɔ:nfulnis] *n* pesar, desconsuelo, duelo, aflicción.
mourning ['mɔ:niŋ] *n* lamentación; duelo, luto; **deep —** luto rigoroso; **to be in —** estar de luto.
mouse [maus] *n* ratón, ratoncito.
moustache [məs'tɑ:ʃ] *n* mostacho, bigote; **heavily —ed** bigotudo.
mouth [mauθ] *n* boca; (*snout*) hocico; entrada, abertura; (*face*) mueca; (*river*) embocadura; **down in the —** deprimido, alicaído; **to make one's — water** hacerse agua la boca; **—wash** enjuagadientes; **by word of —** de palabra.
mouthful ['mauθful] *n* bocado; (*liquid*) bocanada, trago.
mouthpiece ['mauθpi:s] *n* portavoz; (*mus*) boquilla.
movable ['mu:vəbl] *a* movible, móvil; *n pl* mobiliario.
move [mu:v] *n* movimiento; **bold —** temeridad; (*games*) juego, jugada; **on the —** en marcha; *vi* moverse; marchar(se); trasladarse, obrar; *vt* mover, agitar; (*house*) mudar de; (*debate*) presentar; (*emotions*) agitar, excitar, inclinar, conmover, enternecer; **to — along** correr; **to — away** alejarse, quitar; **to — on** (hacer) circular; **to — (a)round** dar vueltas, rodar.
movement ['mu:vmənt] *n* movimiento, meneo; (*mil*) maniobra; juego.
movies ['mu:viz] *n pl* cine; películas.
moving ['mu:viŋ] *a* commovedor, emocionante; patético; (*staircase etc*) movedizo; *n* movimiento; motivo; (*house*) mudanza.
mow [mou] *vt* segar, guadañar.
mower ['mouə] *n* segadora.
much [mʌtʃ] *a ad* mucho, abundante; **as —** tanto; **as — as** tanto como; **so — the better** tanto mejor; **to make — of** festejar.
muck [mʌk] *n* estiércol; porqueríai inmundicia, suciedad; porquería.
mud [mʌd] *n* lodo, barro, fango; (*filthy*) légamo; **to stick in the —** atollarse.
muddle ['mʌdl] *vt* enturbiar, confundir, entontecer; *vi* estar atontado.
muddy ['mʌdi] *a* lodoso, barroso; fangoso, turbio, turbulento.
mudguard ['mʌdgɑ:d] *n* alero, guardabarros.
muezzin [mu:'ezin] *n* almuecín.
muff [mʌf] *n* manguito, cubierta.
muffle ['mʌfl] *vt* envolver, embozar; (*sound*) apagar; **—d** *a* embozado; (*noise*) sordo.
muffler ['mʌflə] *n* bufanda, tapaboca, embozo; silenciador.
mug [mʌg] *n* vaso, pichel.
mulatto [mju'lætou] *n* cuarterón, mulato.
mulberry ['mʌlbəri] *n* mora; **—tree** morera.
mule [mju:l] *n* mula; **pack —** acémila.
muleteer [,mju:li'tiə] *n* arriero, muletero.
multiple ['mʌltipl] *a* múltiple; *n* múltiplo.
multiplication [,mʌltipli'keiʃən] *n* multiplicación.
multiplicity [,mʌlti'plisiti] *n* multiplicidad.
multiply ['mʌltiplai] *vt* multiplicar; *vi* multiplicarse.
multiracial [,mʌlti'reiʃəl] *a* multiracial.
multitude ['mʌlti'tju:d] *n* multitud, sinnúmero, muchedumbre; chusma.
mumble ['mʌmbl] *vti* refunfuñar, rezongar, balbucear, mascullar.
mummy ['mʌmi] *n* momia; (*fam*) mamá.
munch [mʌntʃ] *vti* mascar a dos carrillos.
mundane ['mʌndein] *a* del mundo, mundano.
municipality [mju:,nisi'pæliti] *n* municipalidad, municipio.
munificent [mju:'nifisnt] *a* liberal, munífico, generoso.
munition [mju:'niʃən] *n* municiones, pertrechos.
murder ['mə:də] *n* asesinato; homicidio; *vt* asesinar, matar.
murdered ['mə:dəd] *a* **— person** interfecto.
murderer ['mə:dərə] *n* asesino, matador, homicida.
murderous ['mə:dərəs] *a* homicida, cruel, bárbaro.
murky ['mə:ki] *a* sombrío, obscuro, tenebroso, lóbrego.
murmur ['mə:mə] *n* rumor, murmullo; susurro; (*criticism*) murmuración; *vti* murmurar, susurrar; quejarse de.
muscle ['mʌsl] *n* músculo.

Muscovite ['mʌskəvait] *an* moscovita.
muscular ['mʌskjulə] *a* muscular, musculoso, fornido, membrudo.
muse [mju:z] *n* musa; *vi* meditar, musitar; cavilar; distraerse.
museum [mju'ziəm] *n* museo.
mushroom ['mʌʃrum] *n* seta, hongo.
music ['mju:zik] *n* música; melodía; **— stand** atril; **— stool** taburete; **not to face the —** escurrir el bulto; **to face the —** pagar el pato.
musical ['mju:zikəl] *a* musical, sonoro, armonioso; **— comedy** zarzuela.
musician [mju:'ziʃən] *n* músico.
musing ['mju:ziŋ] *a* pensativo, meditabundo, caviloso.
musket ['mʌskit] *n* fusil, mosquete.
musketeer [.mʌski'tiə] *n* mosquetero.
musketry ['mʌskitri] *n* mosquetería.
muslin ['mʌzlin] *n* muselina, percal.
Mussulman ['mʌslmən] *an* musulmán.
must [mʌst] *vi* deber necesitar.
mustard ['mʌstəd] *n* mostaza.
muster ['mʌstə] *n* revista, reunión, lista; *vi* pasar revista, mostrar, exhibir; reunir.
mustiness ['mʌstinis] *n* humedad, moho.
musty ['mʌsti] *a* mohoso; rancio; mustio.
mute [mju:t] *a* mudo, callado, silencioso; *n* (*mus*) sordina.
muted ['mju:tid] *a* sordo, apagado.
mutilate ['mju:tileit] *vt* mutilar, estropear, truncar, tronchar.
mutilation [.mju:ti'leiʃən] *n* mutilación.
mutineer [.mju:ti'niə] *n* rebelde, amotinado.
mutinous ['mju:tinəs] *a* sedicioso, turbulento.
mutiny ['mju:tini] *n* motín, insurrección; *vi* amotinarse; alzarse.
mutter ['mʌtə] *n* murmullo; gruñido; *vti* murmurar, gruñir, refunfuñar, rezongar, decir entre dientes.
mutton ['mʌtn] *n* carne de (carnero, cordero); **to sell — as lamb** dar gato por liebre.
mutual ['mju:tjuəl] *a* mutuo, recíproco.
muzzle ['mʌzl] *n* (*gag*) bozal, mordaza; (*snout*) hocico, morro; (*gun*) boca; *vt* embozalar, amordazar.
my [mai] *poss* mi, mis.
myopia [mai'oupiə] *n* miopia.
myriad ['miriəd] *n* miríada.
myrtle ['mə:tl] *n* mirto, arrayán.
myself [mai'self] *pn* yo mismo.
mysterious [mis'tiəriəs] *a* misterioso.
mystery ['mistəri] *n* misterio, arcano; **— play** misterio, auto religioso.
mystic ['mistik] *a n* místico.
mysticism ['mistisizəm] *n* misticismo.
mystify ['mistifai] *vt* mistificar, confundir, desconcertar.
myth [miθ] *n* mito, fábula, ficción.
mythological [.miθə'lɔdʒikəl] *a* mitológico.
mythology [mi'θɔlədʒi] *n* mitología.

N

nag [næg] *n* rocín; *vt* regañar, hostigar.
nail [neil] *n* clavo; (*finger*) uña; **wire —** punta de París; **to hit the — on the head** dar en el clavo; **—file** lima para las uñas; *vt* clavar. clavetear; **to — down** sujetar con clavos.
naïve [nɑ:'i:v] *a* cándido, ingenuo.
naïveté [nɑ:'ivtei] *n* candidez, ingenuidad.
naked ['neikid] *a* desnudo, en cueros, en pelota; descubierto; (*land*) pelado; simple; **— eye** simple vista.
nakedness ['neikidnis] *n* desnudez.
name [neim] *n* nombre; (*Christian*) nombre de pila; (*good or bad*) prestigio, reputación, fama; (*of firm*) razón social; denominación; **to give a bad — to** tildar; **in the — of** en nombre de; **to call —s** injuriar, poner motes a; **what is your — ?** ¿cómo se llama vd?; *vt* nombrar, apellidar, llamar, designar; indicar; señalar; (*fix*) fijar.
nameless ['neimlis] *a* sin nombre; innominado; desconocido, anónimo.
namely ['neimli] *ad* a saber, esto es, señaladamente.
namesake ['neimseik] *n* homónimo, tocayo.
nap [næp] *n* siesta, sueño ligero; **to have a —** echar una siesta, descabezar el sueño; (*of cloth*) borra, lanilla; vello; **to catch napping** coger desapercibido.
nape [neip] *n* nuca, cogote.
napkin ['næpkin] *n* (*table*) servilleta.
narrate [næ'reit] *vt* contar, narrar, referir, relatar.
narration [næ'reiʃən] *n* narración, historia, relato.
narrative ['nærətiv] *a* narrativo; *n* narrativa, cuento, relación, relato.
narrow ['nærou] *a* estrecho, angosto, escaso; apretado; (*mean*) tacaño, mezquino; **—minded** intolerante, apocado, mojigato; **— gauge** vía estrecha; *vti* estrechar, limitar; encogerse.
narrowness ['nærounis] *n* estrechez, angostura; pobreza; intolerancia.
nastiness ['nɑ:stinis] *n* suciedad, obscenidad, inmundicia, porquería.
nasty ['nɑ:sti] *a* sucio, asqueroso, indecente, desagradable, malintencionado; sórdido; (*beast etc*) *n* zaino.
nation ['neiʃən] *n* nación, pueblo, país.

national ['næʃənl] *a* nacional.
nationality [ˌnæʃə'næliti] *n* nacionalidad.
nationalization [ˌnæʃənlai'zeiʃən] *n* nacionalización.
native ['neitiv] *a* natural, nativo, oriundo (de), originario (de); habitante (de); natal; *n* indígena, natural.
nativity [nə'tiviti] *n* natividad; **— scene** belén, nacimiento.
natural ['nætʃrəl] *a* natural, nato, sencillo.
naturalist ['nætʃrəlist] *n* naturalista.
naturalize ['nætʃrəlaiz] *vt* naturalizar.
naturally ['nætʃrəli] *ad* naturalmente, desde luego.
naturalness ['nætʃrəlnis] *n* naturalidad.
nature ['neitʃə] *n* naturaleza, índole, constitución; condiciones; natural, temperamento; género, laya; (*drawn*) **from —** del natural; **good natured** afable, bueno, bondadoso, llano.
naught [nɔːt] *n* nada, cero; **to come to —** malograr, naufragar, fracasar.
naughty ['nɔːti] *a* malo, travieso, perverso, pícaro.
nausea ['nɔːziə] *n* náusea, mareo, asco.
nautical ['nɔːtikəl] *a* náutico.
naval ['neivəl] *a* naval.
Navarrese [nævə'riːz] *an* navarro.
navigable ['nævigəbl] *a* navegable.
navigate ['nævigeit] *vti* navegar.
navigation [ˌnævi'geiʃən] *n* navegación.
navigator ['nævigeitə] *n* navegante.
navy [neivi] *n* armada, flota; **— blue** azul marino.
near [niə] *a* cercano, próximo; inmediato, vecino; estrecho; *ad* cerca; casi; **to be —** (*age*) frisar en; **on the — side** citerior; **— by** al lado, a mano; **N— East** Próximo Oriente; *vti* acercar, acercarse.
nearly ['niəli] *ad* aproximadamente, casi, poco más o menos, por poco; íntimamente.
nearness ['niənis] *n* cercanía, proximidad.
neat [niːt] *a* neto, limpio, hermoso, aseado, cuidadoso, repulido; (*clever*) mañoso, hábil, diestro; puro.
neatness ['niːtnis] *n* limpieza, pulcritud, aseo, orden.
necessaries ['nesisəriz] *n pl* utensilios, materias primas, lo esencial.
necessary ['nesisəri] *a* necesario, preciso, esencial, reglamentario, indispensable.
necessitate [ni'sesiteit] *vt* necesitar, ser necesario, requerir.
necessity [ni'sesiti] *n* necesidad, precisión; exigencia; indigencia.
neck [nek] *n* cuello, pescuezo; (*throat*) garganta; (*bottle*) gollete; (*of land*) lengua; **low —** escote; **stiff —** tortícolis.
necklace ['neklis] *n* collar.
necktie ['nek'tai] *n* corbata.
need [niːd] *n* necesidad; penuria; falta; **bodily —s** menesteres; *vt* necesitar, requerir, tener necesidad de, ser necesario, exigir; carecer de; **I — it** me falta, me hace falta; **in —** necesitado; **in — of** falto de.
needful ['niːdful] *a* necesario, preciso, indispensable.
needle ['niːdl] *n* aguja; (*compass*) brújula; **to be on pins and —s** estar en brasas; *vt* incitar, fastidiar, enojar.
needless ['niːdlis] *a* inútil, superfluo.
needlewoman ['niːdlˌwumən] *n* costurera.
needy ['niːdi] *a* necesitado, pobre, indigente.
negative ['negətiv] *n* negativa; *a* negativo; *vt* negar, rechazar, desaprobar.
neglect [ni'glekt] *n* descuido, negligencia; abandono, desaliño; **to fall into —** caer en desuso; *vt* descuidar, dejar de, desatender.
neglectful [ni'glektful] *a* descuidado, negligente.
negligence ['neglidʒəns] *n* descuido, omisión; incuria; dejadez; desaliño.
negligible ['neglidʒəbl] *a* tenue, poquísimo, desdeñable.
negotiate [ni'gouʃieit] *vt* negociar, agenciar.
negotiation [niˌgouʃi'eiʃən] *n* negociación, negocio, gestión.
Negro ['niːgrou] *an* negro.
neigh [nei] *n* relincho; *vi* relinchar.
neighbor ['neibə] *n* (con)vecino, prójimo; matrona.
neighborhood ['neibəhud] *n* vecindad, alrededores, cercanía; **in the —** en los contornos.
neighboring ['neibəriŋ] *a* limítrofe, (con)vecino, rayano, próximo.
neighing ['neiiŋ] *n* relincho.
neither ['naiðə] *cj* ni ... ni; *pn* ni uno ni otro; tampoco.
nephew ['nevjuː] *n* sobrino.
nerve [nəːv] *n* (*med*) nervio; vigor, valor, fortaleza; (*cheek*) descaro; *pl* nerviosidad, ataque de nervios.
nervous ['nəːvəs] *a* temeroso, miedoso, tímido; **—system** sistema nervioso.
nervousness ['nəːvəsnis] *n* nervosidad, nerviosidad, agitación, perturbación.
nest [nest] *n* nido; **— of tables** juego de mesas; *vti* anidar, alojar(se).
nestle ['nesl] *vi* anidarse, apiñarse, acurrucarse.
net [net] *n* red; malla; tul; (*wide-meshed*) manga; **drag —** poliche; (*for tuna*) almadraba; *a* neto, puro, sin descuento; líquido; **— weight** peso neto; *vt* enredar; producir una ganancia neta.
Netherlands ['neðələndz] *n* Holanda, los Países Bajos.

nettle ['netl] *n* ortiga; *vt* picar.
network ['netwə:k] *n* malla; (*roads etc*) red.
neutral ['nju:trəl] *a* neutro, neutral, indiferente.
never ['nevə] *ad* nunca, jamás; en la vida; — **again** nunca jamás; — **failing** inagotable.
nevertheless [ˌnevəðə'les] *cj* no obstante, sin embargo, con todo (eso); todavía.
new [nju:] *a* nuevo; distinto; **brand—** nuevecito, flamante, recién.
New York ['nju:'jɔ:k] *n* Nueva York.
New Zealand [nju:'zi:lənd] *n* Nueva Zelanda.
newborn ['nju:bɔ:n] *a* recién nacido.
newcomer ['nju:'kʌmə] *n* recién llegado; forastero; novato; advenedizo.
newly ['nju:li] *ad* de nuevo, nuevamente, recientemente; — **elected, arrived** *etc* novel.
newness ['nju:nis] *n* novedad.
news [nju:z] *n* noticia(s); novedad; — **film, —reel** (película de) actualidades, noticiero; **to spread** — divulgar la noticia; dar un cuarto al pregonero; **piece of** — noticia.
newspaper ['nju:sˌpeipə] *n* periódico, diario.
newsstand ['nju:zstænd] *n* kiosco.
next [nekst] *a* próximo, siguiente, que sigue, inmediato; *ad* lugeo, en seguida, después; — **door** contiguo, de al lado; — **day** el día siguiente; — **to** junto a, al lado de.
nib [nib] *n* punto, tajo.
nibble ['nibl] *vt* mordiscar, roer, rozar, picar; *n* mordisco, roedura.
nice [nais] *a* agradable, delicado, primoroso; simpático; minucioso; fino, sutil, escrupuloso; — **looking** guapo.
Nice [ni:s] *n* Niza.
nicety ['naisiti] *n* esmero; sutileza, atildamiento, delicadeza; **to a** — con la mayor precisión.
niche [nitʃ] *n* nicho.
Nicholas ['nikələs] *m* Nicolás.
nickel ['nikl] *n* níquel; moneda de cinco centavos.
nickname ['nikneim] *n* apodo, mote, sobrenombre; *vt* motejar.
niece [ni:s] *n* sobrina.
niggardliness ['nigədlinis] *n* parsimonia, tacañería.
niggardly ['nigədli] *a* mezquino, cicatero, miserable.
night [nait] *a* nocturno; — **cap** gorro de dormir; *n* noche; (*of ignorance*) tinieblas; **at, by** — de noche; **last** — anoche; **to—** esta noche; **sleepless** — noche toledana; — **bird** trasnochador; **to be a —bird** (*fam*) correrla; **—dress** camisón.
nightfall ['naitfɔ:l] *n* anochecer; **at** — al anochecer.
nightingale ['naitiŋgeil] *n* ruiseñor, filomela.
nightly ['naitli] *ad* por la(s) noche(s), cada noche.
nightmare ['naitmɛə] *n* pesadilla.
Nile [nail] *n* el Nilo.
nimble ['nimbl] *a* ágil, activo, pronto, veloz, ligero; — **witted** vivo, despierto.
nimbleness ['nimblnis] *n* agilidad, ligereza, expedición, destreza.
nine [nain] *an* nueve.
nineteen ['nain'ti:n] *an* diez y nueve, diecinueve.
ninety ['nainti] *an* noventa.
ninth [nainθ] *a* nono, noveno.
nip [nip] *n* pellizco; rasguño; *vt* morder, pellizcar.
nippers ['nipəz] *n pl* pinzas, tenazas.
nipple ['nipl] *n* teta, pezón.
no [nou] *a* ninguno; *ad* no; — **one** nadie.
nobility [nou'biliti] *n* nobleza, hidalguía; dignidad; (*of heart etc*) caballerosidad; **to prove** — calificarse.
noble ['noubl] *a* noble, hidalgo, ilustre, generoso.
nobleman ['noublmən] *n* caballero, noble.
nobleness ['noublnis] *n* nobleza, magnanimidad, caballerosidad.
nobody ['noubədi] *pn* nadie, ninguno; nulidad.
nocturnal [nɔk'tə:nl] *a* nocturno.
nod [nɔd] *n* seña, signo; (*with sleep*) cabezada; saludo; **a — is as good as a wink** por el hilo se saca el ovillo; *vi* hacer señas con la cabeza; cabecear, dar cabezadas.
noise [nɔiz] *n* ruido, clamor, estrépito, alboroto; rumor; *vt* **to — abroad** propalar.
noised ['nɔizd] **to be — abroad** *a* susurrarse.
noiseless ['nɔizlis] *n* silencioso, callado, sin ruido.
noisiness ['nɔizinis] *n* alboroto, estrépito.
noisome ['nɔisəm] *a* nocivo, fétido; dañino, apestado, apestoso.
noisy ['nɔizi] *a* ruidoso, turbulento.
nomad ['noumæd] *an* nómada; (*of flocks*) trashumante.
nomadic [nou'mædik] *a* errante.
nominate ['nɔmineit] *vt* nombrar, designar, señalar.
nomination [ˌnɔmi'neiʃən] *n* nombramiento, propuesta; adscripción.
nonconformist ['nɔnkən'fɔ:mist] *a n* disidente, inconforme.
none [nʌn] *pn* ninguno, nadie.
nonentity [nɔ'nentiti] *n* persona sin importancia, nulidad, medianía.
nonexistent ['nɔnig'zistənt] *a* que no existe.
nonplus ['nɔn'plʌs] *vt* confundir, dejar (estupefacto, patidifuso).
nonsense ['nɔnsəns] *n* necedad, contrasentido, impertinencia, dis-

parate, desatino, absurdo, adefesio; **what —!** ¡quiá!
nonsensical [nɔn'sensikəl] *a* absurdo, ridículo, disparatado.
non-stop ['nɔn'stɔp] *a* incesante, incesable.
nook [nuk] *n* rincón, rinconcito.
noon [nu:n] *n* mediodía.
noose [nu:s] *n* lazo corredizo; (*halter*) dogal.
nor [nɔ:] *cj* ni; **— neither** tampoco.
normal ['nɔ:məl] *a* normal, usual, regular; **to become —** normalizarse.
normally ['nɔ:məli] *ad* por lo regular.
Norman ['nɔ:mən] *an* normando.
north [nɔ:θ] *n* norte; *a* del norte, septentrional; **N— Star** la polar.
north-east ['nɔ:θ'i:st] *an* nordeste.
northerly ['nɔ:ðəli] *a* septentrional, norteño.
northern ['nɔ:ðən] *a* del norte, septentrional, norteño.
northward ['nɔ:θwəd] *ad* hacia el norte.
north-west ['nɔ:θ'west] *an* noroeste.
Norway ['nɔ:wei] *n* Noruega.
Norwegian [nɔ:'wi:dʒən] *an* noruego.
nose [nouz] *n* nariz, narices; (*animals*) hocico; (*sense of smell*) olfato; **with large —** narigudo; **—bag** morral, cebadera; *vt* olfatear, curiosear.
nostalgia [nɔs'tældʒiə] *n* añoranza.
nostril ['nɔstril] *n* ventana de la nariz.
nosy ['nouzi] *a* curioso, entremetido; **— person** correvedile.
not [nɔt] *ad* no; **— at all** de ningún modo.
notable ['noutəbl] *a* notable, relevante, subido, insigne, aventajado; **— person** notabilidad.
notably ['noutəbli] *ad* sumamente.
note [nout] *n* nota; observación; tono; marca; (*mus*) tecla; (*written*) billete; (*lectures etc*) apunte; **to take —s** sacar apuntes; *vt* notar, anotar, observar, advertir, reparar.
notebook ['noutbuk] *n* cuaderno, memorial.
noted ['noutid] *a* célebre; insigne; notable, señalado, conocido; **let it be — that** conste que.
notepaper ['nout,peipə] *n* papel de escribir.
nothing ['nʌθiŋ] *n* nada; **for —** de balde; **— at all** nonada; friolera; **a bit of —** fruslería; **to come to —** fracasar, malograrse.
notice ['noutis] *n* noticia, advertencia; comunicación, anuncio; consideración, conocimiento; aviso, letrero; **—board** tablón de avisos; **to take — of** notar; **to give —** advertir, avisar; **at the shortest —** en el plazo más breve; tan pronto como sea posible; *vt* notar, caer en la cuenta (de); observar, percatarse, hacer caso de; **it's worth —ing** es de notar.
noticeable ['noutisəbl] *a* notable, perceptible.
notify ['noutifai] *vt* notificar, dar parte, prevenir, avisar.
notion ['nouʃən] *n* noción, idea, concepto; ocurrencia.
notoriety [,noutə'raiəti] *n* notoriedad, fama.
notorious [nou'tɔ:riəs] *a* muy conocido; famoso, de mala fama, ruin.
notoriously [nou'tɔ:riəsli] *ad* notoriamente, públicamente.
notwithstanding [,nɔtwiθ'stændiŋ] *prep cj* no obstante, empero, sin embargo, a despecho de; bien que.
nought [nɔ:t] *n* cero, nada.
noun [naun] *n* substantivo, nombre.
nourish ['nʌriʃ] *vt* alimentar; (*emotion*) cebar; (*hopes*) sustentar, abrigar.
nourishing ['nʌriʃiŋ] *a* nutritivo; **very —** muy alimenticio.
nourishment ['nʌriʃmənt] *n* alimento, alimentación; pábulo; **spiritual —** pasto espiritual.
novel ['nɔvəl] *a* original; *n* novela.
novelist ['nɔvəlist] *n* novelista.
novelty ['nɔvəlti] *n* novedad; **fond of —ies** novelero.
November [nou'vembə] *n* noviembre.
novice ['nɔvis] *n* (*relig*) novicio; principiante; neófito, aprendiz, novato.
now [nau] *ad* ahora; ya; **by —** ya; **from — on** de hoy en adelante; **— and then** de cuando en cuando; **every — and then** a cada momento; **just —** ahora mismo; **— that** ya que, puesto que.
nowadays ['nauədeiz] *ad* hoy día, en la actualidad.
nowhere ['nouwεə] *ad* en ninguna parte.
noxious ['nɔkʃəs] *a* nocivo; (*animal*) dañino; pernicioso, pestífero, malsano.
nucleus ['nju:kliəs] *n* núcleo.
nude [nju:d] *a* desnudo.
nudge [nʌdʒ] *n* codal, codazo; *vt* dar codazos a.
nuisance ['nju:sns] *n* incomodidad, molestia, estorbo, contravención; **what a —!** ¡qué fastidio!
null [nʌl] *a* nulo, sin valor, inválido.
nullify ['nʌlifai] *vt* anular, invalidar.
numb [nʌm] *a* aterido, entumecido, entorpecido; *vt* entumecer, entorpecer.
number ['nʌmbə] *n* número; cifra; suma; (*magazine*) ejemplar; *vt* contar, numerar; sumar.
numberless ['nʌmbəlis] *a* innumerable, innúmero.
numbness ['nʌmnis] *n* torpor, letargo; entumecimiento.
numeral ['nju:mərəl] *n* número, cifra.
numerous ['nju:mərəs] *a* numeroso, muchos.
nun [nʌn] *n* monja, religiosa.

nunnery ['nʌnəri] *n* convento.
nuptial ['nʌpʃəl] *a* nupcial; *n* **—s** nupcias, esponsales.
nurse [nə:s] *n* (*sick*) enfermera; (*children's*) nodriza, ama, aya; **wet —** ama de leche; **—s' home** enfermería; **—maid** niñera; *vt* (*suckle*) amamantar, **criar; cuidar;** (*fig*) fomentar, abrigar.
nursery ['nə:sri] *n* cuarto de niños; (*plants*) pimpollar, criadero, vivero; **—maid** niñera; **— rhymes** cuentos de niños, versos de niños.
nursing ['nə:siŋ] *n* crianza, lactancia; (*of sick*) cuido; **— home** clínica de reposo, sanatorio.
nurture ['nə:tʃə] *n* alimentación; educación, crianza; (*fig*) fomento; *vt* alimentar, nutrir.
nut [nʌt] *n* nuez; (*mech*) hembra, tuerca; (*sl*) crisma; **—brown** castaño, trigueño; **in a —shell** en pocas palabras.
nutcrackers ['nʌt͵krækəz] *n* cascanueces.
nutriment ['nju:trimənt] *n* alimento, nutrición.
nutrition [nju'triʃən] *n* alimentación.
nutritious [nju:'triʃəs] *a* nutritivo, alimenticio.
nymph [nimf] *n* ninfa; zagala, doncella, joven; (*entom*) crisálida.

O

oak [ouk] *n* roble; (*evergreen*) encina.
oar [ɔ:] *n* remo.
oarsman ['ɔ:zmən] *n* remero, remador.
oasis [ou'eisis] *n* oasis.
oat [out] *n* **—s** avena; **—field** avenal; **to sow one's wild —s** correrla.
oath [ouθ] *n* juramento; (*swearword*) taco, improperio, blasfemia; **to take —** prestar juramento.
oatmeal ['outmi:l] *n* harina de avena.
obdurate ['ɔbdjurit] *a* obstinado, inflexible, impertinente, terco.
obedience [ə'bi:diəns] *n* obediencia, sumisión.
obedient [ə'bi:diənt] *a* obediente, sumiso, dócil.
obelisk ['ɔbilisk] *n* obelisco.
obey [ə'bei] *vt* obedecer; (*rules etc*) observar; (*respond*) cumplir con.
obituary [ə'bitjueri] *n* **— notice** necrología; (*in press*) esquela.
object ['ɔbdʒikt] *n* objeto, cosa, asunto; (*purpose*) fin, propósito, intento; (*grammar*) complemento; [əb'dʒekt] *vti* objetar; oponer; oponerse; poner reparos (a), poner tacha (a).
objection [əb'dʒekʃən] *n* objeción, réplica, dificultad, inconveniente; **to raise an —** poner reparos (*a*).
objectionable [əb'dʒekʃnəbl] *a* reprensible, censurable; antipático.
objective [əb'dʒektiv] *a* objetivo; *n* punto, fin, meta, destinación.
obligation [͵obli'geiʃən] *n* obligación, deber, compromiso; **to be under an —** (**to**) deber favores; agradecer.
obligatory [ɔ'bligətəri] *a* obligatorio, forzoso, imprescindible.
oblige [ə'blaidʒ] *vt* obligar, compeler, precisar; (*with favor*) complacer, agradar, servir; **to be —d to** no poder menos de; **I am much —d to you** le estoy muy agradecido.
obliging [ə'blaidʒiŋ] *a* obsequioso, cortés, atento, servicial.
oblique [ə'bli:k] *a* oblicuo, sesgado; diagonal; indirecto; **—ly** *ad* de soslayo.
obliterate [ə'blitəreit] *vt* borrar, cancelar, tachar; (*town etc*) arrasar, destruir; **to be —d** extinguirse, apagarse.
obliteration [ə͵blitə'reiʃən] *n* canceladura; el tachar; el arrasar; destrucción.
oblivion [ə'bliviən] *n* olvido.
oblivious [ə'bliviəs] *a* distraído, olvidadizo; inconsciente (*de*).
obnoxious [əb'nɔkʃəs] *a* dañoso, nocivo, impertinente, ofensivo.
obscene [ɔb'si:n] *a* obsceno, indecente, grosero, verde, sucio.
obscenity [ɔb'seniti] *n* obscenidad, indecencia, suciedad.
obscure [ɔb'skjuə] *a* obscuro, vago, confuso; tenebroso; (*language etc*) enigmático, revesado; (*origin etc*) humilde; *vt* borrar, enturbiar; anublar, obscurecer.
obscurity [əb'skjuəriti] *n* obscuridad; tinieblas; humildad; olvido.
obsequious [əb'si:kwiəs] *a* obsequioso, complaciente, zalamero, servil.
observance [əb'zə:vəns] *n* observancia, respeto; rito, ceremonia; costumbre, práctica.
observant [əb'zə:vənt] *a* perspicaz, observador, atento, vigilante.
observation [͵ɔbzə'veiʃən] *n* (*faculty*) observación; (*act*) examen; (*remark*) reparo; **to be under —** estar vigilado.
observatory [əb'zə:vətri] *n* observatorio.
observe [əb'zə:v] *vt* observar, notar; apuntar, marcar; (*remark*) decir, comentar; (*person*) vigilar; (*festival etc*) celebrar; (*law, order etc*) cumplir.
observer [əb'zə:və] *n* observador.
obsess [əb'ses] *vt* obsesionar.
obsolete ['ɔbsəli:t] *a* inusitado, arcaico, anticuado; pasado de moda; (*matter etc*) atrofiado.
obstacle ['ɔbstəkl] *n* obstáculo, tropezón, contrariedad, inconveniente, estorbo.
obstinacy ['ɔbstinəsi] *n* obstinación, terquedad, porfía.
obstinate ['ɔbstinit] *a* obstinado,

aferrado, tozudo, contumaz, testarudo, rebelde.
obstruct [əb'strʌkt] *vt* (*road etc*) obstruir, poner obstáculos (a); (*scheme etc*) baldar, estorbar, dificultar; (*pipe etc*) atorar.
obstruction [əb'strʌkʃən] *n* obstáculo, obstrucción, estorbo, dificultad.
obtain [əb'tein] *vt* obtener, conseguir; (*desire etc*) lograr; (*for someone*) facilitar; *vi* existir, prevalecer.
obtainable [əb'teinəbl] *a* asequible a mano.
obviate ['ɔbvieit] *vt* obviar, allanar, impedir, evitar.
obvious ['ɔbviəs] *a* obvio, evidente, manifiesto, palpable, transparente.
obviously ['ɔbviəsli] *ad* claro; a todas luces, claramente, bien a las claras.
obviousness ['ɔbviəsnis] *n* evidencia.
occasion [ə'keiʒən] *n* ocasión; oportunidad, coyuntura; sazón, tiempo; causa; motivo, pie; **on —** en caso necesario, a su debido tiempo; **on the — of** con motivo de; **to fit the —** venir a cuento; *vt* ocasionar, mover, causar, dar lugar a, acarrear.
occasional [ə'keiʒənl] *a* ocasional, casual, fortuito; poco frecuente.
occasionally [ə'keiʒnəli] *ad* de tarde en tarde, tal cual vez.
occult [ɔ'kʌlt] *a* oculto, ignoto.
occupant ['ɔkjupənt] *n* ocupante, poseedor; (*house*) inquilino.
occupation [,ɔkju'peiʃən] *n* ocupación, empleo, oficio.
occupy ['ɔkjupai] *vt* ocupar; emplear; entretener; *vi* ocuparse, atarearse.
occur [ə'kə:] *vi* ocurrir, acontecer, suceder.
occurrence [ə'kʌrəns] *n* suceso, acontecimiento; lance.
ocean ['ouʃən] *n* océano.
October [ɔk'toubə] *n* octubre.
octopus ['ɔktəpəs] *n* pulpo.
oculist ['ɔkjulist] *n* oculista.
odd [ɔd] *a* (*queer*) raro, extravagante, fantástico, singular, curioso, estrafalario; extraño; (*uneven*) impar; (*occasional*) suelto; **at — moments** de rato en rato; **an — peseta** tal cual peseta; **— job** chapuza.
oddity ['ɔditi] *n* rareza, singularidad; pajarraco.
odds [ɔdz] *n* desigualdad; ventaja; probabilidades; **against —** desventajosamente, contra la suerte; **— and evens** pares y nones; **— and ends** retazos; **to be at — with** estar reñido con; **to set at —** malquistar.
odious ['oudiəs] *a* odioso, detestable, infame.
odium ['oudiəm] *n* odio, infamia.
odor ['oudə] *n* olor, perfume.
odorless ['oudəlis] *a* inodoro.
of [ɔv] *prep* de, con, tocante a, según; **— late** últimamente.
off [ɔf] *prep* distante de; **day —** día libre; *ad* lejos, a distancia; (*sea*) a la altura de; **well —** acomodado; **—print** suelto, separata; **—shore** a vista de la costa.
offend [ə'fend] *vt* ofender, enfadar, fastidiar, irritar; (*senses etc*) desagradar, herir; *vi* pecar, cometer faltas, disgustar, enojar, deshonrar.
offended [ə'fendid] *a* indignado, lastimado; **to be —** picarse, sentirse herido.
offender [ə'fendə] *n* delincuente, culpado, ofensor.
offense [ə'fens] *n* ofensa, culpa, delito; atentado; **to take —** incomodarse, ofenderse.
offensive [ə'fensiv] *a* ofensivo, injurioso; **— remark** una impertinencia; *n* ofensiva.
offer ['ɔfə] *n* oferta; propuesta, proposición; **to make free — of** franquear; *vt* ofrecer, prometer; (*as candidate*) presentar; (*prospect*) brindar; *vi* ofrecerse, presentarse, prestarse.
offering ['ɔfəriŋ] *n* ofrenda, obsequio; (*church*) oblación; (*votive*) ex-voto; **burnt —** holocausto.
offhand ['ɔf'hænd] *a* informal; *ad* de repente, bruscamente.
office ['ɔfis] *n* oficina, despacho; empleo; oficio; (*eccles*) oficios; **in —** en el poder; **box —** contaduría; **booking —** taquilla; (*doctor's, dentist's*) consultorio.
officer ['ɔfisə] *n* (*mil*) oficial; funcionario; **body of —s** oficialidad.
official [ə'fiʃəl] *a* oficial; **— price** precio de tasa; *n* (*public*) funcionario, empleado.
officiate [ə'fiʃieit] *vti* oficiar; (*eccles*) celebrar; ejercer, desempeñar (*un cargo*).
officious [ə'fiʃəs] *a* oficioso, entremetido.
officiousness [ə'fiʃəsnis] *n* oficiosidad.
offing ['ɔfiŋ] *n* **in the —** mar afuera.
offshoot ['ɔfʃu:t] *n* ramal, renuevo.
offspring ['ɔfspriŋ] *n* prole, linaje, vástago.
oft, often [ɔft, 'ɔfn] *ad* frecuentemente, muchas veces, a menudo, comúnmente.
oil [ɔil] *n* aceite; (*sacramental*) crisma; (*lubricating*) grasa; **— painting** pintura (cuadro) al óleo; **— pan** pozo colector; *vt* engrasar; untar.
oilskin ['ɔilskin] *n* impermeable.
oily ['ɔili] *a* oleaginoso, aceitoso, grasiento; untuoso; craso.
ointment ['ɔintmənt] *n* ungüento, untura.
old [ould] *a* (*pers*) viejo; (*long established etc*) antiguo; **rich —** (*wine*) añejo; **very —** rancio; **—-fashioned** pasado de moda; **— world** muy chapado a la antigua; **the — country** el terruño; (*worn*) usado, gastado; **— man** anciano; **—**

Joe (*etc*) el tío Pepe; **to grow —** envejecer; **to be —** peinar canas.
older ['ouldə] *a* mayor.
oldness ['ouldnis] *n* vejez, ancianidad.
olive ['ɔliv] *n* (*tree*) olivo, (*fruit*) aceituna, oliva; **— grove** olivar; **— oil** aceite de oliva; **— colored** aceitunado; **— branch** rama de oliva.
omelet(te) ['ɔmlit] *n* tortilla.
omen ['oumen] *n* agüero, augurio, presagio, portento; **ill-omened** fatídico.
ominous ['ɔminəs] *a* ominoso, siniestro, nefasto, aciago.
omission [ou'miʃən] *n* omisión, supresión, abstracción, olvido.
omit [ou'mit] *vt* omitir, suprimir, prescindir, pasar por alto, pasar en claro, hacer caso omiso de.
omnibus ['ɔmnibəs] *n* ómnibus.
omnipotent [ɔm'nipətənt] *a* omnipotente, todopoderoso.
omniscient [ɔm'nisiənt] *a* omniscio.
on [ɔn] *ad* sobre, encima; (*en*) adelante; **and so —** y así sucesivamente; *prep* según; por parte de; **later —** más tarde; **what's —?** (*theat*) ¿qué ponen?
once [wʌns] *ad* una vez; antiguamente; **at —** de una vez, sin demora, en el acto, desde luego; **all at —** de (un) golpe; **— for all** de una vez; **for —** una vez siquiera; **once upon a time . . .** érase que se era.
one [wʌn] *a pn* uno, solo, único, cierto; **—-armed** manco; **—-eyed** tuerto; **to be the —** to ser el más indicado para; **— for each** sendos.
oneness ['wʌnnis] *n* unidad.
onerous ['ounərəs] *a* oneroso, pesado.
oneself [wʌn'self] *pn* sí; **to say to —** decir para sí.
one-way ['wʌn'wei] *a* de dirección única.
onion ['ʌnjən] *n* cebolla.
only ['ounli] *ad* solamente, sólo; *a* solo, único.
onset ['ɔnset] *n* asalto, ataque, arremetida.
onward ['ɔnwəd] *ad* hacia adelante.
ooze [u:z] *n* fango, légamo, limo; *vi* rezumar, filtrar, manar.
opaque [ou'peik] *a* opaco.
open ['oupən] *a* abierto; (*fan etc*) extendido; (*disposition*) franco, llano; dispuesto a; susceptible; **half —** entreabierto, entornado; **wide —** de par en par; **— house** puerta franca; **— secret** secreto a voces; **—-minded** sin prejuicios; **in the —** al aire libre, al raso; **to force —** violentar; *vt* abrir; (*exhibition*) inaugurar; empezar; revelar; **to — out** ensanchar; **to — up** franquear; *vi* abrirse; asomarse; **to — on to** dar a, salir a.
open-air ['oupn'ɛə] *a* al aire libre, al raso.
opening ['oupəniŋ] *n* abertura; (*wide*) boquerón; (*of street*) bocacalle; (*in wall*) vano; agujero; (*exhibitions etc*) inauguración; (*in wood*) claro; comienzo; (*opportuntiy*) ocasión, coyuntura.
openly ['oupənli] *ad* abiertamente, con el corazón en la mano.
openness ['oupənnis] *n* confianza, franqueza; frescura.
opera ['ɔpərə] *n* ópera; **comic —** ópera bufa; **— glasses** gemelos.
operate ['ɔpəreit] *vt* manejar, gobernar; efectuar, producir; explotar; *vi* obrar, funcionar; (*med*) operar.
operation [,ɔpə'reiʃən] *n* (*med*) operación; acción, efecto; (*mech*) funcionamiento.
operator ['ɔpəreitə] *n* operador, operario.
opinion [ə'pinjən] *n* opinión, parecer, persuasión: juicio; fama, estimación; **other people's —** el qué dirán.
opponent [ə'pounənt] *n* antagonista, contrario, rival; opositor.
opportune ['ɔpətju:n] *a* oportuno, conveniente.
opportunity [,ɔpə'tju:niti] *n* ocasión, tiempo, caso, coyuntura; pie.
oppose [ə'pouz] *vt* oponer, combatir; hacer frente a; impugnar; *vi* oponerse.
opposed [ə'pouzd] *a* opuesto; encontrado.
opposer [ə'pouzə] *n* adversario, antagonista, rival.
opposite ['ɔpəzit] *a* opuesto; al frente; encontrado, adverso; **directly —** frente por frente.
opposition [,ɔpe'ziʃən] *n* oposición, contradicción, repugnancia; **in —** en contra, en contraste.
oppress [ə'pres] *vt* oprimir, acongojar, agobiar, sofocar, vejar, abrumar.
oppression [ə'preʃən] *n* opresión, yugo; ahogo, pesadez.
oppressive [ə'presiv] *a* opresivo, abrumador; sofocante, gravoso.
oppressor [ə'presə] *n* opresor, tirano.
opprobrium [ə'proubriəm] *n* oprobio, deshonra, ignominia.
optic ['ɔptik] *a* óptico.
optician [ɔp'tiʃən] *n* óptico, optometrista.
optimism ['ɔptimizəm] *n* optimismo.
optimistic [,ɔpti'mistik] *a* optimista.
optional ['ɔpʃənl] *a* facultativo, discrecional.
opulence ['ɔpjuləns] *n* opulencia, riquezas; abundancia.
opulent ['ɔpjulənt] *a* rico, pudiente, acaudalado.
or [ɔ:] *cj* o, sea.
oracle ['ɔrəkl] *n* oráculo.
oral ['ɔ:rəl] *a* verbal, hablado.
orange ['ɔrindʒ] *n* naranja; (*tree*) naranjo; **— blossom** azahar.
oration [ɔ:'reiʃən] *n* oración, discurso, arenga.

orator ['ɔrətə] *n* orador; **eloquent —** pico de oro.
oratorial [ˌɔrə'tɔːriəl] *a* oratorio.
oratory ['ɔrətəri] *n* oratoria, elocuencia; (*eccl*) oratorio.
orb [ɔːb] *n* orbe, esfera.
orbit ['ɔːbit] *n* órbita.
orchard ['ɔːtʃəd] *n* huerto, vergel.
orchestra ['ɔːkistrə] *n* orquesta; **— seat** platea.
ordain [ɔː'dein] *vt* ordenar, establecer, decretar; **to be —ed** (*priest*) ordenarse.
ordeal [ɔː'diːl] *n* prueba.
order ['ɔːdə] *n* orden (*f command, sect, knightly, religious, commercial*); (*m orderliness, comparison*); método, arreglo, mandato; clase, medida; régimen; (*business*) pedido; **— of St James** hábito de Santiago; **Jesuit —** Compañía de Jesús; **in good —** en buen estado; en regla; **till further —s** hasta nueva orden; **out-of-—** descompuesto, no funciona; desarreglado; *pl* **standing—s** reglamento; *vt* (*arrange*) ordenar, arreglar; (*mil*) mandar; disponer; (*com*) pedir, encargar; **to put in —** ordenar, reglamentar; **to be the — of the day** imperar; **to give —s** mandar, preceptuar.
ordinance ['ɔːdinəns] *n* ordenanza, reglamento.
ordinary ['ɔːdnri] *a* ordinario, vulgar, trivial, común; (*wine*) corriente.
ordnance ['ɔːdnəns] *n* artillería.
ore [ɔː] *n* mineral, ganga; **— deposit** yacimiento.
organ ['ɔːgən] *n* órgano; **— player** organista; **— blower** intonador; **barrel —** organillo, manubrio.
organic [ɔː'gænik] *a* orgánico.
organism ['ɔːgənizəm] *n* organismo.
organist ['ɔːgənist] *n* organista.
organization [ˌɔːgənai'zeiʃən] *n* organización, entidad.
organize ['ɔːgənaiz] *vt* organizar, disponer, arreglar.
organizer ['ɔːgənaizə] *n* organizador.
orgy ['ɔːdʒi] *n* orgía.
orient ['ɔːrient] *vt* orientar; *n* **O—** oriente, levante.
Oriental [ˌɔːri'entl] *n* oriental.
orientate ['ɔːrienteit] *vt* orientar(se).
origin ['ɔridʒin] *n* origen, principio, precedencia, procedencia, cuna, raíz; **—s** ascendencia.
original [ə'ridʒənl] *a* original, primitivo, primordial, primero; *n* original; ejemplar.
originality [əˌridʒi'næliti] *n* singularidad, originalidad.
originate [ə'ridʒineit] *vti* originar, causar, provenir; **to — from** derivar de, provenir de.
ornament ['ɔːnəmənt] *n* ornamento; adorno, decoración; **hanging —** colgante; *vt* adornar; embellecer.
ornamental [ˌɔːnə'mentl] *n* ornamental, decorativo.
ornamentation [ˌɔːnəmen'teiʃən] *n* decorado.
ornate [ɔː'neit] *a* adornado; recargado; aparatoso.
orphan ['ɔːfən] *n* huérfano, inclusero.
orphanage ['ɔːfənidʒ] *n* orfelinato, hospicio.
orthodox ['ɔːθədɔks] *a* ortodoxo; admitido.
orthodoxy ['ɔːθədɔksi] *n* ortodoxia.
oscillate ['ɔsileit] *vi* oscilar, vibrar, desviar(se).
ostensible [ɔs'tensəbl] *a* ostensible, aparente, declarado, al aparecer.
ostentation [ˌɔsten'teiʃən] *n* ostentación, aparato, alarde, boato.
ostentatious [ˌɔsten'teiʃəs] *a* ostentoso, suntuoso, fastuoso, pomposo.
ostracism ['ɔstrəsizəm] *n* ostracismo.
ostrich ['ɔstritʃ] *n* avestruz.
other ['ʌðə] *a pn* otro; **every — day** un día sí y otro no, cada tercer día; **this, that and the —** esto lo otro y lo de más allá.
otherwise ['ʌðəwaiz] *ad* de otra manera, de lo contrario; si no.
ought [ɔːt] *vi* deber, convenir, ser menester.
ounce [auns] *n* onza.
our ['auə] *a* nuestro.
ours ['auəz] *pn* nuestro.
ourselves [ˌauə'selvz] *pn* nosotros, nosotros mismos.
oust [aust] *vt* desalojar, echar fuera, desahuciar.
out [aut] *ad* fuera, afuera; *prep* fuera de; *adj* (*book*) terminado, publicado; **just —** reciente; (*the voyage*) **—** de ida; **— and —** de cabo a rabo, acérrimo, incondicional, redomado; **— of** sin, por; **— of doors** al fresco; **— of hand** al momento; **six — of seven,** de cada siete, seis; **— of sight** fuera del alcance de la vista; **— of sorts** indispuesto; **going —** ida; **to be —** esta fuera; haberse apagado; publicarse; **to be — of office** ser un cesante; **to be — of print** estar agotado; **to speak —** hablar claro; **— of place** inadecuado, impropio; **— of the question** inadmisible; **— of the way** (*event etc*) extraordinario, raro, (*place*) inaccesible; **— of the way places** andurriales.
outbreak ['autbreik] *n* erupción, estallido, rompimiento; (*disease*) foco.
outburst ['autbəːst] *n* demasía, desahogo, explosión.
outcast ['autkɑːst] *n* desterrado, desechado, paria.
outcome ['autkʌm] *n* resultado, producto, solución, éxito.
outcry ['autkrai] *n* clamor, gritería, alarido, vocería.
outdo ['aut'duː] *vt* sobrepasar, exceder, sobrepujar.
outdoor ['autdɔː] *a* exterior, al aire libre.

outer ['autə] *a* exterior, de afuera; **—most** extremo.
outfit ['autfit] *n* equipo; avíos, pertrechos; **—ting** habilitación; *vt* equipar.
outgoing [aut'gouiŋ] *a* cesante, saliente.
outgrowth ['autgrouθ] *n* excrecencia; resultado.
outing ['autiŋ] *n* excursión, jira, vuelta, caminata.
outlandish [aut'lændiʃ] *a* extranjero, extraño, raro.
outlaw ['autlɔ:] *n* proscrito, bandido, forajido; *vt* proscribir.
outlay ['autlei] *n* gasto, desembolso.
outlet ['autlet] *n* salida, escape; (*pipe*) toma, desagüe.
outline ['autlain] *n* contorno, traza, silueta; esquema; **to draw — of** perfilar, bosquejar; reseñar.
outlook ['autluk] *n* aspecto, apariencia, prospecto, perspectiva, vista.
outlying ['aut'laiiŋ] *a* lejano, exterior, exéntrico, extrínseco.
outnumber [aut'nʌmbə] *vt* exceder en número.
out of doors ['autəv'dɔ:z] *a* al aire libre.
outpost ['autpoust] *n* avanzada.
output ['autput] *n* producción; rendimiento.
outrage ['autreidʒ] *n* ultraje; desaguisado, atropello; *vt* ultrajar, insultar, violentar.
outrageous [aut'reidʒəs]*a* ultrajante, injurioso, atroz, inaudito, descarado.
outright ['autrait] *a* immediatamente, al instante; sin más ni más; sin vacilar; francamente.
outrun [aut'rʌn] *vt* correr más de prisa que, dejar atrás.
outset ['autset] *n* principio, salida.
outside ['autsaid] *n* (la parte) exterior; (*of vehicle*) imperial; lo de afuera; *a* exterior; *prep* fuera de; *ad* por de fuera; **at the —** a lo sumo, cuando más.
outsider [aut'saidə] *n* forastero, intruso, profano.
outskirts ['autskə:ts] *n* (*town*) suburbio; ensanche, inmediaciones, cercanías, extrarradio; (*wood etc*) lindes, bordes, orilla.
outspoken [aut'spoukən] *a* franco.
outstanding [aut'stændiŋ] *a* (*fin*) por pagar; pendiente; relevante; (*person*) aventajado, sobresaliente; **to be —** brillar.
outstretch [aut'stretʃ] *vt* extender, alargar.
outstrip [aut'strip] *vt* dejar atrás, aventajar.
outward ['autwəd] *a* exterior, externo; aparente; *ad* (hacia, de) fuera, de ida.
outwards ['autwədz] *ad* hacia afuera.
outweigh [aut'wei] *vt* exceder, valer más que.
outworn ['autwɔ:n] *a* usado, gastado; caído en desuso, desechado.
oval ['ouvəl] *n* óvalo; *a* ovalado, oval.
ovation [ou'veiʃən] *n* ovación, aplausos.
oven ['ʌvn] *n* horno.
over ['ouvə] *prep* sobre, encima de; al otro lado de; *ad* sobre, de sobra; a demás; pasado, excesivamente; **— and —** repetidas veces; **— again** de nuevo; **to be —** (*concert etc*) terminar; **to be — and done with** terminar.
overall ['ouvərɔ:l] *n* mono.
overawe [.ouvər'ɔ:] *vt* intimidar; **to be —d** sobrecogerse.
overbalance [.ouvə'bæləns] *n* preponderancia; *vti* preponderar; perder el equilibrio.
overbearing [.ouvə'bεəriŋ] *a* arrogante, dominante; abrumador, agobiante.
overboard ['ouvəbɔ:d] *ad* al agua, al mar.
overburden [.ouvə'bə:dn] *vt* sobrecargar.
overcast ['ouvəkɑ:st] *a* nublado, cerrado; *vt* obscurecer, anublar(se).
overcharge ['ouvə'tʃɑ:dʒ] *n* sobrecarga; (*price*) recargo; *vt* sobrecargar, clavar, hincar la uña; (*price*) recargar.
overcloud [.ouvə'klaud] *vt* anublar, cerrarse.
overcoat ['ouvəkout] *n* abrigo, sobretodo, gabán.
overcome [.ouvə'kʌm] *a* rendido; *vti* vencer, superar, domar, sobreponerse a; dominar, salvar.
overcrowd [.ouvə'kraud] *vt* atestar.
overdo [.ouvə'du:] *vt* exagerar, hacer demasiado.
overestimate ['ouvər'estimeit] *vt* exagerar, estimar en valor excesivo; *n* estimación excisiva.
overfeed ['ouvə'fi:d] *vt* sobrealimentar.
overflow ['ouvəflou] *n* desbordamiento; inundación, riada, superabundancia, desborde; *vt* inundar, desbordar; **to be —ing** superabundar, derramarse.
overgrown ['ouvə'groun] *a* tupido, denso, frondoso.
overhang ['ouvə'hæŋ] *vt* dar sobre, colgar, sobresalir.
overhanging ['ouvə'hæŋiŋ] *a* saledizo, sobresaliente, colgante, pendiente.
overhaul ['ouvəhɔ:l] *n* revisión recorrido; [ouvə'hɔ:l] *vt* repasar, examinar; revisar; reacondicionar; alcanzar; *npl* gastos.
overhead ['ouvə'hed] *ad* superior, elevado, arriba; *n* **—(s)** gastos generales.
overhear [.ouvə'hiə] *vt* entreoír; oír por casualidad.
overjoyed [.ouvə'dʒɔid] *a* gozoso, alborozado, enajenado de alegría.

overland [ˌouvəˈlænd] *ad* por tierra.
overload [ˈouvəˈloud] *n* recargo; *vt* sobrecargar, recargar.
overlook [ˌouvəˈluk] *vt* (*position*) predominar, dominar, mirar de arriba; pasar (en, por) alto, descuidar, hacer caso omiso de; tolerar; hacer la vista gorda; repasar; **I —ed it** se me escapó.
overnight [ˈouvəˈnait] *ad* de la noche a la mañana; una noche.
overpower [ˌouvəˈpauə] *vt* (*person*) sujetar; dominar, forzar, subyugar; sobreponerse a; vencer.
overrate [ˈouvəˈreit] *vt* sobrevalorar.
overrule [ˌouvəˈruːl] *vt* denegar, no admitir.
overrun [ˌouvəˈrʌn] *vt* invadir, asolar, infestar; desbordarse; excederse.
overseer [ˈouvəsiə] *n* inspector, capataz, contramaestre, veedor, mayoral.
overshadow [ˌouvəˈʃædou] *vt* eclipsar, obscurecer, hacer sombra a.
overshoot [ˌouvəˈʃuːt] *vt* exceder, ir demasiado lejos.
oversight [ˈouvəsait] *n* equivocación, omisión, olvido; vigilancia, inspección.
overstep [ˈouvəˈstep] *vt* propasar(se), exceder(se).
overt [ˈouvəːt] *a* abierto, patente, manifiesto.
overtake [ˌouvəˈteik] *vt* sorprender; alcanzar; *vi* tomar la delantera.
overthrow [ˈouvəθrou] *n* vuelco, destronamiento, trastorno; [ˌouvəˈθrou] *vt* echar abajo; destruir; derrocar; vencer.
overture [ˈouvətjuə] *n* preludio, obertura; insinuación, propuesta.
overturn [ˌouvəˈtəːn] *vt* volcar, trastornar, trastrocar.
overweening [ˌouvəˈwiːniŋ] *a* avalentonado, encumbrado, mandón; **— pride** soberbia.
overweight [ˌouvəˈweit] *n* sobrepeso; *a* excesivamente gordo.
overwhelm [ˌouvəˈwelm] *vt* agobiar, reventar, anonadar, abrumar.
overwhelming [ˌouvəˈwelmiŋ] *a* grandioso, abrumador, irrisistible.
owe [ou] *vt* deber; adeudar.
owing [ˈouiŋ] *a* **— to** debido a, a causa de, con motivo de; **it is — to him** le compite; es por causa de él.
owl [aul] *n* búho, mochuelo.
own [oun] *a* propio, suyo propio; peculiar; real; *vt* poseer; confesar; reconocer; **to — up (to)** confesar de plano.
owner [ˈounə] *n* dueño, propietario, patrón, poseedor, teniente; **joint —** condueño.
ownership [ˈounəʃip] *n* propiedad, dominio.
ox [ɔks] *n* buey.
oxygen [ˈɔksidʒən] *n* oxígeno.
oyster [ˈɔistə] *n* ostra.

P

pace [peis] *n* paso; (*speed*) marcha, velocidad; *vti* recorrer, medir a pasos, andar al paso.
pacific [pəˈsifik] *a* pacífico, conciliador; sosegado.
pacify [ˈpæsifai] *vt* pacificar, amansar, apaciguar, sosegar.
pack [pæk] *n* paquete, fardo, lío; (*cards*) baraja; (*on back*) mochila; (*sl*) farándula; (*mules*) recua; (*dogs*) jauría; *vt* empacar, empaquetar, enfardelar, envasar; (*fill*) atestar, colmar; (*in trunk*) embaular; *vi* hacer el equipaje; **to — up** hacer la maleta; **to — off** despachar.
package [ˈpækidʒ] *n* fardo, paquete, bulto; **— holiday, tour** vacación, viaje inclusivo.
packer [ˈpækə] *n* embalador, empacador, envasador.
packet [ˈpækit] *n* paquete, fardo pequeño; (*boat*) paquebote.
packing [ˈpækiŋ] *n* embalaje, envase, empaque; **— case** envase; (*stuffing*) relleno; **to send —** enviar a paseo, despedir a cajas destempladas.
pact [pækt] *n* (con)trato, pacto; *vt* pactar.
pad [pæd] *n* cojinete, cojinillo, colchoncillo; peto; **writing —** bloc de papel; *vt* forrar, rellenar.
padding [ˈpædiŋ] *n* relleno; (*lit*) paja, relleno.
paddle [ˈpædl] *n* canalete; **—wheel** rueda de paleta; *vi* impeler, remar, chapotear.
paddock [ˈpædək] *n* dehesa, cercado.
padlock [ˈpædlɔk] *n* candado.
pagan [ˈpeigən] *an* pagano, idólatra.
page [peidʒ] *n* (*book*) página; (*newspaper*) plana; (*servant*) paje; **—boy** botones; *vt* paginar, numerar.
pageant [ˈpædʒənt] *n* espectáculo, procesión, pompa.
pageantry [ˈpædʒəntri] *n* fasto, parada, pompa.
pail [peil] *n* cubo, pozal, cubeta.
pain [pein] *n* dolor; (*mental, emotional*) pena; (*great*) angustia; tristeza; castigo, pena; *pl* trabajo, fatiga, incomodidad, sinsabores; solicitud; **to feel —** sentir dolor, padecer, sufrir, adolecer; **to be at great —s** esmerarse, apurarse, afanarse; **it —s me** siento (en el alma); *vt* doler, afligir; costar, molestar.
painful [ˈpeinful] *a* penoso, doloroso, trabajoso, angustioso, laborioso.
painfulness [ˈpeinfulnis] *n* pena, dolor.
painless [ˈpeinlis] *a* sin dolor, insensible.
painstaking [ˈpeinzˌteikiŋ] *a* laborioso, esmerado, nimio, cuidadoso.
paint [peint] *n* pintura, color; (*cosmetic*) colorete, arrebol, pig-

mento; *vti* pintar, pintarse; (*favorably*) colorear.
painter ['peintə] *n* pintor; (*house*) pintor (de brocha gorda, de casas).
painting ['peintiŋ] *n* pintura, cuadro; (*action*) el pintar.
pair [pɛə] *n* par, pareja; (*oxen*) yunta; *vti* emparejar, acoplar, igualar.
pajamas [pə'dʒa:məz] *n* pijama.
palace ['pælis] *n* palacio.
palatable ['pælətəbl] *a* sabroso, apetitoso, aceptable; (*pop*) potable.
palate ['pælit] *n* paladar.
pale [peil] *a* pálido, mortecino, claro; *n* estaca; palizada; **to go beyond the —** pasar de la raya; *vti* palidecer.
paleness ['peilnis] *n* palidez.
palisade [,pæli'seid] *n* palizada, estacada, valla.
pall [pɔ:l] *n* paño mortuorio; (*eccl*) palio; *vt* saciar, hartar, empalagar.
palliate ['pælieit] *vt* paliar, excusar, mitigar.
pallid ['pælid] *a* pálido, descolorido.
pallor ['pælə] *n* palidez.
palm [pa:m] *n* (*hand*) palma; (*tree*) palmera; **P— Sunday** Domingo de Ramos; *vt* escamotar; engañar, colar.
palpable ['pælpəbl] *a* palpable, palmario.
palpitate ['pælpiteit] *vi* palpitar, latir, agitarse.
paltry ['pɔ:ltri] *a* mezquino, bajo, despreciable, pobre.
pamper ['pæmpə] *vt* mimar, regalar, consentir.
pamphlet ['pæmflit] *n* folleto, opúsculo, impreso.
pan [pæn] *n* cacerola, caldero, olla, paila; **frying —** sartén; (*of balance*) platillo; (*of musket*) cazoleta.
Panama [,pænə'ma:] *n* Panamá.
Panamanian [,pænə'meiniən] *an* panameño.
pancake ['pænkeik] *n* fruta de sartén, hojuelo.
pane [pein] *n* hoja de vidrio, vidriera; (*window*) cristal.
panegyric [,pæni'dʒirik] *n* panegírico, apología.
panel ['pænl] *n* entrepaño, tablero.
panelled ['pænld] *a* entrepañado; (*ceiling*) artesonado.
pang ['pæŋ] *n* angustia, tormento, congoja; remordimiento, dolor.
panic ['pænik] *n* pánico, consternación.
pansy ['pænzi] *n* pensamiento.
pant [pænt] *n* resuello; *vi* jadear, resollar, palpitar, echar el bofe.
panther ['pænθə] *n* pantera, leopardo.
pantry ['pæntri] *n* despensa.
pants [pænts] *n pl* pantalones.
papa [pə'pa:] *n* papá, padre.
papacy ['peipəsi] *n* papado, pontificado.
papal ['peipəl] *a* pontifical, papal; **— jurisdiction** la curia romana.
paper ['peipə] *n* papel; (*news*) periódico; **brown —** papel de estraza, papel de añafea; **—back** libro en rústica, de bolsillo; **— knife** cortapapel; **—weight** sujetapapeles; *vt* empapelar.
papistry ['peipistri] *n* papismo.
par [pa:] *n* par; **at —** a la par; **to be on a — with** correr parejas con; **below —** bajo par.
parable ['pærəbl] *n* parábola.
parachute ['pærəʃu:t] *n* paracaídas.
parade [pə'reid] *n* desfile, parada, fasto; revista; ostentación, alarde, lucimiento; *vti* desfilar; hacer gala, alardear, lucir, pasear.
paradise ['pærədais] *n* paraíso, edén.
paradox ['pærədɔks] *n* paradoja.
paraffin ['pærəfin] *n* parafina, petróleo de lámpara.
paragon ['pærəgən] *n* dechado, ejemplar.
paragraph ['pærəgra:f] *n* párrafo.
Paraguay ['pærəgwai] *n* el Paraguay.
Paraguayan [,pærə'gwaiən] *an* paraguayo.
parallel ['pærəlel] *a* paralelo, igual; *n* paralelo, semejanza; copia; *vt* correr parejas con; cotejar.
paralysis [pə'rælisis] *n* parálisis, perlesía.
paralytic [,pærə'litik] *an* paralítico.
paralyze ['pærəlaiz] *vt* paralizar; (*speech with emotion*) embargar.
paramount ['pærəmaunt] *a* superior, importante, eminente, supremo.
parapet ['pærəpit] *n* (*mil*) parapeto; pretil, antepecho; *vr* parapetarse.
paraphrase ['pærəfreiz] *n* paráfrasis; *vt* hacer un resumen.
parasite ['pærəsait] *n* parásito.
parcel ['pa:sl] *n* paquete, lío; porción; *vt* **to — out** repartir; **to do up —** liar, empaquetar.
parch ['pa:tʃ] *vt* (re)secar, asolanar, (re)quemar, agostar; (*with thirst*) morirse de sed.
parched ['pa:tʃd] *a* abrasado, quemado; mustio.
parchment ['pa:tʃmənt] *n* pergamino, vitela.
pardon ['pa:dn] *n* perdón, (*law*) indulto, gracia; *vt* perdonar, disculpar, dispensar; **pardon me** dispénseme.
pardonable ['pa:dnəbl] *a* perdonable, venial.
pare [pɛə] *vt* **to — off, down** cercenar; (re)cortar; (*fruit*) mondar; (*potatoes*) pelar.
parent ['pɛərənt] *n* padre, madre; *pl* padres.
parentage ['pɛərəntidʒ] *n* parentela; alcurnia.
parental [pə'rentl] *a* paterno.
Paris ['pæris] *n* París.

parish ['pæriʃ] *n* parroquia; — **priest** párroco, cura.
parishioner [pə'riʃənə] *n* feligrés, parroquiano.
Parisian [pə'riziən] *an* parisiense.
parity ['pæriti] *n* igualdad.
park [pɑ:k] *n* parque, jardín; **car—** parque de estacionamiento; *vtr* estacionar(se).
parking ['pɑ:kiŋ]*n* estacionamiento; **— lot** parque de estacionamiento; **— station** aparcamiento.
parliament ['pɑ:ləmənt] *n* parlamento, cortes; **member of —** miembro, diputado.
parliamentary [,pɑ:lə'mentəri] *a* parlamentario.
parlor ['pɑ:lə] *n* sala de recibo, salón; (*in convent*) locutorio.
parochial [pə'roukiəl] *a* parroquial.
parody ['pærədi] *n* parodia; *vt* parodiar.
parole [pə'roul] *n* **on —** (*mil*) bajo palabra.
paroxysm ['pærəksizəm] *n* paroxismo, arrebato.
parrot ['pærət] *n* loro, cotorra, papagayo.
parry ['pæri] *n* parada, quite, reparo; *vt* parar; evitar.
parsimonious [,pɑ:si'mouniəs] *a* parco, frugal, tacaño.
parsley ['pɑ:sli] *n* perejil.
parson ['pɑ:sn] *n* clérigo, sacerdote, cura, párroco; pastor protestante.
part [pɑ:t] *n* (*share*) parte, porción; (*of book*) entrega; (*actor's*) papel; (*place*) lugar, sitio; cuidado, deber; **for my —** por mi parte; **for the most —** por la mayor parte; **in good —** en buena parte; *vt* partir; (*hair*) hacer la raya; *vi* separarse, desprenderse, despedirse; **to — with** deshacerse de.
partake [pɑ:'teik] *vt* participar de, compartir; **to — of** comer (beber) de.
partial ['pɑ:ʃəl] *a* parcial; **— to** aficionado (a).
partiality [,pɑ:ʃi'æliti] *n* parcialidad; preferencia, predilección.
participant [pɑ:'tisipənt] *n* participante, partícipe.
participate [pɑ:'tisipeit] *vi* participar.
participation [pɑ:,tisi'peiʃən] *n* participación.
participle ['pɑ:tisipl] *n* participio.
particle ['pɑ:tikl] *n* partícula; (*fig*) átomo, grano.
particular [pə'tikjulə] *a* particular; exacto, cuidadoso; quisquilloso; singular; predilecto; detallado; *n* particularidad, detalle, pormenor; **to be very —** hilar delgado, esmerarse, cuidarse.
parting ['pɑ:tiŋ] *n* separación; despedida; (*hair*) raya; (*road*) bifurcación.
partisan [,pɑ:ti'zæn] *a* parcial; *n* partidario. secuaz, devoto, allegado.
partition [pɑ:'tiʃən] *n* partición, división; (*sharing out*) reparto; (*wooden*) tabique; *vt* partir, repartir, cortar.
partly ['pɑ:tli] *ad* en parte, parcialmente, en cierto modo.
partner ['pɑ:tnə]*n* socio, compañero; (*silent*) comanditario; (*dancing*) pareja; (*wife*) consorte, cónyuge.
partridge ['pɑ:tridʒ] *n* perdiz.
party ['pɑ:ti] *n* (*politics, game*) partido; (*hunting*) partida; (*mil*) pelotón; parte; facción; **— to** partícipe en; **evening —** tertulia, velada; sarao; parcialidad; (*pol*) partido, frente, facción.
pass [pɑ:s] *n* (*mountain*) puerto, desfiladero, hoz, paso; (*fencing*) pase, estocada; (*permit*) permiso, salvoconducto, pase; (*theat*) billete de favor; (*exam*) aprobado; **critical —** coyuntura, estorbo; *vt* pasar, llevar; aventajar, superar; (*allow*) consentir, tolerar; (*time*) pasar; (*sentence*) dictar; (*exam*) aprobar; (*counterfeit money etc*) colar; **to — on** (*orders etc*) cursar; **to — over** (*in promotion*) postergar; (*mountains*) cruzar; **to — by** (*coast, on other side etc*) pasar de largo; cruzar, alcanzar; **to — off as** dar como legítimo; **to — on** decidir sobre; **to — through** atravesar; traspasar; atravesar; (*omit*) saltar; omitir; *vi* **to — away** fallecer, expirar; **to come to —** acaecer, acontecer.
passable ['pɑ:səbl] *a* transitable, pasable; practicable; mediano.
passage ['pæsidʒ] *n* paso, pasaje, entrada; (*across rivers etc*) travesía; tránsito; (*in house*) pasillo; (*in story*) episodio; (*book*) trozo.
passenger ['pæsindʒə] *n* pasajero, viajero.
passerby ['pɑ:sə'bai] *n* transeúnte.
passing ['pɑ:siŋ] *n* muerte; paso; fallecimiento; **in —** de paso.
passion ['pæʃən] *n* pasión, ardor, cólera, coraje, enardecimento, furor; **— play** misterio, auto.
passionate ['pæʃənit] *a* apasionado, ardiente, colérico.
passive ['pæsiv] *a* pasivo, inerte.
passport ['pɑ:spɔ:t] *n* pasaporte.
password ['pɑ:swə:d] *n* contraseña, seña, santo y seña.
past [pɑ:st] *a* pasado, último; **— master** consumado; *n* pasado, historia; *prep* más de; **— hope** sin esperanza; (*invalid*) desahuciado.
paste [peist] *n* pasta; argamasa; **sugar —** alfeñique; *vt* pegar.
pastime ['pɑ:staim] *n* pasatiempo, recreo, recreación.
pastor ['pɑ:stə] *n* pastor.
pastoral ['pɑ:stərəl] *a* pastoral; (*novel*) pastoril.
pastry ['peistri] *n* pastelería; pasteles; pastas; **puff —** hojaldre.

pasture ['pɑːstʃə] *n* dehesa, pradera, pasto; *vt* pastar.
pat [pæt] *a* oportuno; *n* caricia; *vt* acariciar, pasar la mano por, tentar.
patch [pætʃ] *n* remiendo, parche; (*on face*) lunar postizo; **elbow —** codera; (*of land*) parcela; *vt* remendar, pegar.
patent ['peitənt] *n* patente, privilegio, diploma; *a* patente, visible, manifiesto; palmario; **— leather** charol, hule; *vt* dar (privilegio, patente).
paternal [pə'təːnl] *a* paternal, paterno.
paternity [pə'təːniti] *n* paternidad.
path [pɑːθ] *n* sendero, senda; (*footpath*) vereda; (*fig*) paso, huella, camino, trayecto; **bridle —** camino de herradura.
pathetic [pə'θetik] *a* patético, tierno, conmovedor.
pathless ['pɑːθlis] *a* intrincado, intransitable.
pathway ['pɑːθwei] *n* senda, vereda, sendero, camino.
patience ['peiʃəns] *n* paciencia, sufrimiento.
patient ['peiʃənt] *a* paciente, sufrido, sumiso; *n* enfermo.
patriarch ['peitriɑːk] *n* patriarca.
patriarchal [ˌpeitri'ɑːkəl] *a* patriarcal.
Patrick ['pætrik] *m* Patricio.
patriot ['peitriət] *n* patriota.
patriotic [ˌpætri'ɔtik] *a* patriótico.
patriotism ['pætriətizəm] *n* patriotismo.
patrol [pə'troul] *n* patrulla; ronda; *vti* (*streets*) rondar, hacer la ronda; (*mil*) patrullar.
patrolman [pə'troulmæn] *n* agente de policía.
patron ['peitrən] *n* patrón, protector, padrino; (*saint*) patrón; protector, mecenas.
patronage ['peitrənidʒ] *n* protección, amparo, patrocinio; (*eccl*) patronato; **under the — of** bajo los auspicios de.
patronize ['pætrənaiz] *vt* patrocinar, proteger, apoyar, fomentar.
pattern ['pætən] *n* modelo, tipo, ejemplar; (*cloth*) muestra; (*dressmaking*) patrón; (*design*) diseño, dibujo; *vti* modelarse sobre.
Paul [pɔːl] *m* Pablo.
Pauline ['pɔːliːn] *f* Paula.
pauper ['pɔːpə] *n* pobre (de solemnidad).
pause ['pɔːz] *n* pausa; hesitación; (*mus*) calderón; (*for response during funeral*) posa; *vi* hacer una pausa, parar(se); detenerse, reflexionar, interrumpirse.
pave [peiv] *vt* pavimentar, adoquinar, enlosar; **to — the way** preparar el terreno.
pavement ['peivmənt] *n* (*traffic*) pavimento; (*sidewalk*) acera; andén.
pavilion [pə'viljən] *n* pabellón, quiosco, cenador.
paw [pɔː] *n* pata; (*sharp*) garra, zarpa; *vti* (*horses*) piafar; **to — about** manosear.
pawn [pɔːn] *n* prenda, empeño; (*chess*) peón; **—shop** casa de préstamos, monte de piedad; *vt* empeñar, dar en prenda.
pawnbroker ['pɔːnˌbroukə] *n* prendero, prestamista.
pay [pei] *n* paga; (*daily*) jornal; (*wages, salary*) sueldo; (*mil*) paga; *vt* pagar; (*debt*) saldar; (*subscription*) abonar(se); **to — attention to** parar mientes en, prestar atención a, atender; **to — back** reembolsar, devolver (con creces); desquitar(se); **to — in advance** adelantar, pagar adelantado; **to — respects** dar los complimientos; **to — off** amortizar, (*scores*) desquitarse; **to — the piper** pagar el pato; **to — out** (*rope*) largar; (*grudge*) ajustarle (a uno) las cuentas.
payable ['peiəbl] *a* pagadero, por pagar, vencido.
payer ['peiə] *n* pagador.
paying ['peiiŋ] *part* **without —** sin pagar.
paymaster ['peiˌmɑːstə] *n* págador, habilitado; **—'s office** pagaduría.
payment ['peimənt] *n* pago, paga; recompensa; **in — for** en pago de; **in full — for** en saldo de.
pea [piː] *n* guisante; **—nut** cacahuete, maní.
peace [piːs] *n* paz, sosiego, reposo, serenidad; *n* **—maker,** *a* **—making** conciliador; **to hold one's —** guardar silencio, callarse.
peaceable ['piːsəbl] *a* pacífico, sosegado; bonachón.
peaceful ['piːsful] *a* tranquilo, apacible, reposado.
peacefulness ['piːsfulnis] *n* tranquilidad, sosiego, quietud.
peach ['piːtʃ] *n* melocotón, durazno; (*tree*) pérsico, melocotonero, alberchiguero,
peacock ['piːkɔk] *n* pavo real, pavón.
peak [piːk] *n* cumbre, cima, peña; (*sharp*) pico, picacho; (*of cap*) visera; (*of achievement*) cúspide.
peal(ing) ['piːl(iŋ)] *n* repique, repiqueteo; (*of laughter*) carcajada; *vi* repicar, echar las campanas a vuelo.
pear [pɛə] *n* pera; **— tree, — orchard** peral.
pearl [pəːl] *n* perla; margarita; **mother of —** nacre, nácar; **to cast —s before swine** echar margaritas a los puercos.
peasant ['pezənt] *n* campesino, labriego, aldeano; villano.
peasantry ['pezəntri] *n* los villanos, los campesinos.
pebble ['pebl] *n* guija, china, guijarro.
peck [pek] *n* (*bird*) picotazo; *vti* picotear.
peculiar [pi'kjuːljə] *a* (*odd*) singular, peculiar; (*to a person*) propio, privativo, particular.

peculiarity [pi,kju:li'æriti] *n* singularidad, peculiaridad, particularidad.
pedagogue ['pedəgog] *n* pedagogo.
pedant ['pedənt] *n* pedante.
pedantic [pi'dæntik] *a* pedante(sco).
pedantry ['pedəntri] *n* pedantería.
pedestal ['pedistl] *n* pedestal, basa.
pedestrian [pi'destriən] *a* pedestre, rastero; *n* peatón; caminante; — **crossing** paso a peatones.
pedigree ['pedigri:] *n* genealogía, linaje, ejecutoria.
peddler ['pedlə] *n* buhonero.
peel [pi:l] *n* (*orange*) cáscara, pellejo; (*fruit*) corteza; (*potato*) peladuras; (*apple*) piel; *vti* pelar, mondar.
peelings ['pi:liŋz] *n pl* mondaduras, peladuras, ralladuras, raspaduras, cortaduras.
peep [pi:p] *n* (*birds*) pío; atisbo, ojeada; —**show** retablo, sombras chinescas; *vi* mirar, atisbar, asomarse; (*birds*) piar.
peer ['piə] *n* par, noble; *vi* **to — at** escrudiñar, fisgar.
peerless ['piəlis] *a* incomparable, sin par, sin igual.
peevish ['pi:viʃ] *a* malhumorado, displicente, enojadizo, mohino, quisquilloso, bronco, desabrido.
peevishness ['pi:viʃnis] *n* displicencia, mal humor, mal genio.
peg [peg] *n* (*mus instrument*) clavija; (*excuse*) pretexto; (*for hanging*) colgadero; **clothes —** pinza; — **leg** pata de palo.
pelican ['pelikən] *n* pelícano, alcatraz.
pell-mell ['pel'mel] *ad* confusamente, a troche y moche, (en) (de) tropel.
pen [pen] *n* pluma; **fountain —** pluma estilográfica; **bull —** (*in ring*) toril; — **holder** mango de pluma, plumero; (*child's*) **play—** pollera; **to — in** *vt* enjaular, encerrar, acorralar.
penalty ['penlti] *n* castigo; multa; (*football*) penálty.
penance ['penəns] *n* penitencia, castigo.
pencil ['pensl] *n* lápiz; —**box** lapicero; — **sharpener** sacapuntas, tajalápiz.
pendent ['pendənt] *a* pendiente, suspendido, colgado.
pendulum ['pendjuləm] *n* péndulo.
penetrable ['penitrəbl] *a* penetrable.
penetrate ['penitreit] *vt* pasar por, entrar a, atravesar; (*deep*) calar; penetrar; (*substance*) horadar; penetrar; **to — inland** internarse.
penetrating ['penitreitiŋ] *a* agudo.
penetration [,peni'treiʃən] *n* penetración, viveza, sutileza, agudeza.
peninsula [pi'ninsjulə] *n* península.
penitence ['penitəns] *n* penitencia, arrepentimiento.
penitent ['penitənt] *an* penitente, compungido.
penitential [,peni'tenʃəl] *a* penitencial; — **garb** sambenito.
penitentiary [,peni'tenʃəri] *a* penitenciario; *n* penitenciaría.
penknife ['pennaif] *n* cortaplumas.
pennant ['penənt] *n* banderola, gallardete, jirón.
penniless ['penilis] *a* sin blanca; sin dinero; (*fam*) a la cuarta pregunta.
penny ['peni] *n* penique.
pension ['penʃən] *n* pensión, subvención; alimentos; **life —** pensión vitalicia; cesantía; (*mil*) retiro; *vt* pensionar.
pensioner ['penʃənə] *n* pensionado, pensionista; (*mil*) inválido.
pensive ['pensiv] *a* pensativo, meditabundo; triste.
pensiveness ['pensivnis] *n* melancolía, meditación.
pentecost ['pentikɔst] *n* pentecostés.
penthouse ['penthaus] *n* piso en lo alto de un edificio.
penury ['penjuri] *n* estrechez, estrecheces, inopia.
people ['pi:pl] *n* pueblo, gente; plebe, gentuza, vulgo; **the (French) —** el pueblo (francés); *vt* poblar.
pepper ['pepə] *n* pimienta; **red —** guindilla; *vt* condimentar, sazonar con pimienta.
per [pə:] *prep* por.
perambulator, (*abbrev*) **pram** ['præmbjuleitə, præm] *n* cochecito para niños.
perceivable [pə'si:vəbl] *ad* perceptible.
perceive [pə'si:v] *vt* notar, percibir; entender; (*dimly*) columbrar.
per cent [pə'sent] *ad* por ciento.
percentage [pə'sentidʒ] *n* tanto por ciento, porcentaje.
perceptibility [pə,septə'biliti] *n* perceptibilidad.
perceptible [pə'septəbl] *n* perceptible, palpable, sensible.
perception [pə'sepʃən] *n* percepción, idea, perspicacia.
perceptive [pə'septiv] *a* perceptivo.
perch [pə:tʃ] *n* percha; (*measure*) pértiga; *vti* posar(se), encaramarse, pararse.
perchance [pə'tʃɑ:ns] *ad* por ventura, acaso, quizá(s).
percolate ['pə:kəleit] *vti* colar, filtrar, rezumarse.
percussion [pə:'kʌʃən] *n* percusión, choque.
perdition [pə:'diʃən] *n* perdición, ruina, infierno.
peremptory [pə'remptəri] *a* perentorio, terminante, absoluto.
perennial [pə'reniəl] *a* perenne, perpetuo; (*bot*) vivaz.
perfect ['pə:fikt] *a* perfecto, completo; acabado, cabal, consumado; (*fruit etc*) maduro, en su punto; [pə'fekt] *vt* perfeccionar, completar, redondear.
perfection [pə'fekʃən] *n* perfección.

perfectly ['pə:fiktli] *ad* perfectamente, a la perfección; a fondo; de perlas, a las mil maravillas, de lo (más) lindo.
perfidious [pə:'fidiəs] *a* pérfido, fementido, traidor.
perfidy ['pə:fidi] *n* perfidia, traición; felonía, alevosía.
perform [pə'fɔ:m] *vt* ejecutar, realizar, desempeñar, llevar a cabo; practicar; (*theat*) representar; (*mus*) tocar.
performance [pə'fɔ:məns] *n* ejecución; representación; (*theat*) función; (*deed*) hazaña.
performer [pə'fɔ:mə] *n* artista.
perfume ['pə:fju:m] *n* perfume; fragancia; [pə'fju:m] *vt* perfumar.
perfumery [pə'fju:məri] *n* perfumería.
perfunctory [pə'fʌŋktəri] *a* superficial, descuidado, rutinario.
perhaps [pə'hæps] *ad* tal vez, acaso.
peril ['peril] *n* peligro, riesgo.
perilous ['periləs] *n* peligroso, arriesgado, expuesto.
period ['piəriəd] *n* período, época; término; punto final; hora (de clase).
periodical [,piəri'ɔdikəl] *an* periódico; *n* revista; **weekly** — semanario; **fortnightly** — quincenal.
perish ['periʃ] *vi* perecer, fenecer.
perishable ['periʃəbl] *a* perecedero, marchitable, frágil.
perjure ['pə:dʒə] *vt* perjurar.
perjury ['pə:dʒəri] *n* perjurio.
permanence ['pə:mənəns] *n* permanencia, duración, estabilidad.
permanent ['pə:mənənt] *a* permanente, estable, duradero, fijo.
permeate ['pə:mieit] *vt* penetrar, calar, impregnar.
permissible [pə'misəbl] *a* permitido, admisible.
permission [pə'miʃən] *n* permiso, permisión, tolerancia, licencia.
permit ['pə:mit] *n* permiso, licencia, pase, guía; [pə'mit] *vt* permitir, consentir, dejar, autorizar, sancionar.
permitted [pə'mitid] *a* licito.
pernicious [pə'niʃəs] *a* pernicioso, pestilente, funesto.
perpendicular [,pə:pən'dikjulə] *a* perpendicular, a plomo.
perpetrate ['pə:pitreit] *vt* perpetrar, cometer.
perpetual [pə'petjuəl] *a* perpetuo, perenne, incesante; **— motion** movimiento continuo.
perpetuate [pə'petjueit] *vt* perpetuar, eternizar.
perpetuity [,pə:pi'tjuiti] *n* perpetuidad.
perplex [pə'pleks] *vt* confundir, aturdir, embrollar, causar perplejidad.
perplexity [pə'pleksiti] *n* perplejidad, embarazo, zozobra, irresolución.
perquisite ['pə:kwizit] *n* percance; **—s** gajes, regalías, buscas.
persecute ['pə:sikju:t] *vt* perseguir, hostigar, acosar; molestar, vejar, acuciar.
persecution [,pə:si'kju:ʃən] *n* persecución.
perseverance [,pə:si'viərəns] *n* persistencia, constancia, firmeza.
persevere [,pə:si'viə] *vi* perseverar, persistir.
persevering [,pə:si'viəriŋ] *a* perseverante, tenaz.
Persia ['pə:ʃə] *n* Persia, Irán.
Persian ['pə:ʃən] *an* persa.
persist [pə'sist] *vi* persistir; porfiar; **to — in** obstinarse en, empeñarse en.
persistence [pə'sistəns] *n* persistencia, porfía; **— in error** contumacia.
persistent [pə'sistənt] *a* pertinaz, porfiado, resuelto.
person ['pə:sn] *n* persona; individuo; (*fam*) tipo, cristiano, sujeto; (*theat*) personaje; **responsible —, — in charge** encargado.
personage ['pə:snidʒ] *n* personaje.
personal ['pə:snl] *a* personal; **lack of — touch** impersonalidad.
personality [,pə:sə'næliti] *n* personalidad.
personify [pə:'sɔnifai] *vt* personificar.
perspective [pə'spektiv] *n* perspectiva.
perspicacious [,pə:spi'keiʃəs] *a* perspicaz, penetrante, sagaz, sutil.
perspicuity [,pə:spi'kjuiti] *n* perspicuidad, lucidez.
perspire [pə'spaiə] *vi* sudar, transpirar.
persuade [pə'sweid] *vt* persuadir, convencer; inducir.
persuasion [pə'sweiʒən] *n* persuasión, creencia.
persuasive [pə'sweisiv] *a* persuasivo, influyente, incitante, convincente.
pert [pə:t] *a* listo, vivo; desparpajado, respondón, fresco, petulante, impertinente.
pertain [pə:'tein] *vi* pertenecer; competer, incumbir.
pertaining [pə:'teiniŋ] *a* pertinente, perteneciente.
pertinacious [,pə:ti'neiʃəs] *a* pertinaz, terco, porfiado.
pertinent ['pə:tinənt] *a* pertinente, oportuno, atinado.
pertness ['pə:tnis] *n* vivacidad; frescura, impertinencia, petulancia.
perturb [pə'tə:b] *vt* perturbar, inquietar, solivantar.
perturbation [,pə:tə:'beiʃən] *n* perturbación, alteración, azoramiento.
Peru [pə'ru:] *n* el Perú.
peruse [pə'ru:z] *vt* recorrer, leer, examinar.
Peruvian [pə'ru:viən] *an* peruano.
pervade [pə:'veid] *vt* ocupar, penetrar.

pervaded [pəː'veidid] *a* **to be —** impregnarse, compenetrarse.
perverse [pə'vəːs] *a* perverso, endiablado, avieso, contumaz, intratable, travieso.
perversion [pə'vəːʃən] *n* corrupción, tergiversación, terquedad, perversión, contrariedad.
perversity [pə'vəːsiti] *n* perversidad, malignidad, contrariedad.
pervert [pə'vəːt] *vt* pervertir, depravar, viciar, infectar, malear; desnaturalizar; ['pəːvəːt] *n* pervertido, renegado.
pessimist ['pesimist] *n* pesimista.
pest [pest] *n* peste; (*of insects*) plaga.
pester ['pestə] *vt* importunar, molestar, cansar, atormentar; (*fam*) dar la lata a.
pestilence ['pestiləns] *n* peste, pestilencia.
pestilential [ˌpesti'lenʃəl] *a* pestilente, pestífero, maligno.
pet [pet] *n* favorito, querido; *vt* mimar, acariciar.
petal [petl] *n* pétalo, hoja.
Peter ['piːtə] *m* Pedro.
petition [pi'tiʃən] *n* solicitud, recurso, instancia; petición; *vt* suplicar; demandar, hacer petición.
petrify ['petrifai] *vti* petrificar(se).
petrol ['petrəl] *n* esencia, gasolina.
petroleum [pi'trouliəm] *n* petróleo, aceite mineral.
petticoat ['petikout] *n* saya, enaguas, zagalejo; **—s** bajos.
petty ['peti] *a* pequeño, mezquino, despreciable; insignificante; **— thief** ratero; **— cash** dinero para gastos menores; **— larceny** hurto; **— officer** subalterno de marina.
pewter ['pjuːtə] *n* peltre.
phantom ['fæntəm] *n* fantasma, coco, espectro, sombra.
phase [feiz] *n* fase, aspecto.
phenomenon [fi'nɔminən] *n* fenómeno.
philanthropy [fi'lænθrəpi] *n* filantropía.
Philip ['filip] *m* Felipe.
Philippines ['filipiːnz] *n* las (Islas) Filipinas.
philologist [fi'lɔlədʒist] *n* filólogo.
philosopher [fi'lɔsəfə] *n* filósofo.
philosophic [ˌfilə'sɔfik] *a* filosófico, sereno.
philosophical [ˌfilə'sɔfikəl] *a* filosófico.
philosophy [fi'lɔsəfi] *n* filosofía.
phlegm [flem] *n* flema.
phlegmatic [fleg'mætik] *a* flemático.
Phoenician [fi'niʃiən] *an* fenicio.
phoenix ['fiːniks] *n* fénix.
phone [foun] *n* teléfono; *vt* telefonear.
phonetics [fou'netiks] *n* fonética.
phosphorous ['fɔsfərəs] *n* fósforo.
photocopy ['foutoukɔpi] *n* fotocopia; *vt* fotocopiar.
photograph ['foutəgrɑːf] *n* foto(grafía); retrato; **to have one's — taken** retratarse; *vt* fotografiar.
photographer [fə'tɔgrəfə] *n* fotógr afo.
photographic [ˌfoutə'græfik] *a* fotográfico.
photography [fə'tɔgrəfi] *n* fotografía.
phrase [freiz] *n* frase, locución; **stock —** frase hecha.
physical ['fizikəl] *a* físico, material.
physician [fi'ziʃən] *n* médico, doctor, facultativo.
physics ['fiziks] *n* física.
physiognomy [ˌfizi'ɔgnəmi] *n* fisonomía; semblante, facciones.
physique [fi'ziːk] *n* presencia, físico; (*fam*) planta.
pianist ['piənist] *n* pianista.
piano [pi'ænou] *n* piano; **upright —** piano vertical; **grand —** piano de cola.
pick [pik] *n* **—ax** pico, azadón; (*fig*) la flor y nata, lo escogido; *vt* picar; escoger; **to — out** entresacar, escoger; **to — up** recoger; pescar; (*stray ears of corn*) espigar; **to — one's nose** hurgarse las narices; **to — clean** mondar, roer; *vi* arrancar.
pickle ['pikl] *n* escabeche, adobo, salmuera; (*sl*) enredo, lío; *pl* encurtido; *vt* escabechar, adobar.
pickpocket ['pikˌpɔkit] *n* ratero, cortabolsas, carterista.
picnic ['piknik] *n* comida de campo, merienda; **to have a —** merendar; *vi* merendar.
picture ['piktʃə] *n* pintura; (*on canvas*) lienzo; cuadro, tela; grabado, imagen; (*of person*) retrato; **the —s** el cine; **word —** (*of person*) semblanza; *vt* pintar, imaginarse.
picturesque [ˌpiktʃə'resk] *a* pintoresco.
pie [pai] *n* (*sweet*) pastel; (*meat, fish*) empanada; **to have finger in —** meter (cuchara, baza).
piece [piːs] *n* pieza, pedazo, fragmento; (*bread*) pedazo, cacho; (*cloth*) retal; (*bits*) añicos; (*fam*) **smart little —** pizpireta; (*of news*) noticia; (*of advice*) consejo; (*of ground*) solar; **to take to —s** desmontar.
pier [piə] *n* muelle, malecón, embarcadero; (*archit*) estribo.
pierce ['piəs] *vt* atravesar, penetrar, taladrar, clavar; acribillar; conmover.
piercing ['piəsiŋ] *a* penetrante, agudo, cortante.
piety ['paiəti] *n* piedad, devoción; **lack of —** impiedad.
pig [pig] *n* puerco; marrano, cerdo.
pigeon ['pidʒin] *n* pichón, paloma; **carrier —** paloma mensajera.
pigeonhole ['pidʒinhoul] *n* casilla.
pig-headed ['pig'hedid] *a* terco, cabezudo.
pigtail ['pigteil] *n* trenza; (*esp bullfighter's*) coleta.

pike ['paik] *n* pica, lanza; (*fish*) lucio.
pile [pail] *n* (*wood*) estaca; (*cloth*) pelo, pelillo; pila, montón, cúmulo; **building —** pilote; *vt* apilar, amontonar; (*arms*) poner en pabellón.
pilfer ['pilfə] *vti* hurtar, ratear; (*esp from housekeeping accounts*) sisar.
pilfering ['pilfəriŋ] *a* ratero; sisón; *n* ratería; sisa.
pilgrim ['pilgrim] *n* peregrino, romero.
pilgrimage ['pilgrimidʒ] *n* peregrinación, romería; **to make a —** peregrinar.
piling ['pailiŋ] **— up** *n* hacinamiento.
pill [pil] *n* píldora; sinsabor.
pillage ['pilidʒ] *n* pillaje; rapiña; *vti* saquear, entrar a saco.
pillar ['pilə] *n* pilar, columna; sostén; **from — to post** de Ceca en Meca; de Herodes a Pilatos.
pillow ['pilou] *n* almohada; cojinete cojín.
pilot ['pailət] *n* piloto, práctico; *vt* pilotear, timonear.
pimple ['pimpl] *n* grano, botón.
pin [pin] *n* alfiler; **like a new —** como una plata; **safety —** imperdible; (*of axle*) clavija; **it's not worth two —s** no vale un comino; **to be on —s** estar impaciente, sobre ascuas; **to have —s and needles** tener agujetas; *vt* prender con alfileres; **to — down** fijar, inmobilizar.
pinafore ['pinəfɔ:] *n* delantal.
pincers ['pinsəz] *n pl* tenazas, pinzas, tenacillas.
pinch [pintʃ] *n* (*nip*) pellizco; (*pain*) aprieto, apuro; **at a —** en caso de apuro; *vt* pellizcar; (*sl*) sisar, hurtar; escatimar.
pine [pain] *n* pino; **—wood** pinar; **— cone** piña, pinocho; **— kernel** piñón; *vi* desfallecer, languidecer; **to — for** anhelar, morirse (por).
pineapple ['pain,æpl] *n* piña, ananá.
ping [piŋ] *n* (*of bullets*) zumbido, silbido.
pink [piŋk] *a* rosado; *n* clavel.
pinnacle ['pinəkl] *n* pináculo; (*archit*) chapitel, remate; cumbre.
pint [paint] *n* pinta.
pioneer [,paiə'niə] *n* (*mil*) zapador; explorador.
pious ['paiəs] *a* pío, piadoso, religioso, devoto.
pipe [paip] *n* (*water*) tubo, tubería, cañón; (*smoking*) pipa, cachimba; (*Moorish*) añafil; **bag—** gaita; (*wine*) carral; *vi* silbar; tocar el caramillo.
piper ['paipə] *n* flautista, gaitero; **to pay the —** pagar el pato.
piping ['paipiŋ] *n* cañería; (*dress*) ribete, guarnición.
piquancy ['pi:kənsi] *n* picante; acrimonia.
pique [pi:k] *n* pique, desazón; rencilla; *vt* picar, irritar, herir; jactarse de.
piracy ['paiərəsi] *n* piratería.
pirate ['paiərit] *n* pirata; *vt* piratear, robar, pillar; (*lit*) contrahacer.
pirated ['paiəritid] *a* **— edition** edición furtiva.
pistol ['pistl] *n* pistola.
pit [pit] *n* foso, hoyo; (*theat*) patio; (*fruit*) hueso; **arm—** sobaco; **coal —** mina; **—-a-pat** tic-tac.
pitch [pitʃ] *n* pez, betún, resina; (*voice etc*) tono; (*ground*) inclinación; (*games*) saque, tiro; extremo; *vt* embrear; tirar, arrojar; **to — forward** caer (de cabeza, de bruces); *vi* (*naut*) cabecear.
pitcher ['pitʃə] *n* cántaro; (*games*) botador, lanzador.
piteous ['pitiəs] *a* lastimoso, lastimero, clamoroso.
pitiful ['pitiful] *n* compasivo; lastimoso, lastimero.
pitiless ['pitilis] *a* desapiadado, encarnizado, cruel, implacable.
pity ['piti] *n* compasión, piedad; **what a —!** ¡qué lástima!; *vt* compadecer, apiadarse de.
pivot ['pivət] *n* gorrón, eje, espigón; yeso mate; *vt* enyesar, emplastar. *vi* girar sobre on eje.
placard ['plæka:d] *n* cartel.
place [pleis] *n* lugar, sitio; puesto; (*of employ*) empleo; (*theat*) localidad; butaca; (*fortified*) plaza; (*ancestral*) solar; (*at table*) cubierto; (*job*) puesto; **dwelling —** hogar, domicilio; (*space*) espacio, asiento; **out of —** impertinente, fuera de lugar, incongruente; **to give — to** ceder el paso; **to take —** tener lugar, verificarse; *vt* colocar, fijar, poner; (*chess*) entablar; acomodar; cifrar en.
placid ['plæsid] *a* plácido; tranquilo, soñoliento.
plague [pleig] *n* peste, plaga; pestilencia; **bubonic —** peste bubónica; *vt* atormentar; dar guerra, atufar.
plain [plein] *a* (*land etc*) llano, plano; (*statement etc*) claro, sin adornos, evidente; (*food etc*) sencillo; (*people, custom etc*) humilde, bueno; (*of appearance*) feo, ordinario; **— and simple** liso y llano; (*mil*) **in — clothes** de paisano; **— truth** pura verdad; **to speak — English** hablar claro, hablar en romance, en cristiano; *n* llano, llanura, vega; planicie; (*SA*) pampa.
plainness ['pleinnis] *n* claridad; sinceridad; llaneza; fealdad.
plaintiff ['pleintif] *n* demandante.
plaintive ['pleintiv] *a* lamentoso, quejoso, dolorido, plañidero, querelloso.
plait [plæt] *n* pliegue; (*hair*) trenza; *vt* trenzar, (entre)tejer, plegar.
plan [plæn] *n* plan, esquema, proyecto; (*fam*) combinación; **rough —** bosquejo; trazado; *vt* proyectar; contemplar; urdir, trazar, bosquejar.

plane [plein] *n* plano; avión; (*carp*) cepillo; — **tree** plátano; *vt* allanar; acepillar, desbastar.
planet ['plænit] *n* planeta.
plank [plæŋk] *n* tablón, tabla, madero.
plant [plɑ:nt] *n* planta; fabrica, taller; instalación; *vt* plantar, establecer; (*line*) comarcar; (*set up*) sentar.
plantation [plæn'teiʃən] *n* plantío, plantación; arboleda.
planter ['plɑ:ntə] *n* plantador, cultivador.
plaster ['plɑ:stə] *n* yeso, emplasto; **adhesive** — esparadrapo.
plastic ['plæstik] *a* plástico; *n* plástico; **—s** plástica.
plate [pleit] *n* plato; tabla; plancha; (*colored*) cromo; (*phot*) placa; (*in book*) lámina; *vt* platear, chapear; blindar; dorar.
plateau ['plætou] *n* meseta.
platform ['plætfɔ:m] *n* plataforma; (*rl*) andén; tablado; (*meeting*) tablado, tribuna, estrado.
platinum ['plætinəm] *n* platino.
platitude ['plætitju:d] *n* perogrullada, verdad de Pero Grullo.
Plato ['pleitou] *m* Platón.
platoon [plə'tu:n] *n* pelotón.
plausible ['plɔ:zəbl] *a* plausible.
play [plei] *n* juego, recreo; (*theat*) comedia, pieza; (*allegorical*) auto; (*mech*) operación; **free** — movimiento libre, libertad; (*reflection*) reflejo; (*on words*) juego de palabras; **fair** — juego limpio; **foul** — trampa; **to give free — to** dar rienda suelta a, dar cuerda a; *vt* (*theat*) hacer un papel, representar; (*mus*) ejecutar, tocar; **to — a trick** engañar, hacer una jugada; **to — truant** hacer novillos; *vi* jugar, divertirse, chancear, holgar.
player ['pleiə] *n* jugador; actor, cómico; **strolling** — cómico de la legua; músico; (*cards*) mano.
playful ['pleiful] *a* juguetón, travieso.
playground ['pleigraund] *n* patio de recreo.
playhouse ['pleihaus] *n* teatro; (*arch*) corral.
playmate ['pleimait] *n* camarada, compañero.
plaything ['pleiθiŋ] *n* juguete.
plea [pli:] *n* alegato, defensa, excusa; pretexto, recurso; instancia.
plead [pli:d] *vi* abogar, argüir, pleitear; **to — for** abogar por.
pleasant ['pleznt] *a* agradable, alegre; (*varied*) ameno; entretenido; gustoso, grato; (*person*) simpático; **very** — encantador; — **journey!** ¡buen viaje!
pleasantness ['plezntnis] *n* contento, agrado.
please [pli:z] *vt* gustar, complacer, contentar, caer en gracia, encantar, causar agrado; *vi* gustar de; querer, agradar, dignarse; — (*request*) sírvase, haga el favor de, por favor; **easy to** — bien contentadizo; **hard to** — mal contentadizo.
pleased ['pli:zd] *a* satisfecho; **to be** — estar contento; **to be — with** estar satisfecho de, pagarse de.
pleasing ['pli:ziŋ] *a* agradable, amable; deleitoso, grato; armonioso; placentero; **to be — to** complacer.
pleasure ['pleʒə] *n* placer, deleite, gusto, agrado, satisfacción.
pleat [pli:t] *n* plegadura, pliegue; *vt* plegar.
plebeian [pli'bi(:)ən] *n* plebeyo, pechero.
pledge [pledʒ] *n* empeño, prenda; arras, rehén; brindis; *vt* empeñar, dar en prenda, prendar; brindar.
plentiful ['plentiful] *a* abundante, copioso, fértil; nutrido.
plenty ['plenti] *n* abundancia, copia, caudal, raudal, fertilidad.
pliable ['plaiəbl] *a* flexible, plegable; dócil.
pliant ['plaiənt] *a* flexible, blando.
plight [plait] *n* condición, apuro, aprieto.
plod [plɔd] *vi* andar con dificultad, adelantar laboriosamente.
plot [plɔt] *n* (*ground*) lote, terreno; (*scheme*) conjuración, complot; (*theat*) enredo, acción, trama, intriga; *vti* tramar, intrigar; trazar.
plotter ['plɔtə] *n* conspirador, intrigante.
plotting ['plɔtiŋ] *n* maquinación, conspiración.
plow [plau] *n* arado; *vti* arar, labrar, surcar; — **share** reja de arado.
plowing ['plauiŋ] *n* labranza.
pluck [plʌk] *n* resolución, ánimo, valor; *vt* (*flowers*) (re)coger; (*birds*) pelar; (*mus*) pulsar; **to — out violently** arrancar; **to — up courage** recobrar el ánimo.
plug [plʌg] *n* taco; tapón; **spark** — bujía; (*el*) enchufe; *vt* tapar; **to — in** (*el*) enchufar.
plum [plʌm] *n* ciruela.
plumage ['plu:midʒ] *n* plumaje.
plumb [plʌm] *a* plomo, recto; **—line** plomada; *vt* aplomar; sond(e)ar.
plumber ['plʌmə] *n* fontanero, plomero.
plume [plu:m] *n* penacho; plumero; gloria; pluma; *vr* vanagloriarse.
plump [plʌmp] *a* gordo, regordete, rollizo; (*cheeks*) cachetudo.
plumpness ['plʌmpnis] *n* gordura; corpulencia.
plunder ['plʌndə] *n* pillaje, botín; *vt* pillar, despojar, saquear, entrar a saco.
plunderer ['plʌndərə] *n* saqueador.
plunge [plʌndʒ] *n* zambullida; *vt* sumergir; chapuzar; *vi* sumergirse, zambullirse.
plural ['pluərəl] *a* plural.

plus [plʌs] *prep, a* más; (*math*) positivo.
ply [plai] *n* pliegue; inclinación; *vt* ejercer; (*needle*) menear; conducir; importunar; *vi* trabajar, ocuparse.
pneumonia [nju(:)'mouniə] *n* pulmonía.
poach [poutʃ] *vi* cazar en vedado; escalfar.
poacher ['poutʃə] *n* cazador furtivo.
pock [pɔk] *n* **—mark** hoyo.
pocket ['pɔkit] *n* bolsillo; receptáculo; **— size** (*book etc*) portátil; **—book** portamonedas; *vt* embolsar.
pod [pɔd] *n* vaina, cápsula.
poem ['pouim] *n* (*epic etc*) poema; (*usu shorter*) poesía, rima; (*mediaeval heroic* —) cantar de gesta.
poet ['pouit] *n* poeta, vate, bardo.
poetic [pou'etik] *a* poético; *n* **—s** poética.
poetry ['pouitri] *n* poesía; (*art of*) poética.
poignancy ['pɔinənsi] *n* resquemor, sentimiento, acerbidad.
poignant ['pɔinənt] *a* sentido, sensible; agudo, amargo, sutil, picante.
point [pɔint] *n* punto; (*tip*) punta; cabo; (*object*) fin, propósito; (*of contact*) toque; (*of character etc*) rasgo; (*sharp*) espigón, punzón; (*time*) sazón, momento; (*in games*) tanto; **knotty —** punto espinoso, (*fam*) busilis; *pl* (*rl*) agujas; **in —** al caso, a propósito; **on the — of** a pique de, a punto de; **to the —** acertado; **to come to the —** dejarse de historias, andar sin ambajes, ir al grano; **to keep to the —** concretarse; **to see the —** caer en la cuenta; *vt* apuntar; (*pencil etc*) apuntar, afilar, sacar punta; **to — at** (*scornfully*) señalar con el dedo; **to — to** señalar.
point-blank ['pɔint'blæŋk] *a* categórico; *ad* a boca de jarro, a quemarropa.
pointed ['pɔintid] *a* (*object*) puntiagudo, afilado; (*remark etc*) intencional, intencionado, malintencionado.
pointer ['pɔintə] *n* aguja, fiel, puntero; (*dog*) perro de muestra.
pointless ['pɔintlis] *a* (*remark*) anodino.
poise [pɔiz] *n* peso, equilibrio; contrapeso; *vi* balancear, equilibrar.
poison ['pɔizn] *n* veneno, tósigo; *vt* envenenar.
poisonous ['pɔiznəs] *a* venenoso, ponzoñoso.
poke [pouk] *vt* hurgar; (*fire*) atizar; *vi* andar a tientas; **to — about** hurgar; **to — one's nose into** (entre)meterse, meter el hocico.
poker ['poukə] *n* hurgón, atizador; (*cards*) póker.
Poland ['poulənd] *n* Polonia.
polar ['poulə] *a* polar; **— bear** oso blanco.
pole [poul] *a* **— star** estrella polar; *n* vara, percha; **greasy —** cucaña; **north —** polo norte; **P—** polaco.
polemics [pɔ'lemiks] *n* polémica.
police [pə'li:s] *n* policía; guardia; **traffic —** agente; **shock —** guardias de asalto; **revenue** *or* **frontier —** carabinero.
policeman [pə'li:smən] *n* agente de policía, guardia.
policy ['pɔlisi] *n* sistema; prudencia; política; (*insurance*) póliza.
Polish ['pouliʃ] *an* polaco.
polish ['pɔliʃ] *n* lustre, nitidez, pulimento; *vt* pulir, lustrar, acicalar, limar; (*shoes*) limpiar, sacar brillo.
polished ['pɔliʃt] *a* ilustrado; urbano; nítido; elegante; pulido; desasnado.
polite [pə'lait] *a* cortés, atento, bien educado, correcto.
politeness [pə'laitnis] *n* cortesía, urbanidad.
politic ['pɔlitik] *a* político.
political [pə'litikəl] *a* político.
politician [ˌpɔli'tiʃən] *n* político.
politics ['pɔlitiks] *n* política.
poll [pɔl] *n* lista, matrícula, elección; padrón; lista electoral; *vt* descabezar; registrar, votar.
polling ['pouliŋ] *n* votación, escrutinio.
pollute [pə'lu:t] *vt* corromper, contaminar, viciar.
Polynesian [ˌpɔli'ni:ziən] *an* polinesio.
pomegranate ['pɔmigrænit] *n* granada.
pommel ['pʌml] *n* pomo; *vt* zurrar, cascar.
pomp [pɔmp] *n* pompa, fasto, atuendo, rumbo.
pompous ['pɔmpəs] *a* pomposo, aparatoso, rumboso; **to be —** darse importancia.
pompousness ['pɔmpəsnis] *n* ostentación, ampulosidad.
pond [pɔnd] *n* (*park*) estanque; charca, alberca; **fish —** vivero.
ponder ['pɔndə] *vti* meditar, pesar; **to — on** meditar sobre.
ponderous ['pɔndərəs] *a* pesado, grave.
poniard ['pɔnjəd] *n* puñal, estoque.
pontiff ['pɔntif] *n* pontífice.
pony ['pouni] *n* haca, jaca, poney.
pool [pu:l] *n* charca, estanque, pozo; (*in card games etc*) polla; **swimming —** piscina; *vt* mancomunar.
poolroom ['pu:lrum] *n* sala de billar.
poop [pu:p] *n* popa.
poor [puə] *a* (*in wealth*) pobre; (*quantity*) escaso; (*origin etc*) humilde, infeliz; mezquino; inútil, viciado; **—spirited** apocado.
pop [pɔp] *a* **— eyes** ojos saltones; **—gun** cerbatana; *n* taponazo, ruido seco; *vt* espetar, disparar; **to — in** (*fam*) caer por.
pope [poup] *n* papa.

poplar ['pɔplə] *n* álamo; (*white*) pobo; (*black*) chopo.
poppy ['pɔpi] *n* amapola, adormidera.
popular ['pɔpjulə] *a* estimado, apreciado; predilecto; (*gathering etc*) concurrido; popular.
popularity [ˌpɔpju'læriti] *n* estimación, reputación, crédito; popularidad.
populate ['pɔpjuleit] *vt* poblar.
population [ˌpɔpju'leiʃən] *n* población.
populous ['pɔpjuləs] *a* populoso.
porcelain ['pɔ:slin] *n* porcelana.
porch [pɔ:tʃ] *n* pórtico, porche; (*church*) atrio; (*house*) entrada, portal.
pore [pɔ:] *n* poro; *vi* **to — over** quemarse las cejas.
pork [pɔ:k] *n* carne de cerdo; **— sausage** longaniza, salchicha.
porridge ['pɔridʒ] *n* gachas (de avena); (*maize*) polenta.
port [pɔ:t] *n* puerto, ensenada; vino de oporto; **—hole** tronera; **—side** babor.
portable ['pɔ:təbl] *a* portátil.
portal ['pɔ:tl] *n* portada, portal.
portend [pɔ:'tend] *vt* pronosticar; amenazar, amagar.
portent ['pɔ:tent] *n* portento; mal agüero.
portentous [pɔ:'tentəs] *a* prodigioso, portentoso.
porter ['pɔ:tə] *n* (*station*) mozo (de cordel); (*in building*) portero; (*esp in University etc*) bedel.
portfolio [pɔ:t'fouliou] *n* cartapacio, carpeta; (*ministerial*) cartera.
portion ['pɔ:ʃən] *n* parte, porción; (*at meals*) consumición; cuota; *vt* (re)partir.
portly ['pɔ:tli] *a* corpulento, grueso; majestuoso, grave.
portmanteau [pɔ:t'mæntou] *n* baúl; maleta, portamanteo.
portrait ['pɔ:trit] *n* retrato; **word —** semblanza; **to make a — of** retratar.
portrayal [pɔ:'treiəl] *n* representación.
Portugal ['pɔ:tjugəl] *n* Portugal.
Portuguese [ˌpɔ:tju'gi:z] *an* portugués, lusitano.
pose [pouz] *n* postura, posición; suposición; pose; *vt* poner, embarazar, proponer; *vi* darse importancia, fingir, echárselas de.
position [pə'ziʃən] *n* posición; (*job*) puesto, situación, colocación; circunstancia; categoría.
positive ['pɔzətiv] *a* positivo, absoluto, cierto, categórico; *n* (*phot*) positiva.
possess [pə'zes] *vt* poseer, tener, haber; (*qualities etc*) reunir.
possessed [pə'zest] *a* poseído; (*by devil*) endemoniado.
possession [pə'zeʃən] *n* posesión; poder; *pl* bienes; **to take — of** apoderarse de; incautar.
possessor [pə'zesə] *n* poseedor.
possibility [ˌpɔsə'biliti] *n* posibilidad, contingencia.
possible ['pɔsəbl] *a* posible; dable; permitido.
possibly ['pɔsəbli] *ad* quizá, acaso, tal vez.
post [poust] *n* (*mail*) correo; (*upright*) poste, pilar; (*job*) puesto, colocación, destino; (*mil*) puesto, avanzada; **— card** (tarjeta) postal; **— office** casa de correos, posta, correos; **small** (*branch*) **— office** estafeta; **— office box number** apartado; **from pillar to —** de Herodes a Pilatos: **by return —** a vuelta de correo; **— free** franco de porte; **— haste** apresurado, con toda urgencia; *vt* (*letters*) echar al correo; (*mil*) mandar; (*bills*) pegar; (*notice*) anunciar; **to keep —ed** tener al corriente; *vi* viajar en silla de posta.
postage ['poustidʒ] *n* porte de carta, franqueo.
postage stamp ['poustidʒ'stæmp] *n* sello, *SA* estampilla, timbre.
postal ['poustəl] *a* postal; **— order** giro.
poster ['poustə] *n* cartel, anuncio, cartelón; **bill—** pegador de carteles.
poste-restante ['poust'restɑ̃:nt] *n* lista de correos.
posterity [pɔs'teriti] *n* posteridad.
posthumous ['pɔstjuməs] *a* póstumo.
postman ['poustmən] *n* cartero.
postmaster ['poustˌmɑ:stə] *n* administrador de correos.
postpone [poust'poun] *vt* posponer, aplazar, demorar, retrasar, postergar.
postponement [poust'pounmənt] *n* aplazamiento.
postscript ['pousskript] *n* posdata, coleta.
posture ['pɔstʃə] *n* postura, actitud, ademán.
pot [pɔt] *n* (*cooking*) olla, marmita, puchero; (*any old* —) cacharro; **to take — luck** hacer penitencia; **flower—** tiesto; **to wash the —s** lavar la vajilla; *vt* envasar; tirar.
potato [pə'teitou] *n* patata; (*sweet*) batata; **French-fried —es** patatas (papas) fritas.
potency ['poutənsi] *n* potencia, poderío, poder.
potent ['poutənt] *a* potente, fuerte, poderoso; influyente.
potentate ['poutənteit] *n* potentado.
potential [pə'tenʃəl] *a* posible, potencial, potente; *n* potencialidad.
pothole ['pɔthoul] *n* (*in road*) bache.
potion ['pouʃən] *n* poción, brebaje, pócima.
potter ['pɔtə] *n* alfarero.
pottery ['pɔtəri] *n* alfarería; loza; cacharros.
pouch [pautʃ] *n* bolsa, zurrón; **game —** escarcela.

poultice ['poultis] *n* cataplasma, compresa, bizma.
poultry ['poultri] *n* volatería, aves de corral.
pounce [pauns] *vi* caer sobre, calar.
pound [paund] *n* libra; depósito; *vt* moler, machacar; aporrear; (*in mortar*) majar.
pour [pɔ:] *vt* derramar, verter; (*wine etc*) escanciar; esparcir; **to — out** vaciar; **to — out (over)** volcar; *vi* llover a cántaros, a chuzos; diluviar; echarse.
pout [paut] *n* pucherito; mueca; *vi* amohinarse, hacer pucheros.
poverty ['pɔvəti] *n* pobreza; (*squalor*) miseria; (*lack*) carencia, poquedad; **— of speech** cortedad; **—stricken** miserable; **the —stricken** los pobres de solemnidad.
powder ['paudə] *n* (*face etc*) polvo(s); **gun—** pólvora; **— bowl** polvera; **to reduce to —** pulverizar, polvorizar; convertirse en polvo; *vr* ponerse polvos.
powdery ['paudəri] *n* polvoriento, empolvado.
power ['pauə] *n* poder; (*physical*) energía; (*math*) potestad; (*of argument etc*) vehemencia; (*over people*) influjo, poderío; mando; (*gift*) facultad; (*rights*) fuero; (*drive*) empuje, pujanza; (*engine, motion*) potencia; fuerza motriz; **reigning —** potentado; **great —s** grandes potencias; **all in one's —** todo lo posible; **— of attorney** poder, procuración; **angelic —s** potestades.
powerful ['pauəful] *a* poderoso, pujante; intenso; (*engine*) potente; (*argument*) contundente, convincente.
powerless ['pauəlis] *a* impotente.
practicable ['præktikəbl] *a* (*road etc*) practicable, transitable; (*action etc*) factible, viable, hacedero; (*idea*) dable.
practical ['præktikəl] *a* práctico.
practically ['præktikli] *ad* casi, punto menos (que).
practice ['præktis] *n* práctica, costumbre, uso; (*professional*) clientela; formalidad; **to put into —** poner en obra.
practice ['præktis] *vt* practicar; (*profession*) profesar; ejercer.
practiced ['præktist] *a* experimentado.
practitioner [præk'tiʃnə] *n* práctico, practicante, médico.
prairie ['prɛəri] *n* pampa, sabana.
praise [preiz] *n* elogio, alabanza; ponderación; (*arch*) loor; *vt* elogiar, celebrar, alabar; ponderar; **to — to the skies** encarecer, poner por las nubes.
praiseworthy ['preizwə:ði] *a* loable, digno de alabanza, honroso, notable, plausible.
prance [prɑ:ns] *vi* encabritarse, hacer corvetas.
pray [prei] *vi* rezar; *vt* rogar, pedir; suplicar.
prayer ['preiə] *n* rezo, oración; ruego; súplica; petición: **— book** devocionario.
preach [pri:tʃ] *vti* predicar; sermonear.
preacher ['pri:tʃə] *n* predicador.
precarious [pri'kɛəriəs] *a* precario, inseguro, azaroso.
precaution [pri'kɔ:ʃən] *n* precaución, cuidado, cautela; desconfianza.
precede [pri:'si:d] *vt* preceder, antepasar; *vi* ir delante.
precedence ['presidəns] *n* precedencia, prioridad.
precedent ['presidənt] *a* precedente, anterior; *n* precedente.
precept ['pri:sept] *n* precepto, regla, mandato.
precinct ['pri:siŋkt] *n* límite, lindero; recinto, distrito.
precious ['preʃəs] *a* precioso; (*style*) rebuscado.
precipice ['presipis] *n* precipicio, despeñadero.
precipitate [pri'sipitit] *an* precipitado; arrebatado; [pri'sipiteit] *vt* precipitar; (*chem*) depositar; **to — oneself** lanzarse; despeñarse.
precise [pri'sais] *a* preciso, exacto, puntual; escrupuloso; singular; clavado.
preciseness [pri'saisnis] *n* precisión, exactitud, rigor.
precision [pri'siʒən] *n* precisión, exactitud.
precocious [pri'kouʃəs] *a* precoz.
precursor [pri:'kə:sə] *n* precursor.
predecessor ['pri:disesə] *n* predecesor, antecesor.
predestine ['pri:'destin] *vt* predestinar.
predicament [pri'dikəmənt] *n* predicamento, apuro, trance, compromiso; categoría.
predict [pri'dikt] *vt* predecir, pronosticar, vaticinar.
prediction [pri'dikʃən] *n* predicción, profecía, pronóstico, adivinanza.
predispose ['pri:dis'pouz] *vt* predisponer.
predominance [pri'dɔminəns] *n* predominio, ascendiente.
pre-eminent [pri:'eminənt] *a* preeminente, supremo, distinguido; sobresaliente, preclaro.
prefabricated ['pri:'fæbrikeitid] *a* prefabricado, desmontable.
preface ['prefis] *n* prefacio, preámbulo, prólogo; proemio; *vt* poner prólogo a; introducir.
prefect ['pri:fekt] *n* prefecto.
prefer [pri'fə:] *vt* preferir, anteponer; ascender.
preferable ['prefərəbl] *a* preferible, preferido.

preferably ['prefərəbli] *ad* preferiblemente, mejor (dicho).
preference ['prefərəns] *n* inclinación, preferencia, predilección.
preferment [pri'fə:mənt] *n* promoción; preferencia.
pregnant ['pregnənt] *a* preñada, encinta; grávido.
prejudice ['predʒudis] *n* prejuicio, prevención; daño, perjuicio; preocupación; **lack of —** imparcialidad; *vt* perjudicar, prevenir, indisponer.
prejudiced ['predʒudist] *a* parcial, que tiene prejuicios.
prejudicial [.predʒu'diʃəl] *a* perjudicial, nocivo.
prelate ['prelit] *n* prelado.
preliminary [pri'liminəri] *a* preliminar.
prelude ['prelju:d] *n* preludio; (*theat*) loa; *vti* preludiar.
premature [.premə'tjuə] *a* prematuro, precoz; temprano.
premier ['premjə] *a* primero; *n* primer ministro; presidente (del consejo de ministros).
premise ['premis] *n* premisa; *pl* local, edificio.
premium ['pri:miəm] *n* premio; (*insurance*) prima; **at a —** sobre la par.
premonition [.premə'niʃən] *n* presentimiento, advertencia.
preoccupation [pri:.ɔkju'peiʃən] *n* preocupación.
preoccupy [pri:'ɔkjupai] *vt* preocupar; **to be preoccupied** estar absorto, estar ocupadísimo.
preparation [.prepə'reiʃən] *n* preparación, apresto; habilitación; (*food*) guiso; (*drug*) confección; **—s** preparativos.
preparative [pri'pærətiv] *a* preparatorio, previo.
prepare [pri'pɛə] *vt* preparar; (*meal*) hacer, guisar; (*person, condition*) acondicionar; *vi* prepararse, aprestarse, disponerse a.
preparedness [pri'pɛədnis] *n* preparación, prevención; prontitud.
prepayment ['pri:'peimənt] *n* pago adelantado; franqueo.
preponderate [pri'pɔndəreit] *vi* preponderar, predominar.
preposition [.prepə'ziʃən] *n* preposición.
prepossessing [.pri:pə'zesiŋ] *a* atractivo, bonito, cautivador.
preposterous [pri'pɔstərəs] *a* absurdo, descabellado.
prerequisite ['pri:'rekwizit] *n* requisito previo.
presage ['presidʒ] *n* presagio; *vt* amagar.
Presbyterian [.prezbi'tiəriən] *an* presbiteriano.
prescribe [pris'kraib] *vt* prescribir, ordenar; (*medicines*) recetar.
prescription [pris'kripʃən] *n* prescripción, orden; receta.
presence ['prezns] *n* presencia; asistencia; (*dignified*) empaque; **fine —** buena planta; **— of mind** entereza, serenidad; **in the — of** delante de, ante.
present ['preznt] *n* regalo, presente; agasajo; (*New Year*) aguinaldo; (*time*) presente, actualidad; *a* presente; **—day** actual; **those —** los presentes, la asistencia; **at —** actualmente, al presente; **to be —** *vi* estar (presente), concurrir; presentarse; **to be — at** presenciar, asistir; **— and future** habido(s) y por haber; **— company excepted** con perdón de los presentes, mejorando lo presente; [pri'zent] *vt* dar, ofrecer; presentar; **to — with** obsequiar; hacer un obsequio; (*occasion*) deparar; (*a case*) exponer, manifestar; (*arms*) presentar; **to — itself** ofrecerse.
presentiment [pri'zentimənt] *n* presentimiento; **to have a —** presentir.
presentation [.prezen'teiʃən] *n* presentación; entrega; *a* con dedicatoria.
presently ['prezntli] *ad* al instante, dentro de poco, en breve, luego.
preservation [.prezə:'veiʃən] *n* conservación; (*grounds etc*) entretenimiento.
preserve [pri'zə:v] *n* conserva, confitura; **—s** (*shooting*) coto; *vt* conservar, preservar.
preside [pri'zaid] *vi* presidir; llevar la batuta.
president ['prezidənt] *n* presidente; **—'s chair** presidencia.
presidential [.prezi'denʃəl] *a* presidencial.
press [pres] *n* (*printing*) prensa; (*clothes*) armario; (*hurry*) prisa, urgencia; **— cutting** recorte de periódico; **—button** botón de presión; *vt* apretar, abrumar, obligar, apremiar; (*troops*) hacer levas; (*grapes*) prensar; (*clothes*) planchar; (*hasten*) instar, apretar; (*print*) imprimir; *vi* urgir; **to — down** apretar, pisar.
pressing ['presiŋ] *a* (*situation*) urgente, apremiante; (*person*) importuno; *n* expresión.
pressure ['preʃə] *n* presión, urgencia; apremio; empuje, impulso; **— gauge** manómetro.
prestige [pres'ti:ʒ] *n* prestigio, renombre, fama.
presume [pri'zju:m] *vt* presumir, suponer, atreverse.
presumption [pri'zʌmpʃən] *n* presunción, arrogancia, orgullo, soberbia; tufo, humos.
presumptuous [pri'zʌmptjuəs] *a* presuntuoso, presumido, encopetado, temerario.
presuppose [.pri:sə'pouz] *vt* presuponer.
pretend [pri'tend] *vti* aparentar, pretextar, fingir; pretender; **to —**

to be hacerse.

pretender [pri'tendə] *n* pretendiente.

pretense [pri'tens] *n* pretensión; pretexto; colorido; designio; **it is a complete —** es una comedia; **under — of** bajo pretexto de, so capa de; **on false —s** ilegalmente.

pretension [pri'tenʃən] *n* pretensión, demanda; **—s** (*to elegance etc*) cursilería.

pretentious [pri'tenʃəs] *a* pretencioso, presumido, cursi.

pretext ['pri:tekst] *n* pretexto; título; especie; **under — of** so color de, con motivo de.

prettiness ['pritinis] *n* lindeza, gracia.

pretty ['priti] *a* bonito; lindo, precioso, mono; **— thing** prenda; *ad* bastante, un poco, algo.

prevail [pri'veil] *vi* prevalecer, predominar, influir, reinar, preponderar; **to — upon** influir, valer, convencer, persuadir.

prevalent ['prevələnt] *a* predominante, corriente.

prevarication [pri,væri'keiʃən] *n* prevaricación, falsedad.

prevent [pri'vent] *vt* impedir, evitar, obstar, imposibilitar, estorbar.

prevention [pri'venʃən] *n* prevención, impedimento, rémora.

preventive [pri'ventiv] *a* preventivo; *n* preservativo.

previous ['pri:viəs] *a* previo, anterior, temprano.

previously ['pri:viəsli] *ad* con anterioridad, previamente, con anticipación.

previousness ['pri:viəsnis] *n* prioridad, anterioridad.

prey [prei] *n* presa; **bird of —** ave de rapiña; *vi* **to — on** pillar, devorar, consumir, remorder, agobiar.

price [prais] *n* precio, valor; **controlled —** precio de tasa; **current —** cotización; **at a high —** caro; **without —** inapreciable; **— list** tarifa; **to set — to** valuar; **of great —** de gran coste; **at any —** cueste lo que cueste; *vt* valuar, tasar, estimar.

priceless ['praislis] *a* inapreciable, sin precio.

prick [prik] *n* punzada; (*of pin*) alfilerazo; **to kick against the —s** dar coces contra el aguijón; *vt* picar, estimular; aguzar, avivar; **to — up one's ears** aguzar las orejas.

pricking ['prikiŋ] *n* **— of conscience** compunción, remordimiento.

prickly ['prikli] *a* espinoso; (*subject*) delicado.

pride [praid] *n* orgullo; soberbia, fiereza, altivez; jactancia; dignidad; *vr* **to — oneself on** preciarse de.

priest [pri:st] *n* sacerdote; (*parish*) cura, párroco; preste; **— in charge** vicario.

priesthood ['pri:sthud] *n* sacerdocio; **to leave the —** colgar los hábitos.

prim [prim] *a* afectado, estirado, peripuesto; **— and proper** relamido.

primary ['praiməri] *a* primario, originario.

prime [praim] *a* principal, primero; escogido, selecto; primitivo.

primeval [prai'mi:vəl] *a* primitivo, pristino.

primitive ['primitiv] *a* primitivo, primordial; radical.

prince [prins] *n* príncipe.

princely ['prinsli] *a* de príncipe, munífico.

princess [prin'ses] *n* princesa.

principal ['prinsəpəl] *a* principal, primario, cardinal; *n* principal, director.

principality [,prinsi'pæliti] *n* principado.

principle ['prinsəpl] *n* principio, fundamento; axioma, máxima; **in —** en principio.

print [print] *n* impresión, marca; grabado; **in —** en letras de molde, impreso; **foot—** huella; **out of —** agotado; **printed matter** impresos; (*cloth*) estampados; *vt* imprimir; (*copies*) tirar; estampar; publicar, dar a la estampa.

printer ['printə] *n* impresor, tipógrafo, cajista.

printing ['printiŋ] *n* (*art, craft of*) imprenta, tipografía; (*act, result*) impresión, tirada; **— works** imprenta; **— press** prensa, rotativa.

prior ['praiə] *a* anterior; previo; **— to** antes de; *n* prior.

priority [prai'ɔriti] *n* (*in time*) anterioridad; prioridad; (*in choice, privilege etc*) preferencia, precedencia.

prism ['prizəm] *n* prisma.

prison ['prizn] *n* cárcel; prisión; **to put in —** encarcelar, llevar a la cárcel.

prisoner ['priznə] *n* (*mil*) prisionero; (*criminal*) preso; **no —s taken** sin cuartel.

pristine ['pristain] *a* primitivo, pristino.

privacy ['privəsi] *n* retiro; secreto.

private ['praivit] *a* privado; **— room** reservado; (*home*) particular; secreto, clandestino; (*land*) vedado; (*views etc*) individual, particular; esotérico; **— home** casa particular; **— road** camino reservado; **—!** (*no entrance*) prohibida la entrada; **in —** en secreto; particularmente; **in — life** en la intimidad; *n* soldado raso.

privation [prai'veiʃən] *n* privación, pérdida, estrechez.

privilege ['privilidʒ] *n* privilegio, título, prerrogativa; **—s** honores.

privileged ['privilidʒd] *pp a* privilegiado, excusado.

privy ['privi] *a* particular, sigiloso, secreto; enterado; *n* letrina, retrete.

prize [praiz] *n* premio; galardón; (*naval*) presa. [praiz] *vt* apreciar, valuar, estimar, reputar.

probability [,prɔbə'biliti] *n* probabilidad.
probable ['prɔbəbl] *a* probable, verosímil.
probation [prə'beiʃən] *n* prueba, ensayo; probación; noviciado.
probe [proub] *n* tienta, sonda, indagación; *vt* sondar, tentar; indagar.
problem ['prɔbləm] *n* problema, cuestión; **what a —!** ¡qué lío!
problematical [,prɔbli'mætikəl] *a* problemático, dudoso.
procedure [prə'si:dʒə] *n* procedimiento, proceder; protocolo.
proceed [prə'si:d] *vi* seguir, avanzar, adelantar; portarse; ponerse a; **to — against** procesar; **to — from** provenir; **to — to** recurrir a.
proceeding [prə'si:diŋ] *n* procedimiento; *pl* proceso, pleito, auto; (*minutes etc*) actas.
proceeds ['prousi:dz] *n pl* productos, renta; rédito.
process ['prouses] *n* proceso; progreso; procedimiento; obra; **in — of time** con el tiempo; *vt* procesar, encausar.
procession [prə'seʃən] *n* (*relig*) procesión; (*for display*) desfile; (*mil*) convoy; (*funeral*) cortejo.
proclaim [prə'kleim] *vt* proclamar, declarar, publicar; declararse.
proclamation [,prɔklə'meiʃən] *n* (*public*) bando, edicto; proclamación.
procrastinate [prou'kræstineit] *vti* dejar para mañana, diferir.
procrastination [prou,kræsti'neiʃən] *n* dilación, tardanza, demora.
procure [prə'kjuə] *vt* procurar, lograr, obtener, gestionar.
prod [prɔd] *n* aguijón; *vt* punzar, picar.
prodigal ['prɔdigəl] *an* pródigo; (*with money*) manirroto, derrochador.
prodigious [prə'didʒəs] *a* prodigioso, portentoso, ingente.
prodigy ['prɔdidʒi] *n* prodigio, portento, pasmo.
produce ['prɔdju:s] *n* producto; (*of earth, labor, thought*) fruto; resultado; víveres; [prə'dju:s] *vt* producir, hacer, llevar, rendir; motivar; fabricar; dar frutos; (*theat*) poner en escena, dirigir.
producer [prə'dju:sə] *n* productor; (*theat*) director de escena.
product ['prɔdəkt] *n* producto, efecto, resultado; rendimiento; **farm —** frutos.
production [prə'dʌkʃən] *n* producción, producto; (*theat*) representación.
productive [prə'dʌktiv] *a* productivo, producente; feraz, prolífico.
profane [prə'fein] *a* profano; impío, sacrílego; *vt* profanar; desprestigiar.
profanity [prə'fæniti] *n* reniegos, impiedad; profanidad.
profess [prə'fes] *vti* profesar; manifestar; asegurar, declarar; hacer profesión de.
professed [prə'fest] *a* declarado; presunto, ostensible.
profession [prə'feʃən] *n* profesión, carrera, declaración.
professional [prə'feʃənl] *a* profesional; (*med*) facultativo.
professor [prə'fesə] *n* profesor; (*Univ*) catedrático.
proficiency [prə'fiʃənsi] *n* pericia, aprovechamiento.
proficient [prə'fiʃənt] *a* aventajado, diestro, experimentado, perito.
profile ['proufail] *n* perfil; corte; silueta.
profit ['prɔfit] *n* provecho, beneficio, ganancia, fruto; utilidad; partido; **— and loss** ganancias y pérdidas; **to make —** beneficiarse; *vt* aprovechar, mejorar; servir; fructificar; **to — by** sacar partido de.
profitable ['prɔfitəbl] *a* provechoso, útil, lucrativo, ventajoso, aventajado, productivo; **— business** negocio redondo.
profound [prə'faund] *a* profundo; (*sleep*) pesado; (*grief*) hondo; (*problem*) recóndito.
profuse [prə'fju:s] *a* abundante, profuso, pródigo.
profusion [prə'fju:ʒən] *n* prodigalidad, exceso.
progeny ['prɔdʒini] *n* progenie, prole, descendientes.
prognosticate [prɔg'nɔstikeit] *vt* pronosticar, predecir, presagiar.
program ['prougræm] *n* programa; plan.
progress ['prougres] *n* progreso; marcha; mejoramiento, carrera; [prə'gres] *vi* avanzar, adelantar, hacer progresos, progresar, marchar.
progressive [prə'gresiv] *an* progresivo; (*pol*) progresista.
prohibit [prə'hibit] *vt* prohibir.
prohibition [,proui'biʃən] *n* proscripción, interdicto; prohibición.
project ['prɔdʒekt] *n* proyecto, designio; plan; [prə'dʒekt] *vt* idear, proyectar; *vi* destacarse, sobresalir; resaltar.
projecting [prə'dʒektiŋ] *a* saliente, saledizo.
projection [prə'dʒekʃən] *n* proyección; salida.
prolixity [prou'liksiti] *n* prolijidad, nimiedad.
prologue ['proulɔg] *n* prólogo, proemio, prefacio; (*to play*) loa.
prolong [prə'lɔŋ] *vt* prolongar, alargar, dilatar.
promenade [,prɔmi'nɑ:d] *n* paseo.
prominence ['prɔminəns] *n* eminencia; altura; influencia, preeminencia.
prominent ['prɔminənt] *a* prominente, saliente; distinguido, notable; conspicuo; (*eyes*) saltones.
promiscuous [prə'miskjuəs] *a*

promiscuo; confuso, mezclado.
promise ['prɔmis] *n* promesa; estipulación, palabra; esperanza; *vt* prometer; pronosticar, augurar, asegurar, ofrecer; brindar, dar la palabra.
promised ['prɔmist] *a* — **land** tierra de promisión.
promising ['prɔmisiŋ] *a* prometedor; lisonjero.
promontory ['prɔməntri] *n* promontorio, cabo.
promote [prə'mout] *vt* (*projects etc*) promover, fomentar, adelantar; (*discussion*) suscitar, acalorar; gestionar, facilitar; (*mil*) ascender.
promotion [prə'mouʃən] *n* (*of activity*) promoción; (*of project etc*) fomento; (*in rank*) ascenso.
prompt [prɔmpt] *a* pronto, presto, veloz; puntual, resuelto; diligente; *vt* sugerir, soplar, incitar, inspirar; (*theat*) apuntar.
promptitude ['prɔmptitju:d] *a* prontitud, puntualidad, rapidez.
promptly ['prɔmptli] *ad* al instante, a prisa.
promptness ['prɔmptnis] *n* prontitud, presteza, puntualidad.
promulgate ['prɔməlgeit] *vt* promulgar, proclamar.
prone [proun] *a* (*temperament*) inclinado, dispuesto, propenso; (*position*) tumbado, postrado.
pronoun ['prounaun] *n* pronombre.
pronounce [prə'nauns] *vt* pronunciar, declarar; (*sentence*) fallar.
pronounced [prə'naunst] *a* marcado, fuerte, notable; (*accent*) clavado.
pronunciation [prə,nʌnsi'eiʃən] *n* pronunciación; articulación.
proof [pru:f] *n* prueba, ensayo; evidencia; probanza, probación, demostración, confirmación; toque; impenetrabilidad; —**reader** corrector; **page** — prueba formada, capilla; *a* — **against** a prueba de.
prop [prɔp] *n* apoyo, sostén; (*mining*) entibo, andema; (*arch*) contrafuerte; *pl* accesorios de teatro; *vt* apoyar, sostener, acodalar; apuntalar.
propaganda [,prɔpə'gændə] *n* propaganda.
propagate ['prɔpəgeit] *vti* propagar; propalar, diseminar.
propel [prə'pel] *vt* impulsar, propulsar, impeler.
propensity [prə'pensiti] *n* propensión.
proper ['prɔpə] *a* propio, idóneo, conveniente; a propósito, adecuado, acertado; pulcro; decente; **prim and** — relamido; **what is** — lo que está bien; **to have a sense of what is** — tener vergüenza.
property ['prɔpəti] *n* propiedad, bienes, hacienda; dominio; cualidad; **man of** — hacendado; (*theat*) aderezo, accesorio.
prophecy ['prɔfisi] *n* profecía, predicción.
prophesy ['prɔfisai] *vti* profetizar.
prophet ['prɔfit] *n* profeta.
prophetic [prə'fetik] *a* profético.
propitious [prə'piʃəs] *a* propicio, feliz.
proportion [prə'pɔ:ʃən] *n* proporción, relación, medida.
proposal [prə'pouzəl] *n* proposición, oferta, propuesta; (*of marriage*) declaración.
propose [prə'pouz] *vt* ofrecer, proponer; pensar; *vi* declararse.
proposition [,prɔpə'ziʃən] *n* proposición; oferta; propósito.
propound [prə'paund] *vt* proponer, asentar.
proprietor [prə'praiətə] *n* propietario, dueño, señor.
propriety [prə'praiəti] *n* conveniencia, decoro, decencia, vergüenza; corrección.
prosaic [prou'zeiik] *a* prosaico, insípido.
proscribe [prəs'kraib] *vt* proscribir, reprobar.
prose [prouz] *a* en prosa; *n* prosa; —**writer** prosista.
prosecute ['prɔsikju:t] *vt* (pro)seguir; continuar; enjuiciar; procesar; encausar.
prosecution [,prɔsi'kju:ʃən] *n* causa, proceso; (*law*) parte actora, fiscal.
prosecutor ['prɔsikju:tə] *n* acusador, actor; **public** — fiscal.
prospect ['prɔspekt] *n* vista; perspectiva; probabilidad; esperanza; — **south** orientación al sur; [prəs'pekt] *vti* explorar.
prospective [prəs'pektiv] *a* probable, por venir, anticipado.
prosper ['prɔspə] *vt* favorecer; *vi* prosperar, medrar.
prosperity [prɔs'periti] *n* prosperidad, bonanza.
prosperous ['prɔspərəs] *a* próspero, floreciente, venturoso.
prostitute ['prɔstitju:t] *n* prostituta, puta, ramera, zorra; *vt* prostituir, vender.
prostrate ['prɔstreit] *a* postrado, tendido, abatido; [prɔs'treit] *vt* humillar, abatir, postrar; *vi* postrarse, prosternarse.
prostration [prɔs'treiʃən] *n* postración, abatimiento.
protect [prə'tekt] *vt* proteger, defender, garantizar; **to** — **from** resguardar, poner al abrigo de.
protection [prə'tekʃən] *n* protección, defensa, apoyo, amparo; — **from** resguardo; (*by patron*) patrocinio; **to claim** — ampararse.
protective [prə'tektiv] *a* protector.
protector [prə'tektə] *n* protector, padrino.
protest ['proutest] *n* protesta; [prə'test] *vti* protestar.
protestant ['prɔtistənt] *an* protestante.

protestation [ˌprɔtes'teiʃən] *n* protesta.
protracted [prə'træktid] *a* largo, prolijo.
protrude [prə'tru:d] *vi* salir fuera, asomarse, sobresalir.
protruding [prə'tru:diŋ] *a* (*eyes*) reventón.
proud [praud] *a* orgulloso, soberbio, engreído, encopetado; altanero, envanecido.
prove [pru:v] *vt* (com)probar; demostrar, acreditar, experimentar, poner a prueba; *vi* dar fe; **to — to be** mostrarse; encontrarse; ser; salir, resultar; **to — the rule** confirmar la regla.
proverb ['prɔvəb] *n* refrán, proverbio, dicho, apotegma.
proverbial [prə'və:biəl] *a* proverbial, famoso, notorio.
provide [prə'vaid] *vt* proporcionar, ofrecer, surtir, apercibir, prevenir; proveer; **to — against** precaver; *vi* abastecer; *vr* proveerse.
provided [prə'vaidid] **— that** *cj* con tal que; dado que.
providence ['prɔvidəns] *n* providencia; provisión.
provident ['prɔvidənt] *a* previsor, prudente, providente, próvido.
province ['prɔvins] *n* provincia; jurisdicción; competencia; **to fall within one's —** incumbir a.
provincial [prə'vinʃəl] *a* provincial, provinciano, campesino.
provision [prə'viʒən] *n* provisión; disposición; **—s** abastecimiento, comestibles.
provisional [prə'viʒənl] *a* provisional, pasajero, interino.
provocative [prə'vɔkətiv] *a* provocativo, sugestivo.
provoke [prə'vouk] *vt* provocar, excitar, irritar, incitar; indignar; promover; *vi* enojar.
provoker [prə'voukə] *n* ofensor, provocador.
provoking [prə'voukiŋ] *a* enojoso, fastidioso; provocativo.
prow [prau] *n* proa, tajamar.
prowess ['prauis] *n* bravura, proeza; **deeds of —** hazañas.
prowl [praul] *vi* rondar, vagar, merodear.
proximity [prɔk'simiti] *n* proximidad, cercanía, inmediación.
proxy ['prɔksi] *n* (*power*) procuración, poder; (*person*) apoderado, comisionado; **by —** mediante apoderado.
prudence ['pru:dəns] *n* prudencia, cordura, decoro, tino.
prudent ['pru:dənt] *a* prudente; precavido, previsor; considerado, sesudo, discreto, recatado.
prudish ['pru:diʃ] *a* mojigato, gazmoño, remilgado.
prune [pru:n] *vti* podar, cortar; adornarse, componerse; *n* ciruela pasa.
pruning ['pru:niŋ] *n* poda; **— knife, — hook** podadera.
Prussian ['prʌʃən] *an* prusiano.
pry [prai] *vi* espiar, acechar, curiosear, fisgar.
psalm [sɑ:m] *n* salmo.
pseudonym ['sju:dənim] *n* seudónimo.
psychiatric [ˌsaiki'ætrik] *a* psiquiátrico *or* siquiátrico.
psychiatrist [sai'kaiətrist] *n* psiquiatra *or* siquiatra.
psychiatry [sai'kaiətri] *n* psiquiatría *or* siquiatría.
psychoanalysis [ˌsaikouə'næləsis] *n* sicoanálisis *or* psicoanálisis.
psychoanalytical [ˌsaikouænə'litikəl] *a* sicoanalítico *or* psicoanalítico.
psychological [ˌsaikə'lɔdʒikəl] *a* sicológico *or* psicológico.
psychologist [sai'kɔlədʒist] *n* psicólogo *or* sicólogo.
psychology [sai'kɔlədʒi] *n* psicología.
psychopath [ˌsaikou'pæθ] *n* sicópata *or* psicópata.
public ['pʌblik] *a* público, notorio; **— convenience** retrete, excusado; **— house** taberna; **— spirit** civismo; *n* público.
publication [ˌpʌbli'keiʃən] *n* publicación; edición.
publicity ['pʌblisiti] *n* publicidad, notoriedad.
publicize ['pʌblisaiz] *vt* dar publicidad a, anunciar.
publish ['pʌbliʃ] *vt* publicar, dar a luz, promulgar, sacar a luz.
publisher ['pʌbliʃə] *n* editor.
pucker ['pʌkə] *n* arruga, pliegue; (*clothes*) buche; *vt* (*eyes*) fruncir; (*dress*) plegar.
puerile ['pjuərail] *a* pueril, infantil.
puerility [pjuə'riliti] *n* puerilidad, niñería.
Puerto Rican ['pwə:tou'ri:kən] *an* puertorriqueño.
puff [pʌf] *n* soplo, bufido; (*of smoke*) bocanada; (*of wind*) racha; *vti* soplar, hinchar; bufar; (*out of breath*) jadear.
puffed [pʌft] *a* hinchado; (*out of breath*) jadeante; **to be — up** hincharse, entumecerse, ensoberbecerse.
pugilist ['pju:dʒilist] *n* boxeador.
pugnacious [pʌg'neiʃəs] *a* belicoso; pendenciero.
pugnacity [pʌg'næsiti] *n* pugnacidad.
pull [pul] *n* (*with hand etc*) sacudida, tirón; (*fam*) buenas aldabas; **a stiff —** estirón; llamada; **bell —** tirador; *vti* tirar; **to — along** arrastrar; **to — away, off, up** tirar, arrancar; **to — out** (*teeth*) extraer, sacar, (*length*) estirar; **to — up** (*roots etc*) extraer; **to — up** (*car*) pararse; tirar; dar un tirón; **to — away** apartar, (*at oars*) remar fuerte; **— down** derrocar,

derribar; abatir; **to — to pieces** despedazar, hacer cisco; **to — up** (*stop*) parar(se), (*interrupt*) atajar; **to — through** (*illness*) salir; **to — someone's leg** tomar el pelo a uno.

Pullman car ['pulmənkɑ:] *n* coche-pullman.

pulp [pʌlp] *n* pulpa, pasta; (*fruit*) carne.

pulpit ['pulpit] *n* púlpito, tribuna.

pulsate [pʌl'seit] *vi* latir, batir.

pulse [pʌls] *n* pulso, pulsación; **to feel the —** tomar el pulso.

pulverize ['pʌlvəraiz] *vt* pulverizar, moler, triturar.

puma ['pju:mə] *n* puma.

pump [pʌmp] *n* bomba; pompa; **village —** mentidero; *vt* darle a la bomba; bombear; sonsacar.

pun [pʌn] *n* equívoco, retruécano; chiste, juego de palabras.

punch [pʌntʃ] *n* (*blow*) puñetazo, revés; (*tool*) punzón; (*drink*) ponche; **P— and Judy show** títeres; **— and Judy showman** titiritero; *vt* (*with holes*) horadar; (*ticket*) picar; (*with fist*) dar puñetazos a.

punctilious [pʌŋktiliəs] *a* puntilloso, etiquetero.

punctiliousness [pʌŋk'tiliəsnis] *n* honrilla, pundonor; puntualidad.

punctual [pʌŋk'tjuəl] *a* puntual, preciso, a la hora.

punctuality [ˌpʌŋktju'æliti] *n* puntualidad, fidelidad.

punctuate ['pʌŋktjueit] *vt* puntuar.

puncture ['pʌŋktʃə] *n* puntura, punzadura; (*tire*) pinchazo; (*skin*) punción; *vt* punzar; pinchar, picar.

pungency ['pʌndʒənsi] *n* resquemor, mordacidad.

pungent ['pʌndʒənt] *a* picante, áspero; (*phrase*) lapidario, corrosivo; (*smell*) acre.

punish ['pʌniʃ] *vt* castigar; (*as example*) escarmentar.

punishable ['pʌniʃəbl] *a* punible.

punishment ['pʌniʃmənt] *n* castigo, pena, penitencia; **capital —** pena capital.

punt [pʌnt] *n* barco llano; batea; *vi* ir en barco llano; apostar.

puny ['pju:ni] *a* pequeño; ruin, mezquino.

pupil ['pju:pl] *n* (*eye*) niña, pupila; (*of teacher*) alumno, discípulo; (*of high school*) colegial.

puppet ['pʌpit] *n* títere, muñeca, fantocha; **—master** titiritero; **— show** títeres, retablo.

purchase ['pə:tʃəs] *n* compra; (*mech*) aparejo; *vt* comprar, lograr.

purchaser ['pə:tʃəsə] *n* comprador.

pure [pjuə] *a* puro, casto, virgen; prístino, depurado; (*style etc*) castizo; (*character*) genuino; (*wine etc*) refinado; (*friendship*) platónico.

purge [pə:dʒ] *vt* purgar, purificar, acrisolar; *vr* purgarse; *n* purga; purgamiento, purgación.

purification [ˌpjuərifi'keiʃən] *n* purificación, depuración; expiación.

purify ['pjuərifai] *vt* purificar; clarificar; (*wine etc*) refinar; purgar, expiar; (*metals*) acrisolar; *vi* purificarse.

Puritan ['pjuəritən] *an* puritano.

purity ['pjuəriti] *n* pureza, honra; (*esp fig of blood*) limpieza.

purple ['pə:pl] *a* purpúreo, de púrpura; **dark —** morado; *n* púrpura.

purport ['pə:pət] *n* intención, intento; sentido, tenor; substancia; [pə:'pɔ:t] *vt* significar; dar a entender; pretender.

purpose ['pə:pəs] *n* intención, voluntad, propósito; **on —** de propósito, de intento; **all to no —** en vano; en balde; *vti* proyectar, determinar, proponer(se).

purposely ['pə:pəsli] *ad* de propósito, adrede, expresamente.

purse [pə:s] *n* bolsa, bolsillo; portamonedas; **— strings** cordones de la bolsa.

pursue [pə'sju:] *vt* perseguir, proseguir, seguir, seguir la pista de, cazar; (*closely*) acosar; (*fiercely*) ensañarse en.

pursuer [pə'sju(:)ə] *n* perseguidor.

pursuit [pə'sju:t] *vt* persecución, seguimiento, busca; interés; **in — of** en pos de.

purvey [pə:'vei] *vti* proveer, suministrar, abastecer.

purveyor [pə:'veiə] *n* abastecedor, proveedor.

push [puʃ] *n* empujón, impulso; energía; (*mil*) ofensiva, avance; *vt* empujar; promover, activar, urgir; apretar; *vi* dar un empujón, esforzarse; apresurarse; **to — away** apartar, rechazar; **to — in** encajar, meter.

pushing ['puʃiŋ] *a* agresivo, emprendedor, entremetido.

put [put] *a* puesto; **— away** arrinconado, guardado; **— out** (*wariness*) escamado; **— out** (*surprise*) estupefacto; **— out** (*irritation*) enojado, incomodado; **to be — out** incomodarse; *vt* poner; (*in position*) colocar; (*in words*) redactar; **to — aside** deponer; **to — away** (*in corner*) arrinconar; apartar; guardar; **to — back** retardar; devolver; **to — between** interponer; **to — by** poner aparte; **to — by** (*money*) ahorrar; reprimir; deprimir; anotar; rebajar; **to — forth** (*leaves*) poblarse, brotar; (*hand*) alargar; (*notice*) publicar; **to — in** insertar, introducir, (*naut*) tocar en; (*claim*) presentar, (*in writing*) poner (por escrito); **to — off** (*in time*) aplazar, demorar, diferir, posponer, (*reject*) desechar, molestar, (*person*) quitar, entretener; **to — on** (*clothes etc*) poner(se), (*shoes, spurs etc*) calzar, (*person*) imponer, (*airs*) echárselas de; **to — out** (*hand etc*) alargar, (*head*) asomar(se), (*tongue*) sacar, (*light*) apagar, matar, (*bone*) dislocar, (*offhand*) fastidiar, contrariar, enojar, desconcertar, (*of temper*) sacar de quicio; **to — right** arreglar, componer; **to — to sea** hacerse a la vela, tomar la mar; **to — two and two together** atar cabos; **to — up** (*building*) construir, (*object*) subir, (*stay*) hospedarse; **to — up to** incitar, instigar; **to — up with** tolerar, aguantar, acomodarse; **to — a stop to** poner coto a; **to — to the test** poner a prueba, acrisolar; **to — together** articular.

putrefaction [ˌpjuːtriˈfækʃən] *n* putrefacción.

putrid [ˈpjuːtrid] *a* podrido, putrefacto, corrompido.

putrify [ˈpjuːtrifai] *vi* pudrirse.

puzzle [pʌzl] *n* embarazo, enigma; (*guessing*) adivinanza; **word —** anagrama; **crossword —** palabras cruzadas, crucigrama; *vt* confundir, embarazar, enmarañar.

puzzling [ˈpʌzliŋ] *a* extraño, enigmático.

pygmy [ˈpigmi] *an* pigmeo.

pyramid [ˈpirəmid] *n* pirámide.

Pyrenees [ˈpirəniːz] *n* los Pirineos.

python [ˈpaiθən] *n* serpiente boa.

Q

quack [kwæk] *n* charlatán, curandero, saltimbanque; (*of duck*) graznido; *vi* graznar.

quadrangle [ˈkwɔdræŋgl] *n* cuadrángulo; patio.

quagmire [ˈkwægmaiə] *n* tremedal, cenagal.

quail [kweil] *n* codorniz; *vi* temblar, acobardarse.

quaint [kweint] *a* raro, típico, pintoresco, anticuado.

quaintness [ˈkweintnis] *n* encanto singular, extrañeza.

quake [kweik] *n* temblor; *vi* temblar, trepidar.

Quaker [ˈkweikə] *an* cuáquero.

qualification [ˌkwɔlifiˈkeiʃən] *n* calificación, requisito; capacidad; restricción.

qualified [ˈkwɔlifaid] *a* habilitado, competente, calificado.

qualify [ˈkwɔlifai] *vt* calificar, moderar; limitar; habilitar; *vi* capacitarse, llenar los requisitos.

quality [ˈkwɔliti] *n* (*type*) clase, calibre, calidad; (*moral*) cualidad; carácter; **first-class —** de la mejor calidad, (*fam*) de marca mayor; *pl* (*moral*) calidades.

qualm [kwɔːm] *n* náusea, desmayo; escrúpulo.

quandary [ˈkwɔndəri] *n* incertidumbre, apuro, perplejidad.

quantity [ˈkwɔntiti] *n* cantidad, número; **unknown —** incógnita.

quarrel [ˈkwɔrəl] *n* (*blows*) pendencia, reyerta; (*words*) querella, altercado, disputa; (*disagreement*) desavenencia; *vi* pelear, querellarse, disputar; batirse; **to — with** meterse con.

quarrelsome [ˈkwɔrəlsəm] *a* pendenciero, querelloso.

quarry [ˈkwɔri] *n* cantera; (*hunting*) presa.

quart [kwɔːt] *n* cuarta, media azumbre; cuarto de quintal.

quarter [ˈkwɔːtə] *n* cuarta parte, cuarto; (*wheat*) arroba, cuartillo; (*in war*) cuartel; cuarto del dólar; *pl* vivienda, morada; (*mil*) cuartel, alojamiento; (*of town*) barrio; (*of year*) trimestre; **— deck** alcázar; *vt* descuartizar; (*mil*) acuartelar; hospedar, alojar.

quarterly [ˈkwɔːtəli] *ad, a* por trimestres.

quartet [kwɔːˈtet] *n* cuarteto.

quash [kwɔʃ] *vt* anular; sofocar.

quaver [ˈkweivə] *n* (*mus*) corchea; *vi* gorjear, trinar; vibrar.

quay [kiː] *n* muelle, malecón.

queen [kwiːn] *n* reina; **— bee** reina; (*cards*) caballo.

queer [kwiə] *a* bizarro, extraño, original, raro; extravagante; extrafalario; **— fellow** extravagante.

queerness [ˈkwiənis] *n* rareza.

quench [kwentʃ] *vt* apagar, extinguir; (*feeling*) ahogar; (*thirst*) calmar.

querulous [ˈkweruləs] *a* quejoso, quejumbroso.

querulousness [ˈkweruləsnis] *n* queja.

query [ˈkwiəri] *n* pregunta, cuestión; *vti* preguntar, inquirir.

quest [kwest] *n* pesquisa, busca, búsqueda.

question [ˈkwestʃən] *n* cuestión, pregunta; asunto; (*fam*) busilis; **burning —** cuestión candente; **out of the —** descartado; *vti* preguntar; interrogar; poner en duda, desconfiar de; cuestionar.

queue [kjuː] *n* cola; (*hair*) coleta; *vi* hacer la cola.

quibble [ˈkwibl] *n* retruécano, juego de palabras; sutileza; *vi* argüir; jugar del vocablo.

quick [kwik] *a* rápido, pronto; vivo, ágil, vivaz; **—tempered** vivo de genio; *n* carne viva; **to cut to the —** herir en lo vivo; vivo.

quicken [ˈkwikən] *vt* vivificar; (re)-animar, acelerar.

quickness [ˈkwiknis] *n* viveza, prontitud, presteza.

quiet [ˈkwaiət] *a* quieto, reposado, tranquilo; pausado; sencillo; suave, retirado; **all —** sin novedad; **on the —** a la sordina; *n* tranquilidad, holganza; *vt* calmar, tranquilizar; **to — down** *vt* callar; *vi* reposarse.

quieten [ˈkwaiətn] *vt* callar, calmar.

quietness [ˈkwaiətnis] *n* quietud,

serenidad, reposo, sosiego, descanso.
quilt [kwilt] *n* sobrecama, cubrecama, cobertor; (*down*) colcha; *vt* estofar.
quintessence [kwin'tesns] *n* quintaesencia.
quip [kwip] *n* pulla; *vi* bromear, echar pullas.
quit [kwit] *a* libre, quito; absuelto; *n* —s en paz; *vt* quitar, dejar, desocupar; absolver; abandonar, cesar.
quite [kwait] *ad* enteramente, completamente; bastante, harto, totalmente; — **a man** todo un hombre.
quiver ['kwivə] *n* (*arrows*) carcaj; temblor; *vi* (re)temblar, palpitar; (*with fear*) estremecer(se).
Quixote, Don ['kwiksout, dɔn] *m* Don Quijote.
quixotic [kwik'sɔtik] *a* quijotesco.
quota ['kwoutə] *n* cuota, contingente.
quotation [kwou'teiʃən] *n* (*lit*) cita, citación; acotación; (*fin*) cotización.
quote [kwout] *vt* citar; (*prices*) cotizar; *n* cuota; *pl* **between —s** entre comillas.

R

rabbi ['ræbai] *n* rabí, rabino.
rabbit ['ræbit] *n* conejo; — **warren** conejero.
rabble ['ræbl] *n* canalla, chusma, gentuza, populacho.
rabid ['ræbid] *a* rabioso, furioso, fanático.
race [reis] *n* raza; casta; linaje; carrera; **horse —** concurso hípico; **—horse** caballo de carrera; **—course** hipódromo; *vi* correr; competir, luchar contra.
Rachel ['reitʃəl] *f* Raquel.
rack [ræk] *n* (*for hanging*) percha, colgadero, tendedor; (*lance*) astillero; (*torture*) potro, tortura; *vt* torturar, atormentar; (*wine*) trasegar; vejar; **to — one's brains** calentarse (devanarse) los sesos.
racket ['rækit] *n* raqueta; (*noise*) estrépito, baraúnda; (*pelota*) cesta, cremallera.
racy ['reisi] *a* (*language*) chispeante, fuerte, rancio.
radiance ['reidiəns] *n* brillo, brillantez, esplendor, claror.
radiant ['reidiənt] *a* radiante, alborozado, resplandeciente.
radiate ['reidieit] *vi* radiar, centellear.
radiator ['reidieitə] *n* radiador, aparato de calefacción.
radical ['rædikəl] *a* radical, fundamental, esencial; *n* radical.
radio ['reidiou] *n* radio; — **station** radioemisora.
radioactive ['reidiou'æktiv] *a* radioactivo.
radioactivity ['reidiouæk'tiviti] *n* radioactividad.
radius ['reidiəs] *n* radio.
raffle ['ræfl] *n* lotería, rifa; (*for charity*) tómbola; *vt* rifar, sortear.
raft [rɑ:ft] *n* balsa.
rafter ['rɑ:ftə] *n* viga, cabrio, traviesa.
rag [ræg] *n* trapo, trapito, harapo, hilacho; **in —s** harapiento; **bundle of —s** estropajo; — **doll** muñeca de trapo; — **market** rastro.
rage [reidʒ] *n* rabia, saña, cólera; enojo; *vi* rabiar, enfurecerse, encolerizarse.
ragged ['rægid] *a* haraposo, harapiento, andrajoso.
raging ['reidʒiŋ] *a* rabioso, bramador.
raid [reid] *n* incursión, irrupción, correría; **air —** ataque aéreo.
rail [reil] *n* (*enclosure*) barrera; (*altar window*) reja; baranda, cerca; (*rl*) riel, carril; *vti* cercar; **to — against** injuriar; burlarse de.
railing ['reiliŋ] *n* reja; baranda, antepecho, pasamano; cerca.
railroad ['reilroud] *n* ferrocarril, vía férrea.
railway ['reilwei] *n* ferrocarril, vía férrea; — **company** campañía ferroviaria; **—man** ferroviario.
raiment ['reimənt] *n* vestidos, ropaje.
rain [rein] *n* lluvia; (*sudden downpour*) chaparrón; (*downpour*) aguacero; **—storm** chubasco; **—bow** arco iris; *vi* llover; (*gently*) lloviznar; **to — cats and dogs, bucketfuls, torrents** llover a cántaros, a chuzos; (*sl*) menudear.
raincoat ['reinkout] *n* impermeable.
rainfall ['reinfɔ:l] *n* aguacero; cantidad de lluvia.
rainwater ['rein,wɔ:tə] *n* agua de lluvia.
rainy ['reini] *a* lluvioso, pluvial.
raise [reiz] *vt* (*on high*) alzar; (*stand up*) poner en pie, enderezar; (*stiffen up*) erguir; (*banner*) enarbolar; (*building*) levantar, erigir; (*hopes etc*) promover, suscitar; excitar, dar lugar a; (*the voice*) hablar alto; (*young*) criar, educar; (*in rank*) ascender; (*siege*) levantar; (*pay*) subir; **to — up** levantar; *vr* **to — oneself up** (*from horizontal*) incorporarse; *n* aumento.
raisin ['reizn] *n* uva pasa.
rake [reik] *n* rastro, rastrillo; (*man*) calavera; *vt* rastrillar; rastrear, hurgar; (*with volley of shots*) barrer.
rally ['ræli] *n* reunión; manifestación; *vti* reanimar(se); reunir(se); (*mil*) replegarse.
ram [ræm] *n* morueco; carnero; (*mil*) ariete; *vt* atacar; **to — down** apisonar, meter a viva fuerza.
ramble ['ræmbl] *n* paseo, excursión; *vi* vagar, divagar, discurrir, andarse por las ramas; (*walking*) salir de excursión.
rambler ['ræmblə] *n* vago; andarín, excursionista.
rampant ['ræmpənt] *a* exuberante;

desenfrenado; (*herald*) rampante.

rampart ['ræmpɑ:t] *n* terraplén; muralla, baluarte.

ramshackle ['ræm.ʃækl] *a* desvencijado.

ranch [rɑ:ntʃ] *n* hacienda, rancho, estancia; **— owner** estanciero, ranchero.

rancid ['rænsid] *a* rancio.

rancor ['rænkə] *n* rencor, inquina, encono.

random ['rændəm] *n* ventura, acaso; **at —** al azar, a la ventura, impensado, al buen tuntún.

range [reindʒ] *n* extensión, alcance; (*of goods*) surtido; (*territory etc*) recorrido; carrera; **cooking —** hornilla, foco, cocina económica; (*line*) fila; **mountain —** cordillera, sierra; **within — of** al alcance de; *vt* ordenar, arreglar, alinear; (*walk etc over*) recorrer; *vi* alinearse; variar; (*shell*) alcanzar.

rank [ræŋk] *n* condición, calidad; rango, grado; (*mil*) promoción; (*row*) fila; (*worldly*) honores; *a* vigoroso; tupido; fétido, rancio; *vti* alinear; alinearse; **to — with** equipararse con; **to — over** tener derecho de precedencia sobre.

rankle ['ræŋkl] *vi* enconar(se), carcomer, mordiscar.

ransack ['rænsæk] *vt* saquear, pillar; rebuscar.

ransom ['rænsəm] *n* rescate; (*prisoner's*) talla; redención; *vt* rescatar, redimir.

rap [ræp] *n* golpe; *vti* golpear; (*out orders*) espetar; criticar.

rapacious [rə'peiʃəs] *a* rapaz.

Raphael ['ræfeiəl] *m* Rafael.

rapid ['ræpid] *a* rápido; veloz; *n* catarata.

rapidity [rə'piditi] *n* rapidez, velocidad, ligereza.

rapier ['reipiə] *n* (*ceremonial*) espadín; (*fencing*) florete; estoque.

rapture ['ræptʃə] *n* transporte, arrebato, rapto, éxtasis, embeleso.

rapturous ['ræptʃərəs] *a* extático, arrebatador, arrobado, entusiástico, apoteósico.

rare [rɛə] *a* raro, exquisito, fénix, bizarro, peregrino, precioso; (*meat*) medio crudo.

rarely ['rɛəli] *ad* rara vez, por rareza.

rarity ['rɛəriti] *n* rareza, fenómeno.

rascal ['rɑ:skəl] *n* bribón, pícaro, galopín, pillo.

rascally ['rɑ:skəli] *a* arrastrado, vil, canallesco; pícaro, tunante.

rash [ræʃ] *a* (*person*) imprudente, arrojado, temerario; arrebatado; (*scheme etc*) precipitado, aventurado; *n* erupción; sarpullido.

rashness ['ræʃnis] *n* temeridad, precipitación, indiscreción.

rasp [rɑ:sp] *vt* raspar, rallar; raer; *n* raspador, rallo.

raspberry ['rɑ:zbəri] *n* frambuesa.

rasping ['rɑ:spiŋ] *a* (*voice*) ronco, áspero; raedor; *n* **—s** raspaduras.

rat [ræt] *n* rata; **I smell a —** aquí hay gato encerrado; **to smell a —** oler el poste.

rate [reit] *n* tasa; proporción, precio; impuesto, contribución; **at the — of** a razón de; **at any —** de todos modos, en todo caso; *vt* valuar, tasar.

rather ['rɑ:ðə] *ad* mejor, primero, más bien; un poco, algo, bastante; **—!** *excl* ¡claro que sí!

ratify ['rætifai] *vt* ratificar, sancionar.

ration ['ræʃən] *n* ración; **— card** cartilla de racionamiento; **—s** suministro; *vt* racionar

rational ['ræʃənl] *a* racional; cuerdo.

rationing ['ræʃəniŋ] *n* racionamiento.

rattle ['rætl] *n* ruido, fracaso; (*dance band etc*) matraca; (*drum*) rataplán; (*child's*) sonajero; **death —** estertor; *vt* (*castanets*) castañetear; zurrir; *vi* rechinar, hacer ruido; **to — on** articular sin parar; **—snake** serpiente cascabel.

rattling ['rætliŋ] *a* ruidoso; magnífico; *n* estertor; ruido.

raucous ['rɔ:kəs] *a* estridente, ronco, bronco.

ravage ['rævidʒ] *n* destrozo; (*of illness etc*) estrago; *vt* asolar, destrozar, talar.

rave [reiv] *vi* delirar, desvariar, encolerizarse; **to — about** morirse por.

raven ['reivn] *n* cuervo; *a* negro.

ravenous ['rævinəs] *a* voraz, hambriento, rapaz.

ravine [rə'vi:n] *n* barranca, garganta, quebrada.

raving ['reiviŋ] *a* furioso, alocado; **— mad** loco rematado, loco de atar; *n* delirio.

ravish ['ræviʃ] *vt* forzar, violar; arrebatar, embelesar.

raw [rɔ:] *a* crudo; verde; (*cotton etc*) en rama; **— material** materia prima; **— recruit** soldado bisoño: soldado raso; **—boned** huesudo; (*weather*) desapacible, crudo; **— flesh** carne viva.

rawness ['rɔ:nis] *n* crudeza.

ray [rei] *n* rayo; **—fish** raya.

Raymond ['reimənd] *m* Raimundo.

raze [reiz] *n* arrasar, asolar; borrar; desmantelar.

razor ['reizə] *n* (navaja, máquina) de afeitar.

reach [ri:tʃ] *n* extensión, alcance, capacidad; (*mil*) potencia; **within — of** al alcance de; *vt* lograr, alcanzar; (*age*) cumplir; **to —out** alargar, tender la mano.

react [ri(:)'ækt] *vi* reaccionar.

reaction [ri(:)'ækʃən] *n* reacción.

reactionary [ri(:)'ækʃnəri] *n* reaccionario, retrógrado; **extreme —** exaltado; **rabid —** cavernícola.

reactor [ri'æktə] *n* reactor.

read [ri:d] *vti* leer, descifrar; (*for degree*) estudiar, cursar; **to — out** leer en alta voz; *pp* [red] **to be well —** ser ilustrado.
reader ['ri:də] *n* lector; corrector (de pruebas).
readily ['redili] *ad* de buena gana, fácilmente, luego.
readiness ['redinis] *n* prontitud, buena disposición, desembarazo.
reading ['ri:diŋ] *n* lectura, lección, modo de entender; **— through** hojeada.
ready ['redi] *a* listo, pronto, preparado, a (la) mano, dispuesto; fácil; (*answer etc*) fácil; **— for action** lanza en ristre; (*money*) contante; **to be —** estar a punto, estar dispuesto; **to be — for** estar a la expectativa; **— made** hecho; **—made clothes** ropa hecha.
reaffirm ['ri:ə'fə:m] *vt* remachar, reiterar.
real [riəl] *a* real, verdadero, positivo, verídico, auténtico; **not —** teórico.
realism ['riəlizəm] *n* realismo.
realist ['riəlist] *n* realista.
reality [ri(:)'æliti] *n* realidad.
realization [,riəlai'zeiʃən] *n* realización, verificación.
realize ['riəlaiz] *vti* realizar, efectuar, darse cuenta, llevar a cabo, verificar(se); cumplirse.
really ['riəli] *ad* realmente, efectivamente, en realidad, de veras.
realm [relm] *n* reino; el estado.
reap [ri:p] *vti* segar, cosechar.
reaping ['ri:piŋ] *n* siega; **— machine** máquina segadora, rastra.
reappear ['ri:ə'piə] *vi* reaparecer.
rear [riə] *a* posterior, trasero, último; *n* (*mil*) retaguardia; parte de atrás; **in the —** (*mil*) en la retaguardia; a la zaga; *vt* criar, cultivar; *vi* encabritarse; (*building*) levantarse.
reason ['ri:zn] *n* razón, argumento; motivo; **for that —** por lo mismo; **to bring to —** meter en cintura; **I see no — why . . . not** no veo inconveniente; *vti* razonar.
reasonable ['ri:znəbl] *a* razonable, discreto, decente; (*price*) módico.
reasonableness ['ri:znəblnis] *n* razón, moderación, racionalidad, sensatez.
reasoning ['ri:zniŋ] *n* razonamiento, raciocinio.
reassemble ['ri:ə'sembl] *vti* reunir(se); volver a armar.
reassure [,ri:ə'ʃuə] *vt* alentar, tranquilizar; *vi* animarse.
rebel ['rebl] *n* rebelde, faccioso, insurgente; [ri'bel] *vi* rebelarse, sublevarse.
rebellion [ri'beljən] *n* rebelión, pronunciamento, sublevación.
rebellious [ri'beljəs] *a* rebelde, faccioso; indómito, indócil.
rebelliousness [ri'beljəsnis] *n* rebeldía.
rebound ['ri:baund] *n* rebote; **on the —** de rechazo; *vi* [ri'baund] rebotar.
rebuke [ri'bju:k] *n* reprensión, censura, reproche; *vt* reprender, increpar, castigar.
recalcitrant [ri'kælsitrənt] *a* refractario, reacio.
recall [ri'kɔ:l] *n* revocación; *vt* revocar, hacer presente; **to — to mind** recordar; (*from position*) deponer.
recapitulate [,ri:kə'pitjuleit] *vt* recapitular.
recapture [ri:'kæptʃə] *n* represa; *vt* represar; volver a tomar.
recasting ['ri:'kɑ:stiŋ] *n* refundición.
recede [ri(:)'si:d] *vi* retirarse, retroceder.
receding [ri(:)'si:diŋ] *a* **— forehead** frente huyente.
receipt [ri'si:t] *n* recibo; entrada; receta; **— book** libro talonario; **—s** ingresos; *vt* dar recibo; **to acknowledge —** acusar recibo.
receive [ri'si:v] *vt* recibir, aceptar, admitir, acoger; (*money*) cobrar.
receiver [ri'si:və] *n* recibidor, receptador, receptor; depositario; recipiente; (*radio*) receptor; (*tele*) auricular.
recent ['ri:snt] *a* reciente; nuevo; **most —** último.
recently ['ri:sntli] *ad* recientemente, ha poco, de nuevo.
receptacle [ri'septəkl] *n* recipiente.
reception [ri'sepʃən] *n* recepción, audiencia, recibo; **royal —** besamanos.
recess [ri'ses] *n* retiro; receso; (*school*) recreo; (*in wall*) nicho; **innermost — of mind** recoveco; **hidden —** entraña, escondrijo; (*mech*) ranura.
recipe ['resipi] *n* receta; (*med*) fórmula.
recipient [ri'sipiənt] *n* recipiente; (*of grant*) concesionario.
reciprocate [ri'siprəkeit] *vti* usar de reciprocidad, corresponder, alternar; (*mech*) oscilar.
recital [ri'saitl] *n* narración; referencia; (*mus*) concierto, recital.
recite [ri'sait] *vt* referir, narrar, relatar; declamar, recitar.
reckless ['reklis] *a* atolondrado, descuidado, temerario, precipitado.
recklessness ['reklisnis] *n* atolondramiento, atrevimiento, descuido, arrojo.
reckon ['rekən] *vti* contar, calcular, tantear; **to — up** computar; **to — on** fiarse de, contar con; estimar.
reckoning ['rekəniŋ] *n* cálculo; reputación; tanteo, cómputo, cuenta; **day of —** día de ajuste de cuentas.
recline [ri'klain] *vti* reclinar(se); recostar(se).
recluse [ri'klu:s] *n* recluso, solitario; eremita.

recognition [ˌrekəg'niʃən] *n* reconocimiento.
recognize ['rekəgnaiz] *vt* reconocer, admitir.
recoil ['riːkɔil] *n* rechazo, reculada; (*gun*) rebufo; [ri'kɔil] *vi* recular, retroceder; (*gun*) rebufar.
recollect [ˌrekə'lekt] *vt* recordar; hacer memoria, acordarse de; *vi* recobrarse, volver en sí.
recollection [ˌrekə'lekʃən] *n* recordación, recuerdo, reminiscencia, memoria.
recommend [ˌrekə'mend] *vt* recomendar, encarecer, encomendar.
recommendation [ˌrekəmen'deiʃən] *n* recomendación.
recompense ['rekəmpens] *n* retribución, recompensa; *vt* recompensar, gratificar, indemnizar.
reconcile ['rekənsail] *vti* reconciliar, componer, avenir(se), compaginar, acomodar(se), allanar(se).
reconciliation [ˌrekənsili'eiʃən] *n* reconciliación.
reconnaissance [ri'kɔnisəns] *n* reconocimiento.
reconnoiter [ˌrekə'nɔitə] *vi* batir, reconocer.
reconstitute ['riː'kɔnstitjuːt] *vt* reconstituir.
record ['rekɔːd] *n* registro; recuerdo, acta; (*gramophone*) disco; (*sport*) récord, marca; *pl* archivos; [ri'kɔːd] *vt* registrar, hacer constar, apuntar; **to break a —** batir el récord.
record player ['rekɔːdˌpleiə] *n* tocadiscos.
recount [ri'kaunt] *vt* relatar, referir, recontar.
recourse [ri'kɔːs] *n* recurso, refugio; **to have — to** recurrir, apelar a.
recover [ri'kʌvə] *vi* restablecerse, convalecer, sanar; *vt* (re)cobrar; (*health*) recuperar; rescatar, redimir; (*money*) reembolsar, cobrar.
recovery [ri'kʌvəri] *n* (*health*) mejoría, convalecencia, cura; (*from prison, vice, loss etc*) redención, rescate; (*money*) reembolso, recobro.
recreate ['riːkri'eit] *vt* recrear; ['rekrieit] *vi* recrearse, divertirse.
recreation [ˌrekri'eiʃən] *n* recreación; esparcimiento, entretenimiento, recreo; distracción.
recruit [ri'kruːt] *n* recluta; **raw —** bisoño; *vt* reclutar; (*by lots*) quintar; *vi* rehacerse.
recruiting [ri'kruːtiŋ] *n* reclutamiento; (*by lot*) quinta; **— depot** banderín.
rectify ['rektifai] *vt* rectificar, corregir.
rector ['rektə] *n* rector; párroco.
recuperate [ri'kuːpəreit] *vt* recuperar, recobrar; *vi* restablecerse, reponerse.
recur [ri'kəː] *vi* repetirse, presentarse de nuevo, acudir.
recurrence [ri'kʌrəns] *n* repetición, retorno, vuelta, reaparición.
red [red] *an* rojo, encarnado, colorado, encendido; (*wine*) tinto; **—hot** candente, extremo; **infra—** infrarrojo; **— tape** balduque, papeleo; **to grow —** colorear, ponerse colorado, sonrojarse.
Red Cross ['red'krɔs] *n* Cruz Roja.
redden ['redn] *vt* enrojecer; *vir* ponerse colorado, ruborizarse.
reddish ['rediʃ] *a* rojizo.
redeem [ri'diːm] *vt* redimir, rescatar, resarcir; (*debt*) amortizar.
redemption [ri'dempʃən] *n* redención, rescate; amortización; **beyond —** sin esperanza.
redness ['rednis] *n* rojez, lo rojo; (*of sky*) arrebol.
redouble [ri'dʌbl] *vt* redoblar, reduplicar.
redoubtable [ri'dautəbl] *a* temible, formidable.
redress [ri'dres] *n* reparación; satisfacción; *vt* reparar, desagraviar, rectificar; (*wrongs*) enderezar.
reduce [ri'djuːs] *vt* reducir, disminuir, menguar; mermar, contraer, marchitar, escatimar; sintetizar; **to — to fact** concretar; **to — to ranks** degradar.
reduction [ri'dʌkʃən] *n* reducción; (*price*) rebaja; contracción; (*fortress*) conquista.
redundance, redundancy [ri'dʌndəns(i)] *n* redundancia; (*wordy*) hojarasca.
redundant [ri'dʌndənt] *a* redundante; superfluo; **to be —** estar de más.
reed [riːd] *n* junco, caña; **— pipe** caramillo; (*mus*) lengüeta.
reef [riːf] *n* arrecife; *vt* rizar.
reel [riːl] *n* devanadera; carrete; *vt* devanar; *vi* titubear, bambolear, tambalear, hacer eses.
re-election ['riːi'lekʃən] *n* reelección.
refer [ri'fəː] *vt* referir; remitir; *vi* referirse (a), hacer alusión (a), concernir, acudir a.
referee [refə'riː] *n* (*sport*) árbitro; ponente, tercero.
reference ['refrəns] *n* referencia, alusión; **— book** libro de consulta; **terms of —** puntos de consulta.
refine [ri'fain] *vt* refinar, purificar; (*sugar*) clarificar; (*metals*) acendrar.
refined [ri'faind] *a* esmerado, pulcro; depurado; exquisito; **over —** decadente.
refinement [ri'fainmənt] *n* refinamiento, delicadeza, esmero; sutileza; gentileza.
reflect [ri'flekt] *vt* reflejar; mirar; (*light*) reverberar; *vi* reflejarse; reflexionar; meditar.
reflection [ri'flekʃən] *n* reflexión, imagen; (*of self*) espejismo; (*light*) reflejo; (*thought*) reconsideración; observación desfavorable, reparo.

reform [ri'fɔ:m] *n* reforma; mejora; *vt* reformar, reconstituir; *vi* reformarse, volver la hoja.
reformation [,refə'meiʃən] *n* (*relig*) reforma; **counter —** contrarreforma; enmienda.
reformer [ri'fɔ:mə] *n* reformador.
refractory [ri'fræktəri] *a* refractorio, contumaz, terco.
refrain [ri'frein] *n* refrán; (*song, poem*) estribillo; *vt* contener, reprimir; *vi* abstenerse, guardarse, reportarse.
refresh [ri'freʃ] *vt* refrescar; aliviar; *vr* cobrar nuevas fuerzas.
refreshing [ri'freʃiŋ] *a* refrescante.
refreshment [ri'freʃmənt] *n* refresco; **— room** cantina.
refrigerator [ri'fridʒəreitə] *n* nevera, frigorífico; **— ship, car** *etc* frigorífico.
refuge ['refju:dʒ] *n* refugio, puerto, amparo, abrigo, (*mountain*) albergue; (*relig*) retiro, asilo; **to take —** refugiarse, acogerse.
refugee [,refju(:)'dʒi:] *n* refugiado, expatriado.
refund [ri'fʌnd] *vt* reembolsar, restituir.
refusal [ri'fju:zəl] *n* repulsa, negativa, negación, desaire; opción.
refuse ['refju:s] *n* desecho, desperdicio; inmundicia, basura; [ri'fju:z] *vt* negarse (a); renunciar a, rehusar, resistirse; *vr* privarse.
refute [ri'fju:t] *vt* refutar, impugnar, rebatir.
regain [ri'gein] *vt* recobrar, recuperar.
regal ['ri:gəl] *a* real, regio.
regalia [ri'geiliə] *n* galas; insignias reales.
regard [ri'gɑ:d] *n* miramiento; consideración, respeto; aprecio, estimación; observancia; **to have — for** considerar; *pl* recuerdos, respetos; **as —s** en cuanto a; **with, in — to** con relación a, con respecto a, por lo que; *vt* estimar, respetar; observar, considerar; **to — as** mirar como; **to — as privilege** honrarse de.
regardless [ri'gɑ:dlis] *a* negligente, sin miramientos; *ad* a troche y moche, prescindiendo de.
regenerate [ri'dʒenərit] *a* regenerado; [,ri:'dʒenəreit] *vt* regenerar.
regent ['ri:dʒənt] *n* regente.
regicide ['redʒisaid] *n* regicidio.
regime [rei'ʒi:m] *n* régimen, sistema; orden, dieta.
regiment ['redʒimənt] *n* regimiento; tercio.
region ['ri:dʒən] *n* región; territorio; comarca, provincia; **in the — of** alrededor de.
register ['redʒistə] *n* registro, inscripción, (*church*) becerro; *vi* inscribir, registrar; (*letters, luggage etc*) certificar, facturar; recomendar; (*as student*) matricular.
registration [,redʒis'treiʃən] *n* registro, inscripción; (*letters*) certificación.
registry ['redʒistri] *n* registro, asiento; (*naut*) matrícula.
regret [ri'gret] *n* pesar, sentimiento; remordimiento; *vt* sentir (pena), lamentar.
regretful [ri'gretful] *a* triste, pesaroso; **to be —** sentir mucho.
regular ['regjulə] *a* regular, ordinario, uniforme; (*attender etc*) asiduo, metódico.
regularity [,regju'læriti] *n* regularidad, orden.
regulate ['regjuleit] *vt* reglamentar, ordenar, gobernar, ajustar, reglar, regular; (*price*) tasar.
regulation [,regju'leiʃən] *a* de reglamento, de rigor; *n* reglamento, arreglo.
rehearsal [ri'hə:səl] *n* ensayo; recitación; **dress —** ensayo general.
rehearse [ri'hə:s] *vt* ensayar, repasar, recitar.
reign [rein] *n* reinado; *vi* reinar; prevalecer.
reimburse [,ri:im'bə:s] *vt* reembolsar.
rein [rein] *n* rienda, freno; **to give free — to** dar rienda suelta a.
reindeer ['reindiə] *n* reno.
reinforce [,ri:in'fɔ:s] *vt* reforzar; estrechar.
reinforced [,ri:in'fɔ:st] *a* reforzado; **— concrete** hormigón armado.
reinforcement ['ri:in'fɔ:smənt] *n* refuerzo; contrafuerte.
reinstate ['ri:in'steit] *vt* restablecer, rehabilitar.
reiterate [ri:'itəreit] *vt* reiterar, reduplicar.
reject [ri'dʒekt] *vt* rechazar, desechar, renunciar a, descartar.
rejection [ri'dʒekʃən] *n* repulsa, repudiación, exclusión, desestimación.
rejoice [ri'dʒɔis] *vti* regocijar(se), alegrar(se).
rejoicing [ri'dʒɔisiŋ] *n* regocijo, fiesta, júbilo.
rejoin ['ri:'dʒɔin] *vti* reunirse con, volver a juntarse con; replicar.
rejoinder [ri'dʒɔində] *n* réplica, respuesta.
rejuvenate [ri'dʒu:vineit] rejuvenecer, remozar.
relapse [ri'læps] *n* recaída; *vi* recaer, reincidir.
relate [ri'leit] *vt* referir; (*story*) narrar, contar; relatar; *vi* relacionarse con, referirse, emparentar con.
related [ri'leitid] *a* **— to** pariente de; **— by blood** consanguíneo; afín, relacionado con.
relating [ri'leitiŋ] *a* **— to** concerniente, referente a.
relation [ri'leiʃən] *n* (*family*) pariente; (*connection*) trato, comunicación: respecto, relación; (*story*) relato; **near —, distant —** cercano, lejano.

relationship [ri'leiʃənʃip] *n* parentesco; trato, intimidad.
relative ['relətiv] *a* relativo; *n* pariente.
relax [ri'læks] *vt* (*rules*) relajar; (*cord*) aflojar; *vi* relajarse, aflojarse, ceder.
relaxation [ˌri:læk'seiʃən] *n* relajación; aflojamiento; (*ease*) recreo, descanso, solaz.
release [ri'li:s] *n* escape; (*from restriction*) soltura, libertad; *vt* libertar, absolver, soltar; (*pressure*) desapretar; (*gas*) desprender; (*tension*) aflojar.
relent [ri'lent] *vi* ablandarse, enternecerse; cejar.
relentless [ri'lentlis] *a* inexorable, implacable, rencoroso; encarnizado.
relevant ['relivənt] *a* pertinente, a propósito.
reliability [riˌlaiə'biliti] *n* seguridad, confianza.
reliable [ri'laiəbl] *a* digno de confianza; serio; puntual; de buena ley; fidedigno; **he is —** es de fiar.
reliance [ri'laiəns] *n* confianza.
relic ['relik] *n* resto, vestigio, rastro; (*holy*) reliquia.
relief [ri'li:f] *n* (*aid*) socorro, alivio, consuelo; (*mil*) relevo; **public —** auxilio social; **to throw into high —** hacer resaltar; (*paint*) relieve, realce.
relieve [ri'li:v] *vt* (*mil*) relevar; (*pain*) aliviar; (*need*) socorrer, aligerar.
religion [ri'lidʒən] *n* religión.
religious [ri'lidʒəs] *a* religioso, devoto, concienzudo; **— house** convento; *n* monje.
relinquish [ri'liŋkwiʃ] *vt* abandonar, ceder, renunciar, desistir de.
relish ['reliʃ] *n* sabor; fruición, goce; *vt* saborear; gustar de, relamerse, saber bien, ser sabroso.
reluctance [ri'lʌktəns] *n* repugnancia, renuencia, desgana; **with —** de mala gana, con reservas, a su pesar.
reluctant [ri'lʌktənt] *a* recalcitrante; reacio, maldispuesto; **to be —** tener pocas ganas, estar poco dispuesto.
reluctantly [ri'lʌktəntli] *ad* de mala gana, a contrapelo, a regañadientes, a su pesar.
rely [ri'lai] *vi* **to — on** descansar en, contar con, fiarse de, confiar en.
remain [ri'mein] *n pl* (*human*) restos; (*civilization etc*) vestigios; (*food*) sobras; (*bits*) desperdicios; cadáver; ruinas; *vi* permanecer, quedar, quedarse.
remainder [ri'meində] *n* resto, residuo; restante, (*arith*) remanente.
remaining [ri'meiniŋ] *a* restante, que queda.
remake ['ri:'meik] *vt* rehacer.
remark [ri'mɑ:k] *n* observación; *pl* comentario; **pointed —** animadversión, reparo; *vti* observar, notar; **to — (unfavorably) on** poner reparos en, hacer notar.
remarkable [ri'mɑ:kəbl] *a* notable, considerable; insigne; marcado.
remedy ['remidi] *n* remedio; cura, medicamento; *vt* remediar, sanar; reparar.
remember [ri'membə] *vt* acordarse de, recordar; hacer memoria, tener presente; **— me to her** dele Vd recuerdos míos.
remembrance [ri'membrəns] *n* recuerdo, conmemoración, memoria.
remind [ri'maind] *vt* recordar, avisar, hacer presente.
reminder [ri'maində] *n* advertencia, aviso.
remiss [ri'mis] *a* remiso, negligente, omiso, descuidado.
remit [ri'mit] *vt* remitir, perdonar; enviar; (*money*) girar.
remnant ['remnənt] *n* resto, residuo; (*cloth*) retal, retazo; *pl* (*food*) bazofia.
remonstrate ['remənstreit] *vt* protestar; objetar, poner reparos, reconvenir.
remorse [ri'mɔ:s] *n* remordimiento, compunción; **to feel —** compungirse, arrepentirse.
remorseful [ri'mɔ:sful] *a* arrepentido, compungido.
remorseless [ri'mɔ:slis] *a* implacable, despiadado.
remote [ri'mout] *a* remoto, ajeno, lejano, apartado; leve.
removal [ri'mu:vəl] *n* eliminación, separación; transporte; (*esp household*) mudanza; (*roots etc*) extirpación; apartamiento.
remove [ri'mu:v] *vt* quitar, trasladar; (*business*) trasladar; (*need*) obviar; sacar, apartar, extraer, substraer; *vi* (*house*) mudarse; alejarse.
remuneration [riˌmju:nə'reiʃən] *n* remuneración; recompensa.
renaissance [rə'neisəns] *n* renacimiento.
render ['rendə] *vt* rendir, lacerar, devolver; (*aid*) prestar; traducir; verter; hacer.
rendezvous ['rɔndivu:] *n* cita, compromiso, punto de reunión.
renew [ri'nju:] *vt* renovar; (*contact*) reanudar.
renewal [ri'nju(:)əl] *n* renovación, prolongación, renuevo, reanudación.
renounce [ri'nauns] *vt* renunciar a, abnegarse, abjurar.
renovate ['renəveit] *vt* renovar, rehacer.
renown [ri'naun] *n* (re)nombre, fama, gloria, nombradía.
renowned [ri'naund] *a* ínclito, renombrado.
rent [rent] *n* (*cloth etc*) desgarradura, raja, desgarrón; (*payment*) renta, alquiler; *vt* alquilar, arrendar, rentar.
renting ['rentiŋ] *n* arrendamiento.
reorganize ['ri:'ɔ:gənaiz] *vt* reorganizar.
repair [ri'pɛə] *n* reparación; restau-

ración; (*shoe*) remiendo; *vt* rehabilitar, reparar; remendar, arreglar; (*losses etc*) subsanar; *vi* encaminarse, recorrer (a).
repartee [ˌrepɑ:'ti:] *n* réplica, agudeza, ocurrencia.
repay [ri:'pei] *vt* reembolsar, pagar, reintegrar.
repayment [ri:'peimənt] *n* reembolso.
repeal [ri'pi:l] *n* revocación, abrogación; *vt* revocar, abrogar, alzar.
repeat [ri'pi:t] *vt* repetir; decorar; repasar.
repeatedly [ri'pi:tidli] *ad* repetidas veces, con empeño, repetidamente.
repel [ri'pel] *vt* repeler, rechazar, repugnar.
repellent [ri'pelənt] *a* repugnante, repelente; repulsivo.
repent [ri'pent] *vi* arrepentirse, dolerse (de).
repentance [ri'pentəns] *n* arrepentimiento.
repentant [ri'pentənt] *a* arrepentido, penitente.
repetition [ˌrepi'tiʃən] *n* repetición, vuelta; insistencia.
replace [ri'pleis] *vt* reemplazar; reponer.
replaceable [ri'pleisəbl] *a* reemplazable, renovable.
replete [ri'pli:t] *a* repleto, lleno, preñado, harto.
reply [ri'plai] *n* respuesta, réplica; *vti* contestar, replicar, responder.
report [ri'pɔ:t] *n* informe, relación, rumor, voz; (*mil*) parte; (*of meeting etc*) memoria; (*newspaper*) crónica; (*gunshot etc*) estampido, cañonazo, estallido; disparo; *vti* referir, informar, divulgar, manifestar; dar parte de, denunciar; **it is reported** corre la voz, se dice.
reporter [ri'pɔ:tə] *n* (*newspaper*) redactor; cronista, reportero.
repose [ri'pouz] *n* reposo; *vti* **to — upon** descansar sobre; *vr* reclinarse.
represent [ˌrepri'zent] *vt* representar, significar, figurarse, suponer.
representation [ˌreprizen'teiʃən] *n* representación; (*theat*) función.
representative [ˌrepri'zentətiv] *a* típico, representativo; *n* representante, portavoz, delegado, encargado.
repress [ri'pres] *vt* reprimir, comprimir; (*smile*) contener, sofocar.
repression [ri'preʃən] *n* represión.
reprieve [ri'pri:v] *n* aplazamiento, indulto, suspensión; *vt* indultar, aliviar.
reprimand ['reprimɑ:nd] *n* regaño, censura, reprensión; *vt* reprender, reñir, regañar.
reprint ['ri:'print] *n* reimpresión; *vt* reimprimir.
reprisal [ri'praizəl] *n* represalia.
reproach [ri'proutʃ] *n* reproche, reconvención, baldón; *vt* reprochar, increpar, dar en cara.
reproduce [ˌri:prə'dju:s] *vt* reproducir.
reproduction [ˌri:prə'dʌkʃən] *n* reproducción; copla; (*exact*) traslado.
reprove [ri'pru:v] *vt* reprender; reprobar, censurar, refregar, reñir.
reptile ['reptail] *n* reptil.
republic [ri'pʌblik] *n* república.
republican [ri'pʌblikən] *an* republicano.
repudiate [ri'pju:dieit] *vt* repudiar, rechazar, desechar.
repugnance [ri'pʌgnəns] *n* repugnancia, desgana, aversión.
repugnant [ri'pʌgnənt] *a* repugnante, antipático, opuesto, incompatible; **to be —** repugnar.
repulse [ri'pʌls] *n* repulsa, rechazo; *vt* rechazar, repulsar, repeler.
repulsive [ri'pʌlsiv] *a* repugnante; (*smell*) hediondo.
reputable ['repjutəbl] *a* honrado, honroso; estimable.
reputation [ˌrepju(:)'teiʃən] *n* reputación, fama, prestigio, nombre, honor, honra.
repute [ri'pju:t] *n* reputación, estimación; **of ill —** de mala fama; *vt* reputar, tener por.
reputed [ri'pju:tid] *a* supuesto, putativo; **to be —** pasar por, tener fama de.
request [ri'kwest] *n* demanda, solicitud, súplica, mandado; **— stop** parada discrecional; *vt* demandar, solicitar, pedir, suplicar.
require [ri'kwaiə] *vt* requerir, pedir, exigir, solicitar, demandar.
requirement [ri'kwaiəmənt] *n* formalidad; requisito, exigencia.
requisite ['rekwizit] *a* necesario, indispensable; preciso; *n* requisito, formalidad.
rescind [ri'sind] *vt* anular, abrogar.
rescue ['reskju:] *n* rescate, salvamento, socorro; *vt* rescatar, salvar, libertar.
rescuer ['reskjuə] *n* libertador, salvador.
research [ri'sə:tʃ] *n* investigación, indagación; *vti* investigar.
resemblance [ri'zembləns] *n* semejanza, parecido, imagen, similitud, afinidad, traslado, analogía.
resemble [ri'zembl] *vt* semejar, parecerse a, salir a.
resent [ri'zent] *vt* ofenderse por; **I — his remark** me (hiere, molesta) su observación.
resentful [ri'zentful] *a* resentido, ofendido.
resentment [ri'zentmənt] *n* resentimiento.
reservation [ˌrezə'veiʃən] *n* reserva, restricción; (*mental*) salvedad.
reserve [ri'zə:v] *n* reserva; *vt* reservar, (*seat*) guardar, retener.
reserved [ri'zə:vd] *a* (*seat*) de preferencia; (*character*) reservado, ce-

rrado, taciturno; sigiloso, circunspecto.
reservoir ['rezəvwɑ:] *n* depósito, surtidero.
reside [ri'zaid] *vi* residir, habitar, morar.
residence ['rezidəns] *n* residencia, domicilio, vivienda, morada.
resident ['rezidənt] *a* residente; *n* habitante, inquilino, vecino.
residue ['rezidju:] *n* residuo, superávit, remanente.
resign [ri'zain] *vt* renunciar, ceder; (*post*) dimitir; *vi* darse de baja; **to — oneself** conformarse, resignarse.
resignation [ˌrezig'neiʃən] *n* (*of mind*) resignación; (*of post*) dimisión, renuncia.
resilient [ri'ziliənt] *a* elástico, resaltante.
resist [ri'zist] *vt* resistir, oponerse a, soportar; sufrir.
resistance [ri'zistəns] *n* resistencia, oposición.
resolute ['rezəlu:t] *a* resuelto, resoluto, denodado.
resolution [ˌrezə'lu:ʃən] *n* resolución, fortaleza, tesón; propósito; (*of meetings*) acuerdo, solución.
resolve [ri'zɔlv] *n* determinación; *vti* resolver(se), decidir(se), tomar un acuerdo, aprobar; dar solución a.
resolved [ri'zɔlvd] *a* resuelto; **it is —** queda acordado.
resonant ['rezənənt] *a* resonante, retumbante, sonoro, hueco.
resort [ri'zɔ:t] *n* concurso; sitio; recurso, medio; **holiday —** lugar de veraneo; *vt* acudir, concurrir; **to — to** acudir a, tener recurso a, recurrir a, echar mano de.
resound [ri'zaund] *vt* repercutir; *vi* resonar, formar eco.
resounding [ri'zaundiŋ] *a* sonoro; famoso, celebrado.
resource [ri'sɔ:s] *n* recurso, expediente; inventiva, ingenio; *pl* recursos, medios.
respect [ris'pekt] *n* respecto, respeto; **out of — for** en obsequio de, en consideración de; **due —** consideración; **to treat with —** considerar; *vt* respetar, acatar, guardar.
respectable [ris'pektəbl] *a* respetable, honrado, decente.
respected [ris'pektid] *a* considerado.
respectful [ris'pektful] *a* respetuoso.
respective [ris'pektiv] *a* respectivo; relativo.
respiration [ˌrespə'reiʃən] *n* respiración, aliento.
respite ['respait] *n* tregua, plazo; respiro, descanso.
resplendent [ris'plendənt] *a* resplandeciente, flamante, refulgente.
respond [ris'pɔnd] *vi* (cor)responder; (*to request*) obedecer; (*in words*) replicar.
response [ris'pɔns] *n* respuesta, réplica; (*welcome*) acogida; **—s** (*relig*) responso.
responsibility [risˌpɔnsə'biliti] *n* responsabilidad, carga, preocupación, fideicomiso; **to take —** cargar (de), hacerse cargo (de), encargarse de.
responsible [ris'pɔnsəbl] *a* responsable; cumplidor; **— person** encargado; **to be — for** cargar con.
rest [rest] *n* reposo; descanso; (*remainder*) residuo; **at —** reposado; en descanso, en paz; resto; (*moment of*) alto, parada; (*support*) apoyo, base; (*others*) los demás; *vi* reposar, holgar, descansar; apoyarse; **to — upon** estribar sobre; **to — on** residir en; **to set at —** tranquilizar.
restaurant ['restərɔ̃:ŋ] *n* fonda, restorán, restaurante.
restful ['restful] *a* sosegado, tranquilo, descansado.
restive ['restiv] *a* alborotadizo, inquieto, nervioso.
restless ['restlis] *a* inquieto, andariego; desasosegado, revoltoso, revuelto; **— night** noche toledana.
restlessness ['restlisnis] *n* inquietud, desazón, turbulencia, desvelo.
restoration [ˌrestə'reiʃən] *n* restauración, devolución.
restore [ris'tɔ:] *vt* restaurar, restituir, devolver, reintegrar; (*spirits*) reanimar; **to be restored** rehacerse.
restrain [ris'trein] *vt* refrenar, moderar, contener, coartar, comprimir.
restrained [ris'treind] *a* **to be —** templarse; (*in speech*) comedirse.
restraint [ris'treint] *n* restricción, dominio de sí mismo, sobriedad, moderación.
restrict [ris'trikt] *vt* restringir, contener, ceñir(se) a.
restricted [ris'triktid] *a* limitado, reducido; **— to** peculiar de, privativo.
restriction [ris'trikʃən] *n* restricción, limitación; cortapisa.
result [ri'zʌlt] *n* resultado; fruto, éxito, secuela, consiguiente; **—s** fruto; **as a —** por consiguiente; *vi* resultar; **to — in** montar a; parar en.
resume [ri'zju:m] *vt* volver a empezar; reanudar, reasumir.
resurrect [ˌrezə'rekt] *vt* resucitar.
retail ['ri:teil] *a* al por menor; [ri:'teil] *vt* revender; vender al por menor.
retain [ri'tein] *vt* retener, guardar, quedarse con, conservar; (*lawyer*) ajustar.
retainer [ri'teinə] *n* deudo; partidario; dependiente.
retaliate [ri'tælieit] *vi* tomar represalias, desquitarse.
retaliation [riˌtæli'eiʃən] *n* represalia, desquite, venganza, talión, desagravio.
retard [ri'tɑ:d] *vt* retardar, demorar.
retention [ri'tenʃən] *n* retención, conservación; retentiva.

reticence ['retisəns] *n* reticencia, reserva.
retina ['retinə] *n* retina.
retinue ['retinju:] *n* séquito, comitiva.
retire [ri'taiə] *vt* recoger, retirar; *vi* retirarse, recogerse; (*from post*) jubilarse.
retired [ri'taiəd] *a* (*place*) recogido, apartado; (*person*) jubilado; — **officer** retirado; — **civil servant** cesante.
retirement [ri'taiəmənt] *n* retiro, reclusión; (*from career*) jubilación; (*mil*) retirada.
retiring [ri'taiəriŋ] *a* retirado, modesto, retraído, recatado.
retort [ri'tɔ:t] *n* réplica; (*chem*) retorta; *vti* redargüir, replicar.
retrace [ri'treis] *vt* (*lines*) volver a trazar; (*steps*) volver sobre sus pasos, desandar; relatar.
retract [ri'trækt] *vti* volver atrás, cantar la palinodia, desmentirse, retractar(se), encoger.
retreat [ri'tri:t] *n* retirada; (*bugle call*) retreta; (*relig*) retiro, clausura; encierra, refugio; *vi* retirarse; (*mil*) batirse en retirada; retroceder; retraerse, refugiarse.
retribution [,retri'bju:ʃən] *n* retribución, justo castigo.
retrieve [ri'tri:v] *vt* recobrar, recuperar; (*hunt*) cobrar.
retrograde ['retrougreid] *a* retrógrado; *vi* retroceder.
retrogression [,retrou'greʃən] *n* retroceso.
return [ri'tə:n] *n* vuelta, regreso, llegada; (*for effort etc*) recompensa, paga; (*election*) acta; (*ticket*) de ida y vuelta; (*of goods etc*) restitución, devolución; (*on investment*) renta; (*for insult*) desagravio; (*mil*) relación; (*tax*) rendimiento; (*to view*) reaparición; (*a form*) hoja, blanco; censo; **by — post** a vuelta de correo; *vt* (*thing lent etc*) devolver; pagar; remitir; corresponder; rendir; *vi* volver, regresar; reaparecer; (*speech*) responder.
reunion ['ri:'ju:njən] *n* reunión; tertulia.
reunite ['ri:ju:'nait] *vti* reunir(se), reconciliarse.
reveal [ri'vi:l] *vt* revelar, patentizar, propalar, manifestar, hacer patente.
revel ['revl] *n* orgía; jarana; borrachera; *vi* regocijarse; gozarse; jaranear.
revelation [,revi'leiʃən] *n* revelación; apocalipsis.
revenge [ri'vendʒ] *n* venganza; desagravio, desquite; *vt* vengarse, desquitarse.
revengeful [ri'vendʒful] *a* vengativo.
revengefulness [ri'vendʒfulnis] *n* encono.
revenue ['revinju:] *n* renta(s), rédito, ingreso(s), entrada; — **police** carabinero(s); **inland —, internal —** rentas públicas.
reverberate [ri'və:bəreit] *vti* reverberar; retumbar; resonar.
revere [ri'viə] *vt* reverenciar, honrar, acatar.
revered [ri'viəd] *a* honorable, venerado.
reverence ['revərəns] *n* reverencia, veneración; acatamiento; *vt* honrar, reverenciar, venerar.
reverend ['revərənd] *a* reverendo.
reverent ['revərənt] *a* reverente, piadoso.
reverie ['revəri] *n* ensueño; meditación, arrobamiento.
reverse [ri'və:s] *n* (*upset*) revés, contrariedad, mudanza, trastorno; (*of paper*) dorso, reverso; **the —** lo contrario, lo opuesto; *vt* trastrocar, invertir, revocar, volcar; *vi* (*aut*) dar marcha atrás.
reversible [ri'və:səbl] *a* revocable; de dos caras.
review [ri'vju:] *n* revista, examen; (*lit*) reseña; *vt* inspeccionar, repasar; (*mil*) revistar; (*book*) reseñar.
revile [ri'vail] *vt* injuriar, ultrajar, denigrar, denostar.
revise [ri'vaiz] *vt* revisar, corregir, rever; (*studies*) repasar; (*play*) refundir.
revision [ri'viʒən] *n* revisión, repaso.
revival [ri'vaivəl] *n* renacimiento, restauración, renovación; (*theat*) reposición.
revive [ri'vaiv] *vt* reanimar, resucitar, avivar, rehacer; *vi* (*hopes*) reverdecer; regenerar; despertar; (*from faint*) volver en sí.
revoke [ri'vouk] *vt* revocar; (*cards*) renunciar.
revolt [ri'voult] *n* rebelión, revuelta, levantamiento, pronunciamiento; *vt* indignar; repugnar; *vi* pronunciarse, rebelarse, levantarse, amotinarse, sublevar.
revolting [ri'voultiŋ] *a* espeluznante, asqueroso; **to be —** dar asco.
revolution [,revə'lu:ʃən] *n* revolución; (*mech*) vuelta, giro.
revolutionary [,revə'lu:ʃnəri] *an* revolucionario.
revolutionize [,revə'lu:ʃnaiz] *vt* revolucionar, trastornar.
revolve [ri'vɔlv] *vti* dar vueltas; girar, revolver; depender de.
revolver [ri'vɔlvə] *n* revólver.
revulsion [ri'vʌlʃən] *n* repugnancia; reacción.
reward [ri'wɔ:d] *n* recompensa; gratificación; premio, galardón; *vt* recompensar, remunerar, premiar.
rhetoric ['retərik] *n* retórica.
rhetorical [ri'tɔrikəl] *a* retórico.
rheumatism ['ru:mətizəm] *n* reumatismo.
Rhine [rain] *n* el Rin.
rhyme [raim] *n* rima, poesía, versos; **without — or reason** sin ton ni son,

a troche y moche, a tontas y a locas; *vti* rimar.
rhythm ['riðəm] *n* ritmo, medida.
rhythmical ['riðmikəl] *a* rítmico.
rib [rib] *n* costilla, varilla; (*vaulting*) nervadura; (*beam*) viga; (*umbrella*) varilla.
ribald ['ribəld] *a* soez, impúdico, obsceno, bajo.
ribbon ['ribən] *n* cinta, listón, banda, filete; (*narrow silk*) colonia.
rice [rais] *n* arroz; **—field** arrozal.
rich [ritʃ] *a* rico, opulento; (*stuff*) precioso, suntuoso, exquisito; (*earth*) fértil; (*in possibilities*) pudiente; (*profits etc*) pingüe; (*food*) suculento; empalagoso; copioso; **to grow —** enriquecerse.
Richard ['ritʃəd] *m* Ricardo.
riches ['ritʃiz] *n pl* riqueza, opulencia, caudales.
richness ['ritʃnis] *n* (*soil*) fertilidad; primor, suntuosidad; sabor.
rickety ['rikiti] *a* desvencijado; destartalado; (*med*) raquítico; **to be —** (*furniture etc*) cojear.
rid [rid] *vt* desembarazar, librar; **to get — of** desembarazarse de, zafarse de, quitarse de encima.
riddle ['ridl] *n* adivinanza, logogrifo; enigma; *vt* (*with bullets etc*) acribillar, cribar.
ride [raid] *n* paseo a caballo; **to take for a —** pasear; *vt* montar; (*waves*) surcar; *vi* montar, ir a caballo, cabalgar; — (*horse to death*) reventar; **to — down** atropellar, pisotear; **to — rough-shod over** imponerse, atropellar.
rider ['raidə] *n* caballero, jinete; adición.
ridge [ridʒ] *n* lomo; cerro, cresta; **mountain —** sierra, serranía; (*along mountain top*) ceja; (*roof*) caballete.
ridicule ['ridikju:l] *n* ridículo; burla, ridiculez; *vt* ridiculizar, mofarse de, rechiflar.
ridiculous [ri'dikjuləs] *a* grotesco; ridículo; **— pretensions** cursilería; **— person** adefesio.
riding ['raidiŋ] *n* equitación; **— boot** bota de montar; **to go —** ir montado, pasear a caballo.
riding school ['raidiŋ'sku:l] *n* escuela de equitación.
rife [raif] *a* frecuente, endémico, reinante; **to be —** reinar, privar, cundir.
rifle ['raifl] *n* fusil; *vt* pillar, robar; rayar, estriar.
rift [rift] *n* hendedura, grieta, rendija.
rig [rig] *vt* ataviar, adornar, equipar; manipular.
rigging ['rigiŋ] *n* aparejo, cordaje, jarcia.
right [rait] *a* (*correct*) correcto, justo, exacto; (*just*) sincero, razonable; (*proper*) indicado, conveniente; (*true*) verdadero, genuino, legítimo; (*straight*) derecho, honrado; (*sane*) cuerdo; **— angle** ángulo recto; **— side** lado derecho, (*of cloth*) haz; **all —** conforme, bueno, bien; *ad* bien, exacto, en derechura; **— or wrong** a tuerto o a derecho, con razón o sin ella; **just —** acertado; (*of food*) en su punto; *n* derecho; justicia; rectitud, dominio; título; autoridad; privilegio; **by —** de derecho; **to the —** a la derecha; **to put to —s** arreglar, reconciliar; *vt* enderezar, hacer justicia; ajustar; **to — a wrong** corregir un abuso; *excl* de acuerdo, muy bien.
righteous ['raitʃəs] *a* justo, equitativo, honrado, probo.
righteousness ['raitʃəsnis] *n* rectitud, equidad, justicia, virtud, honradez.
rightful ['raitful] *a* legítimo, justo.
rightly ['raitli] *ad* bien; **— or wrongly** a tuertas o a derechas.
rigid ['ridʒid] *a* rígido, tieso; (*custom etc*) austero, estricto.
rigor ['rigə] *n* rigor; (*weather*) inclemencia; dureza; exactitud; tesón.
rim [rim] *n* canto; (*of cup*) borde; margen; aro.
rind [raind] *n* peladura; corteza; (*apple*) piel; (*orange*) cáscara.
ring [riŋ] *n* (*finger*) (*jewels*) sortija, (*plain*) anillo; (*larger*) aro, argolla; (*hair*) rizo; (*sport*) circo, arena; (*boxing, bullfight*) plaza, ruedo; (*circle*) círculo; (*of mountains*) cerco; (*under eyes*) ojera; (*of people*) corro; camarilla; (*on door*) llamada; (*bells*) tañido, repique; *vt* cercar; (*bells*) tañer, repicar; (*bell*) tocar; *vi* sonar, resonar; (*in ears*) zumbar; (*telephone*) llamar.
ringing ['riŋiŋ] *n* (*bells*) toque; (*in ears*) zumbido.
ringlet ['riŋlit] *n* rizo, bucle, tirabuzón, sortija.
rinse [rins] *n* enjuague; aclarado; *vt* enjuagar.
riot ['raiət] *n* motín, asonada, bullanga, alboroto; bullicio; *vi* alborotar(se), amotinarse.
rioter ['raiətə] *n* amotinador; alborotador.
riotous ['raiətəs] *a* faccioso; libertino; bullicioso.
rip [rip] *n* rasgadura; descosido; *vt* rasgar, desgarrar; descoser, arrancar.
ripe [raip] *a* maduro; **— for picking** cogedero.
ripen ['raipən] *vti* madurar.
ripeness ['raipnis] *n* madurez.
ripple ['ripl] *n* onda, rizo; murmullo; *vi* encresparse, cabrillear, rizarse.
rise [raiz] *n* (*slope*) cuesta, subida, elevación, altura; (*promotion*) ascenso; (*price*) alza, aumento; (*source*) fuente, origen, principio; (*sun*) salida; **to give — to** motivar, ocasionar; *vi* subir; ponerse (en) (de) pie, levantarse; (*begin*) nacer; suscitarse,

surgir; (*revolt*) alzarse, sublevarse; (*in rank*) ascender, medrar; (*swelling*) hincharse; (*in price*) subir; (*with the lark*) madrugar; **to — above** sobreponerse a; **to — to** estar a la altura de.

rising ['raiziŋ] *n* (*sun*) salida, orto; levantamiento.

risk [risk] *n* riesgo, peligro; **without —** a mansalva; *vt* arriesgar, exponer(se a), aventurar.

risky ['riski] *a* aventurado, arriesgado, temerario.

rite [rait] *n* rito; **funeral —s** exequias.

ritual ['ritjuəl] *an* ritual.

rival ['raivəl] *an* rival; contrincante, competidor; *vt* rivalizar (con), competir, emular.

rivalry ['raivəlri] *n* rivalidad, pugna; **to be in —** pugnar.

river ['rivə] *a* fluvial; *n* río; **up, down —** río arriba, abajo.

road [roud] *n* camino, vía, ruta; (*main*) carretera; (*in town*) calle; (*for vehicles*) calzada; (*side*) camino vecinal; (*way*) paso, curso; *pl* (*naut*) rada, ensenada; **by-—** atajo, trocha; **cross—** encrucijada; **—house** parador; **no —** paso prohibido; **—side** orilla, borde del camino.

roam [roum] *vi* vagar, andar al acaso, errar; **to — the streets** callejear.

roar [rɔ:] *n* rugido, bramido; estruendo; gritería; *vi* rugir, bramar.

roaring ['rɔ:riŋ] *n* (*animals, elements*) bramido.

roast [roust] *an* asado; guiso; *vt* asar, tostar.

rob [rɔb] *vt* robar, hurtar, quitar.

robber ['rɔbə] *n* (*town*) ladrón; (*country*) bandido.

robbery ['rɔbəri] *n* robo, hurto; latrocinio.

robe [roub] *n* manto, vestido; vestidura; (*judge*) toga; **—s** ropaje, hábito; (*eccles*) vestimentas; *vti* vestir(se) de gala, de ceremonia.

Robert ['rɔbət] *m* Roberto.

robin ['rɔbin] *n* petirrojo.

robot ['roubɔt] *n* robot, autómata.

robust [rə'bʌst] *a* robusto, vigoroso, recio, fornido.

rock [rɔk] *n* roca, peña, peñasco; **to be on the —s** estar a la cuarta pregunta; *vt* mecer, arrullar; bambolear; balancear.

rocket ['rɔkit] *n* cohete.

rocking ['rɔkiŋ] *n* balanceo; **— chair** silla mecedora, silla de columpio; **— horse** caballo mecedor.

rocky ['rɔki] *a* rocalloso, rocoso, pedregoso; **— place** roquedal.

rod [rod] *n* varilla, baqueta; (*fishing*) caña, vara; (*of office*) vara; (*punishment*) férula, disciplinas; (*mech*) barra.

Roderick ['rɔdrik] *m* Rodrigo.

roe [rou] *n* corzo; hueva, huevecillos de pescado.

rogue [roug] *n* bribón, pícaro, pillo.

roguish ['rougiʃ] *a* pícaro, picaresco, juguetón, travieso.

role [roul] *n* papel; actuación; **to play a —** hacer un papel.

roll [roul] *n* (*bread*) panecillo, bollo; (*cylinder*) rollo; rodillo; (*turn*) vuelta; (*of names*) lista; (*for promotion*) escalafón; (*of lint*) mecha; (*of drum*) redoble; (*thunder*) retumbo; (*movement*) balanceo; *vt* (*cigarettes*) liar; (*eyes*) entornar, poner en blanco; (*on tongue*) saborear; (*tongue*) vibrar; **to — around, above, back** arrollar; **to — up** arrollar, envolver; **to — up sleeves** arremangarse; **to — out** desenrollar; *vi* rodar; girar; dar vueltas; envolverse; (*waves*) rodar; (*drum*) redoblar; **to — about** revolcarse.

roller ['roulə] *n* rodillo, cilindro, tambor, allanador, arrollador; (*printing*) rulo, rodillo; **— skate** patín de ruedas.

rolling ['rouliŋ] *n* rodadura, rodadero, laminación; **— stock** material móvil.

Roman ['rɔumən] *an* romano.

romance [rə'mæns] *n* novela, historia, fábula, cuento.

romantic [rə'mæntik] *a* romántico; novelesco, pintoresco, sentimental.

romanticism [rə'mæntisizəm] *n* romanticismo.

Rome [roum] *n* Roma.

roof [ru:f] *n* tejado, techo; (*lofty*) techumbre; (*of vehicle*) imperial; (*of mouth*) cielo, paladar; (*flat*) azotea; (*fig*) techo, hogar; *vt* techar.

rook [ruk] *n* grajo; (*chess*) torre, roque.

room [rum] *n* cuarto, habitación, pieza; sala; (*large*) aposento, cámara; (*space*) sitio, espacio, cabida; (*cause*) motivo, ocasión; (*for complaints etc*) margen; **bed—** habitación, alcoba; **lecture —** aula; **to make —** hacer lugar; abrir paso, dar cabida a; **there is —** cabe(n); **—mate** compañero de cuarto.

roomy ['rumi] *a* espacioso, amplio, holgado.

rooster ['ru:stə] *n* gallo.

root [ru:t] *n* raíz, origen, cimiento, base; *vti* arraigar, echar raíces; **to — out** extirpar, dessarraigar.

rope [roup] *n* cuerda; soga; (*naut*) maroma; cable; (*of pearls etc*) hilo, sarta; **to know the —s** (*fam*) conocer el tinglado; *vt* atar, amarrar.

rose [rouz] *n* rosa; **— bush (tree)** rosal; **— window** rosetón; **— bay** adelfa.

rosemary ['rouzməri] *n* tomero.

rosy ['rouzi] *a* rosado, color de rosa, sonrosado; (*prospect etc*) lisonjero.

rot [rɔt] *n* podredumbre; disparate; *vi* pudrir, pudrirse (*or* podrir).

rote [rout] *n* rutina, repetición maquinal; **to learn by —** aprender de memoria, maquinalmente.

rotate [rou'teit] *vt* girar, rodar.

rotten ['rɔtn] *a* podrido, pútrido, corrompido, carcomido.
rottenness ['rɔtnnis] *n* corrupción; mezquindad.
rotter ['rɔtə] *n* canalla, granuja.
rotund [rou'tʌnd] *a* rotundo, redondo.
rouge [ru:ʒ] *n* colorete, arrebol; *vr* arrebolarse, ponerse colorete.
rough [rʌf] *a* (*country*) quebrado, fragoso, desnivelado; (*words*) rudo, duro, agrio, áspero; (*unpolished*) bruto, crudo, grosero, inculto, brusco, tosco; (*weather*) borrascoso, desapacible, tempestuoso; (*indefinite*) aproximado, general, borroso; **— hewn, — and ready** desbastado, de brocha gorda; **— exterior** corteza; *n* **in the —** en bruto, sin pulir; **— draft** boceto, croquis, borrador; *vi* **to — it** pasar apuros.
roughly ['rʌfli] *ad* a bulto; en números redondos; más o menos; ásperamente.
roughness ['rʌfnis] *n* aspereza, dureza, brusquedad, rudeza, escabrosidad; (*of manner*) desabrimiento, brutalidad, grosería.
round [raund] *a* redondo; rollizo; circular, (*statement*) categórico; (*number*) redondo; (*sound*) sonoro; (*dozen etc*) cabal, completo, todo uno; **—-shouldered** cargado de espaldas; *ad* alrededor; a la redonda; **to go — and — a question** dar vueltas a la noria; *n* (*bullets*) descarga, disparo; (*turn*) vuelta, giro; (*dance*) ronda; (*of drinks*) ronda, turno; **to go the —s** rondar, ir de ronda; *vt* doblar; **to — off** dar cima a; **to — out** redondear; **to — up** acorralar.
roundabout ['raundəbaut] *a* indirecto; **— phrases** ambajes; **— way** rodeo; *n* tiovivo.
rounded ['raundid] *a* redondeado; **— off** rematado.
roundly ['raundli] *ad* hecho y derecho; duramente.
roundness ['raundnis] *n* redondez.
roundsman ['raundzmən] *n* mozo de reparto.
rouse [rauz] *vt* despertar, animar, excitar, provocar, levantar.
rout [raut] *n* derrota, asonada; derrota (total); *vt* derrotar.
route [ru:t] *n* ruta, rumbo, vía, derrotero.
routine [ru:'ti:n] *n* rutina.
rove [rouv] *vi* corretear, vagar.
rover ['rouvə] *n* errante, vagamundo.
roving ['rouviŋ] *a* ambulante; (*disposition*) andariego; inquieto.
row [rou] *n* (*seats*) fila; (*houses*) hilera; *vi* (*boat*) remar.
row [rau] *n* querella, pendencia; bronca, alboroto; (*noise*) barullo, escándalo, estrépito; *vi* pelearse con.
rowdiness ['raudinis] *n* escándalo.
rowing ['rouiŋ] *n* remar; **— boat** bote, lancha.
royal ['rɔiəl] *a* real, regio, soberano.
royalist ['rɔiəlist] *an* realista, monárquico.
royalty ['rɔiəlti] *n* realeza, soberanía, dignidad real; derechos (de autor).
rub [rʌb] *n* frotamiento, roce; embarazo; *vti* frotar; **to — against** rozar; (*eyes*) restregar; **to — out** borrar; **to — up against** rozar; **to — shoulders with** rozarse con; **to — the wrong way** frotar a contrapelo.
rubber ['rʌbə] *n* goma, caucho; borrador; *pl* chanclos.
rubbing ['rʌbiŋ] *n* frote, fricción, roce.
rubbish ['rʌbiʃ] *n* porquería, basura, desperdicio; desatino, disparate.
rubble ['rʌbl] *n* ripio, cascote; cantos rodados.
ruby ['ru:bi] *n* rubí, carmín; *a* rubeo, rubicundo, rojo.
rudder ['rʌdə] *n* timón, gobernalle.
ruddy ['rʌdi] *a* rosado; rubicundo; rojizo, encendido.
rude [ru:d] *a* (*manners*) ofensivo, descortés; (*unpolished*) rudo, basto, grosero, tosco; informal.
rudeness ['ru:dnis] *n* grosería, informalidad; ignorancia; rudeza, incivilidad.
rudiment ['ru:dimənt] *n* **—s** nociones, elementos.
rudimentary [ˌru:di'mentəri] *a* rudimentario; elemental; embrionario.
Rudolf ['ru:dɔlf] *m* Rodolfo.
rue [ru:] *vti* llorar, lamentar, arrepentirse.
ruffian ['rʌfjən] *n* rufián, malhechor, ladrón, bruto, asesino, bandolero.
ruffle ['rʌfl] *n* golilla; *vt* (*sew*) fruncir, rizar; arrugar; agitar, descomponer, perturbar.
ruffled ['rʌfld] *a* incomodado, desazonado; **to get —** enojarse, incomodarse.
rug [rʌg] *n* alfombra; alfombrilla; felpo, tapete; **traveling —** manta.
rugged ['rʌgid] *a* escabroso, escarpado, abrupto; tosco, robusto.
ruggedness ['rʌgidnis] *n* tosquedad, escabrosidad, lo escarpado.
ruin ['ru:in] *n* ruina, pérdida, caída, perdición; **—s** escombros, ruinas; *vt* arruinar, perder; asolar, destruir, matar; (*taste*) estragar; (*clothes, fun etc*) estropear, echar a perder.
ruinous ['ruinəs] *a* ruinoso, en ruinas, destartalado; funesto.
rule [ru:l] *n* mando, dominio, régimen; (*of life*) regla, norma, pauta, precepto; reglamento, estatuto; costumbre; regularidad; **as a —** por regla general; *vt* gobernar, regir, mandar; establecer; (*lines*) reglar, trazar rayas; **to — out** no admitir, desestimar.
ruler ['ru:lə] *n* (*person*) gobernador, potentado, soberano; (*instrument*) regla.
ruling ['ru:liŋ] *n* regente, imperante;

decisión; (*law*) fallo; *a* (*classes*) directoras.
rum [rʌm] *n* ron, aguardiente.
rumble ['rʌmbl] *n* ruido sordo, estruendo; *vi* retumbar.
rummage ['rʌmidʒ] *vti* revolver (buscando), registrar, escudriñar.
rumor ['ru:mə] *n* rumor; ruido, fábula; decir, hablilla, voz; **it is rumored** corre la voz, se dice.
run [rʌn] *n* carrera, curso, dirección; (*distance*) recorrido; (*naut*) singladura; (*repetition*) duración; (*freedom*) libre uso; (*theat*) serie; (*of game*) suerte, desarrollo; **chicken —** corral; **in the long —** a la larga, tarde o temprano; *vt* dirigir, sostener; pasar; *vi* correr; funcionar, andar; (*liquids*) verter, manar, fluir, gotear; (*risk*) correr; (*theat*) mantenerse en el cartel; **to — across, into** topar con, tropezar con; **to — up against** dar contra, chocar con; **to — after** seguir, perseguir; **to — aground** encallar; **to — ahead** adelantarse; **to — away** huir, escaparse, (*of horse*) desbocarse, (*of car*) dispararse; **to — away with** arrebatar, fugarse con; **to — counter to** contrariar a, ir en contra; **to — down** (*health*) quebrantar, (*reputation*) difamar, (*accident*) atropellar, (*by police*) acorralar, (*of watch*) acabarse la cuerda; **to — into** extenderse; sumar; chocar con; **to — off** (*liquid*) vaciar(se); repetir; **to — out** salirse; escurrirse; **to — out of** acabarse, agotarse; **to — over** (*accident*) atropellar, (*liquids*) derramarse, (*papers*) repasar, hojear; **to — through** (*book*) hojear, (*money*) derrochar, disipar, (*person*) espetar, penetrar; **to — to** acudir a; tender; alcanzar a; sumar; **to — up** enmendar, incurrir en, (*flag*) izar.
runaway ['rʌnəwei] *a* (*horse*) desbocado; *n* fugitivo.
runner ['rʌnə] *n* corredor, mensajero; peatón, andarín; agente; corredera, muela; (*bot*) serpa; pasador corredizo.
running ['rʌniŋ] *a* corredor, corredizo; *n* carrera, marcha; funcionamiento; marcha, servicio; dirección; **— aground** varada.
Rupert ['ru:pət] *m* Ruperto.
rupture ['rʌptʃə] *n* ruptura; quebradura; desavenencia; (*med*) hernia; *vti* romper; quebrar(se), reventar(se).
rural ['ruərəl] *a* rural, campestre, rústico.
ruse [ru:z] *n* treta, ardid.
rush [rʌʃ] *n* (*bot*) junco; (*forward*) precipitación, ímpetu; embestida; prisa, apuro; (*crowd*) tropel, agolpamiento; *vi* arrojarse, precipitarse, lanzarse; apurar; **to — against** embestir; **to — at** arremeter; (*of people*) agolparse; *vt* activar, despachar al momento.
Russia ['rʌʃə] *n* Rusia.
Russian ['rʌʃən] *an* ruso.
rust [rʌst] *n* orín, herrumbre, moho; *vti* enmohecerse.
rustic ['rʌstik] *a* rústico, campestre, agreste, aldeano; *n* patán, labriego, gañán, palurdo, villano.
rustle ['rʌsl] *n* crujido, susurro; *vi* (*dry leaves etc*) crujir; rechinar; (*leaves in wind*) susurrar, murmurar; *vt* (*cattle*) robar.
rustling ['rʌsliŋ] *n* crujido; susurro; el murmurar.
rusty ['rʌsti] *a* oxidado, mohoso; (*fam*) torpe; **to be —, grow —** enmohecerse.
rut [rʌt] *n* carril; rodada; surco; (*in road*) bache; (*fig*) rutina; *vi* estar en calor.
ruthless ['ru:θlis] *a* desapiadado, inhumano, implacable.
rye [rai] *n* centeno.

S

Sabbath ['sæbəθ] *n* sábado; domingo, día de descanso.
saber ['seibə] *n* sable.
sable ['seibl] *n* (*zool*) cebellina; (*fig*) negro.
sack [sæk] *n* saco, costal, talego; (*of town etc*) saqueo; *vt* (*town*) saquear, poner a saco; embolsar, ensacar, envasar; despedir, (*fam*) mandar de paseo.
sacrament ['sækrəmənt] *n* sacramento; **Holy —** Eucaristía; **to receive the —** comulgar, recibir los (santos) sacramentos.
sacred ['seikrid] *a* sagrado, (sacro)-santo.
sacrifice ['sækrifais] *n* sacrificio; víctima; renunciación; *vt* inmolar, sacrificar; *vi* sacrificarse, abnegarse.
sacrilege ['sækrilidʒ] *n* sacrilegio.
sacrilegious [,sækri'lidʒəs] *a* sacrílego.
sad [sæd] *a* triste, melancólico, sombrío, pesado; lastimoso, lastimero; lóbrego; aciago.
sadden ['sædn] *vt* entristecer, poner triste.
saddle ['sædl] *n* silla; **pack —** albarda; (*hill*) collado; **—bag** alforja; *vt* ensillar; **to — with** cargar con.
sadness ['sædnis] *n* tristeza, pesadumbre, melancolía.
safe [seif] *a* seguro, salvo; ileso, intacto, imperdible; **— conduct** salvoconducto; **— and sound** sano y salvo; *n* caja, arca (de hierro); guardacomidas.
safeguard ['seifgɑ:d] *n* salvaguardia, resguardo; defensa; *vt* proteger, guardar.
safely ['seifli] *ad* sano y salvo, sin daño, sin tropiezo; **to arrive —** llegar sin novedad.
safety ['seifti] *n* seguridad; salvamento; **— pin** prendedor, imperdible, alfiler de seguridad.

sag [sæg] *vi* doblegarse, combarse, hundirse; aflojar(se), flaquear.
sagacious [sə'geiʃəs] *a* sagaz, perspicaz, avisado.
sagacity [sə'gæsiti] *a* sagacidad, penetración, sutileza.
sage [seidʒ] *a* sabio; prudente, cuerdo, sagaz; *n* sabio; (*bot*) salvia.
sail [seil] *n* vela; (*windmill*) aspa; excursión (paseo) en barco; **to set —** hacerse a la vela; *vi* darse a la vela; zarpar, navegar, flotar; (*bird in sky*) cernerse.
sailing ['seiliŋ] *n* navegación; **— boat** barco de vela.
sailor ['seilə] *n* marino, marinero.
saint [seint] *an* santo, bendito.
saintliness ['seintlinis] *n* santidad.
sake [seik] *n* causa, objeto; **for God's —** por (el) amor de Dios; **for mercy's —** por piedad; **for the — of** por, por amor de, en obsequio a.
salable ['seiləbl] *a* vendible, realizable.
salad ['sæləd] *n* ensalada, ensaladilla.
Salamanca ['sælə'mæŋkə] **of —** salmantino.
salaried ['sælərid] *a* asalariado.
salary ['sæləri] *n* sueldo, honorario, paga.
sale [seil] *n* venta; realización; **bargain —** saldo; **public —** almoneda, remate; **ready —** venta fácil; **auction —** subasta; **on —** de venta.
salesman ['seilzmən] *n* vendedor.
salmon ['sæmən] *n* salmón.
saloon [sə'lu:n] *n* salón; taberna, bar; (*naut*) cámara.
salt [sɔ:lt] *a* salado; salobre; *n* sal; **— mine, — pit** salina; (*fig*) ingenio; *vt* salar; (*dry meat*) acecinar; sazonar.
salutary ['sæljutəri] *a* saludable.
salute [sə'lu:t] *n* saludo; *vt* saludar; (*mil*) cuadrarse.
salvage ['sælvidʒ] *n* salvamento.
salvation [sæl'veiʃən] *n* salvación, redención.
salve [sɑ:v] *n* ungüento, remedio, bálsamo; *vt* aplicar ungüentos; socorrer.
same [seim] *a* mismo, idéntico; idem, igual; **the —** igual; **the — to you** igualmente; **to be the — as** valer; **all the —** con todo, sin embargo.
sameness ['seimnis] *n* identidad; igualdad; monotonía.
sample ['sɑ:mpl] *n* muestra, modelo, ejemplar, prueba; *vt* probar.
sanatorium [ˌsænə'tɔ:riəm] *n* sanatorio.
sanctify ['sæŋktifai] *vt* santificar.
sanction ['sæŋkʃən] *n* sanción, beneplácito; *vt* sancionar, ratificar, autorizar.
sanctuary ['sæŋktjuəri] *n* santuario; refugio, sagrado; **to take —** acogerse a sagrado.
sand [sænd] *n* arena; **—bank** arenal, barra; **—shoe** playera; **—paper** papel de lija.
sandal ['sændl] *n* sandalia; (*peasant*) abarca; playera; **hemp-soled —** alpargata; **— factory** alpargatería; **—wood** sándalo.
sandwich ['sænwidʒ] *n* bocadillo, emparedado; *vt* insertar, intercalar.
sandy ['sændi] *a* arenoso, arenisco; sabuloso; rufo.
sane [sein] *a* sano, cuerdo.
sanguinary ['sæŋgwinəri] *a* sanguinario, sangriento.
sanguine ['sæŋgwin] *a* sanguíneo; confiado, esperanzado.
sanitary ['sænitəri] *a* sanitario.
sanity ['sæniti] *n* razón, juicio; cordura; salud mental.
Santander ['sæntən'dɛə] **of the province of —** montañés.
Santiago [ˌsænti'ɑ:gou] **of —** santiagués.
sap [sæp] *n* savia, jugo, zumo; *vti* zapar, socavar; minar; restar.
Saragossa [ˌsærə'gɔsə] *n* Zaragoza.
sarcasm ['sɑ:kæzəm] *n* sarcasmo.
sarcastic [sɑ:'kæstik] *a* sarcástico, mordaz, intencionado.
sardine [sɑ:'di:n] *n* sardina.
Sardinia [sɑ:'diniə] *n* Cerdeña.
Sardinian [sɑ:'diniən] *an* sardo.
sardonic [sɑ:'dɔnik] *a* burlón, con sorna.
sash [sæʃ] *n* faja; banda; cinturón, ceñidor; cíngulo; **— frame** bastidor; (*window*) marco de ventana.
Satan ['seitən] *m* Satanás.
satellite ['sætəlait] *n* satélite.
satiate ['seiʃieit] *vt* saciar, hartar.
satiety [sə'taiəti] *n* saciedad, hartura, colmo.
satin ['sætin] *a* de raso; *n* raso.
satire ['sætaiə] *n* sátira.
satiric [sə'tirik] *a* satírico, mordaz.
satirize ['sætəraiz] *vt* satirizar.
satisfaction [ˌsætis'fækʃən] *n* satisfacción, agrado, complacencia; paga, recompensa; amendación; desquite; **to give — for** desagraviar.
satisfactory [ˌsætis'fæktəri] *a* satisfactorio, suficiente.
satisfied ['sætisfaid] *a* harto; (*duty etc*) cumplido; **to be —** contentarse; **self-—** pagado de sí mismo.
satisfy ['sætisfai] *vt* satisfacer, contentar, gratificar, dar gusto a; cumplir con.
saturate ['sætʃəreit] *vt* saturar; *vr* impregnar, empaparse.
Saturday ['sætədi] *n* sábado.
sauce [sɔ:s] *n* salsa; aderezo; gracia, viveza; (*fam*) impertinencia; **—boat** salsera.
saucer ['sɔ:sə] *n* platillo.
sauciness ['sɔ:sinis] *n* (*fam*) impertinencia, descaro; gracia, desparpajo.
saucy ['sɔ:si] *n* (*fam*) respondón, deslenguado, descarado, impudente.
saunter ['sɔ:ntə] *vi* vagar, pasearse.

sausage ['sɔsidʒ] *n* salchicha, salchichón, embutido; (*pork*) longaniza, chorizo; (*black*) morcilla; (*Catal*) butifarra.
savage ['sævidʒ] *a* salvaje, feroz, fiero; bárbaro, inculto, inhumano; *n* salvaje.
savagery ['sævidʒəri] *n* salvajez; ferocidad; barbarie, brutalidad.
save [seiv] *vt* salvar; (*from sin*) redimir; (*from danger*) preservar, guardar; (*money*) economizar, ahorrar; — **for** excepto, salvo, fuera de.
saving(s) ['seiviŋ(z)] *n* ahorro(s), economía(s); —**s bank** caja de ahorros.
savior ['seivjə] *n* salvador.
savor ['seivə] *n* sabor; gust(ill)o; *vt* saborear; gustar; *vi* **to — of** saber a.
savory ['seivəri] *a* apetitoso, rico, sabroso, salado.
saw [sɔ:] *n* sierra; dicho, refrán, proverbio; *vt* serrar.
sawdust ['sɔ:dʌst] *n* serrín.
sawmill ['sɔ:mil] *n* aserradero.
Saxon ['sæksn] *an* sajón.
say [sei] *n* palabra, dicho; turno; *vt* decir; recitar; (*inscriptions*) rezar; **to — to oneself** decir para sí, decir para su capa.
saying ['seiiŋ] *n* dicho, refrán, proverbio.
scab [skæb] *n* costra; roña; esquirol.
scabbard ['skæbəd] *n* vaina.
scaffold ['skæfəld] *n* (*for execution*) cadalso; (*for building*) andamio.
scaffolding ['skæfəldiŋ] *n* andamio, andamiaje.
scald [skɔ:ld] *n* escaldadura; *vt* escaldar, quemar.
scale [skeil] *n* (*map etc*) escala; (*fish*) escama; (*balance*) platillo; (*mus*) escala; (*of charges*) tarifa; **pair of —s** balanza, báscula; *vt* balancear, pesar; (*mountain*) escalar; **to — down** rebajar; graduar.
scalp [skælp] *n* cuero cabelludo; *vt* escalpar.
scalpel ['skælpəl] *n* escalpelo, bisturí.
scaly ['skeili] *a* escamoso, tiñoso, incrustado.
scamper ['skæmpə] *n* fuga, escapada; *vi* **to — off** escabullirse.
scan [skæn] *vt* escudriñar; (*verse*) medir; (*book*) hojear.
scandal ['skændl] *n* escándalo; calumnia; ignominia; —**monger** correvedile.
scandalize ['skændəlaiz] *vt* escandalizar.
scandalous ['skændələs] *a* escandaloso, indecente, vergonzoso.
Scandinavia [,skændi'neiviə] *n* Escandinavia.
Scandinavian [,skændi'neiviən] *an* escandinavo.
scant [skænt] *a* escaso, corto, insuficiente.
scantiness ['skæntinis] *n* estrechez, insuficiencia.
scanty ['skænti] *a* exiguo, reducido, estrecho, escaso, poco.
scar [skɑ:] *n* cicatriz; (*on face*) chirlo; (*cliff*) farallón; *vi* cicatrizar.
scarce [skɛəs] *a* raro, escaso, contado.
scarcely ['skɛəsli] *ad* con dificultad, no bien, apenas; — **ever** casi nunca.
scarcity ['skɛəsiti] *n* escasez, inopia, carestía; rareza.
scare [skɛə] *n* susto, sobresalto; **to have a —** llevar un susto; *vt* asustar, atemorizar, espantar; **to — out of wits** horripilar; **to — away** ahuyentar.
scarf [skɑ:f] *n* bufanda; banda; tapabocas; pañuelo.
scarlet ['skɑ:lit] *an* escarlata, grana; — **fever** escarlatina.
scatter ['skætə] *vt* dispersar, esparcir, diseminar, derramar; (*seed etc*) sembrar; *vi* esparcirse, huir.
scattered ['skætəd] *a* disperso, desparramado.
scene [si:n] *n* escena; perspectiva; panorama; incidente, escándalo; (*of events*) teatro; (*of action*) escenario; (*of play*) cuadro, escena;—**shifter** tramoyista; **behind the —s** entre bastidores.
scenery ['si:nəri] *n* paisaje, vista; (*theat*) decorado.
scent [sent] *n* olor, perfume; (*track*) rastro, pista; — **bottle** pomar; **to catch — of** olfatear; *vt* perfumar; (*track*) ventear; **to — out** olfatear.
scented ['sentid] *a* oloroso, perfumado.
scepter ['septə] *n* cetro.
schedule ['skedju:l] *n* horario; cédula, inventario, plan; anexo.
scheme [ski:m] *n* proyecto, designio, plan; intriga, ardid; **grandiose —** máquina; **well-laid —** sabia combinación; **colour —** combinación de colores; *vt* proyectar, planear; tramar, intrigar; *vi* urdir, planear.
schism ['sizəm] *n* cisma.
scholar ['skɔlə] *n* (*school*) escolar, estudiante; erudito, sabio.
scholarly ['skɔləli] *a* erudito, sabio, docto.
scholarship ['skɔləʃip] *n* erudición; (*for study*) beca.
school [sku:l] *a* —**fellow,** —**mate** compañero de clase; — **life** escolar; *n* escuela; **boarding —** internado; **grammar —** instituto; — **book** libro de texto; (*of fish*) majal, banco; *vt* enseñar, amaestrar.
schoolhouse ['sku:lhaus] *n* escuela.
schooling ['sku:liŋ] *n* instrucción; enseñanza.
schoolmaster ['sku:l,mɑ:stə] *a* maestro, profesor.
schoolroom ['sku:lrum] *n* sala de escuela, salón de clase.

science ['saiəns] *n* ciencia; sabiduría; pericia; arte (*de*).
scientific [ˌsaiən'tifik] *a* científico.
scientist ['saiəntist] *n* científico, hombre de ciencia.
scintillate ['sintileit] *vi* centellear; chispear.
scion ['saiən] *n* vástago, hijo, hija o desciendente.
scissors ['sizəz] *n pl* tijeras.
scoff [skɔf] *vti* burlarse (*de*), escarnecer, mofarse (*de*).
scold [skould] *vt* reprender, regañar, reñir, increpar.
scone [skɔn] *n* bollo.
scoop ['sku:p] *n* pala de mano; paleta, cuchara; reportaje exclusivo; *vt* cavar, vaciar, ahuecar (*con pala o cuchara*).
scope [skoup] *n* designio; espacio, campo de acción; importancia, radio, extensión, alcance; **full —** amplio campo; carta blanca.
scorch [skɔ:tʃ] *vt* quemar, chamuscar, tostar; agostar, abrasar.
scorching ['skɔ:tʃiŋ] *a* ardiente, abrasador, que quema.
score [skɔ:] *n* (*groove*) muesca, entalladura; motivo; (*games*) tanteo; veintena; **to pay off old —s** ajustar cuentas viejas; *vt* (*carp*) escoplear; (*games*) hacer puntos; marcar; **to — out** rayar; **to — over** llevar una ventaja.
scorn [skɔ:n] *n* desdén, desprecio; escarnio, mofa; *vt* desdeñar, despreciar, menospreciar.
scornful ['skɔ:nful] *a* desdeñoso, insolente, despectivo.
scorpion ['skɔ:piən] *n* escorpión, alacrán.
Scot [skɔt] *n* escocés.
Scotch [skɔtʃ], **Scottish** *an* ['skɔtiʃ] escocés.
scot-free ['skɔt'fri:] *ad* con impunidad.
Scotland ['skɔtlənd] *n* Escocia.
scoundrel ['skaundrəl] *n* bribón, pícaro, malvado, canalla.
scour ['skauə] *vt* fregar, estregar, rascar.
scourge [skə:dʒ] *n* azote; disciplinas; plaga, calamidad; castigo; *vt* azotar, hostigar.
scout [skaut] *n* explorador, batidor; **Boy S—** explorador; *vti* explorar, reconocer; desdeñar.
scowl [skaul] *n* ceño; sobrecejo; *vi* mirar con ceño.
scramble ['skræmbl] *n* trepa; pendencia; *vi* **to — up** trepar, subir gateando; (*eggs*) revolver; **—d eggs** huevos revueltos.
scrap [skræp] *n* pedazo; (*bread*) mendrugo, cacho, fragmento; **— iron** desperdicios de hierro; **not a —** ni pizca; (*fam*) maldito; *pl* despojos, sobras, desperdicios; **—book** álbum de recortes; *vt* deshacerse de, desechar, descartar; *vi* pelear.
scrape [skreip] *n* raedura, raspadura; embarazo, lío, apuro, aprieto; *vt* raer, rascar; (*earth*) escarbar.
scratch [skrætʃ] *n* rasguño, araño; (*deep*) arañazo, (*on stone etc*) estría, raya; *vt* raspar; arañar, rasguñar; (*earth*) escarbar; (*glass*) rayar; **to — out** borrar.
scream [skri:m] *n* alarido, grito, chillido; *vi* chillar, gritar.
screaming ['skri:miŋ] *n* alarido, vocería.
screech [skri:tʃ] *n* chirrido, chillido; *vi* dar gritos, chillar; (*of hinges*) chirriar.
screen [skri:n] *n* biombo; mampara; (*cinema etc*) pantalla; resguardo; (*wooden*) cancel; (*wrought-iron*) reja; (*riddle*) criba, tamiz; *vt* abrigar, ocultar; resguardar; cribar.
screw [skru:] *n* tornillo; (*ship*) hélice; (*nails*) clavos de rosca; **—driver** destornillador.
scripture ['skriptʃə] *n* la Sagrada Escritura, la biblia.
scroll [skroul] *n* rollo de papel o pergamino.
scrub [skrʌb] *n* maleza; *vt* frotar, fregar; *vi* darse trabajo.
scruff [skrʌf] *n* (*of neck*) cogote, pescuezo.
scruple ['skru:pl] *n* escrúpulo; rescoldo, aprensión; *vi* tener escrúpulos, vacilar.
scrupulous ['skru:pjuləs] *a* escrupuloso, delicado, fino, riguroso, concienzudo; exacto; **not very —** ancho de conciencia.
scrupulousness ['skru:pjuləsnis] *n* delicadeza, meticulosidad, escrupulosidad.
scrutinize ['skru:tinaiz] *vt* examinar, escudriñar, atisbar, reconocer.
scrutiny ['skru:tini] *n* escrutinio.
sculptor ['skʌlptə] *n* escultor; (*of religious images*) imaginero.
sculpture ['skʌlptʃə] *n* escultura; estatuaria; *vt* esculpir, cincelar.
scum ['skʌm] *n* lapa; (*of metal*) escoria; (*of pond*) verdoyo; (*people*) hez, heces; *vt* espumar.
scurf [skə:f] *n* caspa, costra.
scythe [saið] *n* guadaña; *vt* guadañar.
sea [si:] *n* mar, océano; (*swell etc*) oleada, marejada, golpe de mar; **open —** mar abierto, piélago; **at —** en el mar; perplejo, perdido; **—horse** hipocampo; **—dog** lobo de mar; **—fight** combate naval; **—side** orilla del mar, playa.
seagull ['si:gʌl] *n* gaviota.
seal [si:l] *n* sello; (*zool*) foca; becerro marino; *vt* (*with seal*) sellar; estampar; (*with wax*) lacrar.
sea level ['si:levl] *n* nivel de mar.
sealing wax ['si:liŋwæks] *n* lacre.
seam [si:m] *n* (*sew*) costura; sutura; filón; (*coal*) capa; (*metal*) venero; *vt* coser.
seaman ['si:mən] *n* marinero.
seamstress ['semstris] *n* costurera.

seaplane ['si:plein] *n* hidroavión.
seaport ['si:pɔ:t] *n* puerto marítimo.
sea power ['si:ˌpauə] *n* fuerza marina.
search [sə:tʃ] *n* busca, pesquisa; indagación, búsqueda, demanda; (*customs etc*) registro; **in — of** en busca de, en demanda de; *vti* buscar, examinar, indagar, tentar; (*below sea surface*) bucear; (*for arms*) cachear.
searching ['sə:tʃiŋ] *a* penetrante, escrutador; completo.
sea shell ['si:'ʃel] *n* concha marina.
seasick ['si:sik] *a* mareado; **to be —** marearse.
seasickness ['si:siknis] *n* mareo.
season ['si:zn] *n* estación, sazón; hora; (*sport, entertainment etc*) temporada; época; **out of —** fuera de temporada; **closed —** veda; **— ticket** abono; **— ticket holder** abonado; *vt* sazonar; habituar; (*food*) condimentar, aliñar.
seasonable ['si:znəbl] *a* oportuno, a propósito.
seasoned ['si:znd] *a* sazonado; **highly —** picante; (*wood*) secado, endurecido.
seasoning ['si:zniŋ] *n* condimento, adobo.
seat [si:t] *n* silla, asiento, sitio; **—s** (*in rows*) gradería; (*theat*) localidad; **judgment —** tribunal; **country —** quinta; (*of war*) teatro; *vt* (a)sentar, colocar, fijar.
sea voyage ['si:'vɔiidʒ] *n* viaje por mar.
sea wall ['si:'wɔ:l] *n* muralla de mar, dique.
seaweed ['si:wi:d] *n* alga marina, asomate, ova.
seaworthy ['si:ˌwə:ði] *a* marinero.
Sebastian [sə'bæstiən] *m* Sebastián.
secluded [si'klu:did] *a* apartado, recogido, desviado.
seclusion [si'klu:ʒən] *n* retiro, retraimiento, reclusión, soledad, recogimiento; **to live in —** encerrarse.
second ['sekənd] *n* segundo; (*duel*) padrino; *a* segundo; **— sight** doble vista; **— hand dealer** prendero; **—hand market** (*Madrid*) Rastro; **— lieutenant** subteniente; **—hand** de segunda mano; de ocasión, usado; *vt* secundar, apoyar; (*in duel*) apadrinar.
secondary ['sekəndəri] *a* secundario, subalterno; **— school** instituto, escuela de segunda enseñanza.
secondly ['sekəndli] *ad* en segundo lugar.
secrecy ['si:krisi] *n* secreto, discreción, sigilo, misterio.
secret ['si:krit] *a* secreto, clandestino; recóndito, privado, oculto; *n* secreto; **dark —** busilis; **confided —** confidencia.
secretary ['sekrətri] *n* secretario.
secrete [si'kri:t] *vt* (*med*) secretar; esconder, ocultar, reservar.
secretive ['si:kritiv] *a* cerrado, sigiloso, callado.
secretly ['si:kritli] *ad* en secreto, a puerta cerrada.
sect [sekt] *n* secta; partido, pandilla.
section ['sekʃən] *n* sección; (*of orange*) gajo; (*of law*) artículo; **cross-—** corte.
secular ['sekjulə] *a* secular, temporal; *n* secular, seglar, laico, profano.
secularize ['sekjuləraiz] *vt* secularizar, exclaustrar.
secure [si'kjuə] *a* seguro, fijo; confiado, descuidado; firme; *vt* asegurar, amarrar, poner en lugar seguro; obtener, lograr, conseguir, procurar; hacerse con; afianzar.
security [si'kjuəriti] *n* seguridad; protección; descuido; afianzamiento, prenda; **to stand — for** salir por; *pl* títulos, valores.
sedateness [si'deitnis] *n* compostura, tranquilidad, formalidad, sosiego.
sediment ['sedimənt] *n* sedimento, asiento, depósito, poso.
sedition [si'diʃən] *n* sedición, tumulto, rebeldía, levantamiento.
seditious [si'diʃəs] *a* sedicioso, turbulento.
seduce [si'dju:s] *vt* seducir, pervertir, burlar; deshonrar.
seduction [si'dʌkʃən] *n* seducción; deshonra.
see [si:] *n* **Holy S—** Santa Sede; *vti* ver; (*glimpse*) columbrar, vislumbrar; percibir; comprender; **to — that** procurar, cuidar de que; **to — about, to** encargarse de; atender a; reflexionar; cuidar de; **to — into** examinar, informarse de; **to — off** despedir(se de); **to — through** (*obstacle, idea, pose*) calar.
seed [si:d] *n* grano, semilla, simiente; germen; **—bed** sementera; **—time** tiempo de siembra; *vi* granar, despepitar; **to sow —** sembrar.
seedling ['si:dliŋ] *n* planta de semillero.
seeing ['si:iŋ] *cj* **— that** visto que.
seek [si:k] *vti* buscar, solicitar; tratar de, intentar; pretender.
seem [si:m] *vi* parecer; **to — like** (*person*) parecerse a, (*name etc*) sonar a.
seeming ['si:miŋ] *a* aparente, parecido; *n* apariencia, fingimiento.
seemly ['si:mli] *a* decente, propio, pulcro, adecuado, decoroso.
seep [si:p] *vi* rezumarse, filtrar.
seethe [si:ð] *vi* hervir.
seething ['si:ðiŋ] *a* hirviente; *n* hervor.
segregate ['segrigeit] *vt* segregar.
Seine [sein] *n* el Sena.
seize [si:z] *vt* (*object*) agarrar, coger, asir; (*power etc*) apoderarse de; (*person*) prender; (*property*) incautar, secuestrar.

seizure ['si:ʒə] *n* secuestro, captura; (*med*) ataque.
seldom ['seldəm] *ad* (pocas, raras) veces, rara vez, de cuando en cuando.
select [si'lekt] *a* selecto, escogido; exquisito; *vt* escoger, elegir, seleccionar; optar por.
selection [si'lekʃən] *n* selección, elección, surtido; muestra.
self [self] *pn* mismo, sí mismo; idéntico, puro; automático; **—same** mismo, mismísimo; **— service** autoservicio; **— -command** dominio sobre sí mismo; **— -satisfied** pagado, engreído; **to have — -respect** tener vergüenza; **— -evident** patente; **— -possession** sangre fría; **— -sacrifice** abnegación.
self-conscious ['self'kɔnʃəs] *a* confuso, tímido, cohibido.
self-consciousness ['self'kɔnʃəsnis] *n* confusión, timidez.
self-contained ['selfkən'teind] *a* completo.
self-control ['selfkən'troul] *n* dominio de sí mismo.
self-defense ['selfdi'fens] *n* defensa propia.
self-governing ['self'gʌvəniŋ] *a* autónomo.
self-government ['self'gʌvnmənt] *n* autonomía.
self-interest ['self'intrist] *n* propio interés.
selfish ['selfiʃ] *a* egoísta, interesado; agarrado.
selfishness ['selfiʃnis] *n* egoísmo, amor propio, tacañería.
sell [sel] *n* (*fam*) chasco; *vti* vender, despachar, traficar, comerciar; **to — cheap** malbaratar; **tickets are sold out** están agotadas las localidades.
seller ['selə] *n* vendedor.
semblance ['sembləns] *n* apariencia, semejanza, semblante; **outward —** exterior; vislumbre; cariz; máscara, ficción; pizca.
semicircle ['semi,sə:kl] *n* semicírculo.
seminary ['seminəri]*n* seminario.
senate ['senit] *n* senado; (*Univ*) profesorado; junta directiva.
senator ['senətə] *n* senador.
send [send] *vt* enviar, mandar, remitir; **to — away** despedir, echar fuera; **to — back** devolver; **to — forth** despachar, enviar; exhalar; **to — out** (*smoke*) emitir, arrojar; despachar, publicar; **to — packing** mandar a paseo; **to — word** mandar recado.
sender ['sendə] *n* remitente, expedidor.
sending ['sendiŋ] *n* envío, remesa.
senile ['si:nail] *a* senil, caduco, chocho.
senior ['si:njə] *a* mayor, de mayor edad, decano; más antiguo; *n* mayor.
seniority [,si:ni'ɔriti] *n* antigüedad.
sensation [sen'seiʃən] *n* sensación, sentimiento, emoción; escándalo.
sensational [sen'seiʃənl] *a* sensacional, colosal.
sense [sens] *n* sentido, razón; juico; **common —** sentido común; **out of one's —s** trastornado; **in any —** por ningún concepto.
senseless ['senslis] *a* sin sentido; sin conocimiento; insensible; insensato, absurdo, disparatado; **— thing** gansada.
sensible ['sensəbl] *a* sensato, razonable, juicioso, cuerdo; **to be — of** estar persuadido de.
sensitive ['sensətiv] *a* sensible, sensitivo; sentido, impresionable, tierno; (*prickly*) quisquilloso; susceptible.
sensory ['sensəri] *a* sensorio.
sensual ['sensjuəl] *a* sensual, carnal.
sensuous ['sensjuəs] *a* sensorio, sensual.
sentence ['sentəns] *n* (*gram*) frase, cláusula, período, oración; (*law*) condenación; fallo, sentencia, juicio; *vt* dar sentencia; sentenciar.
sentiment ['sentimənt] *n* sentimiento, afecto; opinión, concepto; emoción.
sentimental [,senti'mentl] *a* sentimental, tierno, dulzón.
sentry ['sentri] *n* centinela, plantón; **— box** garita.
separate ['seprit] *a* separado; independiente, aparte, distinto; ['sepəreit] *vti* segregar, separar, desprender; alejar, apartar; separarse, desprenderse, desasociarse.
separation [,sepə'reiʃən] *n* separación, excisión, desunión.
September [səp'tembə] *n* se(p)tiembre.
sepulcher ['sepəlkə] *n* sepulcro.
sequel ['si:kwəl] *n* secuela, consecuencia; (*story etc*) continuación.
sequence ['si:kwəns] *n* serie, continuación, sucesión.
serenade [,seri'neid] *n* serenata; **serenading party** ronda.
serene [si'ri:n] *a* sereno; despejado, sosegado, apacible; impávido, impertérrito.
serenity [si'reniti] *n* serenidad, sosiego; sangre fría, presencia de ánimo.
serf [sə:f] *n* siervo, esclavo.
sergeant ['sɑ:dʒənt] *n* sargento.
serial ['siəriəl] *a* en serie; **— story** novela por entregas.
series ['siəri:z] *n* serie; encadenamiento; (*math*) progresión.
serious ['siəriəs] *a* serio, grave, importante, de peso.
seriously ['siəriəsli] *ad* seriamente, en serio.
seriousness ['siəriəsnis] *n* seriedad, gravedad.
sermon ['sə:mən] *n* sermón, prédica, plática.

serpent ['sə:pənt] *n* serpiente, sierpe.
servant ['sə:vənt] *n* criado; servidor, sirviente.
serve [sə:v] *vti* servir; asistir; notificar; ser útil; (*wine*) escanciar, abastecer; (*sentence*) cumplir; (*as soldier*) militar; (*ball*) sacar.
service ['sə:vis] *n* servicio; uso, auxilio; (*tennis*) saque; **at your —** servidor de Vd; **dinner —** vajilla.
serviceable ['sə:visəbl] *a* útil; servicial.
servile ['sə:vail] *a* servil, abyecto, adulador, rastrero.
servility [sə:'viliti] *n* servilismo; bajeza.
servitude ['sə:vitju:d] *n* esclavitud; servidumbre; **penal —** trabajos forzados.
session ['seʃən] *n* sesión, junta.
set [set] *a* reglamentario; prescrito; resuelto, terco; colocado; rígido; yerto; *n* (*cards etc*) serie, juego; (*people*) pandilla, compañía, grupo, los medios; surtido; (*of sun*) ocaso; curso; (*of mind*) tendencia, inclinación; conjunto; **toilet —, perfume —** juego de tocador; (*theat*) decoración; (*dance*) tanda; **radio —** receptor; (*jewels*) aderezo; **— of circumstances** conjunción; **to have a real —to** (*fam*) armarse la de San Quintín; *vt* poner, colocar; fijar; establecer; precisar, definir; (*bones*) reducir; (*saw*) triscar; (*type*) componer; (*jewels*) engarzar; (*music*) poner en; *vi* congelar(se); endurecerse; (*sun*) ponerse; **to — about** ponerse a; emprender; **to — against** malquistar; **to — aside** hacer a un lado; orillar; apartar, dar de mano, destinar; desechar, poner de lado; guardar; **to — before** presentar; **to — down** establecer, formalizar; poner por escrito; poner en tierra; **to — fire to** pegar fuego a; **to — forth** salir; manifestar, exponer; **to — going** operar; poner en marcha, echar a andar; **to — in** (*night*) cerrar; **to — off** salir; poner en relieve, realzar; (*train*) arrancar; **to — on** (*dogs*) azuzar; incitar; **to — in** (*winter etc*) comenzar; **to — out** ponerse en camino, salir, emprender; exponer; señalar; **to — over** tener autoridad sobre; dominar; **to — right** rectificar, encarrilar, enmendar; enderezar, colocar bien; **to — sail** largarse, hacerse a la vela; **to — to** aplicarse, darse a; **to — up** basar, instalar, erigir, instituir, levantar; (*shout*) pegar; instalarse; (*shop*) poner tienda; (*house*) poner casa; **to — up as** constituirse en; echárselas de; **to — upon** acometer; **to — at loggerheads** liar.
setback ['setbæk] *n* revés, contrariedad, rémora, retraso.
settee [se'ti:] *n* canapé, sofá.
setting ['setiŋ] *n* (*sun*) puesta, ocaso; establecimiento; (*jewels*) guarnición, engaste; (*scenery*) fondo, escena, escenario, telón de fondo.
settle ['setl] *n* escaño; *vt* fijar, establecer, colocar; (*disputes etc*) concertar, ajustar; (*debt*) saldar; arreglar; sosegar; **to — on** (*money on*) dotar; (*people*) avecinar; poblar; *vi* establecerse, instalarse; posarse, fijarse, echar raíces; (*chem*) depositar, sedimentar; **to — down** normalizarse, arraigarse.
settled ['setld] *a* arreglado, asentado, determinado; arraigado, establecido.
settlement ['setlmənt] *n* establecimiento; arreglo, ajuste; (*village*) caserío; dotación; acomodo; (*com*) saldo; (*building*) hundimiento.
settler ['setlə] *n* colono.
set-up ['setʌp] *n* sistema, organización, disposición.
seven ['sevn] *an* siete.
seventeen ['sevn'ti:n] *an* diez y siete, diecisiete.
seventh ['sevnθ] *a n* séptimo.
seventy ['sevnti] *an* setenta.
sever ['sevə] *vt* separar; cortar; *vi* romper; cercenar; separarse.
several ['sevrəl] *a* varios, diversos, distintos.
severally ['sevrəli] *ad* cada uno de por sí, separadamente.
severe [si'viə] *a* severo, rígido, austero, recio, áspero, fuerte, intenso.
severity [si'veriti] *n* severidad, rigor, exactitud.
Sevillian [sə'viliən] *an* sevillano.
sew [sou] *vti* coser; **to — up** zurcir; **to — on** pegar.
sewer ['souə] *n* costurera.
sewer ['sju:ə] albañal, cloaca.
sex [seks] *n* sexo; **fair —** bello sexo.
sexual ['seksjuəl] *a* sexual.
shabby ['ʃæbi] *a* raído, mal trajeado, desharrapado; gastado, muy usado; ruin; poco honrado.
shade [ʃeid] *n* sombra; penumbra; (*art*) medio tono; matiz, tono; un poco; (*lamp*) pantalla; fantasma; **to put in the —** hacer sombra a; *vi* sombrear, dar sombra, resguardar; amparar.
shadow ['ʃædou] *n* sombra; oscuridad; aparecido; pizca; amparo; *vti* anublar, obscurecer(se); ensombrecer; **to — forth** anunciar; espiar, seguir.
shadowy ['ʃædoui] *a* umbroso; vago, indefinido, obscuro, tenebroso.
shady ['ʃeidi] *a* sombreado, sombrío, umbroso; sospechoso.
shaft [ʃa:ft] *n* (*arrow*) flecha; (*cart*) vara, eje; (*ie handle*) mango; árbol; (*mine*) tiro; pozo; (*lance*) asta; (*of column*) fuste; virote; (*ventilation*) manguera; (*light*) rayo.
shake [ʃeik] *n* sacudida, meneo, zarandeo; agitación, vibración; (*hands*) apretón; *vti* sacudir, menear;

(*sword*) blandir; (*earth etc*) (re)temblar; (*head*) mover, menear; (*switch*) cimbrear; (*weaken*) debilitar, desalentar, amilanar; (*hands*) estrechar; *vi* (*with fear*) estremecer; (*with laughter*) desternillarse; (*with cold*) tiritar; (*unsteady*) bambolear; **to — off** sacudir(se), zafarse de, deshacerse de; **to — up** remover, descomponer; **difficult to — off** pegajoso.
shaking ['ʃeikiŋ] *n* vibración, sacudimiento, meneo, (re)temblar, traqueteo; *a* oscilante, temblón.
shallow ['ʃælou] *a* (*water*) poco profundo, vadoso; superficial, baladí, ligero; *n* bajío.
shallowness ['ʃælounis] *n* poca profundidad; vanidad, superficialidad.
sham [ʃæm] *a* fingido; supuesto, postizo; *n* impostura, (*battle*) simulacro; *vti* fingir(se), simular.
shame [ʃeim] *n* vergüenza, infamia, bochorno; baldón, afrenta; **to be covered with —** abochornarse; **to lose all sense of —** perder la vergüenza; *vt* avergonzar.
shamefaced ['ʃeimfeist] *a* vergonzoso, tímido.
shameful ['ʃeimful] *a* escandaloso, vergonzoso; ignominioso; impúdico, indecente.
shameless ['ʃeimlis] *a* desvergonzado, impúdico, sinvergüenza; descarado.
shape [ʃeip] *n* forma, figura; configuración, contorno; cuerpo; sesgo; **to give —** configurar; *vt* formar, figurar(se), modelar; dirigir; (*metals etc*) forjar, labrar; ajustar.
shaped ['ʃeipt] *a* hecho; **well-—** bien tallado, torneado.
shapeless ['ʃeiplis] *a* informe, disforme.
shapely ['ʃeipli] *a* bien formado, proporcionado, elegante, simétrico.
share [ʃɛə] *n* (*com*) acción; parte, porción; participación; (*money*) cuota; *vti* dividir, (*com*) partir, participar de, alcanzar; **to — out among** repartir; **to — in** tener parte en, terciar; **to — with** unirse con; **to go —s with** ir a (medias, partes iguales) con.
sharer ['ʃɛərə] *n* participante, partícipe.
sharing ['ʃɛəriŋ] *n* repartición; **— out** reparto.
shark [ʃɑ:k] *n* tiburón; (*fig*) estafador.
sharp [ʃɑ:p] *a* agudo; (*pointed*) puntiagudo; (*edged*) afilado, cortante; (*pain*) agudo, punzante; (*mind etc*) listo, fino, vivo; (*clever*) astuto, mañoso; (*taste*) picante, desabrido, agrio; (*smell*) acre; (*language*) incisivo, mordaz; (*sound*) penetrante, fino; (*outline*) definido; (*harsh*) acerbo; duro; (*mus*) sostenido; **—eyed** lince.
sharpen ['ʃɑ:pən] *vt* afilar, aguzar; (*pencil*) sacar punta a.
sharpness ['ʃɑ:pnis] *n* agudeza, sutileza, viveza.
shatter ['ʃætə] *vt* hacer pedazos, romper, reventar, estrellar; *vi* estrellarse, hacerse pedazos, (*minute pieces*) añicos; (*health*) quebrantar.
shave [ʃeiv] *vt* afeitar; hacer la barba a; **to — off** rapar; *vi* afeitarse, hacerse la barba; (*fig*) pasar rozando.
shaving ['ʃeiviŋ] *n* afeite; afeitada; (*wood*) viruta; acepilladura; *pl* **—s** raspaduras; (*metal*) cizilla.
shawl [ʃɔ:l] *n* toquilla, chal; (*large embroidered*) mantón (*de Manila*); **head —** mantilla.
she [ʃi:] *pn* ella.
sheaf [ʃi:f] *n* haz, gavilla; (*papers*) fajo, lío, pliego; hoja.
shear [ʃiə] *n* **—s** cizalla; *vt* esquilar; recortar, rapar, trasquilar.
shearing ['ʃiəriŋ] *n* esquila, esquileo.
sheath [ʃi:θ] *n* vaina, funda, cubierta; forro.
shed [ʃed] *n* cobertizo, colgadizo, tinglado, sombreja; *vt* derramar, esparcir; mudar; despojarse de.
sheep [ʃi:p] *n* oveja; ganado de lana; carnero; **flock of —** rebaño; **—fold** aprisco, majada; **—dog** perro de pastor.
sheepish ['ʃi:piʃ] *a* vergonzoso, tímido, pusilánime.
sheepishness ['ʃi:piʃnis] *n* timidez, cortedad.
sheer [ʃiə] *a* puro, claro, completo, consumado; escarpado, cortado a pico; *ad* de una vez; *vi* **to — off** alejarse, virar, desviar, zafarse.
sheet [ʃi:t] *n* hoja; (*bed*) sábana; (*water*) extensión; (*metal*) lámina, plancha; (*paper*) cuartilla; **ballad —s** pliegos de cordel.
shelf [ʃelf] *n* anaquel; *pl* (*shelves*) estantería.
shell [ʃel] *n* (*sea*) concha; (*egg*) cáscara, cascarón; **scallop—** venera; (*beetle, turtle etc*) carapacho; (*mil*) bala (*de cañón*), bomba, granada; (*pea*) vaina; **—fish** crustáceo; *vt* pelar, mondar, descortezar, desgranar; bombardear.
shelter ['ʃeltə] *n* abrigo; resguardo; (*ie shed*) colgadizo; cobertizo; (*for tramps*) cotarro; **air-raid —** refugio; (*mountain*) albergue; (*met*) hogar; **to take —** cobijarse; *vt* abrigar, resguardar; encubrir; acoger, albergar; proteger; **to — from** guarecerse de, abrigarse de.
sheltered ['ʃeltəd] *a* **— from** a cubierto de, resguardado.
shelve [ʃelv] *vt* dar carpetazo; postergar; arrinconar; *vi* estar en declive, inclinarse.
shepherd ['ʃepəd] *n* pastor.
sheriff ['ʃerif] *n* alguacil mayor.
sherry ['ʃeri] *n* vino de Jerez; (*very dry type*) manzanilla.

shield [ʃi:ld] *n* escudo; (*leather*) adarga; resguardo, defensa; *vt* proteger, defender, escudar, resguardar; **to — oneself** escudarse.
shift [ʃift] *n* cambio, desviación; recurso; (*of workers*) equipo, tanda; artificio; astucia; trueque; *vt* cambiar; transportar; *vi* variar, mudar; girar; **to — for oneself** bandearse, arreglárselas como pueda.
shifting ['ʃiftiŋ] *a* movedizo; *n* mudanza, transporte.
shilling ['ʃiliŋ] *n* chelín.
shimmer ['ʃimə] *n* reflejo vibrante; *vi* rielar.
shin [ʃin] *n* canilla; **—bone** tibia.
shine [ʃain] *n* brillo, resplandor; *vt* sacar brillo a, lustrar; *vi* brillar, lucir, coruscar, relumbrar; sobresalir.
shining ['ʃainiŋ] *a* brillante, lustroso, reluciente, nítido; resplandeciente, pulido; heroico.
shiny ['ʃaini] *a* lustroso, acharolado.
ship [ʃip] *n* buque, barco; **war—** navío, buque; **merchant —** buque mercante; *vti* embarcar, transportar.
ship building ['ʃip,bildiŋ] *n* construcción naval.
shipment ['ʃipmənt] *n* cargamento, embarque, envío.
shipper ['ʃipə] *n* remitente; importador; exportador.
shipping ['ʃipiŋ] *n* embarque, expedición; buques; **— bill** factura de embarque; **— charges** gastos de embarque.
shipwreck ['ʃiprek] *n* naufragio; siniestro; **to be —ed** naufragar, zozobrar.
shipyard ['ʃip,jɑ:d] *n* astillero.
shirk [ʃə:k] *vt* eludir, rehuir, esquivar, evitar; **to — the consequences** escurrir el bulto.
shirt [ʃə:t] *n* camisa; **— front** pechera; **—maker's shop** camisería; **stuffed —** (*sl*) pelele; **in —sleeves** en mangas de camisa.
shiver ['ʃivə] *n* temblor; **the —s** escalofrío; **to break into —s** romper (en pedazos, en fragmentos); *vti* tiritar, temblar; cascar(se), quebrantar; estrellar(se), hacer(se) (añicos, astillas).
shock [ʃɔk] *n* choque, sacudida; (*med*) shock; sobresalto; (*of hair*) guedeja, madeja, mata; **— troops** tropas de asalto; *vti* sacudir; chocar, causar, sobresaltar; horrorizar; **to be —ed** asombrarse, (*fam*) quedar hecho polvo.
shocking ['ʃɔkiŋ] *a* ofensivo, chocante, horroroso.
shoe [ʃu:] *n* zapato; (*horse*) herradura; **—horn** calzador; *vt* calzar; (*horse*) herrar; **—shine (boy)** *n* limpiabotas.
shoemaker ['ʃu:,meikə] *n* zapatero.
shoot [ʃu:t] *n* retoño, plantón, vástago; **to go out for a —** salir a tirar; *vt* disparar, tirar; (*person*) pasar por las armas, fusilar; **to — down** derribar; **to — off** disparar; **to — out** arrojar; **to — up** *vi* brotar, dar un estirón; (*of pain*) punzar; (*bolt*) correr, echar.
shooting ['ʃu:tiŋ] *n* tiro(s), tiroteo; (*of man etc*) fusilamiento; *a* **— star** exhalación, estrella fugaz.
shop [ʃɔp] *n* tienda; almacén; **back —** trastienda; **—boy** dependiente, mancebo; *vi* hacer compras; **to go shopping** ir a tiendas, ir de compras; (*for food*) ir a la plaza, al mercado.
shopkeeper ['ʃɔp,ki:pə] *n* tendero.
shopwindow ['ʃɔp'windou] *n* escaparate.
shore [ʃɔ:] *n* playa; costa, ribera; (*river*) orilla, margen.
short [ʃɔ:t] *a* corto, reducido, limitado; escaso, breve, sucinto; (*cut —*) seco, brusco; próximo; (*memory*) flaco; (*pastry etc*) quebradizo, vidrioso; **— of breath** corto de resuello; **— cut** atajo; **to go by a — cut** atrochar; **— -lived** efímero; **— -sighted** corto de vista; **— -sightedness** miopía; (*fig*) falta de alcances; **—-tempered** enojadizo; **—hand** taquigrafía; *ad* **in —** en resumen, en una palabra, en suma; **in a — time** luego, pronto; **— of cash** escaso de medios; **— while** rato; **to cut —** cortar en seco, parar, abreviar, atajar; cercenar; abreviar; **to fall — of** no alcanzar, no corresponder; quedarse corto; **to be —** faltar; *n* (*el*) corte.
shortage ['ʃɔ:tidʒ] *n* falta, escasez, carestía.
shortcoming [ʃɔ:t'kʌmiŋ] *n* defecto, descuido, deficiencia.
shorten ['ʃɔ:tn] *vt* acortar, abreviar, reducir.
shortly ['ʃɔ:tli] *ad* dentro de poco, en breve, luego.
shortness ['ʃɔ:tnis] *n* cortedad; brevedad; escasez, insuficiencia.
shot [ʃɔt] *a* (*silk etc*) tornasolado, batido; *n* tiro, descarga; (*in games*) jugada; (*pellets*) perdigones.
shotgun ['ʃɔtgʌn] *n* escopeta.
shoulder ['ʃouldə] *n* hombro, espalda; (*mountain*) lomo; **—blade** omóplato, espaldilla; **—pad** hombrera; **— joint** codillo; **— yoke** charretera; **broad-—ed** ancho de espaldas; **round-—ed** cargado de espaldas; *vt* echar, cargar al hombro; cargar con; **to set one's — to the wheel** arrimar el hombro.
shout [ʃaut] *n* grito, exclamación; *vi* gritar, vociferar, exclamar, dar gritos, hablar a gritos, huchear.
shouting ['ʃautiŋ] *ad* voz en cuello, a gritos; *n* vocería.
shove [ʃʌv] *vti* empujar, impeler; **to — off** alejarse; *n* empellón, empuje.
shovel ['ʃʌvl] *n* pala; *vt* traspalar.
show [ʃou] *n* (*theat*) función, espec-

táculo; (*art*) exposición; (*display*) exhibición; ostentación, boato, aparato; manifestación, promesa, apariencia; demostración; pretexto; **trade —** feria de muestras; **—case** vitrina, escaparate; **—room** sala de exposición; **to make a — of** hacer gala de; *vt* mostrar, enseñar; probar, demostrar; manifestar; (*art*) exponer, exhibir; guiar; **to — to advantage** lucir; *vi* parecer; aparecer; dar señal de; **to — off** lucir, alardear, hacer ostentación de; **to — up** descubrir, poner en ridículo; aparecer; **to — through** transparentarse.

shower ['ʃauə] *n* aguacero, chaparrón; rociada; **a — of money** un chorro de pesetas; **— bath** ducha; *vti* hacer llover, llover; derramar; (*with gifts etc*) llenar.

showery ['ʃauəri] *a* lluvioso, chubascoso.

showman ['ʃoumən] *n* empresario, director de circo, teatro *etc*.

showy ['ʃoui] *a* llamativo, vistoso; rozagante, fastuoso, aparatoso, de postín.

shred [ʃred] *n* jirón, tira; ápice, triza, fragmento; *vt* desmenuzar, hacer tiras.

shrewd [ʃru:d] *a* astuto, sagaz, socarrón, zorro, ladino.

shrewdness ['ʃru:dnis] *n* astucia, sagacidad.

shriek [ʃri:k] *n* grito penetrante, alarido, chillido; *vi* dar chillidos, chillar.

shrill [ʃril] *a* penetrante, chillido, agudo; chillón.

shrine [ʃrain] *n* relicario, urna, templo, capilla.

shrink [ʃriŋk] *vi* encogerse; marchitar(se), contraer(se); (*met*) retroceder, rehuir.

shrivel ['ʃrivl] *vti* arrugar(se), encoger, avellanarse, disminuir(se).

shroud [ʃraud] *n* sudario; mortaja; *vt* amortajar.

shrub [ʃrʌb] *n* arbusto, mata, matorral, maleza.

shrug [ʃrʌg] *vti* (*shoulders*) encoger(se) (de hombros).

shudder ['ʃʌdə] *n* temblor, estremecimiento; escalofrío; *vi* (re)-temblar, estremecerse.

shuffle ['ʃʌfl] *n* evasiva, embuste; (*cards*) barajadura; *vti* (*cards*) barajar; eludir; revolver; (*feet*) arrastrar los pies.

shun [ʃʌn] *vt* esquivar, eludir, rehuir de, retraerse de.

shut [ʃʌt] *vt* cerrar; (*eyes, doors*) entornar; **to — in** (en)cerrar; **to — out** excluir; negar la entrada; **to — up** obstruir; callar(se); tapar la boca; encerrar; recluir; **to — one's eyes to** hacer la vista gorda a.

shutter ['ʃʌtə] *n* postigo, contraventana, puerta ventana; hoja; (*phot*) obturador.

shy [ʃai] *a* asustadizo, huraño, esquivo, hurón, tímido, asombradizo, corto; (*from experience*) escamado; recatado; *vi* asustarse, respingarse.

shyness ['ʃainis] *n* reserva, timidez, recato, cortedad, esquivez.

Siam [sai'æm] *n* Siam, Tailandia.

Siamese [ˌsaiə'mi:z] *an* siamés.

Siberia [sai'biəriə] *n* Siberia.

Siberian [sai'biəriən] *an* siberiano.

Sicilian [si'siliən] *an* siciliano.

Sicily ['sisili] *n* Sicilia.

sick [sik] *a* enfermo, malo; (*sea, air*) mareado; **—bay** enfermería; **— of** fastidiado, harto; **to be —** vomitar; estar enfermo, mareado, marearse.

sicken ['sikn] *vt* marear, enfermar; extenuar; dar asco; *vi* marearse, enfermarse.

sickle ['sikl] *n* hoz, falce, segadera.

sickliness ['siklinis] *n* mareo, achaque; sensiblería.

sickly ['sikli] *a* enfermizo, enclenque, achacoso, doliente; indigesto, nauseabundo, empalagoso.

sickness ['siknis] *n* enfermedad, dolencia; náusea.

side [said] *a* lateral, de lado; **— door** puerta (lateral, accesoria); **— effect** efecto secundario; **—saddle** a sentadillas, a mujeriegas; *n* lado, costado, fase, cara; (*water*) orilla, margen; (*hill*) ladera, vertiente; (*ship*) banda; (*group*) bando, parte, facción, lado; (*billiards*) efecto; (*swagger*) tono; **by the — of** al lado de; **on all —s** por todas partes; **this — up** siempre de canto; *vi* **to — with** tomar partido, ponerse al lado de; decidirse por.

sidelong ['saidlɔŋ] *a* lateral, oblicuo; (*glance*) de soslayo; *ad* lateralmente.

sidewalk ['saidwɔ:k] *n* acera.

sideways ['saidweiz] *ad* de lado, oblicuamente, al través.

siege [si:dʒ] *n* sitio, asedio, cerco.

sieve [siv] *n* cedazo, tamiz, criba; harnero; **to carry water in a —** coger agua en cesto; *vt* acribar.

sift [sift] *vt* cerner, cribar, tamizar; separar; (*grain*) aechar; sondar, indagar.

sigh [sai] *n* suspiro; *vi* suspirar; **to — for** anhelar, ansiar.

sight [sait] *n* vista; espectáculo, escena; cuadro; puntería; **at — a** primera vista; **by —** de vista; **to lose — of** perder de vista; **—s** (*rifle*) alza; **what a —!** (*fam*) ¡qué facha!, ¡qué mamarracho!, ¡qué birria!; *vt* avistar; poner miras (al fusil); **to catch — of** divisar.

sightseeing ['saitˌsi:iŋ] *n* acto de visitar puntos de interés, turismo.

sign [sain] *n* signo; asomo, indicio, señal, indicación, prueba; rastro; sombra; (*written, printed*) letrero; **electric —** anuncio luminoso; **with**

authority to — apoderado; **by —s and spells** por arte de birlibirloque; *vti* firmar, poner firma, rubricar.
signal ['signl] *a* señalado, insigne; *n* señal, signo; (*rl*) banderín; *vt* señalar; *vi* hacer señales.
signature ['signitʃə] *n* firma, rúbrica.
significance [sig'nifikəns] *n* significación; significado, importancia, trascendencia.
significant [sig'nifikənt] *a* significante, considerable, enfático, de peso.
signify ['signifai] *vt* significar, importar, manifestar, hacer saber, dar a entender, simbolizar.
silence ['sailəns] *n* silencio; **to maintain —** guardar silencio; **— gives consent** quien calla, otorga; *vt* silenciar, (mandar, hacer) callar.
silencer ['sailənsə] *n* silenciador.
silent ['sailənt] *a* callado, mudo, sordo, silencioso, tácito; **to be —** callar(se); **to grow —** enmudecer.
silhouette [ˌsilu(:)'et] *n* silueta.
silk [silk] *n* seda; **—worm** gusano de seda; **— hat** sombrero de copa.
silken ['silkən] *a* sedoso, sedeño, de seda; blando, suave.
silky ['silki] *a* de seda, sedeño; suave; lustroso.
silliness ['silinis] *n* tontería, necedad; simpleza.
silly ['sili] *a* mentecato, necio, bobo, imbécil, idiota, abobado, simple.
silver ['silvə] *a* plateado, argentino, de plata; *n* plata; **—work** orfebrería; *vt* platear; azogar.
silvery ['silvəri] *a* plateado, argentino.
similar ['similə] *a* semejante, igual; parejo, parecido; **—ly** *ad* igualmente.
similarity [ˌsimi'læriti] *n* semejanza, homogeneidad; simpatía.
simple ['simpl] *a* simple; mero; ordinario; (*easy*) sencillo, fácil; (*innocent*) simple, bueno, cándido; (*silly*) bobo, tonto; (*manner*) llano, sencillo; familiar.
simpleness ['simplnis] *n* simpleza.
simplicity [sim'plisiti] *n* (*directness, ease*) sencillez; (*silly phrase*) simpleza; (*simple candor*) simplicidad; inocencia; (*of manner*) llaneza; modestia.
simplify ['simplifai] *vt* simplificar.
simulate ['simjuleit] *vt* simular, aparentar, fingir.
simultaneous [ˌsiməl'teiniəs] *a* simultáneo.
sin [sin] *n* pecado, transgresión, falta; **deadly —** pecado capital; *vi* pecar, faltar.
since [sins] *ad* desde (que); *cj* puesto que, como que; *prep* después.
sincere [sin'siə] *a* sincero, leal, franco, cordial; hondo, verdadero; formal.
sincerity [sin'seriti] *n* sinceridad, candor, lealtad, franqueza.
sinecure ['sainikjuə] *n* sinecura; (*fam*) mina, enchufe.
sinew ['sinju:] *n* nervio, tendón; **—s** (*of war*) nervio.
sinewy ['sinju(:)i] *n* nervudo, nervoso, vigoroso.
sinful ['sinful] *n* pecador, pecaminoso; impío, depravado.
sing [siŋ] *n* **—song** sonsonete; *vti* cantar; (*ears*) zumbar.
Singapore [ˌsiŋgə'pɔ:] *n* Singapur.
singe [sindʒ] *vt* chamuscar, sollamar; quemar las puntas del pelo.
singer ['siŋə] *n* cantor, cantante.
singing ['siŋiŋ] *n* canto; (*in the ears*) silbidos, zumbido.
single ['siŋgl] *a* singular; aislado, individual; único; (*person*) célibe, soltero; (*ticket*) sencillo; solo, solitario; *vt* **to — out** separar, escoger; particularizar, distinguir.
singular ['siŋgjulə] *a* singular, insólito, peculiar, extraordinario.
sinister ['sinistə] *a* siniestro; aciago, funesto.
sink [siŋk] *n* (*house*) pila, fregadero; desagüe, albañal; *vt* hundir; (*ship*) hundir, echar a pique; (*shaft*) abrir, cavar; **to —** (*teeth etc*) **into** (*earth etc*) hincar, clavar; (*mark*) grabar; *vi* hundirse, sumirse; (*ship*) naufragar, perderse, zozobrar; **to — down** hundirse, derrumbarse; **to — into** penetrar, grabarse; caer(se) en; **to — in** deprimir, abatir; (*sun*) ponerse; menguar.
sinner ['sinə] *n* pecador.
sinuous ['sinjuəs] *a* sinuoso, tortuoso, serpentino.
sip [sip] *n* sorbo, sorbito; *vti* sorber, chupar, saborear.
sir [sə:] *n* señor; **noble —** su señoría.
sire ['saiə] *n* padre, progenitor, anciano, señor; *vt* (*horse*) engendrar, producir.
siren ['saiərin] *n* sirena.
sister ['sistə] *n* hermana; **—in-law** cuñada, hermana política.
sit [sit] *vi* sentarse, estar sentado; (*hens*) empollar; (*meeting*) celebrar sesión; (*clothes*) sentar (*bien*); **to — down** sentarse; descansar; **to — up** (*in bed*) incorporarse; (*through night*) velar; trasnochar; *vt* sentar, colocar en un asiento.
site [sait] *n* sitio, situación, asiento, planta, local; **building —** solar, terrenos; *vt* situar.
sitting ['sitiŋ] *a* sentado; *n* postura; sesión; (*eggs*) nidada.
sitting room ['sitiŋrum] *n* sala de estar.
situate ['sitjueit] *vt* situar, colocar; *a* situado, colocado.
situated ['sitjueitid] *a* situado, sito; **to be —** ubicarse, estar, hallarse.

situation [ˌsitju'eiʃən] *n* situación; sitio, lugar; posición; (*job*) colocación, puesto; peripecia; **the — being what it is** (a, en) estas alturas.
six [siks] *an* seis; **to set at sixes and sevens** aturrullar.
sixteen ['siks'ti:n] *an* diez y seis, dieciséis.
sixteenth ['siks'ti:nθ] *an* décimosexto.
sixth [siksθ] *a* sexto, seis; *n* sexto.
sixty ['siksti] *an* sesenta.
size [saiz] *n* tamaño; talla; dimensión; (*paper*) cola; (*shoes*) número; *vt* colar; clasificar por tamaños.
skate [skeit] *n* patín; **roller —s** patines de ruedas; *vi* patinar.
skeleton ['skelitn] *n* esqueleto; armazón; esquema; **— key** ganzúa.
skeptic ['skeptik] *a n* escéptico.
skepticism ['skeptisizəm] *n* escepticismo.
sketch [sketʃ] *n* bosquejo, delineación, traza, dibujo, boceto, diseño; *vt* diseñar; bosquejar, delinear, apuntar.
skid [skid] *vi* patinar, arrastrar.
skill [skil] *n* maña, habilidad, destreza; artificio, arte, maestría, soltura; sutileza, gracia; conocimiento; **lack of —** impericia.
skilled [skild] *a* práctico, hábil, experto, versado.
skillful ['skilful] *a* práctico, diestro, hábil, sabio, inteligente, ingenioso, redomado, apañado; industrioso.
skim [skim] *vt* desnatar, espumar; tocar ligeramente, rasar; examinar superficialmente; *vi* deslizarse, razar; (*book*) hojear.
skin [skin] *n* piel; (*complexion*) tez; (*animal*) pellejo; (*pelt*) cuero; (*wine*) odre, pellejo, cuero; (*potato*) cáscara; (*on milk*) nata; **—tight** ajustado como un guante; **to save one's —** salvar el pellejo; *vt* desollar; (*fruit etc*) pelar, mondar; **to — alive** desollar vivo.
skip [skip] *n* salto, brinco; *vt* saltar, omitir, pasar por alto; *vi* saltar a la cuerda.
skipper ['skipə] *n* patrón, capitán; saltador.
skirmish ['skə:miʃ] *n* escaramuza, refriega; *vi* escaramuzar.
skirt [skə:t] *n* falda, saya; (*silk*) brial; (*hooped*) miriñaque; *vt* orillar, ladear; poner cenefa.
skit [skit] *n* libelo, pasquín; burla; paso, boceto cómico.
skull [skʌl] *n* cráneo, calavera.
skunk [skʌŋk] *n* hediondo.
sky [skai] *n* cielo, firmamento; **—scraper** rascacielos; (*to praise*) **to the skies, —high** (*prices*) por las nubes.
skylark ['skailɑ:k] *n* alondra.
skylight ['skailait] *n* claraboya, tragaluz, lumbrera.
slab [slæb] *n* (*stone*) losa; plancha, tabla.
slack [slæk] *a* flojo; (*lax*) negligente, remiso, descuidado; (*in fit*) ancho; *n* (*cool*) cisco; flojedad; *pl* pantalones.
slacken ['slækən] *vt* aflojar, soltar; relajar; retardar, descuidar; (*wind*) amainar; (*speed*) disminuir; *vi* tardarse, entibiarse, cejar.
slackness ['slæknis] *n* relajamiento, flojedad; (*in studies*) desaplicación.
slake [sleik] *vt* extinguir; apagar; (*lime*) azogar, matar.
slam [slæm] *vt* cerrar de golpe; **to — the door in someone's face** dar un portazo a uno.
slander ['slɑ:ndə] *n* calumnia, murmuración; denigración; *vt* calumniar, difamar.
slanderous ['slɑ:ndərəs] *a* calumnioso.
slant [slɑ:nt] *n* oblicuidad, sesgo, declive; *vti* inclinar, sesgar, inclinarse.
slanting ['slɑ:ntiŋ] *a* inclinado, sesgado, oblicuo, de soslayo.
slap [slæp] *n* manotada, palmada; (*on face*) bofetada, cachete; (*with back of hand*) revés; (*fam*) torta; *vt* abofetear; pegar; **—dash** *a* de brocha gorda.
slash [slæʃ] *n* (*knife*) cuchillada; (*whip*) latigazo; *vt* acuchillar; *vi* tirar tajos.
slate [sleit] *n* pizarra, esquisto; *vt* empizarrar; (*fam*) criticar, censurar.
slaughter ['slɔ:tə] *n* mortandad, carnicería; (*by cutting throat*) degüello, degollación; **—house** matadero; (*fam*) degollina; *vt* matar, degollar.
Slav [slɑ:v] *an* eslavo.
slave [sleiv] *n* esclavo; **freed —** liberto; **— traffic** trata; *vi* trabajar como esclavo, sudar tinta.
slavery ['sleivəri] *n* esclavitud.
slavish ['sleiviʃ] *a* servil.
slay [slei] *vt* matar, asesinar.
slaying ['sleiiŋ] *n* matanza; (*by slitting throat*) degollación, degüello.
sled [sled] *n* narria, rastra, trineo.
sledge [sledʒ] *n* trineo.
sleek [sli:k] *a* liso, suave; untuoso, zalamero; *vt* alisar, pulir.
sleep [sli:p] *n* sueño, reposo; adormecer; **light —** duermevela; **—walker** somnámbulo; *vi* dormir(se), descansar; **to — like a top** dormir como un lirón; **to — over, on** (*idea etc*) consultar con almohada.
sleeper ['sli:pə] *n* durmiente; (*rl*) traviesa, travesaño; (*car*) cochecama.
sleepiness ['sli:pinis] *n* somnolencia, sueño, letargo.
sleeping ['sli:piŋ] *a* dormido; **without —** en vela; **— coach, — car** coche-cama; **— partner** comanditario.

sleepless ['sli:plis] *a* desvelado, insomne, en vela.
sleeplessness ['sli:plisnis] *n* insomnio.
sleepy ['sli:pi] *a* soñoliento, amodorrado, soporífero; **to be —** tener sueño.
sleeve [sli:v] *n* manga; **to laugh up one's —** reírse con disimulo.
sleigh [slei] *n* trineo.
slender ['slendə] *a* delgado, sutil, fino, débil, escaso, corto, limitado, remoto.
slenderness ['slendənis] *n* delgadez; (*of hope etc*) tenuidad.
slice [slais] *n* tajada, rebanada; (*bread*) rodaja; (*ham etc*) raja; (*pineapple etc*) rueda; *vt* cortar en lonjas; rebanar; **to — into** tajar.
slide [slaid] *n* resbalón; (*mech*) muesca, encaje; (*geol*) falla; (*phot*) placa; *vi* resbalar, deslizarse.
sliding ['slaidiŋ] *a* resbaladizo, corredizo, movible.
slight [slait] *a* ligero, leve, limitado, fútil, liviano, tenue, flojo; **—est** mínimo; **only —ly** poco; *n* desaire, desprecio; *vt* desairar, desatender, desdeñar, menospreciar.
slim [slim] *a* delgado, esbelto, fino, tenue, escaso.
slimness ['slimnis] *n* delgadez.
slimy ['slaimi] *a* viscoso, fangoso.
sling [sliŋ] *n* honda; (*for arm*) cabestrillo; *vt* lanzar; poner en cabestrillo, eslingar; (*diagonally*) terciar.
slip [slip] *n* (*physically*) resbalón, traspié; (*mistake*) error, lapso; (*moral*) desliz, equivocación; (*paper*) hoja; tira; (*bot*) esqueje, vástago; (*naut*) grada; **—knot** lazo corredizo; **pillow—** funda; **— of tongue** lapsus linguae; **to give the — to** dar esquinazo a; **a — between cup and lip** de la mano a la boca desaparece la sopa; *vt* **to — in** deslizar; **to — off** soltar; (*bone*) dislocarse; *vi* resbalarse, irse los pies; patinar; salirse; cometer un desliz; equivocarse; largarse; **to — away** escurrirse; **to — down** dejarse caer; **to — into** introducirse, caer en, insinuarse; **to — in** colarse; **to — off** quitarse; escabullirse.
slipper ['slipə] *n* (*low heeled*) zapatilla, babucha; (*high heeled*) chinela, chancleta.
slippery ['slipəri] *a* resbaladizo; escurridizo, voluble, evasivo.
slipshod ['slipʃɔd] *a* descuidado.
slit [slit] *n* hendedura, quebradura, hendido; (*for peeping*) raja; resquicio; *vt* rajar, hender, cortar, rasgar; (*cloth*) desgarrar.
slope [sloup] *n* declive, pendiente, inclinación; bajada; sesgo; falda, ladera, vertiente; *vti* sesgar; formar en declive; inclinarse, declinar.
sloping ['sloupiŋ] *a* sesgado, en cuesta, inclinado.
slot [slɔt] *n* ranura, muesca.
sloth [slouθ] *n* pereza; (*zool*) perezoso.
slovenliness ['slʌvnlinis] *n* dejadez, desaseo, desaliño.
slovenly ['slʌvnli] *a* desaliñado, dejado, desastroso, descuidado.
slow [slou] *a* lento, pausado; despacio; (*wits etc*) torpe, pesado, lerdo; (*with difficulty*) premioso; (*behind time*) atrasado, tarde; **—witted** lelo, cerrado de mollera; **— in the uptake** duro de mollera; (*of watch*) **it goes —** atrasa; *vt* retardar, ir más despacio.
slowness ['slounis] *n* lentitud; detención; forma, tardanza, retraso; torpeza.
sluggish ['slʌgiʃ] *a* perezoso, indolente; poltrón; tardo, lento, pesado.
slumber ['slʌmbə] *n* sueño; **heavy —** modorra; *vi* dormir.
slur [slə:] *n* borrón, mancha; reparo; *vt* manchar; **to — over** pasar por encima, desatender, comerse (*syllables etc*).
sly [slai] *a* astuto, bellaco, malicioso, socarrón; redomado; taimado; insidioso; pícaro, cuco; furtivo; **on the —** a hurtadillas; **to get in on the —** colarse; **— bird** pajarraco.
slyness ['slainis] *n* astucia, disimulo; malicia; bellaquería, socarronería.
smack [smæk] *n* (*on face*) cachete; (*whip etc*) chasquido, restallido; (*of taste*) gusto, sabor; (*of speech*) dejo; *vti* saborear; saborearse; (*lips*) relamerse; castañetear; **to — of** saber a.
smacking ['smækiŋ] *n* zurra; *part* **— of** con sus resabios de.
small [smɔ:l] *a* pequeño, chico, menudo, diminuto; poco; corto, de poco bulto; **— fry** gente menuda; **— hours** altas horas; **— change** suelto; **— talk** vulgaridades.
smallness ['smɔ:lnis] *n* pequeñez, insignificancia.
smallpox ['smɔ:lpɔks] *n* viruelas.
smart [smɑ:t] *a* (*clever*) vivo, listo, despejado, hábil; (*sharp taste etc*) picante, acerbo; (*pain*) punzante; de buen tono, elegante; majo; *vi* escocer, doler, resquemar, picar; quedar resentido.
smart(ing) ['smɑ:t(iŋ)] *n* resquemor, escozor, resentimiento.
smartness ['smɑ:tnis] *n* vivacidad; elegancia; inteligencia; agudeza, viveza, ingenio; astucia.
smash [smæʃ] *n* destrozo; fracaso; (*train*) choque; *vt* quebrantar, romper; aplastar; destrozar; hacer pedazos; romperse, saltar en pedazos; (*fin*) fracasar, quebrar; **to — into** chocar con; topar con; darse un tope contra.
smattering ['smætəriŋ] *n* tintura; erudición a la violeta, conocimiento somero.

smell [smel] *n* (*sense of*) olfato; olor; (*animals*) vaho; traza; **to give out (offensive)** — apestar; *vt* oler, olfatear; **to — a rat** oler el poste; **to — out** husmear; percibir; **to — of** oler a.
smelling ['smeliŋ] *a* oloroso, aromático; maloliente.
smile [smail] *n* sonrisa; *vi* sonreír; **to — on** favorecer.
smiling ['smailiŋ] risueño; **— face** cara de Pascua.
smirk [smə:k] *n* visaje, sonriso (boba, afectada); *vi* sonreírse afectadamente.
smite [smait] *vt* golpear, herir; asolar; *vi* aplastar; (*conscience*) remorder.
smith [smiθ] *n* herrero; forjador; artífice.
smithy ['smiði] *n* fragua, forja.
smitten ['smitn] *a* prendado de (*fam*), afligido.
smoke [smouk] *n* humo; **— screen** cortina de humo; **to end in —** volverse (humo, agua de cerrajas); **to have a —** echar un pitillo; *vt* (*cigars etc*) fumar; (*fish etc*) ahumar; sahumar; *vi* humear, echar humo.
smoker ['smoukə] *n* fumador.
smoking ['smoukiŋ] *n* fumar; **— room** cuarto de fumar; **— car** vagón para fumadores; *a* humeante; **no —** se prohibe fumar.
smokeless ['smouklis] *a* sin humo.
smoky ['smouki] *a* humeante; lleno de humo; ahumado; **to be —** humear.
smooth [smu:ð] *a* (*flat*) llano, plano; (*hair*) liso; (*polished*) pulido, terso; (*even*) unido, igual; armonioso; (*easy*) fácil, suave; (*talk etc*) untuoso, fluido, meloso; **—-chinned** barbilampiño; **— shaven** (bien) afeitado; *vt* allanar, igualar; pulir, alisar; (*wood etc*) desbastar; (*way*) facilitar; (*temper*) pacificar, ablandar; **— running** corredizo.
smoothness ['smu:ðnis] *n* suavidad, igualdad; destreza.
smother ['smʌðə] *vt* extinguir, ahogar; apagar; *vi* ahogarse, asfixiarse.
smug [smʌg] *a* relamido, presumido, comodín.
smuggle ['smʌgl] *vt* pasar de contrabando.
smuggler ['smʌglə] *n* contrabandista.
snack [snæk] *n* merienda, refresco, tentempié.
snag [snæg] *n* tropezón.
snail [sneil] *a* **—'s pace** paso de tortuga; *n* caracol.
snake [sneik] *n* culebra, serpiente.
snap [snæp] *n* (*bite*) mordisco; (*fastener*) cierre; (*of fingers*) castañeteo; (*whip etc*) chasquido; (*smartness*) vigor, viveza; (*photo*) instantánea; *a* de golpe, repentino; **—shot** tiro rápido, sin apuntar; *vt* chasquear; romper; (*photo*) sacar una instantánea; *vi* partirse, saltar, quebrarse; estallar; **to — at** mordisquear.
snare [snεə] *n* trampa, lazo; red, trapisonda; (*birds*) orzuelo; asechanza, artimaña: *vt* poner trampas, enmarañar, enredar.
snarl [snɑ:l] *n* gruñido; *vi* regañar, gruñir.
snatch [snætʃ] *vt* **to — away, up** arrebatar, quitar, raptar.
sneak [sni:k] *n* soplón, hombre vil; *vi* **to — away, off** arrastrarse, escabullirse; **to — in** colarse.
sneaking ['sni:kiŋ] *a* bajo, arrastrado, rastrero.
sneer [sniə] *n* desdén, mofa, escarnio; *vi* hablar desdeñosamente; **to — at** escarnecer, burlarse de.
sneeze [sni:z] *n* estornudo; *vi* estornudar.
sniff [snif] *n* sorbetón; *vt* **to — out** husmear, olfatear; *vi* husmear; sorberse los mocos.
snobbishness ['snɔbiʃnis] *n* tufo, esnobismo.
snore [snɔ:] *n* ronquido; *vi* roncar.
snort [snɔ:t] *n* bufido, refunfuño; *vi* resoplar, refunfuñar.
snout [snaut] *n* hocico, trompa, morro.
snow [snou] *n* nieve; **—storm** nevasca; **—drift** ventisquero; *vi* nevar; **to — gently** neviscar.
snowdrop ['snoudrɔp] *n* campanilla de invierno.
snowfall ['snoufɔ:l] *n* nevada.
snowflake ['snoufleik] *n* copo de nieve.
snowshoes ['snou.ʃu:z] *n* raquetas de nieve.
snowy ['snoui] *a* nevoso, de nieve.
snub [snʌb] *n* desaire; **—nosed** chato; *vt* desairar.
snuff [snʌf] *vt* atizar, despabilar; *n* moco, despabiladura; rapé.
snug [snʌg] *a* abrigado, cómodo; (*fit*) ajustado.
so [sou] *ad* así, tan; así como; **— big** así de grande; **— long** (*fam*) hasta luego; **— that** de modo que, de forma que, de suerte que; **— and —** un tal; **Mr. — and —** don Fulano de Tal; Zutano; **and —** conque.
soak [souk] *vti* remojar, saturar, empapar; macerar; (*peas*) poner a remojo; **to — up** chupar, absorber, coger; **to — through** calar.
soaked [soukt] *a* **— to the skin** mojado hasta los huesos, hecho una sopa; **to be — (*in subject*)** empaparse, embeberse.
soap [soup] *n* jabón; *vt* dar jabón.
soapy ['soupi] *a* cubierto de jabón; jabonoso.
soar [sɔ:] *vi* cernerse, remontarse, elevarse, encumbrarse.
sob [sɔb] *n* sollozo, suspiro; *vi* sollozar, suspirar.

sober ['soubə] *a* sobrio, serio, parco, templado; abstemio; (*color*) sombrío, apagado; *vt* desemborrachar; poner grave.

soberness ['soubənis] *n* sobriedad.

sobriety [sou'braiəti] *n* seriedad, gravedad, moderación, cordura.

so-called ['sou'kɔ:ld] *a* así llamado, supuesto.

sociable ['souʃəbl] *a* sociable.

social ['souʃəl] *a* social, sociable; *n* reunión, velada; **— work** asistencia social.

socialist ['souʃəlist] *an* socialista.

society [sə'saiəti] *n* sociedad, asociación, consorcio; compañía.

sociological [,sousiə'lɔdʒikəl] *a* sociológico.

sociologist [,sousi'ɔlədʒist] *n* sociólogo.

sociology [,sousi'ɔlədʒi] *n* sociología.

sock [sɔk] *n* calcetín; golpe fuerte; *vt* golpear.

socket ['sɔkit] *n* (*eye*) cuenca; (*tooth*) alvéolo; (*collarbone*) hoyuela; (*wall*) toma; (*el*) enchufe.

sod [sɔd] *n* cesped; (*cut*) tepe.

soda ['soudə] *n* sosa; **— water** sifón.

sodden ['sɔdn] *a* empapado, saturado, hecho unas papas.

sofa ['soufə] *n* sofá, canapé.

soft [sɔft] *a* suave, blando, muelle, mullido, quedo; (*silly*) tocado de la cabeza; (*shell*) blando; (*water*) dulce; dúctil; manso; débil; afeminado; **— drink** bebida refrescante no alcohólica; **— as silk** como una seda.

soften ['sɔfn] *vt* suavizar, ablandar, endulzar, moderar; (*color*) apagar; templar; enternecer.

softness ['sɔftnis] *n* suavidad, blandura, dulzura; ductilidad; molicie.

soil [sɔil] *n* terreno, tierra, suelo; *vt* ensuciar; manchar, empañar.

soirée ['swɑ:rei] *n* sarao, velada.

sojourn ['sɔdʒə:n] *vi* morar, residir, permanecer; *n* residencia, permanencia.

solace ['sɔləs] *n* solaz, alivio; *vt* solazar, consolar.

sold [sould] *pp of* **sell**; **to be — out** (*edition*) agotarse.

soldier ['souldʒə] *n* soldado, militar, guerrero; (*of Foreign Legion*) legionario.

sole [soul] *a* solo, único; mero; absoluto; **— right** exclusiva; *n* (*shoe*) suela; (*fish*) lenguado; *vt* poner suela, solar.

solemn ['sɔləm] *a* solemne, ponderoso.

solemnity [sə'lemniti] *n* solemnidad, importancia, mesura.

solemnize ['sɔləmnaiz] *vt* solemnizar.

solicit [sə'lisit] *vt* solicitar, pedir, implorar, importunar, demandar.

solicitous [sə'lisitəs] *a* solícito, cuidadoso, ansioso.

solicitude [sə'lisitju:d] *n* solicitud, diligencia.

solid ['sɔlid] *a* sólido, duro, firme, macizo.

solidity [sə'liditi] *n* sustancia, solidez, consistencia.

soliloquy [sə'liləkwi] *n* soliloquio; monólogo.

solitary ['sɔlitəri] *a* solitario, señero; retirado, aislado, único; **in — confinement** incomunicado.

solitude ['sɔlitju:d] *n* soledad.

solution [sə'lu:ʃən] *n* solución.

solve [sɔlv] *vt* (di)solver, resolver, aclarar; (*riddle*) adivinar.

somber ['sɔmbə] *a* tétrico, sombrío, lóbrego.

some [sʌm] *a* algún, alguno; **— sort of** tal cual, un poco de; *pn* algunos; alguna persona.

somebody ['sʌmbədi] *pn* alguien; **— or other** un cualquiera.

somehow ['sʌmhau] *ad* en cierto modo, de algún modo.

someone ['sʌmwʌn] *n* alguien.

somersault ['sʌməsɔ:lt] *n* salto mortal, vuelco, tumbo.

something ['sʌmθiŋ] *n* algo, alguna cosa; **— like** algo como; **— and nothing** un sí es no es; **there is — of the (poet) in him** tiene sus ribetes de (poeta).

sometime ['sʌmtaim] *ad* en algún tiempo, algún día, alguna vez.

sometimes ['sʌmtaimz] *ad* en ocasiones, (a) (algunas) veces.

somewhat ['sʌmwɔt] *ad* algo, algún tanto, en cierto modo.

somewhere ['sʌmwɛə] *ad* en alguna parte.

son [sʌn] *n* hijo; **— and heir** mayorazgo; **—-in-law** yerno.

song [sɔŋ] *n* canto, cantar, cantiga, canción, copla; (*birds*) gorjeo; **— book** cancionero; **S— of S—s** Cantar de los Cantares.

sonnet ['sɔnit] *n* soneto.

sonorous ['sɔnərəs] *a* sonoro, resonante, retumbante.

soon [su:n] *ad* pronto, prontamente, presto; **as — as** en cuanto, así que, no bien; **some time —** un día de estos, temprano.

sooner ['su:nə] *ad* más pronto; **no — than** apenas; **— or later** tarde o temprano, a la larga.

soothe [su:ð] *vt* (*person*) calmar, ablandar, acariciar; (*pain*) aliviar.

soothing ['su:ðiŋ] *a* calmante, sedante, consolador.

sophistry ['sɔfistri] *n* sofistería, argucia.

soporific [,sɔpə'rifik] *an* soporífero, narcótico.

soprano [sə'prɑ:nou] *n* tiple.

sorcerer ['sɔ:sərə] *n* hechicero, brujo, encantador.

sorcery ['sɔ:səri] *n* hechicería, brujería.

sordid ['sɔ:did] *a* sórdido, mezquino, asqueroso, sucio, avariento, interesado.

sordidness ['sɔ:didnis] *n* sordidez, bajeza, vileza.
sore [sɔ:] *a* dolorido; resentido, quejoso; delicado; *n* llaga, úlcera.
soreness ['sɔ:nis] *n* dolor, dolencia, llaga; amargura.
sorrow ['sɔrou] *n* dolor, pena, aflicción; cuita; pesar, sentimiento; **to my —** con gran sentimiento mío; **—-stricken** agobiado de dolor; **to express —** dar el pésame; *vi* afligirse, apenarse.
sorrowful ['sɔrəful] *a* afligido, pesaroso, desconsolado.
sorry ['sɔri] *a* triste, desconsolado, apenado, funesto; (*nag etc*) raquítico, ruin, despreciable; **I am —** lo siento, me pesa; usted dispense; **to be — for** compadecer.
sort [sɔ:t] *n* suerte, clase, especie, condición; **a good —** un buen tipo, buen elemento; **of a —** de cierto modo; **out of —s** indispuesto, malhumorado, deprimido, malucho; *vt* clasificar, separar, repartir, escoger; arreglar.
sortie ['sɔ:ti(:)] *n* rebato; salida.
soul [soul] *n* alma, espíritu, ánima; esencia; corazón; criatura, ser; (*fam*) cristiano, hijo de Dios; **All S—'s Day** Día de las Ánimas.
sound [saund] *a* sano, ileso, perfecto, bueno, entero; autorizado; seguro, firme, válido; cabal; **safe and —** sano y salvo; *n* sonido, son; (*naut*) estuario, ría; **— wave** onda sonora; *vt* sonar; tocar; entonar; (*med*) auscultar; (*take soundings*) fondear, sond(e)ar; (*fig*) tentar el pulso, tantear; *vi* sonar, resonar.
sounding ['saundiŋ] *n* sonda; **to take —s** sondear; *a* sonoro, retumbante; **high-—** rimbombante; campanudo.
soundness ['saundnis] *n* salud; solidez, validez, rectitud, firmeza, seguridad.
soup [su:p] *n* sopa.
sour ['sauə] *a* agrio, ácido; (*fig*) acre, áspero; desabrido, rancio; *vti* agriar(se), (*milk*) cortarse; (*wine*) torcerse; (*land*) malearse; indisponer.
source [sɔ:s] *n* fuente, origen, manantial, germen, procedencia, cuna, foco; **reliable —** buena tinta.
sourness ['sauənis] *n* acedía, acidez; acritud, acrimonia.
south [sauθ] *a* meridional, austral; *n* sud, sur, mediodía.
South America [ˌsauθə'merikə] *n* América del Sur.
south-east ['sauθ'i:st] *n* sudeste; *a* del sudeste.
south-eastern ['sauθ'i:stən] *a* del sudeste.
southern ['sʌðən] *a* del sur, al sur, hacia el sur.
south-west ['sauθ'west] *n* sudoeste; *a* del sudoeste.
south-western ['sauθ'westən] *a* del sudoeste.
souvenir ['su:vəniə] *n* recuerdo.
sovereign ['sɔvrin] *a* soberano, supremo, singular; *n* soberano, potentado, monarca; (*coin*) libra metálica.
sovereignty ['sɔvrənti] *n* soberanía, corona.
soviet ['souviet] *a* soviético.
Soviet Union ['souviət'ju:njən] *n* la Unión Soviética.
sow [sou] *vt* sembrar, esparcir, desparramar; (*seed*) sementar; **to — wild oats** correrla.
spa [spɑ:] *n* balneario.
space [speis] *n* espacio, extensión; intervalo; cabida; plaza; huelgo; ocasión, sazón; *vt* espaciar.
spacious ['speiʃəs] *a* espacioso, extenso, amplio, holgado.
spaciousness ['speiʃəsnis] *n* extensión, amplitud, holgura.
spade [speid] *n* azada; (*mil*) zapa, pala; **to call a — a —** llamar al pan pan y al vino vino.
Spain [spein] *n* España.
span [spæn] *n* palmo; (*bridge*) ojo, luz; tramo, trecho; (*time*) lapso; instante; (*wings*) envergadura; *vt* medir (a palmos); alcanzar, cruzar; tender, extender(se).
spangle ['spæŋgl] *n* lentejuela; (*tinsel*) oropel; **—with stars** estrellado, sembrado de estrellas.
Spaniard ['spænjəd] *n* español.
spaniel ['spænjəl] *n* perro de aguas.
Spanish ['spæniʃ] *a* español, hispano, hispánico; *n* español, castellano; **to talk —** (*fam*) hablar cristiano; **— studies** hispanismo; **— scholar** hispanista.
Spanish America ['spaniʃə'merikə] *n* América Española.
spank [spæŋk] *vt* pegar con la mano.
spar [spɑ:] *n* (*naut*) palo, berlinga; (*min*) espato; (*boxing*) lucha, riña; *vi* boxear.
spare [spεə] *a* escaso; (*body*) enjuto; (*pieces*) de repuesto; (*extra*) disponible; suplementario; de repuesto, de reserva; sobrio; **— time** tiempo desocupado, ratos perdidos; **— parts** piezas de recambio; *vti* ahorrar; escatimar; prescindir de, pasarse sin; hacer gracia de; (*time*) dedicar; disponer de; desistir; refrenarse.
sparing ['spεəriŋ] *a* escaso, frugal, parco; **to be —** escasear, escatimar, ser frugal.
spark [spɑ:k] *n* chispa, centella, chispazo; **— plug** bujía.
sparkle ['spɑ:kl] *n* chisporroteo; centelleo, destello; *vi* chisporrotear, centellear, relampaguear, rutilar.
sparkling ['spɑ:kliŋ] *a* centelleante, rutilante, brillante; (*eyes*) chispeante; (*wine*) espumoso.
sparrow ['spærou] *n* gorrión.
sparse [spɑ:s] *a* desparramado; (*hair, grass*) ralo; frugal.
spasm ['spæzəm] *n* espasmo.

spasmodic [spæz'mɔdik] *a* espasmódico.
spatter ['spætə] *vt* salpicar, rociar.
speak [spi:k] *vti* hablar; articular; proferir; arengar; conversar; interceder por; explicarse; **you may —** Vd tiene la palabra; **to — ill of** murmurar de; **X speaking** (*tel*) habla X; **to — out** hablar claro; **to — up** hablar alto.
speaker ['spi:kə] *n* orador; portavoz.
speaking ['spi:kiŋ] *n* **— trumpet** bocina; **— terms** relaciones superficiales.
spear [spiə] *n* lanza; (*javelin*) venablo; arpón; *vti* alancear; brotar.
special ['speʃəl] *a* especial, particular; notable; privativo; predilecto; sumo, subido.
speciality [ˌspeʃi'æliti] *n* especialidad, particularidad.
species ['spi:ʃi:z] *n* especie, género.
specific [spi'sifik] *a* expreso, preciso, determinado.
specify ['spesifai] *vt* especificar, detallar.
specimen ['spesimin] *n* ejemplar, muestra.
specious ['spi:ʃəs] *a* artificioso; **— arguments** retórica.
speck [spek] *n* mota, mancha, mácula, chispa; peca; pizca; *vt* manchar; espolvorear.
spectacle ['spektəkl] *n* espectáculo, exhibición.
spectacles ['spektəklz] *n pl* anteojos, lentes, gafas; (*horn-rimmed*) quevedos.
spectator [spek'teitə] *n* espectador; **—s** concurrencia, auditorio, público.
speckle ['spekl] *vt* motear, manchar.
specter ['spektə] *n* espectro, visión, fantasma.
speculate ['spekjuleit] *vt* especular, considerar, reflexionar.
speculation [ˌspekju'leiʃən] *n* especulación, raciocinio, meditación, teoría.
speech [spi:tʃ] *n* idioma, habla, lengua; oración, discurso; (*theat*) parlamento; lenguaje; **local —** habla; **to lose one's —** perder el hablar; **after-dinner —** brindis; **part of —** parte de la oración.
speechless ['spi:tʃlis] *a* mudo, cortado, desconcertado; **to leave —** aturdir.
speed [spi:d] *n* velocidad, prisa; (*dispatch*) rapidez, expedición, celeridad, diligencia; marcha, carrera, andar; **at full —** a toda velocidad; a carrera tendida; de corrida, a todo correr; **to make —** apresurarse, darse prisa; *vt* despachar; expedir; ayudar; **to — up** acelerar, activar; *vi* apresurarse; progresar.
speedy ['spi:di] *a* veloz, diligente, expedito, rápido.
spell [spel] *n* (*magic*) hechizo, ensalmo; (*attraction*) fascinación; (*fame*) prestigio; (*turn*) turno, tanda; (*time*) rato, temporada; **—bound** hechizado, arrobado, embobado; *vt* deletrear.
spelling ['speliŋ] *n* deletreo, ortografía; **— mistake** falta de ortografía.
spend [spend] *vt* gastar, disipar, emplear, consumir(se); (*time*) pasar.
spendthrift ['spendθrift] *an* manirroto, pródigo, derrochador.
spent [spent] *a* agotado, rendido.
sphere [sfiə] *n* esfera, bola, orbe; astro.
sphinx [sfiŋks] *n* esfinge.
spice [spais] *n* condimento; especia; picante; *vt* condimentar, aliñar, sazonar.
spick [spik] *a* **— and span** repulido, flamante.
spider ['spaidə] *n* araña.
spike [spaik] *n* espiga; espigón; clavo; *vt* (*gun*) clavar, afianzar.
spill [spil] *n* vuelco, caída; *vti* derramar, verter, esparcir; **to — over** *vi* (*liquids*) rebosar; volcarse en.
spin [spin] *vt* (*thread*) hilar; torcer; (*top*) bailar; hacer girar; **—drier** secadora eléctrica; *vi* **to — out** alargar; girar; **to — around** remolinarse.
spinach ['spinidʒ] *n* espinaca.
spinal ['spainl] *a* **— column** columna vertebral.
spindle ['spindl] *n* huso, eje.
spine [spain] *n* espinazo, espina dorsal.
spineless ['spainlis] *a* sin espina.
spinning ['spiniŋ] *n* filatura, acción de hilar; **— wheel** rueca; **— top** peonza.
spinster ['spinstə] *n* soltera, solterona.
spiral ['spaiərəl] *a* espiral; (*archit*) salomónico; **— staircase** escalera de caracol.
spire ['spaiə] *n* aguja, flecha, chapitel.
spirit ['spirit] *n* espíritu, alma; (*departed*) alma, sombra; (*vigor etc*) ánimo, aliento, brío; (*liveliness*) viveza, fogosidad; (*ghost*) visión, aparecido, espíritu; (*nature*) temple, talento; **to undertake with —** apechugar; *pl* licor, aguardiente; **good —** buen humor; **low —** desalentado; **to pick up —** cobrarse ánimos; *vt* **to — away** arrebatar, hacer desaparecer.
spirited ['spiritid] *a* brioso, fogoso, alentado, animoso, gallardo, valiente, arrogante; **low —** batido, deprimido, amilanado.
spiritual ['spiritjuəl] *a* espiritual.
spiritualist ['spiritjuəlist] *n* espiritista.
spit [spit] *vi* escupir; (*rain*) chispear.
spite [spait] *n* despecho, ojeriza, rencilla, rencor; **in — of** a pesar de, a despecho de; **in — of myself** a pesar mío; *vt* vejar, causar pena.
spiteful ['spaitful] *a* rencoroso, malévolo, maligno.

spitefulness ['spaitfulnis] *n* malevolencia, encono, inquina.
spiv [spiv] *n* (*sl*) holgazán.
splash [splæʃ] *n* salpicadura; chispa; *vt* estrellar, salpicar; chapotear.
splattered ['splætəd] *a* estrellado.
splendid ['splendid] *a* espléndido, heroico; magnífico, fastuoso, lucido; ilustre.
splendidness ['splendidnis] *n* esplendidez, bizarría.
splendor ['splendə] *n* esplendor, brillantez, magnificencia; refulgencia; gloria, fausto.
splint [splint] *n* astilla.
splinter ['splintə] *n* astilla; **to put on a —** entablar; *vt* entablillar; *vt* romperse en astillas.
split [split] *a* partido, hendido; *n* hendedura; grieta; resquebradura; raja; (*among people*) división, rompimiento; *vt* tajar, hender, rajar; partir, dividir, resquebrajar; *vi* grietarse, hendirse; abrirse, estrellarse.
splutter ['splʌtə] *n* chisporroteo; *vi* farfullar; (*candle*) chisporrotear.
spoil [spɔil] *n pl* despojo, botín, trofeo; (*of office*) gajes; *vt* estropear; arruinar, dañar, (*taste*) estragar; (*appearance*) ajar; (*plans*)desbaratar, dar al traste con; (*fruit*) echar a perder, perderse; (*child*) mimar, consentir; (*sack*) despojar, robar; (*by handling*) manosear.
spoiled ['spɔild] **spoilt** ['spɔilt] *a* averiado, roto; estropeado; (*child*) consentido, mimado.
spokesman ['spouksmən] *n* portavoz.
sponge [spʌndʒ] *n* esponja; **to throw in the —, to give up the —** (*fam*) rajarse; *vt* pasar la esponja, lavar con esponja; **to — on** comer (*etc*) de gorra, vivir a costa ajena.
sponsor ['spɔnsə] *n* fiador; (*weddings etc*) padrino.
spontaneity [ˌspɔntə'ni:iti] espontaneidad.
spontaneous [spɔn'teiniəs] *a* espontáneo.
spool [spu:l] *n* bobina.
spoon [spu:n] *n* cuchara; (*tea, coffee etc*) cucharita, cucharilla; (*large*) cucharón.
spoonful ['spu:nful] *n* cucharada; (*tea, coffee etc*) cucharadita.
sport [spɔ:t] *n* deporte; recreo; holgorio; diversión; juego; *vt* (*fam*) gastar; *vi* holgar.
sporting ['spɔ:tiŋ] *a* de caza; deportista.
sportive ['spɔ:tiv] *a* juguetón.
sportsman ['spɔ:tsmən] *n* deportista.
spot [spɔt] *n* (*place*) sitio, lugar, paraje; (*stain*) mancha, lunar, tacha; (*shame*) baldón, tacha; **on the —** en el acto, al punto; *vt* abigarrar, manchar; salpicar; notar, descubrir.
spotless ['spɔtlis] *a* puro, limpio, virgen, sin mancha; inmaculado.
spotted ['spɔtid] *a* manchado, con manchas, con pintas.
spouse [spauz] *n* esposo.
spout [spaut] *n* (*drain*) caño, cañería, tubo; surtidor; (*of water*) chorro; (*teapot*) pico; **water —** tromba; (*sl*) **up the —** acabado, arruinado; *vti* lanzar, arrojar; chorrear.
sprain [sprein] *n* torcedura; *vt* torcer; *vi* dislocarse.
sprawl [sprɔ:l] *vi* tenderse, tumbarse.
spray [sprei] *n* espuma; ramita de árbol; rociada; pulverizador, rociador; *vt* rociar.
spread [spred] *a* extendido, desparramado; *n* extensión, dilatación, amplitud; desarrollo; (*of news*) difusión, diseminación; (*of branches*) ramaje; (*of wings*) envergadura; (*meal*) (*fam*) festín, cuchipanda; **bed—** sobrecama, cobertor; *vt* extender, esparcir; (*wings*) desplegar, desenvolver; (*table*) poner; sembrar, difundir, propalar; *vi* extenderse, popularizarse, generalizarse; (*of news etc*) cundir; (*in speech*) explayarse; **to — abroad** esparcirse, propalar; **to — over, with** untar, dar una capa de; **to — out** separar, extender, distanciar; ramificarse; *vr* esparcirse, ponerse a sus anchas.
spreading ['sprediŋ] *n* propagación.
sprightly ['spraitli] *a* vivo, vivaz, despejado, listo, vivaracho.
spring [spriŋ] *a* primaveral; elástico; *n* (*season*) primavera; (*mech*) resorte, muelle; (*jump*) salto, bote; (*water*) fuente, venero, manantial; (*of action*) móvil, germen; **—board** trampolín; *vt* (*trap*) soltar; (*mine*) volar; (*arch*) arrancar; (*a suggestion etc*) presentar de golpe; **to — over** pasar saltando, saltar por encima; **to — a leak** hacer agua; *vi* saltar, brincar; (*liquid*) manar; (*arise*) provenir, seguirse, hacer; (*rise*) levantar(se), elevarse; **to — at** lanzarse sobre; **to — back** saltar atrás, recular; **to — forth** brotar, precipitarse; **to — up** brotar, desarrollarse, surgir.
springlike ['spriŋlaik] *a* primaveral.
springtime ['spriŋtaim] *n* primavera.
springy ['spriŋi] *a* elástico, muelle, esponjoso.
sprinkle ['spriŋkl] *vt* aspersar, rociar, salpicar, espolvorar.
sprinkling ['spriŋkliŋ] *n* aspersión, rociada; **a — of** unos cuantos.
sprite [sprait] *n* duende, hada.
sprout [spraut] *n* **Brussels —s** col de Bruselas; renuevo, botón; vástago; *vi* brotar, germinar, surgir.
spur [spə:] *n* espuela; (*of cock*) garrón, espolón; (*mountain*) estribación; risco; estímulo; *vt* espolear; impeler, instar, incitar.
spuriousness ['spjuəriəsnis] *a* falsedad.
spurn [spə:n] *vt* desdeñar, despreciar, hollar.

spurt [spəːt] *n* chorro; esfuerzo repentino; *vi* arrojar, brotar, surgir, salir a chorros.

spy [spai] *n* espía; **—glass** catalejo; *vti* espiar; columbrar; **to — on** acechar; **to — out** explorar, reconocer.

squadron ['skwɔdrən] *n* (*naut*) escuadra; (*mil*) escuadrilla aérea.

squalid ['skwɔlid] *a* inmundo, mugriento, escuálido, tiñoso.

squall [skwɔːl] *n* (*cry*) chillido; (*wind, rain*) borrasca, aguacero, racha; *vi* chillar.

squalor ['skwɔlə] *n* escualidez, porquería.

squander ['skwɔndə] *vt* malgastar, disipar, prodigar, despilfarrar, tirar.

square [skwɛə] *a* cuadrado; justo, redondo, íntegro; **— built** cuadrado; **— -dealing** honrado; **— root** raíz cuadrada; **to get — with** desquitarse; **four — feet** cuatro pies cuadrados; **to be —** estar justo, saldado; **to be all —** estar iguales; *n* (*math*) cuadro, cuadrado; (*town*) plaza; (*games*) casilla; (*mil*) cuadro; *vt* cuadrar; elevar al cuadrado; (*com*) saldar; ajustar, arreglar; (*fam*) sobornar; *vi* encajar, ajustarse, acomodar(se).

squash [skwɔʃ] *n* calabaza; *vt* aplastar, magullar.

squat [skwɔt] *a* rechoncho; *vi* agacharse, ponerse en cuclillas, acurrucarse; establecerse.

squeak [skwiːk] *n* chirrido; *vi* crujir, chirriar; restallar; **to have a narrow —** escaparse por un pelo.

squeal [skwiːl] *n* chillido; *vi* chillar, berrear; (*sl*) cantar.

squeamish ['skwiːmiʃ] *a* escrupuloso, delicado, nimio, cosquilloso, fastidioso.

squeeze [skwiːz] *n* presión, apretón; (*fam*) **tight —** aprieto; *vt* apretar, comprimir, oprimir, estrujar; **to — out** exprimir; **to — in** *vi* recalcar; **to — into** pasar apretando.

squint [skwint] *a* bizco; *n* estrabismo, mirada bizca; *vi* bizquear, mirar de través.

squire ['skwaiə] *n* escudero, propietario; *vt* acompañar.

squirm [skwəːm] *vi* retorcerse.

squirrel ['skwirəl] *n* ardilla.

squirt [skwəːt] *n* chorro; jeringazo, jeringa; *vt* jeringar, hacer saltar a chorros.

stab [stæb] *n* herida, puñalada; estocada; *vt* dar de puñaladas, apuñalar.

stability [stə'biliti] *n* estabilidad; firmeza, solidez.

stable ['steibl] *a* estable, firme, fijo; inalterable; *n* establo, caballeriza, cuadra; *vt* poner en la cuadra.

stack [stæk] *n* (*grain etc*) niara; pila; (*arms*) pabellón; (*chimney*) cañón; *vt* hacinar, amontonar.

stadium ['steidiəm] *n* estadio.

staff [stɑːf] *n* (*stick*) báculo, porra; (*shepherd*) cayado; (*flag*) asta; (*of office*) bastón; (*support*) apoyo, sostén; (*mil*) estado mayor; (*household*) servidumbre; (*factory*) plantilla, personal; (*university*) profesorado.

stag [stæg] *n* ciervo, venado.

stage [steidʒ] *n* (*boards*) escenario, tablas; teatro; (*platform*) tablado, plataforma, estrado; (*point*) punto; etapa, jornada, estado; fase; (*in promotion*) escalón; **—coach** diligencia; **— manager** director de escena; **in —s** a tragos, por etapas; **by short —s** a cortas jornadas, poco a poco; *vt* poner en escena, representar.

stagger ['stægə] *vi* hacer eses, tambalear, vacilar, titubear.

staging ['steidʒiŋ] *n* andamiaje, tablado; representación.

stagnant ['stægnənt] *a* encharcado, estancado.

stagnate ['stægneit] *vi* estancar(se), detener(se).

staid [steid] *a* serio, grave, sosegado, (a)sentado, almidonado.

stain [stein] *n* mancha, lunar, mácula, tinte, tintura; (*oil*) lámpara; *vti* manchar, teñir; mancharse; ensuciar, desdorar, empañar.

stained ['steind] *a* **— glass** vidrio de color.

stainless ['steinlis] *a* inmaculado, limpio; (*steel etc*) inoxidable.

stair [stɛə] *n* peldaño, grada; *pl* escalera; **spiral —** escalera de caracol; **flight of —s** tramo; **up—s** arriba, en el piso superior; **down—s** abajo, en el piso inferior.

staircase ['stɛəkeis] *n* escalera; (*stone*) escalinata.

stake [steik] *n* estaca, poste; postura; (*betting*) apuesta, parada, puesta; pira; **at —** en peligro, en juego; *vt* estacar; apostar; parar; arriesgar.

stale [steil] *a* pasado, rancio; (*air*) viciado; (*bread*) duro; (*wine*) picado.

staleness [steilnis] *n* rancidez, vejez, insulsez.

stalk [stɔːk] *n* tallo; tronco, pedúnculo; pezón; *vt* acechar, seguir la pista de.

stall [stɔːl] *n* (*animal*) pesebre; establo; (*shop*) barraca, puesto; **—s** (*eccles*) sillería; *vt* encerrar en establo, poner obstáculos a; atascar(se); (*mech*) atascarse, pararse; **he is —ing** está haciendo la pala.

stalwart ['stɔːlwət] *a* forzudo, fornido; leal.

stamina ['stæminə] *n* fuerza vital, vigor.

stammer ['stæmə] *vi* tartamudear, trabarse la lengua, balbucir.

stamp [stæmp] *n* (*official*) sello, timbre; (*design*) estampa, impresión; (*imprint*) impresión, sello, marca; (*die*) cuño; (*of foot*) pisada; (*quality*) temple, suerte, calaña; (*postage*) sello, *SA* estampilla; (*of truth*) sello; — **duty** de timbre; — **collecting** filatelia; *vt* (*officially*) timbrar, sellar; (*design*) imprimir; (*with die*) acuñar; (*mark*) señalar; (*postage*) poner, pegar un sello; (*with feet*) patear; (*disapprovingly*) patalear; (*with heels*) taconear; (*smash*) triturar; **to — on** pisar, hollar; **to — on** (*mind*) grabar; **to — down** apisonar; **to — out** extirpar, sofocar.

stampede [stæm'pi:d] *n* estampida; *vt* ahuyentar, salir de estampía.

stand [stænd] *n* (*at fairs*) puesto; (*at games*) estrado, tribuna; (*platform*) tarima, plataforma; (*support*) sostén; pedestal, peana; (*stop*) parada, alto; (*resistance*) oposición, resistencia; (*fig*) situación, actitud, posición; **to take a firm —** resistir, mantenerse firme; *vt* (*bear*) resistir, aguantar, tolerar, someterse a; colocar (de pie); **to — up** poner derecho, poner de pie, de canto; **I can't — him** no le puedo ver; *vi* estar de pie; levantarse, erguirse; resistir; detenerse, pararse, quedar suspenso; estar situado; (per)durar, quedar en pie; **to — against** hacer frente a; **to — aloof** mantenerse apartado; **to — aside** apartarse, quitarse de en medio; **to — back** estar apartado, retroceder; **to — by** apoyar, sostener; **to — for** representar, significar; presentarse; tolerar; **to — in need** necesitar; **to — in good stead** servir, militar en (su) favor; **to — in the way** impedir, dificultar, cerrar el paso; **to — on** estar (colocado) sobre; interesar; picarse de; **to — on ceremony** hacerse pedir; **to — on end** ponerse de punta; mantenerse derecho; **to — out** sobresalir, destacar(se), resaltar; oponerse; separarse; **to — up** levantarse, ponerse de pie; **to — up for** abogar por, volver por; abrazar; **to — still** estarse quieto; estancarse.

standard ['stændəd] *a* normal, ejemplar; típico, clásico, de ley; *n* modelo, patrón, orma, tipo; nivel; poste, ilar; (*banner*) pabellón; (*weight*) marco; (*in exam*) calificación; **gold —** patrón de oro; **— bearer** alférez.

standardize ['stændədaiz] *vt* hacer uniforme, controlar.

standing ['stændiŋ] *a* de pie, derecho; duradero, constante; (*law*) vigente; (*water*) encharcado; **— room** (*in theat*) sitio para estar de pie; **— committee** comisión permanente; *n* posición; (*social*) reputación, crédito, rango; sitio; duración; **to be —** estar de pie; **to be still —** quedar todavía; **to remain —** tenerse en pie.

standpoint ['stændpɔint] *n* punto de vista.

standstill ['stændstil] *n* alto, parada; **at a —** parado, en suspenso.

stanza ['stænzə] *n* estrofa, copla, verso.

staple ['steipl] *a* corriente, principal; *n* grampa; aro; **— product** artículo principal, elemento, materia prima.

star [stɑ:] *n* estrella, astro; (*destiny*) sino; (*decoration*) cruz; **shooting —** estrella fugaz; exhalación; **under the —s** al sereno, a cielo raso.

starched ['stɑ:tʃt] *a* almidonado, estirado, tieso, entonado.

stare [stɛə] *n* mirada fija; *vi* mirar; saltar a la vista; **to — at** ojear, clavar los ojos en; **to — straight at** mirar de hito en hito.

stark [stɑ:k] *a, ad* rígido, fuerte; fuertemente; (*truth etc*) desnudo, escueto; **— naked** desnudo, en cueros; **— raving mad** loco rematado, loco de atar.

starling ['stɑ:liŋ] *n* estornino.

starry ['stɑ:ri] *a* estrellado, constelado.

start [stɑ:t] *n* (*surprise*) sobresalto; bote; respingo; (*beginning*) comienzo, principio; salida, ímpetu, arranque; (*advantage*) delantera, ventaja; **by —s** a saltos; **for a —** para empezar; *vt* empezar, comenzar; iniciar; poner en marcha, hacer andar, funcionar; (*task*) suscitar; (*game*) levantar; *vi* sobrecogerse, dar un salto; (*surprise*) botar, sobresaltarse; (*train etc*) arrancar; principiar, salir; emprender; originar, iniciarse; **to — back** emprender el regreso; **to — for** ponerse en marcha hacia; **to — off** marcharse; **to — up** empezar a funcionar.

starter ['stɑ:tə] *n* iniciador; (*race*) starter; (*aut*) arranque.

starting ['stɑ:tiŋ] *a* **— point** punto de partida.

startle ['stɑ:tl] *vt* asustar, espantar, sobresaltar.

starvation [stɑ:'veiʃən] *n* muerte de hambre, inanición.

starve [stɑ:v] *vti* (matar, morir) de hambre.

starving ['stɑ:viŋ] *a* famélico, hambriento.

state [steit] *n* estado, situación, condición; fausto, gala; **in great —** con gran pompa; (*of weather*) temperie; **— paper** documento de estado; **to lie in —** yacer (estar) en capilla ardiente; *vt* exponer, explicar, manifestar, afirmar, declarar, citar; (*problem*) plantear, sentar; (*explicitly*) consignar, poner de bulto.

stated ['steitid] *a* establecido, fijo.

stately ['steitli] *a* magnífico, solemne, imponente, augusto.

statement ['steitmənt] *n* declaración, exposición, expresión, informe; estado, resumen; **self-evident —** perogrullada.

statesman ['steitsmən] *n* estadista, hombre de estado.
station ['steiʃən] *n* (*rl*) estación; (*in life etc*) puesto, situación; **field dressing** — hospital de campaña; apostadero; — **of Cross** estaciones (del Calvario); *vt* apostar, colocar; *vr* situarse.
stationary ['steiʃnəri] *a* estacionario, fijo.
stationery ['steiʃnəri] *n* útiles de escritorio; papelería.
statistics [stə'tistiks] *n* estadística; datos estadísticos.
statue ['stætju:] *n* estatua; (*esp relig*) imagen.
stature ['stætʃə] *n* estatura, tamaño, talla.
status ['steitəs] *n* rango; estado civil; condición; honores.
statute ['stætju:t] *n* ley, acto legislativo, estatuto.
staunch ['stɔ:ntʃ] *a* fiel, acérrimo; *vt* restañar, estancar.
stay [stei] *n* estancia, visita; (*law*) sobreseimiento temporal; freno; apoyo, sostén, demora; *pl* (*corset*) corsé, ballenas de corsé; *vt* impedir, contener, detener, sostener; diferir; *vi* quedar(se); visitar, pasar una temporada, parar; **to — at** hospedarse en; **to — away** ausentarse; **to — up** (*night*) velar, no acostarse.
steadfast ['stedfəst] *a* firme, estable, fijo, resuelto.
steadiness ['stedinis] *n* constancia, firmeza, estabilidad; — **of hand** pulso, firme.
steady ['stedi] *a* constante, fijo, estable, regular; formal; quieto, compasado, sentado; *vt* fijar, sostener.
steak [steik] *n* bistec, filete.
steal [sti:l] *vti* robar, hurtar; **to — away, along** deslizarse, escurrirse; **to — into** (*good graces etc*) insinuarse; colarse.
stealing ['sti:liŋ] *n* latrocinio; robo, hurto.
stealth [stelθ] *n* cautela, recato; **by —** a hurtadillas; a escondidas.
stealthy ['stelθi] *a* furtivo, clandestino; oculto.
steam [sti:m] *n* vapor; (*from animals etc*) vaho; *vti* cocer al vapor; echar vapor.
steamboat ['sti:mbout] *n* vapor.
steamer ['sti:mə] *n* (buque de) vapor.
steamship ['sti:mʃip] *n* buque de vapor.
steed [sti:d] *n* corcel.
steel [sti:l] *n* acero; **cold —** arma blanca; **cast —** acero fundido; *a* acerado; de acero; *vt* acerar; fortalecer.
steep [sti:p] *a* escarpado, en declive; precipitoso, abrupto, acantilado, empinado; *vt* remojar, empapar.
steeple ['sti:pl] *n* campanario; aguja; **—chase** carrera con obstáculos.
steepness ['sti:pnis] *n* declive, precipicio; lo precipitoso.
steer [stiə] *n* novillo; *vt* dirigir, conducir; (*ship*) gobernar; *vi* hacer rumbo a. navegar.
steerage ['stiəridʒ] *n* proa.
steering ['stiəriŋ] *n* (*naut*) gobierno; **— wheel** volante.
stem [stem] *n* tronco, tallo; **from — to stern** de cabo a rabo; *vt* oponerse a; resistir, restañar; contener; navegar contra la corriente.
stench [stentʃ] *n* hediondez, hedor, pestilencia.
stenographer [stə'nɔgrəfə] *n* estenógrafa, taquígrafa.
step [step] *n* (*walk*) paso; (*stair*) peldaño; grada; (*for mounting horse*) estribo; (*door*) umbral; (*sound of*) pisada; (*mark of*) huella; **—child** alnado; **—mother** madrastra; *pl* (*means etc*) diligencias, gestiones; (*terraced*) gradería; (*of stone*) escalinata; **first —** pinitos; **at every —** a cada momento, a cada trinquete; *vt* poner, sentar el pie; (*mast*) plantar; **to — on** pisar; *vi* dar un paso, pisar; avanzar; **to — aside** apartarse; **to — down** bajar; darse de baja; **to — out** apretar el paso; **to — up** (*el*) elevar la tensión.
Stephen ['sti:vn] *m* Esteban.
stepping ['stepiŋ] *a* **— stone** pasadera.
sterile ['sterail] *a* estéril, infecundo, yermo.
sterility [ste'riliti] *n* esterilidad.
sterling ['stə:liŋ] *a* esterlino, de buena ley; **pound —** libra esterlina; **— silver** plata de ley.
stern [stə:n] *a* grave, serio, severo, austero, rigido; *n* popa.
sternness ['stə:nnis] *n* severidad, austeridad, rigidez, seriedad, rigor.
stew [stju:] *n* guisado, cocido, platillo; olla; *vti* guisar, estofar.
stewpan ['stju:pæn] **stewpot** ['stju:pɔt] *n* olla, marmita, cacerola.
steward ['stjuəd] *n* mayordomo; (*of farm*) ranchero; **ship's —** camarero.
stewardess ['stjuədis] *n* camarera.
stewed [stju:d] *a* **— fruit** compota.
stick [stik] *n* (*walking*) caña, bastón; báculo; vara, estaca; (*heavy*) porra, garrote; **broom—** mango; **blind man's —** tiento; *pl* (*fire*) leña; *vt* pegar, unir, fijar; **to — out** (*head etc*) asomarse, sacar; **to — into** hundir, clavar; (*teeth*) hincar; (*to prick*) pinchar, picar, punzar; **to — together** pegar, juntar; *vi* estar (prendido, pegado); **to — at** persistir; **not to — at trifles** no reparar en pelillos, no tener escrúpulos; **to — in** (*throat*) atravesarse(le); **to — in the mud** atascarse; atollarse; **to — to** pegarse; persistir; **to — out** proyectar, (sobre)salir.
sticking ['stikiŋ] *a* **— plaster** esparadrapo.

sticky ['stiki] *a* pegajoso, glutinoso, pegadizo.
stiff [stif] *a* tieso, duro, rígido, tenso; (*of test etc*) difícil, fuerte; (*after exercise*) (músculos) resentidos; (*with cold*) aterido, entumecido; (*clumsy, slow*) torpe, entorpecido; (*manner*) formal, almidonado, estirado, entonado; (*opposition*) duro, terco; (*paste*) espeso; **—necked** estirado, terco, erguido.
stiffen ['stifn] *vti* atiesar, endurecer; ponerse rígido, erguirse; robustecer; (*spirits*) levantar la moral.
stiffness ['stifnis] *n* rigidez, dureza; engreimiento; (*med*) rigor.
stifle ['staifl] *vt* sofocar, ahogar; apagar; suprimir.
stigma ['stigmə] *n* estigma, oprobio, baldón, borrón.
stiletto [sti'letou] *n* estilete; (zapatos de) tacón.
still [stil] *a* inmóvil, fijo, quieto; apacible, quedo, suave, sordo, silencioso, sereno; (*water*) durmiente; **— life** bodegón; **—born** aborto; *ad* todavía, hasta ahora, siempre, no obstante, aún; *n* quietud, calma, sosiego; *vt* acallar, enmudecer, apaciguar, calmar, tranquilizar, detener.
stillness ['stilnis] *n* calma, tranquilidad, quietud, silencio, inactividad.
stilted ['stiltid] *a* hinchado, campanudo, pomposo.
stimulant ['stimjulənt] *n* acicate, estimulante.
stimulate ['stimjuleit] *vt* estimular, incitar, esforzar, excitar, avivar.
stimulating ['stimjuleitiŋ] *a* incitante, inquietante.
stimulation [ˌstimju'leiʃən] *n* excitación.
stimulus ['stimjuləs] *n* aguijón, estímulo, incentivo.
sting [stiŋ] *n* aguijón, picadura; (*of bee*) espigón; (*conscience*) remordimiento; *vt* picar, punzar; (*sl*) clavar, hincar la uña.
stinginess ['stindʒinis] *n* avaricia, tacañería.
stink [stiŋk] *n* mal olor, peste; *vi* apestar.
stipulate ['stipjuleit] *vi* estipular, pactar.
stir [stə:] *n* movimiento, agitación; bulla, alboroto; *vt* mover, remover; (*liquid*) revolver, agitar; **to — up** (*passions etc*) concitar; **to — up** (*rebellion etc*) levantar, fomentar, suscitar, soliviantar; *vi* menearse, agitarse.
stirrup ['stirəp] *n* estribo.
stitch [stitʃ] *n* puntada, punto; (*pain*) punzada, pinchazo; *vt* coser, (*surg*) suturar.
stock [stɔk] *n* (*family*) estirpe; (*tree*) tronco; (*rifle*) caja; (*handle*) mango; (*neck*) collarín; (*cattle*) ganadería; (*store*) provisión, surtido, existencias, acopio; (*fin*) valor, acción; **— broker** bolsista; **— exchange, — market** bolsa de valores; **— farm** rancho; **— farmer** ranchero, ganadero; **— phrase** lugar común, muletilla; *pl* (*for punishment*) cepo; **preferred —** acciones privilegiadas; *vt* proveer, abastecer, surtir; **to — up** almacenar; **to take —** hacer inventario, asesorarse de.
stockade [stɔ'keid] *n* estacada, valla.
stocking ['stɔkiŋ] *n* media; (*knee-length*) calceta.
stocky ['stɔki] *a* rechoncho.
stoic ['stouik] *n* estoico.
stoic(al) ['stouik(əl)] *a* estoico.
stoke [stouk] *vt* cargar.
stoker ['stoukə] *n* fogonero.
stolid ['stɔlid] *a* estólido, insensible, imperturbable.
stomach ['stʌmək] *n* estómago; *vt* digerir, aguantar.
stone [stoun] *a* pétreo, de piedra; *n* piedra; canto; **grave—** lápida; (*rough*) pedrusco; (*fruit*) hueso; **—mason** picapedrero; **—deaf** sordo como una tapia; **corner—** piedra angular; **stepping —** pasadera; **—work** mampostería; **to leave no — unturned** revolver Roma con Santiago; *vt* apedrear, lapidar.
stony ['stouni] *a* pedregoso, pétreo; (*glance*) glacial, de suficiencia; (*fig*) marmóreo, insensible; **— ground** cantorral.
stool [stu:l] *n* taburete, escabel, banqueta.
stoop [stu:p] *n* cargazón de espaldas; (*liquids*) pila; inclinación; *vi* inclinarse, ir encorvado, agacharse; someterse; ser cargado de espaldas.
stop [stɔp] *n* (*bus*) parada; **flag —** parada discrecional; cesación; alto; (*work*) paro; obstáculo, embarazo; (*mus*) tecla; **full —** punto final; **to put a — to** poner (coto, fin) a; **to come to a —** venir a parar, estancarse; **dead —** parada en seco; *vt* parar, detener, interrumpir, terminar, contener, cesar de; (*payment*) suspender; (*flow*) restañar; (*hole*) tapar, cegar, obturar; (*pipe*) atascar; (*tooth*) empastar; *vi* parar(se), plantarse; hacer (alto, punto, parada); acabarse; **to — at** hospedarse a, alojarse; **to — short** pararse en seco.
stoppage ['stɔpidʒ] *n* cesación, detención; suspensión, obstrucción.
stopped [stɔpt] *a* **to be — up** (*pipes etc*) atascarse, estancarse.
stopper ['stɔpə] *n* tapadura, tapón.
store [stɔ:] *n* almacén, tienda; copia; provisión, abundancia; (*private*) escondrijo; **— room** bodega; **dry-goods —** lencería; *pl* pertrechos, provisiones; *vt* proveer, surtir, almacenar; **to — up** amontonar; **to — away** archivar, acumular.
storehouse ['stɔ:haus] *n* almacén; (*fig*) mina, tesoro.

storekeeper ['stɔ:ˌki:pə] *n* tendero.
stor(e)y ['stɔ:ri] *n* piso.
stork [stɔ:k] *n* cigüeña.
storm [stɔ:m] *n* temporal, tormenta; tempestad; **snow—** nevasca; **— in a teacup** tempestad en un vaso de agua; **to take by —** expugnar; *vt* tomar por asalto; **to — at** fulminar.
stormy ['stɔ:mi] *a* tempestuoso, borrascoso.
story ['stɔ:ri] *n* historia, cuento, leyenda, relación; fábula; rondalla; piso; (*sl*) patraña.
story teller ['stɔ:riˌtelə] *n* cuentista.
story telling ['stɔ:riˌteliŋ] *n* acción de contar, narrar.
stout [staut] *a* grueso; robusto; gordo, panzudo; recio, forzudo; resuelto, animoso.
stoutness ['stautnis] *n* robustez, gordura.
stove [stouv] *n* estufa; cocina, fogón.
stowaway ['stouəwei] *n* polizón.
straggle ['strægl] *vi* vagar, estraviarse, rezagarse.
straggler ['stræglə] *n* rezagado; disperso.
straight [streit] *a* derecho, recto; tieso; (*hair*) lacio; (*of drink*) solo; **— ahead** seguido; *ad* directo; **— ahead** enfrente; **— away** de buenas a primeras; **in a — line** rectamente.
straighten ['streitn] *vt* **to — up** enderezar, arreglar; *vi* enderezarse.
straightness ['streitnis] *n* rectitud; probidad.
strain [strein] *n* tensión; (*mus*) tonada, aire; estilo; tema; (*of madness*) vena; (*breed*) raza; (*twist*) torcedura; (*archit*) esguince; *vti* colar, filtrar; esforzar(se); lastimar, torcer, forzar.
strained [streind] *a* violento, forzado; (*relations*) tirante.
strainer ['streinə] *n* colador, filtro, cedazo, tamiz.
strait [streit] *a* angosto; estrecho; exacto; **—laced** estirado; *n* estrecho, aprieto, apuro; (*geog*) **—s** estrecho.
Strait of Magellan *n* Estrecho de Magallanes.
strand [strænd] *n* (*shore*) playa; (*river*) ribera, orilla; (*rope*) cabo, ramal; (*thread*) hebra; (*hair*) trenza; *vt* (*ship*) encallar, varar.
strange [streindʒ] *a* extraño, raro, fantástico, sorprendente, peregrino, desconocido; esquivo.
strangeness ['streindʒnis] *n* extrañeza, novedad, rareza, singularidad, esquivez.
stranger ['streindʒə] *n* extraño, forastero, desconocido, profano; **to be a — to** desconocer.
strangle ['stræŋgl] *vt* estrangular, dar garrote a, ahogar.
strap [stræp] *n* (*leather*) correa; (*waist*) cinturón: (*harness*) contrafuerte; **chin—** carrillera; **shoe—** tirante; precinta; *vt* amarrar con correas.
strapping ['stræpiŋ] *a* gordo, abultado, rozagante; **— youth** mocetón.
Strasburg ['stræzbə:g] *n* Estrasburgo.
stratagem ['strætidʒəm] *n* estratagema, artería, ardid, treta.
strategic [strə'ti:dʒik] *a* estratégico.
strategy ['strætidʒi] *n* estrategia.
stratum ['strɑ:təm] *n* capa, estrato.
straw [strɔ:] *a* pajizo; de paja; *n* paja; **that's the last —** es el colmo; **— loft** pajar; **—colored** pajizo.
strawberry ['strɔ:bəri] *n* fresa.
stray [strei] *a* extraviado, descarriado; (*animal*) mostrenco; *vi* descarriarse, extraviarse; (*of thoughts*) divagar.
streak ['stri:k] *n* raya, lista; (*of light*) rayo; *vt* rayar, listar; abigarrar.
streaky ['stri:ki] *a* abigarrado; listado, rayado.
stream [stri:m] *n* corriente; afluente; arroyo; chorro; (*of words*) flujo; **—lined** aerodinámico; **up—** agua arriba, contracorriente; *vi* fluir, manar, correr, salir a torrentes.
street [stri:t] *n* calle; (*Galicia*) rúa; **—lamp** reverbero.
streetcar ['stri:tkɑ:] *n* tranvía.
strength [streŋθ] *n* fuerza, vigor; fortaleza, energía, solidez, pujanza; brío; (*wine*) cuerpo; nervio, nervosidad; alma; **to gather —** cobrar fuerzas; **by the — of one's arm** a pulso; **on the — of** en atención a; respaldado por, fiándose de.
strengthen ['streŋθən] *vt* fortificar, reforzar, consolidar, cimentar; alentar; fortalecer, robustecer; *vi* fortalecerse.
strengthening ['streŋθəniŋ] *n* refuerzo.
strenuous ['strenjuəs] *a* fuerte, activo, enérgico; agotador, arduo.
strenuousness ['strenjuəsnis] *n* energía, fortaleza, celo.
stress [stres] *n* fuerza, peso, entidad, acento; tensión; coacción; carga; **to lay — on** insistir en, hacer hincapié en, acentuar, recalcar.
stretch [stretʃ] *n* extensión; ensanche; ensanchamiento; (*of time*) tirada; **at a —** de una tirada; (*of land*) llano; *vt* (ex)tender; alargar; ensanchar, forzar; **to — out** tender; *vi* extenderse, desperezarse, estirarse; **to — out** tenderse.
stretcher ['stretʃə] *n* camilla.
strew [stru:] *vt* esparcir, derramar.
stricken ['strikən] *a* agobiado, herido; **— in years** añoso, entrado en años.
strict [strikt] *a* estricto, severo, premioso, riguroso.
strictly ['striktli] *ad* **— speaking** en rigor.
strictness ['striktnis] *n* severidad, rigidez, rigor, exactitud, puntualidad.

stride [straid] *n* tranco, zancada; *vi* **to — along** trancar, pasar a zancadas, andar a trancos, caminar.
strident ['straidənt] *a* estrepitoso, estridente.
strife [straif] *n* lucha, contienda, contención, altercado; disensión; porfía.
strike [straik] *n* huelga; *vt* golpear, pegar, herir; (*colors*) arriar; (*match*) encender; (*coin*) acuñar; (*light*) sacar lumbre; (*attitude*) asumir; (*tent*) desmontar; **to — up** (*conversation*) entablar; **to — up against** chocar con, tropezar con, dar (con, contra), estrellarse contra; **it strikes me** se me ocurre; **it strikes home** me toca de cerca, da en lo vivo; **to go on —** declararse en huelga; *vi* golpear; chocar; (*bell*) sonar; (*ship on reef*) embarrancar; (*of plants*) arraigar; **to — at** acometer; **to — down** derribar; **to — off** borrar, tachar; cercenar; cerrar; **to — out for** arrojarse; **to — through** traspasar, atravesar; **to — up** (*music*) tañer, iniciar.
striker ['straikə] *n* golpeador; huelguista.
striking ['straikiŋ] *a* relevante, llamativo, chocante.
string [striŋ] *n* cuerda, cordón, hilo; (*of people etc*) fila; (*onions*) ristra, horca; (*lies*) sarta; (*curses*) retahila; *vt* encordar, ensartar.
stringed [striŋd] *a* (*instrument*) de cuerda.
stringent ['strindʒənt] *a* estricto, riguroso, apurado.
strip [strip] *n* banda; tira; (*meat etc*) lonja; (*land*) lengua; (*cloth*) tira, jirón; *vt* despojar, quitar, desnudar; (*mech*) desmontar; *vi* desguarnecer, desnudarse, ponerse en cueros.
stripe [straip] *n* raya, lista, banda; (*mil*) galón, galoncillo; veta; (*bruise*) cardenal; *vt* rayar.
striped [straipt] *a* rayado, listado.
strive [straiv] *vi* esforzarse, forcejear, competir, afanarse, apurarse.
stroke [strouk] *n* golpe; pase; (*with whip*) latigazo; (*of bell*) campanada; (*med*) ataque fulminante; caricia; (*of genius etc*) rasgo; (*paint*) pincelada; (*of pen*) plumada; *vt* acariciar.
stroll [stroul] *n* paseo; **to take a —** dar una vuelta.
strolling ['strouliŋ] *a* errante; **— player** cómico de la legua, comediante.
strong [strɔŋ] *a* fuerte, vigoroso, nervioso, recio; intenso, emocionante; violento; vivo, brillante; (*accent*) marcado, pronunciado; generoso; (*colors*) subido; (*liquids*) cargado; **—minded** de creencias arraigadas; **—willed** voluntarioso; cabezudo, decidido.
stronghold ['strɔŋhould] *n* fortaleza.
struck [strʌk] *a* **to be —** (*by idea*) ocurrir(le) (a uno).
structure ['strʌkʃə] *n* construcción, edificio, estructura.
struggle ['strʌgl] *n* lucha, esfuerzo, conflicto; *vi* luchar, debatirse, esforzarse, pugnar; **to — against** resistir.
struggling ['strʌgliŋ] *n* forcejeo, resistencia.
strung [strʌŋ] *a* **highly —** neurasténico, muy nervioso.
strut [strʌt] *n* (*build*) tirante; *vi* pavonearse, contonearse.
Stuart ['stjuət] *m* Estuardo.
stub [stʌb] *n* (*cigarette*) colilla; (*cigar*) chicote.
stubble [stʌbl] *n* rastrojo, rozo.
stubborn ['stʌbən] *a* obstinado, terco, tenaz, testarudo, pertinaz, porfiado; inexpugnable.
student ['stju:dənt] *n* estudiante, alumno; investigador; (*of a course*) cursante; **— band, — merry-making** estudiantina.
studio ['stju:diou] *n* taller; estudio.
studious ['stju:diəs] *a* estudioso, aplicado.
study ['stʌdi] *n* estudio; despacho, oficina, taller; investigación; ensayo; *vti* estudiar, aplicarse; **to — law** cursar leyes; **to — hard** empollarse.
stuff [stʌf] *n* tela; material; (*woolen*) paño; cosa, chisme; *vt* henchir, llenar, atiborrar, atestar; (*foods*) embutir; (*fowl*) rellenar; **to — away** zampar; **to — up** (*pipes*) atorar; *vi* atracarse, llenarse.
stumble ['stʌmbl] *n* traspié, tropezón; desliz; *vi* dar traspiés, tropezar (*con*).
stump [stʌmp] *n* (*tree*) tocón; (*arm, leg*) muñón; (*pencil*) cabo; (*tooth*) raigón; (*cigar*) colilla; *vt* desconcertar.
stun [stʌn] *vt* aturdir, anonadar, pasmar.
stupefied ['stju:pifaid] *a* atontado, turulato; (*fam*) patidifuso.
stupefy ['stju:pifai] *vt* atontar, atolondrar; causar estupor, pasmar.
stupendous [stju(:)'pendəs] *a* prodigioso, sorprendente, estupendo.
stupid ['stju:pid] *a* estúpido, torpe, lelo, abobado, insensato; **to make —** entorpecer; **— action** gansada; **— remark** sandez.
stupidity [stju(:)'piditi] *n* estupidez, insensatez, idiotez, bobería.
stupor ['stju:pə] *n* estupor.
sturdy ['stə:di] *a* fornido, rollizo, robusto, atrevido, vigoroso, porfiado.
stutter ['stʌtə] *n* tartamudeo; balbucear; *vi* tartamudear.
style [stail] *n* (*writing*) estilo, lenguaje; (*type*) género; (*way*) manera; (*construction*) redacción; (*of speech*) tono; (*of address*) tratamiento; (*dress*) moda; **dignified —** empaque;

she has — tiene elegancia; *vt* estilar; nombrar.
stylish ['stailiʃ] *a* elegante, a la moda.
suave [swɑ:v] *a* manso, fino, melifluo.
subdue [səb'dju:] *vt* subyugar, someter, dominar; amansar.
subdued [səb'dju:d] *a* subyugado, sometido; templado; (*tone*) sumiso; (*color*) amortiguado.
subject ['sʌbdʒikt] *a* sujeto, expuesto; supeditado; — **to** sin prejuicio de; propenso a; *n* (*of king*) súbdito; (*of study*) materia, asignatura; (*of talk*) tema, materia; (*of story*) argumento, asunto; — **to fits** cataléptico; **to be — to** (*illness*) adolecer de; [səb'dʒekt] *vt* sujetar, someter, sojuzgar; supeditar, subordinar.
subjection [səb'dʒekʃən] *n* sujeción, sumisión, yugo.
subjugate ['sʌbdʒugeit] *vt* subyugar; dominar.
sublime [sə'blaim] *a* sublime, excelso, exaltado.
submarine ['sʌbməri:n] *an* submarino.
submerge [səb'mə:dʒ] *vt* sumergir, inundar.
submission [səb'miʃən] *n* sumisión, obediencia; sometimiento, humillación.
submissive [səb'misiv] *a* sumiso, rendido, sometido, humilde.
submit [səb'mit] *vi* someter; (*document*) presentar; (*opinion*) exponer; **to — to** deferir; *vi* someterse, conformarse, doblarse, ceder, rendirse; sujetarse a.
subordinate [sə'bɔ:dineit] *a* inferior, subordinado; subalterno; **to be — to** depender de; *vt* posponer.
subscribe [səb'skraib] *vti* subscribir(se), (*to newspaper*) abonarse a.
subscription [səb'skripʃən] *n* suscripción, cuota, abono.
subsequent ['sʌbsikwənt] *a* subsiguiente, posterior.
subsequently ['sʌbsikwəntli] *ad* con posterioridad.
subside [səb'said] *vi* (*noise etc*) apaciguarse, calmarse; (*movement*) bajar; (*ground etc*) hundirse.
subsidence [səb'saidəns] *n* apaciguamiento; submersión; (*ground etc*) desplome, derrumbamiento, hundimiento.
subsidiary [səb'sidiəri] *a* auxiliar, subsidiario, incidental, anejo.
subsidize ['sʌbsidaiz] *vt* subvencionar.
subsidy ['sʌbsidi] *n* subvención.
subsist [səb'sist] *vi* subsistir; vivir, perdurar.
substance ['sʌbstəns] *n* su(b)stancia; materia; esencia, ser, médula; **soft** — (*dough, mud etc*) plasta; (*property*) hacienda, bienes.
substantial [səb'stænʃəl] *a* substancial, importante, de pro; sólido; valioso; cuantioso; esencial.
substantiate [səb'stænʃieit] *vt* comprobar, justificar, atestar, substanciar, fundamentar.
substitute ['sʌbstitju:t] *n* suplente, sustituto; interino, reemplazo; **to act as** — reemplazar, hacer las veces (de); *vt* su(b)stituir, suplir.
substitution [ˌsʌbsti'tju:ʃən] *n* sustitución, reemplazo.
subterfuge ['sʌbtəfju:dʒ] *n* pretexto, subterfugio.
subterraneous [ˌsʌbtə'reiniəs] *a* subterráneo.
subtle [sʌtl] *a* astuto; penetrante, mañoso, ingenioso; sutil, tenue, fino; refinado.
subtlety ['sʌtlti] *n* sutileza, agudeza, argucia.
subtract [səb'trækt] *vt* sustraer, quitar; (*math*) restar.
suburb ['sʌbə:b] *n* suburbio, arrabal; **—s** afueras.
subway ['sʌbwei] *n* galería, paso subterráneo, túnel; metro.
succeed [sək'si:d] *vt* (*inherit*) suceder, reemplazar a; *vi* salir bien, vencer, tener éxito, lograr, conseguir.
success [sək'ses] *n* éxito, prosperidad, bienandanza, triunfo.
successful [sək'sesful] *a* (*person, plan*) próspero; (*scheme*) fructífero; airoso, dichoso; **to be** — tener éxito.
succession [sək'seʃən] *n* sucesión; serie; descendencia.
successive [sək'sesiv] *a* sucesivo.
successively [sək'sesivli] *ad* de seguida, en serie.
successor [sək'sesə] *n* sucesor, heredero.
succinct [sək'siŋkt] *a* conciso, lacónico.
succor ['sʌkə] *n* socorro, asistencia; (*mil*) refuerzo; *vt* socorrer, ayudar, asistir, acudir.
succulent ['sʌkjulənt] *a* suculento, jugoso.
succumb [sə'kʌm] *vi* sucumbir.
such [sʌtʃ] *a* tal; — **and** — (*person*) un tal.
suck [sʌk] *vt* **to — up, away, in** chupar; (*liquids*) sorber; **to — up** (*air etc*) absorber, aspirar; (*as bees*) libar; **to give** — amamantar.
suckle ['sʌkl] *vt* dar de mamar, criar, atetar.
sudden ['sʌdn] *a* repentino, súbito, imprevisto.
suddenly ['sʌdnli] *ad* de repente, repentinamente, de pronto.
suddenness ['sʌdnnis] *n* precipitación.
suffer ['sʌfə] *vt* comportar, sufrir; aguantar; **to — from** aquejar, adolecer de; **to — from the effects of**

resentirse de; sufrir, tener dolor, padecer; consentir.
sufferer ['sʌfərə] *n* paciente, víctima.
suffering ['sʌfəriŋ] *a* **long-—** paciente, sufrido; *n* sufrimiento, calvario; pena, suplicio.
suffice [sə'fais] *vi* bastar, llegar, alcanzar.
sufficiency [sə'fiʃənsi] *n* suficiencia, capacidad; holgura.
sufficient [sə'fiʃənt] *a* suficiente; harto, competente; **to be —** alcanzar, bastar.
suffocate ['sʌfəkeit] *vt* sofocar, asfixiar; *vi* asfixiarse.
suffrage ['sʌfridʒ] *n* sufragio, voto; **to be on —** tolerarse(le).
suffuse [sə'fju:z] *vt* esparcir, bañar.
sugar ['ʃugə] *n* azúcar; **— cane** caña; **— lump** terrón de azúcar; **lump —** azúcar de pilón; **— bowl** azucarero; *vt* azucarar, endulzar; **to — the pill** dorar la píldora.
suggest [sə'dʒest] *vt* sugerir, soplar, insinuar, intimar.
suggestion [sə'dʒestʃən] *n* sugestión, punta, idea.
suicide ['su:isaid] *n* (*act*) suicidio; (*person*) suicida; **to commit —** quitarse la vida, suicidarse.
suit [su:t] *n* (*cards*) palo; serie; (*law*) instancia; pleito, petición; (*in love*) galanteo; petición; (*clothes*) traje; **to follow —** jugar el mismo palo; seguir el ejemplo; *vt* convenir, cuajar; (*appearance*) sentar bien, favorecer; acomodar; contentar; corresponder; concertar; *vi* hacer juego.
suitability [ˌsu:tə'biliti] *n* idoneidad; conveniencia.
suitable ['su:təbl] *a* conveniente, congruente, apropiado, adecuado, propio; idóneo; a propósito; competente; de provecho; **to be —** cuajar, convenir.
suitcase ['su:tkeis] *n* maleta.
suite [swi:t] *n* serie; (*of kings etc*) séquito, tren, comitiva; apartamiento; **three-piece —** tresillo.
suitor ['su:tə] *n* demandante; pretendiente, cortejo.
sulk [sʌlk] *vi* ponerse malhumorado; ser mohino.
sulky ['sʌlki] *a* arisco, huraño.
sullen ['sʌlən] *a* hosco, cazurro, sombrío, tétrico.
sullenness ['sʌlənnis] *n* malhumor, ceño, hosquedad.
sully ['sʌli] *vt* manchar, empañar.
sulphur ['sʌlfə] *n* azufre.
sultan ['sʌltən] *n* sultán.
sultana [sʌl'tɑ:nə] *n* sultana.
sultry ['sʌltri] *a* bochornoso, sofocante.
sum [sʌm] *a* **— total** total; *n* suma, total; cifra; *vt* adicionar, sumar; **to — up** (*argument etc*) concretar, recapitular; *ad* **to — up** en resumidas cuentas.
summary ['sʌməri] *n* sumario, recopilación.
summer ['sʌmə] *a* estival, veraniego, de verano; *n* verano; estío; **Indian —** veranillo de San Martín.
summing ['sʌmiŋ] *n* **— up** recapitulación, epílogo.
summit ['sʌmit] *n* cumbre, cima, cresta, picacho; altura, cúspide.
summon ['sʌmən] *vt* citar, emplazar, convocar; **to — up** requerir.
summons ['sʌmənz] *n* (*police*) citación, requerimiento, intimación, llamamiento.
sump [sʌmp] *n* (*aut*) sumidero del cárter, pozo colector.
sumptuous ['sʌmptjuəs] *a* suntuoso, regio; (*meal*) opíparo.
sun [sʌn] *n* sol; **—beam** rayo de sol; **— blind** toldo; **—dial** cuadrante, reloj de sol; **—stroke** insolación; *vr* **to — oneself** tomar el sol.
sunbathe ['sʌnbeið] *vi* tomar el sol.
sunburn ['sʌnbə:n] *n* solanera, quemadura del sol.
sunburned ['sʌnbə:nd] **sunburnt** ['sʌnbə:nt] tostado, bronceado.
Sunday ['sʌndi] *n* domingo; **Palm —** domingo de Ramos.
sundries ['sʌndriz] *n* varios, varias cosas, géneros diversos.
sundry ['sʌndri] *a* varios, diversos.
sunflower ['sʌnˌflauə] *n* girasol.
sunk [sʌŋk] *a* **to be —** sumirse.
sunlight ['sʌnlait] *n* luz del sol; **in the —** al sol.
sunny ['sʌni] *a* asoleado; alegre.
sunrise ['sʌnraiz] *n* salida del sol, amanecer.
sunset ['sʌnset] *n* puesta del sol, ocaso.
sunshade ['sʌnʃeid] *n* parasol; toldo.
sup [sʌp] *n* sorbo; *vti* sorber; cenar.
superb [su(:)'pə:b] *a* soberbio; magnífico, excelente; (*fam*) estupendo; (*idea etc*) genial.
supercilious [ˌsu:pə'siliəs] *a* altanero, altivo, arrogante.
superficial [ˌsu:pə'fiʃəl] *a* superficial, somero.
superficially [ˌsu:pə'fiʃəli] *ad* por encima; a la ligera.
superfluous [su(:)'pə:fluəs] *a* superfluo; excusado; **to be —** estar de más.
superhuman [ˌsu:pə'hju:mən] *a* sobrehumano.
superintendent [ˌsu:prin'tendənt] *n* superintendente, director; (*police*) subjefe.
superior [su(:)'piəriə] *a* superior, soberbio.
superiority [su(:)ˌpiəri'ɔriti] *n* superioridad, predominio.
supermarket ['su:pəˌmɑ:kit] *n* supermercado.
supernatural [ˌsu:pə'nætʃrəl] *an* sobrenatural.
supersede [ˌsu:pə'si:d] *vt* reemplazar, invalidar.

superstition [ˌsu:pəˈstiʃən] *n* superstición.
superstitious [ˌsu:pəˈstiʃəs] *a* supersticioso.
supervise [ˈsu:pəvaiz] *vt* vigilar, revisar, examinar.
supervision [ˌsu:pəˈviʒən] *n* vigilancia, intervención.
supper [ˈsʌpə] *n* cena; **to have —** cenar.
supplant [səˈplɑ:nt] *vt* suplantar.
supple [ˈsʌpl] *a* flexible, cimbreante.
suppleness [ˈsʌplnis] *n* agilidad, flexibilidad.
supplication [ˌsʌpliˈkeiʃən] *n* suplicación; **—s** preces, votos.
supply [səˈplai] *n* suministro, provisión, abastecimiento; **— and demand** oferta y demanda; *pl* pertrechos, víveres, provisiones, existencias; *vt* surtir, abastecer, suministrar; facilitar; suplir; **to — with** proveer de.
support [səˈpɔ:t] *n* sostén, apoyo, sustento, socorro; respaldo, favor; (*archit*) soporte, estribo, pilar; **in — of** en apoyo de; *vt* sostener, apoyar; proveer; entretener, mantener; respaldar, patrocinar, secundar; abogar por; fortalecer.
supported [səˈpɔ:tid] *a* sostenido; **to be — by** estribar en.
supporter [səˈpɔ:tə] *n* sostén, apoyo; allegado, defensor; apologista; (*sport*) aficionado.
suppose [səˈpouz] *vt* suponer, figurarse, imaginarse, presumir, poner por caso.
supposed [səˈpouzd] *a* presunto, pretendido.
supposition [ˌsʌpəˈziʃən] *n* suposición, supuesto.
suppress [səˈpres] *vt* suprimir, sofocar; ahogar, contener.
suppressed [səˈprest] *a* eliminado, sofocado; **— laughter** el retozo de la risa.
suppression [səˈpreʃən] *n* represión, supresión.
supremacy [su(:)ˈpreməsi] *n* supremacía, dominio.
supreme [su(:)ˈpri:m] *a* supremo.
sure [ʃuə] *a* seguro, cierto, positivo; imperdible, certero, firme; **to make —** cerciorarse de.
surely [ˈʃuəli] *ad* seguramente, con seguridad, en seguridad; cierto.
sureness [ˈʃuənis] *n* seguridad, certidumbre.
surety [ˈʃurəti] *n* fiador, garante; fianza, garantía; **to stand — for** abonar, salir garante.
surf [sə:f] *n* los rompientes; resaca, oleaje, marejada.
surface [ˈsə:fis] *n* superficie; sobrehaz; *vt* allanar, poner una superficie; *vi* salir a la superficie.
surfeit [ˈsə:fit] *n* empacho, ahito, exceso; *vt* empalagar, ahitar, hartar; *vi* hartarse, saciarse.
surge [sə:dʒ] *n* oleaje, oleada; *vi* agitarse, hervir.
surgeon [ˈsə:dʒən] *n* cirujano, quirúrgico.
surgery [ˈsə:dʒəri] *n* cirujía; (*doctor's*) clínica.
surliness [ˈsə:linis] *n* malhumor, murria, desabrimiento.
surly [ˈsə:li] *a* malhumorado, áspero, agrio, arisco.
surmise [ˈsə:maiz] *n* conjetura, vislumbre, sospecha; admiración; [sə:ˈmaiz] *vt* sospechar, conjeturar, presumir, barruntar.
surmount [sə:ˈmaunt] *vt* vencer, sobrepujar, salvar.
surmountable [səˈmauntəbl] *a* superable.
surname [ˈsə:neim] *n* apellido; *vt* apellidar.
surpass [sə:ˈpɑ:s] *vt* (sobre)pasar, prevalecer, superar, exceder, aventajar, descollar sobre.
surpassing [sə:ˈpɑ:siŋ] *a* sobresaliente, eminente, sin par.
surplus [ˈsə:pləs] *n* excedente, superávit, sobrante, remanente.
surprise [səˈpraiz] *n* sorpresa; novedad; (*mil*) copo; *vt* sorprender, admirar, chocar; **to take by —** sobrecoger; (*mil*) copar.
surprised [səˈpraizd] *a* **I am —** me extraña; **to be —** descubrirse, coger(le a uno).
surprising [səˈpraiziŋ] *a* sorprendente, inesperado.
surrender [səˈrendə] *n* rendición, abandono; (*documents etc*) entrega; **— of property** cesión de bienes; renuncia; sumisión.
surrender [səˈrendə] *vt* rendir, renunciar a; (*documents*) entregar; ceder; *vi* rendirse, entregarse, arriar la bandera; darse a.
surreptitious [ˌsʌrəpˈtiʃəs] *a* subrepticio.
surround [səˈraund] *n* rodeo; borde, orilla; *vt* circundar, cercar, ceñir, acompañar, rodear.
surroundings [səˈraundiŋz] *n pl* ambiente; alrededores, contornos.
survey [ˈsə:vei] *n* deslindamiento, reconocimiento, mensura; examen, informe; [səˈvei] *vt* medir, deslindar, inspeccionar; vigilar; pasar en revista, reconocer, registrar.
survival [səˈvaivəl] *n* supervivencia; reliquia; perduración.
survive [səˈvaiv] *vti* sobrevivir, resistir, seguir (vivo, en vida).
survivor [səˈvaivə] *n* sobreviviente.
Susan [ˈsuzn] *f* Susana.
susceptible [səˈseptəbl] *a* sensible, delicado; susceptible; cosquilloso.
suspect [ˈsʌspekt] *n* sospechoso, persona sospechosa; [səsˈpekt] *vti* sospechar, conjeturar, presumir, barruntar; temerse, dudar.
suspend [səsˈpend] *vt* suspender, colgar; interrumpir, aplazar.

suspended [səs'pendid] *a* en vilo; **to be —** colgar.
suspenders [səs'pendəz] *n pl* tirantes.
suspense [səs'pens] *n* suspensión, duda, incertidumbre, suspenso; zozobra; **in —** en vilo, en duda.
suspension [səs'penʃən] *n* suspensión.
suspicion [səs'piʃən] *n* sospecha, recelo, suspicacia, aprensión, escama; sombra, asomo, pizca.
suspicious [səs'piʃəs] *a* (*situation etc*) sospechoso; (*feeling*) suspicaz, desconfiado; (*character*) maleante; **to be — of** recelar.
sustain [səs'tein] *vt* sostener, mantener; resistir, sufrir; apoyar, animar, alimentar.
sustenance ['sʌstinəns] *n* sostenimiento, sustancia, subsistencia; sustento, manutención, alimentos.
swagger ['swægə] *n* fanfarronada; *vi* fanfarronear, echárselas.
swallow ['swɔlou] *n* (*bird*) golondrina; (*drink*) sorbo; trago; (*food*) bocado; *vt* tragar, engullir; ingerir; sorber, deglutir, beber; (*insult*) aguantar; (*one's words*) desdecirse; **to — the bait** tragar el anzuelo.
swamp ['swɔmp] *n* cenagal; *SA* manigua; *vt* sumergir, encenagar, hundir, empantanar, echar a pique.
swampy ['swɔmpi] *a* pantanoso.
swan [swɔn] *n* cisne; **—song** canto del cisne.
swarm [swɔ:m] *n* enjambre; (*people*) hormiguero, gentío; *vi* enjambrar, hervir, pulular, hormiguear; **to — up** trepar a.
swarthy ['swɔ:ði] *a* atezado, tostado.
sway [swei] *n* poder, dominio, imperio; influjo; vaivén, balanceo; *vt* inclinar, influir, inducir; llevar (tras sí); cimbrear; *vi* inclinarse; moverse; oscilar, mecerse.
swear [swɛə] *n* **— word** taco, voto, reniego; juramento; *vt* jurar; renegar; **to — at** maldecir; **to — by** jurar por; **to —in** juramentar.
sweat [swet] *n* sudor; (*fig*) trabajo, fatiga; *vti* sudar.
sweater ['swetə] *n* suéter, jersey, jersé.
sweating ['swetiŋ] *a* (*brow*) sudoroso; *n* transpiración.
Swede [swi:d] *n* sueco.
Sweden ['swi:dn] *n* Suecia.
Swedish ['swi:diʃ] *a* sueco.
sweep [swi:p] *n* extensión, recorrido; curso, carrera; vuelta; barrida; **a clean —** limpieza; **chimney—** deshollinador; (*of wings*) envergadura; *vti* **to — away, up, out** barrer; arrollar, arrebatar, arrastrar; **to — along** pasar (al vuelo, volando, arrastrándose, majestuosamente); **to — the board** (*cards*) dar capote; **to — chimneys** deshollinar.
sweet [swi:t] *a* dulce, azucarado; sabroso; grato; bonito; suave, amable, encantador; (*of babies etc*) rico; **honey —** meloso; **—-toothed** goloso; **— pea** guisante de olor; **— potato** batata; **—-tongued** melifluo; **—-smelling** odorífero, fragante; *n* dulzura, deleite; *pl* dulces, confites; *n* golosinas.
sweeten ['swi:tn] *vt* endulzar; azucarar.
sweetheart ['swi:thɑ:t] *n* novio, amante, galán, cortejo, *f* novia, querida.
sweetness ['swi:tnis] *n* dulzura; suavidad, ternura.
swell [swel] *n* hinchazón; (*sea*) oleada, marejada, oleaje; mar de fondo; prominencia; (*fam*) pisaverde, majo; *vt* hinchar, henchir; (*numbers*) engrosar; *vi* **to — out** hincharse, crecer, subir, dilatarse; (*with pride*) enorgullecerse, envanecerse.
swelling ['sweliŋ] *n* hinchazón, inflación, tumefacción, bollo; (*from below*) chichón.
swelter ['sweltə] *vi* sofocar, abrasarse.
swerve [swə:v] *n* esguince; *vti* desviar(se); apartarse, torcer.
swift [swift] *a* veloz, ligero, presto, raudo, vivo, diligente, repentino; *n* vencejo.
swiftness ['swifnis] *n* velocidad, rapidez, prontitud, celeridad.
swim [swim] *vi* nadar, flotar, sobrenadar; (*of head etc*) tener vértigo; **to — across** pasar a nado.
swimmer ['swimə] *n* nadador.
swimming [swimiŋ] *n* natación; **— bath** piscina; *a* a nado.
swindle ['swindl] *n* estafa, timo; superchería; *vt* timar, estafar, engañar, dar un timo.
swindler ['swindlə] *n* estafador, petardista, timador.
swine [swain] *n* cerdo, puerco.
swing [swiŋ] *n* balanceo, oscilación, vaivén; (*child's*) columpio; **in full —** en plena operación; **—bridge** puente giratorio; *vt* balancear, mecer, columpiar; (*weapon*) blandir; *vi* vibrar, oscilar, columpiarse, balancearse.
swinging ['swiŋiŋ] *a* oscilante; *n* oscilación, vibración, balanceo.
swirl [swə:l] *n* torbellino, remolino; *vi* (*skirt etc*) remolinarse.
Swiss [swis] *an* suizo.
switch [switʃ] *n* (*cane*) varilla, baqueta; (*el*) conmutador, interruptor; (*rl*) cambiavía; apartadero; (*in radio etc*) botón; (*hair*) añadido, postizo; *vt* azotar, fustigar; (*rl*) desviar; **to — on** (*light*) poner; encender; **to — off** (*light*) apagar; (*current*) cerrar; **to — over** conmutar.
Switzerland ['switsələnd] *n* Suiza.
swollen ['swoulən] *a* hinchado, abultado; tumido; (*disease*) entumecido; (*fig*) pomposo.

swoon [swu:n] *n* desvanecimiento; desmayo, soponcio; deliquio; (*relig*) rapto; *vi* desvanecerse, desmayarse.
sword [sɔ:d] *n* espada, acero; (*ceremonial*) espadín; poder militar; **—stick** estoque; **to put to the —** pasar a cuchillo.
sycamore ['sikəmɔ:] *n* sicomoro.
syllable ['siləbl] *n* sílaba.
sylvan ['silvən] *a* silvestre, selvático.
Sylvia ['silviə] *f* Silvia.
symbol ['simbəl] *n* símbolo, emblema; carácter.
symbolize ['simbəlaiz] *vt* simbolizar.
symmetrical [si'metrikəl] *a* simétrico.
symmetry ['simitri] *n* simetría, proporción.
sympathetic [,simpə'θetik] *a* compadecido; simpático; cariñoso; afín; **to feel — with** compadecer con, simpatizar(se) con.
sympathize ['simpəθaiz] *vi* simpatizar; **to — with** (*sorrow*) condolerse; sentir por simpatía; congeniar con.
sympathy ['simpəθi] *n* simpatía; compasión, sentimento; **to be in — with** simpatizarse con; **to express —** (*at loss, illness death, etc*) dar el pésame, condolerse.
symptom ['simptəm] *n* síntoma.
syndicate ['sindikit] *n* sindicato; ['sindikeit] *vt* sindicar.
synonym ['sinənim] *n* sinónimo.
synopsis [si'nɔpsis] *n* sumario, sinopsis.
synthetic [sin'θetik] *a* sintético.
Syria ['siriə] *n* Siria.
Syrian ['siriən] *an* sirio, siríaco.
syringe ['sirindʒ] *n* jeringa, clíster; *vt* jeringar.
syrup ['sirəp] *n* jarabe; almíbar; **fruit —** arrope.
system ['sistim] *n* sistema, régimen; orden, clasificación.
systematic [,sisti'mætik] *a* sistemático.

T

tabernacle ['tæbənækl] *n* tabernáculo; templo; (*on altar*) custodia.
table ['teibl] *n* mesa; catálogo, elenco; cuadro sinóptico; tabla, tablero; **— of contents** índice de materias; **—cloth** mantel; **—spoon** cuchara de sopa; **—land** altiplanicie, meseta; *vt* catalogar; presentar.
tablet ['tæblit] *n* (*writing*) tabla, tableta, tarjeta, bloc; (*commem*) lápida; (*soap*) pastilla.
tack [tæk] *n* tachuela, puntilla; (*sew*) hilván, embaste; (*naut*) amura; *vt* clavar con tachuelas; (*sew*) hilvanar, embastar; *vi* (*naut*) virar.
tackle ['tækl] *n* aparejo, maniobra, jarcia; **fishing —** avíos de pescar; *vt* agarrar, asir; emprender; apechugar; (*football*) atajar.
tact [tækt] *n* tacto, discreción, tino, ten con ten.
tactful ['tæktful] *a* circunspecto, discreto.
tactical ['tæktikəl] *a* táctico.
tactics ['tæktiks] *n* táctica.
tactless ['tæktlis] *a* desmañado, sin tacto, torpe.
tactlessness ['tæktlisnis] *n* indiscreción, torpeza. imprudencia.
taffy ['tæfi] *n* dulce, caramelo.
tag [tæg] *n* (*luggage*) etiqueta; marbete, marca; (*in speech*) muletilla.
Tagus ['teigəs] *n* el Tajo.
tail [teil] *n* cola, rabo; **bushy —** hopo; (*hair*) trenza; (*peacock's*) copete; (*comet's*) cabellera; (*of story etc*) coda; **coat —s** faldillas; **to turn —** volver la espalda.
tailor ['teilə] *n* sastre; **— made** de hechura, hecho a medida.
tailoring ['teilərinŋ] *n* (*cut*) hechura; (*trade*) sastrería.
taint [teint] *n* mancha, infección, borrón; *vt* manchar, viciar, corromper.
take [teik] *n* toma(dura), cogida; **—off** (*av*) despegue; caricatura; *vt* tomar, coger, llevar; (*collect*) percibir, cobrar; (*chess*) comer; (*capture*) posesionarse; prender; (*use*) adoptar; considerar; necesitar; (*catch*) coger, atrapar; (*phot*) sacar; (*exercise*) hacer; (*obstacle*) saltar; *vi* pegar, prender, ser eficaz; **to — after** parecerse a; **to — aim at** apuntar; **to — away** quitar, remover; (*maths*) restar; **to — care of** cuidar de; **to — charge of** encargarse de; **to — down** descolgar; (*mech*) desmontar; humillar, quitar los humos a; **to — for** tomar por; **to — for granted** dar por sentado; **to — from** quitar, privar de; **to — in** acomodar; abarcar; engañar, timar; **to — notice** tomar nota; darse por enterado; **to — off** (*hat*) quitarse; (*mimic*) remedar; (*plane*) despegar; **to — out** sacar (de paseo); quitar; **to — place** sobrevenir, tener lugar, ocurrir; acontecer; **to — as prize** apresar; **to — root** prender; **to — refuge** guarecerse, abrigarse; **to — seriously** tomar a pecho; **to — to** tomar afición a, ponerse a, darse a; **to — to pieces** desmontar, desarmar; **to — a stroll** tomar el fresco, dar un paseo; **to — turns** turnar; **to — in tow** remolcar; **to — up** (*space*) ocupar; abarcar, comprender; (*job*) tomar posesión de; (*criticize*) censurar; empezar; **to — up short** cortar la palabra; **to — upon trust,** tomar a crédito; **to — upon oneself** tomar (a su cargo, por su cuenta), asumir; **to — an hour to get there** tardar una hora en llegar.
takings ['teikiŋz] *n pl* ingresos.
tale [teil] *n* cuento, relación, fábula,

historia, historieta, ficción; embuste; **—teller** cuentista, soplón; **— telling** chismografía; hablilla.
talent ['tælənt] *n* talento, capacidad, cerebro; **—s** prendados.
talented ['tæləntid] *a* talentoso, dotado.
talk [tɔ:k] *n* (*pleasant*) conversación, charla; (*speech*) plática; (*way of talking*) habla; (*between two persons*) coloquio; (*slanderous*) habladuría; (*rumor*) voz común, fama; **big —** fanfarronada; **it was the subject of much —** fué muy comentado; *vt* **to — Spanish** hablar cristiano; **to — nonsense** decir disparates, desbarrar; *vi* hablar, charlar, conversar; (*esp moral talk*) platicar; **to — in whispers** cuchichear; **to — into** convencer; **to — one's head off, through one's ears** hablar por los codos; **to — loudly** hablar alto; **to — for talking's sake** hablar por hablar; **to — out of** disuadir; **to — without rhyme or reason** hablar a tontas y a locas; **to — on** seguir hablando; **to — to** reprender; **to — too much** hablar (más que siete, por los codos).
talkative ['tɔ:kətiv] *a* locuaz, parlero, parlanchín, parlador, charlatán; **— woman** cotorra.
tall [tɔ:l] *a* alto, elevado, grande.
tallness ['tɔ:lnis] *n* altura, estatura.
tally ['tæli] *n* chapa; **— stick** tara; *vti* llevar la cuenta; cuadrar, casar, concordar.
tame [teim] *a* manso; doméstico, domesticado; amansado, domado; *vt* domesticar; domar, amansar, desbravar.
tamer ['teimə] *n* domador.
tamper ['tæmpə] *vi* entremeterse.
tan [tæn] *n* color de tostado; casca; (*sun*) bronceado; *vt* (*leather*) curtir, adobar, aderezar; (*skin*) tostar.
tang [tæŋ] *n* gustillo, sabor.
tangible ['tændʒəbl] *a* tangible, real.
Tangier [tæn'dʒiə] *n* Tánger.
tangle ['tæŋgl] *n* nudo, ovillo; (*fig*) embrollo, enredo; *vt* enredar, embrollar, enmarañar.
tangled ['tæŋgld] *a* revesado.
tank [tæŋk] *n* tanque, depósito de agua, alcubilla, **rain —** cisterna, aljibe; (*mil*) tanque.
tanker ['tæŋkə] *n* petrolero.
tannery ['tænəri] *n* tenería.
tanning ['tæniŋ] *n* curtimiento, curtido.
tantalize ['tæntəlaiz] *vt* atormentar, dar dentera, poner los dientes largos.
tantamount ['tæntəmaunt] *a* equivalente.
tap [tæp] *n* canilla, llave, espita; **water—** grifo; *vt* decentar, perforar, *vi* (*hands*) dar palmaditas; (*with heels*) **to —dance** zapatear.
tape [teip] *n* cinta, galón; **— measure** cinta métrica; **red —** balduque; papeleo, burocracia; **— recorder** magnetofón, magnetófono.
taper ['teipə] *n* bujía, candela, cirio; *vt* afilar, ahusar.
tapering ['teipəriŋ] *a* cónico, afilado.
tapestry ['tæpistri] *n* tapicería; **— worker, — maker** tapicero.
tar [tɑ:] *n* alquitrán, pez, brea; *vt* alquitranar, embrear.
target ['tɑ:git] *n* blanco; **— practice** tiro al blanco.
tariff ['tærif] *a* arancelario; *n* tarifa; (*dues*) arancel.
tarnish ['tɑ:niʃ] *vt* deslustrar, deslucir; empañar, mancillar; *vi* deslucirse, deslustrarse.
tarpaulin [tɑ:'pɔ:lin] *n* lienzo alquitranado, encerado.
tart [tɑ:t] *a* acre, agrio, ácido; mordaz; *n* tarta, pastel.
tartan ['tɑ:tən] *n* tartán; (*vehicle*) tartana.
tartar ['tɑ:tə] *n* tártaro.
task [tɑ:sk] *n* tarea, faena, tanda; **— work** destajo; **to take to —** reprender, regañar.
tassel ['tæsəl] *n* borla, campanilla.
taste [teist] *n* gusto; sabor; (*sip*) sorbo; (*remains*) dejo; (*bit*) pizca; (*sample etc*) muestra; prueba; **— for** afición a, inclinación; (*on palate*) paladar; **in poor —** de mal gusto; cursi; *vt* gustar de; saborear, paladear; (*to try*) probar; (*wine*) catar; *vi* tener gusto; **to — of** saber a.
tasteful ['teistful] *a* sabroso; elegante.
tasteless ['teistlis] *a* insípido, sin gusto, soso, insulso.
tastelessness ['teistlisnis] *n* desabor, insipidez.
tasty ['teisti] *a* sabroso, rico, apetitoso, suculento.
tatter ['tætə] *n* andrajo, harapo; trapo; **in —s** andrajoso, harapiento, desastrado.
tattoo [tə'tu:] *n* (*bugle call*) retreta; (*design*) tatuaje; *vt* tatuar.
tattooing [tə'tu:iŋ] *n* tatuaje.
taunt [tɔ:nt] *n* befa, insulto, reprimenda, vituperio, improperio; *vt* vilipendiar, vituperar.
taut [tɔ:t] *a* tirante, tieso, tenso.
tavern ['tævən] *n* taberna, mesón; (*fam*) tasca; **—keeper** bodegonero, tabernero, mesonero.
tawdry ['tɔ:dri] *a* charro; deslucido, desdorado, cursi.
tax [tæks] *n* contribución(es), impuesto, tributo; **—collector** recaudador; **—payer** pechero; **to pay —es** pechar, tributar; *vt* imponer contribuciones, tasar; (*fig*) cargar, acusar, tachar; **to — with** imputar.
taxation [tæk'seiʃən] *n* impuestos; imposición de contribuciones.
taxi ['tæksi] *n* taxi, coche de punto; **— stand** parada de taxis.

tea [ti:] *n* té; **to have —** tomar (el) té; **afternoon —** merienda; **—cake** bollo; **—set** servicio, juego de té; **—party** té; **—pot** tetera; **—spoon** cucharilla.
teach [ti:tʃ] *vt* enseñar, instruir, inculcar, aleccionar; **to — a lesson to** escarmentar; *vi* ejercer el magisterio.
teacher ['ti:tʃə] *n* (*primary, music etc*) maestro; (*secondary*) profesor; **assistant —, pupil —** pasante.
teaching ['ti:tʃiŋ] *n* instrucción, enseñanza; doctrina.
team [ti:m] *n* (*horses*) pareja, par; (*games*) equipo.
tear [tiə] *n* lágrima.
tear [tɛə] *n* rasgón, roto, descosido; rasgadura; **wear and —** desgaste, desmejoramiento; *vt* romper, rasgar; (*heart*) desgarrar; (*flesh*) lacerar; rasguñar; **to — off, away** arrancar; desgajar; **to — down** demoler, derribar; *vi* rasgarse; **to — along, on, up** volar por, correr a todo trapo; **to — up** (*paper etc*) romper.
tearful ['tiəful] *a* lagrimoso, hecho una magdalena.
tease [ti:z] *vt* enojar, importunar; atormentar, molestar; (*wool*) cardar; (*fam*) jorobar.
technical ['teknikəl] *a* técnico.
technique [tek'ni:k] *n* técnica.
tedious ['ti:diəs] *a* pesado, prolijo, aburrido, cansado, fatigoso.
tediousness ['ti:diəsnis] *n* fatiga, prolijidad, hastío.
tedium ['ti:diəm] *n* tedio.
teem [ti:m] *vi* hormiguear, pulular, rebosar.
teeming ['ti:miŋ] *a* ubérrimo, fecundo.
teetotaler ['ti:'toutlə] *n* abstemio.
telegram ['teligræm] *n* telegrama.
telegraph ['teligrɑ:f] *n* telégrafo; *vt* telegrafiar.
telegraphy [ti'legrəfi] *n* telegrafía.
telephone ['telifoun] *n* teléfono; **— call** llamada; **long-distance — call** conferencia; *vt* telefonear, llamar por teléfono.
telescope ['teliskoup] *n* telescopio, catalejo.
tell [tel] *vt* decir; (*story*) contar, referir; participar, manifestar, determinar, distinguir; **to — off** despachar; reñir; instruir; **it tells** tiene su efecto.
teller ['telə] *n* narrador; (*bank*) pagador.
temerity [ti'meriti] *n* temeridad.
temper ['tempə] *n* mal genio; índole, humor, genio, natural, disposición; **bad —** coraje, atrabilis, berrinche; (*metal*) temple; *vt* templar, moderar, mitigar, atemperar.
temperament ['tempərəmənt] *n* temperamento, humor, disposición, natural.
temperance ['tempərəns] *n* sobriedad; templanza.
temperate ['tempərit] *a* morigerado, abstemio, sobrio; (*climate*) templado; benigno.
temperateness ['tempəritnis] *n* templanza, mesura; serenidad.
temperature ['tempritʃə] *n* temperatura; **high —** calentura; **he has a high —** tiene fiebre.
tempest ['tempist] *n* tempestad, tormenta; temporal.
tempestuous [tem'pestjuəs] *a* tempestuoso, proceloso; turbulento.
templar ['templə] *n* templario.
temple ['templ] *n* templo, iglesia.
temporal ['tempərəl] *a* temporal, transitorio.
temporary ['tempərəri] *a* provisional, interino, improvisado.
temporize ['tempəraiz] *vi* contemporizar, ganar tiempo.
tempt [tempt] *vt* tentar, poner a prueba; inducir; provocar.
temptation [temp'teiʃən] *n* tentación, aliciente.
tempter ['temptə] *n* tentador.
tempting ['temptiŋ] *a* tentador.
ten [ten] *an* diez.
tenable ['tenəbl] *a* sostenible, defensible.
tenacious [ti'neiʃəs] *a* tenaz, porfiado.
tenacity [ti'næsiti] *n* tenacidad, tesón, porfía.
tenant ['tenənt] *n* arrendatario, inquilino; teniente; **joint —** (*of land*) comunero.
tend [tend] *vt* (*look after*) cuidar; (*watch over*) velar, vigilar; guardar; **to — to** tirar a, llevar, dar en, tender a; **to — toward** dirigirse a.
tendency ['tendənsi] *n* tendencia, inclinación, giro, propensión; **natural —** proclividad.
tender ['tendə] *a* tierno, blando; cariñoso; amable, benigno; **—-hearted** compasivo; **— spot** sensible; **— of** cuidadoso de, solícito de; *n* propuesta, oferta; (*boat*) falúa; *vt* ofrecer, presentar, proponer; (*resignation*) presentar; (*thanks*) dar.
tenderness ['tendənis] *n* terneza, ternura; suavidad; cariño, afecto.
tendon ['tendən] *n* tendón, nervio.
tenement ['tenimənt] *n* **— house** casa de vecindad.
Tenerife [,tenə'ri:f] **inhabitant of —** tenerifeño.
tenet ['tenit] *n* dogma, credo, principio.
tennis ['tenis] *n* tenis; **— court** (campo, cancha de) tenis.
tenor ['tenə] *n* tenor.
tense [tens] *n* tiempo; *a* tenso, tirante, tieso; crítico, de mucha emoción.
tension ['tenʃən] *n* tensión, tirantez.
tent [tent] *n* tienda; pabellón; toldo; *vi* acampar.
tentacle ['tentəkl] *n* tentáculo.
tentative ['tentətiv] *a* de prueba, de

ensayo, tentador, tentativo; provisional; *n* prueba, tanteo, ensayo.
tenth [tenθ] *an* décimo.
tenuous ['tenjuəs] *a* tenue, sutil, ingrávido.
tenure ['tenjuə] *n* tenencia, posesión, pertenencia.
tepid ['tepid] *a* tibio, templado.
Terence ['terəns] *m* Terencio.
term [tə:m] *n* (*word*) término, vocablo, voz técnica; (*period*) plazo, período; (*limit*) raya, límite; (*university*) trimestre; (*of imprisonment*) condena; *pl* condiciones, estipulaciones; (*payment*) honorarios; (*of sale*) condiciones; **easy —s** pago a plazos; (*of friendship*) relaciones; familiaridad; **set —s** términos escogidos; **to be on good —s with** llevarse bien con; **to come to —s** llegar a un arreglo, hacer las paces; *vt* nombrar.
terminate ['tə:mineit] *vti* terminar, rematar, poner fin a.
termination [,tə:mi'neiʃən] *n* terminación, final, conclusión.
terminus ['tə:minəs] *n* término; estación final.
terrace ['terəs] *n* terraplén; plataforma, terraza; (*of steps*) escalinata, gradería; (*in amphitheater*) grada; **sun —** solana.
terrain ['terein] *n* terreno.
terrestrial [ti'restriəl] *a* terrestre, terrenal.
terrible ['terəbl] *a* terrible, tremendo, aterrador, pavoroso, hórrido.
terrier ['teriə] *n* perro de busca.
terrific [tə'rifik] *a* terrífico, estupendo, enorme.
terrify ['terifai] *vt* aterrar, espantar, azorar, amilanar.
territory ['teritəri] *n* territorio, comarca, región, dominio.
terror ['terə] *n* terror, espanto, pavor.
terse [tə:s] *a* conciso, sucinto, breve.
test [test] *n* prueba, ensayo, examen; tentativa; piedra de toque, reactivo; **— tube** probeta; **to put to the —** poner a prueba; **to stand the —** soportar la prueba; *vt* probar, ensayar, someter a prueba; (*sight*) graduar.
testament ['testəmənt] *n* testamento.
testify ['testifai] *vti* atestiguar, atestar, dar testimonio, aseverar.
testimonial [,testi'mouniəl] *n* certificado, atestado; (*to distinguished scholar etc*) homenaje.
testimony ['testiməni] *n* testimonio, declaración.
testing ['testiŋ] *n* cata, ensayo.
tête-à-tête ['teitɑ:'teit] *a* cara a cara; *n* momento a solas con.
tether ['teðə] *n* traba, atadura, correa; **to be at the end of one's —** no saber ya qué hacer; *vt* apersogar.
Teutonic [tju'tɔnik] *a* teutónico.
text [tekst] *n* texto; tema; tesis; **—book** libro de texto.
textile ['tekstail] *an* textil.
texture ['tekstʃə] *n* tejido, (con)-textura.
Thames [temz] *n* el Támesis.
than [ðæn] *cj* que.
thank [θæŋk] *n pl* gracias; agradecimiento; *vt* dar gracias, agradecer; **— God** a Dios gracias.
thankful ['θæŋkful] *a* agradecido; **I am — to say** me es grato decir.
thankfulness ['θæŋkfulnis] *n* agradecimiento, gratitud, reconocimiento.
thankless ['θæŋklis] *a* desagradecido, ingrato; (*task*) ímprobo.
thanksgiving ['θæŋks,giviŋ] *n* acción de gracias; *US* **T—** día de gracias.
that [ðæt] *a* ese, aquel; *pn* ése, aquél; **— is** es decir, a saber; *cj* que, a fin de que, para que; *rel* que.
thatch [θætʃ] *n* (*roof*) empaja; (*wall*) barda; *vt* empajar, bardar.
thaw [θɔ:] *n* deshielo; *vti* deshelar, derretir.
the [ði:] *def art* el, la, los, las.
theater ['θiətə] *n* teatro; arte dramático.
theatrical [θi'ætrikəl] *a* teatral.
theft [θeft] *n* hurto, robo, latrocinio.
their [ðɛə] *poss a* su, sus, de ellos, de ellas.
theirs [ðɛəz] *poss pn* (el) suyo, (la) suya, (los) suyos, (las) suyas; de ellos, de ellas.
them [ðem] *pn* ellos, ellas; (*object*) los, las, les.
theme [θi:m] *n* (*study, research, talk etc*) tema, materia, tesis; (*action*) motivo.
themselves [ðəm'selvz] *pn* ellos mismos, ellas mismas; (*refl*) sí, sí mismos, se.
then [ðen] *ad* entonces, en aquel tiempo; luego, después; *cj* pues, en tal caso; por consiguiente, por tanto; **now —** ahora bien; **— and there** en seguida, en el acto; **so —** conque.
thence [ðens] *ad* de allí, por eso, luego, desde aquel momento.
Theodore ['θiədɔ:] *m* Teodoro.
theologian [θiə'loudʒjən] *n* teólogo.
theological [θiə'lɔdʒikəl] *a* teológico.
theology [θi'ɔlədʒi] *a* teología.
theoretical [θiə'retikəl] *a* teórico.
theorist ['θiərist] *n* teórico; hombre de teorías.
theory ['θiəri] *n* teoría; **in —** teóricamente.
there [ðɛə] *ad* allí, allá, ahí; **here and —** acá y acullá, de allá para acá; **— is ,— are** hay.
thereby ['ðɛə'bai] *ad* de este modo, con lo cual.
therefore ['ðɛəfɔ:] *cj ad* por (lo) tanto, (por, en) consecuencia.
Theresa [tə'ri:zə] *f* Teresa.
thereupon ['ðɛərə'pɔn] *ad* por (lo)

tanto, sobre; después de lo cual, por consiguiente.
thermometer [θə'mɔmitə] *n* termómetro.
thermos ['θə:mɔs] *n* — **bottle** termos.
these [θi:z] *a* estos, estas; *pn* éstos, éstas.
thesis ['θi:sis] *n* tesis.
they [ðei] *pn* ellos, ellas.
thick [θik] *a* espeso; (*fat*) grueso, corpulento; (*strong*) fuerte, recio; (*matted*) tupido, apretado; (*fog etc*) denso; (*beard*) poblado, crecido; (*coarse etc*) basto, tosco; torpe; (*indistinct*) borroso, apagado; (*fam*) íntimo; exagerado; — **set** rechoncho; espeso; —**skinned** de pellejo espeso; **through — and thin** incondicionalmente; **to be as — as thieves** ser uña y carne; *n* grueso, espesor.
thicken ['θikən] *vti* engrosar, espesar, aumentar.
thicket ['θikit] *n* maleza, matorral, espesura, monte.
thickness ['θiknis] *n* espesor, grueso, densidad, consistencia.
thief [θi:f] *n* ladrón; **petty** — pillo.
thieving ['θi:viŋ] *n* hurto; *a* rapaz.
thigh [θai] *n* muslo.
thimble ['θimbl] *n* dedal.
thin [θin] *a* (*fine*) delgado, fino, tenue, sutil; (*skinny*) flaco, magro; (*fog etc*) raro, claro, ligero, enrarecido; **very** — consumido; (*fam*) chupado; **as — as a rake** ser un hueso; **to grow** — enflaquecer; afilarse; **to make** — adelgazar; — **skinned** sensible; *vt* enrarecer; aclarar; entresacar; *vi* (*air*) rarificarse.
thing [θiŋ] *n* cosa, objeto, asunto, hecho; tipo; **for one** — en primer lugar; **no such** — no hay tal cosa; **with one — and another** entre unas cosas y otras; **as —s stand** tal como están las cosas.
think [θiŋk] *vt* pensar (en), creer, estimar, meditar, contemplar; discurrir; opinar; *vi* **to — on, of, over** pensar (en), acordarse de; (*imagine*) figurarse; (*of doing something*) pensar, proponerse; **to — little of** tener en poco; **to — well of** tener buen concepto de; **as you — fit** como Vd quiera; **one might** — podría creerse; **I should — so** ya lo creo; **way of —ing** parecer, modo de pensar; **without —ing** maquinalmente.
thinker ['θiŋkə] *n* pensador.
thinness ['θinnis] *n* delgadez, tenuidad, sutileza; flaqueza.
third [θə:d] *an* tercero; (*mus*) tercera; — **part** tercio; — **party rights** tercería.
thirst [θə:st] *n* sed; *vi* tener sed; **to — for** ansiar, codiciar.
thirsty ['θə:sti] *a* sediento; **I am** — tengo sed.
thirteen ['θə:'ti:n] *an* trece.
thirteenth ['θə:'ti:nθ] *an* decimotercero; — **day** el día trece.
thirty ['θə:ti] *an* treinta.
this [ðis] *a* este, esta; *pn* éste, ésta.
thistle ['θisl] *n* cardo.
thither ['ðiðə] *ad* allí, allá; **hither and** — acá y allá.
Thomas ['tɔməs] *m* Tomás.
thong [θɔŋ] *n* correa, tira de cuero.
thorn [θɔ:n] *n* espina, púa, abrojo.
thorny ['θɔ:ni] *a* espinoso, difícil; complicado; (*subject*) escabroso.
thorough ['θʌrə] *a* completo, formal, acabado, perfecto, concienzudo.
thoroughbred ['θʌrəbred] *a* de raza; *ad* por los cuatro costados.
thoroughfare ['θʌrəfɛə] *n* vía pública, calle céntrica; **no** — calle cerrada.
thoroughgoing ['θʌrə,gouiŋ] *a* cabal, perfecto; *ad* por los cuatro costados.
those [ðouz] *a* esos, aquellos; *pn* ésos, aquéllos.
though [ðou] *cj* aunque; bien que, sin embargo, si bien; **as** — como si.
thought [θɔ:t] *pp* **to have** — tener pensado; *n* pensamiento, reflexión, meditación; idea; intención; recuerdo; solicitud; **on second —s** pensándolo mejor, después de pensarlo bien.
thoughtful ['θɔ:tful] *a* pensativo; meditabundo, bien pensado; considerado, precavido; previsor; **to be** — comedirse.
thoughtfulness ['θɔ:tfulnis] *n* cuidado, atención, previsión, reflexión.
thoughtless ['θɔ:tlis] *a* irreflexivo, atolondrado, desatento, incauto.
thoughtlessness ['θɔ:tlisnis] *n* atolondramiento, incuria, ligereza, descuido.
thousand ['θauzənd] *an* mil, un millar; —**s of things** la mar de cosas.
thrash [θræʃ] *vti* trillar, desgranar; (*fam*) zurrar, azotar.
thrashing ['θræʃiŋ] *n* trilla; (*fam*) paliza; — **machine** trilladora; — **floor** era.
thread [θred] *n* hilo, hebra; filete; *vt* enhebrar; (*beads etc*) ensartar.
threadbare ['θredbɛə] *a* raído, gastado.
threat [θret] *n* amenaza, amago.
threaten ['θretn] *vt* amenazar; amagar.
three [θri:] *an* tres.
threshold ['θreʃhould] *n* umbral.
thrice [θrais] *ad* tres veces.
thrift [θrift] *n* ahorro, economía, frugalidad.
thrifty ['θrifti] *a* parco, frugal, económico, aprovechado.
thrill [θril] *n* exaltación, excitación, seducción, emoción; estremecimiento, temblor; *vt* excitar, emocionar; embelesar; *vi* sentir pasión por; temblar, estremecerse, conmoverse.
thrilling ['θriliŋ] *a* emocionante, apasionante, sensacional.
thrive [θraiv] *vi* prosperar, medrar.

throat [θrout] *n* garganta, cuello; **sore —** dolor de garganta; **to cut the — of** degollar.
throb [θrɔb] *n* latido, pulsación, palpitación; *vi* latir, palpitar, vibrar.
throne [θroun] *n* trono; (*canopied*) solio; corona.
throng [θrɔŋ] *n* tropel, turba; hervidero; *vti* atestar, apretar; amontonarse, apiñarse.
thronged [θrɔŋd] *a* concurrido.
throttle ['θrɔtl] *n* gaznate; (*of engine*) regulador, gollete; *vt* estrangular, ahogar, sofocar.
through [θru:] *prep* por, entre, al través de, de un lado a otro, por medio de; *ad* (de, al) través, de parte a parte; **— and —** de pies a cabeza, de cabo a rabo, de una parte a otra; **to carry —** llevar a cabo; **to fall —** fracasar.
throughout [θru:'aut] *prep ad* de todo en todo, a lo largo de; en todas partes; siempre; de parte a parte, de arriba abajo.
throw [θrou] *n* tiro, tirada; jugada, lance; (*unlucky, at cards*) azar; *vt* arrojar, tirar, echar, lanzar; **to — away** tirar, arrojar; (*a chance*) desperdiciar; (*rubbish*) desechar; **to — back** devolver; **to — down** derribar, tender, echar (abajo, por tierra); **to — off** sacudir(se), quitarse, despedir; **to — open** abrir de par en par; **to — out** (*words*) proferir; excluir; **to — up** echar al aire; renunciar a; vomitar; **to — up** (*career*) colgar los hábitos.
thrush [θrʌʃ] *n* tordo, malvís.
thrust [θrʌst] *n* (*archit*) empuje; (*with dagger, sword*) estocada; arremetida; (*machine*) impulso; *vti* empujar, impeler; **to — into** introducir, hundir; clavar; **to — aside** rechazar; **to — out** echar fuera, sacar; **to — through** atravesar de parte a parte; **to — upon** imponer.
thud [θʌd] *n* tras; golpazo.
thumb [θʌm] *n* pulgar; **to — a lift** hacer autostop.
thumbtack ['θʌmtæk] *n* chinche.
thump [θʌmp] *n* golpe, porrazo; *vti* golpear, aporrear.
thunder ['θʌndə] *n* trueno; estampido, estruendo; *vti* tronar; fulminar, retumbar.
thunderbolt ['θʌndəboult] *n* rayo.
thunderstorm ['θʌndəstɔ:m] *n* tempestad y truenos.
thunderstruck ['θʌndəstrʌk] *a* herido de rayo; fulminado, estupefacto, aturdido, helado.
Thursday ['θə:zdi] *n* jueves.
thus [ðʌs] *ad* así, de este modo, en estos términos, siendo así.
thwart [θwɔ:t] *n* banco; *vt* contrarrestar, desbaratar, impedir, frustrar.
thyme [taim] *n* tomillo.
tick [tik] *n* tictac, golpecito, contramarca; momento.
ticket ['tikit] *n* (*theat etc*) billete, localidad; entrada; (*label*) rótulo, etiqueta; **single —** billete sencillo; **return —** billete de ida y vuelta; **season —** abono; **— office** taquilla, despacho.
tickle ['tikl] *vt* hacer cosquillas; halagar; divertir, retozar.
ticklish ['tikliʃ] *a* (*person*) cosquilloso; (*situation*) peliagudo, espinoso; **to be —** tener cosquillas.
tidal ['taidl] *a* de marea.
tide [taid] *n* marea; flujo, marcha; **time and —** tiempo y sazón; **high —** pleamar; **ebb —** bajamar.
tidiness ['taidinis] *n* aseo, pulcritud, atildamiento.
tidings ['taidiŋz] *n pl* noticias, nuevas.
tidy ['taidi] *a* pulcro, decente, aseado, ordenado; **to — up** arreglar.
tie [tai] *n* corbata; lazo; (*bond*) apego, vínculo; (*games*) empate; (*rl*) traviesa, durmiente; *vt* atar, ligar, enlazar, unir; **to — up** (*ships*) abordar, (*parcel etc*) envolver.
tier [tiə] *n* fila, ringlera; **—s** (*of seats*) gradería.
tiger ['taigə] *n* tigre; **—nut** chufa.
tight [tait] *a* estrecho, tirante; (*box*) bien cerrado; (*packed*) apretado; (*clothes*) ajustado; (*situation*) premioso; **water—** impermeable; **air—** herméticamente cerrado; **—rope walker** equilibrista; **to be in a — spot** estar en un aprieto.
tighten ['taitn] *vti* estrechar, apretar.
tightness ['taitnis] *n* tensión, tirantez, impermeabilidad; estrechez; tacañería.
tile [tail] *n* teja, baldosa; (*coloured*) azulejo; *vt* enlosar, tejar.
till [til] *n* (*money*) caja, cajón, gaveta; *vt* labrar, cultivar.
till [til] *prep* hasta; *cj* hasta que.
tiller ['tilə] *n* labrador; (*naut*) caña del timón.
tilt [tilt] *n* inclinación; tienda, toldillo; (*joust*) torneo; *vt* inclinar; (*hat*) ladear; justar.
timber ['timbə] *n* madera (de construcción); árbol de monte.
time [taim] *n* (*measure of*) tiempo, época; plazo; (*occasion*) vez, turno; momento; (*mus*) compás; **what — is it?** ¿qué hora es?; **at —s** a veces; **many —s** a menudo; **in —** a tiempo; **from — to —** de cuando en cuando, a ratos; **at one —** de una vez, de una tirada; **in good —** con tiempo; **in (his) own good —** a (su) tiempo; **— limit** plazo; **— spent in** temporada; **—table** horario; **for some — past** de algún tiempo a esta parte; **at any —** a cualquier hora; **at that —** entonces, en aquel tiempo; **this — a month hence** de aquí a un mes; **for the — being** de momento, por ahora; **behind —** atrasado, retardado; **behind the —s** atrasado; **to**

keep — guardar (el) compás; **to beat** — marcar el compás; **to have a lovely** — pasarlo (bien), divertirse (horrores); *vt* medir el tiempo.
timely ['taimli] *a* oportuno, conveniente.
timetable ['taim.teibl] *n* guía; horario.
timid ['timid] *a* tímido, medroso, espantadizo, corto; temeroso, miedoso.
timidity [ti'miditi] *n* timidez; cortedad; **excessive** — miedo cerval.
Timothy ['timəθi] *m* Timoteo.
tin [tin] *n* estaño; (*manufactured*) hoja de lata, hojalata; (*container*) lata; — **foil** hoja de estaño; *vt* estañar; envasar en lata.
tincture ['tiŋktʃə] *n* tinte, tintura; *vt* teñir, impregnar.
tinder ['tində] *n* yesca.
tinge [tindʒ] *n* tinte, matiz, dejo; punta; *vt* teñir, matizar.
tingle ['tiŋgl] *vi* sentir picazón, hormiguear; **to — with excitement** estremecerse de entusiasmo.
tingling ['tiŋgliŋ] *n* hormigueo.
tinkle ['tiŋkl] *n* retintín; *vti* hacer sonar, sonar.
tinkling ['tiŋkliŋ] *a* resonante; *n* retintín; campanilleo.
tinsel ['tinsəl] *n* oropel.
tint [tint] *n* tinta, tinte; (*painting*) media tinta; *vt* teñir, matizar.
tiny ['taini] *a* minúsculo, menudo; — **fragment of** poquísimo; — **tots** (*fam*) gente menuda.
tip [tip] *n* (*land*) punta, extremidad, cabo; (*tongue*) punta; (*finger*) yema; (*money*) propina, gratificación; (*foil*) botón; (*moon*) cuerno; (*top*) cúspide; (*advice*) aviso; **on —toe** a hurtadillas; **to go on —toe** andar de puntillas; *vt* ladear, inclinar; **to — over** volcar; (*money*) dar propina; (*advice*) dar informes confidenciales.
tipsy ['tipsi] *a* ebrio, achispado, a dos velas.
tiptoe ['tiptou] *n* punta del pie.
tirade [tai'reid] *n* andanada, invectiva, diatriba.
tire ['taiə] *n* llanta, calce, neumático, goma; **flat** — llanta o goma reventada; *vti* fatigar(se); aburrir, fastidiar; **to — out** reventar.
tired ['taiəd] *a* cansado; (*of food*) mustio; — **out** agotado; **to be** — fatigarse.
tiredness ['taiədnis] *n* cansancio, fatiga.
tireless ['taiəlis] *a* incansable, infatigable.
tiresome ['taiəsəm] *a* cansado, aburrido, molesto, fastidioso; **to be** — molestar, fastidiar.
tissue ['tisju:] *n* tejido; — **paper** papel de seda.
tit [tit] *n* (*orni*) paro, nerrerillo; — **for tat** tal para cual, ojo por ojo.
titbit ['titbit] *n* bocado delicado, bocado de rey, golosina, manjar.
title ['taitl] *n* (*person*) título, denominación; (*heading*) epígrafe, rótulo; — **page** portada, frontispicio; (*to*) derecho; **to give a — to** intitular; titular.
titter ['titə] *n* risa entre dientes, risita; *vi* reír entre dientes.
to [tu:] *prep* a, hacia, de, que, hasta, en comparación con.
toad [toud] *n* sapo.
toast [toust] *n* tostada; brindis; *vt* tostar; (*health*) brindar.
toaster ['toustə] *n* tostadera, tostador, parrillas; brindador.
tobacco [tə'bækou] *n* tabaco; **loose** — tabaco picado; — **firm, industry** compañía, industrial tabacalera; — **kiosk** estanco; — **pouch** petaca.
tobacconist [tə'bækənist] *n* vendedor de tabaco; (*small shop, kiosk*) estanquero; **—'s** estanco, tabaquería.
today [tə'dei] *ad* hoy, actualmente.
toe [tou] *n* dedo del pie; (*animal*) pezuña; (*sock*) punta.
toffee ['tɔfi] *n* dulce, caramelo.
together [tə'geðə] *ad* junto, juntos, juntamente, al unísono; a la vez; de seguida, seguido; *vt* **to get** — reunir; *vi* **to come (get)** — convergir, reunirse; **to work** — colaborar.
toil [tɔil] *n* faena, labor, pena, afán(es); *vi* sufrir, sudar, afanarse, matarse.
toilet ['tɔilit] *n* (*grooming*) tocado; — **table** tocador; — **articles** artículos de tocador; — **paper** papel higiénico; (*rest room*) retrete, excusado.
token ['toukən] *n* indicación, señal, muestra; prenda; prueba, favor; recuerdo.
Toledo [tɔ'li:dou] **inhabitant of** — toledano.
tolerable ['tɔlərəbl] *a* pasadero, soportable, llevadero; regular, pasable.
tolerant ['tɔlərənt] *a* tolerante, paciente; despreocupado; **to be — of** admitir.
tolerate ['tɔləreit] *vt* tolerar, aguantar; ver; consentir.
toleration [.tɔlə'reiʃən] *n* tolerancia, indulgencia.
toll [toul] *n* (*to pay*) peaje, pontazgo; (*bell*) clamor, doble, tañido; *vti* sonar, tañer, doblar.
tolling ['touliŋ] *n* son, clamor, doblar.
tomato [tə'mɑ:tou] *n* tomate.
tomb [tu:m] *n* tumba, sepulcro, sepultura.
tombstone ['tu:mstoun] *n* lápida, sepulcral, losa.
tomorrow [tə'mɔrou] *n* mañana; **the day after** — pasado mañana.
ton [tʌn] *n* tonelada.
tone [toun] *n* tono, timbre, tónico; (*of voice*) metal; *pl* (*paint*) matices.
tongs [tɔŋz] *n pl* tenazas, pinzas, tenacillas.
tongue [tʌŋ] *n* lengua; (*speech*) habla;

(*fam*) la sin hueso; (*ie language*) idioma; (*mech*) lengüeta; **to hold one's —** callarse, (*coll*) callar el pico; **—-twister** trabalenguas; **—-tied** premioso; **loose —ed** suelto de lengua.
tonic ['tɔnik] *an* tónico; (*mus*) tónica.
tonight [tə'nait] *ad* esta noche.
tonnage ['tʌnidʒ] *n* tonelaje, porte; derecho de tonelada.
tonsure ['tɔnʃə] *n* tonsura, corona.
too [tu:] *ad* demasiado; asimismo, también, igualmente; **— much** excesivo; **— well** de sobra; **to be — (kind)** pecar de (generoso).
tool [tu:l] *n* herramienta, utensilio, instrumento; *pl* útiles, aperos, aparejos, bártulos.
tooth [tu:θ] *n* diente, (*molar*) muela; (*of comb*) púa; **eye—** colmillo; **to have a sweet —** ser goloso; **— and nail** con tesón.
toothed [tu:θt] *a* dentado; aserrado.
toothless ['tu:θlis] *a* desdentado.
toothpaste ['tu:θpeist] *n* pasta dentífrica, polvos dentífricos.
top [tɔp] *n* (*height*) cima, pico, cumbre; (*height, fig*) punta, cúspide; (*finish*) remate; coronilla; (*lid*) tapa; (*tree*) copa; (*wall*) coronamiento; (*of vehicle*) capota; primero, cabeza; auge; **spinning —** peonza; **from — to bottom** de arriba abajo; **— hat** chistera; **—boots** botas de campaña; **— floor** ático; *vt* descabezar; **to — off** rematar; aventajar.
topic ['tɔpik] *n* asunto, tópico, tema, materia.
topical ['tɔpikəl] *a* actual.
topmost ['tɔpmoust] *a* el más alto; (*stone etc*) remate.
topple ['tɔpl] *vt* derribar; *vi* caer, volcarse, venirse abajo.
torch [tɔ:tʃ] *n* antorcha, hacha, tea.
torment ['tɔ:ment] *n* tormento, martirio, tortura, suplicio; [tɔ:'ment] *vt* atormentar, afligir, dar guerra.
tornado [tɔ:'neidou] *n* huracán, torbellino.
torpedo [tɔ:'pi:dou] *n* torpedo; *vt* torpedear.
torpor ['tɔ:pə] *n* letargo, estupor; torpeza.
torrent ['tɔrənt] *n* torrente, raudal.
torrid ['tɔrid] *a* tórrido, ardiente.
tortoise ['tɔ:təs] *n* tortuga; **—shell** concha; **—shell glasses** quevedos.
tortuous ['tɔ:tjuəs] *a* tortuoso, sinuoso.
torture ['tɔ:tʃə] *n* tortura; tormento, suplicio; *vt* torturar, crucificar.
toss [tɔs] *n* meneo, sacudimiento, sacudida; (*of coin*) cara o cruz; *vt* tirar, lanzar al aire; (*in blanket*) mantear; (*tail etc*) menear, agitar, sacudir; *vi* **to — up** jugar a cara y cruz.
tossing ['tɔsiŋ] *n* traqueteo; agitación, meneo.
total ['toutl] *n* total; *a* entero, todo; **sum —** (*of people*) colectividad; *vt* sumar, ascender a.
totter ['tɔtə] *vi* vacilar, tambalearse, bambolear.
tottering ['tɔtəriŋ] *a* vacilante; ruinoso.
touch [tʌtʃ] *n* tacto, toque, tiento, contacto; (*art*) ejecución, pincelada; (*of pain*) punzada; (*shade of*) punta, sombra; (*proof*) prueba; examen, (*sense of*) tacto; **with a — of** con sus ribetes de; **final —** remate; **to put the final — to** ultimar; **in — with** al tanto de; *vt* tocar; (*with hand*) palpar, manosear; (*brush*) rozar; alcanzar; (*mus*) pulsar, tocar; (*sentiment*) enternecer, conmover; (*prick*) aguijonear; **to — up** adornar, embellecer; *vi* (*at port*) hacer escala; **to — off** descargar.
touching ['tʌtʃiŋ] *n* tiento; *a* conmovedor, tierno, emocionante; *prep* tocante a, en cuanto a.
touchstone ['tʌtʃstoun] *n* toque, piedra de toque.
touchy ['tʌtʃi] *a* irritable, quisquilloso, vidrioso, receloso.
tough [tʌf] *a* duro, arduo, recio, sufrido, tenaz; duradero; (*leathery*) coriáceo; resistente.
toughen ['tʌfn] *vt* curtir, endurecer; **to — up** *vti* endurecer(se).
toughness ['tʌfnis] *n* tenacidad; rigidez; dureza.
Toulouse [tu:'lu:z] *n* Tolosa.
tour [tuə] *n* viaje, vuelta, gira, excursión; *vt* hacer un viaje (por, en); *vi* viajar, hacer una jira, hacer un viaje de turismo.
tourist ['tuərist] *n* turista.
tournament ['tuənəmənt] *n* torneo.
tow [tou] *n* (*rope*) estopa; remolque; *vt* **to —, take in —** remolcar.
toward, towards [tə'wɔ:d(z)] *prep* hacia, del lado de, para con, cosa de.
towel ['tauəl] *n* toalla; **roller —** toalla sin fin.
tower ['tauə] *n* torre; torreón; *vi* elevarse, descollar, dominar.
town [taun] *n* ciudad; población, pueblo; lugar; **my home —** mi pueblo; **— council** cabildo, municipio; **— dweller** ciudadano; **— hall** casa consistorial, casa del concejo, ayuntamiento.
toy [tɔi] *n* juguete, chuchería; *vi* **to — with** jugar, juguetear con, divertirse.
trace [treis] *n* (*trail*) rastro, pista; (*imprint*) huella, pisada; (*sign*) señal, indicio, pizca; *pl* (*of horse*) guarniciones; *vt* (*follow*) rastrear, seguir la pista; (*draw*) trazar, delinear; **to — exactly** calcar; (*derive*) imputar, achacar, inferir; (*study*) descubrir.
track [træk] *n* ruta, rastro, vestigio; (*rl*) vía; (*racing etc*) pista; (*over rough ground*) trocha; **beaten —** camino trillado; **wheel —** rodada; **to**

set on right — encarrilar; *vt* **to — down** rastrear, seguir la pista (a).
trackless ['trækIis] *a* fragoso.
tract [trækt] *n* trecho, región; serie; folleto.
tractable ['træktəbl] *a* tratable, dócil, blando.
trade [treid] *n* comercio, industria, oficio; **he is a ( ) by** — es ( ) de oficio; **free** — libre cambio; — **winds** vientos generales; — **union** gremio, sindicato; *vi* traficar, comerciar, negociar.
trader ['treidə] *n* comerciante.
tradesman ['treidzmen] *n* tendero, artesano, mercader; —**'s entrance** puerta de servicio.
trading ['treidiŋ] *a* mercantil; *n* comercio; — **house** casa, factoría.
tradition [trə'diʃən] *n* tradición.
traditional [trə'diʃənl] *a* tradicional; (*home of family*) solariego.
traffic ['træfik] *n* tráfico, comercio; (*street*) circulación; *vi* comerciar.
tragedy ['trædʒidi] *n* tragedia.
tragic ['trædʒik] *a* trágico.
trail [treil] *n* huella, rastro; pista; cola; (*path*) sendero; — **of powder** reguero de pólvora; *vt* seguir la pista; arrastrar(se); *vi* ir detrás, rezagarse.
train [trein] *n* (*rl*) tren; **through** — tren directo; **mail, excursion, freight, passenger and freight** — tren de correo, de recreo, de mercancías, mixto; (*mules*) recua; (*servants etc*) séquito; (*dress*) cola; *vt* disciplinar, amaestrar, adiestrar; *vi* entrenarse.
training ['treiniŋ] *n* educación, instrucción; (*sport*) entrenamiento; **without** — imperito; — **college** escuela normal; — **ground** (*sport*) estadio; — **ship** buque escuela.
trait [trei] *n* rasgo, toque, característica.
traitor ['treitə] *n* traidor.
traitorous ['treitərəs] *a* pérfido, traicionero, desleal, alevoso.
tramcar ['træmkɑ:] *n* tranvía.
trammel ['træməl] *n* estorbo; traba; *vt* poner trabas a.
tramp [træmp] *n* vagabundo, polizón; marcha, ruido de pisadas.
trample ['træmpl] *vti* **to — on, — underfoot** pisar, hollar, pisotear; pisar.
trance [trɑ:ns] *n* catalepsia; (*relig*) arrobamiento, éxtasis.
tranquil ['træŋkwil] *a* tranquilo, apacible, sosegado, suave.
tranquillity [træŋ'kwiliti] *n* tranquilidad, serenidad, sosiego.
transact [træn'zækt] *vti* llevar a cabo, tramitar, desempeñar; (*business*) evacuar, despachar.
transaction [træn'zækʃən] *n* gestión, negociación, transacción, negocio, trámite; *pl* memorias.
transcend [træn'send] *vt* superar, excedar, rebasar.
transcribe [træns'kraib] *vt* transcribir, copiar.
transfer ['trænsfə] *n* (*goods etc*) transporte; (*title to property*) alienación, traspaso; transbordo; cesión; [træns'fə:] *vt* transferir, transbordar, enajenar, traspasar.
transferable [træns'fə:rəbl] *a* transferible; **not** — inalienable.
transfix [træns'fiks] *vt* traspasar.
transform [træns'fɔ:m] *vt* transformar; (*expression*) demudar, transfigurar; convertir; *vi* transformarse, parar en.
transformation [,trænsfə'meiʃən] *n* transformación; (*of features*) demudación; metamorfosis.
transgress [træns'gres] *vt* violar, contravenir, delinquir, propasarse, transgredir.
transgression [træns'greʃən] *n* transgresión, atentado; pecado; ofensa; extralimitación.
transient ['trænziənt] *a* transitorio, pasajero, transeúnte.
transition [træn'siʒən] *n* transición, paso, mudanza.
transistor [træn'sistə] *n* transistor.
transitory ['trænsitəri] *a* transitorio, fugitivo, fugaz.
translate [træns'leit] *vt* traducir, volver, verter.
translation [træns'leiʃən] *n* traducción; (*eccl*) translación.
translator [træns'leitə] *n* traductor.
transmit [trænz'mit] *vt* transmitir, remitir; (*orders*) cursar.
transmitter [trænz'mitə] *n* transmisor.
transparency [træns'pɛərənsi] *n* transparencia, diafanidad; (*phot*) diapositiva.
transparent [træns'pɛərənt] *a* transparente; cristalino; franco; **to be** — clarear.
transpire [træns'paiə] *vi* transpirar, sudar; divulgarse.
transport ['trænspɔ:t] *n* (*goods etc*) transporte; conducción, acarreo; (*of joy etc*) transporte, éxtasis; acceso; (*mystical*) rapto.
transport [træns'pɔ:t] *vt* (*goods etc*) transportar, acarrear, conducir; (*with joy*) arrebatar, transportar; (*relig*) raptar.
transportation [,trænspɔ:'teiʃən] *n* transporte; transportación.
trap [træp] *n* trampa, cepo; (*ambush*) celada, asechanza; zancadilla; **to lay a** — tender una red; —**s** (*sl*) equipaje; —**door** escotillón; **to be caught in a** — caer en el garlito; *vt* coger en trampa.
trapper ['træpə] *n* cazador.
trappings ['træpiŋz] *n* adorno; arnés, arreos; (*horse*) jaeces.
trash [træʃ] *n* basura, desecho.
trashy ['træʃi] *a* despreciable, sin valor; baladí.
travel ['trævl] *n* viaje; *vi* viajar;

caminar; (*of vehicle*) ir; **to — empty** ir de vacío.
traveler ['trævlə] *n* viajero, viajador, caminante.
traveling ['trævliŋ] *n* (los) viajes; (el) viajar; **— companion** compañero de viaje; **— salesman** agente viajero, viajante de comercio.
traverse ['trævə:s] *vt* atravesar, cruzar; pasar por, recorrer.
travesty ['trævisti] *n* parodia.
tray [trei] *n* bandeja, batea; (*wicker*) azafate.
treacherous ['tretʃərəs] *a* traicionero, traidor, alevoso.
treachery ['tretʃəri] *n* traición, perfidia, defección; deslealtad.
tread [tred] *n* pisada, paso; *vt* **to — down (underfoot)** hollar; **to — on** pisotear, pisar; *vi* dar pasos.
treason ['tri:zn] *n* traición.
treasonable ['tri:znəbl] *a* traidor, pérfido.
treasure ['treʒə] *n* tesoro; caudal; *vt* atesorar; ahuchar.
treasurer ['treʒərə] *n* tesorero.
treasury ['treʒəri] *n* tesoro, tesorería; hacienda pública; **— bill** vale de tesorería.
treat [tri:t] *n* trato, convite; (*fam*) convidada; *vti* tratar, negociar; (*mil*) parlamentar; (*hospitably*) festejar; **to — with** (*chem*) tratar con; **to — on, — of** versar sobre.
treatise ['tri:tiz] *n* tratado.
treatment ['tri:tmənt] *n* trato; (*med*) tratamiento; procedimiento.
treaty ['tri:ti] *n* tratado, asiento, pacto.
treble ['trebl] *a* triple; *n* tiple; *vti* triplicar.
tree [tri:] *n* árbol; **fruit —** árbol frutal.
treeless ['tri:lis] *a* sin árboles.
trellis ['trelis] *n* enrejado; (*plants*) espaldera.
tremble ['trembl] *vi* temblar, estremecerse; trepidar, vibrar.
trembling ['trembliŋ] *a* temblante, trémulo; *n* estremecimiento, temblor.
tremendous [tri'mendəs] *a* tremendo, formidable, estupendo.
tremor ['tremə] *n* temblor, vibración.
tremulous ['tremjuləs] *a* tembloroso, trémulo.
trench [trentʃ] *n* (*mil*) trinchera; cauce; (*foundation*) zanja; (*water*) acequia; *vt* excavar, atrincherar.
trenchant ['trentʃənt] *a* cortante, tajante, mordaz.
trend [trend] *n* tendencia, inclinación, giro, dirección.
trepidation [ˌtrepi'deiʃən] *n* azoramiento.
trespass ['trespəs] *n* transgresión; *vi* **to — upon** violar; (*on time etc*) abusar de; faltar, delinquir.
tresses ['tresiz] *n* trenzas, rizo, (mata) de pelo, bucle.
trial ['traiəl] *n* (*effort*) esfuerzo; prueba, tentativa; (*by taste*) cata; (*by touch*) toque; (*law*) juicio, proceso, vista; experiencia; (*sorrow etc*) desgracia, aflicción; **on —** a prueba; **— shot** tiento; **— trip** viaje de prueba.
triangle ['traiæŋgl] *n* triángulo.
tribe [traib] *n* tribu, casta; horda.
tribulation [ˌtribju'leiʃən] *n* tribulación, pena, congoja.
tribunal [trai'bju:nl] *n* tribunal, juzgado.
tributary ['tribjutəri] *a* tributario; *n* afluente.
tribute ['tribju:t] *n* tributo; impuesto.
trick [trik] *n* trampa, engaño; (*fraud*) timo, fraude, estafa, superchería; (*stratagem*) ardid, maniobra, truco; (*cards*) baza; **smart —** suerte, faena; **skillful —** habilidad, maña; **dirty —** cochinada; **low —** burla pesada, pillería; *vt* engañar, burlar; estafar; camelar; timar; **to — out** ataviar; **to — out of** defraudar.
trickle ['trikl] *n* reguero; *vi* escurrir, gotear.
tricky ['triki] *a* fraudulento, tramposo; vicioso; difícil.
trifle ['traifl] *n* bagatela, niñería, miseria, nada, cosita, insignificancia; **a mere —** una fruslería; **not to stop at —s** no reparar en pelillos; *vi* chancear(se); no tomar en serio; **to — with** jugar con, burlarse de.
trifling ['traifliŋ] *a* insignificante, baladí, fútil.
trigger ['trigə] *n* gatillo, disparador; fiador.
trill [tril] *n* (*mus*) quiebro; (*birds*) trino, gorjeo; *vi* trinar, gorjear.
trim [trim] *a* adornado, ataviado, elegante; ajustado; *vt* adornar; cortar; podar; (*stick etc*) tajar; (*sails*) templar; (*hair*) atusar; (*with studs*) tachonar; (*wick*) despabilar.
trimming ['trimiŋ] *n* (*on dress etc*) guarnición, adorno; (*piece of wood etc*) desbaste; (*of hedge*) poda.
trinket ['triŋkit] *n* baratija, bagatela, miriñaque.
trip [trip] *n* viaje; excursión; tropezón; **to go on a —** viajar, hacer excursiones; *vt* hacer, caer; echar la zancadilla; *vi* tropezar, dar un tropezón; descuidarse.
triple ['tripl] *a* triple; *vt* triplicar.
trite [trait] *a* trivial, común; trillado, gastado, socorrido.
triumph ['traiəmf] *n* triunfo; victoria; *vi* triunfar, vencer, sobreponerse a.
triumphant [trai'ʌmfənt] *a* triunfante.
trivial ['triviəl] *a* trivial, frívolo, baladí.

triviality [ˌtrivi'æliti] *n* menudencia, poca cosa.
trolley ['trɔli] *n* (*el*) trole; (*child's*) carretilla; — **bus** trolebús; — **car** tranvía.
trombone [trɔm'boun] *n* trombón.
troop [tru:p] *n* tropa; turba; cuadrilla; (*soldiers*) mesnada; (*actors*) compañía; *vi* reunirse; formar tropa; ir en tropel; — **ship** barco de transporte de tropas.
trophy ['troufi] *n* trofeo.
tropic ['trɔpik] *n* trópico.
tropical ['trɔpikəl] *a* tropical.
trot [trɔt] *n* trote; *vi* trotar; andar al trote.
troubadour ['tru:bəduə] *n* trovador; **—'s art** gaya ciencia.
trouble ['trʌbl] *n* confusión, trastorno; desazón, desconsuelo; sinsabor, disgusto, aflicción, pena; molestia, incomodidad, apuro; **to be in** — estar afligido, verse en un apuro; *vt* turbar, trastornar, desazonar, incomodar, enfadar; (*be nuisance*) molestar.
troubled ['trʌbld] *a* apenado; (*times etc*) turbulento; **in — waters** a río revuelto.
troublesome ['trʌblsəm] *a* molesto, enfadoso; importuno; penoso; fatigoso; fastidioso.
trough [trɔf] *n* artesa; **food** — comedero; **drinking** — abrevadero.
trousers ['trauzəz] *n* pantalones.
trousseau ['tru:sou] *n* ajuar.
trout [traut] *n* trucha.
truant ['truənt] *a* novillero; **to play** — hacer novillos.
truce [tru:s] *n* tregua; suspensión de hostilidades.
truck [trʌk] *n* camión; — **farmer** hortelano.
truculence ['trʌkjuləns] *n* truculencia, crueldad.
truculent ['trʌkjulənt] *a* cruel, truculento.
trudge [trʌdʒ] *vi* andar trabajosamente.
true [tru:] *a* verdadero, positivo; hecho y derecho; verídico; a plomo; genuino, leal, legítimo.
truism ['tru:izəm] *n* perogrullada; axioma.
trumpery ['trʌmpəri] *n* engaño, fraude: hojarasca; baratija.
trumpet ['trʌmpit] *n* trompa, trompeta, corneta de llaves; *vt* pregonar.
trumpeter ['trʌmpitə] *n* trompetero, trompeta.
truncheon ['trʌntʃən] *n* porra, cachiporra.
trunk [trʌŋk] *n* (*tree*) tronco; (*elephant*) trompa; (*traveling*) baúl; — **call** (*tele*) conferencia.
trust [trʌst] *n* confianza; crédito; cometido; fideicomiso; asociación de compañías; **in** — en administración; **on** — a ojos cerrados; *vti* confiar, tener confianza; fiarse, dar crédito.
trustee [trʌs'ti:] *n* fideicomisario, administrador.
trustful ['trʌstful] *a* confiado.
trustworthiness ['trʌstˌwəðinis] *n* integridad, honradez, probidad.
trustworthy ['trʌstˌwə:ði] *a* digno de confianza; fidedigno, de mucha confianza; — **servant** confidante.
trusty ['trʌsti] *a* fiel, constante, leal, íntegro, seguro.
truth [tru:θ] *n* verdad; fidelidad, veracidad; **the honest** — la pura verdad; **in** — (a la, en) verdad, de veras.
truthful ['tru:θful] *a* verdadero; verídico.
truthfulness ['tru:θfulnis] *n* veracidad.
try [trai] *n* prueba, ensayo, tentativa; *vt* ensayar, probar, tratar de; procurar; poner a prueba, fatigar; (in)-tentar; (*law*) conocer, procesar; juzgar; **to — on** (*clothes etc*) probar; (*for first time*) estrenar; **to — to** tratar (de), esforzarse (a), hacer (por); **to — one's luck** probar fortuna.
trying ['traiiŋ] *a* fatigoso, irritante.
tub [tʌb] *n* cuba, artesón, cubeta.
tube [tju:b] *n* tubo; caño, conducto; metro; **inner** — cámara de aire.
tuberculosis [tjuˌbə:kju'lousis] *n* tuberculosis, tisis.
tuck [tʌk] *n* pliegue (re)cogido; filete; alforza; *vt* **to — up** (*sleeves*) arremangar; **to — into** zampar; **to — up** arregazar; *vt* plegar, hacer alforzas.
Tuesday ['tju:zdi] *n* martes.
tuft [tʌft] *n* (*on hats*) penacho, borla; (*on birds*) cresta; (*of grass*) manojo, mechón.
tug [tʌg] *n* (es)tirón; (*boat*) remolcador; *vti* remolcar; tirar de, halar.
tuition [tju'iʃən] *n* instrucción, enseñanza.
tulip ['tju:lip] *n* tulipán.
tumble ['tʌmbl] *n* caída, tumbo; *vti* caer, dar en tierra; venirse abajo, derrumbarse; (*to an idea*) caer en la cuenta, entender.
tumbledown ['tʌmbldaun] *a* decrépito, destartalado.
tumbling ['tʌmbliŋ] *part* **to come — down** venirse abajo.
tumor ['tju:mə] *n* tumor, apostema; (*small*) buba.
tumult ['tju:mʌlt] *n* tumulto, alboroto, revuelta; conmoción, fragor, bullanga, gritería, motín.
tumultuous [tju'mʌltjuəs] *a* tumultuoso, alborotado.
tuna ['tjunə] *n* atún; **striped** — bonito.
tune [tju:n] *n* tono; tonadilla; tonada; **out of** — destemplado; **in** — templado, afinado; *vt* afinar, templar; acordar, concertar.
tuneful ['tju:nful] *a* melodioso, armonioso.

tunic ['tju:nik] *n* túnica, blusa.
tunnel ['tʌnl] *n* túnel.
turbid ['tə:bid] *a* turbio, espeso; borroso; turbulento.
turbine ['tə:bin] *n* turbina.
turbulent ['tə:bjulənt] *a* turbulento, revoltoso, faccioso.
turf [tə:f] *n* césped; el hipódromo; *vt* encespedar.
turgid ['tə:dʒid] *a* turgente, hinchado, ampuloso.
Turk [tə:k] *n* turco.
turkey ['tə:ki] *n* pavo.
Turkey ['tə:ki] *n* Turquía.
Turkish ['tə:kiʃ] *an* turco.
turmoil ['tə:mɔil] *n* estruendo, disturbio, baraúnda.
turn [tə:n] *n* vuelta; (*walk*) paseo, vuelta; (*mech*) revolución, giro, vuelta; (*duty*) turno, vez, tanda; (*cards*) mano; (*change*) mudanza, marcha; (*character*) genio, inclinación; (*twist*) sesgo, giro; (*of speech*) giro, idiotismo; rodeo; cambio; hechura; proceder; (*good, bad*) pasada, jugada; **good —** favor, servicio; **to do an ill —** hacer un flaco servicio; **at every —** a cada instante; **to take —s** alternar; *vt* volver, dar vueltas a, hacer (rodar, girar); (*years*) cumplir; (*head*) trastornar; (*adrift*) abandonar; (*stomach*) revolver, causar asco; **to — one's coat** cambiar de casaca; **to — aside** desviar; trasladar; **to — away** despedir, apartar; **to — down** doblar; (*gas*) bajar; (*fam*) dar calabazas a; **to — into** transformar en; **to — off** cerrar; **to — on** abrir; depender de; volverse contra; **to — out** despedir; producir; **to — over** volver; revolver; (*in mind*) dar vueltas a; volcar; (*round*) volver; rodar; **to — up** revolver; (*sleeves*) arremangarse; presentarse; **to — upside down** revolver, trastornar, volver patas arriba; **to — upon** fundarse en; recaer sobre; *vi* volver; torcer, desviarse; hacerse, venir a ser; (*tide*) repuntar; **to — away** apartarse; **to — out** salir; **to — out to be** resultar; **to — around** volverse; **to — round and round** dar vueltas; **to — up** (a)parecer, personarse; **to — upon** depender de; **to — over** revolverse; **to — to** recurrir a, tirar hacia.
turning ['tə:niŋ] *n* vuelta, rodeo; cambio, ángulo, esquina; desviación; **— point** punto decisivo, crisis.
turnip ['tə:nip] *n* nabo.
turnout ['tə:naut] *n* (*people*) concurrencia; (*show*) tren.
turnstile ['tə:nstail] *n* torniquete.
turret ['tʌrit] *n* torreón, mirador, torre; **ship's gun —** cúpula.
turtle ['tə:tl] *n* tortuga; **—dove** tórtola.
tusk [tʌsk] *n* colmillo.
tussle ['tʌsl] *n* lucha, pelea.
tutor ['tju:tə] *n* tutor; ayo; *vt* instruir; hacer de tutor.
twang [twæŋ] *n* nasalidad, gangosidad; *vt* rasguear.
twelfth [twelfθ] *an* duodécimo; **T— Night** epifanía, noche de Reyes.
twelve [twelv] *an* doce.
twentieth ['twentiəθ] *a* vigésimo, (*of month*) el veinte.
twenty ['twenti] *an* veinte.
twice [twais] *ad* dos veces.
twig [twig] *n* ramo, varilla, vara; (*small*) vergeta, varita
twilight ['twailait] *n* crepúsculo; **in the —** entre dos luces.
twin [twin] *an* mellizo, gemelo.
twine [twain] *n* cuerda, hilo, pita; guita; *vti* enroscar(se).
twinge [twindʒ] *n* dolor punzante, punzada; *vi* sentir dolor.
twinkle ['twiŋkl] *n* titilación, centelleo; *vt* titilar, rutilar, centellear.
twinkling ['twiŋkliŋ] *n* **in a —** en un santiamén; **in the — of an eye** en un abrir y cerrar de ojos.
twirl [twə:l] *n* giro, vuelta; *vt* enroscar; *vi* girar, dar vueltas.
twist [twist] *n* torsión, quiebro, sacudida; tirón; *vt* (con)torcer, retorcer, enroscar, trenzar, entretejer; *vi* retorcerse, contorcerse.
twisting ['twistiŋ] *n* **— and turning** sinuosidad.
twitch [twitʃ] *n* contracción nerviosa; tirón, sacudida; *vt* crispar; *vi* crispar(se), tirar.
twitter ['twitə] *n* gorjeo; *vi* gorjear, trinar.
two [tu:] *an* dos; **—-edged** de dos filos; **—-faced** de dos caras; **to put — and — together** atar cabos; **—-headed** bicéfalo; **—-syllabled** bisílabo.
type [taip] *n* tipo, modelo, ejemplar; (*print*) carácter, tipo; **—writer** máquina de escribir.
typical ['tipikəl] *a* típico, característico; (*national*) castizo.
typist ['taipist] *n* mecanógrafa.
tyrannical [ti'rænikl] *a* tiránico, tirano.
tyrannize ['tirənaiz] *vt* tiranizar, oprimir.
tyranny ['tirəni] *n* tiranía, despotismo, rigor.
tyrant ['taiərənt] *n* tirano, déspota.

U

ubiquity [ju:'bikwiti] *n* ubicuidad.
ugliness ['ʌglinis] *n* fealdad, deformidad; perversidad.
ugly ['ʌgli] *a* feo, mal parecido; repugnante; (*wound*) peligroso; fiero.
ulcer ['ʌlsə] *n* úlcera, llaga.
ulterior [ʌl'tiəriə] *a* ulterior, posterior.
ultimate ['ʌltimit] *a* último, postrimero; primario; esencial.

ultimately ['ʌltimitli] *ad* al fin y al postre; en fin; a la larga.
Ulysses [ju'lisi:z] *m* Ulises.
umbrage ['ʌmbridʒ] *n* pique; resentimiento; **to take —** incomodarse.
umbrella [ʌm'brelə] *n* paraguas; sombrilla.
unabashed ['ʌnə'bæʃt] *a* descocado, cínico, fresco.
unable ['ʌn'eibl] *a* incapaz, impotente; **to make —** incapacitar.
unacceptable ['ʌnək'septəbl] *a* inaceptable, incompatible, inadmisible.
unaccountable ['ʌnə'kauntəbl] *a* inexplicable, irresponsable, extraño.
unaccustomed ['ʌnə'kʌstəmd] *a* no usual, insólito; no acostumbrado.
unadorned ['ʌnə'dɔ:nd] *a* sencillo, sin adornos, llano.
unadulterated [ˌʌnə'dʌltəreitid] *a* puro, sin mezcla.
unaffected ['ʌnə'fektid] *a* llano, natural.
unafraid ['ʌnə'freid] *a* impertérrito.
unanimity [ˌjunə'nimiti] *n* unanimidad.
unanimous [ju'næniməs] *a* unánime.
unanswerable [ʌn'ɑ:nsərəbl] *a* indisputable, incontrovertible, incontestable.
unarmed ['ʌn'ɑ:md] *a* inerme, desarmado.
unassailable [ˌʌnə'seiləbl] *a* entero, inexpugnable, (*argument*) irrebatible.
unassuming ['ʌnə'sju:miŋ] *a* modesto, sencillo, sin pretensiones.
unauthorized ['ʌn'ɔ:θəraizd] *a* sin autorización, desautorizado.
unavoidable [ˌʌnə'vɔidibl] *a* inevitable, ineludible, ineluctible.
unaware ['ʌnə'wɛə] *a* inconsciente, sin percatarse; **to be — of** ignorar; *ad* —s de sorpresa, inopinadamente, de improviso; **to catch —** sorprender.
unbalanced ['ʌn'bælənst] *a* desequilibrado.
unbearable [ʌn'bɛərəbl] *a* insoportable, insufrible, inaguantable.
unbecoming ['ʌnbi'kʌmiŋ] *a* impropio, que sienta mal.
unbelievable [ˌʌnbi'li:vəbl] *a* increíble.
unbeliever ['ʌnbi'li:və] *n* incrédulo; descreído.
unbend ['ʌn'bend] *vti* enderezar; soltarse.
unbending ['ʌn'bendiŋ] *a* inflexible, estirado.
unbound ['ʌn'baund] *a* suelto; (*book*) sin encuadernar; en rústica.
unbounded [ʌn'baundid] *a* ilimitado, infinito, inconmensurable.
unbreakable [ʌn'breikəbl] *a* irrompible.
unbridled [ʌn'braidld] *a* desenfrenado, licencioso.
unbroken ['ʌn'broukən] *a* intacto, íntegro; (*horse*) indómito, cerril; ininterrumpido.
unburden [ʌn'bə:dn] *vt* descargar; aliviar(se); **to — oneself** franquearse, explayarse, desahogarse.
unbutton ['ʌn'bʌtn] *vt* desabrochar, desabotonar.
uncalled [ʌn'kɔ:ld] *a* **— for** indebido; gratuito; impropio.
uncanny [ʌn'kæni] *a* pavoroso; incauto, raro, misterioso.
unceremoniously ['ʌnˌseri'mouniəsli] *ad* sin empacho, familiarmente.
uncertain [ʌn'sə:tn] *a* incierto, perplejo, dudoso, indeciso, equívoco; indeterminado; precario, irresoluto.
uncertainty [ʌn'sə:tnti] *n* incertidumbre, duda, ambigüedad, irresolución.
unchangeable [ʌn'tʃeindʒəbl] *a* invariable, inalterable, inmutable.
unchanging [ʌn'tʃeindʒiŋ] *a* igual, inmutable, inalterable.
uncharitable [ʌn'tʃæritəbl] *a* poco caritativo.
uncivil ['ʌn'sivl] *a* incivil, descortés, grosero.
uncivilized ['ʌn'sivilaizd] *a* no civilizado, inculto, bárbaro.
uncle ['ʌŋkl] *n* tío.
unclean ['ʌn'kli:n] *a* sucio, desaseado; impuro.
unclouded ['ʌn'klaudid] *a* despejado, claro.
uncomfortable [ʌn'kʌmfətəbl] *a* incómodo, molesto, penoso.
uncomfortableness [ʌn'kʌmfətəblnis] *n* incomodidad, malestar; molestia.
uncommon [ʌn'kɔmən] *a* desusado, poco común, raro.
uncomplimentary ['ʌnˌkɔmpli'mentəri] *a* desfavorable, poco halagüeño.
uncompromising [ʌn'kɔmprəmaiziŋ] *a* inflexible, firme, intransigente.
unconcern ['ʌnkən'sə:n] *n* indiferencia, desapego.
unconcerned ['ʌnkən'sə:nd] *a* indiferente, despreocupado, despegado, desinteresado.
unconditional ['ʌnkən'diʃənl] *a* incondicional.
uncongenial ['ʌnkən'dʒi:niəl] *a* incompatible, antipático.
unconquerable [ʌn'kɔŋkərəbl] *a* indómito, invencible.
unconquered ['ʌn'kɔŋkəd] *a* no vencido.
unconscious [ʌn'kɔnʃəs] *a* inconsciente, insensible; sin sentido.
unconsciously [ʌn'kɔnʃəsli] *ad* inconscientemente, sin saber, sin darse cuenta.
unconsciousness [ʌn'kɔnʃəsnis] *n* inconsciencia, insensibilidad.
uncontrollable [ˌʌnkən'trouləbl] *a* indomable, irrefrenable.
unconventional ['ʌnkən'venʃənl] *a* informal, despreocupado.
unconventionality ['ʌnkənˌvenʃə'næliti] *n* informalidad.

uncork ['ʌn'kɔ:k] *vt* descorchar, destapar.
uncouth [ʌn'ku:θ] *a* torpe, desmañado; tosco, grotesco; extraño.
uncover [ʌn'kʌvə] *vti* descubrir(se), desnudar.
unction ['ʌŋkʃən] *n* unción, ungüento; **extreme —** extremaunción.
uncultivated ['ʌn'kʌltiveitid] *a* inculto, sin cultivar, baldío, yermo.
undamaged ['ʌn'dæmidʒd] *a* indemne, incólume, ileso.
undaunted [ʌn'dɔ:ntid] *a* intrépido, impávido.
undecided ['ʌndi'saidid] *a* indeciso, caviloso.
undefended ['ʌndi'fendid] *a* indefenso.
undefined [,ʌndi'faind] *a* indefinido.
undeniable [,ʌndi'naiəbl] *a* innegable.
under ['ʌndə] *a* inferior, subalterno. bajo; *ad* debajo, abajo, más abajo, menos; *prep* debajo de; menos de; en tiempo de; conforme a; según; **— him** a su mando, a sus órdenes; **— age** menor de edad; **— arms** bajo las armas; **— cover** a cubierto; **— cover of** al abrigo de; **— consideration** en consideración.
underclothes ['ʌndəklouðz] *n* ropa interior; (*fam*) paños menores.
underclothing ['ʌndə,klouðiŋ] *n* ropa interior; paños menores.
undercurrent ['ʌndə,kʌrənt] *n* resaca; **— of gossip** murmuración.
underestimate ['ʌndər'estimeit] *vt* estimar mal; menospreciar.
undergo [ʌndə'gou] *vt* experimentar, sufrir, padecer.
undergraduate [,ʌndə'grædjuit] *n* estudiante (no graduado).
underground ['ʌndəgraund] *a* subterráneo; clandestino; *ad* bajo tierra; oculto; **— railway** (*in city*) metro; *n* subterráneo.
undergrowth ['ʌndəgrouθ] *n* maleza.
underhand ['ʌndəhænd] *a* clandestino; solapado, poco limpio; *ad* clandestinamente, bajo cuerda.
underlie [,ʌndə'lai] *vi* servir de base.
underline ['ʌndə'lain] *vt* subrayar.
undermentioned ['ʌndə'menʃənd] *a* abajo citado.
undermine [,ʌndə'main] *vt* minar, socavar.
underneath [,ʌndə'ni:θ] *prep* bajo; debajo de; *ad* debajo.
underrate [,ʌndə'reit] *vt* rebajar, menospreciar.
undersell ['ʌndə'sel] *vt* vender a un precio más barato que.
underskirt ['ʌndəskə:t] *n* enagua, refajo; (*country girl's*) zagalejo.
understand [,ʌndə'stænd] *vt* entender, comprender, concebir, conocer, sobrentender; sacar (en limpio); *vi* comprender, caer en la cuenta, tener entendido; **that is understood** (está) entendido, por supuesto.
understandable [,ʌndə'stændəbl] *a* comprensible, inteligible.
understanding [,ʌndə'stændiŋ] *n* entendimiento, inteligencia, mente, intelecto, sentido; comprensión, interpretación; presupuesto; *a* entendedor; simpático.
undertake [,ʌndə'teik] *vti* emprender, acometer; comprometerse a.
undertaker [,ʌndə'teikə] *n* director de pompas fúnebres.
undertone ['ʌndətoun] *n* voz baja; rumor; resabio.
undervalue ['ʌndə'vælju:] *vt* menospreciar, despreciar, tasar en menos.
underwear ['ʌndəwɛə] *n* ropa interior.
undeserved ['ʌndi'zə:vd] *a* inmerecido.
undeserving ['ʌndi'zə:viŋ] *a* inmerecedor.
undesirable ['ʌndi'zaiərəbl] *a* indeseable.
undeveloped ['ʌndi'veləpt] *a* sin desarrollar, rudimentario.
undigested ['ʌndi'dʒestid] *a* indigesto, no digerido, sin digerir.
undigestible ['ʌndi'dʒestəbl] *a* indigesto.
undignified [ʌn'dignifaid] *a* poco digno, ordinario, sin dignidad.
undiminished ['ʌndi'miniʃt] *a* íntegro, completo, sin diminución.
undiscovered ['ʌndis'kʌvəd] *a* ignorado, ignoto.
undismayed ['ʌndis'meid] *a* impertérrito.
undisputed ['ʌndis'pju:tid] *a* incontestable.
undisturbed ['ʌndis'tə:bd] *a* impasible, tranquilo, sereno.
undivided ['ʌndi'vaidid] *a* indiviso, entero, íntegro.
undo ['ʌn'du:] *vt* deshacer, arruinar; afligir.
undone ['ʌn'dʌn] *a* sin hacer, deshecho; arruinado.
undoubted [ʌn'dautid] *a* fuera de duda, indubitable, indudable.
undress ['ʌn'dres] *n* desabillé; paños menores; (*mil*) traje de cuartel; *vti* desnudar, desnudarse.
undue ['ʌn'dju:] *a* indebido, desmedido; injusto.
undulate ['ʌndjuleit] *vi* ondular, fluctuar.
undulating ['ʌndju:leitiŋ] *a* ondulante, undoso; (*land*) ondulado, quebrado.
undying [ʌn'daiiŋ] *a* imperecedero, perpetuo.
unearth ['ʌn'ə:θ] *vt* desenterrar.
uneasiness [ʌn'i:zinis] *n* incomodidad, intranquilidad, malestar, desasosiego, desazón.
uneasy [ʌn'i:zi] *a* desasosegado, inquieto, intranquilo, molesto; trabajoso.
uneducated ['ʌn'edjukeitid] *a* poco

instruido, sin educacion, lego; indocto; inculto.
unemployed ['ʌnim'plɔid] *a* parado; sin empleo; (*civil servant*) cesante; desocupado.
unemployment ['ʌnim'plɔimənt] *n* desocupación, paro; (*of white-collar workers*) cesantía.
unending [ʌn'endiŋ] *a* infinito, inacabable, sin fin.
unenviable ['ʌn'enviəbl] *a* poco envidiable.
unequal ['ʌn'i:kwəl] *a* desigual, dispar; parcial; **to be — to** no tener fuerzas para.
unequaled ['ʌn'i:kwəld] *a* inmejorable.
unerring ['ʌn'ə:riŋ] *a* infalible; seguro.
uneven ['ʌn'i:vən] *a* desigual, desnivelado, escabroso, quebrado; (*number*) impar, accidentado.
unevenness ['ʌn'i:vənis] *n* escabrosidad, desigualdad, abolladura, desajuste, desnivel.
unexpected ['ʌniks'pektid] *a* inesperado, de improviso, repentino, inopinado, impensado.
unexpectedly ['ʌniks'pektidli] *ad* inesperadamente, de manos a boca, a la improvista, de rondón.
unfading [ʌn'feidiŋ] *a* inmarcesible; inmarchitable.
unfailing [ʌn'feiliŋ] *a* infalible, indefectible, inagotable.
unfair ['ʌn'fɛə] *a* doble, falso, injusto, sin equidad; (*play*) sucio, tramposo.
unfairness ['ʌn'fɛənis] *n* mala fe, deslealtad.
unfaithful ['ʌn'feiθful] *a* infiel, pérfido.
unfaithfulness ['ʌn'feiθfulnis] *n* infidelidad.
unfamiliar ['ʌnfə'miliə] *a* poco común, desconocido, extraño.
unfasten ['ʌn'fɑ:sn] *vt* soltar, aflojar, desatar.
unfathomable [ʌn'fæðəməbl] *a* insondable, sin fondo.
unfavorable ['ʌn'feivərəbl] *a* desfavorable, contrario, adverso.
unfinished ['ʌn'finiʃt] *a* inacabado, inconcluso, incompleto; imperfecto; crudo.
unfit ['ʌn'fit] *a* impropio; inepto; incapaz, inhábil, inoportuno; *vt* descalificar.
unfitness ['ʌn'fitnis] *n* ineptitud, impropiedad.
unfold ['ʌn'fould] *vt* desplegar; desdoblar; (*system*) desarrollar; (*idea*) exponer, explanar.
unforgettable ['ʌnfə'getəbl] *a* inolvidable.
unforeseen ['ʌnfɔ:'si:n] *a* imprevisto, inopinado.
unforgiving ['ʌnfə'giviŋ] *a* implacable, intransigente.
unfortunate [ʌn'fɔ:tʃnit] *a* (*person*) infortunado, desgraciado, desafortunado; cuitado, malogrado; (*event*) inconveniente, funesto, malhadado.
unfortunately [ʌn'fɔ:tʃnitli] *ad* por desgracia.
unfounded ['ʌn'faundid] *a* sin fundamento; infundado.
unfrequented ['ʌnfri'kwentid] *a* solitario, poco trillado, de poco tránsito.
unfriendly ['ʌn'frendli] *a* poco amistoso, hostil.
unfurl [ʌn'fə:l] *vt* desplegar.
ungainly [ʌn'geinli] *a* torpe, sin gracia, desmañado.
ungentlemanly [ʌn'dʒentlmənli] *a* impropio de un caballero.
ungovernable [ʌn'gʌvənəbl] *a* ingobernable, díscolo.
ungrateful [ʌn'greitful] *a* ingrato, desagradecido.
unguarded ['ʌn'gɑ:did] *a* desguarnecido; indefenso; desprevenido, desapercibido; incauto.
unhappiness [ʌn'hæpinis] *n* desdicha, infortunio, pena, desgracia.
unhappy [ʌn'hæpi] *a* (*person*) infeliz, desdichado, desgraciado; (*event*) infausto, aciago.
unharmed ['ʌn'hɑ:md] *a* incólume, ileso, sano y salvo.
unhealthy [ʌn'helθi] *a* malsano; (*person*) achacoso.
unheard ['ʌn'hə:d] *a* **— of** inaudito.
unheeded ['ʌn'hi:did] *a* inadvertido.
unhesitatingly [ʌn'heziteitiŋli] *ad* sin vacilación, resueltamente.
unhinge [ʌn'hindʒ] *vt* desquiciar; sacar de quicio; quitar los goznes.
unhook ['ʌn'huk] *vt* descolgar, desenganchar; desabrochar.
unhurt ['ʌn'hə:t] *a* indemne, ileso.
uniform ['ju:nifɔ:m] *n* librea; (*mil*) uniforme; *a* igual, uniforme; constante.
unify ['ju:nifai] *vt* unificar, unir.
unimpaired ['ʌnim'pɛəd] *a* inalterado, sin menoscabo, ileso.
unimportant ['ʌnim'pɔ:tənt] *a* insignificante, baladí, trivial.
uninformed ['ʌnin'fɔ:md] *a* inculto, poco al tanto, poco enterado.
uninhabited ['ʌnin'hæbitid] *a* inhabitado.
uninhibited ['ʌnin'hibitid] *a* desahogado.
uninjured ['ʌn'indʒəd] *a* ileso, incólume, intacto, sin dañar.
unintelligible ['ʌnin'telidʒəbl] *a* ininteligible.
unintentional ['ʌnin'tenʃənl] *a* involuntario.
unintentionally ['ʌnin'tenʃənli] *a* sin querer, involuntariamente.
uninteresting ['ʌn'intristiŋ] *a* soso, falto de interés, insípido.
uninterrupted ['ʌn,intə'rʌptid] *a* ininterrumpido, continuo, seguido.
union ['ju:njən] *n* unión, fusión,

enlace; trabazón; mancomunidad; gremio, nudo.
unique [ju:'ni:k] *a* único, excepcional, singular, sin par.
unison ['ju:nizn] *n* armonía, concordancia; *a* unísono.
unit ['ju:nit] *n* unidad.
unite [ju:'nait] *vti* combinar, juntar(se), unir(se), coligarse.
united [ju'naitid] *a* conjunto.
unitedly [ju'naitidli] *ad* a una, de acuerdo, juntamente.
unity ['ju:niti] *n* unidad, unión, concordia.
universal [,ju:ni'və:səl] *a* universal, católico.
universe ['ju:niv:əs] *n* universo.
university [,ju:ni'və:siti] *n* universidad.
unjust ['ʌn'dʒʌst] *a* injusto, inicuo.
unjustifiable [ʌn'dʒʌstifaiəbl] *a* injustificable, sin base.
unkempt ['ʌn'kempt] *a* desgreñado; descuidado.
unkind [ʌn'kaind] *a* áspero, poco amable, antipático, poco generoso, cruel.
unkindness [ʌn'kaindnis] *n* maltrato, falta de compasión; desafecto, malignidad, aspereza.
unknowingly ['ʌn'nouiŋli] *ad* sin saber.
unknown ['ʌn'noun] *a* (*person*) desconocido; incógnito; (*fact*) ignorado; (*work*) inédito; incierto.
unlawful ['ʌn'lɔ:ful] *a* ilegal, ilegítimo, ilícito; — **interest** usura.
unless [ən'les] *conj* a menos que; a no ser que, salvo.
unlike ['ʌn'laik] *a* diferente, distinto, desemejante, dispar.
unlikelihood [ʌn'laiklihud] *n* improbabilidad.
unlikely [ʌn'laikli] *a* improbable, remoto; (*to be true*) inverosímil.
unlimited [ʌn'limitid] *a* ilimitado.
unload ['ʌn'loud] *vt* descargar.
unlock ['ʌn'lɔk] *vt* abrir; dar libre acceso; revelar.
unlooked [ʌn'lukt] *a* — **for** imprevisto, inesperado.
unloose ['ʌn'lu:s] *vt* soltar, desatar, aflojar.
unlucky [ʌn'lʌki] *a* desgraciado, desdichado, infeliz, desafortunado, malogrado; funesto, nefasto.
unmanageable [ʌn'mænidʒəbl] *a* inmanejable, indómito, indomable, ingobernable.
unmannerly [ʌn'mænəli] *a* descortés, grosero, desatento.
unmarried ['ʌn'mærid] *a* soltero, célibe.
unmerited ['ʌn'meritid] *a* inmerecido.
unmindful [ʌn'maindful] *a* olvidadizo, desatento, descuidado.
unmistakable ['ʌnmis'teikəbl] *a* claro, neto, inequívoco, inconfundible.
unmitigated [ʌn'mitigeitid] *a* duro; (*rogue*) redomado.
unmixed ['ʌn'mikst] *a* puro, sin mezcla, sencillo.
unmoved ['ʌn'mu:vd] *a* inmoble, fijo, impasible, sordo.
unnatural [ʌn'nætʃrəl] *a* desnaturalizado, antinatural, monstruoso, inhumano, forzado, ficticio.
unnecessary [ʌn'nesisəri] *a* innecesario, superfluo, gratuito, excusado; **to make** — obviar; **to be** — estar de más.
unnerve ['ʌn'nə:v] *vt* enervar, desalentar; aturdir.
unnoticed ['ʌn'noutist] *a* desapercibido, inadvertido.
unobservant ['ʌnəb'zə:vənt] *a* inobservante, inatento.
unobserved ['ʌnəb'zə:vd] *a* inadvertido; *ad* con disimulación, sin ser visto.
unoccupied ['ʌn'ɔkjupaid] *a* desocupado, vacante, vacío, vacuo.
unofficial ['ʌnə'fiʃəl] *a* no oficial.
unorthodox ['ʌn'ɔ:θədɔks] *a* heterodoxo.
unpack ['ʌn'pæk] *vt* (*luggage*) deshacer; (*goods*) desembalar, desempacar.
unpaid ['ʌn'peid] *a* no pagado; (*post*) honorario; — **bills** cuentas por pagar.
unparalleled [ʌn'pærəleld] *a* incomparable, sin igual, no igualado.
unpardonable [ʌn'pɑ:dnəbl] *a* imperdonable.
unperturbed ['ʌnpə'tə:bd] *a* quieto, sereno.
unpleasant [ʌn'pleznt] *a* desagradable, malsonante, desabrido, enfadoso, ingrato; (*subject*) escabroso.
unpleasantness [ʌn'plezntnis] *n* desagrado, sinsabor, disgusto; (*weather*) desapacibilidad; (*quarrel*) desavenencia.
unpleasing ['ʌn'pli:ziŋ] *a* desagradable, displicente, ofensivo, molesto.
unpolished ['ʌn'pɔliʃt] *a* en bruto, mate, sin brillo; áspero, tosco.
unpopular ['ʌn'pɔpjulə] *a* antipático; malquisto; impopular.
unprecedented [ʌn'presidəntid] *a* inaudito, sin ejemplo.
unprejudiced [ʌn'predʒudist] *a* imparcial, despreocupado.
unprepared ['ʌnpri'pɛəd] *a* sin preparación, desprevenido, descuidado.
unpretentious ['ʌnpri'tenʃəs] *a* modesto, sin pretensiones.
unprincipled [ʌn'prinsəpld] *a* chulo, sin principios, poco escrupuloso.
unproductive ['ʌnprə'dʌktiv] *a* improductivo, estéril, infructífero.
unprofitable [ʌn'prɔfitəbl] *a* desventajoso, poco provechoso, no lucrativo, improductivo.
unprotected ['ʌnprə'tektid] *a* indefenso, desvalido; (*mil*) a cureña rasa.

unpublished ['ʌn'pʌbliʃt] *a* inédito.
unpunished ['ʌn'pʌniʃt] *a* impune.
unqualified ['ʌn'kwɔlifaid] *a* incapaz, desautorizado; incompetente; incondicional, absoluto, entero, inhabilitado.
unquenchable [ʌn'kwentʃəbl] *a* inextinguible, inapagable, insaciable.
unquestionable [ʌn'kwestʃənəbl] *a* incuestionable, indudable, indiscutible.
unravel [ʌn'rævəl] *vt* desenredar, desenmarañar, deshilar.
unreadiness [ʌn'redinis] *n* lentitud, desprevención.
unready ['ʌn'redi] *a* desprevenido, desapercibido.
unreal ['ʌn'riəl] *a* irreal, ilusorio, quimérico, ideal; fantástico, incorpóreo.
unreasonable [ʌn'ri:znəbl] *a* inmoderado; irracional, inconsecuente, exorbitante.
unreasonableness [ʌn'ri:znəblnis] *n* sinrazón, despropósito.
unrecognizable ['ʌn'rekəgnaizəbl] *a* desconocido, irreconocible.
unrelenting ['ʌnri'lentiŋ] *a* inexorable.
unreliable ['ʌnri'laiəbl] *a* caprichoso, poco serio, informal, no fiable.
unrepentant ['ʌnri'pentənt] *a* impenitente.
unrequited ['ʌnri'kwaitid] *a* no correspondido.
unreserved ['ʌnri'zə:vd] *a* ingenuo, sin reserva, comunicativo.
unrest ['ʌn'rest] *n* inquietud, intranquilidad, desazón.
unrestrained ['ʌnris'treind] *a* desenfrenado; *ad* a rienda suelta.
unrestricted ['ʌnris'triktid] *a* sin restricción.
unrewarded ['ʌnri'wɔ:did] *a* sin recompensa.
unripe ['ʌn'raip] *a* verde, crudo, inmaturo.
unrivaled [ʌn'raivəld] *a* sin rival, incomparable.
unroll ['ʌn'roul] *vt* desenrollar, desenvolver.
unruffled ['ʌn'rʌfld] *a* tranquilo, impasible, sin dar(se) por aludido, sereno, sin inmutarse.
unruly [ʌn'ru:li] *a* indócil, rebelde, levantisco; indomable; revoltoso.
unsafe ['ʌn'seif] *a* inseguro.
unsatisfactory ['ʌn,sætis'fæktəri] *a* insuficiente, inconcluso, poco convincente.
unsavory ['ʌn'seivəri] *a* insípido, soso; desabrido; de mala fama, indeseable; (*smell*) hediondo.
unscalable ['ʌn'skeiləbl] *a* infranqueable.
unscathed ['ʌn'skeiðd] *a* ileso.
unscrupulous [ʌn'skrupjuləs] *a* poco escrupuloso, desaprensivo, sin miramientos.
unseal ['ʌn'si:l] *vt* desellar, abrir.
unseasonable [ʌn'si:znəbl] *a* intempestivo, inoportuno.
unseasonably [ʌn'si:znəbli] *ad* en agraz; a deshora, a destiempo.
unseaworthy ['ʌn'si:wə:ði] *a* innavegable, sin condiciones marineras.
unseemly [ʌn'si:mli] *a* indecoroso, indecente.
unseen ['ʌn'si:n] *a* invisible, inadvertido.
unselfish ['ʌn'selfiʃ] *a* desinteresado, desprendido, abnegado.
unsettle ['ʌn'setl] *vt* perturbar, alterar; trastornar.
unsettled ['ʌn'setld] *a* instable, inconstante; incierto; (*weather*) variable; pendiente, revuelto.
unshakable [ʌn'ʃeikəbl] *a* impertérrito, inmóvil.
unsheltered [ʌn'ʃeltəd] *a* desabrigado, desamparado.
unsightliness [ʌn'saitlinis] *n* fealdad, deformidad.
unsightly [ʌn'saitli] *a* disforme, feo, antiestético.
unskilled ['ʌn'skild] *a* inhábil, imperito, lego, torpe.
unsociable [ʌn'souʃəbl] *a* insociable, huraño, intratable; **— person** búho.
unsound ['ʌn'saund] *a* insano, defectuoso; (*beliefs*) heterodoxo; erróneo; **of — mind** extraviado; podrido; inseguro.
unsparing [ʌn'spεəriŋ] *a* pródigo, liberal; implacable.
unspeakable [ʌn'spi:kəbl] *a* inefable, inexpresable; indecible, inaudito.
unstable ['ʌn'steibl] *a* inestable, vacilante, mudable, fugitivo.
unsteadily ['ʌn'stedili] *ad* irregularmente, sin constancia.
unsteadiness ['ʌn'stedinis] *n* inconstancia, ligereza, movilidad.
unsteady ['ʌn'stedi] *a* (*affections*) inconstante; (*belief etc*) incierto; (*ground etc*) movedizo, poco firme.
unsubstantial ['ʌnsəb'stænʃəl] *a* ilusorio, imaginario.
unsuccessful ['ʌnsək'sesful] *a* infeliz, sin efecto, fracasado, desgraciado; **to be —** tener (poco, ningún) éxito.
unsuccessfully ['ʌnsək'sesfuli] *ad* sin éxito.
unsuitability ['ʌn,su:tə'biliti] *n* impropiedad.
unsuitable ['ʌn'su:təbl] *a* inconveniente, inadecuado, impropio, indigno, incongruo.
unsuitableness ['ʌn'su:təblnis] *n* inconveniencia.
unsullied ['ʌn'sʌlid] *a* puro, sin mancha.
unsurmountable ['ʌnsə'mauntəbl] *a* insuperable, infranqueable.
unsurpassable ['ʌnsə'pɑ:səbl] *a* inmejorable.
unsurpassed ['ʌnsə'pɑ:st] *a* insuperado, inmejorable.

unsuspecting ['ʌnsəs'pektiŋ] *a* desprevenido; confiado, sin recelo.
unsympathetic ['ʌn,simpə'θetik] *a* poco simpático, antipático, poco amable.
untamable ['ʌn'teiməbl] *a* indomable.
untamed ['ʌn'teimd] *a* bravío, indomado.
untangle ['ʌn'tæŋgl] *vt* desembarazar.
untasted ['ʌn'teistid] *a* sin (gustar, probar).
untenable ['ʌn'tenəbl] *a* insostenible.
unthinking ['ʌn'θiŋkiŋ] *a* descuidado, desatento.
untidy [ʌn'taidi] *a* desaliñado; (*in dress*) estrafalario; desarreglado, desordenado.
untie ['ʌn'tai] *vt* soltar, desatar.
until [ən'til] *prep cj* hasta, hasta que.
untilled ['ʌn'tild] *a* inculto, baldío; **— land** erial.
untimely [ʌn'taimli] *a* intempestivo; inoportuno; prematuro, inesperado.
untiring [ʌn'taiəriŋ] *a* incansable, infatigable.
untold ['ʌn'tould] *a* no dicho, incalculable; **to leave —** dejar en el tintero.
untouched ['ʌn'tʌtʃt] *a* incólume, sin tocar, íntegro.
untoward [ʌn'touəd] *a* indócil, terco; embarazoso, desgraciado; enojoso; funesto.
untrained ['ʌn'treind] *a* indisciplinado, indócil; inexperto.
untranslatable ['ʌntræns'leitəbl] *a* intraducible.
untrodden ['ʌn'trɔdn] *a* no pisado.
untroubled ['ʌn'trʌbld] *a* tranquilo, apacible.
untrue ['ʌn'tru:] *a* falso, mendaz; pérfido.
untrustworthy ['ʌn'trʌst,wə:ði] *a* indigno de confianza.
untruth ['ʌn'tru:θ] *n* mentira, falsedad.
untutored ['ʌn'tju:təd] *a* ignorante, llano, inculto.
unused ['ʌn'ju:zd] *a* no acostumbrado, desusado.
unusual [ʌn'ju:ʒuəl] *a* insólito, inusitado, extraordinario, excepcional.
unutterable [ʌn'ʌtərəbl] *a* indecible, inefable, imponderable.
unvanquished [ʌn'væŋkwiʃt] *a* invicto.
unvarnished ['ʌn'vɑ:niʃt] *a* sencillo, sin barniz(ar).
unveil [ʌn'veil] *vt* descubrir.
unwariness [ʌn'wɛərinis] *n* imprudencia, imprevisión.
unwarranted ['ʌn'wɔrəntid] *a* injustificado, inmotivado.
unwary [ʌn'wɛəri] *a* incauto, imprudente, aturdido.
unwelcome [ʌn'welkəm] *a* importuno, mal acogido, indeseable.
unwell ['ʌn'wel] *a* indispuesto, enfermizo.
unwieldy [ʌn'wi:ldi] *a* pesado, ingente; **— object** armatoste.
unwilling ['ʌn'wiliŋ] *a* desinclinado, maldispuesto.
unwillingly [ʌn'wiliŋli] *a* sin gana, de mala gana; a regañadientes, con repugnancia.
unwillingness [ʌn'wiliŋnis] *n* mala voluntad; repugnancia.
unwise ['ʌn'waiz] *a* imprudente, indiscreto.
unwitting [ʌn'witiŋ] *a* inconsciente.
unwittingly [ʌn'witiŋli] *ad* sin saber; a ciegas, ignorantemente.
unwonted [ʌn'wountid] *a* raro, no usual, inusitado, desacostumbrado.
unworthiness [ʌn'wə:ðinis] *n* indignidad.
unworthy [ʌn'wə:ði] *a* indigno.
unwounded ['ʌn'wu:ndid] *a* ileso, sin herida.
unwrap ['ʌn'ræp] *vt* desenvolver.
unwritten ['ʌn'ritn] *a* no escrito; **— letters** cartas por escribir.
unyielding [ʌn'ji:ldiŋ] *a* implacable, inflexible, inquebrantable, terco.
up [ʌp] *a* levantado, derecho; **well — in** bien enterado; a la altura de; **— train** tren ascendente; *ad* (hacia) arriba, en lo alto, (en, de) pie; encima; **— to** dispuesto para; capaz de; hasta; **what's —?** ¿qué pasa?, ¿de qué se trata?; **to sit —** (*in bed*) incorporarse; **it's all —** todo se acabó; **drink it —** bébelo todo; **—hill** cuesta arriba; trabajoso; **—stream** río arriba; **—stairs** arriba; **—-to-date** al día; **— and down** por todas partes, arriba y abajo; *interj* arriba; *n* **—s and downs** altibajos, peripecias; *prep* hacia arriba, en lo alto de; **—country** en el interior del país, tierra adentro; **to go —country** internarse; **to sail — a river** remontar un río.
upbraid [ʌp'breid] *vt* reprochar, reconvenir, echar en cara, zaherir.
upheaval [ʌp'hi:vəl] *n* trastorno; sublevación.
uphill ['ʌp'hil] *a* trabajoso; *ad* cuesta arriba.
uphold [ʌp'hould] *vt* sostener, proteger, apoyar.
upholster [ʌp'houlstə] *vt* almohadillar, entapizar, tapizar.
upkeep ['ʌpki:p] *n* entretenimiento.
upland ['ʌplənd] *n* tierras altas, tierra adentro; **bare —s** estepa.
uplift [ʌp'lift] *vt* levantar, alzar, soliviantar.
upon [ə'pɔn] *prep* sobre, encima, en, cerca de; **— oath** bajo juramento; **— pain of death** so pena de muerte.
upper ['ʌpə] *a* superior, más alto; **U— House** cámara alta; **U— Orinoco** el alto Orinoco; *pl* (*shoes*) pala.

uppermost ['ʌpəmoust] *a* supremo, el más alto; predominante.
upright ['ʌprait] *a* vertical, derecho, a plomo; (*person*) probo, íntegro, honrado.
uprising [ʌp'raiziŋ] *n* levantamiento, pronunciamiento.
uproar ['ʌp,rɔ:] *n* tumulto, grita; batahola, alboroto; **to cause —** escandalizar, alborotar.
uproarious [ʌp'rɔ:riəs] *a* tumultuoso, ruidoso, clamoroso.
uproot [ʌp'ru:t] *vt* desarraigar, arrancar de cuajo.
upset [ʌp'set] *a* trastornado, escamado, preocupado; contrariado; *n* trastorno; vuelco; contrariedad; *vt* trastornar, turbar, alterar, inquietar; (*objects*) volcar, tumbar.
upside-down ['ʌpsaid'daun] *ad* boca abajo, en sentido inverso.
upstart ['ʌpstɑ:t] *n* advenedizo.
upward(s) ['ʌpwəd(s)] *ad* hacia arriba, en adelante; en alto.
urban ['ə:bən] *a* urbano, ciudadano.
urbanity [ə:'bæniti] *n* urbanidad, cortesía, civilidad, cultura, comedimiento.
urchin ['ə:tʃin] *n* pillo, pilluelo, granuja, golilla, chiquillo.
urge [ə:dʒ] *n* impulso; *vt* urgir, apremiar, instigar, estimular; **to — on** instar, impelar, apresurar; importunar.
urgency ['ə:dʒənsi] *n* urgencia, premura, insistencia.
urgent ['ə:dʒənt] *a* urgente, premioso, apremiante, perentorio, importante.
urn [ə:n] *n* urna.
us [ʌs] *pn* nos, (*after prep*) nosotros.
usage ['ju:sidʒ] *n* uso, costumbre, usanza; **ill-—** maltrato.
use [ju:s] *n* uso, costumbre, hábito, práctica, empleo; provecho, disfrute; (*law*) usufructo; **out of —** inusitado, fuera de moda; **to be of —** hacer uso de, servirse de, valerse de, prevalerse de; **to make good — of** aprovecharse de; **to make no good — of** desaprovechar; **to put to —** poner en uso, sacar partido de; **to put to full —** explotar; ['ju:z] *vt* usar, emplear, gastar, estilar, valerse de; hacer uso de; tratar; **to — up** gastar, agotar; *vi* acostumbrar; soler.
used [ju:zd] *a* gastado; **to get — to** habituarse a, acostumbrarse a; **to be — to** soler.
useful ['ju:sful] *a* útil, cómodo, de provecho; fructuoso.
usefulness ['ju:sfulnis] *n* utilidad, provecho.
useless ['ju:slis] *a* inútil; inválido; (*person*) inepto, ocioso; (*of no avail*) excusado, vano.
uselessness ['ju:slisnis] *n* inutilidad, vanidad.
user ['ju:zə] *n* el que utiliza.
usher ['ʌʃə] *n* ujier, conserje; (*theat*) acomodador; *vt* introducir; acomodar.
usual ['ju:ʒuəl] *a* usual, acostumbrado, corriente, ordinario.
usually ['ju:ʒuəli] *ad* de ordinario, ordinariamente; **it — happens** suele ocurrir.
usurp [ju:'zə:p] *vt* usurpar; arrogarse.
usurper [ju:'zə:pə] *n* usurpador.
usury ['ju:ʒuri] *n* usura; logro.
utensil [ju:'tensl] *n* utensilio, apero, herramienta.
utility [ju:'tiliti] *n* utilidad, beneficio, partido, provecho.
utilize ['ju:tilaiz] *vt* utilizar; aprovechar, emplear, explotar.
utmost ['ʌtmoust] *a* extremo; el mayor, sumo; **to the —** hasta no más; **the — ends** las extremidades; **to be of the — importance** urgir.
Utopian [ju:'toupiən] *a* utópico, ideal.
utter ['ʌtə] *a* total; cabal, sumo, perentorio; *vt* proferir, articular; manifestar, emitir; **to — a sound** chistar; (*sigh*) exhalar.
utterance ['ʌtərəns] *n* expresión, pronunciación.
utterly ['ʌtəli] *ad* hasta no más, del todo, completamente, enteramente.

V

vacancy ['veikənsi] *n* vacío, hueco; vacuidad, vacancia; (*employment etc*) vacante, vacío.
vacant ['veikənt] *a* vacante, desocupado, libre, vacio, hueco; (*stupid*) vago, estólido.
vacate [və'keit] *vt* evacuar; vaciar; dejar vacante, desocupar.
vacation [və'keiʃən] *n* vacación, asueto; vacaciones.
vacationist [və'keiʃənist] *n* excursionista, turista, veraneante.
vaccinate ['væksineit] *vt* vacunar.
vaccine ['væksi:n] *n* vacuna.
vacuum ['vækjuəm] *n* vacuo; vacío; **—bottle** termos; **—cleaner** aspirador.
vagabond ['vægəbənd] *a* vagabundo, errante, gandul; *n* vago, vagabundo.
vagary ['veigəri] *n* desvarío, capricho, humorada, antojo.
vague [veig] *a* vago, confuso, indefinido, brumoso, dudoso.
vagueness ['veignis] *n* vaguedad.
vain [vein] *a* (*pride*) vano, vanidoso, presumido, presuntuoso; confiado; (*show*) ostentoso; (*useless*) vano, inútil; (*empty*) hueco, fútil; **in —** en vano, de balde; **to grow —** envanecerse.
vale [veil] *n* valle, cañada; **— of tears** valle de lágrimas.
valiant ['væljənt] *a* valiente, valeroso, alentado, esforzado.
valid ['vælid] *a* válido, valedero.

validity [və'liditi] *n* validez.
valise [və'li:z] *n* maleta, valija.
Valladolid [ˌvælədə'lid] (*native*) **of** — vallesoletano.
valley ['væli] *n* valle; **high** — nava; **river** — cuenca.
valor ['vælə] *n* valor, valentía, coraje, ánimo, animosidad, braveza, brío, bizarría.
valuable ['væljuəbl] *a* valioso, costoso, preciado, precioso; **—s** objetos de valor, joyas, alhajas.
valuation [ˌvælju'eiʃən] *n* valuación; valía; (*legal*) tasa(ción), justiprecio, estimación, (*goods at customs*) aforo.
value ['vælju:] *n* valor, valía, mérito; importe, monta; aprecio, estimación; **of great** — de gran coste, valiosísimo; *vt* (a)valuar, valorar, tasar; estimar, apreciar, tener en mucho, dar importancia a.
valued ['vælju:d] *a* apreciable.
valueless ['vælju:lis] *a* sin valor.
valve [vælv] *n* válvula, sopapo; **safety** — válvula de escape.
vampire ['væmpaiə] *n* vampiro; (*fam*) vampiresa.
van [væn] *n* (*motor*) camión; (*horse*) carro; (*mil*) vanguardia.
vanguard ['vængɑ:d] *n* vanguardia.
vanish ['væniʃ] *vi* desvanecerse, disiparse, desaparecer.
vanity ['væniti] *n* vanidad, hinchazón; humos; fatuidad, presunción, engreimiento; alarde.
vanquish ['væŋkwiʃ] *vt* vencer, conquistar, rendir.
vapid ['væpid] *a* insípido, insulso.
vapor ['veipə] *n* vapor; vaho, exhalación; hálito.
vaporous ['veipərəs] *a* vaporoso, etéreo; quimérico.
variable ['vɛəriəbl] *a* variable, vario, inconstante, mudable; veleidoso, versátil.
variance ['vɛəriəns] *n* discrepancia, desavenencia; variación; **at** — en desacuerdo, de punta, discordes.
variation [ˌvɛəri'eiʃən] *n* variación, cambio, variedad.
varied ['vɛərid] *a* ameno.
variegated ['vɛərigeitid] *a* vario, abigarrado, matizado.
variety [və'raiəti] *n* variedad, diversidad; (*goods*) surtido; **to add pleasant — to** amenizar.
various ['vɛəriəs] *a* vario, diverso; mudable.
varnish ['vɑ:niʃ] *n* barniz; *vt* barnizar; vidriar; encubrir.
vary ['vɛəri] *vti* variar, modificar, cambiar; discrepar, estar en desacuerdo.
vase [vɑ:z] *n* vaso, jarrón.
vassal ['væsəl] *n* vasallo, súbdito; esclavo.
vast [vɑ:st] *a* vasto, enorme, inmenso, ilimitado, dilatado.
vastness ['vɑ:stnis] *n* vastedad, inmensidad.
vaudeville ['voudəvil] *n* vaudeville, teatro de variedades.
vault [vɔ:lt] *n* bóveda; cripta; bodega; salto, voltereta; *vti* abovedar; voltear, saltar.
vaulted ['vɔ:ltid] *a* abovedado.
veer [viə] *vi* **to — around** virar, revirar, girar, dirigir.
vegetable ['vedʒitəbl] *n* vegetal, legumbre; — **seller** verdulera; **green —s** verduras; — **garden** huerta.
vegetate ['vedʒiteit] *vi* vegetar.
vegetation [ˌvedʒi'teiʃən] *n* vegetación.
vehemence ['vi:iməns] *n* viveza, impetuosidad, ardor.
vehement ['vi:imənt] *a* vehemente, impetuoso, vivo, caluroso, acalorado, fogoso.
vehicle ['vi:ikl] *n* vehículo; (*any two-wheeled*) carruaje.
veil [veil] *n* velo; cortina; (*heavy*) rebujo; **to take the** — tomar el velo; profesar; *vt* velar, esconder, disfrazar, encubrir, disimular.
vein [vein] *n* (*blood*) vena; (*mineral*) veta, filón; *vt* vetear.
vellum ['veləm] *n* pergamino, vitela.
velocity [vi'lɔsiti] *n* velocidad, celeridad.
velvet ['velvit] *a* aterciopelado; *n* terciopelo.
veneer [vi'niə] *n* chapa; capa exterior, baño, barniz; *vt* (en)chapar; revestir; tapar.
venerable ['venərəbl] *a* venerable.
venerate ['venəreit] *vt* venerar, reverenciar.
veneration [ˌvenə'reiʃən] *n* veneración, culto.
Venetian [vi'ni:ʃən] *a* — **blind** persiana, celosía.
Venezuela [ˌvene'zweilə] *n* Venezuela.
Venezuelan [ˌvenə'zweilən] *an* venezolano.
vengeance ['vendʒəns] *n* venganza.
vengeful ['vendʒful] *a* vengativo, rencoroso.
venial ['vi:niəl] *a* venial, leve.
venison ['venzn] *n* (carne de) venado.
venom ['venəm] *n* veneno, ponzoña; (*fig*) rencor, inquina.
venomous ['venəməs] *a* venenoso, ponzoñoso; maligno, rencoroso.
vent [vent] *n* respiradero; tronera, lumbrera; resolladero; (*artil*) fogón; venteo; **to give — to** dar (rienda suelta a, expresión, salida a), dejar escapar; expresar, desahogar(se); *vt* descargar, desahogar; (*fury*) ensañarse en.
ventilate ['ventileit] *vt* ventilar, airear, orear.
ventriloquist [ven'triləkwist] *n* ventrílocuo.
venture ['ventʃə] *n* riesgo, peligro;

empresa; albur; **at a —** al azar, a la ventura; *vti* aventurar; osar, aventurarse, atreverse, arriesgarse; **to — on** arrojarse a, probar suerte.
venturesome ['ventʃəsəm] *a* atrevido, osado, arrojado, emprendedor.
veracity [ve'ræsiti] *n* veracidad.
veranda [və'rændə] (*around inner court*) cenador; galería, balcón, terraza.
verb [və:b] *n* verbo.
verbatim [və:'beitim] *ad* palabra por palabra, al pie de la letra.
verbose [və:'bous] *a* verboso, locuaz, hinchado, difuso.
verbosity [və:'bɔsiti] *n* ampulosidad, palabrería, labia, verbosidad.
verdant ['və:dənt] *a* verde, fresco.
verdict ['və:dikt] *n* decisión, juicio; (*law*) fallo, sentencia, veredicto.
verdure ['və:dʒə] *n* verdura; lo verde.
verge [və:dʒ] *n* borde, margen; **on the —** a punto de, a dos dedos de, en vísperas de.
verger ['və:dʒə] *n* sacristán, pertiguero.
verify ['verifai] *vt* verificar, comprobar, cerciorarse de; depurar; cumplir.
veritable ['veritəbl] *a* verdadero.
vermilion [və'miljən] *n* bermellón; *a* bermejo.
vermin ['və:min] *n* bichos, sabandija; ratones, parásitos; (*foxes etc*) alimaña.
vernacular [və'nækjulə] *a* vernáculo, nativo.
versatile ['və:sətail] *a* versátil, voluble.
versatility [ˌvə:sə'tiliti] *n* versatilidad; inconstancia.
verse [və:s] *n* verso; copla, estrofa; versículo; **blank —** verso suelto; (*cheap*) aleluya; **to make —s** rimar.
versed [və:st] *a* versado; práctico; **well — in** experto en, conocedor de.
versify ['və:sifai] *vt* trovar, metrificar.
version ['və:ʃən] *n* versión, traducción.
vertical ['və:tikəl] *an* vertical.
vertiginous [və:'tidʒinəs] *a* vertiginoso.
vertigo ['və:tigou] *n* vértigo.
very ['veri] *a* mismo; mismísimo; verdadero, real, idéntico; **— clean** relimpio; **this — night** esta misma noche; **that — moment** aquel mismísimo momento; *ad* muy, sumamente; **— much** muchísimo; **— many** muchísimos.
vespers ['vespəz] *n* vísperas.
vessel ['vesl] *n* (*ship*) barco, buque, bajel, navío; recipiente, vaso.
vest [vest] *n* chaleco; *vt* **to — in** conferir; **to — with** revestir de.
vestibule ['vestibju:l] *n* vestíbulo, zaguán, portal, recibimiento.
vestige ['vestidʒ] *n* vestigio, rastro, huella, señal.
vestment ['vestmənt] *n* vestidura; (*eccl*) vestimenta.
vestry ['vestri] *n* sacristía; vestuario.
veteran ['vetərən] *an* veterano.
veterinary ['vetərinəri] *a* veterinario.
veto ['vi:tou] *n* veto; *vt* poner el veto; vedar, *SA* vetar.
vex [veks] *vt* vejar, molestar, enfadar, hostigar, fatigar, marear, apesadumbrar, atufar, contrariar, baquetear; **to be vexed** incomodarse, picarse.
vexation [vek'seiʃən] *n* vejación, vejamen, enfado, sofoco, quemazón.
viaduct ['vaiədʌkt] *n* viaducto.
vibrate [vai'breit] *vi* vibrar, oscilar; trepidar, retemblar.
vibrating [vai'breitiŋ] *a* palpitante, vibrante.
vibration [vai'breiʃən] *n* vibración, vaivén, trepidación.
vicar ['vikə] *n* vicario.
vicarage ['vikəridʒ] *n* casa del cura.
vicarious [ˌvai'kɛəriəs] *a* vicario, suplente.
vice [vais] *n* vicio; falta, defecto; (*prefix*) vice.
vice-chancellor ['vais'tʃɑ:nsələ] *n* vicecanciller; (*University*) rector.
vice-president ['vais'prezidənt] *n* vicepresidente.
viceroy ['vaisrɔi] *n* virrey.
viceroyalty ['vaisrɔiəlti] *n* virreinato.
vicinity [vi'siniti] *n* vecindad, proximidad, cercanía, contorno, alrededores.
vicious ['viʃəs] *a* vicioso, resabiado, depravado, rencoroso; (*horse*) zaino.
viciousness ['viʃəsnis] *n* resabio, vicio.
vicissitude [vi'sisitjud] *n* vicisitud, vaivén, revés, mudanza, altibajo.
victim ['viktim] *n* víctima; (*of accident etc*) herido; (*law*) interfecto.
victor ['viktə] *n* vencedor.
victorious [vik'tɔ:riəs] *a* vencedor, triunfante; **to be —** triunfar.
victory ['viktəri] *n* victoria, triunfo.
victual ['vitl] *n* víveres, vitualla, comestibles; *vt* abastecer, avituallar.
vie [vai] *vi* **to — with** disputar (con) (a), competir (con), rivalizar (con) (a).
Viennese [ˌviə'ni:z] *an* vienés.
view [vju:] *n* (*look*) ojeada, mirada, inspección; (*sight*) vista, escena, panorama, paisaje, perspectiva; (*opinion*) ver, idea, opinión, parecer; (*aspect*) aspecto; (*intention*) mira, intento, propósito; **sectional —** corte; (*pol*) plataforma; **in — of** en vista de, en atención a; **on —** a la vista, se expone; **with a — to** con vistas a, pensando en, con miras a; **at first —** a primera vista; **point of —** punto de vista; **to have a commanding — over** (pre)dominar; *vt* contemplar, considerar, mirar.

vigil ['vidʒil] *n* vela, vigilia, desvelo.
vigilance ['vidʒiləns] *n* desvelo, vigilancia, precaución.
vigilant ['vidʒilənt] *a* vigilante, despabilado, desvelado, mira.
vigor ['vigə] *n* vigor, fuerza, brío, energía, bravura, nerviosidad; ardor.
vigorous ['vigərəs] *a* vigoroso, recio, fuerte, enérgico, nervioso, nervudo; (*effort*) esforzado.
vile [vail] *a* vil, infame, soez, despreciable, ruin.
vileness [vailnis] *n* vileza, bajeza, infamia.
vilify ['vilifai] *vt* envilecer, vilipendiar.
villa ['vilə] *n* quinta, casa de campo, chalé.
village ['vilidʒ] *n* pueblo, aldea lugar.
villager ['vilidʒə] *n* aldeano, lugareño.
villain ['vilən] *n* malvado, villano, bellaco, pícaro.
villainous ['vilənəs] *a* villano, vil, ruin.
villany ['viləni] *n* villanía, bellaquería, infamia, ruindad.
Vincente ['vinsənt] *m* Vicente.
vindicate ['vindikeit] *vt* vindicar, justificar; *vr* sincerarse.
vindication [ˌvindi'keiʃən] *n* vindicación, justificación, desagravio.
vindictive [vin'diktiv] *a* vengativo.
vindictively [vin'diktivli] *ad* por venganza, con (tanta) inquina.
vine [vain] *n* vid, parra; **— dresser** viñador; **—grower** vinicultor; **— disease** filoxera; **— stock** cepa; **— shoot** codal.
vinegar ['vinigə] *n* vinagre.
vineyard ['vinjəd] *n* viñedo, viña.
vintage ['vintidʒ] *n* vendimia, cosecha.
violate ['vaiəleit] *vt* (*rules etc*) violar, infringir, violentar, quebrantar; forzar; (*town*) entrar a degüello; (*respect etc*) atropellar, profanar.
violation [ˌvaiə'leiʃən] *n* violación, rompimiento, contravención; infracción; estupro.
violence ['vaiələns] *n* violencia, fuerza, ímpetu; **to do oneself —** violentarse.
violent ['vaiələnt] *a* violento, arrebatado, furioso, vehemente; severo, fulminante.
violet ['vaiəlit] *n* violeta.
violin [ˌvaiə'lin] *n* violín.
violinist ['vaiəlinist] *n* violinista.
violoncello [ˌvaiələn'tʃelou] *n* violoncelo.
viper ['vaipə] *n* víbora.
virago [vi'rɑːgou] *n* virago, marimacho.
Virgil ['vəːdʒil] *m* Virgilio.
virgin ['vəːdʒin] *a* virginal, virgen; casto; *n* virgen, doncella.
virginity [və'dʒiniti] *n* virginidad.
virile ['virail] *a* viril, varonil, hombruno, de pelo en pecho.
virility [vi'riliti] *n* virilidad; **to lose —** afeminarse.
virtual ['vəːtjuəl] *a* virtual, en efecto.
virtue ['vəːtjuː] *n* virtud; **by — of** en virtud de.
virtuous ['vəːtjuəs] *a* virtuoso, púdico, honesto.
virulence ['viruləns] *n* virulencia, acrimonia, malignidad.
virulent ['virulənt] *a* virulento, maligno.
visa ['viːzə] *n* visado.
visage ['vizidʒ] *n* semblante, cara, faz, rostro.
viscount ['vaikaunt] *n* vizconde.
viscous ['viskəs] *a* viscoso, pegajoso, glutinoso.
vise [vais] *n* tornillo de banco.
visible ['vizəbl] *a* visible, patente, palmario, manifiesto.
vision ['viʒən] *n* visión, vista; ensueño; perspectiva; fantasma.
visionary ['viʒnəri] *a* visionario, ilusorio, quimérico; *n* visionario.
visit ['vizit] *n* visita, inspección; *vti* visitar, inspeccionar, ir de visita, ir a saludar.
visitation [ˌvizi'teiʃən] *n* visitación, reconocimiento.
visiting ['vizitiŋ] *a* de visita; **— card** tarjeta de visita.
visitor ['vizitə] *n* visita, visitante; (*not from district*) forastero; (*casual, eg at lecture*) oyente; **to be a —** estar de paso.
visor ['vaizə] *n* visera, visor.
vista ['vistə] *n* perspectiva, paisaje, panorama.
visual ['vizjuəl] *a* visual, óptico.
vital ['vaitl] *a* vital, esencial.
vitality [vai'tæliti] *n* vitalidad, vida.
vitiate ['viʃieit] *vt* viciar, corromper; contaminar, invalidar; (*taste*) estragar.
vituperation [viˌtjuːpə'reiʃən] *n* vituperio.
vivacious [vi'veiʃəs] *a* animado, vivaz, resalado, vivaracho, despejado.
vivacity [vi'væsiti] vivacidad, despejo, viveza, vida.
vivid ['vivid] *a* vívido, gráfico; brillante, intenso; **—ness** vivacidad brillo, intensidad.
vivify ['vivifai] *vt* vivificar.
vocabulary [və'kæbjuləri] *n* vocabulario, léxico.
vocalist ['voukəlist] *n* cantor, cantante.
vocation [vou'keiʃən] *n* vocación, carrera, profesión.
vociferate [vou'sifəreit] *vi* vociferar, vocear, desgañitarse.
vociferous [vou'sifərəs] *a* vocinglero, clamoroso, chillón.
vogue [voug] *n* moda, boga.
voice [vɔis] *n* voz, voto; habla; (*fig*) portavoz; (*singing*) cuerda; **loss of**

— afonía; **with one —** al unísono; *vt* expresar, interpretar, hacerse eco de.
void [vɔid] *a* vacío, hueco; inválido, nulo; *n* vacío.
volcano [vɔl'keinou] *n* volcán.
volition [vou'liʃən] *n* volición, voluntad.
volley ['vɔli] *n* descarga, salva; (*tennis*) voleo.
volt [voult] *n* voltio.
voltage ['voultidʒ] *n* voltaje, tensión.
voluble ['vɔljubl] *a* voluble, versátil.
volume ['vɔljum] *n* volumen; masa; bulto; (*book*) tomo; cuantía.
voluminous [və'luminəs] *a* voluminoso, abultado.
voluntary ['vɔləntəri] *a* voluntario, espontáneo.
volunteer [,vɔlən'tiə] *n* voluntario; *vi* ofrecerse, servir como voluntario.
voluptuous [və'lʌptjuəs] *a* voluptuoso, lujurioso.
voluptuousness [və'lʌptjuəsnis] *n* voluptuosidad, sensualidad, lujuria.
vomit ['vɔmit] *n* vómito; *vt* volver, rendir, arrojar, vomitar; *vi* vomitar.
voracious [və'reiʃəs] *a* voraz, tragón.
voracity [vɔ'ræsiti] *n* voracidad, tragazón.
vortex ['vɔ:teks] *n* vórtice, remolino, torbellino.
vote [vout] *n* voto; sufragio; **general —** plebiscito; **to put to the —** poner a votación; **casting —** voto decisivo; *vti* votar, sufragar.
voter ['voutə] *n* votante, elector.
votive ['voutiv] *a* votivo; **— offering** exvoto.
vouch [vautʃ] *vti* atestiguar, afirmar, comprobar, testificar; **to — for** salir garante de, responder de.
voucher ['vautʃə] *n* resguardo; talón, vale, recibo, comprobante.
vow [vau] *n* voto, ofrenda; **to take religious —s** profesar; *vti* hacer votos, jurar.
vowel ['vauəl] *n* vocal.
voyage [vɔiidʒ] *n* viaje; **sea —** navegación, travesía; *vt* navegar, viajar por mar.
vulgar ['vʌlgə] *a* vulgar, común, cursi, chulo, chabacano, ordinario; grosero, tabernario.
vulgarity [vʌl'gæriti] *n* vulgaridad, chocarrería, grosería, mal tono.
vulnerable ['vʌlnərəbl] *a* vulnerable.
vulture ['vʌltʃə] *n* buitre.

W

wad [wɔd] *n* estopa, guata; (*papers*) pliego; (*gun*) taco, rollo.
waddle ['wɔdl] *vt* anadear.
wade [weid] *vi* **to — (across)** vadear.
wading ['weidiŋ] *a* (*bird*) zancudo.
waft [wɑ:ft] *vti* mecer, flotar, llevar por el aire.
wag [wæg] *n* ganso; zumbón; *vt* mover, agitar; (*tail*) sacudir, menear, colear; *vi* moverse, agitarse, menear, colear.
wage [weidʒ] *n* paga, salario, sueldo; **— earner** jornalero; *vt* emprender; **to — war** hacer guerra.
wager ['weidʒə] *n* apuesta; *vti* apostar.
waggish ['wægiʃ] *a* guasón, zumbón.
wagon ['wægən] *n* carro, carreta, coche; chirrión.
waif [weif] *n* niño (desamparado, huérfano, sin hogar, extraviado).
wail [weil] *n* gemido, lamento; *vt* llorar, lamentar; *vi* quejarse, gimotear, clamar.
wailing ['weiliŋ] *a* plañidero; *n* gemido, quejumbre.
waist [weist] *n* cintura, talle; (*sew*) corpiño.
waistcoat ['weiskout] *n* chaleco.
wait [weit] *n* espera; pausa, dilación, tardanza; **in —** al acecho; **to lie in —** acechar, asechar; *vi* **to — for** esperar, aguardar; esperar, estar en expectativa, estar listo; (*at table*) servir; **to — on** servir, presentar sus respetos a; (*in shop*) despachar; seguirse; velar sobre; **— and see** paciencia y barajar.
waiter ['weitə] *n* camarero, mozo; **dumb—** montacargas.
waiting ['weitiŋ] *n* espera, servicio; *ad* **— for** en espera de; **to be — for** estar a la expectativa.
waitress ['weitris] *n* camarera.
waive [weiv] *vt* no tomar en cuenta, desistir de, renunciar.
wake [weik] *n* (*ship*) estela; (*over invalid*) vela, velación; (*feast etc*) verbena, romería; *vt* despertar; *vi* velar; **to — up** despertarse, despabilarse.
wakeful ['weikful] *a* insomne; desvelado; **— nights** vigilia, noches toledanas.
wakefulness ['weikfulnis] *n* insomnio; desvelo, vigilia.
waken ['weikən] *vti* despertar; despertarse.
Wales [weilz] *n* Gales; **Prince of —** Príncipe de Gales.
walk [wɔ:k] *n* paseo, vuelta; (*manner*) andar; (*of horse*) paso; (*place*) paseo, alameda; (*work*) carrera; tipo de vida; **to go for a —** ir de paseo; dar una vuelta; **to take for a —** *vt* pasear; (sacar a) pasear; (*horse*) llevar al paso; *vi* andar, caminar, ir a pie, pasear, ir al paso; portarse; **to — away with** llevarse; **to — quickly** apretar el paso; **to — the streets** callejear; **to — to and fro** andar de un lado para otro.
walker ['wɔ:kə] *n* paseante, peatón, caminante; **a great —** gran andarín.
walking ['wɔ:kiŋ] *n* paseo; **fond of —** andarín; **— stick** bastón, caña.
wall [wɔ:l] *n* muro; (*interior*) pared; **dry —** albarrada; **mud —, garden —**

tapia; (*partition*) tabique; (*fort*) muralla.
wallet ['wɔlit] *n* bolsa; (*for papers*) cartera; (*for game*) zurrón.
wallow ['wɔlou] *vi* revolcarse; **to —** (*in riches*) nadar.
walnut ['wɔ:lnət] *n* nuez; (*tree*) nogal; **— grove** nogueral.
wan [wɔn] *a* pálido, descolorido, desmayado, mortecino.
wand [wɔnd] *n* varita; **magic —** varilla mágica.
wander ['wɔndə] *vi* **to — about** vagar, errar, andar sin objeto; (*mind*) delirar; (*from point*) salirse (del asunto).
wanderer ['wɔndərə] *n* vagabundo; errante, viandante.
wandering ['wɔndəriŋ] *n* viaje; extravío, divagación; aberración, delirio.
wane [wein] *vi* decrecer; (*hopes*) desvanecerse; (*moon*) menguar.
waning ['weiniŋ] *n* mengua, menguante; *a* **— moon** menguante.
want [wɔnt] *n* (*need*) necesidad; (*lack*) falta, carencia; (*scarcity*) escasez, apuro; (*poverty*) privación, indigencia; estrechez; (*requirement*) solicitud; **for — of** por falta de; *vt* necesitar; carecer de; desear, querer; exigir; *vi* estar necesitado; faltar; **wanted** se solicita, se necesita.
wanting ['wɔntiŋ] *a* falto, deficiente; necesitado; de menos; **to be — in** carecer de; **to be —** escasear.
wanton ['wɔntən] *a* desenfrenado, voluntarioso; travieso; lascivo, salaz; suelto; atrevido; inconsiderado; *n* prostituta.
war [wɔ:] *n* guerra; **— without quarter** guerra a muerte; **—horse** corcel de guerra; *vi* guerrear.
warble ['wɔ:bl] *n* trino, gorjeo; *vti* trinar, gorjear.
warbling ['wɔ:bliŋ] *a* melodioso; *n* gorjeo.
ward [wɔ:d] *n* pupilo; pupilaje; tutela; guarda, guardián; (*of city*) barrio; (*hosp*) crujía; (*barrack*) cuadra; *vt* proteger, guardar; **to — off** evitar, desviar, rechazar, conjurar.
warden ['wɔ:dn] *n* custodio, guardián; (*prison*) alcaide.
warder ['wɔ:də] *n* guarda, guardia.
wardrobe ['wɔ:droub] *n* guardarropa, armario; vestuario.
warehouse ['wɛəhaus] *n* almacén, depósito; *vt* almacenar.
wares [wɛəz] *n pl* mercancías.
warfare ['wɔ:fɛə] *n* guerra, operaciones militares.
wariness ['wɛərinis] *n* prudencia, precaución, suspicacia, cautela.
warlike ['wɔ:laik] *a* guerrero, belicoso; bélico.
warm [wɔ:m] *a* (*object*) caliente; (*day, greeting etc*) caluroso, ardiente; (*argument*) acalorado; (*belief*) fervoroso, ardiente; vivo; fogoso; **to be —** (*person*) tener calor; (*weather*) hacer calor; **to get —** calentarse; (*temper etc*) acalorarse; **—hearted** generoso; *vt* **to —** (re)calentar; encender; **to — up** refocilar.
warmth [wɔ:mθ] *n* calor; (*fig*) simpatía, cordialidad, fervor, encarecimiento, ardor.
warn [wɔ:n] *vt* prevenir; avisar, advertir, intimar; encargar, amonestar; **to — against** precaver; *vi* servir de escarmiento.
warning ['wɔ:niŋ] *n* advertencia; amonestación; (*moral*) escarmiento; (*spoken*) reparo; **to give —** advertir.
warp [wɔ:p] *n* alabeo, torcedura; (*weaving*) urdimbre; *vti* alabear, torcer, alabearse; encorvarse, combarse; (*naut*) mover con espía, espiarse.
warrant ['wɔrənt] *n* auto; autorización; orden, boletín, mandato; patente, testimonio, fianza, garantía; citación; *vt* garantizar, asegurar, fiar; justificar; dar pie a.
warren ['wɔrin] *n* conejera.
warrior ['wɔriə] *n* guerrero.
Warsaw ['wɔ:sɔ:] *n* Varsovia.
wary ['wɛəri] *a* prudente, cauto; cauteloso; suspicaz, precavido, escaldado; astuto.
wash [wɔʃ] *n* lavado; ropa (para lavar); loción; (*paint*) lavado; **—bowl** aljofaina, palangana; **—stand** lavabo, aguamanil; **it will all come out in the —** todo saldrá en la colada; *vt* lavar; bañar; dar un baño; (*paint*) lavar; (*dishes*) fregar; *vi* lavarse; **to — one's hands of** lavarse las manos de, desentenderse de.
washerwoman ['wɔʃə,wumən] *n* lavandera.
washing ['wɔʃiŋ] *n* lavamiento, ropa para lavar; (*toilet*) abluciones; **— day** día de colada; **— machine** lavadora, máquina de lavar; **— up** lavado de los platos.
washstand ['wɔʃstænd] *n* aguamanil, palangana.
wasp [wɔsp] *n* avispa; **—'s nest** avispero.
wastage ['weistidʒ] *n* merma, desgaste.
waste [weist] *a* desechado; superfluo; baldío, desolado, desierto; *n* (*misuse*) despilfarro, derroche; disipación; (*lessening*) mengua, consunción; (*wearing away*) desgaste, merma; (*liquid*) derrame, desagüe; (*remains*) desperdicios, despojos, restos; (*bodily etc*) consumo; estrago; (*destruction*) desbarate, asolamiento, destrozo; (*desert*) páramo, estepa, yermo; *SA* **bleak —** pina; **—paper basket** cesto; *vt* malgastar, desperdiciar, tirar; derrochar, derramar; consumir; echar a perder; desbaratar; dar al traste (con); *vi* (des)gastarse; **to — away** (*material*) atrofiarse, mermar;

(*human*) demacrarse, consumirse.
wasteful ['weistful] *a* despilfarrado; pródigo, malgastador.
wastefulness ['weistfulnis] *n* improvidencia, despilfarro.
wastrel ['weistrəl] *n* calavera.
watch [wɔtʃ] *n* (*mil*) vigilia; (*naut*) cuarto, guardia; (*over invalid etc*) vela; (*attention*) desvelo, cuidado, vigilancia; (*group*) ronda, patrulla; (*individual*) vigilante, guardia, sereno, atalaya; (*time*) reloj; **pocket —** reloj de bolsillo; **stop—** cronómetro; **— tower** atalaya, vigía; **to be on the —** estar a la mira; *vt* mirar, observar; (*sport etc*) ver, mirar; (*mil*) hacer (guardia, centinela); asechar; **to — over** velar, vigilar; guardar, celar; *vi* velar.
watchful ['wɔtʃful] *a* vigilante, despabilado, desvelado, cuidadoso.
watchfulness ['wɔtʃfulnis] *n* vigilancia; desvelo.
watchmaker ['wɔtʃ.meikə] *n* relojero; **—'s shop** relojería.
watchman ['wɔtʃmən] *n* sereno.
watchword ['wɔtʃwə:d] *n* consigna; (*mil*) santo y seña; lema.
water ['wɔ:tə] *a* acuático; *n* agua; (*jewel*) agua; **drinking —** agua potable; **cold —** agua fresca; **rain —** agua de lluvia; **spring —** agua de manantial; **mineral—**(agua) gaseosa; **salt —** agua salada; **high —** pleamar, marea alta; **low —** bajamar; **running —** agua corriente; **—bottle** cantimplora; **— closet** (*wc*) retrete, excusado; **— carrier** aguador; **— color** acuarela; **—course** arroyo; madre, lecho; **— jar** tinaja, jarro; **— jug** aguamanil; **— lily** nenúfar; **— line** (*naut*) línea de flotación; **—-mark** (*paper*) filigrana; nivel del agua; **— power** fuerza hidráulica; **—proof** impermeable; **—shed** vertiente; **— tank** aljibe, cisterna; **—wheel** azud, noria; **to carry — in a sieve** coger agua en cesta; *vt* (*plants*) regar, humedecer; (*cattle*) abrevar; (*wine*) aguar; **my mouth —s** se me hace agua la boca.
watercolor ['wɔ:tə.kʌlə] *n* pintura a la aguada, acuarela.
waterfall ['wɔ:təfɔ:l] *n* cascada, salto, catarata.
watering ['wɔ:təriŋ] *n* riego, irrigación; **— can** regadera; **— place** abrevadero, aguadero; balneario.
watermelon ['wɔ:təmelən] *n* sandía.
waterspout ['wɔ:təspaut] *n* tromba.
watertight ['wɔ:tətait] *a* impermeable, estanco.
waterway ['wɔ:təwei] *n* canal, río, ría (navegable).
watery ['wɔ:təri] *a* húmedo, acuoso, aguanoso; insípido.
wave [weiv] *n* ola, onda; **tidal —** aguaje; **permanent —** ondulación permanente; (*of hand*) movimiento, agitación; (*of cold*) ola; (*of sound*) onda sonora; **—length** longitud de onda; **short—** onda corta; *vt* menear; (*hands*) agitar; *vi* flotar, ondear, tremolar.
waver ['weivə] *vi* vacilar, titubear; tambalearse.
waving ['weiviŋ] *n* ondulación.
wavy ['weivi] *a* ondulante, undoso; (*hair*) (*not natural*) ondulado; (*natural*) rizado.
wax [wæks] *n* cera; **shoemaker's —** cerote; (*in ear*) cerilla; **sealing —** lacre; *vt* encerar; *vi* **to — strong** crecer; desarrollarse; aumentar; **to — warm** (*argument*) enardecerse.
way [wei] *n* vía, camino, paso; distancia; (*direction*) rumbo, curso, dirección; (*movement*) marcha, andar, velocidad; (*method*) modo, medio, manera; (*custom*) uso, hábito; conducta; comportamiento; **— in** entrada; **— out** salida; **— through** paso; **to make one's —** orientarse, caminar; abrirse camino; **make —!** ¡paso!; **to get one's (own) —** imponerse, salirse con la suya; **to get in the —** estorbar, estar de más; **to get out of the —** apartarse; **to go out of one's — to** desvivirse por; **there is no — out** no hay (salida, escape); **any —** de cualquier modo; **come this —** ven por acá; **in a —** hasta cierto punto, en cierto modo; **across (over) the —** (justo) enfrente, al otro lado; **by the —** a propósito, incidental, dicho sea de paso; **on the —** en camino; **on the — to** en camino de, con rumbo a; para, en vías de; **out of the —** apartado, aislado, arrinconado, insólito, raro; **in every —** a todas luces; *pl* **—s and means** combinaciones.
wayfarer ['wei.fεərə] *n* caminante, peregrino.
waylay [wei'lei] *vt* asechar; atajar.
wayside ['weisaid] *n* borde del camino.
wayward ['weiwəd] *a* caprichoso; voluntarioso; vacilante.
we [wi:] *pn* nosotros, nosotras.
weak [wi:k] *a* débil, enteco, flojo, flaco; delicado, lánguido; alicaído; (*heart*) cardíaco.
weaken ['wi:kən] *vt* debilitar, enflaquecer; atenuar; *vi* debilitarse.
weakening ['wi:kəniŋ] *n* debilitación; resentimiento.
weakness ['wi:knis] *n* debilidad, achaque; imperfección; futilidad.
weal [wi:l] *n* bienestar, felicidad; **common —** bien público; (*on flesh*) cardenal.
wealth [welθ] *n* riqueza, oro; caudal; opulencia; **worldly —** poderío.
wealthy ['welθi] *a* rico, opulento, caudaloso.
weapon ['wepən] *n* arma.
wear ['wεə] *n* uso, desgaste, deterioro; **— and tear** uso, desgaste; **for evening —** para llevar de noche;

the worse for — bien usado; *vt* (*clothes*) llevar, ponerse; (*for first time*) estrenar; (*sword*) ceñir; exhibir; **to — out** gastar, usar, desgastar; cansar; extenuar; mermar, marchitar; *vi* **to — out, away** deteriorarse, consumirse; **to — oneself out** matarse; (*of clothes*) (per)durar.
wearer ['wɛərə] *n* el que (lleva, usa, gasta) una cosa.
wearied ['wiərid] *a* cansado, fastidiado, aburrido.
weariness ['wiərinis] *n* fatiga, lasitud, cansancio; fastidio.
wearing ['wɛəriŋ] *a* de uso; *n* uso, desgaste, deterioro; **— down** merma.
wearisome ['wiərisəm] *a* aburrido, fastidioso, tedioso, laborioso.
wearisomeness ['wiərisəmnis] *n* fastidio, cansancio, hastío.
weary ['wiəri] *a* cansado, fatigado, rendido; fastidioso; abrumado; *vt* moler, cansar; *vi* fatigarse.
weasel ['wi:zl] *n* comadreja.
weather ['weðə] *n* tiempo; (*harsh*) intemperie; **—beaten** curtido; **—vane** veleta; *vi* aguantar, sobrevivir a; (*wood*) secar al aire; (*a cape*) doblar.
weave [wi:v] *vt* tejer, entretejer; trenzar, urdir; (*plot*) tramar.
weaver ['wi:və] *n* tejedor.
weaving ['wi:viŋ] *n* tejido.
web [web] *n* tela, tejido; (*plot*) urdimbre; **—footed** palmado; **cob—** tela de araña, telaraña.
wed [wed] *vti* casar, casarse con.
wedding ['wediŋ] *n* boda, casamiento; **— ring** anillo nupcial.
wedge [wedʒ] *n* cuña, calce; chaveta; *vt* meter cuñas, atarugar, calzar.
wedlock ['wedlɔk] *n* matrimonio, himeneo; **out of —** ilegítimo.
Wednesday ['wenzdi] *n* miércoles.
wee [wi:] *a* pequeñito, chiquito.
weed [wi:d] *n* mala hierba, cizaña; **— patch** maleza; *vt* desyerbar.
week [wi:k] *n* semana; **—day** día (de trabajo, laborable).
weekend ['wi:k'end] *n* fin de semana.
weekly ['wi:kli] *a* semanal; *n* **— paper** semanario; *ad* semanalmente.
weep [wi:p] *vti* llorar; lamentar.
weeping ['wi:piŋ] *n* llanto; dolor; lágrimas; **— willow** sauce llorón.
weigh [wei] *vti* pesar; (*words*) sopesar; **to — down** gravitar; (*fig*) agobiar; **to — anchor** levar anclas.
weight [weit] *n* peso; carga; momento; **gross —** peso bruto; **by —** al peso; **—s and measures** pesos y medidas; **to give short —** sisar; **to lend — to** militar en (su) favor; *vt* cargar.
weighty ['weiti] *a* pesado, grave, ponderoso; importante, sesudo, poderoso.
weir [wiə] *n* esclusa, presa.
weird [wiəd] *a* ominoso, inquietante; siniestro; extraño, fantástico.
welcome ['welkəm] *a* bienvenido; grato; *excl* ¡bienvenido!; *n* bienvenida, buena acogida; recibimiento; enhorabuena; *vt* dar la bienvenida.
welcoming ['welkəmiŋ] *a* acogedor.
welfare ['welfɛə] *n* bienestar, felicidad, prosperidad.
well [wel] *ad* pues, bien; **as —** inclusivo; **very —** a fondo; de primera; **—-built, —-done** bien hecho; **—-to-do** acomodado, pudiente; **—-worn** cansado; **— and good** enhorabuena; *n* pozo; manantial; **— maker** pocero; *vti* verter, manar.
well-born ['wel'bɔ:n] *a* bien nacido.
well-bred ['wel'bred] *a* bien educado, bien criado.
well-meaning ['wel'mi:niŋ] *a* bien intencionado.
well-off ['wel'ɔf] *a* acomodado, adinerado.
Welsh [welʃ] *a* galés.
west [west] *a* occidental; *n* oeste, occidente; poniente, ocaso; **— wind** poniente.
West Indies ['west'indiz] *n* las Antillas.
westerly ['westəli] *a ad* hacia el occidente.
western ['westən] *a* occidental, del oeste; *n* (*cine*) película de vaqueros.
westward ['westwəd] *a* hacia el oeste.
wet [wet] *a* mojado, húmedo, lluvioso; **to be — through** estar empapado, hecho una sopa; *n* humedad, lluvia; *vt* mojar, empapar.
wetness ['wetnis] *n* humedad.
wet nurse ['wet'nə:s] *n* nodriza.
whale [weil] *n* ballena, cachalote; **—bone** ballena.
wharf [wɔ:f] *n* muelle, andén; malecón; (*loading*) cargadero.
what [wɔt] *pn rel* lo que; **— a . . .!** ¡qué . . .!; **— a lot!** ¡cuánto!; ¿qué?
whatever [wɔt'evə] *pron* cualquiera que, todo lo que.
wheat [wi:t] *n* trigo.
wheedle ['wi:dl] *vt* halagar; sonsacar, embromar, engatusar.
wheel [wi:l] *n* rueda; (*potter's*) torno; **—barrow** carretilla; *vti* hacer rodar, rodar.
wheelwright ['wi:lrait] *n* carretero.
wheeze [wi:z] *vi* roncar, jadear.
wheezing ['wi:ziŋ] *n* resuello.
when [wen] *ad* cuando; al tiempo que, tan pronto como.
whence [wens] *ad* por lo cual, por consiguiente, de donde; ¿dónde?
whenever [wen'evə] *cj* cuandoquiera que, siempre que.
where [wɛə] *ad* donde.
whereabouts ['wɛərəbauts] *n* paradero.
whereas [wɛər'æz] *cj* por cuanto; considerando; mientras que, en vista de que, siendo así que; por el contrario.

whereby [wɛə'bai] *ad* por la cual, por donde.
whereupon [ˌwɛərə'pɔn] *ad* sobre que, entonces.
wherever [wɛər'evə] *ad* dondequiera que.
whet [wet] *vt* amolar, afilar; aguzar; (*appetite*) abrir.
whether ['weðə] *cj* si, sea que.
which [witʃ] *pn* el que, el cual, que; **—?** ¿cuál?
whichever [witʃ'evə] *a pn* cualquier(a) (que), cualesquiera.
whiff [wif] *n* bocanada, soplo, vaho.
while [wail] *n* rato, temporada; **a short — ago** hace poco, hace poco rato; **to be worth —** valer la pena; *cj* en tanto que; a la vez que; mientras (que); al mismo tiempo que, a medida que; (*although*) aunque; *vt* **to — away** (*time etc*) entretener, pasar (el rato).
whim [wim] *n* capricho, antojo, fantasía, manía.
whimper ['wimpə] *n* quejido, queja; *vi* lloriquear, gimotear, plañir.
whimsical ['wimzikəl] *a* caprichoso, antojadizo, fantástico.
whine [wain] *n* quejido; *vi* quejarse; lloriquear, piar.
whinny ['wini] *vi* relinchar.
whip [wip] *n* látigo, zurriago; **—stroke, —lash** latigazo; *vti* azotar, flagelar, zurrar, fustigar; (*cream*) batir.
whipping ['wipiŋ] *n* vapuleo, zurra, tunda.
whirl [wəːl] *n* giro; remolino; *vti* girar, revolotear, remolinar(se), voltear, arremolinar(se).
whirlpool ['wəːlpul] *n* vórtice, remolino.
whirlwind ['wəːlwind] *n* torbellino.
whisk [wisk] *n* cepillo, batidor; movimiento rápido; *vt* batir; (*wag*) menear; **to — away** llevar(se).
whiskers ['wiskəz] *n* patillas; barbas; (*of cats*) bigotes.
whisper ['wispə] *n* cuchicheo; (*leaves etc*) susurro; (*of gossip*) hablilla; *vt* soplar; *vi* cuchichear; musitar; (*leaves*) susurrar.
whispering ['wispəriŋ] *n* cuchicheo, murmullo, susurro.
whistle ['wisl] *n* (*instrument*) silbato; (*penny, tin*) pito; (*sound*) silbo, silbido; (*of disapproval*) rechifla; **to wet one's —** remojar el gaznate; *vt* **to — at** silbar, rechiflar; *vi* silbar.
whit [wit] *n* ápice, jota, pizca.
white [wait] *a* blanco; pálido, lívido; cándido; (*herald*) plata; **— hot** candente; **— lie** mentirilla; **— hair** canas; **— horses** cabrillas; *n* (*egg*) clara; (*of eye*) blanco; blancura; (*half-breed*) **half—** cuarterón; **to go —** blanquearse; ponerse (pálido, lívido).
whiten ['waitn] *vt* blanquear.
whiteness ['waitnis] *n* blancura, albura.
whitewash ['waitwɔʃ] *n* jalbegue; blanqueo, blanquete; *vt* blanquear, encubrir, encalar, enjalbegar; **to — oneself** santificarse.
whither ['wiðə] *ad* adonde; hacia; **—?** ¿hasta dónde?
whitish ['waitiʃ] *a* blanquecino.
Whit Sunday ['wit'sʌndi] *n* domingo de Pentecostés.
Whitsuntide ['witsntaid] *n* Pascua de Pentecostés.
whizz [wiz] *n* zumbido, silbido; *vi* silbar.
who [hu] *pn* quien; **—?** ¿quién?
whoever [hu'evə] *pn* quienquiera que.
whole [houl] *a* todo, total, entero, intacto, íntegro; sano; **as a —** en conjunto; **the — blessed day** todo el santo día; *n* todo; conjunto, totalidad.
wholeness ['houlnis] *n* plenitud, entereza, integridad.
wholesale ['houlseil] *a ad* al por mayor; *n* venta al por mayor.
wholesome ['houlsəm] *a* sano, salubre, saludable.
whom [huːm] *pn* quien, quienes; **to —** a quien, a quienes, al que, a la que, a los que, a las que.
whoop [hup] *n* alarido; *vi* huchear.
whooping ['hupiŋ] *a* **— cough** tos ferina.
whore [hɔː] *n* puta, ramera.
whose [huːz] *pn* cuyo.
whosoever [ˌhuːsou'evə] *pn* quienquiera que.
why [wai] *cj ad* por que, para que; con que; **—?** ¿por qué?; *excl* ¡cómo!, ¡vaya!.
wick [wik] *n* mecha, pabilo.
wicked ['wikid] *a* (*person*) malvado, (*deed, thing*) perverso, impío, inicuo; enorme; malicioso, travieso.
wickedness ['wikidnis] *n* maldad, perversidad; malicia; vicio, impiedad.
wicket ['wikit] *n* portillo, postigo; (*cricket*) terreno, portería; **— gate** postigo de barrera.
wide [waid] *a* ancho, amplio; holgado, dilatado; **one foot —** un pie de ancho; *ad* lejos, a gran distancia; (*of mark*) errado; allá por los cerros de úbeda; **— open** de par en par.
wide-awake ['waidəweik] *a* vigilante, despabilado, alerta.
widen ['waidn] *vti* ensanchar, ampliar, dilatar.
wideness ['waidnis] *n* amplitud, anchura, ancho.
widespread ['waidspred] *a* extenso, extendido; esparcido, generalizado; (*influences etc*) envergadura; **to become —** extenderse.
widow(er) ['widou(ə)] *n* viuda, viudo.

widowhood ['wiďouhud] *n* viudez; (*pension etc*) viudedad.
width [widθ] *n* anchura, ancho; holgura; (*of knowledge*) amplitud.
wield [wi:ld] *vt* manejar, esgrimir; empuñar.
wife [waif] *n* esposa, mujer, cónyuge; (*fam*) costilla.
wig [wig] *n* peluca, cabellera.
wigwam ['wigwæm] *n* tienda de pieles rojas.
wild [waild] *a* (*space, land*) salvaje, agreste, desierto, inculto, despoblado; (*flowers*) silvestre, campestre; selvático; (*animals*) salvaje, bravo; (*fierce*) fiero; feroz, montés; (*in character*) impetuoso, violento, desenfrenado; (*with rage*) furibundo, loco; (*ideas etc*) descabellado, loco. desatinado, estrafalario, extravagante; (*crazy*) alocado, disparatado, insensato; (*untrained*) cerril, bravío, zahareño; (*scene*) alborotado, desenfrenado, desordenado; **—est** (*hopes*) las más lisonjeras.
wilderness ['wildənis] *n* desierto, páramo, yermo.
wildly [waildli] *ad* **to talk —** delirar.
wildness ['waildnis] *n* tosquedad, rusticidad; ferocidad; desvarío.
wile [wail] *n* fraude, supercheria, astucia, treta; *vt* engatusar, embaucar.
will [wil] *n* voluntad, querer; discreción, placer; resolución, ánimo; testamento; **free —** libre albedrío; **at —** a voluntad, a discreción; **against (his) —** a la fuerza; **— power** fuerza de voluntad; **— o' the wisp** fuego fatuo; *vti* legar, dejar en testamento; querer, resolver; disponer.
willful ['wilful] *a* voluntarioso, impetuoso, testarudo; arbitrario, intencionado, premeditado.
willfulness ['wilfulnis] *n* terquedad, obstinación.
William ['wiljəm] *m* Guillermo.
willing ['wiliŋ] *a* gustoso, dispuesto; (*to accept another's opinion*) deferente; complaciente; **to be —** querer; estar dispuesto.
willingly [wiliŋli] *ad* de buena gana, de grado, voluntariamente.
willingness ['wiliŋnis] *n* buena voluntad, complacencia.
willow ['wilou] *n* sauce; **weeping —** sauce llorón.
willowy ['wiloui] *a* esbelto.
willy-nilly ['wili'nili] *ad* a la fuerza.
wily ['waili] *a* astuto, marrullero.
wilt [wilt] *vti* marchitar(se), ajar(se).
win [win] *vti* ganar; vencer; (*after effort*) lograr; (*lottery*) tocar(le a uno); (*sympathy*) captar; (*person*) (*sl*) soplar; (*favor etc*) cazar; **to — over** conquistar, ganar; (*sympathy etc*) granjear; **to — around** sonsacar; *vi* triunfar.
wince [wins] *vi* estremecerse.
wind [wind] *n* viento.
wind [waind] *vt* (*wool*) devanar; (*watch*) dar cuerda a; (*handle*) dar vueltas a; **to — around** enrollar, liar; tejer; *vi* **to — around** enroscarse, serpentear, (re)torcerse; ir con rodeos; hacer meandros.
windfall ['windfɔ:l] *n* ganga; fruta caída del árbol, ganancia repentina.
winding ['waindiŋ] *a* tortuoso, sinuoso; **— sheet** sudario, mortaja; *n* vuelta, revuelta, rodeo; recodo, tortuosidad; *pl* **—s and turnings** recovecos, vueltas y r evueltas.
windmill ['winmil] *n* molino de viento.
window ['windou] *n* ventana; **show —** vidriera; **display —** muestrario; escaparate; **— blinds** persianas; **— glass** cristal; **—sill** antepecho o mesilla de ventana; **— frame** bastidor, marco.
windshield ['windʃi:ld] *n* cortaviento, (*aut*) parabrisa.
windward ['windwəd] *ad* a barlovento.
windy ['windi] *a* ventoso, tempestuoso; (*day*) de (mucho) viento; (*speech*) hinchado; **it is —** hace viento.
wine [wain] *n* vino; **red —** vino tinto; **—shop** taberna; (*fam*) tasca; **—skin** bota, odre, pellejo.
wing [wiŋ] *n* ala; (*mil*) flanco; **—s** (*for swimming*) nadadera, alero; **in the —s** (*theat*) entre bastidores; **on the —** al vuelo; en marcha; **under the — of** bajo la tutela de.
wink [wiŋk] *n* guiño, parpadeo; *vi* guiñar; parpadear; titilar; **as easy as —** es cosa de coser y cantar; **not to have a — of sleep** no cerrar los ojos, pasar la noche de claro en claro; **to — at** (*crime etc*) hacer la vista gorda.
winner ['winə] *n* ganador, vencedor.
winning ['winiŋ] *a* victorioso, triunfante; ganancioso; encantador; *n* triunfo; *n pl* ganancias.
winnow ['winou] *vt* aventar, apalear; entresacar.
winsome ['winsəm] *a* atractivo, simpático, salado.
winter ['wintə] *a* de invierno; *n* invierno; *vi* invernar.
wintry ['wintri] *a* invernal, helado, glacial.
wipe [waip] *vt* limpiar, secar, frotar; **to — dry** enjugar, restregar; **to — out, off** borrar; extirpar; **to — the floor with** poner como un trapo.
wire ['waiə] *n* alambre; telegrama; **—work** filigrana; **barbed —** alambre de púas; **extension —** flexible; **ground —** tierra; *vt* alambrar; *vti* telegrafiar.
wireless ['waiəlis] *a* **— telegraphy** telegrafía sin hilos.
wiry ['waiəri] *a* nervudo, delgado y fuerte, resistente.

wisdom ['wizdəm] *n* sabiduría, prudencia, buen criterio; erudición.
wise [waiz] *a* sabio, docto; cuerdo, prudente; **the three — men** los reyes magos; **to be no —r** quedarse en albis, quedarse en ayunas.
wish [wiʃ] *n* deseo, anhelo; súplica, ruego; *vti* desear, querar, anhelar; **just as one would —** a pedir de boca; **I wish. . . !** ¡ojalá . . . !
wishful ['wiʃful] *a* **— thinking** ilusión; **— thinker** iluso.
wistful ['wistful] *a* anhelante, pensativo, tierno.
wit [wit] *n* chiste, rasgo de ingenio, dicho gracioso; ingenio, gala, sal, gracia, agudeza; (*pers*) conceptista; **to keep one's —s about one** tener ojo; **to lose one's —s** perder la razón; **to — a** saber; esto es; **to live on one's —s** vivir a salto de mata.
witch [witʃ] *n* bruja, hechicera.
witchcraft ['witʃkrɑ:ft] *n* brujería, hechicería, fascinación.
with [wið] *prep* con, de; en compañía de; **— it** moderno.
withdraw [wið'drɔ:] *vt* retirar, quitar, sacar; separar; *vi* retirarse, encerrarse, substraerse, quitarse; (*home*) recogerse; rehuir, esquivarse.
withdrawal [wið'drɔ:əl] *n* (*money*) retiro; (*mil*) retirada; recogida, abandono.
wither ['wiðə] *vti* marchitar, ajar; marchitarse.
withered ['wiðəd] *a* mustio, marchito; seco.
withhold [wið'hould] *vt* retener, contener, rehusar, ocultar, negar.
within [wi'ðin] *prep* dentro de; al alcance de; **— an inch of** poco menos de; por poco; *ad* dentro.
without [wi'ðaut] *prep* sin, falto de, fuera de; *ad* afuera, fuera; *cj* si no, a menos que.
withstand [wið'stænd] *vt* resistir, aguantar, contrarrestar.
witness ['witnis] *n* testigo; declarante; espectador; **in — thereof** en fe de lo cual; **eye—** testigo ocular; *vti* declarar, dar testimonio (como testigo), atestiguar; presenciar; ver; concurrir a.
witticism ['witisizəm] *n* rasgo de ingenio, chiste, agudeza, donaire.
wittiness ['witinis] *n* gracia, gracejo, sal, ingenio.
witty ['witi] *a* chistoso, agudo, ingenioso, ocurrente, chancero; conceptista.
wives' tale ['waivz'teil] *n* **old — —** rondalla.
wizard ['wizəd] *a* (*sl*) estupendo; *n* hechicero, brujo.
woe [wou] *n* dolor, pesar; pena, aflicción; calamidad, miseria.
woebegone ['woubi,gɔn] *a* doloroso, desconsolado; raquítico.
woeful ['wouful] *a* calamitoso, afligido, lastimero.
wolf [wulf] *n* lobo; **—cub** lobato; **—hound** alano.
woman ['wumən] *n* mujer; hembra; **talkative —** cotorra.
womankind ['wuman'kaind] *n* sexo femenino, bello sexo.
womanly ['wumənli] *a* mujeril, femenino.
womb [wu:m] *n* utero, matriz, madre; entrañas.
wonder ['wʌndə] *n* milagro, maravilla; portento; espanto, admiración, prodigio; **to work —s** hacer milagros; **—struck** pasmado, atónito; *vt* desear saber, extrañar, preguntarse; *vi* maravillarse; **I — if he has come?** ¿si habrá venido?
wonderful ['wʌndəful] *a* maravilloso, sorprendente, pasmoso, peregrino, prodigioso.
wondrous ['wʌndrəs] *a* maravilloso, pasmoso; **—ly** a las mil maravillas.
wont [wount] *n* uso, costumbre; **to be — to** soler, acostumbrar.
wonted ['wountid] *a* acostumbrado, usual.
woo [wu:] *vt* cortejar, hacer la corte a, requerir de amores a; pretender; festejar; (*to sleep*) arrullar.
wood [wud] *a* (*material*) madera; (*trees*) bosque, monte; **fire—** leña; **dead—** broza; **—cut** grabado en madera; **— cutter** leñador; **—louse** cochinilla.
wooded ['wudid] *a* arbolado.
wooden ['wudn] *a* de madera, de palo.
woodland ['wudlənd] *n* bosques, monte, selva; *a* silvestre.
woody ['wudi] *a* leñoso; arbolado; (*poet*) nemoroso, boscoso.
wooing ['wu:iŋ] *n* cortejo, festejo.
wool [wul] *n* lana; **— dealer, merchant** lanero; **to be — gathering** estar (en Babia, ensimismado, distraído); **dyed in the —** acérrimo.
woolen ['wulin] *a* de lana, lanar; *n* tejido de lana; género o paña de lana.
woolly ['wu:li] *a* lanudo, lanoso; (*flocks*) lanar; (*ideas*) borroso, vago.
word [wə:d] *n* palabra, vocablo; (*of song*) letra; **by — of mouth** de palabra; **to send —** mandar recado; **on the — of a** (*gentleman etc*) palabra de, a fuer de; **to get a — in** (*edgewise*) meter baza; **not to lose a single —** no perder ripio; **fine —s** galantería; *vt* redactar; expresar, enunciar.
wording ['wə:diŋ] *n* fraseología, redacción, términos.
wordless ['wə:dlis] *a* tácito, mudo.
wordy ['wə:di] *a* verboso, palabrero.
work [wə:k] *n* trabajo, faena, tarea; (*of art*) obra; (*sew*) labor; (*house*) quehaceres; acto, ocupación; **—men** obreros; **fine —** labor fina; *pl* engranaje, motor; fábrica, taller;

dramatic — teatro; *vt* trabajar; (*mine*) explotar; (*dough*) bregar, amasar; (*ground*) laborar; (*sew*) bordar; (*wood*) tallar; (*machine*) operar, manejar, hacer funcionar; poner en juego; obrar, elaborar; **to — on** influir, trabajar; *vi* trabajar, surtir efecto, obrar; (*machine*) funcionar, andar, marchar; (*medicine etc*) obrar, ser eficaz, tener fuerza; (*coll*) pitar; **to — one's way** abrirse camino; **to — one's head off** devanarse los sesos; **to — one's way into** ingerirse; **to — out** agotar; ejecutar; subir; **to — through** horadar; estudiar (*etc*) trabajosamente; **to — up** trabajar; excitar; **to — oneself up** exaltarse; **to — upon** obrar sobre; estar ocupado en; mover a.

workable ['wə:kəbl] *a* factible.

worked ['wə:kt] *a* labrado; **— up** excitado.

worker ['wə:kə] *n* obrero, trabajador, operario.

workhouse ['wə:khaus] *n* asilo.

working ['wə:kiŋ] *n* obra; juego, operación, funcionamiento, marcha; *pl* (*min*) cuenca; **not —** no funciona; **— day** día de trabajo; **— capital** capital de explotación; **— drawing** montea, borrador; **— man** obrero, jornalero; **— class** clase obrera.

workman ['wə:kmən] *n* obrero, trabajador.

workmanlike ['wə:kmənlaik] *a* práctico, experto, trabajado.

workmanship ['wə:kmənʃip] *n* trabajo; pericia, arte, habilidad; confección, hechura; artificio.

workshop ['wə:kʃɔp] *n* taller, fábrica.

workroom ['wə:krum] *n* taller.

world [wə:ld] *n* mundo; **in this —** de tejas abajo; (*relig*) **in the —** en el siglo; **— without end** para siempre jamás.

worldly ['wə:ldli] *a* mundanal, mundano; profano.

worldwide ['wə:ld'waid] *a* mundial, universal.

worm [wə:m] *n* gusano, lombriz; **book—** polilla; **—eaten** carcomido; apolillado; *vt* **to —** (*secrets*) **out of** sonsacar; sacar a (uno) el buche; **to — one's way along** insinuarse, arrastrarse.

worn [wɔ:n] *a* **— (out)** usado; gastado; rendido; agotado; **well-—** cansado; **well-— path** derrotero; **— thin** usado; **to be —** usarse; **to get — out** (*pers*) extenuarse, fatigarse.

worried ['wʌrid] *a* inquieto, preocupado.

worry ['wʌri] *n* cuidado, molestia, zozobra; preocupación, carcoma; quebradero de cabeza; *vt* inquietar, molestar, zozobrar, perturbar; solicitar; apurar; (*dog*) ensañarse; *vi* inquietarse, apurarse, preocuparse.

worrying ['wʌriiŋ] *a* inquietante perturbador.

worse [wə:s] *a ad* peor; ínfimo; **from bad to —** de mal en peor, cada vez peor.

worsen ['wə:sn] *vt* agravar, hacer peor; *vi* agravarse, empeorarse.

worship ['wə:ʃip] *n* (*relig*) culto; veneración; adoración; *vt* adorar, honrar; rendir (culto, reverencia).

worshipping ['wə:ʃipiŋ] *n* adoración, culto.

worst [wə:st] *n* lo peor, lo más malo; **at the —** en el peor de los casos; **to get the — of** llevar la peor parte; *vt* aventajar, vencer.

worsted ['wustid] *an* (de) estambre.

worth [wə:θ] *n* valor, mérito, valía; preciosidad; entidad, monta; *a* equivalente a; **well — seeing** digno de verse, notable; **it is (not) — while** (no) vale la pena; **it is — noting** es de notar.

worthiness ['wə:ðinis] *n* mérito, merecimiento.

worthless ['wə:θlis] *a* inútil, sin valor, baladí, de poca monta, fútil.

worthy ['wə:ði] *a* digno, meritorio, debido, benemérito; acreedor (de); **to be — of** merecer.

would-be ['wudbi] *a* supuesto, que presume de, presunto.

wound [wu:nd] *n* herida; (*sore*) llaga; ofensa; **knife —** cuchillada; **saber —** sablazo; *vt* herir, lastimar; agraviar.

wounded ['wu:ndid] *a* **— man** herido.

wrangle ['ræŋgl] *n* reyerta, camorra, altercado; *vi* reñir.

wrap [ræp] *n* manta; bata; *vt* envolver; **to — around** enroscar; **to — up** empapelar, envolver; **to — oneself up** embozarse, (*in bedclothes*) arrebujarse.

wrapped [ræpt] *a* **to be — up in** (*fig*) ensimismarse en.

wrapper ['ræpə] *n* envoltura, funda, cubierta; (*newspaper*) faja.

wrapping ['ræpiŋ] *a* **— paper** papel de estraza; *n pl* **—s** envolturas.

wrath [rɔθ] *n* cólera, furor.

wrathful ['rɔθful] *a* colérico, encolerizado, rabioso.

wreak [ri:k] *vt* (*anger*) descargar; **to — havoc** hacer estragos, ensañarse en.

wreath [ri:θ] *n* guirnalda; corona (fúnebre).

wreathe [ri:ð] *vt* tejer, enguirnaldar; hacer (guirnalda); enroscar(se).

wreck [rek] *n* desecho, ruina; (*naut*) naufragio; **I am a —** estoy hecho un desastre; *vt* hacer naufragar, echar a pique; *vi* naufragar, zozobrar.

wreckage ['rekidʒ] *n* naufragio, restos.

wren [ren] *n* reyezuelo.

wrench [rentʃ] *n* torcedura; arranque, tirón; llave de tuercas; **monkey —** llave (inglesa); *vt* arrancar, (re)torcer, dislocar; sacar de quicio.

wrest [rest] *vt* arrancar, forzar, arrebatar.

wrestle ['resl] *vi* luchar a brazo partido, combatir; **to — with** bregar; (*to be free*) forcejar.
wretch [retʃ] *n* desgraciado, miserable, menguado.
wretched ['retʃid] *a* (*person*) infeliz, miserable, desgraciado, pobre, cuitado; (*thing etc*) pobre, ruin, mezquino.
wretchedness ['retʃidnis] *n* desdicha, miseria, escualidez.
wriggle ['rigl] *vi* menearse, retorcerse.
wring [riŋ] *vt* (re)torcer(se); (*cloth*) escurrir, estrujar; **to — out** (*water*) exprimir; (*cry*) forzar.
wrinkle ['riŋkl] *n* arruga, surco; *vt* (*brow*) fruncir; arrugar; *vi* arrugarse.
wrist [rist] *n* muñeca; **— watch** reloj de pulsera.
writ [rit] *n* escrito, mandamiento, orden; auto; notificación, ejecución; **Holy W—** Sagrada Escritura.
write [rait] *vt* escribir; (*article etc*) redactar, componer; tener correspondencia con; poner por escrito; **something (nothing) to — home about** (*fam*) cosa (nada) del otro jueves.
writer ['raitə] *n* escritor, autor; literato.
writhe ['raið] *vi* (re)torcer, contorcerse.
writhing ['raiðiŋ] *n* retorcimiento, contorsiones.
writing ['raitiŋ] *n* (*hand*) escritura, letra; (*paper etc*) escrito, documento; (*act, art of*) redacción; **— case** cartera; **— desk** papelera; **in one's own —** de puño y letra.
wrong [rɔŋ] *a* equivocado, erróneo, falso; injusto; inoportuno; **— side** envés, revés, vuelta; **— side out** al revés; *ad* mal, sin causa, al revés; **to go —** extraviarse, malearse, torcerse; **right or —** a tuertas o a derechas; *n* (*insult etc*) injuria, agravio; desaguisado, entuerto; mal, daño; culpa; error; **to be (in the) —** no tener razón, estar equivocado; equivocarse; **—doer** malhechor; *vt* injuriar; perjudicar, causar perjuicio, ofender.
wrong-doing ['rɔŋ'duiŋ] *n* maldad, maleficencia, pecado, injusticia.
wrongful ['rɔŋful] *a* inicuo, injusto.
wroth [rouθ] *a* colérico.
wrought [rɔ:t] *a* labrado, trabajado; **highly —** depurado; **— iron** hierro batido, hierro forjado; **over—** sobreexcitado.
wry [rai] *a* torcido; **— face** mueca; **—-mouthed** boquituerto.

X

X-ray(s) ['eks'rei(z)] *n* rayo(s) X.
xylophone ['zailəfoun] *n* xilófono.

Y

yacht [jɔt] *n* yate.
yachting ['jɔtiŋ] *n* excursión en yate.
yam [jæm] *n* ñame, camote, boniato.
Yankee ['jæŋki] *an* yanqui.
yard [jɑ:d] *n* (*measure*) yarda; (*equiv*) vara; corral, patio; (*naut*) verga.
yarn [jɑ:n] *n* hilaza, hilo; (*coll*) cuento.
yawn [jɔ:n] *n* bostezo; *vi* bostezar.
yawning ['jɔ:niŋ] *a* bostezante; *n* bostezo.
year [jə:] *n* año; **leap —** año bisiesto.
yearling ['jə:liŋ] *a* primal, añal, añojo; **— lamb** borrego.
yearly ['jə:li] *a* anual; *ad* anualmente, una vez al año, cada año.
yearn [jə:n] *vi* anhelar, ambicionar, suspirar por.
yearning ['jə:niŋ] *n* anhelo, prurito.
yeast [ji:st] *n* levadura, fermento.
yell [jel] *n* alarido, aullido; *vi* vociferar, gritar, chillar, decir (hablar) a gritos.
yellow ['jelou] *a* amarillo, gualdo.
yellowish ['jelouiʃ] *a* amarillento.
yellowness ['jelounis] *n* amarillez.
yeoman ['joumən] *n* hacendado, labrador rico, terrateniente.
yes [jes] *ad* sí; **— it is** sí tal.
yesterday ['jestədi] *ad* ayer; **the day before —** anteayer.
yet [jet] *cj* aunque, sin embargo, con todo; *ad* todavía, hasta ahora, hasta aquí; **not —** todavía no.
yew [ju:] *n* tejo.
yield [ji:ld] *n* (*fin*) rendimiento, rédito; beneficio; (*crops*) cosecha, cogida; *vt* (*produce*) producir, rendir, rentar, dar de sí; (*give away*) dar, ceder; deferir; (*give up*) entregar, devolver, conceder; *vi* rendir, ceder, sucumbir; conformarse, consentir; doblegarse.
yoke [jouk] *n* yugo; **—strap** coyunda; *vt* enyugar, uncir, acoyundar; someter al yugo, oprimir; **to throw off the —** sacudir el yugo.
yokel ['joukəl] *n* patán, pelo de la dehesa.
yolk [jouk] *n* yema.
yon, yonder [jɔn, 'jɔndə] *a ad* allá, a lo lejos.
you [ju:] *pn* (*subject*) tú, vosotros, vosotras, usted, ustedes; (*object*) le, la, les, las, te, os; (*after prep*) sí, ti; (*refl*) se, te.
young [jʌŋ] *a* joven; juvenil; tierno, verde, fresco; **very —** imberbe; **— man, fellow** (*fam*) pollo, pollito; **— blood** pimpollo; **—er son** segundón; **with —** encinta, preñada; *n* (*of animals*) cría; los jóvenes.
youngish ['jʌŋiʃ] *a* juvenil.
youngster ['jʌŋstə] *n* mocito; jovencito; **—s** gente menuda.

your [jɔ:] *a* tu, tus; su, sus; de Vd; vuestro.
yours [jɔ:z] *pn* el tuyo, el suyo, de Vd, el vuestro.
yourself [jɔ:'self] *pn* tú mismo, Vd, vosotros.
yourselves [jɔ:'selvz] *pn* vosotros mismos, vosotras mismas, ustedes mismos, ustedes mismas.
youth [ju:θ] *n* (*abstract*) juventud, mocedad; (*person*) joven, mozo; pollo, pollito; **country —** zagal.
youthful ['ju:θful] *a* juvenil, joven.
youthfulness ['ju:θfulnis] *n* mocedad, juventud.
Yugoslavia ['ju:gou'slɑ:viə] *n* Yugoeslavia.
Yugoslavian ['ju:gou'slɑ:viən] *an* yugoeslavo.
yule [ju:l] *n* tiempo de Navidad.

Z

Z [zi:] (*letter*) zeta.
zeal [zi:l] *n* celo, ardor; furia.
zealot ['zelət] *n* fanático.
zealous ['zeləs] *a* celoso, fervoroso, apasionado; (*in work*) hacendoso.
zebra ['zi:brə] *n* cebra.
zenith ['zeniθ] *n* cenit; **at the — of** al apogeo de.
zephyr ['zefə] *n* céfiro.
zero ['ziərou] *n* cero; **below —** bajo cero.
zest [zest] *n* gusto, sabor, deleite; aliciente.
zigzag ['zigzæg] *n* zigzag; *a* **— course** meandro; *vi* zigzaguear, mover en zigzag; andar haciendo eses; (*of horses, going uphill*) cuartear.
zinc [ziŋk] *n* cinc.
zip, zipper [zip, 'zipə] *n* cremallera.
zodiac ['zoudiæk] *n* zodíaco.
zone [zoun] *n* zona.
zoo [zu:] *n* parque (jardín) zoológico.
zoological [,zouə'lɔdʒikəl] *a* zoológico.
zoologist [zou'ɔlədʒist] *n* zoólogo.
zoology [zou'ɔlədʒi] *n* zoología.
zoom [zu:m] *n* zumbido; *vi* zumbar.
zulu ['zu:lu:] *n* zulú.

Spanish Grammar—Gramática Española

THE DEFINITE ARTICLE (the)

	Singular	*Plural*
masculine	el, *e.g.* el toro	los, *e.g.* los toros
feminine	la, *e.g.* la casa	las, *e.g.* las casas

THE INDEFINITE ARTICLE (a, some)

	Singular	*Plural*
masculine	un (a), *e.g.* un toro	unos (some), *e.g.* unos toros
feminine	una (a), *e.g.* una casa	unas (some), *e.g.* unas casas

DEMONSTRATIVE ADJECTIVES (this, that, those)

Masc. Singular	*Fem. Singular*	*Masc. Plural*	*Fem. Plural*
este	esta	estos	estas
ese	esa	esos	esas
aquel	aquella	aquellos	aquellas

DEMONSTRATIVE PRONOUNS (this one, that one, those ones)

Masc. Singular	*Fem. Singular*	*Masc. Plural*	*Fem. Plural*
éste	ésta	éstos	éstas
ése	ésa	ésos	ésas
aquél	aquélla	aquéllos	aquéllas

PLURAL OF NOUNS AND ADJECTIVES

1. Ending in a vowel, add S, *e.g.*
   carta, cartas
   duro, duros
2. Ending in a consonant, add ES, *e.g.*
   virtud, virtudes
   holgazán, holgazanes

FEMININE OF ADJECTIVES

1. Ending in O, change O to A, *e.g.*
   duro, dura
2. Any other ending, no change, *e.g.*
   cortés, azul, dulce

Exceptions

1. Ending in a consonant and signifying geographical origin, etc., add A, *e.g.*
   inglés, inglesa
   alemán, alemana
   andaluz, andaluza

2. Ending in OR which are not words of comparison, add A, *e.g*

hablador, habladora

3. Ending in ÁN, ÓN, ÍN, add A, *e.g.*

holgazán, holgazana
preguntón, preguntona
pequeñín, pequeñina

4. Ending in OTE, ETE, change E to A.

ADVERBS

In general, adverbs are formed by adding -MENTE to the feminine singular form of the adjective, *e.g.*

absoluto, absoluta—absolutamente
útil, útil—útilmente

There are many irregular adverbs and adverbial phrases, *e.g.* ahora, now; detrás, behind; a gatas, on all fours; a más no poder, with all one's might; etc.

PUNCTUATION

Note that in questions and exclamations, Spanish requires an inverted sign, ¡ or ¿ at the beginning, *e.g.*

¿ Dónde está mi paraguas?
¡ Qué traje tan elegante!

PRONOUNS—LOS PRONOMBRES

	Subject	*Direct object*	*Indirect object*
	Singular		
1	yo, I	me, me	me, to me
2	tú, you	te, you	te, to you
3	él, he	le, (persons) him	le, to him
		lo, (things) it	
	ella, she	la, her	le, to her
	usted, you	le, you	le, to you
		la, you	
	Plural		
1	nosotros, we	nos, us	nos, to us
	nosotras, we	nos, us	nos, to us
2	vosotros, you	os, you	os, to you
	vosotras, you	os, you	os, to you
3	ellos, they	los, them	les, to them
	ellas, they	las, them	les, to them
	ustedes, you	los, you	les, to you
		las, you	

	Reflexive	*With preposition*
	Singular	
1	me, myself	para mí, for me
2	te, yourself	para ti, for you
3	se, himself	para él, for him
	se, herself	para ella, for her
	se, yourself	para usted, for you
	Plural	
1	nos, ourselves	para nosotros, for us
	nos, ourselves	para nosotras, for us

2	**os,** yourselves	**para vosotros,** for you
	os, yourselves	**para vosotras,** for you
3	**se,** themselves	**para ellos,** for them
	se, themselves	**para ellas,** for them
	se, yourselves	**para ustedes,** for you

N.B. **Tú** and **vosotros** are used when talking to persons whom we would normally address by their first name.

Usted and **ustedes** are more formal.

POSSESSIVE PRONOUNS

when noun is	*Masculine singular*	*Feminine singular*	*Meaning*
	(el) mío	(la) mía	mine
	(el) tuyo	(la) tuya	yours
	(el) suyo	(la) suya	his, hers, yours
	(el) nuestro	(la) nuestra	ours
	(el) vuesto	(la) vuestra	yours
	(el) suyo	(la) suya	their, yours

when noun is	*Masculine Plural*	*Feminine Plural*	*Meaning*
	(los) míos	(las) mías	mine
	(los) tuyos	(las) tuyas	yours
	(los) suyos	(las) suyas	his, hers, yours
	(los) nuestros	(las) nuestras	ours
	(los) vuestros	(las) vuestras	yours
	(los) suyos	(las) suyas	their, yours

POSSESSIVE ADJECTIVES

when noun is	*Masculine singular*	*Feminine singular*	*Meaning*
	mi	mi	my
	tu	tu	your
	su	su	his, her, your
	nuestro	nuestra	our
	vuestro	vuestra	your
	su	su	their, your

when noun is	*Masculine plural*	*Feminine plural*	*Meaning*
	mis	mis	my
	tus	tus	your
	sus	sus	his, her, your
	nuestros	nuestras	our
	vuestros	vuestras	your
	sus	sus	their, your

Spanish Verbs-Verbos Españoles

Regular

There are three classes of conjugations of regular verbs in Spanish:

First Conjugation—Verbs ending in -ar, e.g. habl-ar
Second Conjugation—Verbs ending in -er, e.g. com-er
Third Conjugation—Verbs ending in -ir, e.g. viv-ir

Most parts of regular verbs are formed by adding the appropriate endings to the stem, e g. habl-, com-, viv- For the future and conditional tenses, the endings are added to the whole of the infinitive.

First Conjugation -ar

Model Verb: HABLAR =to speak

INFINITIVE hablar STEM habl-
PRESENT PARTICIPLE hablando
PAST PARTICIPLE hablado

PRESENT INDICATIVE

	Singular	*Plural*
1.	hablo	hablamos
2.	hablas	habláis
3.	habla	hablan

IMPERFECT INDICATIVE

	Singular	*Plural*
1.	hablaba	hablábamos
2.	hablabas	hablábais
3.	hablaba	hablaban

PRETERITE OR PAST DEFINITE

	Singular	*Plural*
1.	hablé	hablamos
2.	hablaste	hablasteis
3.	habló	hablaron

FUTURE

	Singular	*Plural*
1.	hablaré	hablaremos
2.	hablarás	hablaréis
3.	hablará	hablarán

CONDITIONAL

	Singular	*Plural*
1.	hablaría	hablaríamos
2.	hablarías	hablaríais
3.	hablaría	hablarían

IMPERATIVE

	Singular	*Plural*
1.	—	hablemos
2.	habla	hablad
3.	hable	hablen

PRESENT SUBJUNCTIVE

	Singular	*Plural*
1.	hable	hablemos
2.	hables	habléis
3.	hable	hablen

IMPERFECT SUBJUNCTIVE

	Singular	*Plural*
1.	hablase	hablásemos
2.	hablases	habláseis
3.	hablase	hablasen

CONDITIONAL SUBJUNCTIVE

	Singular	*Plural*
1.	hablara	habláramos
2.	hablaras	hablárais
3.	hablara	hablaran

Second Conjugation -er

Model Verb: COMER =to eat

INFINITIVE comer — STEM com-
PRESENT PARTICIPLE comiendo
PAST PARTICIPLE comido

PRESENT INDICATIVE

	Singular	*Plural*
1.	como	comemos
2.	comes	coméis
3.	come	comen

CONDITIONAL

	Singular	*Plural*
1.	comería	comeríamos
2.	comerías	comeríais
3.	comería	comerían

IMPERFECT INDICATIVE

	Singular	*Plural*
1.	comía	comíamos
2.	comías	comíais
3.	comía	comían

IMPERATIVE

	Singular	*Plural*
1.	—	comamos
2.	come	comed
3.	coma	coman

PRETERITE OR PAST DEFINITE

	Singular	*Plural*
1.	comí	comimos
2.	comiste	comisteis
3.	comió	comieron

PRESENT SUBJUNCTIVE

	Singular	*Plural*
1.	coma	comanos
2.	comas	comáis
3.	coma	coman

FUTURE

	Singular	*Plural*
1.	comeré	comeremos
2.	comerás	comeréis
3.	comerá	comerán

IMPERFECT SUBJUNCTIVE

	Singular	*Plural*
1.	comiese	comiésemos
2.	comieses	comieseis
3.	comiese	comiesen

CONDITIONAL SUBJUNCTIVE

	Singular	*Plural*
1.	comiera	comiéramos
2.	comieras	comierais
3.	comiera	comieran

Third Conjugation -ir

Model Verb: VIVIR =to live

The formation of parts of verbs of the third conjugation follows the patterns given for the second conjugation except in the first and second persons plural of the present: *vivimos*, *vivis*; and in the second person plural of the imperative: *vivid*.

INFINITIVE vivir — STEM viv-
PRESENT PARTICIPLE viviendo
PAST PARTICIPLE vivido

PRESENT INDICATIVE			IMPERATIVE	
	Singular	*Plural*	*Singular*	*Plural*
1.	vivo	vivimos	—	vivamos
2.	vives	vivís	vive	vivid
3.	vive	viven	viva	vivan

IMPERFECT INDICATIVE
vivía *etc*

PRETERITE vivi *etc*

FUTURE viviré *etc*

CONDITIONAL viviría *etc*

PRESENT SUBJUNCTIVE
vivía *etc*

IMPERFECT SUBJUNCTIVE
viviese *etc*

CONDITIONAL SUBJUNCTIVE
viviera *etc*

Radical-Changing Verbs

In these verbs the vowel of the stem undergoes slight changes when the stress falls on that vowel. There are three classes of such verbs.

Class 1

-E changes to -IE and -O to -UE when the stress falls on the vowel of the stem.

This occurs in the 1st, 2nd and 3rd persons singular and the 3rd person plural of the Present Indicative and the Present Subjunctive, e.g.

perder = to lose mostrar = to show

PRESENT INDICATIVE		PRESENT SUBJUNCTIVE	
pierdo	muestro	pierda	muestre
pierdes	muestras	pierdas	muestres
pierde	muestra	pierda	muestre
perdemos	mostramos	perdamos	mostremos
perdéis	mostráis	perdáis	mostréis
pierden	muestran	pierdan	muestren

All class 1 verbs end in -ar or -ir

Class 2

(a) -E changes to -IE and -O to -UE when the stress falls on the vowel of the stem.

This occurs in the 1st, 2nd and 3rd persons singular and the 3rd person plural of the Present Indicative and the Present Subjunctive, e.g.

sentir = to feel dormir = to sleep

PRESENT INDICATIVE		PRESENT SUBJUNCTIVE	
siento	duermo	sienta	duerma
sientes	duermes	sientas	duermas
siente	duerme	sienta	duerma
sentimos	dormimos	sintamos*	durmamos*
sentís	dormís	sintáis*	durmáis*
sienten	duermen	sientan	duerman

*see (b)

(b) -E changes to -I and -O to -U before -IE, -IÓ, or stressed -A. This occurs in the Present Participle, the 3rd persons singular and plural of the Preterite, and 1st and 2nd persons plural of the Present Subjunctive (see above), all of the Imperative Subjunctive and the Conditional Subjunctive.

PRESENT PARTICIPLE
sintiendo durmiendo

PRETERITE

sentí	dormí
sentiste	dormiste
sintió	durmió
sentimos	dormimos
sentisteis	dormisteis
sintieron	durmieron

IMPERFECT SUBJUNCTIVE
sintiese *etc* durmiese *etc*

CONDITIONAL SUBJUNCTIVE
sintiera *etc* durmiera *etc*

All class 2 verbs end in -ir.

Class 3

-E changes to -I when the stress falls on the vowel of the stem and before -IE, -IÓ and stressed A.

This occurs in the Present Participle, the 1st, 2nd, 3rd persons singular and 3rd person plural of the Present Indicative, 3rd persons singular and plural of the preterite, all of the Present Subjunctive, the Imperfect Subjunctive and the Conditional Subjunctive.

Model Verb: PEDIR = to ask

PRESENT PARTICIPLE pidiendo

PRESENT INDICATIVE

	Singular	*Plural*
1.	pido	pedimos
2.	pides	pedís
3.	pide	piden

PRETERITE

	Singular	*Plural*
1.	pedí	pedimos
2.	pediste	pidisteis
3.	pidió	pidieron

PRESENT SUBJUNCTIVE
pida *etc*

IMPERFECT SUBJUNCTIVE
pidiese *etc*

CONDITIONAL SUBJUNCTIVE
pidiera *etc*

All Class 3 verbs end in -ir.

The change which takes place in any radical-changing verb is indicated in the dictionary as follows: **(ie), (ue), (i).**

Verbs in which Spelling Changes occur

Ending in	*Change*	*Tenses affected*	
-car	-c to -qu	1st person sing.	whole of pres.
e.g. colocar	before -e	pret.	subj.
to place		coloqué	coloque

-gar e.g. cargar to load	-c to -gu before -e	1st person sing. pret. cargué	whole of pres. subj. cargue
-zar e.g. organizar to organize	-z to -c before -e	1st person sing. pret. organicé	whole of pres. subj. organice
-cer -cir e.g. esparcir to scatter (when -c is preceded by a consonant)	-c to -z before -o or -a	1st person sing. pres. ind. esparzo	whole of pres. subj. esparza
-cer -cir e.g. conocer to know (when -c is preceded by a vowel)	-z is inserted before -c when this is followed by -o or -a	1st person sing. pres. ind. conozco	whole of pres. subj. conozca
-ger -gir e.g. dirigir to direct	-g to -j before -o or -a	1st person sing. pres. ind. dirijo	whole of pres. subj. dirija
-quir e.g. delinquir to offend	-qu to -c before -o or -a	1st person sing. pres. ind. delinco	whole of pres. subj. delinca
-guir e.g. seguir to follow	-gu to g before -o or -a	1st person sing. pres. ind. sigo	whole of pres. subj. siga

Other Changes

-uir excluding those ending in -quir and -guir but including -güir e.g. constituir = to constitute	Add -y between the stem and the ending in the Pres. Indic. and Pres. Subj. before -o, -e, -a. Constituyo, constituye, constituya. Unaccented -i changes to -y in the Pres. Part., 3rd person sing. and plural pret., whole of imp. subj. and cond. subj. Constituyendo, constituyó, constituyeron, constituyese, constituyera.
-llir -ñir e.g. bullir = to boil gruñir = to grunt	Omit the unaccented -i of the ending in the Pres. Part., 3rd person sing. and plural pret., whole of Imp. Subj. and plural Pret., whole of Imp. Subj. and Cond. Subj. Bullendo, bulló, bulleron, bullese, bullera. Gruñendo, gruñó, gruñeron, gruñese, gruñera.

-eír when the verb is radical-changing of Class III e.g. reír = to laugh	Omit the unaccented i of the ending in the Pres. Part., 3rd person sing. and plural Pret., whole of Imp. Subj. and Cond. Subj. Riendo, rió, rieron, riese, riera.

When the stem of a verb of the first conjugation ends in a weak vowel (i, u) this vowel often takes the stress and requires a written accent before endings which are not stressed and begin with a vowel, e.g. variar, continuar.

Pres. Ind.	varío etc.	but	variamos
	continúo etc.	„	continuamos
Pres. Subj.	varíe etc.	„	variemos
	continúe etc.	„	continuemos
Imperative	varía		variad
	continúa		continuad

Verbs having Irregular Past Participles

abrir	*to open*	abierto
cubrir	*to cover*	cubierto
describir	*to describe*	descrito
descubrir	*to discover*	descubierto
devolver	*to give back*	devuelto
escribir	*to write*	escrito
envolver	*to wrap*	envuelto
freír	*to fry*	frito
imprimir	*to print*	impreso
morir	*to die*	muerto
oprimir	*to oppress*	oprimido *or* opreso
prender	*to seize*	prendido *or* preso
proveer	*to provide*	provisto *or* proveído
romper	*to break*	roto *or* rompido
suprimir	*to suppress*	suprimido *or* supreso
transcribir	*to transcribe*	transcrito
volver	*to return*	vuelto

Irregular verbs—Verbos irregulares

Infinitive	*Present Indicative*	*Future; Conditional*	*Imperfect Indicative*	*Preterite*	*Present Subjunctive*	*Imperfect and Conditional Subjunctive*	*Imperative*
andar to walk	ando *etc*	andaré *etc* andaría *etc*	andaba *etc*	anduve anduviste anduvo anduvimos anduvisteis anduvieron	ande *etc*	anduviese *etc* anduviera *etc*	anda ande
caber to be contained, to fit	quepo cabes cabe cabemos cabéis caben	cabré *etc* cabría *etc*	cabía *etc*	cupe cupiste cupo cupimos cupisteis cupieron	quepa *etc*	cupiese *etc* cupiera *etc*	cabe quepa *etc*
caer to fall	caigo caes cae caemos caéis caen	caeré *etc* caería *etc*	caía *etc*	caí caiste cayó caimos caisteis cayeron	caiga *etc*	cayese *etc* cayera *etc*	cae caiga *etc*

Infinitive	*Present Indicative*	*Future; Conditional*	*Imperfect Indicative*	*Preterite*	*Present Subjunctive*	*Imperfect and Conditional Subjunctive*	*Imperative*
conducir	conduzco	conduciré *etc*	conducía *etc*	conduje	conduzca *etc*	condujese *etc*	conduce
to lead	conduces	conduciría *etc*		condujiste			conduzca
similarly	conduce			condujo		condujera *etc*	*etc*
deducir	conducimos			condujimos			
inducir	conducís			condujisteis			
introducir	conducen			condujeron			
producir							
traducir							
dar	doy	daré *etc*	daba *etc*	di	dé	diese *etc*	da
to give	das	daría *etc*		diste	des	diera *etc*	dé *etc*
	da			dio	dé		
	damos			dimos	demos		
	dais			disteis	deis		
	dan			dieron	den		
decir	digo	diré *etc*	decía *etc*	dije	diga	dijese *etc*	di
to say	dices	diría *etc*		dijiste	digas	dijera *etc*	diga
	dice			dijo	diga		decid
	decimos			dijimos	digamos		digan
	decís			dijisteis	digáis		
	dicen			dijeron	digan		

Infinitive	*Present Indicative*	*Future; Conditional*	*Imperfect Indicative*	*Preterite*	*Present Subjunctive*	*Imperfect and Conditional Subjunctive*	*Imperative*
estar	estoy	estaré *etc*	estaba *etc*	estuve	esté	estuviese *etc*	está
to be	estás	estaría *etc*		estuviste	estés	estuviera *etc*	esté
	está			estuvo	esté		estad
	estamos			estuvimos	estemos		estén
	estáis			estuvisteis	estéis		
	están			estuvieron	estén		
haber	he	habré *etc*	había *etc*	hube	haya *etc*	hubiese *etc*	he
to have	has	habría *etc*		hubiste		hubiera *etc*	haya
	ha			hubo			habed
	hemos			hubimos			hayan
	habéis			hubisteis			
	han			hubieron			
hacer	hago	haré *etc*	hacía	hice	haga *etc*	hiciese *etc*	haz
to do, make	haces	haría *etc*		hiciste		hiciera *etc*	haga
similarly	hace			hizo			haced
satisfacer	hacemos			hicimos			hagan
to satisfy	hacéis			hicisteis			
	hacen			hicieron			

Infinitive	*Present Indicative*	*Future; Conditional*	*Imperfect Indicative*	*Preterite*	*Present Subjunctive*	*Imperfect and Conditional Subjunctive*	*Imperative*
ir	voy	iré *etc*	iba	fui	vaya *etc*	fuese *etc*	ve
to go	vas	iría *etc*	ibas	fuiste		fuera *etc*	vaya
	va		iba	fue			id
	vamos		íbamos	fuimos			vayan
	vais		ibais	fuisteis			
	van		iban	fueron			
oír	oigo	oiré *etc*	oía *etc*	oí	oiga *etc*	oyese *etc*	oye
to hear	oyes	oiría *etc*		oíste		oyera *etc*	oiga
	oye			oyó			oíd
	oímos			oímos			oigan
	oís			oísteis			
	oyen			oyeron			
poder	puedo	podré *etc*	podía *etc*	pude	pueda *etc*	pudiese *etc*	
to be able	puedes	podría *etc*		pudiste		pudiera *etc*	
	puede			pudo			
	podemos			pudimos			
	podéis			pudisteis			
	pueden			pudieron			

Infinitive	*Present Indicative*	*Future; Conditional*	*Imperfect Indicative*	*Preterite*	*Present Subjunctive*	*Imperfect and Conditional Subjunctive*	*Imperative*
poner to put, place *similarly* **exponer** to expose **imponer** to impose **proponer** to propose **suponer** to suppose	pongo pones pone ponemos ponéis ponen	pondré *etc* pondría *etc*	ponía *etc*	puse pusiste puso pusimos pusisteis pusieron	ponga *etc*	pusiese *etc* pusiera *etc*	pon ponga poned pongan
querer to want, wish, love	quiero quieres quiere queremos queréis quieren	querré *etc* querría *etc*	quería *etc*	quise quisiste quiso quisimos quisisteis quisieron	quiera *etc*	quisiese *etc* quisiera *etc*	quiere quiera quered quieran

Infinitive	*Present Indicative*	*Future; Conditional*	*Imperfect Indicative*	*Preterite*	*Present Subjunctive*	*Imperfect and Conditional Subjunctive*	*Imperative*
saber	sé	sabré *etc*	sabía *etc*	supe	sepa *etc*	supiese *etc*	sabe
to know	sabes	sabría *etc*		supiste		supiera *etc*	sepa
	sabe			supo			sabed
	sabemos			supimos			sepan
	sabéis			supisteis			
	saben			supieron			
salir	salgo	saldré *etc*	salía *etc*	salí	salga *etc*	saliese *etc*	sal
to go out	sales	saldría *etc*		saliste		saliera *etc*	salga
	sale			salió			salid
	salimos			salimos			salgan
	salís			salisteis			
	salen			salieron			
ser	soy	seré *etc*	era *etc*	fui	sea *etc*	fuese *etc*	sé
to be	eres	sería *etc*		fuiste		fuera *etc*	sea
	es			fue			sed
	somos			fuimos			sean
	sois			fuísteis			
	son			fueron			

Infinitive	*Present Indicative*	*Future; Conditional*	*Imperfect Indicative*	*Preterite*	*Present Subjunctive*	*Imperfect and Conditional Subjunctive*	*Imperative*
tener	tengo	tendré *etc*	tenía *etc*	tuve	tenga *etc*	tuviese *etc*	ten
to have	tienes	tendría *etc*		tuviste		tuviera *etc*	tenga
similarly	tiene			tuvo			tened
contener	tenemos			tuvimos			tengan
to contain	tenéis			tuvisteis			
detener	tienen			tuvieron			
to stop							
entretener							
to entertain							
mantener							
to maintain							
obtener							
to obtain							
sostener							
to support							
traer	traigo	traeré *etc*	traía *etc*	traje	traiga *etc*	trajese *etc*	trae
to bring	traes	traería *etc*		trajiste		trajera *etc*	traiga
	trae			trajo			traed
	traemos			trajimos			traigan
	traéis			trajisteis			
	traen			trajeron			

Infinitive	*Present Indicative*	*Future; Conditional*	*Imperfect Indicative*	*Preterite*	*Present Subjunctive*	*Imperfect and Conditional Subjunctive*	*Imperative*
valer	valgo	valdré *etc*	valía *etc*	valí *etc*	valga *etc*	valiese *etc*	val
to be worth	vales	valdría *etc*				valiera *etc*	valga
similarly	vale						valed
equivaler	valemos						valgan
to be equivalent to	valéis						
	valen						
venir	vengo	vendré *etc*	venía *etc*	vine	venga *etc*	viniese *etc*	ven
to come	vienes	vendría *etc*		viniste		viniera *etc*	venga
similarly	viene			vino			venid
convenir	venimos			vinimos			vengan
to suit	venís			venisteis			
prevenir	vienen			vinieron			
to prevent							
ver	veo	veré *etc*	veía *etc*	vi	vea *etc*	viese *etc*	ve
to see	ves	vería *etc*		viste		viera *etc*	vea
	ve			vio			ved
	vemos			vimos			vean
	veis			visteis			
	ven			vieron			

Verbos ingleses fuertes e irregulares—English Strong and Irregular Verbs

Infinitivo	*Pretérito*	*Participio pasado*
abide	abode	abode
arise	arose	arisen
awake	awoke, awaked	awakened, awoke
be	was	been
bear	bore	born(e)
beat	beat	beaten
become	became	become
befall	befell	befallen
begin	began	begun
behold	beheld	beheld
bend	bent	bent
bereave	bereft	bereft
beseech	besought	besought
bet	bet	bet
bid	bade, bid	bidden
bid	bid	bid
bind	bound	bound
bite	bit	bitten
bleed	bled	bled
blow	blew	blown
break	broke	broken
breed	bred	bred
bring	brought	brought
build	built	built
burn	burned, burnt	burned, burnt
burst	burst	burst
buy	bought	bought
cast	cast	cast
catch	caught	caught
chide	chid	chid(den)
choose	chose	chosen
cleave	cleft, clove	cleft, cloven
cling	clung	clung
come	came	come
cost	cost	cost
creep	crept	crept
cut	cut	cut
deal	dealt	dealt
dig	dug	dug
do	did	done
draw	drew	drawn
dream	dreamed, dreamt	dreamed, dreamt

Infinitivo	*Pretérito*	*Participio pasado*
drink	drank	drunk
drive	drove	driven
dwell	dwelt, dwelled	dwelt, dwelled
eat	ate	eaten
fall	fell	fallen
feed	fed	fed
feel	felt	felt
fight	fought	fought
find	found	found
flee, fly	fled	fled
fling	flung	flung
fly	flew	flown
forbid	forbade	forbidden
forget	forgot	forgotten
forgive	forgave	forgiven
forsake	forsook	forsaken
freeze	froze	frozen
get	got	got, gotten
give	gave	given
go	went	gone
grind	ground	ground
grow	grew	grown
hang	hung	hung
have	had	had
hear	heard	heard
hew	hewed	hewn
hide	hid	hid(den)
hit	hit	hit
hold	held	held
hurt	hurt	hurt
inlay	inlaid	inlaid
keep	kept	kept
kneel	knelt, kneeled	knelt, kneeled
know	knew	known
lay	laid	laid
lead	led	led
leap	leaped, leapt	leaped, leapt
leave	left	left
lend	lent	lent
let	let	let
lie	lay	lain
light	lighted, lit	lighted, lit
lose	lost	lost
make	made	made
may	might	—
mean	meant	meant
meet	met	met
mow	mowed	mown
pay	paid	paid
put	put	put

Infinitivo	*Pretérito*	*Participio pasado*
quit	quit	quit
read	read	read
rend	rent	rent
rid	rid	rid
ride	rode	ridden
ring	rang	rung
rise	rose	risen
run	ran	run
saw	sawed	sawn, sawed
say	said	said
see	saw	seen
seek	sought	sought
sell	sold	sold
send	sent	sent
set	set	set
sew	sewed	sewn, sewed
shake	shook	shaken
shall	should	—
shave	shaved	shaved, shaven
shed	shed	shed
shine	shone	shone
shoe	shod	shod
shoot	shot	shot
show	showed	shown
shrink	shrank	shrunk
shrive	shrove	shriven
shut	shut	shut
sing	sang, sung	sung
sink	sank, sunk	sunk
sit	sat	sat
slay	slew	slain
sleep	slept	slept
slide	slid	slid
sling	slung	slung
slink	slunk	slunk
slit	slit	slit
smell	smelled, smelt	smelled, smelt
smite	smote, smit	smitten, smit
sow	sowed	sown
speak	spoke	spoken
speed	sped, speeded	sped, speeded
spend	spent	spent
spill	spilt	spilt
spin	spun, span	spun
spit	spat, spit	spat, spit
split	split	split
spoil	spoiled, spoilt	spoiled, spoilt
spread	spread	spread
spring	sprang	sprung
stand	stood	stood

Infinitivo	*Pretérito*	*Participio pasado*
steal	stole	stolen
stick	stuck	stuck
sting	stung	stung
stink	stank, stunk	stunk
stride	strode	stridden, strode
strike	struck	struck
string	strung	strung
strive	strove	striven
swear	swore	sworn
sweep	swept	swept
swell	swelled	swollen
swim	swam	swum
swing	swung	swung
take	took	taken
teach	taught	taught
tear	tore	torn
tell	told	told
think	thought	thought
thrive	throve	thriven
throw	threw	thrown
thrust	thrust	thrust
tread	trod	trodden
understand	understood	understood
wake	woke, waked	waked
wear	wore	worn
weave	wove	woven, wove
weep	wept	wept
wet	wet	wet
win	won	won
wind	wound	wound
withdraw	withdrew	withdrawn
withhold	withheld	withheld
withstand	withstood	withstood
wring	wrung	wrung
write	wrote	written

Numerals—Los Números

NÚMEROS CARDINALES		CARDINAL NUMBERS
cero	**0**	zero
uno	**1**	one
dos	**2**	two
tres	**3**	three
cuatro	**4**	four
cinco	**5**	five
seis	**6**	six
siete	**7**	seven
ocho	**8**	eight
nueve	**9**	nine
diez	**10**	ten
once	**11**	eleven
doce	**12**	twelve
trece	**13**	thirteen
catorce	**14**	fourteen
quince	**15**	fifteen
dieciseis	**16**	sixteen
diecisiete	**17**	seventeen
dieciocho	**18**	eighteen
diecinueve	**19**	nineteen
veinte	**20**	twenty
veintiuno	**21**	twenty-one
veintidós	**22**	twenty-two
veintitrés	**23**	twenty-three
treinta	**30**	thirty
cuarenta	**40**	forty
cincuenta	**50**	fifty
sesenta	**60**	sixty
setenta	**70**	seventy
ochenta	**80**	eighty
noventa	**90**	ninety
noventa y cinco	**95**	ninety-five
cien	**100**	one hundred
ciento uno	**101**	hundred and one
ciento diez	**110**	hundred and ten
doscientos	**200**	two hundred
quinientos cuarenta	**540**	five hundred and forty
mil	**1000**	one thousand

setenta mil doscientos ochenta	**70,280**	seventy thousand two hundred and eighty
quinientos mil	**500,000**	five hundred thousand
un millón	**1,000,000**	one million
mil millones	**1,000,000,000**	one billion

NÚMEROS ORDINALES		ORDINAL NUMBERS
primero	**1**st	first
segundo	**2**nd	second
tercero	**3**rd	third
cuarto	**4**th	fourth
quinto	**5**th	fifth
sexto	**6**th	sixth
séptimo	**7**th	seventh
octavo	**8**th	eighth
noveno	**9**th	ninth
décimo	**10**th	tenth
undécimo	**11**th	eleventh
duodécimo	**12**th	twelfth
decimotercero	**13**th	thirteenth
decimocuarto	**14**th	fourteenth
decimoquinto	**15**th	fifteenth
decimosexto	**16**th	sixteenth
decimoséptimo	**17**th	seventeenth
decimoctavo	**18**th	eighteenth
decimonoveno	**19**th	nineteenth
vigésimo	**20**th	twentieth
vigésimo primero	**21**st	twenty-first
vigésimo segundo	**22**nd	twenty-second
vigésimo tercero	**23**rd	twenty-third
trigésimo	**30**th	thirtieth
cuadrigésimo	**40**th	fortieth
quincuagésimo	**50**th	fiftieth
sexagésimo	**60**th	sixtieth
septuagésimo	**70**th	seventieth
octuagésimo	**80**th	eightieth
nonagésimo	**90**th	ninetieth
nonagésimo quinto	**95**th	ninety-fifth
centésimo	**100**th	(one) hundredth
bicentésimo	**200**th	two hundredth
milésimo	**1000**th	(one) thousandth
(el) un millón	**1,000,000**th	millionth

Dinero, Pesos y Medidas Españoles—Spanish Weights, Measures and Money

LONGITUD—LENGTH

1 milímetro	·001 meter	=·0394 inch
1 centímetro	·01 meter	=·394 inch
1 metro	39·4 inches	1 yard
1 kilómetro	1000 meters	1094 yards or ⅝ mile
8 kilómetros	5 miles	

SUPERFICIE—AREA

1 hectárea	=11960·11 square yards
1 kilómetro cuadrado	247·11 acres

CAPACIDAD—CAPACITY

1 centilitro	·01 liter	=·0176 pint
1 litro	1¾ pints	·2201 gallon
1 hectolitro	100 liters	22 gallons 2¾ bushels
1 kilolitro	1000 liters	220 gallons 27½ bushels

PESO—WEIGHT

1 miligramo	·001 gram	=·0154 grain
1 centigramo	·01 gram	=·1543 grain
1 gramo		=15·43 grains
1 hectogramo	100 grams	*=3½ oz
1 kilogramo	1000 grams	*=2 lbs 3 oz
1 tonelada	1000 kilograms	*=1 ton

EL TERMÓMETRO—THE THERMOMETER

Punto de Congelamiento	Centigrade 0° Fahrenheit 32°	Freezing point
Punto de Ebullición	Centigrade 100° Fahrenheit 212°	Boiling point

DINERO—MONEY

Una peseta=cien centésimos de peseta=céntimos

* aproximadamente—* roughly

Dinero, Pesos y Medidas Ingleses — English Weights, Measures and Money

LONGITUD—LENGTH

Pulgada	25 milímetros	inch
pie	·304 metro	foot
yarda	·914 metro	yard
	1·828 metros	fathom
milla	1,609 metros	mile
nudo, milla náutica	1,853 metros	nautical mile, knot
5 millas	8 kilómetros	8 miles

MEDIDAS DE CAPACIDAD—CAPACITY

pinta	=0·567 litre	pint
cuarto	=1·543 litre	quart
galón	4·53 litres	gallon
peck	9·086 litres	peck
bushel	290·781 litres	bushel
quarter	36,348 litres	quarter

PESOS—WEIGHT

onza	28·35 grams	ounce
libra	453·59 grams	pound
	6·35 kilos	stone
quarter	12·7 kilos	

DINERO—MONEY

(Estados Unidos)

un dólar = 100 centavos	one dollar = 100 cents

(Reino Unido)

una libra=100 peniques	one pound=100 pence

Spanish Abbreviations — Abreviaturas Españolas

A

a área (*area*)
(a) alias (*alias*)
A alteza (*highness*)
ab abad (*abbot*)
abr abril (*April*)
a/c a cuenta (*on account*)
aC antes de Cristo (*before Christ*)
AC año de Cristo (*year of Our Lord*); Acción Católica (*Catholic Action*)
a de JC, aJC antes de Jesucristo (*before Jesus Christ*)
admón administración (*administration*)
AECE Asociación Española de Cooperación Europea (*Spanish Association for European Cooperation*)
afmo, affmo afectísimo (*affectionate, loving*)
A.D.G. a Dios gracias (*thanks to God*)
ago agosto (*August*)
ALRP a los reales pies (*at the royal feet*)
ap aparte (*aside*); apóstol (*apostle*)
Apoc Apocalipsis (*Apocalypse*)
APRA Alianza Popular Revolucionaria Americana (*American People's Revolutionary Alliance*)
art artículo (*article*)
arz arzobispo (*archbishop*)
atto atento (*attentive*)

B

B beato (*blessed*); bien (*well*)
Barna Barcelona
BO bolétin oficial (*official bulletin*)
BOE Boletín Oficial del Estado (*official state bulletin*)
Bón batallón (*battalion*)
Br bachiller (*bachelor*)
Bs As Buenos Aires
Bto Beato (*blessed*)

C

c/ cuenta (*account*)
C Celsius='centígrado' (*centigrade*); compañía (*company*)
cal caloría (*calorie*)
Cal California
cap capítulo (*chapter*)
cc centímetros cúbicos (*cubic centimeters*)
c/c cuenta corriente (*current account*)

CCEI Comisión Católica Española de la Infancia (*Spanish Catholic Commission for Children*)
CECA Comunidad Europea del Carbón y del Acero (*European Coal and Steel Community*)
cént, cénts, cts céntimo(s), centavo(s) (*cent*)
cf confesor (*confessor*)
CF club de fútbol (*football club*)
cfr confer, compárese, confróntese (*compare*)
cg centigramo (*centigram*)
cgo cargo (*load*)
CGS cegesimal (*centimeter gram second*)
Cía compañía (*company*)
CIME Comité intergubernamental de Migraciones Europeas (*Intergovernmental Committee for European Migration*)
cje corretaje (*agency*)
cl centilitro(s) (*centiliter*)
cm centímetro(s) (*centimeter*)
CMB cuyas manos besa (*kisses your hands*)—formal salutation in letter
CPB cuyos pies besa (*kisses your feet*)—formal salutation in letter
col columna (*column*)
cos coseno (*cosine*)
cosec cosecante (*cosecant*)
cotg cotangente (*cotangent*)
cta cuenta (*account*)
cte corriente (*current*)
ctg cotangente (*cotangent*)
cts céntimos (*cents*)
c/u cada uno (*each one*)
CV caballos de vapor (*horse power*)
ch cheque (*check*)

D

D Don (*Sir, Mr*)
Da Doña (*Lady, Mrs*)
dcha derecha (*right*)
DDT dicloro-difenil-tricloroetano (insecticida) (*dichloro-diphenyl-trichloro-ethane* (*insecticide*)
d/f, d/fha días fecha (*date*(*d*))
dg decigramo(s) (*decigram*)
Dg decagramo(s) (*decagram*)
dicbre, dic diciembre (*December*)
dl decilitro(s) (*deciliter*)
Dl decalitro(s) (*decaliter*)
dm decímetro(s) (*decimeter*)
Dm decámetro(s) (*decameter*); Dios mediante (*God willing*)
Dr doctor (*doctor*)
dupdo duplicado (*duplicate*)
dv días vista (*days after sight*)

E

E este (*east*)
ECOSOC Consejo Económico y Social de las Naciones Unidas (*United Nations Economic and Social Council*)

ed	edición (*edition*); editor (*publisher*); editorial (*publishing*)
EE UU	Estados Unidos (*United States*)
EM	Estado Mayor (*General Staff*)
Ema	eminencia (*eminence*)
Emmo	eminentísimo (*most eminent*)
ene	enero (*January*)
ENE	estenordeste (*east-north-east*)
entlo	entresuelo (*mezzanine, entresol*)
EPD	en paz descanse (*rest in peace*)
EPM	en propia mano (*in our possession*)
ESE	estesudeste (*east-south-east*)
etc	etcétera (*etcetera*)
Ex	Exodo (*Exodus*)
Exc	excelencia (*excellency*)
Excmo, Excma	Excelentísimo -ma (*most excellent*)

F

fa	factura (*invoice*)
F	faradio (*farad*)
FC	Ferrocarril (*railway*); fútbol club (*football club*)
F (de T)	Fulano (de Tal) (*so-and-so*)
Fdez	Fernández
feb	febrero (*February*)
fec	fecit (*made by*)
FET	Falange Española Tradicionalista (*Spanish Traditional Falange*)
fha	fecha (*date*)
FIFA	Federación Internacional de Fútbol Asociación (*International Federation of Football Associations*)
FF CC	ferrocarriles (*railways*)
fol	folio
Fr	fray (*father, brother* (*eccles*))
fr, frs	franco(s) (*franc*(*s*))
fra	factura (*invoice*)

G

g	gramo (*gram*)
g/	giro (*draft*)
Ga	García
Gen, Gén	Génesis (*Genesis*)
g/p, gp	giro postal (*money order*)
gr(s)	gramo(s) (*gram*)
gral	general (*general*)
gv	gran velocidad (*express*)

H

h	hora(s) (*hour*)
Ha	hectárea(s) (*hectare*)
Hg	hectogramo(s) (*hectogram*)
Hl	hectolitro(s) (*hectoliter*)
Hm	hectómetro(s) (*hectometer*)
hnos	hermanos (*brothers*)
Hz	hertzio (*hertz*)

Ilmo, Ilma	ilustrísimo -ma (*most illustrious*)
Imp	imprenta (*printing, printed*)
INI	Instituto Nacional de Industria (*National Industrial Institute*)
INLE	Instituto Nacional del Libro Español (*Spanish National Book Institute*)
ITRAP	Instituto Técnico para la Racionalización de la Administración Pública (*Technical Institute for the Rationalization of Public Administration*)
izq, izqda	izquierdo, izquierda (*left*)

J

JC	Jesucristo (*Jesus Christ*)
Jhs	Jesús (*Jesus*)
JONS	Juntas de Ofensiva Nacional-Sindicalista (*National-Sindicalist Movement (groups)*)
jul	julio (*July*)
jun	junio (*June*)

K

Kc, kc	kilociclo (*kilocycle*)
Kg, kg	kilogramo (*kilogram*)
khz	kilohertzio (*kilohertz*)
Kl	kilolitro (*kiloliter*)
Km, km	kilómetro(s) (*kilometer(s)*)
Kw, kw	kilovatio(s) (*kilowatt(s)*)
Kwh, kwh, kw/h	kilovatios-hora (*kilowatt hours*)

L

l	litro(s) (*liter*); libro (*book*)
L	licenciado (*bachelor*)
L/	Letra (*draft letter*)
Ldo, Lda	licenciado (*bachelor*)
LECE	Liga europea de cooperación económica (*European League for Economic Cooperation*)
Lib	Libro (*book*); libra (*pound*)
Lic	licenciado (*bachelor*)

M

m	metro(s) (*meter(s)*); minutos (*minutes*)
m/	mi (*my*); mes (*month*)
M	madre (*mother*); marco (*mark*);
Ma	María (*Mary*)
mar	marzo (*March*)
my	mayo (*May*)
mb	milibar (*millibar*)
m/c	mi cuenta (*my account*)
Mc	megaciclo (*megacycle*)
mg	miligramo(s) (*milligram(s)*)
M I Sr	Muy Ilustre Señor (*Dear Sir*)
ml	mililitro (*milliliter*)

mm, m/m	milímetro (*millimeter*)
m/n	madres (*mothers*); moneda nacional (*national currency*); motonave (*ship*)
MS, ms	manuscrito (*manuscript*)
MSS, mss	manuscritos (*manuscripts*)

N

n/	nuestro -a (*our*)
N	norte (*north*)
Na, Sa	Nuestra Señora (*Our Lady*)
NE	nordeste (*north-east*)
no	número (*number*)
NO	noroeste (*north-west*)
nov, novbre	noviembre (*November*)
NS	Nuestro Señor (*Our Lord*)
NSJC	Nuestro Señor Jesucristo (*Our Lord Jesus Christ*)
NT	Nuevo Testamento (*New Testament*)
núm	número (*number*)

O

o/	orden (*order*)
O	oeste (*west*)
OC	Orden Carmelita (*Order of Carmelites*)
OCED	Organización de Cooperación Económica y Desarrollo (*Organization for Economic Cooperation and Development*)
O Cist	Orden Cisterciense (*Order of Cistercians*)
oct	octubre (*October*)
OEA	Organización de los Estados Americanos (*Organization of American States*)
OECE	Organización europea de cooperación económica (*Organization for European Economic Cooperation*)
OIT	Organización Internacional del Trabajo (*International Labor Organization*)
OM	orden ministerial (*ministerial order*)
ONO	oesnoroeste (*west-north-west*)
ONU	Organización de las Naciones Unidas (*United Nations Organization*)
op	opus (*work*)
OP	Orden de Predicadores (*Order of Preachers*)
OSO	oessudoeste (*west-south-west*)
OTAN	Organización del Tratado del Atlántico Norte (*North Atlantic Treaty Organization*)

P

p	página (*page*); por (en representación de) (*for=representing*)
pa, PA	por autorización (*by authority*); por ausencia (*by (in) absence*)
pág	página (*page*)
Pat	patente (*patent*)
PC	Partido Comunista (*Communist party*)
PD	posdata (*postcript*)
p ej	por ejemplo (*for example*)
PO	por orden (*by order*)

PP	padres (*fathers*)
pral	principal (*principal*)
pról	prólogo (*prologue*)
prova	provincia (*provincial*)
pta, ptas	peseta, pesetas
pv	pequeña velocidad (*slow not express*)
PVP	precio de venta al público (*retail price*)

Q

qbsm	que besa su mano (*who kisses your hand*)
qbsp	que besa sus pies (*who kisses your feet*)
qDg	que Dios guarde (*God protect him*)
qege	que en gloria esté (*may he be in glory*)
qepd	que en paz descanse (*may he rest in peace*)
qesm	que estrecha su mano (*who offers his hand*)

R

R	Réaumur (*degrees of temperature*); reverendo (*reverend*)
RAE	Real Academia Española (*Spanish Academy*)
RAU	República Árabe Unida (*United Arab Republic*)
RENFE	Red Nacional de los Ferrocarriles Españoles (*Spanish Railways*)
RO	Real orden (*royal order*)
Rte	remitente (*sender*)

S

s	siguiente (*following*)
S	San (*Saint*); sur (*south*)
$	dólares (*dollars*); pesos, escudos
SA	sociedad anónima (*stock company*); su alteza (*his/her/your highness*)
sdad	sociedad (*society*)
SDM	su divina majestad (*his divine majesty*)
SE	sudeste (*south east*) su excelencia (*his/her/your excellency*)
S en C	sociedad en comandita (*silent partnership, private company*)
sep, sept, sepbre	septiembre (*September*)
SEU	sindicato español universitario (*Spanish union of students*)
seuo	salvo error u omisión (*errors or omissions excepted*)
sig, sgte	siguiente (*following*)
sl	sus labores (*his/her/your works*)
SL	sociedad limitada (*limited company*)
SM	su majestad (*his/her/your majesty*)
SMC	su majestad católica (*his catholic majesty*)
SMI	su majestad imperial (*his/her/your imperial majesty*)
Smo	santísimo (*most holy*)
s/n	sin número (*number*)
SN	servicio national (*national service*)
SO	sudoeste (*south west*)
Sr	señor (*Mr*)
Sra	señora (*Mrs*)
Srta	señorita (*Miss*)

SRM	su real majestad (*his/her/your royal majesty*)
ss	seguro servidor (*faithful servant*)
SS	su santidad (*his holiness*)
ss, sigs	siguientes (*following*)
SSE	sud sudeste (*south south east*)
SSO	sud sudoeste (*south south west*)
sss	su seguro servidor (*your faithful servant*)
Sto, Sta	santo, santa (*saint*)

T

t	tomo (*volume*)
T	tara (*tare*)
tel, telef	teléfono (*telephone*)
tg	tangente (*tangent*)
tít	título (*title*)
Tm	tonelada métrica (*metric ton*)
TNT	trinitrotolueno (*trinitrotoluene*)
TV	televisión (*television*)

U

Ud, Uds	usted, ustedes (*you*)
URSS	Unión de Repúblicas Socialistas Soviéticas (*Soviet Union*)

V

v	véase (*see*); verso (*back*)
V	usted (*you*); voltio (*volt*); véase (*see*)
VA	vuestra alteza (*your highness*)
Vd, Vds	usted, ustedes (*you*)
Vda	viuda (*widow*)
vgr, vg	verbigracia (*for instance*)
VI	vuestra (senoría) ilustrísima (*his/her your illustrious lordship*)
vid	vide (*see*)
VM	vuestra majestad (*his/her/your majesty*)
vol	volumen (*volume*)
VS	vuestra señoría (*your lordship*)
VV	ustedes (*you*)

X

Xto	Cristo (*Christ*)

Abreviaturas Inglesas — English Abbreviations

A

A	adults (*adultos*)
AA	Alcoholics Anonymous (*Asociación para la ayuda a los alcohólicos*)
AAA	American Automobile Association (*Asociación americana de automovilistas*)
AC	alternating current (*corriente alternativa*)
A/C	account (current) (*a cuenta*)
AD	in the year of our Lord (*L: anno Domini*) (*de la era cristiana*)
AF of L	American Federation of Labo r (*Federación americana de trabajo*)
A1	first class (*de primera categoría*)
am	before noon (*L: ante meridiem*) (*antes del mediodía*)
AMA	American Medical Association (*Asociación americana de médicos*)
approx	approximate(ly) (*aproximadamente*)
assn	association (*asociación*)
asst	assistant (*auxiliar, adjunto*)
av	average (*promedio*)
Ave	avenue (*avenida*)

B

b	born (*nacido*)
BA	Bachelor of Arts (*Licenciado en Filosofía y Letras*)
BBC	British Broadcasting Corporation (*Sociedad británica de radiofusión*)
BC	before Christ (*antes de Jesucristo*); British Columbia (*la Columbia Británica*)
BD	Bachelor of Divinity (*Licenciado en teología*)
Bd	Board (*consejo, comité*)
BDS	Bachelor of Dental Surgery (*Licenciado en cirugía dental*); bomb disposal squad (*grupo de hombres entendidos en la explosión de bombas*)
B/E	bill of exchange (*letra de cambio*)
BEA	British European Airways (*Líneas Aéreas Europeas Británicas*)
B.Litt	Bachelor of Letters (*Licenciado en Letras*)
B.Mus	Bachelor of Music (*Bachiller en Música*)
BOAC	British Overseas Airways Corporation (*Compañía Británica de Líneas Aéreas Transatlánticas*)
Brit	Britain (*Gran Bretaña*); British (*británico*)
Bros	Brothers (commercial); (*hermanos (comercial)*)
B/S	Bill of Sale (*Escritura de venta*)
BSc	Bachelor of Science (*Licenciado en ciencias*)
Bt	Baronet (*Barón*)

C

C	Cape (*cabo*); centigrade (*centigrado*); central (*central*)
c	cent (*céntimo*); centigram (*centigramo*); centime (*céntimo*); centimeter (*centímetro*); century (*siglo*); chapter (*capítulo*); about (*L: circa*) (*cerca, approximadamente*)
cap	capital letter (*mayúscula*); chapter (*capítulo*)
cf	compare (*compárese, confróntese*)
CIA	Central Intelligence Agency (*Agencia central de Inteligencia*)
CID	Criminal Investigation Department (*sección de la policía británica que se ocupa de la investigación de actos criminales*)
cif	Cost, insurance and freight (*precio que incluye el coste, el seguro y el flete*)
CIO	Congress of Industrial Organizations (*Congreso de organizaciones industriales*)
CND	Campaign for Nuclear Disarmament (*Campaña de Desarme Nuclear*)
CO	Commanding Officer (*comandante*); conscientious objector (*persona que rehusa a hacer el servicio militar por razones de conciencia*)
Co	Company (*Compañía*)
c/o	care of (*para entregar a*)
COD	cash on delivery (*pagar contra recepción*)
CP	Communist Party (*Partido comunista*)
cwt	hundredweight(s) (*vigésima parte de una tonelada, 50 kilos aproximadamente*)

D

d	died (*muerto*); date (*fecha*); daughter (*hija*); penny (*penique*)
DA	district attorney (*fiscal*)
DC	District of Columbia (*Distrito de Columbia*); Direct Current (*corriente continua*)
DD	Doctor of Divinity (*Doctor en Teología*)
DDT	Dichloro-diphenyl-trichloro-ethane (an insecticide) (*Dicloro-difenil-tricloroetano* (*insecticida*))
dept	department (*departamento*); deponent (*deponente*)
do	ditto (the same) (*lo mismo*)
doz	dozen (*docena*)

E

EEC	European Economic Community (Common Market) (*Comunidad Económica Europea* (*Mercado Común*))
EFTA	European Free Trade Association (*Asociación Europea de Libre Cambio*)
eg	for example (*L: exampli gratia*) (*por ejemplo*)
EP	extended play (*de duración reducida* (*disco de* 45 *r.p.m.*))
esp	especially (*especialmente*)
est	established (*establecido*)
etc	and the rest (*L: et cetera*) (*etcétera*)

F

FAO	Food and Agriculture Organization (*Organizacion para la Alimentacion y la Agricultura*)
FBI	Federal Bureau of Investigation (*Oficina Federal de Investigacion*)
FO	Foreign Office (*Departamento de Asuntos Exter ores*)
fob	free on board (*precio de la mercancia puesta a bordo*)
ft	foot, feet (*pie(s)*); fort (*fortaleza*); fortification (*fortificación*)

G

gal	gallon(s) (*medida*=4.546 *litros*)
GATT	General Agreement on Tariffs and Trade (*Acuerdo general sobre Aranceles e Intercambio Comercial*)
GB	Great Britain (*Gran Bretaña*)
GI	goverment issue (American private soldier) (*soldado americano*)
GMT	Greenwich Mean Time (*hora oficial del meridiano de Greenwich*)
GOP	Republican Party (*Partido republicano*)
Govt	Government (*Gobierno*)
GP	general practitioner (*médico general*)
GPO	General Post Office (*Correos*)

H

h & c	hot and cold (water) ((*agua*) *caliente y fria*)
HE	His Excellency (*Su excelencia*); His Eminence (*Su eminencia*); high explosive (*explosivo peligroso*)
HM	His (Her) Majesty (*Su majestad*)
HMS	His (Her) Majesty's Service/or His (Her) Majesty's Ship (*Servicio de su majestad; barco de su majestad*)
Hon	Honorary (*honorario*); Honorable (*honorable*)
hp	horsepower (*caballos de vapor*); hire purchase (*pago a plazos*)
HQ	headquarters (*sede central*)
HRH	His (Her) Royal Highness (*su majestad*)

I

I, Is	island(s) (*isla(s)*)
ib, ibid	in the same place (*L. ibidem*) (*en el mismo lugar*)
ICBM	Intercontinental Ballistic Missile (*misil balistico intercontinental*)
CEM	Intergovernmental Committee for European Migration (*Comité Intergubernamental para la Migracion Europea*)

ie	that is; namely (*L. id est*) (*es decir; esto es*)
ILO	International Labor Organization (*Organización Internacional de Trabajo*)
IMF	International Monetary Fund (*Fondo Monetario Internacional*)
in	inch, inches (*pulgada (medida)*)
Inc, Incorp	incorporated (*incorporado*)
incl	included, including, inclusive (*incluido, inclusivo*)
INS	International News Service (*Servicio Internacional de Noticias*)
Inst	Institute (*Instituto*)
IOU	I owe you (*pagaré*)
IQ	intelligence quotient (*cociente de inteligencia*)
IRA	Irish Republican Army (*ejército irlandés republicano*)

J

JP	Justice of the Peace (*juez, magistrado*)
jr	junior (*menor, hijo, el más joven*)

K

KKK	Ku Klux Klan (*sociedad racista*)
KO	(boxing) knockout (*fuera de combate*)
Kt	Knight (*caballero (título)*)
kw	kilowatt (*kilovatio*)

L

L	Latin (*latín*); Law (*Ley*)
l	lake (*lago*); left (*izquierda*); lira (*lira*)
£	pound (*libra(s) esterlina(s)*)
lb	pound (*libra (medida de peso* = ⅘ *kilo)*)
LLB	Bachelor of Laws (*Licenciado en Derecho*)
LP	Long playing (record) (*disco de larga duración*); Labor Party (*Partido laborista*)
LSD	lysergic acid diethylamide; pounds, shillings, pence (*libras, chelines, peniques*)
Ltd	Limited (Company) ((*Sociedad*) *Anónima*)

M

m	male (*masculino*); meter (*metro*); minute (*minuto*) married (*casado*); mile (*milla*); month (*mes*)
MA	Master of Arts (*Maestro en Artes*)
MB, ChB	Bachelor of Medicine (*Licenciado en Medicina*); Bachelor of Surgery (*Licenciado en Cirugía*)
MC	Master of Ceremonies (*Maestro de Ceremonias*); Member of Congress (*Miembro del congreso*); Military Cross (*Cruz Militar*)
MD	Doctor of Medicine (*Doctor en Medicina*)
Messrs	the plural of Mr, used before the name of a business firm or in a list referring to the names of several men (*Srs (Señores)*)
MI	Military Intelligence (*Inteligencia Militar*)

MP	Member of Parliament (*miembro del Parlamento*); Military Police (*Policía militar*)
mph	miles per hour (*millas por hora*)
Mr	Mister (*Señor*)
Mrs	Mistress (*Señora*)
MS(S)	manuscript(s) (*manuscrito(s)*)
Mt	mount, mountain (*monte, montaña*)

N

N	Nitrogen (*nitrógeno*); North, Northern ((*del*) *Norte*)
n	name (*nombre*); noun (*sustantivo*); neuter (*neutro*); noon (*mediodia*); nephew (*sobrino*); born (*L: natus*) (*nacido*)
NAM	National Association of Manufacturers (*Asociación Nacionale de Fabricantes*)
Nat	National (*nacional*); Nationalist (*nacionalista*)
NATO	North Atlantic Treaty Organization (*Organización del tratado del atlántico norte*)
NB	note well (*L. nota bene*) (*observa bien*); New Brunswick
NCO	Non-commissioned officer (*Oficial sin comisión* (*ejército*))
NE	north-east (*nordeste*); New England (*Nueva Inglaterra*)
NHS	National Health Service (*Servicio Nacional de Salud*)
no(s)	number(s) (*L: numero*) (*número(s)*)
NW	north-west (*noroeste*)
NY	New York (*Nueva York*)
NZ	New Zealand (*Nueva Zelanda*)

O

OAS	Organization of American States (*Organización de los Estados Americanos*)
OECD	Organization for Economic Cooperation and Development (*Organización de cooperación económica y desarrollo*)
OED	Oxford English Dictionary (*diccionario inglés publicado por la prensa de la Universidad de Oxford*)
OEEC	Organization for European Economic Cooperation (*Organización europea de cooperación económica*)
OK	all correct (*todo correcto*); all right (*bien, de acuerdo*)
OM	Order of Merit (*Orden de Mérito*)
OXFAM	Oxford Committee for Famine Relief (*Comité de Oxford para combatir el hambre*)
Oxon	Oxford, Oxfordshire, of Oxford (*L. Oxoniensis*) (*Ciudad/universidad de Oxford*)
oz	ounce(s) (*onza(s)*)

P

p	page (*página*); participle (*participio*)
pa	per annum, by the year (*por año*)
P & O	Peninsular and Oriental (Steam Navigation Company) ((*Compañia de Navegación*) *Peninsular y Oriental*)

PhD Doctor of Philosophy (*Doctor en Filosofía*)
PM Prime Minister (*primer ministro*); Past Master (*maestro*)
pm afternoon (*L. post meridiem*) (*después del mediodía*); after death (*L. post mortem*) (*después de la muerte*)
PO Post Office (*Correos*); Postal Order (*giro postal*)
POB Post Office Box (*apartado, casilla postal*)
POW prisoner of war (*prisionero de guerra*)
pp on behalf of (*por cuenta, autorización de*); pages (*páginas*)
Pres President (*Presidente*)
PRO Public Relations Officer (*Oficial de relaciones públicas*)
PS Postscript (*post scriptum, posdata*)
PTO Please Turn Over (*Continuación*)

Q

qt quart (*medida de líquido=2 pints=1 litro aproximadamente*)
qv which see (*L. quod vide*) (*véase*)

R

RA Royal Academy (*Real Academia*)
RAF Royal Air Force (*Reales Fuerzas Aéreas (de Gran Bretaña)*); Royal Aircraft Factory (*Fábrica Real de Aviones*)
RC Roman Catholic (*católico romano*); Red Cross (*Cruz Roja*)
Rd road (*calle*)
regd registered (*registrado*)
Rep Representative (*representativo*); Republic (*república*); Republican (*republicano*); Repertory (*repertorio*); Reporter (*reportero*)
Rev Reverend (*Reverendo*); Revelations (*Bib*) (*Revelaciones*)
RN Royal Navy (*Marina Real*); Registered nurse (*enfermera matriculada*)
Rt Hon Right Honorable (*Honorable*)

S

S sulfur (*azufre*); south (*sud*); Saint (*Santo*); Socialist (*Socialista*); Society (*Sociedad*)
s second (*segundo*); shilling (*chelín*); son (*hijo*); singular (*singular*); substantive (*sustantivo*); solubility (*solubilidad*)
Sch School (*escuela*)
SE south-east (*sudeste*)
SEATO South-East Asia Treaty Organization (*Organización del tratado del sudeste asiático*)
Sec, Secy secretary (*secretario*)

SHAPE	Supreme Headquarters Allied Powers, Europe (*Sede Suprema de las Fuerzas Aliadas en Europa*)
St	Saint (*Santo*); Strait (*Estrecho*); Street (*Calle*)
SW	south-west (*sudoeste*)

T

TB	tuberculosis (*tuberculosis*)
TNT	trinitrotoluene (explosive) (*trinitrotolueno* (*explosivo*))
TT	total abstainer (teetotal) (*abstemio total*); tuberculin-tested (*que ha sufrido la prueba de tuberculina*)
TUC	Trades Union Congress (*Congreso de Sındicatos*)
TV	television (*televisıón*)
TWA	Trans World Airlines (*Líneas Aéreas Trans World*)

U

UK	United Kingdom (*Reino Unido* (*Gran Bretaña*))
UN(O)	United Nations (Organization) (*Organización de las Naciones Unidas*)
UNESCO	United Nations Educational, Scientific and Cultural Organization (*Organización de las Naciones Unidas para la Educación, la Ciencia y la Cultura*)
UNICEF	United Nations International Children's Emergency Fund (*Fondo Internacional de las Naciones Unidas de Socorro a la Infancia*)
US(A)	United States (of America) (*Estados Unidos* (*de América*))
USAF	United States Air Force (*Fuerzas Aéreas de los Estados Unidos*)
USN	United States Navy (*Armada de los Estados Unidos*)
USSR	Union of Socialist Soviet Republics (*Unıón de Repúblicas Socialistas Soviéticas*)

V

VD	venereal disease (*enfermedad venereal*)
VHF	very high frequency (*alta frecuencia*)
VIP	(*fam*) very important person (*persona muy importante*)
viz	namely (*L. videlicet*) (*es decir*)

W

W	west (*oeste*); western ((*del*) *oeste*); Welsh (*galés*)
WHO	World Health Organization (*Organización Mundial de Salud*)
wk	week (*semana*)
wp	weather permitting (*si lo permıte el tiempo*)

Y

yd	yard(s) (*yarda*(*s*))
YHA	Youth Hotels Association (*Asociación de albergues para la juventud*)
YMCA	Young Men's Christian Association (*Asociación cristiana de hombres jovenes*)
yr	year (*año*); younger (*menor*); your (*tu, su*)
YWCA	Young Women's Christian Association (*Asociación cristiana de mujeres jovenes*)